THE ENGLISH LEGAL SYSTEM

Fourteenth Edition

2013–2014

Gary Slapper, LLB, LLM, PhD, PGCE (Law)

Global Professor at New York University, and Director of New York
University in London; Door Tenant, 36 Bedford Row, the Chambers of Richard
Wilson QC and William Harbage QC; Visiting Professor of Law at The Open
University, and The Chinese University, Hong Kong

David Kelly, BA, BA (Law), PhD

Previously Principal Lecturer in Law, Staffordshire University

Routledge
Taylor & Francis Group

LONDON AND NEW YORK

Fourteenth edition published 2013
by Routledge
2 Park Square, Milton Park, Abingdon, Oxon OX14 4RN

Simultaneously published in the USA and Canada
by Routledge
711 Third Avenue, New York, NY 10017

Routledge is an imprint of the Taylor & Francis Group, an informa business

First edition published by Cavendish Publishing 1994
Thirteenth edition published by Routledge 2012

British Library Cataloguing in Publication Data
A catalogue record for this book is available from the British Library

Library of Congress Cataloging in Publication
A catalog record for this book has been requested

ISBN: 978–0–415–63999–6 (hbk)
ISBN: 978–0–415–63998–9 (pbk)
ISBN: 978–0–203–52292–9 (ebk)

Typeset in Simoncini Garamond
by RefineCatch Limited, Bungay, Suffolk

MIX
Paper from
responsible sources
FSC
www.fsc.org FSC® C004839

Printed in Great Britain by Bell & Bain Ltd., Glasgow

CONTENTS

1 LAW AND LEGAL STUDY — 1

2 THE RULE OF LAW AND HUMAN RIGHTS — 23

3 SOURCES OF LAW — 83

PREFACE

In a law lecture delivered on 25 October 1758, William Blackstone described law as 'this most useful and most rational branch of learning'. With the growth and pervasion of law in the succeeding two and a half centuries, the importance of legal study has risen accordingly.

Law permeates into every cell of social life. It governs everything from the embryo to exhumation. It governs the air we breathe, the food and drink that we consume, our travel, sexuality, family relationships, our property, the world of sport, science, employment, business, education, health, everything from neighbour disputes to war. Taken together, the set of institutions, processes, laws and personnel that provide the apparatus through which law works, and the matrix of rules that control them, are known as the legal system.

This system has evolved over a long time. Today it contains elements that are very old, such as the coroner's courts which have an 800-year history, and elements that are very new, such as electronic law reports and judges using laptops.

A good comprehension of the English legal system requires knowledge and skill in a number of disciplines. The system itself is the result of developments in law, economy, politics, sociological change and the theories which feed all these bodies of knowledge. This book aims to assist students of the English legal system in the achievement of a good understanding of the law, and its institutions and processes. We aim to set the legal system in a social context, and to present a range of relevant critical views.

Being proficient in this subject also means being familiar with contemporary changes and proposed changes and this new edition has been comprehensively revised and updated to take these into account.

Since the thirteenth edition of this book, the changes to the English legal system have been many and varied. We have included in the text a wide range of legislative, common law, constitutional, and European developments that have occurred in the last year.

We are once again very grateful to all those who advanced suggestions for improvement of the book since the previous edition; many of those suggestions have been implemented in this edition.

Gary Slapper
David Kelly
1 November 2012

THE ENGLISH LEGAL SYSTEM – AN OVERVIEW

This book is about the English legal system. It is helpful to note, right at the very beginning, that the system was never designed in full at one point. It is over a thousand years old and it evolved over that time.

Even some of the elements within the system which appear to run all the way through, such as the monarchy, have changed considerably over the centuries. Monarchs in the tenth century, for example, did not rule over the whole of what would be today seen as the UK, and their powers were not limited by conventions as they are in modern times.

It is also important to note that the system has not come to a stop today. It is still growing and developing and always will do. At one time in the long history of the legal system, there was no democratic parliament to make law, but now there is. At one time, law could be declared by the monarch, but now that is impossible.

For a long time before the twentieth century there was no organised system of appeals in criminal cases but today there is such a system. In its early stages of development, the legal system had no organised law reporting so, in law courts, previous cases were analysed only in an oral way with lawyers and judges giving accounts of previous cases from memory, whereas today we have libraries full of voluminous law reports and all major decisions published in full online. Indeed, communications technology is completely altering the way the system works by allowing for new relationships between lawyers and their clients to exist in an electronic sphere. Precedents (previous cases which are relevant to the one in dispute) from all around the world can be consulted instantly in court using a computer, and mobile telephony can be used to summon witnesses to legal cases.

The pen and parchment allowed law to work in one particular way; the printing press meant law could be developed to a higher level of sophistication; the prevalence of the typewriter and photocopying facilities changed things further; and the internet and mobile telephony take law into a different sphere. It is clear that the story has not stopped here and that law will continue to develop in relation to technology.

Law, though, is also affected by the politics and the economy that surround it. New laws affecting the way the legal system works can be passed by one parliament but subsequently repealed when a different group of politicians gain power and want to change the legal system in accordance with their political views. In this text book we aim not only to explain the law and mechanisms of the legal system but to situate those changes in the context of such matters as *how the law came to be what it is* and *what social, economic and political issues arise from the legal system.*

In *Chapter 1* we examine the different approaches to legal study and the way that this book engages with such study. We also examine basic questions affecting the study of the legal system such as what is meant by law and how law can be classified according to different criteria.

In *Chapter 2* we examine the rule of law and human rights. These are very important ideas at the centre of the modern legal system. They are always in the thinking of lawyers, judges and legislators and civil servants and quite often they are ideas which are explicitly part of legal discussions. In its briefest form, the 'rule of law' is the idea that everyone is governed by the existing law, that no one is above it, and that random or capricious decisions in law courts are undesirable. The rule of law refers to an idea by which people are governed by rules, not by the whim of rulers.

The story of 'human rights' is a long one whose origins can be traced back many centuries, but such rights were systematically enshrined in documents by the United Nations and in Europe only from the middle of the last century. Since then they have become democratically implanted in many countries such as the UK. They cover basic unalterable rights, such as that no one should be tortured; and other rights such as the right to freedom of expression, which can only be taken away where there is a compelling need under such criteria that it is in the interests of a democracy.

In *Chapter 3* we examine the sources of law. In general language people speak about 'the law' as if it were one single thing, but in fact there are various sorts of law, including law that we follow from being a member of the European Union, legislation direct from the UK Parliament, and the judicial decisions of the higher level courts in the UK.

In *Chapters 4* and *5* we examine the civil courts and the civil process. In general terms 'civil law' means the law which governs the relationship *between* organisations like companies, and *between* individuals and organisations, and *between* individuals. This is different from the criminal process and courts which we look at in Chapters 6, 7 and 8, where one of the parties is the state and that party is prosecuting an individual or organisation for committing a crime.

In one sense, the civil courts and civil process are sub-compartments of the English legal system. It is, though, not quite as straightforward as that. It is not the case that the buildings and people who work in the civil side of law are entirely separate from the people and buildings concerned with the criminal side of the system. Some judges and lawyers, and some of the court and governmental buildings, deal with both civil and criminal matters. The civil courts have their own system of procedures and rules and their own special set of court orders and remedies. Typically, for example, a litigant in the civil process wishes to have an award of damages to compensate them for some harm or loss, or an order (an injunction) to stop someone from doing something legally wrong.

In *Chapters 6, 7* and *8* we examine the Criminal Courts and criminal process. Prosecutions for crimes are brought by the state against individuals or groups of individuals or organisations such as companies. To be convicted of a crime is a serious matter and, where the crime is a serious one, conviction can result in a life-changing sentence for the convict. Of all prosecutions brought each year, of which there are over 1.5 million, 98 per cent are carried out in magistrates' courts, with the remainder being held as trials before a jury in Crown Courts.

The state is mighty and powerful and highly resourced, whereas the individual is comparatively weak and poorly resourced. So, over time, rules about what evidence can be heard in court have evolved to prevent the state getting a conviction where the evidence would not sustain a fair conviction. No one, for example, can be convicted on the basis of a confession alone – there must be other credible evidence against them. That rule is to prevent confessions being extracted from suspects by improper means. Today, there are debates about whether defendants in criminal trials have too many rights; we examine these issues in these chapters.

In *Chapter 9* we examine the judiciary. Much of modern law comes from democratically passed legislation but these laws will often only be given clear meaning once they are interpreted and applied by judges in law courts (we examine the rule of statutory interpretation in Chapter 3). So, as the judiciary plays such a critically important role in 'making law', it becomes very important to analyse and evaluate this body of people, this legal institution. In this chapter we examine the constitutional role of the judiciary and such elements as how judges are selected and trained, and how their conduct is regulated.

In *Chapter 10* we examine the role of judicial reasoning and politics. The scientific study of how judges arrive at the judgments in cases is of momentous importance because it is through that route that so much of English law is made real.

In *Chapter 11* we examine the jury. The system of the jury trial has ancient origins and has been an indispensable part of the English legal system ever since. It is now replicated in over 50 countries of the commonwealth and is, according to one theory, the most important element in a legal system that guarantees against the tyranny of the state.

In *Chapter 12* we examine arbitration, tribunal adjudication and alternative dispute resolution. Going through the law courts to resolve a civil dispute or family law dispute is almost always a very long, expensive and confrontational event. There is considerable doubt about whether that approach is the best in all cases. In this chapter we look at the alternative mechanisms to standard law court hearings. These began as adventurous innovations on the outskirts of the legal system but their success in various ways has given them a progressively large and important role within the legal system. Arbitration, tribunal adjudication and alternative dispute resolution are now a central part of the legal system.

In *Chapter 13* we examine legal services. For most citizens the legal system's main manifestation is through its lawyers. This chapter examines and evaluates the systems through which legal advice and representation in court are provided. We examine the different types of lawyer, such as solicitors and barristers, and the changing structure of legal services. Recently we have moved into an era where lawyers can be involved in offering legal services in businesses which combine with other professionals such as accountants, and where commercial companies (even supermarkets) can own law firms.

In *Chapter 14* we examine the funding of legal services. Most citizens, of course, do not know any more about the law than they know about chemistry or medicine. It is therefore problematic if they have to try to defend themselves against a criminal or civil action without a lawyer. How should legal services be provided to people who could not otherwise afford to pay for a lawyer? In this chapter we examine the rules of the legal aid system and its changing features in the light of the economic and political environment.

In 1950, 85 per cent of the English population was covered by the legal aid system whereas by 2012 the proportion of people covered had fallen to 25 per cent. The significance and consequences of access to law are covered in this chapter.

Finally, in *Chapter 15* we examine the European context of the English legal system. As one of the 27 Member States of the European Union and one of the 47 Member States of the Council of Europe (and thus a signatory to the European Convention on Human Rights), the UK is governed significantly by law which does not emanate from the UK courts or the Parliament of the UK. In this chapter we examine the sources of European law and the institutions of the European Union – the way that laws are made and implemented.

ACKNOWLEDGMENTS

We owe a immeasurable gratitude to many people for the work and expertise that contributed to this book. We owe a particular debt to Suzanne, Hannah, Emily, Charlotte, Jane and Michael for their patience and support, again, while we researched, read and wrote.

We have again greatly benefited from the encouragement and sustained, meticulous professionalism of Fiona Briden at Routledge. Her thoughtful approach to guiding the redesign of this book has been superb. We are very grateful to Damian Mitchell, at Routledge, and to Karen Davies for her expertise on the diagrams. We are indebted to Mel Dyer at RefineCatch for his vigilant professionalism and to Jackie Day for expertly managing the production at Routledge. The book benefited greatly from the punctilious copy-editing of Ian Howe. We owe great thanks again to the outstanding professionalism of Vicki Scoble in civil process, the legal professions, and civil law. The work of Martha Spurrier on the criminal justice and courts has, once again, been superb. The work of Stephanie Pywell on statutory instruments was very helpful. We are indebted to Professor Dame Hazel Genn QC, Carolyn Bracknell, Lulu Phillips, Professor Michael Furmston, Miceál Barden, HH Judge Lynn Tayton QC, John Cooper QC, and Professor Wayne Morrison. In respect of human rights, we should particularly like to acknowledge the ongoing support of the Celtic connections: Miceál Barden, Angus McDonald, and Dewi Williams.

Others have offered uplifting encouragement, observations and assistance, or have stimulated our thinking in a helpful way. Thanks are thus due to Doreen and Ivor Slapper, Clifford, Maxine, Pav, Anish, the late Raie Schwartz, David and Julie Whight, Professor Robert Reiner, Hugh McLaughlan, Bèn Fitzpatrick, Eric Sneddon, Abigail Carr, Robert Zimmerman, Carol Howells, Professor Sir Jeffrey Jowell QC, Professor Ian Dennis, Professor Matthew Weait, Professor Tony Lentin, Frances Thomas, Alison Morris, Patrick Whight, Malcolm Park, Sheriff Andrew M Cubie, Frances Gibb, Legal Editor of *The Times*, Sir Stephen Sedley, and The Rt Hon The Lord Woolf.

Guide to Using the Book

The English Legal System contains a number of features designed to support and reinforce your learning. This Guided Tour shows you how to make the most of your textbook by illustrating each of the features used by the authors.

3.1   INTRODUCTION

This chapter considers where law comes find it. As was stated in Chapter 1, in civ priate code to find the law relating to th has not only to look at the legislation, bu but one also has to look in the cases for t common law. Nor should it be forgotter of the law of the European Union.

Chapter Introductions

These Introductions are a brief overview of the core themes and issues you will encounter in each chapter.

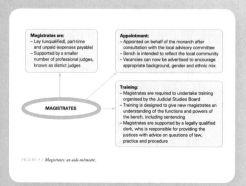

FIGURE 9.1 *Magistrates: an aide-mémoire.*

Diagrams

Visual learners are catered for via a series of diagrams and tables, which help facilitate the understanding of concepts and interrelationships within key topics.

CHAPTER SUMMARY: ARBITRATION, T
ALTERNATIVE DISPUTE RESOLUTION

ALTERNATIVE DISPUTE RESOLUTION
ADR has many features that make it prefe

Chapter Summaries

The essential points and concepts covered in each chapter are distilled into concise summaries at the end of each chapter in order to provide you with an at-a-glance reference point for each topic.

Food for Thought

Key questions are included at the end of each chapter to inform further study and to help deepen your understanding of important topics.

FURTHER READING

Baldwin, J, 'The social composition of magistra
Blom-Cooper, L, 'Bias: malfunction in judicial
Browne-Wilkinson, N (Sir), 'The independenc
Clayton, R, 'Decision-making in the Supreme (
PL 682–5
Crawford, L, 'Race awareness training and the
Griffith, JAG, *The Politics of the Judiciary*, 5th

Further Reading and Useful Websites

Selected further reading and useful websites are included at the end of each chapter to provide a pathway for further study.

COMPANION WEBSITE

Now visit the companion website to:

- test your understanding of the key terms us
- revise and consolidate your knowledge of '
  investigation of crime' using our Multiple (
- view all of the links to the Useful Websites

www.routledge.com/cw/slapper

Companion Website

Signposts to relevant material available on the book's popular Companion Website are included at the end of each chapter.

Guide to the Companion Website

www.routledge.com/cw/slapper

'One of the best sets of online resources I have ever seen.' *Richard Lee, Senior Lecturer, Manchester Metropolitan University*

For Lecturers

Visit *The English Legal System*'s Companion Website to discover a comprehensive range of resources designed to enhance the teaching and learning experience for both students and lecturers.

A free suite of exclusive resources developed to help you to teach the English legal system.

Testbank

Download a fully customisable bank of questions which test your students' understanding of the English legal system. These can be migrated to your university's Visual Learning Environment so that they can be customised and used to track student progress.

Diagrams

Use diagrams from the text in your own lecture presentations with our PowerPoint slides.

For Students

Audio Introduction to The English Legal System

Listen to Gary Slapper describe the authors' aims and intentions in his audio introduction to *The English Legal System*.

Legal Skills Guide

Improve your essential legal skills with our practical guides to Mooting, Negotiation, Finding Legal Information, Legal Writing and more.

Test your understanding of the English legal system with more than 200 online questions, each including hints, commentary and links back to the textbook.

Search over 100 essential legal terms in our handy online Glossary or check your knowledge with our interactive Flashcards.

Glossary Terms and Flashcards

LIST OF FIGURES

TABLE OF CASES

TABLE OF STATUTES

TABLE OF STATUTORY INSTRUMENTS

TABLE OF EUROPEAN LEGISLATION

TABLE OF ABBREVIATIONS

ABH	actual bodily harm
ABS	alternative business structures
ACAS	Advisory, Conciliation and Arbitration Service
ADR	alternative dispute resolution
AJTC	Administrative Justice and Tribunals Council
AOE	attachment of earnings orders
ARM	Automatic Referral to Mediation
ASBO	anti-social behaviour order
BCS	British Crime Survey
BIS	Bail Information Schemes
BME	black and minority ethnic
BSB	Bar Standards Board
BVT	best value tendering
CAB	citizen's advice bureau
CC	Competition Commission
CCP	Chief Crown Prosecutor
CCRC	Criminal Cases Review Commission
CCU	Complex Crime Unit
CDS	Criminal Defence Service
CJC	Civil Justice Council
CJEU	Court of Justice of the European Union
CJPOA	Criminal Justice and Public Order Act
CJR	Civil Justice Review
CJSSS	Criminal Justice; Simple, Speedy, Summary
CLAC	Community Legal Advice Centre
CLCC	Central London County Court
CLS	Community Legal Service
CLSP	Community Legal Service Partnership
CNR	cell nuclear replacement
CPD	continuing professional development
CPR	Civil Procedure Rules
CPS	Crown Prosecution Service
CRAR	Commercial Rent Arrears Recovery
CRB	Criminal Records Bureau
Crim PRC	Criminal Procedure Rule Committee
CSO	Community Support Officers

DCA	Department for Constitutional Affairs
DFB	deductions from benefits
DPP	Director of Public Prosecutions
DTI	Department of Trade and Industry
EC	European Community
ECHR	European Convention on Human Rights
ECJ	European Court of Justice
ECtHR	European Court of Human Rights
EEC	European Economic Community
EMS	European Monetary System
JSB	Judicial Studies Board
KPI	key performance indicators
LCD	Lord Chancellor's Department
LCF	Law Centres' Federation
LCS	Legal Complaints Service
LDP	Legal Disciplinary Partnership
LLP	limited liability partnership
LO	Legal Ombudsman
LPC	Legal Practice Course
LSB	Legal Services Board
LSC	Legal Services Commission
LSO	Legal Services Ombudsman
LSRC	Legal Services Research Centre
MCC	magistrates' courts committees
MDP	multidisciplinary practices
MFR	minimum funding requirement
MNP	multinational partnership
MOJ	Ministry of Justice
NAFIS	National Automated Fingerprint Identification System
NAO	National Audit Office
OFT	Office of Fair Trading
OJC	Office for Judicial Complaints
OLC	Office for Legal Complaints
OSS	Office for the Supervision of Solicitors
PAP	pre-action protocol
PC	practising certificate (solicitors)
PCA	Parliamentary Commissioner for Administration
PDS	Public Defenders' Service
PNC	police national computer
QBD	Queen's Bench Division
QC	Queen's Counsel
SDT	Solicitors' Disciplinary Tribunal
SFO	Serious Fraud Office
SIA	Security Industry Authority
SIAC	Special Immigration Appeals Commission

STV	single transferable vote
TPIMs	terrorism prevention and investigation measures
UNCITRAL	United Nations Commission on International Trade Law
VHCC	very high cost cases
VOL	voluntary mediation scheme

LAW AND LEGAL STUDY 1

There are a number of possible approaches to the study of law. One such is the traditional or formalistic approach. This approach to law is posited on the existence of a discrete legal universe as the object of study. It is concerned with establishing a knowledge of the specific rules, both substantive and procedural, which derive from statute and common law and which regulate social activity. The essential point in relation to this approach is that study is restricted to the sphere of the legal without reference to the social activity to which the legal rules are applied. In the past, most traditional law courses and the majority of law textbooks adopted this 'black letter' approach. Their object was the provision of information on what the current rules and principles of law were, and how to use those rules and principles to solve what were, by definition, legal problems. Traditionally, English legal system courses have focused attention on the institutions of the law, predominantly the courts, in which legal rules and principles are put into operation, and here too the underlying assumption has been as to the closed nature of the legal world – its distinctiveness and separateness from normal everyday activity. This book continues that tradition to a degree, but also recognises, and has tried to accommodate, the dissatisfaction with such an approach that has been increasingly evident among law teachers and examiners in this area. To that end, the authors have tried not simply to produce a purely expository text, but have attempted to introduce an element of critical awareness and assessment into the areas considered. Potential examination candidates should appreciate that it is just such critical, analytical thought that distinguishes the good student from the mundane one.

Additionally, however, this book goes further than traditional texts on the English legal system by directly questioning the claims to distinctiveness made by, and on behalf of, the legal system and considering law as a socio-political institution. It is the view of the authors that the legal system cannot be studied without a consideration of the values that law reflects and supports, and again, students should be aware that it is in such areas that the truly first-class students demonstrate their awareness and ability.

1.2   THE NATURE OF LAW

One of the most obvious and most central characteristics of all societies is that they must possess some degree of order to permit the members to interact over a sustained period of time. Different societies, however, have different forms of order. Some societies are highly regimented with strictly enforced social rules, whereas others continue to function in what outsiders might consider a very unstructured manner with apparently few strict rules being enforced.

Order is therefore necessary, but the form through which order is maintained is certainly not universal, as many anthropological studies have shown (see Mansell and Meteyard, 2004).

In our society, law plays an important part in the creation and maintenance of social order. We must be aware, however, that law as we know it is not the only means of creating order. Even in our society, order is not solely dependent on law, but also involves questions of a more general moral and political character. This book is not concerned with providing a general explanation of the form of order. It is concerned more particularly with describing and explaining the key institutional aspects of that particular form of order that is *legal* order.

The most obvious way in which law contributes to the maintenance of social order is the way in which it deals with disorder or conflict. This book, therefore, is particularly concerned with the institutions and procedures, both civil and criminal, through which law operates to ensure a particular form of social order by dealing with various conflicts when they arise.

Law is a *formal* mechanism of social control and, as such, it is essential that the student of law be fully aware of the nature of that formal structure. There are, however, other aspects to law that are less immediately apparent, but of no less importance, such as the inescapable political nature of law. Some textbooks focus more on this particular aspect of law than others, and these differences become evident in the particular approach adopted by the authors. The approach favoured by this book is to recognise that studying the English legal system is not just about learning legal rules, but is also about considering a social institution of fundamental importance.

1.2.1   LAW AND MORALITY

There is an ongoing debate about the relationship between law and morality and as to what exactly that relationship is or should be. Should all laws accord with a moral code, and, if so, which one? Can laws be detached from moral arguments? Many of the issues in this debate are implicit in much of what follows in the text, but the authors believe that, in spite of claims to the contrary, there is no simple causal relationship of dependency or determination, either way, between morality and law. We would rather approach both morality and law as ideological, in that they are manifestations of, and seek to explain and justify, particular social and economic relationships. This essentially materialist approach, to a degree, explains the tensions between the competing ideologies of law and morality and explains why they sometimes conflict and why they change, albeit asynchronously, as underlying social relations change.

Law and Morality

At first sight it might appear that law and morality are inextricably linked. There at least appears to be a similarity of vocabulary in that both law and morality tend to see relationships in terms of rights and duties and much of law's ideological justification comes from the claim that it is essentially moral. However, that is not necessarily the case and much modern law is of a highly technical nature (such as rules of evidence or procedure) dealing with issues that have very little, if any, impact on issues of morality as such. Opinions about the relationship between law and morality diverge between two schools of thought:

- One side adopts a 'natural law' approach which claims that law must be moral in order to be law, and that 'immoral law' is a contradiction in terms. Natural lawyers usually base their ideas of law on underlying religious beliefs and texts which are in the very literal sense sacrosanct, but this is not a necessity and opposition to specific law may be based on pure reason or political ideas.
- The other side can be characterised as 'legal positivists'. They argue that law has no necessary basis in morality and that it is simply impossible to assess law in terms of morality.

These issues feed into debates as to what is connoted by the rule of law, which will be considered in some detail in Chapter 2 of this text.

The Legal Enforcement of Morality: the Hart v Devlin Debate

This aspect of the law and morality debate may be reduced to the question: does the law have a responsibility to enforce a moral code, even where the alleged immorality takes place in private between consenting adults? Consider this example: in Britain there are over two million cohabiting gay couples. Homosexual sex was legalised in 1967 (for 21-year-olds, lowered to 18-year-olds in 1994), and consensual heterosexual anal intercourse was decriminalised by s 143 of the Criminal Justice and Public Order Act 1994. In British legal debate the moral issue was fought out in the 1960s by Lord Devlin and Professor HLA Hart. Devlin argued that 'the suppression of vice is as much the law's business as the suppression of subversive activities'. A shared morality, he argued, is the cement of society, without which there would be aggregates of individuals but no society. Hart argued that people should not be forced to adopt one morality for its own sake. He repudiated the claim that the loosening of moral bonds is the first stage of social disintegration, saying that there was no more evidence for that proposition than there was for Emperor Justinian's statement that homosexuality was the cause of earthquakes.

In any event it might be said that Hart 'won' the debate in the sense that it was his influence that led to the passing of the 1960s legislation liberalising the law on abortion, prostitution, homosexuality, and abolishing capital punishment. However, such issues can still arise – as was seen in the *Brown* case, considered later, and the ongoing issue of the 'rights' relating to assisted suicide as considered in *R (on the application of Purdy) v Director of Public Prosecutions* (2009).

The Morality of the Law Maker

One particular aspect of the debate that will be repeatedly highlighted in what follows is the way in which certain individuals, particularly judges, have the power not just to make and mould law, but to make and mould law in line with their own ideologies, i.e. their individual values, attitudes and prejudices – in other words their moralities.

> Morality *vis à vis* the law constitutes an external environment which inter-acts with the lawmaking process, not because law makers are blessed with divine insight into the 'general will', but rather because laws tend to be based on value-loaded information which percolates to the law-makers (*whose own individual values have a disproportionate influence upon the process*). [L Bloom-Cooper and G Drewry, *Law and Morality* (1976), p. xiv]

This issue is central to the Royal College of Nursing case considered in Chapter 3 and on the companion website at: www.routledge.com/cw/slapper.

1.3   CATEGORIES OF LAW

There are various ways of categorising law, which initially tend to confuse the non-lawyer and the new student of law. What follows will set out these categorisations in their usual dual form, while at the same time trying to overcome the confusion inherent in such duality. It is impossible to avoid the confusing repetition of the same terms to mean different things and, indeed, the purpose of this section is to make sure that students are aware of the fact that the same words can have different meanings, depending upon the context in which they are used.

1.3.1   COMMON LAW AND CIVIL LAW

In this particular juxtaposition, these terms are used to distinguish two distinct legal systems and approaches to law. The use of the term 'common law' in this context refers to all those legal systems that have adopted the historic English legal system. Foremost among these is, of course, the United States, but many other Commonwealth and former Commonwealth countries retain a common law system. The term 'civil law' refers to those other jurisdictions that have adopted the European continental system of law derived essentially from ancient Roman law, but owing much to the Germanic tradition.

The usual distinction to be made between the two systems is that the common law system tends to be case-centred and hence judge-centred, allowing scope for a discre-tionary, *ad hoc*, pragmatic approach to the particular problems that appear before the

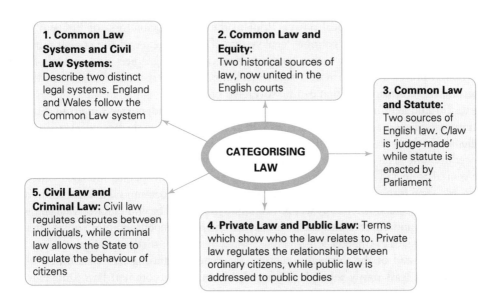

1. **Common Law Systems and Civil Law Systems:** Describe two distinct legal systems. England and Wales follow the Common Law system

2. **Common Law and Equity:** Two historical sources of law, now united in the English courts

3. **Common Law and Statute:** Two sources of English law. C/law is 'judge-made' while statute is enacted by Parliament

CATEGORISING LAW

5. **Civil Law and Criminal Law:** Civil law regulates disputes between individuals, while criminal law allows the State to regulate the behaviour of citizens

4. **Private Law and Public Law:** Terms which show who the law relates to. Private law regulates the relationship between ordinary citizens, while public law is addressed to public bodies

FIGURE 1.1 *Categorising Law.*

courts, whereas the civil law system tends to be a codified body of general abstract principles which control the exercise of judicial discretion. In reality, both of these views are extremes, with the former overemphasising the extent to which the common law judge can impose his discretion and the latter underestimating the extent to which continental judges have the power to exercise judicial discretion. It is perhaps worth mentioning at this point that the Court of Justice of the European Union (CJEU), established, in theory, on civil law principles, is in practice increasingly recognising the benefits of establishing a body of case law.

It has to be recognised, and indeed the English courts do so, that, although the CJEU is not bound by the operation of the doctrine of *stare decisis* (see below, 3.6) it still does not decide individual cases on an *ad hoc* basis and, therefore, in the light of a perfectly clear decision of the CJEU, national courts will be reluctant to refer similar cases to its jurisdiction. Thus, after the ECJ, as it was then referred to, decided in *Grant v South West Trains Ltd* (1998) that Community law, now referred to as Union law, did not cover discrimination on grounds of sexual orientation, the High Court withdrew a similar reference in *R v Secretary of State for Defence ex p Perkins (No 2)* (1998) (see below, 15.3, for a detailed consideration of the CJEU).

1.3.2 COMMON LAW AND EQUITY

In this particular juxtaposition, the terms refer to a particular division within the English legal system.

The common law has been romantically and inaccurately described as the law of the common people of England. In fact, the common law emerged as the product of a particular struggle for political power. Prior to the Norman Conquest of England in 1066, there was no unitary, national legal system. The emergence of the common law represents the imposition of such a unitary system under the auspices and control of a centralised power in the form of a sovereign king; in that respect, it represented the assertion and affirmation of that central sovereign power.

Traditionally, much play is made about the circuit of judges travelling round the country establishing the 'King's peace' and, in so doing, selecting the best local customs and making them the basis of the law of England in a piecemeal but totally altruistic procedure. The reality of this process was that the judges were asserting the authority of the central State and its legal forms and institutions over the disparate and fragmented State and legal forms of the earlier feudal period. Thus, the common law was common *to* all in application, but certainly was not common *from* all. (The contemporary meaning and relevance and operation of the common law will be considered in more detail later in this chapter and in Chapter 3.)

By the end of the thirteenth century, the central authority had established its precedence at least partly through the establishment of the common law. Originally, courts had been no more than an adjunct of the King's Council, the *Curia Regis*, but gradually the common law courts began to take on a distinct institutional existence in the form of the Courts of Exchequer, Common Pleas and King's Bench. With this institutional autonomy, however, there developed an institutional sclerosis, typified by a reluctance to deal with matters that were not, or could not be, processed in the proper *form of action*. Such a refusal to deal with substantive injustices because they did not fall within the particular parameters of procedural and formal constraints, by necessity, led to injustice and the need to remedy the perceived weaknesses in the common law system. The response was the development of *equity*.

Plaintiffs unable to gain access to the three common law courts might directly appeal to the sovereign, and such pleas would be passed for consideration and decision to the Lord Chancellor, who acted as the king's conscience. As the common law courts became more formalistic and more inaccessible, pleas to the Chancellor correspondingly increased and eventually this resulted in the emergence of a specific court constituted to deliver 'equitable' or 'fair' decisions in cases that the common law courts declined to deal with. As had happened with the common law, the decisions of the Courts of Equity established principles that were used to decide later cases, so it should not be thought that the use of equity meant that judges had discretion to decide cases on the basis of their personal idea of what was just in each case.

The division between the common law courts and the Courts of Equity continued until they were eventually combined by the Judicature Acts (JdA) 1873–75. Prior to this legislation, it was essential for a party to raise an action in the appropriate court – for example, the courts of law would not implement equitable principles; the Acts, however, provided that every court had the power and the duty to decide cases in line with common law and equity, with the latter being paramount in the final analysis.

Some would say that, as equity was never anything other than a gloss on common law, it is perhaps appropriate, if not ironic, that now both systems have been effectively subsumed under the one term: common law.

Common law remedies are available as of right. Remedies in equity are discretionary: in other words they are awarded at the will of the court and depend on the behaviour and situation of the party claiming such remedies. This means that, in effect, the court does not have to award an equitable remedy where it considers that the conduct of the party seeking such an award has been such that the party does not deserve it (*D & C Builders v Rees* (1965)).

1.3.3 COMMON LAW AND STATUTE LAW

This particular conjunction follows on from the immediately preceding section, in that the common law here refers to the substantive law and procedural rules that have been created by the judiciary through the decisions in the cases they have heard. Statute law, on the other hand, refers to law that has been created by parliament in the form of legislation. Although there has been a significant increase in statute law in the twentieth and twenty-first centuries, the courts still have an important role to play in creating and operating law generally and in determining the operation of legislation in particular. The relationship of this pair of concepts is of central importance and is considered in more detail in Chapter 3.

1.3.4 PRIVATE LAW AND PUBLIC LAW

Private law deals with relations between individuals with which the state is not directly concerned nor involved in. Public law, on the other hand, relates to the interrelationship of the state and the general population, in which the state itself is a participant. Somewhat confusingly, under the English legal system the state can enter into private law relationship with individuals, so the term public law is more accurately restricted to those aspects where the State is acting in a public capacity.

There are two different ways of understanding the division between private and public law. At one level, the division relates specifically to actions of the state and its functionaries vis-à-vis the individual citizen, and the legal manner in which, and form of law through which, such relationships are regulated: public law. In the nineteenth century, it was at least possible to claim, as AV Dicey did, that under the common law there was no such thing as public law in this distinct administrative sense and that the powers of the state with regard to individuals were governed by the ordinary law of the land, operating through the normal courts. Whether such a claim was accurate or not when it was made – and it is unlikely – there certainly can be no doubt now that public law constitutes a distinct and growing area of law in its own right. The growth of public law in this sense has mirrored the growth and increased activity of the contemporary state, and has seen its role as seeking to regulate such activity. The crucial role of judicial review in relation to public law will be considered in some detail in Section 10.5, and the content and impact of the Human Rights Act 1998 will be considered later in Chapter 2.

There is, however, a second aspect to the division between private and public law. One corollary of the divide is that matters located within the private sphere are seen as purely a matter for individuals themselves to regulate, without the interference of the state, whose role is limited to the provision of the forum for deciding contentious issues and mechanisms for the enforcement of such decisions. Matters within the public sphere, however, are seen as issues relating to the interest of the state and general public, and as such are to be protected and prosecuted by the state. It can be seen, therefore, that the category to which any dispute is allocated is of crucial importance to how it is dealt with. Contract may be thought of as the classic example of private law, but the extent to which this purely private legal area has been subjected to the regulation of public law, in such areas as consumer protection, should not be underestimated. Equally, the most obvious example of public law in this context would be criminal law. Feminists have argued, however, that the allocation of domestic matters to the sphere of private law has led to a denial of a general interest in the treatment and protection of women. By defining domestic matters as private, the state and its functionaries have denied women access to its power to protect themselves from abuse. In doing so, it is suggested that, in fact, such categorisation has reflected and maintained the social domination of men over women.

1.3.5   CIVIL LAW AND CRIMINAL LAW

Civil law is a form of private law and involves the relationships between individual citizens. It is the legal mechanism through which individuals can assert claims against others and have those rights adjudicated and enforced. The purpose of civil law is to settle disputes between individuals and to provide remedies; it is not concerned with punishment as such. The role of the state in relation to civil law is to establish the general framework of legal rules and to provide the legal institutions to operate those rights, but the activation of the civil law is strictly a matter for the individuals concerned. Contract, tort and property law are generally aspects of civil law.

Criminal law, on the other hand, is an aspect of public law and relates to conduct which the State considers with disapproval and which it seeks to control and/or eradicate. Criminal law involves the *enforcement* of particular forms of behaviour, and the state, as the representative of society, acts positively to ensure compliance. Thus, criminal cases are brought by the state in the name of the Crown and cases are reported in the form of *Regina v* . . . (*Regina* is simply Latin for 'queen' and case references are usually abbreviated to *R v* . . .) whereas civil cases are referred to by the names of the parties involved in the dispute, for example, *Smith v Jones*. In criminal law, a prosecutor prosecutes a defendant (or 'the accused'). In civil law, a claimant sues (or 'brings a claim against') a defendant.

In distinguishing between criminal and civil actions, it has to be remembered that the same event may give rise to both. For example, where the driver of a car injures someone through their reckless driving, they will be liable to be prosecuted under the Road Traffic legislation, but at the same time, they will also be responsible to the injured party in the civil law relating to the tort of negligence.

Standard of proof

A crucial distinction between criminal and civil law is the level of proof required in the different types of cases. In the criminal case, the prosecution is required to prove that the defendant is guilty beyond reasonable doubt, whereas in a civil case, the degree of proof is much lower and has only to be on the balance of probabilities. This difference in the level of proof raises the possibility of someone being able to succeed in a civil case, although there may not be sufficient evidence for a criminal prosecution. Indeed, this strategy has been used successfully in a number of cases against the police where the Crown Prosecution Service (CPS) has considered there to be insufficient evidence to support a criminal conviction for assault. A successful civil action may even put pressure on the CPS to reconsider its previous decision not to prosecute (see, further, below, 8.2, for an examination of the CPS). In June 2009 relatives of the victims of the Omagh bombing in Northern Ireland, which killed 29 people in 1998, won the right to take a civil case against members of the real IRA, following the failure of a criminal prosecution to secure any convictions. In approving the action the Judge in the case held that there was overwhelming evidence against four members of the terrorist group in relation to the atrocity.

Burden of proof

It is essential not to confuse the standard of proof with the burden of proof. The latter refers to the need for the person making an allegation, be it the prosecution in a criminal case or the claimant in a civil case, to prove the facts of the case. In certain circumstances, once the prosecution/claimant has demonstrated certain facts, the burden of proof may shift to the defendant/respondent to provide evidence to prove their lack of culpability. The reverse burden of proof may be either *legal* or *evidential*, which in practice indicates the degree of evidence they have to provide in order to meet the burden they are under.

It should also be noted that the distinction between civil and criminal responsibility is further blurred in cases involving what may be described as hybrid offences. These are situations where a court awards a civil order against an individual, but with the attached sanction that any breach of the order will be subject to punishment as a criminal offence. As examples of this procedure may be cited the Protection from Harassment

	Criminal law:	Civil law:
Courts:	Magistrates' and Crown Court	County Court and High Court
Aims:	Enforce standards of behaviour, protect, punish and rehabilitate	Resolve disputes between individuals
Outcomes:	Sentences include imprisonment and community service	To compensate for loss or harm caused
Terminology:	Prosecute, guilt, etc	Action, liability, etc
Standard of proof:	Beyond reasonable doubt	On the balance of probability
Procedure:	Arrest and charge by police, prosecution by CPS	Decision to bring an action made by claimant

FIGURE 1.2 *Differences between Criminal and Civil law.*

Act 1997 and the provision for the making of Anti-Social Behaviour Orders available under s 1(1) of the Crime and Disorder Act 1998. Both of these provisions are of considerable interest and deserve some attention in their own right. The Protection from Harassment Act was introduced as a measure to deal with 'stalking', the harassment of individuals by people continuously following them, and allowed the victim of harassment to get a court order to prevent the stalking. Whereas stalking may have been the high-profile source of the Act, it is possible, however, that its most useful provision, if it is used appropriately, may actually lie in providing more protection for women who are subject to assault and harassment from their partners than is available under alternative criminal or civil law procedures. In March 2001, a black clerk in a City of London police station used the Act successfully against *The Sun* newspaper in an action. The newspaper had published three articles about the woman after she had reported four police officers in her station for making racist comments about a Somali asylum seeker and as a consequence had received hate mail. The paper admitted that the articles were 'strident, aggressive and inflammatory' and the judge held that they were also racist. In his view, the Protection from Harassment Act gave the claimant 'a right to protection from harassment by all the world including the press'. The Court of Appeal subsequently refused an application by the newspaper to strike out the action (*Thomas v News Group Newspapers* (2001)) and consequently it can be concluded that the Act potentially offers significant protection to the ordinary members of the public who have been the object of what many see as press harassment. Such protection is, of course, additional to any other protection provided under the Human Rights Act 1998.

While there certainly is potential for the Protection from Harassment Act to be used positively, many have claimed that in practice it has been used in a repressive way to prevent otherwise legitimate demonstrations. Perhaps significantly, the definition of harassment was extended by s 125 of the Serious Organised Crime and Police Act (SOCPA) 2005, to include 'a course of conduct . . . which involves harassment of two or more persons'. And as conduct is defined as including speech, this means that a person need only address someone once to be considered to be harassing them, as long as they have also addressed someone else in the same manner. Another such allegedly antidemocratic provision is contained in s 132 of SOCPA.

Anti-social behaviour orders

Anti-social behaviour orders (ASBOs) were introduced under the Crime and Disorder Act 1998 and have been extended in the Police Reform Act (PRA) 2002 and the Anti-social Behaviour Act 2003. ASBOs are available against individuals aged 10 or over. Their purpose is to control and minimise persistent problematic behaviour that seriously inconveniences other individuals or communities. ASBOs are currently issued for a minimum period of two years but may remain in force 'until further notice'.

What amounts to anti-social behaviour is not defined in specific terms, but the sort of behaviour that is subject to this form of control includes, although it is not limited to:

● harassment of residents or passers-by;

● verbal abuse;

- criminal damage;
- vandalism;
- noise nuisance;
- writing graffiti;
- engaging in threatening behaviour in large groups;
- racial or homophobic abuse;
- smoking or drinking alcohol while under age;
- drug or alcohol abuse;
- begging;
- prostitution;
- kerb-crawling;
- throwing missiles;
- assault;
- vehicle crime.

An application for an ASBO is not made by individuals who are subjected to the anti-social behaviour, for the obvious reason that they might be subjected to further victimisation. It is the function of local authorities, police forces, including the British Transport Police, and registered social landlords to collect the evidence and put it to the magistrates' court. Initially the ASBO was a purely civil action distinct from, and an alternative to, criminal actions. However, the PRA 2002 introduced the possibility of such orders being made on conviction in criminal proceedings, in addition to, but separate from, any sentence imposed. The Serious Crime Act 2007 introduced the possibility of courts awarding Serious Crime Prevention Orders (SCPO). These civil behaviour orders were designed to be used against those involved in serious crime with the stated purpose of protecting the public by preventing, restricting or disrupting involvement in serious crime. Such orders could be made on application to the High Court, or the Crown Court upon conviction for a serious offence, and breach of the order is a criminal offence.

Subsequently, the Criminal Justice and Immigration Act (CJIA) 2008, amongst many changes (e.g. s 79 abolished the common law offences of blasphemy and blasphemous libel in England and Wales), introduced new control orders and powers in relation to anti-social behaviour. Thus Part 7 of the Act, ss 98 to 117, introduced the concept of the violent offender orders (VOO). As the name indicates, these orders, similar in effect to ASBOs and SCPOs, are imposed where it is '*necessary for the purpose of protecting the public from the risk of serious violent harm caused by the offender*' in addition to sentencing in the case of conviction for specific violent offences. The person to be made subject to such an order must be at least 18, have been convicted of a 'specified offence' and have received a sentence of at least one year in prison or a psychiatric hospital.

The 'specified offences' are manslaughter, attempted murder, conspiracy to murder and other violent offences under the Offences against the Person Act 1861.

Section 118 of the CJIA inserted a new Part 1A into the Anti-social Behaviour Act 2003, which made provision for closure orders in respect of premises associated with persistent disorder or nuisance. The provisions are similar to those in Part 1 of that Act, which relate to closure orders in respect of premises where Class A drugs are used unlawfully and permits police and local authorities to apply for a court order to close, for a period of three months, business or residential premises associated with anti-social behaviour in terms of 'significant and persistent disorder or persistent serious nuisance to members of the public'. It is an offence to remain in or re-enter the premises for the duration of the order.

R (on the application of McCann) v Manchester Crown Court

The exact legal categorisation of these orders and their consequences was considered by the House of Lords in two conjoined cases: *R (on the application of McCann) v Manchester Crown Court; Clingham v Kensington and Chelsea RLBC* (2002). The *McCann* case raised three related issues: the first related to the exact legal nature of the orders, whether they were civil in nature, as contended by the State, or criminal, as lawyers for the appellants argued. The answers to two further related questions depended upon the answer to that primary question. The first of these related to the difference in the way in which the rules of hearsay evidence operated in civil and criminal cases, with the former being less stringent than in criminal cases. The second related to the issue of what the appropriate standard of proof required to support the issuing of the order was: was it the civil law standard, on the balance of probabilities, or the criminal standard of beyond all reasonable doubt?

The House of Lords answered the questions as follows:

> Proceedings for an anti-social behaviour order were civil under domestic law. In support of this conclusion the court relied on a number of factors. Firstly, the Crown Prosecution Service was not involved in applications for the making of such an order as they were in criminal proceedings. Secondly, there was no need to show *mens rea*, or the guilty mind required to establish criminal liability. Thirdly, the issuing of the ASBO was not a penalty as such, as would be the outcome of a criminal case.

As the House found no contrary cases in the European Court of Human Rights it concluded that ASBO procedures could not be seen to be criminal for the purposes of Art 6 of the Human Rights Act 1998.

Following on from the first determination, that the proceedings were civil in nature, the Civil Evidence Act 1995 and the Magistrates' Courts (Hearsay Evidence in Civil Proceedings) Rules 1999 permitted the introduction of hearsay evidence. However, as regards the weight given to such evidence, that depended on the facts of each case, but its cumulative effect could be sufficient to support the issuing of the order.

As regards the issue of the standard of proof, however, the House held that the criminal standard should be applied. For the purposes of s 1(1)(a) of the Crime and Disorder Act, it would suffice for the magistrates '*to be sure*' that the defendant had acted in an anti-social manner. In the words of Lord Steyn '[the magistrates] must in all cases under section 1 apply the criminal standard ... it will be sufficient for the magistrates, when applying section 1(1)(a) to be sure that the defendant has acted in an anti-social manner, that is to say in a manner which caused or was likely to cause harassment, alarm, or distress to one or more persons not of the same household as himself.'

Lord Steyn went on to point out that when considering whether, for the purposes of s1(1)(b) of the Act, an order was necessary to protect persons from further anti-social acts, the magistrates needed only to exercise their judgment and no standard of proof was involved: 'it [was] an exercise of judgement or evaluation.'

Whereas these Acts may seem initially to offer a welcome additional protection to the innocent individual, it has to be recognised that such advantage is achieved in effect by criminalising what was, and remains, in other circumstances non-criminal behaviour, and deciding its applicability on the basis of the lower civil law burden of proof.

For more information on ASBOs and the related 'Acceptable Behaviour Contracts', reference can be made to the Home Office document 'A Guide to Antisocial Behaviour Orders and Acceptable Behaviour Contracts' available at http://webarchive. nationalarchives.gov.uk/20110220105210/http://rds.homeoffice.gov.uk/rds/antisocial1. html.

Anti-social behaviour orders have been subject to much criticism for the way they have been used in an attempt to define wider social problems as problems merely relating to social order. Of particular concern is the way that they and related orders are used to deal with political protestors, those suffering from mental health problems and young people generally.

As one commentator has put it:

The reality is that ASBOs are being used far beyond their initial remit of dealing with vandals and nuisance neighbours. Behaviour that is overtly non-criminal is being criminalised and society's vulnerable groups are being targeted. Increasingly it is behaviour that is different rather than 'antisocial' that is being penalised. The form such punishment takes is perhaps of even greater concern because ASBOs effectively bypass criminal law and operate within their own shadow legal system. In effect, we no longer need to break the law to go to jail. In this sense they typify a growing abandonment of the rule of law. [Max Rowlands, ECLN Essays no 9: 'The state of ASBO Britain – the rise of intolerance']

ASBO statistics

The Home Office provides detailed cumulative statistics on the operation of the ASBO regime on an annual basis. The most recent statistics available relate to the period 1 April to 31 December 2010 (http://www.homeoffice.gov.uk/publications/science-research-statistics/research-statistics/crime-research/asbo-stats-england-wales-2010/).

In relation to ASBOs issued, the statistics reveal that:

- During the period covered, a total of 20,335 ASBOs were issued. The highest number of ASBOs issued in any calendar year was 4,122 in 2005, since when there has been a year-on-year fall in the number issued, with 1,664 being issued in 2010 (Table 1).
- Since 1 June 2003, 86 per cent of ASBOs have been issued to males, 17,396 as against 2,835 issued to females (Table 2).
- Since 2004, more ASBOs have been issued following conviction for a criminal offence rather than following a simple application. Thus in 2010, 58.2 per cent of ASBOs were issued following a conviction for a criminal offence (Table 3).

As regards breaches of ASBOs, the statistics show that:

- There have been a total of 51,976 separate breaches of ASBOs during the period covered. However, it should be noted that individual ASBOs tend to be breached on numerous occasions, on average 4.5 times (Table 10).
- The breach rate (by year of issue) shows that on average 29.2 per cent of ASBOs are breached within the year of issue.
- The rate of breaches shows a steady decrease over time from 2003. Thus in 2003, 69.6 per cent of ASBOs issued were breached at least once. However, during 2010 only 30.6 per cent of ASBOs issued were breached (Table 16b).
- Immediate custodial sentences were given to 6,007 offenders for breaches of ASBOs with an average custodial sentence length of 5.2 months (Table 13).

As with many of the previous government's initiatives, the ASBO and its related orders did not find favour with the newly elected coalition government and in July 2010 the Home Secretary, Theresa May, announced her wish to see ASBOs replaced by simpler sanctions that would be easier to obtain and to enforce and that, where possible, 'should be rehabilitating and restorative, rather than criminalising and coercive'.

In February 2011 the Home Office announced its proposals, which included:

- The Criminal Behaviour Order, a civil order available on conviction for any offence, that it could be given to anyone over the age of criminal responsibility and would replace the CRASBO. The Criminal Behaviour Order would be additional to the court's sentence for the offence, not a substitute for it.
- The Crime Prevention Injunction, a civil court order that agencies can secure quickly to stop an individual's anti-social behaviour. As a civil order it would be issued on the civil rather than the criminal standard of proof, i.e. the balance of probabilities. However, any subsequent breach of the CPI would need to be proved 'beyond reasonable doubt'. Although such a breach would not be a criminal offence and would not result in a criminal record, the consequences of breaking it could result in an action for contempt of court, if the CPI was issued in the County

Court. CPIs could include both prohibitions on behaviour and positive requirements to address underlying issues, and would replace a range of current orders.

The Home Office indicated its ongoing commitment to the reform of the ASBO regime in the criminal justice White Paper, 'Putting victims first: more effective responses to antisocial behaviour', which it issued in May 2012 (http://www.official-documents.gov.uk/document/cm83/8367/8367.asp).

The White Paper continued the drive to reduce the existing 19 distinct anti-social behaviour orders to just six, including the Criminal Behaviour Order and the Crime Prevention Injunction as set out in the original proposals. The White Paper also proposed the introduction of a 'community trigger' to ensure that the public had the power to demand that appropriate authorities take action in the event of a complaint about anti-social behaviour. Although there was no proposal to spell out in legislation exactly how local areas should implement such a trigger, the scheme to be piloted by Manchester City Council and Greater Manchester was cited as a possible indication of how it would work. Under the Manchester scheme, the threshold for the trigger will be behaviour causing 'harassment, alarm and distress', based on either:

- three or more complaints from one individual about the same problem, where no action has been taken; or
- five individuals complaining about the same problem where no action has been taken by relevant agencies.

Victims will be able to activate the trigger through a simple online form (accessible on all relevant authorities' websites), by letter or by telephone, describing the anti-social behaviour they are experiencing, and when it was previously reported. They will receive an acknowledgement within 24 hours, setting out a clear timeline for the response. If the complaint meets the threshold, a single lead professional will pool information from all the relevant authorities to build up a full picture of the case and identify any action that could resolve the problem, including support for the victim(s). The Chair of the Community Safety Partnership will then reply to the complainant, setting out what agencies propose to do.

A further example of the relationship between criminal law and civil law may be seen in the courts' power to make an order for the confiscation of a person's property under the Proceeds of Crime Act 2002 (see below, at 2.5.1.1).

Private prosecutions
It should not be forgotten that although prosecution of criminal offences is usually the prerogative of the State, it remains open to the private individual to initiate a private

prosecution in relation to a criminal offence. It has to be remembered, however, that even in the private prosecution, the test of the burden of proof remains the criminal one requiring the facts to be proved beyond reasonable doubt. An example of the problems inherent in such private actions can be seen in the case of Stephen Lawrence, the young black man who was gratuitously stabbed to death by a gang of white racists whilst standing at a bus stop in London. Although there was strong suspicion, and indeed evidence, against particular individuals, the CPS declined to press charges against them on the basis of insufficiency of evidence. When the lawyers of the Lawrence family mounted a private prosecution against the suspects, the action failed for want of sufficient evidence to convict. As a consequence of the failure of the private prosecution, the rule against double jeopardy meant that the accused could not be retried for the same offence at any time in the future, even if the police subsequently acquired sufficient new evidence to support a conviction. The report of the Macpherson Inquiry into the manner in which the Metropolitan Police dealt with the Stephen Lawrence case gained much publicity for its finding of 'institutional racism' within the service, but it also made a clear recommendation that the removal of the rule against double jeopardy be considered. Subsequently, a Law Commission report recommended the removal of the double jeopardy rule and provision to remove it, under particular circumstances and subject to strict regulation, was contained in ss 75–79 of the Criminal Justice Act 2003.

In September 2010 two men, Gary Dobson and David Norris, were arrested for the murder of Stephen Lawrence. Dobson had been one of the people originally charged in the private prosecution, but the Court of Appeal held that there was sufficient new scientific evidence to justify a retrial under the Criminal Justice Act 2003. Following another review of the scientific evidence, and the discovery of new and substantial evidence, Dobson and Norris were prosecuted in 2011 and convicted of Stephen Lawrence's murder (3rd January 2012).

In considering the relationship between civil law and criminal law, it is sometimes thought that criminal law is the more important in maintaining social order, but it is at least arguable that, in reality, the reverse is the case. For the most part, people come into contact with the criminal law infrequently, whereas everyone is continuously involved with civil law, even if it is only the use of contract law to make some purchase. The criminal law of theft, for example, may be seen as simply the cutting edge of the wider and more fundamental rights established by general property law. In any case, there remains the fact that civil and criminal law each has its own distinct legal system. The nature of these systems will be considered in detail in later chapters. The structure of the civil courts is considered in Chapter 4 and that of the criminal courts in Chapter 6.

1.4 APPROACHES TO LAW AND LEGAL STUDY

There are a number of possible approaches to the study of law, each of which has its own implications for how law is understood, located and studied.

1.4.1   BLACK LETTER LAW

The first is the traditional/formalistic approach. This 'black letter' approach to law, as it is commonly referred to, is posited on the existence of a discrete legal universe as the object of study. It is concerned with establishing a knowledge of the specific legal rules that regulate social activity. The essential point in relation to this approach is that study tends to be restricted to the sphere of the legal without reference to the social activity to which the legal rules are applied.

However, as well as learning the law in the foregoing sense as simply a body of rules and principles and techniques to be mastered, it is important to learn something *about* law. The reason for this and the justification for this course is that law is considerably more than just the trade of lawyers.

1.4.2   CONTEXTUALISM

The second approach to the study of law is the contextualist approach. This is by far the most common approach to law in modern academic institutions, and the intention behind it is to recognise that law is a *social* phenomenon and operates within a social context. Society requires particular tasks to be undertaken, be it the maintenance of order or the regulation of economic activity, and it is the function of *law* to perform those tasks.

The move from the black letter approach to the contextualist one involves an important shift in emphasis. No longer is law seen as simply a matter to be explained and justified in its own terms. It no longer constitutes its own discrete universe, but is analysed and perhaps more importantly it can actually be assessed within its socio-economic context and its performance can be evaluated in relation to the supposed purposes within that socioeconomic context.

1.4.3   CRITICAL LEGAL THEORY

The contextualist approach may therefore be seen as an advance on the sterile legalism of the black letter approach to the extent that it takes cognisance of, and seeks to accommodate human behaviour within, the real world. I would suggest, however, that there is still one major shortcoming in its approach. True, it seeks to place law in its context, but what exactly is the context into which law is to be fitted? In our particular society the context is, and without any pejorative overtones, advanced capitalism. The difficulty with the contextualist approach is that it tends to take that particular context for granted; as a given, the assumed, unproblematic, and to that extent unquestioned, background in relation to which law has to operate. To that extent the concern of the contextualist is still the *legal* regulation of particular behaviour, without any great detailed consideration of the actual behaviour to which the legal rules are addressed.

It is only a third type of approach to the study of law that attempts to remedy that shortcoming in the contextualist approach; that third type of approach, and the one espoused by this particular text, is the critical/theoretical approach to law. From this latter perspective, not only is law in context an object of study, but equally, if not more essentially, the context within which law functions is itself an object of study. Neither law nor its social context is taken for granted, and the actual social relations and activity to which law is applied are examined in order to try to account for the existence of law in the first place.

In our society, as has been stated previously, law appears to, and does, play an important part in the creation and maintenance of social order, its centrality being typified in the very phrase 'law and order', with its underlying suggestion that the two go together, with the latter, order, depending on the existence of the former, law. We must be aware, however, that law, as we know it, is not the only means of creating order. [Even in our society order is not solely dependent on law, and we are not continuously having recourse to the courts in order to solve our problems.]

Critical legal study is concerned with seeking a general explanation of the form of order, but more particularly it is concerned with a search for the explanation of why our society has developed its particular form of *legal* order. In stressing the contribution that law makes to determining what we accept as order in our society, we are implicitly asserting the point that there can be no single universal idea of order, but rather that there are different versions of order. The version operating in our society, an order essentially shaped by law, is but one specific type of order; it is both culturally and historically specific to our present society.

Whichever approach one adopts to legal study – and each is valid within its own terms – will depend not just upon the individual student's approach and the ideological framework they operate within, but also the area of law that the student wishes to research. Some projects may be open to a merely expository analysis, while others, by the very nature of the subject, will demand a more critical analysis and explanation.

1.5   SKILLS

At the centre of any law student's course will be the law library, although, increasingly, paper-based resources are being supported by internet and other electronic sources. As well as general academic skills, law students need to develop particular skills relating to the finding and reading of legal texts. They are also required to develop the specific skills of writing legal essays and answering problem questions. The online Legal Skills Guide website that supports this text encourages the development of such skills, see at www. routledge.com/cw/slapper.

THE STUDY OF LAW

The study of law is not just a matter of learning rules. It is a general misconception that learning the law is about learning a mass of legal rules. Critical, analytical thought should inform the work of the good student.

THE NATURE OF LAW

Legal systems are particular ways of establishing and maintaining social order. Law is a formal mechanism of social control. Studying the English legal system involves considering a fundamental institution in our society.

CATEGORIES OF LAW

Law may be categorised in a number of ways, although the various categories are not mutually exclusive.

Common law and civil law relate to distinct legal systems. The English legal system is a common law one as opposed to continental systems, which are based on civil law.

Common law and equity distinguish the two historical sources and systems of English law. Common law emerged in the process of establishing a single legal system throughout the country. Equity was developed later to soften the formal rigour of the common law. The two systems are now united, but in the final analysis, equity should prevail.

Common law and statute relate to the source of law. Common law is judge made; statute law is produced by parliament.

Private law and public law relate to whom the law is addressed. Private law relates to individual citizens, whereas public law relates to institutions of government.

Civil law and criminal law distinguish between law, the purpose of which is to facilitate the interaction of individuals and law that is aimed at enforcing particular standards of behaviour.

APPROACHES TO LEGAL STUDY

Students of law can adopt a number of distinct approaches to legal study. Prominent among these are the traditional 'black letter' approach, the more evaluative 'contextualist' approach or the more radical 'critical legal studies' approach.

SKILLS

This textbook is supported by a Legal Skills Guide that can be found at www.routledge.com/cw/slapper skills. There you can improve the skills you'll need to be a successful law student, and ultimately a successful lawyer.

1.   When asked to think of a law, most people immediately think of that archetypal public form of law, criminal law. However, although important, that is only one aspect of law and one that doesn't affect most people in the way that other elements of the law do. Most people can go through a day without the criminal law impinging on them, but it is almost certain that they will enter into contractual relationships, even if it is only riding on a bus or buying a sandwich. Equally the private law of property structures our society and is essential to its operation. Consider what other areas of law have an impact on how our society functions. If you are studying for a law degree, think of all the legal subjects you might possibly study.

2.   Consider the relationship between law and morality. Is there any underpinning moral basis to law?

3.   Consider the relationship of law and society and the following questions:

      Does law exist independently of society?

      Does law create society or does society create law?

      Is law simply a matter of legal rules and legal reasoning?

      What does law actually do?

4.   Consider the roles of a law student, lawyer, judge:

      What essential skills are required to perform these roles satisfactorily?

      Do these skills differ, and if so, why?

FURTHER READING

Barnett, H, *Constitutional and Administrative Law*, 9th edn, 2011, Abingdon: Routledge

Bradney, A *et al, How to Study Law*, 5th edn, 2005, London: Sweet & Maxwell

Clinch, P, *Using a Law Library*, 2nd edn, 2001, London: Blackstone

Fitzpatrick, P (ed), *Dangerous Supplements*, 1991, London: Pluto

Mansfield, M, *Memoirs of a Radical Lawyer*, Bloomsbury, 2009

Slapper, G, and Kelly, D, *Questions and Answers on the English Legal System*, 2012 & 2013, Abingdon: Routledge

Susskind, R, *The End of Lawyers?*, 2009, Oxford: OUP

SOCIAL AND LEGAL ORDER

Mansell, W and Meteyard, B, *A Critical Introduction to Law*, 3rd edn, 2004, London: Cavendish Publishing

Roberts, S, *Order and Dispute*, 1979, Harmondsworth: Penguin

LEGAL LANGUAGE

Friedman, L, 'On interpretation of laws' (1988) 11(3) Ratio Juris 252

Goodrich, P, *Reading the Law*, 1986, Oxford: Basil Blackwell

Jackson, B, *Making Sense in Law*, 1995, London: Deborah Charles

The constant impingement of legal issues on all aspects of social and individual life should be tracked and explored at:

www.bbc.co.uk
www.guardian.co.uk
www.timesonline.co.uk
www.independent.co.uk
www.ft.com
www.intute.ac.uk/socialsciences/law

A free online service that helps you to find the best web resources for your studies and research.
www.ukcle.ac.uk/index.html
The website for the UK Centre for Legal Education.

www.justice.gov.uk
The official website of the Ministry of Justice.

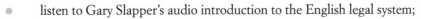

Now visit the companion website to:

- listen to Gary Slapper's audio introduction to the English legal system;
- test your understanding of the key terms using our Flashcard Glossary;
- revise and consolidate your knowledge of 'Law and legal study' using our Multiple Choice Question testbank;
- view all of the links to the Useful Websites above;
- access legal news from around the world via a feed from the Lawdit reading room;
- access the supporting Legal Skills Guide, which discusses eight key skills.

www.routledge.com/cw/slapper

THE RULE OF LAW AND HUMAN RIGHTS

2.1 INTRODUCTION

This chapter considers two concepts that are not always, or indeed usually, dealt with in English Legal System textbooks: the two interrelated concepts are 'the rule of law' and 'human rights'. However, it is the contention of the authors that ideas about the rule of law and human rights are, and always should have been, at the core of our understanding and assessment of any, and certainly our own, legal system, and further that they are assuming a more apparent and increased centrality and importance in relation to its operation and justification. However, it has to be recognised from the outset that any consideration of the specific ideas inherent in these general concepts cannot be approached satisfactorily from the purely 'black letter' legal perspective, but must engage the student in a related consideration of the socio-political context from which they derive and to which they relate and on which they operate. Further, the concepts themselves are fluid and as will be seen, different commentators have adopted widely varying approaches to them.

2.2 THE RULE OF LAW

The 'rule of law' represents a symbolic ideal against which proponents of widely divergent political persuasions measure and criticise the shortcomings of contemporary state practice. This varied recourse to the rule of law is, of course, only possible because of the lack of precision in the actual meaning of the concept; its meaning tends to change over time and, as will be seen below, to change in direct correspondence with the beliefs of those who claim its support and claim, in turn, to support it. It is undeniable that the form and content of law and legal procedure have changed substantially in the course of the twentieth and twenty-first centuries. It is usual to explain such changes as being a consequence of the way in which, and the increased extent to which, the modern state intervenes in everyday life, be it economic or social. As the state increasingly took over the regulation of many areas of social activity, it delegated wide-ranging discretionary powers to various people and bodies in an attempt to ensure the successful implementation of its policies. The assumption and delegation of such power on the part of the state brought it into potential conflict with previous understandings of the rule of law, which had entailed a strictly limited ambit of state activity. The impact of this on the understanding and operation of the principle of the rule of law and its implications in relation to the judiciary are traced out below and will be returned to in Chapter 9.

Some might consider that it is not appropriate to have a section such as this in a textbook on the English legal system and that its proper place would be in a text on constitutional law or legal theory. However, it is essential to appreciate the central importance of the concept of the rule of law to the whole structure and operation of the English legal system. The fundamental nature of the concept of the rule of law is and always has been central, although perhaps implicit, in all the aspects of the legal system that are considered in this text. However, the Constitutional Reform Act 2005 has for the first time recognised this centrality in the form of a statutory provision. As s 1 of the Act simply and clearly states, it does not adversely affect:

(a)   the existing constitutional principle of the rule of law, or
(b)   the Lord Chancellor's existing constitutional role in relation to that principle.

This very point was taken up by the former most senior judge in the House of Lords, the late Lord Bingham, whose speech on the issue will be considered in detail below.

As has been stated, although the idea of the rule of law is difficult to give a substantive definition of, that has not prevented a number of legal and social theorists from attempting to do just that. However, as will be seen and as has already been hinted at, the various explanations of what is, or should be, understood by the concept differ considerably and are different in accord with the socio-political approach adopted by the individual writers.

2.2.1 AV DICEY

According to AV Dicey in *An Introduction to the Study of the Law of the Constitution* (1885), the UK had no such thing as administrative law as distinct from the ordinary law of the land. Whether he was correct or not when he expressed this opinion – and there are substantial grounds for doubting the accuracy of his claim even at the time he made it – it can no longer be denied that there is now a large area of law that can be properly called administrative, that is, related to the pursuit and application of particular state policies, usually within a framework of statutory powers.

According to the notoriously chauvinistic Dicey, the rule of law was one of the key features that distinguished the English constitution from its Continental counterparts. Whereas foreigners were subject to the exercise of arbitrary power, the Englishman was secure within the protection of the rule of law. Dicey suggested the existence of three distinct elements, which together created the rule of law as he understood it:

An absence of arbitrary power on the part of the state: the extent of the state's power, and the way in which it exercises such power, is limited and controlled by law. Such control is aimed at preventing the state from acquiring and using wide discretionary powers, for, as Dicey correctly recognised, the problem with discretion is that it can be exercised in an arbitrary manner, and that above all else is to be feared, at least as Dicey would have us believe.

Equality before the law: the fact that no person is above the law, irrespective of rank or class. This was linked with the fact that functionaries of the state are subject to the same law and legal procedures as private citizens.

Supremacy of ordinary law: the fact that the English constitution was the outcome of the ordinary law of the land and was based on the provision of remedies by the courts rather than on the declaration of rights in the form of a written constitution.

It is essential to recognise that Dicey was writing at a particular historical period but, perhaps more importantly, he was writing from a particular political perspective that saw the maintenance of *individual* property and *individual* freedom to use that property as one chose as paramount. He was opposed to any increase in state activity in the pursuit of collective interests. In analysing Dicey's version of the rule of law, it can be seen that it venerated *formal* equality at the expense of *substantive* equality. In other words, he thought that the law and the state should be blind to the real concrete differences that exist between people, in terms of wealth or power or connection, and should treat them all the same, as possessors of *abstract* rights and duties.

There is an unaddressed, and certainly unresolved, tension in Dicey's work. The rule of law was only one of two fundamental elements of the English polity; the other was parliamentary sovereignty. Where, however, the government controls the legislative process, the sovereignty of parliament is reduced to the undisputed supremacy of central government. The tension arises from the fact that, whereas the rule of law was aimed at controlling arbitrary power, parliament could, within this constitutional structure, make provision for the granting of such arbitrary power by passing appropriate legislation.

This tension between the rule of law and parliamentary sovereignty is peculiar to the British version of liberal government. Where similar versions of government emerged on the Continent, and particularly in Germany, the power of the legislature was itself subject to the rule of law. This subordinate relationship of state to law is encapsulated in the concept of the *Rechtsstaat*.

This idea of the *Rechtsstaat* meant that the state itself was controlled by notions of law, which limited its sphere of legitimate activity. Broadly speaking, the state was required to institute general law and could not make laws aimed at particular people.

The fact that this strong *Rechtsstaat* version of the rule of law never existed in England reflects its particular history. The revolutionary struggles of the seventeenth century had delivered effective control of the English state machinery to the bourgeois class, who exercised that power through parliament. After the seventeenth century, the English bourgeoisie was never faced with a threatening state against which it had to protect itself; it effectively was the state. On the Continent, this was not the case and the emergent bourgeoisie had to assert its power against, and safeguard itself from, the power of a state machinery that it did not control. The development of *Rechtsstaat* theory as a means of limiting the power of the state can be seen as one of the ways in which the Continental bourgeoisie attempted to safeguard its position. In England, however, there was not the same need in the eighteenth and nineteenth centuries for the bourgeoisie to protect itself behind a *Rechtsstaat* version of the rule of law. In England, those who

benefited from the enactment and implementation of general laws as required by
Rechtsstaat theory – the middle classes – also effectively controlled parliament and could
benefit just as well from its particular enactments. Thus, in terms of nineteenth-century
England, as Franz Neumann stated, the doctrines of parliamentary sovereignty and the
rule of law were not antagonistic, but complementary.

2.2.2 FA VON HAYEK

FA von Hayek followed Dicey in seeing the essential component of the rule of law as
being the absence of arbitrary power in the hands of the state. As Hayek expressed it in
his book *The Road to Serfdom* (1971):

> Stripped of all technicalities the Rule of Law means that government in all
> its actions is bound by rules fixed and announced beforehand.

Hayek, however, went further than Dicey in setting out the form and, at least in a
negative way, the content that legal rules had to comply with in order for them to be
considered as compatible with the rule of law. As Hayek expressed it:

> The Rule of Law implies limits on the scope of legislation, it restricts it to the
> kind of general rules known as formal law; and excludes legislation directly
> aimed at particular people.

This means that law should not be particular in content or application, but should be
general in nature, applying to all and benefiting none in particular. Nor should law
be aimed at achieving particular goals: its function is to set the boundaries of personal
action, not to dictate the course of such action.

Hayek was a severe critic of the interventionist state in all its guises, from the
fascist right wing to the authoritarian left wing and encompassing the contemporary
welfare state in the middle. His criticism was founded on two bases:

Efficiency: from the microeconomic perspective – and Hayek was an economist
– only the person concerned can fully know all the circumstances of their situation. The
state cannot wholly understand any individual's situation and should, therefore, as a
matter of efficiency leave it to the individuals concerned to make their own decisions
about what they want or how they choose to achieve what they want, so long as it is
achieved in a legal way.

Morality: from this perspective, to the extent that the state leaves the individual
less room to make individual decisions, it reduces their freedom.

It is apparent, and not surprising considering his Austrian background, that
Hayek adopted a *Rechtsstaat* view of the rule of law. He believed that the meaning of the

rule of law, as it was currently understood in contemporary English jurisprudence, represented a narrowing from its original meaning, which he believed had more in common with *Rechtsstaat* than it presently did. As he pointed out, the ultimate conclusion of the current weaker version of the rule of law was that, so long as the actions of the state were duly authorised by legislation, any such act was lawful, and thus a claim to the preservation of the rule of law could be maintained. It should be noted that Hayek did not suggest at any time that rules enacted in other than a general form are not laws; they are legal, as long as they are enacted through the appropriate and proper mechanisms; they simply are not in accordance with the rule of law as he understood that principle.

Hayek disapproved of the change he claimed to have seen in the meaning of the rule of law. It is clear, however, that, as with Dicey, his views on law and the meaning of the rule of law were informed by a particular political perspective. It is equally clear that what he regretted most was the replacement of a free market economy by a planned economy, regulated by an interventionist state. The contemporary state no longer simply provided a legal framework for the conduct of economic activity, but was actively involved in the direct coordination and regulation of economic activity in the pursuit of the goals that it set. This had a profound effect on the form of law. Clearly stated and fixed general laws were replaced by open-textured discretionary legislation. Also, whereas the Diceyan version of the rule of law had operated in terms of abstract rights and duties, formal equality and formal justice, the new version addressed concrete issues and addressed questions of substantive equality and justice.

Hayek's views in relation to law and economics were extremely influential on conservative political thinking in the last quarter of the twentieth century and, in particular, on the Conservative government of Margaret Thatcher, which was elected in 1979 with the overt policy of reducing the impact and influence of the central state on economic activity and individuals. Thatcher was famous/infamous for, amongst other things, her declaration that there was no such thing as society, 'only individuals and families'.

2.2.3   EP THOMPSON

The rule of law is a mixture of implied promise and convenient vagueness. It is vagueness at the core of the concept that permits the general idea of the rule of law to be appropriated by people with apparently irreconcilable political agendas in support of their particular political positions. So far, consideration has been given to Dicey and Hayek, two theorists on the right of the political spectrum who saw themselves as proponents and defenders of the rule of law; however, a similar claim can be made from the left. The case in point is EP Thompson, a Marxist historian, who also saw the rule of law as a protection against, and under attack from, the encroaching power of the modern state.

Thompson shared Hayek's distrust of the encroachments of the modern state and he was equally critical of the extent to which the contemporary state intervened in the day-to-day lives of its citizens. From Thompson's perspective, however, the problem arose not so much from the fact that the state was undermining the operation of the market economy, but from the way in which the state used its control over the legislative process to undermine civil liberties in the pursuit of its own concept of public interest.

In *Whigs and Hunters* (1975), a study of the manipulation of law by the landed classes in the eighteenth century, Thompson concluded that the rule of law is not just a necessary means of limiting the potential abuse of power, but that:

> . . . the Rule of Law, itself, the imposing of effective inhibitions upon power and the defence of the citizen from power's all-intrusive claims, seems to me an unqualified human good.

In reaching such a conclusion, Thompson clearly concurs with Hayek's view that there is more to the rule of law than the requirement that law be processed through the appropriate legal institutions. He too argued that the core meaning of the rule of law involved more than mere procedural propriety and suggested that the other essential element is the way, and the extent to which, it places limits on the exercise of state power.

2.2.4 JOSEPH RAZ

Some legal philosophers have recognised the need for state intervention in contemporary society and have provided ways of understanding the rule of law as a means of controlling discretion without attempting to eradicate it completely. Joseph Raz ('The Rule of Law and its virtue' (1977) 93 LQR 195), for example, recognised the need for the government of men as well as laws, and that the pursuit of social goals may require the enactment of particular, as well as general, laws. Indeed, he suggested that it would be impossible in practical terms for law to consist solely of general rules. Raz even criticised Hayek for disguising a political argument as a legal one in order to attack policies of which he did not approve. Yet, at the same time, Raz also saw the rule of law as essentially a negative value, acting to minimise the danger that could follow the exercise of discretionary power in an arbitrary way. In that respect, of seeking to control the exercise of discretion, he shares common ground with Thompson, Hayek and Dicey.

Raz claimed that the basic requirement from which the wider idea of the rule of law emerged is the requirement that the law must be capable of guiding the individual's behaviour. He stated some of the most important principles that may be derived from this general idea:

> Laws should be prospective rather than retroactive. People cannot be guided by or expected to obey laws that have not as yet been introduced. Laws should also be open and clear to enable people to understand them and guide their actions in line with them.

Laws should be stable and should not be changed too frequently as this might lead to confusion as to what was actually covered by the law.

There should be clear rules and procedures for making laws.

The independence of the judiciary has to be guaranteed to ensure that they are free to decide cases in line with the law and not in response to any external pressure.

The principles of natural justice should be observed, requiring an open and fair hearing to be given to all parties to proceedings.

The courts should have the power to review the way in which the other principles are implemented to ensure that they are being operated as demanded by the rule of law.

The courts should be easily accessible as they remain at the heart of the idea of making discretion subject to legal control.

The discretion of the crime preventing agencies should not be allowed to pervert the law.

It is evident that Raz saw the rule of law being complied with if the procedural rules of law-making were complied with, subject to a number of safeguards. It is of no little interest that Raz saw the courts as having an essential part to play in his version of the rule of law. This point will be considered further in section 10.5 in relation to judicial review.

2.2.5   ROBERTO UNGER

In *Law and Modern Society* (1976), the American critical legal theorist Roberto Unger set out a typology of social order, one category of which is essentially the rule of law system. Unger distinguished this form of social order from others on the basis of two particular and unique characteristics. The first of these is *autonomy*: the fact that law has its own sphere of authority and operates independently within that sphere without reference to any external controlling factor. Unger distinguished four distinct aspects of legal autonomy, which may be enumerated as follows:

> *substantive autonomy*: this refers to the fact that law is not explicable in other, non-legal terms. To use the tautological cliché – the law is the law. In other words, law is self-referential, it is not about something else; it cannot be reduced to the level of a mere means to an end, it is an end in itself;
>
> *institutional autonomy*: this refers to the fact that the legal institutions such as the courts are separate from other state institutions and are high-lighted in the fundamental principle of judicial independence;

> *methodological autonomy*: this refers to the fact that law has, or at least lays claim to having, its own distinct form of reasoning and justifications for its decisions;
>
> *occupational autonomy*: this refers to the fact that access to law is not immediate, but is gained through the legal professions, who act as gatekeepers and who exercise a large degree of independent control over the working of the legal system.

The second distinguishing feature of legal order, according to Unger, is its *generality*: the fact that it applies to all people without personal or class favouritism. Everyone is equal under the law and is treated in the same manner.

In putting forward this typology of social order, Unger recognised the advantages inherent in a rule of law system over a system that operates on the basis of arbitrary power, but he was ultimately sceptical as to the reality of the equality that such a system supports and questioned its future continuation. The point of major interest for this book, however, is the way in which each of the four distinct areas of supposed autonomy is increasingly being challenged and undermined, as will be considered at the end of the next section.

2.2.6 MAX WEBER

Unger saw the development of the rule of law as a product of Western capitalist society and, in highlighting the distinct nature of the form of law under that system, he may be seen as following the German sociologist Max Weber. Weber's general goal was to examine and explain the structure and development of Western capitalist society. In so doing, he was concerned with those unique aspects of that society which distinguished it from other social formations. One such distinguishing characteristic was the form of law that he characterised as a formally rational system, which prefigured Unger's notion of legal autonomy (see Weber, *Wirtschaft und Gesellschaft* (trans 1968)).

Weber's autonomous legal system was accompanied by a state that limited itself to establishing a clear framework of social order and left individuals to determine their own destinies in a free market system. In the course of the twentieth century, however, the move from a free market to a basically planned economy, with the state playing an active part in economic activity, brought about a major change in both the form and function of law.

2.2.7 THE RULE OF LAW AND THE CONTEMPORARY FORM OF LAW

While the state remained apart from civil society, its functions could be restricted within a limited sphere of activity circumscribed within the doctrine of the rule of law. However, as the state became increasingly involved in actually regulating economic activity, the form of law had by necessity to change. To deal with problems as and when they arose, the state had to assume discretionary powers rather than be governed by fixed predetermined rules. Such discretion, however, is antithetical to the traditional idea of the rule of law, which was posited on the fact of limiting the state's discretion. Thus emerged the tension between the rule of law and the requirements of regulating social activity that FA von Hayek, for one, saw as a fundamental change for the worse in our society.

With specific regard to the effect of this change on law's previous autonomy, there is clear agreement among academic writers that there has been a fundamental alteration in the nature of law. Whereas legislation previously took the form of fixed and precisely stated rules, now legislation tends be open-textured and to grant wide discretionary powers to particular state functionaries, resulting in a corresponding reduction in the power of the courts to control such activity. The courts have resisted this process to a degree, through the expansion of the procedure for judicial review, but their role in the area relating to administration remains at best questionable. The growth of delegated legislation, in which parliament simply passes enabling Acts, empowering ministers of state to make regulations, as they consider necessary, is a prime example of this process (considered in detail in section 3.5). In addition, once made, such regulations tend not to be general but highly particular, even technocratic, in their detail.

The increased use of tribunals with the participation of non-legal experts rather than courts to decide disputes, with the underlying implication that the law is not capable of resolving the problem adequately, also represents a diminishment in law's previous power, as does the use of planning procedures as opposed to fixed rules of law in determining decisions. (Tribunals will be considered in Chapter 12.)

Legislation also increasingly pursues substantive justice rather than merely limiting itself to the provision of formal justice as required under the rule of law. As an example of this, consumer law may be cited: thus, in the Unfair Contract Terms Act 1977, contract terms are to be evaluated on the basis of reasonableness and, under the Consumer Credit Act 1974, agreements may be rejected on the basis of their being extortionate or unconscionable. Such provisions actually override the market assumptions as to formal equality in an endeavour to provide a measure of substantive justice.

All the foregoing examples of a change can be characterised as involving a change from 'law as end in itself' to 'law as means to an end'. In Weberian terms, this change in law represents a change from *formal rationality*, in which law determined outcomes to problems stated in the form of legal terms through the application of abstract legal concepts and principles, to a system of *substantive rationality*, where law is simply a mechanism to achieve a goal set outside of law.

In other words, law is no longer seen as completely autonomous as it once was. Increasingly, it is seen as merely instrumental in the achievement of some wider purpose, which the state, acting as the embodiment of the general interest, sets. Paradoxically, as will be seen later, even when the law attempts to intervene in this process, as it does through judicial review, it does so in a way that undermines its autonomy and reveals it to be simply another aspect of political activity.

The return to a more Hayekian, free-market-based economy and polity since the election of the Thatcher Conservative government in 1979, and its continuation by all other governments, of whatever persuasion, since then has certainly changed the rhetoric and ideology about the relationship of the individual and the state. Whether it has changed the reality of state action in relation to individuals, and the role of law in mediating that relationship, is a matter of doubt and debate, especially in light of the emergence of the threat of terrorist activity. The immediate actions and proposals of the current Conservative/Liberal Democrat coalition government, such as their much-heralded 'bonfire of the quangos', appear to signal their intention to pursue the practical reduction of state intervention interference, with a corresponding passage of power to market mechanisms, although the actual results remain to be seen and assessed.

2.3   THE RULE OF LAW AND THE JUDICIARY

The commentators considered above came from a variety of academic backgrounds, but the essential practical importance of the concept of the rule of law was highlighted in a speech delivered by the former most senior Law Lord, the late Lord Bingham of Cornhill, in November 2006 under the deceptively simple title 'The Rule of Law' (the sixth *Sir David Williams Lecture* delivered at the Centre for Public Law at the University of Cambridge).

As has already been indicated, the Constitutional Reform Act (CRA) 2005 provides, in s 1, that the Act does not adversely affect 'the existing constitutional principle of the rule of law' or 'the Lord Chancellor's existing constitutional role in relation to that principle'. That provision is further reflected in the oath to be taken by Lord Chancellors under s 17(1) of the Act, to respect the rule of law and defend the independence of the judiciary. However, as Lord Bingham pointed out, the Act does not actually define what is meant by the rule of law, or indeed the Lord Chancellor's role in relation to it. He also recognised the difficulty in fixing a single meaning or in fact any substantive content to the principle, citing various different academic references to it, some of which have been considered above, but nonetheless he felt it appropriate to offer his own understanding of the rule of law.

In Lord Bingham's view, the authors of the 2005 Act apparently also recognised the difficulty of formulating a succinct and accurate definition suitable for inclusion in a statute, and consequently left the task of definition to the courts, if and when the occasion arose. The importance of such a task of definition cannot be underestimated for it places an essential duty on, and considerable power in the hands of, the judiciary. If, as the CRA recognises, the rule of law is an existing constitutional principle, then the judges will be required to construe statutes in relation to that principle in such a way as to ensure that they do not infringe that constitutional principle. A further implication of the CRA is that the Lord Chancellor's conduct, in relation to role and duty to the rule of law, would be open to judicial review, were he to be challenged in that regard. As the rule of law already is an existing constitutional principle of the UK and one that may be more contentious in the future, it becomes imperative to attempt to define what it actually means. It is this task that Lord Bingham sets himself in the lecture under consideration and he suggests that at its core is the idea that 'all persons and authorities within the state, whether public or private, should be bound by and entitled to the benefit of laws publicly and prospectively promulgated and publicly administered in the courts'.

Bingham rests his basic understanding on John Locke's dictum that 'Wherever law ends, tyranny begins'. Yet, even in that regard, he demurs by admitting that in some proceedings justice can only be done if they are *not* dealt with in public.

However, the main importance is the detail that Lord Bingham introduces through his consideration of the eight implications, or sub-rules, that he holds are particular aspects of the general principle of the rule of law. These sub-rules are:

- The law must be accessible and so far as possible intelligible, clear and predictable.

The reasoning behind this requirement is that if everyone is bound by the law they must be able without undue difficulty to find out what it is, even if that means taking advice from their lawyers. Equally the response should be sufficiently clear that a course of action can be based on it. However, for this to be achieved, there has to be an end to what Lord Bingham refers to as the 'legislative hyperactivity which appears to have become a permanent feature of our governance'. This excessive legislation, exacerbated by baffling parliamentary draftsmanship, is particularly problematic in relation to the 'torrent of criminal legislation', not all of which is 'readily intelligible'.

However, Lord Bingham does not leave his fellow judges in doubt about their responsibilities in the creation of legal uncertainty and criticises 'the length, complexity and sometimes prolixity of modern common law judgments, particularly at the highest level'. However, on consideration he rejects the supposed benefit of single opinion decisions in the House of Lords, with only one judgment and four decisions in agreement with that, in favour of multiple judgments 'where the well-considered committee of five or more, can bring to bear a diversity of professional and jurisdictional experience which is valuable in shaping the law.'

As Lord Bingham saw it, the benefit of multiple decisions in shaping the law was, however, subject to the three caveats:

(i)   whatever the diversity of opinion the judges should recognise a duty, not always observed, to try *to ensure that there is a clear majority ratio*. Without that, no one can know what the law is until Parliament or a later case lays down a clear rule.

(ii) excessive innovation and adventurism by judges had to be avoided. Without challenging the value or legitimacy of judicial development of the law, taken to extremes, such judicial creativity can itself destroy the rule of law.

(iii) all these points apply with redoubled force in the criminal field with the conclusion that judges should create new offences or widen existing offences so as to make punishable conduct that was not previously subject to punishment.

- Questions of legal right and liability should ordinarily be resolved by application of the law and not the exercise of discretion.

Lord Bingham does not share Dicey's complete antipathy to the exercise of discretion, and cites immigration law as an example where it has been advantageous. Nonetheless he does believe that the essential truth of Dicey's insight stands and that 'the broader and more loosely-textured a discretion is, *whether conferred on an official or a judge*, the greater the scope for subjectivity and hence for arbitrariness, which is the antithesis of the rule of law'. However, he is satisfied that the need for discretion to be narrowly defined, and its exercise to be capable of reasoned justification, are requirements which UK law almost always satisfies.

- The laws of the land should apply equally to all, save to the extent that objective differences justify differentiation.

However, if the law is to apply to all, then governments should also accept the converse, that the rule of law does not allow for any distinction between British nationals and others. Unfortunately, the second part of the reciprocal link did not appear to have been considered when parliament passed Part 4 of the Anti-terrorism, Crime and Security Act 2001, which was held to be incompatible with the Human Rights Act in the *Belmarsh* cases (see 2.5.2).

- The law must afford adequate protection of fundamental human rights.

This sub-rule goes beyond the formalistic approaches of both Dicey and Raz to insist that the rule of law does in fact connote a substantive content, although Lord Bingham is less certain as to the particular detail of that content. In response to Raz he states:

> A state which savagely repressed or persecuted sections of its people could not in my view be regarded as observing the rule of law, even if the transport of the persecuted minority to the concentration camp or the compulsory exposure of female children on the mountainside were the subject of detailed laws duly enacted and scrupulously observed. So to hold would, I think, be to strip the existing constitutional principle affirmed by section 1 of the 2005 Act of much of its virtue and infringe the fundamental compact which, as I shall suggest at the end, underpins the rule of law.

But he also recognises that this is a difficult area and that there is not even a standard of human rights universally agreed among 'so-called' civilised nations. However, although he admits to this element of vagueness about the content of this sub-rule, he maintains that 'within a given state there will ordinarily be a measure of agreement on where the lines are to be drawn, and in the last resort (subject in this country to statute) the courts are there to draw them'.

Consequently, the rule of law must require the legal protection of such human rights as are recognised in that society.

- Means must be provided for resolving, without prohibitive cost or inordinate delay, bona fide civil disputes which the parties themselves are unable to resolve.

As a corollary of the principle that everyone is bound by and entitled to the benefit of the law is the requirement that people should be able, in the last resort, to go to court to have their rights and liabilities determined. In stating this sub-rule Lord Bingham makes it clear that he is not seeking to undermine arbitration, which he sees as supremely important, rather he is looking to support the provisions of a properly funded legal aid scheme, the demise of which he clearly regrets, as may be seen from the following:

Whether conditional fees, various pro bono schemes and small claims procedures have filled the gap left by this curtailment I do not myself know. Perhaps they have, and advice and help are still available to those of modest means who deserve it. But I have a fear that tabloid tales of practitioners milking the criminal legal aid fund of millions, and more general distrust of lawyers and their rewards, may have enabled a valuable guarantee of social justice to wither unlamented.

Lord Bingham is equally concerned about the fact that successive governments have insisted that the civil courts, judicial salaries usually aside, should be self-financing: the cost of running the courts being covered by fees recovered from litigants. The danger with such an approach is that the cost of going to court in order to get redress may preclude some people from gaining access to the legal system.

- Ministers and public officers at all levels must exercise the powers conferred on them reasonably, in good faith, for the purpose for which the powers were conferred and without exceeding the limits of such powers.

As Lord Bingham saw it:

> The historic role of the courts has of course been to check excesses of executive power, a role greatly expanded in recent years due to the increased complexity of government and the greater willingness of the public to challenge governmental (in the broadest sense) decisions. Even under our constitution the separation of powers is crucial in guaranteeing the integrity of the courts' performance of this role.

This judicial role has of course been met through judicial review.

However, Lord Bingham is conscious, and unarguably so it would appear, of a shift away from the traditional relationship of the courts and the executive, under which the convention was that ministers, however critical of a judicial decision, and exercising their right to appeal against it or, in the last resort, legislate to reverse it retrospectively, did not engage in any public attack on the judiciary. In a muted, although nonetheless threatening, rejoinder to the present government Lord Bingham states his view that:

> This convention appears to have worn a little thin in recent times, as I think unfortunately, since if ministers make what are understood to be public attacks on judges, *the judges may be provoked to make similar criticisms of ministers*, and the rule of law is not, in my view, well served by public dispute between two arms of the state.

●   Adjudicative procedures provided by the state should be fair.

The rule of law would seem to require no less. The general arguments in favour of open hearings are familiar, summed up on this side of the Atlantic by the dictum that justice must manifestly and undoubtedly be seen to be done and on the American side by the observation that 'Democracies die behind closed doors'.

While he sees application of this sub-rule to ordinary civil processes to be largely unproblematic, he does recognise that there is more scope for difficulty where a person faces adverse consequences as a result of what he is thought or said to have done or not done, whether in the context of a formal criminal charge or in other contexts such as deportation, precautionary detention, recall to prison or refusal of parole. The question in those circumstances is what does fairness ordinarily require? Lord Bingham's first response to the question is that, first and foremost, decisions must be taken by adjudicators who are:

> independent and impartial: independent in the sense that they are free to decide on the legal and factual merits of a case as they see it, free of any extraneous influence or pressure, and impartial in the sense that they are, so far as humanly possible, open-minded, unbiased by any personal interest or partisan allegiance of any kind.

But additionally a second element is involved, which relates to the presumption that any issue should not be finally decided against a person until they have had an adequate opportunity for their response to the allegation to be heard. In effect this means that:

> a person potentially subject to any liability or penalty should be adequately informed of what is said against him; that the accuser should make adequate disclosure of material helpful to the other party or damaging to itself; that where the interests of a party cannot be adequately protected without the benefit of professional help which the party cannot afford, public assistance should so far as practicable be afforded; that a party accused should have an adequate opportunity to prepare his answer to what is said against him; and that the innocence of a defendant charged with criminal conduct should be presumed until guilt is proved.

In the context of criminal law this raises two pertinent issues:

(i) *Disclosure* This relates to material in the possession of the prosecutor, which they are for reasons of public interest unwilling to disclose to the defence. As the law stands at present, material need not be disclosed if in no way helpful to the defence; if helpful to the point where the defence would be significantly prejudiced by non-disclosure, the prosecutor must either disclose the material or abandon the prosecution.

(ii) *Reverse burden of proof* Some statutory offences place a reverse burden on the defendant; i.e. the defendant has to show that they did not commit the offence alleged. In Lord Bingham's opinion such reversals in the normal burden of proof are 'not in themselves objectionable, but may be so if the burden is one which a defendant, even if innocent, may in practice be unable to discharge'.

However, of much more concern to Lord Bingham in this regard was the increase in the instances, outside the strictly criminal sphere, in which parliament has provided that the full case against a person, put before the adjudicator as a basis for decision, should not be disclosed to that person or indeed to their legal representative. One example of this procedure is of course the non-derogation control orders issued under the Prevention of Terrorism Act 2005. A further inroad in relation to this issue is to be found in the provisions of the Justice and Security Bill 2012 (see p 73). In his Rule of Law lecture he expressed the view that:

Any process which denies knowledge to a person effectively, if not actually, accused of what is relied on against him, and thus denies him a fair opportunity to rebut it, must arouse acute disquiet. But these categories reflect the undoubted danger of disclosing some kinds of highly sensitive information, and they have been clearly identified and regulated by Parliament, which has judged the departure to be necessary and attempted to limit its extent.

In *SSHD v E* (2007) he was required to provide a practical consideration of and decision in relation to the concerns raised above.

- The existing principle of the rule of law requires compliance by the state with its obligations in international law.

This particular section of Lord Bingham's lecture is interesting for the indirect way in which he examines the involvement of the UK in the ongoing war in Iraq, while as he said 'not for obvious reasons touch[ing] on the vexed question whether Britain's involvement in the 2003 war on Iraq was in breach of international law and thus, if this sub-rule is sound, of the rule of law'.

The way he achieved this was through a comparison between the procedures followed in 2003 and those followed at the time of the Suez invasion of 1956. While he concluded that the comparison suggests that over the period the rule of law has gained ground in the UK, it also allowed him to make some pointed comments in relation to the way the current war was initiated. In this regard he considered the different roles assumed by the law officers in both situations, and while he welcomed the involvement of the Attorney General in providing legal advice to the government, he raised doubts about to whom the Attorney General ultimately owed his duty – the government, as the then Attorney General had seen it, or the public at large, which Lord Bingham, personally, appears to support, as is evident from the following passage (the role of the Attorney General will be considered further at 9.3.2):

There seems to me to be room to question whether the ordinary rules of client privilege, appropriate enough in other circumstances, should apply to a law officer's opinion on the lawfulness of war: it is not unrealistic in my view to regard the public, those who are to fight and perhaps die, rather than the government, as the client . . . [a]nd the case for full, contemporaneous, disclosure seems to me even stronger when the Attorney General is a peer, not susceptible to direct questioning in the elected chamber.

In conclusion Lord Bingham correlated the rule of law with a democratic society based on 'an unspoken but fundamental bargain between the individual and the state, the governed and the governor, by which both sacrifice a measure of the freedom and power which they would otherwise enjoy. The individual living in society implicitly accepts that he or she cannot exercise the unbridled freedom enjoyed by Adam in the Garden of Eden, before the creation of Eve, and accepts the constraints imposed by laws properly made because of the benefits which, on balance, they confer. The state for its part accepts that it may not do, at home or abroad, all that it has the power to do but only that which laws binding upon it authorise it to do. If correct, this conclusion is reassuring to all of us who, in any capacity, devote our professional lives to the service of the law. For it means that we are not, as we are sometimes seen, mere custodians of a body of arid prescriptive rules but are, with others, the guardians of an all but sacred flame which animates and enlightens the society in which we live'. – A true Lockean view of the rule of law if there ever was one.

2.3.1 THE SEPARATION OF POWERS

Inherent in Lord Bingham's speech is a tension between the judges and the other elements in the constitution – the executive/government and parliament – with Lord Bingham seeing the role of the judges as protecting the society from unlawful inroads into its liberties and rights. This tension has been heightened by the enactment of the Human Rights Act 1998, to be considered in the following section; however, before that can be done it is necessary to examine the concept of the separation of powers and related concepts such as parliamentary sovereignty and judicial independence. Although the idea of the separation of powers can be traced back to ancient Greek philosophy, it was advocated in early modern times by the English philosopher Locke and the later French philosopher Montesquieu, and found its practical expression in the constitution of the United States. The idea of the separation of powers is posited on the existence of three distinct functions of government (the legislative, executive and judicial functions) and the conviction that these functions should be kept apart in order to prevent the centralisation of too much power. Establishing the appropriate relationship between the actions of the state and the legal control over those actions crucially involves a consideration of whether there is any absolute limit on the authority of the government of the day. Answering that question inevitably involves an examination of the general constitutional structure of the UK and, in particular, the inter-relationship of two doctrines: parliamentary sovereignty and judicial independence. It also requires an understanding of the role of judicial review and the effect of the Human Rights Act 1998, and has caused no little friction between the judiciary and the executive, especially in the person of the Home Secretary.

There is, in any case, high judicial authority for claiming that the separation of powers is an essential element in the constitution of the UK (see *R v Hinds* (1979), p 212, in which Lord Diplock, while considering the nature of different Commonwealth constitutions in a Privy Council case, stated that 'It is taken for granted that the basic principle of the separation of powers will apply . . .'). In any case, the point of considering the doctrine at this juncture is simply to highlight the distinction and relationship between the executive and the judiciary and to indicate the possibility of conflict between the two elements of the constitution. This relationship assumes crucial importance if one accepts, as some have suggested, that it is no longer possible to distinguish the executive from the legislature as, through its control of its majority in the House of Commons, the executive (that is, the government) can legislate as it wishes and in so doing, can provide the most arbitrary of party political decisions with the form of legality. The question to be considered here is to what extent the judiciary can legitimately oppose the wishes of the government expressed in the form of legislation, or to what extent they can interfere with the pursuit of those wishes. As will be seen below, the power of the judiciary in relation to legislative provisions has been greatly enhanced by the passage of the Human Rights Act 1998.

The Separation of Powers and the Constitutional Reform Act 2005

The details of this major constitutional reform Act will be considered in detail in due course, but it cannot be denied that the force that drove the government to introduce the Act was an understanding of the imperatives of the separation of powers and the wish to regularise the constitution of the United Kingdom within that framework. Consequently, the anomalous position of the Lord Chancellor, who was a member of all three branches of the political structure, was to be resolved and the House of Lords, as the supreme court, was to be removed from its location within the legislative body.

2.3.2 PARLIAMENTARY SOVEREIGNTY

As a consequence of the victory of the parliamentary forces in the English revolutionary struggles of the seventeenth century, parliament became the sovereign power in the land. The independence of the judiciary was secured, however, in the Act of Settlement 1701. The centrality of the independence of the judges and the legal system from direct control or interference from the state in the newly established constitution was emphasised in the writing of John Locke, who saw it as one of the essential reasons for, and justifications of, the social contract on which the social structure was assumed to be based. It is generally accepted that the inspiration for Montesquieu's *Spirit of Law* (*De L'Esprit des Lois*) was the English constitution, but if that is truly the case, then his doctrine of the separation of powers was based on a misunderstanding of that constitution, as it failed to take account of the express *superiority of parliament* in all matters, including its relationship with the judiciary and the legal system.

It is interesting that previous conservative thinkers have suggested that the whole concept of parliamentary sovereignty is itself a product of the self-denying ordinance of the common law. Consequently, they suggested that it was open to a subsequent, more robust judiciary, confident in its own position and powers within the developing constitution, to reassert its equality with the other two elements of the polity. Just such an approach may be recognised as implicit in a number of the judgments of the augmented nine-person House of Lords in *Jackson v HM Attorney General* (2005). The case concerned the use of the Parliament Acts to pass legislation banning hunting with dogs, and in that respect it will be considered in detail at 3.3, but in doing so it by necessity raised, without the requirement to deal definitively with, the essential constitutional question as to the relationship of the courts and parliament. While the majority of the judges, at the least, express reservations as to the power of the House of Commons under the Parliament Acts, the most overtly challenging statement can be seen in the judgment of Lord Steyn. His view of parliamentary sovereignty may be deduced from the following passage, in which he considers the argument of the Attorney General that the application of the Parliament Acts effectively is subject to no limitation:

> If the Attorney General is right the 1949 Act could also be used to introduce oppressive and wholly undemocratic legislation . . . The classic account given by Dicey of the doctrine of the supremacy of Parliament, pure and absolute as it was, can now be seen to be out of place in the modern United Kingdom. Nevertheless, the supremacy of Parliament is still the *general* principle of our constitution. It is a construct of the common law. The judges created this principle. If that is so, it is not unthinkable that circumstances could arise where the courts may have to qualify a principle established on a different hypothesis of constitutionalism. In exceptional circumstances involving an attempt to abolish judicial review or the ordinary role of the courts, the Appellate Committee of the House of Lords or a new Supreme Court may have to consider whether this is a constitutional fundamental which even a sovereign Parliament acting at the behest of a complaisant House of Commons cannot abolish.

Lord Steyn's reasoning was subsequently questioned, and the traditional view of parliamentary sovereignty was reasserted by the former Master of the Rolls and current President of the Supreme Court, Lord Neuberger, in his Weedon Lecture in April 2011. As he put it:

> Ultimately, it might be said that Lord Steyn's point that the courts had invented Parliamentary sovereignty and could therefore remove or qualify it involves an intellectual sleight of hand: Parliamentary sovereignty *was acknowledged* rather than *bestowed* by the courts. They acknowledged what had been clearly established by civil war, the Glorious Revolution of 1688, the Bill of Rights 1689 and the Act of Settlement 1701 (emphasis added).

Lord Neuberger went on:

> [Parliament] can, if it chooses, and clearly and expressly states that it is so doing, enact legislation which is contrary to the rule of law . . . neither the Convention nor the Human Rights Act goes nowhere near to imposing a limit on Parliamentary legal sovereignty.
>
> It is true that membership of the Convention imposes obligations on the state to ensure that judgments of the Strasbourg court are implemented, but those obligations are in international law, not domestic law. And, ultimately, the implementation of a Strasbourg, or indeed a domestic court judgment is a matter for Parliament. If it chose not to implement a Strasbourg judgment, it might place the United Kingdom in breach of its treaty obligations, but as a matter of domestic law there would be nothing objectionable in such a course. It would be a political decision, with which the courts could not interfere.

European Union Act 2011

In September 2011, Parliament passed the European Union Act 2011. The main purpose of the Act was to make provision for the application of the post-Lisbon treaties. However, s 18 of the Act, for the first time, places the common law principle of parliamentary sovereignty on a statutory footing and states that all EU law takes effect in the UK only by virtue of the will of Parliament, as provided in the ECA 1972. The issue of parliamentary sovereignty in relation to the European Union will be considered at 15.1.1.

2.3.3 JUDICIAL INDEPENDENCE

The exact meaning of 'judicial independence' became a matter of debate when some members and ex-members of the senior judiciary suggested that the former Conservative Lord Chancellor, Lord Mackay of Clashfern, had adopted a too restrictive interpretation of the term, which had reduced it to the mere absence of interference by the executive in the trial of individual cases. They asserted the right of the legal system to operate independently, as an autonomous system apart from the general control of the state, with the judiciary controlling its operation, or at least being free from the dictates and strictures of central control.

According to Lord Mackay, in the first of his series of Hamlyn lectures entitled 'The Administration of Justice' (1994):

> The fact that the executive and judiciary meet in the person of the Lord Chancellor should symbolise what I believe is necessary for the administration of justice in a country like ours, namely, a realisation that both the

judiciary and the executive are parts of the total government of the country with functions that are distinct but which must work together in a proper relationship if the country is to be properly governed . . . It seems more likely that the interests of the judiciary in matters within the concerns covered by the Treasury are more likely to be advanced if they can be pursued within government by a person with a lifetime of work in law and an understanding of the needs and concerns of the judiciary and who has responsibility as Head of the Judiciary, than if they were to be left within government as the responsibility of a minister with no such connection with the judiciary.

The tension inherent in the relationship between the courts and the executive government took on a more fundamental constitutional aspect with the passing of the Human Rights Act 1998. By means of that Act, the courts were given the right to subject the actions and operations of the executive and, indeed, all public authorities to the gaze and control of the law, in such a way as to prevent the executive from abusing its power. If the Human Rights Act represented a shift in constitutional power towards the judiciary, the Act was nonetheless sensitive to maintain the doctrine of parliamentary sovereignty. In the United States, with its written constitution, the judiciary in the form of The Supreme Court has the power to declare the Acts of the legislature unconstitutional and consequently invalid. No such power was extended to the UK courts under the Human Rights Act, although some commentators saw the Human Rights Act as eventually leading to a similar outcome in the UK. Such tension was further heightened when, in June 2003, the government announced its intention to radically alter the constitution, and the judges' role within it, at an apparent single stroke by the expedient of removing the role of Lord Chancellor.

Given the judiciary's suspicion of Lord Mackay as Lord Chancellor, it is not a little ironic that the government's announcement of its intention to abolish the position of Lord Chancellor was met by strong judicial reaction, in language very similar to that used by that former holder of the office. The judges, supported by many parliamentarians and commentators, made it absolutely clear that they thought that their independence would best be protected by a strong, legally qualified, champion within the cabinet. Such a role had been performed by the Lord Chancellor. Consequently, the judiciary generally regretted, not to say resisted, the abolition of the office as originally provided for in the Constitutional Reform Bill 2003. Although such resistance succeeded in retaining the office of the Lord Chancellor, its functions were greatly reduced and s 2 of the Constitutional Reform Act of 2005 provides that the holder of the office should be 'qualified by experience', which need not include legal experience. Neither will the holder of the office necessarily sit in the House of Lords. However, in recognition of the sensitivities of the judiciary, s 3 of the Act, for the first time, places a legal duty on government ministers to uphold the independence of the judiciary and specifically bars them from trying to influence judicial decisions through any special access to judges.

When Gordon Brown replaced Tony Blair as Prime Minister in the summer of 2007, the resulting Cabinet reshuffle resulted in the abolition of the Department for Constitutional Affairs and its being replaced by a new Justice Ministry headed by Jack Straw, who also replaced Lord Falconer as Lord Chancellor, although remaining a member of the House of Commons. The new ministry, which is ultimately responsible for looking after the interests of the judiciary and courts, also assumed responsibility for the prison service, which caused the judges great concern as they feared that their allocation from the joint ministerial budget would be under pressure from the ever-expanding prison budget.

Following the General Election of 2010, the new coalition Justice Minister was the extremely experienced MP Kenneth Clarke QC, although his experience did not save him from being replaced in the Cabinet reshuffle in September 2012. The current minister is Chris Grayling, who is the first non-lawyer to hold the office of Lord Chancellor.

In July 2007 the House of Lords Select Committee on the Constitution issued an extensive, and certainly not uncritical, report entitled 'Relations between the executive, the judiciary and Parliament'. As its title suggests, the report focused on the these fundamental constitutional issues in the context of the rule of law generally and in the light of the particular changes introduced by the Human Rights Act, Constitutional Reform Act and the replacement of the Department for Constitutional Affairs by the new Justice Ministry. The report may be located at www.parliament.uk/hlconstitution/, the government's response at www.justice.gov.uk/publications/response-relations.htm and the judiciary's reply at http://www.judiciary.gov.uk/Resources/JCO/Documents/Consultations/const_committee_response.pdf.

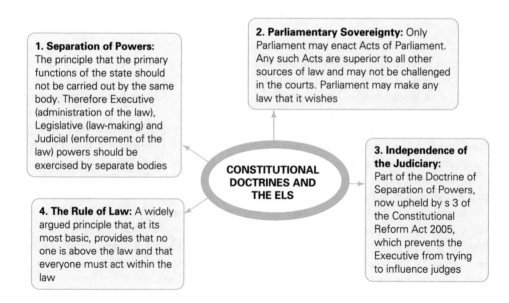

1. Separation of Powers: The principle that the primary functions of the state should not be carried out by the same body. Therefore Executive (administration of the law), Legislative (law-making) and Judicial (enforcement of the law) powers should be exercised by separate bodies

2. Parliamentary Sovereignty: Only Parliament may enact Acts of Parliament. Any such Acts are superior to all other sources of law and may not be challenged in the courts. Parliament may make any law that it wishes

3. Independence of the Judiciary: Part of the Doctrine of Separation of Powers, now upheld by s 3 of the Constitutional Reform Act 2005, which prevents the Executive from trying to influence judges

4. The Rule of Law: A widely argued principle that, at its most basic, provides that no one is above the law and that everyone must act within the law

CONSTITUTIONAL DOCTRINES AND THE ELS

FIGURE 2.1 *Constitutional Doctrines and the English Legal System.*

2.4   HUMAN RIGHTS DISCOURSE AND THE RULE OF LAW

In an article published in the *London Review of Books* and *The Guardian* newspaper in May 1995, three years before the enactment of the Human Rights Act, the High Court judge, as he then was, Sir Stephen Sedley, made explicit the links and tensions between the doctrine of the rule of law and the relationship of the courts and the executive, and the implications for the use of judicial review as a means of controlling the exercise of executive power. In his view:

> Our agenda for the 21st century is not necessarily confined to choice between a 'rights instrument' interpreted by a judiciary with a long record of illiberal adjudication, and rejection of any rights instrument in favour of Parliamentary government. The better government becomes, the less scope there will be for judicial review of it.
>
> But, for the foreseeable future, we have a problem: how to ensure that as a society we are governed within a law which has internalised the notion of fundamental human rights. Although this means adopting the Rule of law, like democracy, as a higher-order principle, we do have the social consensus which alone can accord it that primacy. And, if in our own society the Rule of law is to mean much, *it must at least mean that it is the obligation of the courts to articulate and uphold the ground rules of ethical social existence which we dignify as fundamental human rights* . . . There is a potential tension between the principle of democratic government and the principle of equality before the law . . . The notion that the prime function of human rights and indeed the Rule of law is to protect the weak against the strong is not mere sentimentality. It is the child of an era of history in which equality of treatment and opportunity has become perceived . . . as an unqualified good, and of a significant recognition that you do not achieve equality merely by proclaiming it . . . fundamental human rights to be real, have to steer towards outcomes which invert those inequalities of power that mock the principle of equality before the law.

Such talk of fundamental human rights denies the absolute sovereignty of parliament in its recognition of areas that are beyond the legitimate exercise of state power. It also recognises, however, that notions of the rule of law cannot be satisfied by the provision of merely formal equality as Dicey and Hayek would have it and previous legal safeguards would have provided. For Sedley, the rule of law clearly imports, and is based on, ideas of substantive equality that market systems and legal formalism cannot provide and in fact undermine. His version of the rule of law clearly involves a reconsideration of the relationship of the executive and the judiciary, and involves the latter in a further reconsideration of their own previous beliefs and functions.

2.5   THE HUMAN RIGHTS ACT 1998

As is evident in the quotation from Sir Stephen Sedley above, some judges, at least, saw their role in maintaining the rule of law as providing protection for fundamental human rights. In attempting to achieve this end, they faced a particular problem in relation to the way in which the unwritten English constitution was understood, and was understood to operate. The freedom of individual action in English law was not based on ideas of positive human rights which could not be taken away, but on negative liberties: that is, individual subjects were entitled to do whatever was not forbidden by the law. This was particularly problematic when it was linked to the doctrine of the sovereignty of parliament, which, in effect, meant that parliament was free to restrict, or indeed remove, individual liberties at any time merely by passing the necessary legislation.

It is generally accepted that the courts developed the procedure of judicial review, as an aspect of the rule of law, in an attempt to protect individuals from the excesses of an over-powerful executive (see below, at 10.5, for a detailed consideration). But, in so doing, they were limited in what they could achieve by the very nature of the procedure available to them. They could not directly question the laws produced by parliament on the basis of substance, as constitutional courts in other systems could, but were restricted essentially to questioning the formal or procedural proprieties of such legislation. There was, however, an alternative forum capable of challenging the substance of English law, and one that was based on the assumption of positive rights rather than negative liberties. That forum was the European Court of Human Rights (ECtHR).

It has to be established and emphasised from the outset that the substance of this section has absolutely nothing to do with the European Union as such; the Council of Europe is a completely distinct organisation and, although membership of the two organisations overlap, they are not the same. The Council of Europe is concerned not with economic matters, but with the protection of civil rights and freedoms (the nature of these institutions and the operation of the ECtHR will be considered in detail in Chapter 15).

The UK was one of the initial signatories to the European Convention on Human Rights and Fundamental Freedoms (hereafter the ECHR) in 1950, which was instituted in postwar Europe as a means of establishing and enforcing essential human rights. In 1966, the UK recognised the power of the European Commission on Human Rights to hear complaints from individual UK citizens and, at the same time, recognised the authority of the ECtHR to adjudicate in such matters. It did not, however, at that time incorporate the ECHR into UK law.

The consequence of non-incorporation was that the Convention could not be directly enforced in English courts. In *R v Secretary of State for the Home Department ex p Brind* (1991), the Court of Appeal decided that ministerial directives did not have to be construed in line with the ECHR, as that would be tantamount to introducing the ECHR into English law without the necessary legislation. UK citizens were therefore in the position of having to pursue rights, which the state endorsed, in an external forum rather than through their own court system and, in addition, having to exhaust the domestic judicial procedure before they could gain access to that external forum. Such a situation was extremely unsatisfactory, and not just for complainants under the ECHR. Many members of the judiciary, including the then Lord Chief Justice Lord Bingham, were in favour of incorporation, not merely on general moral grounds, but equally on the ground that they resented having to make decisions in line with UK law which they knew full well would be overturned on appeal to the European Court. Equally, there was some discontent that the decisions in the European Court were being taken, and its general jurisprudence was being developed, without the direct input of the UK legal system. The courts, however, were not completely bound to decide cases in presumed ignorance of the ECHR, and did what they could to make decisions in line with it. For example, where domestic statutes were enacted to fulfil ECHR obligations, the courts could, of course, construe the meaning of the statute in the light of the ECHR. It was also possible that, due to the relationship of the ECHR with European Community law, the courts could find themselves applying the former in considering the latter. More indirectly, however, where the common law was uncertain, unclear or incomplete, the courts ruled, wherever possible, in a manner which conformed with the ECHR or, where statute was found to be ambiguous, they presumed that parliament intended to legislate in conformity with the UK's international obligations under the ECHR. As the late Lord Bingham put it:

> In these ways, the Convention made a clandestine entry into British law by the back door, being forbidden to enter by the front [Earl Grey Memorial Lecture, http://webjcli.ncl.ac.uk/1998/issue1/bingham1.html].

Even allowing for this degree of judicial manoeuvring, the situation still remained unsatisfactory. Pressure groups did agitate for the incorporation of the ECHR into the UK legal system, but when in 1995 a Private Member's Bill moving for incorporation was introduced in the House of Lords, the Home Office minister, Lady Blatch, expressed the then government's view that such incorporation was 'undesirable and unnecessary, both in principle and practice'. The Labour opposition, however, was committed to the incorporation of the ECHR into UK law and, when it gained office in 1997, it immediately set about the process of incorporation. This process resulted in the Human Rights Act (HRA) 1998.

Rights Provided Under the European Convention on Human Rights

The Articles incorporated into UK law, and listed in Sched 1 to the Act, cover the following matters:

- the right to life. Article 2 states that 'Everyone's right to life shall be protected by law';

- prohibition of torture. Article 3 actually provides that 'No one shall be subjected to torture or to inhuman or degrading treatment or punishment';
- prohibition of slavery and forced labour (Art 4);
- the right to liberty and security. After stating the general right, Article 5 is mainly concerned with the conditions under which individuals can lawfully be deprived of their liberty;
- the right to a fair trial. Article 6 provides that 'everyone is entitled to a fair and public hearing within a reasonable time by an independent and impartial tribunal established by law';
- the general prohibition of the enactment of retrospective criminal offences. Article 7 does, however, recognise the *post hoc* criminalisation of previous behaviour where it is 'criminal according to the general principles of law recognised by civilised nations';
- the right to respect for private and family life. Article 8 extends this right to cover a person's home and their correspondence;
- freedom of thought, conscience and religion (Art 9);
- freedom of expression. Article 10 extends the right to include 'freedom ... to receive and impart information and ideas without interference by public authority and regardless of frontiers';
- freedom of assembly and association. Article 11 specifically includes the right to form and join trade unions;
- the right to marry (Art 12);
- prohibition of discrimination in relation to the enjoyment of the rights and freedoms set forth in the convention (Art 14);
- the right to peaceful enjoyment of possessions and protection of property (Art 1 of Protocol 1);
- the right to education (subject to a UK reservation (Art 2 of Protocol 1));
- the right to free elections (Art 3 of Protocol 1);
- the right not to be subjected to the death penalty (Arts 1 and 2 of Protocol 6).

The rights listed can be relied on by any person, non-governmental organisation or group of individuals. Importantly, they also apply, where appropriate, to companies that are incorporated entities and hence legal persons. However, they cannot be relied on by governmental organisations, such as local authorities.

The Nature of Rights Under the Act, Proportionality and Derogation

The rights listed above are not all seen in the same way. Some are absolute and inalienable and cannot be interfered with by the state. Others are merely contingent and are subject to derogation, that is, signatory states can opt out of them in particular circumstances. The ECtHR also recognised the concept of 'a margin of appreciation', which allows for countries to deal with particular problems in the context of their own internal circumstances (see below, at 15.4). The absolute rights are those provided for in Arts 2, 3, 4, 7 and 14. All the others are subject to potential limitations. In particular, the rights provided for under Arts 8, 9, 10 and 11 are subject to legal restrictions such as are:

> . . . necessary in a democratic society in the interests of national security or public safety, for the prevention of crime, for the protection of health or morals or the protection of the rights and freedoms of others [Art 11(2)].

The UK entered such a derogation in relation to the extended detention of terrorist suspects without charge, under the Prevention of Terrorism (Temporary Provisions) Act 1989, subsequently replaced and extended by the Terrorism Act 2000. Those powers had been held to be contrary to Art 5 of the Convention by the ECtHR in *Brogan v UK* (1989). The UK also entered a derogation with regard to the Anti-Terrorism, Crime and Security Act 2001, which was enacted in response to the attack on the World Trade Center building in New York on 11 September of that year. The Act allowed for the detention without trial of foreign citizens suspected of being involved in terrorist activity (see, further, below, at 2.5.2).

In deciding the legality of any derogation, courts are required not just to be convinced that there is a need for the derogation, but they must also be sure that the state's action has been proportionate to that need. In other words, the state must not overreact to a perceived problem by removing more rights than is necessary to effect the solution. With further regard to the possibility of derogation, s 19 of the 1998 Act requires a minister, responsible for the passage of any Bill through parliament, either to make a written declaration that it is compatible with the Convention or, alternatively, to declare that although it may not be compatible, it is still the government's wish to proceed with it.

The Structure of the Human Rights Act

The HRA has profound implications for the operation of the English legal system. However, to understand the structure of the HRA, it is essential to be aware of the nature of the changes introduced by the Act, especially in the apparent passing of fundamental powers to the judiciary. Under the doctrine of parliamentary sovereignty, the legislature could pass such laws as it saw fit, even to the extent of removing the rights of its citizens. The 1998 Act reflects a move towards the entrenchment of rights recognised under the Convention, but, given the sensitivity of the relationship between the elected parliament and the unelected judiciary, it has been thought expedient to minimise the change in the constitutional relationship of parliament and the judiciary.

Section 2 of the Act requires future courts to take into account any previous decision of the ECtHR. This provision impacts on the operation of the doctrine of precedent within the English legal system, as it effectively sanctions the overruling of any previous English authority that was in conflict with a decision of the ECtHR.

However, in *Price v Leeds City Council* (2006), the House of Lords held that where there were contradictory rulings from it and the European Court of Human Rights, English courts were required to follow the ruling of the House of Lords. The case is considered in detail at 3.6.3.

Section 3 requires all legislation to be read, so far as possible, to give effect to the rights provided under the Convention. As will be seen, this section provides the courts with new and extended powers of interpretation. It also has the potential to invalidate previously accepted interpretations of statutes that were made, by necessity, without recourse to the Convention (see *Mendoza v Ghaidan* (2002)).

Section 4 empowers the courts to issue a declaration of incompatibility where any piece of primary legislation is found to conflict with the rights provided under the ECHR. This has the effect that the courts cannot invalidate primary legislation, essentially Acts of Parliament but also Orders in Council, which are found to be incompatible; they can only make a declaration of such incompatibility, and leave it to the legislature to remedy the situation through new legislation. Section 10 provides for the provision of remedial legislation through a fast-track procedure, which gives a minister of the Crown the power to alter such primary legislation by way of statutory instrument.

Section 5 requires the Crown to be given notice where a court considers issuing a declaration of incompatibility and the appropriate government minister is entitled to be made a party to the case.

Section 6 declares it unlawful for any public authority to act in a way that is incompatible with the ECHR, and consequently the Human Rights Act does not *directly* impose duties on private individuals or companies unless they are performing public functions. Whether or not a private company is performing a public function can prove problematic, there are instances where they would clearly be considered as doing so: such as privatised utility companies providing essential services, or if a private company were to provide prison facilities then clearly it would be operating as a public authority. However, at the other end of an uncertain spectrum, it has been held that, where a local authority fulfils its statutory duty to arrange the provision of care and accommodation for an elderly person through the use of a private care home, the functions performed by the care home are not to be considered as of a public nature. At least that was the decision of the House of Lords by a majority of three to two in *YL v Birmingham City Council* (2007), a surprisingly conservative decision, and one that met with much dismay, given that there was the expectation that the public authority test would be applied generously.

Section 6(3), however, *indirectly* introduces the possibility of horizontal effect into private relationships. As s 6(3)(a) specifically states that courts and tribunals are public authorities they must therefore act in accordance with the Convention. The consequence of this is that although the HRA does not introduce new causes of action between private individuals, the courts, as public authorities, are required to recognise and give effect to their Convention rights in any action that can be raised.

In *R v (on the application of Al-Skeini) v Secretary of State for Defence* (2007), which related to the conduct of the armed forces in Iraq, the House of Lords held that s 6 applies to a public body even if it is acting outside the United Kingdom territory, as long as it is acting within the jurisdiction of the United Kingdom, and jurisdiction depends upon control of the relevant location.

Where a public authority is acting under the instructions of some primary legislation, which is itself incompatible with the ECHR, the public authority will not be liable under s 6.

Section 7 allows the 'victim of the unlawful act' to bring proceedings against the public authority in breach. However, this is interpreted in such a way as to permit relations of the actual victim to initiate proceedings.

Section 8 empowers the court to grant such relief or remedy against the public authority in breach of the Act as it considers just and appropriate.

Where a public authority is acting under the instructions of some primary legislation, which is itself incompatible with the ECHR, the public authority will not be liable under s 6.

Section 19 of the Act requires that the minister responsible for the passage of any Bill through parliament must make a written statement that the provisions of the Bill are compatible with ECHR rights. Alternatively, the minister may make a statement that the Bill does not comply with ECHR rights, but that the government nonetheless intends to proceed with it.

Reactions to the introduction of the HRA have been broadly welcoming, but some important criticisms have been raised. First, the ECHR is a rather old document and does not address some of the issues that contemporary citizens might consider as equally fundamental to those rights actually contained in the document. For example, it is silent on the rights to substantive equality relating to such issues as welfare and access to resources. Also, the actual provisions of the ECHR are uncertain in the extent of their application, or perhaps more crucially in the area where they can be derogated from, and at least to a degree they are contradictory. The most obvious difficulty arises from the need to reconcile Art 8's right to respect for private and family life with Art 10's freedom of expression. Newspaper editors have expressed their concern in relation to this particular issue, and fear the development, at the hands of the court, of an overly limiting law of privacy that would prevent investigative journalism. This leads to a further difficulty – the potential politicisation, together with a significant enhancement in the power, of the judiciary. Consideration of this issue will be postponed until some cases involving the HRA have been examined.

Perhaps the most serious criticism of the HRA was the fact that the government did not see fit to establish a Human Rights Commission to publicise and facilitate the operation of its procedures. Many saw the setting up of such a body as a necessary step in raising human rights awareness and assisting individuals, who might otherwise be unable to use the Act, to enforce their rights. However, on 1 October 2007, a new Equality and Human Rights Commission (EHRC) came into operation. The new commission brought together and replaced the former Commission for Racial Equality, the Equal Opportunities Commission and the Disability Rights Commission, with the remit of promoting 'an inclusive agenda, underlining the importance of equality for all in society as well as working to combat discrimination affecting specific groups'. The unified commission did not meet with universal approval as is evidenced in Jackie Ashley's acerbic writing in *The Guardian* newspaper:

> Ministers thought that if you brought lesbians, wheelchair users and Afro-Caribbean people into the same organisation, they would all share the same view of equality and human rights, and campaign for one another. That is not entirely naïve. It happens, but in political parties where such people share a philosophical outlook. To think that because people are gay, Asian or blind they must agree about each other's condition is patronisingly anti-political. David Cameron's Tories remind us how many gay people are right wing; there are many homophobic members of black Evangelical churches; a man in a wheelchair may not necessarily believe in equal pay for women. They may share the same view of human rights. They may not. A body that tries to blend together different group interests as if they were all part of the same cause is trying to take the politics out of issues that remain inescapably political, and subject to argument. It's like saying that because the National Farmers' Union, the National Trust and the Ramblers Association are all involved in the countryside they should be the same organisation.

It should be noted that just as the EHRC brought together a number of previous institutions under one body, so the government brought together all discrimination law under one piece of legislation, the Equality Act 2010.

The stated aim of the Act is to promote fairness and equality of opportunity, tackle disadvantage and discrimination, and modernise and strengthen the law relating to discrimination. In pursuit of these ends it created one piece of discrimination legislation by consolidating existing discrimination legislation, together with over 100 statutory instruments and more than 2,500 pages of guidance and statutory codes of practice.

The main elements of the Act are:

- banning age discrimination in the provision of goods, facilities or services and public functions;
- establishing a single equality duty for public bodies;
- extending positive action measures to allow employers to make their organisation or business more representative;
- allowing political parties to use all-women shortlists;
- reducing nine major pieces of legislation, and around 100 statutory instruments into a single Act, making the law more accessible and easier to understand, so that everyone can be clear on their rights and responsibilities.

2.5.1 JUDICIAL INTERPRETATION AND APPLICATION OF THE HUMAN RIGHTS ACT

Before and subsequent to the coming into effect in England of the HRA on 2 October 2000, the newspapers were full of dire warnings as to the damaging effect that the Act would have on accepted legal principles and practices. However, an examination of some of the earliest cases to reach the higher courts may serve to dispel such a view.

Although the HRA was enacted in 1998, it did not come into force generally until October 2000. The reason for the substantial delay was the need to train all members of the judiciary, from the highest Law Lord to the humblest magistrate, in the consequences and implications of the new Act. However, the Act was in force before that date in Scotland as a consequence of the devolution legislation, the Scotland Act, which specifically applied the provisions of the HRA to the Scottish Parliament and executive. It is for that reason that the earliest cases under the Human Rights provisions were heard in the Scottish courts.

2.5.1.1 Restriction of non-absolute rights and proportionality

Road Traffic Act 1988

In *Brown v Stott* (2001), the claimant had been arrested at a supermarket on suspicion of the theft of a bottle of gin. When the police officers noticed that she smelled of alcohol, they asked her how she had travelled to the store. Brown replied that she had driven and pointed out her car in the supermarket car park. Later, at the police station, the police used their powers under s 172(2)(a) of the Road Traffic Act 1988 to require her to say who had been driving her car at about 2.30 pm, that is, at the time when she would have travelled in it to the supermarket. Brown admitted that she had been driving. After a positive breath test, Brown was charged with drink-driving, but appealed to the Scottish High Court of Justiciary for a declaration that the case could not go ahead on the grounds that her admission, as required under s 172, was contrary to the right to a fair trial under Art 6 of the ECHR.

In February 2000, the High Court of Justiciary supported her claim on the basis that the right to silence and the right not to incriminate oneself at trial would be worthless if an accused person did not enjoy a right of silence in the course of the criminal investigation leading to the court proceedings. If this were not the case, then the police could require an accused person to provide an incriminating answer which subsequently could be used in evidence against them at their trial. Consequently, the use of evidence obtained under s 172 of the Road Traffic Act 1988 infringed Brown's rights under Art 6(1).

Even before the HRA was in operation in England, the Scottish case was followed by a similar ruling in Birmingham Crown Court in July 2000.

The implication of these decisions was extremely serious, not just in relation to drink-driving offences, but also in relation to fines following the capture of speeding cars by traffic cameras. As can be appreciated, the film merely identifies the car; it is s 172 of the Road Traffic Act that actually requires the compulsory identification of the driver. If

Brown v Stott stated the law accurately, then the control of speeding cars and drink-driving was in a parlous state.

However, on 5 December 2000, the Privy Council reversed the judgment of the Scottish appeal court in *Brown*. The Privy Council reached its decision on the grounds that the jurisprudence of the ECtHR, established through previous cases, had clearly established that while the overall fairness of a criminal trial could not be compromised, the constituent rights contained in Art 6 of the ECHR were not themselves absolute and could be restricted in certain limited conditions. Consequently, it was possible for individual states to introduce limited qualification of those rights, so long as they were aimed at 'a clear public objective' and were 'proportionate to the situation' under consideration. The ECHR had to be read as balancing community rights with individual rights. With specific regard to the Road Traffic Act, the objective to be attained was the prevention of injury and death from the misuse of cars, and s 172 was not a disproportionate response to that objective.

Subsequently, in a majority decision in *O'Halloran v UK* (2007), the European Court of Human Rights approved the use of s 172 in order to require owners to reveal who had been driving cars caught on speed cameras.

See also the related decision of the House of Lords in *Sheldrake v Director of Public Prosecutions* (2004), which concerned s 5(2) of the Road Traffic Act 1988 relating to the offence of being in charge of a vehicle after consuming excess alcohol. The court held that s 5(2) did not require the prosecution to prove that the defendant was likely to drive while intoxicated. Rather, the effect of s 5(2) was to allow the defendant to escape liability if they could prove, on a balance of probabilities, that there was no likelihood of their driving in their intoxicated condition. The House accepted that this interpretation of s 5(2) infringed the presumption of innocence and introduced a reverse burden of proof, but it considered that such a provision was neither arbitrary nor did it go beyond what was reasonably necessary, given the need to protect the public from the potentially lethal consequences of drink-driving. As Lord Bingham explained the matter:

> The defendant has a full opportunity to show that there was no likelihood of his driving, a matter so closely conditioned by his own knowledge and state of mind at the material time as to make it much more appropriate for him to prove on the balance of probabilities that he would not have been likely to drive than for the prosecutor to prove, beyond reasonable doubt, that he would. I do not think that imposition of a legal burden went beyond what was necessary.

Confiscation Cases

Prior to the Proceeds of Crime Act 2002, a number of Acts of Parliament allowed for the property of individuals to be confiscated where it was assumed that such assets were the result of criminal activity. That legislation included the Criminal Justice Act 1988, as amended by the Proceeds of Crime Act 1995, the Drug Trafficking Act 1994 and the Terrorism Act 2000.

In allowing the court to make such an assumption, the Acts reversed the usual burden of proof to the extent that the person against whom the powers are used is required to demonstrate, on the balance of probabilities, that their assets are not the product of criminal activity. Section 1(1) of the Proceeds of Crime (Scotland) Act 1995 also allows for individuals' assets to be confiscated on the basis of similar assumptions.

In October 2000, in *McIntosh v AG for Scotland*, it was argued that the assumption made under s 3(2) of the 1995 Act displaced the presumption of innocence in Art 6(2) of the ECHR and hence was unlawful. McIntosh had been convicted for supplying heroin and the Crown had applied for a confiscation order under the 1995 Act. The Crown submitted that, since confiscation orders did not constitute a separate criminal offence, Art 6(2) of the Convention could not grant him the presumption of innocence in respect of such an action.

The High Court of Justiciary, Lord Kirkwood dissenting, approved McIntosh's submission and issued a declaration to that effect and, in so doing, threatened the efficacy of the whole confiscation policy.

In December 2000, the Court of Appeal in England, sitting with Lord Chief Justice Woolf on the panel, had the opportunity to consider the effect of the HRA on the assumptions relating to confiscation powers in the case of *R v Benjafield and Others* (2001). In the Court of Appeal's opinion, the express reversal of the burden of proof in confiscation proceedings amounted to a substantial interference with the normal presumption of innocence. However, it held that parliament had adequately balanced the defendant's interests against the public interest and cited the fact that the question of confiscation only arose after conviction and that the court should not make a confiscation order when there was a serious risk of injustice. It also considered that the court's role in the appeal procedure ensured that there was no unfairness to the individual concerned. As in the Privy Council's decision in *Brown*, the Court of Appeal held that where the discretion given to the court and prosecution was properly exercised, it was justifiable as a reasonable and proportionate response to a substantial public interest. In so doing, it declined to apply the High Court of Justiciary's decision in *McIntosh*, preferring the approach of the Privy Council in *Brown*.

When the further appeal in the *McIntosh* case came before the Privy Council in February 2001, the decision of the Scottish appeal court was unanimously overturned on two grounds:

- the confiscation order was not by way of a criminal action and therefore the assumptions were not in contravention of Art 6(2). An application for a confiscation order did not, of itself, lay a criminal charge against the convicted defendant. Although the court could assume that such a defendant had been involved in drug trafficking, there were no statutory assumptions as to a defendant's guilt for drug-trafficking offences;

- in addition, and more generally, Art 6(2) was not an absolute right and therefore, following *Brown*, could justifiably be encroached upon by the proportionate enactment of a democratically elected Parliament in the pursuit of its anti-crime policy.

In reaching this decision, the Privy Council expressly approved the Court of Appeal's decision in *R v Benjafield*.

Subsequently, in *Phillips v UK*, decided in July 2001, the ECtHR concurred with the decision of the Privy Council in *McIntosh* by holding, by a majority of 5:2, that the confiscation procedure under the Drug Trafficking Act 1994 was not contrary to European Convention rights and, unanimously, that in any event the provisions of the Act represented a proportionate response to the problem under consideration.

Finally, when *R v Benjafield* came on appeal to the House of Lords, it felt comfortable in following the decisions and reasoning in both *McIntosh* and *Phillips*. At the same time, the House of Lords also applied that reasoning to confiscation procedure under the Criminal Justice Act 1988 in *R v Rezvi* (2002).

The courts' power to make confiscation orders was extended under the Proceeds of Crime Act (PCA) 2002, which came into full effect in March 2003.

2.5.1.2   Judicial interpretation of statutes under s 3 of the HRA

R v A (2001)

It has long been a matter of concern that in cases where rape has been alleged, the common defence strategy employed by lawyers has been to attempt to attack the credibility of the woman making the accusation. Judges had the discretion to allow questioning of the woman as to her sexual history where this was felt to be relevant, and in all too many cases this discretion was exercised in a way that allowed defence counsel to abuse and humiliate women accusers. Section 41 of the Youth Justice and Criminal Evidence Act (YJCEA) 1999 placed the court under a restriction that seriously limited evidence that could be raised in cross-examination of a sexual relationship between a complainant and an accused. Under s 41(3) of the 1999 Act, such evidence was limited to sexual behaviour 'at or about the same time' as the event giving rise to the charge that was 'so similar' in nature that it could not be explained as a coincidence.

In *R v A*, the defendant in a case of alleged rape claimed that the provisions of the YJCEA 1999 were contrary to Art 6 of the ECHR to the extent that they prevented him from putting forward a full and complete defence. In reaching its decision, the House of Lords emphasised the need to protect women from humiliating cross-examination and prejudicial but valueless evidence in respect of their previous sex lives; it nonetheless held that the restrictions in s 41 of the 1999 Act were *prima facie* capable of preventing an accused from putting forward relevant evidence that could be crucial to his defence.

However, rather than make a declaration of incompatibility, the House of Lords preferred to make use of s 3 of the HRA to allow s 41 of the YJCEA 1999 to be read as permitting the admission of evidence or questioning relating to a relevant issue in the case where it was considered necessary by the trial judge to make the trial fair. The test of admissibility of evidence of previous sexual relations between an accused and a complainant under s 41(3) of the 1999 Act was whether the evidence was so relevant to the issue of consent that to exclude it would be to endanger the fairness of the trial under Art 6 of the ECHR. Where the line is to be drawn is left to the judgment of trial judges. In reaching its decision, the House of Lords was well aware that its interpretation of s 41 did a violence to its actual meaning, but it nonetheless felt it within its power so to do. The words of Lord Steyn are illustrative of this process:

> In my view section 3 requires the court to subordinate the niceties of the language of section 41(3)(c), and in particular the touchstone of coincidence, to broader considerations of relevance judged by logical and common sense criteria of time and circumstances. After all, it is realistic to proceed on the basis that the legislature would not, if alerted to the problem, have wished to deny the right to an accused to put forward a full and complete defence by advancing truly probative material. It is therefore possible under section 3 to read section 41, and in particular section 41(3)(c), as subject to the implied provision that evidence or questioning which is required to ensure a fair trial under Article 6 of the Convention should not be treated as inadmissible.

In this way, the House of Lords restored judicial discretion as to what can be raised in cross-examination in rape cases. It is to be hoped, sincerely but without much conviction on the basis of past history, that it is a discretion that will be exercised sparingly and sympathetically.

Re S (2002)

In *Re S*, the Court of Appeal used s 3 of the HRA in such a way as to create new guidelines for the operation of the Children Act 1989, which increased the courts' powers to intervene in the interests of children taken into care under the Act. This extension of the courts' powers in the pursuit of the improved treatment of such children was achieved by reading the Act in such a way as to allow the courts increased discretion to make interim rather than final care orders, and to establish what were referred to as 'starred milestones' within a child's care plan. If such starred milestones were not achieved within a reasonable time, then the courts could be approached to deliver fresh directions. In effect, what the Court of Appeal was doing was setting up a new, and more active, regime of court supervision in care cases.

The House of Lords, however, although sympathetic to the aims of the Court of Appeal, felt that it had exceeded its powers of interpretation under s 3 of the HRA and, in its exercise of judicial creativity, it had usurped the function of parliament.

Lord Nicholls explained the operation of s 3:

> The Human Rights Act reserves the amendment of primary legislation to Parliament. By this means the Act seeks to preserve parliamentary sovereignty. The Act maintains the constitutional boundary. Interpretation of statutes is a matter for the courts; the enactment of statutes are matters for Parliament ... [but that any interpretation which] departs substantially from a fundamental feature of an Act of Parliament is likely to have crossed the boundary between interpretation and amendment.

Unfortunately, the Court of Appeal had overstepped that boundary.

Mendoza v Ghaidan (2002)

In *Mendoza v Ghaidan* (2002), the Court of Appeal used s 3 to extend the rights of same-sex partners to inherit a statutory tenancy under the Rent Act 1977. In *Fitzpatrick v Sterling Housing Association Ltd* (1999), the House of Lords had extended the rights of such individuals to inherit the lesser assured tenancy by including them within the deceased person's family. It declined to allow them to inherit statutory tenancies, however, on the grounds that they could not be considered to be the wife or husband of the deceased as the Act required. In *Mendoza*, the Court of Appeal held that the Rent Act, as it had been construed by the House of Lords in *Fitzpatrick*, was incompatible with Art 14 of the ECHR on the grounds of its discriminatory treatment of surviving same-sex partners. The court, however, decided that the failing could be remedied by reading the words 'as his or her wife or husband' in the Act as meaning 'as if they were his or her wife or husband'. *Mendoza* is of particular interest in the fact that it shows how the HRA can permit lower courts to avoid previous and otherwise binding decisions of the House of Lords. It also clearly shows the extent to which s 3 increases the powers of the judiciary in relation to statutory interpretation.

In spite of this potential increased power, the House of Lords found itself unable to use s 3 in *Bellinger v Bellinger* (2003). The case related to the rights of transsexuals and the court found itself unable, or at least unwilling, to interpret s 11(c) of the Matrimonial Causes Act 1973 in such a way as to allow a male to female transsexual to be treated in law as a female. Nonetheless, the court did issue a declaration of incompatibility (see below for explanation).

2.5.1.3   Declarations of incompatibility under s 4 of the HRA

As has been stated previously, the courts are not able to declare primary legislation invalid, but, as an alternative, they may make a declaration that the legislation in question is not compatible with the rights provided by the ECHR.

The first declaration of incompatibility was actually issued in *R v (1) Mental Health Review Tribunal, North & East London Region (2) Secretary of State for Health ex p H* in March 2001. In that case, the Court of Appeal held that ss 72 and 73 of the Mental

Health Act 1983 were incompatible with Art 5(1) and (4) of the ECHR inasmuch as they reversed the normal burden of proof, by requiring the detained person to show that they should not be detained rather than the authorities to show that they should be detained.

R v Secretary of State for the Environment, Transport and the Regions ex p Holding & Barnes plc and Others (2001)

In this case, the House of Lords overturned an earlier decision of the Administrative Court that had called into question the operation of the planning system under the Town and Country Planning Act 1990. Under the Act, the ultimate arbiter in relation to planning decisions was the Secretary of State. The Administrative Court held that, as a member of the executive, determining policy, the Secretary of State should not be involved in the quasi-judicial task of deciding applications. It followed, therefore, that the operation of the planning system was contrary to the right to a fair hearing by an independent tribunal as provided for under Art 6 of the ECHR.

In overturning that decision, the House of Lords unanimously decided that the planning process was human rights compatible. In their Lordships' view, the possibility of judicial review was sufficient to ensure compliance with Art 6(1) of the ECHR, even though it could only remedy procedural rather than substantive deficiencies.

Indeed, their Lordships showed some displeasure at the manner in which Art 6 had been deployed in an attempt to undermine the democratically elected Secretary of State by seeking to pass the power to make policy decisions from him to the courts. Both Lords Slynn and Hoffmann quoted the words of the European Commission in *ISKCON v UK* (1994) with approval:

> It is not the role of Article 6 of the Convention to give access to a level of jurisdiction which can substitute its opinion for that of the administrative authorities on questions of expediency and where the courts do not refuse to examine any of the points raised . . .

Even more pointedly, Lord Hoffmann commented that:

> The Human Rights Act 1998 was no doubt intended to strengthen the rule of law but not to inaugurate the rule of lawyers.

The Coalition Government and the Human Rights Act

Historically, the Conservative Party argued against the enactment of the Human Rights Act (HRA) by the Labour government in 1998, on the grounds that it diminished the power of parliament and gave too much power to the unelected judiciary. In October 2009, in an article in the tabloid paper *The Sun*, the leader of the then opposition party, David Cameron, reaffirmed the Conservative Party's opposition to the HRA and promised that, if elected, he would replace it with a British Bill of Rights. However, subsequently, on forming a coalition government with the Liberal Democrat Party, which was committed to the HRA, Cameron appeared to drop any proposals to repeal the Act and instead set up a Commission for a Bill of Rights, chaired by Sir Leigh Lewis.

The Commission's remit was to examine the operation and implementation of ECHR obligations in the UK, and to consider ways to promote a 'better' understanding of the true scope of these obligations and liberties. It was also charged with providing interim advice to the government on the ongoing Interlaken process to reform the Strasbourg court ahead of the UK's Chairmanship of the Council of Europe and to date that has been the focus of its attention (see below, 15.4).

Protection of Freedoms Act 2012

The Protection of Freedoms Act was passed in May 2012. It looks to relax a number of provisions introduced by the previous government. Among other measures (it has 121 sections and 10 schedules), the Act:

- brings in a new framework for police retention of fingerprints and DNA data, and requires schools to get parents' consent before processing children's biometric information;
- introduces a code of practice for surveillance camera systems and provides for judicial approval of certain surveillance activities by local authorities;
- provides for a code of practice to cover officials' powers of entry, with these powers being subject to review and repeal;
- outlaws wheel-clamping on private land;
- introduces a new regime for police 'stop and searches' under the Terrorism Act 2000;
- reduces the maximum pre-charge detention period under the Terrorism Act from 28 to 14 days;
- enables those with convictions for consensual sexual relations between men aged 16 or over (which have since been decriminalised) to apply to have them disregarded;
- extends Freedom of Information rights by requiring datasets to be available in a reusable format;
- repeals provisions (never brought into force) which would have allowed trial without a jury in complex fraud cases;
- removes time restrictions on when marriage or civil partnership ceremonies may take place.

In October 2011, at the Conservative Party annual conference, the Home Secretary, Theresa May, reasserted her party's antagonism to the HRA, stating that it 'had to go'. In her notorious 'catgate' speech she justified the attack on the Act as follows:

> We all know the stories about the Human Rights Act. The violent drug
> dealer who cannot be sent home because his daughter – for whom he pays
> no maintenance – lives here. The robber who cannot be removed because he
> has a girlfriend. The illegal immigrant who cannot be deported because –
> **and I am not making this up** – he has a pet cat.

Regrettably for the Home Secretary and the truth, an examination of the transcripts of
the case in point revealed that ownership of a cat was not actually the ground for refusing
the deportation order and her claims were ridiculed as laughable by the then Justice
Secretary Ken Clarke. Clarke subsequently had to apologise. It has to be noted that
Clarke's replacement as Justice Minister, Chris Grayling, while in opposition – and like
his leader David Cameron – famously announced that he was in favour of tearing up the
HRA and replacing it with a British document.

2.5.2   HUMAN RIGHTS AND ANTI-TERRORISM LEGISLATION

It is almost commonplace that the recognition of human rights is most sorely tested
when those claiming the protection of those rights might not otherwise meet with sympathetic treatment. Thus it is the argument of those who would repeal the Human Rights
Act that it is used as a block on the pursuit of substantive law and order by shyster
lawyers who recognise its utility as a means of protecting the rights of criminals,
prisoners, illegal immigrants and other supposedly blameworthy or morally dubious
individuals at the expense of the rights of the good, and no doubt God-fearing (in a non-
Islamic way), moral majority. However, it is precisely the universality and non-contingent
nature of human rights, the fact that they are, or at least should be, an attribute of every
person, irrespective of status, class, race, gender, religion or political belief, that provides
the foundation for the very theory of human rights. It might also be said that the
extent to which the universality of human rights is recognised and applied to even 'the
undeserving' is the test of the very humanity of a society and its legal system.

What follows requires a consideration of perhaps the most essential tension
between the courts, in their recognition and application of human rights, and the state
in its desire to protect what it perceives as the public interest through controlling those
it considers a threat to that public interest: a tension between judiciary and legislature,
and perhaps one that prefigures future tension between the newly established Supreme
Court and parliament.

Anti-Terrorism, Crime and Security Act 2001

Following the terrorist attack on the World Trade Center on 11 September 2001, the UK
parliament introduced the Anti-Terrorism, Crime and Security Act (ACSA) 2001. This
Act allowed for the detention, without charge, of non-UK citizens suspected of terrorist
activities, but who could not be repatriated to their own countries because of fear for
their wellbeing.

While a person who would otherwise be detained was free to leave the United Kingdom, the Act provided that a person certificated as a suspected international terrorist under s 21 might be detained in circumstances where their safe removal or departure from the UK was not practical (s 23(1)).

Such a provision was clearly contrary to Art 5 of the ECHR. Consequently, the government was required to enter a derogation from the Convention by virtue of the Human Rights Act 1998 (Designated Derogation) Order 2001, the justification for the derogation being that the prospect of terrorism following 11 September 2001 threatened the life of the nation.

SIAC Hearings and Special Advocates

The Special Immigration Appeals Commission (SIAC) was empowered under the ACSA 2001 to hear appeals in relation to decisions taken under it. The SIAC originally had been established by the Special Immigration Appeals Commission Act 1997 in response to a decision of the ECtHR in *Chahal v UK* (1997), in relation to the political deportations. Hearings before the SIAC are conducted on both an open basis and a closed basis. In the former, anyone can attend, but in the latter, which deal with matters of state security, not only the public but the detained persons and their lawyers are excluded and therefore have no access to, let alone the possibility of challenging, the evidence used against them. In closed session, the detainees are represented by Special Advocates who are lawyers with clearance to access secret and security documents. These Special Advocates are neither appointed by the people they represent, nor are they at liberty to divulge any information to them. (See further, Justice & Security Bill p 73.)

The Belmarsh Cases

This title refers to a number of cases that focused on the issues of the compatibility of ACSA 2001 with the European Convention on Human Rights and the compliance with the convention of orders made under its auspices.

A v Secretary of State for the Home Department (SIAC and the Court of Appeal) (2002)

In July 2002, the SIAC held that the ACSA 2001 was not in compliance with the anti-discriminatory provisions of Art 14 of the Convention to the extent that it treated non-nationals differently from UK nationals. Somewhat surprisingly the government/parliament had not scheduled any derogation for the purposes of Art 14 of the Convention. However, according to Collins J, merely submitting a derogation would not have solved the shortcoming as, in any event, the provisions of the Act were disproportionate, there being no reasonable relationship between the means employed and the aims sought to be pursued by the state. Collins J did raise some general concern with his conclusion that it was open to parliament to remedy the incompatibility by extending the power of detention to cover nationals as well as non-nationals.

The then Home Secretary, David Blunkett, attacked the SIAC decision and it was subsequently overturned by the Court of Appeal. In so doing, the Court of Appeal emphasised that, as the case related to matters of national security, it was self-evidently of a nature in which the courts should show considerable deference towards the executive. Consequently, as the Home Secretary was better qualified than the courts to decide what action had to be taken to safeguard national security, the courts should not intervene. According to the Court of Appeal, the case concerned an example of what has become known as the 'area of deference' within which the courts will 'defer on democratic grounds to the considered opinion of the elected body or person whose actual decision is said to be incompatible with the Convention'.

The approach of the Court of Appeal in this case was reminiscent of the quiescent attitude of previous courts when faced with the exercise of executive power. Perhaps the classic example of such subservience is to be found in *Liversidge v Anderson* (1942) in which a majority of the House of Lords approved the power of the Home Secretary to imprison a person without trial under wartime defence regulations. Lord Atkin, in the minority, famously railed against the granting of such uncontrolled power to the Home Secretary and accused his fellow members of the House of Lords of being '. . . more executive-minded than the executive'.

Subsequently, in May, June and July 2003, the SIAC heard appeals brought by 10 individuals against their certification by the Home Secretary, and consequently their detention without trial. The appeal hearings consisted of both open and closed sessions. Neither the internees, nor the lawyers of their choice, were permitted to attend the closed sessions and their interests were represented by Special Advocates.

Judgments on the 10 appeals were handed down in a public session on 29 October 2003. Each judgment confirmed the certification of the individual concerned and dismissed their appeal. This open judgment indicated the generic evidence of general relevance to all the appellants. The evidence relating to each of the individuals, which was considered in the closed sessions, was dealt with in a separate closed judgment, which was not made public or disclosed to the appellants or their lawyers.

A v Secretary of State for the Home Department (House of Lords) (2004)

When the original case of the detainees under the Anti-Terrorism, Crime and Security Act ultimately came before the House of Lords, it resulted in a crushing judgment against the Act and an undisguised and unmitigated rebuke to the government and its anti-terrorism policies. The strength of the decision was almost startling, especially in the light of the previously more accommodating decisions of the Court of Appeal in relation to state policy. The case was heard by a panel of nine Law Lords, Lord Steyn having stood down from the appeal because he had previously expressed the view that the derogation was unjustified, and it was decided by a majority of 8:1, only Lord Walker dissenting, that the ACSA was incompatible with the provisions of the ECHR.

Although the House of Lords recognised the deference due to the government and parliament and accepted that the government had been entitled to conclude that there was a public emergency, it nonetheless concluded that the response to the perceived threat had been disproportionate and incompatible with the rights under the ECHR.

It held that the prohibition on grounds of nationality or immigration status, under Art 14, had not been the subject of derogation. Further, it held that the decision to detain one group of suspected international terrorists, defined by nationality or immigration status, and not another could not be justified, and violated Art 14 of the ECHR. In relation to the discriminatory effect of the Act, the House pointed out the illogicality at its heart for, if the potential threat to the security of the UK *by UK nationals* suspected of being Al Qa'ida terrorists could be addressed without infringing their right to personal liberty, then why could not similar measures be used to deal with any threat presented by *foreign nationals*.

The House of Lords also held that ss 21 and 23 of the Act were disproportionate for the general reason that the provisions did not rationally address the threat to the security of the UK presented by Al Qa'ida terrorists. This general conclusion was supported by a number of particular shortcomings within the Act, such as the facts that:

> it did not address the threat presented by UK nationals;

> it permitted foreign nationals suspected of being Al Qa'ida terrorists to pursue their activities abroad if there was any country to which they were able to go.

As a result of this reasoning, the House of Lords decided that s 23 of the ACSA was incompatible with Art 5 and Art 14 of the ECHR and appropriately quashed the Derogation Order 2001, as it was secondary rather than primary legislation.

While the preceding report of *A v Secretary of State for the Home Department* provides an objective account of the House of Lords' decision, it does little to reflect the intensity of feeling expressed in the individual judgments of those involved in the case, which can only be appreciated through the words of the judges involved. While the leading judgment of Lord Bingham, the senior Law Lord, was delivered in measured, if critical, terms, it cannot but be recognised that some of the other members of the judicial panel expressed themselves in such florid language as to lay themselves open to the accusation of 'showboating' – an expression used to indicate a mixture of self- and over-indulgence.

That being said, even Lord Bingham felt free to express his view that the judiciary were an essentially democratic part of the modern UK political system. As he put it:

> . . . I do not accept the full breadth of the Attorney General's submissions. *I do not in particular accept the distinction which he drew between democratic institutions and the courts. It is of course true that the judges in this country are not elected and are not answerable to Parliament. It is also of course true, as pointed out in para. 29 above, that Parliament, the executive and the courts have different functions. But the function of independent judges charged to interpret and apply the law is universally recognised as a cardinal feature of the modern democratic state, a cornerstone of the rule of law itself.* The Attorney General is fully entitled to insist on the proper limits of judicial authority, but he is wrong to stigmatise judicial decision-making as in some way undemocratic . . . The effect is not, of course, to override the sovereign legislative authority of the Queen in Parliament, since if primary legislation is

declared to be incompatible the validity of the legislation is unaffected (section 4(6)) and the remedy lies with the appropriate minister (section 10), who is answerable to Parliament. The 1998 Act gives the courts a very specific, wholly democratic, mandate. (emphasis added)

However, the most patently (over-)rhetorical judgment was delivered by Lord Hoffmann, of which the following quotation is merely one example:

95. . . . Of course the government has a duty to protect the lives and property of its citizens. But that is a duty which it owes all the time and which it must discharge without destroying our constitutional freedoms. There may be some nations too fragile or fissiparous to withstand a serious act of violence. But that is not the case in the United Kingdom. When Milton urged the government of his day not to censor the press even in time of civil war, he said:

'Lords and Commons of England, consider what nation it is whereof ye are, and whereof ye are the governors'

96. This is a nation which has been tested in adversity, which has survived physical destruction and catastrophic loss of life. I do not underestimate the ability of fanatical groups of terrorists to kill and destroy, but they do not threaten the life of the nation. Whether we would survive Hitler hung in the balance, but there is no doubt that we shall survive Al-Qa'ida.

However, perhaps the most overtly political speech was that of Lord Scott, which contained the following passages:

142. . . . The making of such a declaration [of incompatibility] will not, however, affect in the least the validity under domestic law of the impugned statutory provision. *The import of such a declaration is political not legal.*

154. . . . The Secretary of State is unfortunate in the timing of the judicial examination in these proceedings of the 'public emergency' that he postulates. It is certainly true that the judiciary must in general defer to the executive's assessment of what constitutes a threat to national security or to 'the life of the nation'. But judicial memories are no shorter than those of the public and the public have not forgotten the faulty intelligence assessments on the basis of which United Kingdom forces were sent to take part, and are still taking part, in the hostilities in Iraq.

> 155. ... Indefinite imprisonment in consequence of a denunciation on grounds that are not disclosed and made by a person whose identity cannot be disclosed is the stuff of nightmares, associated whether accurately or inaccurately with France before and during the Revolution, with Soviet Russia in the Stalinist era and now associated, as a result of section 23 of the 2001 Act, with the United Kingdom. (emphasis added)

It is significant to note that these speeches were delivered before the murderous bombings in London on 7 July 2005, or perhaps the rhetorical flourishes might have been more controlled. In any event, the House of Lords' decision, in what has become known as the *Belmarsh* case, represented a general exercise in judicial activism in relation to the executive power, but its declaration of incompatibility together with the quashing of the Derogation Order left the government with a particular problem: whether it would be able to renew the provisions of the ACSA in March 2005, as was required by the Act itself. When it became apparent that there was no such possibility, the government introduced new procedures for dealing with suspected terrorists under the Prevention of Terrorism Act 2005 (PTA 2005). The initial Prevention of Terrorism Bill was subjected to the most rigorous game of parliamentary ping pong in almost 100 years, before it was eventually passed with many of its original provisions having been removed or mitigated (see 3.3 for an explanation of this concept). Perhaps most astonishingly to outsiders, the clock of parliament stopped during this process and the morning of Thursday 10 March melded without recognition into the late afternoon of 11 March, which was treated technically as a continuation of 10 March. This is because the 'day' continued, technically, for as long as parliament was engaged in debate.

Prevention of Terrorism Act 2005 and Control Orders

The Act as eventually passed dealt with one of the shortcomings of the ACSA by widening the provisions of the previous legislation to control all terrorist-related activity, *irrespective of nationality* or indeed the particular cause the terrorists supported. But perhaps even more essentially, neither did it attempt to continue the detention without trial regime under the ACSA, which was replaced with a new system of 'control orders'. These control orders were to be of two distinct types; derogating and non-derogating in relation to the ECHR.

Derogating control orders

As its title suggests, this type of control order requires derogation from ECHR because it deprives the person affected of their liberty by requiring them to remain in a particular place at all times. It is equivalent to house arrest and consequently it clearly infringes the person's rights under Art 5 of the ECHR.

In any event no derogation orders were ever sought.

Non-derogating control orders

This type of control order allows the Home Secretary to impose a range of controls over people's activities. Section 1(4) states that these controls may include any one or more of a list of 16 different kinds of restrictions. The possible restrictions relate to the imposition of curfews and the use of tagging for the purposes of monitoring those curfews. They also allow for the restriction and control of the movement of the individuals concerned, or restrictions on association with other named individuals. They also provide for the possibility of a ban on the use of mobile phones or the internet. The government claimed that, even if the non-derogational control orders affected other Convention rights, such as the right to private and family life (Art 8), the right to freedom of expression (Art 10), or the right to freedom of association (Art 11), as they very well might, nonetheless they would not require derogation because they did not engage the right to liberty (Art 5). Thus the argument runs that, as this type of order does not lead to the detention of those subjected to it, it does not require any derogation procedure to validate any action taken in line with its provisions.

In order to make a non-derogating control order the Home Secretary is normally required to apply for leave from a judge of the High Court (s 3(1)). However, in an emergency situation, where it is not possible to wait for judicial approval, the Home Secretary may certify as to the urgency of the case for the order and it will take effect immediately. In the latter circumstances, the order must be referred to the Court for confirmation within seven days, and if confirmed, it will be referred for a full hearing. Alternatively, if the order is not confirmed it will be quashed (s 3(6)).

In the case of non-derogating control orders, the standard of proof for making the order is less than that for the derogating control order. The test is that the Home Secretary has reasonable grounds for suspecting that the individual is or was so involved (s 2(1)(a)) and that the order is necessary to protect the public (s 2(1)(b)).

The 2005 Act retained the role of the *Special Advocate*, who is expected to support the interests of the suspect in regard to material that neither the accused nor his chosen legal representatives is allowed access to.

Section 9(4) provides that any breach of a control order, without reasonable excuse, is a criminal offence punishable on indictment by imprisonment of up to five years.

The legal effect of non-derogation control orders issued under the PTA 2005 were considered by the House of Lords in a series of related appeals, the decisions in which were delivered in three judgments at the end of October 2007.

The maximum length of control orders

In the first, *Secretary of State for the Home Department v JJ and others* (2007), the issue was whether an order imposing an 18-hour curfew, coupled with other restrictions on the activities of those subject to the orders, amounted to deprivation of liberty and consequently was contrary to Art 5 of the ECHR. In deciding the question the court recognised the distinction between the *unqualified* right to liberty and the *qualified* rights of freedom of movement, communication and association provided under the ECHR as previously expressed by the ECtHR.

The general effect of the particular control orders in question were summarised by the Court of Appeal in para 4 of its judgment as follows:

> The obligations imposed by the control orders are set out in annex I to Sullivan J's judgment. They are essentially identical. Each respondent is required to remain within his 'residence' at all times, save for a period of six hours between 10 am and 4 pm. In the case of GG the specified residence is a one-bedroom flat provided by the local authority in which he lived before his detention. In the case of the other five respondents the specified residences are one-bedroom flats provided by the National Asylum Support Service. During the curfew period the respondents are confined in their small flats and are not even allowed into the common parts of the buildings in which these flats are situated. Visitors must be authorised by the Home Office, to which name, address, date of birth and photographic identity must be supplied. The residences are subject to spot searches by the police. During the six hours when they are permitted to leave their residences, the respondents are confined to restricted urban areas, the largest of which is 72 square kilometres. These deliberately do not extend, save in the case of GG, to any area in which they lived before. Each area contains a mosque, a hospital, primary health care facilities, shops and entertainment and sporting facilities. The respondents are prohibited from meeting anyone by pre-arrangement who has not been given the same Home Office clearance as a visitor to the residence.

In addition, the controlled persons were required to wear an electronic tag and to report to a monitoring company on first leaving their flat after a curfew period and on returning to it before a curfew period. They were forbidden to use or possess any communications equipment of any kind except for one fixed telephone line in their flat maintained by the monitoring company. They were at liberty to attend a mosque of their choice if it was in their permitted area and approved in advance by the Home Office. A request by JJ to study English at a college outside his area was refused.

At first instance Sullivan J held that the cumulative effect of the obligations placed on the respondents went far beyond the mere restriction of liberty, recognised as potentially legitimate by the ECtHR, and was such as to deprive them of their liberty in breach of Art 5 of the Convention. As a result, Sullivan J held that the Secretary of State had had no power to make an order that was incompatible with Art 5 of the ECHR and any such purported order had to be treated as a nullity and totally ineffective.

Sullivan J's decision was subsequently approved by the Court of Appeal and, on further appeal to the House of Lords, it was decided by a majority of 3:2 that neither the judge at first instance nor the Court of Appeal had erred in their legal reasoning and the House of Lords expressly approved their rulings. In the view of the House, the effect of the 18-hour curfew, coupled with the effective exclusion of social visitors meant that the men subject to the control orders were practically in solitary confinement for an indefinite duration. Further, the House of Lords confirmed that as the control orders were a nullity, the defects in them could not be cured by the court simply amending the content of the provisions as was argued for by the Secretary of State.

Of the majority of the House of Lords who held that the control orders amounted to a deprivation of liberty, Lord Bingham and Baroness Hale were content simply to hold that the 18-hour curfew was contrary to Art 5 without considering the possibility of an alternative period that would count as merely a restriction on, rather than a deprivation of, liberty and hence be lawful. However, Lord Brown suggested that a 16-hour curfew period would be an acceptable limit.

The second of the linked cases, *Secretary of State for the Home Department v MB & AF* (2007) also concerned the issues considered in *JJ* and on this occasion the House of Lords unanimously held that a curfew of 14 hours with related restrictions did not amount to a deprivation of liberty. Consequently, if 14 hours did not count as a deprivation of liberty on the basis of *AF*, and 18 hours did amount to such a deprivation as in *JJ*, then Lord Brown's 16 hours appeared to be the appropriate time limit for curfews under PTA 2005 control orders.

However, in *Secretary of State for the Home Department v AP* (2010), which concerned someone subject to a control order confined to a flat for 16 hours a day in a Midlands town 150 miles away from his family in London, Lord Brown subsequently clarified/retracted his original suggestion.

In *AP* the Supreme Court unanimously decided that conditions that might be proportionate restrictions upon Art 8 rights to respect for private and family life can 'tip the balance' in relation to Art 5, which guarantees the right to liberty and security. In other words the court should take account of the *effect* of any restrictions in deciding whether a control order amounts to a deprivation of liberty. However, in the leading judgment Lord Brown stated that:

> I nevertheless remain of the view that for a control order with a 16-hour curfew (*a fortiori* one with a 14-hour curfew) to be struck down as involving a deprivation of liberty, the other conditions imposed would have to be *unusually destructive* of the life the controlee might otherwise have been living. (emphasis added)

The use of torture to extract evidence

After their release from Guantanamo Bay (see immediately below), former detainees brought civil claims against UK ministers and intelligence agencies, claiming that they had been complicit in their unlawful imprisonment and the abuse they received while in captivity. Initially, the High Court allowed the possibility of the state raising a defence to the civil action based on evidence that could not be openly disclosed to the claimants. However, the Court of Appeal forcefully rejected such a possibility as being a fundamental breach of the common law.

This topic has assumed increased importance since it was first considered as a subsidiary issue in the earlier anti-terrorist related cases, and caused a furore when it was announced in November 2010 that the state would be paying millions of pounds to a number of individuals who had claimed to have been tortured, with either the knowledge or collusion of the UK security services.

A v Secretary of State for the Home Department (2005)

During the hearing relating to the appeals against their detention under the provisions of ACSA in October 2003, SIAC stated that the fact that evidence against the detainees had, or might have been, obtained through torture inflicted by foreign officials, but without the complicity of the British authorities, could be used in determining the outcome of the cases. SIAC held that while the use of torture might affect the weight to be given to the evidence, its source did not render it legally inadmissible.

On appeal the claimants argued that SIAC should not have considered any evidence, unless it was shown not to have been obtained as a result of a breach of Art 3 of the ECHR. They also argued that the burden of proof should fall on the Secretary of State to show that the relevant evidence was not obtained in breach of Art 3. The Court of Appeal, however, confirmed the approach previously taken by SIAC, holding by a majority that it would be contrary to the exercise of the statutory power and unrealistic to expect the Home Secretary to investigate each statement relied on, in order to determine whether it had been produced as a result of torture.

In December 2005 a seven-strong panel of the House of Lords delivered its decision on the further appeal, in spite of the previous repeal of part 4 of ACSA 2001. There were two issues before the House of Lords. The first related to the question as to whether evidence produced through torture could be used in any circumstances. The second related to the burden of proof in relation to showing whether or not torture had been used to produce the evidence in question.

In relation to the first issue, the House was unanimous in its disapproval of the previous approaches of SIAC and the Court of Appeal. It was clear under the common law and under international law that no evidence obtained as a result of torture could be used, even if the torture was conducted by another state, without the complicity of the United Kingdom authorities. While parliament might have the power to approve the use of torture evidence, it had not done so through ACSA. This general view is encapsulated in the words of Lord Bingham at para 52:

> ... it would of course be within the power of a sovereign Parliament (in breach of international law) to confer power on SIAC to receive third-party torture evidence. But the English common law has regarded torture and its fruits with abhorrence for over 500 years, and that abhorrence is now shared by over 140 countries which have acceded to the Torture Convention. I am startled, even a little dismayed, at the suggestion (and the acceptance by the Court of Appeal majority) that this deeply-rooted

tradition and an international obligation solemnly and explicitly undertaken can be overridden by a statute and a procedural rule which make no mention of torture at all.

However, as to the second issue the House of Lords divided 4:3, with the majority holding that SIAC should not admit evidence if it concluded, on a balance of probabilities, that it was obtained by torture. If the commission was in doubt as to whether the evidence was obtained by torture, then it should admit it, but it should bear its doubt in mind when evaluating the evidence. On the other hand, a strongly argued minority opinion held that SIAC should refuse to admit the evidence if it was unable to conclude that there was not a real risk that the evidence had been obtained by torture. If it was in doubt whether the evidence had been procured by torture, then the commission should exclude the evidence.

The majority position was based on a literal reading of Art 15 of the International Convention against Torture and other Cruel Inhuman or Degrading Treatment or Punishment 1984. That article provided that a statement could not be used as evidence if it was 'established' to have been made as a result of torture. As the majority rightly held, that provision did not say that the statement had to be excluded if there was an unrebutted suspicion of torture, but equally, as Lord Hoffmann pointed out, 'Article 15 of the Torture Convention, which speaks of the use of torture being "established", could never have contemplated a procedure in which the person against whom the statement was being used had no idea of what it was or who had made it', as was the situation with regard to the operation of SIAC.

The majority did, however, consider that point in holding that the individual defendant would not be expected to shoulder the entire burden of demonstrating that a particular piece of evidence stated to justify his certification and detention was obtained by torture. According to Lord Hope the defendant would only be required to raise the issue that the information used against him might have come from a country suspected of practising torture, after which the task of assessing the matter would be passed to SIAC itself.

Lord Rodger, rather naïvely, described how 'those in the relevant department who were preparing a case for an SIAC hearing would sift through the material, *on the lookout for anything that might suggest torture had been used*', and as he later pointed out (para 143, emphasis added):

> The Home Secretary accepted that he was under a duty to put any such material before the Commission. *With the aid of the relevant intelligence services, doubtless as much as possible will be done.* And SIAC itself will wish to take an active role in suggesting possible lines of inquiry.

Consequently defendants could rest assured, confident in the understanding that those who were seeking to have them detained would do everything in their power to ensure that the evidence against them was free from any taint of torture. Perhaps Lord Bingham deserves the final cutting comment on the flawed reasoning of the majority in the House of Lords:

> My noble and learned friend Lord Hope proposes, in paragraph 121 of his opinion, the following test: is it *established*, by means of such diligent enquiries into the sources that it is practicable to carry out and on a balance of probabilities, that the information relied on by the Secretary of State *was* obtained under torture? This is a test which, in the real world, can never be satisfied. The foreign torturer does not boast of his trade. The security services, as the Secretary of State has made clear, do not wish to imperil their relations with regimes where torture is practised. The special advocates have no means or resources to investigate. The detainee is in the dark. It is inconsistent with the most rudimentary notions of fairness to blindfold a man and then impose a standard which only the sighted could hope to meet. *The result will be that, despite the universal abhorrence expressed for torture and its fruits, evidence procured by torture will be laid before SIAC because its source will not have been 'established'.* (at para 59, emphasis added)

The full extent of Lord Hope's naïvety and Lord Bingham's realism about the security services' approach to torture became apparent in a number of cases relating to individuals who had been held and questioned as suspected Al Qa'ida terrorists by foreign powers including the United States of America. After the bombing of the World Trade Center in New York in 2001, the government of the United States in its pursuit of its war on terrorism generally, and Al Qa'ida in particular, adopted a number of strategies. Amongst these were the process of 'extraordinary rendition' and the establishment of a camp to detain suspected Al Qa'ida members at Guantanamo Bay, a US base on Cuban soil.

Extraordinary rendition is the extra-judicial process of passing detainees from one country to another in order to facilitate their questioning without their being able to access legal redress. The implicit suspicion is that such rendition was to countries where torture was routinely used as a means of extracting information from detainees. Guantanamo Bay was established as a non-sovereign American site specifically to prevent those detained there from demanding rights of access to the United States' legal system.

Perhaps the most prominent of those subject to rendition and detention at Guantanamo Bay was Binyam Mohamed. Mohamed was born in Ethiopia and was granted refugee status in Britain in 1994. He travelled to Afghanistan in 2001 and was subsequently detained in Pakistan in 2002 on suspicion of involvement in terrorism. Following his detention he was 'rendered' to Morocco and Afghanistan before eventually being taken to Guantanamo in September 2004. He was subsequently returned to the UK in February 2009, when he instituted proceedings, not only alleging that he suffered torture and abuse during his time as a detainee, but that such torture was conducted with the complicity of the UK intelligence forces.

Following a number of embarrassing cases, requiring the release of damaging documents, the Justice Minister, Kenneth Clarke, announced on 16 November 2010 that 16 former detainees, including Mohamed, would be paid an undisclosed sum in compensation for their treatment while in detention. Clarke announced to the House of Commons that the cost of the mediated payments would be less than the cost of defending the cases through the courts and would avoid the publication of any further damaging security documents. However, in early August 2011 *The Guardian* revealed that it had come into possession of a document setting out the UK's previous interrogation policy in relation to the use of mistreatment and torture during the interrogation of terrorist suspects by other authorities. The document instructed intelligence officers not to carry out any action 'which it is *known*' would result in torture. However, they could proceed when they foresaw 'a real possibility [that] their actions will result in an individual's mistreatment' *as long as they first sought assurances from the agency conducting the interrogation.* Where, in spite of assurances to the contrary, there was still a real possibility of unlawful mistreatment of the detainee, any continued activity by the UK agents required authority at a senior level. Allegedly, the document stated that in deciding whether to give permission, senior MI5 and MI6 management would balance the risk of mistreatment and the risk that the officer's actions could be judged to be unlawful against the need for the proposed action and that, in some cases, government ministers might need to be consulted to get the necessary approval. The document stated that in deciding the case the senior management should weigh 'the operational imperative for the proposed action, such as if the action involves passing or obtaining life-saving intelligence', against 'the level of mistreatment anticipated and how likely those consequences are'.

Previously in July 2010, a new and more rigorous set of interrogation instructions applying to suspected terrorists detained in foreign regimes was drafted and published on the orders of Prime Minister David Cameron. The new code was issued on the grounds that the new coalition government 'was determined to resolve the problems of the past' and 'wished to give greater clarity about what is and what is not acceptable in the future'. Unfortunately in October 2011, in *R (Al Bazzouni) v Prime Minister*, the High Court, in a judicial review case, held that the provisions in the guidance allowing the use of 'hooding' of prisoners were unlawful as being contrary to Article 3 of the ECHR.

Also in July 2010 the newly appointed Prime Minister David Cameron announced that a judicial inquiry would take place into the UK's role in torture and rendition since the Al Qa'ida attacks of September 2001 (see further below).

The Justice and Security Bill 2012

The embarrassment suffered by the government as a result of the consideration of sensitive security-related material in open court, without question, fostered its determination to prevent such embarrassment in the future. The result was a Justice and Security Green Paper issued in October 2011, which allowed a relatively short time for consultation, closing in January 2012. Although the Green Paper was subject to much criticism, rather than issue a White Paper to allow further consideration, the government preferred to publish its Justice and Security Bill in May 2012.

The parliamentary summary of the bill states three purposes:

- the oversight of the Security Service, the Secret Intelligence Service, the Government Communications Headquarters and other activities relating to intelligence or security matters;
- the provision for closed material procedure in relation to certain civil proceedings;
- the prevention of making certain court orders for the disclosure of sensitive information; and for connected purposes.

Part 2 of the Bill contains the most immediately controversial material, in that s 6 makes provision to enable the Secretary of State to apply to the court for a 'closed material procedure' (CMP) in certain civil proceedings in the courts. This is essentially an extension to other civil courts of the procedure previously considered in relation to SIAC under which the detained person and their legal representatives are prevented from hearing, and of course challenging, evidence presented to the court in their absence. Section 8 similarly allows for the appointment of Special Advocates to protect the interest of the detained person (see p62). The Minister triggers the process by deciding that a closed material procedure is needed, and applying to the judge, who decides whether to allow it or not. The judge *must* grant the application if one of the parties to the proceedings would be required to disclose material in the proceedings and the disclosure would be damaging to national security.

It has been suggested by supporters of the CMP that it will improve accountability and oversight on the ground that it will actually allow highly sensitive intelligence information to be heard in private as opposed to being completely excluded under a public interest immunity certificate, as is the case at present. A Ministry of Justice spokesperson was reported as claiming that:

> These proposals will extend civil justice so that cases which are currently not heard by the courts can be. They will mean that allegations made against the government will be fully examined by an independent court, and that the government will no longer have to pay out taxpayers' money settling cases which it believes have no merit. Closed material procedures, which are at the heart of our proposed reform, are already used in the UK justice system in several areas – including immigration and employment cases. (http://www.guardian.co.uk/law/2012/may/09/queen-speech-secret-hearings-courts)

Section 13 of the Bill relates to what are known as Norwich Pharmacal orders (NPOs). Such court orders apply in civil proceedings where one party seeks the disclosure of information from another party in order to identify the proper defendant, support their case or establish their defence to an action (*Norwich Pharmacal Co. & Others v Customs and Excise Commissioners* (1974)). The essential point, however, is that the involvement of the party required to provide the information may well be completely innocent, but nonetheless they are still required to supply the information, where it is deemed necessary in the interests of justice. It was on the basis of such a Norwich Pharmacal order that Binyam Mohamed had gained access to the documents required to support his action against the UK security services.

If enacted, subsection 13(2) will require that a court may not order the disclosure of information sought if the information is sensitive information.

What is covered by the term 'sensitive information' is defined in subsection 13(3) as information:

(a)   held by an intelligence service;

(b)   obtained from, or held on behalf of, an intelligence service;

(c)   derived in whole or part from information obtained from, or held on behalf of, an intelligence service;

(d)   relating to an intelligence service; or

(e)   specified or described in a certificate issued by the Secretary of State, in relation to the proceedings, as information which should not [be] ordered to disclose[d].

Such a provision goes a very long way to completely emasculating the operation of Norwich Pharmacal orders in matters relating to state security, much, one can only imagine, to the great delight of the government and the security services.

In considering the potential effect of s 13, Fiona Londras of University Dublin School of Law commented:

> It is true that the certification is subject to review [s 14], and it is quite possible that the courts would impose a demanding standard on the government to justify any decision ruling that certain information is sensitive, but that notwithstanding, section 13 is difficult to describe as anything but an affront. Its purpose is unquestioningly to ensure yet another avenue towards discovering the depth and breadth of the UK's involvement in what might charitably be called unsavoury activities is blocked.
>
> Even if the certification process – itself a stunning provision of quasi-judicial power to a government minister – were to disappear in the legislative process (and I don't believe it will), the remainder of section 13 is still a matter of extreme concern. (http://www.guardian.co.uk/law/2012/may/29/justice-security-section-13)

The Coalition Government and Terrorism

In July 2010, the new coalition Home Secretary, Theresa May, announced a full review of anti-terrorism laws and procedures to be conducted by former Director of Public

Prosecutions Lord Macdonald. On announcing the review the Home Secretary claimed that it would focus on which powers could be scaled back in order to restore the balance between civil liberties and security. This proposal was in no little way a result of the decision in January 2010, of the European Court of Human Rights in *Gillan & Quinton v UK*, in which the court ruled that police powers, under section 44 of the Terrorism Act 2000, to arbitrarily stop and search people without the need for any grounds for suspicion, were contrary to the European Convention on Human Rights. The court held that the powers themselves, and the way they were authorised, were 'neither sufficiently circumscribed, nor subject to adequate legal safeguards against abuse'. The problems with the section 44 powers were further compounded in June 2010 when it was revealed that even such authorisation procedures as there were, had not been complied with, either because the authorisation given had exceeded the maximum 28-day limit or had not been properly approved by ministers within 48 hours. As has been seen, these issues were addressed in the Protection of Freedoms Act 2012.

The Terrorism Prevention and Investigation Measures Act 2011

In January 2011 the Home Secretary announced the government's intention with regard to the future of the control order regime, after some reportedly tense negotiations with her coalition partners in the Liberal Democrat party. The generally accepted assessment of the proposals was that they were a political compromise, which did little to live up to promises of the previous rhetorical claims as to a more liberal regime, with some commentators referring to the proposal as 'control order lite'.

The subsequent Terrorism Prevention and Investigation Measures Act 2011 included the following provisions:

- the new laws will be permanent, doing away with the requirement for parliament to renew them on an annual basis;
- the replacement for the control order regime will be known as Terrorism Prevention and Investigation Measures (TPIMs);
- there will be a two-year limitation on TPIMs, but they may be extended if new information emerges that leads the Home Secretary to believe that the person is still a danger;
- the secretary of state must now have 'reasonable grounds to believe' rather than 'reasonable grounds to suspect' that a person may pose a terrorist threat;
- the secretary of state is required to seek the court's permission before imposing the measures, except in the most urgent cases where the notice must be referred immediately to the court for confirmation;
- the current curfew requirements will be replaced by 'overnight residence' requirements;
- electronic tagging and restrictions on travel will be retained;
- greater access to the internet, phones and personal meetings will be allowed.

The Terrorism Prevention and Investigation Measures Act 2011 retains the power to relocate individuals to another part of the country without consent under powers for the secretary of state to impose enhanced TPIM notices. This, essentially emergency power may only be used, when Parliament is not in session, i.e. between the dissolution of a Parliament and the first Queen's Speech of the next Parliament.

As has been already mentioned, in July 2010, the Prime Minister announced that a judicial inquiry would take place into the UK's role in torture and rendition since the Al Qa'ida attacks of September 2001. This inquiry was to be conducted by a three-person inquiry panel led by Sir Peter Gibson, a former appeal court judge. Immediately, some doubts were raised about the appointment of Sir Peter Gibson, as he was currently commissioner for the intelligence services and thus might be seen as already having an interest in the issue. In August 2011, lawyers representing Britons detained in Guantánamo Bay, and 10 non-governmental organisations, wrote to the inquiry saying they would not co-operate with it. The grounds of the refusal were allegations that:

- evidence was to be heard largely in secret;
- the government would decide what would be published;
- the victims would not be able to question, or even identify, witnesses from MI5, MI6 or other agencies;
- the government had excluded from disclosure evidence from foreign intelligence agencies, including the CIA.

The NGOs, which include Amnesty, Liberty, Justice, and Human Rights Watch, claim that the way the inquiry has been set up fails to comply with Article 3 ECHR.

At the time, the inquiry was widely seen as designed to halt the growing number of extremely expensive and time-consuming, not to say politically damaging, civil claims by those who had been subjected to detention. On announcing the inquiry, Cameron pointed out that it could not begin until civil claims had been resolved through mediation or settled by compensation and Scotland Yard's investigation into the possible criminal conduct of two intelligence officers, one an MI5 operative and the other from MI6, had been concluded. As has been stated above, the then current civil cases were settled through mediation, and in early January 2012, the Crown Prosecution Service announced that it would not be bringing charges in relation to the original criminal allegations. However, the announcement also contained information that there would be a further criminal investigation into the alleged rendition of Libyan subjects to the former Gadhafi regime where they had been subjected to torture. Given the necessarily protracted nature of such criminal investigation into this latter allegation, the then Justice Secretary, Kenneth Clarke, was left with little choice but to announce the discontinuation of the Gibson inquiry. In making the announcement to parliament he emphasised that the government remained committed to a judge-led inquiry in the future, when the criminal investigations were complete. In a subsequent statement Sir Peter Gibson pointed out that the time had not all been wasted:

> The Inquiry regrets the fact that we are not able to complete the task we were asked to do by the Prime Minister (as set out in his letter to me of 6 July 2010). However we recognise that it is not practical for the Inquiry to continue for an indefinite period to wait for the conclusion of the police investigations. The Inquiry has, however, already done a large amount of preliminary work, including the collation of many documents from Government departments and the Security and Intelligence Agencies. We welcome therefore the opportunity to bring together the work we have done to date. The Inquiry will therefore produce a report of our work, highlighting themes which might be subject to further examination. (http://www.detaineeinquiry.org.uk/2012/01/statement-by-the-chairman-of-the- detainee-inquiry/)

CHAPTER SUMMARY: THE RULE OF LAW AND HUMAN RIGHTS

Various writers have different understandings of what the concept actually means, but see it essentially as involving a control of arbitrary power – Dicey, Hayek, Thompson, Raz, Unger and Weber.

The essential question is whether the UK is still governed under the rule of law, and of course the conclusion depends on the original understanding of the rule of law: Hayek and Thompson would have said not; Raz would say it was. Sir Stephen Sedley has a view as to the continued operation of the rule of law, which is based on substantive equality and challenges previous legal thought. Current judicial thought may be taken from the detailed consideration of the rule of law provided by the late Lord Bingham.

SEPARATION OF POWERS

The judges and the executive in the separation of powers have distinct but interrelated roles in the constitution. The question arises as to the extent to which the courts can act to control the activities of the executive through the operation of judicial review. The position of the Lord Chancellor as judge and member of the government has been questioned by many, including the current government.

THE HUMAN RIGHTS ACT 1998

The HRA incorporates the ECHR into domestic UK law. The Articles of the ECHR cover the following matters:

the right to life (Art 2);
prohibition of torture (Art 3);

prohibition of slavery and forced labour (Art 4);

the right to liberty and security (Art 5);

the right to a fair trial (Art 6);

the general prohibition of the enactment of retrospective criminal offences (Art 7);

the right to respect for private and family life (Art 8);

freedom of thought, conscience and religion (Art 9);

freedom of expression (Art 10);

freedom of assembly and association (Art 11);

the right to marry (Art 12);

prohibition of discrimination (Art 14).

The incorporation of the ECHR into UK law means that UK courts must decide cases in line with the above Articles. This has the potential to create friction between the judiciary and the executive/legislature.

THE STRUCTURE OF THE HUMAN RIGHTS ACT 1998

Section 2 requires future courts to take into account any previous decision of the ECtHR.

Section 3 requires all legislation to be read so far as possible to give effect to the rights provided under the Convention.

Section 4 empowers the courts to issue a declaration of incompatibility where any piece of primary legislation is found to conflict with the rights provided under the Convention.

Section 6 declares it unlawful for any public authority to act in a way that is incompatible with the Convention.

Section 7 allows the 'victim of the unlawful act' to bring proceedings against the public authority in breach.

Section 8 empowers the court to grant such relief or remedy against the public authority in breach of the Act as it considers just and appropriate.

Section 10 provides for fast-track remedial legislation where an Act of Parliament has been declared incompatible with Convention rights.

Section 19 of the Act requires that the minister responsible for the passage of any Bill through Parliament must make a written statement as to whether its provisions are compatible with Convention rights.

CASES DECIDED UNDER THE HUMAN RIGHTS ACT 1998

Cases relating to s 3 powers:

R v A (2001);

Re S (2002);

Mendoza v Ghaidan (2003).

Cases relating to declarations of incompatibility:

R v (1) Mental Health Review Tribunal, North & East London Region (2001);

Wilson v Secretary of State for Trade and Industry (2003);

A v Secretary of State for the Home Department (2004).

Cases relating to sentencing:

> *R v Secretary of State for the Home Department ex p Anderson and Taylor* (2002);
> *A v Secretary of State for the Home Department* (2005).

Cases relating to anti-terrorism legislation:

> *A v Secretary of State for the Home Department* (2002) & (2004);
> *Secretary of State for the Home Department v JJ and others* (2007);
> *Secretary of State for the Home Department v AP* (2010);
> *Secretary of State for the Home Department v MB & AF* (2007);
> *Al Rawi & Ors v Security Service & Ors* (2010);
> *A v Secretary of State for the Home Department* (2005);
> *Mohamed, R (on the application of) v Secretary of State for Foreign & Commonwealth Affairs* 1 & 2 (2010).

FOOD FOR THOUGHT

1. Consider what exactly is meant by the rule of law. Is it simply a matter of legal rules or does it connote something else? For example, Nazi Germany was notoriously legalistic, but were the legal rules it introduced and applied really the outcome of the rule of law?

2. Consider the distinction between the form and substance of the law. Is law 'right' simply because it has been introduced in the appropriate manner? If not, what grounds are there for criticising such law?

3. Consider the nature of human rights. What are they exactly and where do they come from? Would people have no human rights if there were no formal legal provisions, such as the Human Rights Act, recognising them?

4. Is it ever justifiable to torture suspects to acquire information? If not, why not? If it is, what limits can/should be placed on its use and who should regulate its use?

5. Some commentators and politicians complain that the Human Rights Act has increased the power of the judges. To what extent is this correct, and if it is correct, how has that been achieved, and is it a matter to be concerned about?

6. Human rights are currently politically controversial, with many members of the Conservative Party actively seeking the repeal and replacement of the Human Rights Act with a purely domestic Bill of Rights. To what extent is this proposal welcome, or feasible, in the current political/social context?

FURTHER READING

LAW, POLITICS AND THE RULE OF LAW

Anti-Social Behaviour Orders: Analysis of the First Six Years, 2004, London: National Association of Probation Officers

Bennion, F, 'A naked usurpation?' (1999) 149 NLJ 421

Bingham, T (Lord), *The Rule of Law*, 2010, London: Allen Lane

Dicey, AV, *Introduction to the Law of the Constitution*, 1897, London: Macmillan

Feldman, D, 'The Human Rights Act and constitutional principles' (1999) 19(2) JLS, June

Fenwick, H, *Civil Liberties and Human Rights*, 4th edn, 2007, Abingdon: Routledge-Cavendish

Fenwick, H, Masterman, R and Phillipson, G (eds), *Judicial Reasoning under the UK Human Rights Act*, 2007, Cambridge: CUP

Fine, R, *Democracy and the Rule of Law*, 1984, London: Pluto

Hayek, F von, *The Road to Serfdom*, 1962, London: Routledge

Hill, C, *Liberty Against the Law*, 1996, Harmondsworth: Penguin

Horowitz, MJ, 'The Rule of Law: an unqualified good?' (1977) 86 Yale LJ 561

Kairys, D (ed), *The Politics of Law: A Progressive Critique*, 1990, London: Pantheon

Kavanagh, A, 'Judging the judges under the Human Rights Act: deference, disillusionment and the "war on terror" ' [2009] PL 287–304

Keating, D, 'Upholding the Rule of Law' (1999) 149 NLJ 533

Laws, J (Sir), 'Law and democracy' [1995] PL 72

Locke, J, *The Treatises of Government*, 1988, Cambridge: CUP

Raz, J, 'The Rule of Law and its virtue' (1977) 93 LQR 195

Rozenberg, J, 'Upholding the Rule of Law' (2009) 106(6) Law Soc Gazette 8

Sedley, S (Sir), *Freedom, Law and Justice*, 1998, Hamlyn Lectures, London: Sweet & Maxwell

Sedley, S (Sir), 'Human rights: a 21st century agenda' [1995] PL 386

Steiner, H and Alston, P, *International Human Rights in Context*, 3rd edn, 2007, Oxford: OUP

Steyn (Lord), 'Civil liberties in modern Britain' [2009] PL 228–36

Thompson, A, 'Taking the right seriously: the case of FA Hayek', in Fitzpatrick, P (ed), *Dangerous Supplements*, 1991, London: Pluto

Thompson, E, *Whigs and Hunters*, 1977, Harmondsworth: Penguin

Wadham, J, 'Rights and responsibilities' (2009) 106(39) Law Soc Gazette 8

Young, J, 'The politics of the Human Rights Act' (1999) 26(1) JLS 27

Zander, M, 'The Prevention of Terrorism Act 2005' (2005) 155 NLJ 438

USEFUL WEBSITES

www.echr.coe.int/ECHR

The Council of Europe site – it includes all the decisions of the Commission on Human Rights, the Court of Human Rights and the Committee of Ministers back to 1951.

www.cpl.law.cam.ac.uk/past_activities/the_rt_hon_lord_bingham_the_rule_of_law.php

An audio archive of '*The Rule of Law*', a lecture given in 2006 by The Rt Hon Lord Bingham of Cornhill KG, House of Lords.

www.equalityhumanrights.com

The official website for the Equality and Human Rights Commission.

www.lse.ac.uk/collections/LSEPublicLecturesAndEvents/pdf/20060222-Goldsmith.pdf

An online transcript of '*Government and the Rule of Law in the Modern Age*', a lecture given in 2006 by The Rt Hon The Lord Goldsmith QC, Attorney General.

COMPANION WEBSITE

Now visit the companion website to:

- test your understanding of the key terms using our Flashcard Glossary;
- revise and consolidate your knowledge of 'The rule of law and human rights' using our Multiple Choice Question testbank;
- view all of the links to the Useful Websites above.

www.routledge.com/cw/slapper

SOURCES OF LAW

3

This chapter considers where law comes from and where students of law have to look to find it. As was stated in Chapter 1, in civil law systems one only has to look in the appropriate code to find the law relating to that area. However, in a common law system one has not only to look at the legislation, both primary and secondary, made by parliament, but one also has to look in the cases for the judicial statement that actually constitute that common law. Nor should it be forgotten that much of English law is now a restatement of the law of the European Union.

Ever since the UK joined the European Economic Community, now the European Union, it has progressively, but effectively, passed the power to create laws that have effect in this country to the wider European institutions. In effect, regarding Union matters, the UK's legislative, executive and judicial powers are now controlled by, and can only be operated within, the framework of European Union (EU) law. It is essential, therefore, even in a text that is primarily concerned with the English legal system, that the contemporary law student is aware of the operation of the legislative processes of the EU. Chapter 15 of this book will consider the EU and its institutions in some detail; the remainder of this chapter will concentrate on internal sources of law.

If the institutions of the EU are sovereign within its boundaries, then within the more limited boundaries of the UK, the sovereign power to make law lies with parliament. Under UK constitutional law, it is recognised that parliament has the power to enact, revoke or alter such, and any, law as it sees fit. Even the Human Rights Act (HRA) 1998 reaffirms this fact in its recognition of the power of parliament to make primary legislation that is incompatible with the rights provided under the European Convention on Human Rights (ECHR). Whether this will remain the case in the future is, however, a moot point. Coupled with this wide power is the convention that no one parliament can bind its successors in such a way as to limit their absolute legislative powers.

This absolute power is a consequence of the historical struggle between parliament and the Stuart monarchy in the seventeenth century. In its conflict with the Crown, parliament claimed the power of making law as its sole right. In so doing, parliament curtailed the royal prerogative and limited the monarchy to a purely formal role in the legislative procedure. In this struggle for ultimate power, the courts sided with parliament and, in return, parliament recognised the independence of the courts from its control. Prerogative powers still exist and remain important, but are now mainly exercised by the government in the name of the Crown, rather than by the Crown itself. In October 2009 the Ministry of Justice published a review of the remaining prerogative powers available to government ministers and the Crown (www.justice.gov.uk/about/docs/royal-prerogative.pdf). Some of the general prerogative powers are extremely important, such as the declaration of war and the power to issue, refuse or withdraw passport facilities, but others are less so, such as powers connected with prepaid postage stamps.

Although we still refer to our legal system as a common law system, and although the courts still have an important role to play in the interpretation of statutes, it has to be recognised that legislation is the predominant method of law-making in contemporary times. It is necessary, therefore, to have some knowledge of the workings of the legislative process.

3.3.1   THE PRE-PARLIAMENTARY PROCESS

Any consideration of the legislative process must be placed in the context of the political nature of parliament. Most statutes are the outcome of the policy decisions taken by government, and the actual policies pursued will of course depend upon the political persuasion and imperatives of the government of the day. Thus, a great deal of law creation and reform can be seen as the implementation of party political policies.

For example, the previous Labour governments, first elected in May 1997, introduced considerable constitutional reform as proposed in its manifesto. Thus, the Scottish Parliament and the Welsh Assembly have been instituted and many hereditary peers have been removed from the House of Lords. As the last election, in May 2010, resulted in no one party having an overall majority of Members of Parliament, the government had to be formed by a coalition of the larger Conservative and smaller Liberal Democrat parties. As the basis for this coming together, the parties had to fashion a compromise programme, rather than insist on pursuing their individual manifesto promises. This has already generated some disquiet among some people who voted for a particular party on the basis of a specific manifesto promise, only to see that promise subsequently denied. This was particularly the case with some Liberal Democrat voters who expressed anger when their party subsequently supported an increase in university fees, in spite of its pre-election promise not to do so.

As, by convention, the government is drawn from the party controlling a majority in the House of Commons, it can effectively decide what policies it wishes to implement and trust to its majority to ensure that its proposals become law. Accusations have been made that when governments have substantial majorities, they are able to operate without taking into account the consideration of their own party members, let alone the views of opposition members. It is claimed that their control over the day-to-day procedure of the House of Commons, backed with their majority voting power, effectively reduces the role of parliament to that of merely rubber-stamping their proposals.

It is certainly true, as the experience of the previous Conservative administration in the UK demonstrated, that governments with small majorities, if not actually in a minority, have to be circumspect in the policies they pursue through parliament. The fact that the elections of 1997 and 2001 returned the Labour Party to power, with much larger majorities than even they expected, once again raised the prospect of an over-powerful executive forcing its will through a politically quiescent parliament. Even the large vote against the war with Iraq in March 2003 was not sufficient to derail the will of the executive. One outstanding example where the previous government could not secure an overall majority was in relation to the vote on the proposal in the Terrorism Bill 2006 for the extension of the period of detention of suspected terrorists from 28 to 90 days.

The establishment of the coalition government clearly involves an increase in fissile tendencies, as the government faces not only the difficulty of controlling members of more than one party, but faces the much harder task of holding together two discrete memberships with sometimes incompatible political views. In response to this perceived potential difficulty one of the first decisions taken by the coalition was to introduce the constitutionally controversial *Fixed-term Parliaments Act 2011*. The stated purpose of this Act is to provide for five-year fixed-term parliaments. It actually fixes the date of the next General Election at 7 May 2015, although it allows the Prime Minister some leeway to alter the date by up to two months before or after that date. It also provides only two ways in which an election could be triggered before the end of the five-year term:

- if a motion of no confidence is passed and no alternative government is found;
- if a motion for an early General Election is agreed either by at least two-thirds of the House or without division.

The government generates most of the legislation that finds its way into the statute book, but individual Members of Parliament may also propose legislation in the form of Private Members' Bills.

There are in fact three ways in which an individual Member of Parliament can propose legislation:

- through the ballot procedure, by means of which 20 backbench Members get the right to propose legislation on the 10 or so Fridays in each parliamentary Session specifically set aside to consider such proposals;
- under Standing Order 39, which permits any Member to present a Bill after the 20 balloted Bills have been presented;

- under Standing Rule 13, the 10-minute rule procedure, which allows a Member to make a speech of up to 10 minutes in length in favour of introducing a particular piece of legislation.

Of these procedures, however, only the first has any real chance of success and even then success will depend on securing a high place in the ballot and on the actual proposal not being too contentious. Examples of this include the Abortion Act 1967, which was introduced as a Private Member's Bill to liberalise the provision of abortion, and the various attempts that have subsequently been made by Private Members' Bills to restrict the original provision. In relation to particular reforms, external pressure groups or interested parties may very often be the original moving force behind them. When individual Members of Parliament are fortunate enough to find themselves at the top of the ballot for Private Members' Bills, they may well also find themselves the focus of attention from such pressure groups proffering pre-packaged law reform proposals in their own particular areas of interest.

The decision as to which government Bills are to be placed before parliament in any Session is under the effective control of two Cabinet committees:

- the *Future Legislation Committee* determines which Bills will be presented to parliament in the *following* parliamentary Session;
- the *Legislation Committee* is responsible for the legislative programme conducted in the *immediate* parliamentary Session. It is the responsibility of this Committee to draw up the legislative programme announced in the Queen's Speech, delivered at the opening of the parliamentary Session.

Green Papers are consultation documents issued by the government, which set out and invite comments from interested parties on particular proposals for legislation. After considering any response, the government may publish a second document in the form of a White Paper, in which it sets out its firm proposals for legislation.

The publication of draft Bills is a third way through which pre-legislative consultation and scrutiny can take place. In recent years it has become common for government departments to issue such draft Bills to allow for consultation and for more detailed scrutiny of the proposed text to take place before the Bill is formally introduced into the legislative process. Such draft Bills are made available on the UK Parliament website and are examined either by select committees in the House of Commons or in the House of Lords or by a joint committee of both Houses of Parliament.

3.3.2   THE LEGISLATIVE PROCESS

Parliament consists of three distinct elements: the House of Commons with 650 directly elected members; the House of Lords with approximately 800 unelected members; and the monarch.

Before any legislative proposal, known at that stage as a Bill, can become an Act of Parliament, it must proceed through, and be approved by, both Houses of Parliament and must receive the Royal Assent. The ultimate location of power, however, is the House of Commons, which has the authority of being a democratically elected institution.

A Bill must be given three readings in both the House of Commons and the House of Lords before it can be presented for the Royal Assent. It is possible to commence the procedure in either House, although money Bills must be placed before the Commons in the first instance.

When a Bill is introduced in the Commons, it undergoes five distinct procedures:

- *First reading.* This is purely a formal procedure in which its title is read and a date set for its second reading.
- *Second reading.* At this stage, the general principles of the Bill are subject to extensive debate. The second reading is the critical point in the process of a Bill. At the end, a vote may be taken on its merits and, if it is approved, it is likely that it will eventually find a place in the statute book.
- *Committee stage.* After its second reading, the Bill is passed to a standing committee whose job it is to consider the provisions of the Bill in detail, clause by clause. The committee has the power to amend it in such a way as to ensure that it conforms with the general approval given by the House at its second reading. Very occasionally, a Bill may be passed to a special standing committee which considers the issues involved before going through the Bill in the usual way as a normal standing committee. Also, the whole House may consider certain Bills at committee stage. In general, these are Bills of constitutional importance, such as the House of Lords Bill, which proposed the reformation of the Upper House in 1999. Other Bills that need to be passed very quickly and certain financial measures, including at least part of each year's Finance Bill, are also considered by the committee of the whole House.
- *Report stage.* At this point, the standing committee reports the Bill back to the House for consideration of any amendments made during the committee stage.
- *Third reading.* Further debate may take place during this stage, but it is restricted to matters relating to the content of the Bill; questions relating to the general principles of the Bill cannot be raised.

When a Bill has completed all these stages, it is passed to the House of Lords for its consideration. After consideration by the Lords, the Bill is passed back to the Commons, which must then consider any amendments to the Bill that might have been introduced by the Lords. Where one House refuses to agree to the amendments made by the other, Bills can be repeatedly passed between them but, as Bills must usually complete their process within the life of a particular parliamentary Session, a failure to reach agreement within that period might lead to the total loss of the Bill. However, in 1998, the House of Commons Modernisation Committee agreed that, in defined circumstances and subject to certain safeguards, government Bills should be able to be carried over from one Session to the next, in the same way that Private and Hybrid Bills may be. The first Bill to be treated in this way was the Financial Services and Markets Bill 1998–99, which the House agreed to carry over into the 1999–2000 Session after a debate on 25 October 1999. The effect was to stay proceedings on the Bill in standing committee at the end of the 1998–99

Session and to carry it over into the next Session, when the committee resumed at the point in the Bill it had previously reached. In October 2004, a contested vote in the Commons made the carry-over process a permanent Standing Order of the House.

Surprisingly, and to no little opposition anger, on 13 September 2010 the coalition government announced that the current session of parliament would be extended into 2012 and that the next State Opening of Parliament would not take place until May 2012. The opposition claimed that by doubling the usual 12-month length of the parliamentary session, which previously had begun in October/November unless there was a General Election, the coalition government had allowed itself more time to ensure the passage of its legislative proposals, some of which are of a highly contentious nature.

The Parliament Acts

Given the need for legislation to be approved in both Houses of Parliament, it can be seen that the House of Lords has considerable power in the passage of legislation. However, the fact that it was never a democratically accountable institution, together with the fact that until 2005 it had an in-built Conservative party majority reflecting its previous hereditary composition, meant that its legislative powers had to be curtailed. Until the early years of the twentieth century, the House of Lords retained its full power to prevent the passage of legislation. However, Lloyd-George's Liberal budget of 1909 brought the old system to breaking point when the House of Lords originally refused to pass it. Although the budget was eventually passed after a General Election in 1910, a second election was held on the issue of reform of the House of Lords. As a result of the Liberal victory the Parliament Act of 1911 was introduced, which removed the House of Lords' power to veto a Bill. As a matter of interest, the 1911 Act also reduced the maximum lifespan of a parliament from seven years to its current five years and specifically retained the House of Lords' power to block any attempt to prolong the lifetime of a parliament. The Parliament Act of 1911 reduced the power of the Lords of the ability to delay a Bill by up to two years. In 1949 the Parliament Act of that year further reduced the Lords' delaying powers to one year, but it is significant that the 1949 Act was itself only introduced through the use of the previous Parliament Act of 1911.

Since 1949 the delaying powers of the House of Lords have been as follows:

- a 'Money Bill', that is, one containing only financial provisions, can be enacted without the approval of the House of Lords after a delay of one month;
- any other Bill can be delayed by one year.

Only four substantive Acts have been passed into law without the consent of the House of Lords:

- The *War Crimes Act 1991*
- The *European Parliamentary Elections Act 1999*
- The *Sexual Offences (Amendment) Act 2000*
- The *Hunting Act 2004*.

The last piece of legislation, the Hunting Act, was introduced to prohibit the hunting of mammals with dogs and was particularly designed to outlaw the tradition of fox-hunting.

However, of essential importance in relation to this Act was that the use of the Parliament Act 1949 to pass it, in the face of the refusal of the House of Lords, gave rise to a consideration of the legality of the Act itself in *Jackson v HM Attorney General* (2005).

Jackson v HM Attorney General (2005)

The appellants argued that the 1949 Act was itself invalid on the basis that it did not receive the consent of the House of Lords, and the Parliament Act 1911 did not permit an Act such as the 1949 Act to be enacted without the consent of the House of Lords. Thus, although the Hunting Act gave rise to the case, the essential underlying issue related to the validity of the 1949 Act, which in turn depended on the effect of the 1911 Parliament Act. As Lord Bingham put it, 'The merits and demerits of the Hunting Act, on which opinion is sharply divided, have no bearing on the legal issue which the House, sitting judicially, must resolve.'

In its reading of the Parliament Acts, the Court of Appeal concluded that under the 1911 Act the House of Commons had the power to make a 'relatively modest and straightforward amendment'. The Court of Appeal went on to conclude that the Parliament Act of 1949 was within that ambit, as an example of a 'relatively modest' amendment, as was the Hunting Act. However, the Court of Appeal raised doubts as to the power of the House of Commons, acting without the agreement of the House of Lords, to make changes 'of a fundamentally different nature to the relationship between the House of Lords and the Commons from those which the 1911 Act had made'. Thus the Court of Appeal raised the fundamental constitutional question relating to the ultimate power of the House of Commons.

Once again an augmented nine-member panel of the House of Lords was required to deal with these fundamental constitutional issues. In doing so, the House of Lords unanimously held that the reasoning of the Court of Appeal could not be sustained. In reaching that conclusion the House of Lords rejected the argument that the Parliament Act of 1911 was an exercise in the *delegation* of powers from parliament to the House of Commons, which could not later be used to extend those powers. Rather, as Lord Bingham stated:

> The overall object of the 1911 Act was not to delegate power: it was to restrict, subject to compliance with the specified statutory conditions, the power of the Lords to defeat measures supported by a majority of the Commons . . .

The House of Lords, however, did differ in their assessment of the extent of the power extended to the House of Commons under the Parliament Acts. It is clear that a majority of the House of Lords were of the view that the House of Commons could use the powers given to it under the Parliament Acts to force through such legislation as it wished, but a number of the judges were of the view that the Commons could not extend its own lifetime through such a procedure, as that would be in direct contradiction to the provisions of the Parliament Act 1911. Also, as has been pointed out at 2.3.2, although the decision in *Jackson* exemplifies the traditional deference of the courts to the supremacy of laws of parliament, the possibility of future changes in the relationship between the two institutions was at least hinted at in the judgment of Lord Steyn.

The Royal Assent is required before any Bill can become law. There is no constitutional rule requiring the monarch to assent to any Act passed by parliament. There is, however, a convention to that effect, and refusal to grant the Royal Assent to legislation passed by parliament would place the constitutional position of the monarchy in jeopardy. The procedural nature of the Royal Assent was highlighted by the Royal Assent Act 1967, which reduced the process of acquiring Royal Assent to a formal reading out of the short title of any Act in both Houses of Parliament.

An Act of Parliament comes into effect on the date of the Royal Assent, unless there is any provision to the contrary in the Act itself. It is quite common either for the Act to contain a commencement date for some time in the future, or for it to give the appropriate Secretary of State the power to give effect to its provisions at some future time by issuing statutory instruments. The Secretary of State is not required to bring the provisions into effect and it is not uncommon for some parts of Acts to be repealed before they are ever in force.

A current example of this is the massive, and hugely complex, Criminal Justice Act (CJA) 2003. As yet, not all of its provisions have come into effect, and full implementation will only take place over an extended timescale, if at all. One instance of this, which raises a number of issues that will be considered further in various sections of this book, relates to the provisions of s 43 of the CJA, which provides for the prosecution of certain serious and complex fraud cases to be conducted without a jury. Unusually, by virtue of s 330(5) of the CJA, any statutory instrument seeking to bring s 43 into force requires an affirmative resolution of both Houses of Parliament. Following the failure of the Jubilee extension fraud cases the government announced its intention to implement s 43, and to that end a draft commencement order was produced. However, in July 2007 the House of Lords effectively killed off a Fraud (Trials without a Jury) Bill by postponing its consideration for six months and subsequently it never re-appeared. Section 111 of the Protection of Freedoms Bill 2010–2011 proposes the repeal of s 43 of the CJA.

A more recent example of this failure to implement legislative provisions may be seen in the Equality Act 2010, one of the last pieces of legislation passed by the previous government. Although the new coalition Home Secretary and Minister for Women and Equalities brought most of the provisions into effect through commencement orders, she let it be known that she would not do so with all its provisions and certainly not s 1 of the Act, which *imposed a duty on public bodies* to have due regard when making strategic decisions to reducing the inequalities of outcome that result from socio-economic disadvantage. In response, critics accused her of rendering the Act 'virtually toothless'.

The 1997 Labour Government was elected on the promise of the fundamental reform of the House of Lords, which it saw as undemocratic and unrepresentative. After establishing a Royal Commission, the government embarked on a two-stage process of reform. The first stage of reform was achieved through the House of Lords Act 1999, which removed the right of the majority of hereditary peers to sit in the House of Lords. The second stage of reform was set out, towards the end of 2001, in a White Paper entitled 'Completing the Reform'.

The most controversial aspect of the White Paper was the relatively small proportion of directly elected members it proposed, especially when compared with the large proportion of members who would be nominated rather than elected. The government, faced with much criticism, even from its own MPs, set up a joint committee of both Houses of Parliament to consider the course of future reform. Somewhat surprisingly, that committee made no recommendation and merely listed seven possible options for determining the membership of a reformed House of Lords. The options were:

- a fully appointed house;
- a fully elected house;
- 80 per cent appointed, 20 per cent elected;
- 80 per cent elected, 20 per cent appointed;
- 60 per cent appointed, 40 per cent elected;
- 60 per cent elected, 40 per cent appointed;
- 50 per cent appointed, 50 per cent elected.

Even more surprisingly, in February 2003, the House of Commons voted against all of the options and thus failed to approve any of them. The closest vote, for an 80 per cent elected house, fell narrowly by 284 votes against to 281 in favour.

On coming to power the Conservative/Liberal Democrat coalition passed the Conservative-inspired Parliamentary Voting System and Constituencies Act (PVSCA) 2011, which provided for a future reduction in the number of MPs to 600 while equalising the numerical size of constituencies. The Act, at the behest of the Liberal Democrats, also provided for a referendum on an alternative voting system, which was subsequently rejected in May 2011.

The coalition government's policy on reform of the House of Lords faced the initial problem of combining the two parties' manifesto proposals, the Conservatives preferring a 'mainly elected' second chamber and the Liberal Democrats a 'fully elected' second chamber. In May 2011 the government published a White Paper and draft Bill containing proposals for a smaller, reformed House of Lords. The draft Bill provided for:

- the powers of the reformed House of Lords to remain the same;
- the reformed House to be limited to 300 members, each eligible for a single term of 15 years;

- elections to use the single transferable vote (STV), electing a third of members each time with elections normally taking place at the same time as General Elections;
- multi-member electoral districts, to be drawn up independently based on national and county boundaries;
- a continuation of the presence of Bishops of the Church of England in the House of Lords, but reducing their number from 26 to 12;
- a transition staggered over the course of three electoral cycles.

Crucially, the draft Bill proposed a reformed House of Lords with 80 per cent of elected members (240), with the remaining 20 per cent (60 members) appointed independently to sit as cross-benchers.

However, in July 2012, 91 Conservative MPs effectively killed off any possibility of the reform Bill being passed by aligning, and voting, with the Labour Party against a 'programme motion' which would have set a timetable for debate on the measure. Without such a limit on debate there was no real chance of the Bill being passed and Nick Clegg, the Liberal Democrat leader and deputy prime minister, who had been pushing for the reform, had to recognise defeat and effectively withdraw the Bill.

In retaliation, Clegg and his Liberal Democrats withdrew their support for the reduction of the number of MPs. Although Prime Minster Cameron has insisted that he will proceed with the vote necessary to implement the reform to the House of Commons, the withdrawal of Liberal Democrat support effectively means that the necessary vote will not be passed. This defeat has been recognised tacitly in the declaration of the chairman of the Conservative party that candidates for the next election will be selected on the basis of existing parliamentary boundaries. In any event the PVSCA 2011 will remain on the statute book, perhaps to be implemented at a later date.

Consequently, although all three major parties had included reform of the House of Lords in their election manifestos, it now seems apparent that no such reform will take place in the near future, nor will the redrawing of constituency boundaries with the resultant reduction in MPs' seats take place.

3.3.3 THE DRAFTING OF LEGISLATION

In 1975, in response to criticisms of the language and style of legislation, the Renton Committee on the Preparation of Legislation (Cmnd 6053) examined the form in which legislation was presented. Representations were made to the Committee by a variety of people ranging from the judiciary to the lay public. The Committee divided complaints about statutes into four main headings relating to:

- obscurity of language used;
- over-elaboration of provisions;
- illogicality of structure;
- confusion arising from the amendment of existing provisions.

It was suggested that the drafters of legislation tended to adopt a stylised archaic legalism in their language and employed a grammatical structure that was too complex and convoluted to be clear, certainly to the layperson and even, on occasion, to legal experts. These criticisms, however, have to be considered in the context of the whole process of drafting legislation and weighed against the various other purposes to be achieved by statutes. The actual drafting of legislation is the work of parliamentary counsel to the Treasury, who specialise in this task. The first duty of the drafters must be to give effect to the intention of the department instructing them, and to do so in as clear and precise a manner as is possible. These aims, however, have to be achieved under pressure, and sometimes extreme pressure, of time. An insight into the various difficulties faced in drafting legislation was provided by a former parliamentary draftsman, Francis Bennion, in an article entitled 'Statute law obscurity and drafting parameters' ((1978) British JLS 235). He listed nine specific parameters which the drafter of legislation had to take into account. These parameters are as follows:

- *Legal effectiveness*. This is the need for the drafters to translate the political wishes of those instructing them into appropriate legal language and form.
- *Procedural legitimacy*. This refers to the fact that the legislation must conform with certain formal requirements if it is to be enacted. For example, it is a requirement that Acts be divided into clauses, and Bills not assuming this form would not be considered by parliament.
- *Timeliness*. This refers to the requirement for legislation to be drawn up within particularly pressing time constraints. The effect of such pressure can be poorly drafted and defective provisions.
- *Certainty*. It is of the utmost importance that the law be clearly set down so that individuals can know its scope and effect and can guide their actions within its provisions. The very nature of language, however, tends to act against this desire for certainty. In pursuit of certainty, the temptation for the person drafting the legislation is to produce extremely long and complex sentences consisting of a series of limiting and refining sub-clauses. This process in turn, however, tends merely to increase the obscurity of meaning.
- *Comprehensibility*. Ideally, legislation should be comprehensible to the layperson, but given the complex nature of the situation that the legislature is dealing with, such an ideal is probably beyond attainment in practice. Nonetheless, legislative provisions certainly should be open to the comprehension of the Members of Parliament who are asked to vote on them, and they certainly should not be beyond the comprehension of the legal profession who have to construe them for their clients. Unfortunately, some legislation fails on both these counts.
- *Acceptability*. This refers to the fact that legislation is expected to be couched in uncontentious language and using a traditional prose style.
- *Brevity*. This refers to the fact that legislative provisions should be as short as is compatible with the attainment of the legislative purpose. The search for brevity in legislation can run counter to the wish for certainty in, and acceptability of, the language used.

- *Debatability*. This refers to the fact that legislation is supposed to be structured in such a way as to permit it, and the policies that lie behind it, to be debated in parliament.
- *Legal compatibility*. This refers to the need for any new provision to fit in with already existing provisions. Where the new provision alters or repeals existing provisions, it is expected that such effect should be clearly indicated.

A consideration of these various desired characteristics shows that they are not necessarily compatible; indeed, some of them, such as the desire for clarity and brevity, may well be contradictory. The point remains that those people charged with the responsibility for drafting legislation should always bear the above factors in mind when producing draft legislation, but if one principle is to be pursued above others, it is surely the need for clarity of expression and meaning.

3.3.4 TYPES OF LEGISLATION

Legislation can be categorised in a number of ways. For example, distinctions can be drawn between the following:

- *Public Acts*, which relate to matters affecting the general public. These can be further subdivided into either government Bills or Private Members' Bills.
- *Private Acts*, on the other hand, relate to the powers and interests of particular individuals or institutions, although the provision of statutory powers to particular institutions can have a major effect on the general public. For example, companies may be given the power to appropriate private property through compulsory purchase orders.
- *Enabling legislation* gives power to a particular person or body to oversee the production of the specific details required for the implementation of the general purposes stated in the parent Act. These specifics are achieved through the enactment of statutory instruments. (See below, at 3.5 for a consideration of delegated legislation.)

Acts of Parliament can also be distinguished on the basis of the function they are designed to carry out. Some are *unprecedented* and cover new areas of activity previously not governed by legal rules, but other Acts are aimed at *rationalising* or *amending* existing legislative provisions.

- *Consolidating legislation* is designed to bring together provisions previously contained in a number of different Acts, without actually altering them. The Companies Act of 1985 was an example of a consolidating Act. It brought together provisions contained in numerous amending Acts that had been introduced since the previous consolidation Act of 1948. The new Companies Act 2006 also consolidated some previous legislation passed since the 1985 Act, but as it also contains previous common law provisions it may also be seen as an example of the next category.

- *Codifying legislation* seeks not just to bring existing statutory provisions under one Act, but also looks to give statutory expression to common law rules. The classic examples of such legislation are the Partnership Act of 1890 and the Sale of Goods Act 1893 (now 1979).

- *Amending legislation* is designed to alter some existing legal provision. Amendment of an existing legislative provision can take two forms:

  (i)   a *textual amendment* is one where the new provision substitutes new words for existing ones in a legislative text or introduces completely new words into that text. Altering legislation by means of textual amendment has one major drawback, in that the new provisions make very little sense on their own, without the contextual reference of the original provision they are designed to alter;

  (ii)   *non-textual amendments* do not alter the actual wording of the existing text, but alter the operation or effect of those words. Non-textual amendments may have more immediate meaning than textual alterations, but they too suffer from the problem that, because they do not alter the original provisions, the two provisions have to be read together to establish the legislative intention.

Neither method of amendment is completely satisfactory, but the Renton Committee on the Preparation of Legislation favoured textual amendments over non-textual amendments.

3.4 STATUTORY INTERPRETATION

So far, attention has focused on the procedure through which the legislature makes law, but once it has come into being the law has to be applied and given effect, and ultimately that is the role of the judges. Parliament might have said what the law is; the task for the judges is to make sense of parliament's words.

3.4.1 PROBLEMS IN INTERPRETING LEGISLATION

The accepted view is that the constitutional role of the judiciary is simply to *apply* the law. The function of creating law is the prerogative of parliament. As will be seen, such a view is simplistic to the extent that it ignores the potential for judicial creativity in relation to the operation of the common law and the doctrine of judicial precedent. Equally, however, it ignores the extent to which the judiciary have a measure of discretion and creative power in the manner in which they interpret the legislation that comes before them.

Section 3.3.3 has already considered the general difficulties involved in drafting legislation from the point of view of the person carrying out the drafting; equally, however, it has to be recognised that determining the actual meaning of legislation presents judges with a practical difficulty. In order to *apply* legislation, judges must ascertain the meaning of the legislation, and in order to ascertain the meaning, they are faced with the difficulty of interpreting the legislation.

Before considering the way in which judges interpret legislation, it is pertinent to emphasise that, in spite of the best endeavours of those who draft legislation to be precise in communicating the meaning of what they produce, the process of interpretation is inescapable and arises from the nature of language itself. Legislation can be seen as a form of linguistic communication. It represents and passes on to the judiciary what parliament has determined the law should be in relation to a particular situation. Legislation, therefore, shares the general problem of uncertainty inherent in any mode of communication. One of the essential attributes of language is its fluidity; the fact that words can have more than one meaning and that the meaning of a word can change depending on its context. In such circumstances, it is immediately apparent that understanding is an active process. Faced with ambiguity, the recipient of information has to decide which of various meanings to assign to specific words, depending upon the context in which they are used.

Legislation gives rise to additional problems in terms of communication. One of the essential requirements of legislation is generality of application, the need for it to be written in such a way as to ensure that it can be effectively applied in various circumstances, without the need to detail those situations individually. This requirement, however, gives rise to particular problems of interpretation, for, as has been pointed out in 3.3.3, the need for generality can only really be achieved at the expense of clarity and precision of language. A further possibility that is not as uncommon as it should be is that the legislation under consideration is obscure, ambiguous, or indeed meaningless, or fails to achieve the end at which it is aimed, simply through being badly drafted. The task facing the judge in such circumstances is to provide the legislation with some effective meaning.

Legislation therefore involves an inescapable measure of uncertainty that can only be made certain through judicial interpretation. To the extent, however, that the interpretation of legislative provisions is an active process, it is equally a creative one, and inevitably it involves the judiciary in making law through determining the meaning and effect to be given to any particular piece of legislation. There is a further possibility that has to be considered: that judges might actually abuse their role as necessary interpreters of legislation in such a way as to insinuate their own particular personal views and prejudices into their interpretations, and in so doing misapply the legislation and subvert the wishes of the legislature.

3.4.2 APPROACHES TO STATUTORY INTERPRETATION

Having considered the problems of interpreting language generally and the difficulties in interpreting legislation in particular, it is appropriate to consider in detail the methods and mechanisms that judges bring to bear on legislation in order to determine its meaning. There are, essentially, two contrasting views as to how judges should go about determining the meaning of a statute – the restrictive, literal approach and the more permissive, purposive approach:

1.   *The literal approach*

The literal approach is dominant in the English legal system, although it is not without critics, and devices do exist for circumventing it when it is seen as too restrictive. This view of judicial interpretation holds that the judge should look primarily to the words of the legislation in order to construe its meaning and, except in the very limited circumstances considered below, should not look outside of, or behind, the legislation in an attempt to find its meaning.

2.   *The purposive approach*

The purposive approach rejects the limitation of the judges' search for meaning to a literal construction of the words of legislation itself. It suggests that the interpretative role of the judge should include, where necessary, the power to look beyond the words of statute in pursuit of the reason for its enactment, and that meaning should be construed in the light of that purpose and so as to give it effect. This purposive approach is typical of civil law systems. In these jurisdictions, legislation tends to set out general principles and leaves the fine details to be filled in later by the judges who are expected to make decisions in the furtherance of those general principles.

European Union (EU) legislation tends to be drafted in the continental, civil law manner. Its detailed effect, therefore, can only be determined on the basis of a purposive approach to its interpretation. This requirement, however, runs counter to the literal approach that is the dominant approach in the English system. The need to interpret such legislation, however, has forced a change in that approach in relation to EU legislation and even with respect to domestic legislation designed to implement Community legislation. Thus, in *Pickstone v Freemans plc* (1988), the House of Lords held that it was permissible, and indeed necessary, for the court to read words into inadequate domestic legislation in order to give effect to EU law in relation to provisions relating to equal pay for work of equal value. (For a similar approach, see also the House of Lords' decision in *Litster v Forth Dry Dock* (1989) and the decision in *Three Rivers DC v Bank of England (No 2)* (1996), considered below at 3.4.4.2.)

3.4.2.1   The purposive approach and updating construction

It has to be recognised that for some time there has been a move away from the over-reliance on the literal approach to statutory interpretation to a more purposive approach. As Lord Griffiths put it in *Pepper v Hart* [1993] 1 All ER 42 at 50:

> The days have long passed when the court adopted a strict constructionist view of interpretation which required them to adopt the literal meaning of the language. The courts now adopt a purposive approach which seeks to give effect to the true purpose of legislation and are prepared to look at much extraneous material that bears on the background against which the legislation was enacted.

Such a shift has been necessitated, to no little degree, by the need for the courts to consider matters that were not within the original contemplation of parliament at the time when the legislation was passed, but which have since been brought into play by the effect of technological advances. As Lord Steyn in *R (Quintavalle) v Secretary of State for Health* [2003] 2 All ER 113 at 123 put it:

> The pendulum has swung towards purposive methods of construction. This change was not initiated by the teleological approach of European Community jurisprudence, and the influence of European legal culture generally, but it has been accelerated by European ideas . . .

That process may be traced through a number of controversial cases starting with *Royal College of Nursing of the United Kingdom v Department of Health and Social Security* (1981) (considered in detail at 3.4.3). In his minority judgment Lord Wilberforce, in that case, had expressed the view that ([1981] AC 800 at 822):

> In interpreting an Act of Parliament it is proper, and indeed necessary, to have regard to the state of affairs existing, and known by Parliament to be existing, at the time. It is a fair presumption that Parliament's policy or intention is directed to that state of affairs. Leaving aside cases of omission by inadvertence . . . *when a new state of affairs, or a fresh set of facts bearing on policy, comes into existence, the courts have to consider whether they fall within the Parliamentary intention. They may be held to do so, if they fall within the same genus of facts as those to which the expressed policy has been formulated. They may also be held to do so if there can be detected a clear purpose in the legislation which can only be fulfilled if the extension is made.* How liberally these principles may be applied must depend upon the nature of the enactment, and the strictness or otherwise of the words in which it has been expressed . . . In any event there is one course which the courts cannot take, under the law of this country; they cannot fill gaps; they cannot by asking the question 'What would Parliament have done in this current case – not being one in contemplation – if the facts had been before it?' attempt themselves to supply the answer, if the answer is not to be found in the terms of the Act itself. (emphasis added)

In other words, Lord Wilberforce thought that legislation *may not* be construed so as to cover new states of affairs, if the new construction required the court to fill gaps, or to ask what parliament would have done in relation to situations that it could not have had any knowledge of, and hence were outside the ambit of the actual text of the legislation.

However, the court *could* use a purposive reading to extend the law to new situations where one of two things applied:

(i)   the genus of subject matter encompassed the new subject matter; or

(ii)   parliament's purpose was clear and an extended reading was necessary to give effect to it.

Given that Lord Wilberforce actually decided that the *Royal College of Nursing* case was not one in which the court should use the purposive approach, it is perhaps not a little ironic that his exposition of the appropriate circumstances under which the courts can adopt a purposive approach has been generally accepted, and, in many cases, used to extend the application of statutes in a way that he himself might very well not have agreed with.

In *R (Quintavalle) v Secretary of State for Health* (2003) the courts were asked to declare whether embryos created by cell nuclear replacement (CNR), a form of human cloning involving a human egg and a cell from a donor's body, were regulated under the Human Fertilisation and Embryology Act (HFE) 1990, which had been passed at a time when embryos were only ever created by fertilisation of an egg by a sperm. Section 1(1) (a) of the Act defines embryos as 'a live human embryo where fertilisation is complete'.

An organisation opposed to cloning and embryo experimentation, the Pro-Life Alliance, contested a statement from the government that therapeutic cloning research was permitted under the HFE Act 1990, subject to licensing by the regulatory authority, the Human Fertilisation and Embryology Authority (HFEA). The Alliance sought a declaration that the authority had no power to license such research on the grounds that an embryo created by cell nuclear replacement did not fall within the statutory definition of 'embryo'. The argument for the Alliance was that as cloned embryos created by CNR were never fertilised, as commonly understood, they could not be subject to the Act and, more importantly for them, the HFEA could not have any authority to license any such activity.

At first instance the declaration sought by the Alliance was granted 'with some reluctance', the judge saying that the government's argument to have the statute take account of new technology involved 'an impermissible rewriting and extension of the definition'. However, the Court of Appeal set aside the declaration, which decision the House of Lords subsequently confirmed, holding that the purposive interpretation argued for by the government did *not* require the court to assume the mantle of legislator. In so doing both Lord Bingham and Lord Steyn referred to the importance of a purposive approach in enabling the courts to give effect to the intention of parliament in areas where legislative provisions need to be considered in the context of rapid scientific and technological change.

In deciding *Quintavalle*, the House of Lords based its decision on Lord Wilberforce's comments in the *Royal College of Nursing* case, which in the opinion of Lord Bingham 'may now be treated as authoritative'. In so doing the House of Lords held that embryos created by CNR, notwithstanding the fact that they were unfertilised, were within the same '*genus of facts*' as embryos created naturally or fertilised *in vitro*. In putting Lord Wilberforce's proposition into operation, the House of Lords held that CNR organisms were, in essence, sufficiently like other embryos to be considered as belonging to the same '*genus of facts*'. Parliament could not rationally have been assumed to have intended to exclude such embryos from the regulation; consequently, the fact of fertilisation was not to be treated as integral to the s 1 definition. Consequently, they were subject to the control of the HFE Act 1990 and the HFEA could authorise research using such embryos.

In reaching his decision, Lord Bingham considered the purpose and procedure of statutory interpretation and concluded that ([2003] 2 All ER 113 at 118):

> The basic task of the court is to ascertain and give effect to the true meaning of what Parliament has said in the enactment to be construed. But that is not to say that attention should be confined and a literal interpretation given to the particular provisions which give rise to difficulty. Such an approach not only encourages immense prolixity in drafting, since the draftsman will feel obliged to provide expressly for every contingency which may possibly arise. It may also (under the banner of loyalty to the will of Parliament) lead to the frustration of that will, because undue concentration on the minutiae of the enactment may lead the court to neglect the purpose which Parliament intended to achieve when it enacted the statute . . . The court's task, within the permissible bounds of interpretation, is to give effect to Parliament's purpose. So the controversial provisions should be read in the context of the statute as a whole, and the statute as a whole *should be read in the historical context of the situation which led to its enactment*. (emphasis added)

With regard to the specific question of whether words in statutes should retain their original meaning, or whether they may be interpreted in the light of contemporary social factors, Lord Bingham concluded that legislation is akin to a living text, the meaning of which speaks differently as the social context in which it speaks changes. In his view (at 118):

> There is, I think, no inconsistency between the rule that statutory language retains the meaning it had when Parliament used it and the rule that a statute is always speaking . . . The meaning of 'cruel and unusual punishments' has not changed over the years since 1689, but many punishments which were not then thought to fall within that category would now be held to do so.

The impact of the preference for the purposive approach over the literal one may be seen in *R v Z and others* (2005) in which four men were charged with being members of a proscribed organisation contrary to s 11(1) of the Terrorism Act 2000. Schedule 2 of the Act listed the organisations proscribed under the Act. It referred to the IRA but did not specifically mention the 'Real IRA', which the men were allegedly members of. At first instance the judge found no case to answer, but following a reference by the Attorney-General for Northern Ireland, the Northern Ireland Court of Appeal disagreed, concluding that it was the intention of the legislature to include the 'Real IRA' within the term 'the IRA' and that the legislation therefore had to be construed in such a way as to include that organisation.

In the House of Lords, counsel for the accused argued that the task of the court was 'to interpret the provision which parliament has enacted and not to give effect to an inferred intention of parliament not fairly to be derived from the language of the statute'. The House of Lords rejected that argument, holding that the historical context of the legislation was of fundamental importance. It decided that all the Westminster and Stormont statutes were directed towards the elimination of Irish-related terrorism and that the general approach in legislation had been to proscribe the IRA, using that title as a blanket description that 'embraced all emanations, manifestations and representations of the IRA, whatever their relationship to each other'.

The effect of *Pepper v Hart* (1993), permitting access to *Hansard*, will be considered at 3.4.4.2 below, but for the moment, it is still the case that the judges remain subject to the established rules of interpretation of which there are three primary rules of statutory interpretation, together with a variety of other secondary aids to construction.

3.4.3 RULES OF INTERPRETATION

In spite of the content of the preceding section, it is still necessary to consider the traditional and essentially literally based approaches to statutory interpretation. What follows in this and the following two sections should be read within the context of the Human Rights Act (HRA) 1998, which requires all legislation to be construed in such a way as, if at all possible, to bring it within the ambit of the European Convention on Human Rights (ECHR). The effect of this requirement is to provide the judiciary with powers of interpretation much wider than those afforded to them by the more traditional rules of interpretation, as can be seen from *R v A* (2001), considered above at 2.5.1.2. However, to quote Lord Steyn further in this particular context ([2001] 3 All ER 1 at 16):

> ... the interpretative obligation under section 3 of the 1998 Act is a strong one. It applies even if there is no ambiguity in the language in the sense of the language being capable of two different meanings ... [s]ection 3 places a duty on the court to strive to find a possible interpretation compatible with Convention rights. Under ordinary methods of interpretation a court may depart from the language of the statute to avoid absurd consequences: section 3 goes much further. Undoubtedly, a court must always look for a contextual and purposive interpretation: section 3 is more radical in its effect ... In accordance with the will of Parliament as reflected in section 3 it will sometimes be necessary to adopt an interpretation which linguistically may appear strained.
>
> The techniques to be used will not only involve the reading down of express language in a statute but also the implication of provisions. A declaration of incompatibility is a measure of last resort. It must be avoided unless it is plainly impossible to do so.

Nonetheless, where the HRA is not involved, the courts still have to interpret legislative provisions. The three traditional rules of statutory interpretation are as follows:

1   *The literal rule*

Under this rule, the judge is required to consider what the legislation actually says rather than considering what it might mean. In order to achieve this end, the judge should give words in legislation their literal meaning – that is, their plain, ordinary, everyday meaning – even if the effect of this is to produce what might be considered an otherwise unjust or undesirable outcome. The literal rule appears at first sight to be the least problematic method of interpreting legislation. Under this rule, the courts most obviously appear to be recognising their limitations by following the wishes of parliament as expressed in the words of the legislation under consideration. When, however, the difficulties of assigning a fixed and unchallengeable meaning to any word is recalled, the use of the literal rule becomes less uncontroversial. A consideration of the cases reveals examples where the literal rule has been used as a justification for what otherwise might appear as partial judgments on the part of the court concerned in the case.

Inland Revenue Commissioners v Hinchy (1960) concerned s 25(3) of the Income Tax Act 1952, which stated that any taxpayer who did not complete their tax return was subject to a fixed penalty of £20 plus *treble the tax which he ought to be charged under the Act*. The question that had to be decided was whether the additional element of the penalty should be based on the total amount that should have been paid, or merely the unpaid portion of that total. The House of Lords adopted a literal interpretation of the statute and held that any taxpayer in default should have to pay triple their original tax bill.

In *R v Goodwin* (2005) the rider/driver of a jet-ski in the sea off Weymouth, crashed into another jet-ski, causing serious injuries to the rider/driver of the other machine.

The defendant was prosecuted under s 58 of the Merchant Shipping Act 1995, which makes it an offence for 'the master of . . . a United Kingdom ship' negligently to do any act which causes or is likely to cause serious injury to any person. Section 313 of the Act defines a ship as including every description of vessel 'used in navigation'. At first instance it was decided that a jet-ski was a ship for the purposes of the Merchant Shipping Act 1995 and as a result the defendant pleaded guilty.

On appeal, however, the Court of Appeal quashed his conviction, deciding that a jet-ski is not 'used in navigation' for the purpose of travel from one place to another and as s 58 only applies to sea-going ships and the jet-ski was used only within the port of Weymouth, it could not really be described as 'sea-going'.

A further problem with regard to the literal rule, relating to the difficulty judges face in determining the literal meaning of even the commonest of terms, can be seen in *R v Maginnis* (1987). The defendant had been charged under the Misuse of Drugs Act 1971, with having drugs in his possession and *with intent to supply them*. He claimed that, as he had intended to return the drugs to a friend who had left them in his car, he could not be guilty of *supplying* as charged. In this case, the judges, from first instance, through the Court of Appeal to the House of Lords, disagreed as to the literal meaning of the common word 'supply'. Even in the House of Lords, Lord Goff, in his dissenting judgment, was able to cite a dictionary definition to support his interpretation of the word. It is tempting to suggest that the majority of judges in the House of Lords operated in a totally disingenuous way by justifying their decision on the literal interpretation of the law whilst, at the same time, fixing on a non-literal meaning for the word under consideration. In actual fact, in *R v Maginnis*, each of the meanings for 'supply' proposed by the various judges could be supported by dictionary entries. That fact, however, only highlights the essential weakness of the literal rule, which is that it wrongly assumes that there is such a thing as a single, uncontentious, literal understanding of words. While *R v Maginnis* concerned the meaning of 'supply', *Attorney General's Reference (No 1 of 1988)* (1989) concerned the meaning of 'obtained' in s 1(3) of the Company Securities (Insider Dealing) Act 1985, since replaced by the Criminal Justice Act 1993, and led to similar disagreement as to the precise meaning of an everyday word. *Bromley LBC v GLC* (1983) may be cited as an instance where the courts arguably took a covert politic decision under the guise of applying the literal meaning of a particular word in a piece of legislation.

In *Owens v Dudley Metropolitan Borough Council* (2011) the Court of Appeal confirmed that, where statute does not define a term, it should be given its ordinary meaning. In this case the claimant was employed as a special needs teacher and counsellor. Although her contract of employment described her as a teacher, her employer claimed that she was not in fact a teacher and consequently could not be a member of the Teachers' Pension scheme. At first instance the High Court held that she was not a teacher as she merely provided services ancillary to teaching. The Court of Appeal held that, as there was no specific definition of 'teacher' in the Teachers' Pension Scheme, the dictionary definitions of the term should be referred to. As the dictionary definition was wide and went beyond people who stand in front of pupils in a classroom, the claimant was held to come within the definition.

2   *The golden rule*

This rule is generally considered to be an extension of the literal rule. In its general expression, it is used in circumstances where the application of the literal rule is likely to result in what appears to the court to be an obviously absurd result. The golden rule was first stated by Lord Wensleydale in *Grey v Pearson* (1857), but its operation is better defined by the words of Lord Blackburn in *River Wear Commissioners v Adamson* (1877) as follows:

> [W]e are to take the whole statute and construe it all together, giving the words their ordinary signification, unless when so applied they produce an inconsistency, or an absurdity or inconvenience so great as to convince the Court that the intention could not have been to use them in their ordinary signification, and to justify the Court in putting them in some other signification, which, though less proper, is one which the Court thinks the words will bear.

It should be emphasised, however, that the court is not at liberty to use the golden rule to ignore, or replace, legislative provisions simply on the basis that it does not agree with them; it must find genuine difficulties before it declines to use the literal rule in favour of the golden one. How one determines or defines genuine difficulty is of course a matter of discretion and, therefore, dispute. As Lord Blackburn's definition makes clear, the use of the rule actually involves the judges in finding what they consider the statute should have said or provided, rather than what it actually did state or provide. As will be seen below, the justification for this judicial activity is based on that extremely wide, amorphous, not to say spurious, legal concept: public policy. However, such a justification immediately raises the questions of the judges' understanding of, and right to determine, public policy, which will be considered in the next section of this chapter.

It is sometimes stated that there are two versions of the golden rule:

(a)   *The narrow meaning* This is used where there are two apparently contradictory meanings to a particular word used in a legislative provision or the provision is simply ambiguous in its effect. In such a situation, the golden rule operates to ensure that preference is given to the meaning that does not result in the provision being an absurdity. An example of the application of the golden rule in this narrow sense is *Adler v George* (1964). The defendant had been charged, under the Official Secrets Act 1920, with obstruction in the vicinity of a prohibited area, whereas she had actually carried out the obstruction inside the area. The court preferred not to restrict itself to the literal wording of the Act and found the defendant guilty as charged.

(b)   *The wider meaning* This version of the golden rule is resorted to where, although there is only one possible meaning to a provision, the court is of the opinion that to adopt such a literal interpretation will result in Lord Blackburn's 'inconsistency, absurdity or inconvenience'. The classic example of this approach is to be found in *Re Sigsworth* (1935), in which the court introduced common law rules into legislative provisions, which were silent on the matter, to prevent the estate of a murderer from benefiting from the property of the party he had murdered. Just as it was contrary to public policy to allow a murderer to benefit directly from the proceeds of his offence, so it would equally be contrary to public policy to allow the estate of a murderer to benefit from his offence. However, the public policy issue becomes less certain when one realises that there was actually no question of the murderer benefiting directly in this case, as he had committed suicide. In that light, the decision can be seen as punishing those who would have benefited on his death for an offence that they had nothing to do with – effectively cutting them out from what had been a legitimate expectation before the murder. In October 2003, the Law Commission recommended a change in the rule in *Sigsworth* and proposed a change in the law to allow children to inherit from grandparents who have been murdered by the children's father or mother. As the report states, the law should penalise killers, not their children. Its provisional view was that the law should operate as though the killer had died, allowing the children to inherit the property.

Another example of this approach is found in *R v National Insurance Commissioner ex p Connor* (1981), in which the court held, in spite of silence in the actual legislation, that Connor was not entitled to a widow's pension on the grounds that she had been the actual cause of her widowed status by killing her husband. Once again, when taken at face value, the decision in *Connor* appears perfectly justifiable on the grounds of public policy as the court stated, but appears less so when it is pointed out that Connor was actually found guilty of manslaughter and sentenced merely to a two-year period of probation.

Subsequent to the *Connor* case, the Forfeiture Act 1982 was passed, giving courts the discretionary power to ignore the rule of public policy that precludes a person who has unlawfully killed another from acquiring a benefit as a consequence of the killing. The Act does not apply in relation to murder, but nonetheless it does give the courts discretion to mitigate the effects of the rule applied in *Connor* where they are of the opinion that the circumstances of the case merit it. Thus, in *Dunbar v Plant* (1997), the Court of Appeal held that the forfeiture rule applied to the survivor of a suicide pact who had abetted the death of her partner. The court, however, applied the Forfeiture Act to permit her to benefit from his share in their jointly owned house and to claim against his life insurance policy.

In deciding whether or not to make use of the Forfeiture Act, the courts will look at the behaviour of both the killer and the person killed, so it might be expected that it would be used in relation to cases where the killing has been as a result of long-term abuse or some other mitigating circumstances. However, as the introduction of the public policy rule was itself a product of the common law, so the courts have in any case felt free to distinguish and limit the strict application of the rule in *Connor* (see, for example, *Re K (Deceased)* (1985)).

3   *The mischief rule*

At one level, the mischief rule is clearly the most flexible rule of interpretation, but in its traditional expression it is limited by being restricted to using previous common law rules in order to decide the operation of contemporary legislation. It is also, at least somewhat, paradoxical that this most venerable rule, originally set out in *Heydon's Case* (1584), is also the one which most obviously reveals the socio-political nature of judicial decisions.

In *Heydon's Case*, it was stated that in making use of the mischief rule, the court should consider the following four things:

(a)   What was the common law before the passing of the statute?

(b)   What was the mischief in the law which the common law did not adequately deal with?

(c)   What remedy for that mischief had parliament intended to provide?

(d)   What was the reason for parliament adopting that remedy?

It has to be remembered that, when *Heydon's Case* was decided, it was the practice to cite in the preamble of legislation the purpose for its enactment, including the mischief at which it was aimed. (An example where the preamble made more sense than the actual body of the legislation is the infamous Bubble Act of 1720.) Judges in this earlier time did not, therefore, have to go beyond the legislative provision itself to implement the mischief rule. With the disappearance of such explanatory preambles, the question arises as to the extent to which judges can make use of the rule in *Heydon's Case* to justify their examination of the policy issues that underlie particular legislative provisions. Contemporary practice is to go beyond the actual body of the legislation. This, however, raises the question as to what courts can legitimately consider in their endeavour to determine the purpose and meaning of legislation, which will be considered separately below.

The example usually cited of the use of the mischief rule is *Corkery v Carpenter* (1950), in which a man was found guilty of being drunk in charge of a 'carriage', although he was in fact only in charge of a bicycle. A much more controversial application of the rule is to be found in *Royal College of Nursing v DHSS* (1981), where the courts had to decide whether the medical induction of premature labour to effect abortion, under the supervision of nursing staff, was lawful. In this particularly sensitive area, whether one agrees with the ultimate majority decision of the House of Lords in favour of the legality of the procedure or not probably depends on one's view of abortion. This fact simply serves to highlight the socio-political nature of the question that was finally determined by the House of Lords under the guise of merely determining the legal meaning of a piece of legislation.

3.4.3.1   The relationship of the rules of interpretation

It is sometimes suggested that the rules of interpretation form a hierarchical order. On that basis, the first rule that should be applied is the literal rule, and that rule only cedes to the golden rule in particular circumstances where ambiguity arises from the application of the literal rule. The third rule, the mischief rule, it is suggested, is only brought into use where there is a perceived failure of the other two rules to deliver an appropriate result. On consideration, however, it becomes obvious that no such hierarchy exists. The literal rule is supposed to be used unless it leads to a manifest absurdity, in which case it will give way to the golden rule. The immediate question this supposition gives rise to is – what is to be considered as an absurdity in any particular case, other than the view of the judge deciding the case? The three rules are contradictory, at least to a degree, and there is no way in which the outsider can determine in advance which of them the courts will make use of to decide the meaning of a particular statute. Many may welcome the fact that the courts have moved towards a more explicitly purposive approach as outlined previously and as was recommended by the Law Commission report in 1969. It has to be recognised, however, that such a shift in approach provides the judiciary with additional power in relation to determining the meaning and effect of legislation. Cynics might say that such change merely makes overt the power that the judiciary always had, but previously exercised in a covert way.

3.4.4 AIDS TO CONSTRUCTION

In addition to the three main rules of interpretation, there are a number of secondary aids to construction. These can be categorised as either intrinsic or extrinsic in nature:

3.4.4.1 Intrinsic assistance

Intrinsic assistance is derived from the statute, which is the object of interpretation; the judge uses the full statute to understand the meaning of a particular part of it. The *title*, either long or short, of the Act under consideration may be referred to for guidance (*Royal College of Nursing v DHSS* (1981)). It should be noted, however, that a general intention derived from the title cannot overrule a clear statement to the contrary in the text of the Act.

It was a feature of older statutes that they contained a *preamble*, which was a statement, preceding the actual provisions of the Act, setting out its purposes in some detail and to which reference could be made for purposes of interpretation. Again, however, any general intention derived from the preamble could not stand in the face of express provision to the contrary within the Act.

Whereas preambles preceded the main body of an Act, schedules appear as additions at the end of the main body of the legislation. They are, however, an essential part of the Act and may be referred to in order to make sense of the main text.

Some statutes contain section headings and yet others contain marginal notes relating to particular sections. The extent to which either of these may be used is uncertain, although *DPP v Schildkamp* (1969) does provide authority for the use of the former as an aid to interpretation.

Finally, in regard to intrinsic aids to interpretation, it is now recognised that punctuation has an effect on the meaning of words and can be taken into account in determining the meaning of a provision.

3.4.4.2 Extrinsic assistance

Extrinsic assistance, that is, reference to sources outside of the Act itself, may on occasion be resorted to in determining the meaning of legislation – but which sources? Some external sources are unproblematic. For example, judges have always been entitled to refer to *dictionaries* in order to find the meaning of non-legal words. They also have been able to look into *textbooks* for guidance in relation to particular points of law, and in using the mischief rule, they have been able to refer to *earlier statutes* to determine the precise mischief at which the statute they are trying to construe is aimed. The Interpretation Act 1978 is also available for consultation with regard to particular difficulties. Unfortunately, its title is somewhat misleading, in that it does not give general instructions for interpreting legislation, but simply defines particular terms that are found in various statutes.

Other extrinsic sources, however, are more controversial. In 3.3, the various processes involved in the production of legislation were considered. As was seen, there are many distinct stages in the preparation of legislation. Statutes may arise as a result of reports submitted by a variety of commissions. In addition, the preparation of the precise structure of legislation is subject to consideration in working papers, known as *travaux préparatoires*. Nor should it be forgotten that in its progress through parliament, a Bill is the object of discussion and debate, both on the floor of the Houses of Parliament and in committee. Verbatim accounts of debates are recorded and published in *Hansard*.

Each of these procedures provides a potential source from which a judge might discover the specific purpose of a piece of legislation or the real meaning of any provision within it. The question is, to which of these sources are the courts entitled to have access?

Historically, English courts have adopted a restrictive approach to what they are entitled to take into consideration. This restrictive approach has been gradually relaxed, however, to the extent that judges are allowed to use extrinsic sources to determine the mischief at which particular legislation is aimed. Thus, they have been entitled to look at Law Commission reports, Royal Commission reports and the reports of other official commissions. Until fairly recently, however, *Hansard* literally remained a closed book to the courts, but in the landmark decision in *Pepper v Hart* (1993), the House of Lords decided to overturn the previous rule. The issue in the case was the tax liability owed by teachers at Malvern College, a fee-paying school. Employees were entitled to have their sons educated at the school while paying only 20 per cent of the usual fees. The question was as to the precise level at which this benefit in kind was to be taxed. In a majority decision, it was held that where the precise meaning of legislation was uncertain or ambiguous or where the literal meaning of an Act would lead to a manifest absurdity, the courts could refer to *Hansard*'s reports of parliamentary debates and proceedings as an aid to construing the meaning of the legislation.

The operation of the principle in *Pepper v Hart* was extended in *Three Rivers DC v Bank of England (No 2)* (1996) to cover situations where the legislation under question was not in itself ambiguous but might be ineffective in its intention to give effect to some particular EC directive. Applying the wider purposive powers of interpretation open to it in such circumstances (see 3.4.2 above), the court held that it was permissible to refer to *Hansard* in order to determine the actual purpose of the statute. The *Pepper v Hart* principle only applies to statements made by ministers at the time of the passage of legislation, and the courts have declined to extend it to cover situations where ministers subsequently make some statement as to what they consider the effect of a particular Act to be (*Melluish (Inspector of Taxes) v BMI (No 3) Ltd* (1995)).

It is essential to bear in mind that *Pepper v Hart* was not intended to introduce a general purposive approach to the interpretation of non-European Community legislation. Recourse to *Hansard* is to be made only in the context of the mischief rule, as a further method of finding out the mischief at which the particular legislation is aimed.

The way in which *Pepper v Hart* should be used in relation to the HRA was considered by the House of Lords in *Wilson v Secretary of State for Trade and Industry* in 2003. This case was remarkable in that neither of the parties to the original issue took part in the House of Lords case. However, as it followed a previous declaration of incompatibility delivered by the Court of Appeal, it was pursued by the Attorney General on behalf of the Secretary of State. In addition, and for the first time ever, both the Speaker of the House of Commons and the Clerk of the Parliaments intervened in relation to the manner in which the Court of Appeal had scrutinised *Hansard* in order to determine the purpose of the legislation in question. The House of Lords proved much more sensitive than the Court of Appeal had been as to the tension between the courts and parliament in regard to the exercise of the powers of the courts in relation to compatibility issues under the HRA and equally restrictive in the use that could be made of *Hansard* in relation to the exercise of those powers. As Lord Nicholls put it:

> I expect the occasions when resort to Hansard is necessary as part of the statutory 'compatibility' exercise will seldom arise. The present case is not such an occasion. Should such an occasion arise the courts must be careful not to treat ministerial or other statements as indicative of the objective intention of Parliament. Nor should the courts give a ministerial statement, whether made inside or outside Parliament, determinative weight. It should not be supposed that members necessarily agreed with the minister's reasoning or his conclusions.

Consequently, it can be seen that the initial and primary role of the judge is to interpret the legislation as it stands and only, in limited circumstances, to have recourse to *Hansard* to look for enlightenment as to the meaning of the Act, and even then it must be done with circumspection.

3.4.5 PRESUMPTIONS

In addition to the rules of interpretation, the courts may also make use of certain presumptions. As with all presumptions, they are rebuttable. The presumptions operate:

- *Against the alteration of the common law.* Parliament is sovereign and can alter the common law whenever it decides to do so. In order to do this, however, parliament must expressly enact legislation to that end. If there is no express intention to that effect, it is assumed that statute does not make any fundamental change to the common law. With regard to particular provisions, if there are alternative interpretations, one of which will maintain the existing common law situation, then that interpretation will be preferred. In *R (Rottman) v Commissioner of Police* (2002), the claimant was arrested on a warrant issued under the Extradition Act 1989, and the police searched his house and seized various items that they believed to be evidence. The House of Lords affirmed the legality of this search and seizure. The common law power to search an arrested person's premises was not extinguished in relation to extradition offences by the Police and Criminal Evidence Act (PACE) 1984. According to Lord Hutton, while that Act clearly replaced the pre-existing common law in relation to domestic offences, it made no reference to extradition offences and so must be supposed to have left the common law intact in relation to them.

● *In favour of the assumption that a mental element is required for criminal offences.* It is a general requirement of the criminal law that, in order for a person to be convicted of a crime, he is proved not only to have committed the relevant act or conduct (or sometimes to have failed to do something), but also to have done this with a blameworthy state of mind. This state of mind is known by the Latin tag *mens rea* (the mental element).

The necessary mental element can include: (a) intention; (b) gross negligence; (c) recklessness; (d) inadvertence; or (e) simple knowledge of a state of affairs. Because the consequences of being convicted of a criminal offence are very serious and include a possible custodial sentence and a life-ruining conviction, there was always the assumption in the common law (judge-made law) that criminal law offences require some form of *mens rea* before a person can be convicted.

Today, more criminal law offences have been created through parliamentary legislation than those which existed by virtue of the common law. When interpreting statutes, the court will presume that parliament intended that no criminal liability should arise without a requirement that *mens rea* be proven.

In some areas of social concern, however, like traffic accidents or underage drinking, parliament has seen fit to pass what are known as 'strict liability' offences. These are criminal offences for which it is *not* necessary for the prosecution to prove that the defendant had a particular attitude towards the crime in question, for example, that he intended to commit it, but merely that the relevant conduct took place. The thinking behind such criminalisation of conduct is that because defendants will not be able to escape liability by pleading that they did not intend to produce a particular result or that they did not have relevant knowledge, everyone will be encouraged to be that much more vigilant that they do not offend that particular law.

Sometimes, someone comes before the criminal law courts accused of an offence created by statute, and the courts must decide whether the words of the statute imply that it is necessary for the prosecution to prove the defendant had a mental element. The general rule here is that parliament will be presumed not to have wanted to create a strict liability criminal offence unless it has been explicit about wanting to do so. There are, though, a number of factors to be taken into account in answering this question, including the nature of the language used, the subject matter of the activity and the overall framework of the Act. In *Sweet v*

Parsley (1970), the accused had a house just outside of Oxford, which she rented out and visited only occasionally. She was convicted of being concerned in the management of premises used for the purpose of smoking cannabis, contrary to s 5(b) of the Dangerous Drugs Act 1965; however, she had had no knowledge that the house was being used in this way. The House of Lords held that her conviction should be quashed, since it had to be proved that it was the accused's 'purpose' that the premises were used for smoking cannabis (that is, that she intended the premises to be so used). In the case, Lord Reid said that:

> . . . whenever a section is silent as to *mens rea* there is a presumption that . . . we must read in words appropriate to require *mens rea*.

In *R v Hussain* (1981), the Court of Appeal decided that possessing a firearm without a certificate is, under s 1 of the Firearms Act 1968, an offence of strict liability, so that the prosecution is not required to prove that the accused knew the article he had was a firearm. Similarly, the Court of Appeal decided in *R v Bradish* (1990) that, under s 5(1) of the Firearms Act 1968, the offence of being in possession of a prohibited weapon (a spray canister containing CS gas) is a crime of strict liability. It was therefore not a defence for the accused to argue that because the gas was concealed within the canister, he did not know, and could not reasonably have been expected to know, that the article in his possession was a prohibited weapon. The court's choice in these cases to impose strict liability is in furtherance of the general purpose of the firearms legislation, that is, to put everyone on their guard that so wrong is the possession of firearms that those who have them without the appropriate licence will effectively be deemed automatically to be guilty of an offence.

In another case, the Court of Appeal decided that the offence created by s 11 of the Company Directors (Disqualification) Act 1986 of acting as a director of a company while an undischarged bankrupt, except with the leave of the court, was one of strict liability. Thus, a mistaken but genuinely held belief that the bankruptcy had been discharged was no defence to the crime (*R v Brockley* (1994)). The court took the view that the mischief sought to be tackled by s 11 of the Act was of wide social concern and that, therefore, the creation of strict liability would promote the object of the Act by obliging bankrupts themselves to ensure that their bankruptcy was in fact discharged before they acted again as company directors.

In *R v K* (2001), the defendant was charged with indecently assaulting a 14-year-old girl, who had in fact consented and who had told him she was over 16. Section 14(1) of the Sexual Offences Act 1956 was silent as to *mens rea* so far as knowledge of the girl's age was concerned. On the other hand, s 14(4) expressly stated that genuine belief was to be a defence where an adult woman lacked the mental capacity to consent. Consequently, the Court of Appeal could legitimately infer that parliament had *not* intended genuine belief to be a defence for 14(1), otherwise it would have said so. The House of Lords reversed the finding of the Court of Appeal holding that, as the 1956 Act was a consolidating Act, drawing together provisions from several previous Acts without making any substantive changes to them, the inference suggested by the Court of Appeal was not appropriate and the common law presumption against strict liability should prevail.

- *Against retrospective effect of new law.* The courts operate a presumption of interpretation that statutes will not operate retrospectively. It is one thing for parliament to legislate that, for example, as from next year all fox-hunting is illegal. It would be quite another thing for parliament to legislate that not only will fox-hunting be illegal if carried on in future, but that anyone who participated in such an event during the last five years is open to prosecution today. Such a presumption against retrospective effect is important in relation to crimes, but is relevant in other areas too, such as contractual arrangements and taxation. This principle operates not only to stop people whose conduct was innocent at the time from being convicted by a backward-looking Act, but also to stop people whose conduct was guilty at any given time from being free from blame just because an Act decriminalises certain conduct. So, if an Act abolishes an offence by repealing a statutory provision, then the repeal will not affect the punishment of someone who has been convicted of this crime at an earlier stage, nor the continuation of legal proceedings in respect of crimes that were committed before the law was changed. The presumption against retrospective effect was considered by the Court of Appeal in *Home Secretary v Wainwright* (2002). Two relatives visiting a prisoner were strip-searched as a condition of entry to the prison, and subsequently claimed a violation of their right to respect for private life. The court held that since the events in question had happened before the HRA 1998 came into force, s 3 of that Act could not be relied on. As parliament had expressly made s 22(4) of the Act retroactive, its failure to do the same for s 3 must be taken to have been intentional. See also *R v Lambert* (2001) and *R v Kansal* (2001).

  As parliament is supreme, there being no body with higher constitutional powers, it can pass retrospective legislation if it wishes, but it must do so using express words to achieve this end. The War Damage Act 1965 was passed specifically to overrule the decision of the House of Lords in *Burmah Oil Co Ltd v The Lord Advocate* (1965), and to deprive Burmah Oil of the results of having won that case. The oil company's installations in Burma, which was then a British colony, had been destroyed by the British Forces in 1942 in order to prevent them being captured by Japanese forces. The company, which was registered in Scotland, sued the Crown for compensation. The Crown contended that no compensation was payable when property was destroyed under the Royal Prerogative. The House of Lords decided that compensation was payable. The Act of Parliament was then passed to override the House of Lords' decision and to prevent the burden of compensation having to be met by the taxpayer. An example of modern legislation which has been made expressly retrospective is the War Crimes Act 1991. This Act allows the Attorney General to authorise criminal proceedings for homicide committed in Germany or German-occupied territory during World War II. The prosecution can be against a person in the UK regardless of his nationality at the time of the alleged offence. The relaxation of the 'double jeopardy' rule by s 75 of the Criminal Justice Act 2003 has retrospective effect (s 75(6)).

- *Against deprivation of liberty.* The law courts work on the assumption that parliament does not intend to deprive a person of his liberty unless it is explicitly making provision for such a punishment. Thus, Lord Scarman has stated that:

> ... if Parliament intends to exclude effective judicial review of the exercise of a power in restraint of liberty, it must make its meaning crystal clear [*R v Secretary of State for the Home Department ex p Khawaja* (1983)].

The House of Lords ruled that an immigration Act that it was examining did not have the effect of placing the burden of proof on an immigrant to show that the decision of the Home Office to detain him was unjustified. In other words, one could not read the Act in a way that allowed someone to be deprived of their liberty unless and until they proved that such imprisonment was unjustified.

- *Against application to the Crown.* Unless the legislation contains a clear statement to the contrary, it is presumed not to apply to the Crown.
- *Against breaking international law.* Where possible, legislation should be interpreted in such a way as to give effect to existing international legal obligations.
- *In favour of words taking their meaning from the context in which they are used.* This final presumption refers back to, and operates in conjunction with, the major rules for interpreting legislation considered previously. The general presumption appears as three distinct sub-rules, each of which carries a Latin tag. The *noscitur a sociis* rule is applied where statutory provisions include a list of examples of what is covered by the legislation. It is presumed that the words used have a related meaning and are to be interpreted in relation to each other. (See *IRC v Frere* (1969), in which the House of Lords decided which of two possible meanings of the word 'interest' was to be preferred by reference to the word's location within a statute.) The *ejusdem generis* rule applies in situations where general words are appended to the end of a list of specific examples. The presumption is that the general words have to be interpreted in line with the prior restrictive examples. Thus, a provision which referred to a list that included 'horses, cattle, sheep and other animals' would be unlikely to apply to domestic animals such as cats and dogs. (See *Powell v Kempton Park Racecourse* (1899), in which it was held that, because a statute prohibited betting in a specified number of *indoor* places, it could not cover an *outdoor* location.) The *expressio unius exclusio alterius* rule simply means that where a statute seeks to establish a list of what is covered by its provisions, then anything not expressly included in that list is specifically excluded.

(See *R v Inhabitants of Sedgley* (1831), where rates expressly stated to be payable on *coal* mines were held not to be payable in relation to *limestone* mines.)

For further examples and resources illustrating the way statutory interpretation is carried out, exercises and technical guidance, please go to: www.routledge.com/cw/slapper where you will find a guide to Using Legislation.

3.5   DELEGATED OR SUBORDINATE LEGISLATION

Delegated legislation is of particular importance. Generally speaking, delegated legislation is law made by some person or body to whom parliament has delegated its general law-making power. A validly enacted piece of delegated legislation has the same legal force and effect as the Act of Parliament under which it is enacted but, equally, it only has effect to the extent that its enabling Act authorises it.

It should also be recalled that s 10 of the HRA 1998 gives ministers power to amend primary legislation by way of statutory instrument where a court has issued a declaration that the legislation in point is incompatible with the rights provided under the ECHR.

The output of delegated legislation in any year greatly exceeds the output of Acts of Parliament. For example, in the parliamentary year 2011 only 25 public general Acts were passed, as against 3133 statutory instruments.

In statistical terms, therefore, it is at least arguable that delegated legislation is actually more significant than primary Acts of Parliament.

There are various types of delegated legislation:

● *Orders in Council.* Consideration of this type of legislation is confused by the interplay of related and overlapping concepts and the historical process that saw parliament exercise control over the power of the crown.

Historically, orders in council were the result of the exercise of the royal prerogative in consultation with the Privy Council, the monarch's close advisors. As has already been mentioned, some aspects of these prerogative powers remain and are excised through the issuing of Orders in Council. Orders in Council made under prerogative powers are primary legislation. However, distinct from such exercise of prerogative powers are the statutory orders which arise from the fact that parliament, through statute, has given the Crown powers to make law through the issuing of Orders in Council. It is this latter type of Orders in Council that is correctly referred to as delegated legislation. The passing of statutory Orders in Council may also involve a Parliamentary procedure, depending on the Act from which they stem. Consequently some Orders may need to be laid before Parliament in draft before being made, or after they have been made. Alternatively, the Act may require the Order to be approved by Parliament before it comes into force. The importance of this distinction lies in the fact that, as has already been explained, under the HRA 1998 the courts have greater power in relation to secondary legislation than they do in regard to primary legislation.

The Privy Council is nominally a non-party-political body of eminent parliamentarians, but in effect it is simply a means through which the government, in the form of a committee of ministers, can introduce legislation in the form of Orders in Council, without the need to go through the full parliamentary process. Although it is usual to cite situations of state emergency as exemplifying occasions when the government will resort to the use of Orders in Council, the use of this statutory form is far from uncommon. Perhaps the widest scope for Orders in Council is to be found in relation to EU law, for under s 2(2) of the European Communities Act 1972, ministers can give effect to provisions of Union law which do not have direct effect (see further section 15.2 below).

Ministers may also be given statutory power to make orders to introduce or alter exiting provisions, but such orders are not to be confused with Orders in Council. To add further potential confusion, since 1946, under s 1 of the Statutory Instruments Act (SIA) 1946, every power to make an Order in Council conferred by an Act of Parliament passed after 1 January 1948 must be in the form of a statutory instrument. Consequently, most Orders in Council are also statutory instruments, but there still exists the possibility of Orders in Council that are not to be issued as SIs, either being the result of the exercise of prerogative power or deriving from a pre-1948 statute.

- *Statutory instruments* are the means through which government ministers introduce particular regulations under powers delegated to them by parliament in enabling legislation.

- *Bylaws* are the means through which local authorities and other public bodies can make legally binding rules. Bylaws may be made by local authorities under such enabling legislation as the Local Government Act 1972.

- *Court Rule Committees* are empowered to make the rules which govern procedure in the particular courts over which they have delegated authority, under such Acts as the Senior Courts Act 1981 (originally passed as The Supreme Court Act 1981 but changed in name by the Constitutional Reform Act 2005, Sched 11), the County Courts Act 1984 and the Magistrates' Courts Act 1980.

- *Professional regulations* governing particular occupations may be given the force of law under provisions delegating legislative authority to certain professional bodies who are empowered to regulate the conduct of their members. An example is the power given to The Law Society, under the Solicitors' Act 1974, to control the conduct of practising solicitors.

3.5.1 ADVANTAGES IN THE USE OF DELEGATED LEGISLATION

The advantages of delegated legislation include the following:

- *Time saving*

  Delegated legislation can be introduced quickly, where necessary in particular cases, and can permit rules to be changed in response to emergencies or unforeseen problems.

The use of delegated legislation, however, also saves parliamentary time generally. Given the pressure on debating time in parliament and the highly detailed nature of typical delegated legislation, not to mention its sheer volume, parliament would not have time to consider each individual piece of law that is enacted in the form of delegated legislation. It is considered of more benefit for parliament to spend its time in a thorough consideration of the principles of the enabling Act, leaving the appropriate minister or body to establish the working detail under its authority.

● *Access to particular expertise*

Related to the first advantage is the fact that the majority of Members of Parliament simply do not have sufficient expertise to consider such provisions effectively. Given the highly specialised and extremely technical nature of many of the regulations that are introduced through delegated legislation, it is necessary that those authorised to introduce the legislation should have access to the necessary external expertise required to formulate such regulations. With regard to bylaws, it practically goes without saying that local and specialist knowledge should give rise to more appropriate rules than reliance on the general enactments of parliament.

● *Flexibility*

The use of delegated legislation permits ministers to respond on an *ad hoc* basis to particular problems, as and when they arise, and provides greater flexibility in the regulation of activity subject to the minister's overview.

3.5.2 DISADVANTAGES IN THE PREVALENCE OF DELEGATED LEGISLATION

The disadvantages in the use of delegated legislation include the following:

● *Accountability*

A key issue involved in the use of delegated legislation concerns the question of accountability and erosion of the constitutional role of parliament. Parliament is presumed to be the source of legislation, but with respect to delegated legislation, the individual members are not the source of the law. Certain people, notably government ministers and the civil servants who work under them to produce the detailed provisions of delegated legislation, are the real source of such regulations. Even allowing for the fact that they are, in effect, operating on powers delegated to them from parliament, it is not beyond questioning whether this procedure does not give them more power than might be thought appropriate, or indeed constitutionally correct, while at the same time disempowering and discrediting parliament as a body.

● *Scrutiny*

The question of general accountability raises the need for effective scrutiny, but the very form of delegated legislation makes it extremely difficult for ordinary Members of Parliament to fully understand what is being enacted and to monitor it effectively. This difficulty arises in part from the tendency for such regulations to be highly specific, detailed and technical. This problem of comprehension and control is compounded by the fact that regulations appear outside the context of their enabling legislation, but only have any real meaning within that context.

- *Bulk*

  The problem faced by ordinary Members of Parliament in effectively keeping abreast of delegated legislation is further increased by the sheer mass of such legislation. If parliamentarians cannot keep up with the flow of delegated legislation, how can the general public be expected to do so?

3.5.3   THE LEGISLATIVE AND REGULATORY REFORM ACT 2006

In previous editions of this book the authors have, to a greater or lesser degree, focused on the increase in the power of Ministers of State to alter Acts of Parliament by means of statutory instruments in the pursuit of economic, business and regulatory efficiency.

The first of these (dis)empowering Acts of Parliament that brought this situation about was the De-regulation and Contracting Out Act (DCOA) 1994, introduced by the last Conservative government. It was a classic example of the wide-ranging power that enabling legislation can extend to ministers in the attack on such primary legislation as was seen to impose unnecessary burdens on any trade, business or profession. Although the DCOA 1994 imposed the requirement that ministers should consult with interested parties to any proposed alteration, it nonetheless gave them extremely wide powers to alter primary legislation without the necessity of having to follow the same procedure as was required to enact that legislation in the first place. For that reason, deregulation orders were subject to a far more rigorous procedure (sometimes referred to as 'super-affirmative') than ordinary statutory instruments. The powers were extended in its first term in office by the Labour government under the Regulatory Reform Act (RRA) 2001.

It was, however, only with the proposed Legislative and Regulatory Reform Bill 2006 that alarm bells started to ring generally. This critical reaction was based on the proposed power contained in the Act for ministers to create new criminal offences, punishable with less than two years' imprisonment, without the need for a debate in parliament.

The proposals under the Legislative and Regulatory Reform Bill 2006 were constitutionally dangerous to the extent that they gave to the executive powers that should be a function of the legislature.

As a result of opposition, the government amended the legislation to ensure that its powers could only be used in relation to business and regulatory efficiency.

Similar fears were raised in relation to the Public Bodies Act 2011. Although not as wide-ranging as was originally proposed, the Act still gives government ministers wide powers to abolish non-government bodies and agencies, referred to as quangos.

3.5.4   CONTROL OF DELEGATED LEGISLATION

The foregoing difficulties and potential shortcomings in the use of delegated legislation are, at least to a degree, mitigated by the fact that specific controls have been established to oversee it:

3.5.4.1   Parliamentary control over delegated legislation

Power to make delegated legislation is ultimately dependent upon the authority of parliament and parliament retains general control over the procedure for enacting such law. New regulations in the form of delegated legislation are required to be laid before parliament. This procedure takes two forms depending on the provision of the enabling legislation. Some regulations require a positive resolution of one or both of the Houses of Parliament before they become law. Most Acts, however, simply require that regulations made under their auspices be placed before parliament. They automatically become law after a period of 40 days unless a resolution to annul them is passed.

The problem with the negative resolution procedure is that it relies on Members of Parliament being sufficiently aware of the content, meaning and effect of the detailed provisions laid before them. Given the nature of such statutory legislation, such reliance is unlikely to prove secure.

Since 1973, there has been a *Joint Select Committee on Statutory Instruments* whose function it is to scrutinise all statutory instruments. The Joint Committee is empowered to draw the special attention of both Houses to an instrument on any one of a number of grounds specified in the Standing Orders (No 151 of the House of Commons and No 74 of the House of Lords) under which it operates, or on any other ground *which does not relate to the actual merits of the instrument or the policy it is pursuing.*

The House of Commons has its own *Select Committee on Statutory Instruments*, which is appointed to consider all statutory instruments laid *only* before the House of Commons. This committee is empowered to draw the special attention of the House to an instrument on any one of a number of grounds specified in Standing Order No 151; or on any other ground. However, as with the joint committee, it is not empowered to consider the merits of any statutory instrument or the policy behind it. As an example of its operation, after considering two statutory instruments, namely *Personal Equity Plan (Amendment No 2) Regulations 2005 (SI 2005/3348) and Individual Savings Account (Amendment No 3) Regulations 2005 (SI 2005/3350)*, the Committee considered that they should be drawn to the attention of the House of Commons on the ground that there appeared to be a doubt whether they were *intra vires.*

EU legislation is overseen by a specific committee – as are local authority bylaws. In 2003 the House of Lords established a *Committee on the Merits of Statutory Instruments*, the task of which is to consider the policy implications of statutory instruments. It has wide-ranging remit and is specifically charged with the task of deciding whether the attention of the House should be drawn to a particular statutory instrument on any one of the following grounds:

- that it is politically or legally important or gives rise to issues of public policy likely to be of interest to the House;

- that it is inappropriate in view of the changed circumstances since the passage of the parent Act;

- that it inappropriately implements EU legislation;

- that it imperfectly achieves its policy objectives.

http://www.publications.parliament.uk/pa/ld200405/ldselect/ldmerit/92/5030101.htm

3.5.4.2 Judicial control of delegated legislation

It is possible for delegated legislation to be challenged through the procedure of judicial review, on the basis that the person or body to whom parliament has delegated its authority has acted in a way that exceeds the limited powers delegated to them. Any provision outside this authority is *ultra vires* and is void. Additionally, there is a presumption that any power delegated by parliament is to be used in a reasonable manner, and the courts may on occasion hold particular delegated legislation to be void on the basis that it is unreasonable. The process of judicial review will be considered in more detail in Chapter 10. However, an interesting example of this procedure may illustrate the point. In January 1997, the Lord Chancellor raised court fees and, at the same time, restricted the circumstances in which a litigant could be exempted from paying such fees. In March, a Mr John Witham, who previously would have been exempted from paying court fees, successfully challenged the Lord Chancellor's action. In a judicial review, it was held that Lord Mackay had exceeded the statutory powers given to him by parliament. One of the judges, Rose LJ, stated that there was nothing to suggest that parliament ever intended 'a power for the Lord Chancellor to prescribe fees so as to preclude the poor from access to the courts'.

The power of the courts in relation to delegated legislation has been considerably increased by the enactment of the HRA 1998. As has been seen, the courts cannot directly declare primary legislation invalid, but can only issue a declaration of incompatibility. However, no such limitation applies in regard to subordinate legislation, which consequently may be declared invalid as being in conflict with the rights provided under the ECHR. This provision significantly extends the power of the courts in relation to the control of subordinate legislation, in that they are no longer merely restricted to questioning such legislation on the grounds of procedure, but can now assess it on the basis of content, as measured against the rights provided in the ECHR. It should be noted that some Orders in Council, as expressions of the exercise of the royal prerogative, are not open to challenge and control in the same way as other subordinate legislation.

A Case Study on ultra vires: HM Treasury v Mohammed Jabar Ahmed (2010)

In this, the first substantive case heard by the Supreme Court, it quashed fully the Terrorism (United Nations Measures) Order 2006 and quashed parts of the Al Qa'ida and Taliban (United Nations Measures) Order 2006 as being *ultra vires* the powers extended to the Treasury under the United Nations Act 1946.

Both Orders had been made by the Treasury under power conferred by s 1 of the United Nations Act (UNA) 1946, which was enacted to facilitate the taking of measures to implement decisions of the UN Security Council. In each case the Orders were made to give effect to resolutions of the United Nations Security Council, which were designed to suppress and prevent the financing and preparation of acts of terrorism.

The Orders specifically provided for the freezing of the funds, economic resources and financial services available to individuals who had been included on a United Nations list of associates of Usama Bin-Laden, or were involved in international terrorism, or were reasonably suspected of involvement with international terrorism.

In delivering the leading judgment, Lord Hope (with the agreement of Lord Walker and Lady Hale) emphasised the far-reaching and serious effect of the asset-freezing measures on not just the individuals concerned, but also their families. Using the scope afforded by the rule in *Pepper v Hart*, he concluded that the legislative history of the 1946 Act demonstrated that Parliament 'did not intend that the 1946 Act should be used to introduce coercive measures which interfere with UK citizens' fundamental rights'. The crucial question for the court to consider was whether s 1 of UNA conferred power on the executive, *without any Parliamentary scrutiny*, to give effect in this country to decisions of the Security Council, which are targeted against individuals. And the answer to that question was a clear no.

In answering the question in that way, the Supreme Court was at pains to emphasise that it was in no way usurping the role of the legislature. Indeed as Lord Phillips put it:

> Nobody should form the impression that in quashing the TO and the operative provision of the AQO the Court displaces the will of Parliament. On the contrary, the Court's judgment vindicates the primacy of Parliament, as opposed to the Executive, in determining in what circumstances fundamental rights may legitimately be restricted.

3.6   CASE LAW

Case law refers to the creation and refinement of law in the course of judicial decisions. The foregoing has highlighted the increased importance of legislation in its various guises in today's society but, even allowing for this and the fact that case law can be overturned by legislation, the UK is still a common law system and the importance and effectiveness of judicial creativity and common law principles and practices cannot be discounted.

3.6.1   PRECEDENT

The doctrine of binding precedent, or *stare decisis*, lies at the heart of the English legal system. The doctrine refers to the fact that, within the hierarchical structure of the English courts, a decision of a higher court will be binding on a court lower than it in that hierarchy. In general terms, this means that when judges try cases, they will check to see if a similar situation has come before a court previously. If the precedent was set by a court of equal or higher status to the court deciding the new case, then the judge in the present case should follow the rule of law established in the earlier case. Where the precedent is from a lower court in the hierarchy, the judge in the new case may not follow, but will certainly consider, it. (The structure of the civil courts will be considered in detail in Chapter 4 and that of the criminal courts in Chapter 5.)

3.6.2 LAW REPORTING

It is apparent that the operation of binding precedent is reliant upon the existence of an extensive reporting service to provide access to previous judicial decisions. This section briefly sets out where one might locate case reports on particular areas of the law. This is of particular importance to counsel, who are under a duty to bring all relevant case authority to the attention of the court, whether it advances their case or not. Consequently, they are expected to make themselves thoroughly aware of the current reports.

The Year Books

The earliest reports of particular cases appeared between 1275 and 1535 in what are known as *The Year Books*. These reports are really of historical interest as they were originally written in that peculiar language that was, and to a degree still is, the bane of law students and to the incomprehension of French students, Legal French. As with the common law generally, the focus was on procedural matters and forms of pleading. Those who are engaged in the study of legal history will find the most important cases translated and collected together in the Seldon Society series or the Rolls series but, for the main part, they represent a backwater little navigated by those whose concern is modern law.

Private Reports (1535–1865)

These reports bear the name they do because they were produced by private individuals and cited by the name of the person who collected them. They were, however, published commercially for public reference. The ongoing problem with the private reports relates to their accuracy. At best it can be said that some were better, that is, more accurate than others. Of particular importance among the earlier reports were those of Plowden, Coke and Burrows, but there are many other reports that are of equal standing in their own right, with full and accurate reports of the cases submitted by counsel, together with the reason for the decisions in the particular case. A substantial number of the private reports have been collated and published as the *English Reports*. The series comprises 178 large volumes – 176 volumes being reports and the last two volumes providing an index of all the cases reported. In addition, the reports are accompanied by a useful wall chart to assist location of individual reports.

Modern Reports (1865 to present)

As has been seen, the private reports were not without their problems. In addition to at least occasional inaccuracy, their publication could be both dilatory and expensive. This situation was at last remedied by the establishment of the Council for Law Reporting in 1865, subsequently registered as a corporate body in 1870 under the name of The Incorporated Council of Law Reporting for England and Wales. The Council was established under the auspices of the Inns of Court and The Law Society with the aim of producing quicker, cheaper and more accurate reports than had been available previously.

The Law Reports

These are the case reports produced by the Council. They have the distinct advantage of containing summaries of counsels' arguments and, perhaps even more importantly, they are subject to revision by the judges in the case before they are published. Not surprisingly, the *Law Reports* are seen as the most authoritative of reports, and it is usual for them to be cited in court cases in preference to any other report.

The current series of Law Reports from 1891 is issued annually in four parts:

- Appeal Cases (AC);
- Chancery Division (Ch);
- Family Division (Fam);
- King's/Queen's Bench (KB/QB).

Delays in reporting can obviously mean that cases decided in one year are not reported until the following year. Since the start of the current series, individual volumes of reports carry the year of publication in square brackets together with a volume number if there is a need for more than one. Cases are cited, therefore, in relation to the year and volume in which they are published, rather than the year they were decided.

Weekly Law Reports (citation WLR)

These have also been published by the Council since 1953 and, although they are not reports of cases decided in the current week as the name might suggest, they are produced much more quickly than the Law Reports. The need for speed means that these reports do not contain counsels' arguments, nor do they enjoy the benefit of judicial correction before printing. There are three volumes of reported cases, the last two containing the cases that will also appear in the Law Reports.

All England Law Reports (citation All ER)

These reports are produced by the legal publishers, Butterworths, and, although they do enjoy judicial revision, they do not contain counsels' arguments. They are published weekly and are then collated annually in volumes.

Legal Periodicals and Newspapers

The *Solicitors Journal* (Sol Jo or SJ) has been reporting cases since 1851 and some cases are only to be found in its reports. In such circumstances, the reports may be cited in court. The same is also true for cases reported in other journals such as the *New Law Journal* or the other specialist legal journals.

The reports in the broadsheet newspapers *The Times* and *The Independent* may also be cited in such circumstances, as long as they have been produced by appropriately qualified individuals (the Courts and Legal Services Act 1990 extended the right to solicitors as well as barristers). It has to be recognised, however, that some of these reports are rather insubstantial in nature.

Specialist Reports

There are a number of specialist reports. Indeed, there are more than can be mentioned here, but amongst the most important of these are:

- Industrial Relations Law Reports (IRLR);
- Knight's Local Government Reports (LGR);
- Lloyd's Law Reports (Lloyd's Rep);
- Report on Tax Cases (TC or Tax Cas);
- Criminal Appeal Reports (Cr App R).

European Community Reports

Although European cases may appear in the reports considered above, there are two specialist reports relating to EC cases:

- *European Court Reports (ECR)*

  These are the official reports produced by the European Court of Justice (ECJ). As such, they are produced in all the official languages of the Community and consequently suffer from delay in reporting.

- *Common Market Law Reports (CMLR)*

  These are unofficial reports published weekly in English by the European Law Centre.

Reports of the European Court of Human Rights in Strasbourg are provided in the European Human Rights Reports (EHRR).

CD-ROMs and Internet Facilities

As in most other fields, the growth of information technology has revolutionised law reporting and law finding. Many of the law reports mentioned above are available both on CD-ROM and on the Internet. See, for example, Justis, Lawtel, Lexis-Nexis and Westlaw UK among others. Indeed, members of the public can now access law reports directly from their sources in the courts, both domestically and in Europe. The first major electronic cases database was the Lexis system, which gave immediate access to a huge range of case authorities, some unreported elsewhere. The problem for the courts was that lawyers with access to the system could simply cite lists of cases from the database, without the courts having access to paper copies of the decisions. The courts soon expressed their displeasure at this indiscriminate citation of unreported cases trawled from the Lexis database (see *Stanley v International Harvester Co of Great Britain Ltd* (1983)).

The British and Irish Legal Information Institute (Bailii http://www.bailii.org/) is a charitable institution which provides online access to cases and legislation in the UK, Ireland and Europe. In October 2011, *The Guardian* started a campaign to make the site more accessible to the general public by making it searchable using Google.

Neutral Citation

In line with the ongoing modernisation of the whole legal system, the way in which cases are to be cited has been changed. Thus, from January 2001, following *Practice Direction (Judgments: Form and Citation)* [2001] 1 WLR 194, a new neutral system was introduced and extended in the following year in a further Practice Direction in April 2002. Cases in the various courts are now cited as follows:

Supreme Court	[year]	UKSC case no
House of Lords	[year]	UKHL case no
Court of Appeal (Civil Division)	[year]	EWCA Civ case no
Court of Appeal (Criminal Division)	[year]	EWCA Crim case no

High Court

Queen's Bench Division	[year]	EWHC case no (QB)
Chancery Division	[year]	EWHC case no (Ch)
Patents Court	[year]	EWHC case no (Pat)
Administrative Court	[year]	EWHC case no (Admin)
Commercial Court	[year]	EWHC case no (Comm)
Admiralty Court	[year]	EWHC case no (Admlty)
Technology & Construction Court	[year]	EWHC case no (TCC)
Family Division	[year]	EWHC case no (Fam)

Within the individual case, the paragraphs of each judgment are numbered consecutively, and where there is more than one judgment, the numbering of the paragraphs carries on sequentially. Thus, for example, the neutral citation for the House of Lords' decision in *Jackson v HM Attorney General* considered above at 3.3.2 is [2005] UKHL 56 and the citation for the quotation from Lord Bingham in the case is at paragraph 25. The specific law report series within which the case is reported is cited after the neutral citation; thus, the decision may be found at [2005] 3 WLR 733 or [2005] 4 All ER 1253.

Citing authorities in court

In March 2012, Judge LCJ issued a Practice Direction to clarify the practice and procedure governing the citation of authorities in the Senior Courts of England and Wales. Consequently:

- where a judgment is reported in the Official Law Reports (AC, QB, Ch, Fam) published by the Incorporated Council of Law Reporting for England and Wales, that report must be cited. Other series of reports and official transcripts of judgment may only be used when a case is not reported in the Official Law Reports;

- if a judgment is not, or not yet, reported in the Official Law Reports but it is reported in the Weekly Law Reports (WLR) or the All England Law Reports (All ER), that report should be cited. If the case is reported in both the WLR and the All ER, either report may properly be cited;

- if a judgment is not reported in the Official Law Reports, the WLR or the All ER, but it is reported in any of the authoritative specialist series of reports which contain a headnote and are made by individuals holding a Senior Courts qualification, the specialist report should be cited;

- where a judgment is not reported in any of the reports referred to above, but is reported in other reports, they may be cited;

- where a judgment has not been reported, reference may be made to the official transcript if that is available. Handed-down text of the judgment should not be used as that may have been subject to late revision after the text was handed down. In any event an unreported case should not usually be cited unless it contains a relevant statement of legal principle not found in reported authority.

3.6.3 PRECEDENT WITHIN THE HIERARCHY OF THE COURTS

Supreme Court

Perhaps the most significant change to have taken place in the English legal system in recent times is the replacement of the judicial committee of the House of Lords by the Supreme Court. The Supreme Court began its work on 1 October 2009 and was officially opened by the Queen on 16 October 2009. The court will be considered in much more detail in later chapters, but as the replacement for the House of Lords it now clearly sits at the pinnacle of the English court hierarchy and as such its future decisions will have the same effect and binding power as those of its predecessor. Given the novelty of the Supreme Court, with the related lack of actual judgments, the decision has been taken that it would be wrong simply to delete references to the House of Lords and tedious to continually refer to the House of Lords as the House of Lords/Supreme Court. Consequently all future, and indeed previous, references to the House of Lords will be assumed to apply to the Supreme Court. However, it is inescapable that what follows will contain a mixture of the two titles as is considered appropriate. It should also be mentioned that the Supreme Court carries on the previous double existence of the House of Lords as the Privy Council as a distinct institution.

Supreme Court Decisions

The decisions of the Supreme Court are binding on all other courts in the legal system, except the House of Lords itself. The House of Lords was bound by its own previous decisions until it changed this practice in 1966. The old practice had been established in the nineteenth century and was reaffirmed in a famous case in 1898 – *London Tramways Co Ltd v London County Council*. The rationale for the old practice was that decisions of the highest court in the land should be final so that there would be certainty in the law and a finality in litigation.

The rule, however, did not appear to create certainty and had become very rigid by the end of the nineteenth century. The practice was eventually changed in July 1966 when Lord Gardiner, the Lord Chancellor, made a statement on behalf of himself and his fellow Law Lords. This *Practice Statement* [1966] 3 All ER 77 runs as follows:

> Their Lordships regard the use of precedent as an indispensable foundation upon which to decide what is the law and its application to individual cases. It provides at least some degree of certainty upon which individuals can rely in the conduct of their affairs as well as a basis for orderly development of legal rules.
>
> Their Lordships nevertheless recognise that too rigid adherence to precedent may lead to injustice in a particular case and also unduly restrict the proper development of the law. They propose, therefore, to modify their present practice and, while treating former decisions of this House as normally binding, to depart from a previous decision when it appears right to do so.
>
> In this connection they will bear in mind the danger of disturbing retrospectively the basis on which contracts, settlements of property, and fiscal arrangements have been entered into and also the special need for certainty as to the criminal law.
>
> This announcement is not intended to affect the use of precedent elsewhere than in this house.

The current practice enables the Supreme Court to adapt English law to meet changing social conditions and to pay attention to the decisions of superior courts in the Commonwealth. It was also regarded as important at the time that the House of Lords' practice be brought into line with that of superior courts in other countries, like the United States Supreme Court and State supreme courts elsewhere, which are not bound by their own previous decisions. It also has the effect of bringing the practice of the UK's highest domestic court into line with the practice of both the ECJ and the European Court of Human Rights (ECtHR), neither of which is bound by a rigid doctrine of precedent, although in practice, they do not wilfully ignore previous decisions they have made. The possibility of the Supreme Court changing its previous decisions is a recognition that law, whether expressed in statutes or cases, is a living, and therefore changing, institution that must adapt to the circumstances in which and to which it applies if it is to retain practical relevance.

Any appellant who intends to ask the Supreme Court to depart from its own previous decision must draw special attention to this in the appeal documents (*Practice*

Direction (House of Lords: Preparation of Case) [1971] 1 WLR 534). After 1966, the House used this power quite sparingly and no doubt the Supreme Court will continue this reluctance. It will not refuse to follow its earlier decision merely because that decision was wrong. A material change of circumstances will usually have to be shown.

In *Conway v Rimmer* (1968), the House of Lords unanimously overruled *Duncan v Cammell Laird and Co* (1942) on a question of the discovery of documents. *Duncan v Cammell Laird and Co* concerned the question of whether a plaintiff could get the defendant to disclose documents during wartime, which related to the design of a submarine. *Conway v Rimmer* concerned whether a probationary police officer could insist on getting disclosure of reports written about him by his superintendent. In the earlier case, the House of Lords held that an affidavit sworn by a government minister was sufficient to enable the Crown to claim privilege not to disclose documents in civil litigation, without those documents being inspected by the court. In the later case, their Lordships held that the minister's affidavit was not binding on the court. The second decision held that it is for the court to decide whether or not to order disclosure. This involves balancing the possible prejudice to the State if disclosure is ordered against any injustice that might affect the individual litigant if disclosure is withheld. Today, the minister's affidavit will be considered by the court, but it is no longer the sole determinant of the issue.

In *Herrington v British Railway Board* (1972), the House of Lords overruled *Addy and Sons v Dumbreck* (1929). In the earlier case, the House of Lords had decided that an occupier of premises was only liable to a trespassing child if that child was injured by the occupier intentionally or recklessly. In its later decision, the House of Lords changed the law in line with the changed social and physical conditions since 1929. Their Lordships felt that even a trespasser was entitled to some degree of care, which they propounded as a test of 'common humanity'.

In *R v United Railways of the Havana and Regla Warehouses Ltd* (1961), the House of Lords decided that damages awarded in an English civil case could only be awarded in sterling. The issue came up for reconsideration in 1976, by which time there had been significant changes in foreign exchange conditions, and the instability of sterling at the later date was of much greater concern than it had been in 1961. In the second case, *Miliangos v George Frank (Textiles) Ltd* (1976), the House of Lords overruled the earlier decision, stating that damages could be awarded in other currencies.

In *R v Secretary of State for the Home Department ex p Khawaja* (1983), the House of Lords departed from its own previous decision made two years earlier – *R v Secretary of State for the Home Department ex p Zamir* (1980). The earlier case had put the main burden of proof on an alleged illegal immigrant to show that his detention was not justified. In its decision two years later, the House of Lords expressed the view that the power of the courts to review the detention and summary removal of an alleged illegal immigrant had been too narrowly defined in the 1980 decision. It held that continued adherence to the precedent would involve the risk of injustice and would obstruct the proper development of law.

In *Murphy v Brentwood District Council* (1990), the House of Lords overruled its earlier decision in *Anns v Merton London Borough Council* (1978) on the law governing the liability of local authorities for the inspection of building foundations. In the earlier decision, the House of Lords held that a local authority was under a legal duty to take reasonable care to ensure that the foundations of a building complied with building regulations. The duty was owed to the owner and occupier of the building who had a legal action if the duty was broken. This created a very wide and extensive duty of care for local authorities, which was out of kilter with the development of this area of law (negligence) in relation to other property-like goods. There was considerable academic and judicial resistance to the decision in *Anns*. In overruling it, the House of Lords in *Murphy* cited the reluctance of English law to provide a remedy for pure economic loss, that is, loss that is not consequential upon bodily injury or physical damage.

If a person commits a murder or assists someone to do so under duress, that is, while under threat that unless he kills or helps, he himself will be murdered, should this afford him a legal defence? In *DPP for Northern Ireland v Lynch* (1975), the House of Lords decided that duress was available as a defence to a person who had participated in a murder as an aider and abettor. Twelve years later, the House of Lords overruled that decision. It held in *R v Howe* (1987) that the defence of duress is not available to a person charged with murder or as an aider and abettor to murder. Some people might regard it as unjust that a person who kills, or assists in a killing, while under duress should be so severely punished under the criminal law, but in taking away the defence of duress from murderers and those who assist them, the House of Lords founded its decision partly upon considerations of social policy (it made references to a rising tide of crimes of violence and terrorism that needed a strict response from the law) and a recognition that, where people killed others or assisted in such events while under duress, their conviction could be addressed by other mechanisms, such as the availability of parole and the royal prerogative of mercy.

Another significant example of the House of Lords recognising and accommodating changed circumstances can be seen in *Hall v Simons* (2000), in which it declined to follow the previous authority of *Rondel v Worsley* (1969), which had recognised the immunity of barristers against claims for negligence in their presentation of cases (see below, at 13.5.1 for an extended analysis of this case).

The final case to consider at this point is *R v G* (2003) in which the House of Lords disapproved of the Lord Diplock's objective explanation of recklessness in relation to criminal law as stated previously in *R v Caldwell* (1982).

A Case Study: The House of Lords, the Practice Statement and the Limitation Act 1980

Under s 2 of the Limitation Act 1980, the general rule is that the period of limitation for an action in tort is six years from the date on which the cause of action accrues.

However, ss 11 to 14 establish a different regime for actions for damages for negligence, nuisance or breach of duty where the damages are in respect of personal injuries. In these latter cases, the limitation period is three years from either the date when the cause of action accrued or the 'date of knowledge' as defined in s 14, whichever is the later. In addition, s 33 gives the court discretion to extend the period within which a claim can be lodged when it appears that it would be equitable to do so. It can be seen that the latter regime is much more liberal than the strictly constrained s 2 procedure, and in recent cases the House of Lords has been required to consider the extent to which the more liberal s 11 regime should be applied. In doing so, however, it has had to consider the extent to which its own previous restrictive judgments should continue to apply or whether it should exercise its powers under the 1966 practice statement in order to overrule those previous authorities.

The first such decision, *Horton v Sadler* (2007), concerned the circumstances under which a court might exercise its discretion to allow an out-of-time claim under s 33 of the Act. In *Walkley v Precision Forgings Ltd* (1979) the House had previously decided that the exercise of such discretion was not possible where a writ had been issued before the limitation period expired, but the action had not been pursued to completion. The reasoning of the court appeared to be that, as the action had actually been started within the limitation period, it could not be argued that it was the limitation period as such that prevented its completion. However, in *Horton v Sadler* the House of Lords revealed the flaw in the earlier reasoning in *Horton*, which had focused on the first action to the exclusion of the later action. In the opinion of the House in *Horton* it was the circumstances of the later case, begun after the expiration of the limitation period, that had to be examined in deciding whether or not the s 33 discretion could be exercised. For that reason the House of Lords overruled its previous ruling in *Walkley v Precision Forgings Ltd*.

The next issue relating to the operation of the Limitation Act 1980 arose in a series of unrelated cases in which six appellants, all of whom alleged that they had been victims of sexual abuse during their childhood, appealed against decisions of lower courts that their claims were statute-barred under s 2 of the Limitation Act 1980. The cases assumed a level of notoriety in the popular press due to the linked case of *A v Hoare* (2008) in which the defendant had been convicted in 1989 of an attempted rape of the claimant, involving a serious and traumatic sexual assault. He was sentenced to life imprisonment, but in 2004, while still serving his sentence, he won £7m on the UK national lottery. Subsequently the claimant started proceedings for damages in December 2004.

In each of the cases, the respective judges had been constrained by judicial precedent to follow the previous House of Lords' judgment in *Stubbings v Webb* (1993), which had decided unanimously that s 11 of the Limitation Act 1980 did not apply in cases of deliberate assault, including indecent assault. The House clearly considered that an action for an intentional trespass to the person did not amount to an action for 'negligence, nuisance or breach of duty' within the meaning of s 11(1) of the Act. As a consequence of *Stubbings*, such claimants were subject to the three-year limitation period rather than the more generous provisions in ss 11–14 and s 33 which allowed for claims to be brought out of time if the court considered this was equitable.

In *A v Hoare* the House of Lords, again unanimously, held that *Stubbings v Webb* had been wrongly decided and concluded that ss 11 and 33 of the Limitation Act 1980 did extend to claims for damages in tort arising from trespass to the person, including sexual assault. As Baroness Hale pointed out, it is a common feature of claims for sexual abuse that they are instituted many years after the events complained of and thus very often after a limitation period of six years has passed. To subject such claims to the rigours of s 2 limitations effectively would be to deny access to justice to those who had suffered such abuse.

A's case was remitted to the Queen's Bench Division to decide whether the discretion under s 33 should be exercised in her favour and subsequently, and not very surprisingly, in June 2008 Mr Justice Coulson exercised the s 33 discretion in favour of A.

The Supreme Court, the Human Rights Act and the European Court of Human Rights

The effect of the Human Rights Act on the operation of the doctrine of precedent, and in particular the impact of decisions of the ECtHR on the Supreme Court, has already been mentioned in Chapter 2. Reference may well be made to the stark expression of that relationship made by Lord Rodger in *Secretary of State for the Home Department v AF* (2009). However, a more considered, if no less resigned, expression of the relationship, with the ECtHR being clearly the superior court with its judgments overruling those of the domestic English court, may be found in Lord Hoffman's pragmatic judgment in the same case. As he put it:

> I agree that the judgment of the European Court of Human Rights ('ECtHR') in *A v United Kingdom* (Application No 3455/05) requires these appeals to be allowed. I do so with very considerable regret, because I think that the decision of the ECtHR was wrong and that it may well destroy the system of control orders which is a significant part of this country's defences against terrorism. Nevertheless, I think that your Lordships have no choice but to submit. It is true that section 2(1)(a) of the Human Rights Act 1998 requires us only to 'take into account' decisions of the ECtHR. As a matter of our domestic law, we could take the decision in *A v United Kingdom* into account but nevertheless prefer our own view. But the United Kingdom is bound by the Convention, as a matter of international law, to accept the decisions of the ECtHR on its interpretation. To reject such a decision would almost certainly put this country in breach of the international obligation which it accepted when it acceded to the Convention. I can see no advantage in your Lordships doing so.

Mistakes by the Supreme Court

The following tautology may be applied in relation to the Supreme Court: as the ultimate authority on the law, it says what the law is; and as what it says is the law, it cannot be wrong. However, what happens if the Supreme Court subsequently believes that what it said the law was, was wrong? On rare occasions decisions of the House of Lords have almost immediately been recognised to have been wrong. Just such a situation arose in *Anderton v Ryan* (1985), when the House of Lords interpreted the Criminal Attempts Act 1981 in such a way as to virtually make the Act ineffective. Following much academic criticism, the House of Lords acknowledged its error and in *R v Shivpuri* (1986), after only one year, it overruled *Anderton v Ryan*. The leading judgment in *Shivpuri* was delivered by Lord Bridge, as was only fitting as he had also been a member of the erroneous majority in *Anderton v Ryan*. As he stated:

> I have made clear my own conviction, which as a party to the decision . . . I
> am the readier to express, that the decision was wrong. What then is to be
> done? If the case is indistinguishable, the application of the strict doctrine
> of precedent would require that the present appeal be allowed. Is it permis-
> sible to depart from precedent under the Practice Statement (Judicial
> Precedent) [1966] 1 WLR 1234 notwithstanding the especial need for
> certainty in the criminal law? The following considerations lead me to
> answer that question affirmatively. First, I am undeterred by the considera-
> tion that the decision in *Anderton v Ryan* was so recent. *The Practice
> Statement is an effective abandonment of our pretension to infallibility. If a
> serious error embodied in a decision of this House has distorted the law, the
> sooner it is corrected the better.* (emphasis added)

The foregoing was done in line with the operation of the doctrine of precedent within the
English legal system, as a result of which only the House of Lords could overrule a
previous decision of that court. However, it was fortunate that in *Shivpuri*, the House had
an early opportunity to reconsider its previous exposition of the law. The question arises
as to what would happen if an earlier legal determination by the House of Lords/Supreme
Court were subsequently to be generally accepted as wrong. In strict terms, as all other
courts are bound by the rules of precedent to follow the House of Lords/Supreme Court,
no change could be considered until a similar case returned to the House of Lords/
Supreme Court. Just such a situation arose in relation to the issue of provocation as a
defence to a charge of murder. However, before considering the details of the situation it
is necessary to explain the role of the Privy Council in regard to the doctrine of precedent.

The Judicial Committee of the Privy Council (see 4.12), although essentially made
up of the Justices of the Supreme Court, is not actually a part of the English legal system.
Consequently its decisions do not fit within the hierarchical structure of the English
system and are not binding on any English court, although its decisions are of extremely
strong persuasive authority. On the other hand, it has been previously accepted that
decisions of the House of Lords are nonetheless to be followed by the Privy Council.
Thus in *Tai Hing Ltd v Liu Chong Hing Bank* (1986) the Committee (per Lord Scarman,
p 14) stated that:

> Once it is accepted . . . that the applicable law is English, their Lordships of
> the Judicial Committee will follow a House of Lords' decision which covers
> the point in issue. The Judicial Committee is not the final judicial authority
> for the determination of English law. That is the responsibility of the House
> of Lords in its judicial capacity. Though the Judicial Committee enjoys a
> greater freedom from the binding effect of precedent than does the House
> of Lords, it is in no position on a question of English law to invoke the
> Practice Statement pursuant to which the House has assumed the power to
> depart in certain circumstances from a previous decision of the House.

Thus the traditional situation was that the House of Lords was supreme and in matters of English law it bound the Privy Council, which was never any more than of persuasive authority in relation to English law. However, this traditional view has been radically undermined by a series of cases relating to the interpretation of provocation as a defence under s 3 of the Homicide Act 1957.

Section 3 of the Homicide Act 1957 provides that a jury must decide two issues in assessing whether a defendant can make use of the defence of provocation:

(i)   whether the killer lost self-control in their reaction to words or acts, and

(ii)   whether a 'reasonable man' would have acted in that way.

Difference of opinion, not to say controversy, has arisen in relation to the second element of his test. In the House of Lords' decision in *R v Camplin* (1978), Lord Diplock stated that when considering whether the defendant's reaction to provocation had been that of a reasonable man, the jury should have regard to the fact that the reasonable man referred to:

was a person having the power of self-control, to be expected of an ordinary person of the sex and age of the accused, but in other aspects *sharing such of the accused's characteristics* as they think would affect the gravity of the provocation to him. (emphasis added)

However, the actual meaning of the words italicised in the above quotation has proved fertile ground for legal debate. Thus in *Luc Thiet Thuan v R* (1997), in the Privy Council the majority held that the standard of self-control to be applied was that of the ordinary person, not that of a brain-damaged person, as was involved in the case. In the minority, Lord Steyn suggested that the particular characteristics possessed by the defendant must be attributed to the reasonable man.

In two later decisions the Court of Appeal declined to follow the majority in *Luc Thiet Thuan*, holding that, as the majority decision in that case was in conflict with decisions of the Court of Appeal, the doctrine of precedent required the Court of Appeal to follow its own decisions (see *R v Campbell* (1997) and *R v Parker* (1997)). However, in *R v Smith (Morgan)* (2001) a majority of the House of Lords held that *Luc Thiet Thuan* had been wrongly decided and by a majority of 3:2 held that juries could take account of the personal characteristics of defendants that made them particularly susceptible to losing self-control. As with *Anderton v Ryan*, this decision met with concentrated academic attack and it became generally, if certainly not universally, accepted that the House of Lords had got it wrong. The problem, however, was that no immediate opportunity presented itself for the House of Lords to reverse the decision in *Morgan Smith*. Instead, the Law Lords elected to make use of an appeal to the Privy Council in a case from Jersey, which has its own legal jurisdiction, but with a murder law based on English law. The case was *Attorney General for Jersey v Holley* (2005).

More in recognition of the potential consequences of their actions than the importance of the case *per se*, 9 of the total of 12 Law Lords sat on the Privy Council hearing and ruled. As Lord Nicholls, in the majority, stated (para 1):

> The decision of the House in (*Morgan Smith*) is in direct conflict with the decision of their Lordships' board in *Luc Thiet Thuan v the Queen*. And the reasoning of the majority in the *Morgan Smith* case is not easy to reconcile with the reasoning of the House of Lords in *R v Camplin* . . . *This appeal, being heard by an enlarged board of nine members, is concerned to resolve this conflict and clarify definitively the present state of English law*, and hence Jersey law, on this important subject.

Such an intention was also accepted by the minority, who acknowledged the effect of the majority decision was to clarify the state of English law in relation to the partial defence of provocation. The conclusion, by a majority of six to three, was that the *Morgan Smith* case had been wrongly decided. Thus the Privy Council had made its decision; what remained was to consider the impact of that ruling in relation to the operation of the doctrine of precedent within the English court structure. The opportunity to do so came when the joined appeals in *R v James and R v Karimi* came before the Court of Appeal in January 2006.

The issue before the court was simple: was the Court of Appeal bound to follow the House of Lords' decision in *Morgan Smith*, or was the decision of the Privy Council in *Holley* to be preferred? Once again, a strengthened bench of the Court of Appeal, made up of five rather than the usual three members, indicated the importance of the case. In reaching its decision, the Court of Appeal was extremely sensitive to the manner in which *Holley* had been used as a device for subverting the traditional operation of the doctrine of precedent, but in an exercise of judicial realism it both raised, and dealt with, the central issues relating to precedent; thus per Lord Phillips, Chief Justice, paras 41–2:

> it is not this court, but the Lords of Appeal in Ordinary who have altered the established approach to precedent. There are possible constitutional issues in postulating that a Board of the Privy Council, however numerous or distinguished, is in a position on an appeal from Jersey to displace and replace a decision of the Appellate Committee on an issue of English law. Our principles in relation to precedent are, however, common law principles. Putting on one side the position of the European Court of Justice, the Lords of Appeal in Ordinary have never hitherto accepted that any other tribunal could overrule a decision of the Appellate Committee. Uniquely a majority of the Law Lords have on this occasion decided that they could do so and have done so in their capacity as members of the Judicial Committee of the Privy

Council. We do not consider that it is for this court to rule that it was beyond their powers to alter the common law rules of precedent in this way.

The rule that this court must always follow a decision of the House of Lords and, indeed, one of its own decisions rather than a decision of the Privy Council is one that was established at a time when no tribunal other than the House of Lords itself could rule that a previous decision of the House of Lords was no longer good law. *Once one postulates that there are circumstances in which a decision of the Judicial Committee of the Privy Council can take precedence over a decision of the House of Lords, it seems to us that this court must be bound in those circumstances to prefer the decision of the Privy Council to the prior decision of the House of Lords.* That, so it seems to us, is the position that has been reached in the case of these appeals.

As a consequence of the preceding cases it is now apparent that the Privy Council can in exceptional circumstances overrule precedents of the House of Lords. According to the Court of Appeal in *James*, those exceptional circumstances arose as a result of the following attributes in the case:

- All nine of the Lords of Appeal in Ordinary sitting in *Holley* agreed in the course of their judgments that the result reached by the majority clarified definitively English law on the issue in question.

- The majority in *Holley* constituted half the Appellate Committee of the House of Lords. We do not know whether there would have been agreement that the result was definitive had the members of the Board divided five/four.

- In the circumstances, the result of any appeal on the issue to the House of Lords is a foregone conclusion.

It might not be over-cynical to suggest that such 'exceptional' circumstances will occur as and when the Justices of the Supreme Court (a) agree with advocates who in a case make such a suggestion, and (b) deem it desirable to change the law in such a case. It certainly cannot be denied that the decisions in *Holley* and *James* fundamentally alter the previous understanding of the way in which the doctrine of precedent operates within the English legal system and affords the Justices of the Supreme Court a second way of altering their previous decisions in addition to the Practice Statement of 1966.

The Court of Appeal

In civil cases, the Court of Appeal is generally bound by previous decisions of the House of Lords. Although the Court of Appeal, notably under the aegis of Lord Denning, attempted on a number of occasions to escape from the constraints of *stare decisis*, the House of Lords repeatedly reasserted the binding nature of its decisions on the Court of Appeal. The

House of Lords emphasised the balance between the need for certainty in the law against the need to permit scope for the law to develop, and in so doing, it asserted its function, as the court of last resort at the head of the hierarchy, to undertake necessary reform. The relationship between and functions of the House of Lords and the Court of Appeal was clearly stated by Lord Diplock in *Davis v Johnson* [1978] 1 All ER 1132 at 1137–8:

> In an appellate court of last resort a balance must be struck between the need on the one side for legal certainty resulting from the binding effect of previous decisions and on the other side the avoidance of undue restriction on the proper development of law. In the case of an intermediate appellate court, however, the second desideratum can be taken care of by an appeal to a superior court, if reasonable means of access to it are available; while the risk to the first desideratum, legal certainty, if the court is not bound by its own previous decisions grows ever greater with increasing membership and the number of three-judge divisions in which it sits . . . So the balance does not lie in the same place as the court of last resort.

The decision to be taken by the Court of Appeal when faced with conflicting precedents from the Supreme Court and the Privy Council has been considered previously. The more general relationship between the Court of Appeal and the Privy Council was clarified by Lord Neuberger MR in *Sinclair Investments (UK) Ltd v Versailles Trade Finance Ltd* (2011). In explaining the situation of the Court of Appeal he stated:

> We should not follow the Privy Council decision . . . in preference to decisions of this court, unless there are domestic authorities which show that the decisions of this court were *per incuriam*, or at least of doubtful reliability. Save where there are powerful reasons to the contrary, the Court of Appeal should follow its own previous decisions . . . It is true that there is a powerful subsequent decision of the Privy Council which goes the other way, but that of itself is not enough to justify departing from the earlier decisions of this court. . . . I do not suggest that it would always be wrong for this court to refuse to follow a decision of the Privy Council in preference to one of its own previous decisions, but the general rule is that we follow our previous decisions, leaving it to the Supreme Court to overrule those decisions if it is appropriate to do so. Two recent cases where this court preferred to follow a decision of the Privy Council rather than an earlier domestic decision which would normally be regarded as binding (in each case a decision of the House of Lords) are *R v James* and *Abou-Rahmah v Abacha*. In each case, the decision was justified, based as it was on the proposition that it was a foregone conclusion that, *if the case had gone to the House of Lords, they would have followed the Privy Council decision* (paras 72–74, emphasis added).

However, as has been seen in 2.5.1.2 above, the Court of Appeal in *Mendoza v Ghaidan* (2002) used s 3 of the HRA to extend the rights of same-sex partners to inherit a statutory tenancy under the Rent Act 1977. In so doing, it extended the earlier decision of the House of Lords in *Fitzpatrick v Sterling Housing Association Ltd* (1999), which had been decided before the HRA came into force. Thus, it can be seen that the HRA gives the Court of Appeal latitude to effectively overrule decisions of the House of Lords which were decided before the HRA came into effect and in conflict with the ECHR.

See also the reasoning of the Court of Appeal in *D v East Berkshire Community NHS Trust* (2004) in which the Court of Appeal held that the decision of the House of Lords in *X (Minors) v Bedfordshire County Council* (1995) could not be maintained after the introduction of the Human Rights Act 1998 as that Act had undermined the policy consideration that had largely dictated the House of Lords' decision. That approach was directly approved in *Kay v London Borough of Lambeth* (2005) (see below).

Similarly, decisions of the ECJ, which effectively overrule previous decisions of the House of Lords, will also be followed by the Court of Appeal.

The Court of Appeal generally is also bound by its own previous decisions in civil cases. There are, however, a number of exceptions to this general rule. Lord Greene MR listed these exceptions in *Young v Bristol Aeroplane Co Ltd* (1944):

- Where there is a conflict between two previous decisions of the Court of Appeal. In this situation, the later court must decide which decision to follow and, as a corollary, which to overrule. Such a situation arose in *Tiverton Estates Ltd v Wearwell Ltd* (1974). In that case, which dealt with the meaning of s 40 of the Law of Property Act 1925 (subsequently repealed), the court elected to follow older precedents rather than follow the inconsistent decision in *Law v Jones* (1974). The decision in *Tiverton Estates Ltd v Wearwell Ltd* can be justified as the mere working out of the rules of precedent. As *Law v Jones* must have been made in ignorance of, or based on a failure to properly understand, the earlier decisions (see *per incuriam*, below), it could have been ignored on that ground alone. However, this particular exception is wider than that, in that it allows the current Court of Appeal to choose between the previous conflicting authorities. Hence, the Court of Appeal could have decided to follow *Law v Jones* if it preferred.

- Where a previous decision of the Court of Appeal has been overruled, either expressly or impliedly, by the House of Lords. An express overruling would obviously occur where the House of Lords actually considered the Court of Appeal precedent, but it is equally possible that the *ratio* in a precedent from the Court of Appeal could be overruled without the actual case being cited and considered. In this situation, the Court of Appeal, in line with the normal rules of precedent, is required to follow the decision of the House of Lords. Thus, in *Family Housing Association v Jones* (1990), the Court of

Appeal felt obliged to ignore its own precedents on the distinction
between a licence and a tenancy in property law where, although they
had not been expressly overruled, they were implicitly in conflict
with later decisions of the House of Lords in *AG Securities Ltd v
Vaughan* (1988) and *Street v Mountford* (1985).

Where the previous decision was given *per incuriam* or, in other
words, that previous decision was taken in ignorance of some
authority, either statutory or case law, that would have led to a
different conclusion. In this situation, the later court can ignore the
previous decision in question. It is important to emphasise, however,
that the missing authority must be such that it must have led to a
different conclusion; the mere possibility is not enough. There are so
many case authorities that it is simply not possible to cite all of them.
However, the essential authorities, those that lead to a particular decision, must be considered. It is the absence of any such of these
authorities that renders a decision *per incuriam*. As will be appreciated, the instances of decisions being ignored on the basis of a ruling
of *per incuriam* are 'of the rarest occurrence' (*Morelle Ltd v Wakeling*
(1955)). One example, however, may be seen in *Williams v Fawcett*
(1985), in which the Court of Appeal did find such exceptional
circumstances as would permit it to treat its previous decisions as
having been made *per incuriam*. The facts of the case involved an
appeal against a decision to commit a person to prison for contempt
of court in breaching a non-molestation order. Previous decisions of
the Court of Appeal had held that any such committal order had to
be signed by the court officer who issued it. However, the present
court found that the law as stated in the Criminal Court Rules did not
allow for appeal simply on the grounds that the order was not signed
by a proper officer as long as the seal of the court was applied. Of
crucial importance among the circumstances that led to the finding of
per incuriam in relation to the earlier decisions was the fact that, given
the expense involved, the case would be unlikely to go to the House
of Lords for its final determination of the legal situation. It should be
noted that this justification can be seen to fit with the previous quotation from Lord Diplock in *Davis v Johnson*, to the extent that the
Court of Appeal decided that, in this instance, there was no 'reasonable means of access to' the court of last resort. A similar justification
for another finding of *per incuriam* can be found in *Rickards v Rickards*
(1989), in which the Court of Appeal held that its previous decision
in *Podberry v Peak* (1981) had misunderstood and wrongly applied
the House of Lords' decision in *Laine v Eskdale* (1891). In overruling
Podberry, the court held that it had the power to hear an appeal

against a refusal to extend the time limit within which a person could appeal against the award of a lump sum in a clean-break divorce settlement. The court once again held that as the issue involved was so serious, and as it was unlikely to go to the House of Lords, then the Court of Appeal should itself remedy the earlier misunderstanding stated in its own previous decision. An interesting example of the principle can be found in *R (on the Application of W) v Lambeth LBC* (2002), in which the Court of Appeal overruled its earlier judgment of only six months previously in *R (A) v Lambeth LBC* (2001) as regards the interpretation and effect of s 17 of the Children Act 1989. The matter of interest is not so much that the later court held that the earlier one would have reached a different conclusion had the law been fully explained to it, but that one of the judges in the unanimous decision in *R (W) v Lambeth LBC* was Laws LJ, who had delivered a minority judgment to the same effect in *R (A) v Lambeth LBC*.

There used to be a further exception to the general rule that the Court of Appeal was bound by its own earlier decisions and that was in relation to an interlocutory or interim decision made by a panel of only two judges (*Boys v Chaplin* (1968)); even interim decisions by a full panel of three judges were still binding. However, as a consequence of the Woolf reforms and under the Civil Procedure Rules 1998, the distinction between interlocutory and final appeals was removed. Consequently, it was held in *Cave v Robinson, Jarvis and Rolf* (2002) that the decision in *Boys v Chaplin* was no longer sustainable, although the Court of Appeal stated that it might be possible to adjust the reasoning in *Boys v Chaplin* where the later court was satisfied that the earlier decision of the two-person court was 'manifestly wrong'.

Although on the basis *of R v Spencer* (1985) it would appear that there is no difference in principle between the operation of the doctrine of *stare decisis* between the criminal and civil divisions of the Court of Appeal, it is generally accepted that in practice, precedent is not followed as strictly in the former as it is in the latter. Courts in the Criminal Division are not bound to follow their own previous decisions that they subsequently consider to have been based on either a misunderstanding or a misapplication of the law. The reason for this is that the criminal courts deal with matters involving individual liberty and therefore require greater discretion to prevent injustice.

The European courts and domestic precedent

The foregoing list deals with all the exceptions set out in *Young v Bristol Aeroplane Co Ltd*, but the following additional exceptions to the rule have become apparent since that decision:

● There is also the possibility/likelihood that, as a consequence of s 3 of the European Communities Act 1972, the Court of Appeal can ignore a previous decision of its own which is inconsistent with EC law or with a later decision of the ECJ. As s 3 requires courts either to refer cases dealing with Community law to the ECJ, or alternatively to decide the cases themselves in the light of the previous decision of the ECJ, it would appear that the section gives the Appeal Court grounds for ignoring any of its previous decisions which conflict with subsequent decisions of the ECJ. This effectively fits the ECJ into the traditional hierarchical structure of precedence as the court of last resort in relation to Community law matters.

- It has taken some time for the precise effect of the HRA 1998 to be seen, but as has been explained above at 2.5, s 2 of the Act requires all courts and tribunals to take into account any judgment, decision, declaration or advisory opinion of the ECtHR. As previously the decisions of the European Court of Human Rights were not directly binding on the UK courts, this means that the decisions and jurisprudence of the ECtHR will affect the way in which the UK courts reach decisions in cases involving the rights provided under the European Convention.

In *Director General of Fair Trading v Proprietary Association of Great Britain (No 2)* (2001) (see below, at 9.2.3), the Court of Appeal felt able to refine the decision of the House of Lords in *R v Gough* (1993) to bring it into line with ECtHR jurisprudence, and it is almost without doubt that it will overrule its own decisions where those are in conflict with the provisions of the ECHR. The issue of the effect of s 2 of the HRA in relation to the domestic rules of precedent was considered extensively in *Lambeth London Borough Council v Kay; Price v Leeds City Council* (2006). These combined appeals, in essence, related to the effectiveness of orders to take possession of land owned by public authorities but occupied by the appellants, without right under domestic law. The argument that the appellants could rely on Art 8 of the ECHR was rejected by all the courts from the first instance to the House of Lords. In reaching its decision, the House of Lords, by a majority, held that it was not necessary for a local authority to prove that domestic law complied with Art 8. Courts could and should proceed on the assumption that domestic law was compatible with Art 8. The onus was on the occupier to show that there were highly exceptional circumstances to support their case. Much was made of the House of Lords' decision in these cases, especially as *Kay* related to the rights of travellers to occupy land. However, the cases also raised fundamental issues relating to the operation of precedent within the court hierarchy, with specific relevance to the authority of the ECtHR within the domestic structure.

In the *Kay* case, the Court of Appeal had held that it was bound by the decision of the House of Lords in *Harrow London Borough Council v Qazi* (2004), but it also expressed the opinion that the *Qazi* decision was incompatible with the later decision of the ECtHR in *Connors v United Kingdom* (2004). However, as neither the precise effect of s 2 of the Human Rights Act, nor the hierarchical authority of competing decisions of the ECtHR and the House of Lords, had previously received a definitive consideration in the English courts, the Court of Appeal granted leave to appeal to the House of Lords on the issue of precedent. On that issue Lord Bingham delivered the leading judgment, with which the other members of the court concurred. As Lord Bingham explained, there is a distinct difference in the consequences of decisions of the European Court of Justice and those of the European Court of Human Rights: the former are binding, the latter are not. As Lord Bingham put it (para 28):

> The mandatory duty imposed on domestic courts by section 2 of the 1998 Act is to take into account any judgment of the Strasbourg Court and any opinion of the Commission. Thus they are not strictly required to follow Strasbourg rulings, as they are bound by section 3(1) of the European Communities Act 1972 and as they are bound by the rulings of superior courts in the domestic curial hierarchy.

As regards the effect of decisions of the ECtHR within the English legal system of precedent, Lord Bingham addressed the fundamental issue of authority head-on (para 40):

> Reference has already been made to the duty imposed on United Kingdom courts to take Strasbourg judgments and opinions into account and to the unlawfulness of courts, as public authorities, acting incompatibly with Convention rights. The questions accordingly arise whether our domestic rules of precedent are, or should be, modified; whether a court which would ordinarily be bound to follow the decision of another court higher in the domestic curial hierarchy is, or should be, no longer bound to follow that decision if it appears to be inconsistent with a later ruling of the Court in Strasbourg.

His conclusion, with which the other members of the judicial panel concurred, was equally forthright in maintaining the integrity of the existing structure of binding precedent within the domestic hierarchical structure (para 43):

> . . . certainty is best achieved by adhering, even in the Convention context, to our rules of precedent. It will of course be the duty of judges to review Convention arguments addressed to them, and if they consider a binding precedent to be, or possibly to be, inconsistent with Strasbourg authority, they may express their views and give leave to appeal, as the Court of Appeal did here. Leap-frog appeals may be appropriate. In this way, in my opinion, they discharge their duty under the 1998 Act. But they should follow the binding precedent . . .

However, Lord Bingham did allow for one *exceptional* set of circumstances. As previously mentioned, he and the other members of the House of Lords specifically acknowledged that in such circumstances as occurred in *D v East Berkshire Community NHS Trust*, where the previous authority had been set without reference to the Human Rights Act, the Court of Appeal would be at liberty to avoid following the previous decision of the House of Lords.

Subsequently, in its judgment in *McCann v United Kingdom* (2008), the ECtHR disagreed with the majority of the House of Lords in *Kay* (2005), holding that *Connors* (2004) was not confined to cases involving the eviction of travellers, nor was it limited to cases where the applicant was seeking to challenge the law itself rather than its application or procedure in a particular case. However, in *Doherty v Birmingham City Council* the House of Lords decided that the basic rule in this area remained as laid down by the majority in *Qazi v Harrow* (2004) and reaffirmed by the majority in *Kay*. Although in *McCann* the European Court of Human Rights had endorsed the reasoning of the minority in *Kay*, the House of Lords in *Doherty* decided that the approach of the ECtHR could best be implemented by applying and developing the reasoning of the majority, rather than the minority, view expressly supported by the ECtHR.

In September 2010, when the *Kay* case reached the ECtHR, that court followed its own reasoning in *McCann* and reasserted its preference for the minority opinions in the House of Lords' judgments in *Kay*. The ECtHR judgment in *Kay* was handed down while the House of Lords was hearing another case relating to the same issue in *Manchester City Council v Pinnock*. The ECtHR's *Kay* decision was actually handed down after the oral hearing of the *Pinnock* case and the House of Lords asked for written submissions on its effect. The judgment of the House of Lords was delivered by Lord Neuberger, who was still sitting as a member of that court before taking up his position as Master of the Rolls and represents a falling in line, if ever so slightly hesitantly, with the jurisprudence of the ECtHR:

48. This Court is not bound to follow every decision of the ECtHR. Not only would it be impractical to do so: it would sometimes be inappropriate, as it would destroy the ability of the Court to engage in the constructive dialogue with the ECtHR which is of value to the development of Convention law. Of course, we should usually follow a clear and constant line of decisions by the ECtHR. But we are not actually bound to do so or (in theory, at least) to follow a decision of the Grand Chamber. As Lord Mance pointed out in *Doherty v Birmingham* [2009] 1 AC 367, para 126, section 2 of the HRA requires our courts to 'take into account' ECtHR decisions, not necessarily to follow them. Where, however, there is a clear and constant line of decisions whose effect is not inconsistent with some fundamental substantive or procedural aspect of our law, and whose reasoning does not appear to overlook or misunderstand some argument or point of principle, we consider that it would be wrong for this Court not to follow that line.

49. In the present case there is no question of the jurisprudence of the ECtHR failing to take into account some principle or cutting across our domestic substantive or procedural law in some fundamental way. That is clear from the minority opinions in *Harrow v Qazi* [2004] 1 AC 983 and *Kay v Lambeth* [2006] 2 AC 465, and also from the fact that our domestic law was already moving in the direction of the European jurisprudence in

> *Doherty v Birmingham* [2009] 1 AC 367. *Even before the decision in* Kay v
> UK *(App no 37341/06), we would, in any event, have been of the opinion that
> this Court should now accept and apply the minority view of the House of
> Lords in those cases. In the light of* Kay, *that is clearly the right conclusion.*
>
> Therefore, if our law is to be compatible with Article 8, where a
> court is asked to make an order for possession of a person's home at the suit
> of a local authority, the court must have the power to assess the proportion-
> ality of making the order, and, in making that assessment, to resolve any
> relevant dispute of fact (emphasis added).

Divisional Courts

The Divisional Courts, each located within the three divisions of the High Court, hear
appeals from courts and tribunals below them in the hierarchy. They are bound by the
doctrine of *stare decisis* in the normal way and must follow decisions of the House of Lords
and the Court of Appeal. In turn, they bind the courts below them in the hierarchy, including
the ordinary High Court cases. The Divisional Courts are also normally bound by their
own previous decisions, although in civil cases, they may make use of the exceptions open
to the Court of Appeal in *Young v Bristol Aeroplane Co Ltd* (1944) and, in criminal appeal
cases and cases relating to judicial review, the Queen's Bench Divisional Court may refuse
to follow its own earlier decisions where it feels the decision to have been made wrongly.

In *R v Greater Manchester Coroner ex p Tal* (1984), the Divisional Court held that
it had supervisory jurisdiction in relation to coroners' courts, although this was contrary
to its previous decision in *R v Surrey Coroner ex p Campbell* (1982). In so doing, the
court stated that its power to depart from its previous decisions was conferred under the
Senior Courts Act 1981, but it also held, on the basis of the House of Lords' decision in
O'Reilly v Mackman (1982), that *Campbell* had wrongly applied *Anisminic v Foreign
Compensation Commission* (1969). *Tal*, therefore, may also be seen as an example of the
normal exceptions in *Young v Bristol Aeroplane Co Ltd*.

In *R v Stafford Justices ex p Commissioners of Customs and Excise* (1990), the
Queen's Bench Divisional Court held that its previous decision in *R v Ealing Justices ex
p Dixon* (1990) had been wrongly decided. Both cases related to the rights to undertake
prosecutions where individuals had been charged, as required under s 37 of the Police
and Criminal Evidence Act (PACE) 1984, by the police. Contrary to the *Ealing Justices*
case, the Divisional Court in the *Stafford Justices* case held that merely being charged by
the police did not require that the police should pursue the prosecution and that Customs
and Excise could undertake the prosecution. In a similar case, although this time relating
to the powers of the Inland Revenue to undertake prosecutions on indictment without
the consent of the Attorney General, the Divisional Court approved the *Stafford Justices*
decision and stated clearly that the *Ealing Justices* case should no longer be followed
(*R v Criminal Cases Review Commission ex p Hunt* (2001)).

The House of Lords implicitly approved the Divisional Court's power to overrule
its own previous decisions in *DPP v Butterworth* (1994). This case was the culmination
of a number of cases relating to the refusal to provide a breath specimen contrary to

s 7(6) of the Road Traffic Act 1988. In *DPP v Corcorran* (1993), a Divisional Court held that where a person was not informed for which of two potential offences he was being required to provide a specimen, any prosecution was undermined for duplicity. However, in *DPP v Shaw* (1993), a differently constituted Divisional Court subsequently held that *Corcorran* was wrongly decided and was an example of a *per incuriam* decision. *Shaw* rather than *Corcorran* was followed in the later Divisional Court decision in *DPP v Butterworth*. That decision was expressly approved by the House of Lords.

High Court

The High Court is also bound by the decisions of superior courts. Decisions by individual High Court judges are binding on courts inferior in the hierarchy, but such decisions are not binding on other High Court judges, although they are of strong persuasive authority and tend to be followed in practice. The simple reason for this is that different judgments would lead to confusion in relation to exactly how the particular law in question was to be understood. It is possible, however, for High Court judges to disagree and for them to reach different conclusions as to the law in a particular area. The question then becomes, how is a later High Court judge to select which precedent to follow? It is usually accepted, although it is not a rule of law, that where the later decision has actually considered the previous one and has provided cause for not following it, then that is the judgment which later High Court judges should follow (*Colchester Estates v Carlton Industries plc* (1984)).

Conflicting decisions at the level of the High Court can, of course, be authoritatively decided by reference upwards to the Court of Appeal and then, if necessary, to the House of Lords, but when the cost of such appeals is borne in mind, it is apparent why, even on economic grounds alone, it is important for High Court judges not to treat their discretion as a licence to destabilise the law in a given area.

In relation to conflicting judgments at the level of the Court of Appeal, the High Court judge is required to follow the later decision.

Crown Courts cannot create precedent and their decisions can never amount to more than persuasive authority.

County courts and magistrates' courts do not create precedents.

It has to be particularly noted that the HRA now requires courts in the UK to take into consideration all previous decisions of the ECtHR, which now become precedents for the UK courts to follow. This is the case even where the ECtHR decision was in conflict with previous UK law. Equally, any English precedent that was in conflict with a decision of the ECtHR is now invalidated.

3.6.4 BINDING PRECEDENT

Not everything in a case report sets a precedent. The contents of a report can be divided into two categories:

- *Ratio decidendi*

  It is important to establish that it is not the actual decision in a case that sets the precedent; that is set by the rule of law on which the decision is founded.

This rule, which is an abstraction from the facts of the case, is known as the *ratio decidendi* of the case. The *ratio decidendi* (Latin for 'reason for deciding') of a case may be understood as the statement of the law applied in deciding the legal problem raised by the concrete facts of the case.

- *Obiter dictum*

  This phrase is Latin for 'a statement by the way'. Any statement of law that is not an essential part of the *ratio decidendi* is, strictly speaking, superfluous, and any such statement is referred to as an *obiter dictum* (*obiter dicta* in the plural), that is, said 'by the way'. Although *obiter dicta* do not form part of the binding precedent, they are persuasive authority and can be taken into consideration in later cases if the judge in the later case considers it appropriate to do so.

The division of cases into these two distinct parts is a theoretical procedure. Unfortunately, judges do not actually separate their judgments into the two clearly defined categories, and it is for the person reading the case to determine what the *ratio* is. In some cases, this is no easy matter, and it may be made even more difficult in appellate cases where each of the judges may deliver their own lengthy judgments with no clear single *ratio*. (The potential implications of the way in which later courts effectively determine the *ratio* in any particular case will be considered below and in section 10.4.2.) Students should always read cases fully; although it is tempting to rely on the headnote at the start of the case report, it should be remembered that this is a summary provided by the case reporter and merely reflects what that person thinks the *ratio* is. It is not unknown for headnotes to miss an essential point in a case.

3.6.5   ADVANTAGES OF CASE LAW

There are numerous perceived advantages of the doctrine of *stare decisis*, among which are the following:

- *Consistency*. This refers to the fact that like cases are decided on a like basis and are not apparently subject to the whim of the individual judge deciding the case in question. This aspect of formal justice is important in justifying the decisions taken in particular cases.

- *Certainty*. This follows from, and indeed is presupposed by, the previous item. Lawyers and their clients are able to predict what the outcome of a particular legal question is likely to be in the light of previous judicial decisions. Also, once the legal rule has been established in one case, individuals can orientate their behaviour with regard to that rule, relatively secure in the knowledge that it will not be changed by some later court.

- *Efficiency*. This refers to the fact that it saves the time of the judiciary, lawyers and their clients for the reason that cases do not have to be reargued. In respect of potential litigants, it saves them money in court expenses because they can apply to their solicitor/barrister for guidance as to how their particular case is likely to be decided in the light of previous cases on the same or similar points. (It should of course be recognised that the vast bulk of cases are argued and decided on their facts rather than on principles of law, but that does not detract from the relevance of this issue and is a point that will be taken up later in Chapter 10.)

- *Flexibility*. This refers to the fact that the various mechanisms by means of which the judges can manipulate the common law provide them with an opportunity to develop law in particular areas without waiting for parliament to enact legislation. In practice, flexibility is achieved through the possibility of previous decisions being either overruled or distinguished, or the possibility of a later court extending or modifying the effective ambit of a precedent. (It should be re-emphasised that it is not the decision in any case which is binding, but the *ratio decidendi*. It is correspondingly and equally incorrect to refer to a decision being overruled.)

This apparently small measure of discretion, in relation to whether later judges are minded to accept the validity of *obiter* statements in precedent cases, opens up the possibility that judges in later cases have a much wider degree of discretion than is originally apparent in the traditional view of *stare decisis*. It is important in this respect to realise that it is the judges in the later cases who actually determine the *ratio decidendi* of previous cases.

Judges, as has been noted previously, in delivering judgments in cases do not separate and highlight the *ratio decidendi* from the rest of their judgment, which can lead to a lack of certainty in determining the *ratio decidendi*. This uncertainty is compounded by the fact that reports of decisions in cases may run to considerable length, and where there are a number of separate judgments, although the judges involved may agree on the decision of a case, they may not agree on the legal basis of the decision reached. This difficulty is further compounded where there are a number of dissenting judgments. In the final analysis, it is for the judge deciding the case in which a precedent has been cited to determine the *ratio* of the authority and thus to determine whether he or she is bound by the case or not. This factor provides later courts with a considerable degree of discretion in electing whether to be bound or not by a particular authority.

The main mechanisms through which judges alter or avoid precedents are as follows:

- *Overruling*

  This is the procedure whereby a court higher up in the hierarchy sets aside a legal ruling established in a previous case. It has generally been accepted that overruling acts retrospectively, that is to say that the law as stated in the higher court is held to have always been the law. Thus not only is the new precedent effective as to future situations, but it is deemed to have applied equally to situations in the past. This may be seen as an outcome of the declaratory theory of law, in which judges were seen as merely stating rather than making the law. Thus the judges in the court that overrules a precedent made by a lower court are understood to be merely removing a mistaken understanding of what the law was, rather than actually changing that law. Equally, when a higher court ruled that a previous interpretation of a statutory provision was wrong, there was no question of that court changing the law: it was merely correcting an error of interpretation (for a further consideration of this point see *R v R* below).

However, the possibility of a change in this traditional approach to precedent was considered by the House of Lords in *National Westminster Bank plc v Spectrum Plus Ltd* (2005).

Spectrum had opened an account with National Westminster Bank, and obtained an overdraft facility. As part of that procedure the company issued a debenture to secure its debt to the bank. As security, the debenture purported to provide a specific charge over the company's book debts and a floating charge over its property and undertaking. As regards the book debts, the company had to pay them into a special account with the bank, the use of which was limited. However, as long as the overdraft limit was not exceeded, the company was free to draw on the account for its business purposes. When the company went into voluntary liquidation the bank applied for a declaration that the debenture had created a fixed charge over the company's book debts, with the effect that it would receive payment from those funds before other preferred creditors, such as the company's former employees and, at that time, importantly the Commissioners of HM Revenue and Customs. However, were the security to be considered as merely a floating charge the bank would lose priority in relation to the preferred creditors, although it would still stand in front of ordinary unsecured creditors. At first instance the Vice Chancellor held that the charge granted to the bank was only a floating charge but the Court of Appeal allowed the bank's appeal.

In the House of Lords the main substantive issue related to the nature of the security provided by the book debts, whether a fixed or floating charge. The bank relied on the precedent set by the High Court in *Siebe Gorman and Co Ltd v Barclays Bank Ltd* (1979). In that case Slade J had decided that arrangements of the kind under consideration were of the nature of fixed charges. That precedent had been accepted and extended by the Court of Appeal in *re New Bullas Trading Ltd* (1994) and was accepted and followed in the Court of Appeal in the present case. Nonetheless, the House of Lords unanimously held that the particular security given over Spectrum's book debts were not in the nature of fixed charges and in so doing overruled the precedent of *Siebe Gorman and Co Ltd v Barclays Bank Ltd* and consequentially the precedent in *re New Bullas Trading Ltd*.

However, as a subsidiary issue in the case but a more essential one for the operation of the doctrine of precedent in the English legal system, the question as to whether the House of Lords had power to deliver prospective rulings, that is, decisions applicable only in the future, was considered. The argument put forward on behalf of the bank on this issue was that *Siebe Gorman* had stood unchallenged for many years and banks generally had followed it and organised their business relationships on the basis that it was an accurate statement of the law. Consequently it was argued that, even if *Siebe Gorman* was to be overruled, the effect of that decision should only be prospective, and should not provide grounds for invalidating the very many cases that had been settled in reliance upon *Siebe Gorman* precedent. The argument against prospective overruling was that it amounted to the judicial usurpation of the legislative function of parliament, to the extent that the judiciary would be deciding how and when law was to have effect, and consequently it was outside the constitutional limits of judicial power.

The leading and wide-ranging decision in relation to the matter of prospective overruling was delivered by Lord Nichols, who concluded that (para 39):

> The objections in principle and difficulties in practice mentioned above have substance, particularly in respect of the traditional interpretation of statutes. These objections are compelling pointers to what should be the normal reach of the judicial process. But, even in respect of statute law, they do not lead to the conclusion that prospective overruling can never be justified as a proper exercise of judicial power. *In this country the established practice of judicial precedent derives from the common law. Constitutionally the judges have power to modify this practice.*
>
> Instances where this power has been used in courts elsewhere suggest there could be circumstances in this country where prospective overruling would be necessary to serve the underlying objective of the courts of this country: to administer justice fairly and in accordance with the law. *There could be cases where a decision on an issue of law, whether common law or statute law, was unavoidable but the decision would have such gravely unfair and disruptive consequences for past transactions or happenings that this House would be compelled to depart from the normal principles relating to the retrospective and prospective effect of court decisions.*
>
> If, altogether exceptionally, the House as the country's supreme court were to follow this course I would not regard it as trespassing outside the functions properly to be discharged by the judiciary under this country's constitution. Rigidity in the operation of a legal system is a sign of weakness, not strength. It deprives a legal system of necessary elasticity. Far from achieving a constitutionally exemplary result, it can produce a legal system unable to function effectively in changing times. *'Never say never' is a wise judicial precept, in the interest of all citizens of the country.*

Six of the other judges in the seven-strong panel of the House of Lords accepted Lord Nicholls' 'never say never' proposition; Lady Hale did consider the issue, but of that number most adopted the more conservative approach of Lord Hope when he stated that (para 126):

> I would respectfully agree with his comment about the wisdom of a 'never say never' approach but find myself unable to visualise circumstances in which it would be proper for a court, having reached a conclusion as to the correct meaning of a statute, to decline to apply to the case in hand the statute thus construed.

However, even though the House of Lords held open the possibility that in an exceptional case it could decide that its decision should only take effect for the future, in the instant case it decided that there was no good reason for postponing the effect of overruling *Siebe Gorman*. As a consequence of that decision it has been suggested that for those involved in previous cases, in which book debts were treated in accordance with what was then believed to be the law, apart from arguments of limitation, they may be able to seek further redress in the light of the restatement of the law. Alternatively, they may be able to rely on a defence that they have changed their position and therefore argue that their case should not now be reopened.

It is somewhat anomalous that, within the system of *stare decisis*, precedents gain increased authority with the passage of time. As a consequence, courts tend to be reluctant to overrule long-standing authorities even though they may no longer accurately reflect contemporary practices or morals. In addition to the wish to maintain a high degree of certainty in the law, the main reason for judicial reluctance to overrule old decisions would appear to be the fact that overruling operates retrospectively, with the effect that the principle of law being overruled is held never to have been law. Overruling a precedent might, therefore, have the consequence of disturbing important financial arrangements made in line with what were thought to be settled rules of law. It might even, in certain circumstances, lead to the imposition of criminal liability on previously lawful behaviour. It has to be emphasised, however, that the courts will not shrink from overruling authorities where they see them as no longer representing an appropriate statement of law.

The decision in *R v R* (1992) to recognise the possibility of rape within marriage may be seen as an example of this, although, even here, the House of Lords felt constrained to state that it was not actually altering the law, but was merely removing a misconception as to the true meaning and effect of the law. As this demonstrates, the courts are rarely ready to challenge the legislative prerogative of parliament in an overt way. For example, in *Curry v DPP* (1994), the Divisional Court attempted to remove the presumption that children between the ages of 10 and 14, who were charged with a criminal offence, did not know that what they did was seriously wrong and the prosecution had to provide evidence to rebut that presumption. Mann LJ justified reversing the presumption by claiming that although it had often been assumed to be the law, it had never actually been specifically considered by earlier courts. On such reasoning, he felt justified in departing from previous decisions of the Court of Appeal which otherwise would have bound him. The House of Lords subsequently restored the previous presumption. Although their Lordships recognised the problem, and indeed appeared to sympathise with Mann LJ's view, they nonetheless thought that such a significant change was a matter for parliamentary action rather than judicial intervention. The doctrine of *doli incapax* was finally removed by s 34 of the Crime and Disorder Act 1998. Of perhaps even greater concern is the fact that s 35 extended s 35 of the Criminal Justice and Public Order Act 1994 to cover all persons aged 10 or over. Thus, courts are now entitled to draw (adverse) inferences from the failure of such children to either give evidence or answer questions at their trial.

Bellinger v Bellinger (2003), considered at 2.5.1.2 above, provides a contemporary example of the courts' reluctance to overrule cases and change the law where parliament is the appropriate forum for such change. In response to the House of Lords' decision in *Bellinger*, the complex issues relating to trans-sexual people were taken up in the Gender Recognition Bill, which had its first reading in November 2003 only seven months later. The subsequent Gender Recognition Act 2004 came into full effect in April 2005.

Overruling should not be confused with *reversing*, which is the procedure whereby a superior court in the hierarchy reverses the decision of a lower court in the same case. As 'overruling' refers to the *ratio* of a case and not its decision, it is quite possible for a higher court to overrule the *ratio* for a decision of a lower court yet still reach the same decision for a different reason. Equally, it is possible for the higher court to approve the *ratio* yet not agree with its application by the lower court and consequently reverse that court's decision.

- *Distinguishing*

In comparison to the mechanism of overruling which is rarely used, the main device for avoiding binding precedents is that of distinguishing. As was previously stated, the *ratio decidendi* of any case is an abstraction from, and is based upon, the material facts of the case. This opens up the possibility that a court may regard the facts of the case before it as significantly different from the facts of a cited precedent and thus, consequentially, it will not find itself bound to follow that precedent. Judges use the device of distinguishing where, for some reason, they are unwilling to follow a particular precedent and the law reports provide many examples of strained distinctions where a court has quite evidently not wanted to follow an authority that it would otherwise have been bound by.

3.6.6 DISADVANTAGES OF CASE LAW

It should be noted that the advantage of flexibility at least potentially contradicts the alternative advantage of certainty, but there are other disadvantages in the doctrine, which have to be considered. Among these are the following:

- *Uncertainty*

This refers to the fact that the degree of certainty provided by the doctrine of *stare decisis* is undermined by the absolute number of cases that have been reported and can be cited as authorities. This uncertainty is increased by the ability of the judiciary to select which authority to follow through use of the mechanism of distinguishing cases on their facts. A further element leading to uncertainty was highlighted by James Richardson, the editor of *Archbold* (1995), the leading practitioners' text on criminal law, who has claimed that the lack of practical experience of some judges in the Criminal Appeal Court is:

... compounded by an apparent willingness, on occasion, to set aside principle in order to do what the court feels to be right (either way) in the individual case.

As Richardson suggests:

In the long run, this can only undermine a system which claims to operate on the basis of a hierarchy of binding precedent.

● *Fixity*

This refers to the possibility that the law in relation to any particular area may become ossified on the basis of an unjust precedent, with the consequence that previous injustices are perpetuated. An example of this is the possibility of rape within marriage, which has only relatively recently, given its long history, been recognised (*R v R* (1992)).

● *Unconstitutionality*

This is a fundamental question that refers to the fact that the judiciary are over-stepping their theoretical constitutional role by actually *making law* rather than restricting themselves to the role of simply applying it. This possibility requires a close examination of the role of the courts in the process of law-making.

The traditional *declaratory theory of law* claims that judges do not make law, they simply state what it is. This view, however, gives rise to two particular conceptual difficulties:

(a)   *Innovation*: legal rules, as social institutions and creations, cannot be subject to infinite regression; they must have had a beginning at some time in the past when some person or group of people made or recognised them. Every common law rule must have had an origin. To put this in a simpler way, if a particular law was not created by statute, it must have been created by a judge; even if the level of creative activity was no more than recognising the legitimacy, or otherwise, of the practice in question, as was the role of the original circuit judges. Where an issue arises before a court for the first time, it follows, as a matter of course, that there can be no precedent for the court to follow and, given the rapid change in contemporary society, it can only be suggested that such innovations and potentially innovatory court cases are increasingly likely. In such novel circumstances, courts are faced with the choice of either refusing to decide a case, or stating what the law should be. In earlier times, judges did not shirk from this task and, even in modern times, courts are required on occasion to consider situations for the first time. Such cases are described as cases of first impression and inevitably involve judges in the creation of new law.

(b)   *Reform*: the question arises as to how the law is to develop and change to cater for changed circumstances if cases are always to be decided according to precedent.

These considerations raise the question that if the law, as represented in either common law or statute law, is out of line with current social beliefs and practices, then should it not be incumbent upon the judiciary to decide cases in line with the currently prevailing standards, even if this means ignoring previous decisions and interpretations? Not to do so leaves the judges open to the charge of being out of touch with social reality. To overtly change the law, however, opens them up to the alternative charge of acting beyond their powers and of usurping the role and function of the legislature. Opinions on this matter range from those that would deny completely the right of judges to make or change the law, to those that would grant the judges the right to mould the law in line with their conception of justice. Others would recognise the fact that the common law was judge-made and restrict judicial creativity to the development of established common law principles. There is an important corollary to this latter position which links it with those who limit judicial creativity, for the implicit assertion is that judges have no place in reforming statutory provisions. They may signal the ineffectiveness of such provisions and call for their repeal or reform, but it would be a usurpation of the legislature's function and power for the courts to engage in such general reform.

In any case, this question unavoidably raises the issue of the actual extent of judicial creativity (compare and contrast *R v R* (1992) and *DPP v C* (1995) in this light). The previous consideration of distinguishing has demonstrated how the doctrine of *stare decisis* can be avoided by the judiciary. A further way in which judges have a creative impact on the law is in the way in which they adapt and extend precedent in instant cases. In addition, judicial reasoning, which will be considered in detail in Chapter 10, tends to be carried out on the basis of analogy, and judges have a large degree of discretion in selecting what are to be considered as analogous cases. They also have a tendency to extend, continuously, existing precedents to fit new situations, as the evolution of the tort of negligence will show.

It is now probably a commonplace of legal theory that judges do make law. Perhaps the more interesting question is not whether judges make law, but why they deny that they do so. In spite of the protestations of the judiciary, law and judicial decision-making is a political process to the extent that it is deciding which values are to be given priority within society. Through their choice of values, the judiciary sanction or prohibit particular forms of behaviour. Due to their position in the constitution, however, judges have to be circumspect in the way in which, and the extent to which, they use their powers to create law and impose values. To overtly assert or exercise the power would be to challenge the power of the legislature. For an unelected body to challenge a politically supreme parliament would be unwise to say the least. It is for that reason that the courts on occasion take refuge behind the cloak of a naïve declaratory theory of law.

The Practical Importance of Precedent

The foregoing has set out the doctrine of binding precedent as it operates in theory to control and indeed limit the ambit of judicial discretion. It has to be recognised, however, that the doctrine does not operate as stringently as it appears at first sight and that there are particular shortcomings in the system that have to be addressed in weighing up the undoubted advantages with the equally undoubted disadvantages.

Nonetheless, the practical importance of the doctrine of precedent can be seen in the history of three conjoined cases, *Fairchild v Glenhaven Funeral Services Ltd and Others* (2002).

The cases related to claims for compensation for injury – mesothelioma, a terminal lung disease caused by the exposure of workers to asbestos fibre – during the course of their working lives with more than one employer. Both the High Court and the Court of Appeal held that the claimants' cases could not succeed, as they could not prove which exposure to asbestos fibre had actually caused the resultant disease. As they could not prove which employer was at fault, no employer could be held liable.

Only a matter of days before the House of Lords was due to hear the appeal, a consortium of insurance companies, which would have had to provide any recompense in the final analysis, offered to settle the present cases on a voluntary basis and set up a compensation scheme for the hundreds of other claimants who were waiting for the outcome of those cases. The point, however, was that the payments to be made would have been significantly less than would have been awarded if the claimants won their case in the House of Lords. The insurers decided that they would rather not risk an adverse decision in the House of Lords, and actually told the Lords' judicial office that the settlement had been reached, thus removing the need to hear the final appeal. In reality, no such settlement had been reached.

The representative of the claimants stated that the settlement scheme was a 'sordid attempt to manipulate the judicial process, the whole objective [being] to ensure that the Court of Appeal's decision remains intact'. The representative of the insurers stated that it was 'not cynical – it was practical'. Lord Bingham, the senior judge in the House of Lords, stated that the episode had been 'entirely regrettable'.

When the cases subsequently came before the House of Lords, the fears of the insurance companies were proved justified by that court overruling the decision of the Court of Appeal, thus laying the insurers open to significantly more liability than they would have had to meet under their voluntary scheme.

It has to be admitted, however, that this sort of manoeuvring also occurs in relation to trade union and other civil rights cases, where the specialist lawyers who deal with such issues attempt to ensure that potentially ground-breaking issues are argued in relation to relatively stronger cases rather than very weak ones. The practicality is that once a positive precedent, the legal rule, is established in the strong case, it can be extended into a wider area. It would, however, be much more difficult to overturn a contrary precedent handed down in a weak case.

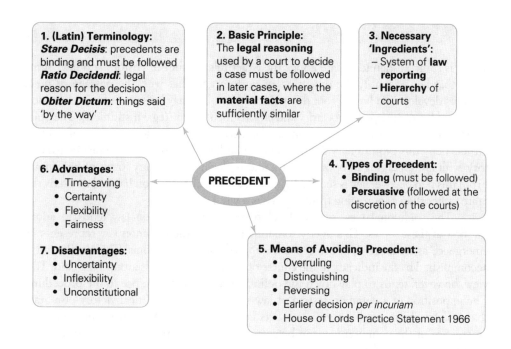

1. (Latin) Terminology:
Stare Decisis: precedents are binding and must be followed
Ratio Decidendi: legal reason for the decision
Obiter Dictum: things said 'by the way'

2. Basic Principle:
The **legal reasoning** used by a court to decide a case must be followed in later cases, where the **material facts** are sufficiently similar

3. Necessary 'Ingredients':
– System of **law reporting**
– **Hierarchy** of courts

6. Advantages:
- Time-saving
- Certainty
- Flexibility
- Fairness

7. Disadvantages:
- Uncertainty
- Inflexibility
- Unconstitutional

PRECEDENT

4. Types of Precedent:
- **Binding** (must be followed)
- **Persuasive** (followed at the discretion of the courts)

5. Means of Avoiding Precedent:
- Overruling
- Distinguishing
- Reversing
- Earlier decision *per incuriam*
- House of Lords Practice Statement 1966

FIGURE 3.1 *Precedent: an aide-mémoire.*

3.7 BOOKS OF AUTHORITY

When a court is unable to locate a precise or analogous precedent, it may refer to legal textbooks for guidance. Such books are subdivided, depending on when they were written. In strict terms, only certain works are actually treated as authoritative sources of law. Among the most important of these works are those by Glanvill from the twelfth century, Bracton from the thirteenth century, Coke from the seventeenth century and Blackstone from the eighteenth century. When cases such as *R v R* are borne in mind, it might be claimed, with justification, that the authority of such ancient texts may be respected more in the breach than in the performance. Given the societal change that has occurred in the intervening time, one can only say that such a refusal to fetishise ancient texts is a positive, and indeed necessary, recognition of the need for law to change in order to keep up with its contemporary sphere of operation. Legal works produced after Blackstone's *Commentaries* of 1765 are considered to be of recent origin, and they cannot be treated as authoritative sources. The courts, however, will look at the most eminent works by accepted experts in particular fields in order to help determine what the law is or should be. See, for example, the citation of Shetreet's *Judges on Trial*, and De Smith, Wolf and Jowell, *Judicial Review of Administrative Action*, in Lord Browne-Wilkinson's decision in *Re Pinochet* (1999), Bennion's *Statutory Interpretation* in *Wilson v Secretary of State for Trade and Industry* (2003), and Bruno Simma's *The Charter of the United Nations, A Commentary* in *HM Treasury v Mohammed Jabar Ahmed* (2010).

3.8   CUSTOM

There is some academic debate about the exact relationship of custom and law. Some claim that law is simply the extension of custom and that with the passage of time, customs develop into laws. From this point of view, law may be seen as the redefinition of custom for the purposes of clarity and enforcement by the legal institutions. The State institutions are seen as merely refining the existing customary behaviour of society. Others deny this evolutionary link and claim that law and custom are in fact contradictory, with law emerging in opposition to, and replacing, customary forms of behaviour. From this perspective, law is seen as being a new form of regulation handed down by the State rather than as emerging from society as a whole.

The traditional view of the development of the common law tends to adopt the first of these views. This overly romantic notion of the common law represents its emergence as no more than the crystallisation of common customs. This distillation is accomplished by the judiciary in the course of their historic travels around the land. This view, however, tends to play down the political process that gave rise to the procedure. The imposition of a common system of law represented the political victory of a State that had fought to establish and assert its central authority. Viewed in that light, the emergence of the common law can be seen actually to support the second of the two approaches suggested above.

Although some of the common law may have had its basis in general custom, a large proportion of these so-called customs were invented by the judges themselves and represented what they wanted the law to be, rather than what people generally thought it was.

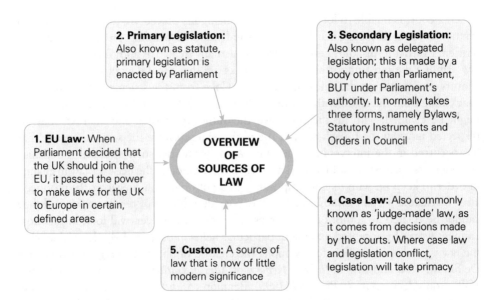

FIGURE 3.2 *Overview of Sources of Law.*

One source of customary practice that undoubtedly did find expression in the form of law was business and commercial practice. These customs and practices originally were constituted in the distinct form of the law merchant, but gradually this became subsumed under the control of the common law courts and ceased to exist apart from the common law.

Notwithstanding the foregoing, it is still possible for specific local customs to operate as a source of law. In certain circumstances, parties may assert the existence of customary practices in order to support their case. Such local customs may run counter to the strict application of the common law and, where they are found to be legitimate, they will effectively replace the common law. Even in this respect, however, reliance on customary law as opposed to common law, although not impossible, is made unlikely by the stringent tests that have to be satisfied. The requirements that a local custom must satisfy in order to be recognised are that:

- it must have existed from 'time immemorial', that is, 1189;
- it must have been exercised continuously within that period;
- it must have been exercised peaceably without opposition;
- it must also have been felt to be obligatory;
- it must be capable of precise definition;
- it must have been consistent with other customs;
- it must be reasonable.

Given this list of requirements, it can be seen why local custom is not an important source of law. However, the courts will have recourse to custom where they see it as appropriate, as may be seen in *Egerton v Harding* (1974), in which the courts upheld a customary duty to fence land against cattle straying from an area of common land.

3.9 LAW REFORM

At one level law reform is either a product of parliamentary or judicial activity, as has been considered previously. Parliament tends, however, to be concerned with particularities of law reform, and the judiciary are constitutionally and practically disbarred from reforming the law in anything other than an opportunistic and piecemeal way. Therefore, there remains a need for the question of law reform to be considered generally and a requirement that such consideration be conducted in an informed but disinterested manner.

Reference has already been made to the use of consultative Green Papers by the government as a mechanism for gauging the opinions of interested parties to particular reforms. More formal advice may be provided through various advisory standing committees. Amongst these is the *Law Reform Committee*. The function of this Committee is to consider the desirability of changes to the civil law which the Lord Chancellor may refer to it. The *Criminal Law Revision Committee* performs similar functions in relation to criminal law.

Royal Commissions may be constituted to consider the need for law reform in specific areas. The Commission on Criminal Procedure (1980) led to the enactment of the Police and Criminal Evidence Act 1984, and the recommendation of the 1993 Royal Commission on Criminal Justice (Runciman Commission) informed subsequent reform of the criminal law system.

Committees may be set up in order to review the operation of particular areas of law, the most significant of these being the Woolf review of the operation of the civil justice system. Similarly, Sir Robin Auld conducted a review of the whole criminal justice system and Sir Andrew Leggatt reviewed the tribunal system. Detailed analysis of the consequences flowing from the implementation of the recommendations of these reviews will be considered subsequently.

If a criticism is to be levelled at these Committees and Commissions, it is that they are all *ad hoc* bodies. Their remit is limited and they do not have the power either to widen the ambit of their investigation or to initiate reform proposals.

The *Law Commission* fulfils the need for some institution to concern itself more generally with the question of law reform. It was established under the Law Commissions Act 1965 and its general function is to keep the law as a whole under review and to make recommendations for its systematic reform to ensure that the law is as fair, modern, simple and cost-effective as possible.

As part of its goal to make the law as simple as possible, the Commission has adopted three interrelated approaches: codification, consolidation and revision.

Codification

The Commission looks toward the codification of the law. Codification has already been mentioned in respect of Civil Law in Chapter 1 and the Commission has expressed its view that the law would be more accessible to the citizen, and easier for the courts to understand, if the English system also adopted a series of statutory codes. The Commission has had a long-established aim of working towards a codification of criminal law; however, the tenth programme of law reform signals a change in approach, reflecting a more realistic recognition of the difficulties involved in such a project and the need to reform the law before it can be successfully codified.

As the Commission stated in its 10th programme:

> The complexity of the common law in 2007 is no less than it was in 1965. Further, the increased pace of legislation, layers of legislation on a topic being placed one on another with bewildering speed, and the influence of European legislation, continue to make codification ever more difficult. The Commission continues to believe that codification is desirable, but considers that it needs to redefine its approach to make codification more achievable.
>
> Accordingly the Commission has decided that:
>
> (1)   It will continue to use the definition of codification used by Gerald Gardiner in *Law Reform Now*, that is, 'reducing to one statute, or a

small collection of statutes, the whole of the law on any particular subject'.

(2)   Consistently with Gardiner's concerns in 1964, the Commission's main priority is first to reform an area of the law sufficiently to enable it to return and codify the law at a subsequent stage. If it can codify at the same time as reforming, it will do so.

The first direct effect of these decisions is that the Commission has removed from this programme, mention of a codification project in relation to criminal law. The duty in reforming the criminal law, as elsewhere, is to identify reform projects that will make the law accessible, remove uncertainties and bring it up to date with the aim that in the future we will return and codify the area if we cannot do so as part of the project. Rather than specifically referring to codification as the intended outcome, we have introduced a new item which seeks to undertake projects to simplify the criminal law. We see this work as the necessary precursor to any attempts to codify the criminal law.

Consolidation

This process brings together all existing statutory provisions, previously located in several different pieces of legislation, under one Act. As explained in Chapter 3 above, under this procedure the law itself remains unchanged, but those who use it are able to find it all in one place. An example, cited by the Commission, is the Powers of Criminal Courts (Sentencing) Act 2000, which brought together in a single piece of legislation sentencing powers which were previously to be found in more than a dozen Acts.

Statute Law Revision

The Commission continuously keeps under review the need to remove antiquated and/ or anachronistic laws from the statute book, the continued existence of which make it subject to derision, even if they do not bring it into disrepute. As the Commission states, the purpose of its statute law repeals work is to modernise and simplify the statute book, reduce its size and save the time of lawyers and others who use it. Implementation of the repeal proposals is by means of special Statute Law (Repeals) Acts and 18 such Acts have been introduced since 1965, repealing more than 2,000 Acts either completely or partially.

It was as a result of this process, and following a 1995 Law Commission Report (No 230), that the Law Reform (Year and a Day Rule) Act was introduced in 1996. This Act removed the ancient rule which prevented killers being convicted of murder or manslaughter if their victim survived for a year and a day after the original offence. The Statute Law (Repeals) Act 2004 removed a Victorian Act which empowered the Metropolitan Police to license shoeblacks and commissionaires and, in so doing, removed the offence of fraudulently impersonating a shoeblack or commissionaire. The eighteenth and most recent Statute Law (Repeals) Act of 2008 repealed 260 whole Acts and part-repealed 68 others. Amongst the obsolete laws removed were Acts relating to local prisons, London workhouses and turnpike roads, together with 12 Acts relating to the former East India Company. An 1839 law, requiring street musicians to leave an area if required to do so by irritated householders, was also removed. A nineteenth report, recommending the repeal of more than 800 statutes and the partial repeal of 50 others, was issued in May 2012 and subsequently enacted in 2013.

The Commission is a purely advisory body and its scope is limited to those areas set out in its current programme of law reform, which has to be approved by the Lord Chancellor. It recommends reform after it has undertaken an extensive process of consultation with informed and/or interested parties. At the conclusion of a project a report is submitted to the Lord Chancellor and Parliament for their consideration and action.

Although the scope of the Commission is limited to those areas set out in its programme of law reform, its ambit is not unduly restricted, as may be seen from the range of matters covered in its eleventh programme set out in July 2011.

Among the areas to be covered in the new programme are:

- charity law, examining a range of issues concerning the constitution and regulation of charities and their activities;

- conservation covenants, investigating the case for a new statutory interest in land that would enable a conservation obligation to be enforceable against a landowner by someone who is not a neighbour;

- contempt, reviewing the law on contempt to take into account use of the internet and other technologies and to ensure courts have the powers they need to deal with contempt in the face of the court;

- data sharing between public bodies, clarifying the existence and nature of legal obstacles to data sharing;

- electoral law, rationalising the complicated framework of rules governing electoral processes and taking account of advances in technology;

- electronic communications code, considering whether the Code can be made more transparent, user-friendly and efficient in resolving disputes;

- European contract law, assessing the impact of the EC-generated optional instrument that sets out which laws apply to contracts made between businesses (and between businesses and consumers) from different Member States;

- family financial orders, considering how court orders for financial provision following divorce or the end of a civil partnership and orders concerning financial arrangements for children are enforced;

- misconduct in a public office, simplifying and clarifying this common law offence, and ensuring the law takes into account the fact that functions traditionally considered to be public in nature are now often discharged by private individuals and volunteers;

- offences against the person, restructuring the law, probably by creating a new hierarchy of offences, and modernising and simplifying the language used to define offences against the person;

- rights to light, assessing whether this area of law correctly balances a right to receive light against the right of neighbours affected by it to develop their land; including examining the relationship with planning law and the range of remedies available where a right is interfered with;

- taxis and private hire vehicles, reviewing and simplifying the existing complex and separate regulatory systems, removing geographical inconsistencies and modernising to reflect advances in technology;

- trademark and design litigation, unjustified threats, considering whether to repeal, reform or extend four provisions that impose liability to pay damages on the makers of an unjustified threat of intellectual property litigation;

- wildlife, modernising the law on wildlife management, simplifying it and making it easier to understand.

The Eleventh Programme of Law Reform is available on the Commission's website at: http://www.justice.gov.uk/lawcommission/docs/lc330_eleventh_programme.pdf

In addition to these programme projects, ministers may refer matters of particular importance to the Commission for its consideration. As was noted in Chapter 1, it was just such a referral by the Home Secretary, after the Macpherson Inquiry into the *Stephen Lawrence* case, that gave rise to the Law Commission's recommendation that the rule against double jeopardy be removed in particular circumstances. An extended version of that recommendation was included in the Criminal Justice Act 2003.

Annual reports list all Commission publications. The Law Commission claims that, in the period since its establishment in 1965, over 100 of its law reports have been implemented. Examples of legislation following from Law Commission reports are: the Contracts (Rights of Third Parties) Act 1999, based on the recommendations of the Commission's Report No 180, *Privity of Contract;* and the Trustee Act 2000, based on the Commission's Report No 260. In February 2002 the Land Registration Act was passed, which has had a major impact on the land registration procedure. The Act implemented the draft Bill which was the outcome of the Commission's largest single project.

Current judicial review procedures are very much the consequence of a 1976 Law Commission report, and a review of their operation and proposals for reform was issued in October 1994.

In the area of criminal law, the preparatory work done by the Commission on several aspects of the criminal justice system (bail, double jeopardy and the revelation of an accused person's bad character) was incorporated into the Criminal Justice Act 2003.

In addition, ss 5 and 6 of the Domestic Violence, Crime and Victims Act 2004 reflect the recommendations of an earlier Commission report. The issue investigated related to situations where a child is non-accidentally killed or seriously injured, and it is apparent that one or more of a limited number of defendants must have committed the crime, but there is no evidence that allows the court to identify which of the defendants actually committed the offence. The Domestic Violence, Crime and Victims Act 2004 also contains provisions reflecting the Commission report relating to the prosecution of people charged with multiple offences.

In August 2004 the Commission published its Report on Partial Defences to Murder, recommending the reform of the defence of provocation, with particular reference to murders committed in the context of domestic violence. That report also included a recommendation that the Home Office undertake a wholesale review of the law of murder, including sentencing regimes, and subsequently in December 2005 the Commission published its proposals for reforming the law of murder, *Bringing the Law of Murder into the 21st Century*. Its initial conclusion was that the current law on murder 'is a mess' and in an attempt to remedy that situation it provisionally recommended that there should be three tiers of homicide:

- In the top tier would be cases where there is an intention to kill. This is the worst category and would retain the mandatory life sentence.

- In the second tier would be cases of killing through reckless indifference to causing death and intention to do serious harm but not to kill. This tier would also include revised versions of provocation, diminished responsibility and duress. The sentence would depend on the details of the case.

- In the third tier (manslaughter) would be cases of killing by gross negligence or intention to cause harm but not serious harm.

In November 2006 the Law Commission published its final report setting out recommendations for reform of the law of homicide proposing the adoption of the three-tier structure, comprising first-degree murder, second-degree murder and manslaughter. Although the recommendations on partial defences were implemented to a substantial extent in the Coroners and Justice Act 2009, in January 2011 the new government let it be known that it would not implement the remainder of the recommendations on the grounds that the time was not right to take forward such a substantial reform of the criminal law.

The Commission's recommendations in relation to the offence of corporate killing were incorporated in the Corporate Manslaughter and Corporate Homicide Act 2007, and its recommendations on inchoate liability for assisting and encouraging crime were enacted in the Serious Crime Act 2007. Finally the Commission's report and draft Bill on bribery led to the passing of the Bribery Act 2010, which came into force in July 2011.

Having emphasised the role of the Law Commission as a source of new law, it remains a fact that at the end of 2007, 31 of its reports recommending reform remained to be implemented, even though a number of them had been accepted by the government. In response to this failure of implementation the former Law Lord, Lord Lloyd of Berwick, introduced the Law Commission Bill 2008–09 in the House of Lords. In support of the Bill Lord Kingsland pointed out that: 'Over the years . . . [the Law Commission] has been tasked with many seemingly intractable problems, has grappled with them and produced a solution, only to find that solution spurned by the political classes.'

The resultant Act contains provisions to amend the Law Commission Act 1965 so as to:

- require the Lord Chancellor to prepare an annual report, to be laid before parliament, on the implementation of Law Commission proposals;
- require the Lord Chancellor to set out plans for dealing with any Law Commission proposals which have not been implemented and provide the reasoning behind decisions not to implement proposals;
- allow the Lord Chancellor and Law Commission to agree a protocol about the Law Commission's work. The protocol would be designed to provide a framework for the relationship between the UK government and the Law Commission, and the Lord Chancellor would have to lay the protocol before parliament.

The second report on the implementation of Law Commission proposals was issued in March 2012 and revealed that 18 reports remained to be implemented.

Mention should also be made of the relatively new Civil Justice Council (CJC), established under the Civil Procedure Act 1997. The remit of this Council, which is made up of a variety of judges, lawyers, academics and those representing the interests of consumers and others, under the chair of the Master of the Rolls, currently Lord Dyson, is to:

- keep the civil justice system under review;
- consider how to make the civil justice system more accessible, fair and efficient;
- advise the Lord Chancellor and the judiciary on the development of the civil justice system;
- refer proposals for change to the civil justice system to the Lord Chancellor and the Civil Procedure Rule Committee;
- make proposals for research.

Given the massive upheaval that has resulted from the implementation of Lord Woolf's review of the civil justice system, it is to be hoped that the CJC will function effectively to bring about smaller alterations in the system as soon as they become necessary.

Access to Justice for Litigants in Person (or self-represented litigants)

In November 2011 the Civil Justice Council released a critical report entitled: *Access to Justice for Litigants in Person (or self-represented litigants)*. The report followed an examination of how litigants in person are likely to be affected by reductions to public funding for legal advice and representation, and ways in which public and voluntary bodies could best respond to the challenges arising as a result of this cutback in funding. The working party found that the numbers of litigants representing themselves will increase, giving rise to the fear that:

Many of them will not know how to bring or defend legal proceedings in the absence of legal advice and representation and will either suffer a reduction in the quality of justice or they will entirely abandon their efforts to enforce or defend their rights or will try to take their cases to court but not do so properly.

The CJC report makes ten recommendations for immediate action:

1. Improving the accessibility, currency and content of existing online resources;
2. Producing a 'nutshell' guide for self-represented litigants (SRPs);
3. Improving judicial and court services for SRPs;
4. Advice for judges on the availability of legal pro bono services;
5. Guidance for court staff when dealing with SRPs;
6. Guidance for legal professionals, and what SRPs can expect from lawyers;
7. Notice of McKenzie Friends; these are people who volunteer to assist unrepresented parties;
8. Introducing a code of conduct for McKenzie Friends;
9. Freeing up in-house lawyers to provide pro bono services; and
10. A call for leadership from major advice and pro bono agencies across England and Wales to drive collaboration.

The report went on to make recommendations to be addressed in the medium term:

(a) A systematic review should be undertaken of court leaflets, forms and information, involving consultation with experts in the field;
(b) Making a primary website available that pulls together and maintains the best independent guidance;
(c) Increasing the number of courts that offer Personal Support Units and information officers to assist SRPs;
(d) Producing a user-friendly guide to the Small Claims Court;
(e) Improving access to legal advice;
(f) Developing Law works early electronic advice for SRPs and agencies;
(g) Finding new means of funding the administration of pro bono and other voluntary legal services;
(h) Offering surgeries and after-hours court information sessions for SRPs;
(i) Keeping records of numbers and circumstances of SRPs, and ensuring court user committees address their needs; and
(j) Reviewing the question of access to appeals after refusals by a judge on the 'paper' application.

The EC is increasingly a source of law for the UK.

LEGISLATION

Legislation is law produced through the parliamentary system. The government is responsible for most Acts, but individual Members of Parliament do have a chance to sponsor Private Members' Bills. The passage of a Bill through each House of Parliament involves five distinct stages: first reading; second reading; committee stage; report stage; and third reading. It is then given Royal Assent. The Supreme Court only has limited scope to delay legislation.

Among the problems of drafting Acts is the need to reconcile such contradictory demands as brevity and precision. Legislation can be split into different categories: public Acts affect the general public; private Acts relate to particular individuals; consolidation Acts bring various provisions together; codification Acts give statutory form to common law principles; amending Acts alter existing laws and amendments may be textual, which alters the actual wording of a statute, or non-textual, in which case the operation rather than the wording of the existing law is changed.

DELEGATED LEGISLATION

Delegated legislation appears in the form of: Orders in Council; statutory instruments; bylaws; and professional regulations.

The main advantages of delegated legislation relate to: speed of implementation; the saving of parliamentary time; access to expertise; and flexibility.

The main disadvantages relate to: the lack of accountability of those making such law; the lack of scrutiny of proposals for such legislation; and the sheer amount of delegated legislation.

Controls over delegated legislation are: in parliament, the Joint Select Committee on Statutory Instruments; and, in the courts, *ultra vires* provisions may be challenged through judicial review.

CASE LAW

Case law is that law created by judges in the course of deciding cases. The doctrine of *stare decisis* or binding precedent refers to the fact that courts are bound by previous decisions of courts equal to or above them in the court hierarchy. The Supreme Court can now overrule its own previous rules; the Court of Appeal cannot.

It is the reason for a decision, the *ratio decidendi*, that binds. Everything else is *obiter* and not bound to be followed.

Judges avoid precedents through either overruling or distinguishing them.

The advantages of the doctrine relate to: saving the time of all parties concerned; certainty; flexibility; and the meeting of the requirements of formal justice.

The disadvantages relate to: uncertainty; fixity; and unconstitutionality.

CUSTOM

Custom is of arguable historic importance as a source of law and is of very limited importance as a contemporary source.

LAW REFORM

Law reform in particular areas is considered by various standing committees particularly established for that purpose and Royal Commissions may also be established for such purposes. The Law Commission, however, exists to consider the need for the general and systematic reform of the law.

FOOD FOR THOUGHT

1.   In relation to the concept of the separation of powers mentioned in Chapter 2, consider the extent to which Parliament as a whole decides on law. The ideal is of the legislature, the actual Members of Parliament, debating issues in order to produce the best possible legislation. However, is that really the case? Consider where most legislation comes from, who proposes it and who ensures that it is enacted. It has been suggested that the executive controls parliament through its control of party politics. On that basis, the issue to consider is the extent to which the parliamentary process is just a rubber-stamping exercise for party political programmes.

2.   Consider the current structure of the Houses of Parliament, an issue of some contemporary and long-standing debate. In particular, consider the function and membership of the House of Lords. What additional function does it perform over that of the House of Commons and how should its membership be decided?

3.   Generally, law applies to everyone and ignorance of the law is no excuse for breaking it. Yet, to most new law students, let alone ordinary members of the public, certain pieces of legislation are almost totally incomprehensible. This raises certain issues for consideration as follows:

Why can legislation not be written in ordinary language?

Who is legislation actually written for?

Why do judges have to interpret legislation?

To what extent is interpretation creation?

4.   There is a huge amount of law generated every year and lots of it comes in the form of delegated legislation. To what extent is this just a fact of contemporary political life, or is it a matter of concern?

5.   The common law is the law made by judges, but under the separation of powers judges are not supposed to make law. Judges are bound by precedent but can develop the law. How can both of these, apparently contradictory, sentences be reconciled?

6. The *ratio decidendi* in any case represents the binding precedent that has to be followed in later cases. However, who actually states the ratio?

FURTHER READING

Boulton, C (ed), *Erskine May's Treatise on the Law, Privileges, Proceedings and Usage of Parliament*, 1989, London: Butterworths

Cross, R, *Cross, Harris and Hart, Precedent in English Law*, 4th edn, 1991, Oxford: Clarendon

Elliot, M and Perreau-Saussine, A, 'Pyrrhic public law: Bancoult and the sources, status and content of common law limitations on prerogative power' [2009] PL 697–722

Goodhart, A, 'The *ratio decidendi* of a case' (1959) 22 MLR 117

Holdsworth, W, 'Case law' (1934) 50 LQR 180

Jenkins, C, 'Helping the reader of Bills and Acts' (1999) 149 NLJ 798

MacCormick, N, *Legal Rules and Legal Reasoning*, 1978, Oxford: Clarendon

Masterman, R, 'Interpretations, declarations and dialogue: rights protection under the Human Rights Act and Victorian Charter of Human Rights and Responsibilities' [2009] PL 112–31

Mora, PD, 'The compatibility with art. 10 ECHR of the continued publication of a libel on the Internet: *Times Newspapers Ltd (Nos 1 and 2) v The United Kingdom*' (2009) 20(6) Ent LR 226–8

Simpson, A, 'The *ratio decidendi* of a case' (1957) 20 MLR 413;(1958) 21 MLR 155

The following are also relevant to the issues in Chapter 3:

Bates, T, 'The contemporary use of legislative history in the United Kingdom' (1995) 54(1) CLJ 127

Bell, J and Engle, G (Sir), *Cross: Statutory Interpretation*, 3rd edn, 1995, London: Butterworths

Bennion, F, 'Statute law: obscurity and drafting parameters' (1978) 5 British JLS 235

Bennion, F, *Statutory Interpretation*, 2nd edn, 1992, London: Butterworths

Committee on the Preparation of Legislation, *Renton Committee Report*, Cmnd 6053, 1975, London: HMSO

Editorial, 'Disability discrimination: tribunal interprets DDA to cover discrimination by association' (2008) 869 IDS Emp L Brief 3–5

Eskridge, W, *Dynamic Statutory Interpretation*, 1994, Cambridge, MA: Harvard UP

Friedman, L, 'On interpretation of laws' (1988) 11(3) Ratio Juris 252

Manchester, C, *Exploring the Law: The Dynamics of Precedent and Statutory Interpretation*, 2006, London: Sweet & Maxwell

Stone, J, 'The Ratio of the Ratio Decidendi' (1959) 22 MLR 597

Watson-Brown, A, 'In Search of Plain English – The Holy Grail or Mythical Excalibar of Legislative Drafting (2011) 33(1) Statute Law Review

USEFUL WEBSITES

www.uk-legislation.hmso.gov.uk/acts.htm

An extensive collection of Acts of Parliament.

www.lawcom.gov.uk

The Law Commission's website is a valuable resource because it carries scores of reports that provide very useful critical digests of whole areas of law.

www.legislation.gov.uk

The UK Statute Law database.

www.lawcom.gov.uk

The official website of the Law Commission.

www.parliament.uk

The official website of Parliament.

www.hmcourts-service.gov.uk

The official website of Her Majesty's Courts Service.

www.supremecourt.gov.uk

The official website of the Supreme Court.

COMPANION WEBSITE

Now visit the companion website to:

- test your understanding of the key terms using our Flashcard Glossary;
- revise and consolidate your knowledge of 'Sources of law' using our Multiple Choice Question testbank;
- view all of the links to the Useful Websites above;
- read further about using cases and legislation in the Legal Skills Guide;
- view a sample exam question and answer on sources of law, taken from the authors' latest Questions & Answers book on The English Legal System.

www.routledge.com/cw/slapper

THE CIVIL COURTS

4

The first part of this chapter looks at the civil court structure and at which type of cases are heard in which trial courts, the rules relating to transfer of cases from one level of court to another, the system of appeals and the criticisms that have been made of the various aspects of these systems.

What is the difference between a criminal and civil case? There are several key distinctions.

Criminal cases are brought by the State against individual or corporate defendants, whereas civil cases are brought by one citizen or body against another such party. The State here involves the police (or possibly Customs and Excise officers or tax inspectors), who investigate the crime and collect the evidence, and the Crown Prosecution Service, which prepares the Crown's case. In civil cases, the State is not involved (although it may be a party to the case, such as in a judicial review claim), except insofar as it provides the courts and personnel so that the litigation can be judged. If a party refuses, for example, to be bound by the order a court makes in a civil case, then that party may be found in contempt of court and punished, that is, imprisoned or fined.

The outcomes of civil and criminal cases are different. If a criminal case is successful from the point of view of the person bringing it (*the prosecutor*) because the magistrate or jury finds *the defendant* (sometimes called *the accused*) guilty as charged, then the result will be a sentence. There is a wide range of sentences available, from absolute or conditional discharges (where the convicted defendant is free to go without any conditions or with some requirement, for example, that the defendant undertakes never to visit a particular place) to life imprisonment. Criminal sentences, or 'sanctions', are imposed to mark the State's disapproval of the defendant's crime. There is often a considerable cost in imposing a punishment. The prison population was 86,048 in June 2012. The male prison population increased by 1 per cent to 81,925 and the female prison population fell by 1 per cent to 4,123 in the period 30 June 2011 to 30 June 2012 (*Offender Management Statistics Quarterly Bulletin*, Ministry of Justice, 24 July 2012). At an average cost of £102 per prisoner per day (*Hansard*, 27 March 2012, col 1070W), the average cost to the state is £37,000 per prisoner per year. By contrast, fines (the most common sentence or 'disposal') can often bring revenue to the State. In any event, the victim of a crime never gains from the sanction imposed on the criminal. A criminal court can order a convicted person to pay the victim compensation, but this will be in addition to and separate from the sentence for the crime.

If a civil case is successful from the point of view of the person bringing the claim (the *claimant*), the outcome will be one of a number of civil remedies which are designed to benefit the *claimant* and in which the State, or wider community, has no direct interest. Civil remedies include damages, court orders like injunctions, orders of prohibition and specific performance. So, in civil proceedings, the *claimant* will sue the *defendant* and a successful claim will result in *judgment for* the *claimant*. In matrimonial cases, the party who brings an action is called the *petitioner* and the other party is known as the *respondent*.

Civil and criminal cases are processed differently by the English legal system. They use different procedures and vocabulary, and they are dealt with, on the whole, by different courts. It is very important not to confuse the vocabularies of the different systems and speak, for example, about a claimant 'prosecuting' a company for breach of contract. The law of contract is civil law, so the defendant would be 'sued' or 'litigated against' or have 'a claim taken against' him, her or it.

The following question then arises: 'What is the difference between a crime and a civil wrong; how am I to tell into which category a particular wrong falls?' The answer will be found simply by building up a general legal knowledge. There is nothing inherent in any particular conduct that makes it criminal. One cannot say, for example, that serious wrongs are crimes and that lesser transgressions will be civil wrongs: some crimes are comparatively trivial, like some parking offences, while some civil wrongs can have enormously harmful consequences, as where a company in breach of a contract causes financial harm to hundreds or thousands of people.

Sometimes a single event can be both a crime and a civil wrong. If you drive at 50 mph in a 30 mph zone and crash into another vehicle, killing a passenger, you may be prosecuted by the State for causing death by dangerous driving and, if convicted, imprisoned or fined. Additionally, you may be sued for negligence (a tortious civil wrong) by a dependant of the killed passenger and the driver.

4.2 HER MAJESTY'S COURTS AND TRIBUNALS SERVICE

The Courts Act 2003 provided for a new unified courts administration to be created, by combining the functions of the court service and the magistrates' courts committees. The new organisation, Her Majesty's Courts Service (HMCS), was established in April 2005. The aim of the agency was to deliver improved services to the community, taxpayer, victims, witnesses and all other users of the courts and to develop best practice with the most effective use of resources.

The proposal to set up a new system of courts administration in England and Wales derived from Sir Robin Auld's review of the criminal courts published in October 2001 (*A Review of the Criminal Courts of England and Wales*, The Right Honourable Lord Justice Auld, 2001). He recommended that a 'single centrally funded executive agency, as part of the former Lord Chancellor's Department (now the Ministry of Justice) should be responsible for the administration of all courts, civil, criminal and family (save for what was then the House of Lords), replacing the court service and magistrates' courts committees'.

The government accepted Sir Robin's proposals for a unified system of courts administration in the White Paper 'Justice for All', published in July 2002. The Courts Act 2003 was passed to implement the changes and Her Majesty's Courts Service was later launched in 2005.

On 1 April 2011 Her Majesty's Courts Service and the Tribunals Service were amalgamated into one integrated agency, Her Majesty's Courts and Tribunals Service (HMCTS), providing support for the administration of justice in courts (up to and including the Court of Appeal) and most tribunals. HMCTS remains a separate agency of the Justice Ministry.

The courts are not in a good economic state. In 2008 the then Lord Chief Justice announced that the maintenance backlog in the courts had risen from £38m in 2000 to £200m, stating that it would remain at this level for three years. More recently the Lord Chief Justice has observed that the courts remain under 'enormous pressure' (The Lord Chief Justice's Report 2010–2012). The current economic situation poses significant challenges to the justice system; the Coalition Government intends to cut £350 million from the legal aid budget alone and, following a consultation in 2010, 129 courts have been closed (The Lord Chief Justice's Report 2010–2012).

Grave concerns about the civil court system have been raised by District Judge David Oldham, president of the Association of Her Majesty's District Judges (Woolf reforms and cost-cutting have led to acute shortages and a 'deficient' system, F Gibb, *The Times*, 16 April 2009). He argues that the civil courts are woefully under-resourced – a problem ever more acute in times of hardship. He has stated:

> My mission is to persuade the Government to return to funding our civil courts to a realistic level and as the recession brings more and more individuals to the county courts, to ensure that all who need it have access to free and efficient expert advice and assistance from a duty solicitor or advice agency independent of the Courts Service.

Judge Oldham notes that the civil court system receives a smaller slice of public funds than criminal or family courts, and fees charged to court users have risen to 'draconian levels' under the policy of making civil courts pay for themselves.

One result, according to the judge, has been a fall in care applications (for vulnerable children) by local authorities. They were given extra funds for such cases but it was not ring-fenced. The range of the increase, he argues, from £150 to £4,000, was something the local authorities just could not cope with. Concerns remain that local authorities may not bring care proceedings and because cost is a factor, Judge Oldham argues, the authorities 'will look at alternative ways of dealing with a child. That is potentially putting that child at risk'. On top of this, civil legal aid has, he says, 'virtually disappeared', and the number of people acting for themselves has soared – such as in family disputes over the residence of a child or contact. 'Where emotions run high, it is very difficult for people to deal with these cases themselves' (*The Times*, 16 April 2009). The Commission of Inquiry into Legal Aid has estimated that the legal aid cuts to the civil system are a false economy; according to figures supplied to the Inquiry by Citizens Advice, for every £1.00 of legal aid spent on benefits advice, the State saves up to £8.80, and for every £1.00 of legal aid spent on employment advice, the State saves up to £7.13 (see http://www. guardian.co.uk/law/2011/jun/14/legal-aid-cuts-false-economy).

Judge Oldham also observed that the recession has resulted in a steep rise in bankruptcy proceedings by local authorities over council tax arrears: 'there's not much we can do by the time it gets to us after several opportunities to pay and the councils have an obligation to their ratepayers'; plus a rise in housing repossession claims. The electronic system for such claims by mortgage companies allows only a five-minute hearing, which, Oldham says, is often inadequate. About half those in arrears are unrepresented: legal aid is limited and few solicitors have a franchise to do the work.

Professor Dame Hazel Genn argued in her 2009 Hamlyn Lectures that the main thrust of civil justice reform in the last decade was not primarily about greater access, nor about greater justice, 'It is simply about diversion of disputants away from the courts' (F Gibb, *The Times*, 23 June 2009). She argued that:

> In England, we are witnessing the decline of civil justice, the degradation of court facilities and the diversion of civil cases to private dispute resolution – accompanied by an anti-court, anti-adjudication rhetoric that interprets these developments as socially positive.

She argued that a principal threat to civil justice was the 'unstoppable burgeoning of criminal justice' including the demands of human rights laws and costs of a growing prison population. The battle for resources was heightened at a time of economically imposed financial restraint. With a unified budget for all parts of the justice system now established under the Ministry of Justice, the importance of civil justice is, Genn has argued, obscured and under-rated. Unlike any other common law system the civil courts in England are self-financing, paid for by litigants. However, Genn noted, any surplus generated from litigants' fees is not invested in the civil courts: instead it is 'redirected into the gaping maw of criminal justice'. Lady Hale, Justice of the Supreme Court, has contributed to this debate. In a speech in 2011 she observed that the Coalition Government's plans for cutting legal aid would 'of course have a disproportionate effect on the poorest and most vulnerable in society. Indeed the government's own equality impact statement accepts that they will have a disproportionate impact on women, ethnic minorities and people with disabilities' ('Equal Access to Justice in the Big Society', speech by Lady Hale to The Law Society, 27 June 2011).

4.3 MAGISTRATES' COURTS

Magistrates' courts have a significant civil jurisdiction. They hear family proceedings under the Domestic Proceedings and Magistrates' Courts Act (DPMCA) 1978 and the

Children Act (CA) 1989. Here, the court is termed a 'family proceedings court' or 'FPC'. A family proceedings court must normally be composed of not more than three justices, including, as far as is practicable, both a man and a woman. Justices who sit on such benches must be members of the 'family panel', which comprises people specially appointed to deal with family matters. The magistrates' court deals with adoption proceedings, applications for residence and contact orders (the CA 1989), and maintenance relating to spouses and children. Under the DPMCA 1978, these courts also have the power to make personal protection orders and exclusion orders in cases of domestic violence. They have powers of recovery in relation to council tax and charges for water, gas and electricity.

4.4 COUNTY COURTS

The county courts were introduced in 1846 to provide local, accessible fora for the adjudication of relatively small-scale litigation. There are 173 county courts. These courts are served by circuit judges and district judges, the latter appointed by the Lord Chancellor from persons who have a seven-year qualification (s 71 of the CLSA 1990).

The Civil Procedure Rules (CPR), which we examine in Chapter 5, operate the same process irrespective of whether the case forum is the High Court or the county court. Broadly speaking, county courts will hear small claims and fast-track cases, while the more challenging multi-track cases will be heard in the High Court.

Over the past 10 years, the numbers of cases being resolved by the county court has increased as the financial limit of cases within its jurisdiction has increased. Also during this period, the profile of county court work has changed. The numbers both of full trials and of small claims arbitrations have fallen sharply since the 1990s. In 1994, there were 24,219 trials and 87,885 small claims arbitrations. In 2011, there were 15,941 trials and 36,719 small claims arbitrations. The small claims limit is £5,000, except for personal injury claims, which carry a £1,000 limit. At the time of writing there is a proposal to raise the small claims limit to £10,000.

A *Practice Direction* ([1991] 3 All ER 722) states that certain types of actions set down for trial in the High Court are considered too important for transfer to a county court. These are cases involving:

- professional negligence;
- fatal accidents;
- allegations of fraud or undue influence;
- defamation;
- malicious prosecution or false imprisonment;
- claims against the police.

The civil courts are under great pressure from the cutbacks being made as part of governmental budget strategy. Governmental plans announced in 2010 will see the

Ministry of Justice's budget cut from £9 billion to £7 billion, with £450 million coming out of administrative areas alone. The staffing of the law courts is already, by common judicial consent, quite inadequate but 14,250 of these frantically demanding jobs will be cut, along with a possible 15,000 at the Ministry of Justice itself, leaving the residual workforce to toil in a hopeless Sisyphean challenge.

In 2007, Judge Paul Collins, London's most senior county court judge, said that low pay and high turnover among staff meant that serious errors were commonplace and routinely led to incorrect judgments in court. He said that with further cuts looming 'we run the risk of bringing about a real collapse in the service we're able to give to the people using the courts'.

The 2012 Judicial and Court Statistics give the following profile of court activity for 2011 (Judicial and Court Statistics, Ministry of Justice, June 2012):

Key findings

Appeals

- There were 77 appeals presented to the UK Supreme Court during 2011, while 81 appeals were determined.

- During 2011 a total of 7,475 applications for leave to appeal were received, of which 1,535 were against conviction in the Crown Court and 5,623 against the sentence imposed.

- A total of 2,576 appeals were heard by the Court of Appeal Criminal Division during 2011, of which 503 appeals against conviction and 2,073 appeals against sentence were heard.

- A further 1,269 appeals were filed in the Court of Appeal Civil Division.

- There were 11,200 applications for permission to apply for judicial review received in the Administrative Court of the High Court in 2011, the majority of which, as in previous years, concerned asylum and immigration matters.

- Of the 396 substantive applications for judicial review which were dealt with at the Administrative Court during 2011, 174 (44 per cent) were allowed, 213 (54 per cent) were dismissed and the remaining 2 per cent were withdrawn.

County Court

- Some 1,553,983 civil (non-family) cases started in 2011, a fall of 4 per cent compared to 2010, continuing the general downward trend seen since 2006.

- The fall in 2011, compared to 2010, was mainly due to decreases in specified money claims (typically related to debt issues) of 4 per cent, mortgage-related claims of 3 per cent, unspecified money claims (typically related to personal injury) of 6 per cent and insolvency petitions of 25 per cent.

- There were 275,920 defences made in 2011, 5 per cent fewer than in 2010 and the lowest number since 2006.

- Defended cases which are not settled or withdrawn generally result in a hearing or trial. In total there were 15,941 fast- and multi-track trials in 2011, a fall of 9 per cent from 2010. Fast-track and multi-track trials took place an average 56 weeks after the claim was originally made, up from 54 weeks in 2010 and 53 weeks in 2009. These trials lasted between four and a half and five hours on average.

- In 2011, 36,719 small claims hearings were disposed of, a decrease of 14 per cent from 2010. On average, small claims hearings occurred 30 weeks after the claim was originally made, a week less than in 2010, and lasted approximately 1 hour 20 minutes.

- There were 275,938 applications for enforcement in 2011 (of which the majority were for warrants, and the remainder for orders such as for attachment of earnings, which oblige the debtor's employer to deduct a set sum from the debtor's pay and forward it to the court). This was a decrease of 13 per cent compared with 2010 and of 49 per cent compared with 2008. These falls reflect the large falls in claims issued for a specified amount of money and repossession of property and also the large increases in court fees for enforcement applications since 13 July 2009.

- A total of 59,338 repossessions of property were made by county court bailiffs, a rise of 10 per cent on the previous year; 25,487 of the properties were on behalf of mortgage lenders, 8 per cent more than in 2010 but still 29 per cent lower than the 2008 peak.

Regarding remedies, the county court cannot grant the prerogative remedies; that is, they cannot grant search orders (an interim mandatory injunction obtained without notice to prevent the defendant from removing, concealing or destroying evidence in the form of documents or moveable property, formerly known as the Anton Piller order) and neither, generally, can they grant freezing orders (formerly Mareva injunctions) to prevent the defendant from removing his assets out of the jurisdiction of the English courts or dissipating them. For recent authoritative guidance of both of these orders, see *Practice Direction ex p Mareva Injunctions and Anton Piller Orders* (1994).

The main advantage to litigants using the small claims process is the fact that, if sued, they can defend themselves without the fear of incurring huge legal costs, since the costs that the winning party can claim are strictly limited. The average waiting period for trial was 30 weeks (as opposed to 56 weeks for fast- and multi-track cases). Although successful claimants are unable to recover costs of legal representation, the small claims procedure does not exclude litigants from seeking legal advice or engaging such legal representation. If a litigant is unrepresented, the district judge may assist him or her by putting questions to witnesses or to the other party, and by explaining any legal terms or expressions.

A litigant simply needs to complete a claim form, available from any county court, and send it to the court with the issue fee appropriate to the amount claimed (ranging from £80 to £230, depending on the value of the claim). If the case is defended, it will be dealt with at an informal hearing, sitting around a table in the district judge's office. This avoids the need for a trial in open court, which many litigants find daunting.

The working of the small claims system is looked at in greater detail in Chapter 5.

4.5 THE HIGH COURT OF JUSTICE

The High Court was created in 1873 as a part of the Supreme Court of Judicature. The Constitutional Reform Act 2005 established a new Supreme Court of the United Kingdom (which has been operational from 2009) to replace the House of Lords as the highest court of appeal. The new official collective name for the High Court, the Court of Appeal and the Crown Court (previously called 'The Supreme Court of Judicature') is the Senior Courts of England and Wales. The Supreme Court of Judicature of Northern Ireland was renamed the Court of Judicature of Northern Ireland.

The High Court has three administrative divisions: the Court of Chancery, the Queen's Bench Division (QBD) and the Family Division (Divorce and Admiralty and Exchequer and Common Pleas were merged with the QBD in 1880 and 1970). High Court judges sit mainly in the Royal Courts of Justice in the Strand, London, although it is possible for the High Court to sit anywhere in England or Wales. Current directions from the Lord Chancellor mean that the court sits in 27 provincial cities and towns.

The High Court judiciary comprises the Vice Chancellor; the Lord Chief Justice who presides over the QBD; the President, who presides over the Family Division; the Senior Presiding Judge (s 72 of the CLSA 1990); and 108 High Court judges or *'puisne judges'* (pronounced 'pewnee' and meaning 'lesser'). The number of High Court judges is fixed by statute.

To be qualified for appointment as a *puisne* judge, a person must have 10 years' qualification within the meaning of s 71 of the CLSA 1990 – essentially, someone who has had a general right of audience on all matters in that court for at least 10 years. The Constitutional Reform Act 2005 established the Judicial Appointments Commission. This body, with 14 members drawn from the judiciary, the lay magistracy, the legal professions and the public, was launched in 2006. It is responsible for selecting candidates to recommend for judicial appointment to the Secretary of State for Justice (formerly the Secretary of State for Constitutional Affairs). This ensures that while merit will remain the sole criterion for appointment, the appointments system will be placed on a fully modern, open and transparent basis.

4.5.1 THE QUEEN'S BENCH DIVISION

The Queen's Bench Division – the main common law court – takes its name from the original judicial part of the general royal court, which used to sit on a bench in the Palace of Westminster. It is the division with the largest workload and has some criminal jurisdiction and appellate jurisdiction. The main civil work of this court is in contract and tort cases, as well as hearing more specialist cases such as applications for judicial review. The court has 72 judges and the *Judicial and Court Statistics 2012* show total claims and originating proceedings. In 2011, 13,928 claims and originating proceedings were issued, down 16 per cent on 2010 and therefore continuing the downward trend from 2009. In London (at the Royal Courts of Justice), of the 4,726 proceedings issued, 1,178 related to a debt (25 per cent), 969 related to breach of contract (21 per cent), 805 were personal injury actions (17 per cent) and 805 were clinical negligence actions (21 per cent). In London (at the Royal Courts of Justice), the number of judgments given either in default of a response by the defendant or as summary judgments during 2011 totalled 1,280.

The Commercial Court is part of the QBD, being served by up to 15 judges with specialist experience in commercial law and presiding over cases concerning banking and insurance matters. The formal rules of evidence can be abandoned here, with the consent of the parties, to allow testimony and documentation that would normally be inadmissible. This informality can be of considerable benefit to the business keen to settle its dispute as quickly and easily as possible. Proceedings in the Commercial Court are governed by Part 58 of the Civil Procedure Rules. The QBD also includes an Admiralty Court to deal with the, often esoteric, issues of law relating to shipping. Commercial Court judges are sometimes appointed as arbitrators.

The Enterprise Act 2002 provides that the Office of Fair Trading (OFT), which investigates markets where it has reasonable grounds to suspect that competition is being prevented, restricted or distorted, may refer cases to the Competition Commission (CC). Decisions of the OFT and the CC can be reviewed by the Competition Appeal Tribunal.

The Employment Appeal Tribunal is presided over by a High Court judge and either two or four laypersons, and hears appeals from employment tribunals. It is not part of the High Court, but is termed a superior court of record.

It is important to remember that most civil claims are settled out of court; only about 1 per cent of cases where claim forms are issued result in civil trials.

4.5.2   THE QUEEN'S BENCH DIVISIONAL COURT

The nomenclature can be puzzling here. This court, as distinct from the QBD, exercises appellate jurisdiction. Here, two or sometimes three judges sit to hear appeals in the following circumstances:

- appeals on a point of law by way of case stated from magistrates' courts, tribunals and the Crown Court (there were 79 such appeals in 2011, 73 per cent of which were appeals from magistrates' courts);

- by exercising judicial review of the decisions made by governmental and public authorities, inferior courts and tribunals. Leave to apply for judicial review is granted or refused by a single judge. Claims for judicial review can be heard by a single judge (there were 11,200 applications for permission to apply for judicial review in 2011, the majority of which concerned asylum and immigration matters. This was a 6 per cent increase on the number of applications in 2010);

- applications for the writ of *habeas corpus* from persons who claim they are being unlawfully detained (there were 34 such cases in 2010).

4.5.3   THE CHANCERY DIVISION

The Chancery Division is the modern successor to the old Court of Chancery, the Lord Chancellor's court from which equity was developed. It has 18 judges. Its jurisdiction includes matters relating to:

- the sale or partition of land and the raising of charges on land;
- the redemption or foreclosure of mortgages;
- the execution or declaration of trusts;
- the administration of the estates of the dead;
- bankruptcy;
- contentious probate business, for example, the validity and interpretation of wills;
- company law;
- partnerships;
- revenue law.

Like the QBD, the Chancery Division contains specialist courts; these are the Patents Court and the Companies Court. The Chancery Division hears its cases in London or in one of eight designated provincial High Court centres. The work is very specialised and there is a Chancery Bar for barristers who practise in this area. Chancery judges are normally appointed from this Bar. In 2011 there were 35,328 proceedings started in the Chancery Division, an increase of 6 per cent on 2010 following a sharp fall between 2009 and 2010.

4.5.4   THE CHANCERY DIVISIONAL COURT

Comprising one or two Chancery judges, this appellate court hears appeals from the Commissioners of Inland Revenue on income tax cases, and from county courts on certain matters like bankruptcy. It disposed of 52 appeals in 2011, which included 28 being dismissed and five being struck out or withdrawn.

4.5.5   THE FAMILY DIVISION

The Family Division of the High Court was created by the Administration of Justice Act 1970. It deals with:

- all matrimonial matters, both at first instance and on appeal;
- matters relating to minors, proceedings under the CA 1989;
- legitimacy;
- adoption;

- proceedings under the Domestic Violence and Matrimonial Proceedings Act 1976 and s 30 of the Human Fertilisation and Embryology Act 1990.

4.5.6 THE FAMILY DIVISIONAL COURT

The Family Divisional Court, consisting of two High Court judges, hears appeals from decisions of magistrates' courts and county courts in family matters. Commonly these involve appeals against orders made about financial provision under the DPMCA 1978. The court disposed of 121 appeals in 2011, the highest number since 2006.

4.5.7 THE COURT OF PROTECTION

The Court of Protection is a specialist court established by the Mental Capacity Act 2005. It is a supreme court of record with the same rights, privileges and authority as the High Court. The Court of Protection makes decisions, and appoints others (called deputies) to make decisions, on behalf of people who lack mental capacity under the Mental Capacity Act 2005. These decisions relate to incapacitous people's financial affairs, property, health and welfare. The Court sits at the Royal Courts of Justice in London as well as in a number of regional courts, including Newcastle, Bristol, Manchester and Cardiff. The Court is served by five High Court judges, 33 district judges and 40 circuit judges. The Court of Protection has powers to:

- decide whether a person has the capacity to make a particular decision for themselves;
- make declarations, decisions or orders on financial or welfare matters affecting people who lack capacity to make these decisions;
- appoint a deputy to make ongoing decisions for people lacking capacity to make those decisions;
- decide whether a Lasting Power of Attorney (LPA) or Enduring Power of Attorney (EPA) is valid;
- remove deputies or attorneys who fail to carry out their duties; and
- hear cases concerning objections to the registration of an LPA or EPA.

In 2011 there were 23,538 applications made to the Court of Protection.

4.6 APPEALS FROM THE HIGH COURT

Appeals from decisions made by a judge in one of the three High Court Divisions will go to the Court of Appeal (Civil Division). An exception to this rule allows an appeal to miss out or 'leapfrog' a visit to the Court of Appeal and go straight to the Supreme Court (ss 12–15 of the Administration of Justice Act 1969). In order for this to happen, the trial judge must grant a 'certificate of satisfaction' and the Supreme Court must give leave to appeal. For the judge to grant a certificate, he or she must be satisfied that the case involves a point of law of general public importance, either concerned mainly with statutory interpretation or one where he or she was bound by a Court of Appeal or a Supreme Court decision. Also, both parties must consent to the procedure.

4.7   THE COURT OF APPEAL (CIVIL DIVISION)

The Court of Appeal was established by the Judicature Act (JdA) 1873. Together with the High Court of Justice, the Court of Appeal formed part of the Supreme Court of Judicature. Why is it called 'Supreme' if the House of Lords was a superior court? The answer is that the JdA 1873 abolished the House of Lords in its appellate capacity, hence the Court of Appeal became part of the Supreme Court but, after a change of government, the House of Lords was reinstated as the final court of appeal by the Appellate Jurisdiction Act 1876.

The Constitutional Reform Act 2005 established a new Supreme Court of the United Kingdom (operational from 2009) to replace the House of Lords as the highest court of appeal. The new official collective name for the High Court, Court of Appeal and Crown Court (previously called 'The Supreme Court of Judicature') is the Senior Courts of England and Wales.

The Court of Appeal is served by senior judges – currently 37 – termed Lord Justices of Appeal. Additionally, the President of the Family Division of the High Court, the Vice Chancellor of the Chancery Division and High Court judges can sit in the Court of Appeal. The court hears appeals from the three divisions of the High Court, the Divisional Courts, the county courts, the Employment Appeal Tribunal, the Immigration and Asylum Upper Tribunal, the Lands Tribunal, the Transport Tribunal and the Court of Protection. The most senior judge is the Master of the Rolls. Usually, three judges will sit to hear an appeal, although for very important cases, five may sit. In the interests of business efficiency, some matters can be heard by two judges. These include:

- applications for leave to appeal;
- an appeal where all parties have consented to the matter being heard by just two judges;
- any appeal against an interim order or judgment (that is, one which is provisional).

Where such a court is evenly divided, three or five judges must rehear the case before it can be further appealed to the Supreme Court.

There may be four or five divisions of the court sitting on any given day. The court has a heavy workload. In the Court of Appeal Civil Division, there were a total of 3,758 applications filed/set down and 3,709 disposed of in 2011. This was an increase of

12 per cent and 17 per cent, respectively, on 2010, both figures being at the highest level since 2005. There has been an increase in the number of applications issued from 3,006 in 2007 to 3,353 in 2010 and 3,758 in 2011 (*Judicial and Court Statistics 2011*, Ministry of Justice, 28 June 2012). In cases of great urgency, this court is often *de facto* the final court of appeal, so that a party can act in reliance on its decision without waiting to see the outcome of any possible appeal to the Supreme Court. In *C v S and Others* (1987), a case concerning a putative father's right to prevent a prospective mother from having an abortion, the woman was between 18 and 21 weeks' pregnant and her termination, if it was to be carried out, had to be performed within days of the Court of Appeal's decision. The hospital concerned was reluctant to carry out the operation in case the father appealed to the House of Lords and won. To have earlier terminated the pregnancy might then, the hospital believed, have been the crime of infanticide. Leave to appeal to the Lords was refused and the termination was performed but, in the Court of Appeal, Sir John Donaldson MR said ([1987] 1 All ER 1230 at 1243):

> It is a fact that some thousand appeals are heard by this court every year, of which about 50 go to the House of Lords . . . So, in practical terms, in the everyday life of this country, this court is the final court of appeal and it must always be the final court of appeal in cases of real urgency. In those circumstances, no one could be blamed in any way, *a fortiori* could they as a practical matter be prosecuted, for acting on a judgment of this court. If that be wrong, which it is not, the life of the country in many respects would grind to a halt. The purpose of any supreme court, including the House of Lords, is to review historically and on a broad front; it is not to decide matters of great urgency which have to be decided once and for all.

4.8 THE APPEAL PROCESS

4.8.1 THE ACCESS TO JUSTICE ACT 1999 (PART IV)

In relation to civil appeals, the Access to Justice Act (AJA) 1999 made several changes:

- provided for permission to appeal to be obtained at all levels in the system (s 54);
- provided that, in normal circumstances, there will be only one level of appeal to the courts (s 55);
- introduced an order-making power to enable the Lord Chancellor to vary appeal routes in secondary legislation, with a view to ensuring that appeals generally go to the lowest appropriate level of judge (s 56);
- ensured that cases which merit the consideration of the Court of Appeal reach that court (s 57);

- gave the Civil Division of the Court of Appeal flexibility to exercise its jurisdiction in courts of one, two or more judges (s 59).

Together, these measures are intended to ensure that appeals are heard at the right level, and dealt with in a way which is proportionate to their weight and complexity; that the appeals system can adapt quickly to other developments in the civil justice system; and that existing resources are used efficiently, enabling the Court of Appeal (Civil Division) to tackle its workload more expeditiously. The provisions relating to the High Court (ss 61–65) allow judicial review applications.

4.8.2 RIGHT TO APPEAL

The AJA 1999 provides for rights of appeal to be exercised only with the permission of the court, as prescribed by rules of court. Previously, permission was required for most cases going to the Civil Division of the Court of Appeal, but not elsewhere. Under the Act, with three exceptions, permission to appeal must be obtained in all appeals to the county courts, High Court or Civil Division of the Court of Appeal. The exceptions are appeals against committal to prison, appeals against a refusal to grant *habeas corpus*, and appeals against the making of secure accommodation orders under s 25 of the Children Act 1989 (a form of custodial 'sentence' for recalcitrant children). There is no appeal against a decision of the court to give or refuse permission, but this does not affect any right under rules of court to make a further application for permission to the same or another court.

The Act provides that, where the county court or High Court has already reached a decision in a case brought on appeal, there is no further possibility of an appeal of that decision to the Court of Appeal, unless (s 55) the Court of Appeal considers that the appeal would raise an important point of principle or practice, or there is some other compelling reason for the court to hear it. This is known as the second appeals test.

4.8.3 DESTINATION OF APPEALS

Section 56 of the AJA 1999 enables the Lord Chancellor to vary, by order, the routes of appeal for appeals to and within the county courts, the High Court and the Civil Division of the Court of Appeal. Before making an order, the Lord Chancellor will be required to consult the Heads of Division, and any order will be subject to the affirmative resolution procedure. The following appeal routes are specified by order:

- In fast-track cases heard by a district judge, appeals will be to a circuit judge.
- In fast-track cases heard by a circuit judge, appeals will be to a High Court judge.

- In multi-track cases, appeals of interim decisions made at first instance by a district judge will be to a circuit judge, by a master or circuit judge to a High Court judge, and by a High Court judge to the Court of Appeal.

- In multi-track cases, appeals of final orders, regardless of the court of first instance, will be to the Court of Appeal.

- The Heads of Division are the Lord Chief Justice, the Master of the Rolls, the President of the Family Division and the Vice Chancellor.

- A decision is interim where it does not determine the final outcome of the case.

The legislation provides for the Master of the Rolls or a lower court to direct that an appeal that would normally be heard by a lower court be heard instead by the Court of Appeal. This power would be used where the appeal raises an important point of principle or practice, or is a case that, for some other compelling reason, should be considered by the Court of Appeal.

4.8.4 CIVIL DIVISION OF COURT OF APPEAL

The 1999 Act makes flexible provision for the number of judges of which a court must be constituted in order for the Court of Appeal to be able to hear appeals. Section 54 of the Senior Courts Act 1981 provided that the Court of Appeal was constituted to exercise any of its jurisdiction if it consisted of an uneven number of judges not less than three. In limited circumstances, it provided that a court could be properly constituted with two judges. The 1999 Act allows the Master of the Rolls, with the concurrence of the Lord Chancellor, to give directions about the minimum number of judges of which a court must consist for given types of proceedings. Subject to any directions, the Act also allows the Master of the Rolls, or a Lord Justice of Appeal designated by him for the purpose, to determine the number of judges who will sit to hear any particular appeal.

4.8.5 JURISDICTION OF SINGLE JUDGE OF HIGH COURT

The 1999 Act allows certain applications to be routinely heard by a single judge of the High Court. It does this by removing an obstacle that existed in the earlier legislation by which the route of appeal for these cases was to the House of Lords, but the Administration of Justice Act 1960 provides that the Supreme Court will only hear appeals in these matters from a Divisional Court (that is, more than one judge) of the High Court. The 1999 Act amends the 1960 Act so that the Supreme Court can hear appeals from a single High Court judge.

Under Part 52 of the CPR, the general rule is that permission to appeal in virtually all cases is mandatory. It should be obtained immediately following the judgment from the lower court or appellate court. Permission will only be given where the court considers that the appellant shows a real prospect of success or there is some other compelling reason for the court to hear the appeal.

All appeals will now be limited to a review rather than a complete rehearing and the appeal will only be allowed if the decision of the lower court was wrong or unjust due to a serious procedural or other irregularity.

The rule now is that there should be only one appeal. Lord Justice Brooke emphasised in the leading case of *Tanfern v Cameron MacDonald and Another* (2000), 'the decision of the first appeal court is now to be given primacy'. An application for a second or subsequent appeal (from the High Court or county court) must be made to the Court of Appeal, which will not accede unless the appeal raises an important point of principle or practice, or there is some other compelling reason to hear the appeal.

The general rule is that an appeal lies to the next level of judge in the court hierarchy, that is, district judge to county court judge to High Court judge. The main exception relates to an appeal against a final decision in a multi-track claim, which will go straight to the Court of Appeal.

Great emphasis is placed on ensuring that cases are dealt with promptly and efficiently, and on weeding out and deterring unjustified appeals. The result is that the opportunity to appeal a decision at first instance in a lower court is much more restricted. It is vital, therefore, that practitioners be properly prepared at the initial hearing. For more on this, see Richard Harrison ((2000) 150 NLJ 1175–6).

The Courts Act 2003 governs several aspects of the jurisdiction of the civil courts.

Section 52 of the Magistrates' Courts Act 1980 limits the jurisdiction of justices to deal with civil complaints to anything done (or neglected to be done) within the commission area for which the justice acts. The Courts Act 2003 amends this provision to reflect lay magistrates being given a national jurisdiction.

There were previously no provisions that allowed the transfer of civil proceedings from one magistrates' court to another. The Courts Act 2003 introduced such provisions to match the arrangements for criminal cases. There were already detailed provisions allowing for the transfer of family proceedings between magistrates' courts and also to the county courts and the High Court. This Act made no changes to those provisions.

Section 49: Family Proceedings Courts

This section of the 2003 Act sets out the framework whereby lay magistrates and district judges (Magistrates' Courts) are authorised to hear family proceedings. The Lord Chancellor must authorise a Justice of the Peace before he or she can sit as a member of a family proceedings court. These personal authorisations are valid throughout England and Wales. The Lord Chancellor has power to make rules regarding (a) the allocation and removal of authorisations for justices to sit as members of family proceedings courts, (b) the appointment of chairmen of family proceedings courts, and (c) the composition of such family proceedings courts. District judges (Magistrates' Courts) are required to be 'ticketed' for this work.

Section 62: Head and Deputy Head of Civil Justice

This section requires the Lord Chancellor to appoint a Head of Civil Justice, and gives power to appoint a deputy. It has been recognised that there is an ongoing need for a Head of Civil Justice to provide consistency and an overview, although it is accepted that the level of work may decrease as the Woolf reforms (the reforms to the civil justice system contained in the *Access to Justice* Report) continue to settle down. Therefore, the need for support from a deputy may decline.

Those eligible for appointment are the Master of the Rolls, the Vice Chancellor and any ordinary judge of the Court of Appeal. The Head of Civil Justice and the Deputy Head of Civil Justice, where there is one, will be *ex officio* members of the Civil Procedure Rule Committee (Civil PRC) as provided for in s 83. No other specific functions, duties or powers to be attached to these posts are to be provided in statute.

Section 63: Ordinary Judges of the Court of Appeal

This section deals with a specific problem: s 2(3) of the Senior Courts Act 1981 required an ordinary judge of the Court of Appeal to be styled a 'Lord' Justice of Appeal, whatever his or her gender. This section removes this anomaly. In 2012, only four of the 37 Appeal Court judges are female: Dame Heather Hallett, Dame Jill Black, Dame Anne Rafferty and Dame Mary Arden. Male members of the Court of Appeal are knighted (they are knighted upon elevation to the High Court), and are therefore known off the Bench, for example, as Sir David Keene. Senior female judges are invested as Dames of the British Empire (DBE). In their capacity as Appeal Court judges, the judges are known by their judicial titles, such as Lady Justice Hallett and Lord Justice Keene.

Section 64: Power to Alter Judicial Titles

Although s 63 amends one title – Lord Justice of Appeal – s 64 provides the Lord Chancellor with a power to amend the other titles listed (which encompasses all of the judicial titles in the Supreme Court and county courts) in the future to avoid similar problems arising. Some titles may need modernisation, to make them more easily understandable to court users. The acceptance commanded by titles containing a presumption of male gender might also change. Such orders may only be made after consultation with the Lord Chief Justice, Master of the Rolls, President of the Family Division and Vice Chancellor.

4.9   THE SUPREME COURT

In October 2009, the UK Supreme Court assumed the jurisdiction of the Appellate Committee of the House of Lords and the devolution jurisdiction of the Judicial Committee of the Privy Council. It is an independent institution, presided over by 12 independently appointed judges known as Justices of the Supreme Court. The Court is housed in the refurbished Middlesex Guildhall on London's Parliament Square – opposite the Houses of Parliament and alongside Westminster Abbey and the Treasury – a fitting location for the apex of the justice system.

The official website of the Supreme Court (www.supremecourt.gov.uk) notes that 'Courts are the final arbiter between the citizen and the state, and are therefore a fundamental pillar of the constitution'. The new court has been established to achieve a complete separation between the United Kingdom's senior judges and the Upper House of Parliament, emphasising the independence of the Law Lords and increasing the distance between Parliament and the courts. As with the previous decisions of the House of Lords, when it was the highest court in the land, the impact of Supreme Court decisions will extend far beyond the parties involved in any given case, shaping society and directly affecting our everyday lives. In their previous role as the Appellate Committee of the House of Lords the Justices gave many landmark rulings about such matters as marital rape, the defence of provocation, the detention without trial of alleged terrorists, the legality of the Hunting Act 2004 under European law, and whether or not a schoolgirl could be prevented from wearing traditional cultural dress.

The Supreme Court, as well as being the final court of appeal, plays an important role in the development of United Kingdom law. It has given a number of landmark rulings on subjects including police powers of stop and search, the territorial application of the Human Rights Act 1998, the legal status of prenuptial agreements and age discrimination in the workplace. As an appeal court, the Supreme Court cannot consider a case unless a relevant order has been made in a lower court.

The Supreme Court:

- is the final court of appeal for all United Kingdom civil cases, and criminal cases from England, Wales and Northern Ireland;
- hears appeals on arguable points of law of general public importance;
- concentrates on cases of the greatest public and constitutional importance; and
- maintains and develops the role of the highest court in the United Kingdom as a leader in the common law world.

The Supreme Court hears appeals from the following courts in each jurisdiction:

- against certain schemes of the Church Commissioners under the Pastoral Measure 1983.

In 2011, 37 appeals were entered, including eight from Jamaica, eight from Mauritius, seven from the Bahamas and four from Trinidad and Tobago, while 45 cases were dealt with (some of which may have originated from a previous year). The Committee also hears appeals on devolution issues.

CHAPTER SUMMARY: THE CIVIL COURTS

THE DIFFERENCES BETWEEN CIVIL AND CRIMINAL LAW

There is no such thing as inherently criminal conduct. A crime is whatever the State has forbidden on pain of legal punishment. The conduct that attracts criminal sanctions changes over time and according to different social systems. The terminology and outcomes of the two systems are different. In criminal cases, the *prosecutor prosecutes the defendant* (or *accused*); in civil cases, the *claimant sues the defendant*.

HER MAJESTY'S COURTS AND TRIBUNALS SERVICE

Her Majesty's Courts and Tribunals Service was created in April 2011. It brings together Her Majesty's Courts Service and the Tribunals Service into one integrated agency providing support for the administration of justice in courts and tribunals.

   HM Courts and Tribunals Service is an agency of the Ministry of Justice. It uniquely operates as a partnership between the Lord Chancellor, the Lord Chief Justice and the Senior President of Tribunals.

   The agency is responsible for the administration of the criminal, civil and family courts and tribunals in England and Wales and non-devolved tribunals in Scotland and Northern Ireland. Its aim is to provide for 'a fair, efficient and effective justice system delivered by an independent judiciary'.

   HM Courts and Tribunals Service aims to ensure that all citizens receive 'timely access to justice according to their different needs, whether as victims or witnesses of crime, defendants accused of crimes, consumers in debt, children at risk of harm, businesses involved in commercial disputes or as individuals asserting their employment rights or challenging the decisions of government bodies'. See: http://www.justice.gov.uk/about/hmcts/

   The agency employs approximately 20,770 staff and operates from around 650 locations. It has a gross annual budget of around £1.7 billion, approximately £585 million of which is recovered in fees and income from service users. It handles over 1.8 million criminal cases, 1.6 million civil claims, more than 141,000 family law disputes and almost 800,000 tribunal cases annually.

MAGISTRATES' COURTS

Magistrates' courts have a significant civil jurisdiction. They hear some family proceedings and deal with non-payment of council tax.

COUNTY COURTS

The county courts deal with various types of civil case including professional negligence; fatal accidents; and allegations of fraud or undue influence. Over two million proceedings are started each year. The main advantage to litigants using the small claims process is the fact that, if sued, they can defend without fear of incurring huge legal costs, since the costs that the winning party can claim are strictly limited.

HIGH COURT

The High Court has three administrative divisions: the Court of Chancery, the Queen's Bench Division (QBD) and the Family Division. High Court judges sit mainly in the Courts of Justice in the Strand, London, although it is possible for the High Court to sit anywhere in England or Wales. Each branch also has a divisional court which is an appeal court, mainly for the magistrates' and county courts. The Court of Protection that deals exclusively with matters arising under the Mental Capacity Act 2005 has the same powers as the High Court.

THE COURT OF APPEAL (CIVIL DIVISION)

The court hears appeals from the three divisions of the High Court, the Divisional Courts, the county courts, the Employment Appeal Tribunal, the Asylum and Immigration Upper Tribunal, the Lands Tribunal, the Transport Tribunal and the Court of Protection. The most senior judge is the Master of the Rolls.

RIGHT TO APPEAL

Rights of appeal can be exercised only with the permission of the court, as prescribed by rules of court. There are three exceptions: appeals against committal to prison, appeals against a refusal to grant *habeas corpus* and appeals against the making of secure accommodation orders under s 25 of the Children Act 1989.

THE SUPREME COURT

In 2009 the Supreme Court assumed the jurisdiction of the Appellate Committee of the House of Lords and the devolution jurisdiction of the Judicial Committee of the Privy Council. It is an independent institution, presided over by 12 independently appointed judges, known as Justices of the Supreme Court.

FOOD FOR THOUGHT

1.   A contingency fee agreement is one under which the client's lawyer is paid a percentage of the settlement sum or damages award, if, but only if, their claim is successful. If the claim is unsuccessful, the lawyer does not get paid. Contingency fee agreements are common in the US but are not currently permitted in the UK.

The Supreme Court of the United Kingdom, created by the Constitutional Reform Act 2005, has replaced the House of Lords as the final court of appeal in the UK. The Court has jurisdiction to hear appeals from the Court of Appeal (Civil and Criminal Divisions) and, in limited circumstances, the High Court. It is served by judges known as Justices of the Supreme Court

The Court of Appeal (Civil Division) is one of the 'Senior Courts of England and Wales', hearing appeals from the High Court, the County Courts and the Employment Appeal Tribunal. The Court is largely staffed by senior judges known as Lord Justices of Appeal

The Judicial Committee of the **Privy Council** is the final court of appeal for UK overseas territories, Crown Dependencies and some Commonwealth countries

The High Court is one of the 'Senior Courts of England and Wales' and is staffed by High Court (or *Puisne*) Judges. It hears more complex and higher value civil disputes (plus some criminal jurisdiction) and is divided into three 'divisions':

The **Queen's Bench Division** hears actions in contract & tort and has three courts attached: Commercial, Admiralty and Technology & Construction. The QB Divisional Court has appellate jurisdiction and also hears actions relating to Judicial Review and writs of *habeas corpus*

The **Family Division** has jurisdiction in family matters including matrimony, proceedings under the Children Act 1989 and non-contentious probate cases. Attached to it is the Family Divisional Court, which has appellate jurisdiction

The **Chancery Division** hears cases principally related to business such as insolvency, mortgages, administration of estates, partnership disputes and intellectual property. The Companies and Patents Courts are attached to it, while the Chancery Divisional Court has appellate jurisdiction in regard to tax and bankruptcy matters

County courts have jurisdiction in claims including contract, tort and landlord & tenant disputes (and, sometimes, uncontested divorce petitions). There are geographical and financial limitations on their jurisdiction and more complex cases should be heard by the High Court. The Court is staffed by Circuit & District Judges and Recorders (p/time)

Magistrates' courts, although thought of as criminal courts, have civil jurisdiction that includes granting licences in regard to betting, and 'family' matters, including orders for protection against violence, maintenance orders and proceedings concerning the welfare of children, including adoption

It should be remembered that not all civil disputes reach trial. Most are dealt with through statutory or voluntary complaints procedures, or through **mediation**, **negotiation** or **arbitration**. In addition, **Ombudsmen** have the power to determine complaints in the public sector and, on a voluntary basis, in some private-sector activities – for example, banking. In addition, the relevance of **tribunals** to the machinery of justice in the UK should not be forgotten

FIGURE 4.1 *The Structure of the Civil Courts.*

Lord Justice Jackson's January 2010 report on costs in civil litigation argues that contingency fee agreements should be introduced into the UK. Do you agree? Would such agreements compromise the integrity and independence of the lawyer?

2.   In 2009, 36 per cent of the UK population were eligible for legal aid. Since 2004, civil legal aid expenditure has decreased by 15 per cent. What are the access to justice issues that arise when legal aid is cut? Are there other ways of improving access to justice in times of economic strife?

3.   The justice system in the UK is adversarial. Should litigants be forced to use mediation before they go to court in order to reduce costs and alleviate the backlog in the court system?

FURTHER READING

Blackstone's Civil Practice, 2012, Oxford: OUP

Gibb, F, 'Age of secrecy ends as family courts are opened to media scrutiny', *The Times*, 28 April 2009

Gold, S, 'Civil way' (2009) 159 NLJ 7378

Millett, T, 'A marked improvement' (2008) 158 NLJ 7321

Ministry of Justice, *Judicial and Court Statistics 2012*, June 2012

New Law Journal, 'New charter for civil courts' [2007] 138

Parpworth, N, 'The hunt goes on' (2008) 158 NLJ 8118

USEFUL WEBSITES

www.hmcourts-service.gov.uk
The official site of Her Majesty's Courts Service.

http://www.judiciary.gov.uk/about-the-judiciary/advisory-bodies/cjc
The site of the Civil Justice Council.

www.supremecourt.gov.uk
The new website for the Supreme Court.

COMPANION WEBSITE

Now visit the companion website to:

● test your understanding of the key terms using our Flashcard Glossary;

● revise and consolidate your knowledge of 'The civil courts' using our Multiple Choice Question testbank;

● view all of the links to the Useful Websites above.

www.routledge.com/cw/slapper

THE CIVIL PROCESS

5

Jarndyce [v] Jarndyce drones on. This scarecrow of a suit has, in the course of time, become so complicated that no man alive knows what it means. The parties to it understand it least; but it has been observed that no two Chancery lawyers can talk about it for five minutes without coming to a total disagreement as to all the premises. Innumerable children have been born into the cause; innumerable young people have married into it; innumerable old people have died out of it. Scores of persons have deliriously found themselves made parties in Jarndyce [v] Jarndyce, without knowing how or why; whole families have inherited legendary hatreds with the suit. The little plaintiff or defendant, who was promised a new rocking horse when Jarndyce [v] Jarndyce should be settled, has grown up, possessed himself of a real horse, and trotted away into the other world. Fair wards of court have faded into grandmothers; a long procession of Chancellors has come in and gone out . . . there are not three Jarndyces left upon the earth perhaps, since old Tom Jarndyce in despair blew his brains out at a coffee-house in Chancery Lane; but Jarndyce [v] Jarndyce still drags its dreary length before the Court, perennially hopeless [*Bleak House*, 1853, Charles Dickens].

Many critics believe that the adversarial system has run into the sand, in that, today, delay and costs are too often disproportionate to the difficulty of the issue and the amount at stake. The solution now being followed to that problem requires a more interventionist judiciary: the trial judge as the trial manager [Henry LJ, *Thermawear v Linton* (1995) CA].

5.1 INTRODUCTION

The extent of delay, complication and therefore expense of civil litigation may have changed since the time of Dickens' observations about the old Court of Chancery, but how far the civil process is as efficient as it might be is a matter of some debate. In

October 2010, governmental plans proposed that the Ministry of Justice's budget be cut by 23 per cent. The staffing of courts is already inadequate but 14,250 of these frantically demanding jobs will go, leaving the residual workforce to toil in an arguably hopeless Sisyphean challenge.

In 2007, Judge Paul Collins, London's most senior county court judge, said (February, *Law in Action*, BBC Radio 4) that low pay and high turnover among staff meant that serious errors were commonplace and routinely led to incorrect judgments in court. He said that with further cuts looming 'we run the risk of bringing about a real collapse in the service we're able to give to the people using the courts'.

5.2 THE NEED FOR REFORM

A survey by the National Consumer Council in 1995 found that three out of four people in serious legal disputes were dissatisfied with the civil justice system (*Seeking Civil Justice: A Survey of People's Needs and Experiences*, 1995, NCC). Of the 1,019 respondents, 77 per cent claimed the system was too slow, 74 per cent said it was too complicated and 73 per cent said that it was unwelcoming and outdated.

According to the Civil Justice Review (CJR) 1988, delay in litigation 'causes continuing personal stress, anxiety and financial hardship to ordinary people and their families. It may induce economically weaker parties to accept unfair settlements. It also frustrates the efficient conduct of commerce and industry'. Despite some of the innovations in the five years following that CJR, the problems continued.

Historically, change has come very slowly and gradually to the legal system. The report of the CJR was largely ignored and, with the exception of a shift in the balance of work from the High Court to the county court (under the Courts and Legal Services Act (CLSA) 1990), no major changes came from its recommendations. The whole process began again with the Woolf Review of the civil justice system. In March 1994, the Lord Chancellor set up the Woolf Inquiry to look at ways of improving the speed and accessibility of civil proceedings, and of reducing their cost. Lord Woolf was invited by the government to review the work of the civil courts in England and Wales. He began from the proposition that the system was 'in a state of crisis . . . a crisis for the government, the judiciary and the profession'. The recommendations he formulated – after extensive consultation in the UK and in many other jurisdictions – form the basis of major changes to the system that came into effect in April 1999. David Gladwell, head of the Civil Justice Division of the Lord Chancellor's Department (LCD), stated (*Civil Litigation Reform*, 1999, LCD, p 1) that these changes represent 'the greatest change the civil courts have seen in over a century'.

In the system that Lord Woolf examined, the main responsibility for the initiation and conduct of proceedings rested with the parties to each individual case, and it was normally the plaintiff (now claimant) who set the pace. Thus, Lord Woolf also noted:

Without effective judicial control . . . the adversarial process is likely to encourage an adversarial culture and to degenerate into an environment in which the litigation process is too often seen as a battlefield where no rules apply. In this environment, questions of expense, delay, compromise and fairness have only a low priority. The consequence is that the expense is often excessive, disproportionate and unpredictable; and delay is frequently unreasonable [*Access to Justice*, Interim Report, 1995, p 7].

The system had degenerated in a number of other respects. Witness statements, a sensible innovation aimed at 'cards on the table', began after a very short time to follow the same route as pleadings, with the drafter's skill often used to obscure the original words of the witness. In addition, the use of expert evidence under the old system left a lot to be desired:

The approach to expert evidence also shows the characteristic range of difficulties: instead of the expert assisting the court to resolve technical problems, delay is caused by the unreasonable insistence on going to unduly eminent members of the profession and evidence is undermined by the partisan pressure to which party experts are subjected.

When Lord Woolf began his examination of the civil law process, the problems facing those who used the system were many and varied. His Interim Report published in June 1995 identified these problems. He noted, for example, that:

. . . the key problems facing civil justice today are cost, delay and complexity. These three are interrelated and stem from the uncontrolled nature of the litigation process. In particular, there is no clear judicial responsibility for managing individual cases or for the overall administration of the civil courts. Just as the problems are interrelated, so too the solutions, which I propose, are interdependent. In many instances, the failure of previous attempts to address the problem stems not from the solutions proposed but from their partial rather than their complete implementation [*Access to Justice*, Interim Report of Lord Woolf, 1995].

Many potential litigants are deterred from taking action by the high costs. It is also relevant to remember that whichever party loses the claim must pay for his own expenses and those of the other side; a combined sum which will, in many cases, be more than the sum in issue. An appeal to the Court of Appeal will increase the costs even further (in effect, fees and expenses for another claim) and the same may be true again if the case is taken to the Supreme Court (formerly House of Lords). There is in such a system a great pressure for parties to settle their claims. The CJR found that 90–95 per cent of cases were settled by the parties before the trial.

The cost of taking legal action in the civil courts has been gigantic. Two cases cited by Adrian Zuckerman in an address to Lord Woolf's Inquiry illustrate the point. In one, a successful claim by a supplier of fitted kitchens to stop a £10,000-a-year employee from taking up a job with a competitor cost the employer £100,000, even though judgment was obtained in under five weeks from the start of the proceedings. The expense of this case was in fact double the stated amount when the cost of the Legal Aid Fund's bill for the employee's defence was added to the total. In another case, a divorced wife had to pay £34,000 in costs for a judgment that awarded her £52,000 of the value of the family home.

It was the spiralling costs of civil litigation, to a large extent borne by the taxpayer through legal aid, which prompted the Lord Chancellor to move to cap the Legal Aid Fund. The legal aid budget rose from £426 million in 1987–88 to £1,526 million in 1997–98.

The system of civil procedure entails a variety of devices. Very complex cases may require the full use of many of these devices, but most cases could be tried without parties utilising all the procedures. Exorbitant costs and long delays often resulted from unduly complicated procedures being used by lawyers acting for parties to litigation. Zuckerman has argued that this problem arose from the fact that the legal system was evolved principally by lawyers with no concern for cost efficiency. In both the High Court and the county court, the system allowed parties to quarrel as much over procedural matters as the actual merits of the substantive dispute. In one case, for example, the issue of whether a writ had been properly served on the other side had to be considered by a Master (the High Court judicial officer empowered to deal with procedural matters) and then on appeal, by a judge, and then on another appeal, by the Court of Appeal. Thus, cost and delay could build up before the parties even arrived at the stage of having their real argument heard. If a claim or defence was amended, the fate of the amendment could take two appeal hearings to finally resolve. The pre-trial proceedings often degenerated into an intricate legal contest separate from the substantive issue.

The CJR 1988 recommended unification of the county courts and the High Court. It accepted the need for different levels of judiciary, but argued that having different levels of courts was inefficient. This recommendation carried what Roger Smith, then director of the Legal Action Group, called an 'unspoken sting', namely, that a divided legal profession could hardly survive a unified court. The Bar rebelled and the judiciary were solidly opposed to such change. The recommendation was not legislated.

The CLSA 1990, following other recommendations in the CJR, legislated for large numbers of cases in the High Court being sent down to the county courts to expedite their progress. No extra resources were given to the county courts to cope with the influx of cases and so, not surprisingly, there has been a growing backlog of cases and a poorer quality of service in the county courts. This problem may well have worsened rather than been helped by the introduction of the Civil Procedure Rules (CPR), as more cases are now heard in the county courts.

There were tactical reasons why parties were tempted to use the full panoply of procedural rules. The rule that 'costs follow success' (that is, the losing side usually has to pay the legal costs of the other side) can operate to encourage the building up of expense. Wealthy litigants could employ protracted procedures in an effort to worry poorer opponents to settle on terms determined by the former. Conditional fee arrangements

THE NEW CIVIL PROCESS

(see below, at 14.11) have made very little impact on the system, so lawyers who are paid by the hour regardless of success are unlikely to be especially anxious about the speed and efficiency of their work.

5.3 THE NEW CIVIL PROCESS

Following the Civil Procedure Act 1997, the changes have been effected through the new Civil Procedure Rules (CPR) 1998, which came into force on 26 April 1999. These rules replaced the Rules of the Supreme Court 1965 and the County Court Rules 1981. The Rules are divided into parts and practice directions. There are also pre-action protocols. Each part deals with a particular aspect of procedure and within each part is a set of rules laying down the procedure relating to that aspect. Also, under most parts can be found new practice directions that give guidance on how the rules are to be interpreted. In addition, the rules are kept under constant review and there are regular updates; in January 2010, the fifty-first update was issued and in March 2010 the fifty-second. The former introduced many changes and the latter a small number. The fifty-third update was issued on 1 October 2010 and the fifty-fourth was introduced on 20 October 2010 with minor changes. The fifty-fifth update was introduced on 6 April 2011. This update has introduced a number of changes, which include part 45 to allow HM Revenue and Customs (HMRC) a fixed costs award for the recovery of money in the county court where the matter is conducted by an HMRC officer. The latest, being the fifty-eighth update, was introduced on 6 April 2012 and incorporated rules to facilitate the processing of the early stages of all money claims work through the County Court Money Claims Centre in Salford. Of major importance has been the accessibility of the CPR, which can be found on the LCD website, including practice directions and updates. A further method of improving the civil process has been the introduction of pre-action protocols for certain types of case, which are designed to increase the opportunity for settling cases as early in the proceedings as possible by improving communication between the parties and their advisers. The rules are quoted as, for example, 'rule 4.1', which refers to Part 4, r 1 of the CPR.

The reforms work towards conflict resolution as the main purpose for civil legal proceedings, rather than a case being a prolonged opportunity for lawyers to demonstrate a range of legalistic skills.

The principal parts of all of these new rules and guidelines are examined below.

The main features of the new civil process are as follows.

The Case Control

The progress of cases is monitored by using a computerised diary monitoring system. Parties are encouraged to co-operate with each other in the conduct of the proceedings; which issues need full investigation and trial are decided promptly and others disposed of summarily.

Court Allocation and Tracking

The county courts retain an almost unlimited jurisdiction for handling contract and tort claims. Where a matter involves a claim for damages or other remedy for libel or slander, or a claim where the title to any toll, fair, market or franchise is in question, then the proceedings cannot start in the county court unless the parties agree otherwise. On 9 February 2012 The Ministry of Justice announced that non-personal injury claims under £100,000 cannot be heard in the High Court.

Issuing proceedings in the High Court is now limited to personal injury claims with a value of £50,000 or more; other claims with a value of more than £100,000 and equity claims where the property is worth at least £350,000; claims where an Act of Parliament requires a claim to start in the High Court; or specialist High Court claims.

Cases are allocated to one of three tracks for a hearing, that is, small claims, fast track or multitrack, depending on the value and complexity of the claim.

The Documentation and Procedures

Most claims will be begun by a multipurpose form and the provision of a response pack, and the requirement that an allocation questionnaire is completed is intended to simplify and expedite matters.

5.3.1   THE CIVIL PROCEDURE RULES

The CPR are the same for the county court and the High Court. The vocabulary is more user-friendly, so, for example, what used to be called a 'writ' will be a 'claim form' and a *guardian ad litem* will be a 'litigation friend'.

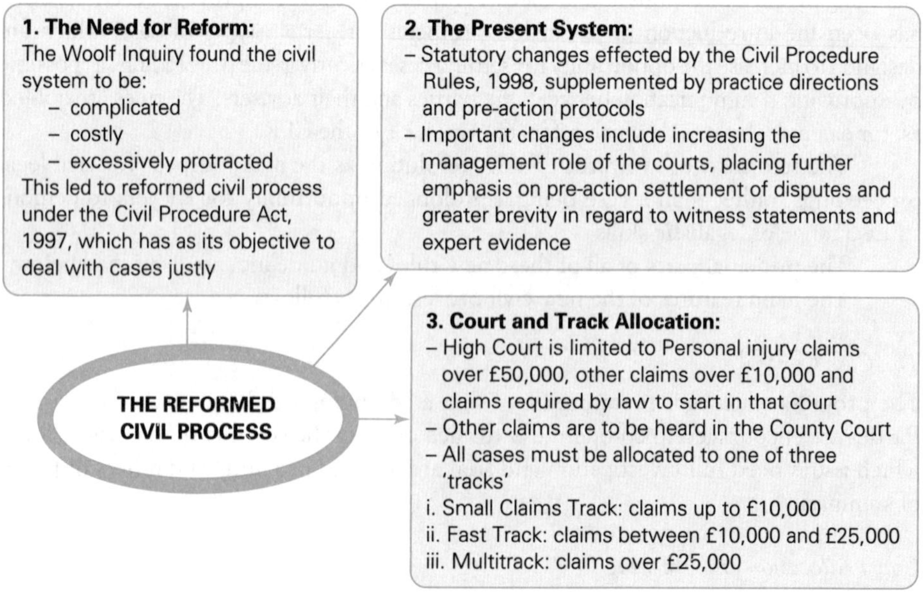

1. The Need for Reform:
The Woolf Inquiry found the civil system to be:
- complicated
- costly
- excessively protracted
This led to reformed civil process under the Civil Procedure Act, 1997, which has as its objective to deal with cases justly

2. The Present System:
- Statutory changes effected by the Civil Procedure Rules, 1998, supplemented by practice directions and pre-action protocols
- Important changes include increasing the management role of the courts, placing further emphasis on pre-action settlement of disputes and greater brevity in regard to witness statements and expert evidence

THE REFORMED CIVIL PROCESS

3. Court and Track Allocation:
- High Court is limited to Personal injury claims over £50,000, other claims over £10,000 and claims required by law to start in that court
- Other claims are to be heard in the County Court
- All cases must be allocated to one of three 'tracks'
i. Small Claims Track: claims up to £10,000
ii. Fast Track: claims between £10,000 and £25,000
iii. Multitrack: claims over £25,000

FIGURE 5.1 *The Reformed Civil Process.*

Although in some ways all the fuss about the new CPR being so far-reaching creates the impression that the future will see a sharp rise in litigation, the truth may be different. During the last ten years, the sort of civil litigation that people mean when they speak about 'compensation culture' has gone down, not up. There are, incontrovertibly, thousands fewer such claims in the courts now than ten years ago. The Queen's Bench Division of the High Court is the court that deals with all substantial claims in personal injury, breach of contract, and negligence actions. According to official figures (*Judicial and Court Statistics 2011*, Ministry of Justice, 28 June 2012), 153,624 writs and originating summonses were issued by the court in 1995. By 2011, however, the number of annual actions issued was down to 13,928. The number of claims issued in the county courts (which deal with less substantial civil disputes in the law of negligence) has also fallen. In 1998, the number of claims issued nationally was 2,245,324 but in 2011 it was 1,553,983.

5.3.2 THE OVERRIDING OBJECTIVE (CPR PART 1)

The overriding objective of the CPR is to enable the court to deal justly with cases. It applies to all of the rules and the parties to a case are required to assist the court in pursuing the overriding objective. Further, when the courts exercise any powers given to them under the CPR, or in interpreting any rules, they must consider and apply the overriding objective. The first rule reads:

> 1.1(1) These rules are a new procedural code with the overriding objective of enabling the court to deal with cases justly.

This objective includes ensuring that the parties are on an equal footing and saving expense. When exercising any discretion given by the CPR, the court must, according to r 1.2, have regard to the overriding objective and a checklist of factors, including the amount of money involved, the complexity of the issue, the parties' financial positions, how the case can be dealt with expeditiously and fairly, and by allotting an appropriate share of the court's resources while taking into account the needs of others. In future, as Judge John Frenkel observes ('On the road to reform' (1998)), 'the decisions of the Court of Appeal are more likely to illustrate the application of the new rules to the facts of a particular case as opposed to being interpretative authorities that define the meaning of the rules'.

5.3.3 PRACTICE DIRECTIONS

Practice directions (official statements of interpretative guidance) play an important role in the new civil process. In general, they supplement the CPR, giving the latter fine detail. They tell parties and their representatives what the court will expect of them in respect of documents to be filed in court for a particular purpose, and how they must co-operate with the other parties to their action. They also tell the parties what they can expect of the court, for example, they explain what sort of sanction a court is likely to impose if a particular court order or request is not complied with. Almost every part of the new rules has a corresponding practice direction. They supersede all previous practice directions in relation to civil process.

5.3.4   PRE-ACTION PROTOCOLS

The pre-action protocols (PAPs) are an important feature of the reforms. They exist for cases of *clinical disputes* (formerly called medical/clinical negligence, but now extended to cover claims against dentists, radiologists and so on) and *personal injury, disease and illness, construction and engineering disputes, defamation, professional negligence, housing disrepair, housing possession following rent arrears, housing possession following mortgage arrears, low value personal injury claims in road traffic accidents, dilapidations at end of lease or tenancy of a commercial property and judicial review*. Further protocols are likely to follow.

In the *Final Report on Access to Justice* (1996), Lord Woolf stated (Chapter 10) that PAPs are intended to 'build on and increase the benefits of early but well-informed settlements'. The purposes of the PAPs, he said, are:

(a)   to focus the attention of litigants on the desirability of resolving disputes without litigation;

(b)   to enable them to obtain the information they reasonably need in order to enter into an appropriate settlement;

. . .

(d)   if a pre-action settlement is not achievable, to lay the ground for expeditious conduct of proceedings.

The protocols were drafted with the assistance of The Law Society, the Clinical Disputes Forum, the Association of Personal Injury Lawyers and the Forum of Insurance Lawyers. Most clients in personal injury and clinical dispute claims want their cases settled as quickly and as economically as possible. The new spirit of co-operation fostered by the Woolf reforms should mean that fewer cases are pushed through the courts. The PAPs are intended to improve pre-action contact between the parties and to facilitate better exchange of information and fuller investigation of a claim at an earlier stage. Both clinical disputes and personal injury PAPs recommend:

●   the claimant sending a reasonably detailed letter of claim to the proposed defendant, including details of the accident/medical treatment/negligence, a brief explanation of why the defendant is being held responsible, a description of the injury and an outline of the defendant's losses. Where the matter involves a road traffic accident, the name and address of the hospital where treatment was received along with the claimant's hospital reference number should be provided. Unlike a 'pleading' in the old system (which could not be moved away from by the claimant), there will be no sanctions applied if the proceedings differ from the letter of claim. However, as Gordon Exall has observed ('Civil litigation brief' (1999) SJ 32, 15 January), letters of claim should be drafted with care because any variance between them and the claim made in court will give the defendant's lawyers a fruitful opportunity for cross-examination;

- the defendant in personal injury cases should reply to the letter within 21 days of the date of posting, identify insurers if applicable and if necessary identify specifically anything omitted from the letter. The healthcare provider in clinical dispute cases should acknowledge the letter within 14 days of receipt and should identify who will be dealing with the matter. The defendant/healthcare provider then has a maximum of three months to investigate/provide a reasoned answer and tell the claimant whether liability is admitted. If it is denied, reasons must be given;

- within that three-month period or on denial of liability, the parties should organise disclosure of key documents. For personal injury cases, the protocol lists the main types of defendant's documents for different types of cases. If the defendant denies liability, then he should disclose all the relevant documents in his possession, which are likely to be ordered to be disclosed by the court. In clinical dispute claims, the key documents will usually be the claimant's medical records, and the protocol includes a *proforma* application to obtain these;

- the personal injury PAP also includes a framework for the parties to agree on the use of expert evidence, particularly in respect of a condition and prognosis report from a medical expert. Before any prospective party instructs an expert, he should give the other party a list of names of one or more experts in the relevant specialty that he considers are suitable to instruct. Within 14 days, the other party may indicate an objection to one or more of the experts; the first party should then instruct a mutually acceptable expert. Only if all suggested experts are objected to can the sides instruct experts of their own. The aim here is to allow the claimant to get the defendant to agree to one report being prepared by a mutually agreeable non-partisan expert. The clinical dispute PAP encourages the parties to consider sharing expert evidence, especially with regard to quantum (that is, the amount of damages payable);

- both PAPs encourage the parties to use alternative dispute resolution (ADR) or negotiation to settle the dispute during the pre-action period.

At the early stage of proceedings, when a case is being allocated to a track (that is, small claims, fast track or multi-track), after the defence has been filed, parties will be asked whether they have complied with a relevant protocol, and if not, why not. The court will then be able to take the answers into account when deciding whether, for example, an extension of time should be granted. The court will also be able to penalise poor conduct by one side through costs sanctions – an order that the party at fault pay the costs of the proceedings or part of them.

5.4   CASE CONTROL (CPR PART 3)

Case control by the judiciary, rather than leaving the conduct of the case to the parties, is a key element in the reforms resulting from the Woolf Review. The court's case management powers are found in Part 3 of the CPR, although there is a variety of ways in which a judge may control the progress of the case. A judge may make a number of orders to give opportunities to the parties to take stock of their case-by-case management conferences, check they have all the information they need to proceed or settle by pre-trial reviews, or halt the proceedings to give the parties an opportunity to consider a settlement. When any application is made to the court, there is an obligation on the judge to deal with as many outstanding matters as possible. The court is also under an obligation to ensure that witness statements are limited to the evidence that is to be given if there is a hearing, and expert evidence is restricted to what is required to resolve the proceedings. Judges receive support from court staff in carrying out their case management role. The court monitors case progress by using a computerised diary monitoring system which:

- records certain requests, or orders made by the court;
- identifies the particular case or cases to which these orders/requests refer, and the dates by which a response should be made; and
- checks on the due date whether the request or order has been complied with.

Whether there has been compliance or not, the court staff will pass the relevant files to a procedural judge (a Master in the Royal Courts of Justice, a district judge in the county court), who will decide if either side should have a sanction imposed on them.

In the new system, the litigants have much less control over the pace of the case than in the past. They will not be able to draw out proceedings, or delay in the way that they once could have done, because the case is subject to a timetable. Once a defence is filed, the parties get a timetable order that includes the prospective trial date. The need for pre-issue preparation is increased, and this benefits litigants because, as Professor Hazel Genn's research has shown (*Hard Bargaining: Out of Court Settlement in Personal Injury Claims* (1987)), in settled personal injury actions, 60 per cent of costs were incurred before proceedings. The court now has a positive duty to manage cases. Rule 1.4(1) states that 'The court must further the overriding objective by actively managing cases'. The rule goes on to explain what this management involves:

1.4(2) Active case management includes –

(a)   encouraging the parties to co-operate with each other in the conduct of the proceedings;

(b)   identifying the issues at an early stage;

(c)   deciding promptly which issues need full investigation and trial and accordingly disposing summarily of the others;

(d)   deciding the order in which issues are to be resolved;

(e)   encouraging the parties to use an alternative dispute resolution procedure if the court considers that appropriate . . .;

(f)   helping the parties to settle the whole or part of the case;

(g)   fixing timetables or otherwise controlling the progress of the case;

(h)   considering whether the likely benefits of taking a particular step justify the cost of taking it;

(i)   dealing with as many aspects of the case as it can on the same occasion;

(j)   dealing with the case without the parties needing to attend court;

(k)   making use of technology; and

(l)   giving directions to ensure that the trial of a case proceeds quickly and efficiently.

It is worth noting here that district judges and deputy district judges have had extensive training to promote a common approach (see above, at 5.4). Training is being taken very seriously by the judiciary. District judges now occupy a pivotal position in the civil process.

Part 3 of the CPR gives the court a wide range of substantial powers. The court can, for instance, extend or shorten the time for compliance with any rule, practice direction or court order, even if an application for an extension is made after the time for compliance has expired. It can also hold a hearing and receive evidence by telephone or 'by using any other method of direct oral communication'.

The Association of District Judges, the Association of Personal Injury Lawyers and the Forum of Insurance Lawyers, who meet at six-monthly intervals to discuss how the operation of the CPR might be improved ((2000) 13 LSG 11), agreed that telephone hearings work very well (on the whole), but contested interim applications are often not suitable for telephone hearings and should not be disguised as case management conferences. Furthermore, not all courts have yet received the right equipment to be able to conduct a telephone hearing. The district judge cannot be put in the role of a go-between, which happens in some judges' rooms where there is no conference facility but one party has attended in person and the opponent is on the other end of a standard telephone.

Part 3 of the CPR also gives the court powers to:

- strike out a statement of case;
- impose sanctions for non-payment of certain fees;
- impose sanctions for non-compliance with rules and practice directions;
- give relief from sanctions.

There is, though, a certain flexibility built into the rules. A failure to comply with a rule or practice direction will not necessarily be fatal to a case. Rule 3.10 of the CPR states:

> Where there has been an error of procedure such as a failure to comply with a rule or practice direction:
>
> (a)   the error does not invalidate any step taken in the proceedings unless the court so orders; and
>
> (b)   the court may make an order to remedy the error.

The intention of imposing a sanction will always be to put the parties back into the position they would have been in if one of them had not failed to meet a deadline. For example, the court could order that a party carries out a task (like producing some sort of documentary evidence) within a very short time (for example, two days) in order that the existing trial dates can be met.

5.4.1 CASE MANAGEMENT CONFERENCES

Case management conferences may be regarded as an opportunity to 'take stock'. Many of these are now conducted by telephone. There is no limit to the number of case management conferences that may be held during the life of a case, although the cost of attendance at such hearings against the benefits obtained will always be a consideration in making the decision. They will be used, among other things, to consider:

- giving directions, including a specific date for the return of a listing questionnaire;
- whether the claim or defence is sufficiently clear for the other party to understand the claim they have to meet;
- whether any amendments should be made to statements of case;
- what documents, if any, each party needs to show the other;
- what factual evidence should be given;
- what expert evidence should be sought and how it should be sought and disclosed; and
- whether it would save costs to order a separate trial of one or more issues.

5.4.2   PRE-TRIAL REVIEWS

Pre-trial reviews will normally take place after the filing of listing questionnaires and before the start of the trial. Their main purpose is to decide a timetable for the trial itself, including the evidence to be allowed and whether this should be given orally; instructions about the content of any trial bundles (bundles of documents including evidence, such as written statements, for the judge to read) and confirming a realistic time estimate for the trial itself.

Rules require that, where a party is represented, a representative 'familiar with the case and with sufficient authority to deal with any issues likely to arise must attend every case management conference or pre-trial review'.

Both the Chancery Guide and the Queen's Bench Guide provide that where it is estimated that a case will last more than 10 days or where a case warrants it the court may consider directing a pre-trial review.

5.4.3   STAYS FOR SETTLEMENT (CPR PART 26) AND SETTLEMENTS (CPR PART 36)

Under the new CPR, there is a greater incentive for parties to settle their differences. Part 36 sets out the procedure for either party to make offers to settle. A Part 36 offer can be made before the start of proceedings and also in appeal proceedings.

The party making the offer is called the 'offeror' and the party receiving it is called the 'offeree'. Under the revised Part 36 rule where an offer relates to settlement of a money claim it is no longer possible to accompany the offer with the payment of funds into court. This provision applies irrespective of who the offeror is and whether that party has the means or assets to pay. When a Part 36 offer is accepted by the claimant the defendant must pay the sum offered within 14 days (unless the parties agree to extend the time period), failing which the claimant can enter judgment.

The court will take into account any pre-action offers to settle when making an order for costs. Thus, a side that has refused a reasonable offer to settle will be treated less generously in the issue of how far the court will order their costs to be paid by the other side. For this to happen, the offer must be one which is made to be open to the other side for at least 21 days after the date it was made (to stop any undue pressure being put on someone with the phrase 'take it or leave it, it is only open for one day then I shall withdraw the offer').

If an offer to settle is to be made in accordance with Part 36 it must be made in writing and state that it is intended to have the consequences of Part 36. Where the defendant makes the offer, it must specify a period of not less than 21 days within which the defendant will be liable for the claimant's costs if the offer is accepted. In addition either party's offer must state whether it relates to the whole or part of the claim, or to an issue which arises in it and if so to which part or issue and whether any counterclaim is taken into account. The revised Part 36 rule allows the parties to withdraw any offer after the expiry of the 'relevant period' as defined in Rule 36.3.1.c without the court's permission. However, before the expiry of the 'relevant period' it is possible for a Part 36 offer to be withdrawn or its terms changed to be less advantageous to the 'offeree' only with the court's permission.

Several aspects of the new rules encourage litigants to settle rather than take risks in order (as a claimant) to hold out for unreasonably large sums of compensation, or try to get away (as a defendant) with paying nothing rather than some compensation. The system of Part 36 payments or offers does not apply to a claim allocated to the small claim track but, for other cases, it seems bound to have a significant effect. Part 36 applies prior to a small claims track allocation and on reallocation from this track to the other two tracks.

Thus, if at the trial, a claimant does not get more damages than a sum offered by the defendant, or obtain a judgment more favourable than a Part 36 offer, the court will, unless it considers it unjust to do so, order the claimant to pay any costs incurred by the defendant after the latest date for accepting the payment or offer without requiring the court's permission, together with interest on those costs.

Similarly, where at trial, a defendant is held liable to the claimant for a sum at least equal to the proposals contained in a claimant's Part 36 offer (that is, where the claimant has made an offer to settle), the court may order the defendant to pay interest on the award at a rate not exceeding 10 per cent above the base rate for some or all of the period, starting with the date on which the defendant could have accepted the offer without requiring the court's permission. In addition, the court may order that the claimant be entitled to his costs on an indemnity basis together with interest on those costs at a rate not exceeding 10 per cent above base rate for the period from the latest date when the defendant could have accepted the offer without requiring the court's permission.

The court has a general and overreaching discretion to make a different order for costs than the normal order under Part 44.

District Judge Frenkel has given the following example:

> Claim, £150,000 – judgment, £51,000 – £50,000 paid into court. The without prejudice correspondence shows that the claimant would consider nothing short of £150,000. The claimant may be in trouble. The defendant will ask the judge to consider overriding principles of Part 1 'Was it proportional to incur the further costs of trial to secure an additional £1,000?'. Part 44.3 confirms the general rule that the loser pays but allows the court to make a different order to take into account offers to settle, payment into court, the parties' conduct including pre-action conduct and exaggeration of the claim [(1999) 149 NLJ 458].

Active case management imposes a duty on the courts to help parties settle their disputes. A 'stay' is a temporary halt in proceedings, and an opportunity for the court to order such a pause. Either party to a case can also make a written request for a stay when filing their completed allocation questionnaire. Where all the parties indicate that they have agreed on a stay to attempt to settle the case, provided the court agrees, they can have an initial period of one month to try to settle the case. If the court grants a stay, the claimant must inform the court if a settlement is reached, otherwise at the expiry of the stay it will effectively be deemed that a settlement has not been reached and the file will be referred to the judge for directions as considered appropriate.

The court will always give the final decision about whether to grant the parties more time to use a mediator or arbitrator or expert to settle, even if the parties are agreed they wish to have more time. A stay will never be granted for an indefinite period.

5.4.4 APPLICATIONS TO BE MADE WHEN CLAIMS COME BEFORE A JUDGE (CPR PART 1)

The overriding objective in Part 1 requires the court to deal with as many aspects of the case as possible on the same occasion. The filing of an allocation questionnaire, which is to enable the court to judge in which track the case should be heard, is one such occasion. Parties should, wherever possible, issue any application they may wish to make, such as an application for summary judgment (CPR Part 24), or to add a third party (CPR Part 20), at the same time as they file their questionnaire. Any hearing set to deal with the application will also serve as an allocation hearing if allocation remains appropriate.

5.4.5 WITNESS STATEMENTS (CPR PART 32)

In the *Final Report on Access to Justice*, Lord Woolf recognised the importance of witness statements in cases, but observed that they had become problematic because lawyers had made them excessively long and detailed in order to protect against leaving out something that later proved to be relevant. He said 'witness statements have ceased to be the authentic account of the lay witness; instead they have become an elaborate, costly branch of legal drafting' (para 55).

Witness statements must contain the evidence that the witness will give at trial. They should be drafted in lay language and should not discuss legal propositions. Witnesses will be allowed to amplify on the statement or deal with matters that have arisen since the report was served, although this is not an automatic right and a 'good reason' for the admission of new evidence will have to be established.

5.4.6 EXPERTS (CPR PART 35)

The rules place a clear duty on the court to ensure that 'expert evidence is restricted to that which is reasonably required to resolve the proceedings'. That is to say that expert evidence will only be allowed either by way of written report, or orally, where the court gives permission. Equally important is the rules' statement about experts' duties. Rule 35.3 states that it is the clear duty of experts to help the *court* on matters within their expertise, bearing in mind that this duty overrides any obligation to the person from whom they have received instructions or by whom they are paid.

There is greater emphasis on using the opinion of a single expert. Experts are only to be called to give oral evidence at a trial or hearing if the court gives permission.

Experts' written reports must contain a statement that they understand and have complied with, and will continue to comply with, their duty to the court. Instructions to experts are no longer privileged and their substance, whether written or oral, must be set out in the expert's report. Thus, either side can insist, through the court, on seeing how the other side phrased its request to an expert.

5.5   COURT AND TRACK ALLOCATION (CPR PART 26)

Part 7 of the CPR sets out the rules for starting proceedings. A new restriction is placed on which cases may be begun in the High Court. The county courts retain an almost unlimited jurisdiction for handling contract and tort claims (that is, negligence cases, nuisance cases but excluding a claim for damages or other remedy for libel or slander unless the parties agree otherwise). Issuing proceedings in the High Court is now limited to:

- personal injury claims with a value of £50,000 or more; other claims with a value of more than £100,000;
- claims where an Act of Parliament requires proceedings to start in the High Court;
- specialist High Court claims which need to go to one of the specialist 'lists', like the Commercial List, the Technology and Construction List; or
- equity claims where the property is worth at least £350,000.

The new civil system works on the basis that the court, upon receipt of the defence, requires the parties to complete 'allocation questionnaires' (giving all the relevant details of the claim, including how much it is for and an indication of its factual and legal complexity). Under Part 26 of the CPR, the case will then be allocated to one of three tracks for a hearing. These are: (a) small claims track; (b) fast track; and (c) multi-track. Each of the tracks offers a different degree of case management. The multi-track has, since 6 April 2009, a minimum limit of £25,000.01.

The small claims limit is £10,000, although personal injury and housing disrepair claims for over £1,000, illegal eviction and harassment claims will be excluded from the small claims procedure. The limit for cases going into the fast track system is £25,000. Applications to move cases 'up' a track on grounds of complexity will have to be made on the allocation questionnaire (see below). All small claims up to £5,000 will now be dealt with by mediation.

Directions (instructions about what to do to prepare the case for trial or hearing) will be proportionate to the value of the claim, its importance, complexity and so on. Each track requires a different degree of case monitoring, that is, the more complex the claim, the more milestone events there are likely to be (that is, important points in the process, like the date by which the allocation questionnaire should be returned). Time for carrying out directions, no matter which track, may be extended or shortened by agreement between parties, but must not, as a result, affect any of the milestones relevant to that track. The time for carrying out directions will be expressed as calendar dates rather than periods of days or weeks. Directions will include the court's directions concerning the use of expert evidence.

There is no longer any 'automatic reference' to the small claims track. Claims are allocated to this track in exactly the same way as to the fast track or multi-track. The concept of an *'arbitration'* therefore disappears and is replaced by a *small claims hearing*. Aspects of the old small claims procedure that are retained include their informality, the interventionist approach adopted by the judiciary, the limited costs regime and the limited grounds for appeal (misconduct of the district judge or an error of law made by the court).

Key features of the small claims are:

- *jurisdiction of claims limited to no more than £10,000* (with the exception of claims for personal injury where the damages claimed for pain and suffering and loss of amenity do not exceed £1,000 and the financial value of the whole claim does not exceed £10,000; and for housing disrepair where the claim for repairs and other work does not exceed £1,000 and the financial value of any other claim for damages is not more than £1,000);

- *all small claims up to £5,000 to be dealt with by mediation*;

- *hearings to be generally public hearings* – but subject to some exceptions (CPR Part 39);

- *paper adjudication, if parties consent* – where a judge thinks that paper adjudication may be appropriate, parties will be asked to say whether or not they have any objections within a given time period. If a party does object, the matter will be given a hearing in the normal way;

- *parties need not attend the final hearing* – a party not wishing to attend the final hearing will be able to give the court written notice before the hearing that they will not be attending. The notice must be filed with the court seven days before the start of the hearing. This will guarantee that the court will take into account any written evidence that the party has sent to the court. A consequence of this is that the judge must give reasons for the decision reached which will be included in the judgment;

- *use of experts* – expert witnesses will only be allowed to give evidence with the permission of the court;

- *costs* – these are not generally awarded, but a small award may be made to cover costs in issuing the claim, court fees, for legal advice and assistance relating to proceedings which included a claim for an injunction or an order for specific performance, the costs assessed by summary procedure in relation to an appeal and expenses incurred by the successful party, witnesses and experts. Under r 44.14 of the CPR, additional costs may be awarded against any party who has behaved unreasonably;

- *preliminary hearings* – these may be called:

  (a) where the judge considers that special directions are needed to ensure a fair hearing and where it appears necessary that a party should attend court so that it can be ensured that the party understands what he is required to do to comply with the special directions;

(b)   to enable the judge to dispose of the claim where he is of the view that either of the parties has no real prospect of success at a full hearing;

(c)   to enable the judge to strike out either the whole or part of a statement of case on the basis that it provides no reasonable grounds for bringing such a claim.

- *the introduction of tailored directions* – to be given for some of the most common small claims, for example, spoiled holidays or wedding videos, road traffic accidents, building disputes.

Parties can consent to use the small claims track even if the value of their claim exceeds the normal value for that track, but subject to the court's approval. The limited cost regime will not apply to these claims, but trial costs are at the discretion of the court and will be limited to the costs that might have been awarded if the claim had been dealt with in the fast track. Generally, the parties will be restricted to a maximum one-day hearing.

The milestone events for the small claims track are the date for the return of the allocation questionnaire and the date of the hearing.

5.5.2 THE FAST TRACK (CPR PART 28)

The fast track provides a streamlined procedure for the handling of cases not suitable for small claims track and where the value of the claim does not exceed £25,000. It is appropriate where:

> the trial is likely to last for no longer than one day; and oral expert evidence at trial will be limited to –
>
> (i)   one expert per party in relation to any expert field; and
> (ii)   expert evidence in two expert fields.

The procedures will ensure that the costs remain proportionate to the amount in dispute. The features of the procedure which aim to achieve this are:

- standard directions for trial preparation which avoid complex procedures and multiple experts, with minimum case management intervention by the court;

- a standard limited period between directions and the start of the trial, it will not be more than 30 weeks;

- a maximum of one day (five hours) for trial;

- trial period must not exceed three weeks and parties must be given 21 days' notice of the date fixed for trial unless in exceptional circumstances the court directs shorter notice;

- normally, no oral expert evidence is to be given at trial, but where allowed, will be limited to one expert per party in any expert field and expert evidence in two expert fields; and
- costs allowed for the trial are fixed depending on the level of advocacy.

Directions given to the parties by the judge will normally include a date by which parties must file a listing questionnaire. As with allocation questionnaires, the procedural judge may impose a sanction where a listing questionnaire is not returned by the due date. Listing questionnaires will include information about witnesses, confirm the time needed for trial, parties' availability and the level of advocate for the trial.

The milestone events for the fast track are *the date for the return of allocation* and *listing questionnaires* and *the date for the start of the trial or trial period.*

5.5.3 THE MULTI-TRACK (CPR PART 29)

The multi-track is intended to provide a flexible regime for the handling of claims over £25,000 or lower, more complex claims if not appropriate for the fast track.

This track does not provide any standard procedure, such as those for small claims or claims in the fast track. Instead, it offers a range of case management tools – *standard directions, case management conferences* and *pre-trial reviews* – which can be used in a 'mix and match' way to suit the needs of individual cases. Whichever of these is used to manage the case, the principle of setting a date for trial, or a trial period at the earliest possible time, no matter that it is some way away, will remain paramount.

Where a trial period is given for a multi-track case, this will be one week. Parties will be told initially that their trial will begin on a day within the given week. The rules and practice direction do not set any time period for giving notice to the parties of the date fixed for trial.

5.6 DOCUMENTATION AND PROCEDURES

One of the main aims of the Woolf reforms is to simplify court forms. Under the old system, there were various forms that needed to be completed at the outset of a claim – different types including summonses, originating applications, writs and petitions. Under the new system, most claims will be begun by using a 'Part 7' claim form.

5.6.1 HOW TO START PROCEEDINGS – THE CLAIM FORM (CPR PART 7)

A Part 7 claim form has been designed for multipurpose use. It can be used if the claim is for a *specified* amount of money (the old term was *liquidated* damages) or an *unspecified* amount (replacing the term *unliquidated* damages). The form can also be used for non-monetary claims, for example, where the claimant just wants a court order, not money. The person issuing the claim form is called a claimant (plaintiff in old vocabulary) and the person at whom it is directed will continue to be known as a defendant.

Under the new rules, the court can grant any remedy to which the claimant is entitled, even if the claimant does not specify which one he wants. It is, though, as Gordon Exall has observed ((1999) SJ 162, 19 February), dangerous to start a claim without having a clear idea of the remedy you want. The defendant might be able to persuade the court not to allow the claimant a certain part of his costs if he (the defendant) finds himself having to consider a remedy that had not been mentioned prior to the trial.

In the longer term, it seems clear that a plain set of language forms designed all at one time as a part of one coherent system will provide a more efficient system than that afforded by a collection of outdated forms which have been generated reactively over a long period. The most important change to come out of the twenty-first CPR update was the new allocation questionnaire. All the questions were revised in the light of experience since April 1999.

5.6.2   ALTERNATIVE PROCEDURE FOR CLAIMS (CPR PART 8)

Part 8 of the rules introduced the *alternative procedure for claims*. This procedure is commenced by the issue of a Part 8 claim form. It is intended to provide a speedy resolution of claims that are not likely to involve a substantial dispute of fact, for example, applications for approval of infant settlements, or for orders enforcing a statutory right such as a right to have access to medical records (under the Access to Health Records Act 1990). The Part 8 procedure is also used where a rule or practice direction requires or permits its use.

The main differences between this and the Part 7 procedure are as follows:

- a hearing may be given on issue or at some later stage if required;
- only an acknowledgment of service is served with the claim form by way of a response document;
- a defendant must file an acknowledgment of service to be able to take part in any hearing;
- a defendant must serve a copy of the acknowledgment on the other parties, as well as filing it with the court;
- no defence is required;
- default judgment is not available to the claimant; the court must hear the case;
- there are automatic directions for the exchange of evidence (in this case, in the form of witness statements);
- Part 8 claims are not formally allocated to a track; they are automatically multi-track cases.

The 'value' of a claim is the amount a claimant reasonably expects to recover. Unless the amount being claimed is a specified amount, a claimant will be expected (Part 16) to state the value band into which the claim is likely to fall. The value bands reflect the values for the different tracks (for example, £1 to £10,000 for small claims). Value is calculated as the amount a claimant expects to recover, ignoring any interest, costs, contributory negligence, or the fact that a defendant may make a counterclaim or include a set-off in the defence. If a claimant is not able to put a value on the claim, the reasons for this must be given.

Particulars of claim may be included in the claim form, attached to it, or may be served (that is, given or sent to a party by a method allowed by the rules) separately from it. Where they are served separately, they must be served within 14 days of the claim form being served. The time for a defendant to respond begins to run from the time the particulars of claim are served.

Part 16 is entitled *Statements of case* (replacing the term *pleadings*). Statements of case include documents from both sides: claim forms, particulars of claims, defences, counterclaims, replies to defences and counterclaims, Part 20 (third party) claims and any *further information* provided under CPR Part 18 (replacing the term *further and better particulars*). Part 16 also sets out what both particulars of claim and defences should contain.

Part 16 states:

(1)   The claim form must –

    (a)   contain a concise statement of the nature of the claim;

    (b)   specify the remedy which the claimant seeks;

    (c)   where the claimant is making a claim for money, contain a statement of value in accordance with rule 16.3;

    (cc)   where the claimant's only claim is for a specified sum, contain a statement of the interest accrued on that sum; and

    (d)   contain such other matters as may be set out in a practice direction.

The Woolf Report was against obliging the claimant to state the legal nature of the claim as this would prejudice unrepresented defendants. If the nature of the claim is uncertain, then the court can take its own steps to clarify the matter.

Where a claimant is going to rely on the fact that the defendant has been convicted for a crime arising out of the same circumstances for which the claimant is now suing, then the particulars of claim must contain details of the conviction, the court which made it, and exactly how it is relevant to the claimant's arguments.

It is optional for the claimant also to mention any point of law on which the claim is based and the names of any witnesses which he proposes to call. All statements of case must also contain a statement of truth.

5.6.5   STATEMENTS OF TRUTH (CPR PART 22)

A statement of truth is a statement that a party believes that the facts or allegations set out in a document, which they put forward, are true. It is required in statements of case, witness statements and expert reports. Any document that contains a statement of truth may be used in evidence. This will avoid the previous need to swear affidavits in support of various statements made as part of the claim.

Any document with a signed statement of truth that contains false information given deliberately, that is, without an honest belief in its truth, will constitute a contempt of court (a punishable criminal offence) by the person who provided the information. Solicitors may sign statements of truth on behalf of clients, but on the understanding that it is done with the clients' authority, and with clients knowing that the consequences of any false statement will be personal to them.

5.6.6   RESPONSE TO PARTICULARS OF CLAIM (CPR PART 9)

When a claim form is served, it will be served with a response pack. The response pack will contain an acknowledgment of service, a form of admission and a form of defence and counterclaim. The response pack will be served with a claim form containing the particulars of claim, which are attached to it or, where particulars of claim are served after the claim form, with the particulars. A defendant must respond within 14 days of service of the particulars of claim. If a defendant ignores the claim, the claimant may obtain judgment for the defendant to pay the amount claimed. A defendant may:

- pay the claim;
- admit the claim, or partly admit it;
- file an acknowledgment of service; or
- file a defence.

Requirements have also been introduced regarding the content of a defence. A defence that is a simple denial is no longer acceptable and runs the risk of being struck out by the court (that is, deleted so that it may no longer be relied upon). A defendant must state in any defence:

- which of the allegations in the particulars of claim are denied, giving reasons for doing so and must state his own version of the events if he intends to put forward a different version to that of the claimant;

- which allegations the defendant is not able to admit or deny but which the claimant is required to prove;

- which allegations are admitted; and

- if the defendant disputes the claimant's statement of value, the reasons for doing so and, if possible, stating an alternate value.

These rules mark a significant change of culture from the old civil procedure rules. Under the old rules, a defendant could, in his defence, raise a 'non-admission' or a 'denial'. The first meant that the defendant was putting the plaintiff (now claimant) to proof, that is, challenging him to prove his case on the balance of probabilities. The second meant that the defendant was raising a specific defence, for example, a 'development risks defence' under the Product Liability Act 1988. Defendants were allowed under the old rules to keep as many avenues of defence available for as long as possible. Under the new rules, the defendant must respond according to the choices in the four options above. According to r 16.5(5), if the defendant does not deal specifically with an allegation, then it will be deemed to be admitted. However, where a defendant does not specifically deal with an allegation, but in any event sets out in his defence the nature of his case on that issue, it will be deemed that the matter be proved.

5.6.7 SERVICE (CPR PART 6)

Where the court is to serve any document (not just claim forms), it is for the court to decide the method of service. This will generally be by first-class post. The deemed date of service is two days after the day of posting for all defendants, including limited companies. Where a claim form originally served by post is returned by the Post Office, the court will send a notice of non-service to the claimant stating the method of service attempted. The notice will tell the claimant that the court will not make any further attempts at service. Service therefore becomes a matter for claimants. The court will return the copies of the claim form, response pack and so on, for claimants to amend as necessary and re-serve.

Claimants may serve claim forms, having told the court in writing that they wish to do so, either personally, by post, by fax, by document exchange (a private courier service operated between law firms) or by email or other electronic means. A claimant who serves the claim form must file a certificate of service within seven days of service with a copy of the document served attached.

5.6.8 ADMISSIONS AND PART ADMISSIONS (CPR PART 14)

The possibility of admitting liability for a claim for a specific amount and making an offer to pay by instalments, or at a later date, applies to both county court and High

Court cases. Where the claim is for a specific amount, the admission will be sent direct to the claimant. However, if a claimant objects to the rate of payment offered, there are changes that affect the determination process, that is, the process by which a member of a court's staff or a judge decides the rate of payment.

Cases involving a specific amount where the balance outstanding, including any costs, is less than £50,000, will be determined by a court officer. Those where the balance is £50,000 or more, or for an unspecified amount of any value, must be determined by a Master or district judge. The Master or judge has the option of dealing with the determination on the papers without a hearing or at a hearing.

A defendant in a claim for an unspecified amount of money (damages) will be able to make an offer of a specific sum of money in satisfaction of a claim, which does not have to be supported by a payment into court. A claimant can accept the admission and rate of payment offered as if the claim had originally been for a specific amount. The determination procedure described above will apply where a claimant accepts the amount offered, but not the rate of payment proposed.

If a claimant does not accept the amount offered, a request that judgment be entered for liability on the strength of the defendant's admission may be made to the court. This is referred to as *judgment for an amount and costs to be decided by the court* (replacing *interlocutory judgment for damages to be assessed*). Where judgment is entered in this way, the court will, at the same time, give case management directions for dealing with the case.

Where a request for such a judgment is received, the court file will be passed to a procedural judge. The judge may allocate the case to the small claims track and give directions if it is of appropriate value; ask that the case be set down for a *disposal* hearing; or where the amount is likely to be heavily disputed, order a trial. Directions will be given as appropriate. A disposal hearing in these circumstances may either be a hearing at which the court gives directions, or at which the amount and costs are decided.

5.6.9   DEFENCE AND AUTOMATIC TRANSFER (CPR PART 26)

Claims for specified amounts will be transferred automatically to the defendant's 'home court' where the defendant is an individual who has filed a defence. The defendant's home court will be the court or district registry, including the Royal Courts of Justice, for the district in which the defendant's address for service as shown on the defence is situated. This means that, where a solicitor represents the defendant, this will be the defendant's solicitor's business address.

Where there is more than one defendant, it is the first defendant to file a defence who dictates whether or not automatic transfer will take place. For example, if there were two defendants to a claim, one an individual and one a limited company, there would be no automatic transfer if the limited company was the first defendant to file a defence.

5.6.10   ALLOCATION QUESTIONNAIRE (FORM N150)

The purpose of this document is to enable the judge to allocate in which track the case should be heard. When a defence is filed, the issuing court will send out a copy of the defence to all other parties to the claim, together with an allocation questionnaire, a notice setting out the date for returning it, and the name and address of the court (or district registry or the Royal Courts of Justice (that is, High Court), as appropriate) to which the completed allocation questionnaire must be returned. A notice of transfer will also be sent if the case is being automatically transferred.

The allocation questionnaire will not be served on the parties when a defendant files a defence if r 14.5 or r 15.10 applies or if the court decides to dispense with its service.

When all the parties have filed their allocation questionnaire, or at the end of the period for returning it, whichever is the sooner (providing the questionnaires have not been dispensed with or the case stayed under r 26.4), the court will allocate the claim to a track. If there is sufficient information, the judge will allocate the case to a track and a notice of allocation and directions will be sent out to each party. Where the judge has insufficient information, an order may be made for a party to provide further information. In particularly complex cases, for those allocated to the multi-track, the judge may first list the matter for a case management conference to formulate directions.

Where only one party has filed a questionnaire the judge may allocate the claim to a track, providing he has enough information, or will order that an allocation hearing be listed and that all parties must attend. Where none of the parties has filed a questionnaire, the file will be returned to the judge who will usually decide to impose a sanction by ordering that the claim and any counterclaim be struck out unless a completed questionnaire is filed within three days from service of the order.

The questionnaire asks a number of questions, for example:

- Do you wish there to be a one-month stay to attempt to settle this case?
- Which track do you consider most suitable for your case (small claims, fast track or multi-track)? A party wishing a case to be dealt with on a track that is not the obviously suitable track must give reasons.
- At this stage, you are asked whether you have complied with any relevant protocols, and if not, why not and the extent of the non-compliance.
- You are asked for an estimate of costs to date and the overall costs up to trial.
- You are asked if you wish to use expert evidence at the trial, whether expert reports have been copied to the other side, who the expert is and, if the parties have not agreed upon a common expert, why not.

The purpose of this questionnaire is to make both sides have a clear overview of the case at an early stage, so it becomes very difficult for lawyers to bumble along buffeted by developments in a case. To reduce delays and therefore costs, it is desirable that a lawyer should be able to purposefully stride through a case along a planned route.

5.6.11 DEFAULT JUDGMENT (CPR PART 12)

If a defendant (to a Part 7 claim) files an acknowledgment stating an intention to defend the claim, this extends the period for filing a defence from 14 to 28 days from the date of service of the particulars. Failure to file an acknowledgment with the court or, later, failure to file a defence can result in 'default judgment'. That means the court will, without a trial, find in favour of the claimant, so the defendant will lose the case.

If the defendant does not to reply to the claim, a claimant may apply for default judgment for the amount claimed if the amount claimed is a specified amount, or on liability if the amount claimed is unspecified, after the 14-day period from service has elapsed.

There are a number of cases in which it is not possible to obtain judgment in default, notably in claims for delivery of goods subject to an agreement controlled by the Consumer Credit Act 1974.

5.6.12 SUMMARY JUDGMENT (CPR PART 24)

Summary judgment is available to both claimants and defendants. Where either party feels that the other does not have a valid claim or defence, they can apply to the court for the claim or defence to be struck out and for judgment to be entered in their favour. The applicant, either claimant or defendant, must prove to the court's satisfaction that the other party has no real prospect of success and that there is no other compelling reason why the case or issue should be dealt with at trial.

Application for summary judgment cannot be made without the court's permission (replacing the term 'leave') or where a practice direction provides otherwise, before an acknowledgment of service or defence has been filed. Where the claimant makes an application before a defendant files a defence, the defendant against whom it is made need not file a defence. If a claimant's application is unsuccessful, the court will give directions for the filing of a defence.

5.7 PUBLIC AND PRIVATE HEARINGS (CPR PART 39)

Under the rules, the distinction between 'public' and 'private' hearings is not whether a claim or application is heard in a courtroom or the *judge's room* (formerly called *chambers*), but whether members of the public are allowed to sit in on the hearing wherever it takes place.

Courts are not required to make any special arrangements to accommodate members of the public, for example, if the judge's room is too small to accommodate more than those directly concerned with the claim. However, where a hearing is 'public', anyone may obtain a copy of the order made upon payment of the appropriate fee.

Rule 39.2 states that:

(1)   The general rule is that a hearing is to be in public.
(2)   The requirement for a hearing to be in public does not require the court to make special arrangements for accommodating members of the public.

(3)   A hearing, or any part of it, may be in private if –

(a)   publicity would defeat the object of the hearing;

(b)   it involves matters relating to national security;

(c)   it involves confidential information (including information relating to personal financial matters) and publicity would damage that confidentiality;

(d)   a private hearing is necessary to protect the interests of any child or protected party;

(e)   it is a hearing of an application made without notice and it would be unjust to any respondent for there to be a public hearing;

(f)   it involves uncontentious matters arising in the administration of trusts or in the administration of a deceased person's estate; or

(g)   the court considers this to be necessary, in the interests of justice.

5.8 APPEALS (CPR PART 52)

The appeal system is covered in Chapter 4 above.

There is generally no automatic right to appeal under the CPR, except as provided for in r 52.3 or statute. The exceptions include situations where the appeal is against –

(i)   a committal order;

(ii)   a refusal to grant *habeas corpus*; or

(iii)   a secure accommodation order.

Generally, parties need permission to appeal and this will be granted only where:

(a)   the court considers that the appeal would have a real prospect of success; or

(b)   where there is some other compelling reason why the appeal should be heard.

Permission to appeal will usually be made to the lower court at the hearing against which it is to be appealed. Alternatively, an appeal can be made to the appeal court in an appeal notice usually within 14 days after the date of the decision to be appealed unless directed otherwise by the lower court.

The important procedural points and the routes to appeal will vary depending on whether the matter involves a final decision.

Generally, an appeal will lie to the next court above. From a district judge of the county court, appeal lies to a circuit judge; from a Master or district judge of the High Court, or a circuit judge, appeal lies to a High Court judge; and from a High Court judge, appeal lies to the Court of Appeal. In almost all cases, permission is needed in order to appeal.

Paragraph 2A.1 of the Practice Direction to Part 52 provides:

Where the decision to be appealed is a final decision –

1   in a Part 7 claim allocated to the multi-track; or
2   made in specialist proceedings (under the Companies Act 1985 or 1989 or to which sections I, II, or III of Part 57 or any of Parts 58 to 63 apply)

the appeal is to be made to the Court of Appeal (subject to obtaining any necessary permission).

A final decision 'is a decision of a court that would finally determine (subject to any possible appeal or detailed assessment of costs) the entire proceedings whichever way the court decides the issues before it'. A decision will not be deemed a final decision where an order is made on a summary or detailed assessment of costs or on an application to enforce a final decision. In these circumstances the appeal will follow the general appeal route.

If a decision of a circuit judge is in relation to fast-track claims, claims on the multitrack except for final decisions, and Part 8 claims including final decisions but excluding final decisions in specialist proceedings, appeal lies to the High Court. However, a Part 8 claim that is a final decision and is treated as allocated to the multi-track may be sent direct to the Court of Appeal if the court considers appropriate.

Under CPR 52.14 a lower court may order the appeal to be sent directly to the Court of Appeal, where it considers that the appeal would raise an important point of principle or practice or there is some other compelling reason for the Court of Appeal to hear it.

Generally an appeal will be limited to a review of the decision of the lower court unless a practice direction provides otherwise or the court considers that in the circumstances of the particular appeal it would be in the interests of justice to order a re-hearing. The appeal court will not hear any oral evidence or new evidence unless it orders otherwise. An appeal will be allowed where the decision in the lower court was wrong, or unjust due to a serious procedural or other irregularity in the lower court's proceedings.

When the court deals with appeals it must have regard to the overriding objective in CPR 1.1. Consequently, the appeal court is only likely to deal with appeals where they are founded on an error of law, against a finding of fact, in respect of the exercise of a discretion, involving new evidence or a change of circumstances or where a serious procedural or other irregularity arises causing injustice.

Appeals from the Court of Appeal lie to the Supreme Court, but the appellant must be granted leave either by the Court of Appeal or by the Supreme Court. The application for leave must first be made to the Court of Appeal, and then if refused, by petition for leave to appeal, which will be heard by the Supreme Court sitting in public. Only cases involving points of public importance reach the Supreme Court and there are usually fewer than 50 civil appeals heard by the Supreme Court each year. It is possible, under the Administration of Justice Act 1969, for the Supreme Court to hear an appeal direct from the High Court, 'leapfrogging' the Court of Appeal. The agreement of both parties and the High Court judge is required. Such cases must concern a point of statutory interpretation (including the construction of a statutory instrument), which has been fully explored by the High Court judge, or concern a point that he was bound by precedent to follow.

5.9 REMEDIES

The preceding sections of this chapter have examined the institutional and procedural framework within which individuals pursue civil claims. What it has not addressed is the question why people pursue such claims. Taking a claim to court can be expensive, time-consuming and very stressful, but people accept these costs, both financial and personal, because they have a grievance that they require to be settled. In other words, they are seeking a remedy for some wrong they have suffered, or at least that they believe they have suffered. In practice, it is the actual remedy available that the litigant focuses on, rather than the finer points of law or procedure involved in attaining that remedy; those are matters for the legal professionals. It is appropriate, therefore, to offer a brief explanation of remedies, although students of the law will engage with the details of remedies in the substantive legal subjects, such as contract and tort. As will be seen, it is essential to distinguish between the common law remedy of damages, available as of right, and equitable remedies, which are awarded at the discretion of the court (see above, at 1.3.2).

5.10 DAMAGES

As has been said, the whole point of damages is compensatory: to recompense someone for the wrong they have suffered. There are, however, different ways in which someone can be compensated. For example, in contract law, the object of awarding damages is to put the wronged person in the situation they would have been in had the contract been completed as agreed; that is, it places them in the position they would have been after the event. In tort, however, the object is to compensate the wronged person, to the extent that a monetary award can do so, for injury sustained; that is, to return them to the situation they were in before the event.

5.10.1   TYPES OF DAMAGES

(a)   *Compensatory damages*: these are the standard awards considered above, intended to achieve no more than to recompense the injured party to the extent of the injury suffered. Damages in contract can only be compensatory.

(b)   *Aggravated damages*: these are compensatory in nature, but are additional to ordinary compensatory awards and are awarded in relation to damage suffered to the injured party's dignity and pride. They are, therefore, akin to damages being paid in relation to mental distress. In *Khodaparast v Shad* (2000), the claimant was awarded aggravated damages after the defendant had been found liable for the malicious falsehood of distributing fake pictures of her in a state of undress, which resulted in her losing her job.

(c)   *Exemplary damages*: these are awarded in tort in addition to compensatory damages. They may be awarded where the person who committed the tort intended to make a profit from their tortious action. The most obvious area in which such awards might be made is in libel cases, where the publisher issues the libel to increase sales. Libel awards are considered in more detail at 11.6.1 below, but an example of exemplary awards can be seen in the award of £50,000 (originally £275,000) to Elton John as a result of his action against *The Mirror* newspaper (*John v MGN Ltd* (1996)).

(d)   *Nominal damages*: these are awarded in the few cases which really do involve 'a matter of principle', but where no loss or injury to reputation is involved. There is no sct figure in relation to nominal damages; it is merely a very small amount.

(e)   *Contemptuous damages*: these are extremely small awards made where the claimant wins their case, but has suffered no loss and has failed to impress the court with the standard of their own behaviour or character. In *Reynolds v Times Newspaper Ltd* (1999), the former Prime Minister of Ireland was awarded one penny in his libel action against *The Times* newspaper; this award was actually made by the judge after the jury had awarded Reynolds no damages at all. Such an award can be considered nothing if not contemptuous.

5.10.2   DAMAGES IN CONTRACT

The estimation of what damages are to be paid by a party in breach of contract can be divided into two parts: remoteness and measure.

Remoteness of Damage

What kind of damage can the innocent party claim? This involves a consideration of causation, and the remoteness of cause from effect, in order to determine how far down a chain of events a defendant is liable. The rule in *Hadley v Baxendale* (1854) states that damages will only be awarded in respect of losses that arise naturally, that is, in the natural course of things, or which both parties may reasonably be supposed to have contemplated, when the contract was made, as a probable result of its breach.

The effect of the first part of the rule in *Hadley v Baxendale* is that the party in breach is deemed to expect the normal consequences of the breach, whether they actually expected them or not.

Under the second part of the rule, however, the party in breach can only be held liable for abnormal consequences where they have actual knowledge that the abnormal consequences might follow. In *Victoria Laundry Ltd v Newham Industries Ltd* (1949), the defendants contracted to deliver a new boiler to the plaintiffs, but delayed in delivery. The plaintiffs claimed for normal loss of profit during the period of delay, and also for the loss of abnormal profits from a highly lucrative contract, which they could have undertaken had the boiler been delivered on time. In this case, it was decided that damages could be recovered in regard to the normal profits, as that loss was a natural consequence of the delay. The second claim failed, however, on the grounds that the loss was not a normal one, but was a consequence of an especially lucrative contract, about which the defendant knew nothing.

As a result of the test for remoteness, a party may be liable for consequences which, although within the reasonable contemplation of the parties, are much more serious in effect than would be expected.

In *H Parsons (Livestock) Ltd v Uttley Ingham and Co* (1978), the plaintiffs, who were pig farmers, bought a large food hopper from the defendants. While erecting it, the defendants failed to unseal a ventilator on the top of the hopper. Because of lack of ventilation, the pig food stored in the hopper became mouldy. The pigs that ate the mouldy food contracted a rare intestinal disease and died. It was held that the defendants were liable for the loss of the pigs. The food affected by bad storage caused the illness as a natural consequence of the breach, and the death from such illness was not too remote.

Measure of Damages

Damages in contract are intended to compensate an injured party for any financial loss sustained as a consequence of another party's breach. The object is not to punish the party in breach, so the amount of damages awarded can never be greater than the actual loss suffered. The aim is to put the injured party in the same position they would have been in had the contract been properly performed. Where the breach relates to a contract for the sale of goods, damages are usually assessed in line with the market rule. This means that, if goods are not delivered under a contract, the buyer is entitled to go into the market and buy similar goods, and pay the market price prevailing at the time. They can then claim the difference in price between what they paid and the original contract price as damages. Conversely, if a buyer refuses to accept goods under a contract, the seller can sell the goods in the market and accept the prevailing market price. Any difference between the price they receive and the contract price can be claimed in damages.

Non-Pecuniary Loss

At one time, damages could not be recovered where the loss sustained through breach of contract was of a non-financial nature. The modern position is that such non-pecuniary damages can be recovered. In *Jarvis v Swan Tours Ltd* (1973), the defendant's brochure stated that various facilities were available at a particular ski resort. The facilities available were in fact much inferior to those advertised. The plaintiff sued for breach of contract. The court decided that Jarvis was entitled to recover not just the financial loss he suffered, which was not substantial, but also for loss of entertainment and enjoyment. The Court of Appeal stated that damages could be recovered for mental distress in appropriate cases, and this was one of them.

5.10.3   DAMAGES IN TORT

Remoteness of Damage

Even where causation is established, the defendant will not necessarily be liable for all of the damage resulting from the breach. The question to be asked in determining the extent of liability is whether the damage is of such a kind as the reasonable person should have foreseen, but this does not mean that the defendant should have foreseen precisely the sequence or nature of the events. The test for remoteness of damage in tort was set out in *The Wagon Mound (No 1)* (1961). The defendants negligently allowed furnace oil to spill from a ship into Sydney Harbour. The oil spread and came to lie beneath a wharf owned by the plaintiffs. The plaintiffs had been carrying out welding operations and, on seeing the oil, they stopped welding in order to find out whether it was safe to continue. They were assured that the oil would not catch fire and resumed welding. However, cotton waste that had fallen into the oil caught fire, which in turn ignited the oil, and the resultant fire spread to the plaintiff's wharf. It was held that the defendants were liable in tort, as they had breached their duty of care. However, they were only held liable for the damage caused to the wharf and slipway through the fouling of the oil. They were not liable for the damage caused by fire because that damage was unforeseeable due to the high ignition point of the oil.

Economic Loss

There are two categories of economic loss that may form the basis of a claim in negligence. First, there is economic loss arising out of physical injury or damage to property and, second, there is what is known as 'pure economic loss', which is unconnected with physical damage. Following recent developments, only the former is recoverable unless the claimant can show that there was 'a special relationship' between them and the defendant (*Williams v Natural Life Health Foods Ltd* (1998)).

5.11   EQUITABLE REMEDIES

Equitable remedies are not available as of right and are only awarded at the discretion of the court. They will not be granted where the claimant has not acted properly. There are a number of maxims that relate to the awarding of equitable remedies. Thus, for example, it is frequently stated that '*He who comes to equity must come with clean hands*', which simply means that persons looking for the remedy must have behaved properly themselves (*D & C Builders v Rees* (1966)). The actual remedies are as follows.

Specific Performance

It will sometimes suit a party to break their contractual obligations and pay damages; however, through an order for specific performance, the party in breach may be instructed to complete their part of the contract. An order of specific performance will only be granted in cases where the common law remedy of damages is inadequate, and providing the matter does not fall into a category where the courts will not order specific performance. It is not usually applied to contracts concerning the sale of goods where replacements are readily available. It is most commonly granted in cases involving the sale of land, where the subject matter of the contract is unique.

Generally, specific performance will not be available in respect of contracts of employment or personal service. However, in light of *C H Giles & Co Ltd v Morris and others* (1972), it would appear that the courts may be prepared to depart from this principle in certain circumstances.

Specific performance will not be granted if the court has to constantly supervise its enforcement. In *Ryan v Mutual Tontine Westminster Chambers Association* (1893), the landlords of a flat undertook to provide a porter, who was to be constantly in attendance to provide services such as cleaning the common passages and stairs, and delivering letters. The person appointed spent much of his time working as a chef at a nearby club. During his absence, his duties were performed by a cleaner or by various boys. The plaintiff sought to enforce the contractual undertaking. It was held that, although the landlords were in breach of their contract, the court would not award an order of specific performance.

The reason given was that to enforce the contract would require constant supervision by the court. In addition, it was held that damages were an adequate remedy and hence the only available course of action. By comparison, in *Posner and others v Scott-Lewis and others* (1986) an order for specific performance was granted. In this case, the landlord had covenanted (so far as it was in his power) with the tenants to employ a resident porter to carry out certain specified tasks. The court held that the covenant was specifically enforceable as they could order the landlord to employ a resident porter within a specified time, as this would not require constant supervision by the court. If the landlord failed to adhere to the order the tenants could go back to the court and take appropriate action.

Injunction

This is the term used in relation to the courts' powers to order someone to either do something or, alternatively, to refrain from doing something. Injunctions are governed by s 37 of the Senior Courts Act 1981 and they may be granted on an interim or a permanent basis. Breach of an injunction is a contempt of court. Examples of specific injunctions are 'freezing orders', formerly known as Mareva injunctions, which are interim orders that prevent defendants from moving their assets out of the jurisdiction of the English courts before their case can be heard. Another well-known order is the search order, formerly known as an Anton Piller order, which prevents the concealment or disposal of documents that might be required in evidence at a later time. It can also authorise the searching of premises for such evidence.

In contrast, an injunction directs a person not to break their contract. It can have the effect of indirectly enforcing contracts for personal service. In *Warner Bros v Nelson* (1937), the defendant, the actress Bette Davis, had entered a contract that stipulated that she was to work exclusively for the plaintiffs for a period of one year. When she came to England, the plaintiffs applied for an injunction to prevent her from working for someone else. The court granted the order to Warner Bros. In doing so, the court rejected Nelson's argument that granting it would force her either to work for the plaintiffs or not to work at all. An injunction will only be granted to enforce negative covenants within the agreement, and cannot be used to enforce positive obligations (*Whitwood Chemical Co v Hardman* (1891)).

Rectification

This award allows for the alteration of contractual documents. It is generally assumed that written contractual documents accurately express the parties' terms, especially where the document has been signed. There are occasions, however, when the court will allow the written statement to be altered where it does not represent the true agreement (*Joscelyne v Nissen* (1970)).

Rescission

This action sets aside the terms of a contractual agreement and returns the parties to the situation they were in before the contract was entered into. The right to rescind a contract may be available as a result of fraud, misrepresentation of any type or the exercise of undue influence. The right can be lost, however, for a number of reasons, such as it being impossible to return the parties to their original position, affirmation, delay or the intervention of third-party rights.

5.12   COSTS (CPR PARTS 44–48)

Fixed Costs (CPR Part 45)

There are rates for the fixed costs allowed on issue of a claim and on entry of judgment where a party is represented by a solicitor.

The fee structure is designed so that fees become payable as the various stages of a claim are reached (a 'pay as you go' regime).

Courts are proactive in collecting fees, in particular those that are payable at allocation and listing stages, but *without interrupting* a case's progress. There are sanctions for non-payment of allocation and listing questionnaire fees, which could lead to a party's statement of case being struck out.

Assessment (CPR Part 47)

The terms *taxed* costs and *taxation* (which were previously used to denote that costs a lawyer was claiming had been approved by a senior officer of the court) are now redundant and have been replaced by assessment. Costs will either be assessed summarily, that is, there and then, or there will be a *detailed assessment* at some later stage where one party has been ordered to pay another's costs.

Summary Assessment

Judges will normally summarily assess costs at the end of hearings, both interim and final, and particularly at the end of fast track trials. Parties will be expected to bring any necessary documentation to the hearing for this purpose. In this way, the need for detailed assessment of costs is avoided so far as possible.

5.13   WHAT HAS THE NEW SYSTEM ACHIEVED?

The new CPR, the most fundamental changes in civil process for over 100 years, have radically altered the operation of civil justice. Since the new rules came into force (26 April 1999), they have been regularly reformed. The fifty-second update came into force in March 2010, the fifty-third in October 2010 and the fifty-eighth in April 2012.

Part of the rationale of the new rules was to expedite the way cases were dealt with and to allow more cases to be settled early through negotiation between the parties or ADR. In this respect, there was some early evidence of success. During the May to August period in 1999, there was a 25 per cent reduction in the number of cases issued in the county courts compared with the same period the previous year. By the end of January 2000, there was a further fall of 23 per cent. Mr Justice Burton of the QBD presented an interesting assessment of the new rules. Speaking at the City law firm, Kennedys, he outlined five benefits of the reforms, five problems, and what he referred to as 'one big question mark' ((2000) Law Soc Gazette, 10 February).

The five problems with the reforms were: the courts' inflexibility in not allowing parties to agree extensions of time between themselves; the danger of the judiciary pushing time guillotines onto parties; the risk that lawyers and clients could exploit 'standard' disclosure to conceal important documents; single joint experts possibly usurping the role of judges; and summary assessments of costs leading to judges making assumptions replacing detailed costs analysis. The benefits were listed as: pre-action protocols; emphasis on encouraging settlement; judicial intervention; Part 24 strike-out provisions; and Part 36 offers to settle.

Mr Justice Burton said there had been three options for reforming appeals:

1. to extend the present system in order to discourage more than one appeal;
2. to refuse appeals without leave; or
3. to abolish the present system, giving no right to re-hearings, only appeals.

He said he regretted that all three had been adopted (in the Access to Justice Act 1999). The consequence will be pressure on judges 'to get it right first time' and higher costs for parties.

It is now more than 15 years since the publication of Lord Woolf's 'Access to Justice report'. So have the reforms been a success? Reynolds Porter Chamberlain (RPC) a large city law firm analysed statistics from the Department of Constitutional Affairs, which showed that High Court commercial proceedings had more than halved since 1999. RPC found that in the first year of the reforms there was a 41.3 per cent drop in cases being litigated and over the following five years this had gradually declined to a drop of 1.7 per cent in 2005.

Edward Mann, a partner at RPC, commented that:

> the most important aim of Lord Woolf's report was to avoid litigation wherever possible, by making claimants consider the merits and costs of their case at an early stage and by encouraging them to settle out of court. Ten years on we can see that there has clearly been a decline in the number of civil court cases and that the reforms were undeniably successful in this respect if not others, notably the aim of reducing the complexity and cost of litigation has not been realised.

The issue of costs is a re-occurring theme that has been commented upon by many notable people in the legal world. Ted Greeno, a partner at Herbert Smith, believed that the Woolf reforms would result in higher costs for commercial cases. He is of the opinion that the rise in costs has nothing to do with the court's adversarial system but 'is a result of the introduction of pre-action protocols, case management and unnecessary bureaucracy, as well as unrealistic timetables and the unpredictable threat of costs sanctions which cause lawyers to practise "defensively".'

Lord Phillips has commented that the Woolf reforms 'have been effective in changing the whole ethos of litigation', but has criticised the reforms for not reducing costs. He said: 'there is still a problem with the cost of civil litigation – it is extremely expensive. Professional people – barristers and solicitors – are expensive. Although the Woolf reforms hoped to reduce costs, this hasn't happened. A sensible person would look in horror at the risks involved' ((2005) Law Soc Gazette, 13 October).

Sir Anthony Clarke has commented that 'unless you are an extremely rich individual, a corporation or an organ of the state, no one can afford to litigate'. He believes that 'the most important issue that the civil justice system needs to worry about is control over costs' ((2006) Law Soc Gazette, 21 April).

Clearly, there is concern over the high costs of litigation since the introduction of the Woolf reforms. This will need to be looked into in the not too distant future if the reforms are to continue to be an overall success and it will be interesting to see how the problem will be cured, if at all.

Apart from the problems with costs, have the courts found any particular problems with the CPR in practice? District Judge Terence John has identified eight problems that he has found re-occurring ((2006) New Law Journal, 7 April), which are:

- routine requests for stays;
- requests for trial at the court of issue typically 'for the convenience of parties and witnesses', when the parties live and the cause of action arose at the other end of the country;
- non-committal answers about witnesses;

- routine unsubstantiated requests for permission to use experts;
- misleading references to experts as 'single joint' when clearly they are not;
- proposal for allocation to inappropriate tracks without explanation;
- proposed directions that are inapplicable, typically fast-track directions that make no provision for trial within the 30-week period; and
- inaccurate estimates of costs.

These issues may recede as time goes by, especially as DJ John argues that one of the reasons for the above problems could be that courts 'have routinely slipped into prescribing a 14-day period for the return of the allocation questionnaire, when under the rules, that is only a prescribed minimum period'. Perhaps if a more realistic timescale is given at the outset, fewer of the above problems will occur.

However, despite identifying the above problems, DJ John believes Woolf reforms are here to stay and have changed the civil legal world for the better. DJ John has observed how the court system has changed with county courts dealing with about 70 per cent of claims through the small claims track and a further 20 per cent dealt with by the fast track. Clearly most claims are destined for the small claims track and if it were not for the Woolf reforms, parties would not have recourse to justice, as there would be no realistic means of resolution. As DJ John stated ((2006) New Law Journal, 22 September), 'too often its significance is understated by those who fail to appreciate how the complexities and costs would otherwise deter litigants and, in effect, frustrate their access to justice'.

Overall, it could be argued that the Woolf reforms can be seen as a triumphant step in the right direction as they have resulted in a wider proportion of society being able to achieve greater access to justice especially where the problem is of a relatively small nature and can be dealt with quickly and cheaply in the lower courts. However, the reforms may not be so good where, for example, the problem involves complex commercial issues and/or where a matter goes to appeal as costs rack up very quickly with the parties requiring the assistance of solicitors, barristers and experts and with the length of time it can take to resolve the more complex case. However, the Woolf reforms have been criticised by Dame Hazel Genn in her Hamlyn lectures (F. Gibb, 'Woolf v Genn: the decline of civil justice', *The Times*, 23 June 2009). Dame Hazel believed that the civil justice reforms were not about greater access or greater justice to society but rather as a route to divert litigants away from the courts and instead direct them to mediation. Part of this rationale, she believes, was due to the self-financing of the civil court system and the government's lack of commitment to civil justice in favour of the criminal justice system. Going forward, Dame Hazel considers that the criminal justice system is a drain on the public purse, particularly in light of current financial constraints, the importance of human rights law and the increasing prison population. Dame Hazel believed that whilst society had strong views on civil justice it was not picked up due to 'a lack of solid empirical evidence'. Lord Woolf has publicly commented upon Dame Hazel's views and expressed dissatisfaction with her argument that not enough empirical evidence was put forward (F. Gibb, 'Woolf v Genn: the decline of civil justice', *The Times*, 23 June 2009).

This is because Dame Hazel was one of Lord Woolf's review team when he was looking at proposed reforms to the civil justice system. In expressing criticism of Dame Hazel, Lord Woolf acknowledged that one commentator, Professor Michael Zander, was critical of his reforms but remained consistent with his views. Professor Zander did not consider that the government's intention was to utilise the reforms to reduce resources to the civil justice system and his proposed reforms required directly the opposite, namely proper resourcing. Whilst Lord Woolf acknowledges that the civil justice system is not high profile as far as government is concerned compared to the criminal justice system, he emphasises that this has nothing to do with judges. Lord Woolf also believes that mediation is a 'proper functioning part of the justice system that does help in certain cases to achieve justice'.

5.14   ENFORCEMENT OF CIVIL REMEDIES

It is one thing to be awarded a remedy by the court against another party, but it is another thing to actually enforce that remedy. Consequently, an effective enforcement system is essential to providing access to justice. Statistics in the 2001 Green Paper, *Towards Effective Enforcement*, reveal that as regards warrants of execution, which account for about 85 per cent of all enforcement effort, only 35 per cent of all warrants issued are paid. It was also estimated that the value of unpaid post-judgment debt is more than £600 million per year. With specific regard to small claims, once again 35 per cent of successful claimants had received no part of the sum awarded to them, several months after judgment.

In March 2003, the LCD issued the White Paper, *Effective Enforcement*, in which it claimed to set out a strategy for reforming the current system by:

- improving methods of recovering civil debt; and
- establishing a more rigorous system of controls for enforcement agents, previously known as bailiffs.

In announcing the White Paper, Baroness Scotland, Civil Justice Minister, said:

> Society wants those who owe money judgments to pay their dues but also wants to protect the vulnerable. It's about getting the balance right in a system that is firm but fair in enforcing decisions of the court. So the system we propose will utilise the full weight of the law on those who won't pay while at the same time safeguarding vulnerable individuals who simply can't pay.

On 12 June 2003 the Department for Constitutional Affairs (DCA) was created and took over the LCD's responsibilities for the court system and judiciary. In July 2006, the DCA published the draft Tribunals, Courts and Enforcement Bill and on 19 July 2007 the Tribunals, Courts and Enforcement Act 2007 received Royal Assent. The provisions dealing with the recovery of rent arrears and the enforcement of judgments and orders are not yet in force, and are to be brought into force by the Lord Chancellor.

The 2007 Act provides for the abolition of the right of distress for rent. This is a common law right that allows landlords to recover unpaid rent from tenants without using the courts. Landlords can seize control of goods in the tenanted premises and sell them, utilising the money raised to offset against the rent arrears.

When Part 3 of the 2007 Act comes into force (it is expected to commence in 2013), it will create a statutory right for the landlord of tenanted commercial premises to recover unpaid rent. The new system will be known as Commercial Rent Arrears Recovery (CRAR). As the name suggests, this procedure will not apply to residential premises, only leases of commercial premises.

Only the landlord (who will be the person entitled to the immediate reversion of the commercial premises) will be able to exercise CRAR. Where the reversion is mortgaged, the mortgagee of the landlord's interest will be able to exercise CRAR, providing the mortgagee has given notice of its intention to take possession or enter into receipt of rent and profits and the lease is binding on the mortgagee. A receiver will also be able to exercise CRAR in the name of the landlord where the receiver is appointed by a court in relation to the landlord's interest.

The landlord (or mortgagee or receiver) must satisfy the criteria for being an 'enforcement agent', if it is to exercise CRAR, otherwise an enforcement agent will need to be appointed to carry out the task of CRAR on its behalf.

The rent that can be recovered under CRAR is the amount payable under the lease for possession and use of the premises together with interest on that amount and value added tax on that amount and the interest. Rent does not include any sum in respect of rates, council tax, services, repairs, maintenance, insurance or other ancillary matters, irrespective of whether these amounts are reserved as rent in the lease.

CRAR cannot be exercised unless, before a notice of enforcement is given, the tenant is in arrears of rent and the amount of the rent arrears is certain or capable of being calculated with certainty. Further, CRAR cannot be exercised unless the 'net unpaid rent' is at least the minimum amount to be prescribed by regulations before both the time when the notice of enforcement is given and the first time that goods are taken control of after the notice.

CRAR will only apply if the lease is in writing. Any reference to lease will include the lease as varied, however, the variation need not be in writing. A lease will not be a commercial lease if any of the following apply to the premises (or any part):

- it is let under the immediate lease as a dwelling;
- it is let under an inferior lease as a dwelling;
- it is occupied as a dwelling.

A lease will be deemed a commercial lease and thus within the ambit of CRAR if the occupation of the dwelling is in breach of the terms of the lease or any superior lease.

The Act also makes a number of changes to existing court-based methods of enforcing debts in the civil courts. Part 4 contains new provisions, including powers to obtain information about debtors (see the Act's *Explanatory Notes*, Office of Public Sector Information, 2008).

Attachment of Earnings Orders

An attachment of earnings order (AEO) is a means of securing payment of certain debts by requiring an employer to make deductions direct from an employed debtor's earnings. Currently, the rate of deductions under an AEO made to secure payment of a judgment debt is calculated by a county court using information provided by the debtor. The Government identified weaknesses in the system and in particular the fact that information provided by debtors is often unreliable. The Act tackles this by making provision for a new method of calculation of deductions from earnings based on fixed rates, similar to the system used for council tax AEOs. Another weakness of the AEO system is that if a debtor changes job and does not inform the court of his new employer's details, the AEO lapses. The Act therefore enables the High Court, county courts, magistrates' courts and fines officers to request the name and address of the debtor's new employer from Her Majesty's Revenue and Customs (HMRC), for the purpose of redirecting the AEO.

Charging Orders

A charging order is a means of securing payment of a sum of money ordered to be paid under a judgment or order of the High Court or a county court by placing a charge on to the debtor's property (usually a house or land or securities such as shares). A charging order can be made absolute or subject to conditions. Once an order is in place, a creditor can subsequently apply to court seeking an order for sale of the charged property. Under the old law, the court could not make a charging order when payments due under an instalment order made to secure that same sum were not in arrears. In certain instances this could prejudice the creditor, allowing for example a debtor with large judgment debts, who is meeting his regular instalments, to benefit from the sale of a property without paying off the debt. The Tribunals, Courts and Enforcement Act 2007 removes this restriction and enables access to charging orders in circumstances where a debtor is not yet in arrears with an instalment order. As a safeguard, the Act allows the Lord Chancellor to set financial thresholds beneath which a court cannot make a charging order or order for sale, in order to ensure that charging orders are not used to secure payment of disproportionately small judgment debts.

CHAPTER SUMMARY: THE CIVIL PROCESS

THE NEED FOR REFORM

The Woolf Inquiry into the civil justice system was set up by the government in 1994 to examine why civil litigation was generally very costly, protracted, complicated and subject to long delays.

Starting Proceedings: Claimant commences proceedings by completing:
- *Claim form* to which may be attached the '*particulars of claim*' statement of case, which must include a '*statement of truth*'
- Court will serve documents on the defendant, who may provide a defence, counterclaim or fail to respond
- Once a defence is filed, an *allocation questionnaire* may be completed. The judge may then allocate the case to the appropriate 'track' (Where the defendant has failed to respond, the court may issue a judgment in default.)

Pre-trial Process: The judiciary now have an enhanced management role (case control), which involves encouraging greater co-operation between the parties, including the use of alternative dispute resolution (ADR) and giving directions in order that the case proceeds quickly and efficiently, involving:
- case management conferences
- pre-trial reviews
- consideration of pre-action offers to settle (known as Part 36 payments)

Courts have a duty to help parties settle their disputes, including the use of 'stays', which provide more time for the parties to settle

Court and Track Allocation:
- Where a case has been allocated to the **'small claims track'**, parties are under no obligation to attend and 'paper adjudication' may be heard by agreement. As the procedure is intended to be quick and less formal, legal representation, use of expert witnesses and the awarding of costs are less common than under other tracks
- Where a case has been allocated to the **'fast track'**, the period between directions and the start of the trial cannot be more than *30 weeks*, while the trial time is limited to *one day*. Advocacy costs will also be capped
- Where a case has been allocated to the **'multi-track'**, a range of cases management tools may be used in a 'mix and match' to suit the needs of the individual case

Remedies: Claimants initiate actions in order to seek a remedy for a wrong that they have suffered. The **common law** remedy available is damages
- **Equitable remedies** are only available at the discretion of the court and include specific performance and injunction

Costs: assessed by the judge at the end of a hearing
Court Fees: payable on a 'pay as you go' basis

FIGURE 5.2 *An Overview of Civil Process.*

The Inquiry published its final report in 1996 and its proposals resulted in the Civil Procedure Act 1997 and the Civil Procedure Rules 1998. The new Civil Procedure Rules (CPR) are the same for the county court and the High Court.

THE NEW CIVIL PROCESS

The changes are effected through the Civil Procedure Act 1997 and the CPR 1998. These have been supplemented by new practice directions and pre-action protocols.

THE OVERRIDING OBJECTIVE (CPR PART 1)

The overriding objective of the new CPR is to enable the court to deal justly with cases.

The first rule reads:

> 1.1(1) These rules are a new procedural code with the overriding objective of enabling the court to deal with cases justly.

PRACTICE DIRECTIONS

Practice directions (official statements of interpretative guidance) play an important role in the new civil process. In general, they supplement the CPR, giving the latter fine detail. They tell parties and their representatives what the court will expect of them in respect of documents to be filed in court for a particular purpose, and how they must co-operate with the other parties to their action. They also tell the parties what they can expect of the court.

THE PRE-ACTION PROTOCOLS

The pre-action protocols (PAPs) are an important feature of the reforms.

They exist for cases of clinical disputes, personal injury, disease and illness, construction and engineering disputes, defamation, professional negligence, housing disrepair, housing repossession following rent arrears, housing possession following mortgage arrears, low value personal injury claims in road traffic accidents, dilapidations at end of lease or tenancy of a commercial property and judicial review.

They are likely to be followed, over time, with similar protocols for cases involving other specialisms like debt.

CASE CONTROL (CPR PART 3)

Judges will receive support from court staff in carrying out their case management role. The court will monitor case progress by using a computerised diary monitoring system.

Active case management includes:

(a)   encouraging the parties to co-operate with each other in the conduct of the proceedings;

(b)   identifying the issues at an early stage;

(c)   deciding promptly which issues need full investigation and trial and, accordingly, disposing summarily of the others;

(d)   deciding the order in which issues are to be resolved.

CASE MANAGEMENT CONFERENCES

Case management conferences may be regarded as an opportunity to 'take stock'. There is no limit to the number of case management conferences that may be held during the life of a case, although the cost of attendance at such hearings measured against the benefits obtained will always be a consideration in making the decision.

PRE-TRIAL REVIEWS

Pre-trial reviews will normally take place after the filing of listing questionnaires and before the start of the trial. Their main purpose is to decide a timetable for the trial itself (including the evidence to be allowed and whether this should be given orally), instructions about the content of any trial bundles (bundles of documents including evidence such as written statements, for the judge to read) and confirming a realistic time estimate for the trial itself.

STAYS FOR SETTLEMENT (CPR PART 26) AND SETTLEMENTS (PART 36)

Under the new CPR, there is a greater incentive for parties to settle their differences.

The court will take into account any pre-action offers to settle when making an order for costs. Thus, a side that has refused a reasonable offer to settle will be treated less generously in the issue of how far the court will order their costs to be paid by the other side. For this to happen, the offer, though, must be one that is made open to the other side for at least 21 days after the date it was made (to stop any undue pressure being put on someone with the phrase: 'take it or leave it; it is only open for one day, then I shall withdraw the offer').

WITNESS STATEMENTS (CPR PART 32)

Under the new rules, witness statements must contain the evidence that the witness will give at trial, but they should be briefer than those drafted under the previous rules; they should be drafted in lay language and should not discuss legal propositions. Witnesses will be allowed to amplify on the statement or deal with matters that have arisen since the report was served, although this is not an automatic right and a 'good reason' for the admission of new evidence will have to be established.

EXPERTS (CPR PART 35)

New rules place a clear duty on the court to ensure that 'expert evidence is restricted to that which is reasonably required to resolve the proceedings'. That is to say, expert evidence will only be allowed either by way of written report or orally, where the court gives permission. Equally important is the rules' statement about experts' duties.

COURT AND TRACK ALLOCATION (CPR PART 26)

Part 7 of the CPR sets out the rules for starting proceedings. A new restriction is placed on which cases may be begun in the High Court. County courts retain an almost unlimited jurisdiction for handling contract and tort claims (that is, negligence cases, nuisance cases, but excluding a claim for damages or other remedy for libel or slander unless the parties agree otherwise). Issuing proceedings in the High Court is now limited to:

- personal injury claims with a value of £50,000 or more;
- other claims with a value of more than £100,000;
- equity claims where the property is worth at least £350,000;
- claims where an Act of Parliament requires an action to start in the High Court; or
- specialist High Court claims that need to go to one of the specialist 'lists', like the Commercial List, the Technology and Construction List.

The new civil system works on the basis of the court, upon receipt of the claim (accompanied by duly filled in forms giving all the relevant details of the claim, including how much it is for and an indication of its factual and legal complexity), allocating the case to one of three tracks for a hearing. These are:

- small claims;
- fast track;
- multi-track.

The new small claims limit is £10,000, although personal injury and housing disrepair claims for over £1,000, illegal eviction and harassment claims will be excluded from the small claims court. The limit for cases going into the fast-track system is £25,000, and only claims for over £100,000 can be issued in the High Court. Applications to move cases 'up' a track on grounds of complexity will have to be made on the new allocation questionnaire.

DOCUMENTATION AND PROCEDURES

HOW TO START PROCEEDINGS – THE CLAIM FORM (CPR PART 7)

Under the new system, most claims will be begun by using a 'Part 7' claim form – a form which has been designed for multi-purpose use. It can be used if the claim is for a *specified* amount of money (the old term was *liquidated* damages) or an *unspecified* amount (replacing the term *unliquidated* damages) and for non-monetary claims.

Under the new rules, the court can grant any remedy to which the claimant is entitled, even if the claimant does not specify which one he wants.

ALTERNATIVE PROCEDURE FOR CLAIMS (CPR PART 8)

Part 8 of the new rules introduces the alternative procedure for claims. This procedure is commenced by the issue of a Part 8 claim form. It is intended to provide a speedy resolution of claims that are not likely to involve a substantial dispute of fact, for example, applications for approval of infant settlements, or for orders enforcing a statutory right such as a right to have access to medical records (under the Access to Health Records Act 1990). The Part 8 procedure is also used where a rule or practice direction requires or permits its use.

STATEMENT OF CASE – PARTICULARS OF CLAIM (CPR PART 16)

Particulars of claim may be included in the claim form, attached to it, or may be served (that is, given or sent to a party by a method allowed by the rules) separately from it. Where they are served separately, they must be served within 14 days of the claim form being served. The time for a defendant to respond begins to run from the time the particulars of claim are served.

Part 16 of the CPR is entitled 'statements of case' (replacing the word 'pleadings'). Statements of case include documents from both sides: claim forms, particulars of claims, defences, counterclaims, replies to defences and counterclaims, Part 20 (third-party) claims and any further information provided under Part 18 of the CPR (replacing the term 'further and better particulars'). Part 16 of the rules also sets out what both particulars of claim and defences should contain.

STATEMENTS OF TRUTH (CPR PART 22)

A statement of truth is a statement that a party believes that the facts or allegations set out in a document, which they put forward, are true. It is required in statements of case, witness statements and expert reports. Any document that contains a statement of truth may be used in evidence. This will avoid the previous need to swear affidavits in support of various statements made as part of the claim.

DEFENCE AND AUTOMATIC TRANSFER (CPR PART 26)

Claims for specified amounts will be transferred automatically to the defendant's 'home court' where the defendant is an individual who has filed a defence. The defendant's home court will be the court or district registry, including the Royal Courts of Justice, for the district in which the defendant's address for service as shown on the defence is situated. This means that where a solicitor represents the defendant, this will be the defendant's solicitor's business address.

Where there is more than one defendant, it is the first defendant to file a defence who dictates whether or not automatic transfer will take place. For example, if there were two defendants to a claim, one an individual and one a limited company, there would be no automatic transfer if the limited company was the first defendant to file a defence.

ALLOCATION QUESTIONNAIRE (FORM N150)

The purpose of this document is to enable the judge to allocate in which track the case should be heard. When a defence is filed, the issuing court will send out a copy of the defence to all other parties to the claim together with an allocation questionnaire, a notice setting out the date for returning it and the name and address of the court (or district registry or the Royal Courts of Justice – that is, High Court – as appropriate) to which the completed allocation questionnaire must be returned. A notice of transfer will also be sent if the case is being automatically transferred.

The allocation questionnaire will not be served on the parties when a defendant files a defence if r 14.5 or r 15.10 applies or if the court decides to dispense with its service.

When all the parties have filed their allocation questionnaire, or at the end of the period for returning it, whichever is the sooner (providing the questionnaires have not been dispensed with or the case stayed under r 26.4), the court will allocate the claim to a track. If there is sufficient information, the judge will allocate the case to a track and a notice of allocation and directions will be sent out to each party. Where the judge has insufficient information, an order may be made for a party to provide further information.

Where only one party has filed a questionnaire the judge may allocate the claim to a track providing he has enough information or will order that an allocation hearing be listed and that all parties must attend.

DEFAULT JUDGMENT (CPR PART 12)

If a defendant (to a Part 7 claim) files an acknowledgment stating an intention to defend the claim, this extends the period for filing a defence from 14 to 28 days from the date of service of the particulars. Failure to file an acknowledgment or, later, failure to file a defence can result in default judgment, that is, the court will find for the claimant, so the defendant will lose the case.

REMEDIES

It is essential to distinguish between the common law remedy of damages, available as of right, and equitable remedies, which are awarded at the discretion of the court.

DAMAGES

Damages are compensatory, to recompense someone for the wrong they have suffered. There are, however, different ways in which someone can be compensated.

In contract law, the object of awarding damages is to put the wronged person in the situation they would have been in had the contract been completed as agreed: that is, it places them in the position they would have been after the event. In tort, however, the object is to compensate the wronged person, to the extent that a monetary award can do so, for injury sustained: that is, to return them to the situation they were in before the event.

EQUITABLE REMEDIES

Specific performance

This remedy will only be granted in cases where the common law remedy of damages is inadequate. It is not usually applied to contracts concerning the sale of goods where replacements are readily available. It is most commonly granted in cases involving the sale of land, where the subject matter of the contract is unique.

Injunction

This is the term used in relation to the courts' powers to order someone either to do something or, alternatively, to refrain from doing something.

Rectification

This award allows for the alteration of contractual documents.

Rescission

This action sets aside the terms of a contractual agreement and returns the parties to the situation they were in before the contract was entered into.

COURT FEES

A new fee structure takes account of the different procedures, a movement towards a 'pay as you go' fees regime and the need for full cost recovery. 'Pay as you go' means that parties will be expected to contribute more in fees, the more court and judicial time they use, for example, if they do not settle and carry on to trial.

FOOD FOR THOUGHT

1. The English legal system has always been categorised as an adversarial system with the judge sitting as an umpire rather than a participant in cases. As a consequence the conduct of cases was to a large degree in the hands of the lawyers. Consider the consequences of such lack of judicial control for all the parties concerned in the case. Then consider how the Woolf reforms were designed to overcome these problems by instituting a process of greater judicial control.

2. To what extent is it fair to claim that the reforms have been about saving time and money, both clients' and the State's? How exactly have these savings been pursued?

3. Although referred to as the 'new' civil process, the Woolf reforms have been in operation for more than 15 years. Is it not time to assess how successful they have been? How would such an assessment be made?

4. In relation to the fast-track procedure, consider why there are different financial limits: £10,000 for the majority of claims but £1,000 for personal injury claims and housing disrepair actions. Why are the latter considered to need more judicial attention, and does this imply anything about possible shortcomings in the fast-track procedure?

5. It is accepted that 'justice delayed is justice denied', but can the same not be said in relation to a failure to provide adequate enforcement of remedies?

FURTHER READING

Blackstone's Civil Procedure (HH Judge William Rose (ed)), 2013, Oxford: OUP
Burns, R, 'A view from the ranks' (2000) 150 NLJ 1829–30
Genn, H, *Hamlyn Lectures 2008: Judging Civil Justice*
Genn, H, *Hard Bargaining: Out of Court Settlements in Personal Injury Claims*, 1987, Oxford: OUP
Gold, S, 'Civil Way' (2008) 158 NLJ 1370
Gold, S, 'Civil Way' (2008) 158 NLJ 1412
Harrison, R, 'Cry Woolf' (1999) 149 NLJ 1011
Kinley, A, 'Preparing the way' (2009) 153(40) SJ 8
Miller, F, 'The adversarial myth' (1995) 145 NLJ 743
New Law Journal, Increase in Civil Cases in High Court [2007] 1628
Sime, S, *A Practical Approach to Civil Procedure*, 2007, Oxford: OUP
Solon, M, 'Selecting the best' (2008) 158 NLJ 1299
Squire, G, 'No more hired guns' (2009) 153(40) SJ 20
Thacker, R, 'The new Supreme Court' (2009) Legal Action 20–21
Zander, M, 'Are there any clothes for the emperor to wear?' (1995) 145 NLJ 154
Zuckerman, AAS, 'A reform of civil procedure – rationing procedure rather than access to justice' (1995) 22 JLS 156

USEFUL WEBSITES

www.justice.gov.uk/civil/procrules_fin/menus/rules.htm
This site, hosted by the Ministry of Justice, contains all the Civil Procedure Rules, and is regularly updated.

www.civiljusticecouncil.gov.uk
The official website of the Civil Justice Council.

COMPANION WEBSITE

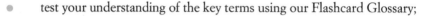

Now visit the companion website to:

- test your understanding of the key terms using our Flashcard Glossary;
- revise and consolidate your knowledge of 'The civil process' using our Multiple Choice Question testbank;
- view all of the links to the Useful Websites above.

www.routledge.com/cw/slapper

THE CRIMINAL COURTS   6

There are over 12,000 different criminal offences in English law, 3,700 of which have been created since 1997. Professors Andrew Ashworth and Lucia Zedner recently identified that criminalisation is no longer a last resort but has become 'a routine system for management disorder' (A. Ashworth and L. Zedner (2008) 'Defending the criminal law: reflections on the changing character of crime', 2 *Criminal Law and Philosophy* 21). These offences can be classified in different ways. You could, for example, classify them according to whether they are offences against people or property; you could classify them according to the type of mental element (*mens rea*) required for the offence, for example, 'intention' or 'recklessness'. Another type of classification, and the one that concerns us here, is whether the offence is triable *summarily*, that is, in a magistrates' court (for relatively trivial offences like traffic offences), or is an *indictable* offence (the more serious offences like murder, manslaughter, rape and robbery are *indictable only*), triable in front of a judge and jury in a Crown Court.

From the mid-nineteenth century, magistrates were empowered to hear some indictable cases in certain circumstances. Today, there is still a class of offence that is triable 'either way', that is, summarily or in a jury trial. A typical example would be a potentially serious offence such as theft, but one that has been committed in a minor way, as in the theft of a milk bottle. These offences now account for about 80 per cent of those tried in Crown Courts. Most defendants, however, opt for summary trial. The magistrates' court has the power to refuse jurisdiction – that means to refuse to deal with the matter – if it thinks, having considered the facts of the case, that its powers of sentencing would be insufficient if the case resulted in a conviction.

Where several defendants are charged together with either-way offences, each defendant's choice can be exercised separately. So, if one elects for trial in the Crown Court, the others may still be tried summarily if the magistrates agree (*R v Brentwood Justices ex p Nicholls* (1991)).

An estimated 1.62 million defendants were proceeded against in criminal cases in magistrates' courts in 2011 (excluding breaches) (*Judicial and Court Statistics 2011*, Ministry of Justice, June 2012). This amounts to a fall compared with the 1.68 million defendants in 2010 and the 1.79 million defendants in 2009.

The office of magistrate or Justice of the Peace (JP) dates from 1195, when Richard I first appointed 'keepers of the peace' to deal with those who were accused of breaking 'the King's peace'. The JPs originally acted as local administrators for the king in addition to their judicial responsibilities. Apart from the 24,267 lay justices who sit in some 330 courts, there are also 137 district judges (magistrates' courts) (formerly known as stipendiary magistrates) and 143 deputy district judges (magistrates' courts) who sit in cities and larger towns (*Judicial and Court Statistics 2011*, Ministry of Justice, July 2012). They are qualified, experienced lawyers who are salaried justices. A Practice Direction from the Lord Chief Justice sets out details concerning the classification and allocation of Crown Court business, and some of this is relevant to the magistrates' courts. For example, upon sending someone for trial at the Crown Court, the magistrates should, if the offence is a class I offence (for example murder, manslaughter or treason) specify the most convenient location of the Crown Court where a High Court judge or a circuit judge authorised to try such cases regularly sits: *Practice Direction (Criminal proceedings: Classification and allocation of business)* (2005).

It became evident in 2009 that the workload of many magistrates' courts was being diverted away from the court system. Magistrates complained that increasing numbers of offenders were being dealt with by 'on-the-spot' fines and cautions – almost half of all offences are now dealt with in this way (*The Times*, 10 July 2009). John Thornhill, chairman of the Magistrates' Association, said: 'Magistrates are reporting to us cancelled sittings across the country, either because of no work, or disposing of the case out of court'. Costs were not saved in the long term, however, because nearly half of such fines went unpaid. Mr Thornhill observed that 'Many of these cases come back to the courts in the end, because the offender has failed to pay'. The use of out-of-court penalties has risen sharply in recent times. In 2011, across England and Wales, 91,910 cases were sent for trial in the Crown Court. Enforcement of financial penalties in England and Wales in 2011, in terms of the amount actually paid, was £277 million, representing a 1 per cent decrease on 2010 (*Judicial and Court Statistics 2011*, Ministry of Justice, July 2012).

In May 2010, plans to build a new magistrates' court in Birmingham were deferred as part of 'additional budget savings', according to a Ministry of Justice press release (http://www.justice.gov.uk/news/newsrelease280510a.htm). This represents part of the £95 billion cut in public spending that the government plans to make over the next five years, with the Ministry of Justice needing to reduce its budget by £1 billion.

6.2.1 SUMMARY TRIAL

Summary offences are created and defined by statute. There are thousands of different summary offences. They include traffic offences, common assault, taking a motor vehicle without consent and driving while disqualified: about 90 per cent of all cases are dealt with in the magistrates' court (*Judicial and Court Statistics 2011*, Ministry of Justice, July 2012).

Cases are heard in the court for the district in which the offence is alleged to have been committed. In most cases, the defendant will be in court, but it is possible for the accused in road traffic offences to plead guilty by post and not to attend court.

Two or three magistrates whose powers of sentencing are limited by the Acts that govern the offences in question will hear the cases. A district judge (magistrates' courts) may sit without lay magistrates. The maximum sentence that magistrates can impose on a private individual is a Level 5 fine (current maximum £5,000) and/or a 12-month prison sentence for more than one either-way offence (see below), or six months for one offence. Businesses may be fined up to £20,000 for certain offences. The maximum sentences for many summary offences are much less than these limits. Where a defendant is convicted of two or more offences at the same hearing, the maximum custodial sentence for any one offence is 12 months (s 154 of the Criminal Justice Act 2003, to be brought into law at a date to be appointed). Several sentences to be served concurrently, including more than one 12-month sentence, will be permitted. Consecutive sentences amounting to more than 12 months are not permitted, but will be limited to 65 weeks once s 155 of the Criminal Justice Act 2003 is brought into force. A date for its coming into force has still not yet been appointed.

Many statutory offences are given particular 'levels' according to their seriousness. This means that if a government minister wishes to raise fines (say to be in line with inflation), he does not have to go through hundreds of different offences, altering the maximum fine in relation to each one separately; the maxima for each level are simply altered. The 2010 figures are as follows: Level 5 up to £5,000; Level 4 up to £2,500; Level 3 up to £1,000; Level 2 up to £500; and Level 1 up to £200: s 37 of the Criminal Justice Act 1982.

The Criminal Justice Act (CJA) 1991 (the framework statute for many of the sentencing powers of the courts until the enactment of a consolidating statute, the Powers of the Criminal Courts (Sentencing) Act 2000) provided for a new system of fining in magistrates' courts: the 'unit fine' system. Under this system, fines were linked to the offender's income. The idea was that the rich should pay more than the poor for the same offence. Crimes were graded from 1 to 10 and the level of crime was then multiplied by the offender's weekly disposable income. The system's figures, however, resulted in many anomalies and it was eventually abolished. Nevertheless, in fixing the appropriate amount for a convicted defendant's fine, the magistrates must still take into account his income. Other sentences that the court may use include absolute discharge, conditional discharge, community orders (replacing the old probation orders, community service/punishment orders and curfew orders, and including many new types of requirements which can be included in community orders), and compensation orders.

After a conviction, the magistrates will hear whether the defendant has a criminal record and, if so, for what offences. This is to enable them to pass an appropriate sentence. If, after hearing that record, they feel that their powers of sanction are insufficient to deal with the defendant, then the defendant may be sent to the Crown Court for sentencing.

A bench of lay magistrates is legally advised by a justices' clerk who is legally qualified and guides the justices on matters of law, sentencing and procedure. The justices' clerk may give advice even when not specifically invited to do so. It is an established principle of English law that 'justice should not only be done but manifestly and undoubtedly be seen to be done' (*R v Sussex Justices ex p McCarthy* (1924), *per* Lord Hewart CJ). This is not about the proceedings being visible from a public gallery! It means there must be nothing in the appearance of what happens in a trial that might create an impression that something improper happened. In the *Sussex Justices* case, Mr McCarthy had been convicted of dangerous driving. He found out that the clerk to the magistrates, the person giving them legal advice, was a solicitor who happened to be representing someone who was suing him as a result of the car accident. Even though the solicitor might have been perfectly professional, there was the appearance that he *could* have framed his advice to the magistrates (even subconsciously) to help secure a conviction because such an outcome would have assisted his client in the civil case. The clerk had retired with the magistrates when they went to consider their verdict. The conviction was quashed because of the possibility of bias.

The magistrates are independent of the clerks and thus the clerks should not *instruct* the magistrates as to what decision to make on any point, nor should they appear to be doing so. The clerk should not, therefore, normally retire with the justices when they go to consider their verdict in any case, although they may be called on by the magistrates to give legal advice on any point. The clerk should not give any judgment on matters of fact. The justices' clerk will employ legally qualified assistants to sit in court with magistrates – they are known as court legal advisers and carry out the advisory role described above. Court legal advisers have been given 'delegated powers' to deal with straightforward unopposed applications in the absence of the magistrates – for example, where both prosecution and defence agree an adjournment of a case or where a warrant for the arrest of the accused is to be issued in his/her absence. As these are formal matters the attendance of the magistrates in court is not required if the legal adviser is happy to deal with them in this way.

The court is required in certain cases to consider a compensation order and to give reasons if it decides not to make such an order. Compensation orders are governed by the provisions of ss 130–34 of the Powers of the Criminal Courts (Sentencing) Act (PCC(S)A) 2000. Section 130 states that a court before which a person is convicted, in addition to dealing with him in any other way, may make a compensation order. The order is to compensate personal injury, loss or damage resulting from the offence in question or any other offence 'taken into consideration' (that is, admitted by the defendant) by the court. The defendant can also be ordered to make payments for funeral expenses or bereavement in respect of a death resulting from an offence (other than a death due to a motor accident). The court, s 130(3) states, 'shall give reasons, on passing sentence, if it does not make such a compensation order in a case where this section empowers it to do so'. Unlike a fine, the compensation will go to the victim rather than to the State, so these orders save victims of crime from having to claim damages against defendants in the civil courts. They are not intended as an alternative to punishment, enabling the defendant to buy his way out of the penalties for the crime. Even so, s 130(12) gives priority to the issue of a compensation order over a fine. In 2010, the

Crown Court and magistrates' courts issued 154,428 compensation orders. The total cost in 2010 was £44,620,426 (*Hansard*, 20 June 2011, col 86W).

Alongside any such compensation order, an offender may also be required to pay prosecution costs, currently set at £85, and a so-called 'Victim Surcharge', currently priced at £15. This surcharge is statutorily imposed regardless of whether or not there was a victim or victims. In this way, it can be understood as a tax on the cost of a prosecution.

6.2.2 OFFENCES TRIABLE 'EITHER WAY'

Where the defendant is charged with an offence triable 'either way', two preliminary decisions have to be made: first, should he be tried summarily (by magistrates) or on indictment (in the Crown Court by a judge and jury)? The procedures by which this matter is resolved are known as plea before venue and mode of trial hearings.

In a plea before venue hearing, that is, one where the accused is charged with an either-way offence, he is first asked if he wishes to indicate a guilty plea. If he does, the magistrates will hear the facts of the case and see details of his previous convictions. They retain the power to commit him for sentence to the Crown Court if they feel that their powers of punishment are inadequate (this is dealt with later in more detail). If they feel that they have enough power to deal with the accused, then they proceed to sentence him.

If the defendant pleads not guilty or declines to indicate his plea then a mode of trial hearing is held. In this hearing the prosecution and defence make submissions about whether the case should be heard at the magistrates' or Crown Court. The magistrates then decide whether to agree to hear the case or decline to do so and commit it to the Crown Court. If they agree to hear the case then the accused can still choose (elect) to have his case heard by a jury and – if he so chooses – the case will be committed for Crown Court trial. If he decides in favour of the magistrates' court, then it will fix a date for a summary trial.

Secondly, if the determination is in favour of trial on indictment (by either method), the question is asked whether there is a sufficient *prima facie* case to go before the Crown Court. This question is answered at a hearing known as *committal proceedings*. Changes to this system have been made by the Criminal Justice Act 2003 Sched 3, and in December 2011 the government announced that the changes would be brought into force. These changes abolish committal hearings in a large number of cases where the offence is triable either way. The changes came into force in a number of locations on 18 June 2012 but have not yet been rolled out across the country.

Most defendants charged with 'either-way' offences are tried by magistrates: 42,981 cases were committed to the Crown Court in 2011 because the magistrates considered their sentencing powers to be inadequate and on average 4 per cent of cases go to the Crown Court because the defendants elect trial by jury (*Judicial and Court Statistics 2011*, Ministry of Justice, July 2012).

The defendant therefore can insist on trial on indictment, but cannot insist on being tried summarily if the magistrates decline jurisdiction. Similarly, the magistrates can decide that the defendant should be tried on indictment, but cannot insist that he be tried summarily. Prosecutions conducted by the Attorney General, the Solicitor General or the Director of Public Prosecutions must be tried on indictment if so requested by the prosecutor.

The Act will make various changes to this area but its provisions have not yet been fully implemented.

Section 41 of the Criminal Justice Act 2003, via para 5 of Sched 3, substitutes s 19 of the Magistrates' Courts Act 1980, which makes provision for the procedure to be followed by a magistrates' court in deciding whether a case involving an offence triable either way to which the defendant has not indicated a guilty plea should be tried summarily or on indictment. The new procedure ('allocation') differs from the present one in that the court is to be informed about, and take account of, any previous convictions of the defendant in assessing whether the sentencing powers available to it are adequate. The court is to have regard, not only (as now) to any representations made by the prosecution or defence, but also to allocation guidelines, which may be issued by the Sentencing Guidelines Council under s 170. This section is partially in force.

Section 41: Allocation of Offences Triable either Way and Sending Cases to the Crown Court

Section 41 introduces Sched 3, Part 1 of which sets out (through amendments to existing statutes) how it is to be decided whether cases triable either way should be tried summarily or on indictment, and provides for the sending to the Crown Court of those cases that need to go there.

Amendments to the Magistrates' Courts Act 1980

Paragraphs 3 and 4 of Sched 3 to the 2003 Act clarify that the preliminary stages of an either way case, including the plea before venue and allocation procedures, may take place at a hearing before a single justice. However, a single justice may *not* conduct a contested trial, nor – while he may take a guilty plea – may he impose a sentence on the offender. Paragraph 3 also limits the sentence that may be imposed where a person pleads guilty to a low-value offence.

Paragraph 5 substitutes s 19 of the Magistrates' Courts Act 1980, which makes provision for the procedure to be followed by a magistrates' court in deciding whether a case involving an offence triable either way to which the defendant has not indicated a guilty plea should be tried summarily or on indictment. The new procedure ('allocation') differs from the previous one in that the court is now to be informed about, and take account of, *any previous convictions* of the defendant in assessing whether the sentencing powers available to it are adequate. The court is to have regard not only (as previously) to any representations made by the prosecution or defence, but also to allocation guidelines which may be issued by the Sentencing Council (formerly the Sentencing Guidelines Council) under s 170.

Paragraph 6 substitutes s 20 of the Magistrates' Courts Act 1980, which sets out the procedure to be followed by the magistrates' court where it decides that a case is suitable for summary trial. As previously, defendants will be told that they can either consent to be tried summarily or, if they wish, be tried on indictment. In making that decision, they may be influenced by the knowledge that, since it will generally no longer be possible to be committed for sentence to the Crown Court once the magistrates have accepted jurisdiction, they cannot receive a sentence beyond the magistrates' powers. Moreover, defendants now have the opportunity of requesting an indication from the magistrates as to whether, if they pleaded guilty at that point, the sentence would be custodial. The magistrates' court now has a discretion whether or not to give such an indication to a defendant. The magistrates may refuse to give an indication and are not required to give reasons for doing so. Where an indication is given, defendants have the opportunity to reconsider their original indication as to plea. Where a defendant then decides to plead guilty, the magistrates' court will proceed to sentence. A custodial sentence will be available only if such a sentence was indicated, and if so – unlike after a guilty plea indication under s 17A or 17B – the option of committal to the Crown Court for sentence under s 3 of the PCC(S)A 2000 will not be available, although committal for sentence under s 3A of that Act will be available where the criteria for an extended sentence or a sentence for public protection appear to be met.

If this is not the case (that is, where the defendant declines to reconsider his plea indication, or where no sentence indication is given), the defendant will be given the choice between accepting summary trial or electing for trial on indictment, as at present. Where an indication of sentence is given and the defendant does not choose to plead guilty on the basis of it, the sentence indication is not binding on the magistrates who later try the case summarily, or on the Crown Court if the defendant elects trial on indictment.

Paragraph 7 substitutes s 21 in the Magistrates' Courts Act 1980 so that, where the court decides that trial on indictment is more suitable, it will proceed to send the case to the Crown Court in accordance with s 51(1) of the Crime and Disorder Act 1998.

Paragraph 10 adds four new sections (24A–24D) to the Magistrates' Courts Act 1980, which apply a procedure akin to that in ss 17A–17C ('plea before venue') to cases involving defendants who are under 18. It would apply in certain cases where it falls to the court to decide whether the defendant should be sent to the Crown Court for trial, whether in his own right, or for joint trial with an adult defendant.

Paragraph 11 amends s 25 of the Magistrates' Courts Act 1980. The previous power to switch between summary trial and committal proceedings is abolished, and in its place there is a new power for the prosecution to apply for an either-way case which has been allocated for summary trial to be tried on indictment instead.

Sending Cases to the Crown Court

Paragraphs 15–20 amend the Crime and Disorder Act 1998. Paragraph 17 sets out the order in which a magistrates' court is to apply various procedures in respect of either-way offences.

Paragraph 18 substitutes s 51 of the Crime and Disorder Act 1998 (see below, at 5.2.4.3) so that it applies not only to indictable-only offences (and cases related to such offences), but also where an either-way case involving an adult defendant is allocated for trial on indictment. The provisions for sending to the Crown Court related cases against the same defendant or another defendant (including one under 18) are preserved.

Paragraphs 21–28 amend the PCC(S)A 2000. The most important of these concerns the committal to the Crown Court for sentence of offences triable either way. This power is no longer available in cases where the magistrates' court has dealt with the case having accepted jurisdiction (whether as a contested case or a guilty plea), but is limited to cases where a guilty plea has been indicated at plea before venue.

If a defendant charged with a number of related either-way offences pleads guilty to one of them at plea before venue and is sent to the Crown Court to be tried for the rest, the power in s 4 of the PCC(S)A 2000 – to send the offence to which he has pleaded guilty to the Crown Court for sentence – still exists.

6.2.3 YOUTH COURTS

The procedures previously discussed apply only to those aged at least 18. Defendants under 18 years of age will normally be tried by a youth court, no matter what the classification of the offence (summary, either way, indictable only). However, a defendant under 18 must be tried on indictment where the charge is homicide, and may be tried on indictment where:

- the offence charged is punishable with at least 14 years' imprisonment, or is indecent assault, or (if the defendant is at least 14 years of age) is causing death by dangerous driving or causing death by careless driving while under the influence of drink or drugs;
- the defendant is jointly charged with an adult who is going to be tried on indictment and the court considers that it is in the interests of justice that both should be tried on indictment.

A defendant under 18 may be tried summarily in an adult magistrates' court where:

- he is to be tried jointly with an adult. This is subject to the power to commit both for trial on indictment, and also subject to a power to remit the defendant under 18 for trial to a youth court where the adult pleads guilty, or is discharged or committed for trial on indictment, but the defendant is not;
- he is charged as a principal offender and an adult is charged with aiding, abetting, etc;
- he is charged separately from, but at the same time as, an adult, and the charges against each arise out of the same or connected circumstances;
- it appears during the course of a summary trial that, contrary to the initial belief, he is under the age of 18.

There is likely to be a significant reduction in the number of defendants aged under 18 tried at the Crown Court following the introduction of s 41 of the Criminal Justice Act

2003 which, through Sched 3 to the Act, reframes the rules to produce the foregoing principles.

When defendants under 18 are tried by magistrates in the youth court, there will generally be three justices to hear the case, of whom one must be a man and one a woman. These justices will have had special training to deal with such cases. There are special provisions relating to punishment for this age group. The current maximum fine for a child (under 14 years of age) is £250, and for a young person (under 18) £1,000 (s 36 MCA 1980, as amended by s 17(2) CJA 1991 and Sched 13). Members of both groups may be made the subject of supervision orders and compensation orders. A sentence of imprisonment may be imposed only on a defendant who is at least 21 years old. A sentence of detention in a young offenders' institution may be imposed only on a defendant who is at least 18 years old (the intention is to bring all those aged at least 18 within the imprisonment regime). For those under 18, the custodial sentence is a detention and training order, which may be imposed only where an adult could have been sentenced to imprisonment. Where the defendant is under 15, a detention and training order can be imposed only if he is a 'persistent' offender. In measures under Part III of the PCC(S)A 2000, the youth court will on some occasions be obliged, and on others will have the discretion, to refer the young offender to a youth offender panel, the members of which will agree with the young offender and his family a course of action designed to tackle the offending behaviour and its causes. This could involve actions such as making apologies, carrying out reparation, doing community work or taking part in family counselling.

Traditionally, the aim of the youth court system has been to take the young offender out of the normal criminal court environment, and this has involved strict rules about public access to the court. In general, members of the public have not been permitted to attend and reporting restrictions have been very tight. Parents can be required to attend, and must attend in the case of any person under the age of 16, unless such a requirement would be unreasonable in the circumstances. The name or photograph of any person under 18 appearing in a case must not be printed in any newspaper or broadcast without the authority of the court or the Home Secretary. Also the youth justice system has introduced a system of warnings and reprimands (formerly known as cautions) that are issued instead of court proceedings for many offenders in an attempt to divert them from the youth court system.

The Criminal Justice and Immigration Act 2008 made many changes to the operation of the youth justice system. Sections 1 to 8 (and Scheds 1 to 4) introduce youth rehabilitation orders (YROs), a new generic community sentence for children and young people. Section 9 sets out the purposes of sentencing in relation to young offenders. It says a sentencing court must have regard to 'the principal aim of the youth justice system' which is to 'prevent offending (or re-offending) by persons aged under 18'. It identifies the purposes of sentencing as:

(a)   the punishment of offenders;

(b)   the reform and rehabilitation of offenders;

(c)   the protection of the public; and

(d)   the making of reparation by offenders to persons affected by their offences.

Section 10 clarifies courts' sentencing powers to make it clear that a court is not *required* to impose a community sentence in cases where the offence is serious enough to justify such a sentence. Section 11 restricts the community order to imprisonable offences only. This will apply to offenders aged 18 and over only.

6.2.4 INDICTABLE OFFENCES – COMMITTAL PROCEEDINGS

Traditionally, where the magistrates decide that an offence triable either way should be tried in the Crown Court, they held committal proceedings. However, following the partial implementation of Sched 3 of the Criminal Justice Act 2003 (following the Criminal Justice Act 2003 (Commencement No. 28 and Saving Provisions) Order 2012, which came into force on 18 June 2012), committal proceedings for either-way offences going to the Crown Court have been abolished in many areas of England and Wales. The government intends to abolish committal proceedings everywhere in due course.

6.2.4.1 Old and new committals

Under the old system there were two sorts of committals under the Magistrates' Courts Act s 6(1) (known as 'old style') and s 6(2) ('new style'). The different possibilities gave the defendant a tactical choice. Under the old-style committal, the hearing was contested. The magistrates heard and examined the evidence although the prosecution just read out its witness statements and exhibits with the defendant's lawyer asking the magistrates to rule that there is insufficient evidence to proceed, that is, that there is no *prima facie* (Latin for 'at first sight') case to answer. By contrast in a new committal, the magistrates did not hear evidence or submissions. This was opted for if the defence did not wish to contest the evidence at the first stage, or if it was clear that there was a *prima facie* case to answer. The overwhelming majority of committal proceedings before magistrates were under s 6(2), that is, the case was 'sent up' to the Crown Court by the magistrates on the basis of the papers alone.

    Committal proceedings have now largely been abolished by the partial bringing into force of Sched 3 to the Criminal Justice Act 2003 (see above). Where committal proceedings have been abolished, 'either-way' offences that are to proceed to Crown Court trial will be sent there directly.

6.2.4.2 Reporting committal proceedings

In the old-style committal proceedings, it was generally only the prosecution that would give evidence, with the defence reserving its arguments. Until 1967, the prosecution case was frequently reported on in the press so that it was virtually impossible to find an unbiased jury for the trial. A notorious instance of this was the case of Dr John Bodkin Adams in 1957. During the committal, deaths of patients other than the one for which he was to stand trial were referred to, but were not afterwards part of the evidence at the trial (*The Times*, 15 January 1957). The law on reporting was eventually changed by the CJA 1967 and is now found in the MCA 1980. There are now restrictions on any application for dismissal put in by the defence. It is thus an offence to report on any aspect of the case if reporting restrictions have not been lifted by the bench. The bare matters that may as a matter of course be reported are:

- the identity of the court and the names of the examining magistrates;
- the names, ages, addresses and occupations of the accused and witnesses;
- the offence charged;
- the names of the lawyers engaged in the case;
- the decision of the court whether to commit or not and, if so, details of the committal, for example, to which court;
- any arrangements for bail;
- whether public funding was granted.

These restrictions, however, must be lifted by the magistrates if requested to do so by the accused. Where there are two or more accused and one objects to the reporting restrictions being lifted, then the magistrates must not lift them unless they regard it to be in the interests of justice to do so.

6.2.4.3 Section 51 of the Crime and Disorder Act 1998

This statute applies where the defendant is charged with an indictable-only offence – one which can only be tried by a Crown Court (for example, murder, manslaughter, rape or robbery). Section 51 of the Crime and Disorder Act (CDA) 1998 states that, where an adult is charged with an offence triable only on indictment, the court shall send him directly to the Crown Court for trial. He is 'sent forthwith'. Where he is also charged with an either-way offence or a summary offence, he may be sent directly to the Crown Court for that as well, provided the magistrates believe that it is related to the indictable offence and, in the case of a summary offence, it is punishable with imprisonment or involves obligatory or discretionary disqualification from driving. Under this procedure, the accused may apply to a Crown Court judge for the charge(s) to be dismissed, and the judge should so direct if it appears that the evidence would be insufficient to convict the accused (Sched 3 to the CDA 1998). When Sched 3 to the CJA 2003 comes fully into force, this procedure will be amended (see above 6.2.2.1).

6.2.4.4 Consistency of sentencing

Concern is often expressed at what sometimes appear to be quite notable discrepancies in sentencing practices employed by different benches of magistrates. It might be that these variations are unavoidable in circumstances where the rigidity of fixed penalties is unacceptable for most offences and regional differences in types of prevalent crime prompt justices to have certain attitudes to particular offences. Media reports from courtrooms are also unlikely to pick out the full detail and nuances of cases; there is clearly a difference between following a case in the press and watching it from the public gallery. There are several research surveys that demonstrate the discrepancies in magistrates' sentencing. Tarling, for example (*Sentencing and Practice in Magistrates' Courts*, 1979, Home Office Study 98), showed that in the 30 courts he surveyed, the use of probation (as it was then called) varied between 1 per cent and 12 per cent, suspended sentences between 4 per cent and 16 per cent, and fines between 46 per cent and 76 per cent. In one study, it was found that custody rates, average custodial sentence lengths (ACSL) and the use of life and Indeterminate sentences for Public Protection (IPPs) vary significantly across the 42 Criminal Justice Areas (CJAs) in England and Wales. For example, of those CJAs with custody rates in the top five for 2006, three (Essex, Bedfordshire and London) were consistently in the top five for 2003, 2004 and 2005. Similarly for those CJAs with custody rates in the bottom five for 2006, two (Dyfed–Powys and Lincolnshire) were consistently in the bottom five for 2003, 2004 and 2005 (T Mason, N de Silva, N Sharma, D Brown, G Harper, *Local Variation in Sentencing in England and Wales*, 2007, Ministry of Justice).

6.2.4.5   Committals for sentence

Currently, cases committed to the Crown Court for sentence must be heard in the Crown Court by a bench composed of a High Court judge, circuit judge or recorder sitting with between two and four JPs. The Powers of the Criminal Courts (Sentencing) Act 2000 ss 3–7 state that where, on a summary trial of an offence triable 'either way' a person aged 18 or over is convicted, the magistrates can commit the convicted person to the Crown Court for sentence if the magistrates are of the opinion that the offence was so serious that greater punishment should be inflicted for it than they have power to impose, or, in the case of a violent or sexual offence, that a custodial sentence for a period longer than the magistrates have power to impose is necessary to protect the public from serious harm.

6.2.5   WARRANT EXECUTION AND FINE DEFAULT POWERS

The police used to be primarily responsible for arresting fine defaulters and those in breach of community sentences. Increasingly, however, some police forces have given this work a low priority. The Courts Act 2003 extended the use of the Department for Work and Pensions' longstanding Third Party Deduction Scheme, which allows deductions from benefits to enforce payment of fines. The level of deductions is contained in the Social Security Fines (Deductions from Income Support) (Amendment) Regulations 2004.

Deductions can be applied when the offender is first sentenced, subsequently applied if the offender defaults as part of a resetting of payment terms, or used as a further sanction by the fines officer. While £5 is the maximum amount that can be deducted from benefits automatically to pay a fine, the overall cap on deductions remains at £8.40. Other deductions can include council tax, rent arrears, fuel costs, housing costs and water charges.

The Crown Court sits in 92 locations in England and Wales. The *Judicial and Court Statistics 2011* (Ministry of Justice, July 2012) shows that:

- around 91,910 cases were committed/sent for trial to the Crown Court in 2011. This represents a decrease of 6 per cent compared to 2010. Disposals of cases committed/sent for trial increased by 6 per cent to 93,960 in 2011;
- some 42,981 cases were committed to the Crown Court for sentence in 2011, an increase of 5 per cent on the previous year, while appeals against magistrates' decisions decreased by 3 per cent to 13,359;
- guilty pleas as a proportion of all defendants where a plea was entered remained at 70 per cent in 2011, the same as in 2010;
- in 2011, the cracked trial rate decreased by three percentage points to 40 per cent while the ineffective trial rate remained at 14 per cent.

Until 1971, the main criminal courts were the Assizes and the Quarter Sessions. These courts did not sit continuously and were not held in locations that corresponded with centres of population, as had been the case when they developed. The system was very inefficient as circuit judges wasted much time simply travelling from one town on the circuit to the next, and many defendants spent long periods in gaol awaiting trial.

Change was made following the *Report of the Beeching Royal Commission on Assizes and Quarter Sessions* (1969). The Courts Act 1971 abolished the Assizes and Quarter Sessions. These were replaced by a single Crown Court, a part of the Supreme Court of Judicature. The Crown Court is not a local court like the magistrates' court, but a single court which sits in over 90 centres. England and Wales are divided into six circuits, each with its own headquarters and staff. The centres are divided into three tiers. In first-tier centres, High Court judges hear civil and criminal cases, whereas circuit judges and recorders hear only criminal cases. Second-tier centres are served by the same types of judge, but hear criminal cases only. At third-tier centres, recorders and circuit judges hear just criminal cases.

Criminal offences are divided into four classes according to their gravity. Class 1 offences are the most serious, including treason and murder, and are usually tried by a High Court judge; exceptionally he may transfer a murder case (including attempts) to be heard by a circuit judge approved for this purpose by the Lord Chief Justice. Class 2 offences include manslaughter and rape and are subject to similar provisions. Class 3 offences include all remaining offences, triable only on indictment, and are usually tried by a High Court judge, although releases of cases to circuit judges are more common here. Class 4 offences include robbery, grievous bodily harm and all offences triable 'either way', and are not normally tried by a High Court judge.

6.3.1   THE JUDGES

High Court judges are usually from the Queen's Bench Division (QBD). Circuit judges are full-time appointments made by the Queen on the advice of the Lord Chancellor. They are drawn from advocates with at least 10 years' experience of Crown Court practice (s 71 of the CLSA 1990) or lawyers who have been recorders. Appointment is also possible for someone who has had three years' experience in a number of other judicial offices like that of the district judge (magistrates' courts). Circuit judges retire at the age of 72, or 75 if the Lord Chancellor thinks it in the public interest.

A circuit judge may be removed from office by the Lord Chancellor on the grounds of incapacity or misbehaviour (s 17(4) of the Courts Act 1971). This right has not been exercised since 1983, when Judge Bruce Campbell, an Old Bailey judge, was removed from office a week after being convicted of two charges of smuggling.

To qualify for appointment as a recorder, a person must have 10 years' experience of advocacy in the Crown Court or county courts. JPs may also sit in the Crown Court, provided they are with one of the types of judge mentioned above. It is mandatory for between two and four JPs to sit when the Crown Court is hearing an appeal or dealing with persons committed for sentence by a magistrates' court.

6.3.2   JURISDICTION

The Crown Court hears all cases involving trial on indictment. It also hears appeals from those convicted summarily in the magistrates' courts. At the conclusion of an appeal hearing, it has the power to confirm, reverse or vary any part of the decision under appeal (s 48(2) of the Senior Courts Act 1981). If the appeal is decided against the accused, the Crown Court has the power to impose any sentence that the magistrates could have imposed, including one that is harsher than the one originally imposed on the defendant.

6.3.3   DELAY AND OTHER CONCERNS REGARDING CROWN COURT PROCEEDINGS

Defendants committed to the Crown Court to be tried might have to wait a long time. The *Judicial and Court Statistics 2011* (Ministry of Justice, July 2012) show that:

- in 2011, the average waiting time for defendants on bail in committed for trial cases was 15.3 weeks and 8.6 weeks for those held in custody;
- in sent for trial cases the average waiting time in 2011 for defendants on bail was 23.5 weeks and 15.5 weeks for those held in custody;
- the average hearing time for defendants who pleaded not guilty decreased from 19.5 hours in 2010 to 18.9 hours in 2011 in sent for trial cases, and rose from 7.3 hours in 2010 to 7.9 hours in 2011 in committed for trial cases.

Ever since the Streatfield Committee Report recommended in 1961 that the maximum time a defendant should have to wait after committal for trial should be eight weeks, there have been many schemes to help achieve this aim, but none has been particularly successful. Since 1985, for example, a person charged with an offence triable 'either way' can request the prosecution to furnish him with information (in the form of witness statements, a summary of the case, etc) of the case against him. This was aimed at increasing the number of guilty pleas by showing to the defendant at an early stage the strength of the prosecution's case. Of course, if a defendant has chosen trial in the Crown Court he has long been entitled to have the entire prosecution case served on him at committal proceedings at the Magistrates' Court.

As at 2 October 2012, there were 660 circuit judges in England and Wales, compared with 680 as at 1 April 2010. This represents what the Ministry of Justice has described as 'a fluctuating trend' (http://www.justice.gov.uk/downloads/statistics/courts-and-sentencing/jcs-2011/judicial-court-stats-2011.pdf). The number of recorders and district judges remained at about the same level as in 2010, at 1,233 and 447, respectively, in 2012. Most Crown Court cases are heard by Circuit Judges. In 2011, they sat in 89 per cent of all trial cases dealt with in the Crown Court. Less complex or serious cases can be heard by Recorders; in 2011 they sat in 9 per cent of all trial cases dealt with in the Crown Court. High Court judges deal with the more complex and difficult cases. In 2011 they sat in 2 per cent of all trial cases dealt with in the Crown Court. They try the most serious criminal cases in the Crown Court and in 2011 they sat in 26 per cent of all Class 1 cases compared to only 2 per cent in each of Class 2 and Class 3 cases. In October 2010, there were 1,233 Recorders sitting in the courts, a marginal drop of two fewer judges than in 2008 (updated figures have not been published for 2011).

When one remembers that the average time to try a case on a plea of 'not guilty' is about 18 hours, the burden of work on the Crown Court – dealing with over 90,000 trials and 170,346 defendants each year – is considerable. The consequent delay has very serious repercussions for the criminal justice system: justice delayed is justice denied. The accuracy of testimony becomes less reliable the longer the gap between the original reception of the data by a witness and his account of it in court. Also important is the stress and pain for those innocent defendants who have to wait so long before their case can be put to a jury.

The largest ever study of Crown Court cases, undertaken by Zander and Henderson for the Runciman Commission, made some worrying findings. Their research was based on responses to questionnaires by more than 22,000 people involved in 3,000 Crown Court cases. The views of lawyers, judges, clerks, jurors, police and defendants were all canvassed. There were convictions in 8 per cent of cases that defence lawyers thought weak, 6 per cent that prosecution barristers thought weak and 4 per cent that judges thought weak, suggesting that innocent people were still being convicted in significant numbers. Further, 31 defendants said that they had pleaded guilty to offences they had not committed. Their reasons were varied: to avoid a trial; to gain a less severe sentence; or because they had been advised to do so by their lawyers.

Another worrying discovery, since poor defence lawyers have recently been cited as contributing to miscarriages of justice, is the large number of Crown Court cases (about one-third) that were being dealt with by unqualified clerks attending on the barrister at Court rather than trained, qualified solicitors. Some defendants met with their barrister for the first time on the morning of their trial, and for about one-third of these cases, the conference lasted for just 15 minutes. In about one-third of all cases, the barristers only received their instructions the day before the trial.

6.4   MAGISTRATES' COURTS v CROWN COURTS

For offences triable 'either way', there has been much debate about the merits of each venue. The introduction of the 'plea before venue' procedure previously described has significantly reduced the number of cases committed for trial to the Crown Court and significantly increased the number committed for sentence. In 2011 the proportion of all defendants (including those who did not enter a plea) who entered a not guilty plea in committed/sent for trial cases was 30 per cent, an increase of one percentage point from 2010. The guilty plea rate (the number of guilty pleas as a proportion of all defendants who pled) was 70 per cent, the same as in 2010. Since 2001 the guilty plea rate has steadily risen from 56 per cent to the current rate of 70 per cent. Initiatives in the Crown Court and other agencies, such as offering an early plea sentencing discount (a more lenient sentence if the defendant pleads guilty early) and providing early charging advice from the Crown Prosecution Service at police stations, have helped to increase the guilty plea rate. Moreover, other initiatives have not only helped to reduce the number of extraneous hearings, but have promoted early guilty plea decisions (*Judicial and Court Statistics 2011*, Ministry of Justice, July 2012).

One of the reasons defendants choose to have their cases tried at the Crown Court is that prosecution cases sometimes fall apart during the delay before a Crown Court hearing, allowing the defendant to go free. Another is that juries cannot be compelled to give reasons for convicting, unlike magistrates, who can be required to justify their reasons in writing for review in the High Court, which can overturn convictions or acquittals. Thus, there is a greater chance with jury convictions that an appeal court will regard a conviction (should there be one) as unsafe and unsatisfactory because the jury's reasons for having convicted will not be known. Thus, a defendant who suspects that he might be convicted can reasonably prefer to be convicted by a jury than by a magistrate because the former do not and cannot give reasons for their verdicts and are therefore perhaps easier to appeal. Jury verdicts are arguably more likely to be regarded as unsafe on appeal because it will not be known whether some improper factor (like a judge's misdirection) had entered their deliberation. The reports of the Court of Appeal (Criminal Division) contain many cases where the court states that a conviction should be quashed because a misleading statement from the judge might have influenced the jury. It might be said that a defendant should prefer the magistrates' court as the sentencing is generally lower, but when the defendant's antecedents are known (after a conviction), he can still be committed to the Crown Court for sentence, so the magistrates' courts are not really preferable to a defendant with a criminal record who fears another conviction is likely.

However, it is worth remembering that the Crown Court has more draconian powers of sentence compared to the magistrates' court – for example on a burglary it can sentence a defendant to 14 years' imprisonment whereas a magistrates' court's limit is six months.

6.5   CRIMINAL APPEALS

The process of appeal depends upon how a case was originally tried, whether summarily or on indictment. The system of criminal appeals underwent some changes during 2005 as a result of the Criminal Justice Act 2003.

6.5.1   APPEALS FROM MAGISTRATES' COURTS

Two routes of appeal are possible. The first route allows only a defendant to appeal. The appeal is to a judge and between two and four magistrates sitting in the Crown Court and can be: (a) against conviction (only if the defendant pleaded not guilty) on points of fact or law; or (b) against sentence. Such an appeal will take the form of a new hearing of the entire case (a trial *de novo*). In 2011, 44 per cent of appellants to the Crown Court had their appeals allowed or their sentences varied (*Judicial and Court Statistics 2011*, Ministry of Justice, July 2012).

Alternatively, the defendant can appeal 'by way of case stated' to the High Court (the Divisional Court of the QBD). This court consists of two or more judges (usually two), of whom one will be a Lord Justice of Appeal. Here, either the defence or the prosecution may appeal, but the grounds are limited to: (a) a point of law; or (b) that the magistrates acted beyond their jurisdiction. If the prosecution succeeds on appeal, the court can direct the magistrates to convict and pass the appropriate sentence. There is also an appeal by way of case stated from the Crown Court to the Divisional Court when the Crown Court has heard an appeal from the magistrates' court.

Appeal from the Divisional Court is to the Supreme Court. Either side may appeal, but only on a point of law and only if the Divisional Court certifies the point to be one of general public importance. Leave to appeal must also be granted either by the Divisional Court or the Supreme Court. Some magistrates' court decisions (not including conviction and sentence) can be appealed by way of a judicial review to the High Court if the magistrates were acting unlawfully, irrationally, in a way that was procedurally unfair, as a result of bias or in breach of the Human Rights Act 1998. Such decisions include a refusal to grant an adjournment, a decision to amend a charge or a decision to refuse bail.

6.5.2   APPEALS FROM THE CROWN COURT

Appeals from the Crown Court lie to the Court of Appeal (Criminal Division), which hears appeals against conviction and sentence. This court, replacing the Court of Criminal Appeal, was established in 1966. The Division usually sits in at least two courts – one composed of the Lord Chief Justice sitting with two judges of the QBD and the other of a Lord Justice of Appeal and two Queen's Bench judges. During 2010, a total of 7,475 applications for leave to appeal were received, of which 1,535 were against conviction in the Crown Court and 5,623 against the sentence imposed. Of the total applications for leave to appeal (permission to appeal) which were considered by a single judge, numbering 4,606 in 2011, 221 applications were granted in respect of appeals against conviction and 1,063 against sentence.

Of the appeals heard by the Full Court during 2011, nearly 200 applications to appeal against conviction were allowed. The Full Court also allowed 1,386 appeals against sentence. The number of retrials ordered by the Full Court in 2010 was 56, a continuation of the marked decrease on the 59 retrials ordered in 2009 and the 72 in 2008 (at the time of writing figures for 2011 had not been provided).

Until 1996, s 2 of the Criminal Appeal Act (CAA) 1968 permitted the Court of Appeal to allow an appeal against conviction where it felt:

> (a)   that the verdict of the jury should be set aside on the ground that, under all the circumstances of the case, it is unsatisfactory or unsafe; or
>
> (b)   that the judgment of the court of trial should be set aside on the ground of a wrong decision of any question of law; or
>
> (c)   that there was a material irregularity in the course of the trial, and in any other case shall dismiss the appeal;
>
> provided that the court may, notwithstanding that they are of opinion that the point raised in the appeal might be decided in favour of the appellant, dismiss the appeal if they consider that no miscarriage of justice has actually occurred.

January 1996 saw the introduction of the Criminal Appeal Act (CAA) 1995. The introduction of ss 1, 2 and 4 of the Act brought particularly significant changes to the criminal appeal system.

Section 1 amended the CAA 1968 so as to bring an appeal against conviction, an appeal against a verdict of not guilty by reason of insanity and an appeal against a finding of disability, *on a question of law alone*, into line with other appeals against conviction and sentence (that is, those involving questions of fact, or mixtures of law and fact). Now, all appeals against conviction and sentence must first have leave of the Court of Appeal or a certificate of fitness for appeal from the trial judge before the appeal can be taken. Before the 1995 Act came into force, it was possible to appeal without the consent of the trial judge or Court of Appeal on a point of law alone. In parliament, the reason for this change was given as the need to 'provide a filter mechanism for appeals on a ground of law alone which are wholly without merit' (HC Official Report, SC B (Criminal Appeal Bill) Col 6, 21 March 1995).

Section 2 changed the grounds for allowing an appeal under the CAA 1968. Under the old law, the Court of Appeal was required to allow an appeal where: (1) the conviction, verdict or finding should have been set aside on the ground that, under all the circumstances, it was unsafe or unsatisfactory; or (2) that the judgment of the court of trial or the order of the court giving effect to the verdict or finding should be set aside on the ground of a wrong decision of law; or (3) that there was a material irregularity in the course of the trial. In all three situations, the Court of Appeal was allowed to dismiss the appeal if it considered that no miscarriage of justice had actually occurred. The law now requires the Court of Appeal to allow an appeal against conviction under s 1 of the CAA 1968, an appeal against verdict under s 12 (insanity) or an appeal against a finding of disability if it thinks that the conviction, verdict or finding is 'unsafe' (as opposed to the old law, which used the 'unsafe or *unsatisfactory*' formula).

During the parliamentary passage of the Act, there was much heated debate about whether the new provisions were designed to narrow the grounds of appeal. That would amount to a tilt in favour of the State in that it would make it harder for (wrongly) convicted people to appeal. Government ministers insisted that the effect of the new law was simply to restate or consolidate the practice of the Court of Appeal. One government spokesman said that:

> In dispensing with the word 'unsatisfactory', we agree with the Royal Commission on criminal justice that there is no real difference between 'unsafe' and 'unsatisfactory'; the Court of Appeal does not distinguish between the two.
>
> Retaining the word 'unsatisfactory' would imply that we thought there was a real difference and would only lead to confusion.

There were many attempts during the legislation's passage to insert the words 'or may be unsafe' after the word 'unsafe'. The Law Society, the Bar, Liberty and JUSTICE called on the government to make such a change. Also opposed to the use of the single word 'unsafe' was the eminent criminal law expert Professor JC Smith. The late Professor Smith argued cogently that there were many cases where a conviction was seen as 'unsatisfactory' rather than 'unsafe', so that there was a need for both words. Sometimes, the Court of Appeal might be convinced that the defendant is guilty (so the conviction is 'safe') but still wishes to allow the appeal because fair play, according to the rules, must be seen to be done. Accepting improperly extracted confessions (violating s 76 of the Police and Criminal Evidence Act (PACE) 1984) simply because it might seem obvious that the confessor is guilty will promote undesirable interrogation practices, because police officers will think that even if they break the rules, any resulting confession will nevertheless be allowed as evidence.

Professor Smith gave the example ((1995) 145 NLJ 534) of where there has been a serious breach of the rules of evidence. In *Algar* (1954), the former wife of the defendant testified against him about matters during the marriage. The Court of Appeal allowed his appeal against conviction, but Lord Goddard said: 'Do not think that we are doing this because we think that you are an innocent man. We do not. We think that you are a scoundrel.' (*The Times*, 17 November 1953) The idea behind such remarks is that rules are rules, and the rules of evidence must be obeyed in order to ensure justice. Once you start to accept breaches of the rules as being justified by the outcome (ends justifying means), then the whole law of evidence could begin to collapse.

The proposal to include 'or might be unsafe' was rejected for the reason probably best summarised by Lord Taylor, the then Lord Chief Justice, who argued in the Lords that there was no merit in including the words 'or may be unsafe', as the implication of such doubt is already inherent in the word 'unsafe'.

Cases decided since the new formula was introduced have tended to indicate that the Court of Appeal has not adopted a restrictive interpretation. Thus, a conviction was quashed as unsafe in *Smith (Patrick Joseph)* (1999) because of irregularities at trial, even though the accused had admitted his guilt during cross-examination. The Human Rights Act (HRA) 1998, incorporating the European Convention on Human Rights (ECHR), introduced a further significant element into the consideration of this issue. Article 6 ECHR, to which English courts must give effect unless incompatible with an Act of Parliament, gives the defendant a right to a fair trial. Irregularities in a trial, including misdirections by the judge, admission of improperly obtained evidence and so on, might cast doubt on the fairness of the trial without necessarily making the conviction unsafe on a narrow view of that word. In *Davis* (2001), the Court of Appeal suggested that since a conviction might be unsafe even where there was no doubt about guilt, but there were serious irregularities at the trial, English rules on appeals were compatible with Art 6. However, it went on to argue that a violation of Art 6 did not necessarily imply that the conviction must be quashed. Subsequently, Lord Woolf CJ argued in *Togher* (2000) that obligations under the ECHR meant that it was almost inevitable that if the accused had been denied a fair trial, his conviction would have to be regarded as unsafe. Confusingly the European Court of Human Rights itself does not always follow the restrictive approach, appearing to use consequentialist reasoning to justify using evidence obtained in violation of Art 3 ECHR (the prohibition against torture and inhuman and degrading treatment) in a criminal trial in the case of *Gäfgen v Germany* (2011).

The *Davis* decision was appealed to the House of Lords, where the reasoning and approach of the appellate court was confirmed as correct (2008). The *Davis* decision on the compatibility of anonymous witnesses with the demands of Art 6 ECHR should now be read in conjunction with the *Horncastle* decision of the UK Supreme Court ([2009] UKSC 14) and the affirmation of the Supreme Court's decision by the Grand Chamber of the European Court of Human Rights in *Al-Khawaja v United Kingdom* (2012). The upshot of these decisions is that Art 6 will not *automatically* be breached where hearsay statements amount to the 'sole and decisive' evidence in a criminal trial.

The Court is also vigilant about the operation of s 78 of the Police and Criminal Evidence Act 1984, which allows a court to exclude unfair evidence or unfairly obtained evidence. Section 78 operates as a so-called 'exclusionary discretion' rule.

Section 4 provides a unified test for the receipt of fresh evidence in the Court of Appeal. Under the old law, the Court of Appeal had a discretion under s 23(1)(c) of the CAA 1968 to receive fresh evidence of any witness if it was thought necessary or expedient in the interests of justice. Section 23(2) added a duty to receive new evidence that was relevant, credible and admissible, and which could not reasonably have been adduced at the original trial. There was often much argument about whether new evidence should be received under the court's discretion or its duty. Gradually, the 'duty' principles came to be merged into the 'discretion' principles. The aim of the latest amendment is to reflect the current practice of the court. The general discretion under s 23(1) has been retained, but the 'duty' principle has been replaced with a set of criteria which the court must consider. They are:

- whether the evidence appears to the court to be capable of belief;
- whether it appears to the court that the evidence may afford any ground for allowing the appeal;
- whether the evidence would have been admissible at the trial on the issue under appeal; and
- whether there is a reasonable explanation for the failure to adduce the evidence at trial.

Only the accused may appeal. No leave to appeal is required if the appeal is against conviction on a point of law, but it is needed for appeals on points of fact or mixed fact and law. Leave is also required for appeals against sentence. Under s 36 of the CJA 1972, the Attorney General can refer a case which has resulted in an acquittal to the Court of Appeal where he believes the decision to have been questionably lenient on a point of law. The Court of Appeal deals just with the point of law and the defendant's acquittal is not affected even if the court decides the point against the defendant. It merely clarifies the law for future cases.

Sections 35–36 of the CJA 1988 allow the Attorney General to refer indictable-only cases to the Court of Appeal where the sentence at trial is regarded as unduly lenient. The Court can impose a harsher sentence. Following the determination of an appeal by the Court of Appeal or by the Divisional Court, either the prosecution or the defence may appeal to the Supreme Court. Leave from the court below or the Supreme Court must be obtained and two other conditions fulfilled according to s 33 of the CAA 1968:

1. the court below must certify that a point of law of general public importance is involved; and
2. either the court below or the Supreme Court must be satisfied that the point of law is one which ought to be considered by the Supreme Court.

The High Court can quash tainted acquittals under s 54 of the CPIA 1996. An acquittal is 'tainted' where someone has since been convicted of conspiring to pervert the course of justice in the case by interfering with the jury.

6.5.2.1 The Criminal Justice Act 2003

Section 57: Introduction

This section sets out certain basic criteria for a prosecution appeal under this Part of the Act. The right of appeal arises only in trials on indictment and lies to the Court of Appeal.

Sub-section (2) sets out two further limitations on appeals under this Part. It prohibits the prosecution from appealing rulings on discharge of the jury and those rulings that may be appealed by the prosecution under other legislation, for example, appeals from preparatory hearings against rulings on admissibility of evidence and other points of law.

Sub-section (4) provides that the prosecution must obtain leave to appeal, either from the judge or the Court of Appeal.

Section 58: General Right of Appeal

This section sets out the procedure that must be followed when the prosecution wishes to appeal against a terminating ruling. The section covers both rulings that are formally terminating and those that are *de facto* terminating in the sense that they are so fatal to the prosecution case that, in the absence of a right of appeal, the prosecution would offer no or no further evidence. It applies to rulings made at an applicable time during a trial (which is defined in sub-s (13) as any time before the start of the judge's summing up to the jury).

Where the prosecution fails to obtain leave to appeal or abandons the appeal, the prosecution must agree that an acquittal follow by virtue of sub-ss (8) and (9).

Section 59: Expedited and Non-Expedited Appeals

This section provides two alternative appeal routes: an expedited (fast) route and a non-expedited (slower) route. The judge must determine which route the appeal will follow (sub-s (1)). In the case of an expedited appeal, the trial may be adjourned (sub-s (2)). If the judge decides that the appeal should follow the non-expedited route, he may either adjourn the proceedings or discharge the jury, if one has been sworn (sub-s (3)). Sub-section (4) gives both the judge and the Court of Appeal power to reverse a decision to expedite an appeal, thus transferring the case to the slower non-expedited route. If a decision is reversed under this sub-section, the jury may be discharged.

Section 61: Determination of Appeal by Court of Appeal

This section sets out the powers of the Court of Appeal when determining a prosecution appeal. This needs to be read in conjunction with s 67.

Sub-section (1) authorises the Court of Appeal to confirm, reverse or vary a ruling that has been appealed against. The section is drafted to ensure that, after the Court of Appeal has ordered one or other of these disposals, it must then always make it clear what is to happen next in the case.

When the Court of Appeal confirms a ruling, sub-ss (3) and (7) provide that it must then order the acquittal of the defendant(s) for the offence(s) which are the subject of the appeal.

When the Court of Appeal reverses or varies a ruling, sub-ss (4) and (8) provide that it must either order a resumption of the Crown Court proceedings or a fresh trial, or order the acquittal of the defendant(s) for the offence(s) under appeal. By virtue of sub-ss (5) and (8), the Court of Appeal will only order the resumption of the Crown

Court proceedings or a fresh trial where it considers it necessary in the interests of justice to do so.

Section 68: Appeals to the Supreme Court

Sub-section (1) amends s 33(1) of the Criminal Appeal Act 1968 to give both the prosecution and defence a right of appeal to the Supreme Court from a decision by the Court of Appeal on a prosecution appeal against a ruling made under this Part of the Act.

Sub-section (2) amends s 36 of the Criminal Appeal Act 1968 to prevent the Court of Appeal from granting bail to a defendant who is appealing, or is applying for leave to appeal, to the Supreme Court from a Court of Appeal decision made under this Part of the Act. Bail will continue to be a matter for the trial court.

In 2011 the Supreme Court had an overall caseload of 77 appeals from various courts within England and Wales. The Privy Council had a caseload of 37 appeals.

Section 69: Costs

Sub-sections (2) and (3) amend ss 16(4A) and 18 of the Prosecution of Offences Act 1985 to give the Court of Appeal power, on an appeal under this Part, to award costs to and against the defendant.

The Criminal Justice Act also allows for the retrial of serious offences.

Section 75: Cases that may be Retried – Changes to the Rule against 'Double Jeopardy'

Section 75 sets out the cases that may be retried under the exception to the normal rule against *double jeopardy*. These cases all involve serious offences which in the main carry a maximum sentence of life imprisonment, and which are considered to have a particularly serious impact either on the victim or on society more generally. The offences to which the provisions apply are called 'qualifying offences' and are listed in Sched 5 to the Act. They include murder, manslaughter, rape and arson endangering life.

The cases that may be retried are those in which a person has been acquitted of one of the qualifying offences, either on indictment or following an appeal, or of a lesser qualifying offence of which he could have been convicted at that time. This takes into account cases of 'implied acquittals', in which, under the current law, an acquittal would have prevented a further prosecution being brought for a lower level offence on the same facts. For example, an acquittal for murder may also imply an acquittal for the lower level offence of manslaughter, but new evidence may then come to light, which would support a charge of manslaughter. A person may only be retried in respect of a qualifying offence.

In certain circumstances, cases may also be tried where an acquittal for an offence has taken place abroad, so long as the alleged offence also amounted to a qualifying offence and could have been charged as such in the UK. This would include, for example, offences such as war crimes, and murder committed outside the UK, for which the courts in England and Wales have jurisdiction over British citizens abroad. Such cases are likely to be rare. Subsection (5) recognises that offences may not be described in exactly the same way in the legislation of other jurisdictions.

Section 76: Application to the Court of Appeal

Section 76 allows a prosecutor to apply to the Court of Appeal for an order that quashes the person's acquittal and orders him to be retried for the qualifying offence. A 'prosecutor' means a person or body responsible for bringing public prosecutions, such as the Crown Prosecution Service or HM Customs and Excise. Where a person has been acquitted outside the UK, the court will need to consider whether or not the acquittal would act as a bar to a further trial here and, if it does, the court can order that it must not be a bar.

Applications to the Court of Appeal require the personal written consent of the Director of Public Prosecutions (DPP). This provides a safeguard to ensure that only those cases in which there is sufficient evidence are referred to the Court of Appeal. The DPP will also consider whether it is in the public interest to proceed. This section also recognises any international obligations arising under the Treaty of the European Union, under which negotiations are taking place to support the mutual recognition of the decisions of the courts in other EU Member States.

Applications may also be brought by public prosecuting authorities if new evidence arises in cases that have previously been tried by means of a private prosecution.

Only one application for an acquittal to be quashed may be made in relation to any acquittal. In March 2006, a man accused of a 1989 murder became the first person to have his case referred to the Court of Appeal under this procedure. The body of Julie Hogg, 22, from Teesside, was found hidden behind her bath by her mother, Ann Ming. William Dunlop, 42, was acquitted of Ms Hogg's murder. In April 2005, police said they were to re-examine the case of Ms Hogg. William Dunlop previously faced two murder trials, but each time the jury failed to reach a verdict and he was formally acquitted in 1991. The then Director of Public Prosecutions, Ken Macdonald, said that after looking at submissions from the Chief Crown Prosecutor for Cleveland, Martin Goldman, he was satisfied the Crown Prosecution Service should apply to the Court of Appeal for a retrial. The Court of Appeal heard this application and ordered a retrial of Dunlop under s 75. In October 2006 he pleaded guilty to murdering Ms Hogg and was sentenced to life imprisonment. The Court of Appeal had applied s 75 when the CPS applied for a re-hearing of Dunlop's case and felt that: (1) a jury could be selected which would not have any prior knowledge of Dunlop's earlier conviction; (2) that any such recollection was outweighed by the fact that Dunlop had repeatedly confessed to Ms Hogg's murder since his acquittals in 1991 and that he had been convicted of perjury in relation to his denial of that offence; (3) the delay did not render a retrial unfair; (4) the new evidence under s 78 was both compelling and overwhelming (it consisted of Dunlop's repeated confessions) and he was in no position to rebut the new evidence; (5) justice required that he face a retrial.

As the first example of this new procedure these comments by the Court of Appeal are clearly important. This provision was subsequently invoked by the Court of Appeal to quash the acquittal of Gary Dobson for the murder of the black teenager Stephen Lawrence in 1993 (*R v Dobson* (2011)) (see also 1.3.5). Following Dobson's second trial in 2011, he was convicted of murder.

Section 77: Determination by the Court of Appeal

Section 77 sets out the decisions that the Court of Appeal may make in response to an application for an acquittal to be quashed. The court must make an order quashing an acquittal and ordering a retrial if it considers that the requirements set out in ss 78 and 79 of the Act are satisfied, namely that there is new and compelling evidence in the case, and that it is in the interests of justice for the order to be made. The court must dismiss an application where it is not satisfied as to these two factors.

Section 78: New and Compelling Evidence

Section 78 sets out the requirement for there to be new and compelling evidence against the acquitted person in relation to the qualifying offence, and defines evidence which is 'new and compelling'. Evidence is 'new' if it was not adduced at the original trial of the acquitted person. Evidence is 'compelling' if the court considers it to be reliable and substantial and, when considered in the context of the outstanding issues, the evidence appears to be highly probative of the case against the acquitted person. The court is thus required to make a decision on the strength of the new evidence. So, for example, new evidence relating to identification would only be considered 'compelling' if the identity of the offender had been at issue in the original trial. It is not intended that relatively minor evidence, which might appear to strengthen an earlier case, should justify a retrial.

Section 79: Interests of Justice

Section 79 sets out the requirement that in all the circumstances it is in the interests of justice for the court to quash an acquittal and order a retrial. In determining whether it is in the interests of justice, the court will consider in particular: whether there are existing factors that make a fair trial unlikely (for example, the extent of adverse publicity about the case); the length of time since the alleged offence was committed; and whether the police and prosecution acted with due diligence and expedition in relation to both the original trial and any new evidence. The court may take into account any other issues it considers relevant in determining whether a retrial will be in the interests of justice.

The Criminal Justice and Immigration Act 2008 alters the test for ordering a retrial in England and Wales (or that the trial should resume) where the Court of Appeal allow a prosecution appeal against a terminating ruling. The original CJA 2003 provided that a court should not order a resumed or fresh trial unless it considered it necessary in the interests of justice to do so. Now, under s 44 of the 2008 Act, the court may not order that the defendant be acquitted unless it considers that he could not receive a fair trial/retrial.

6.6 THE ACCESS TO JUSTICE ACT 1999 – JURISDICTION

Section 61 of the Access to Justice Act 1999 establishes the jurisdiction of the High Court to hear cases stated by the Crown Court for an opinion of the High Court. This part of the Act (Part IV) enables these and certain other applications to the High Court to be listed before a single judge. It provides for the appointment of a Vice President of the QBD. It also prohibits the publication of material likely to identify a child involved in proceedings under the Children Act 1989, before the High Court or a county court, and allows for those under 14 years old to attend criminal trials.

6.7 JUDICIAL COMMITTEE OF THE PRIVY COUNCIL

The Judicial Committee of the Privy Council was created by the Judicial Committee Act 1833. Under the Act, a special committee of the Privy Council was set up to hear appeals from the Dominions. The cases are heard by the judges (without wigs or robes) in a committee room in London. The Committee's decision is not a judgment but an 'advice' to the monarch, who is counselled that the appeal be allowed or dismissed.

The Committee is the final court of appeal for certain Commonwealth countries that have retained this option, and from some independent members and associate members of the Commonwealth. The Committee comprises Privy Councillors who are Justices of the Supreme Court.

Most of the appeals heard by the Committee are civil cases. In the rare criminal cases, it is only on matters involving legal questions that appeals are heard. The Committee does not hear appeals against criminal sentence.

The decisions of the Privy Council are very influential in English courts because they concern points of law that are applicable in this jurisdiction and they are pronounced upon by Lords of Appeal in Ordinary in a way that is tantamount to a Supreme Court ruling. These decisions, however, are technically of persuasive precedent only, although English courts normally follow them; see, for example, the criminal appeal case *Abbot v R* (1977).

This was an appeal from Trinidad and Tobago. The Privy Council ruled that duress is no defence to the perpetrator of murder.

6.8 ROYAL COMMISSION ON CRIMINAL JUSTICE

Research undertaken for the Royal Commission by Kate Malleson of the London School of Economics found that judges' mistakes are by far the most common ground for successful appeals against conviction. The research discovered that in about 80 per cent of cases where convictions were quashed, there had been an error at the trial and, in most instances, it was judicial error.

Of 300 appeals in 1990, just over one-third were successful. Of those appealing, almost two-thirds of defendants appealed against conviction on the ground that the trial judge had made a crucial mistake and, of those, 43 per cent succeeded in having their convictions quashed. Sixteen defendants were vindicated by the Court of Appeal in claims that the judge's summing up to the jury was biased or poor; a further 42 convictions were quashed because the judge was wrong about the law or evidence.

This research was critical of the way the Court of Appeal failed to consider cases where fresh evidence had emerged since the trial or where there was a 'lurking doubt' about the conviction. The Report urged that the court be given a new role allowing it to investigate the events leading up to a conviction.

The Royal Commission was set up, under the chairmanship of Viscount Runciman, in March 1991, after the release of the Birmingham Six (an important case in a series of notorious miscarriages of justice in which people were found to have been wrongly convicted and sentenced for serious crimes). It reported in July 1993, with 352 recommendations largely designed to prevent wrongful conviction. Several of the recommendations are relevant to discussion of the criminal courts. The numbers here refer to those of the recommendations in the Report.

The Commission recommended (331) that the Home Secretary's power to refer cases to the Court of Appeal under s 17 of the CAA 1968 should be removed and a new body – the Criminal Cases Review Authority – should be set up to consider allegations (332) that a miscarriage of justice might have occurred. The Authority should have 'operational independence' (333), with a chairman appointed by the Queen on the advice of the Prime Minister. The Authority should be independent of the court structure (336) and should refer meritorious cases directly to the Court of Appeal. There should be neither a right of appeal nor a right to judicial review (340) in relation to decisions reached by the Authority. The Authority should consist of both lawyers and lay people, should be supported by a staff of lawyers (344) and should devise its own rules and procedures. It should be able to discuss cases directly with applicants (345) and should have powers (347) to direct its own investigations. These recommendations were largely met by the terms of the CAA 1995.

The latest data show that between January and July 2010, 10 criminal appeals were presented to the Supreme Court of which five were allowed outright (*Judicial and Court Statistics 2010*, Ministry of Justice, July 2011 – data for 2011 has not yet been produced). All those appeals were brought from the criminal division of the Court of Appeal.

6.9   CRIMINAL CASES REVIEW COMMISSION

The Criminal Cases Review Commission (CCRC) is an independent body set up under the CAA 1995. The CCRC came into being on 1 January 1997. It employs 90 staff members, including a core of 50 specialist caseworkers. It is responsible for investigating suspected miscarriages of criminal justice in England, Wales and Northern Ireland. This function was previously carried out through the office of the Home Secretary. He would make occasional referrals of cases back to the Court of Appeal when a unit of civil servants in the Home Office evaluated a case (which had otherwise exhausted the formal court appeal system) as warranting further consideration. Over 250 cases were transferred from the Home Office around 31 March 1997, when the Commission took over responsibility for casework.

The CCRC cannot overturn convictions or sentences itself. Instead, it may refer to the Court of Appeal a conviction for an offence tried on indictment, or a finding of not guilty by reason of insanity, or a finding that a person was under a disability when he did the act or made the omission, and may also refer cases in respect of sentence where they were tried on indictment (s 9 of the CAA 1995). Additionally, the CCRC may refer to the Crown Court convictions and sentences imposed by magistrates' courts, though the Crown Court may not impose any punishment more severe than that of the court from which the decision is referred (s 11 of the CAA 1995). The Court of Appeal itself may direct the CCRC to carry out an investigation and it must report to the court when finished or as required to do so by the court. Once the reference has been made, it will be treated as an appeal for the purposes of the CAA 1968.

The Commission is given power by ss 17–21 of the CAA 1995 to obtain information and carry out investigations, including appointing investigating officers (who are likely to be police officers where there have been previous police investigations).

Any decision to refer a case to the relevant appellate court has to be taken by a committee of at least three members. The CCRC considers whether or not there is a real possibility that the conviction, finding, verdict or sentence would not be upheld were a reference to be made.

In order to establish that there is a real possibility of an appeal succeeding regarding a conviction, there has to be: an argument or evidence which has not been raised during the trial or at appeal; or exceptional circumstances.

In order to establish that there is a real possibility of an appeal succeeding against a sentence, there has to be a legal argument or information about the individual or the offence which was not raised in court during the trial or at appeal.

Other than in exceptional circumstances, the Commission can only consider cases in which an appeal through the ordinary judicial appeal process has failed and, once a decision is taken to refer a case to the relevant court of appeal, the Commission has no other involvement.

The CCRC referred the notorious case of Derek William Bentley to the Court of Appeal. Mr Bentley was convicted at the Central Criminal Court on 11 December 1952 of the murder of PC Sidney Miles. Mr Bentley did not actually shoot the officer. His accomplice fired the gun in a failed burglary attempt, but Mr Bentley was convicted under the principles of 'joint enterprise', even though he was being held under arrest by a police officer, metres away from where his accomplice fired the pistol. An appeal against conviction was heard by the Court of Criminal Appeal on 13 January 1953 and dismissed. Mr Bentley was hanged on 28 January 1953.

Bentley's conviction and sentence were the subject of numerous representations to the Home Office. In July 1993, on the recommendation of the Home Secretary, Her Majesty The Queen, in the exercise of the Royal Prerogative of Mercy, granted to Mr Bentley a posthumous pardon limited to sentence.

Following submissions from the applicants' solicitors and the completion of its own inquiries, the CCRC concluded that the Court of Appeal should reconsider Mr Bentley's conviction. The trial was seen as unfair in a number of respects, for example, the fact that, although 18, Bentley had a mental age of 11 was kept a secret from the jury, and the judge's summing up to the jury was astonishingly biased in favour of the police. In August 1998, on a momentous day in legal history, the Court of Appeal cleared Bentley of the murder for which he was hanged 46 years earlier. In giving judgment, the Lord Chief Justice, Lord Bingham, said: '. . . the summing up in this case was such as to deny the appellant that fair trial which is the birthright of every British citizen.'

The latest figures (CCRC *Case Statistics*, figures to 30 July 2012) show the following data:

Total applications*:	15,002 (total applications includes 279 cases transerred from the Home Office when the Commission was set up in 1997)
Cases waiting:	255
Cases under review:	638
Completed:	14,280 (including ineligible) 504 referrals
Heard by Court of Appeal:	462 (325 quashed, 137 upheld, 0 reserved)

Taking a global perspective on legal systems, it is unusual for any machinery of justice to provide as many opportunities for appeal and challenge as exist in the English system. The CCRC website is easy to use and well maintained (www.ccrc.gov.uk). Within the 'Case Library' tab, you can go to the hyperlink 'Cases we have referred'. From there, there are links to 'previous 20 cases', 'first 20 cases' and also a search engine comprehensively pooling information on referrals to the CCRC. The details of past referrals are displayed as follows:

Name:	UNDERWOOD Dennis Bernard
Reference Number:	963/97
Date Referred to Court:	20/10/2000
Offence:	Murder
Appeal Outcome:	Upheld
Date of Appeal Outcome:	22/05/2003
Judgment:	Available

6.10 A MISCARRIAGE OF JUSTICE

One of the English legal system's worst miscarriages of justice cases in recent history was exposed in the Court of Appeal in February 1998. In 1979, Vincent Hickey, Michael Hickey, Jimmy Robertson and Pat Molloy, who became known as the Bridgewater Four, were convicted of the murder of a 13-year-old boy, Carl Bridgewater. Although the men were not angelic characters (and two had serious criminal records), they strenuously protested that they were not guilty of the horrific child murder.

Eighteen years later, and after two earlier failed visits to the Court of Appeal and seven police investigations, three of the men were released on 21 February on unconditional bail in anticipation of an appeal hearing in April. The fourth defendant, Mr Molloy, died in jail in 1981. The appeal was eventually allowed.

The Crown has conceded that the case against the men was 'flawed' by evidence falsified and fabricated by police officers. There has also come to light significant fingerprint evidence, tending to exonerate the four, which was not disclosed to the defence by the prosecution. Mr Molloy was questioned for 10 days without access to a solicitor, and a fabricated statement from Vincent Hickey was used to persuade Mr Molloy to confess to the crime. Before he died, Mr Molloy claimed he had been beaten by police officers in the course of his interrogation. The former police officers alleged to have falsified the evidence were investigated but not prosecuted.

The case was given extensive coverage in the print and broadcast media in February 1997 and made a significant impact upon public consciousness. This major case raises many points germane to the operation of the criminal justice system. The following are of particular importance:

The case was originally investigated in 1978, before PACE 1984 had been passed. The requirements under PACE 1984 for suspects to be given access to legal advice (s 58, Code C) and for interviews to be recorded (s 60, Code E) may have reduced or eliminated the opportunity for police malpractice of the sort which occurred in the *Bridgewater* case.

Although the criminal justice system ultimately corrected an injustice, this result was achieved primarily through the indefatigable efforts of a few dedicated family members, campaigning journalists and Members of Parliament who would not let the issue disappear from the public forum. The case attracted attention because of the terrible nature of the crime – a child murder. It is quite possible that many other unjust convictions in cases with more mundane facts are never propelled into public discussion or overturned.

Miscarriages of justice cases involve two types of insult to notions of legal fairness: (a) the wrongly imprisoned endure years of incarceration; (b) the real culprits (a child killer in the *Bridgewater* case) are never identified and could well go on to commit other offences.

The men were released due to the discovery of evidence that had been fabricated and falsified; yet the CPIA 1996 restricts defence access to prosecution evidence.

The CCRC was established to re-evaluate alleged cases of miscarriages of justice. One criticism of it has been that it does not have its own independent investigators, but must rely on police officers to re-examine cases.

The jury is only as good as the information and arguments put before it allows it to be. After the prosecution's case had been devastated by the discovery of new scientific evidence in 1993 (a forensic psychiatrist showed that Molloy's 'confession' used language the suspect would not have used), the foreman of the jury from the 1979 trial risked prosecution for contempt of court by issuing a statement to say that he thought that the men were not guilty. He, along with another juror, said they regretted that they had not been given all the evidence that was available at the time of the trial.

6.11 REFORM OF THE CRIMINAL COURTS

An impetus for reform came in December 1999 from the desire on the part of the government to subject the criminal courts to a process of review to parallel that undertaken by

Lord Justice Woolf in relation to the civil courts earlier in the 1990s. The Lord Chancellor appointed Lord Justice Auld to conduct on his own an independent review of the working of the criminal courts. His terms of reference required him to inquire into and report on:

> [. . .] the practices and procedures of the criminal courts at every level, with a view to ensuring that they deliver justice fairly, by streamlining all their processes, increasing their efficiency and strengthening the effectiveness of their relationships with others across the whole of the criminal justice system, and having regard to the interests of all parties including victims and witnesses, thereby promoting confidence in the rule of law.

Lord Justice Auld's review of the criminal courts was published in September 2001. It contained a number of controversial proposals. Many of these proposals were adopted by the government and were legislated in the Courts Act 2003, which received Royal Assent on 20 November 2003. The most important features are addressed below.

The Act is divided into nine Parts. The key parts are as follows:

Part 1: Maintaining the Court System

- This places the Lord Chancellor under the general duty of maintaining an efficient and effective court system and gives him power to make appropriate arrangements for staff and accommodation. This Part also abolishes magistrates' courts committees (MCCs) and establishes courts' boards.

The Lord Chancellor's duty now concerns all the main courts in England and Wales, namely the Court of Appeal, the High Court, the Crown Court, the county courts and the magistrates' courts. This responsibility is discharged, in practice, by Her Majesty's Courts Service.

Part 2: Justices of the Peace

- This makes provision for Justices of the Peace and other matters relating to magistrates' courts. It replaces commission areas and petty session areas with local justice areas and provides for fines officers. This Part also makes provision about the effect of the Act of Settlement 1701 on the appointment of lay magistrates.

Lay magistrates are appointed to a local justice area on the basis of the place where they reside, and most summary offences must be tried in the local justice area where the alleged offence took place. Lay magistrates are appointed for England and Wales. This, coupled with changes in Part 3 of the Act, has the effect of giving lay magistrates a national jurisdiction. The Lord Chancellor is, however, placed under a statutory duty to assign lay magistrates to a local justice area.

The Act creates the role of a 'fines officer' to take enforcement action in certain circumstances, thus removing the need for all enforcement decisions to be taken by a court. A fines collection system (Sched 5) has been set up, which introduces financial incentives to offenders to pay their fines, as well as providing a range of new disincentives for fine default, including wider powers to make attachments of earnings orders (AOE) and deductions from benefits (DFB). The system is designed to encourage payment, but includes new penalties for those who have the means and will not pay. The Act also introduces new sanctions for failing to provide information necessary to make AOE orders and DFB applications. For those who are unable to pay a fine, the Act introduces (in Sched 6) a system for discharging fines by unpaid work.

Section 21 of the Act requires the Lord Chancellor to take all reasonable and practicable steps to ensure that lay justices are kept informed on matters that affect them in the performance of their duties in a local justice area, and that their views will be taken on such matters.

Section 22 makes similar provision to s 10A(1), (3) and (4) of the Justices of the Peace Act (JPA) 1997 (as amended by the Administration of Justice Act (AJA) 1999). These provide for the appointment by the Lord Chancellor of district judges (magistrates' courts), qualification requirements, payment of allowances and removal from office. This section also replaces provisions in s 69 of the JPA 1997, which provides for the swearing-in of district judges (magistrates' courts) – consequential amendments will require them to be sworn in by a circuit judge or High Court judge.

Section 23 of the 2003 Act replaces s 10A(2) of the JPA 1997 (as amended by the AJA 1999), which deals with the appointment of a senior district judge and a deputy senior district judge. The section allows the Lord Chancellor to appoint one of the district judges (magistrates' courts) to be the senior district judge and, if the Lord Chancellor decides to do this, he may appoint another district judge (magistrates' courts) to be his deputy. The main function of the senior district judge is judicial administration. This section says that the Lord Chancellor will have a discretion, rather than a duty, to appoint a senior district judge (chief magistrate) and deputy. This is because the government accepted the Auld Review's recommendation that the role of the senior district judge should be reviewed, both as to its functions and its necessity.

Part 3: Magistrates' Courts
- This deals with jurisdiction and procedure in criminal, civil and family proceedings in magistrates' courts.

Section 50 of the Act deals with youth courts. This section sets out the framework whereby lay magistrates and district judges (magistrates' courts) are to be authorised to hear youth cases. The Act also enables the higher judiciary including circuit judges and recorders to hear these cases, without particular authorisation, in consequence of the extension of their jurisdiction to include that of a district judge (magistrates' courts) by s 66.

Part 4: Judges
- This allows for alterations to the names of judicial titles and offices. This Part also allows district judges (magistrates' courts) to sit as Crown Court judges and gives

judges of the higher courts all the powers of Justices of the Peace, to give increased flexibility in judicial deployment.

Flexibility in Deployment of Judicial Resources

Section 65: District Judges (Magistrates' Courts) as Crown Court Judges

Unification of the administration of the criminal courts provides scope for rationalising the work of the magistrates' and Crown Courts. For example, district judges can deal with and make orders in relation both to allocation and to other interim issues in cases reserved to the Crown Court. This is further eased by the revised allocation of cases provided by the Criminal Justice Act 2003. Revised allocation of cases ensures that cases are dealt with by the court at the appropriate level with regard to the complexity, value and proportionality of the case.

Section 66: Judges having Powers of District Judges (Magistrates' Courts)

Under this section, a Crown Court judge can make orders and sentence in relation to cases normally reserved to magistrates' courts when disposing of related cases in the Crown Court. As part of implementing the policy of greater flexibility in judicial deployment, this section provides that High Court judges, circuit judges and recorders should be able to sit as magistrates when exercising their criminal and family jurisdiction. The same applies to deputy High Court judges and deputy circuit judges. This provision is not used extensively, but it is possible for a circuit judge in the Crown Court to deal with a summary offence without the case having to go back to a magistrates' court. Historically, certain summary offences could be included in an indictment. If the person was convicted on the indictment, the Crown Court could sentence him if he pleaded guilty to the summary offence, but if he pleaded not guilty, the powers of the Crown Court ceased. Now the judge of the Crown Court can deal with the summary offences then and there as a magistrate, following magistrates' courts' procedure.

Section 67: Removal of Restrictions on Circuit Judges Sitting on Certain Appeals

This section provides for the repeal of s 56A of the Senior Courts Act (SCA) 1981 (as inserted by s 52(8) of the Criminal Justice and Public Order Act 1994). Repeal enables the selected circuit judges who sit in the Criminal Division of the Court of Appeal to hear or determine any appeal against either a conviction before a judge of the High Court or a sentence passed by a judge of the High Court.

Part 5: Procedure Rules and Practice Directions

The Criminal Courts

The government recognised in the White Paper, *Justice for All*, that the benefits the Auld Review identified from a fully unified criminal court could be realised through closer alignment of the criminal courts. This could be achieved without a complete reordering of the courts system or the introduction of an 'intermediate tier'.

The White Paper announced that the government would legislate to bring the magistrates' courts and the Crown Court closer together and that these courts, when exercising their criminal jurisdiction, would be known as 'the criminal courts'. This part of the Act addresses this change.

Practice Directions

The Heads of Division (the Lord Chief Justice, Master of the Rolls, President of the Family Division and Vice Chancellor) have power under the High Court's inherent jurisdiction to make directions as to practice and procedure. Section 74A of the County Courts Act (CCA) 1984, amended under the Constitutional Reform Act 2005, gives the President of the Courts of England and Wales overall control over practice directions to be followed in county courts. He, and any person authorised by him, may make directions as to the practice and procedure of county courts, but there is no statutory provision about practice directions for magistrates' courts. The President can make directions as to the practice and procedure of the criminal courts. It will also provide statutory authority for the President of the Family Division, with the concurrence of the Lord Chancellor, to be able to issue practice directions in his or her own name which are binding on the magistrates' courts and county courts when hearing family proceedings.

Criminal Procedure Rule Committee

The creation of the Criminal Procedure Rule Committee (Crim PRC) established a forum for the development of rules, to determine the practices and procedures to be used in all criminal courts in England and Wales. The Committee identifies itself as being 'responsible for modernising court procedure and practice and making the Criminal Procedure Rules' (http://www.justice.gov.uk/about/moj/advisory-groups/criminal-procedure-rule-committee). The work of the Committee complements and coexists alongside other agencies for criminal justice reform, including the Law Commission. This work involves 'engaging with partners across the criminal justice system . . . ensuring that proposals are practicable and that effective consultation takes place before new rules are made'. Having consulted beforehand, the Committee meets to discuss proposals and consider drafted rules. The Committee is currently chaired by the Lord Chief Justice of England and Wales, Lord Judge; the deputy chairman is Lady Justice Rafferty.

There were previously two committees with different purposes and differing powers: the Magistrates' Courts' Rule Committee (under s 144 of the MCA 1980) and the Crown Court Rule Committee (under ss 84 and 86 of the SCA 1981). They each dealt with rules concerning criminal and civil business. Neither Committee had overarching responsibility for ensuring consistency across the courts. They rarely met. The Crim PRC now has responsibilities that were exercised by the Magistrates' Courts' Rule Committee and the Crown Court Rule Committee, insofar as they relate to rules of criminal practice and procedure.

Part 6: Miscellaneous

- This amends the procedures for appeals to the House of Lords (now the Supreme Court) and the Court of Appeal.

Provisions Relating to Criminal Procedure and Appeals

Appeals to Court of Appeal: Procedural Directions

Section 87 of the Courts Act 2003 inserts new sections into the Criminal Appeal Act (CAA) 1968 to extend the powers of: (a) a single judge in the Court of Appeal (Criminal Division); and (b) the Registrar of the Court of Appeal (Criminal Division) prior to determination by the full court of an appeal or application for leave to appeal. Section 31B enables either a single judge or the Registrar to give procedural directions that need not trouble the full court, thus reducing delay. Section 31C provides, in the case of a decision of a single judge, for the appellant or, under specified circumstances, the prosecution to apply to the full court to review such a direction. Section 31C also provides for the decision by the Registrar to be reviewed by a single judge in the first instance or, if the defence or prosecution so wish, further reviewed by the full court.

In the Court of Appeal (Criminal Division), single judges consider applications for leave to appeal and act as a 'filter' by carrying out certain specified functions of the full Court of Appeal. Section 31 of the CAA 1968 lists the powers of the Court of Appeal, which may be exercised by a single judge. However, the inability of the single judge to make a broader range of procedural directions for the conduct and progress of an appeal can lead to delay and unnecessary complication.

The Auld Review recommended that a judge of the Court of Appeal should be empowered, when considering applications for leave to appeal, to give procedural directions for the hearing of the application or of the appeal that need not trouble the full court, subject to a right on the part of the applicant or the prosecution, as the case may be, to renew the application to the full court.

The Registrar of Criminal Appeals (who also holds the posts of Master of the Crown Office and Queen's Coroner and Attorney) has ultimate responsibility for the management and running of the Criminal Appeal Office, which has a staff of 150. The Registrar also provides a key reference point for the judiciary in the criminal justice system. He or she undertakes the judicial responsibilities listed in s 31A of the CAA 1968.

The Registrar has the power (among other things) to give procedural directions for the preparation or hearing of the application or of the appeal, to determine applications for an extension of time and to identify which Court of Appeal judges are to sit in the criminal division.

Prosecution Appeals from the Court of Appeal

The Act amends s 2 of the Administration of Justice Act 1960 and s 34 of the CAA 1968 by extending the time in which an application by either the defence or the prosecution for leave to appeal from a decision of the Court of Appeal (Criminal Division) can be made. It also makes clear that time begins to run against either the prosecution or the defendant from the date of the Court of Appeal's reasoned judgment, rather than from the date of its decision. The Act makes provision with the same effect in relation to Northern Ireland by amending para 1 of Sched 1 to the Judicature (Northern Ireland) Act 1978 and s 32 of the Criminal Appeal (Northern Ireland) Act 1980.

The Auld Review recommended that s 34(2) of the CAA 1968 should be amended to empower the House of Lords (as it then was) and Court of Appeal, as the case may be, to extend the time within which a prosecutor may apply for leave to appeal, as it does in the case of a defendant. There is a disparity between a defendant and a prosecutor as to the operation of the time limits within which each may petition the Supreme Court for leave to appeal where the Court of Appeal, having certified a point of law of general public importance, has refused leave. Both have 14 days from the decision of the Court of Appeal to apply to it for leave and, if leave is refused by the court, a further 14 days from the date of refusal to petition the Supreme Court. While the Supreme Court or the Court of Appeal have power at any time to extend a defendant's time for application for leave, neither has power to do so if the prosecutor wishes leave but fails to apply within time. The Act gives both the defence and the prosecution an extra 14 days. However, it was not considered appropriate to accept the recommendation that the prosecution should be able to apply for an extension of time – this would leave a defendant with the indefinite possibility of the original conviction being restored by the Supreme Court.

6.12 CORONERS' COURTS

The coroners' courts are one of the most ancient parts of the English legal system, dating back to at least 1194. They are not, in modern function, part of the criminal courts, but because of historical associations, it makes more sense to classify them with the courts in this chapter rather than that dealing with civil courts. The coroner was an appointment originally made as *custos placitorum coronae*, keeper of the pleas of the Crown. They had responsibility for criminal cases in which the Crown had an interest, particularly a financial interest.

Today, there are 157 coroners' courts, of which 21 sit full-time. These are presided over by 138 full-time coroners and 240 deputy and assistant coroners and a Chief Coroner. The Chief Coroner is a new office, created by the Coroners and Justice Act 2009, intended to give national leadership to the coroner service across England and Wales. HHJ Peter Thornton QC has been appointed the first Chief Coroner. Coroners are usually lawyers (with at least a five-year qualification within s 71 of the Courts and Legal Services Act (CLSA) 1990), although about 25 per cent are medical doctors with an appropriate legal qualification. The main jurisdiction of the coroner today concerns unnatural and violent deaths (including those under Article 2 of the European Convention on Human Rights where the death in question may have been caused by State agents), although treasure trove is also something occasionally dealt with.

The classifying of types of death is clearly of critical importance, not just to the State, politicians and policy-makers, but also to the sort of campaign groups that exist in a constitutional democracy to monitor suicides, drug-related deaths, deaths in police custody and prison, accidental deaths, deaths in hospitals and deaths through industrial diseases.

There were 222,371 deaths reported to coroners in 2011, a fall of 3.6 per cent from 2010. Inquests were opened on 30,981 of the deaths that were reported and the most common verdicts were deaths from natural causes (29.5 per cent) and deaths from accident or misadventure (26 per cent). Verdicts of suicide rose by 7 per cent in 2011 (*Coroners Statistics 2011 England and Wales*, Ministry of Justice, May 2012). If death occurs in any of the following circumstances, it should routinely be reported to the coroner who has jurisdiction (see http://www.direct.gov.uk/en/Governmentcitizensandrights/Death/WhatToDoAfterADeath/DG_066713):

- after an accident or injury;
- following an industrial disease;
- during a surgical operation;
- before recovery from an anaesthetic;
- if the cause of death is unknown;
- if the death occurred in prison or police custody, or otherwise while a person was being detained by a State authority;
- if the death was violent or unnatural – for example, suicide, accident or drug or alcohol overdose;
- if the death was sudden and unexplained – for example, a sudden infant death (cot death);
- if the deceased was not seen by the doctor issuing the medical certificate after he or she died, or during the 14 days before the death.

Anyone who is concerned about the cause of a death can inform a coroner about it, in the same way that members of the public are encouraged to report suspected crimes to the police. In practice, however, a death will be reported to the coroner by a doctor or the police.

The coroner will order a post-mortem and this may reveal a natural cause of death that can be duly registered. If not, or in certain other circumstances, such as where the death occurred in prison or police custody or if the cause is unknown, there will be an inquest. The proportion of all registered deaths reported to coroners remained at an estimated 47 per cent in 2011, the same as in 2010. This percentage has been relatively consistent over the last few years. The percentage of cases involving post-mortem examinations, as a proportion of all deaths reported to coroners, fell slightly from just above 44 per cent in 2010 to 42 per cent in 2011. This continues the existing downward trend in the number of post-mortems being undertaken (*Coroners Statistics 2011 England and Wales*, Ministry of Justice, May 2012).

Nearly all inquests concluded in 2011, as in other years, were held without juries. The number of inquests held with juries in 2010 was 482, a rise of 40 compared with 2010. Both the number and proportion of inquests held with juries have shown a downward trend in recent years but the trend appears now to have halted. The proportion of inquests held with juries has fallen from 3.6 per cent of inquests concluded in 1999 to just over 1.5 per cent in 2011 (*Coroners Statistics 2011 England and Wales*, Ministry of Justice, May 2012). The State, however, has historically been insistent that certain types of case must be heard by a jury in order to promote public faith in government. When, in 1926, legislation for the first time permitted inquests to be held without juries, certain types of death were deliberately marked off as still requiring jury scrutiny and these included deaths in police custody, deaths resulting from the actions of a police officer on duty and deaths in prison. This was seen as a very important way of fostering public trust in potentially oppressive aspects of the State. In 1971, the Brodrick Committee Report on the coronial system saw the coroner's jury as having a symbolic significance and thought that it was a useful way to legitimate the decision of the coroner.

In order to comply with Article 2 of the European Convention on Human Rights, and according to domestic legislation, a jury must be summoned where the death occurred:

(a)   in prison, or in such a place or such circumstances as to require an inquest under another Act;

(b)   in police custody, or resulted from an injury caused by a police officer in the purported execution of his or her duty;

(c)   where there are certain statutory reporting obligations under the Health and Safety Act 1974 or any other Act, and in certain other circumstances, especially where there may be a continuing or recurring danger to the public.

The coroner's court is unique in using an inquisitorial process. There are no 'sides' in an inquest. There may be representation for people such as the relatives of the deceased, insurance companies, prison officers, car drivers, companies (whose policies are possibly implicated in the death) and train drivers, etc, but all the witnesses are the coroner's witnesses. The coroner decides who shall be summoned as witnesses and in what order they shall be called.

Historically, an inquest jury could decide that a deceased had been unlawfully killed and then commit a suspect for trial at the local assizes. When this power was taken away in 1926 the main bridge over to the criminal justice system was removed. There then followed, in stages, an attempt to prevent inquest verdicts from impinging on the jurisdictions of the ordinary civil and criminal courts. Now, an inquest jury is exclusively concerned with determining who the deceased was and 'how, when and where he came by his death'. The court is forbidden to make any wider comment on the death and must not determine or appear to determine criminal liability 'on the part of a named person'.

Nevertheless, the jury may still now properly decide that a death was unlawful (that is, a crime). The verdict 'unlawful killing' is on a list of options (including 'suicide', 'accidental death' and 'open verdict') made under legislation and approved by the Home Office.

Highly contentious provisions contained in the Coroners and Justice Act 2009 (in force since 1 February 2010) change and clarify important aspects of both criminal justice and coronial law. Policy circulars (numbers 2010/02 and 2010/03), produced by the Criminal Law Policy Unit within the Ministry of Justice in January 2010, provide a useful overview of the key changes effected by the 2009 Act: http://www.justice.gov.uk/publications/docs/circular-02-2010-coroners-justice-act.pdf. Among key changes brought in by the 2009 Act, s 59 amends s 2 of the Suicide Act 1961 so as to replace the substantive offence of aiding, abetting, counselling or procuring suicide. The separate offence of attempting to commit the s 2 offence is replaced by the 2009 Act with a single offence cast in modern, familiar language. The Criminal Attempts Act 1981, therefore, no longer applies to s 2 of the 1961 Act. However, the scope of the law remains the same: these changes do not render liable to prosecution anyone who would not have been liable before. Instead, the purpose of these changes is to clarify the scope and application of criminal offences in this area.

A full copy of the Coroners and Justice Act 2009 is available at http://www. legislation.gov.uk/ukpga. The accompanying 'explanatory notes' on the 2009 Act are available at http://www.legislation.gov.uk/ukpga/2009/25/notes/contents

CHAPTER SUMMARY: THE CRIMINAL COURTS

THE MAIN COURTS

The trial courts are the magistrates' courts and Crown Courts. In serious offences, known as *indictable offences*, the defendant is tried by a jury in a Crown Court; for *summary offences*, he is tried by magistrates; and for 'either-way' offences, the defendant can be tried by magistrates if they agree, but he may elect jury trial in the Crown Court.

The main issues here concern the distribution of business between the magistrates' court and Crown Courts: what are the advantages of trial in the magistrates' court: (a) for the State; and (b) for the defendant? Conversely, what are the disadvantages?

APPEALS

Criminal appeals from the magistrates go to the Crown Court or to the QBD Divisional Court 'by way of case stated' on a point of law or that the JPs went beyond their proper powers, or by way of judicial review. If the prosecution succeeds on appeal, the court can direct the magistrates to convict and pass the appropriate sentence. There is also an appeal by way of case stated from the Crown Court to the Divisional Court when the Crown Court has heard an appeal from the magistrates' court. From the Crown Court, appeals against conviction and sentence lie to the Court of Appeal (Criminal Division). Note the powers of the Attorney General under s 36 of the CJA 1972 and his powers under ss 35 and 36 of the CJA 1988.

Part IV of the Access to Justice Act 1999 establishes the High Court's jurisdiction to hear cases stated by the Crown Court for an opinion. It enables these cases stated to be heard by a single judge.

The Judicial Committee of the Privy Council hears final appeals from some Commonwealth countries and its decisions are of persuasive precedent in English law.

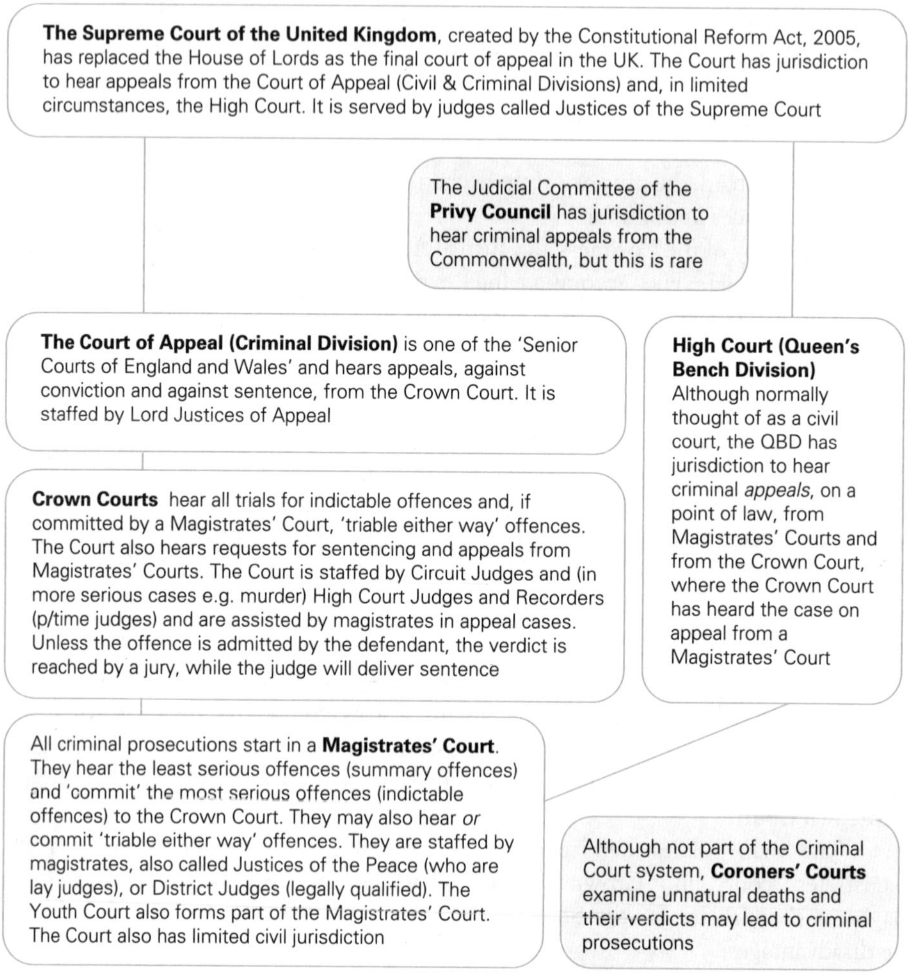

The **Supreme Court of the United Kingdom**, created by the Constitutional Reform Act, 2005, has replaced the House of Lords as the final court of appeal in the UK. The Court has jurisdiction to hear appeals from the Court of Appeal (Civil & Criminal Divisions) and, in limited circumstances, the High Court. It is served by judges called Justices of the Supreme Court

The Judicial Committee of the **Privy Council** has jurisdiction to hear criminal appeals from the Commonwealth, but this is rare

The Court of Appeal (Criminal Division) is one of the 'Senior Courts of England and Wales' and hears appeals, against conviction and against sentence, from the Crown Court. It is staffed by Lord Justices of Appeal

High Court (Queen's Bench Division) Although normally thought of as a civil court, the QBD has jurisdiction to hear criminal *appeals*, on a point of law, from Magistrates' Courts and from the Crown Court, where the Crown Court has heard the case on appeal from a Magistrates' Court

Crown Courts hear all trials for indictable offences and, if committed by a Magistrates' Court, 'triable either way' offences. The Court also hears requests for sentencing and appeals from Magistrates' Courts. The Court is staffed by Circuit Judges and (in more serious cases e.g. murder) High Court Judges and Recorders (p/time judges) and are assisted by magistrates in appeal cases. Unless the offence is admitted by the defendant, the verdict is reached by a jury, while the judge will deliver sentence

All criminal prosecutions start in a **Magistrates' Court**. They hear the least serious offences (summary offences) and 'commit' the most serious offences (indictable offences) to the Crown Court. They may also hear *or* commit 'triable either way' offences. They are staffed by magistrates, also called Justices of the Peace (who are lay judges), or District Judges (legally qualified). The Youth Court also forms part of the Magistrates' Court. The Court also has limited civil jurisdiction

Although not part of the Criminal Court system, **Coroners' Courts** examine unnatural deaths and their verdicts may lead to criminal prosecutions

FIGURE 6.1 *The Structure of the Criminal Courts.*

REVIEW AFTER APPEAL

In an attempt to deal with possible miscarriages of justice, and following the recommendations of the Royal Commission on Criminal Justice in 1993 (the Runciman Commission), the Criminal Appeal Act 1995 established the Criminal Cases Review Commission (CCRC). The CCRC has power to investigate and to refer cases to the Court of Appeal (or, where appropriate, the Crown Court) where it considers that there is a real possibility of an appeal succeeding.

THE CORONERS' COURTS

These are not part of the criminal justice system. Their main function is to decide the cause of unnatural deaths. Verdicts such as unlawful killing, might result with other legal processes like criminal prosecutions or human rights claims.

1.   The age of criminal responsibility in the UK is 10. This is one of the lowest ages of criminal responsibility in the world. Where an adult defendant with the mental age of a 10-year-old could establish a defence of diminished responsibility or insanity, does it make sense for an actual 10-year-old to be tried as an adult?

2.   Evidence obtained using oppressive techniques is not admissible in criminal proceedings. But what about the situation where the police believe that a child's life is in immediate danger and so threaten a suspect with physical violence if he does not tell them where the child is? If the suspect confesses and the child is found dead, should that confession be admissible evidence?

3.   The bench of three magistrates in a youth court must be made up of at least one woman and one man. Currently there is only one woman in the Supreme Court; of 107 judges at the high court, only three are from ethnic minorities and only 16 are women. Is it important that the judiciary reflect the diversity of the population? And if it is, what can be done to diversify the bench?

FURTHER READING

Archbold: *Criminal Pleading, Evidence and Practice*, 2012, Richardson, P J (ed), London: Sweet & Maxwell

Bates, T, 'The contemporary use of legislative history in the United Kingdom' (1995) 54(1) CLJ 127

Bell, J and Engle, G (Sir), *Cross: Statutory Interpretation*, 3rd edn, 1995, London: Butterworths

Bennion, F, 'Statute law: obscurity and drafting parameters' (1978) 5 British JLS 235

Bennion, F, *Statutory Interpretation*, 2nd edn, 1992, London: Butterworths

Burrows, D, 'Enforcement matters: Part 1' (2009) 159 NLJ 334–5; Part II (2009) 159 NLJ 415

Carlen, P, *Magistrates' Justice*, 1976, Oxford: Martin Robertson

Committee on the Preparation of Legislation, *Renton Committee Report*, Cmnd 6053, 1975, London: HMSO

Dugg, A, Farmer, L, Marshall, S and Tadros, V (eds), *The Trial on Trial – Truth and Due Process*, 2004, Oxford: Hart Publishing

Eskridge, W, *Dynamic Statutory Interpretation*, 1994, Cambridge, MA: Harvard UP

Fitzpatrick, B, *Going to Court*, 2006, Oxford: OUP

Friedman, L, 'On interpretation of laws' (1988) 11(3) Ratio Juris 252

Gibb, F, 'The highest court in the land opens its doors to the public', *The Times*, 1 October 2009

Grove, T, *The Magistrates' Tale*, 2002, London: Bloomsbury

Hillman, M, 'For the public good?' (2008) 158 NLJ 661

Manchester, C, *Exploring the Law: The Dynamics of Precedent and Statutory Interpretation*, 2006, London: Sweet & Maxwell

Matthews, P and Foreman, J (eds), *Jervis: On the Office and Duties of Coroners*, 1993, London: Sweet & Maxwell

Moxon, D and Hedderman, C, 'Mode of trial decisions and sentencing differences between courts' (1994) 33(2) Howard J of Criminal Justice 97

New Law Journal, 'Increase in cases to CCRC' [2007] 1060

Richardson, J (ed), *Archbold on Criminal Pleading, Evidence and Practice*, 2012, London: Sweet & Maxwell

Stone, J, 'The Ratio of the Ratio Decidendi' (1959) 22 MLR 597

USEFUL WEBSITES

www.hmcourts-service.gov.uk
The official website of Her Majesty's Courts Service.

www.magistrates-association.org.uk
The official website of the Magistrates' Association.

http://www.justice.gov.uk/index.htm
The official website of the Criminal Justice System.

COMPANION WEBSITE

Now visit the companion website to:

- test your understanding of the key terms using our Flashcard Glossary;

- revise and consolidate your knowledge of 'The criminal courts' using our Multiple Choice Question testbank;

- view all of the links to the Useful Websites above.

www.routledge.com/cw/slapper

THE CRIMINAL PROCESS: (1) THE INVESTIGATION OF CRIME

7

The criminal justice system has unceasingly been the subject of widespread heated debate in parliament, the broadcast media and the print media, and in academic and professional journals. The Criminal Justice Act 2003, for example, had 339 sections and made hundreds of quite significant changes to the operation of the criminal justice system. It was followed shortly afterwards by the Serious Organised Crime and Police Act 2005. The changes made by these statutes span many areas, including those of criminal evidence, bail, juries and appeals. We examine some of these, where relevant, in this chapter and in Chapter 8.

Police-recorded crime may not adequately represent all crime. The Crime Survey for England and Wales (CSEW), which replaces the British Crime Survey, is based on interviews conducted throughout the year, and includes crimes that are not reported to the police. Nevertheless, police-recorded crime in England and Wales has been falling; in 2011/2012 there were just under 4 million police-recorded crimes, compared with 4.3 million in 2010/11. This puts police-recorded crime at its lowest since the National Crime Recording Standard was introduced in April 2002: police-recorded crime in 2011/2012 represents a drop of a third since 2002/2003 and is 50 per cent lower than the mid-1990s peak of 19.1 million crimes per annum (Crime Survey for England and Wales, Office of National Statistics, July 2012). According to the CSEW, crime now remains around the lowest level ever reported. The majority of both CSEW crimes (in the 2011/12 survey) and crimes recorded by the police in 2011/12 were theft, violence and vandalism or criminal damage offences.

The rise in crime through the 1980s followed an economic downturn and rising unemployment. Many commentators therefore expected the current economic downturn to lead to increases in acquisitive crime. However, since the onset of the current economic downturn in late 2008, there has not been a rise in overall acquisitive crime, and many types of acquisitive crime (such as domestic burglary and vehicle theft) continue to show a flat or downward trend. However, there is evidence of more recent increases in some categories of theft. One of the most marked rises in recent years has been in the recorded crime category of 'Other theft or unauthorised taking', which is up 2 per cent in 2011/12 compared with 2010/11 following a 10 per cent rise between 2009/10 and 2010/11. Although recorded crime statistics do not allow for the breakdown of this category by type of item stolen, it is known to include thefts of metal and metal cable. It is thought that metal theft has been an important contributor to rises in 'other theft or unauthorised taking' and this type of crime has also occurred in other countries, such as the USA, and is closely linked to metal commodity prices (Sidebottom et al, 'Theft in Price-volatile Markets (2011) *Journal of Research in Crime and Delinquency*, 48(3), pp 396–418).

It is possible that the rise in metal theft is now slowing. This is supported by the latest figures from British Transport Police (BTP) which suggest the large increases in metal theft from the rail network between 2009/10 and 2010/11 are now reducing, with the BTP reporting a fall in theft of railway property, which is likely to be driven by metal theft.

A special data subset pertaining to knife crime was started in 2007/08. In 2011/12, for the selected offences of attempted murder, GBH with intent, GBH without intent, robbery, threats to kill, ABH, sexual assault and rape, the police recorded 30,999 offences. Where a knife or sharp instrument was involved, a fall of 5 per cent was seen from 2011/12, following a fall of 3 per cent from the previous year (Crime Survey for England and Wales, Office of National Statistics, July 2012).

The CSEW is a face-to-face victimisation survey in which people resident in households in England and Wales are asked about their experiences of crime in the 12 months prior to interview. Respondents to the survey are also asked about their attitudes towards different crime-related issues, such as the police, criminal justice system, and perceptions of crime and anti-social behaviour. Until recently, the British Crime Survey (the predecessor to the CSEW) did not cover crimes against those aged under 16 (see the submissions made during the consultation process by The Children's Society, http://www.childrenssociety.org.uk/resources/documents/Policy/8683_full.pdf). Since January 2009, interviews have been carried out with children aged as young as 10. For the first time, in 2011, the BCS provided statistics on crimes against children. In the most recent survey it is estimated that there were one million offences against 10- to 15-year-olds in 2011/12 and that children were more likely than adults to be the victims of violent crime (Crime Survey for England and Wales, Office of National Statistics, July 2012). The CSEW provides a better reflection of the true extent of crime because it includes incidents that are not reported to the police and crimes which are not recorded by them.

Crime involving weapons (such as knives and guns) represents a sample area in which the rate of crime has consistently dropped since 2005/06; gun crime has fallen by 39 per cent since 2005/06 and knife crime also demonstrates a downward trend (Crime Survey for England and Wales, Office of National Statistics, July 2012).

This chapter and the following one refer to the 'criminal justice system'. This has been for many years an accepted descriptive term used by social scientists, journalists and, occasionally, lawyers. Officially, however, there is no such thing as the 'criminal justice system'. Governmental responsibilities, for example, overlap in this area. The Home Secretary is responsible for the Metropolitan Police, criminal statistics, the probation service and the Crown Prosecution Service (CPS) (and, more broadly, for 'law and order'). The Lord Chancellor is responsible for all the criminal law courts, the appointment of magistrates and the judges. Nonetheless, in recent times, there has been increasing governmental recognition of something called the 'criminal justice system'. On 30 December 1998, for example, a single official statement entitled 'Joint Press Release on the Criminal Justice System Public Service Agreement' was issued on behalf of the Home Office, the Lord Chancellor's Department (LCD) (now the Ministry of Justice) and the Attorney General's Office. It stated:

> The overarching aims, objectives and performance measures for the criminal justice system have been published for the first time in a cross-departmental Public Service Agreement. The three Departments, and their respective services, will be working more closely than ever before to ensure that the criminal justice system protects the public and delivers justice. Inter-agency co-operation will be promoted at regional, local, as well as at the national level. Ministers believe that these arrangements are a good example of 'joined-up government' in practice.

The aims and objectives of the criminal justice system have now been refined. The official statement says (for more information see http://www.justice.gov.uk):

> The purpose of the Criminal Justice System (CJS) is to deliver justice for all, by convicting and punishing the guilty and helping them to stop offending, while protecting the innocent. It is responsible for detecting crime and bringing it to justice; and carrying out the orders of court, such as collecting fines, and supervising community and custodial punishment.

The key goals for the CJS were stated as being:

- to improve the effectiveness and efficiency of the CJS in bringing offences to justice;
- to increase public confidence in the fairness and effectiveness of the CJS;
- to increase victim satisfaction with the police, and victim and witness satisfaction with the CJS;
- to consistently collect, analyse and use good quality ethnicity data to identify and address race disproportionality in the CJS; and
- to increase the recovery of criminal assets.

7.2 MISTRUST OF THE SYSTEM

There exists mistrust of the criminal justice system from both those who believe innocent people have been convicted and those who think guilty people escape justice.

The number of exposed miscarriages of justice involving malpractice and disastrous errors by agencies of the criminal justice system has grown rapidly. On 19 March 1991, the day the Birmingham Six were released from prison having wrongly served 16 years in jail, the Home Secretary announced a Royal Commission on Criminal Justice to examine the system with a view to reducing the chances of wrongful conviction. The Commission published its report with 352 recommendations in July 1993. Some of these recommendations have been implemented in subsequent legislation (like the establishment of the Criminal Cases Review Commission (CCRC) by the Criminal Appeal Act (CAA) 1995). For a useful discussion of these issues, see Annabelle James, 'Miscarriages of justice in the 21st century' (2002) 66(4) *Journal of Criminal Law*, pp 326–37. Great concern was expressed by pressure groups about the government's rejection of the Royal Commission's findings in relation to the so-called 'right to silence'.

This right was effectively undermined by ss 34–37 of the Criminal Justice and Public Order Act (CJPOA) 1994, and this change will arguably increase the chances of miscarriages occurring rather than reduce them. Confidence in the criminal justice system appears to be in decline. In a national survey for the 1962 Royal Commission on the Police (Cmnd 1728, 1962, HMSO), 83 per cent of respondents indicated that they had 'a great deal of respect' for the way the police operated. In a national poll in 1993, conducted by MORI for *The Sunday Times* and the Police Federation, under 50 per cent of respondents indicated that they had 'a great deal of respect' for the way the police operated. The poll also showed that one in six adults (7 million people) actually distrust the police (*The Sunday Times*, 25 July 1993). In another nationwide poll (*The Independent*, 21 June 1993), 28 per cent of respondents indicated that they would be 'concerned at what might be going to happen' if stopped by the police, with only 36 per cent of respondents indicating they would be confident that they would be treated fairly. More recently, two criminologists have challenged the current government's proposed policy to cut 'red tape' associated with stop-and-search paperwork. As announced by Theresa May, the Home Secretary, the government's appetite to slash the bureaucracy of stop-and-searches has been hailed by Ben Bowling and Rebekah Delsol as removing a monitoring system that has rendered policing more accountable. (See 'Reducing stop-and-search paperwork undermines fairness', guardian.co,uk, 26 May 2010, http://www.guardian.co.uk/commentisfree/liberty-central/2010/may/26/stop-and-search-reform-theresa-may.)

Unlike its predecessor (the BCS), the CSEW does not report on public confidence in aspects of the criminal justice system (CJS). The 2007/08 BCS shows that, compared with 2006/07, public confidence in the CJS had improved in five of the seven aspects covered. These increases follow a period where confidence fell in most aspects of the CJS between 2005/06 and 2006/07. Prior to this there had been general improvements between 2002/03 and 2005/06. The report *Crime in England and Wales 2009/10* (Tenth report, Home Office, July 2011) noted that:

- According to the 2010/11 BCS, 61 per cent of people thought that the CJS as a whole was fair, an increase from 59 per cent in 2009/10, and 43 per cent were confident in the effectiveness of the CJS in bringing people who commit crimes to justice, an increase from 41 per cent in 2009/10. The disparity in these figures for fairness and effectiveness is itself interesting: it suggests that the public generally value a State prosecution service that is fair, even if it is not at all times effective. This observation needs to fit, however, within a system that recognises that delay in awaiting trial is a ground of unfairness – for defendants (especially those remanded in custody) and witnesses alike.

● The 2010/11 BCS showed that 59 per cent of people thought the police in their local area were doing a good or excellent job, a significant improvement on the 56 per cent who held that view in 2009/10 and the 53 per cent in 2008/09. Overall confidence in the local police in 2010/11 rose to 72 per cent, as compared with 69 per cent in 2009/10. Levels of confidence in the CJS varied by demographic and socio-economic characteristics: the proportion of participants who had confidence in stating that the CJS is fair or effective was higher amongst younger people.

7.2.1 A CONTRADICTION

There is a friction between the sorts of policies that these two concerns generate – that is, first, that people seem to want the police to have greater powers to combat crime. Yet, contradictorily, the public want greater controls on the police and evidence so as to avoid more miscarriages of justice. Unjust convictions lay against the Winchester Three, the Guildford Four, the Birmingham Six, the Maguire Seven, the Tottenham Three, Stefan Kiszko, Judith Ward and the Bridgewater Three (*The Guardian*, 21, 22 February 1997). It is argued that, if we wish to avoid similar instances of injustice, we should tighten the rules of evidence and procedure that govern the investigation and prosecution of crime. Against this, it has been argued that the police should have greater powers and that the trial process should be tilted less in favour of the defendant. (For example, see Charles Pollard, Chief Constable of the Thames Valley Police: letter, *The Times*, 12 April 1995; article, *The Sunday Times*, 9 July 1995.) The rules on disclosure of evidence in criminal trials, for example, were radically changed by the Criminal Procedure and Investigations Act (CPIA) 1996. In particular, the material the prosecution has to disclose to the defence is staged (albeit that the CPS have a duty of continuous review) and brought within a more restrictive framework.

The defence has a duty to disclose its case in advance of trial, in the form of what is called a Defence Statement or commonly but incorrectly called a 'DCS'. It is incumbent on all defendants to comply with the requirements of ss 5(5) and 6A of the Criminal Procedure and Investigations Act 1996, even if no positive defence is asserted by them (and so their case is conducted solely by means of putting the prosecution to proof). Failure to comply with these provisions may lead a jury to draw an adverse inference against a defendant should they wish to do so. A defendant is statutorily obliged to set out the nature of their defence ahead of trial. It is wrong for a barrister or solicitor (or for a barrister to advise his professional client, the solicitor) to advise a defendant not to prepare or co-operate in the writing of a Defence Statement. However, where a defendant chooses not to set out the nature of his defence, neither he nor his legal representative are liable for contempt of court proceedings (*R v Rochford* (2010)).

One problem, therefore, in this area of the English legal system is that as the growing problems of crime, and the fear of crime, become more important concerns of government, there are emerging two lobbies for change. Those lobbies are diametrically opposed.

The criminal process is examined here in three chapters. This chapter considers the law relating to important pre-trial matters up to and including the admissibility of confession evidence in court. Chapters 8 and 11 look at institutional and procedural aspects of prosecution and matters relating to bail, the classification of offences, trials, plea bargaining and the jury. In examining all these topics, it is important to keep in mind the various aims of the criminal justice system and the extent to which the existing law serves these aims. Among the aims to be borne in mind are the following:

- to detect crime and convict those who have committed it;
- to have rules relating to arrest, search, questioning, interrogation and admissibility of evidence which do not expose suspects to unfair treatment likely to lead to unjust convictions;
- to have rules as above which do not unnecessarily impede the proper investigation of crime;
- to ensure that innocent persons are not convicted;
- to maintain public order;
- to maintain public confidence in the criminal justice system;
- to properly balance considerations of justice and fair procedure with those of efficiency and funding.

7.2.2 CONTEMPORARY ISSUES

The criminal justice system is bearing signs of strain as it tries to cope with a society in the throes of major transitions. These include: changes in the pattern of family life; changes in the nature of employment expectations; the economic downturn; and a revolution in information and communications technology.

In 1993, the prison population of England and Wales was 42,000 (this includes those incarcerated in young offender institutions). In June 2012 the prison population was 85,697 (Population and Capacity briefing for 22 June 2012, London: Ministry of Justice) and the Prison Reform Trust has reported that 83 out of 134 prisons in England and Wales are overcrowded.

The Police and Magistrates' Courts Act 1994 amended the Police Act 1964, permitting Home Secretaries to 'determine objectives for the policing of all of the areas of all police authorities'. Under this power, a new police mission statement was announced in 1999. The purpose of the police according to this is 'to help secure a safe and just society in which the rights and responsibilities of individuals, families and communities are properly balanced'. This raises many contentious issues. The determination of, for example, what is a 'just society' has become something that is more overtly a matter for policing policy than in previous times. The police role was more simply, in the words of Robert Peel, the nineteenth-century founder of modern policing, to 'prevent and detect crime'.

Can 134,000 police officers do well enough to retain credibility in a society of 60 million people undergoing all sorts of social upheavals? In 1998, the police had to respond to 17.8 million incidents and 7.5 million 999 calls. The racist canteen culture revealed in the wake of the Stephen Lawrence Inquiry (see above, at 1.3.5), and the recognition in 1998 by the Commissioner for the Metropolitan Police that he probably had 250 corrupt officers on his force, did not help raise public confidence. In October 2003, BBC1 broadcast an extremely disturbing undercover documentary titled *Secret Policeman*. It revealed strong evidence of racism among new recruits at a police training centre in Cheshire.

The main thrust of governmental policy in relation to the criminal justice system at the moment appears to be an unusual cocktail consisting of several privatisation measures, heavy cuts and a good dose of centralisation.

Criminal justice has historically been regarded by government as a matter for the State. Recently, however, first under the Conservative government in the early 1990s, then under Labour, and now under the Coalition Government, various parts of the system have been privatised. Such moves have not generally been seen as runaway successes. In November 1998, there was public scandal at the extent of injury to prison officers and trainers and damage to the premises of the country's leading private institution for young offenders. It was revealed that over £100,000 of damage had been wrought by wild 12- to 14-year-olds at the Medway Secure Training Centre in Kent. After more than one fiasco, privatised prison escort services have come in for severe criticism. A provision of the CJPOA 1994 allowing for private sponsorship of police equipment has been a boon for satirical cartoonists.

By contrast, there are several ways in which aspects of the criminal justice system, historically all independent from each other and detached from governmental control, have been drawn within the influence of central government. It has, for example, been a hallowed precept of the British constitution that police forces are local and not governmental agencies. Yet, under Conservative legislation, the Home Secretary became allowed to 'determine objectives for the policing of the areas of all police authorities'.

There is also reason for disquiet about the law contained in the Terrorism Act 2000, which makes the opinion of a police officer admissible evidence in court. Proof of membership of a proscribed organisation may be based in part upon the opinion of a senior police officer. Considerable evidence – from miscarriage of justice cases, especially those involving suspects of terrorism from Northern Ireland – showed that some police officers were apparently prepared to lie and falsify evidence to secure convictions. The new law has hence caused some people to become alarmed at the prospect that a person could be convicted of a serious offence on evidence taken mainly from the opinion of a police officer.

Proactive 'intelligence-led' policing has become increasingly commonplace in recent years, especially in relation to drugs and organised crime. Such techniques inevitably involve deception by police officers and their informers (see C Dunnighan and C Norris, 'A risky business: the recruitment and running of informers by English police officers' (1996) 19 Police Studies 1). This may involve testing whether a person is willing to commit an offence. Although English law has never recognised a defence of entrapment, entrapment may be a mitigating factor and a ground for excluding evidence: *R v Looseley; Attorney General's Reference (No 3 of 2000)* (2002). (See A. Ashworth, 'Re-drawing the boundaries of entrapment' [2002] Crim LR 161–79.)

Until recently, foreign persons – that is, non-British nationals – suspected of involvement in terrorist activities could be detained without trial under the provisions of Part 4 of the Anti-terrorism, Crime and Security Act 2001. Detention without trial obviously breached Art 5(1) of the European Convention on Human Rights. The policy was justified under Art 15 which permits derogation from Art 5(1) in time of war 'or other public emergency threatening the life of the nation'. The House of Lords addressed the issue in 2004: *A and X and Others* [2004] UKHL 56. Their Lordships decided the case against the government. Lord Hoffmann rejected the view that modern terrorists were a threat to the life of the nation (and therefore that a 'state of emergency' was appropriate): 'The real threat to the life of the nation [. . .] comes not from terrorism but from laws such as these' (see P Mendelle, 'No detention please, we're British?' (2005) 155 NLJ 77). Although the government could (theoretically) have ignored this decisive rebuff, it accepted the constitutional reality that the law had to change and introduced legislation providing for control orders. Control orders were extremely controversial. According to Doug Jewell, Liberty's campaign director: 'The Prevention of Terrorism Act 2005 is a fundamentally flawed piece of legislation. No one knows how [the orders] are going to be enacted . . . It's going to be a policing nightmare.' See ' "Profound unease" over control orders' (2005) 155 NLJ 394. The coalition government has subsequently re-branded control orders as 'terrorist prevention and investigation measures', which will have a qualified limitation period of two years in the Protection of Freedoms Act 2012, which received Royal Assent on 1 May 2012.

7.3 ARREST

According to AV Dicey, 'individual rights are the basis not the result of the law of the constitution' (*Law of the Constitution*, 6th edn, p 203; cited by Judge LJ in *R v Central Criminal Court ex p The Guardian, The Observer and Bright* (2002)). Before considering the rights of the citizen and the law governing arrest and detention, what happens in the police station and what evidence is admissible in court, it is appropriate to look first at what the citizen can do if those rights are violated.

7.3.1 REMEDIES FOR UNLAWFUL ARREST

Like other areas of law where the liberty of the subject is at stake, the law relating to arrest is founded upon the principle of *justification*. If challenged, the person who has attempted to make an arrest must justify his actions and show that the arrest was lawful. Failing this, the arrest will be regarded as unlawful. In *Roberts v Chief Constable of Cheshire Police* (1999), the Court of Appeal held that a failure to carry out a review of detention in accordance with s 40 of PACE 1984 rendered a subsequent period of detention unlawful.

There are four possible remedies:

- The person, or someone on his behalf, can bring proceedings of *habeas corpus*. This ancient prerogative writ used to begin with the words 'habeas corpus', meaning 'you must have the body' and 'produce the body'. It is addressed to the detainer and asks him to bring the detainee in question before the court at a specified date and time. The remedy protects the freedom of those who have been unlawfully detained in prison, hospital, police station or private custody. The writ is applied for from a judge in chambers and can, in emergencies, be made over the telephone. It must be issued if there is *prima facie* evidence that the detention is unlawful. As every detention is unlawful, the burden of proof is on the detainer to justify his conduct. If issued, the writ frees the detainee and thus allows him to seek other remedies (below) against the detainer.

- To use the illegality of the detention to argue that any subsequent prosecution should fail. This type of argument is very rarely successful as illegally obtained evidence is not, *ipso facto, automatically rendered* inadmissible. The House of Lords ruled in *R v Sang* (1979) that no discretion existed to exclude evidence simply because it had been illegally or improperly obtained. A court could only exclude relevant evidence where its effect would be 'unduly prejudicial'. This is reflected in s 78(1) of the Police and Criminal Evidence Act (PACE) 1984. This perhaps surprising rule was supported by the Royal Commission on Criminal Justice (although the argument there was chiefly focused on the admissibility of confession evidence). Professor Zander, however, in a note of dissent, contested the idea that a conviction could be upheld despite serious misconduct by the prosecution if there is other evidence against the convicted person. He states: 'I cannot agree. The moral foundation of the criminal justice system requires that, if the prosecution has employed foul means, the defendant must go free if he is plainly guilty [. . .] the conviction should be quashed as an expression of the system's repugnance.' An extreme case might involve the admissibility of confession evidence obtained by torture by the authorities in another country (see for example *Gäfgen v Germany* (2011)). Since the Human Rights Act (HRA) 1998 became fully operative in October 2000, it has no longer been possible to treat such issues merely as involving interpretation of s 78(1) of PACE 1984 itself. Additionally, any court must take Art 6 of the European Convention on Human Rights (ECHR) into account in appropriate circumstances. For further discussion of this aspect, see above, at 2.5.1.1–2.5.1.2, and below, at 15.4.

- An action for damages for false imprisonment. In some cases, the damages for such an action would be likely to be nominal if the violation by the detainer does not have much impact on the detainee. Consider cases under this heading like *Christie v Leachinsky* (1947). Damages can, however, be considerable. In *Reynolds v Commissioner of Police for the Metropolis* (1982), a jury awarded £12,000 damages to the plaintiff. She had been arrested in the early hours in connection with charges of arson for gain, that is, that insured houses, which had been set alight deliberately, would be the subject of 'accidental fire' insurance claims. She was taken by car to a police station, a journey which took two and a half hours. She was detained until about 8.00 pm when she was told there was no evidence against her. She arrived home about 11.00 pm. The judge, Caulfield J, ruled that the police had no reasonable grounds for suspecting the plaintiff of having committed an arrestable offence and he directed the jury in relation to damages. The jury awarded £12,000 and the defendant's appeal against this sum as excessive was dismissed.

- A judicial review of the detention. A judicial review of a decision to detain someone can be brought in the High Court on the ground that the detention is unlawful. The judicial review may include a claim under the Human Rights Act 1998 that the detention is in violation of Art 5 ECHR. If the High Court finds in favour of the detainee, it has the power to quash the decision to detain, order that the detainee be released and, in some limited circumstances, to award damages.

In a review of trends in actions against the police, S Khan and M Ryder ((September 1998) Legal Action 16) comment on two cases in relation to damages. In *Goswell v Commissioner of Police for the Metropolis* (1998), a jury awarded damages totalling £302,000 to Mr Goswell, comprising £120,000 for assault, £12,000 for false imprisonment and £170,000 exemplary damages. On appeal, Simon Brown LJ held that £100 was an appropriate award for basic damages for false imprisonment for 20 minutes. He allowed for the fact that the unlawfulness of the detention was a consequence of a breach of s 28 of PACE 1984 and expressed the opinion that the case 'does not in the fullest sense involve a wrongful deprivation of liberty'. Basic damages were assessed at £22,500, aggravated damages at £10,000 and £15,000 for exemplary damages. Overall, the figure was reduced from £302,000 to £47,500. In a second case against the police, *Commissioner of Police for the Metropolis v Gerald* (1998), an initial award by a jury of £125,000 for assault, false imprisonment and malicious prosecution was reduced to £50,000 on appeal by the Commissioner.

Apart from the question of civil remedies, it is important to remember the following:

- If the arrest is not lawful, there is the right to use reasonable force to resist it: *R v Waterfield* (1964); *Kenlin v Gardiner* (1967). This is a remedy, however, of doubtful advisability, as the legality of the arrest will only be properly tested after the event in a law court. If a police officer was engaged in what the courts decide was a lawful arrest or conduct, then anyone who uses force against the officer might have been guilty of an offence of assaulting an officer in the execution of his duty, contrary to s 89(1) of the Police Act 1996.

- That, for our purposes in considering the consequences for an unlawfully arrested person faced with prosecution, s 78 of PACE 1984 states:

> 78(1) In any proceedings, the court may refuse to allow evidence on which the prosecution proposes to rely to be given if it appears to the court that, having regard to all the circumstances, including the circumstances in which the evidence was obtained, the admission of the evidence would have such an adverse effect on the fairness of the proceedings that the court ought not to admit it.

7.3.2 GENERAL POWERS OF ARREST

In *Spicer v Holt* (1977), Lord Dilhorne stated:

> Whether or not a person has been arrested depends not upon the legality of the arrest, but on whether he has been deprived of his liberty to go where he pleases.

So, a person detained by the police against his will is arrested. Whether this arrest is lawful will depend on whether the conditions for a lawful arrest have been satisfied.

Lawful arrests are those: (1) under warrant; (2) without warrant at common law; or (3) without warrant under legislation.

7.3.3 ARREST UNDER WARRANT

The police lay a written information on oath before a magistrate that a person 'has, or is suspected of having, committed an offence' (s 1 of the Magistrates' Courts Act 1980). The Criminal Justice Act (CJA) 1967 provides that warrants should not be issued unless the offence in question is indictable or is punishable with imprisonment.

Until recently, complex extradition arrangements existed between the Member States of the European Union (EU). In December 2001, the EU agreed in principle to introduce European arrest warrants. The decision was formally adopted in June 2002. The traditional approach (found in extradition agreements) embodied the principle of 'dual criminality' – that is, a person would not be extradited from one State to another unless his alleged offence was an extraditable crime in both countries. This requirement has now been removed from a list of 32 offences. The inclusion of 'racism and xenophobia' has aroused some controversy. (See S Allegre, 'The myth and the reality of a modern European judicial space' (2002) 152 NLJ 986–7).

7.3.4 COMMON LAW ARRESTS

The only power to arrest at common law is where a breach of the peace has been committed and there are reasonable grounds for believing that it will be continued or renewed, or where a breach of the peace is reasonably apprehended. Essentially, it requires *conduct* related to violence, real or threatened. A simple disturbance does not, in itself, amount to a breach of the peace unless it results from violence, real or threatened.

In 1981, two cases decided within months of each other offered definitions of a breach of the peace, in an attempt to bring some clarification to an area of law that previously was in doubt. In *R v Howell* (1981), the defendant was arrested after being involved in a disturbance at a street party in the early hours of the morning. Watkins LJ, who delivered the judgment of the court, observed that there was a power of arrest for anticipated breach of the peace, provided the arrestor had been witness to the earlier shouting and swearing of H. It followed that there must be reasonable grounds for belief, and the arrestor must believe at the time that the defendant's conduct, either alone or as part of a general disturbance, was likely to lead to the use of violence by the defendant or someone else in the officer's presence.

The court adopted the following definition of 'breach of the peace'. It occurs:

> Wherever harm is actually done or is likely to be done to a person or in his presence his property or a person is in fear of being so harmed through an assault, an affray, a riot, unlawful assembly or other disturbance.

In the second of the two cases, *R v Chief Constable of the Devon and Cornwall Constabulary ex p Central Electricity Generating Board (CEGB)* (1981), Lord Denning MR suggested that breach of the peace might be considerably wider than this. This case involved a group of protesters who had occupied private land in order to prevent CEGB employees from carrying out a survey to assess its suitability for a nuclear power station. The protest was intended to be peaceful and non-violent. Lord Denning MR suggested that:

> There is a breach of the peace whenever a person who is lawfully carrying out his work is unlawfully and physically prevented by another from doing it ... If anyone unlawfully and physically obstructs the worker, by lying down or chaining himself to a rig or the like, he is guilty of a breach of the peace.

He appears to have been saying (Feldman, *Civil Liberties and Human Rights in England and Wales* (1993), pp 788–9) not that a breach of the peace is automatic in such circumstances. Instead, in the context of the *CEGB* case, any obstruction or unlawful *resistance* by the trespasser could give the police a reasonable apprehension of a breach of the peace, in the sense of violence.

However, in cases that have followed (such as *Parkin v Norman* (1982); *Percy v DPP* (1995); and *Foulkes v Chief Constable of Merseyside Police* (1998)), it is the definition in *R v Howell* that has been preferred. Despite earlier doubts, argues Parpworth ('Breach of the peace: breach of human rights?' (1998) 152 JP 6, 7 November), the decision of the European Court of Human Rights (ECtHR) in *Steel and Others v UK* (1998) brings clear and authoritative clarification to this area of law. This case represents 'a clear endorsement by a court largely unfamiliar with the common law concept of a breach of the peace that such a concept is in accordance with the terms of the European Convention on Human Rights'.

At common law, a constable may arrest a person for conduct that he genuinely suspects might be likely to cause a breach of the peace even on private premises where no member of the public is present: *McConnell v Chief Constable of Manchester* (1990). Although mere shouting and swearing alone will not constitute a breach of the peace, it is an offence under s 28 of the Town Police Causes Act 1847 and could lead to an arrest under s 25 of PACE 1984 (general arrest conditions). If it causes harassment, alarm or distress to a member of the public, it may constitute an offence under s 5 of the Public Order Act 1986.

7.3.5 ARREST UNDER LEGISLATION

The right to arrest is generally governed by s 24 of PACE 1984 (as amended by SOCPA below).

Serious Organised Crime and Police Act 2005 (SOCPA)

Part 3 of this Act, which came into force in January 2006, makes a number of changes to police powers set out in the Police and Criminal Evidence Act 1984 (PACE) and extends the powers of Community Support Officers (CSOs) and other persons designated or accredited under the provisions of the Police Reform Act 2002.

Sections 110, 111, 113 and 114 and Sched 7 revise the framework of arrest and search powers in PACE. In particular they provide, in the case of a constable's power of arrest, for all offences to be 'arrestable' subject to a necessity test. This means that someone who has committed a relatively low order criminal offence, like littering, could, in theory, be arrested if an officer deemed it necessary and was able to satisfy his or her desk sergeant at the police station that this was so. That might occur, for example, if the person being requested to pick up the litter refused to do so, and then refused to give his or her name to the officer.

Section 110 states:

(1) For section 24 of PACE (arrest without warrant for arrestable offences) substitute—

24 Arrest without warrant: constables
(1) A constable may arrest without a warrant—

    (a) anyone who is about to commit an offence;

(b)　anyone who is in the act of committing an offence;

(c)　anyone whom he has reasonable grounds for suspecting to be about to commit an offence;

(d)　anyone whom he has reasonable grounds for suspecting to be committing an offence.

(2)　If a constable has reasonable grounds for suspecting that an offence has been committed, he may arrest without a warrant anyone whom he has reasonable grounds to suspect of being guilty of it.

(3)　If an offence has been committed, a constable may arrest without a warrant—

(a)　anyone who is guilty of the offence;

(b)　anyone whom he has reasonable grounds for suspecting to be guilty of it.

(4)　But the power of summary arrest conferred by subsection (1), (2) or (3) is exercisable only if the constable has reasonable grounds for believing that for any of the reasons mentioned in subsection (5) it is necessary to arrest the person in question.

(5)　The reasons are—

(a)　to enable the name of the person in question to be ascertained (in the case where the constable does not know, and cannot readily ascertain, the person's name, or has reasonable grounds for doubting whether a name given by the person as his name is his real name);

(b)　correspondingly as regards the person's address;

(c)　to prevent the person in question—

(i)　causing physical injury to himself or any other person;

(ii)　suffering physical injury;

(iii)　causing loss of or damage to property;

(iv)　committing an offence against public decency (subject to subsection (6)); or

(v)　causing an unlawful obstruction of the highway;

(d)　to protect a child or other vulnerable person from the person in question;

(e)　to allow the prompt and effective investigation of the offence or of the conduct of the person in question;

(f)   to prevent any prosecution for the offence from being hindered by the disappearance of the person in question.

(6)   Subsection (5)(c)(iv) applies only where members of the public going about their normal business cannot reasonably be expected to avoid the person in question.

24A Arrest without warrant: other persons

(1)   A person other than a constable may arrest without a warrant—

(a)   anyone who is in the act of committing an indictable offence;

(b)   anyone whom he has reasonable grounds for suspecting to be committing an indictable offence.

(2)   Where an indictable offence has been committed, a person other than a constable may arrest without a warrant—

(a)   anyone who is guilty of the offence;

(b)   anyone whom he has reasonable grounds for suspecting to be guilty of it.

(3)   But the power of summary arrest conferred by subsection (1) or (2) is exercisable only if—

(a)   the person making the arrest has reasonable grounds for believing that for any of the reasons mentioned in subsection (4) it is necessary to arrest the person in question; and

(b)   it appears to the person making the arrest that it is not reasonably practicable for a constable to make it instead.

(4)   The reasons are to prevent the person in question—

(a)   causing physical injury to himself or any other person;

(b)   suffering physical injury;

(c)   causing loss of or damage to property; or

(d)   making off before a constable can assume responsibility for him.

Section 112 introduces a new offence of failing to obey a police direction to leave an exclusion area. Section 115 extends the powers of the police, in s 1 of PACE, to stop and search persons suspected of carrying prohibited fireworks.

Sections 116 to 118 enable the police to take photographs and fingerprints of persons away from a police station and to take impressions of a person's footwear at a police station (although note that there are amendments pending for ss 117 and 118). The power to take photographs is extended to Community Support Officers (CSOs) and accredited persons in limited circumstances. Section 116(3) amends s 64A of PACE to allow the police to pass a photograph to the court for the purposes of enforcing the orders of the court. This new power is in addition to that which already allows the police to pass a photograph to the court for the purposes of prosecution. Section 119 amends the definition of an intimate and non-intimate sample.

Section 120 was repealed before it came into force and s 121, which enables police staff to undertake custody functions previously restricted to police officers, has not yet been brought into force.

Sections 122 and 123 and Scheds 8 and 9 extend the powers of CSOs, other designated police staff and accredited persons. Those provisions enable police staff to access certain information relating to drivers, vehicle registration plate suppliers and motor insurance.

These are highly controversial new powers. The case to extend powers for the police is built on the idea that those who have done nothing wrong will have nothing to fear from the exercise of the powers. The extension of police powers is also defended on the grounds that any arrest, to be lawful, must be 'necessary' (see s 24(5) of PACE as amended, above, by s 110 of the Serious Organised Crime and Police Act).

There are, however, clear reasons for concern at this development. A society in which the police have unlimited powers can be described as a 'police state', and such tyranny is almost universally disfavoured. That, of course, is very far from the position now in the UK, a country that has what are among the best-protected liberties in the world. However, the closer that law in the UK moves towards giving the police very wide powers to arrest, the greater the need for concern. A society in which people can be arrested for any offence, in which CCTV is ubiquitous (Surveillance UK, *The Independent*, 22 December 2005), and in which police 'success' is progressively measured by how many arrests and crimes solved, might reduce certain sorts of offending (although many sorts of criminality are not reduced by such policies). But how comfortable a place would it be to live? The inhabitants of many countries in which there are dictatorial governments and no respect for civil liberties do not seem to rejoice in the crime-free streets. At all events, the most desirable balance between freedom not to be interfered with by police officers, and policing that improves society by effectively reducing crime, is ultimately a political question for the public, rather than the small section of the public comprised by judges, lawyers and police officers. The cases below are included to illustrate the operation of s 24 of PACE (although note that they were decided before SOCPA came into force).

7.3.6   G v DPP (1989)

In *G v DPP* (1989), the appellant (G) with other juveniles, including a co-accused, Gill, went to a police station to complain about being ejected from a public service vehicle. On being asked for their names and addresses by the officer, G, the appellant, refused to do so; some of the others gave false particulars, but Gill gave his real name and address. The officer did not accept that Gill's particulars were correct because in his experience people who committed offences did not give correct details (even though the juveniles had only gone to the police station to complain about the way they had been treated on the bus). The juveniles would not accept the officer's advice about their complaint and became threatening and abusive. Gill was arrested for 'disorderly behaviour in a police station' and he struggled and resisted; the appellant joined in, punching the officer and causing him to lose hold of Gill. Both Gill and G were convicted of assaulting a police officer in the execution of his duty. The Divisional Court quashed their convictions. The offence of 'violent behaviour' or 'disorderly behaviour' under the Town Police Causes Act 1847 was not an arrestable offence. The only power the officer therefore had to arrest Gill was under s 25(3) of PACE 1984, if there were genuine doubts about Gill's name and address. But the ground given by the officer – an account about people who commit offences not giving their proper name, and so on – was not a proper ground because there was no evidence that the youths had committed any offences; they had gone to the police simply to complain. Therefore, in purporting to arrest Gill, the officer had not been acting in the execution of his duty and the appellant could not, therefore, have been guilty of obstructing him in the performance of such duty.

It should be noted, in particular that, under s 24(6), no offence need actually have been committed. All that is required is that the police officer *reasonably believes* that an arrestable offence has been committed.

The differences in the powers of arrest in s 24 are based on whether an offence:

- *is being* committed: anyone may make the arrest; see s 24(4);
- *has been* committed: anyone may make the arrest; see s 24(5) on the wider powers of the police (s 24(6)) who can arrest where they have 'reasonable grounds for suspecting that an arrestable offence has been committed' whether one has in fact been committed or not;
- is *about to be* committed: only a police officer may act here; see s 24(7).

PACE 1984 preserves an old common law distinction in respect of the powers of constables and private individuals when making such arrests. Where an arrest is being made *after* an offence is thought to have been committed, then PACE 1984 confers narrower rights upon the private individual than on the police officer.

7.3.7 WALTERS v WH SMITH & SON LTD (1914)

In *Walters v WH Smith & Son Ltd* (1914), the defendants had reasonably suspected that Walters had stolen books from a station bookstall. At his trial, Walters was acquitted, as the jury believed his statement that he had intended to pay for the books. No crime had therefore been committed in respect of any of the books. Walters sued the defendants, *inter alia*, for false imprisonment, a tort which involves the wrongful deprivation of personal liberty in any form, as he had been arrested for a crime that had not in fact been committed. The Court of Appeal held that, to justify the arrest, a private individual – as opposed to police officer – had to show not only reasonable suspicion but *also* that the offence for which the arrested person was given over into custody had in fact been committed, even if by someone else. A police officer making an arrest in the same circumstances could legally justify the arrest by showing 'reasonable suspicion' alone, without having to show that an offence was, in fact, committed.

This principle is now incorporated in s 24 of PACE 1984. It is worthy of note that the less prudent arrestor who acts against a suspect when the latter is suspected of being in the act of committing an arrestable offence (s 24(4)) can justify his conduct simply by showing that there were 'reasonable grounds' on which to base the suspicion. They need not show that an offence was in fact being committed. If the arrestor waits until he thinks the crime has been committed, then, whereas a police officer will only have to show 'reasonable grounds for suspecting that an arrestable offence has been committed' (s 24(6)), a citizen can only justify his behaviour if an offence 'has been committed' (s 24(5)).

7.3.8   *R v SELF* (1992)

This analysis is supported by the decision in *R v Self* (1992). The defendant was seen by a store detective in Woolworths to pick up a bar of chocolate and leave the store without paying. The detective followed him out into the street and, with the assistance of a member of the public, she arrested the suspect under the powers in s 24(5) of PACE 1984. The suspect resisted the arrest and assaulted both his arrestors. He was subsequently charged with theft of the chocolate and with offences of assault with intent to resist lawful apprehension or detainer, contrary to s 38 of the Offences Against the Person Act 1861. At his trial, he was acquitted of theft (apparently for lack of *mens rea*), but convicted of the assaults. These convictions were quashed by the Court of Appeal on the grounds that, as the arrest had not been lawful, he was entitled to resist it. The power of arrest conferred upon a citizen (s 24(5)) in circumstances where an offence is thought to *have been committed* only applies when an offence *has* been committed. As the jury decided that Mr Self had not committed any offence, there was no power to arrest him.

It is not easy to justify the considerable legal protection available to police officers when compared with the near total lack of protection available to ordinary British subjects/citizens. In the article mentioned above, Professor Spencer states: '[I]f a citizen, reacting to the words "Stop thief!" tackles someone who looks for all the world like a fleeing robber, he has no defence if it later turns out that no robbery has actually occurred. The person he tackles can hit him with impunity, and sue him for damages at leisure later' ('Extending the Police State', *ibid*). This seems far from satisfactory.

7.3.9   *JOHN LEWIS & CO v TIMS* (1952)

In *John Lewis & Co v Tims* (1952), Mrs Tims and her daughter were arrested by store detectives for shoplifting four calendars from the appellant's Oxford Street store. It was a regulation of the store that only a managing director or a general manager was authorised to institute any prosecution. After being arrested, Mrs Tims and her daughter were taken to the office of the chief store detective. They were detained there until a chief detective and a manager arrived to give instructions whether to prosecute. They were eventually handed over to police custody within an hour of arrest. In a claim by Mrs Tims for false imprisonment, she alleged that the detectives were obliged to give her into the custody of the police immediately upon arrest. The House of Lords held that the delay was reasonable in the circumstances. There were advantages in refusing to give private detectives a 'free hand' and leaving the determination of such an important question as whether to prosecute to a superior official.

7.3.10   WHAT IS THE MEANING OF 'REASONABLE GROUNDS FOR SUSPECTING'?

Many of the powers of the police in relation to arrest, search and seizure are founded upon the presence of reasonable 'suspicion', 'cause' or 'belief' in a state of affairs, usually that a suspect is involved actually or potentially in a crime.

In *Castorina v Chief Constable of Surrey* (1988), detectives reasonably concluded that the burglary of a company's premises was an 'inside job'. The managing director told them that she had recently dismissed someone (the plaintiff), although she did not think it would have been her, and that the documents taken would be useful to someone with a grudge. The detectives interviewed the plaintiff, having found out that she had no criminal record, and arrested her under s 2(4) of the Criminal Law Act (CLA) 1967 (which has now been replaced by s 24(6) of PACE 1984). She was detained at the police station for almost four hours, interrogated and then released without charge. On a claim for damages for wrongful arrest and detention, a jury awarded her £4,500. The trial judge held that the officers had had a *prima facie* case for suspicion, but that the arrest was premature. He had defined 'reasonable cause' (which the officers would have needed to show they had when they arrested the plaintiff) as 'honest belief founded upon reasonable suspicion leading an ordinary cautious man to the conclusion that the person arrested was guilty of the offence'. He said an ordinary man would have sought more information from the suspect, including an explanation for any grudge on her part. In this, he relied on the *dicta* of Scott LJ in *Dumbell v Roberts* (1944) that the principle that every man was presumed innocent until proved guilty also applied to arrests. The Court of Appeal allowed an appeal by the chief constable. The court held that the trial judge had used too severe a test in judging the officers' conduct.

Purchas LJ said that the test of 'reasonable cause' was objective and therefore the trial judge was wrong to have focused attention on whether the officers had 'an honest belief'. The question was whether the officers had had reasonable grounds to suspect the woman of the offence. There was sufficient evidence that the officers had had sufficient reason to suspect her.

Woolf LJ thought there were three things to consider in cases where an arrest is alleged to be unlawful:

- Did the arresting officer suspect that the person who was arrested had committed the offence? This was a matter of fact about the officer's state of mind.

- If the answer to the first question is yes, then was there reasonable proof of that suspicion? This is a simple objective matter to be determined by the judge.

- If the answers to the first two questions are both yes, then the officer did have a discretion to arrest, and the question then was whether he had exercised his discretion according to *Wednesbury* principles of reasonableness.

This case hinged on the second point and, on the facts, the chief constable should succeed on the appeal.

Note: The *Wednesbury* principles come from *Associated Provincial Picture Houses Ltd v Wednesbury Corp* (1948). Lord Greene MR laid down principles to determine when the decision made by a public authority could be regarded as so perverse or unreasonable that the courts would be justified in overturning that decision. The case actually concerned whether a condition imposed by a local authority on cinemas operating on Sundays was reasonable. Lord Greene MR said:

> [. . .] a person entrusted with a discretion must, so to speak, direct himself properly in law. He must call his own attention to matters which he is bound to consider. He must exclude from his consideration matters which are irrelevant to what he has to consider. If he does not obey those rules, he may be truly said, and often is said, to be acting 'unreasonably'.

Sir Frederick Lawton, the third judge in the Court of Appeal in *Castorina*, agreed. The facts on which 'reasonable cause' was said to have been founded did not have to be such as to lead an ordinary cautious man to conclude that the person arrested *was* guilty of the offence. It was enough if they could lead an ordinary person to *suspect* that he was guilty.

This creates quite some latitude for the police. Additionally, the House of Lords has decided in *Holgate-Mohammed v Duke* (1984) that, where a police officer reasonably suspects an individual of having committed an arrestable offence, he may arrest that person with a view to questioning him at the police station. His decision can only be challenged on *Wednesbury* principles if he acted improperly by taking something irrelevant into account. The police arrested a former lodger for theft of jewellery from the house where she had lived in order to question her at the police station. The trial judge awarded her £1,000 damages for false imprisonment. The Court of Appeal set aside the award and the decision was upheld by the House of Lords. The following passage from a judgment in the Court of Appeal in *Holgate-Mohammed* was approved in the House of Lords:

> As to the proposition that there were other things which [the police officer] might have done. No doubt there were other things which he might have done first. He might have obtained a statement from her otherwise than under arrest to see how far he could get. He might have obtained a specimen of her handwriting and sent that off for forensic examination

against a specimen of the writing of the person who had obtained the money by selling the stolen jewellery, which happened to exist in the case. All those things he might have done. He might have carried out fingerprint investigations if he had first obtained a print from the plaintiff. But, the fact that there were other things which he might have done does not, in my judgment, make that which he did do into an unreasonable exercise of the power of arrest if what he did do, namely, to arrest, was within the range of reasonable choices open to him.

It has been forcefully contended, however, that, in some circumstances, a failure to make inquiries before making an arrest could show that there were insufficient grounds for the arrest. See Clayton and Tomlinson, 'Arrest and reasonable grounds for suspicion' (1988) Law Soc Gazette, 7 September.

Note, however, that the powers are *discretionary*. See *Simpson v Chief Constable of South Yorkshire Police* (1991).

7.3.11 DETENTION SHORT OF ARREST

For there to be an arrest, the arrestor must regard his action as an arrest. If he simply detains someone to question him without any thought of arrest, the action will be unlawful. It is often reported in criminal investigations that a person is 'helping police with their inquiries'. In *R v Lemsatef* (1977), Lawton LJ said:

It must be clearly understood that neither customs officers nor police officers have any right to detain somebody for the purposes of getting them to help with their inquiries.

There is no police power to detain someone against his will in order to make inquiries about that person. See also *Franchiosy* (1979). This is confirmed by s 29 of PACE 1984, which states that where someone attends a police station 'for the purpose of assisting with an investigation', he is entitled to leave at any time unless placed under arrest. He must be informed at once that he is under arrest 'if a decision is taken by a constable to prevent him from leaving at will'. There is, however, no legal duty on the police to inform anyone whom they invite to the station to help with their inquiries that he may go.

7.3.12 SUSPECTS STOPPED IN THE STREET

In *Kenlin v Gardiner* (1967), a police officer took hold of the arm of a boy he wanted to question about the latter's suspicious conduct. The boy did not believe the man was a policeman, despite having been shown a warrant card, and punched the officer in order to escape. The other boy behaved similarly but their convictions for assaulting an officer in the execution of his duty were quashed by the Divisional Court. The court held that the boys were entitled to act as they did in self-defence as the officer's conduct in trying to physically apprehend them had not been legal. There is no legal power of detention short of arrest. As Lawton LJ observed in *R v Lemsatef* (see above), the police do not have any powers to detain somebody 'for the purposes of getting them to help with their inquiries'.

It is important, however, to examine the precise circumstances of the detaining officer's conduct. There are cases to suggest that if what the officer does amounts to only a *de minimis* interference with the citizen's liberty, then forceful 'self-defence' by the citizen will not be justified. In *Donnelly v Jackman* (1970), an officer approached a suspect to ask some questions. The suspect ignored the request and walked away from the officer. The officer followed and made further requests for the suspect to stop and talk. He tapped the suspect on the shoulder and the suspect reciprocated by tapping the officer on the shoulder and saying 'Now we are even, copper'. The officer tapped the suspect on the shoulder again, which was replied to with a forceful punch. Mr Donnelly's conviction was upheld and the decision in *Kenlin v Gardiner* was distinguished as, in the earlier case, the officer had actually taken hold of the boys and detained them. The court stated that, 'it is not every trivial interference with a citizen's liberty that amounts to a course of conduct sufficient to take the officer out of the course of his duties'.

In *Bentley v Brudzinski* (1982), the facts were very close to those above. A constable stopped two men who had been running barefoot down a street in the early hours. He questioned them about a stolen vehicle as they fitted the description of suspects in an earlier incident. They waited for about 10 minutes while the officer checked their details over a radio and then they began to leave. Another constable, who had just arrived on the scene, then said, 'Just a minute', and put his hand on the defendant's shoulder. The defendant then punched that officer in the face. Unlike the decision in *Donnelly v Jackman*, the Divisional Court held that the officer's conduct was more than a trivial interference with the citizen's liberty and amounted to an unlawful attempt to stop and detain him. The respondent was thus not guilty of assaulting an officer in the execution of his duty.

Note, also, that a person may be arrested for being silent or misleading under s 25 of PACE 1984, if the officer has reasonable doubts about the suspect's name and address or whether the summons procedure can be used at the address given.

7.3.13 STOP AND SEARCH

PACE 1984 gives the police power to search 'any person or vehicle' and to detain either for the purpose of such a search (s 1(2)). A constable may not conduct such a search 'unless he has reasonable grounds for suspecting that he will find stolen or prohibited articles' (s 1(3)). Any such item found during the search can be seized (s 1(6)). An article is 'prohibited' if it is either an offensive weapon or it is 'made or adapted for use in the course of or in connection with burglary, theft, taking a motor vehicle without authority or obtaining property by deception or is intended by the person having it with him for such use by him or by some other person' (s 1(7)). An offensive weapon is defined as meaning 'any article made or adapted for use for causing injury to persons or intended by the person having it with him for such use by him or by some other person' (s 1(9)). This definition is taken from the Prevention of Crime Act 1953. It has two categories: things that are offensive weapons *per se* (that is, in themselves), like a baton with a nail through the end or knuckle-dusters, and things that are not offensive weapons, like a spanner, but which are intended to be used as such. If the item is in the first category, then the prosecution need prove only that the accused had it with him to put the onus onto the accused to show that he had a lawful excuse. Stop and search powers can now also be exercised under s 8A regarding items covered by s 139 of the CJA 1988. These items are any article that has a blade or is sharply pointed, except folding pocket knives with a blade of less than three inches. It is an offence to possess such items without good reason or lawful authority, the onus of proof being on the defendant. The courts will not accept the carrying of offensive weapons for generalised self-defence unless there is some immediate, identifiable threat.

Under s 2 of PACE 1984, a police officer who proposes to carry out a stop and search must state his name and police station, and the purpose of the search. A plain-clothes officer must also produce documentary evidence that he is a police officer. The officer must also give the grounds for the search. Such street searches must be limited to outer clothing; the searched person cannot be required to remove any article of clothing other than a jacket, outer clothes or gloves. The officer is required to make a record of the search immediately, or as soon as is reasonably practicable afterwards (s 3). The record of the search should include the object of the search, the grounds of the search and its result (s 3). A failure to give grounds as required by s 2(3)(c) will render the search unlawful (*R v Fennelley* (1989)).

On 7 March, 2011, s 1 of the Crime and Security Act 2010 was brought into force to amend s 3 of PACE 1984 to reduce recording requirements where a search is conducted under s 2. These amendments are reflected in the revisions to Code A that were brought into effect on the same day (paras 4.1–4.10). There is no longer a require-ment to record the person's name or description, whether anything was found or whether any injury or damage was caused as a result of the search. However, the police are obliged to record:

- ethnicity
- objective of search
- grounds for search
- identity of the officer carrying out the stop and search
- date
- time
- place.

One case involved a protester who wore a skeleton-type mask at a demonstration. A police officer asked her to remove it. When she failed to do so, he tried to remove it himself. The protester responded by hitting him in the face. She was charged with assaulting a police officer in the course of his duty. The charge was dismissed by magistrates (partly because the policeman had failed to give his name, the location of his police station, or the reason why he wanted the mask to be removed). The Divisional Court took the view that an assault had been committed: *DPP v Avery* (2002).

Section 1 CJA 2003 extended powers to stop and search – and extended the definition of prohibited articles under s 1 of PACE 1984. It now includes articles made, adapted or intended for use in causing criminal damage. It does this by amending the list of offences in s 1(8) of PACE 1984 to include offences under s 1 of the Criminal Damage Act 1971. The effect is to give police officers power to stop and search where they have reasonable suspicion that a person is carrying, for example, a paint spray can, which they intend to use in producing graffiti.

Section 1(1) of the Criminal Damage Act 1971 made it a criminal offence for a person to destroy or damage any property belonging to another without lawful excuse if he intends to destroy or damage that property. Where a person is reckless as to whether that property would be destroyed or damaged, this provision also comes into play. Section 1(2) of that Act created a related offence of destroying or damaging property with intent to endanger life.

Stop and search powers that do not require reasonable suspicion include those under the CJPO 1994 ss 60 and 60AA and the CJA 1988 s 139B. Section 60 of the CJPO gives the police the power to stop and search where an officer of the rank of inspector or above has given the appropriate authorisation under s 60(1). These powers can be exercised for a maximum of 24 hours if the officer reasonably believes:

(a)   that incidents involving serious violence may take place in any locality in his police area, and that it is expedient to give an authorisation under this section to prevent their occurrence;

(aa) that–

(i)   an incident involving serious violence has taken place in England and Wales in his police area;

(ii)   a dangerous instrument or offensive weapon used in the incident is being carried in any locality in his police area by a person; and

(iii) it is expedient to give an authorisation under this section to find the instrument or weapon; or

(b)   that persons are carrying dangerous instruments or offensive weapons in any locality in his police area without good reason,

7.3.14 THE CODE OF PRACTICE FOR THE EXERCISE OF STATUTORY POWERS OF STOP AND SEARCH

In view of the wide powers vested in the police in the exercise of stop and search, Code A was revised in 2010 to reflect the recent legislation and to clarify how searches under stop and search powers are to be conducted. Codes B, D and F were revised in 2008. The latest versions took effect on 31 January 2008 (for details see http://www.homeoffice.gov.uk/police/powers/pace-codes/). Codes C, G and H were revised in 2012 (for details see http://www.homeoffice.gov.uk/publications/about-us/parliamentary-business/written-ministerial-statement/codes-practice-ct-wms/?view=Standard&pubID=1027808).

The primary purpose of stop and search powers is to enable officers to allay or confirm suspicions about individuals without exercising their powers of arrest. The Code applies to powers of stop and search and states at para 2.1(a) that these are 'powers which require reasonable grounds for suspicion before they may be exercised; that articles unlawfully obtained or possessed are being carried'.

Reasonable suspicion can never be supported on the basis of personal factors alone. For example, a person's race, age, appearance, or the fact that the person is known to have a previous conviction cannot be used alone or in combination with each other as the reason for searching that person, and nor can generalisations or stereotypical images of certain groups or categories of people (para 2.2). Paragraph 2.6 states that:

> Where there is reliable information or intelligence that members of a group or gang habitually carry knives unlawfully or weapons or controlled drugs, and wear a distinctive item of clothing or other means of identification to indicate their membership of the group or gang, that distinctive item of clothing or other means of identification may provide reasonable grounds to stop and search.

Other means of identification might include jewellery, insignias, tattoos or other features that are known to identify members of the particular gang or group (Note 9).

Any search involving the removal of more than an outer coat, jacket, gloves, headgear or footwear, or any other item concealing identity, may only be made by an officer of the same sex as the person searched and may not be made in the presence of anyone of the opposite sex unless the person being searched specifically requests it (para 3.6). All searches involving exposure of intimate parts of the body shall be conducted in accordance with para 11 of Annex A to Code C. All stops and searches must be carried out with courtesy, consideration and respect for the person concerned. Every reasonable effort must be made to reduce to the minimum the embarrassment that a person being searched may experience (para 3.1).

The revised Code A at para 2.15 introduces new powers to require removal of face coverings. These powers were added by s 60A of the Criminal Justice and Public Order Act 1994. Paragraph 2.15 states:

The officer exercising the power must reasonably believe that someone is wearing an item wholly or mainly for the purpose of concealing identity. There is also a power to seize such items where the officer believes that a person intends to wear them for this purpose. There is no power for stop and search for disguises. An officer may seize any such item which is discovered when exercising a power of search for something else, or which is being carried, and which the officer reasonably believes is intended to be used for concealing anyone's identity.

7.3.15   SEARCH OF ARRESTED PERSONS

The power to search after arrest somewhere other than at the police station is governed by s 32 of PACE 1984 (searches of detained persons are dealt with by s 54 and Code C, para 4.1). Section 32(1) allows the police to search someone arrested where there are grounds for believing that he may present a danger to himself or to others. Section 32(2) allows a search for anything that might be used to effect an escape or which might be evidence relating to any offence. Additionally, s 32(2)(b) gives the police power to enter and search the premises he was in when arrested, or immediately before he was arrested, for evidence relating to the offence for which he was arrested. Unlike the power to search under s 18, this is not limited to arrestable offences, nor do the searched premises need to be occupied or controlled by him. Such searches, however, are only lawful where there are reasonable grounds for believing that the search might find something for which a search is permitted under s 18(5) and (6). Random or automatic searching is not lawful. Section 32(4) states that a person searched in public cannot be required to take off more than outer garments like coats, jackets and gloves.

7.3.16   SEARCH ON DETENTION

Section 54 of PACE 1984 and Code C, para 4.1 require the custody officer (a particular officer with special responsibilities in police stations) to take charge of the process of searching detainees. He must ascertain what the suspect has with him unless he is to be detained for only a short time and not put in a cell. The person detained can be searched to enable this to happen, but the custody officer needs to believe it to be necessary; it is not an automatic right (s 54(6)). Anything the detainee has can be seized and retained, although clothes and personal effects can only be kept if the custody officer *believes* that the detained person *may* use them to escape, interfere with evidence, or cause damage or injury to himself, to others or to property. The police are not permitted, however, to retain anything protected by legal professional privilege, that is, private legal communications between the detainee and his legal adviser. The police can also seize things they *reasonably believe* to be evidence of an offence. A search must be carried out by a constable who is the same sex as the person to be searched. Strip searches can only be made where the custody officer thinks it necessary to get some item that the detainee would not be allowed to keep. The officer must make a record of the reason for the search and its result. Section 8 CJA removed the requirement of the custody officer to record or cause to be recorded everything a detained person has with him on entering custody. The custody officer is under a duty to ascertain what the person has with him, but the nature and detail of any recording is at the custody officer's discretion. He also has a discretion as to whether the record is kept as part of the custody record or as a separate record. This seeks to reduce the serious burden on officers, which can arise from recording large volumes of property. Clearly, it is still necessary to make records, not least to ensure against claims that property has been mishandled or removed. However, it is open to the police to make judgements about how to balance the need for recording against the amount of administrative work involved.

7.3.17 PROCEDURE ON ARREST

At common law (that is, before PACE 1984), it was necessary for the arrestor to make it clear to the arrestee that he was under compulsion either: (a) by physical means, such as taking him by the arm; or (b) by telling him, orally, that he was under compulsion. There was a danger, where words alone were used, that they might not be clear enough. Consider *Alderson v Booth* (1969). Following a positive breathalyser test, the officer said to the defendant: 'I shall have to ask you to come back to the station for further tests.' D did accompany the officer to the station. Lawful arrest was a condition precedent to anyone being convicted of driving with excess alcohol in their blood. At his trial, the defendant said he had not been arrested. He was acquitted and the prosecution appeal failed. Compulsion is a necessary element of arrest and the magistrates were not convinced that it was present in this case. The Divisional Court was not prepared to contradict the factual finding of the magistrates.

Additionally, where words alone were used, it was necessary for the arrestee to accede to the detention. There was no arrest where the arrestor said 'I arrest you' and the arrestee ran off before he could be touched (see *Sandon v Jervis* (1859)).

These principles remain good law after PACE 1984; see, for example, *Nichols v Bulman* (1985).

According to s 28(3) of PACE 1984, no arrest is lawful unless the arrestee is informed of the ground for the arrest at the time of, or as soon as reasonably practicable after, the arrest. Where a person is arrested by a constable, this applies (s 28(4)) regardless of whether the ground for the arrest is obvious.

The reasons for this rule were well put by Viscount Simon in *Christie v Leachinsky* (1947):

> . . . a person is *prima facie* entitled to personal freedom [and] should know why for the time being his personal freedom is being interfered with . . . No one, I think, would approve of a situation in which when the person arrested

> asked for the reason, the policeman replied 'that has nothing to do with you: come along with me' . . . And there are practical considerations . . . If the charge . . . is then and there made known to him, he has the opportunity of giving an explanation of any misunderstanding or of calling attention to other persons for whom he may have been mistaken, with the result that further inquiries may save him from the consequences of false accusation . . .

An arrest, however, becomes lawful once the ground is given. In *Lewis v Chief Constable of the South Wales Constabulary* (1991), the officers had told the plaintiffs of the fact of arrest, but delayed telling them the grounds for 10 minutes in one case and 23 minutes in the other. The Court of Appeal said that arrest was not a legal concept but arose factually from the deprivation of a person's liberty. It was also a continuing act and therefore what had begun as an unlawful arrest could become a lawful arrest. The remedy for the plaintiffs was the damages they had been awarded for the 10 minutes and 23 minutes of illegality: £200 each.

In *DPP v Hawkins* (1988), the Divisional Court held that an exception to the rule requiring information to be given to the arrestee exists where the defendant makes it impossible (for example, by his violent conduct) for the officer to communicate the reasons for the arrest to him. In that situation, the arrest is lawful and remains lawful until such a time as the reasons should have been given. The fact that the reasons were not given then does not invalidate the original arrest. The arrest would only become unlawful from the moment when the reasons for it should have been given to the arrested person.

In *R v Telfer* (1976), a police officer knew that the defendant was wanted for questioning about certain burglaries. The officer checked that the suspect was wanted, but not for which particular burglaries. He then stopped the defendant and asked him to come back to the station; when the defendant refused, he was arrested 'on suspicion of burglary'. The arrest was held to be unlawful. The person arrested was entitled to know the particular burglary of which he was suspected.

In *Nicholas v Parsonage* (1987), N was seen riding a bicycle without holding the handlebars by two police officers. They told him twice to hold the bars and then he did so. When they drove off, N raised two fingers. They then stopped N and PC Parsonage asked him for his name, telling him it was required as he had been riding his bicycle in a dangerous manner. N refused. P then informed him of his powers under PACE 1984 and requested N's name and address. N again refused. P then arrested him for failing to give his name and address. N attempted to ride off and a struggle ensued. N was subsequently convicted of, *inter alia*, assaulting a police officer in the execution of his duty, contrary to s 51(1) of the Police Act 1964. His appeal was dismissed by the Divisional Court, which held that the arrest under s 25 of PACE 1984 had been lawful as a constable exercising power under s 25(3) was not required to say why he wanted the suspect's name and address. N had been adequately informed of the ground of arrest under s 28(3) of PACE 1984. N was not arrested for failing to give his name and address; he was arrested because, having committed the minor offence of 'riding in a dangerous manner', it then became necessary to arrest him because the conditions in s 25(3)(a) and (c) were satisfied. These conditions were that an arrest for a minor offence is possible where the officer believes that the service of a summons is impracticable because he has not been given a proper name and address.

As to the extent of the explanation that has to be given on arrest under s 28 of PACE 1984, *Christie v Leachinsky* (above) was considered in *R v Chalkley and Jeffries* (1998). In this case, an arrest for an alleged credit card fraud was made for an ulterior motive, namely, to place recording equipment in the arrested defendant's house in order to record his discussions about planned robberies. The Court of Appeal held that, as there were reasonable grounds for suspecting the arrested defendant's involvement in the credit card frauds, and given that the police had informed him of this, the trial judge had been correct to rule that the arrest was lawful notwithstanding the ulterior motive.

Is it necessary for an arrestor to indicate to the arrestee the grounds on which his 'reasonable suspicion' was based? In *Geldberg v Miller* (1961), the appellant parked his car outside a restaurant in London while he had a meal. He was asked by police officers to move the car. He refused, preferring to finish his meal first. On being told that the police would remove the car, he removed the rotor arm from the distributor mechanism. He also refused to give his name and address or show his driving licence and certificate of insurance. He was arrested by one of the officers for 'obstructing him in the execution of his duty by refusing to move his car and refusing his name and address'. There was no power to arrest for obstruction of the police as no actual or apprehended breach of the peace was involved. The court held, however, that the arrest was valid for 'obstructing the thoroughfare', an offence under s 56(6) of the Metropolitan Police Act 1839, an offence the officer had not mentioned. Lord Parker CJ said:

> In my judgment, what the appellant knew and what he was told was ample to fulfil the obligation as to what should be done at the time of an arrest without warrant.

An arrest will be unlawful, however, where the reasons given point to an offence for which there is no power of arrest (or for which there is only qualified power of arrest) and it is clear that no other reasons were present in the mind of the officer: *Edwards v DPP* (1993). This principle was confirmed in *Mullady v DPP* (1997). A police officer arrested M for 'obstruction', an offence with the power of arrest only if the defendant's conduct amounted to a breach of the peace (for which there is a common law power of arrest) or if one of the general arrest conditions as set out in s 25 is satisfied. The police argued that the officer could have arrested M for a breach of the peace and merely gave the wrong reason. The Divisional Court held that the officer had acted unlawfully and that it would be wrong for the justices to go behind the reason given and infer that the reason for the arrest was another lawful reason.

In some circumstances, the court may infer a lawful reason for an arrest if the circumstantial evidence points clearly to a lawful reason (*Brookman v DPP* (1997)). However, if there is insufficient evidence to determine whether a lawful or unlawful reason was given for the arrest, then the police will fail to show that the arrest was lawful (*Clarke v DPP* (1998)). The issue seems to be what degree of evidence is necessary to allow the court to infer a lawful reason for arrest (see further, Khan and Ryder (September 1998) Legal Action 16).

7.3.18   POLICE POWERS UNDER S 60 OF THE CRIMINAL JUSTICE AND PUBLIC ORDER ACT 1994

Section 60 of the CJPOA 1994 provides for a stop and search power in anticipation of violence, and was introduced to deal with violent conduct, especially by groups of young men (note that this section has amendments pending). The section provides that, where authorisation for its use has been granted:

(4) A constable in uniform may:

    (a) stop any pedestrian and search him or anything carried by him for offensive weapons or dangerous instruments;

    (b) stop any vehicle and search the vehicle, its driver and any passenger for offensive weapons or dangerous instruments.

(5) A constable may, in the exercise of those powers, stop any person or vehicle and make any search he thinks fit whether or not he has any grounds for suspecting that the person or vehicle is carrying any weapons or articles of that kind.

(6) If, in the course of such a search under this section, a constable discovers a dangerous instrument or an article which he has reasonable grounds for suspecting to be an offensive weapon, he may seize it.

The authorisation required by s 60 must be given by a police officer of, or above, the rank of superintendent (or a chief inspector or inspector where such an officer reasonably believes that incidents involving serious violence are imminent and no superintendent is available). The authorising officer must reasonably believe that:

(a) incidents involving serious violence may take place in any locality in his area; and

(b) it is expedient to grant an authorisation to prevent their occurrence.

Such an authorisation, which must be in writing, will permit the exercise of stop and search powers within that locality for a period up to 24 hours. The authorisation could conceivably be given in fear of a single incident, even though the CJPOA 1994 requires fear of 'incidents'. This is because s 6 of the Interpretation Act 1978 states that the plural includes the singular unless a contrary intention is shown.

There are several aspects of this section that have been drafted in what appears to be a deliberately vague way. 'Serious violence' is not defined and this will be very much within the judgment of the senior officer concerned, provided of course that his view is based upon reasonable belief. Richard Card and Richard Ward, in a commentary on the Act (*The Criminal Justice and Public Order Act 1994* (1994)), have noted that the dictionary includes 'force against property' as within the definition of violence, and this may well become an important matter for decision by the courts.

The word 'locality' is left undefined in the CJPOA 1994. It could be an area outside a particular club or pub, or it might extend to a large estate. The courts have the power to declare an authorisation invalid because of an overly expansive geographical area; they are unlikely to substitute their own view for that of the operational officer.

7.3.19 OTHER ASPECTS OF S 60 OF THE CRIMINAL JUSTICE AND PUBLIC ORDER ACT 1994

'Offensive weapon' (s 60(4), (11)) means the same as for s 1(9) of PACE 1984. It is: (a) any article made or adapted for use for causing injury to persons; or (b) intended by the person having it with him for such use by him or some other person. There is no provision for reasonable excuse for the possession of such weapons.

'Dangerous instruments' (s 60(4)) will often be caught within the definition of offensive weapons, but the definition extends to cover instruments that have a blade or are sharply pointed (s 60(11)).

The authorising officer must reasonably believe that it is 'expedient' to give an authorisation in order to prevent the occurrence of incidents of serious violence. Thus, the authorisation need not be the only way in which such incidents may be prevented. Various policing factors may have to be balanced, including the ability of the police force to remain effective and efficient if it were to use other methods.

There is no power to detain especially conferred on officers by s 60 in order to carry out the search, but it does make failure to stop a summary offence. As it stands, there is nothing in s 60 that would permit an officer to use any force to conduct a nonconsensual search. It is possible that the courts could imply such a power. When conducting the search, the officer must give the suspect his name, the police station to which he is attached, the authorisation for the search and the reason for the search. It seems that failure to comply with these conditions will make the search unlawful. (See *Fennelley* (1989), a case where the defendant was not told why he was stopped, searched and arrested in the street. Evidence from the search, some jewellery, was excluded at the trial. Evidence of drugs found on him at the police station was also excluded.)

The scope of s 60 and police powers to stop and search are being incrementally extended through various Acts of Parliament. They include the following: s 8 of the Knives Act 1997 amended s 60 to allow *initial* authorisations by an officer of the rank of inspector or above, thus obviating the need for an officer of at least the rank of superintendent. Section 60(1)(b) extends the criteria under which an authorising officer may invoke this power to include reasonable belief that incidents involving serious violence may take place or that such instruments or weapons are being carried in a particular area. Section 60(3) provides that authorisations may be extended up to 24 hours instead of six, although only an officer of the rank of superintendent or above may do this. A new sub-s (11A) was inserted under s 60 by s 8 of the Knives Act 1997 and states that, 'for the purposes of this section, a person carries a dangerous instrument or an offensive weapon if he has it in his possession'.

These amendments are intended to deal with anticipated violence in situations where gangs or persons may be 'tooled-up' and travelling through various police areas en route to an intended scene of confrontation. Thus, the power may be invoked even where it is believed that the actual anticipated violence may occur in another police jurisdiction, for example, by football hooligans travelling to and from matches.

Further amendments to s 60 have been made under the CDA 1998. This is mainly to deal with the problem of troublemakers deliberately wearing facial coverings to conceal their identities, especially when the police are using CCTV cameras. Section 25 of the CDA 1998 inserted a new sub-s 4A under s 60, which conferred a power on any constable in uniform to demand the removal of, or seize, face coverings where authority had been given under s 60, if the officer reasonably believed that the face covering was being worn, or was intended to be used, to conceal a person's identity. The Anti-Terrorism, Crime and Security Act 2001 replaced s 60(4A) with s 60AA. This is broader than the earlier sub-section and provides for the removal of 'disguises'. Section 25 also extends s 60(8) and makes it a summary offence if a person fails to stop, or to stop a vehicle, or to remove an item worn by him, when required by the police in the exercise of their powers under s 60. This is punishable by a term of imprisonment not exceeding one month and/or a maximum fine of £1,000. Section 60A inserted by s 26 of the CDA 1998 provides that things seized under s 60 may be retained in accordance with regulations made by the Secretary of State. (See L Jason-Lloyd (1998) 162 JP 836, 24 October.)

7.3.20   ACCOUNTABILITY AND S 60 OF THE CRIMINAL JUSTICE AND PUBLIC ORDER ACT 1994

There are dangers that the powers under s 60 could be misused, as no reasonable suspicion is required and the requirements for authorisation are rather nebulous.

The safeguards against misuse include the fact that the admissibility of evidence gained through the use of a dubious stop and search event may be in doubt if there are serious breaches of the revised Code A. Someone charged with obstructing a police officer in the exercise of duty may raise breaches of the Code in defence. Unlawful search or seizure may also provide a basis for an application for exclusion of evidence thus obtained under s 78 of PACE 1984.

As the police have a common law power to take whatever action is necessary in order to prevent an imminent breach of the peace (*Moss v Mclachlan* (1985)), then, even if a challenge to the use of a s 60 power is technically successful, the police conduct in question may often be thus justified.

7.3.21 THE TERRORISM ACT 2000

The Terrorism Act 2000 gave exceptional powers of stop and search to uniformed police constables. A person of at least the rank of commander or assistant chief constable, who considered it expedient to do so for the prevention of acts of terrorism, could issue an authorisation specifying a particular area or place (to last for not more than 28 days). This gave a constable power to stop vehicles and pedestrians within that area or place and search the vehicle, driver, passengers, pedestrians (and anything with them) for articles of a kind that could be used in connection with terrorism. These powers could be exercised whether or not the constable had grounds for suspecting the presence of articles of that kind. The constable could seize and retain an article that he discovered in the course of such a search and that he reasonably suspected was intended to be used in connection with terrorism (ss 44 and 45). By s 47, it was an offence to fail to stop a vehicle when required to do so, fail to stop when required to do so, and willfully to obstruct a constable in the exercise of these powers. The offences are punishable with six months' imprisonment and/or a fine of up to £5,000.

These provisions were not confined to terrorism in connection with Northern Ireland or international terrorism. 'Terrorism' means the use or threat of action involving serious violence against a person, serious damage to property, endangering the life of a person other than the 'terrorist'. This must be coupled with creating a serious risk to the health or safety of the public or a section of the public, or designing seriously to interfere with or seriously to disrupt an electronic system. The above action(s) must be designed to influence the government or to intimidate the public or a section of the public, and made for the purpose of advancing a political, religious or ideological cause. However, where the use or threat of action involves the use of firearms or explosives, it need not be designed to influence the government or to intimidate the public or a section of the public.

In *Gillan and Quinton v UK* (2010) the ECtHR held that the requirement on a person to submit to a stop and search under s 44 of the TA 2000 represented a clear interference with the right to respect for private life under Art 8 ECHR, finding that the provisions of the TA 2000 had been neither sufficiently circumscribed nor subject to adequate safeguards against abuse. The court was also influenced by the massive increase in the use of the power since it had been introduced and the fact that it was disproportionately used against ethnic minorities. As a result of the judgment the coalition government made a remedial order under the Human Rights Act 1998 (the Terrorism Act 2000 (Remedial) Order 2011), which has the effect of repealing ss 44, 45, 46 and most of s 47. The new Protection of Freedoms Act 2012 now provides the police with more circumscribed powers to authorise stop and search of persons and vehicles without reasonable suspicion (s 47A) in exceptional circumstances. This places the powers provided by the Terrorism Act 2000 Remedial Order 2011 on a permanent footing. The Protection of Freedoms Act 2012 also changes stop and search powers in the Terrorism Act 2000 (ss 43 and 43A) which require reasonable suspicion to enable searches of vehicles or their occupants. Codes of practice supporting the new legislation were laid before Parliament in May 2012 in the form of the Terrorism Act 2000 (Codes of Practice for the Exercise of Stop and Search Powers) Order 2012. In addition PACE codes of practice C, G and H have been amended to introduce a new code of practice for the video recording with sound of interviews carried out under s 41 of, and Sched 7 to, the Terrorism Act 2000 and post-charge questioning of terrorist suspects under the Counter-Terrorism Act 2008.

7.3.22   THE USE OF FORCE TO EFFECT AN ARREST

The use of force by a member of the public when arresting someone is governed by s 3 of the CLA 1967. This states:

(1)   A person may use such force as is reasonable in the circumstances in the prevention of crime, or in effecting or assisting in the lawful arrest of offenders or suspected offenders or of persons unlawfully at large.

Reasonable force will generally mean the minimum necessary to effect an arrest. The use of force by police officers is governed by s 117 of PACE 1984. This states:

Where any provision of this Act:

(a)   confers a power on a constable; and

(b)   does not provide that the power may only be exercised with the consent of some person, other than a police officer, the officer may use reasonable force, if necessary, in the exercise of the power.

7.3.23   DUTIES AFTER ARREST

A person arrested by a constable, or handed over to one, must be taken to a police station as soon as is 'practicable', unless his presence elsewhere is 'necessary in order to carry out such investigations as it is reasonable to carry out immediately' (s 30(1), (10) of PACE 1984). Where a citizen makes an arrest, he 'must, as soon as he reasonably can, hand the man over to a constable or take him to the police station or take him before a magistrate', *per* Lord Denning in *Dallison v Caffery* (1965). There is no requirement, however, that this be carried out immediately: *John Lewis & Co v Tims* (see above, at 7.3.9).

7.4 INTERROGATION, CONFESSION AND ADMISSIBILITY OF EVIDENCE

Before moving into the specific provisions of PACE 1984 and the Codes of Practice, it is important to be aware of the general issues at stake in this area of law. Are the rights of suspects being interrogated by the police sufficiently protected by law? Is there scope for abuse of power by the police? Are the police burdened by too many legal requirements when trying to induce a suspect to confess to a crime? What effects are likely to flow from the undermining of the right to silence (see ss 34–37 of the CJPOA 1994, 7.4.3–8 below)?

Once again, it is also necessary to bear in mind the significance of the ECHR in this context. Unless impossible because of conflicting primary legislation, English courts must interpret rules of law so as to be compatible with obligations under the ECHR. Article 5 guarantees a right to liberty. To justify depriving a person of his liberty before conviction for an offence, for example, Art 5 requires that there be a lawful arrest or detention for the purpose of bringing the person before a competent authority on a reasonable suspicion of having committed an offence, or that arrest or detention is considered reasonably necessary to prevent him from committing an offence. Moreover, every person arrested shall be informed promptly in a language that he understands of the reasons for his arrest. The arrested person shall be informed of any charge against him, shall be brought promptly before a judge and shall be entitled to trial within a reasonable time or to release pending trial. Clearly, PACE requirements in relation to arrest and detention must be measured against Art 5. Equally, Art 6 requires a fair trial and declares a presumption of innocence, matters that bear on the conduct of the trial, the evidence presented, and the obligation to offer explanations or risk the consequences of adverse inferences being drawn from silence.

7.4.1 TIME LIMITS ON DETENTION WITHOUT CHARGE

Under s 40 of PACE 1984, the Custody Officer is obliged to review the detention of a suspect held at the police station as follows:

(a) the first review shall be not later than six hours after the detention was first authorised;

(b) the second review shall be not later than nine hours after the first;

(c) subsequent reviews shall be at intervals of not more than nine hours. The purpose of such reviews is to reduce the possibility that the suspect is being held for too long or unnecessarily while the investigation is ongoing. Both the suspect and/or his solicitor are allowed to make representations about the termination or continuation of the detention.

Section 6 of the CJA 2003 introduces a new innovation – the use of telephones for review of police detention. This provision enables reviews of the continuing need for detention without charge carried out under s 40 of PACE 1984 to be conducted over the telephone rather than in person at the police station. Such reviews have to be carried out by an officer of at least inspector rank. PACE 1984 currently only allows telephone reviews where it is not reasonably practicable for the reviewing officer to be present at the police station.

The new s 40A(1) allows a review to be carried out by means of a discussion over the telephone with one or more persons at the police station where the arrested person is held. In practice, the reviewing officer would normally speak to the custody officer at the police station, as well as to the detained person or their legal representative if they wanted to exercise their right to make representations about the continuing need for detention.

The new s 40A(2) specifies that telephone reviews are not applicable where it is reasonably practicable to carry out the review using video-conferencing facilities in accordance with regulations under s 45A of PACE 1984. Where such video-conferencing facilities are readily available, it is appropriate that they should be used.

Under s 41 of PACE 1984, a suspect can be held without being charged for 24 hours before any further authorisation needs to be given. At this point, the situation must be reviewed and further detention must be authorised by an officer of at least the rank of superintendent (s 42). The period is measured from arrival at the police station. If he is arrested by another force, the time runs from his arrival at the station of the area where he is wanted. If further detention is authorised, this can continue for up to the 36-hour point. After 36 hours from the beginning of the detention, there must be a full hearing in a magistrates' court with the suspect and, if he wishes, legal representation (s 43). The magistrates can grant a warrant of further detention for up to a further 60 hours – making a total of 96 hours (ss 43 and 44). However, the police could not be granted the 60-hour period as a whole because the maximum extension that a magistrates' court can grant at one time is 36 hours (ss 43(12) and 44). The magistrates can only grant such extensions if the offence being investigated is an indictable offence (s 116) and is being investigated diligently and expeditiously. Moreover, it must be shown that the further detention is necessary to secure or preserve evidence relating to an offence for which the suspect is under arrest or to obtain such evidence by questioning him (s 43(4)).

Section 38 states that, *after being charged*, the arrested person must be released with or without bail, unless:

- it is necessary to hold him so that his name and address can be obtained; or
- the custody officer reasonably thinks that it is necessary to hold him for his own protection or to prevent him from causing physical injury to anyone or from causing loss of or damage to property; or
- the custody officer reasonably thinks that he needs to be held because he would otherwise fail to answer bail or to prevent him from interfering with witnesses or otherwise obstructing the course of justice; or
- the custody officer believes that it is necessary for him to be detained in order that a sample under s 63B can be obtained; or
- he is a juvenile and ought to be held 'in his own interests'.

If the suspect is charged and not released, he will have to be brought before a magistrates' court 'as soon as practicable' – and not later than the first sitting after being charged (s 46(2)). Section 7 of the CJA 2003 amended limits on police powers on periods of detention without charge. This provision extends the scope for an officer of at least superintendent rank to authorise detention without charge up to a maximum of 36 hours. As the law previously stood, an officer of superintendent rank or above could extend detention without charge up to an overall period of 36 hours. This can only be done if an officer of sufficient rank is satisfied that detention is necessary to secure, preserve or obtain evidence, that the investigation is being conducted diligently and expeditiously, and that the relevant offence was an indictable offence.

The amendment allows detention to be extended for up to an overall period of 36 hours where the relevant offence is an arrestable offence, provided the other conditions are satisfied.

This broadened capacity for extended detention without charge assists the police in dealing effectively with a range of offences, for example, robbery, where it will sometimes be extremely difficult or impossible to complete the necessary investigatory processes within 24 hours.

7.4.2 SEARCHES OF DETAINED PERSONS

Searches of people detained at police stations are governed by s 54 and Code C (revised May 2012). The Act also allows 'speculative searches' in which fingerprints, samples or information in respect thereof can be checked against other similar data held by the police. Section 82 of the CJPA 2001 retrospectively amended s 64 of PACE 1984, giving the police the right to retain DNA samples and fingerprints. In *S and Marper v UK* (2009) the ECtHR held that holding DNA samples of people who were arrested but later acquitted or had the charges against them dropped was a violation of the right to privacy under Art 8 ECHR. This provision has therefore been amended retrospectively by way of the Crime and Security Act 2010, brought into force on 7 March 2011. This provision contains the requirement to destroy all DNA samples after six months. However, the ability to retain DNA *profiles* for six years, even if the person has never been charged, prosecuted or convicted of an offence, remains.

A person may only be searched if the custody officer considers this necessary in order to make a complete list of his property (s 54(6)). There is no automatic right to search all suspects as a matter of routine. The police can, however, search anyone to ascertain whether he has with him anything that he could use to cause physical injury, damage property, interfere with evidence or assist him to escape (s 55, as amended). Section 65 deals with intimate searches:

> [. . .] a search which consists of the physical examination of a person's body orifices other than the mouth.

A physical examination of the mouth is therefore allowed in the circumstances where a non-intimate search of the person may occur, subject to the ordinary safeguards (Code of Practice A, para 3, Code C). A search of the mouth for drugs is not the taking of a sample as defined by s 65 of PACE 1984, so the restrictions that apply to the taking of samples do not apply here. A search of an arrested person's mouth may thus be carried out by a police officer at the station, subject to the safeguards in Code C. The officer carrying out the search must be of the same sex as the arrested person (s 54(9)). Nonetheless, an officer of either sex may search the arrested person's mouth at the time of the arrest if he or she has reasonable grounds to believe that the arrested person is concealing therein evidence related to the offence (s 32(2)(b)). The powers to take fingerprints and non-intimate samples have recently been extended: revised Code A paras 4.1–4.10 and revised Code D para 4.3 (see below).

Intimate searches must be authorised by an officer of the rank of superintendent or above, on the basis of reasonable belief that the arrested person in police detention has concealed on himself anything that could be used to cause physical injury to himself or to others and that he might so use it. Intimate searches for weapons can, if a doctor or registered nurse is not available, be carried out by a police officer of the same sex as the suspect. If the search is for drugs, it can only be carried out by a doctor or registered nurse. It cannot be carried out at a police station (s 55(4)). Intimate searches for drugs are limited to those for hard drugs, defined as Class A drugs in Sched 2 to the Misuse of Drugs Act 1971.

Section 9 CJA 2003 covers taking fingerprints without consent. This section has extended the circumstances in which the police may take a person's fingerprints without consent, to include taking fingerprints from a person arrested for a recordable offence and detained in a police station.

Sub-section (2) replaces the existing provisions about the taking of fingerprints on the authority of an inspector with a *wider power* to take fingerprints *from any person detained in consequence of his arrest for a recordable offence.*

The requirement to give a person whose fingerprints are taken without consent reasons for doing so and for recording the reason as soon as practical applies to the new power (see s 9(5)).

This amendment to s 61 of PACE 1984 prevents persons who come into police custody and who may be wanted on a warrant or for questioning on other matters from avoiding detection by giving the police a false name and address. Using LiveScan technology, which enables the police to take fingerprints electronically and which is linked to the national fingerprint database (NAFIS), the police are able to confirm a person's identity while he is still in police detention if his fingerprints have been taken previously. It will also assist in enabling vulnerable or violent people to be identified more quickly and dealt with more effectively. A speculative search of the fingerprint crime scene database can also reveal if the person may have been involved in other crimes.

Section 10 CJA covers where the police propose taking non-intimate samples without consent. This section extends the circumstances in which the police may take a non-intimate sample without consent from a person in police detention to include taking such a sample from a person arrested for a recordable offence.

Section 63 of PACE 1984 provides powers for taking a non-intimate sample without consent from a person in the following circumstances:

- following charge with a recordable offence or notification that the person will be reported for such an offence;
- if the person is in police detention (or is being held in custody by the police on the authority of a court), on the authority of an inspector, which can only be given where the officer has reasonable grounds for believing the suspect is involved in a recordable offence and the sample will tend to confirm or disprove his involvement;
- following conviction for a recordable offence.

On 7 March 2011 ss 2–7 of the Crime and Security Act came into force amending ss 61 and 63 of PACE to enable fingerprints and non-intimate samples to be taken from people who have been arrested for a recordable offence, either if they have been released on bail before the data have been taken or if the data that were taken subsequently proved to be inadequate for analysis. Also on 7 March 2011 s 117 of the Serious Organised Crime and Police Act (SOCPA) was brought into force, further amending ss 61, 63A and 64 of PACE. This provision now permits a police officer to take a person's fingerprints without his consent even though he has not been arrested. In order to do so the officer must reasonably suspect that he is committing or attempting to commit an offence. In addition, the officer must either not know or not be able to readily ascertain his name, or have reasonable grounds for doubting whether the name given by the person is his real name.

In relation to a person in police detention, sub-ss (2) and (3) replace the existing provisions about the taking of a non-intimate sample on the authority of an inspector with a wider power to take a non-intimate sample from any person in police detention in consequence of his arrest for a recordable offence. This is conditional on him not having had a sample of the same type and from the same part of the body taken already in the course of the investigation or, if one has been taken, that it proved insufficient for the analysis.

The new power is available whether or not the sample is required for the investigation of an offence in which the person is suspected of being involved. However, the police will of course be able to use the new power to obtain samples in cases where, under the present law, an inspector's authorisation would have to be given (for example, in a rape investigation, to obtain a foot impression, a hair sample and a mouth swab).

The requirement to give a person from whom a non-intimate sample is taken without consent the reason for doing so and for recording the reason as soon as practicable applies to the new power (see s 10(5)).

The amendments do not affect the existing powers to take samples from persons held in custody by the police on the authority of a court.

DNA profiles extracted from non-intimate samples taken from arrested persons will be added to the samples already held on the national DNA database and checked for matches with DNA taken from crime scenes.

7.4.3   ANSWERING POLICE QUESTIONS AND THE RIGHT TO SILENCE

The police are free to ask anyone any questions. The only restriction is that all questioning is supposed to cease once a detainee has been charged. Code C, para 11.6 states that:

> The interview or further interview of a person about an offence with which that person has not been charged or for which they have not been informed they may be prosecuted must cease when the officer in charge of the investigation:
>
> (a)   is satisfied all the questions they consider relevant to obtaining accurate and reliable information about the offence have been put to the suspect, this includes allowing the suspect an opportunity to give an innocent explanation and asking questions to test if the explanation is accurate and reliable, eg, to clear up ambiguities or clarify what the suspect said;
>
> (b)   has taken account of any other available evidence; and
>
> (c)   the officer in charge of the investigation, or in the case of a detained suspect, the custody officer, see *paragraph 16.1*, reasonably believes there is sufficient evidence to provide a realistic prospect of conviction for that offence if the person was prosecuted for it. See Note 11B.
>
> This paragraph does not prevent officers in revenue cases or acting under the confiscation provisions of the Criminal Justice Act 1988 or the Drug Trafficking Act 1994 from inviting suspects to complete a formal question and answer record after the interview is concluded.

There is no *obligation* on a citizen to answer police questions. A person cannot be charged, for example, with obstructing the police in the execution of their duty simply by failing to answer questions. Although a judge or prosecutor cannot suggest to the jury that such silence is evidence of guilt, adverse inferences might be drawn in court from a defendant's earlier refusal to answer police questions if he has been given the police caution (see below – s 34 of the CJPOA 1994). 'Adverse inferences' can be drawn, the logic runs, on the basis that failure to answer questions suggests there is something to hide, or there is no explanatory, adequate answer. Judges seem to have interpreted this section rather narrowly. Lord Bingham CJ, for example, said in *R v Bowden* (1999):

> Proper effect must of course be given to these provisions . . . But since they restrict rights recognised at common law as appropriate to protect defendants against the risk of injustice, they should not be construed more widely than the statutory language allows.

It could be argued that s 34 is difficult to reconcile with the fair trial guarantees found in Art 6 of the ECHR. The Strasbourg Court has said, for example, that 'the very fact that an accused is advised by his lawyer to maintain his silence must be given appropriate weight by the domestic court. There may be good reason why such advice is given'; *Condron and Condron v UK* (2001). See generally, Ian Dennis, 'Silence in the police station: the marginalisation of section 34' [2002] Crim LR 25–38 and 7.4.6 below. What is clear, however, is that a conviction cannot be founded on silence alone in the absence of any other evidence.

In *Rice v Connolly* (1966), the appellant was seen by officers in the early hours of the morning behaving suspiciously in an area where house-breaking had taken place on the same evening. On being questioned, he refused to say where he was going or where he had come from. He refused to give his full name and address, though he did give a name and the name of a road which were not untrue. He refused to accompany the officer to a police box for identification purposes, saying: 'If you want me, you'll have to arrest me.' He was arrested and charged with willfully obstructing a police officer contrary to s 51(3) of the Police Act 1964.

His appeal against conviction succeeded. Lord Parker CJ noted that the police officer was acting within his duty in inquiring about the appellant and that what the appellant did was obstructive. The critical question, though, was whether the appellant's conduct was 'willful' within the meaning of s 51. Lord Parker CJ, in the Divisional Court, took that word to mean 'intentional [and] without lawful excuse'. He continued:

> It seems to me quite clear that, though every citizen has a moral duty or, if you like, a social duty to assist the police, there is no legal duty to that effect, and, indeed, the whole basis of the common law is the right of the individual to refuse to answer questions put to him by persons in authority, and to refuse to accompany those in authority to any particular place; short, of course, of arrest.

The court was unanimous, although one judge, James J, cautioned that he would not go as far as to say that silence coupled with conduct could not amount to obstruction. It would depend on the particular facts of any given case.

7.4.4 DUTIES TO ANSWER

There are certain circumstances where the citizen is under a duty to answer police questions. Where a constable has reasonable grounds for believing that a vehicle has been involved in an accident and he seeks the particulars of the driver, he may arrest that person if the information is not given. With the Home Secretary's consent, and on the authority of a chief constable, coercive questioning (that is, where a suspect's silence can be used in evidence against him) can be used in matters under s 11 (as amended) of the Official Secrets Act 1911. There are also wide powers under the Companies Act 1985 to require officers and agents of companies to assist inspectors appointed to investigate the company. Refusal to answer questions can be sanctioned as a contempt of court (s 431) and as a criminal offence (s 447). A person can also be required to answer questions put to him by a liquidator of a company (*Bishopsgate Management Ltd v Maxwell Mirror Group Newspapers* (1993)). However, following the ECtHR case of *Saunders v UK* (1996), s 59 and Sched 3 of the YJCEA 1999 restricted the provisions of the Companies Act 1985 in relation to evidence; the powers of investigation are not affected but the prosecution will not be able to adduce evidence, or put questions, about the accused's answers to inspectors conducting an investigation using their powers of compulsion unless the evidence is first adduced, or a question asked, by or on behalf of the accused in the proceedings.

Under s 2 of the CJA 1987, the Director of the Serious Fraud Office (SFO) (dealing with frauds worth over £5 million) can require anyone whom he has reason to think has relevant information to attend to answer questions and to provide information including documents and books. Such statements, however, cannot be used in evidence against the persons who make them unless they go into the witness box and give inconsistent testimony. Even this power, though, does not require the breach of legal professional privilege. Failure to comply with s 2 requests is a criminal offence and can result in an application for a magistrates' search warrant. These powers have been widely used. The SFO Annual Report for 2009–2010 revealed that 55 cases had been investigated, nine had been successfully prosecuted and 22 had been the subject of restraint or compensation orders, with 91.7 per cent of defendants being convicted at trial (*Serious Fraud Office Annual Report,* 1 April 2009 – 31 March 2010, available at www.sfo.gov.uk). In *R v Director of the Serious Fraud Office ex p Smith* (1993), the House of Lords held that the SFO could compel a person to answer questions relating to an offence with which he had already been charged. It followed that in relation to such questions, the suspect did not have to be further cautioned.

Other powers to compel answers on pain of penalties for refusal exist under the Terrorism Act 2000, and refusal to answer certain allegations from the prosecutor can be treated as acceptances of them under the Drug Trafficking Act 1994.

The closest English law comes to creating a duty to give one's name and address is the power given to the police under s 25(3) of PACE 1984. This is the power to arrest for a non-arrestable offence where the officer cannot find out the suspect's particulars for the purpose of serving a summons on him.

There is no duty to offer information about crime to the police. However, s 19 of the Terrorism Act 2000 makes it an offence for a person who believes or suspects that another person has committed an offence under any of ss 15–18 (offences involving funding of terrorism), and bases his belief or suspicion on information that comes to his attention in the course of a trade, profession, business or employment to not disclose to an officer as soon as is reasonably practicable his belief or suspicion, and the information on which it is based. Additionally, s 5 of the CLA 1967 creates the offence of accepting money or other consideration for not disclosing information that would lead to the prosecution of an arrestable offence. The House of Lords has also held that it is the duty of every citizen in whose presence a breach of the peace is being committed to attempt to stop it, if necessary by detaining the person responsible. It is, however, except in the case of a citizen who is a police officer, 'a duty of imperfect obligation' (*Albert v Lavin* (1982), *per* Lord Diplock).

7.4.5 WHAT CAN BE SAID IN COURT ABOUT SILENCE IN THE FACE OF POLICE QUESTIONING

There is an established common law rule that neither the prosecution nor the judge should make adverse comment on the defendant's silence in the face of questions. The dividing line, however, between proper and improper judicial comment was a matter of great debate. In Scotland, a trial judge may not comment on a defendant's failure to answer questions. It is suggested that the position in England and Wales, whereby a judge may comment, not only undermines the right to silence but also provides fertile ground for judicial misdirections to the jury, in turn increasing the opportunities for appeal on points that arise simply in default of lack of judicial restraint. There are many reasons why a suspect might remain silent when questioned (for example, fear, confusion, reluctance to incriminate another person) and the 'right to silence' enjoyed the status of a long-established general principle in English law. Thus, in *R v Davis* (1959), a judge was ruled on appeal to have misdirected the jury when he told them that 'a man is not obliged to say anything but you are entitled to use your common sense . . . [C]an you imagine an innocent man who had behaved like that not saying anything to the police . . . He said nothing.'

An exception, though, was that some degree of adverse suggestion was permitted where two people were speaking on equal terms and one refused to comment on the accusation made against him by the other. In *R v Parkes* (1974), the Privy Council ruled that a judge could invite the jury to consider the possibility of drawing adverse inferences from silence from a tenant who had been accused by a landlady of murdering her daughter. The landlady and tenant, for the purposes of this encounter, were regarded as having a parity of status unlike a person faced with questions from the police. It was held in *R v Chandler* (1976) that the suspect was on equal terms with the police officer where the former was in the company of his solicitor. Chandler had refused to answer some of the questions he had been asked by the police officer before the caution. The judge told the jury that they should decide whether the defendant's silence was attributable to his wish to exercise his common law right or because he might incriminate himself. The Court of Appeal quashed Chandler's conviction since the judge had gone too far in suggesting that silence before a caution could be evidence of guilt.

It was proper for the judge to make some comment on a defendant's reticence before being cautioned, provided that the jury were directed that the issue had to be dealt with in two stages: (i) was the defendant's silence an acceptance of the officer's allegations? and, if so, (ii) could guilt of the offence charged be reasonably inferred from what the defendant had implicitly accepted? The court said that it did not accept that a police officer always had an advantage over a suspect. Everything depended on the circumstances. In an inquiry into local government corruption, for example, a young officer might be at a distinct disadvantage when questioning a local dignitary. That type of interview was very different from a 'tearful housewife' being accused of shoplifting.

The Court of Appeal's decision in *Chandler* asserted that silence might only be taken as acquiescence to police allegations before a caution. The court excluded silence after the caution as being something from which anything adverse can be inferred, because a suspect could not be criticised for remaining silent having been specifically told of that right. This, however, seemed like an irrational dichotomy. If the suspect did, in fact, have a legal right to silence whether or not he had been cautioned, it is very odd that full enjoyment of the right could only be effective from the moment of it being announced by the police. Additionally, any questioning of a suspect at a police station prior to a caution being given is probably in contravention of Code C, para 10, which requires a caution to be given at the beginning of each session of questioning. Violation of the Code affords grounds for an appeal under s 78 of PACE 1984. Cautions need not be given according to para 10.1:

> [. . .] if questions are for other necessary purposes, eg:
>
> (a)   solely to establish their own identity or ownership of any vehicle;
>
> (b)   to obtain information in accordance with any relevant statutory requirement, see *paragraph 10.9*;
>
> (c)   in furtherance of the proper and effective control of a search, eg, to determine the need to search in the exercise of powers of stop and search or to seek co-operation while carrying out a search . . .

These cases must now all be read in the light of s 34 of the CJPOA 1994.

7.4.6   RIGHT TO SILENCE IN COURTS

Before the changes to the right to silence that were made by the CJPOA 1994, the value of maintaining the traditional approach was subjected to considerable scrutiny. Since 1988, the right to silence was effectively abolished in Northern Ireland. It became possible for a court to draw adverse inferences from a defendant's silence when he was arrested. Adverse inferences could also be drawn from the defendant's failure to provide an explanation for any 'object, substance or mark' on his clothing, footwear or in his possession, which the arresting officer found suspicious and questioned the suspect about (Criminal Justice (Evidence etc) (Northern Ireland) Order 1988).

Similar recommendations were made by the Home Office Working Group on the Right to Silence in 1989. The question was also considered by the Runciman Royal Commission on Criminal Justice. It had to decide whether to adopt a practice like the Northern Ireland system and the one recommended by the Home Office, or whether to retain the right to silence, as the Philips Royal Commission on Criminal Procedure had recommended in 1981. In evidence to the Runciman Royal Commission, the proposal to retain the right to silence was supported by The Law Society, the Bar Council and the Magistrates' Association. It was opposed by the police, the CPS, HM Council of circuit judges and several senior judges.

Professor Michael Zander's research on this issue suggested that the role of the right to silence in the real workings of the criminal justice system was in fact not as significant as often argued. In one of his studies, 'Investigation of crime' [1979] Crim LR 211, he looked at 150 cases randomly drawn from those heard at the Old Bailey. According to police statements, of the 286 defendants (in many cases, there was more than one defendant), only 12 were said to have relied on their right to silence when confronted by police accusations. Of these, nine were convicted. Zander has also made the following points:

- Most defendants plead guilty, so the right to silence is unimportant in such a context.

- Common law rules permit the judge to *mention* the defendant's silence and, in some limited circumstances, to comment on it.

- In any event, the jury may draw adverse conclusions about the defendant's silence to police questions, that is, whether the judge is permitted to comment on this or not.

In a study commissioned by the LCD, only 2 per cent of 527 suspects exercised their right to silence; see Sanders *et al, Advice and Assistance at Police Stations and the 24 Hour Duty Solicitor Scheme*, 1989, LCD.

In a study by Stephen Motson, Geoffrey Stephenson and Tom Williamson ((1992) 32 *British Journal of Criminology* 23–40), the researchers looked at 1,067 CID interviews carried out in nine London police stations in 1989. Their method was to carefully match cases where the right to silence had been exercised with like cases where it had not, and then compare the outcomes. The researchers found that decisions as to whether to prosecute were based on factors like the strength of the evidence against the suspect and the seriousness of the offence. They were not correlated with whether the suspect responded to questions or not. There was no evidence that silence at the police station gave the suspect any advantage at court. They commented:

> The high proportion of silence cases who ultimately plead guilty might be taken to suggest that the use of silence is a ploy – adopted for the most part by previously convicted offenders, [it] is abandoned in favour of a guilty plea when prosecution, probable conviction and (especially) sentencing are nigh.

The Runciman Royal Commission eventually decided to recommend retaining the right to silence. Its Report (1993) states (para 82):

> The majority of us believe that adverse inferences should not be drawn from silence at the police station and recommend retaining the present caution and trial direction.

The Commission did, however, recommend (para 84) the retention of the current law regarding silence in investigations of serious and complex fraud under which adverse consequences can follow from silence. The Report notes that a large proportion of those who use the right to silence later plead guilty. The majority of the Commission felt that the possibility of an increase in convicting the guilty by abolishing the right would be outweighed by the considerable extra pressure on innocent suspects in police stations. The Commission did, however, meet the police and CPS concern about 'ambush defences', where a defence is entered late in a trial, thus leaving the prosecution no time to check and rebut the defence. The Commission recommended that if the defence introduces a late change or departs from the strategy it has disclosed in advance to the prosecution, then it should face adverse comment (para 136). Professor Zander, however, issued a note of dissent that the principle must remain that the burden of proof always lies with the prosecution. He states:

> The fundamental issue at stake is that the burden of proof throughout lies with the prosecution. Defence disclosure is designed to be helpful to the prosecution and, more generally, to the system. But, it is not the job of the defendant to be helpful either to the prosecution or the system.

Since the abolition of the court of Star Chamber in 1641, no English court has had the power to use torture or force to exact confessions from suspects. The so-called 'right to silence' really meant that a suspect could remain silent when questioned by police or in court without prosecution counsel or the judge being allowed to make adverse comment to the jury about such a silence. Traditionally, silence could not be used in court as evidence of guilt.

In support of the old rule, it could be said that:

- people are innocent until proven guilty of a crime by the State;

- people should never be under force to condemn themselves;

- there are several reasons other than genuine guilt why someone may wish to remain silent in the face of serious accusations – they might be terrified, confused, lacking capacity, mentally ill, wishing to protect someone else or fearful that the truth might get them in some other type of trouble. The 11th Report of the Criminal Law Revision Committee (1972) gives several examples. The accused might be so shocked at an accusation that he forgets a vital fact which would acquit him of blame; his excuse might be embarrassing, like being in the company of a prostitute; or he may fear reprisals from another party;

• the 'right' is widely protected in other aspects of society: the police, for example, when facing internal disciplinary charges, are not bound to answer questions or allegations put to them.

7.4.7 LIMITATIONS ON THE RIGHT TO SILENCE

The government ignored the recommendations of the Runciman Commission and, in ss 34–37 of the CJPOA 1994, curtailed the right to silence. Everyone still has the right to remain silent in the same circumstances as they did before the CJPOA 1994 but what changed was the entitlement of a judge or prosecuting counsel to make adverse comment on such a silence.

Notwithstanding the 1994 Act, therefore, any person may refuse to answer questions put to him out of court. There are only a few exceptions to this (as with s 2 of the CJA 1987, which concerns the investigation of serious fraud, and requires certain questions to be answered under pain of punishment for refusal) and they existed before the Act. The CJPOA 1994 does not alter the position of the accused person as a witness – he remains a competent but not compellable witness in his own defence (s 35), although now the prosecution as well as the judge may comment upon such a failure to give evidence (s 168).

Except in so far as the new law makes changes, the old law still applies.

In enacting ss 34–37 of the CJPOA 1994, the government was adopting a particular policy. The general purpose of the Act was to assist in the fight against crime. The government took the view that the balance in the criminal justice system had become tilted too far in favour of the criminal and against the public in general, and victims in particular. The alleged advantage of the change in law is that it helps convict criminals who, under the old law, used to be acquitted because they took advantage of the right to keep quiet when questioned without the court or prosecution being able to comment adversely upon that silence. Introducing the legislation, the Home Secretary said that change in law was desirable because 'it is professional criminals, hardened criminals and terrorists who disproportionately take advantage of and abuse the present system'. There was also a feeling that defendants would wait until the last possible moment to formulate their defence, effectively 'ambushing' the prosecution.

Section 34 states that where anyone is questioned under caution by a police officer, or charged with an offence, then a failure to mention a fact at that time which he later relies on in his defence will allow a court to draw such inferences as appear proper about that failure. Inferences may only be drawn if, in the circumstances, a suspect could reasonably have been expected to mention the fact when he was questioned. The inferences that can be drawn can be used in determining whether the accused is guilty as charged. The section, however, permits adverse inferences to be drawn from silence in situations that do not amount to 'interviews' as defined by Code C of PACE 1984, and thus which are not subject to the safeguards of access to legal advice and of contemporaneous recording that exist where a suspect is interviewed at the police station. The caution to be administered by police officers is as follows (with appropriate variants for ss 36 and 37):

> You do not have to say anything. But, it may harm your defence if you do not mention when questioned something which you later rely on in court. Anything you do say may be given in evidence.

Section 58 of the Youth Justice and Criminal Evidence Act (YJCEA) 1999 amends s 34 by adding a new s 34(2A). This restricts the drawing of inferences from silence in an interview at a police station (or similar venue) where the suspect was not allowed an opportunity to consult a solicitor prior to being questioned or charged (see Code D, Annex C). This amendment is intended to meet the ruling of the ECtHR in *Murray v UK* (1996) that delay in access to legal advice, even if lawful, could amount to a breach of Art 6, given the risk of adverse inferences being drawn.

An interesting illustration of the principle at work can be found in *R v Maguire (Glen)* (2008). The appellant offender (M) appealed against his conviction for two offences of wounding contrary to the Offences against the Person Act 1861 s 20. M was accused, following an argument in a public house, firstly, of committing an unprovoked attack on a victim in a street with a rice flail, which he had allegedly taken from his pocket, and, secondly, of emerging from his house with a meat cleaver later the same evening, with which he struck a second victim on the arm. M gave two different accounts of the evening's events, one during a police interview and the other in evidence at the trial. Both versions raised the issue of self-defence. On the Crown's application, the trial judge gave a direction under the Criminal Justice and Public Order Act 1994 s 34 in conventional form, in which he identified two sets of facts on which M had relied at trial but which he had not mentioned in police interview, namely, (i) that there had been no real gap between the incidents, that he had been confronted by a mob of people outside his house and that his need to act in self-defence arose at the same time in fending off what was a joint attack by the purported victims, and, (ii) that, having emerged from his house, he was naked when obliged to confront the mob. M was convicted but appealed saying his convictions were unsafe because the judge was wrong to give a direction under s 34 of the 1994 Act.

His appeal was dismissed. The Court of Appeal ruled that:

> With or without such a direction, the Crown's case was plainly going to be that M's evidence had been shown to be untruthful, partly by other contradictory evidence in the case, and also by the way that his account had changed. The judge was virtually certain to refer to it, and he would no doubt have told the jury that it was up to them to say whether the explanation for the change in account might be an innocent one, or whether it was that M's evidence was untruthful. The s 34 direction was a formalised way of saying precisely the same. Section 34 did no more than seek to apply common sense.

Such a direction always raised the question whether the omission to refer to something in interview which appeared later in evidence was or was not an indication that the new material was untruthful. The object of the section and of the direction was to enable the jury to decide that question. In the instant case, the matters identified by the judge were capable of being facts within the meaning of s 34, but even if they were not, the judge's direction would have been substantially the same. The fact that the s 34 direction included the proposition that the jury were entitled to infer some additional support for the Crown from the change of evidence did not alter that. The jury had had the issues which arose in the case properly before them, and the convictions were safe.

The court also said that prosecutors should be cautious about too readily seeking to invite formalised directions under s 34. Anything that over-formalised common sense was to be discouraged.

Section 35 allows a court or jury to infer what appears proper from the refusal of an accused person to testify in his own defence, or from a refusal without good cause to answer any question at trial. In para 44 of the *Practice Direction (Criminal: Consolidated)* (2002), the Lord Chief Justice indicated that where the accused is legally represented, the following should be said by the judge to the accused's lawyer at the end of the prosecution case if the accused is not to give evidence:

Have you advised your client that the stage has now been reached at which he may give evidence and, if he chooses not to do so or, having been sworn, without good cause refuses to answer any question, the jury may draw such inferences as appear proper from his failure to do so?

If the lawyer replies to the judge that the accused has been so advised, then the case will proceed. If the accused is not represented, and still chooses not to give evidence or answer a question, the judge must give him a similar warning, ending: '[. . .] the jury may draw such inferences as appear proper. That means they may hold it against you'.

Section 36 permits inferences to be drawn from the failure or refusal of a person under arrest to account for any object, substances or mark in his possession, on his person, in or on his clothing or footwear, or in any place at which he is at the time of arrest. Section 37 permits inferences to be drawn from the failure of an arrested person to account for his presence at a particular place where he is found.

Thus, as the late Lord Taylor, the then Lord Chief Justice, observed, the legal changes do not, strictly speaking, abolish the right to silence:

> If a defendant maintains his silence from first till last, and does not rely on any particular fact by way of defence, but simply puts the prosecution to proof, then [ss 34–37] would not bite at all.

The change was widely and strongly opposed by lawyers, judges and legal campaign groups. Liberty, for example, said that drawing adverse inferences from silence undermines the presumption of innocence. Silence is an important safeguard against oppressive questioning by the police, particularly for the weak and vulnerable.

John Alderson, former chief constable of Devon and Cornwall (1973–82) and a respected writer on constitutional aspects of policing, has written of the impending danger when police are able to 'exert legal and psychological pressure on individuals held in the loneliness of their cells'. He stated (*The Independent*, 1 February 1995) that:

> History tells us that, when an individual has to stand up against the entire apparatus of the modern State, he or she is very vulnerable. That is why, in criminal cases, the burden of proof has always rested on the State rather than on the accused. The Founding Fathers of America amended their constitution to that effect in 1791.

An example might be persons detained indefinitely at the Home Secretary's discretion at HMP Belmarsh and HMP Woodhill (see J Cooper, 'Guantanamo Bay, London' (2004) 154 NLJ 41).

Undermining the right to silence may constitute a significant constitutional change in the relationship between the individual and the State. It may be doubted whether the majority of suspects should be put under greater intimidation by the system because of the conduct of a few 'hardened criminals' – the justification for the legislation given by the then Home Secretary when he introduced it.

7.4.8 DIRECTIONS TO THE JURY ON SILENT DEFENDANTS

Following the enactment of the CJPOA 1994, there has been a steady stream of case law about the correct judicial practice when directing the jury about the drawing of adverse inferences under ss 34 and 35.

In *R v Cowan* (1995), the Court of Appeal considered what should be said in the summing up if the defendant decides not to testify. The jury must be directed that (as provided by s 38(3) of the CJPOA 1994) an inference from failure to give evidence could not on its own prove guilt. The jury had to be satisfied (on the basis of the evidence called by the prosecution) that the prosecution had established a case to answer before inferences could be drawn from the accused's silence. The jury could only draw an adverse inference from the accused's silence if that silence could only be sensibly attributed to the accused having no answer to the charge or none that could stand up to cross-examination.

The difficult issue as to correct judicial practice when the accused remains silent during interview on the advice of his solicitor was considered in *R v Condron* (1997) and *R v Argent* (1997). These cases make it clear that such advice was only one factor to be taken into consideration, along with all the other circumstances, in any jury determination as to whether adverse inferences could be drawn from a 'no comment' interview. In *Condron*, the Court of Appeal considered the guidelines set out in *Cowan* (above) and concluded that they were equally applicable to failure to answer questions (s 34) and failure to testify (s 35).

Stuart-Smith LJ, giving the judgment of the court, went on to say that it was desirable to direct the jury that if, despite any evidence relied upon to explain the failure (to answer questions), or in the absence of such evidence, it concluded that the failure could only sensibly be attributed to the accused having fabricated the evidence, the jury might draw an adverse inference.

More detailed guidance was given in *Argent*, where Lord Bingham set out the conditions that had to be met before s 34 could operate. They include:

(a)   the failure to answer had to occur before the defendant was charged;

(b)   the alleged failure must occur during questioning under caution;

(c)   the questioning must be directed at trying to discover whether and by whom the offence has been committed;

(d)   the failure must be a failure to mention any fact relied on in the person's defence;

(e)   the fact the defendant failed to mention had to be one which this particular defendant could reasonably be expected to have mentioned when being questioned, taking account of all the circumstances existing at that time (for example, the time of day, the defendant's age, experience, mental capacity, state of health, sobriety, personality and access to legal advice).

The Court of Appeal in *Argent* took a similar view to that of the Judicial Studies Board (JSB) as regards the relevance of legal advice to remain silent. This, of course, puts the solicitor who attends the interview under some difficulty, especially as The Law Society guidelines suggest that to remain silent is appropriate when the police have made less than full disclosure of the evidence available. However, Lord Bingham in *Argent* added that the jury is neither concerned with the correctness of the solicitor's advice, nor with whether it complies with The Law Society guidelines, but with the reasonableness of the defendant's conduct in all circumstances.

The court approved the trial judge's direction to the jury:

> You should consider whether or not he is able to decide for himself what he should do or having asked for a solicitor to advise him he would not challenge that advice [at p 34].

In *R v Daniel (Anthony Junior)* (1998), it was held that the *dicta* of Stuart-Smith LJ in *Condron* (1997) need not be confined to a subsequent fabrication. In addition to the JSB specimen direction, it is desirable for the judge in an appropriate case to include a passage to the effect that, if the jury conclude that the accused's reticence could only sensibly be attributed to his unwillingness to be subjected to further questioning, or that he had not thought about all the facts, or that he did not have an innocent explanation to give, they might draw an adverse inference. This was upheld soon after by the Court of Appeal in *R v Beckles and Montague* (1999), when the defendant gave a 'no comment' interview on legal advice. It was held that the proper inference under s 34 was not limited to recent fabrication.

In three cases – *R v Beckles* (2004), *R v Hoare & Pierce* (2004) *and R v Howell* (2005) the Court of Appeal arrived at the following position:

- Where an accused gives evidence that they remained silent on the advice of their solicitor, the question for the jury/court is whether – the situation existing at the time – it is reasonable to expect the accused to have mentioned the relevant fact(s);

- The fact that the court/jury accepts that the accused genuinely relied on legal advice when staying silent and not revealing facts that are subsequently relied on in court does not mean that the jury are obliged to conclude that it was reasonable for the accused not to mention those facts;

- A court might be more likely to conclude that reliance on legal advice not to put forward facts was reasonable if there was a sound foundation for it – examples being: little or no police disclosure; the case is too complex or too old to expect immediate answers from the accused; the accused has personal problems (for example, mental disability, shock, intoxication);

- A court might be less likely to conclude that reliance on legal advice not to put forward facts was reasonable if the advice was not based on a sound foundation – examples that The Law Society Guidance sets out are: a belief that the detention is unlawful; the victim has not made a written statement; a belief that the victim might withdraw the complaint; a belief that the police will charge anyway, whatever the accused says.

Where, however, a judge concludes that the requirements of s 34 have not been satisfied and therefore that it is not open to him to leave to the jury the possibility of drawing adverse inferences, he must direct the jury that it should not in any way hold against the accused the fact that he did not answer questions in interview (*R v McGarry* (1998)).

The provisions as to silence must also meet the requirements of Art 6 of the ECHR. The ECtHR held in *Murray v UK* (1996) that this right is not absolute and that a system under which inferences could be drawn from silence did not in itself constitute a breach of Art 6, though particular caution when drawing inferences was necessary. This was reaffirmed in *Condron v UK* (2001), where the Court asserted that though silence could not be the only, or even the main, basis for any conviction, it was right that it should be taken into account in circumstances which clearly called for an explanation from the accused (examples might be having to account for presence at the scene of the crime, or having to account for the presence of fibres on clothing). It should be noted that although the specimen direction issued by the JSB and used by judges emphasises that silence cannot be the only basis for a conviction, it does not make any reference to whether it can be the *main basis* for conviction. Thus, there is a possible conflict between the approach under the ECHR and that currently adopted in English courts.

The ECtHR considers that legal advice is of great significance in this system. Thus, both *Murray v UK* and *Condron v UK* stressed the importance of access to legal advice at the time of any interview. As explained earlier, the finding in *Murray v UK* that denial of access to legal advice, in conjunction with the drawing of inferences, amounted to a breach of Art 6 led to the amendment to the CJPOA 1994 contained in s 34(2A). However, access in itself is not the end of the matter. The question which then arises is whether the drawing of inferences may be improper under the ECHR where silence results from legal advice. The approach of the English courts to this has been discussed above. The ECtHR held in both *Condron v UK* and *Averill v UK* (2000) that legal advice may be a proper reason for declining to answer questions and that it may not be fair to draw adverse inferences in such cases. A solicitor representing a young or otherwise vulnerable person may recognise that the evidence against the client is very weak. Advising such a client to 'say nothing' will often make good sense (see A Keogh, 'The right to silence – revisited again' (2003) 153 NLJ 1352–3).

The jury should be informed that no adverse inference should be drawn where a defendant 'genuinely and reasonably' relies on a solicitor's advice to remain silent in interview: *R v Beckles* (2004).

In *R v Robert Webber* (2004), the House of Lords decided that, for the purposes of working out whether a silent defendant in court was 'relying on a fact' used in his defence (and therefore something that could prompt the judge to allow the jury to draw adverse inferences about the defendant's silence), answers given by a witness for the prosecution who was being cross-questioned by the defendant's counsel were facts.

A positive suggestion put to a witness by or on behalf of a defendant could amount to a fact relied on in his defence for the purpose of s 34 of the CJPOA 1994, even if that suggestion was not accepted by a witness.

The defendant (W) appealed from a decision (summarised below) that the trial judge was correct to give a direction under s 34 of the CJPOA 1994. W and two co-defendants had been charged with conspiracy to murder. The prosecution case against W was based on three incidents. When interviewed by police about each incident, W had either denied involvement in any conspiracy or said that he was not present. At trial, W's counsel put it to several prosecution witnesses that their evidence relating to the incidents was wrong. The witnesses rejected counsel's suggestions. The certified question for the House of Lords was whether a suggestion put to a witness by or on behalf of a defendant could amount to a 'fact relied on in his defence' for the purpose of s 34 of the Act, if that suggestion was not adopted by the witness. W submitted that s 34 was directed to evidence and that suggestions of counsel were not evidence unless or until accepted by a witness. The prosecution submitted that such suggestions were matters on which a defendant relied, whether or not he supported them by his own or other evidence, and whether or not prosecution witnesses accepted them.

The court held that a positive suggestion put to a witness by or on behalf of a defendant could amount to a fact relied on in his defence for the purpose of s 34 even if that suggestion was not accepted by a witness. The word 'fact' in s 34 covered any alleged fact that was in issue and was put forward as part of the defence case. If the defendant advanced at trial any pure fact or exculpatory explanation or account that, if true, he could reasonably have been expected to advance earlier, s 34 was potentially applicable. A defendant relied on a fact or matter in his defence not only when he gave or adduced evidence of it, but also when counsel, acting on his instructions, put a specific and positive case to prosecution witnesses, as opposed to asking questions intended to probe or test the prosecution case. That was so, whether or not the prosecution witness accepted the suggestion put. The appeal was dismissed.

7.4.9   TAPE-RECORDING OF INTERROGATIONS

The police were initially very hostile to the recommendation of the Philips Royal Commission on Criminal Procedure that there should be tape-recording of interviews with suspects. After a while, however, the police became more enthusiastic when it became apparent that the tape-recording of the interrogations increased the proportion of guilty pleas and reduced the challenges to prosecution evidence. Tape-recording of interviews is conducted in accordance with Code of Practice E. The tapes are time-coded so that they cannot be interfered with. It is now compulsory for all police stations to record all interviews with suspects interrogated in connection with indictable offences and are used as a matter of course with all offences where an interview is held.

7.4.10   CONFESSIONS AND THE ADMISSIBILITY OF EVIDENCE

It was long established by the common law that a confession would not be admitted in evidence if it was 'involuntary' in the sense that it was obtained by threat or promise held out by a person in authority. This would include 'even the most gentle, if I may put it that way, threats or slight inducements', *per* Lord Parker CJ in *R v Smith* (1959). In that case, a sergeant major had put the whole company on parade and told them no one would be allowed to move until one of them gave details about which of them had been involved in a fight resulting in a stabbing. A confession resulting from this incident was ruled to have been something that should not have been admitted (although the conviction was not quashed as there was other evidence against the defendant).

In *R v Zavekas* (1970), a conviction was quashed where it had resulted from an improper promise. Z was told that the police were arranging an identification parade and that he would be free to go if he was not picked out. He asked whether he could be allowed to go at once if he made a statement. The officer agreed and then Z made a statement admitting guilt. The admission was given in evidence and Z was convicted. His conviction was quashed even though the inducement had not been proffered by the police. Similarly, the Court of Appeal regarded it a 'fatal inducement' for a police officer to have agreed to a request by the defendant, in *R v Northam* (1968), for a second offence to be taken into account at a forthcoming trial rather than tried as a separate matter.

Apart from threats and promises, 'oppression' leading to a confession would render such a statement inadmissible. The Judges Rules were a set of guidelines made by Divisional Court judges for excluding unreliable evidence, but they left it as discretionary whether violation of the rules should result in the exclusion of any resultant evidence.

There had been a significant change in the approach of the courts by the 1980s. The new approach was to ask, even where there had been promises or threats, as a matter of fact and causation, had there been an involuntary confession? In *R v Rennie* (1985), Lord Lane CJ stated that even where a confession was made 'with a hope that an admission may lead to an earlier release or a lighter sentence' and the hope was prompted by something said or done by a person in authority, the confession would not automatically be regarded as involuntary. The same applied where, as in the present case, a confession was prompted by a fear that otherwise the police would interview and perhaps charge the defendant's sister and mother. The judge should apply his 'common sense' and assume that voluntary meant 'of one's own free will'.

This approach was much criticised as it was often impossible for even trained psychologists to realise which pressures on a suspect being questioned were the ones that prompted him to confess.

The law is now contained in s 76 of PACE 1984, which renders inadmissible any confession (i) obtained as a result of oppression (s 76(2)(a)) or (ii) which was obtained in consequence of something 'likely in the circumstances to render unreliable any confession which might be made by the accused in consequence thereof' (s 76(2)(b)).

'Oppression' is defined by s 76(8) to include 'torture, inhuman or degrading treatment, and the use or threat of violence'.

7.4.11 OPPRESSION

The judge rules on whether evidence is admissible on these lines: if it is admitted, then the jury decides whether to believe it. There should be a 'trial within a trial' – without the jury – to determine whether the evidence is admissible (*R v Liverpool Juvenile Court ex p R* (1988)).

The courts have not found much evidence of 'oppression' in police questioning. In *Miller* (1986), a paranoid schizophrenic had confessed to killing his girlfriend. He had admitted the killing in an interview which contained both reliable and unreliable matter. He later retracted his confession. It was argued for him at trial that the confession should be excluded under s 76(2)(a) – that it had been obtained by 'oppression of the person who made it', as it had come as the result of protracted and oppressive interviews that had caused him to suffer an episode of 'schizophrenic terror'. Medical evidence was given that the style and length of questioning had produced a state of voluntary insanity in which his language reflected hallucinations and delusion. The judge would not exclude the evidence and the defendant was convicted of manslaughter. The Court of Appeal held that the mere fact that questions triggered off hallucinations in the defendant was not evidence of oppression.

In *R v Fulling* (1987), the Court of Appeal held that it was not oppression for the police to tell the defendant that her lover had been having an affair with another woman, which so affected her that she made a confession. The word 'oppression', the court held, should be given its ordinary dictionary meaning as stated in the *Oxford English Dictionary*:

> The exercise of authority or power in a burdensome, harsh or wrongful manner; unjust or cruel treatment of subjects, inferiors, etc; the imposition of unreasonable or unjust burdens.

In *R v Anthony Paris R v Yusuf Abdullahi* and *R v Stephen Wayne Miller* (1993), it was held that it was perfectly legitimate for police officers to pursue their interrogation of a suspect with the intention of eliciting an account or gaining admissions, and they were not required to give up after the first denial or even a number of denials. However, it was undoubtedly oppressive within the meaning of s 76(2) of the Police and Criminal Evidence Act 1984 to shout at a suspect. That had occurred in the case of *Miller*, after he had denied involvement over 300 times. Thus the confessions obtained were unreliable, particularly in view of the fact that Miller was on the borderline of mental handicap. Accordingly, considering the tenor and length of the police interviews, those interviews ought not to have been admitted in evidence.

7.4.12 UNRELIABILITY

Evidence of a confession can be excluded if it was given:

> [. . .] in consequence of anything said or done which was likely in the circumstances existing at the time, to render unreliable any confession which might be made by him in consequence thereof [. . .] [s 76(2)(b)].

The phrase 'anything said or done' means by someone other than the suspect. In *R v Goldenberg* (1988), G, a heroin addict, was arrested on a charge of conspiracy to supply diamorphine. He requested an interview five days after his arrest and during this he gave information about a man who he said had supplied him with heroin. It was argued for G at trial that he had given the statement to get bail and thus to be able to feed his addiction. G contended that the words 'in consequence of anything said or done' included things said or done by the suspect and that the critical things here were the things G had said and done, namely, requested the interview and given any statement that would be likely to get him out of the station. G was convicted and his appeal was dismissed. Neill LJ stated:

> In our judgment, the words 'said or done' in s 76(2)(b) of the 1984 Act do not extend so as to include anything said or done by the person making the confession. It is clear from the wording of the section and the use of the words 'in consequence' that a causal link must be shown between what was said or done and the subsequent confession. In our view, it necessarily follows that 'anything said or done' is limited to something external to the person making the confession and to something which is likely to have some influence on him.

The reasoning in cases like *R v Zavekas* (see above, at 7.4.10) has now clearly been rejected. This view is confirmed by Code C; if a suspect asks an officer what action will be taken in the event of his answering questions, making a statement or refusing to do either, the officer may inform him what action he proposes to take in that event 'provided that the action is itself proper and warranted' (para 11.3).

7.4.13   *R v HEATON* (1993)

In *R v Heaton* (1993), the appellant was convicted of manslaughter of his 26-day-old son. The evidence of the mother, who was of limited intelligence, was that the appellant had shaken the child hard to quieten him and that the child subsequently went limp and breathless. She had also said that she had given the child Calpol (a children's medicine containing paracetamol).

   Due to difficulties in contacting the appellant's solicitor, he had been in custody overnight for some fifteen and a half hours by the time he was able to see a solicitor. As he said he had been ill, he was examined by a doctor who said he was fit to be interviewed. He was interviewed for about 75 minutes in the presence of the solicitor and the interview was tape-recorded. The first part of the interview dealt with his background details. When asked about the events leading up to the child's death, he at first denied that he had held the child. Later, he admitted holding the child but denied holding him up in the air. Under further questioning, he admitted holding the child up in the air and finally conceded that he had shaken the child about four times to and fro to keep him quiet and that the child's head was flopping.

   The defence case was that the death could have been caused solely by the administration of the wrong drug by the mother. Although she claimed to have given the child Calpol, which contained paracetamol, no evidence of any paracetamol was found in the child's body on postmortem. However, promethazine was found in the blood and was the active ingredient of Phenergen, a drug which the mother also had in the house for the older children. In his evidence, the appellant said that he came downstairs to find the baby purplish in the face and breathless and had seen the mother giving him some medicine, following which she became hysterical and shook the baby. In the interview he had been upset and as the police would not believe what he was saying, in the end he had told them that he had shaken the child. He denied that he had done so violently or in order to quieten the child.

A *voir dire* was convened on this particular issue – a *voir dire* is a trial within a trial where the judge, having asked the jury to go out, decides a dispute between counsel as to whether certain evidence is admissible. The defence, on the *voir dire*, sought to exclude the evidence of the appellant's interview under ss 76 and 78 of PACE 1984. An application was made to call a psychiatrist, Dr Z, on the *voir dire*. The trial judge ruled against admitting Dr Z's evidence and ruled that the interview should be admitted.

On appeal, it was argued on the appellant's behalf that the trial judge was wrong to exclude the evidence of Dr Z, and that the trial judge should have excluded the interview because the officers concerned had applied pressure to the appellant, raising their voices and repeating their questions.

The Court of Appeal dismissed the appeal, holding:

- The trial judge had considered Dr Z's report, which was based upon a single interview with the appellant, sight of the case papers, hearing of the interview tapes and a conversation with the probation officer. Dr Z had noted in particular: 'My impression is that he is not exceptionally bright and is possibly of dull normal intelligence and is very suggestible.' In *R v Turner* (1975), Lawton LJ had said at p 83:

  [. . .] an expert's opinion is admissible to furnish the court with scientific information which is likely to be outside the experience and knowledge of a judge or jury. If, on the proven facts, a judge or jury can form their own conclusions without help, then the opinion of an expert is unnecessary. In such a case, if it is given dressed up in scientific jargon, it may make judgment more difficult. The fact that an expert witness has impressive scientific qualifications does not, by that fact alone, make his opinion on matters of human nature or behaviour within the limits of normality any more helpful than that of the jurors themselves; but there is a danger that they may think it does.

  In the more recent case of *R v Raghip, Silcott and Braithwaite* (1991), the Court of Appeal had drawn a distinction between psychiatric or psychological evidence going to *mens rea* and such evidence going to the reliability of a confession, but had not criticised the general principle laid down in *Turner*. The court had rejected a 'judge for yourself' approach by the judge in respect of the jury and, it would seem, in respect of his own task on a *voir dire*, where there was expert evidence which would have been of assistance in assessing the defendant's mental condition. In that case, Alliott J said:

> [...] the state of the psychological evidence before us [...] is such that the jury would have been assisted in assessing the mental condition of Raghip and the consequent reliability of the alleged confessions. Notwithstanding that Raghip's IQ was at 74 just in the borderline range, a man chronologically aged 19 years seven months at the date of the interview with a level of functioning equivalent to that of a child of nine years, and the reading capacity of a child of six years, cannot be said to be normal. It would be impossible for the layman to divide that data from Raghip's performance in the witness box, still less the abnormal suggestibility of which [the expert witness] spoke.

- There was in *Heaton* no suggestion of mental handicap or low intelligence; the appellant was within the normal range of intelligence, albeit towards the duller end of it. There was nothing more than Dr Z's bare impression that the appellant was very suggestible; there were no data on which to found that assertion nor was it clear that 'very suggestible' was outside the normal range. The judge expressly indicated that he should be told if there was anything more to Dr Z's evidence than was contained in his report and he was not informed of anything else. In those circumstances, he concluded that there was nothing in the doctor's impression which complied with the tests laid down in *Turner* and illustrated by *Raghip*; in the court's judgment, he was justified in ruling as he did. Unless the medical evidence sought to be introduced on an issue of this kind was truly based on some scientific data or expert analysis outside the experience of judge and jury, a mere impression, even of a highly qualified doctor, that the defendant 'is not exceptionally bright' or was 'very suggestible' was not admissible for the reasons set out by Lawton LJ.

- The court had read the transcript of the interview and heard the tape-recordings. The appellant had a full opportunity to consult with a solicitor before the interview and the solicitor was present throughout. A doctor had examined the appellant and pronounced him fit to be interviewed. The questioning lasted only 75 minutes and much of the first two tapes was concerned merely with taking the appellant's history. Voices were slightly raised but there was no shouting and no oppressive hostility; the pace of the interview was slow and the appellant was given time to consider his replies. Some questions were repeated several times but not inappropriately. In *R v Paris, Abdullahi and Miller* (1994), where similar arguments were raised, the court said:

> Of course, it is perfectly legitimate for officers to pursue their interrogation of their suspect with a view to eliciting his account or gaining admissions. They are not required to give up after the first denial or even after a number of denials.

In that case, the questioning had continued for some 13 hours and the tapes had shown hostility and bullying on the part of the interviewing officers. In the present case, the situation was wholly different, with the appellant changing his story gradually over a comparatively short period and providing further details without the police putting them in. The judge had been right to conclude that the prosecution had discharged the burden upon them to exclude oppression and the possibility that the circumstances might have rendered the admission unreliable.

In a commentary on *Heaton* in the *Criminal Law Review*, it is pointed out that the law on confessions is developing in a number of ways to prevent, as far as is possible, the conviction of weak-minded and suggestible persons on the basis of their own unreliable statements. In addition to the exclusionary rule in s 76(2)(b) of PACE 1984 and the discretion in s 78, defendants labouring under a 'significant degree of mental handicap' are protected by the rule in *McKenzie* (1993), which requires an unconvincing case based solely on confessions to be withdrawn from the jury.

'Confessions' made to fellow prisoners are particularly controversial. In 1996, Lin, Megan and Josie Russell were attacked while taking their dog for a walk. Lin and Megan were killed; Josie suffered serious injuries. Michael Stone was arrested and charged with the murders. He was then remanded into custody. At his trial in 1998, two fellow inmates, Damien Daley and Harry Thompson, were called as witnesses. Both alleged that Stone had 'confessed' to them. Stone was convicted. The next day, Thompson contacted national newspapers. He said that he had lied in court because of police pressures. In 2001, Stone's convictions were quashed by the Court of Appeal. At his retrial, the prosecution used Daley's evidence and Stone was reconvicted. A strong argument could be made for excluding such dubious evidence under s 78 of PACE. The central problem has been described by Gwyn Morgan in 'Cell confessions' (2002) 152 NLJ 453:

> There may be a strong incentive for 'grasses' to come up with their incriminating stories. Deals may be done with the police as to the withdrawal of

charges. Even where this is not the case, those on remand may well feel –
even if they are wrong – that giving evidence for the prosecution will ease
the way when their own cases come up. And where the grasses are already
convicted, they may be anxious (again rightly or wrongly) to give a favourable impression to the prison authorities or the parole board. What's more,
in contrast to most witnesses, coming to court does not adversely interfere
with their lives; it's a day out.

See also 'Cell confessions – no stone left unturned' (2005) 155 NLJ 550–51.

7.4.14   CAN A SOLICITOR PROVIDE THE 'SOMETHING SAID OR DONE'?

In *R v Wahab* (2003) the accused was arrested on suspicion that he was involved in a
conspiracy to supply drugs. He was interviewed in the presence of his solicitor. After the
third interview he authorised his solicitor to approach the police to see whether
his family, who were also in custody, might be released if he confessed his guilt.
In accordance with those express instructions his solicitor approached the police
who made it clear that no promises could be made or guarantees given. The solicitor
told W that if he made admissions the police would look at the whole picture and
that if the evidence against the family was 'borderline' they would be released. At
a fourth interview W confessed to his involvement in the conspiracy, but only as a
middleman.

The accused dismissed his solicitor and employed a different one for his trial
where he sought the exclusion of the fourth interview. The Court of Appeal held that
advice properly given to a defendant by his solicitor did not normally provide a basis for
excluding a subsequent confession under s 76(2) of the Police and Criminal Evidence
Act 1984. The Court further held that one of the duties of a legal advisor, whether at a
police station, or indeed at a pre-trial conference, or during the trial itself, is to give the
client realistic advice. That emphatically did not mean that the advice had to be directed
to 'getting the client off, or simply making life difficult for the prosecution; though
it had to be sensibly robust considering the advantages that the client might derive
from evidence of remorse and a realistic acceptance of guilt, or the corresponding
disadvantages of participating in a no-comment interview.

7.5   REVISED PACE CODES

In January 2008, revised PACE Codes of Practice A–E came into force. In addition,
The Police and Criminal Evidence Act 1984 (Codes of Practice) (Revision of
Codes C, G and H) Order 2012 makes changes to PACE Codes C, G and H.
Although the essential structure remains substantially intact, there are numerous
amendments.

Code A – stop and search.

The revised Code A makes it clear beyond doubt that searches must not take place unless the necessary legal power exists. If an officer asks a member of the public to account for his 'actions, behaviour, presence in the area or possession of anything', a record must be made. The person stopped will be entitled to a copy. As of March 2011 Code A has been further amended to reflect the significant reduction in the quantity of information the police are required to record after a stop and search of a vehicle. While officers are still required to record the ethnicity of the occupant, they are no longer required to record their details, the registration number of the vehicle or even any injury or damage caused. The 2011 amendments to Code A also remove the requirement for officers to record 'stops'. Police forces are now free to decide in consultation with their local communities whether to continue monitoring the stops on a local level.

Code A has also been amended to introduce detailed guidance on the use of the stop and search powers under s 60 of the CJPOA 1994. These powers allow a senior police officer to authorise the stop and search of people and vehicles without reasonable grounds for up to 24 hours and within a defined locality. In order for these powers to be granted, there must be reasonable belief that to do so would help prevent serious violence or that a person is carrying offensive weapons.

The previous Code A did not set out any explicit restrictions, nor did it give any guidance regarding the identification of who may be stopped under these powers. Additional provisions in Code A now provide guidance as to the risks of unlawful discrimination and draw attention to the 'protected characteristics' as set out in s 4 of the Equality Act 2010. These provisions must now be read in light of the 2011 Remedial Order issued under the Human Rights Act 1998 (see above).

Code B – entry and search of premises. Paragraph 1.3 states:

> The right to privacy and respect for personal property are key principles of the Human Rights Act 1998. Powers of entry, search and seizure should be fully and clearly justified before use because they may significantly interfere with the occupiers' privacy. Officers should consider if the necessary objectives can be met by less intrusive means.

Paragraph 7.7 states:

> The Criminal Justice and Police Act 2001, Part 2, gives officers limited powers to seize property from premises or persons so that they can sift or examine it elsewhere. Officers must be careful they only exercise these powers when it is essential and they do not remove any more material than necessary. The removal of large quantities of material, much of which may not ultimately be retainable, may have serious implications for the owners [. . .] Officers must carefully consider if removing copies or images of relevant material or data would be a satisfactory alternative to removing originals.

As of March 2011 amendments to Code B have extended the conditions which must be met in order for a search under s 18 of PACE to be authorised. Under the previous version of the Code, paragraph 4.3 required that the authorising officer (of the rank of inspector or above) be satisfied that the necessary grounds under s 18 existed. This paragraph has now been extended to require the inspector to be satisfied, in addition to the grounds set out in s 18, 'that the premises are occupied or controlled by the arrested person'. This reflects the judgment in *Khan v Commissioner of Police of the Metropolis* (2008). A suspect had falsely provided Mr Khan's address as his own upon arrest. Entry and search of this address was duly authorised and undertaken under s 18. The Commissioner argued that s 18 should be interpreted so as to qualify the requirement of occupation and control by the suspect by reference to the belief of knowledge of the officer. The Court of Appeal rejected this submission and, dismissing the Commissioner's appeal, found that there was no justification for such a reading and that 'the requirement for occupation or control is central and fundamental to the operation of section 18'. The amended Code A is an attempt to achieve what the Metropolitan Police Commissioner failed to do in *Khan*: that is, to circumvent the clear wording of s 18 to protect the police from claims for damages in circumstances where the wrong address is searched in good faith.

Code C – treatment and questioning in the police station.

The revised version of Code C restricts the drawing of adverse inferences by a detainee's decision to remain silent until he has received legal advice. This has implications for the cautioning of suspects. The revisions are largely a response to *Murray v UK* (1996). In addition, the changes made to Code C in 2012 increase the safeguards in the procedure to be followed by the police where a detainee changes their mind about wanting legal advice.

Code D – identification procedures.

These have been amended partly to take account of the increasing use of video evidence. Amendments have also been made to Code D of the PACE codes to reflect the changes implemented by the Crime and Security Act regarding the power to take fingerprints and samples. Section 117 of SOCPA 2005 came into force in March 2011 and amends s 61 of PACE. Section 117 allows fingerprints to be taken on the street following arrest by officers using mobile fingerprint technology in circumstances when identification is in issue. Code D has been revised to reflect this amendment. However, unlike the standard provision for the taking of fingerprints in the course of an investigation pursuant to s 61(6C) of PACE, under Code D such samples cannot be retained after they have been checked. Code D also provides additional guidance regarding the circumstances in which the police may use the fingerprint technology, including what might constitute reasonable doubt about identity and when identity cannot reasonably be ascertained.

A new safeguard has been introduced under Code D for identification procedures to minimise the risks of collusion and mistaken recognition. Witnesses are now to be asked whether they recognise the individual and records are to be kept of information provided in advance of any identification process.

Code E – tape recordings.

Revisions to Code E largely reflect changes to cautioning procedures.

Code F – video recording of suspects' interviews (pilot schemes are ongoing).
Code G – guidance for the extended police powers of arrest.

The 2012 amendments to Code G reflect s 149 of the Legal Aid, Sentencing and Punishment of Offenders Act 2012 by giving guidance to police officers considering making an arrest on how to consider whether the individual was acting in self-defence, to protect another or to maintain discipline in a school.

Code H – detention, treatment and questioning of suspected terrorists.

The changes made to Code H in 2012 allow the police to undertake post-charge questioning in certain circumstances in line with the provisions contained in the Counter-Terrorism Act 2008.

In addition, the Terrorism Act 2000 (Video Recording with Sound of Interviews and Associated Code of Practice) Order 2012 and the Counter-Terrorism Act 2008 (Code of Practice for the Video Recording with Sound of Post-Charge Questioning) Order 2012 introduce a new code of practice for the video-recording with sound of interviews carried out under s 41 of, and Sched 7 to, the Terrorism Act 2000 and post-charge questioning of terrorist suspects under the Counter-Terrorism Act 2008.

7.6   THE CRIMINAL JUSTICE ACT 2003 AMENDMENTS OF THE POLICE AND CRIMINAL EVIDENCE ACT 1984

The following changes were made by the 2003 Act in addition to those set out in the body of the text above.

Section 11 CJA 2003: Codes of Practice

This section makes fundamental changes to the process for establishing and amending codes of practice under PACE 1984. At present, there are codes covering stop and search, searching of premises, detention, identification and the recording of interviews. The amendments provide for a less bureaucratic and more targeted consultation process for new and revised codes and for a simpler process of seeking parliamentary approval for minor or straightforward changes to existing codes. The amendment to s 67 of PACE 1984 will maintain the requirement for an order bringing a new code into operation to be laid before parliament and approved by each House.

Sub-section (1) establishes a new procedure whereby orders bringing revisions into operation to the codes may be either laid before parliament or subject to the draft affirmative procedure. The government has undertaken (see *Hansard*, 7 July 2003, col 45) to be bound by the advice of the Home Affairs Select Committee on the appropriate procedure to be followed for proposed changes.

Sub-sections (2)–(4) amend the procedure for making and revising codes of practice applicable to the military police to require codes and revisions simply to be laid before parliament.

At the beginning of the twenty-first century, we can see the first governmental recognition of something called a 'criminal justice system'.

REMEDIES

Remedies for unlawful arrest include: (1) an action for *habeas corpus*; (2) that any subsequent prosecution arising from the arrest should fail – s 78 of the Police and Criminal Evidence Act (PACE) 1984; (3) a claim for damages for false imprisonment. If the arrest is not lawful, then reasonable force may be used to resist it; (4) judicial review and human rights.

ARREST

Arrest can be: (1) under police warrant; (2) under common law for breach of the peace; or (3) under legislation, principally PACE 1984. The details in ss 24 and 25 of PACE 1984 and connected cases are very important. Detention short of arrest does not exist. Note this confirmation by s 29 of PACE 1984.

SUSPECTS STOPPED IN THE STREET

Suspects stopped in the street are not legally obliged to help police with inquiries. Note the distinction between *Kenlin v Gardiner* (1967) and *Donnelly v Jackman* (1970). Note also that a person may be arrested for being silent or misleading under s 25 if the officer has reasonable doubts about the suspect's name and address, or whether the summons procedure can be used at the address given. Note the enlarged powers of stop and search under s 60.

PROCEDURE ON ARREST

Procedure on arrest involves the arrestor having to inform the suspect of the grounds for arrest (s 28(3)). Note, though, that an arrest becomes lawful from when the information is given. The extent of the required information to the suspect is important (see *Geldberg v Miller* (1961); *R v Telfer* (1976)).

THE USE OF FORCE

The use of force to effect an arrest must be 'reasonable in all the circumstances' (s 3 of the Criminal Law Act 1967 (citizens); s 117 of PACE 1984 (police officers)).

STOP AND SEARCH

Stop and search is governed by s 1 and Code A of PACE 1984. The judge can exclude evidence obtained in breach of the Codes (s 67(7) of PACE 1984). There are legal obligations on an officer conducting a search (ss 2 and 3 of PACE 1984). Note that the Code is quite specific about what indices can be grounds for reasonable suspicion and which, individually or combined, may not.

Section 60 of the Criminal Justice and Public Order Act (CJPOA) 1994 has provided a new stop and search power in anticipation of violence. Under it, with authorisation, an officer can stop any pedestrian and search him for offensive weapons or dangerous instruments, or even stop vehicles. The authorising officer must reasonably believe that incidents involving serious violence may take place in the area. Section 81 of the same Act creates a new power of stop and search of people and vehicles where it is expedient to do so to prevent certain acts of terrorism.

SEARCH OF ARRESTED PERSONS

Search of arrested persons is governed by s 32 of PACE 1984. The person arrested cannot be required to take off more than outer garments. The place where he was arrested, or where he was immediately before, can also be searched under s 32. Note the differences between this power and those under s 18 regarding premises.

SEARCH ON DETENTION

Search on detention is governed by s 54 of PACE 1984 and Code C, para 4.1, which require the custody officer to take charge of the process of searching the detained person.

INTERROGATION, CONFESSION AND ADMISSIBILITY OF EVIDENCE

The main problem here is for the law to strike the proper balance between giving the police sufficient power to interrogate and protecting the interests of suspects. Too few rules governing how the police can conduct an interrogation and too few rules restricting the sort of evidence that can be put to a jury might easily lead to oppressive behaviour by the police interviewing suspects. Too many restrictive rules, conversely, will thwart the police in their endeavours to prosecute offenders successfully. The general rule in this area is that the courts have discretionary exclusionary powers under s 78 of the 1984 Act (the general overriding exclusionary provision) and s 76 (specifically pertaining to the admissibility of evidence derived from a purported confession by a defendant).

THE RIGHT TO HAVE SOMEONE INFORMED

The right to have someone informed after arrest is given to all suspects after arrest. It can be delayed, however, under s 116. The case must involve a 'serious arrestable offence' and it must be authorised by a superintendent on certain grounds, for example, the arrested person would alert others involved in a crime.

ACCESS TO LEGAL ADVICE

Access to legal advice is provided for under s 58 and Code C. The notification must accord with details set out in Code C. Note the criticisms of the Duty Solicitor Scheme. Is it adequately staffed? Note also the circumstances in which legal advice can be delayed under s 116, Code C, Annex B. In certain circumstances, questioning can begin before the detainee's legal advisor arrives.

TIME LIMITS

Note ss 42 and 38 of PACE 1984 for time limits operational before and after charges. Delayed access to legal advice is possible in cases of serious arrestable offences. A suspect can be held for up to 24 hours without being charged; up to 36 hours with authorisation from the superintendent and up to 96 hours with magistrates' permission.

THE RIGHT TO SILENCE

The right to silence means that a person cannot be charged with obstructing the police in the execution of their duty simply by failing to answer questions. Note the important difference between *Rice v Connolly* (1966) and *Ricketts v Cox* (1982). There are some circumstances where the suspect does have to answer on pain of penalty (s 2 of the Criminal Justice Act 1987). Section 2 pertains to a category of persons who (perceive that they) owe a duty of confidence to the suspect(s) and are interviewed under circumscribed compulsory powers. Section 2(2) CJA 1987 provides that: 'The Director [of the SFO] may by notice in writing require the person whose affairs are to be investigated ("the person under investigation") or any other person whom he has reason to believe has relevant information to answer questions or otherwise furnish information with respect to any matter relevant to the investigation at a specified place and either at a specified time or forthwith' (published April 2010; see the Serious Fraud Office webpage, http://www.sfo.gov.uk/about-us/history—legislation/section-2—and-legislative-tools. aspx). This gives the Director the right to compel people to answer questions. However, other legislation, including notably the Human Rights Act 1998, provides that a person cannot be *forced* to incriminate themselves (by means not just of threat but statutory compulsion). Therefore, the information obtained under s 2 CJA 1987 cannot be used in criminal proceedings against that person, except in a prosecution for failure to comply with s 2 CJA 1987. There are, hence, a number of statutory safeguards Statements made in s 2(2) CJA 87. Interviews may not be used in evidence against the maker at his/her subsequent trial unless:

> the trial is for the offence of giving false or misleading statements in the interview (s 2(14) CJA 87); or
>> evidence relating to the interview is adduced, or a question relating to it is asked, by the defendant-interviewee during the trial. In that event the SFO may, under s 2(8)(b) CJA 87, cross-examine on inconsistencies.

Interviews under s 2 will commonly be used for bank representatives, professional advisors with a duty of confidentiality to their clients, and witnesses who refuse a voluntary interview. While suspects can, in principle, be interviewed using s 2 powers, the circumstances where this is appropriate are vanishingly rare, due to the limited manner in which evidence obtained this way can be used.

Under ss 34–37 of the CJPOA 1994, certain adverse inferences may be drawn from a suspect's failure to answer police questions, or his failure to answer them in court.

THE CRIMINAL JUSTICE ACT 2003

This piece of legislation makes a number of important changes to the criminal justice system. The Act extends the definition of prohibited articles under s 1 of PACE 1984 so that it includes articles made, adapted or intended for use in causing criminal damage. Section 3 adds new offences to the list of specified offences which are arrestable offences: the offence of making a false application for a passport; the offence of possession of cannabis or cannabis resin; and the offence of making a false application for a driving licence. The Act also makes fundamental changes to the process for establishing and amending codes of practice under PACE 1984.

FOOD FOR THOUGHT

1.   When a person is detained they have a right to legal advice. But what about the motorist who is pulled over and questioned by police at the side of the road? Or the protestor who is interrogated by the police while he is on a march? Should people have a right to legal advice even when their liberty has not been limited?

2.   Arrangements are currently being made for the appointment of directly elected politicians as police commissioners who would oversee local police forces and hire and fire chief constables. Does this make the police force more accountable? Or does it compromise the independence of the police by making them serve a political agenda?

3.   Do you think that the requirement to retain for six years the DNA profiles of individuals who have never been charged, prosecuted or convicted of any offence is proportionately justified? Should there be a mechanism for the independent review of the decisions to destroy or retain DNA profiles?

FURTHER READING

Ashworth, A and Redmayne, M, *The Criminal Process*, 2005, Oxford: OUP

Baldwin, J and McConville, M, *Jury Trials*, 1979, Oxford: Clarendon

Buckland, R, 'Update: police and criminal evidence' (2009) 153(9) SJ 20–23

Cape, E, 'Police station law and practice update', May (2009) Legal Action 10–15

Committee on Fraud Trials, *Roskill Report*, 1986, London: HMSO

Darbyshire, P, 'The lamp that shows that freedom lives – is it worth the candle?' [1991] Crim LR 740

Davies, M, Croall, H and Tyrer, J, *Criminal Justice: An Introduction to the Criminal Justice System in England and Wales*, 2010, Longman

Devlin, P, *Trial by Jury*, 1956, London: Stevens

Findlay, M and Duff, P, *The Jury Under Attack*, 1988, London: Butterworths

Greer, S, 'The right to silence: defence disclosure and confession evidence' (1994) 21 JLS 103

Office of National Statistics, *Crime in England and Wales 2010/2011*, July 2012

Parpworth, N, 'Under control?' (2008) NLJ 1061

Royal Commission on Criminal Justice, *Runciman Report*, Cm 2263, 1995, London: HMSO

Sanders, A and Young, R, *Criminal Justice*, 2006, Oxford: OUP

Sidebottom, A, Belur, J, Bowers, K, Tompson, L and Johnson, SD, Theft in Price-Volatile Markets: On the Relationship between Copper Price and Copper Theft. (2011) 48(3) Journal of Research in Crime and Delinquency 396–418

Zander, M, 'Out of order' (2008) NLJ 1121

Zander, M, *The Police and Criminal Evidence Act 1984*, 6th edn, 2008, London: Sweet & Maxwell

USEFUL WEBSITES

www.cjsonline.gov.uk

The official website of the Criminal Justice System–very useful across a range of subjects.

www.homeoffice.gov.uk

The website of the Home Office – very useful on matters of policing and crime.

COMPANION WEBSITE

Now visit the companion website to:

- test your understanding of the key terms using our Flashcard Glossary;
- revise and consolidate your knowledge of 'The criminal process: (1) the investigation of crime' using our Multiple Choice Question testbank;
- view all of the links to the Useful Websites above.

www.routledge.com/cw/slapper

THE CRIMINAL PROCESS: (2) THE PROSECUTION 8

The classification of offences and matters relating to transfers for trial, summary trial, and trial on indictment are dealt with in Chapter 6.

Until 1986, England was one of only a few countries that allowed the police to prosecute rather than hand over this task to a State agency like the office of the district attorney in the United States, or the procurator fiscal in Scotland (an office established in the fifteenth century). The Crown Prosecution Service (CPS) was established by the Prosecution of Offences Act (POA) 1985. As a result the police now play only a limited part in prosecutions beyond the stage of charging the suspect. It is a prosecutor who takes the charging decision, though their decision may be – and invariably is – informed by representations from the relevant officer, who is the Custody Officer involved with a case. The Custody Officer must determine, to the satisfaction of the Crown Prosecutor reviewing the case, that there is sufficient evidence to charge a person with an offence. That officer must do this in accordance with the Threshold Test as to evidential sufficiency. Formerly, police officers alone had decided what charge, if any, was appropriate on the basis of the evidence in a case. The principle now prevailing is that Crown Prosecutors – not the Custody Officer – will determine whether a person is to be charged in all indictable only, either way or summary offences, subject to those cases specified in this guidance which the police may continue to charge. The rationale is that the decision as to charge is a distinctly legal one, given the requirement to consider and apply the law as to the seriousness of the alleged offence (see the guidance of the Director of Public Prosecutions on charging (4th edn, January 2011), issued under s 37A of the Police and Criminal Evidence Act 1984, http://www.cps.gov.uk/publications/directors_guidance/dpp_guidance_4.html).

However, the tide may be set to turn on this arrangement. Two London boroughs, Barking and Dagenham, and Havering, are piloting a new initiative to test the return of some charging decisions from the Crown Prosecution Service (CPS) to the police as part of the CPS 'Modernising Charging' programme, as announced in May 2004: http://lcjb.cjsonline.gov.uk/area23/library/Briefing%20Notes/ModernisingCharging2BN.pdf.   In May 2011 the Home Secretary announced that the Home Office will pilot doubling the number of charges transferred to the police from the CPS, making them responsible for 80 per cent of charging decisions, including shoplifting cases. This is a drive to cut 'red tape' in response to Jan Berry's report on Reducing Bureaucracy in Policing (available at http://www.policesupers.com/uploads/news/reducing-bureaucracy-policing.pdf), and the Home Secretary hopes that the pilot will save 2.5 million police hours per year (see Catherine Baksi's article in the *Law Gazette* on 9 May 2011: http://www.lawgazette. co.uk/news/charging-powers-passed-cps-police). No report on the progress of these initiatives has been forthcoming in 2012.

There used to be five different forms of prosecution, those by:

- the police, who prosecuted most offences;
- the Attorney General/Solicitor General, whose permission was needed to prosecute for many serious crimes and who could enter a *nolle prosequi* to stop certain prosecutions or give a *fiat* to disallow them from the beginning;
- the Director of Public Prosecutions (DPP), who prosecuted in very serious cases and cases brought to him by the government;
- public bodies like local authorities. These used to amount to about 25 per cent of all prosecutions, most having been brought by the Post Office for television licence offences;
- private prosecutions, which involved having to persuade a magistrate of the propriety in issuing a summons. The Attorney General and the DPP both had the power to take over a private prosecution and then drop it for reasons of public policy. Private bodies like stores and the RSPCA most regularly brought prosecutions. A study in 1980 showed that only 2.4 per cent of prosecutions were private (Lidstone, *Prosecutions by Private Individuals and Non-Police Agencies* (1980)). The right to bring private prosecutions was retained by s 6(1) of the POA 1985.

Today, the first three of the above list are conducted by the CPS. This chapter examines the workings of the State prosecution service.

8.2 THE CROWN PROSECUTION SERVICE

The move to establish a CPS was precipitated by a report from JUSTICE, the British section of the International Commission of Jurists, in its 1970 Report, *The Prosecution Process in England and Wales*. It argued that the police were not best suited to be prosecutors because they would often have a commitment to winning a case even where the evidence was weak, given the investment in a case that its investigation invariably represents. They were also not best placed to consider the public policy aspects of the discretion not to prosecute. The police were firmly opposed to such a change. They argued that statistics showed that the police were not given to pursuing cases in a way that led to a high rate of acquittal. They also showed that in cases involving miscarriages of justice, the decision to prosecute had been taken by a lawyer.

The question was referred to the Philips Royal Commission on Criminal Procedure, which judged the then existing system according to its fairness, openness and accountability. It proposed a new system based on several distinct features, including the following:

- that the initial decision to charge a suspect should rest with the police;
- that thereafter all decisions as to whether to proceed, alter or drop the charges should rest with another State prosecuting agency;
- this agency would provide advocates for all cases in the magistrates' courts apart from guilty pleas by post. It should also provide legal advice to the police and instruct counsel in all cases tried on indictment.

The POA 1985 established a national prosecution service under the general direction of the DPP. The 1985 Act gives to the DPP and the CPS as a whole the right to institute and conduct any criminal proceedings where the importance or difficulty of the case make that appropriate (s 3(2)(b)). This applies to cases that could also be started by the police or other bodies like local authorities. It can also, in appropriate circumstances, take over and then discontinue cases. The CPS relies on the police for the resources and machinery of investigation.

In the period following its launch, the CPS experienced severe problems of staff shortage related to the general funding of the service. This improved over the years, and by March 1993, the full lawyer staff quotient had almost been met. It was apparently difficult to recruit staff of an adequate standard for the available pay and there has been considerable use of agents, that is, lawyers in private practice working for the CPS on a fee-for-case basis.

As employed solicitors or barristers, Crown Prosecutors were originally unable to conduct cases in the higher courts. Changes to the rules on rights of audience in the higher courts for employed lawyers, introduced by the Access to Justice Act 1999, now permit them to do so. Consequently, any Crown Prosecutor who is qualified to appear before the higher courts is able to do so. At the end of March 2012, the CPS employed around 7,464 people. It prosecuted 787,613 cases in the Magistrates' Courts and 107,268 in the Crown Courts, with higher conviction than in 2010–11. Over 94 per cent of all staff are engaged in, or support, front-line prosecutions. The CPS has 945 prosecutors able to appear in the Crown Court and on cases in the Higher Courts (*Annual Report and Resource Accounts 2011–2012*, Crown Prosecution Service). In October 2010, the CPS identified a new strategy for enhancing its role as 'an independent prosecution service that delivers a valued public service' (http://www.cps.gov.uk/publications/reports/2009/resource_accounts.html). This new strategy takes account of the budget cuts that the CPS has to make: by 2014–15. The CPS budget will have fallen by 25 per cent in real terms from its 2009–10 budget and its expenditure on its headquarters will be 50 per cent lower than in 2008–09. Within the new strategy, there are five strategic objectives contained in what the CPS has billed its 'business plan':

- Focus the CPS's support to victims, witnesses and communities.
- Embed its advocacy strategy.
- Improve performance in the magistrates' courts.
- Ensure that CPS people are well led, managed and engaged.
- Contribute to the wider Criminal Justice System.

Additionally, changes to the POA 1985, introduced by the Crime and Disorder Act (CDA) 1998, permit some lower court work to be undertaken by designated caseworkers, called Associate Prosecutors, who are not Crown Prosecutors. To be able to do so, they must have undergone specified training and have at least three years' experience of casework or have a legal qualification. They are able to review and present straightforward magistrates' court cases, which raise no technical issues and which are uncomplicated in terms of fact and law. Essentially, this involves cases where there is an anticipated guilty plea, bail applications, or minor road traffic offences where the proof in absence procedure is used. They cannot deal with cases such as indictable-only offences, contested trials, where there is election for jury trial and cases which raise sensitive issues. In 2007/08, Associate Prosecutors dealt with 20.4 per cent of magistrates' courts' sessions. This was a significant increase on the figure of 14.7 per cent for 2006/07 (http://www.cps.gov.uk/careers/other_legal_professionals/associate_prosecutor/). (These are the latest data available in October 2012.)

From its inception, the CPS was criticised for a variety of alleged faults, principally that it was inefficient and had a low success rate in prosecutions. Many police officers expressed doubts about the rigour with which cases were handled by the CPS, and dubbed it the 'Criminal Protection Society'. The Bar Council passed a motion in 1993 condemning the service for being too ready to abandon cases 'fearing defeat or cost'. (On 'fearless advocacy,' see the Bar's Code of Conduct, produced by the Bar Standards Board, 8th edn., in force 31 October 2004. See the full text of the Code, hosted by the Bar Standards Board at http://www.barstandardsboard.org.uk/standardsandguidance/codeofconduct//). Significant changes have been made to the Code of Conduct in 2010. At para 303(a) of the Code, it is stated that a barrister 'must promote and protect fearlessly and by all proper and lawful means the lay client's best interests and do so without regard to his own interests or to any consequences to himself or to any other person . . .'. (See, also, the 2010–11 Bar Handbook, setting out guidance as to 'a barrister's professional obligations, parameters of work, permitted charging arrangements, ability to get paid, getting redress when not paid, tax and VAT liabilities, insurance, practice planning and good practice advice, and relevant statutory and regulatory references, for all barristers be they self-employed or sole practitioners, employed, publicly or privately funded', www.barcouncil.org.uk/memberservices/BarHandbook2010-11/.) The rate of convictions appeared to have levelled between 2008/09 and 2009/10, but it has grown significantly in 2010/11. At the close of March 2012, the conviction rate was over 86 per cent, compared with 80.7 per cent in 2009/10 and 80.9 per cent in 2008/09. In previous years, the rate was 76.7 per cent in 2005/06, 77.3 per cent in 2006/07 and 79.3 per cent in 2007/08 (*Annual Report and Resource*

Accounts 2011–2012, Crown Prosecution Service, http://www.cps.gov.uk/publications/reports/2011/index.html).

   There are currently 13 areas into which the Crown Prosecution Service is divided, not including the specialised casework handled by the central Casework Divisions. During 2011/12, 68.4 per cent of defendants pleaded guilty in the Magistrates' Court and 72.8 per cent pleaded guilty in the Crown Court (*Annual Report and Resource Accounts 2011–2012*, Crown Prosecution Service). In terms of magistrates' casework, the number of defendants prosecuted by the CPS fell by 6.0 per cent during 2009/10, by 3.6 per cent in 2010/11 and by 6.4 per cent in 2011/2012. The CPS has identified that 'several factors may affect this figure, including the number of arrests, the impact of the early involvement of prosecutors, the number of offences cleared up by the police, and the number of offenders cautioned by the police. The present fall in caseload may also be related to lower levels of recorded crime, and to the increased number of comparatively minor offences now dealt with by way of a fixed penalty without CPS involvement' (http://www.cps.gov.uk/publications/reports/2011/index.html).

8.2.1   THE CODE FOR CROWN PROSECUTORS

This Code is issued under s 10 of the POA 1985. The Code was substantially reviewed in February 2010 by Keir Starmer QC, the Director of Public Prosecutions, and will be reviewed again in 2012/13. The Code can be viewed in full at www.cps.gov.uk/code. At the time of introducing the recent revisions to the Code, Keir Starmer QC said (http://www.cps.gov.uk/news/press_releases/108_10/index.html):

> The Code is a core document for the Crown Prosecution Service (CPS) and an invaluable tool for ensuring that the right principles are applied fairly and consistently when making our decisions in every case. These changes will help everyone understand how prosecutors make decisions, underpinning our commitment to openness at every stage of the prosecution process.
>
>   [. . .]
>
>   The role of the prosecutor is constantly evolving. The CPS and the Revenue & Customs Prosecutions Office recently merged and we are liaising much more closely with our local communities. It is critical that the Code is kept as relevant and clear as possible to assist prosecutors in their increasingly diverse roles and specialties.

The issue of the new Code reflects changes to legislation and practice since the previous Code was issued in 2004. Changes to the Code are intended to set out more clearly the principles that prosecutors must follow when they decide whether or not to prosecute. Those guiding principles include:

- a clearer explanation of the public interest factors tending in favour and against prosecution;

- a clearer explanation of how the public interest stage of the Full Code Test is applied;

- prosecutors having a discretion to stop a prosecution in the public interest, in exceptional circumstances, before all of the evidence is available;

- a fuller section explaining the use of out-of-court disposals for both adults and youths;

- prosecutors being able to conduct pre-trial witness interviews when it is needed to assess the reliability of witness evidence or better understand complex evidence.

8.2.2   THE DISCRETION TO PROSECUTE

The police have a very significant discretion as to what to do when a crime has possibly been committed. They could turn a blind eye, caution the suspect or charge the suspect, in which case they must decide what is the most appropriate charge or charges commensurate with the facts and seriousness of the alleged conduct. Environmental health officers, the Health and Safety Executive, and the Environment Agency inspectors, as officers statutorily charged with investigative powers, are in a similar position.

As is very cogently argued by McConville, Sanders and Leng in *The Case for the Prosecution* (1991), prosecution cases are constructed from the evidence and testimony of many people including lay witnesses, victims, the police, CPS lawyers and expert witnesses. Each of these parties is fallible and prone to perceive events in line with their own sorts of experience. The net result of this is that the prosecution case is normally nothing more than an *approximation* of 'the truth'. In crude terms, we move further towards an explanatory account if we understand truth *as* proof. In their preface to *Reconstructing Reality in the Courtroom* (1981), Bennett and Feldman asserted that: 'the use of stories to reconstruct the evidence in cases casts doubt on the common belief about justice as a mechanical and objective process'. Stories, their argument runs, serve as tools in the task of selecting from a glut of information what material will in fact be presented as evidence. Bennett and Feldman also contend that narrative devices like stories also serve to plug gaps. William Twining has, however, doubted this account of the somewhat subjective cherry-picking of stories in putting together a case. In particular, Twining argues, facts in issue, materiality, relevance, burdens of proof and presumptions, are peculiarly *lawyers'* concepts. Coupled with these, he continues, is the advocate's marshalling of 'the theory of the case' (see *Twining's Rethinking Evidence: Exploratory Essays*, Cambridge University Press (Law in Context series), 2nd edn, 2006).

The most influential role in what can neutrally be put as the narrative of a case is that of the police, as it is they who ultimately decide whether to charge anyone, and if so, whom and for what. Once these discretions have been exercised, there is a relatively narrow band of data on which the CPS can work.

In 1951, the Attorney General, Lord Shawcross, noted that:

> It has never been the rule in this country – I hope it never will be – that suspected criminal offences must automatically be the subject of prosecution [House of Commons Debates, vol 483, col 681, 29 January 1951].

This *dictum* has been almost universally accepted within the criminal justice system.

There is evidence, however, that the police do (for operational or social reasons) tend to focus their attention on particular types of conduct. Research, for example, by Andrew Sanders has shown a tendency for there to be a bias in favour of prosecuting working-class offenders as opposed to middle-class offenders. He compared the police response to offences with that of the Factory Inspectorate's response to violation of the health and safety laws, and found that the police were much more likely to initiate prosecutions against working-class suspects than were the factory inspectors against businesses and business executives. For the police, there was an institutional bias in favour of prosecution reflected in the principle 'let the court decide', whereas for the Factory Inspectorate, prosecution was a last resort pursued only after an attempt at negotiated compliance had failed. In 1980, there were 22,000 serious cases of tax evasion, but only one in 122 cases was prosecuted. By contrast, there were 107,000 social security frauds, of which one in four was prosecuted. Tax evasion resulted in a loss to the public purse 30 times larger than that caused by social security fraud, yet there was more State money spent on prosecuting people for social security fraud. (See Sanders, 'Class bias in prosecutions' (1985) 24 Howard J 176.) There is also evidence that the Environment Agency has a 'bottom-heavy' enforcement policy, that is, it is more concerned to prosecute minor offenders than large companies. Anglers who catch fish without licences are far more likely to appear in court than the directors of companies that pollute the environment. (See P de Prez, 'Biased enforcement or optimal regulation: Reflections on recent Parliamentary scrutiny of the Environment Agency' (2001) 13(3) Environmental Law and Management 145–50.)

8.2.3 POLICE CAUTIONING OF OFFENDERS

Prior to changes introduced by the Crime and Disorder Act (CDA) 1998, cautioning of both adult and young offenders was a possible alternative to prosecution and was particularly encouraged in the case of the latter. Following implementation of the changes introduced by the 1998 Act, cautions are now available only for adult offenders, with a new system of reprimands and warnings applying to young offenders. The Criminal Justice Act 2003 introduced several changes in this area; these are addressed below.

Cautioning of Adults
The Home Office provided guidance on when to caution in 1990 and 1994 (see Home Office Circulars 1990/59 and 1994/18). Further guidance has since been supplied in February 2007, by way of the 3rd edition of the Director of Public Prosecutions

guidance to police officers and Crown Prosecutors as to charging practices (www.cps. gov.uk/publications/directors_guidance/dpp_guidance.html#_09; see also the factsheet on charging decisions available at http://www.cps.gov.uk/news/fact_sheets/decision_ to_charge/). In overview, a system of cautions, reprimands and final warnings has been instituted as a mechanism of diverting from prosecution. Where the police consider that the Threshold Test is met in a case, a caution may be appropriate in the case of adults.

Other than an indictable-only offence, a caution may be an appropriate, proportionate means of disposal by way of diversion from prosecution. This is conditional on the police having determined that it is in the public interest to administer a simple caution. In such cases, the police may issue that caution, reprimand or final warning as appropriate, without referring the case to a Crown Prosecutor. In the case of youths, the police may administer a reprimand or final warning (www.cps.gov.uk/publications/ directors_guid-ance/dpp_guidance.html#_09).

A caution is not a conviction, but, if put as a formal caution, it remains on an offender's record for a minimum of five years and may be used at the sentencing stage if he is subsequently convicted of another offence. A caution must be administered by an officer of the rank of inspector or above, and attendance at the police station is usually required. Three conditions must be met:

- There must be sufficient evidence to have justified a prosecution.
- The offender must admit guilt.
- The offender must agree to the procedure.

Cautioning may be particularly appropriate where an offender is old or infirm, mentally ill, suffering from severe physical illness or suffering from severe emotional distress.

It may also be considered appropriate to give a conditional caution. Unlike the simple caution, the decision whether or not to offer a conditional caution can only be taken by a prosecutor either as part of the statutory charging process or on review of a case charged by the police (see below).

Reprimands and Warnings for Young Offenders

Sections 65–66 of the CDA 1998 introduced a new scheme that includes police reprimands and warnings, accompanied by intervention to reduce the likelihood of reoffending (note that amendments are pending to these sections). A first offence can result in a reprimand, final warning or criminal prosecution, depending on its seriousness. A further offence following a reprimand will lead to a warning or a charge. A further offence after a warning will normally lead to a charge, a second warning only being possible in limited circumstances where the latest offence is not serious and more than two years have elapsed since the first warning was given. Reprimands and warnings will be issued at a police station and a police officer may only issue them where:

- there is sufficient evidence for prosecution;
- guilt is admitted;

- there are no previous convictions; or
- prosecution is not in the public interest.

After a warning has been issued, the young offender will be referred to a youth offending team (as established by s 39 of the CDA 1998), which will assess the offender to determine whether a rehabilitation programme to prevent reoffending is appropriate, and to provide one where it is. Conditional discharge of a young offender who commits an offence within two years of receiving a warning is not possible unless there are exceptional circumstances relating to the offence or the offender. Any reprimand, warning or recorded noncompliance with a rehabilitation programme may be cited in court in the same way as previous convictions.

The Criminal Justice Act 2003 and Changes to the System

The Criminal Justice Act 2003 made several changes to this area. The changes are in Part 3 of the Act (note that amendments are pending to a number of these sections).

Section 22: Conditional Cautions

Section 22 defines a conditional caution and provides that it may be given to an adult offender if the five requirements in s 23 are met. The conditions that may be imposed are restricted to those aimed at reparation for the offence, or at the rehabilitation of the offender. A conditional caution may be given by an authorised person as defined in sub-s (4).

Section 23: The Five Requirements

Section 23 sets out the requirements that need to be met for a conditional caution to be given. The requirements are: that there is evidence against the offender; that a 'relevant prosecutor' (as defined in s 27) considers that the evidence would be sufficient to charge him and that a conditional caution should be given; that the offender admits the offence; that the offender has been made aware of what the caution (and failure to comply with it) would mean; and that he signs a document containing details of the offence, the admission, the offender's consent to the caution, and the conditions imposed.

Section 24: Failure to Comply with the Conditions

Section 24 provides that if the offender fails without reasonable excuse to satisfy the conditions attached to the conditional caution, he may be prosecuted for the offence. If proceedings are commenced, the document referred to in s 23 is admissible in evidence, and the conditional caution ceases to have effect.

Section 25: Code of Practice

This section makes provision for the Home Secretary, with the consent of the Attorney General, to publish a Code of Practice setting out the criteria for giving conditional cautions, how they are to be given and who may give them, the conditions that may be imposed and for what period, and arrangements for monitoring compliance.

The Code for Crown Prosecutors (promulgated on behalf of the DPP) sets out the official criteria governing the discretion to prosecute.

The revised Code issued in 2004 requires two tests to be satisfied before a prosecution is brought: there must be a 'realistic prospect of conviction' (the evidential test); and the prosecution must be 'in the public interest'. The further revised Code (February 2010) does not change the operation of this two-stage approach but serves to clarify what constitutes 'the public interest' in this context.

The evidential test requires prosecutors to predict what a jury or bench, properly directed, would be likely to decide. The guidelines require prosecutors to assess the reliability of evidence, not just its admissibility, hence the questions (para 5.4b): 'Is there evidence which might support or detract from the reliability of a confession? Is the reliability affected by factors such as the defendant's age, intelligence or level of understanding?' As Glanville Williams ([1985] Crim LR 115) and Andrew Sanders ((1994) 144 NLJ 946) have argued, this test favours people who are well-respected in society – like police officers and businessmen – in whose favour juries and magistrates might be biased. It disfavours the sort of victims who are unlikely to make good witnesses. Sanders proposes a better test: whether, on the evidence, a jury or bench ought (on the balance of probabilities) to convict.

The public interest must be considered in each case where there is enough evidence to provide a realistic prospect of conviction. In cases of any seriousness, a prosecution will usually take place unless there are public interest factors tending against prosecution which clearly outweigh those tending in favour.

Announcing the revised Code that was published in 2004, the Attorney-General noted (*Hansard*, HL Deb, 16 November 2004 vol. 666 c50WS) that the fundamental evidential and public interest considerations remained the same as in the earlier 2001 Code. However, the Code was amended to reflect the then new role played by the Crown Prosecution Service in statutory charging, whereby Crown Prosecutors, rather than the police, normally decide whether or not to charge a suspect and determine the appropriate charge or charges. The new Code also reflected other key developments in the four years since its earlier iteration. These include: the developing role of prosecutors in assisting the sentencing court, and seeking post-conviction orders, such as anti-social behaviour orders; alternatives to prosecution, such as conditional cautioning; and public interest factors in favour of prosecution, relating to confiscation and any other orders, children, and community confidence.

The Code lists some 'public interest factors in favour of prosecution' (para 5.9) and some against (para 5.10). The former include cases where:

- a conviction is likely to result in a significant sentence;
- a weapon was used or violence was threatened during the commission of the offence;
- the offence was committed against a person serving the public, like a police officer or a nurse;

- the offence, although not serious in itself, is widespread in the area where it was committed;

- there is evidence that the offence was carried out by a group;

- the offence was motivated by any form of discrimination against the victim's ethnic or national origin, sex, religious beliefs, political views or sexual orientation; or the suspect demonstrated hostility towards the victim based on any of those characteristics.

A prosecution is less likely to proceed, we are told (para 5.10), where (*inter alia*):

- the court is likely to impose a very small or nominal penalty;

- the offence was committed as a result of a genuine mistake or misunderstanding (judged against the seriousness of the offence);

- the loss or harm can be described as minor and was the result of a single incident, particularly if it was caused by a misjudgment;

- a prosecution is likely to have a very bad effect on the victim's physical or mental health, always bearing in mind the seriousness of the offence;

- details could be made public that could harm sources of information, international relations or national security.

Crown Prosecutors and others must balance factors for and against prosecution, carefully and fairly. Deciding on the public interest is, the Code says (para 5.11), 'not simply a matter of adding up the number of factors on each side'.

The Attorney-General has commended the Code to prosecutors outside the CPS. This may help to correct inconsistent approaches between the police and CPS on the one hand and, on the other, prosecutors like HMRC and the Health and Safety Executive. As Sanders (see above) has observed, if you illegally gain a fortune or maim someone, you will probably be treated more leniently than ordinary disposals for such offences if the crimes are, technically, tax evasion and operating an unsafe place of work. Local authorities and the Environment Agency seem generally reluctant to prosecute environmental offenders. This can lead to a situation in which environmental crime, for example, makes good business sense. See M Watson, 'Offences against the environment: the economics of crime and punishment' (2004) 16(4) Environmental Law and Management 2003–04. For the Health and Safety Executive, see G Slapper, *Blood in the Bank*, (1999).

8.2.5 CPS INDEPENDENCE FROM THE POLICE

The CPS is institutionally separate from the police. The police are no longer in a client–lawyer relationship with the prosecutor, able to give instructions about how to proceed. The police are still, however, in the most influential position as it is only once they have taken the decision to charge a suspect that the CPS will be called on to look at the case. The CPS in practice exercises no supervisory role over the police investigation of cases;

it simply acts on the file presented after the investigation by the police. It cannot instruct the police to investigate a particular incident.

The power of the CPS to discontinue prosecutions (under s 23 of the POA 1985), or the continuing power to withdraw or offer no evidence, is an important feature of its independence. However, McConville makes the argument that '[t]he system is dominated throughout its stages by the interests and values of the police, with the CPS playing an essentially subordinate and reactive role' in *The Case for the Prosecution* (1991).

The Report of the Runciman Royal Commission on Criminal Justice (1993) recommended that the CPS should play a greater role in the investigative process. It stated (para 93):

> The police should seek the advice of the CPS at the investigation stage in appropriate cases in accordance with guidelines to be agreed between the two services.

The Report also stated (para 95):

> Where a chief officer of police is reluctant to comply with a request from the CPS to investigate further before a decision on discontinuance is taken, HM Chief Inspector of Constabulary in conjunction with the Director of Public Prosecutions should bring about a resolution of the dispute.

Oddly, however, the rationale underlying the establishment of the CPS (independence from the police) appears to have been undermined since 1998, when many police stations have had CPS liaison officers working in the stations themselves.

Further evidence of encouragement of the relationship between the CPS and the police appears in the response to recommendations made by the Glidewell Committee in 1998. The Committee recommended that the CPS should take responsibility for the prosecution process immediately following charge. There should be a single integrated unit to assemble and manage case files, combining the current police Administrative Support Units and those parts of the CPS branch which deal with file preparation and review. The Committee proposed as a model a 'Criminal Justice Unit' in the charge of a CPS lawyer with mainly CPS staff, although many of these might be the civilian police staff currently employed in Administrative Support Units. The Committee suggested that such a unit would need to be able to call on the police to take action in obtaining more evidence. This would require that a senior police officer would need to be part of the unit, housed in or near the relevant police station. The unit would deal with fast-track cases in their entirety and with simple summary cases, that is, with both the file preparation and the necessary advocacy. The CPS should primarily be responsible, in the magistrates' courts, for the timely disposal of all cases prosecuted by its lawyers, and share with the court one or more performance indicators related to timeliness. The

Committee recommended the formation of 'trial units' to deal with advocacy in some trials in the magistrates' courts. This was also recommended for the management and preparation of all cases in the Crown Court. The intention was to lead to a shift in the centre of gravity of the CPS towards the Crown Court.

These recommendations were put into effect in six pilot areas. A report by the Glidewell Working Group in February 2001 found that, following a study carried out in September and October 2000, the recommendations had important effects, in that they:

- eliminated unnecessary work through improved communications;
- speeded up notification of proposed discontinuance;
- improved notification of case results to victims and witnesses;
- freed up staff to take on additional functions;
- established a single contact point for the public on the prosecution of magistrates' court cases.

8.2.6 JUDICIAL CONTROL OF PROSECUTION POLICY

There is a very limited way in which the courts can control the exercise of prosecutorial discretion by the police. Lord Denning MR gave the example in one case of a chief constable issuing a directive to his men that no person should be prosecuted for stealing goods worth less than £100 (around £2,000 at 2011 prices), and said 'I should have thought the court could countermand it. He would be failing in his duty to enforce the law'. More generally, the courts had no control, *per* Lord Denning MR, *R v Metropolitan Police Commissioner ex p Blackburn* [1968] 1 All ER 763 at 769:

> For instance, it is for the Commissioner of Police of the Metropolis, or the Chief Constable, as the case may be, to decide in any particular case whether inquiries should be pursued, or whether an arrest should be made or a prosecution brought. It must be for him to decide on the disposition of his force and the concentration of his resources on any particular crime or area. No court can or should give him directions on such a matter.

Apart from this, there is the doctrine of constabulary independence (see *Fisher v Oldham Corp* (1930)), which regards the constable as an independent office-holder under the Crown who cannot be instructed by organisational superiors or by governmental agency about how to exercise his powers. The constable is accountable only to law. The judiciary has shown a marked reluctance to interfere with decisions made by police chiefs concerning, in particular, the allocation of resources and direction of police officers (see *Harris v Sheffield United Football Club Ltd* (1987); *R v Chief Constable of Sussex ex p International Trader's Ferry Ltd* (1997)).

An interesting instance of the courts being used to attack a use of police discretion is *R v Coxhead* (1986). The appellant was a police sergeant in charge of a police station. A young man was brought into the station to be breathalysed and the sergeant recognised him as the son of a police inspector at that station. The sergeant knew the inspector to be suffering from a bad heart condition. In order not to exacerbate this condition, the sergeant did not administer the test and allowed the motorist to go free. The sergeant was prosecuted and convicted for conduct tending and intended to pervert the course of justice. The sergeant's defence was that his decision came within the legitimate scope of discretion exercised by a police officer. The trial judge said the matter should be left for the jury to determine; they must decide the extent of any police discretion in accordance with the facts. The jury convicted the sergeant and his conviction was upheld by the Court of Appeal. In minor cases, the police had a very wide discretion whether to prosecute, but in major cases they had no discretion or virtually none. Thus, in a serious case like drink-driving, there was no discretion which the sergeant could have been exercising legitimately. It is odd, however, that this is left for the jury to decide after the event rather than being subject to clear rules to anticipate the proper exercise of police discretion.

It is possible to bring a judicial review of the decision to prosecute or not to prosecute. The courts are likely to direct the CPS to review its prosecutorial decisions where:

- it is apparent that the law has not been properly understood and applied (*R v DPP, ex p Jones (Timothy)* [2000]);

- it can be demonstrated on an objective appraisal of the case that some serious evidence supporting a prosecution has not been carefully considered (*R (on the application of Joseph) v DPP* [2001]; *R (on the application of Peter Dennis) v DPP* [2006]);

- it can be demonstrated that in a significant area, a conclusion as to what the evidence is to support a prosecution is irrational (*R v DPP, ex p Jones (Timothy)* [2000]);

- the decision is perverse, that is, one at which no reasonable prosecutor could have arrived (*R v DPP, ex p C* [1995]);

- CPS policy, such as that set out in the Code for Crown Prosecutors, has not been properly applied and/or complied with (*R v DPP, ex p C* [1995]; *R v DPP, ex p Manning* [2001]; *R v Chief Constable of Kent, ex p L; R v DPP, ex p B* (1991));

- the decision has been arrived at because of an unlawful policy (*R v DPP, ex p C* [1995]);

- it can be demonstrated that the decision was arrived at as a result of fraud, corruption or bad faith (*R v DPP, ex p Kebilene* [2000]; *R v Panel on Takeovers and Mergers, ex p Fayed* [1992]).

Reference has already been made to the fact that Crown Prosecutors are now able to appear in the higher courts if they are suitably qualified. This has caused a great deal of concern in some quarters. The basis of the worry is that, as full-time salaried lawyers working for an organisation, CPS lawyers will sometimes be tempted to get convictions using dubious tactics or ethics because their own status as employees and prospects of promotion will depend on conviction success rates. Where, as now, barristers from the independent Bar are used by the CPS to prosecute, there is (it is argued) a greater likelihood of the courtroom lawyer dropping a morally unsustainable case.

Section 42 of the Access to Justice Act 1999 tries to overcome any possible difficulties with a provision (amending s 27 of the Courts and Legal Services Act (CLSA) 1990) that every advocate 'has a duty to the court to act with independence in the interests of justice', in other words, a duty that overrides any inconsistent duty that might lie, for example, to an employer. Professor Michael Zander QC has contended, however, that these are 'mere words'. He has said (letter to *The Times*, 29 December 1998) that they are unlikely to exercise much sway over CPS lawyer employees concerned with performance targets set by their line managers, and that:

> The CPS as an organisation is constantly under pressure in regard to the proportion of discontinuances, acquittal and conviction rates. These are factors in the day-to-day work of any CPS lawyer. It is disingenuous to imagine they will not have a powerful effect on decision making.

The Bar was also very wary of this change, an editorial in *Counsel* (the journal of the Bar of England and Wales) saying:

> [. . .] we are gravely concerned about the extent to which prosecutions will be done in-house by the CPS when the need for independent prosecutors is so well established in our democracy [(1999) Counsel 3, February].

It is important to set the arguments in a wider context. What are the social, economic or political debates surrounding this issue of how best to run a system of courtroom prosecutors? The change to having Crown Court prosecutions carried out by salaried CPS lawyers might well be expected to be more efficient, as the whole prosecution can be handled in-house, without engaging the external service of an independent barrister. This assumption has recently been discredited, however: CPS in-house cases are in fact more expensive to run than instructing chambers-based barristers (see website of the Bar Council, 27 July 2009: 'Independent Study Heavily Criticises CPS Claims about In-House Advocates are Based on "Alice in Wonderland Accounting" '). Some will argue that justice is being sacrificed to the deity of cost-cutting. On the other hand, it could be argued that justice and efficiency are not mutually exclusive phenomena and – as has been shown above – the CPS has been actively recruiting HCAs to prosecute in the Crown Court. Keir Starmer QC, the Director of Public Prosecutions, has committed himself to the view that 'in-house advocacy is here to stay for the CPS' (9 January 2009). However, the real-term costs of Higher Court Advocates (HCAs) has been effectively queried, with recent Bar Council meetings discussing the relative expense of independent and in-house barristers (www.barcouncil.org.uk/aboutthebar-council/meetings/minutes/BarCouncilMeeting17July2010/). This has culminated in a turf war between in-house CPS advocates and independent practitioners at the Bar. (See the article by Frances Gibb, 'Bar Council says Crown Prosecution Service wasting millions with in-house prosecutions', 27 July 2009, *The Times* (http://business.timeson-line. co.uk/tol/business/law/article6728772.ece). See also the annual report for 2010 of the Chairman of the Criminal Bar Association, Paul Mendelle QC: www. criminalbar.com/86/records/376/Chairmans%20Report%20for%20the%20CBA%20 June%20 2010.pdf.) It remains to be seen what effect the new CPS Panel Advocate Scheme, which commenced in autumn 2011, will have on this debate.

8.3 BAIL

Bail is the release from custody, pending a criminal trial, of an accused. The relevant statute is the Bail Act (BA) 1976. Bail may be with or without conditions. Conditional bail may granted, for example, on the promise that an accused will not contact witnesses or co-defendants in a case; that he will co-operate with probation or other State agencies; that he will adhere to reporting or so-called 'doorstep' or curfew conditions. Other conditions of remand on bail might include the promise that money will be paid to the court by a 'surety' (the person 'standing' the bail money) if he absconds. All decisions on whether to grant bail therefore involve delicate questions of balancing interests, but the exercise begins with the presumption that an accused should be at liberty until proven guilty. The test to be applied is a threshold one. Where there are 'substantial grounds' for believing that the exceptions to bail in the Bail Act 1976 are met, a court may be satisfied that deprivation of the liberty of an accused can be justified.

A person is presumed innocent of a criminal charge unless he is proved guilty of it; this implies that no one should ever be detained unless he has been found guilty. It follows that there is a presumption of liberty, which the prosecution may oppose only by establishing 'substantial grounds' to overturn that presumption. For several reasons, however, it can be regarded as undesirable to allow some accused people to go back to society before the case against them is tried in a criminal court. Indeed, about 12 per cent of offenders who are bailed to appear in court fail to appear for their trials. In January 2005, the Attorney General called for a crack-down on defendants who skip bail. At the time in question, 60,000 'failed to appear' (FTA) warrants were outstanding. Lord Goldsmith said: 'They will see that they can't thumb their nose at the criminal justice system. Turning up at court is not optional. It is a serious obligation and we will enforce it' (C Dyer, 'Bail bandits blitz begins today', *The Guardian*, 14 January 2005).

In 2008, it was revealed that nearly one in seven people charged with murder and awaiting trial was released on bail. A survey by the Courts Service disclosed that at least 60 of the 455 people accused of murder were on the streets on 31 January 2008, while 35 out of 41 of those awaiting trial for manslaughter were bailed. (That survey has not been updated.) The disclosure came after Gary Weddell murdered Traute Maxfield, his mother-in-law, before killing himself. At the time, he was on bail charged with the murder of his wife (*The Times*, 25 February 2008). The Coroners and Justice Act 2009 has since reformed the law relating to the application and grant of bail. In particular, s 115 of that Act provides that a defendant who is charged with murder (and other offences) may not be granted bail except by a judge of the Crown Court. The power of magistrates to consider bail in murder cases – whether at the first hearing or after a breach of an existing bail condition – is thus removed. A bail decision in such cases must be made as soon as reasonably practicable. In any event, a decision must be made within 48 hours (excluding public holidays), beginning the day after the defendant's appearance in the magistrates' court.

To refuse bail to an accused might involve depriving someone of liberty who is subsequently found not guilty or convicted, but given a non-custodial sentence. Such a person will probably have been kept in a police cell or in a prison cell for 23 hours a day. Unlike the jurisdictions in the Netherlands, Germany and France, no compensation is payable in these circumstances. On the other hand, to allow liberty to the accused pending trial might be to allow him to abscond, commit further offences, interfere with witnesses and obstruct the course of justice. A suspected terrorist might commit further outrages (a controversial issue following the explosions in London on 7 July 2005).

The difficulties involved in finding the proper balance have been highlighted by several cases of serious assault and rape being committed by persons who were on bail, and by the fleeing of Asil Nadir to Northern Cyprus in May 1993. Mr Nadir skipped his £3.5 million bail to travel to a jurisdiction that would not extradite him to England. He claimed that he would not be given a fair trial for the offences of theft and false accounting with which he was charged, and went on the public record as saying that his sureties would not suffer hardship as he would repay those who had put up bail for him.

The basic way in which the law currently seeks to find the right balance in such matters is by operating a general presumption in favour of bail, a presumption that can be overturned if one or more of a number of indices of suspicion exist in respect of a particular defendant. Even where bail is granted, it may be subject to certain conditions to promote public safety and the interests of justice. The Criminal Justice Act 2003 makes several changes to the law of bail. All the changes are addressed in 8.3.3 below.

8.3.1 THE CRIMINAL JUSTICE AND PUBLIC ORDER ACT 1994

In the 1990s, the government took the view that bail was too easily granted and that too many crimes were being committed by those on bail who ought to be in custody while awaiting trial. The Bail (Amendment) Act 1993 and the Criminal Justice and Public Order Act (CJPOA) 1994 (ss 25–30) emanate from that philosophy, their aim being to restrict the granting of bail. A case that caught public sympathy for this view involved a young man who had many convictions for car crime and joyriding. While on bail, he was joyriding in a vehicle when he smashed into a schoolgirl. She clung to the bonnet but he shook her off and thus killed her. The Home Secretary commented publicly that the new legislative measures would prevent such terrible events.

Each year prior to the Acts, about 50,000 offences were committed by people on bail. A study by the Metropolitan Police in 1988 indicated that 16 per cent of those charged by that force were already on bail for another offence. Another study in 1993, from the same force, showed that, of 537 suspects arrested in one week during a clampdown on burglary, 40 per cent were on bail. Some had been bailed 10 or 15 times during the preceding year (figures from Robert Maclennan MP, HC Committee, col 295, 1994). A recent survey revealed that males in prison for motor vehicle theft who had previous experience of bail claimed on average to have committed a similar offence *each month* while on bail (*Justice for All*, Cm 5563, 2002, The Stationery Office).

In the criminal process, the first stage at which bail is usually raised as an issue is at the police station. If a person is arrested on a warrant, this will indicate whether he is to be held in custody or released on bail. If the suspect is arrested without a warrant, then the police will have to decide whether to release the suspect after he has been charged. After a person has been charged, s 38(1)(a) of the Police and Criminal Evidence Act (PACE) 1984 states that a person must be released unless: (a) his name and address are not known; or (b) the custody officer reasonably thinks that his detention is necessary for his own protection; or (c) to prevent him from injuring someone or damaging property, or because he might abscond, or interfere with the course of justice. Most arrested people are bailed by the police. In 1990, 83 per cent of those arrested in connection with indictable offences and 88 per cent of those arrested for summary offences (other than motoring offences) were released. This area has been amended by s 28 of the CJPOA 1994. A custody officer can now, in the case of an imprisonable offence, refuse to release an arrested person after charge if the officer has reasonable grounds for believing that the detention of that person is necessary to prevent him from committing any offence. Previously, many cases were caught by (b) (above), but some likely conduct, for example drink-driving, was not.

Section 27 of the CJPOA 1994 amends PACE 1984 (ss 38 and 47) so as to allow the police to grant conditional bail to persons charged. The conditions can be whatever is required to ensure that the person surrenders to custody, does not commit an offence while on bail, or does not interfere with witnesses or otherwise obstruct the course of justice. The new powers of the custody officer, however, do not include a power to impose a requirement to reside in a bail hostel. By amending Part IV of PACE 1984, s 29 of the CJPOA 1994 gives the police power to arrest without warrant a person who, having been granted conditional police bail, has failed to attend at a police station at the appointed time.

The Bail Act 1976 created a statutory presumption of bail. It states (s 4) that, subject to Sched 1, bail shall be granted to a person accused of an offence and brought before a magistrates' court or a Crown Court, and also to people convicted of an offence who are being remanded for reports to be made. The court must therefore grant bail (unless one of the exceptions applies), even if the defendant does not make an application. Schedule 1 provides that a court need not grant bail to a person charged with an offence punishable with imprisonment if it is satisfied that there are 'substantial grounds' (the relevant test) for believing that, if released on bail, the defendant would:

- fail to surrender to custody;
- commit an offence while on bail; or
- interfere with witnesses or otherwise obstruct the course of justice.

The court can also refuse bail if it believes that the defendant ought to stay in custody for his own protection, or if it has not been practicable, for want of time, to obtain sufficient information to enable the court to make its decision on bail, or he has previously failed to answer to bail (Sched 1, Part I, paras 2–6).

When the court is considering the grounds stated above, all relevant factors must be taken into account. These include: the nature and seriousness of the offence, the character, antecedents, associations and community ties of the defendant, and his record for satisfying his obligations under previous grants of bail.

If the defendant is charged with an offence not punishable with imprisonment, Sched 1 provides that bail may only be withheld if he has previously failed to surrender on bail and if the court believes that, in view of that failure, he will again fail to surrender if released on bail.

Section 25 of the CJPOA 1994 provided that, in some circumstances, a person who had been charged with or convicted of murder, attempted murder, manslaughter, rape or attempted rape must not be granted bail. The circumstances were simply that the conviction must have been within the UK, and that, in the case of a manslaughter conviction, it must have been dealt with by way of a custodial sentence. The word 'conviction' is given a wide meaning and includes anyone found 'not guilty by way of insanity'.

There was debate about whether the changes wrought by s 25 were justifiable. A Home Office Minister, defending the section, stated that it would be worth the risk if it prevented just one murder or rape, even though there might be a few 'hard cases', that is, people eventually acquitted of crime, who were remanded in custody pending trial (David Maclean MP, Minister of State, Home Office, HC Committee, col 282, 1994). As Card and Ward remarked in a commentary on the CJPOA 1994, the government, when pushed, was unable to cite a single case where a person released on bail, in the circumstances covered by s 25, reoffended in a similar way. There is no time limit on the previous conviction and there is no requirement of any connection between the previous offence and the one in question. Card and Ward suggest that there is a world of difference between a person who was convicted of manslaughter 30 years ago on the grounds of complicity in a suicide pact and who is now charged with attempted rape (of which he must be presumed innocent), and the person who was convicted of rape eight years ago and now faces another rape charge. The first person is not an obvious risk to society and it is, they argue, regrettable that bail will be denied to him. There is also argument to be had with the contents of the s 25 list. Why should some clearly dangerous and prevalent crimes like robbery be omitted from it? In any case, it might have been better had the offences in the list raised a strong presumption against bail as opposed to an absolute ban, as the former could be rebutted in cases where there was, on the facts, no risk.

A further significant difficulty with this approach was that it appeared to be incompatible with the requirements of Art 5(3) of the European Convention on Human Rights (ECHR), decisions of the court on which make it clear that the decision to remand a defendant in custody before trial must be a decision of the court based on the merits after a review of the facts. By precluding bail in the specified circumstances, s 25 denied the court the opportunity to take a decision based on the merits. Thus, in *CC v UK* (1999) (subsequently confirmed by the European Court of Human Rights in *Caballero v UK* (2000)), the European Court found that s 25 violated rights under Art 5(3) where the claimant had been denied bail on a rape charge in 1996 because of a conviction for manslaughter in 1987.

Anticipating this decision, s 25 was amended by the CDA 1998 to provide that bail should only be granted in homicide and rape cases if the court is 'satisfied that there are exceptional circumstances which justify it'. However, doubts have been expressed by the Law Commission and others about whether this change achieves compliance with obligations under the ECHR. The argument is that the presumption required by the ECHR is innocence and therefore that the defendant should be released, while the presumption under the amended s 25 is that the defendant should not be released. Nevertheless, what effectively operates as a presumption *against* bail in s 25 of the Criminal Justice and Public Order Act 1994 has been found by the courts as not incompatible with Art 5(3) (the liberty guarantee) of the ECHR, provided the overall burden is not on the defendant to prove that bail should be granted (see *R (O) v Harrow Crown Court* (2006)).

Bail can be granted as conditional or unconditional. Where it is unconditional, the accused must simply surrender to the court at the appointed date. Failure to appear without reasonable cause is an offence under the BA 1976 (s 6) and can result, if tried in a Crown Court, in a sentence of up to 12 months' imprisonment or a fine. Conditions can be attached to the granting of bail where the court thinks that it is necessary to ensure that the accused surrenders at the right time and does not interfere with witnesses or commit further offences. There is no statutory limit to the conditions the court may impose. The most common include requirements that the accused reports daily or weekly to a police station, resides at a particular address, surrenders his passport, or does not go to particular places or associate with particular people.

Section 7 of the BA 1976 gives the police power to arrest anyone on conditional bail whom they reasonably suspect is likely to break the conditions or has already done so. Anyone arrested in these circumstances must be brought before a magistrate within 24 hours. The magistrate may then reconsider the question of bail.

Personal recognisances, by which the suspect agreed to pay a sum if he failed to surrender to the court, were abolished by the BA 1976 (s 3(2)), except in cases where it is believed that the defendant might try to flee abroad. The Act did retain the court's right to ask for sureties as a condition of bail. By putting sureties in a position where they can have large sums of money 'estreated' if the suspect does not surrender to the court, significant pressure (not using the resources of the criminal justice system) is put on the accused. The proportion of those who do not answer to bail is about 12 per cent of those given bail. Section 9 of the BA 1976 strengthens the surety principle by making it a criminal offence to agree to indemnify a surety. This sort of thing could happen, for example, if the accused agreed to reimburse the surety in the event that he skipped bail and the surety was requested to pay.

The CDA 1998 makes further changes to the law relating to bail. Section 54, which amended ss 3 and 3A of the BA 1976, provides for increased powers to require security or impose conditions (by taking away the requirement that the defendant must appear unlikely to remain in Great Britain). The amendment also allows courts to be able to require defendants to attend interviews with a legal representative as a condition of bail.

8.3.2 APPEALS AND REAPPLICATIONS

The rules that govern how someone who has been refused bail might reapply and appeal have also been framed with a view to balancing the interests of the accused with those of the public and justice. The original refusal should not be absolute and final but, on the other hand, it is seen as necessary that the refusals are not reversed too easily.

If the court decides not to grant the defendant bail, then Sched 1, Part IIA (inserted by s 154 of the Criminal Justice Act (CJA) 1988) provides that it is the court's duty to consider whether the defendant ought to be granted bail at each subsequent hearing. At the first hearing after the one at which bail was first refused, he may support an application for bail with any arguments, but at subsequent hearings, the court need not hear arguments as to fact or law which it has heard before. The CJA 1988 enables a court to remand an accused, in his absence, for up to three successive one-week remand hearings provided that he consents and is legally represented. Such repeated visits are costly to the State and can be unsettling for the accused, especially if he has to spend most of the day in a police cell, only to be told the case has been adjourned again without bail. If someone does not consent, they are prevented from applying for bail on each successive visit if the only supporting arguments are those that have been heard by the court before (*R v Nottingham JJ ex p Davies* (1980)).

To avoid unproductive hearings, that is, to promote courts being able to adjourn a case for a period within which reasonable progress can be made on it, s 155 of the CJA 1988 allows for adjournments for up to 28 days provided the court sets the date for when the next stage of the proceedings should take place. What began as an experiment under this section has now been extended to all courts by statutory order (SI 1991/2667).

The interests of the accused are also served by the variety of appeals he may make if bail has been refused. If bail has been refused by magistrates then, in limited circumstances, an application may be made to another bench of magistrates. Applications for reconsideration can also be made to a judge in chambers (through a legal representative) or to the Official Solicitor (in writing). Appeal can also be made to a Crown Court in respect of bail for both pre-committal remands and where a defendant has been committed for trial or sentence at the Crown Court.

Section 3 of the BA 1976 allows for an application to vary the conditions of court bail to be made by the person bailed, the prosecutor or a police officer. Application may also be made for the imposition of conditions on unconditional court bail. As amended by the CJPOA 1994, s 3 of the BA 1976 now allows for the same thing in relation to police bail, although the new provisions do not allow the prosecutor to seek reconsideration of the decision to grant bail itself. Under the Bail (Amendment) Act 1993, however, the prosecution does now have a right to appeal against the grant of bail by a court. This right applies to offences that carry a maximum sentence of imprisonment of five years or more, and to offences of taking a vehicle without consent (joyriding). When this right of appeal is exercised, the defendant will remain in custody until the appeal is heard by a Crown Court judge who will decide whether to grant bail or remand the defendant in custody within 48 hours of the magistrate's decision. Parliament was concerned that this power could be abused and has stated that it should be reserved 'for cases of greatest concern, when there is a serious risk of harm to the public' or where there are 'other significant public interest grounds' for an appeal. Section 18 of the Criminal Justice Act 2003 has changed the law so as to allow the prosecution to appeal against bail in all cases of imprisonable offences (see below, at 8.3.3).

Section 67(1) of the CJA 1967 states that time spent in custody pre-trial or pre-sentence can generally be deducted from the ultimate sentence. (If the relevant provisions of ss 87 and 88 of the Powers of Criminal Courts (Sentencing) Act 2000 are brought into force, s 67 will be repealed.) No compensation, however, is paid to people who have been remanded in custody but are subsequently found not guilty.

Section 240A of the Criminal Justice Act 2003, as inserted by s 21 of the Criminal Justice and Immigration Act 2008, provides for a deduction from the ultimate sentence if the offender has spent time on bail subject to a curfew of nine hours or more in any given day, coupled with an electronic monitoring condition. The defendant will generally be entitled to an order to the effect that half the number of days spent on bail subject to those conditions should count as time served by the prisoner as part of his sentence.

This area of law was subject to a comprehensive revision after a Home Office special working party reported in 1974, and has been legislatively debated and modified twice since the BA 1976. It is, however, still a matter of serious concern, both to those civil libertarians who consider the law too tilted against the accused, and to the police and commentators, who believe it too lenient in many respects. This criticism of the law from both sides of the debate might indicate a desirable state of balance reached by the current regulatory framework:

- *Opposition to the current arrangements – the civil liberties perspective*
  It is a cause for concern that, in the 1990s, of those dealt with summarily after being remanded in custody, about 50 per cent received non-custodial sentences and a further 25 per cent were acquitted.

  There are wide variations in the local policies of different courts. One study has shown, for instance, that the number of indictable custodial remands per 1,000 indictable proceedings was 111 in Brighton, as against 313 in Bournemouth (B. Gibson, 'Why Bournemouth?' (1987) 151 JP 520, 15 August).

  In 2012, the remand prison population was somewhere between 12,000 and 13,000, 15 per cent of the prison population (*Remand Prisoners: Thematic Review*, HM Inspectorate of Prisons, August 2012: http://www.justice.gov.uk/

downloads/publications/inspectorate-reports/hmipris/thematic-reports-and-research-publications/remand-thematic.pdf).

- *Opposition to the current arrangements – the police/public perspective*
  There are arguments that point to the number of people who commit offences while on bail. A study conducted in Bristol, for example, showed that over one-third of all defendants charged with burglary were on bail for another offence at the time of their arrest. Following some dreadful cases of serious offences being committed while the perpetrator was on bail, s 153 of the CJA 1988 required magistrates to give reasons if they decided to grant bail against police objections in cases of murder, manslaughter or rape.

  The percentage of people who skip bail is too high, especially for the more minor offences. Note: the annual figure, however, of those who do not answer to bail is consistently under 12 per cent.

Positive developments in recent years have been the use of Bail Information Schemes (BIS) for courts (about 100 courts now operate such schemes) and government attempts to increase the number of bail hostels. The BIS resulted from pilot schemes organised by the Vera Institute of Justice of New York. They give courts verified information from the probation service about defendants' accommodation or community ties. The evidence suggests that the courts using such schemes make greater use of bail than those which do not have the schemes.

8.3.3   BAIL AND THE CRIMINAL JUSTICE ACT 2003

The Criminal Justice Act 2003 made many changes to the law of bail. First we need to discuss those relating to police bail at the point at which someone is arrested.

Section 4: Bail Elsewhere than at a Police Station

This section amends s 30 of PACE (creating a new s 30A) to enable police officers to grant bail to persons following their arrest without the need to take them to a police station. It provides the police with additional flexibility following arrest and the scope to remain on patrol where there is no immediate need to deal with the person concerned at the station. It is intended to allow the police to plan their work more effectively by giving them new discretion to decide exactly when and where an arrested person should attend a police station for interview. See A Hucklesby, 'Not necessarily a trip to the police station: the introduction of police bail' (2004) CrimLR 803–13.

Sub-sections (2)–(6) amend s 30 to take account of the new power to grant bail. The basic principle remains that a person arrested by a constable or taken into custody by a constable after being arrested by someone else must be taken by a constable to a police station as soon as is practicable. However, this is subject to the provisions dealing with release either on bail or without bail.

Sub-section (4) expands existing s 30(7) of PACE 1984 to provide that a constable must release the person concerned without bail if, before reaching the police station, he is satisfied that there are no grounds for keeping him under arrest or releasing him on bail under the new provisions.

Sub-section (5) replaces existing s 30(10) and (11) of PACE 1984 to make it clear that a constable may delay taking an arrested person to a police station or releasing him on bail if that person's presence elsewhere is necessary for immediate investigative purposes. The reason for such delay must be recorded either on arrival at the police station or when the person is released on bail.

Sub-section (7) inserts a series of new sections into PACE 1984, which provide police officers with the framework of powers to grant bail following arrest. Section 30A provides that a constable has power to release a person on bail at any time prior to arrival at a police station. It specifies that the person released on bail must be required to attend a police station and that any police station may be specified for that purpose. No other requirement may be imposed on the person as a condition of bail.

Section 30B requires that the constable must give the person bailed a written notice, prior to release, setting out the offence for which he was arrested and the ground on which that arrest was made. It must tell him that he is required to attend a police station and may specify the relevant station and time. If these details are not specified in that initial notice, they must be set out in a further notice provided to the person at a later stage. The police have the capacity to change the specified station or time if necessary and the person concerned must be given written notice of any such change.

Section 30C contains various supplemental provisions. Section 30C(1) allows for the police to remove the requirement to attend a police station to answer bail, provided they give the person a written notice to that effect.

Section 30C(2) makes it clear that where someone attends a non-designated police station to answer bail following arrest, he must be released or taken to a designated police station within six hours of his arrival. Designated stations are those nominated by chief officers as suitable for detention purposes and are generally stations with appropriate facilities to cater for extended periods of custody.

Section 30C(3) specifies that nothing in the BA 1976 applies in relation to bail under these new arrangements. The law that applies to this form of bail is set out in PACE 1984 as amended by the Criminal Justice Act 2003.

Section 30C(4) clarifies that a person who has been released under the new bail provisions may be re-arrested if new evidence justifying such a course of action has come to light since their release.

Section 30D deals with failure to answer to bail under the new arrangements. Section 30D(1) allows a constable to arrest without a warrant a person who fails to attend the police station at the specified time. Section 30D(2) states that a person arrested in such circumstances must be taken to a police station as soon as practicable after the arrest. Section 30D(3) defines the station relevant for the purposes of sub-s (1) as whichever station is defined in the latest notice provided to the person concerned. Section 30D(4) clarifies that such an arrest for failure to answer to bail is to be treated as an arrest for an offence for certain PACE purposes.

The Act also addresses bail other than at the immediate point someone is arrested, such as in court, where it has to be decided whether the defendant should be kept in custody or let free before the next court appearance.

Section 13: Grant and Conditions of Bail

Sub-section (1) makes a number of changes to s 3(6) of the BA 1976 to enable bail conditions to be imposed for a defendant's own protection or welfare, in the same circumstances that he might have been remanded in custody for that purpose.

Sub-section (4) amends para 5 of Part II of Sched 1 to the BA 1976 so that, where a defendant charged with a non-imprisonable offence is arrested under s 7, bail may be refused only if the court is satisfied that there are substantial grounds for believing that if released on bail (whether subject to conditions or not) he would fail to surrender to custody, commit an offence while on bail, or interfere with witnesses or otherwise obstruct the course of justice.

Section 14: Offences Committed on Bail

Sub-section (1) requires the court to refuse bail to an adult defendant who was on bail in criminal proceedings at the date of the offence, unless the court is satisfied that there is no significant risk that he would commit an offence if released on bail. This replaces para 2A of Part I of Sched 1 to the BA 1976 (which provides that a defendant need not be granted bail if he was on bail at the time of the alleged offence).

Section 15: Absconding by Persons Released on Bail

Sub-section (1) requires the court to refuse bail to an adult defendant who failed without reasonable cause to surrender to custody in answer to bail in the same proceedings, unless the court is satisfied that there is no significant risk that he would so fail if released.

Sub-section (2) requires the court, in the case of defendants under 18, to give particular weight to the fact that they have failed to surrender to bail, in assessing the risk of future absconding.

Sub-section (3) disapplies s 127 of the Magistrates' Court Act 1980 (which prevents summary proceedings from being instituted more than six months after the commission of an offence) in respect of offences under s 6 of the Bail Act, and instead provides that such an offence may not be tried unless an information is laid either within six months of the commission of the offence, or within three months of the defendant's surrender to custody, arrest or court appearance in respect of that offence. This will ensure that a defendant cannot escape being prosecuted for the Bail Act offence merely by succeeding in absconding for more than six months.

Section 16: Appeal to the Crown Court

Section 16 creates a new right of appeal to the Crown Court against the imposition by magistrates of certain conditions of bail. The conditions that may be challenged in this way are requirements relating to residence, provision of a surety or giving a security, curfew, electronic monitoring or contact. This complements the removal by s 17 of the existing High Court power to entertain such appeals.

Section 18: Appeal by the Prosecution

Section 18 amends s 1 of the Bail (Amendment) Act 1993 so that the prosecution's right of appeal to the Crown Court against a decision by magistrates to grant bail is extended to cover all imprisonable offences.

Section 19: Drug Users: Restriction on Bail

Evidence accepted by the Home Office suggests that there is a link between drug addiction and offending. In addition, it is widely accepted that many abusers of drugs fund their misuse through acquisitive crime. There is thus a real concern that, if such offenders who have been charged with an imprisonable offence are placed on bail, they will merely reoffend in order to fund their drug use.

Under this section, an alleged offender aged 18 or over, who has been charged with an imprisonable offence, will not be granted bail (unless the court is satisfied that there is no significant risk of his committing an offence while on bail) where the three conditions below exist:

● there is drug test evidence that the person has a specified Class A drug in his body (by way of a lawful test obtained under s 63B of PACE or s 161 of this Act); and

● either the offence is a drugs offence associated with a specified Class A drug or the court is satisfied that there are substantial grounds for believing that the misuse of a specified Class A drug caused or contributed to that offence or provided its motivation; and

● the person does not agree to undergo an assessment as to his dependency upon or propensity to misuse specified Class A drugs, or has undergone such an assessment but does not agree to participate in any relevant follow-up action offered.

The assessment will be carried out by a suitably qualified person, who will have received training in the assessment of drug problems. If an assessment or follow-up is proposed and agreed to, it will be a condition of bail that it be undertaken. This provision can only apply in areas where appropriate assessment and treatment facilities are in place.

8.4 PLEA BARGAINING

'Plea bargaining' has been defined as 'the practice whereby the accused enters a plea of guilty in return for which he will be given some consideration that results in a sentence concession' (Baldwin and McConville, *Negotiated Justice: Pressures on Defendants to Plead Guilty* (1977)). In practice, this can refer to:

● a situation either where there has been a plea arrangement for the accused to plead guilty to a lesser charge than the one with which he is charged (for example, charged with murder, agrees to plead guilty to manslaughter). This is sometimes called 'charge bargaining'; or

- where there is simply a sentencing discount available on a plea of guilty by the accused. This has been given statutory force by s 144 CJA 2003, which requires a court to award a reduced sentence for a timely guilty plea.

Plea bargaining is widespread in some common law countries, for example, the United States.

In the *Marine Hose* case (2007), the Office of Fair Trading (OFT) brought its first charges under the Enterprise Act 2002 when it charged three businessmen with cartel offences. The men were arrested in Texas in May 2007. As part of a landmark plea bargaining agreement with the US Department of Justice, the three men were allowed to return to the United Kingdom to face charges. Under the terms of that agreement, the men pleaded guilty to violations of US antitrust law following which their sentences in the United States were deferred so that they could return to the United Kingdom to plead guilty to charges under the Enterprise Act. The men served their prison sentences in the United Kingdom (B Summers, 'Update on Recent Fraud Cases' (2008) 29(11) Comp Law 342–44).

Summers has cogently presented this case as an example of the importance of plea bargaining in the US criminal justice system. This differs from the informal post-charge discussions between the prosecution and the defence which currently take place in England and Wales. In 2008, the Attorney General's office launched a consultation on the *Introduction of a Plea Negotiation Framework for Fraud Cases in England and Wales* to examine the possible advantages in offering parties to fraud cases the opportunity to reach a court-sanctioned agreement at an early stage.

The consultation presented a framework for plea negotiation whereby the parties enter into pre-charge discussions with a view to agreeing a basis of plea. It envisaged discussions taking place on the presumption that nothing said by the suspect could be used against him in any subsequent proceedings (although a written agreement to the contrary would be possible). The framework included guidelines for prosecutors on when to accept a guilty plea. If accepted, the basis of plea would then be recorded in a written plea agreement to go before the Crown Court at the defendant's first appearance. The judge could accept or reject the agreement, or defer a decision pending further information; he could also give an indication of a maximum sentence. (Summers, 'Update' (2008), as above.) Summers raised the question of whether the framework was actually in the public interest. Of particular importance is that, as drafted, the framework did not differentiate between corporations and individuals. This meant that the unavailability of legal aid pre-charge could leave unfunded individuals in a position where they do not have access to independent legal advice.

On 5 May 2009 a system of plea negotiation in fraud cases was introduced by the Attorney General (the guidelines for prosecutors are available at: http://www.sfo.gov.uk/media/111905/ag_s_guidelines_on_plea_discussions_in_cases_of_serious_or_complex_fraud.pdf). The General Principles for prosecutors undertaking plea negotiations are as follows:

1. In conducting plea discussions and presenting a plea agreement to the court, the prosecutor must act openly, fairly and in the interests of justice.

2. Acting in the interests of justice means ensuring that the plea agreement reflects the seriousness and extent of the offending, gives the court adequate sentencing powers, and enables the court, the public and the victims to have confidence in the outcome. The prosecutor must consider carefully the impact of a proposed plea or basis of plea on the community and the victim, and on the prospects of successfully prosecuting any other person implicated in the offending. The prosecutor must not agree to a reduced basis of plea which is misleading, untrue or illogical.

3. Acting fairly means respecting the rights of the defendant and of any other person who is being or may be prosecuted in relation to the offending. The prosecutor must not put improper pressure on a defendant in the course of plea discussions, for example, by exaggerating the strength of the case in order to persuade the defendant to plead guilty, or to plead guilty on a particular basis.

4. Acting openly means being transparent with the defendant, the victim and the court. The prosecutor must:

    - ensure that a full and accurate record of the plea discussions is prepared and retained;

    - ensure that the defendant has sufficient information to enable him or her to play an informed part in the plea discussions;

    - communicate with the victim before accepting a reduced basis of plea, wherever it is practicable to do so, so that the position can be explained; and

    - ensure that the plea agreement placed before the court fully and fairly reflects the matters agreed. The prosecutor must not agree additional matters with the defendant which are not recorded in the plea agreement and made known to the court.

8.4.1   R v TURNER (1970)

A plea of guilty by the accused must be made freely. The accused must only be advised to plead guilty if he has committed the crime in question. In *R v Turner* (1970), Lord Parker CJ set out guidelines on plea bargaining. He stated that:

(1)   it may sometimes be the duty of counsel to give strong advice to the accused that a plea of guilty with remorse is a mitigating factor which might enable the court to give a lesser sentence (displays of remorse following a not-guilty plea tend to be unconvincing);

(2)   the accused must ultimately make up his or her own mind as to how to plead;

(3) there should be open access to the trial judge and counsel for both sides should attend each meeting, preferably in open court; and

(4) the judge should never indicate the sentence which he is minded to impose, nor should he ever indicate that on a plea of guilty he would impose one sentence, but that on a conviction following a plea of not guilty he would impose a severer sentence.

The judge could say what sentence he would impose on a plea of guilty (where, for example, he has read the depositions and antecedents) but without mentioning what he would do if the accused were convicted after pleading not guilty. Even this would be wrong, however, as the accused might take the judge to be intimating that a more severe sentence would follow upon conviction after a guilty plea. The only exception to this rule is where a judge says that the sentence will take a particular form, following conviction, whether there has been a plea of guilty or not guilty.

8.4.2 COURT OF APPEAL PRACTICE DIRECTION

These guidelines were subsequently embodied in a Court of Appeal *Practice Direction* [1976] Crim LR 561, which are now included in *Practice Direction (Criminal: Consolidated)* [2002] 1 WLR 2870, para 45. A number of difficulties have been experienced in applying these principles. Perhaps the greatest problem has resulted from the fact that, although the principles state (No 45.4) that a judge should never say that a sentence passed after a conviction would be more severe than one passed after a guilty plea, it is a generally known rule that guilty pleas lead to lesser sentences (and see above for the effect of s 144 CJA 2003). In *R v Cain* (1976), it was stressed that, in general, defendants should realise that guilty pleas attract lesser sentences. Lord Widgery said, 'Any accused person who does not know about it should know about it.' The difficulty is that the trial judge must not mention it; otherwise he could be construed as exerting pressure on the accused to plead guilty.

In *R v Turner*, the defendant pleaded not guilty to a charge of theft. He had previous convictions and during an adjournment he was advised by counsel in strong terms to change his plea. After having spoken with the judge, whom the defendant knew, counsel advised that in his opinion a plea of guilty would result in a non-custodial sentence, whereas if he persisted with a not-guilty plea and thereby attacked police witnesses, there was a real possibility of receiving a custodial sentence. The defendant changed his plea to guilty and then appealed on the ground that he did not have a free choice in changing his plea. His appeal was allowed on the basis that he might have formed the impression that the views being expressed to him by his counsel were those of the judge, particularly as it was known by the accused that counsel had just returned from seeing the judge when he gave his advice to the accused.

The advantages for the prosecution in gaining a guilty plea are obvious, but justice demands that the court should be able to pass a proper sentence consistent with the gravity of the accused's actions, and if a plea is accepted, then the defendant can only be sentenced on the basis of the crime that he has admitted. The Farquharson Committee on the Role of Prosecuting Counsel thought that there is a general right for the prosecution to offer no evidence in respect of any particular charge, but that where the judge's opinion is sought on whether it is desirable to reassure the public at large that the right course is being taken, counsel must abide by the judge's decision. Where the judge thinks that counsel's view to proceed is wrong, the trial can be halted until the DPP has been consulted and given the judge's comments. In the notorious case of *R v Sutcliffe* (1981), the 'Yorkshire Ripper' case, the prosecution and defence had agreed that Sutcliffe would plead guilty to manslaughter on the grounds of diminished responsibility, but the trial judge rejected that agreement and, after consultations with the DPP, Sutcliffe was eventually found guilty of murder.

8.4.3   *R v PITMAN* (1991)

The extent of the difficulties in framing rules on plea bargaining which achieve clarity and fairness can be judged by the remark of Lord Lane CJ in the case of *R v Pitman* [1991] 1 All ER 468 at 470:

> There seems to be a steady flow of appeals to this court arising from visits by counsel to the judge in his private room. No amount of criticism and no amount of warnings and no amount of exhortation seems to be able to prevent this from happening.

In this case, on counsel's advice, the appellant pleaded not guilty to causing death by reckless driving. On Cup Final day in 1989, he had driven, having been drinking all afternoon, in a car without a rear view mirror. He had crashed into another car, killing one of its passengers, while having double the permitted level of alcohol in his blood.

During the trial, the judge called both counsel to his room and stated that he did not think there was a defence to the charge. Counsel for the appellant explained that although the appellant had admitted that his carelessness caused the accident, the advice to plead not guilty was based on the fact that the prosecution might not be able to prove the necessary recklessness. The trial judge replied that the appellant's plea was a matter for the appellant himself and not counsel, and that if the appellant accepted responsibility for the accident, he ought to plead guilty and if he did so, he would receive 'substantial credit' when it came to sentencing.

Counsel for the appellant then discussed this with the appellant who changed his plea to guilty and was sentenced to nine months' imprisonment and disqualified from driving for four years. His appeal was allowed as the judge had put undue pressure on the appellant and his counsel to change his plea to guilty. The remarks passed had suggested that his chances of acquittal were slight if he pleaded not guilty and that if he was found guilty, he would certainly be sentenced to imprisonment. Lord Lane CJ emphasised that a judge should not initiate discussions in private and that where, at the behest of counsel, they are absolutely necessary, they should be recorded by shorthand or on a recording device.

Another problem here concerns framing the guidelines so that they are sufficiently permissive to allow counsel access to the judge in his private room in deserving instances, but avoiding the problems of confidentiality. As Mustill LJ said in *R v Harper-Taylor and Barker* (1988): 'The need to solve an immediate practical problem may combine with the more relaxed atmosphere of the private room to blur the formal outlines of the trial.' There is a risk that counsel and solicitors may hear something said to the judge which they would rather not hear, putting them into a state of conflict between their duties to their clients and their obligations to maintain the confidentiality of the private room. Reviewing the current state of the law, Curran has written that the effect of cases like *R v Bird* (1977) and *R v Agar* (1990) (the latter not a plea bargaining case but one that hinged on a judge's ruling in his private room as complied with by counsel to the appellant's detriment) is that defence counsel has a duty to disclose to his client any observations made by the judge in his room, which significantly affect the client's case, whether or not the judge expresses them to be made confidentially.

The difficulties in this area of law stem largely not from deficient rules, but rather from the wish that the rules should achieve diverse aims. As Zander has observed, the fundamental problem is that the Court of Appeal wants to have it both ways: 'On the one hand, it wants defendants to appreciate that, if they plead guilty, they will receive a lesser sentence. On the other hand, it does not want judges to provide defendants with solid information as to how great the discount will be.'

8.5 THE SENTENCING PROCESS, THE SEPARATION OF POWERS AND THE HRA

One area of criminal law that throws the relationship between the executive and the judiciary into particularly sharp focus is that of sentencing individuals who have been found guilty of particular offences. It is equally one that involves the interplay of judicial review, the ECHR and the HRA.

8.5.1 AUTOMATIC LIFE SENTENCE UNDER S 2 OF THE CRIME (SENTENCES) ACT 1997

In 1997, immediately prior to the election of that year, Parliament, in the guise of the former Conservative Home Secretary Michael Howard, required the provision of automatic life sentences for those found guilty of a second serious offence. Thus, s 2 of the Crime (Sentences) Act 1997 required judges to pass indeterminate life sentences for those found guilty of a range of offences including attempted murder, rape, manslaughter, wounding, causing grievous bodily harm with intent and robbery with a real or imitation firearm, where the guilty person had been previously convicted of another offence on the list. Given their discontent with the provisions for mandatory sentencing in relation to convictions for murder, it can be appreciated that many of the judiciary, led by the late Lord Justice Taylor, saw the Act as a dangerous party-politicisation of the criminal justice system and an unwarranted interference by the legislature with the scope of judicial power and discretion, and were vociferous in their opposition to it.

However, even when the Act came into force, it still left some scope for judicial discretion whereby they could identify such 'exceptional circumstances' as could justify the non-application of the mandatory sentence. Until the implementation of the HRA, the question was as to what properly constituted such exceptional circumstances, and different courts tended to reach different conclusions of a more or less liberal nature. Thus, in *R v Stephens* (2000), the defendant, who already had a previous serious conviction, was found guilty of grievous bodily harm with intent and was consequently given an automatic life sentence. At his trial, the prosecution had offered, and Stephens had rejected, the opportunity to plead guilty to a lesser charge, which would not have led to the imposition of the automatic life sentence. When it emerged that his counsel had not advised him as to the possible consequences of his decision to defend the more serious charge, the Court of Appeal held that that fact amounted to sufficient exceptional circumstances to quash the life sentence. However, in *R v Turner* (2000), where the defendant was also found guilty of causing grievous bodily harm with intent, the court felt obliged to impose the automatic life sentence, even though a period of some 30 years had elapsed since his previous conviction for manslaughter at the age of 22. The court could find no exceptional circumstances.

This unsatisfactory situation was resolved by reference to the HRA in *R v Offen and Others* (2001), in which the Court of Appeal considered five related claims that the imposition of automatic life sentences was contrary to the ECHR. The facts of Offen's case provide a context for the decision.

Offen had robbed a building society using a toy gun. The cashiers thought the gun was real and placed £960 in his bag. During the robbery, he was nervous and shaking, and apologised to the staff as he left the building. A customer grabbed the bag with the money in it and gave it back to the building society. When he was arrested, Offen admitted the offence, but claimed he had not taken the medication he needed to deal with his schizophrenia. His previous conviction for robbery had been committed in similar circumstances. At his trial, he was subsequently sentenced automatically to life imprisonment.

In delivering its judgment, the Court of Appeal was extremely circumspect in considering its relationship with Parliament and its new powers under the HRA. It was equally firm, however, in its removal of the mandatory element from this aspect of the sentencing process.

As regards its relationship with Parliament, the court stressed that it was of the greatest importance to bear in mind Parliament's intention in establishing the automatic life sentences. In the present instance, it understood that intention as being to protect the public against a person who had committed two serious offences. The Court of Appeal went on, however, to draw the conclusion that, on the basis of that concentration on the importance of protecting the public, it could be assumed that the Act was not intended to apply to anyone who did not pose a future risk.

Focusing on the future danger posed by the offender to the public rather than on the mere fact of their having committed two offences would allow the court to decide each case on the basis of its own particular facts, and if the facts of any particular case showed that the statutory assumption was misplaced, then that would constitute exceptional circumstances for the purposes of s 2 of the 1997 Act. As examples, the committing of different offences, the age of the offender and the lapse of time between the offences could give rise to exceptional circumstances in the context of a particular case that could override the assumption as to the imposition of the mandatory life sentence.

The court's identification of Parliament's intention in passing the Act cannot be doubted. The supposed corollary of this intention is, however, much less certain. However, its process of logic allowed the Court of Appeal to interpret the Act in such a way as to support its own preferred approach, which was effectively to remove the automatic element in the sentencing process and to reintroduce an element of judicial discretion. The foregoing interpretation of the Act was supported by the court's marshalling of the HRA. In their judgments, the three members of the Court of Appeal stated that s 2 of the 1997 Act did not contravene Arts 3 and 5 of the ECHR so long as, and only to the extent that, exceptional circumstances were construed in such a way that it did not result in offenders being sentenced to life imprisonment when they did not constitute a significant risk to the public: that is, as the Court of Appeal had already decided it should be construed. In reaching this conclusion, the Court of Appeal can be seen to be employing s 3 of the HRA, in that it was interpreting the primary legislation of the Crime (Sentences) Act 1997 in such a way as to make it compatible with the ECHR rights. In so doing, the judiciary achieved its preferred end without having to issue a declaration of incompatibility and without having to rely on the government introducing an amendment to its own Powers of Criminal Courts (Sentencing) Act 2000, s 109 of which had re-enacted s 2 of the 1997 Act.

Section 109 of the Powers of Criminal Courts (Sentencing) Act 2000 has itself been repealed by s 332 of the Criminal Justice Act 2003. Parliament has replaced the relatively simple provision of two serious offences leading to an 'automatic' life sentence with an apparently more flexible concept of dangerousness. By s 229 of the Criminal Justice Act 2003, the courts are obliged to consider whether an offender has fallen into a category of dangerousness by virtue of being convicted of a 'specified offence' and it requires the courts to consider degrees of risks of serious harm from further offences by such an offender. A substantial amount of discretion appears to be given to the sentencing court by s 229:

229 The assessment of dangerousness

(1) This section applies where—

    (a) a person has been convicted of a specified offence, and

    (b) it falls to a court to assess under any of sections 225 to 228 whether there is a significant risk to members of the public of serious harm occasioned by the commission by him of further such offences.

(2) . . . the court in making the assessment referred to in subsection (1)(b)—

(a) must take into account all such information as is available to it about the nature and circumstances of the offence,

[(aa) may take into account all such information as is available to it about the nature and circumstances of any other offences of which the offender has been convicted by a court anywhere in the world,]

(b) may take into account any information which is before it about any pattern of behaviour of which [any of the offences mentioned in paragraph (a) or (aa)] forms part, and

(c) may take into account any information about the offender which is before it.

[(2A) The reference in subsection (2)(aa) to a conviction by a court includes a reference to—

(a) a finding of guilt in service disciplinary proceedings, and

(b) a conviction of a service offence within the meaning of the Armed Forces Act 2006 ('conviction' here including anything that under section 376(1) and (2) of that Act is to be treated as a conviction).]

(3) . . .

(4) . . .

[Amendment
Sub-s (2): words omitted repealed by the Criminal Justice and Immigration Act 2008, ss 17(1), (2)(a), 149, Sch 28, Pt 2, Date in force: 14 July 2008: see SI 2008/1586, art 2(1), Sch 1, paras 8, 50(1), (2)(c).]

However, when the section is read more closely it can be seen that – when sentencing 18-year-olds and older defendants (the majority of the cases) – the courts will be obliged to make assumptions about the presence of serious risk in sub-s (2). See sub-s (3) – 'the court MUST assume,' and so on. Thus the courts are bound by a similar test as under s 109 of the Powers of Criminal Courts (Sentencing) Act 2000.

The new provisions came into force for offences committed after 4 April 2005.

8.5.2 MANDATORY LIFE SENTENCES IN RELATION TO MURDER

When the death penalty for murder was removed in 1965, it was replaced by a mandatory life sentence, that is, if an individual is found guilty of murder, the court has no
alternative but to sentence them to a period of life imprisonment. By definition, a 'life
sentence' is for an indeterminate period, but the procedure is for a period to be specified, which the person must serve before they can be considered for release on parole.
The problematic question of who sets this tariff is considered below. The judiciary have
been consistently opposed to this fettering of their discretion; a number of leading
judges, including the past Lord Chief Justices Bingham and Taylor, have spoken out
against it, and in 1993 Lord Chief Justice Lane led a committee that recommended that
the mandatory sentence be removed. In 1989, a Select Committee of the House of Lords,
appointed to report on murder and life imprisonment, recommended the abolition of
the mandatory life sentence. Lord Lane, formerly Lord Chief Justice, chaired a
Committee on the Penalty for Homicide, which also produced a critical report in 1993:

> (1) The mandatory life sentence for murder is founded on the assumption
> that murder is a crime of such unique heinousness that the offender forfeits
> for the rest of his existence his right to be set free. (2) That assumption is a
> fallacy. It arises from the divergence between the legal definition of murder
> and that which the lay public believes to be murder. (3) The common law
> definition of murder embraces a wide range of offences, some of which are
> truly heinous, some of which are not. (4) The majority of murder cases,
> though not those which receive the most publicity, fall into the latter cate-
> gory. (5) It is logically and jurisprudentially wrong to require judges to
> sentence all categories of murderer in the same way, regardless of the partic-
> ular circumstances of the case before them. (6) It is logically and constitu-
> tionally wrong to require the distinction between the various types of murder
> to be decided (and decided behind the scenes) by the executive as is, gener-
> ally speaking, the case at present . . .

As their Lordships correctly pointed out, there can be degrees of heinousness, even in
regard to murder, and not all of those convicted deserve to be sentenced to life imprisonment. Mercy killers surely should not be treated in the same way as serial killers. This
desire of the judges to remove the restriction in their sentencing power has, however, run
up against the wish of politicians to be seen as tough on crime, or at least not soft on
crime.

The uncomfortable relationship between criminal justice and party politics can
be seen in the conviction for murder of Norfolk farmer Tony Martin in April 2000.
Martin had used a shotgun to shoot two people who had broken into his farmhouse.
One was injured and the other, 16-year-old Fred Barras, was killed. Martin was charged
with murder and at his trial, evidence was introduced to show that he had lain in wait for
his victims, had set traps in his house and had used an illegal pump-action shotgun to

shoot Barras in the back as he was attempting to run away. By a majority of 10:2 the jury found him guilty of murder and, as required, the judge sentenced him to life imprisonment. Much of the press considered the sentence to be outrageously severe on a man whom they portrayed as merely protecting his property against the depredations of lawless louts. (It has to be stated that Barras and his accomplice did have 114 previous convictions between them.) In focusing attention on the right of individuals to use force to protect their property – which, in any case, they already had so long as they did not use more than reasonable force – the press displaced attention from where it could best be focused. Had the court not been required to pass a mandatory sentence, then it would have been able to pass a more suitable sentence, if that had been appropriate in the circumstances. The press, however, would not countenance the granting of such discretionary sentencing power to the courts which, in other circumstances, they persistently characterise as being out of touch and dangerously soft on criminals.

The subsequent provision of s 76 of the Criminal Justice and Immigration Act 2008 did no more than provide a gloss on the existing law of self-defence. It maintained the existing common law test established in *Palmer v R* (1971), to the effect that the defence is only available to someone if they honestly believed it was necessary to use force and if the degree of force used was not disproportionate in the circumstances as they viewed them. Consequently a person who uses force is to be judged subjectively, on the basis of the circumstances as they saw them, and in the heat of the moment they will not be expected to have judged exactly what action was called for, and that a degree of latitude may be given to a person who only did what they honestly or instinctively thought was necessary.

In *R v Hussain* (2010) Munir Hussain had discovered three masked men in his house. The burglars tied up and threatened to kill him and his family. However, Hussain's son managed to escape and told his uncle what had happened. When help arrived, the intruders ran away, but Hussain and his brother chased and caught one of them. He was Walid Salem, a criminal with more than 50 previous convictions. The brothers then subjected Salem to what the judge described as a 'dreadful, violent attack'.

The revenge attack left Salem with a permanent brain injury after he was struck with a cricket bat so hard that it broke into three pieces. At their trial it was decided that the brothers' reaction was disproportionate and Munir Hussain was sentenced to 30 months' detention and his brother to 39 months' detention. The case caused a furore in the press and eventually, on appeal, Hussain and his brother were given suspended sentences on the ground that the assault on Salem was 'totally out of character'.

The coalition government currently has plans to revise s 76 of the Criminal Justice and Immigration Act 2008 in order to allow home owners to use disproportionate force against intruders. It remains to be seen whether these plans will be implemented.

A case study: women and infanticide

The issue of mandatory life sentences for those convicted of murder came to prominence in relation to Sally Clark, a mother convicted and subsequently exonerated of the killing of her two infant children, one of whom died in 1996 and the other of whom died in 1998. Originally convicted on the spurious statistical evidence of an expert witness, she was released by the Court of Appeal when her husband discovered evidence that the second of their children had been suffering from a severe, and probably terminal, bacterial infection that had entered his cerebral and spinal fluid. Astonishingly, the existence of the infection had been known by the prosecution pathologist, but was never revealed to the defence.

It may be claimed, as it has been previously when other miscarriages of justice have come to light, that the outcome of the Sally Clark case demonstrates the essential validity of the English legal system. It should be emphasised, however, that the result only emerged due to the tenacity, skill and good luck of her husband. The conduct of the original case actually highlights problems in the reliance on the testimony of expert witnesses and the deficiency in the information provided to the defence by those involved in the prosecution.

The case also raises the general issue of women convicted of killing their babies. Under the Infanticide Act 1938, where a woman kills her child of under 12 months, what would ordinarily be murder is reduced to manslaughter if, at the time of the killing, 'the balance of her mind was disturbed by reason of her not having fully recovered from the effect of giving birth to the child or by reason of the effect of lactation'. As a result of this reduction in the severity of the charge, the judge, in the case of a conviction, will be in a position to exercise discretion in the sentence handed down. However, where women refuse to plead guilty to the lesser charge of manslaughter on the basis of their mental condition, they have on conviction to face the full force of the law in the form of the mandatory life sentence for murder. Following the Sally Clark appeal case, it is not unlikely that some of them had been convicted on doubtful evidence.

In June 2003, Trupti Patel was accused of killing her three babies, none of whom survived beyond the age of three months. All three died suddenly in separate incidents between 1997 and 2001. Although expert evidence for the prosecution claimed that the deaths pointed to the mother having killed her children, another expert for the defence claimed that the three deaths, rather than pointing to guilt, strongly suggested that there was a genetic disorder in her family that could account for the sudden deaths of the children. This suggestion was supported by evidence relating to the unexplained deaths of a number of Mrs Patel's maternal grandmother's children. The jury unanimously declared Mrs Patel innocent of killing her children.

In December 2003, the Court of Appeal overturned the murder conviction of Angela Cannings, who had been found guilty of smothering two of her babies, seven-week-old Jason in 1991 and 18-week-old Matthew in 1999, a previous child having died at the age of 13 weeks in 1989. Once again, the evidence for the original conviction had been produced by the same expert witness for the prosecution, Professor Sir Roy Meadow, and once again the evidence for the overturning of the conviction, on the basis of the likelihood of a underlying genetic disorder in the children, was provided by Professor Michael Patton. Angela Cannings had served 20 months of a mandatory life sentence because she would not admit to something she had not done. At her original trial, Mrs Justice Hallett, the presiding judge, had had no choice but to jail her for life, but clearly expressed her dissatisfaction with the situation (*The Guardian*, 14 May 2002):

> There was no evidence before the court that suggested there was anything wrong with you when you killed your children. I have no doubt that for a woman like you to suffocate these babies there must have been something seriously wrong with you. You wanted these babies and you cherished them.
>
> It's no coincidence, in my view, that you committed these acts in the weeks after their births. It is not my decision when you will be released, but I intend to make it known in my remarks that in my view you will never be a threat to anyone in future.

Such a statement from the judge, although intended to be sympathetic, reflects a *post hoc* rationalisation, on spurious medical grounds, of Cannings' supposed actions. However, it also reflects the unwillingness of the court to countenance any challenge to the authority of the mistaken male expert. There is no doubt that some women may be serving life sentences for actions carried out in a state of *postpartum* depression, a well-recognised and potentially severely debilitating medical condition, and should not be serving such long-term sentences. However, the crucial point that the *Cannings* case demonstrates is that many women were locked up, or had their children taken away from them, on the testimony of an expert of extremely questionable authority.

The Court of Appeal gave its reason for quashing Angela Cannings' conviction in January 2004. In so doing, Judge LJ recognised that medical science was 'still at the frontiers of knowledge' about unexplained infant deaths and stated that prosecutions should not be proceeded with where experts disputed the cause of death, 'unless there is additional cogent evidence'.

Following the *Cannings* judgment, the Attorney General announced a review of the 258 cases in the previous 10 years in which parents were convicted of killing a child under two, and 15 pending prosecutions involving unexplained infant deaths. However, in addition to those women who had been wrongly locked up as a consequence of at least controversial expert evidence, there were also thousands of cases in which mothers suspected of harming their children, but who had not been prosecuted, had had their children removed by court order in care proceedings brought by local authorities. In many of the cases, mothers thought to have harmed an older child had their subsequent children taken into care at birth. Most of the children concerned were probably fostered, but many would have been legally adopted and become parts of their new families. The necessary legal proceedings to remove the children from their mothers were conducted through the family justice system, which operates on the lower civil standard of proof: the balance of probabilities.

Also in January 2004, the Solicitor General, Harriet Harman, confirmed that civil cases in which children had been taken into care would be reviewed along with those cases that had resulted in criminal prosecution. In a statement to the House of Commons, Ms Harman said (*The Guardian*, 21 January 2004):

> We are not in a position to say in how many care proceedings the evidence of experts was decisive. We will make sure that we recognise that not only injustices done in the criminal justice system but any potential injustices in care proceedings are identified and acted on. We should recognise that for women who have lost a child and then have had another child taken away [. . .] prison is nothing of a penalty compared to the terrible suffering that they have endured. While we are getting on straight away to the issue of those in prison and criminal processes, we bear in mind the absolute, utmost gravity and seriousness of those whose injustice is not in the hands of the criminal justice system but as a result of the family justice system.

In preparation for the review, the Solicitor General consulted Dame Elizabeth Butler-Sloss, President of the High Court Family Division, and the Children's Minister, Margaret Hodge, as to how the review of care cases could be handled. Subsequently, in February 2004, Hodge announced that the number of reviews in relation to civil cases would be in 'the low hundreds'. In her statement she said (*The Guardian*, 24 February 2004):

> I recognise [. . .] there will be concerns in cases where an adoption order followed on from a care order made on the basis of disputed expert medical evidence. But to suggest that cases could be reopened would give false hope to those who might wish to argue that the original adoption was based on flawed evidence.

It is extremely rare for the courts to reopen the case of a child who has been officially adopted. An adoption order will only be set aside in the most exceptional of circumstances, for example, if there had been fraud or some procedural error in the proceedings. As family courts are required to treat the child's best interests as the paramount principle, they will rarely move a child who is settled and well cared for. Such is the law and perhaps there is validity in it, but it provides a resolution that can never have closure for those concerned, particularly the parents of children the law has unfairly taken away from them. It also resonates discordantly with the significantly less severe sentences received by men who kill their partners and plead guilty to the less severe crime of manslaughter, especially when it is supported by alleged but unsubstantiated claims of provocation or temporary diminished responsibility.

8.5.3   SENTENCE TARIFFS

In relation to mandatory life sentences, the Home Secretary formerly had the power to set what is known as the tariff, whereas in relation to other, non-mandatory life sentences, it was for the trial judge to set the tariff. The tariff was that part of the sentence that must be served before the person serving the prison sentence could be considered for release, on licence, by the Parole Board. Release after the tariff period was not automatic and depended on the decision of the Parole Board, which in turn depended on the behaviour of the individual while in prison and the extent to which they posed a threat to the public. The justification of the tariff was that it served to establish a minimum period of punishment and retribution. The question, however, was whether such a period should be determined by a member of the executive, the Home Secretary, or by the judiciary. As has been stated, the working out of this question involved an interplay of judicial review, the ECHR and the HRA, and demonstrated the way in which the HRA increased the powers of the courts in relation to the executive in a way that judicial review could never encompass.

There had been substantial criticism of the process of setting the tariff. In 1996, the Home Affairs Select Committee of the House of Commons took evidence and deliberated on the relevant issues. Their report (*Murder: The Mandatory Life Sentence*) recommended that the tariff and release decisions be removed from the Home Secretary and left with the trial judge and the Parole Board.

Before examining the situation in England, it should be noted that in Scotland, the Convention Rights (Compliance) (Scotland) Act 2001 now provides that in the case of mandatory life sentences, the trial judge fixes the 'punishment part' of the sentence, on the expiry of which the Parole Board decides on possible release on licence. The test applied to determine suitability for release is identical to that applied to discretionary life prisoners in England and Wales, namely, that the Parole Board is satisfied that the prisoner does not present a substantial risk of reoffending in a manner that is dangerous to life or limb, or of committing serious sexual offences.

The situation is similar in Northern Ireland: there, the Life Sentences (Northern Ireland) Order 2001 provides that the trial judge decides the tariff for a mandatory life prisoner and that release after serving the tariff is determined by Life Sentence Review Commissioners (with a status and functions very similar to those of the Parole Board operating in England and Wales). The test applied by the Commissioners is one of protection of the public from 'serious harm', this term meaning the risk of harm from violent or sexual offences.

There are in effect three distinct elements in a mandatory life sentence: the minimum term, the period after the minimum term has been served until the recommendation of the Parole Board to release the person on licence, and the overhanging possibility that the person might be recalled to prison if they breach the conditions of their release on licence at a later date. The first part – the minimum term – is punitive. The other elements are preventive and intended for public protection.

However, the question still arises as to what should happen where there is no need for any preventive element to a sentence. Precisely such situations arose in the related cases of *R v Lichniak* (2002) and *R v Pyrah* (2002). The two individuals concerned had been found guilty of murder, but in both cases the sentencing judges had clearly stated that neither of them represented a future danger to the community, nor was there any likelihood of their committing such offences in the future. Both were nonetheless subject to the mandatory life sentence for murder and appealed unsuccessfully to both the Court of Appeal and the House of Lords. Both courts held that the imposition of the mandatory life sentence did not violate Arts 3 or 5 of the ECHR and that such sentences were neither arbitrary nor disproportionate.

The decision of the House of Lords is, to say the least, somewhat surprising, especially when it is compared with the decision of the Privy Council in *Reyes v the Queen* (2002). In *Reyes*, it was held that a mandatory death sentence, operative in the jurisdiction of Belize, amounted to inhuman and degrading punishment. Among the grounds for that decision was the fact that the mandatory nature of the sentence precluded proper judicial consideration of the appropriate penalty. Although the Privy Council did expressly limit its reasoning to the Belize legal system in *Reyes*, and although the death penalty does stand alone as the harshest of penalties, it is nonetheless arguable that the mandatory life sentence in the United Kingdom achieves a similar, if less severe, consequence in limiting proper judicial consideration of the appropriate sentence to apply in different circumstances. It is apparent in both the *Lichniak* and *Pyrah* cases that the judges deciding the sentences did not really think that life sentences were appropriate, yet they had no choice but to pass such sentences. Can the imposition of an inappropriate sentence be anything other than arbitrary and disproportionate?

As will be considered below, perhaps Lichniak and Pyrah were unfortunate in the timing of their appeals. Those appeals followed a number of highly sensitive decisions in which the courts had used their powers under the HRA to remove the powers of the Home Secretary to set the punitive tariff in mandatory life sentences. Perhaps, given the highly charged, not to say antagonistic, nature of the relationship between the courts and past Home Secretaries, removing the mandatory sentence altogether was a step too far for the courts, or at least a step further than they thought it wise to take under current political circumstances.

Juveniles

Just as in the cases of adults sentenced to a mandatory life sentence, so the Home Secretary used to have the power to set the tariff for juveniles sentenced to detention at Her Majesty's pleasure, that is, for an indeterminate period. However, in 1999, the European Court of Human Rights held that the exercise of that power by the Home Secretary was in contravention of the ECHR. The Home Secretary subsequently relinquished the power. The path to such a resolution is traced below.

In 1993, Jon Venables and Robert Thompson, two 10-year-old boys, were found guilty of the murder of two-year-old James Bulger. As juveniles, they were both sentenced, as required under s 53(1) of the Children and Young Persons Act (CYPA) 1933, to be detained at Her Majesty's pleasure. The trial judge recommended a tariff of eight years as an appropriate period for retribution and deterrence, although, on review, Lord Chief Justice Taylor recommended that the tariff should be increased to 10 years. However, the ultimate decision as to the length of the tariff lay with the then Conservative Home Secretary, Michael Howard. Given the particularly brutal manner of the killing, there was very considerable public interest in the case and the sentencing of the two boys. *The Sun* newspaper organised a public petition to the effect that they should be 'locked up for life' or serve at least 25 years. Some 306,000 people signed and submitted petitions to that effect to the Home Secretary, who ultimately decided that the tariff should be set at 15 years. Doubts were raised as to whether, in ignoring the recommendations of the judges in reaching his decision, the Home Secretary had taken a (party) political rather than quasi-judicial decision to assuage the concerns of potential voters by demonstrating a willingness to be tough on crime and criminals.

R v Secretary of State for the Home Department ex p Venables and Thompson (1997)

Lawyers for Venables and Thompson successfully sought judicial review of the Home Secretary's decision. On final appeal to the House of Lords (*Secretary of State for the Home Department v V (A Minor) and T (A Minor)* (1997)), the Home Secretary having lost all the previous cases, it was held that in setting the tariff at 15 years, he had not taken into account the welfare of the children as required by s 44 of the CYPA 1933. Additionally, the House of Lords stated that although the Home Secretary was entitled to take into account considerations of a public character, he must distinguish between legitimate public concern and mere public clamour. The Home Secretary had therefore misdirected himself and his decision was unlawful and should be quashed. The mechanism of judicial review therefore allowed the court to insist that, even if statute permitted the executive, in the form of the Home Secretary, to take sentencing decisions, in reaching any such decision, he must act in a judicial rather than a political manner. As Lord Steyn expressed it ([1997] 3 All ER 97 at 147):

> In fixing a tariff the Home Secretary is carrying out, contrary to the constitutional principle of the separation of powers between the executive and the judiciary, a classic judicial function.

What judicial review could not achieve, however, was either the removal of the Home Secretary's general power or the substitution of the courts' decision for his particular decision. It would still have been for the Home Secretary to take the new decision as to the appropriate tariff, had the Strasbourg Court not intervened before such a decision could be taken.

T v UK; V v UK (1999)

Lawyers for Thompson and Venables had appealed to the ECtHR, claiming that many aspects of their clients' cases had been conducted in a manner that was contrary to the ECHR. In December 1999, the ECtHR delivered its judgment and found that although many of the grounds for appeal were unfounded, the applicants had been denied a fair trial in accordance with Art 6 of the ECHR, as they had not been able to participate effectively in the proceedings. The reason for this finding was that the conduct of the case in the Crown Court must have been at times incomprehensible and frightening to the two boys, and it was not sufficient that they were represented by skilled and experienced lawyers. The Court also held that there had been a violation of Art 6 on the grounds that they had been denied a fair hearing by 'an independent and impartial tribunal'. The fixing of the tariff was tantamount to a sentencing procedure and therefore should have been exercised by an impartial judge, rather than a member of the executive, as the Home Secretary clearly was.

Subsequent to, and consequent upon, this decision, the Home Secretary, by this time the Labour politician Jack Straw, announced in March 2000 that legislation would be introduced to provide that tariffs for juveniles should be set by trial judges, in open court, in the same way as they are for adults sentenced to discretionary life sentences. Until that legislation was passed by parliament, the Home Secretary undertook that in using his statutory power, he would follow the recommendations of the Lord Chief Justice. In July 2000, Lord Chief Justice Woolf issued a practice statement setting out the criteria to be applied in establishing the tariff for juvenile offenders, and in October of that year, in line with those criteria, he set the tariff for both Thompson and Venables at eight years, which meant that they were immediately open to the operation of the normal parole system. Lord Woolf's decision did not go without challenge both in the media and the courts, a subsequent application for judicial review being rejected, but perhaps the last words on the matter should remain with him ([2001] 1 All ER 737 at 741):

> The one overriding mitigating feature of the offence is the age of the two boys when the crime was committed. However grave their crime, the fact remains that if that crime had been committed a few months earlier, when they were under 10, the boys could not have been tried or punished by the courts. In addition, account has to be taken of the fact that the last seven years, the period of their adolescence, has been passed in custody.

In January 2001, Dame Butler-Sloss, President of the Family Division, granted a permanent injunction banning the media in England from revealing any information about the new identities that Thompson and Venables would live under when they were eventually released from custody. In the light of the many threats that had been made against Thompson and Venables, the order, the first of its kind, was made on the basis of the HRA and Art 2 of the ECHR, in that the court held that it was necessary in order to protect their right to life.

In June 2001, the new Home Secretary, David Blunkett, announced that the Parole Board had agreed to the release on life licence of Thompson and Venables. On 2 March 2010 it was confirmed by the Ministry of Justice that Jon Venables had been recalled to custody following a breach of his licence conditions (see http://www.guardian.co.uk/uk/feedarticle/8970918).

Adults

As has been pointed out above, the regime that once applied to juveniles sentenced to indeterminate sentences also applied to adults who were sentenced to mandatory, but indeterminate, life sentences. Not only did the courts accept the Home Secretary's general power to determine a tariff, but, more contentiously, it had been accepted that the Home Secretary could set an 'all life' tariff in appropriate circumstances, such as those in *R v Secretary of State for the Home Department ex p Myra Hindley* (2000).

Hindley had been convicted of murder in 1966 and was sentenced as required by the Murder (Abolition of Death Penalty) Act 1965 to life imprisonment. As the House of Lords later stated, she was subject to a mandatory life sentence, itself subject to a discretionary executive power, vested in the Home Secretary to direct her release on licence at any time. The fact that the Home Secretary had such a discretion to release on licence led to the conclusion that he equally had the discretion not to release her, as long as he complied with the duty to reconsider his decision at reasonable intervals.

Hindley's case was decided prior to the coming into effect of the HRA and, therefore, in deciding it, the courts considered themselves not at liberty to apply that Act. Subsequently, in an interview in the journal the *New Statesman*, Lord Chief Justice Woolf, who, as the then Master of the Rolls, had sat in the Court of Appeal in the *Hindley* case, expressed the view that, in reaching his decision in that case, he had been constrained by the law as it then was. He did concede, however, that the HRA had altered the situation. Consequently, it was likely that in the future domestic courts would follow the ECtHR in *T v UK* and *V v UK*, and hold that it would be in breach of Art 6 for the Home Secretary to continue to determine the tariff in murder cases, on the grounds that such a procedure would be a denial of the right to a fair hearing by 'an independent and impartial tribunal'. Lord Woolf's interview was widely reported in the news media, with the strong implication that the courts in the future might sanction the release of Myra Hindley.

Subsequent to his interview in the *New Statesman*, however, the Lord Chief Justice seemed to reconsider the wisdom of a direct challenge to the Home Secretary's power to set the tariff in mandatory life sentences.

R v Secretary of State for the Home Department ex p Anderson and Taylor (2001)

In November 2001, two convicted murderers complained that the Home Secretary had fixed their tariffs higher than had been recommended by the judges at their trial: 20 years instead of 15 years for the first, and 30 years instead of 16 years for the second. They argued that it was incompatible with Art 6(1) of the ECHR for a member of the executive to carry out what was in fact a sentencing exercise. The Court of Appeal, made up of Lord Woolf and Simon Brown and Buxton LJJ, rejected their arguments. In doing so, the Court of Appeal's disapproving views on mandatory life sentences in general were expressed by Simon Brown LJ, who stated that ([2001] EWCA Civ 1968 para 56):

> [. . .] I accept of course that the mandatory life sentence is unique. But not all the offences for which it is imposed can be regarded as uniquely grave. Rather the spectrum is a wide one with multiple sadistic murders at one end and mercy killings at the other. Lifelong punitive detention will be appropriate only exceptionally.

Nonetheless, the Court of Appeal felt itself constrained by case law from the ECtHR and, in particular, the authority of *Wynne v UK* decided in 1994 and *T v UK* and *V v UK*.

In *Wynne*, the ECtHR decided that no violation arose under Art 5(4) in relation to the continued detention after release, and recall to prison, of a mandatory life prisoner convicted of an intervening offence of manslaughter, the tariff element of which had expired. The ECtHR held that the sentence constituted a *punishment* for life. In *T v UK* and *V v UK*, while citing the *Wynne* judgment, the ECtHR reiterated that an adult mandatory life sentence constituted punishment for life. On the face of those authorities, the Court of Appeal in *Anderson and Taylor* declined to challenge the Home Secretary's power in relation to mandatory life sentences.

Perhaps the Court of Appeal's reluctance to challenge the executive's power head-on was based on the realisation that, as the court noted, a decision on the same point was expected within the following year in the ECtHR (*Stafford v UK* (2002)). It is perhaps not overly cynical to suggest that the Court of Appeal adopted its conservative approach in the realisation that, in the context of the prevailing tense relationship between the Home Secretary and the courts, it was perhaps politic to leave the final decision to remove the Home Secretary's power to the ECtHR, which decision their Lordships clearly expected.

Stafford v UK (2002)

Derek Stafford was convicted of murder in 1967 and released on licence in April 1979. His licence required him to remain in the United Kingdom, but he left to live in South Africa. In April 1989 he was arrested in the United Kingdom, having returned from South Africa on a false passport. Although the possession of a false passport only led to a fine, he remained in custody due to the revocation of his life licence. He was released in March 1991, once again on a life licence. In 1994 he was convicted of conspiracy to forge travellers' cheques and passports and sentenced to six years' imprisonment. In 1996 the Parole Board recommended his release on life licence, having reached the conclusion that he did not present a danger of violent reoffending. The Secretary of State rejected the Board's recommendation. But for the revocation of his life licence, the applicant would have been released from prison on the expiry of the sentence for fraud in July 1997, and in June 1997, he sought judicial review of the Secretary of State's decision to reject the Board's recommendation for immediate release. He was successful at first instance, but both the Court of Appeal and the House of Lords denied his claim and upheld the power of the Home Secretary to revoke his licence and thus effectively detain him under ss 39(1) and 35(2) of the Criminal Justice Act 1991 (the latter subsequently replaced by s 29 of the Crime (Sentences) Act 1997), even though there was no prospect of his committing any violent crime in the future. Both courts, however, expressed unease at their decisions. As Lord Bingham CJ stated in the Court of Appeal ([1998] 1 WLR 503 at 518):

> The imposition of what is in effect a substantial term of imprisonment by the exercise of executive discretion, without trial, lies uneasily with ordinary concepts of the Rule of Law. I hope that the Secretary of State may, even now, think it right to give further consideration to the case.

When the case came before the Grand Chamber of the ECtHR in May 2002, and as the Court of Appeal in *Anderson* had expected, it held that it was no longer in the interest of justice to follow its previous decision in *Wynne*. The ECtHR stated that although it was not formally bound to follow any of its previous judgments, it was 'in the interests of legal certainty, foreseeability and equality before the law that it should not depart, without cogent reason, from precedents laid down in previous cases'. However, it felt that the fixing of the tariff for mandatory life sentences was clearly a sentencing exercise, and that it was no longer possible to distinguish between mandatory life prisoners, discretionary life prisoners and juvenile murderers as regards the nature of that sentencing process. The ECtHR also held that the finding in *Wynne* that the mandatory life sentence constituted punishment for life could no longer be maintained. It was therefore open to the court to decide that the Secretary of State's role in fixing the tariff was a sentencing exercise and not merely a matter relating to the administrative implementation of the sentence. As a result, it concluded that the exercise of such power by the Home Secretary was contrary to Art 5(1) and (4) of the ECHR.

When the decision of the ECtHR in *Stafford* was delivered, the UK press immediately returned to the possibility of the imminent release of the child killer Myra Hindley. What they failed to indicate was that the ECtHR itself, in line with previous statements of the UK courts, had actually recognised the validity of 'whole life' tariffs in exceptional circumstances. Its decision was merely that it was for the courts rather than the executive to make such recommendations. In any event, Hindley died in prison in November 2002.

The first person actually to benefit from the *Stafford* decision was Satpal Ram, who was released from prison in June 2002 after having served more than 15 years for a murder he claimed was committed in self-defence in a racial attack. The previous Home Secretary had overturned a Parole Board recommendation to release Mr Ram in 2000. The succeeding Home Secretary preferred to release him rather than contest an action for judicial review of his predecessor's decision, recognising that *Stafford* made any argument to the contrary untenable.

R v Secretary of State for the Home Department ex p Anderson and Taylor (2002)

By November 2002, the appeals in the *Anderson and Taylor* cases had reached the House of Lords and were considered by a seven-member panel, indicating their importance. The essential issue under consideration was the effect that the *Stafford* decision in the ECtHR would have on English law, s 35(2) and (3) of the Criminal Justice Act 1991 having been replaced by similar provisions under s 29 of the Crime (Sentences) Act 1997. In the event, the House of Lords followed the decision of the ECtHR and held that the fixing of the tariff for a convicted murderer was legally indistinguishable from the imposition of sentence. Consequently, to ensure compatibility with Art 6(1), any such tariff should be set by an independent and impartial tribunal and not the Home Secretary, who was part of the executive. It was therefore incompatible with Art 6 for the Home Secretary to fix the tariff of a convicted murderer. However, the House of Lords went on to decide that it was not possible to interpret s 29 of the Crime (Sentences) Act 1997 in such a way as to make it compatible with the rights provided under the ECHR. As a result, the House of Lords issued a declaration of incompatibility to the effect that s 29 was contrary to the right under Art 6 to have a sentence imposed by an independent and impartial tribunal.

The above series of cases demonstrates how the implied wishes of the Court of Appeal in *Anderson* could be given express effect in the later House of Lords' decision, without the possibility of any direct accusation of political interference on the part of the judiciary.

The political sensitivity of the preceding cases, and the extent to which they challenge executive power, may go some way to explain the apparent conservatism of the decision of the House of Lords in the *Lichniak* and *Pyrah* cases, considered previously. A close reading of the cases certainly reveals grounds for the House of Lords to overturn those decisions and to remove mandatory life sentences altogether.

The foregoing analysis has used the term 'tariff' to refer to the period that a person sentenced to a life term must serve for the purposes of punishment. It should be noted, however, that, in a Practice Statement issued in May 2002, the Lord Chief Justice accepted the recommendation of the Sentencing Advisory Panel that it should be replaced by the clearer expression 'minimum term'.

The political tension around the issue of sentencing was further heightened when, in May 2003, Home Secretary Blunkett announced his intention to introduce proposals that would introduce a new statutory system in relation to sentencing in murder cases, together with a new Sentencing Guidelines Council to advise judges on appropriate sentencing. The Home Secretary made it clear that he considered that the judges had failed to provide clear and consistent sentencing. Indeed, the proposal can be seen as a direct attack on the Lord Chief Justice, Lord Woolf, whose directive on sentencing, issued in 2002, had indicated that the previous 14-year minimum 'starting point' should be replaced by 16 years for more serious cases and 12 years for lesser crimes such as mercy killings. The Home Secretary was quoted as saying: 'I share public concern that some very serious criminals seem to be serving a relatively short spell in prison [. . .] It will be Parliament that decides the structure. It will be judges that act within it.' Not surprisingly, the Bar Council described the proposal as 'constitutionally a leap in the dark' and said that the Home Secretary was trying to 'institutionalise the grip of the executive around the neck of the judiciary'.

The proposed scheme was subsequently attacked by Lord Woolf in a speech on the Bill in the House of Lords in June of that year and in the background notes for which he stated that:

> The indirect, knock-on effect of the proposed minimum period is highly undesirable [. . .] Sentencing, particularly in relation to murder, should be removed from the political arena. The present proposal will have the effect of increasing political involvement.

The Lord Chief Justice also took exception to the proposal to appoint a senior police officer to the Sentencing Council (formerly the Sentencing Guidelines Council) and more generally highlighted the logical contradiction in the Home Secretary's approach, as Lord Woolf stated:

> It is surely extraordinary to propose a council to make guidelines and at the same time include your own guidance in the legislation establishing the council.

Nonetheless, both the Council and the sentencing guidelines in relation to murder were implemented in the Criminal Justice Act 2003, and were the first of its major changes in the criminal justice system to be brought into effect in January 2004.

Section 269 of the Act applies to any murders for which sentence is passed on or after 18 December 2003. It introduces a three-tier system and requires the courts to apply the following sentencing principles:

Level 1: whole life sentences will be the starting point for murderers:

- multiple murders, that is, two or more, that show a substantial degree of premeditation, involve abduction of the victim prior to the killing or are sexual or sadistic;
- murder of a child following abduction or involving sexual or sadistic conduct;
- murder carried out through acts of terrorism;
- murder where the offender has been previously convicted of murder.

Level 2: attracting a 30-year minimum sentence for:

- murders of police and prison officers in the course of duty;
- murder involving the use of a firearm or explosive;
- killing done for gain (burglary, robbery, etc, including professional or contract killing);
- killing intended to defeat ends of justice (killing of a witness);
- race/religion/sexual orientation motivated murder;
- single sadistic or sexual murder of an adult;
- multiple murders (other than those above).

Level 3: a 15-year minimum sentence will apply for:

- other murders by adults and all murders by children under 17.

The whole life recommendation does not apply to offenders below the age of 21, but offenders aged 18 to 20 years of age will be subject to either the 15- or 30-year starting points.

Those aged 17 years or under will be subject to a 12-year starting point.

It should be emphasised that the above recommendations state starting points in sentencing, and once trial judges have determined the starting point by applying the above principles, they may consider aggravating and mitigating factors (examples of which are set out in the Act) and may move up or down from the starting point to arrive at the appropriate minimum term.

In *R v Jones; R v Chandi, Multani, Khangura and Dosanjh; R v Ashman; R v Hobson* (2005), the Court of Appeal held that the guidance in the Criminal Justice Act 2003 was provided to help a court assess the appropriate sentence. Although a court was to have regard to this guidance, each case would depend crucially on its particular facts and a court, proposing to depart from the guidelines, would have to set out its reasoning.

In the light of previous experience in the courts, and in a clear endeavour to ensure compliance with the ECHR, s 269 provides that the scheme is not compulsory. However, s 270 requires any judge who departs from the recommended sentences to explain their reasons for so doing in open court. In any event, the Attorney General has the power to challenge unduly lenient sentences and will be able to challenge any minimum term that he considers to be unduly lenient under the Criminal Justice Act principles (for further consideration of the Criminal Justice Act 2003, see above, at 8.5.1).

The Home Secretary has – therefore – since the *Anderson* case in 2003 played no role in the setting of the minimum term to be served by an offender sentenced to life imprisonment for murder. If an offender sentenced to life imprisonment for murder wishes to appeal against the minimum term fixed then he can do so to the Court of Appeal.

There were 86,420 prisoners in custody at 5 October 2012, up 2,776 from a year earlier (*Ministry of Justice Prison Population Bulletin*, 5 October 2012, available at: http://www.justice.gov.uk/statistics/prisons-and-probation/prison-population-figures). In July 2010, the Prison Reform Trust published its Bromley Briefings Prison Factfile (http://www.prisonreformtrust.org.uk/uploads/documents/FactFileJuly2010.pdf). That file stated that from 2000 to 2008 the average time served in prison increased by 14 per cent (from 8.1 to 9.3 months) for those released from determinate sentences. The proportion of the prison population serving indeterminate sentences (life sentences and IPPs) increased from 9 per cent in 1995 to 18 per cent in 2010 (*Ministry of Justice (2009) Story of the prison population 1995–2009, England and Wales*, London, Ministry of Justice). If those longer sentences were included, the average time served would be higher.

Hirst v UK (No. 2)

Convicted prisoners are currently barred by s 3 of the Representation of the People Act 1983 from voting in parliamentary or local elections. In March 2004, the ECtHR ruled in *Hirst v UK (No. 2)* that the UK Government's blanket ban prohibiting sentenced prisoners from voting was unlawful. Despite rejection in 2005 of the appeal against this judgment, which was mounted by the UK Government – two protracted public consultation exercises – the same exclusionary policy remains in place. In an open letter (dated 21 May 2010) addressed to the Committee of Ministers at the Council of Europe, Juliet

Lyon CBE, Director of the Prison Reform Trust, stated that up to 73,000 prisoners had been unlawfully denied the right to vote in the UK general and local elections on 6 May 2010. Nineteen of the 47 countries in the Council of Europe – which include all 27 EU Member States – have no restrictions on prisoners voting. In France and Germany courts have the power to impose loss of voting rights as an additional punishment, while Sweden, Switzerland and Denmark are among countries with no ban at all on voting for prisoners. Ireland ended a voting ban five years ago, giving all prisoners a postal vote in the constituency where they would normally live. In July 2011, the ECtHR Grand Chamber accepted a referral in the case of *Scoppola v Italy* involving issues analogous to those which arose in *Hirst*. The UK Government successfully applied to intervene in that case and the Court granted an extension of six months from the date of the final decision in the *Scoppola* judgment before the Government had to comply with its obligations to change the current law as it applies to prisoners. During this time a further 2,500 applications from prisoners in the UK were submitted to the ECtHR.

The Grand Chamber of the ECtHR has now handed down judgment in *Scoppola*. The judgment does not overrule *Hirst* but substantially increases the margin of appreciation afforded to governments to implement the decision. The ECtHR reaffirmed the principles set out in *Hirst*, in particular that disenfranchisement which affects a group of people generally, automatically and indiscriminately, based solely on the fact that they are serving a prison sentence, irrespective of the length of the sentence and irrespective of the nature or gravity of their offence and their individual circumstances, is not compatible with Art 3 of Protocol No.1. However, the ECtHR held that proportionality did not require that the decision to deprive a convicted prisoner of the vote be taken by a judge. The clock is now ticking again for the UK Government to implement the decision of the ECtHR.

CHAPTER SUMMARY: THE CRIMINAL PROCESS: (2) THE PROSECUTION

THE CROWN PROSECUTION SERVICE

The Crown Prosecution Service (CPS) was introduced in 1986. It is important to understand the five types of prosecution that existed before this time and how the CPS was supposed to resolve the criticisms of the old system. What sort of biases can occur in the use of prosecutorial discretion and why? Why were the police regarded as unsuitable to exercise the prosecutorial discretion? What were the police defences to those criticisms? The police argued that conviction rates vindicated the way they exercised their discretion. The Code for Crown Prosecutors (2010) specifies factors that should weigh for and against a prosecution.

CAUTIONING OFFENDERS

Cautioning and conditionally cautioning offenders is now applicable only to adults, with a new system of reprimands and warnings applying to young offenders. The CPS guidelines on prosecution require a 'realistic prospect of conviction' and that the 'public interest' is served by any prosecution. What difficulties are caused by such formulae?

JUDICIAL CONTROL

Judicial control of prosecution policy is very limited and amounts to being able to correct only irrational, unlawful or fraudulent decisions or those contrary to CPS policy (see *R v Metropolitan Police Commissioner ex p Blackburn* (1968)).

BAIL

Bail is the release from custody (whether after arrest, police interview or remand in a prison), pending a criminal trial, of an accused. Bail may be granted with or without conditions. For example, conditional bail might include that a person connected with a defendant in some way stands *surety*, on the promise that money will be paid into the court if the defendant does not turn up for his trial or otherwise absconds. Other conditions that might be attached to the grant of bail include reporting at a police station at specified times or so-called 'doorstep' conditions, whereby the police can turn up at any time to check that a defendant is in a place (his home or workplace, usually) at a time when he should be. Not contacting witnesses, living at a specified address and surrendering a passport or otherwise not applying for travel documents are all other possible bail conditions. The important issue raised here is how best the bail regulations should be framed so as to balance the conflicting interests of public safety and the liberty of the defendant, who enjoys the presumption of innocence until and in the event of his guilt being proven in a court of law. Public safety would perhaps be best served by keeping everyone accused of a crime in custody until their trial. This, though, would clearly be unnecessarily draconian. Conversely, civil liberty and the presumption of innocence might be best served by allowing every suspect to remain free, however heinous the crime of which they have been accused and whatever their past record. The important statutory provisions are s 38 of the Police and Criminal Evidence Act 1984 and ss 3, 4 and 6 of and Sched 1 to the Bail Act 1976.

Changes made by the Bail (Amendment) Act 1993 and the Criminal Justice and Public Order Act 1994 allow prosecutors to appeal against the granting of bail, restrict some aspects of it being granted and afford greater opportunities for police bail.

PLEA BARGAINING

Plea bargaining is the practice where the accused enters a plea of guilty in return for which he will be given a sentence concession. It can also refer to 'plea arrangements' where the accused agrees to plead guilty to a lesser charge than the one with which he is, or is to be, charged. Note the recommendation of the Runciman Commission to introduce sentence discounting as a means to avoid 'cracked trials'. Dangers arising from such procedures include innocent persons being pressurised to 'take a plea' and serious offenders being processed for minor offences. In a system where the vast majority of cases in the Crown Court and magistrates' courts result in guilty pleas (72.5 per cent and 67.8 per cent, respectively), the operation of the plea bargain becomes very important as an 'efficient' means of disposing of cases. However, the CPS should only accept lesser pleas in the pursuit of 'efficiency' where, on the facts of a case, a lesser plea fits the evidence and is commensurate with the seriousness of the offence. Plea bargaining then operates as a rational means by which to dispose of cases.

THE RUNCIMAN REPORT

The Runciman Report makes the following recommendations. Section 8 of the Contempt of Court Act 1981 should be amended. Attempts have been made to improve the representative nature of juries. The operation of disqualification procedures should be tightened and extended to those on bail. The ethnic mix of a jury should be open to adjustment. In complex fraud trials, judges should be permitted to explain the nature of the matters involved at the outset of the trial. Magistrates should have the final say in where offences triable 'either way' are heard – rather than, as currently, a defendant in an 'either-way' matter either accepting summary trial or else 'electing' Crown Court trial.

THE CRIMINAL JUSTICE ACT 2003

The Act made a number of changes, most of which were implemented in 2004–06. It introduced the 'conditional caution', and changed the law relating to bail. It amended s 30 of PACE 1984 to enable police officers to grant bail to persons following their arrest without the need to take them to a police station. It provided the police with additional flexibility following arrest and the scope to remain on patrol where there is no immediate need to deal with the person concerned at the station. It also required the court to refuse bail to an adult defendant who was on bail in criminal proceedings at the date of the offence, unless the court is satisfied that there is no significant risk that he would commit an offence if released on bail.

THE SENTENCING PROCESS, THE SEPARATION OF POWERS AND THE HRA

Cases relating to s 3 powers:

- *R v A* (2001);
- *Re S* (2002);
- *Mendoza v Ghaidan* (2004).

Cases relating to declarations of incompatibility:

- *R v (1) Mental Health Review Tribunal, North & East London Region* (2001);
- *Wilson v Secretary of State for Trade and Industry* (2003).

Cases relating to sentencing:

- *R v Offen and Others* (2001);
- *R v Secretary of State for the Home Department ex p Anderson and Taylor* (2002).

By s 229 of the Criminal Justice Act 2003, the courts are obliged to consider whether an offender has fallen into a category of dangerousness by virtue of being convicted of a 'specified offence' and it requires the courts to consider degrees of risks of serious harm from further offences by such an offender.

1. Currently one in 10 of the prison population are serving an imprisonment for public protection sentence (see the Prison Reform Trust report *Unjust Deserts: Imprisonment for Public Protection*, 2010). This imprisonment is based on an assessment of 'dangerousness'. In 2010 these indeterminate sentences cost the public purse in excess of £100 million. Are indeterminate sentences ethically and practically justifiable?

2. In the UK juries are selected at random with no regard for gender or ethnic diversity. Is a more diverse jury a fairer jury? Is it important for the race or gender of a defendant to be represented in the 12 people that try him or her?

3. On 5 October 2012, the prison population in England and Wales was 86,420. When Ken Clarke was Home Secretary for the first time (from 1992 to 1993), the average prison population was 44,628. According to the government, the overall cost of the criminal justice system has risen from 2 per cent of GDP to 2.5 per cent over the last 10 years. That is a higher per capita level than the US or any EU country. Court-ordered community sentences were more effective (by seven percentage points) at reducing one-year proven reoffending rates than custodial sentences of less than 12 months for similar offenders. Prison has a poor record for reducing reoffending – 49 per cent of adults are reconvicted within one year of being released. For those serving sentences of less than 12 months, this increases to 59 per cent. For those who have served more than 10 previous custodial sentences the rate of reoffending rises to 77 per cent (see The Bromley Briefing, June 2011). Should short custodial sentences be abolished?

FURTHER READING

Archbold: *Criminal Pleading, Evidence and Practice*, 2012, James Richardson (ed), London: Sweet & Maxwell

Ashworth, A, *Sentencing and Criminal Justice*, 2010, Cambridge: CUP

Ashworth, A and Redmayne, M, *The Criminal Process*, 2005, Oxford: OUP

Baldwin, J and McConville, M, *Negotiated Justice: Pressures on Defendants to Plead Guilty*, 1977, Oxford: Martin Robertson

Bindaman, D, 'Crown duals' (1999) Law Soc Gazette 22–8

Buxton, R, 'The private prosecutor as a minister of justice' [2009] 6 Crim LR 427–32

Carkeek, L, 'Assisted suicide guidance' (2009) 159 NLJ 1391

Cockburn, JS and Green, TA, *Twelve Good Men and True*, 1988, Princeton: Princeton UP

Devlin, P, *Trial by Jury*, 1956, London: Stevens

Findlay, M and Duff, P, *The Jury Under Attack*, 1988, London: Butterworths

Hastie, R, *Inside the Juror: The Psychology of Juror Decision Making*, 1993, Cambridge: CUP

Lawrence, J, O'Kane, M, Rab, S and Nakhwal, J, 'Hardcore bargains: what could plea bargaining offer in UK criminal cartel cases?' (2008) 7(1) Comp LJ 17–42

Padfield, N, 'The Criminal Justice and Immigration Act 2008', Legislative Comment, Arch News 2008, 7

Rose, D, *In the Name of the Law – The Collapse of Criminal Justice*, 1996, London: Jonathan Cape

Sanders, A, 'Class bias in prosecutions' (1985) 24 Howard J 176

Sanders, A and Young, R, *Criminal Justice*, 2000, London: Butterworths

Thompson, EP, *Writing by Candlelight*, 1980, London: Merlin

Uglow, S, Cheney, D and Dickson, L, *Criminal Justice*, 2nd edn, 2002, London: Sweet & Maxwell

Wurtzel, D, *Spotlight on the CPS*, Counsel (2009)

USEFUL WEBSITE

www.cps.gov.uk

This is the website of the Crown Prosecution Service.

COMPANION WEBSITE

Now visit the companion website to:

● test your understanding of the key terms using our Flashcard Glossary;

● revise and consolidate your knowledge of 'The criminal process: (2) the prosecution' using our Multiple Choice Question testbank;

● view all of the links to the Useful Websites above.

www.routledge.com/cw/slapper

THE JUDICIARY

9

The importance of the courts and the judges within the common law has already been considered in previous chapters of this book. It has been suggested that the judges have considerable scope for determining the meaning and effect of law through their marshalling, not to say manipulation, of the rules of precedent and statutory interpretation. The purpose of the present chapter is further to consider those issues but more essentially to consider the actual roles of judges, how they are appointed and how the operation of their judicial functions may raise constitutional issues as to the interests the judiciary represent.

　　The recent past has seen what can only be seen as enormous changes in relation to the judiciary. Not only has the new Supreme Court replaced the House of Lords as the highest court in the United Kingdom, but there has also been a change in the way in which judges are appointed and a reduction in the central role of the Lord Chancellor. Each of these changes has already had an impact on the constitution of the United Kingdom and it is at least arguable that they will have an even greater impact in the future, as will be considered below.

9.2　THE CONSTITUTIONAL ROLE OF THE JUDICIARY

Central to the general idea of the rule of law (see Chapter 2 above) is the specific proposition that it involves the rule of *law* rather than the rule of *people*. Judges hold a position of central importance in relation to the concept of the rule of law. They are expected to deliver judgment in a completely impartial manner through a strict application of the law, without allowing their personal preference, or fear or favour of any of the parties to the action, to affect their decision in any way.

　　This desire for impartiality is reflected in the constitutional position of the judges. In line with Montesquieu's classic exposition of the separation of powers, the judiciary occupy a situation apart from the legislative and executive arms of the State, and operate independently of them. Prior to the English revolutionary struggles of the seventeenth century between Parliament and the monarch, judges held office at the king's pleasure.

Not only did this mean that judges could be dismissed when the monarch so decided, but it highlighted the lack of independence of the law from the State in the form, and person, of the monarch. With the victory of Parliament and the establishment of a State based on popular sovereignty, and limited in its powers, the independence of the judiciary was confirmed in the Act of Settlement 1701. The centrality of the independence of the judges and the legal system from direct control or interference from the State in the newly established constitution was emphasised in the writing of the English philosopher, John Locke, who saw it as one of the essential reasons for, and justifications of, the social contract on which the social structure was assumed to be based.

In order to buttress the independence of the judiciary and remove them from the danger of being subjected to political pressure, it has been made particularly difficult to remove senior judges once they have been appointed. Their independence of thought and opinion is also protected by the doctrine of judicial immunity. Both of these principles will be considered in more detail below, as will the change in the procedure for appointing judges, which cannot but have had an impact on their perceived independence from politics and politicians.

9.2.1   THE CONSTITUTIONAL ROLE OF THE LORD CHANCELLOR

The following brief historical consideration of the constitutional position of the Lord Chancellor and the Appellate Committee of the House of Lords, as the highest court in England was correctly referred to, has to be placed within the immediate context of the changes made by the Constitutional Reform Act 2005, which radically altered both institutions. The point of it is to highlight why those changes were, and arguably had to be, made.

The Lord Chancellor always held an anomalous position in respect of the separation of powers in the contemporary State, in that the holder of that position played a key role in each of the three elements of the State. The Lord Chancellor was the most senior judge in the English court structure, sitting as he did in the House of Lords. At the same time, however, the Lord Chancellorship was a party-political appointment, and the occupant of the office owed his preferment to the Prime Minister of the day. Not only was the incumbent a member of the executive, having a seat in the Cabinet, but he was also responsible for the operation of his own government department. In addition to these roles, it should not be overlooked that the Chancellor was also the Speaker of the House of Lords in its general role as a legislative forum.

The party-political role of the Lord Chancellor gave rise to a furore when, in February 2001, Lord Irvine, the then New Labour appointee, personally wrote to lawyers who were known sympathisers of the Labour Party, asking them to donate at least £200 to the party at a fundraising dinner he was to host. His political critics made much of the fact that, as the person ultimately responsible for appointing the judiciary, his soliciting of party funds from those who might apply for such positions in the future could be represented as improper. As such, the press immediately entitled it the 'cash for wigs' affair, echoing the previous 'cash for questions' scandal in the House of Commons and the subsequent 'cash for peerages' scandal. The Lord Chancellor, however, refused to apologise for his action. In a statement to the House of Lords, delivered in his political persona and therefore two paces apart from the woolsack on which he sat when acting as the Speaker of the House of Lords, he stated that:

> I do not believe I have done anything wrong nor do I believe that I have broken any current rules. If I did I would be the first to apologise.

According to Lord Irvine, it was misconceived to claim that the Lord Chancellor was not a party-political post, and that every minister from the Prime Minister down was involved in fundraising. The best that could be said for the Lord Chancellor was that, although he had done nothing unlawful, he had acted in an unwise, politically naïve and injudicious manner, and one that once again brought the anomalous constitutional role of his office to the political foreground and renewed calls for its reformation, if not removal.

In addition to difficulties arising directly from his responsibility for implementing political policies in relation to the legal system, the Lord Chancellor's judicial role also came into question. As a consequence of the fact that the appointment of the Lord Chancellor is a purely political one, there is no requirement that the incumbent should have held any prior judicial office. Indeed, in the case of Lord Irvine, he had never served in any judicial capacity, making his reputation as a highly successful barrister. Nonetheless, as Lord Chancellor, he was the most senior judge and was entitled to sit, as he thought appropriate (see 9.2.2 below for further observations about the Lord Chancellor's residual powers).

There was, however, a much more fundamental issue relating to the manner in which the Lord Chancellor's former multifunctional role may be seen as having breached the doctrine of the separation of powers. There cannot but be doubts as to the impropriety of a member of the executive functioning as a member of the judiciary and Lord Irvine himself withdrew from sitting in a case in March 1999 in which he recognised the possibility of a conflict of interest. That case involved an action by the family of a man who had died in police custody. The suggestion was made that the Lord Chancellor's participation in the judicial panel raised doubts as to whether the case would be decided by an independent and impartial tribunal. Given his recent guidelines warning the judiciary about the need to be sensitive to issues of conflict of interest, the Lord Chancellor clearly felt himself required to stand down from hearing the case.

In *McGonnell v UK* (2000), the European Court of Human Rights (ECtHR) confirmed the previous decision of the Commission (see Chapter 15) in relation to the judicial function of the Bailiff of the island of Guernsey. It was held that the fact that the Bailiff had acted as the judge in a case in which he had also played an administrative role was in breach of Art 6 of the European Convention on Human Rights (ECHR). In the words of the Commission decision:

> It is incompatible with the requisite appearance of independence and impartiality for a judge to have legislative and executive functions as substantial as those carried out by the Bailiff.

Although those words could apply equally to the Lord Chancellor, the actual court decision was limited to the situation of the Bailiff, and Lord Irvine made it clear that he considered its application to be limited to the particular facts of the Guernsey situation. Nonetheless, the Lord Chancellor continued not to sit on cases where there might appear to be a conflict between his judicial and other roles. In February 2003, the Lord Chancellor's dual role as judge and member of the executive came under attack in the parliamentary assembly of the Council of Europe, which oversees the operation of the ECHR (see Chapter 15). A Dutch member, Erik Jurgens, a vice president of the assembly, tabled a motion that stated that:

> The assembly . . . has repeatedly stressed that judges should be a completely independent branch of government. It is undeniable that combining the function of judge with functions in other branches of government calls that independence seriously into question.

Mr Jurgens was quoted as saying that he was advising eastern European countries seeking entry to the Council of Europe that they would not be admitted unless their judges were totally independent, so it was an anomaly that one of the original members had a figure like the Lord Chancellor, and further that:

> Sooner or later a case is going to come to the European Court of Human Rights at Strasbourg, and I think they will certainly say that this is an unacceptable combination.

In April 2003, Lord Irvine defended the unique position of the Lord Chancellor in an appearance before the parliamentary select committee with oversight of the Lord Chancellor's Department. Questioned on the conflict inherent in his power to make law and still sit as a judge, he responded that he had 'difficulty seeing why this issue is so important', and argued against changing a legal system that had an enviable international reputation, simply for the sake of constitutional purity. As he put it:

> The basic point is that the higher judiciary accept this role – they believe profoundly that it is a superior system to any other.

9.2.1.1   The Constitutional Reform Act 2005

While Lord Irvine preferred to maintain his position rather than bow to constitutional purity, his views were apparently not shared by his colleagues in government and most importantly the Prime Minister, who sacked him in June 2003. As part of a Cabinet reshuffle, which appeared to involve a power struggle between the Home Secretary and the Lord Chancellor, which the former won, Lord Irvine was not only removed from office, but it was announced that his office itself was to disappear. A new ministry, the Department for Constitutional Affairs, was to replace the Lord Chancellor's Department and Lord Falconer was appointed Secretary of State for Constitutional Affairs to replace Lord Irvine as Lord Chancellor. It would appear that the announcement was made without anyone having thought through the constitutional implications, or indeed practicalities, of simply abolishing the position of the Lord Chancellor. Initially, Lord Falconer said he was not the Lord Chancellor and that he would not be assuming all of the functions of his predecessor. However, the realisation soon dawned that it was simply impossible to eradicate the role of the Lord Chancellor by simple diktat. Lord Falconer had to be Lord Chancellor even if by default, as someone had to perform the constitutional functions attached to the Lord Chancellor's office. So, on the first day in his new role, Lord Falconer was to be seen in wig and tights sitting on the woolsack in the House of Lords, for the simple reason that someone had to do it. As a consequence, Lord Falconer was, at least for the time being, both Secretary of State for Constitutional Affairs and Lord Chancellor, although in the former role he was charged with the duty of abolishing the latter role. It should be noted that from the outset Lord Falconer made it clear that he would not, and never did, sit as a judge. As regards his legislative role in chairing sessions of the House of Lords, the CRA subsequently provided for the election of an independent Lord Speaker and in July 2006 the House of Lords elected Baroness Hayman as the first office holder.

The proposal of the original Constitutional Reform Bill for the complete abolition of the officer of the Lord Chancellor was extremely controversial. Reference has already been made to the concerns of the judiciary as to the abolition of the role of the Lord Chancellor and those concerns were also shared by politicians and social commentators. Many of the latter argued against what they saw as the ditching of hundreds of years of history and practice for the sake of dressing up a Cabinet reshuffle as a matter of constitutional importance.

The government, nonetheless, insisted on pursuing its reforms, and justifying them on the basis of transparency and the recognition that it was no longer appropriate for one person to perform the disparate functions of the Lord Chancellor in clear contradiction of the doctrine of the separation of powers. However, as many correctly pointed out, the constitution of the UK never actually incorporated a strict separation of powers. Nonetheless, that recognition cannot be taken as justifying a situation that, as preceding analysis has shown, was clearly founded on fundamental conflicts of interest and was almost certainly contrary to the European Convention on Human Rights. In this regard, the changes introduced by the Constitutional Reform Act 2005 can be seen to be not only pertinent, but also timely, in their endeavour to address an issue before it became a problem. Nonetheless, as was explained above, the government did submit to the wish to retain the ancient office of Lord Chancellor, although the importance of the role was significantly reduced. Following a Cabinet reshuffle in 2007, which also involved the replacement of the Department of Constitutional Affairs by a new Justice Ministry, the Justice Minister, Jack Straw, became the first member of the House of Commons to assume the role and title of Lord Chancellor. The current Justice Minister and Lord Chancellor is Chris Grayling MP.

As part of the reform of the office of Lord Chancellor its former judicial functions transferred to President of the Courts of England and Wales who is currently Lord Judge, who succeeded Lord Phillips as Lord Chief Justice in October 2008. In this new position, he is responsible for the training, guidance and deployment of judges. He is also responsible for representing the views of the judiciary of England and Wales to Parliament and ministers.

9.2.2   THE CONSTITUTION AND THE ROLE OF THE HOUSE OF LORDS AND THE SUPREME COURT

As has been mentioned previously, by virtue of the Constitutional Reform Act 2005, the Supreme Court replaced the House of Lords as the highest court in the United Kingdom in October 2009. The Judicial Committee of the Privy Council remains as a distinct entity, but follows the Supreme Court to its new location.

Consequently the Supreme Court is the final court of appeal for all United Kingdom civil cases, and criminal cases from England, Wales and Northern Ireland and hears appeals on arguable points of law of general public importance. However, once again, the explanation for this event requires a brief consideration of its historical and constitutional context. A number of issues came together to raise questions about the operation of the House of Lords as the final court of appeal in the English legal system and the role of the Privy Council. Among these were the devolution of parliamentary power to the Scottish Parliament and Welsh Assembly, the previous and proposed further reform of the House of Lords, the enactment of the Human Rights Act and the role of the House of Lords itself in the *Pinochet* case (see below). However, of far greater significance was the proposal in the Constitutional Reform Act 2005 to replace the currently constituted Appeal Committee of the House of Lords with a new Supreme Court.

The case for the reform of the Lord Chancellor's position and against the location of the most senior judges in the House of Lords was presented to the commission examining the reform of the House of Lords, by JUSTICE, the civil rights organisation. Both aspects of the challenges were strongly rejected by the then Lord Chancellor Irvine in a speech to the Third Worldwide Common Law Judiciary Conference in Edinburgh, delivered in July 1999. Nonetheless, spring 2002 saw a spate of speeches and interviews highlighting disagreement, if not actual tension, between the Lord Chancellor and some of the most senior members of the judiciary. In March of that year, Lord Steyn, then the second longest serving Law Lord, expressed the view that Lord Irvine's insistence on sitting as a judge in the House of Lords was a major obstacle to the creation of a Supreme Court to replace the House of Lords. In April, the Lord Chancellor's response was reported in the *Financial Times* newspaper. The article stated that, 'Lord Irvine may have an impressive intellect, but his lack of diplomacy means he will seldom be short of enemies'. The point of that comment was supported by the Lord Chancellor's reaction to Lord Steyn's previous comments, dismissing them in a tone of effete arrogance, as 'rather wearisome . . . he's not a political scientist, he knows nothing about the internal workings of government – or very little'. As reported, he reduced Lord Steyn's argument to a demand for 'a grand new architectural venture', stating that the argument that 'the

Lord Chancellor, because of his desire to continue sitting, is preventing the judges from having a new building – that's just nonsense'.

Lord Irvine's views should, however, be contrasted with those of the former senior Law Lord, Lord Bingham, expressed in the Spring Lecture given at the Constitution Unit at University College London in May 2002. In a paper entitled *A New Supreme Court for the UK*, Lord Bingham directly addressed all of the issues raised above, except for the role of the Lord Chancellor, before stating his preference for:

> . . . a supreme court severed from the legislature, established as a court in its own right, re-named and appropriately re-housed, properly equipped and resourced and affording facilities for litigants, judges and staff such as, in most countries of the world, are taken for granted.

As to the views and future role of the Lord Chancellor, the reduction of his direct judicial powers was implicit in the speech. As Lord Bingham concluded: '. . . inertia . . . is not an option.'

Once again, Lord Irvine's political antennae appear to have lacked acuity, in that, not only was he replaced as Lord Chancellor by Lord Falconer, but as has been seen, his successor proposed the establishment of a Supreme Court much along the lines of that suggested by Lord Bingham. Thus Part 2 of the Constitutional Reform Act 2005 contained provisions for the following:

- The establishment of a new, independent Supreme Court, separate from the House of Lords with its own independent appointments system, its own staff and budget and its own building: Middlesex Guildhall. This new Supreme Court should not be confused with the old Supreme Court, which was the title previously given to the High Court and Court of Appeal. In future those courts will be known as the Senior Courts of England and Wales.

- The 12 judges of the Supreme Court will be known as Justices of the Supreme Court and will no longer be allowed to sit as members of the House of Lords. As a matter of fact, all of the present members are life peers and as a result will be able to sit in the House of Lords on their retirement from their judicial office, but this may not always be the case in the future.

- The current Law Lords will become the first 12 Justices of the Supreme Court, and the most senior will be appointed President of the Supreme Court. Lord Phillips, the former Lord Chief Justice, was appointed the first President of the new court and when it actually sat for the first time in October 2009 there were only 11 justices in office.

These measures can be considered in two parts: first, the creation of a Supreme Court, distinct from the House of Lords; and second, the removal of the right of the members of that new Supreme Court to sit as members of the Upper House. Neither of these proposals found favour with a majority of the members of the Law Lords; indeed, in their collective response to the Consultation Paper on constitutional reform, six of the 12 expressed their opposition to the creation of a Supreme Court and eight supported the retention of at least some judicial representation in the House of Lords. The minority supported the complete separation of judicial and legislative activity, as did Lord Falconer, who explained the need for reform thus:

> The present position is no longer sustainable. It is surely not right that those responsible for interpreting the law should be able to have a hand in drafting it. The time has come for the UK's highest court to move out from under the shadow of the legislature.

The relevance of Lord Falconer's argument was given added power by the decision of the Scottish Court of Sessions, the equivalent of the Court of Appeal, in *Davidson v Scottish Ministers (No 2)* (2002). The case involved a challenge to a previous court decision, on the grounds of Art 6 of the ECHR, for the reason that one of the judges in the earlier case, the former Lord Advocate Lord Hardie, had spoken on the issue before the court while a member of the Scottish Assembly. The Court of Sessions held that Lord Hardie should at least have declared his previous interest in the matter and that, in the light of his failure to do so, there was at least the real possibility of bias, and ordered the case to be retried.

In other constitutional systems, both civil, as in France, or common law, as in the United States of America, not only is there a clear separation of powers between the judiciary, the executive and the legislature, there is also a distinct Constitutional Court, with the power to strike down legislation on the grounds of its being unconstitutional. It has to be emphasised that the UK Supreme Court will not be in the nature of these other supreme courts, in that it will not be a constitutional court as such and it will not have the powers to strike down legislation. Consequently, although the proposed alterations clearly increase the appearance of the separation of powers, the doctrine of parliamentary sovereignty remains unchallenged. It was presumably the lack of such power that led Lord Woolf to comment that the new court would effectively replace a first-class appeal court (the House of Lords) with a second-class Supreme Court.

It remains to be seen, however, whether, under the changed circumstances of the contemporary constitution, the Supreme Court, as the highest court in the land, will simply assume the previously limited role of the House of Lords, or whether it will, with the passage of time, assume new functions and increased powers as are consonant with Supreme Courts in other jurisdictions. This issue arose in September 2009 when Lord Neuberger, the current President of the Supreme Court, spoke on a BBC radio programme and expressed the opinion that the advent of the Supreme Court was not unproblematic: as he put it; 'The danger is that you muck around with a constitution like the British constitution at your peril because you do not know what the consequences of any change will be', and that there was a real risk of 'judges arrogating to themselves greater power than they have at the moment'. Former Lord Chancellor, Lord Falconer, also expressed the view that the Supreme Court 'will be bolder in vindicating both the freedoms of individuals and, coupled with that, being willing to take on the executive', but Lord Phillips, the first President of the Supreme Court, was more conciliatory towards the executive expressing the view that, although he could not predict how the court would function in the future, he did not foresee it changing in the way suggested by Lord Neuberger.

It is a commonplace of politics that the devolution of power from the UK Parliament in London, particularly to the Scottish Parliament in Edinburgh, will give rise to disputes as to the relationship between the two bodies. Eventually, such issues will have to be resolved in the courts. Jurisdiction was originally with the Privy Council but has been subsequently transferred to the Supreme Court. During 2010 and 2011 there was considerable tension between the Supreme Court and the Scottish Executive in relation to the court's powers under the Human Rights Act, as a UK rather than a Scottish court, to determine criminal cases in relation to Scots law (see *Cadder v HM Advocate* (2010) and *Fraser v MH Advocate* (2012). In *AXA General Insurance Limited v The Lord Advocate (Scotland)* (2011) the Supreme Court considered the constitutional position of the Scottish Parliament and concluded, in the words of Lord Hope:

> As a result of the Scotland Act, there are thus two institutions with the power to make laws for Scotland: the Scottish Parliament and, as is recognised in section 28(7), the Parliament of the United Kingdom. The Scottish Parliament is subordinate to the United Kingdom Parliament: its powers can be modified, extended or revoked by an Act of the United Kingdom Parliament. Since its powers are limited, it is also subject to the jurisdiction of the courts.

Lord Hope's judgment in *AXA* is also of general interest with respect to the constitutional relationship between parliament and the courts.

Nor should it be forgotten that the Human Rights Act has, for the first time, given the courts clear power to declare the UK Parliament's legislative provision contrary to essential human rights (see above, at 2.5). Even allowing for the fact that the HRA has been introduced in such a way as to maintain the theory of parliamentary sovereignty, in practice, the courts will inevitably become involved in political/constitutional issues. Once the courts are required to act in constitutional matters, it is surely a mere matter of time before they become Constitutional Courts, as distinct from ordinary courts, with specialist judges with particular expertise in such matters.

Re Bow Street Metropolitan Stipendiary Magistrate ex p Pinochet Ugarte (1999)

No consideration of the operation of the judiciary generally, and the House of Lords in particular, can be complete without a detailed consideration of what can only be called the *Pinochet* case (the various cases are actually cited as *R v Bartle* and *R v Evans* (House of Lords' first hearing); *Re Pinochet* (House of Lords' appeal against Lord Hoffmann); *R v Bartle* and *R v Evans* (final House of Lords' decision)).

In September 1973, the democratically elected government of Chile was overthrown in a violent army coup led by the then General Augusto Pinochet Ugarte; the President, Salvador Allende, and many others were killed in the fighting. Subsequently, in the words of Lord Browne-Wilkinson, in the final House of Lords' hearing ([1999] 2 All ER 97 at 100):

> There is no doubt that, during the period of the Senator Pinochet regime, appalling acts of barbarism were committed in Chile and elsewhere in the world: torture, murder and the unexplained disappearance of individuals on a large scale.

Although it was not suggested that Pinochet had committed these acts personally, it was claimed that he was fully aware of them and conspired to have them undertaken.

In 1998, General Pinochet, by now Senator for life and recipient of a Chilean amnesty for his actions (extracted as the price for his returning his country to democracy), came to England for medical treatment. Although he was initially welcomed, he was subsequently arrested on an extradition warrant issued in Spain for the crimes of torture, murder and conspiracy to murder allegedly orchestrated by him in Chile during the 1970s. Spain issued the international warrants, but Pinochet was actually arrested on warrants issued by the metropolitan stipendiary magistrate under s 8(1)(b) of the Extradition Act 1989. The legal question for the English courts was whether General Pinochet, as Head of State at the time when the crimes were committed, enjoyed diplomatic immunity. In November 1998, the House of Lords rejected Pinochet's claim by a 3:2 majority, Lord Hoffmann voting with the majority but declining to submit a reasoned judgment.

Prior to the hearing in the House of Lords, Amnesty International, which campaigns against such things as State mass murder, torture and political imprisonment, and in favour of general civil and political liberties, had been granted leave to intervene in the proceedings, and had made representations through its counsel, Geoffrey Bindman QC. After the *Pinochet* decision, it was revealed, although it was hardly a secret, that Lord Hoffmann was an unpaid director of the Amnesty International Charitable Trust, and that his wife also worked for Amnesty. On that basis, Pinochet's lawyers initiated a very peculiar action: they petitioned the House of Lords about a House of Lords' decision; for the first time, the highest court in the land was to be subject to review, but review of itself, only itself differently constituted. So, in January 1999, another panel of

Law Lords set aside the decision of the earlier hearing on the basis that Lord Hoffmann's involvement had invalidated the previous hearing. The decision as to whether Pinochet had immunity or not would have to be heard by a new, and differently constituted, committee of Law Lords.

It has to be stated in favour of this decision that the English legal system is famously rigorous in controlling conflicts of interest, which might be seen to affect what should be a neutral decision-making process. The rule, which applies across the board to trustees, company directors and other fiduciaries as well as to judges, is so strict that the mere possibility of a conflict of interest is sufficient to invalidate any decision so made, even if in reality the individual concerned was completely unaffected by their own interest in coming to the decision. In the words of the famous *dictum* of Lord Hewart, it is of fundamental importance that 'justice must not only be done but should manifestly and undoubtedly be seen to be done' (*R v Sussex Justices ex p McCarthy* (1924)). With regard to the judicial process, it has been a long-established rule that no one may be a judge in his or her own cause, that is, they cannot judge a case in which they have an interest. This is sometimes known by the phrase *nemo judex in causa sua*. Thus, for example, judges who are shareholders in a company appearing before the court as a litigant must decline to hear the case (*Dimes v Grand Junction Canal* (1852)). It is therefore astonishing that Lord Hoffmann did not withdraw from the case, or at least declare his interest in Amnesty when it was joined to the proceedings. The only possible justification is that Lord Hoffmann assumed that all of those involved in the case, including the Pinochet team of lawyers, were aware of the connection. Alternatively, he might have thought that his support for a charitable body aimed at promoting civil and political liberties was so worthy in itself as to be unimpeachable: could not, and indeed should not, every English judge subscribe, for example, to cl 3(c) of the Amnesty International Charitable Trust memorandum, which provides that one of its objects is 'to procure the abolition of torture, extra-judicial execution and disappearance'?

In either case, Lord Hoffmann was wrong.

Once it was shown that Lord Hoffmann had a relevant interest in its subject matter, he was disqualified without any investigation into whether there was a likelihood or suspicion of bias. The mere fact of his interest was sufficient to disqualify him unless he had made sufficient disclosure. Hitherto, only pecuniary or proprietary interests had led to automatic disqualification. But, as Lord Browne-Wilkinson stated, Amnesty, and hence Lord Hoffmann, plainly had a non-pecuniary interest sufficient to give rise to an automatic disqualification for those involved with it.

The House of Lords therefore decided that Lord Hoffmann had been wrong, but it remained for the House of Lords to extricate itself, with whatever dignity it could manage, from the situation it had, through Lord Hoffmann, got itself into. This it endeavoured to do by reconstituting the original hearing with a specially extended committee of seven members. Political and legal speculation was rife before the decision of that court. It was suggested that the new committee could hardly go against the decision of the previous one without bringing the whole procedure into disrepute, yet the earlier court had actually contained the most liberal, and civil liberties minded, of the Lords. It was assumed that the new hearing would endorse the earlier decision, if with reluctance, but what was not expected was the way in which it would actually do so.

In reaching the decision that General Pinochet could be extradited, the House of Lords relied on, and established, Pinochet's potential responsibility for the alleged crimes from the date on which the UK incorporated the United Nations Convention on Torture into its domestic law through the Criminal Justice Act 1988 – 29 September 1988. Consequently, he could not be held responsible for any crimes committed before then, but was potentially liable for any offences after that date. Thus, although the later House of Lords' committee provided the same decision as the first one, it did so on significantly different, and much more limited, grounds from those on which Lords Steyn and Nicholls, with the support of Lord Hoffmann, relied. Such a conclusion is neither satisfactory in law nor political practice, and did nothing to deflect the unflattering glare of unwanted publicity that had been visited on the House of Lords.

It is important not to overstate what was decided in *Re Pinochet*. The facts of that case were exceptional and it is unlikely that it will lead to a mass withdrawal of judges from cases; however, there might well be other cases in which the judge would be well advised to disclose a possible interest. Finally, with regard to *Re Pinochet*, whatever one's views about the merits, sagacity or neutrality of the current judiciary, there is considerable evidence to support the proposition that, historically, judges have often been biased towards certain causes and social classes. For example, JAG Griffith's book, *The Politics of the Judiciary* (1997) (see 10.7.1 below), is brimming with concrete examples of judges who have shown distinctly conservative and illiberal opinions in cases involving workers, trade unions, civil liberties, Northern Ireland, police powers, religion and other matters. Lord Hoffmann was wrong, but it is nonetheless ironic that the first senior judge to have action taken against him for possible political bias was someone whose agenda was nothing more than being against torture and unjudicial killings.

Locabail (UK) Ltd v Bayfield Properties Ltd (1999)

Following a number of other cases in which lawyers sought to challenge a judgment on the grounds that through a social interest or remote financial connection the judge was potentially biased, the Court of Appeal delivered authoritative guidance on the matter in *Locabail (UK) Ltd v Bayfield Properties Ltd and Another* (1999).

The Court of Appeal ruled that all legal arbiters were bound to apply the law as they understood it to the facts of individual cases as they found them without fear or favour, affection or ill will: that is, without partiality or prejudice. Any judge, that term embracing every judicial decision-maker, whether judge, lay justice or juror, who allowed any judicial decision to be influenced by partiality or prejudice deprived the litigant of his important right and violated one of the most fundamental principles underlying the administration of justice. The law was settled in England and Wales by the House of Lords in *R v Gough* (1993), establishing that the relevant test was whether there was in relation to any given judge a real danger or possibility of bias. When applying the real danger test, it would often be appropriate to inquire whether the judge knew of the matter relied on as appearing to undermine his impartiality. If it were shown that he did not, the danger of its having influenced his judgment was eliminated and the appearance of possible bias dispelled. It was for the reviewing court, not the judge concerned, to assess the risk that some illegitimate extraneous consideration might have influenced his decision.

There was one situation where, on proof of the requisite facts, the existence of bias was effectively presumed and in such cases, it gave rise to automatic disqualification, namely, where the judge was shown to have an interest in the outcome of the case which he was to decide or had decided: see *Dimes v Proprietors of the Grand Junction Canal* (1852), *R v Rand* (1866) and *R v Camborne Justices ex p Pearce* (1955). However, it would be dangerous and futile to attempt to define or list factors which might, or alternatively might not, give rise to a real danger of bias, since everything would depend on the particular facts. Nonetheless, the court could not conceive of circumstances in which an objection could be soundly based on the religion, ethnic or national origin, gender, age, class, means or sexual orientation of the judge. Nor, at any rate ordinarily, could an objection be soundly based on his social, educational, service or employment background or history; nor that of any member of his family; nor previous political associations, membership of social, sporting or charitable bodies; nor Masonic associations; nor previous judicial decisions; nor extracurricular utterances, whether in textbooks, lectures, speeches, articles, interviews, reports or responses to consultation papers; nor previous receipt of instructions to act for or against any party, solicitor or advocate engaged in a case before him; nor membership of the same Inn, circuit, local Law Society or chambers.

By contrast, a real danger of bias might well be thought to arise if there existed personal friendship or animosity between the judge and any member of the public involved in the case; or if the judge were closely acquainted with any such member of the public, particularly if that individual's credibility could be significant in the decision of the case; or if in a case where the credibility of any individual were an issue to be decided by the judge, he had in a previous case rejected that person's evidence in such outspoken terms as to throw doubt on his ability to approach such a person's evidence with an open mind on any later occasion.

It might well be thought that the Court of Appeal was bound to come to this conclusion. Had it ruled that membership of certain societies, or a particular social background, or the previous political associations of a trial judge were grounds for appeal, two consequences would follow. First, there would be a rapid expansion of the use by law firms of special units that monitor and keep files on all aspects of judges' lives. Second, there would be a proliferation of appeals in all departments of the court structure at the very time when there is such a concerted effort to reduce the backlog of appeals. The decision in *Locabail* leaves the question of profound jurisprudential importance: how far can judges judge in an entirely neutral and socially detached manner?

Locabail was decided before the HRA 1998 came into force, but the Court of Appeal soon had the opportunity to assess the rules in *R v Gough* against the requirements of the European Court's approach to bias in relation to Art 6 of the ECHR. *Director General of Fair Trading v Proprietary Association of Great Britain (re Medicaments and Related Classes of Goods (No 2))* (2001) related to a case before the Restrictive Practices Court. Six weeks into the trial, one of the lay members of the panel hearing the case, an economist, disclosed that, since the start of the case, she had applied for a job with one of the main witnesses employed by one of the parties to the case. On learning this, the respondents argued that such behaviour must imply bias on her part and that consequently, the whole panel should stand down, or at least the member in question should stand down. The Restrictive Practices Court rejected the argument. On appeal, the Court of Appeal took the opportunity to refine the common law test as established in *R v Gough*. Previously, the court determining the issue had itself decided whether there had been a real danger of bias in the inferior tribunal. Now, in line with the jurisprudence of the ECtHR, the test was whether a fair-minded observer would conclude that there was a real possibility of bias. In other words, the test moved from being a subjective test on the part of the court to an objective test from the perspective of the fair-minded observer. In the case in question, the Court of Appeal held that there was sufficient evidence for a fair-minded observer to conclude bias on the part of one member of the panel and that consequently, at the stage the trial had reached, her discussions would have contaminated the other two members, who should also have been stood down. The approach adopted by the Court of Appeal in *re Medicaments and Related Classes of Goods (No 2))* was subsequently approved by the House of Lords in *Porter v Magill* (2001) and in the words of Lord Hope the test for bias is 'whether the fair-minded and informed observer, having considered the facts, would conclude that there was a real possibility that the tribunal was biased'.

Subsequently, in *Lawal v Northern Spirit Ltd* (2003), the House of Lords stated that 'public perception of the possibility of unconscious bias is the key' and while not finding it necessary to delve into the characteristics to be attributed to the fair-minded and informed observer, did suggest that such a person would adopt a balanced approach 'neither complacent nor unduly sensitive or suspicious'.

Finally, in *Meerabux v The Attorney General of Belize* (2005), Lord Hope in delivering the report of the Privy Council raised the possibility that had the House of Lords been able to apply the refined version of the test for apparent bias, rather than the test set out in *Gough*, then it is unlikely that it would have found it necessary to find a solution to the problem that it was presented with by applying the automatic disqualification rule. Not a little ironically, Lord Hoffman himself was a member of this particular Privy Council panel.

9.3 JUDICIAL OFFICES

Although not required to know the names of present incumbents, students should at least be aware of the various titles of judges and equally know which courts they operate in.

Lord Chancellor. The history of this particular office has been considered previously and it only remains to state that in its contemporary, reduced state, the office-holder is the current Justice Minister Chris Grayling MP.

Lord Chief Justice. The holder of this position is now President of the Courts of England and Wales and the most senior member of the judiciary. As President of the Courts of England and Wales, the Lord Chief Justice is responsible for representing the views of the judiciary of England and Wales to Parliament, the Minister (that is, the Secretary of State for Justice) and Ministers of the Crown generally. He is also to be responsible, within the resources made available by the Minister, for maintaining appropriate arrangements for the welfare, training and guidance of the judiciary of England and Wales, and for maintaining appropriate arrangements for the deployment of the judiciary of England and Wales and allocating work within courts. The Lord Chief Justice is the President of the Criminal Division of the Court of Appeal and is formally the senior judge in the Queen's Bench Division of the High Court. The present Lord Chief Justice is the appropriately named Lord Judge.

President of the Supreme Court and Deputy President of the Supreme Court. The senior member of the new court and his deputy will fill these roles. They will sit on the appointment commission for any new members of the Supreme Court. Lord Phillips was the first president and his deputy was Lord Hope. In October 2011, Lord Phillips announced his intention to retire from the Supreme Court, effective from the summer of 2012. His successor is Lord Neuberger.

Master of the Rolls. The holder of this office is regarded as second in judicial importance to the Lord Chief Justice. He is President of the Civil Division of the Court of Appeal and is responsible for the allocation and organisation of the work of the judges of the Division, as well as presiding in one of its courts. At present, this position is held by Lord Dyson, who stood down from the House of Lords to take up this position.

President of the Family Division of the High Court of Justice. This person is the senior judge in the Family Division and is responsible for organising the operation of the Court. The current president is Lord Justice Munby.

President of the Queen's Bench Division and Judge in Charge of the Administrative Court. This post was instituted by the Constitutional Reform Act 2005 and the functions of the holder are apparent in the title. The current incumbent is Sir Roger Thomas.

Chancellor of the High Court. This post was also created under the CRA 2005 and replaced the former office of Vice Chancellor of the Supreme Court. Although the Lord Chancellor is nominally the head of the Chancery Division of the High Court, the actual function of organising the Chancery Division falls to the Chancellor. The current incumbent is Sir Andrew Morritt.

Senior Presiding Judge for England and Wales. The Courts and Legal Services Act (CLSA) 1990 recognised the existing system and required that each of the six separate Crown Court circuits should operate under the administration of two presiding judges appointed from the High Court. In addition, a senior presiding judge is appointed from the Lords Justices of Appeal. The current office-holder is LJ Sir John Goldring.

9.3.1 JUDICIAL HIERARCHY

The foregoing are specific judicial offices. In addition, the various judges who function at the various levels within the judicial hierarchy are referred to in the following terms:

Justices of the Supreme Court. When all appointed, these 12 judges now constitute the highest court in the United Kingdom and have been considered in some detail previously. *The qualifications and procedure for appointment will be considered below.*

Lords of Appeal in Ordinary. These were the people normally referred to as the Law Lords for the simple reason that they were ennobled when they were appointed to their positions and sat in the House of Lords. Historically, they constituted the highest court in the United Kingdom and have been replaced by the Supreme Court as considered above.

Lords Justices of Appeal. This category, of which there are 38 incumbents, constitutes the majority of the judges in the Court of Appeal, although the other specific office-holders considered previously may also sit in that court, as may High Court judges specifically requested to do so. They all used to be known as Lord Justice, even if they were female. The first female member of the Court of Appeal, Elizabeth Butler-Sloss, had to be referred to by the male title because the Senior Courts Act 1981 had not considered the possibility of a woman holding such high judicial office. The rules were changed subsequently to allow female judges in the Court of Appeal to be referred to as Lady Justices, and whereas their male counterparts receive knighthoods on their elevation, the women become Dames.

High Court judges. These are sometimes referred to as '*puisne*' (pronounced 'pewnee') judges, in reference to their junior status in relation to those of superior status in the Supreme Court. There are currently 110 such judges appointed. Judges are appointed to particular divisions depending on the amount of work needing to be conducted by that division, although they may be required to hear cases in different divisions and may be transferred from one division to another by the Lord Chancellor. Others, such as former High Court and Court of Appeal judges, or former circuit judges or recorders, may be requested to sit as judges in the High Court. High Court judges are referred to by their name followed by the initial 'J'.

The Lord Chancellor may also appoint deputy judges of the High Court on a purely temporary basis, in order to speed up the hearing of cases and to reduce any backlog that may have built up. The Heilbron Report on the operation of the civil justice system was critical of the use of deputy judges and recommended that more permanent High Court judges should be appointed if necessary. The maximum numbers were subsequently increased to their present level, but the use of deputy judges has continued to provide grounds for criticism of the operation of the legal system, and has led to suggestions that the use of 'second-rate' judges might eventually debase the whole judicial currency.

Circuit judges. Although there is only one Crown Court, it is divided into six distinct circuits, which are serviced, in the main, by circuit judges who also sit as county court judges to hear civil cases. There are currently 665 circuit judges, each being addressed as 'Your Honour'.

Recorders are part-time judges appointed to assist circuit judges in their functions in relation to criminal and civil law cases. There are currently 1,155 recorders in post.

District judges. This category of judge, previously referred to as registrars, is appointed on a full-time and part-time basis to hear civil cases in the county court. There are currently 447 district judges.

All judicial statistics are available on the Ministry of Justice website at http://webarchive.nationalarchives.gov.uk/+/http://www.justice.gov.uk/publications//judicialandcourtstatistics.htm

The situation of *magistrates* will be considered separately at 9.9 below and the situation of *chairmen of tribunals* and *tribunal judges* will be considered at 12.5.

9.3.2 LEGAL OFFICES

In addition to these judicial positions, there are three legal offices that should be noted:

- The *Attorney General*, like the Lord Chancellor, is a political appointee and a member of the executive, whose role is to act as the legal adviser to the government. For example, in March 2003, the former Attorney General, Lord Goldsmith, controversially advised the government that there was a legal basis for its use of military force against Iraq. Subsequently, in November 2006 Lord Goldsmith had to decide whether there were any grounds for pursuing criminal charges against individuals who had allegedly paid money to the Labour party in order to benefit from the awarding of honours such as peerages – inevitably once again 'the cash-for-honours scandal'. The suggestion was that Goldsmith, as a political appointee, was in no position to decide the fate of those who had appointed him to his office. He, however, insisted on his right to take the ultimate decision, although he offered the assurance that he did so on the basis of independent legal advice. The final *cause célèbre* to emerge in Goldsmith's time as Attorney General emerged in December 2006 when he announced that a Serious Fraud Office investigation into alleged bribery, involving payments from the arms firm BAE to members of the Saudi Arabian royal family, would be stopped at the alleged instigation of the then Prime Minister Tony Blair.

  The current holder of the office of Attorney General is the Conservative MP Dominic Grieve.

  As to the functions carried out by the Attorney General, he alone has the authority to prosecute in certain circumstances and appears for the Crown in important cases. As may be recalled from 6.5 above the Attorney General also has powers to appeal against points of law in relation to acquittals under the Criminal Justice Act (CJA) 1972 and can also appeal against unduly lenient sentences under the CJA 1988. The crucially important decision of the House of Lords that DNA evidence, acquired in regard to another investigation and which should have been destroyed under s 64 of the Police and Criminal Evidence Act (PACE) 1984, could nonetheless be used, was taken as the result of a reference by the Attorney General (*Attorney General's Reference (No 3 of 1999)*).

- The *Solicitor General* is the Attorney General's deputy and the office is currently held by the Conservative MP Oliver Heald.

- The *Director of Public Prosecutions* (DPP) is the head of the national independent Crown Prosecution Service (CPS) established under the Prosecution of Offences Act 1985 to oversee the prosecution of criminal offences. The decision of the DPP whether to prosecute or not in any particular case is subject to judicial review in the courts. In *R v DPP ex p C* (1994), it was stated that such powers should be used sparingly and only on grounds of unlawful policy, failure to act in accordance with policy and perversity. Nonetheless, successful actions have been taken against the DPP in relation to decisions not to prosecute in *R v DPP ex p Jones* (2000) and in *R v DPP ex p Manning* (2000) (see 8.2 for an examination of the CPS). The position is currently held by Kier Starmer QC.

9.4   APPOINTMENT OF JUDICIARY

The somewhat astonishing fact is that there are nearly 40,000 judicial office-holders in England and Wales if one includes judges, tribunal members and magistrates. This section of this book considers how such a number of people actually come to hold these judicial positions.

In the first of his Hamlyn Lectures of 1993, the then Lord Chancellor, Lord Mackay, stated that the pre-eminent qualities required by a judge are:

> . . . good sound judgment based upon knowledge of the law, a willingness to study all sides of an argument with an acceptable degree of openness, and an ability to reach a firm conclusion and to articulate clearly the reasons for the conclusion.

Although the principal qualification for judicial office was experience of advocacy, Lord Mackay recognised that some people who have not practised advocacy may well have these necessary qualities to a great degree. This was reflected in the appointment of an academic and member of the Law Commission, Professor Brenda Hoggett, to the High Court in December 1993. Professor Hoggett, who sat as Mrs Justice Hale, was the first High Court judge not to have had a career as a practising barrister, although she qualified as a barrister in 1969 and was made a QC in 1989. As Dame Brenda Hale, she sat in the Court of Appeal; now as Lady Hale of Richmond, she is the first female member of the Law Lords.

The Courts and Legal Services Act (CLSA) 1990 introduced major changes into the qualifications required for filling the positions of judges. Judicial appointment is still essentially dependent upon the rights of audience in the higher courts, but at the same time as the CLSA 1990 effectively demolished the monopoly of the Bar to rights of audience in such courts, it opened up the possibility of achieving judicial office to legal practitioners other than barristers.

The Tribunals, Courts and Enforcement Act 2007 extended the possibility of holding judicial office to Fellows of the Institute of Legal Executives. This provision came into effect in November 2010.

9.4.1   QUALIFICATIONS

The main qualifications for appointment are as follows (the CLSA 1990 is dealt with in detail at 13.6 below):

● *Lord of Appeal in Ordinary*

  (a)   the holding of high judicial office for two years; or

  (b)   possession of a 15-year Supreme Court qualification under the CLSA 1990.

The Constitutional Reform Bill retains the same qualifications for members of the new Justices of the Supreme Court. There is, however, a new statutory appointments procedure under the proposed legislation, which is considered below.

- *Lord Justice of Appeal*

  (a)   the holding of a post as a High Court Judge; or

  (b)   possession of a 10-year High Court qualification under the CLSA 1990.

- *High Court judges*

  (a)   the holding of a post as a circuit judge for two years;

  (b)   possession of a 10-year High Court qualification under the CLSA 1990.

- *Deputy judges* must be qualified in the same way as permanent High Court Judges.

- *Circuit judges*

  (a)   the holding of a post as a recorder;

  (b)   possession of either a 10-year Crown Court qualification or a 10-year county court qualification under the CLSA 1990;

  (c)   the holding of certain offices, such as district judge, Social Security Commissioner, chairman of an industrial tribunal, stipendiary magistrate for three years.

- *Recorders* must possess a 10-year Crown Court or county court qualification under the CLSA 1990.

- *District judges* require a seven-year general qualification under the CLSA 1990.

9.4.2   SELECTION OF JUDGES

So far, attention has concentrated on the specific requirements for those wishing to fulfil the role of judge, but it remains to consider the more general question relating to the process whereby people are deemed suitable and selected for such office. Although the appointment procedure for judges has changed as a consequence of the Constitutional Reform Act 2005, with the establishment of the Judicial Appointments Commission, it is still necessary briefly to examine the former appointment procedure in order to explain the need for the reforms introduced by that Act.

Senior Judicial Positions

All judicial appointments remain, theoretically, at the hands of the Crown. Previously, however, the Crown was guided, if not actually dictated to, in regard to its appointment by the government of the day. Thus, as has been seen, the Lord Chancellor was a direct political appointment and the Prime Minister also advised the Crown on the appointment of other senior judicial office-holders such as the Law Lords and Appeal Court judges. Such apparent scope for patronage in the hands of the Prime Minister did not go without criticism.

Also under the previous system judges at the level of the High Court and Circuit
Bench were appointed by the Crown on the advice of the Lord Chancellor, and the Lord
Chancellor personally appointed district judges, lay magistrates and the members of
some tribunals. This system did not go without challenge either, the question being
raised as to how the Lord Chancellor actually reached his decision to recommend or
appoint individuals to judicial offices.

High Court Bench

In the past, appointment to the High Court Bench was by way of invitation from
the Lord Chancellor. However, in 1998, the LCD issued an advertisement inviting
applicants to apply for such positions. However, the Lord Chancellor retained his
right to invite individuals to become High Court judges. As regards the system of
invitation, the question immediately raised was as to exactly how the Lord Chancellor
selected the recipients of his favour. There being no system as such, there could be
no transparency and without transparency there had to be doubts as to the fairness of
the process. Even where a candidate applied for the post of High Court judge, the
procedure was different from applications at a lower level, for the reason that the
candidate was not interviewed after the usual consultation process with the senior
judiciary and the candidate's own referees. The Lord Chancellor simply decided whom
to appoint on the basis of that consultation process. Thus doubts about the secretive
nature of the consultancy procedure were compounded as regards applicants for the
High Court Bench.

Former Lord Chancellor Irvine's repeated insistence on the objectivity of the
judicial appointments process did little to remove the suspicion that, because it relied on
the sounding of the senior members of the judiciary and professions, it remained in the
final analysis restrictive, conservative and unfair, especially to minority groups.

The previous procedure of appointment to the High Court was subject to some
sharp criticism in a review conducted for the Bar Council under the chairmanship of the
former Appeal Court judge, Sir Iain Glidewell. The main review concluded that the
system of appointment was not sufficiently transparent. More contentiously, however, it
suggested that, given the increased role of the judiciary in matters relating to the review
of administrative decisions, devolution issues and human rights, it was no longer constitutionally acceptable for judges to be appointed by the government of the day, a member
of which the Lord Chancellor is. Consequently, the Glidewell review recommended that:

- the Lord Chancellor should cease to be responsible for the selection and appointment of High Court judges;
- the responsibility for such appointments should be transferred to a newly created
  independent body, a High Court Appointments Board; and
- the appointments to the High Court should only be made from among people
  who have made application for the position.

As a least favoured option, the review recommended that, if the Lord Chancellor
continued to be responsible for appointments to the High Court, he should reach his

decisions only after receiving the report and advice of a panel that should have the task of shortlisting and interviewing candidates, as is done for other judicial offices.

Circuit Judges and Below

All appointments up to and including circuit judges were made on the basis of open competition run by the Department for Constitutional Affairs (DCA).

The first stage was an advertisement for a particular judicial vacancy, which appeared in the national press and/or legal journals. The candidates were required to provide the names of three members of the judiciary or the legal profession as referees. Written assessments of candidates were then sought from those people whose names were given by the candidates themselves but in addition comments were solicited from 'a wide range of other judges and lawyers who were approached for assessments on the Lord Chancellor's behalf'.

The DCA, and indeed the previous Lord Chancellor himself, was adamant that there was no secrecy about those who were consulted, as lists detailing this latter group were given in the application packs and every person on that list was invited to comment on each applicant.

All assessments were made against stated criteria but were provided in confidence, which the DCA pointed out, with justification, is a common practice where references are sought by prospective employers.

A panel of three – a judge, a layperson and one of the Lord Chancellor's senior officials – carried out shortlisting of candidates. The panel also conducted the formal interviews, although the Lord Chancellor personally considered the situation of those interviewed before reaching a final decision. The DCA provided feedback and advice to unsuccessful candidates, including, on a non-attributed basis, information about matters contained in the assessments received.

Relying on the recommendations and opinions of the existing judiciary as to the suitability of the potential candidates might appear sensible at first sight. However, it brought with it the allegation, if not the fact, that the system was over-secretive and led to a highly conservative appointment policy. Judges were suspected, perhaps not unnaturally, of favouring those candidates who have not been troublesome in their previous cases and who have shown themselves to share the views and approaches of the existing office-holders.

In his 1993 Hamlyn Lecture Lord Mackay stated that the arrangements in the UK for the collection of data about candidates for the judiciary were comparatively well developed, and provided those who have to take the decisions, essentially the Lord Chancellor himself, with fuller information than would otherwise be available to them. The reasoning behind this claim would appear to be that, because the procedure was secret and limited, people commenting on the suitability of candidates would be willing to be more frank and open than would otherwise be the case were the references open to wider inspection. Such spurious justification is worrying in its complacency and its refusal to recognise that the secretive nature of the process might permit referees to make unsubstantiated derogatory comments that they would otherwise not feel free to make.

One of Lord Irvine's earliest actions as Lord Chancellor had been to declare the government's intention to inquire into the merits of establishing a Judicial Appointments

Commission. However, rather than carry out that intention, he announced in 1999 that Sir Leonard Peach, the former Commissioner for Public Appointments, would be conducting an independent scrutiny of the way in which the current appointment processes for judges operated. In December of that year, Sir Leonard reported that he had been:

> ...impressed by the quality of work, the professionalism and the depth of experience of the civil servants involved [LCD Press Release, 3 December 1999].

Sir Leonard did recommend that a Commission for Judicial Appointments be established, whose role would be to monitor the procedures and act as an Ombudsman for disappointed applicants. However, it was also recommended that the Commission should not have any role in the actual appointments, but should merely maintain an independent oversight of the procedure.

Not surprisingly, Lord Irvine was most happy to accept such findings and Sir Leonard's proposals, and the system of appointing the judiciary remained essentially unchanged. The appointment of Sir Colin Campbell, Vice Chancellor of Nottingham University, as the first Commissioner was announced in March 2001. Nonetheless, the work of the Commission proved salutary in relation to the appointments process and its reports did not hold back on providing a constant flow of restrained if sometimes acerbic criticism of the process and indeed the continued role of the Lord Chancellor within that process.

Somewhat surprisingly, in April 2003 Lord Irvine announced – before the select committee with oversight of his department – that he intended to issue three separate consultation documents relating to:

- whether judges and lawyers should continue to wear wigs and gowns in court;
- whether the status of Queen's Counsel should be retained and the related appointment process; and
- the role of the Judicial Appointments Commission.

Once again, Lord Irvine's actions were forestalled by his dismissal from office and his replacement in June 2003 by Lord Falconer, who immediately issued a consultation paper on the establishment of a full-blown Judicial Appointments Commission, which subsequently formed the basis of the proposals in regard to judicial appointments contained in the Constitutional Reform Act 2005.

In his last annual report before the Commission for Judicial Appointments (CJA) gave way to the Judicial Appointments Commission (JAC) under the Constitutional Reform Act 2005, Sir Colin Campbell pointed out that although the judicial appointments process had improved significantly from the perceived 'closed shop' of five years previously, there was still a lot of work to be done. In listing the history of the previous procedures, he detailed the many shortcomings it had found. These problems were listed as:

- inconsistencies in the ways in which candidates were selected;
- differences between the treatment of nominees and applicants;
- a lack of clear criteria as the basis for appointments, especially with reference to silk;
- a lack of clarity as to the role played by automatic consultation ('secret soundings');
- obscurity as to how the information gathered was treated and weighted;
- mechanisms for assessing candidates that were unrelated to the core competencies required for a post;
- poor interviewing techniques;
- systemic bias against less visible candidates: often solicitors, women and ethnic minorities;
- poor record keeping, which obstructed reliable audit trails; and
- a culture of unquestioning deference towards established judicial attitudes.

However, the report was both positive and admonitory in its conclusion that:

> the judicial appointments system today looks very different from the one we inherited just five years ago. Nevertheless, it is a work in progress, not the finished article. In five years' time we hope and expect it to look different again, encompassing appraisal, targeted and structured referencing, better feedback and career planning . . . The challenge for the future is to continue the momentum towards achieving a fair, open, transparent and accountable appointments process, which will in turn deliver a judiciary selected on merit and reflective of society, in which we can all have full confidence.

That challenge was passed on to the Judicial Appointments Commission in April 2006.

9.4.3 THE JUDICIAL APPOINTMENTS COMMISSION

Part 4 of the Constitutional Reform Act created a new independent Judicial Appointments Commission (JAC), which was in due course to assume responsibility for the process of selecting all judges for appointment in England and Wales from magistrates to members of the Supreme Court. However, following an agreement between the Lord Chancellor, the Judicial Appointments Commission (JAC), the Lord Chief Justice and the Magistrates' Association, it was decided that the JAC will not take responsibility for the recruitment and selection of magistrates. Consequently that function will remain with the Lord Chancellor's Advisory Committees on Justices of the Peace for the foreseeable future.

The Judicial Appointments Commission makes recommendations to the Lord Chancellor and no one may be appointed whom the Commission has not selected. The Lord Chancellor may reject a candidate, once, and ask the Commission to reconsider, once. However, if the Commission maintains its original recommendation, the Lord Chancellor must appoint or recommend for appointment whichever candidate is selected. The appointments of Lords Justices and above will continue to be made by the Queen formally, after the Commission has made a recommendation to the Lord Chancellor. The Act makes special provision for the appointment of the Lord Chief Justice, Heads of Division and Lords Justices of Appeal. In these cases the Commission will establish a selection panel of four members, consisting of two senior judges, normally including the Lord Chief Justice, and two lay members of the Commission.

Members of the Judicial Appointments Commission are appointed by the Queen, on the recommendation of the Lord Chancellor. Schedule 12 of the Act sets out the membership of the Judicial Appointments Commission, together with its powers and responsibilities. Of the total of 15 Commissioners:

- six must be lay members;
- five must be members of the judiciary (three judges of the Court of Appeal or High Court, including at least one Lord Justice of Appeal and at least one High Court judge, one circuit judge and one district judge);
- two must be members of the legal profession;
- one must be a tribunal member; and
- one must be a lay magistrate.

Significantly, the Chair of the Commission is one of the lay members. The Act requires that all candidates must be of good character and that selection shall be made strictly on merit. In addition it gives the Lord Chancellor power to issue guidance to the Commission in regard to what considerations to take into account in assessing merit, which the Commission must have regard to. However, the Act does not prescribe detailed appointments procedures and makes it clear that any such procedures are a matter for the Commission to decide.

It can be seen that although the Lord Chancellor retains the ultimate power to decide whom to appoint, or to recommend to the Queen for appointment, and thus maintains Parliamentary accountability, his discretion has been tightly circumscribed by the provisions of the Act.

The Act also provides for the establishment of a Judicial Appointments and Conduct Ombudsman to whom unsuccessful or disgruntled applicants for judicial office can apply for a consideration of their case. As the full title suggests the Ombudsman also will have a role to play in relation to matters of a disciplinary nature and s 110 allows complaints to be made to the Judicial Appointments and Conduct Ombudsman about judicial disciplinary cases.

JAC has identified five core qualities and abilities that are required for any judicial office, although they may be adapted for different posts; thus for example a High Court judge would be expected to display a high level of legal knowledge, whereas a lay tribunal member would be expected to display expertise in their professional field.

1.   *Intellectual capacity*

   ● high level of expertise in your chosen area or profession;

   ● ability quickly to absorb and analyse information;

   ● appropriate knowledge of the law and its underlying principles, or the ability to acquire this knowledge where necessary.

2.   *Personal qualities*

   ● integrity and independence of mind;

   ● sound judgment;

   ● decisiveness;

   ● objectivity;

   ● ability and willingness to learn and develop professionally.

3.   *An ability to understand and deal fairly*

   ● ability to treat everyone with respect and sensitivity whatever their background;

   ● willingness to listen with patience and courtesy.

4.   *Authority and communication skills*

   ● ability to explain the procedure and any decisions reached clearly and succinctly to all those involved;

   ● ability to inspire respect and confidence;

   ● ability to maintain authority when challenged.

5.   *Efficiency*

   ● ability to work at speed and under pressure;

   ● ability to organise time effectively and produce clear reasoned judgments expeditiously;

   ● ability to work constructively with others (including leadership and managerial skills where appropriate).

While JAC is 'committed to widening the range of applicants for judicial appointment and to ensuring that the very best eligible candidates are drawn from a wider range of backgrounds', this goal is to be achieved by encouraging a wider range of applicants and through the provision of a fair and open selection process. That being said, all appointments will be made purely on merit. However, the first appointments of the Commission were subjected to criticism in the newspapers in early 2008 when it was discovered that the first 10 High Court judges appointed under the new system were all men and thus not very different from those appointed under the old system.

JAC's role in the judicial appointments process begins when they receive a request from Her Majesty's Courts Service (HMCS), the Tribunals Service or on behalf of a tribunal outside the Tribunals Service. It then seeks out the best candidates, using the processes described below as measured against the qualities and abilities relevant to that post. The JAC's website (www.judicialappointments.gov.uk/index.htm) provides the following outline of the procedures leading to judicial appointment:

Stage 1: Application

Most positions are advertised widely in the national press, legal publications, the professional press and online. The application form is tailored for each individual selection exercise. Alongside the form, an information pack is available to applicants, which includes details of the eligibility criteria and guidance on the application process. This too is tailored for each exercise. Both documents can be downloaded from our website or are sent out to candidates on request. Once JAC has received a completed application form, it is required under s 63(3) of the Constitutional Reform Act to select people for appointment who are of 'good character' and has established guidance to help people to decide whether there is anything in their past conduct, or present circumstances (for example business connections) which might affect their application for judicial appointment. The essential principles in determining in good character are:

- the overriding need to maintain public confidence in the standards of the judiciary; and
- that public confidence will only be maintained if judicial office-holders and those who aspire to such office maintain the highest standards of behaviour in their professional, public and private lives.

Stage 2: Assessment

Candidates are asked on their application form to nominate up to three referees normally, or in some cases six. The Commission may also seek references from a list of Commission-nominated referees, which is published for each selection exercise. The time at which references are sought will depend on the assessment method used for shortlisting:

- If a qualifying test is used, references are taken up after the qualifying test and before interviews take place.
- If a paper sift is used, references are taken up before the sift and used to make the shortlisting decisions.

In all cases, references will form part of the information that JAC uses to make final selection recommendations to the Lord Chancellor.

Shortlisting

This may be done on the basis of qualifying tests or paper sift, using the application form and references. For senior appointments, where candidates will usually have an extensive track record, shortlisting will normally be done on information supplied by the candidate and from references.

Interviews and Selection Days

The next stage of the assessment will vary depending on the nature of the post to be filled. Candidates might be asked to attend a selection day, which may entail a combination of role-plays and an interview. For some specialist and the most senior appointments, there might be only a panel interview.

Panel Reports

Panel members assess all the information about each candidate, prepare reports on their findings and agree which candidates best meet the required abilities.

Statutory Consultation

As required under ss 88(3) and 94(3) of the CRA, the panel's reports on candidates likely to be considered by the Commission are sent to the Lord Chief Justice and another person who has held the post, or has relevant experience.

Stage 3: Selection and Recommendation

Recommendation to the Lord Chancellor

The Commissioners consider all the information gathered on the candidates and select candidates to be recommended to the Lord Chancellor for appointment.

Final Checks

For existing judicial office-holders, we check with the Office for Judicial Complaints (OJC) that there are no complaints outstanding against them. For all other candidates recommended for appointment, a series of good character checks are done with the Police, Her Majesty's Revenue and Customs and relevant professional bodies.

The Lord Chancellor may also require candidates to undergo a medical assessment before their appointment is confirmed. JAC recommends to the Lord Chancellor one candidate for each vacancy. The Lord Chancellor can reject that recommendation but he is required to provide his reasons to the Commission. He cannot select an alternative candidate.

Appointment to the Supreme Court

As regards future appointments to the Supreme Court, s 25 of the Constitutional Reform Act (CRA) sets out three possible routes to qualification. These are:

1. having held high judicial office, for at least two years;
2. having satisfied the judicial-appointment eligibility condition on a 15-year basis;
3. having been a qualifying practitioner for at least 15 years.

Although appointment to office is by the Crown, ss 26, 27, 28, 29, 30 and 31 and Sched 8 CRA 2005 set out the procedure for appointing a member of the Supreme Court. The

Lord Chancellor must convene an *ad hoc* selection commission if there is, or is likely to be, a vacancy. Subsequently, the Lord Chancellor will notify the Prime Minister of the identity of the person selected by that commission and under s 26(4), the Prime Minister *must* recommend the appointment of that person to the Queen.

Schedule 8 contains the rules governing the composition and operation of the selection commission, which will consist of the President of the Supreme Court, who will chair the commission, the Deputy President of the Supreme Court and one member from each of the territorial judicial appointment commissions (see below), one of whom must be a person who is not legally qualified. The next most senior ordinary judge in the Supreme Court will take the unfilled position on the selection commission if either the President or Deputy President is unable to sit.

Section 27 sets out the process that must be followed in the selection of a justice of the Supreme Court. The commission decides the particular selection process to be applied, the criteria or competences against which candidates will be assessed, but in any event the requirement is that any selection must be made solely on merit. However, sub-s 27(8) does require that the commission must take into account the need for the Court to have among its judges generally at least two Scottish judges and usually one from Northern Ireland. The Lord Chancellor, as provided for by sub-s 27(9), may issue non-binding guidance to the commission about the vacancy that has arisen, for example on the jurisdictional requirements of the Court, which the commission must have regard to.

Under sub-ss 27(2) and (3) the commission is required to consult:

(i)   senior judges who are neither on the commission nor willing to be considered for selection;

(ii)   the Lord Chancellor;

(iii)   the First Minister in Scotland;

(iv)   the Assembly First Secretary in Wales; and

(v)   the Secretary of State for Northern Ireland.

Sub-section 28(1) provides that after a selection has been made the commission must submit a report nominating one candidate to the Lord Chancellor, who then must also consult the senior judges (or other judges) who were consulted by the commission, the First Minister in Scotland, the Assembly First Secretary in Wales and the Secretary of State for Northern Ireland.

Section 29 sets out the Lord Chancellor's options after he has received a name from the commission and carried out the further consultation under s 28. The procedure may be divided into three possible stages.

1.   Stage 1, where a person has been selected and recommended by the appointments commission. At this stage the Lord Chancellor may:

(i)   accept the nomination and notify the Prime Minister;

    (ii)   reject the selection;

    (iii)   require the commission to reconsider its selection.

2.   Stage 2, where a person has been selected following a rejection or reconsideration at stage 1. In this event the Lord Chancellor can:

    (i)   accept the nomination and notify the Prime Minister;

    (ii)   reject the selection but only if it was made following a reconsideration at stage 1;

    (iii)   require the commission to reconsider the selection, but only if it was made following a rejection at stage 1.

3.   Stage 3, where a person has been selected following a rejection or reconsideration at stage 2. At this point, the Lord Chancellor *must* accept the nomination unless he prefers to accept a candidate who had previously been reconsidered but not subsequently recommended for a second time.

    In effect this means that the Lord Chancellor's options are as follows. He can:

    (i)   accept the recommendation of the commission;

    (ii)   ask the commission to reconsider; or

    (iii)   reject the recommendation.

Where the Lord Chancellor requires the commission to *reconsider* its original selection, the commission can still put forward the same name with additional justifications for its selection. In such circumstance the Lord Chancellor will either accept the recommendation or reject it. Alternatively the commission can recommend another candidate, whom the Lord Chancellor can accept, reject or require reconsideration of.

    However, if the Lord Chancellor *rejects* the original name provided by the selection commission, it must submit an alternative candidate giving reasons for its choice.

    At this point the Lord Chancellor can either:

(i)   accept the second candidate; or

(ii)   ask the selection commission to reconsider.

On reconsideration the commission can either resubmit the second candidate or propose an alternative candidate. At this point the Lord Chancellor must make a choice. He can either accept the alternative candidate or he can then choose the reconsidered candidate.

    Under sub-s 30(1), the Lord Chancellor's right of rejection is only exercisable where in his opinion the person selected is not suitable for the office concerned. The right to require reconsideration is exercisable under three conditions:

    (i)   where he feels there is not enough evidence that the person is suitable for office;

(ii)   where he feels there is not enough evidence that that person is the best candidate on merit; or

(iii)   where there is not enough evidence that the judges of the Court will between them have enough knowledge of, and experience in, the laws of each part of the United Kingdom, following the new appointment.

Should the Lord Chancellor exercise either of these options he must provide the commission with his reasons in writing (s 30(3)).

The current position of the Supreme Court

When the Supreme Court commenced operation in October 2009, there were only 11 justices, rather than the full complement of 12. One former member of the Judicial Committee of House, Lord Neuberger, had stepped down to take up the position of Lord of the Rolls in the Court of Appeal. At the time it was thought that the final place would be filled by Jonathan Sumption QC. Although Sumption had never held high judicial office he did qualify under the third, and perhaps surprising, criterion set out in s 25, that of having 15 years' qualification as a practitioner. However, it was suggested that Sumption withdrew his application, after some concern was expressed amongst the senior judiciary. Subsequently the former Court of Appeal judge Sir John Dyson was appointed to be the twelfth justice of the Supreme Court.

Following the appointment of Sir John, it was announced that he and all future holders of the office of Justice of the Supreme Court would be given the courtesy title of Lord or Lady.

In May 2011, following the retirement of Lords Saville and Collins, it was announced that Jonathan Sumption would, after all, be joining the Supreme Court together with Sir Nicholas Wilson. Lord Wilson assumed his position almost immediately, but, again rather surprisingly, Sumption's appointment was postponed to permit him to act as a barrister in several cases he was already committed to.

In July 2011, following the death of Lord Rodger and with the imminent retirement of Lord Brown in 2012, an *ad hoc* selection commission was established under s 27 and Sched 8 of the Constitutional Reform Act 2005 to select candidates to replace both justices. This was followed in October by the announcement that Lord Phillips was to resign at the end of the summer in 2012, several months before his required date of retirement, the reason being to facilitate a smooth handover to his replacement, during the time when the court was not actually sitting.

The illness and subsequent death of Lord Rodger, together with the delay in Jonathan Sumption taking up his position, meant that for an extended period in 2011 the Supreme Court had to function with only 10 justices.

On his retirement Lord Phillips was replaced as President by Lord Neuberger, who resumed his position in the Supreme Court, but Lord Dyson moved in the other direction to take up the role of Master of the Rolls.

In April 2009, the then Lord Chancellor, Jack Straw, set up an Advisory Panel on Judicial Diversity. As the final report of that committee stated:

> the establishment of the panel reflected the Lord Chancellor's concern, shared by the Lord Chief Justice, Lord Judge, and the Chairman of the Judicial Appointments Commission, Baroness Prashar, that, despite efforts over many years, significant progress on judicial diversity has not been made.

In February 2010, the advisory panel submitted its report (http://www.equality-ne. co.uk/downloads/759_advisory-panel-judicial-diversity-2010.pdf). It observed that traditionally the judiciary has been drawn from well-educated, middle-class, white male barristers and suggested that the under-representation of certain well-qualified groups, essentially women and members of ethnic minorities, might be due to 'factors other than pure talent' which might 'be influencing either people's willingness to apply or the selection process'.

The report suggested that, previously, there had never been a coherent, comprehensive strategy to promote diversity in relation to the appointment of the judiciary. To deal with this shortcoming it suggested the deployment of systematic, career-long strategies to promote diversity throughout general, as well as specifically judicial, legal careers, together with consistent monitoring and evaluation of such strategies.

The panel made a total of 53 recommendations to achieve the desired outcome. Amongst these were:

- Judges and members of the legal profession should engage with schools and colleges to ensure that students from under-represented groups understand that a judicial career is open to them.

- The legal profession, including law firms, should actively promote judicial office amongst those who are currently not coming forward, and, together with the judiciary, support and encourage talented candidates from under-represented groups to apply.

- There should be open and transparent selection processes at all levels.

- The Judicial Appointments Commission should revise its criteria for assessing merit, to support and underline with greater clarity its commitment to diversity.

- There should be no quotas or targets for recruiting under-represented groups, but, in line with s 159 of the Equality Act 2010, the use of positive selection in favour of particular minority candidates, where candidates for judicial office are seen to have equal abilities.

- The promotion of flexible working arrangements with exceptions needing to be justified.

- The requirement for candidates for judicial office to be able to demonstrate experience of diversity in either their private or professional lives.
- The Judicial Studies Board should evolve into a Judicial College.

In support of the specific recommendations the panel recommended the creation of a Judicial Diversity Taskforce to oversee an agreed action plan for change. Baroness Neuberger, chair of the panel, expressed her confidence that the proposals would result in the judiciary accurately reflecting society within 10 years.

In May 2011 the House of Lords Constitution Committee announced an inquiry into the judicial appointments system and in its report of March 2012, although it stated that a more diverse judiciary would increase confidence in the justice system, it concluded that 'we support the current appointments model and believe that no fundamental changes should be made.'

Nonetheless the committee did make the following recommendations:

- The Lord Chancellor should have no power to determine the JAC's membership or to issue directions as to how it should act; this would be damaging both to its independence and to the perception of its independence.
- The Lord Chancellor should continue to have only a limited role in the appointment of senior members of the judiciary.
- Parliamentarians should not hold pre- or post-appointment hearings of judicial candidates, nor should they sit on selection panels.
- Merit must continue to remain the sole criterion for appointment, but s 159 of the Equality Act 2010 should be used as part of the appointments process.
- A formal appraisal system for the judiciary should be introduced.

The committee did not consider that sufficient steps had yet been taken to increase judicial diversity. Accordingly, its recommendations included suggestions that:

- the recommendations of the Advisory Panel on Judicial Diversity should be implemented more rapidly;
- appointments panels must include laypersons who can bring a different perspective to the assessment of candidates' abilities;
- all selection panels should themselves be gender and, wherever possible, ethnically diverse;
- all those involved in the appointments process must be required to undertake diversity training;
- there needed to be an increased commitment to flexible working and the taking of career breaks within the judiciary and that the Senior Courts Act 1981 should be amended to allow part-time appointments to be made at High Court level and above;
- there needed to be a greater commitment on the part of the government, the judiciary and the legal professions to encourage applications for judicial posts from lawyers other than barristers.

Subsequently, in November 2011, the Ministry of Justice published a consultation document entitled *Appointments and Diversity: A Judiciary for the 21st Century* (http://www.justice.gov.uk/downloads/consultations/judicial-appointments-consultation-1911.pdf). The consultation sought views on legislative changes 'to achieve the proper balance between executive, judicial and independent responsibilities and to improve clarity, transparency and openness in the judicial appointments process'. In addition, the consultation also sought views on creating a more diverse judiciary that is reflective of society. The government's response to the consultation process was published in May 2012 and found expression in clause 18 of, and Schedule 12 to, the Crime and Courts Bill 2012.

However, in June 2012 Baroness Neuberger, the chair of the original Advisory Panel on Judicial Diversity, attacked the then Lord Chancellor, Ken Clarke, for giving himself too big a role in the appointment of senior judiciary in the Crime and Courts Bill, declaring the proposals a disgrace. As she pointed put, although the Lord Chancellor would relinquish his role in the appointment of judges below the rank of High Court to the Lord Chief Justice, he would need to be consulted on senior appointments to the Court of Appeal and above. He would also sit on selection panels for the Lord Chief Justice and president of the Supreme Court, although both panels would have a lay chair. Baroness Neuberger was reported as saying 'I think the Lord Chancellor is trying to fudge it, and he should know better.' As she correctly pointed out, the proposals to extend the powers of the Lord Chancellor went directly against the recommendation of the House of Lords' constitution committee, as reported above.

It should be noted that the Crime and Courts Bill also amends s 63 of the Constitutional Reform Act 2005 to provide that neither the requirement to select candidates for judicial office solely on merit, nor Part 5 of the Equality Act 2010, prevents the selecting body from preferring one candidate over another, where two persons are judged to be of equal merit, for the purposes of increasing diversity within the judiciary.

In September 2012 the second report of the Judicial Diversity Taskforce indicated that 20 of the 53 recommendations from the Advisory Panel report had been implemented in full with the remainder underway (http://www.justice.gov.uk/downloads/publications/policy/moj/judicial-diversity-taskforce-annual-report-2012.pdf). However, the taskforce was rightly cautious about claiming huge success.

> These are all notable achievements; however, it is not the time to rest on our laurels. The Taskforce must continue to provide focus, energy and strong, visible leadership to this ambitious programme of change.

Perhaps the size of the task that still lies ahead may be evidenced in the latest judicial diversity statistics. Currently, there is one woman in the House of Lords and only four in the Court of Appeal. In the High Court, the number is 17 out of 110 and, of 665 circuit judges, 114 are women. At the level of recorders, there are 118 women from a total of 1,155; and at district judge level, the number is 117 from 447 (as at April 2012).

The Justice Ministry has collated statistics on the ethnic origin of the judiciary, but it warns that the information they provide may be inaccurate as it is supplied only on a voluntary basis. However, using the statistics provided, it is apparent that if one restricts analysis to the black and Asian ethnic communities, for which groups statistics are available, then there are only five members of those groups in the High Court. At the level of circuit judge the ethnic minority representation is 1.7 per cent. At the level of recorder, the percentage is 5.1 per cent; at district judge level, it is also 5.1 per cent; and at deputy district judge level, it is 5.0 per cent. In the magistrates' courts, black and Asian people make up 2.8 per cent of the complement of full-time district judges. All statistics are available on the Judiciary of England website at http://www.judiciary.gov.uk/publications-and-reports/statistics/.

Case study: Does the gender of the judge matter? Radmacher v Granatino

In *Radmacher (formerly Granatino) v Granatino* (the clue of the substance being in the full title of the case), for the first time the highest court in England was required to consider the issue of prenuptial agreements in which the parties, as a precursor to their marriage, establish a limit on subsequent claims on the event of the marriage breaking up. The question before the court was whether such 'freely entered into' contractual agreements are binding in law to the degree that they override the usual principles of fairness at the time of divorce in such a way as to limit the rights of the parties that the courts would otherwise apply.

There were two particular twists in the case:

- Whereas usually it is the husband looking to protect his interests upon divorce, in this instance it was the ex-wife who was trying to enforce the agreement.
- In recognition of the importance of the case the Supreme Court heard it as a panel of nine justices, including the first and, to date, only woman member of the UK's highest court, Baroness Hale.

In a judgment of 69 pages and 195 paragraphs the court, by a majority of eight to one, determined that such prenuptial agreements were legal and enforceable. The one dissenting voice was Lady Hale. Whilst seven of the justices produced a single majority judgment of 123 paragraphs, and Lord Mance delivered his own judgment, in essential agreement, in seven paragraphs, Hale delivered her minority judgment in 69 extensive paragraphs. However, the core of her difference may be found in paragraph 137:

> Above all, perhaps, the court hearing a particular case can all too easily lose sight of the fact that, unlike a separation agreement, the object of an ante-nuptial agreement is to deny the economically weaker spouse the provision to which she – it is usually although by no means invariably she – would

otherwise be entitled . . . This is amply borne out by the precedents available in recent text-books . . . Would any self-respecting young woman sign up to an agreement which assumed that she would be the only one who might otherwise have a claim, thus placing no limit on the claims that might be made against her, and then limited her claim to a pre-determined sum for each year of marriage regardless of the circumstances, as if her wifely services were being bought by the year? Yet that is what these precedents do. *In short, there is a gender dimension to the issue which some may think ill-suited to decision by a court consisting of eight men and one woman* (emphasis added).

The questions that cannot be avoided in relation to this case are whether Baroness Hale's gender gave her an insight/awareness that was not shared with, or indeed open to, the other eight male judges and if so, whether this awareness should have been allowed to influence her judgment (this last could of course be rewritten to question the privileging of the assumedly male perspective of the majority of the judges).

As a matter of coincidence, and no doubt one much appreciated by the authors, a book entitled *Feminist Judgments: From Theory to Practice* (Hunter, McGlynn, & Rackley) had come out in September 2010 and had set itself the task of reconsidering and 're-judging' several notable cases from a feminist perspective, the application of which, they argued, would have led to very different decisions. Ironically, Baroness Hale's judgments were not found to be beyond criticism.

9.4.5   ALTERNATIVE APPROACHES TO APPOINTING JUDGES

A different approach, following the example of the USA, might be for the holders of the higher judicial offices to be subjected to confirmation hearings by, for example, a select committee of the House of Commons. Lord Mackay dismissed any such possibility as follows:

The tendency of prior examination . . . is to discover and analyse the previous opinions of the individual in detail. *I question whether the standing of the judiciary in our country, or the public's confidence in it, would be enhanced by such an inquiry*, or whether any wider public interest would be served by it [emphasis added].

It is perhaps unfortunate that the italicised words in the above passage can be interpreted in a way that no doubt Lord Mackay did not intend but which, nonetheless, could suggest a cover-up of the dubious opinions of those appointed to judicial office. The 2011 House of Lords Constitution Committee report also expressly rejected the possibility of parliamentarians being involved in pre- or post-appointment hearings of judicial candidates (see immediately above).

An even more radical alternative would be to open judicial office-holding to election as they also do in the USA, although in this case, one might well agree with Lord Mackay that:

> The British people would not feel that this was a very satisfactory method of appointing the professional judiciary.

Alternatively, and following Lord Mackay's emphasis on the professional nature of the judiciary, the UK could follow continental examples and provide the judiciary with a distinct professional career structure as an alternative to legal practice.

As has been seen, the changes made under the Constitutional Reform Act were subjected to many criticisms from the judges to the Commons Committee on Constitutional Affairs, with many social commentators and journalists joining in the attack. It is true that the reforms were an unlooked-for consequence of an ill-thought-out Cabinet reshuffle, and equally true that the proposed alterations provided the possibility of political interference with the independence and operation of the judiciary, especially with the future possibility of a weak Secretary of State for Justice and an overly strong Home Secretary. Nonetheless, it was surely not appropriate, indeed it was inconsistent, for those concerned to resort to an uncritical pragmatic defence of the *status quo* on the basis that it had worked so far. The system may have worked, but did it do so in an open and transparent manner, and in whose interests did it operate? The opportunity for more radical reforms may not have been taken, but the measures that have been taken surely represent an improvement in the structure and operation of the judicial system.

9.5 TRAINING OF THE JUDICIARY

Following the Constitutional Reform Act 2005, two new judicial institutions were established: the Judicial Office and the Judicial College, both of which operate as independent judicial bodies within the Judicial Office for England and Wales and are funded directly by the Ministry of Justice.

Judicial Office (JO)

This was set up in 2006 to support the judiciary in discharging its responsibilities under the CRA 2005. It reports to the Lord Chief Justice who, as Head of the Judiciary, has the responsibility for:

- representing the views of the judiciary of England and Wales to Parliament, the Lord Chancellor and ministers generally;

- maintaining arrangements for the welfare, training and guidance of the judiciary, within the resources made available by the Lord Chancellor;
- maintaining arrangements for the deployment of judges and the allocation of work within the courts.

The creation of the JO brought together and replaced several units that had previously existed independently, including the Judicial Studies Board (JSB) and the Judicial Communications Office. In 2010 it assumed responsibility for providing secretariat support and sponsorship of the Family and Civil Justice Councils, both of which provide independent advice to government and in 2011 it assumed responsibility for the work of the Office for Judicial Complaints. Also in 2011 the JO took over responsibility for the Tribunals Judicial Office and for provision of judicial training for the courts' and tribunals' judiciary through a new body, the Judicial College, which replaced the Judicial Studies Board.

The JO provides a broad range of support to the judiciary, including:

- administrative support and advice for training and development for judicial office-holders;
- research, analysis, legal and secretarial support for the senior judiciary and its governance bodies on a wide range of jurisdictional, constitutional and other strategic matters;
- dealing with official complaints against judicial office-holders through the Office for Judicial Complaints;
- HR and welfare support services;
- communication and media advice and information.

Judicial College

In April 2011, the newly established Judicial College brought together and replaced the Judicial Studies Board and the Tribunals Judicial Training Group and assumed responsibility for training judicial office-holders in the courts and in most tribunals. The Judicial College ensures that high-quality training is provided to enable judicial office-holders to carry out their duties effectively and in a way which preserves judicial independence and supports public confidence in the justice system.

The Judicial College aims to meet the highest professional standards in judicial learning and development.

The College is directly responsible for the development and delivery of training to judges in the Crown, county and higher courts in England and Wales and to tribunals, judges and members who come under the leadership of the Senior President of Tribunals.

The Senior President's responsibilities extend to judges and members within reserved tribunals across the UK. The College also provides some direct training to those who exercise judicial functions in the magistrates' courts (in England and Wales), as well as training materials, advice and support to those providing training in the magistrates' courts.

Prior to the establishment of the JSB, now the JC, the training of judges in the UK was almost minimal, especially when considered in the light of the continental practice where being a judge, rather than practising as an advocate, is a specific and early career choice, which leads to specialist and extensive training.

The Judicial College's activities fall under three main headings (what follows is taken from the publications of the JSB, but remains pertinent to the operation of the JC):

- initial training for new judicial office-holders and those who take on new responsibilities;

- continuing professional education to develop the skills and knowledge of existing judicial office-holders;

- delivering change and modernisation by identifying training needs and providing training programmes to support major changes to legislation and the administration of justice.

The Judicial College provides training and instruction to all part-time and full-time judges in judicial skills. An essential element of the philosophy of the College is that the training is provided by judges for judges. The training requirements of the different jurisdictions are the responsibility of distinct committees:

- The Judicial Training Committee delivers the training programmes for the Circuit and District Bench. It oversees training in the civil, family and criminal jurisdictions (the latter including District Judges in the magistrates' courts).

- The Magisterial Committee organises the training of newly elected chairmen of magistrates' benches and induction and continuation training for deputy district judges (magistrates' courts) and district judges (magistrates' courts). It is also responsible for advising on, developing and monitoring the training of lay magistrates and justices' clerks, which is delivered locally by magistrates' courts committees.

- The Tribunals Committee is responsible for the training needs of judicial office-holders in tribunals (see 12.5). The committee is chaired by a High Court judge and includes Tribunal Presidents, judicial training heads and academic trainers from a wide range of tribunal jurisdictions.

- The Equal Treatment Advisory Committee provides advice and support for the other committees with the overall function of supporting all judges and judicial office-holders 'to recognise the many ways in which social, cultural and other differences may have a bearing on the conduct of cases and the wider judicial role'.

Assistant recorders are required to attend seminars on procedure and sentencing before they can sit on their own in the Crown Court. Later, training takes the form of further, intermittent seminars focusing primarily on sentencing. Those sitting in the Crown Court benefit specifically from the advice contained in the *Crown Court Bench Book of Specimen Directions*. In the preface to the 1999 edition, although it was last updated in March 2010, Mr Justice Kay, then the Chair of the JSB Criminal Committee, explained its function thus:

> This . . . has become one of the most useful tools available to judges, experienced and inexperienced, in preparing a summing up. They are increasingly referred to by the Court of Appeal, Criminal Division as a starting point for a correct direction on matters of law and it is important that they are understood in that context and not simply repeated without being adapted to the facts and circumstances of a particular case. The Judicial Studies Board does not seek to lay down legal principles or to resolve difficult questions of law. It attempts to do no more than reflect the law and interpretation of the law as laid down by the courts and to that end every decision of the Court of Appeal, Criminal Division referring to these directions is studied to see if change is necessary.

The specific nature of the Specimen Directions is a delicate matter, as they do not, and indeed cannot, represent an unconditional statement of what the law and judicial practice is. They always have to be adapted by the judges to fit particular circumstances. Such a fact has to be recognised, and indeed it is enforced by an injunction not to reproduce the Directions as a part of any commercial activity. A civil law Bench Book has also been produced, and there are other Bench Books for reference in family law proceedings, youth court proceedings and for the guidance of district judges (magistrates' courts). There is also an *Equal Treatment Bench Book* for use by all members of the judiciary (see further immediately below).

Judicial training has probably never been of greater public concern or been executed with such rigour since the JSB was established in 1979. For example, the judiciary were subject to thorough retraining in the new civil procedure. This training included residential seminars for all full-time and part-time judges dealing with civil work, local training and conferences held at various national locations. In an interview in October 2009, Judge John Phillips, who was involved in devising the JSB's new programme, emphasised a change in judicial training, 'with less emphasis on the letter of the law and more on the acquisition of judicial skills'. As he added 'There are, in any event, many ways for judges to keep pace with developments in the law – via JSB e-learning packages and e-letters, and other channels of communication such as professional legal publications, websites, law reports, judgments, textbooks and other sources.'

9.5.1 EQUAL TREATMENT TRAINING

Law is supposed to operate on the basis of formal equality: everyone is assumed to be equal before the law and to be treated equally, regardless of their personal attributes or situation (see Chapter 2). In the past, however, accusations have been levelled at the judiciary that allege that, at the very least, they themselves are insensitive to the sensitivities of others, particularly in matters of race, gender, sexual orientation and in relation to people with disabilities. Not only have they been accused of lacking understanding and sympathy towards others with different values or practices from their own, but it has also been claimed that many of them have been resistant to changing their attitudes.

However, such resistance runs the danger of alienating large sections of the population over which the judiciary exercises its power and, when law is reduced to the level of mere power rather than legitimate authority, its effectiveness is correspondingly reduced. In the light of the recognition that something had to be done to forestall such potential damage, the JSB instituted seminars for training part-time and circuit judges in racial awareness, for example, reminding them that, in a multicultural/multi-faith society, it is offensive to ask for people's 'Christian' names, as well as warning them as to the dangers of even more crassly offensive language and racial stereotyping that appears to be so much a part of the English use of metaphor.

In 1999, for the first time, JSB training included new guidance for all judges on equal treatment issues such as disability, gender and sexual orientation, and litigants in person. In announcing that equal treatment training was to be integral to all induction courses, Lord Justice Waller (the then chairman of the JSB) stated:

> There is absolutely no room for complacency in these areas. And I am not going to say just because someone has been on our course, they will be perfect, but I hope that, as a result, judges are better equipped to do their jobs [*The Times*, 13 July 1999].

A key component in the JSB's strategy of overcoming the appearance of insensitivity and related perception of prejudice was the production of the *Equal Treatment Bench Book* (last updated in October 2009), which it has to be said provides a truly comprehensive first-class guide for the judiciary in ensuring awareness of the need to treat all those who come before them equally and with sensitivity and civility.

Ethnic Minorities in the Criminal Court

An opportunity to assess the success of the then JSB's policy in assuring equality of treatment was provided in March 2003 by the publication of a research report entitled *Ethnic Minorities in the Criminal Court: Perceptions of Fairness and Equality of Treatment*.

The research project investigated the extent to which ethnic minority defendants and witnesses in Crown Courts and magistrates' courts perceived their treatment to have been unfair and whether those who did perceive unfairness attributed it to racial bias. The experience of the ethnic minority group was compared with that of white defendants. The study also took into account the views of court staff, judges, magistrates and lawyers. Altogether, 1,252 people were interviewed in Manchester, Birmingham and London, and the proceedings in more than 500 cases were observed.

As Regards Defendants:

- The proportion who said their treatment had been unfair in court was about one-third in the Crown Court and about a quarter in the magistrates' courts.
- There was little difference between ethnic minority and white defendants (33 per cent of black, 27 per cent of Asian and 29 per cent of white defendants).
- One in five black defendants in the Crown Court and one in 10 in the magistrates' courts, and one in eight Asian defendants in both types of court, thought that their unfair treatment in court related to their ethnicity.
- Very few perceived racial bias in the conduct or attitude of judges or magistrates (only 3 per cent in the Crown Court and 1 per cent in the magistrates' courts).
- There were no complaints about racist remarks from the bench.
- Most complaints about racial bias concerned sentences perceived to be more severe than those imposed on a similar white defendant.
- 31 per cent of ethnic minority defendants in the Crown Court and 48 per cent in the magistrates' courts said they would like more people from ethnic minorities sitting in judgment and among the staff of the courts.

As Regards Witnesses:

- None complained of racial bias in the Crown Court.
- 7 per cent perceived racial bias in the magistrates' courts.

As Regards the Judges and Magistrates:

- All the judges and two-thirds of the magistrates had received training in ethnic awareness.
- Only two judges and three magistrates said that it had 'added nothing' or been 'unhelpful'.

As Regards Court Officials and Lawyers:

- 98 per cent of white clerks and ushers thought there was equal treatment of ethnic minorities by the courts, compared with:
  - (a)   71 per cent of Asian staff; and
  - (b)   28 per cent of black staff.
- 69 per cent of white lawyers thought there was equal treatment of ethnic minorities by the courts; compared with:
  - (a)   63 per cent of Asian lawyers; and
  - (b)   43 per cent of black lawyers.

- 30 per cent of black lawyers said they had personally witnessed incidents in court that they regarded as 'racist'; as opposed to:

  (a)　　13 per cent of white lawyers; and

  (b)　　11 per cent of Asian lawyers.

The conclusion of the research project was that there had been:

> . . . a substantial change for the better in perceptions of ethnic minorities of racial impartiality in the criminal courts. Several judges mentioned that attitudes had altered markedly in recent years and magistrates reported a substantial decline in the frequency of racially inappropriate remarks. Many lawyers also reported that racial bias or inappropriate language was becoming 'a thing of the past'. These positive findings, taken together with the much lower than expected proportion of defendants complaining of racial bias, may be a reflection of both general social improvements in the treatment of ethnic minorities and the specific efforts begun by the Lord Chancellor's Department in the early 1990s to heighten the awareness of all involved in the system of the need to guard against racial bias.

Nonetheless, the report warned against complacency and emphasised that the fact that one in five black and one in eight Asian defendants definitely perceived racial bias in the Crown Court, and at least 1 in 10 in the magistrates' courts, combined with the fact that black lawyers and staff were more likely to perceive racial bias than others, was sufficient cause to continue the efforts towards eliminating the vestiges of perceived unequal treatment.

Perceptions of racial bias, more frequently held by black defendants in the Crown Court, may well arise from a belief that the disproportionately large number of black people caught up by the criminal justice and prison systems must, at least to some extent, be a reflection of racism. Every effort therefore should be made when passing sentence to demonstrate and convince defendants that no element of racial stereotyping or bias has entered into the decision.

Among black defendants and lawyers in particular, there was a belief that the authority and legitimacy of the courts, and confidence in them, would be strengthened if more personnel from ethnic minorities were seen to be playing a part in the administration of criminal justice. Indeed, in the Crown Court, many judges agreed that more could be done to avoid the impression of the courts as 'white dominated institutions'.

However, there is an undercurrent in the report, which supports a more critical reading. While it was concerned with '*perceptions* of racial bias', such perceptions may not wholly comprehend the underlying reality. Eliminating inappropriate language may well be a good thing in itself, but if it merely provides camouflage for a system that remains fundamentally biased in terms of its outcomes, then doubts have to be raised about its fundamental worth. The difference in perception of the black lawyers and court staff as to the true nature of the system would seem to provide grounds to support such a possibility. Given that differential sentencing remains the major ground of complaint relating to allegations of ethnic bias, that surely remains the most pressing issue in relation to equality. As the report states:

> The findings of this study may go some way to dispelling the view that most minority ethnic defendants believe that their treatment by the courts has been racially biased. But *if it could be shown that the 'cultural change' which this study has identified has had a real impact on eliminating differential sentencing of white and ethnic minority defendants*, this would further encourage the confidence of ethnic minorities in the criminal courts [emphasis added].

9.6 RETIREMENT OF JUDGES

All judges are now required to retire at 70, although they may continue in office at the discretion of the Lord Chief Justice and the approval of the Lord Chancellor. The Judicial Pensions and Retirement Act 1993 reduced the retirement age from the previous 75 years for High Court judges and 72 years for other judges, although a judge already serving on the implementation of the Act (31 March 1995) retains the pre-existing retirement age. Part-time members of the judiciary were customarily required to retire at 65, but following an initial finding by an employment tribunal in February 2008 that such a policy was discriminatory, the Lord Chancellor announced that the retirement age for part-time judges would be increased to bring it in line with the general judicial retirement age of 70. The 2011 House of Lords Constitution Committee, previously considered, recommended that the retirement age for Court of Appeal judges and Supreme Court justices should be raised to 75.

The reduction of the retirement age may have been designed to reduce the average age of the judiciary, but of perhaps even more significance in this respect is the change that was introduced in judicial pensions at the same time. The new provision requires judges to have served for 20 years, rather than the previous 15, before they qualify for full pension rights. This effectively means that if judges are to benefit from full pension rights, they will have to take up their appointments by the time they are 50. Given that judges are predominantly appointed from the ranks of high-earning QCs, this will either reduce their potential earnings at the Bar or reduce their pay package as judges by approximately 7.5 per cent. This measure led to a great deal of resentment within both the Bar and the judiciary, Lord Chief Justice Taylor referring to its unfairness and meanness, and it was one of the issues that fuelled the antagonism between Lord Mackay and the other members of the judiciary.

With regard to compulsory retirement, many people thought it particularly regrettable that Lord Bingham's age meant that he could not assume the role of the first President of the new Supreme Court. That honour passed to Lord Philips who was a sprightly 71 when he assumed the office.

In the summer of 2005, Sir Hugh Laddie, a High Court Chancery Judge of some 10 years' standing, announced his intention to resign from his position and return to legal practice. He was the first judge to return to private practice for over 30 years and it is reported that his resignation upset the Lord Chancellor by breaking the 'unwritten rule that joining the judiciary is a one-way street'. Sir Hugh compounded the difficulties in the situation when, in February 2006, he delivered a lecture at the University of London, in which he told the audience that although he was an expert in intellectual property law, he was frequently asked to sit on tax and insolvency cases. As he admitted (*Law Society Gazette*, 23 February 2006):

> I knew nothing about tax, except that that it came as a nasty shock at the end of the year. I had never studied it or did it at the bar, or insolvency . . . I had colleagues who said that it was marvellous to do cases outside their own field, that it was stimulating. When I resigned, I felt a certain sensitivity about deciding cases about which I had no knowledge. It would have been better to use a roulette wheel.

9.7   JUDICIAL CONDUCT AND DISCIPLINE

In August 2011 a revised *Guide to Judicial Conduct* was published by the Judges' Council after wide consultation with members of the judiciary. The guide:

- offers assistance to judges on issues rather than prescribing a detailed code; and
- sets up principles from which judges can make their own decisions and so maintain their judicial independence.

The guide accepts, as a basis for its more detailed consideration, what are referred to as the Bangalore principles, which were established following a United Nations initiative. The Bangalore principles may be understood as six underlying values with the stated intention of:

> . . . establish[ing] standards for ethical conduct of judges. They are designed to provide guidance to judges and to afford the judiciary a framework for regulating judicial conduct. They are also intended to assist members of the Executive and Legislature, and lawyers and the public in general, to better understand and support the judiciary.

The essential principles are:

(i) Judicial independence is a prerequisite to the rule of law and a fundamental guarantee of a fair trial. A judge shall therefore uphold and exemplify judicial independence in both its individual and institutional aspects.

(ii) Impartiality is essential to the proper discharge of the judicial office. It applies not only to the decision itself but also to the process by which the decision is made.

(iii) Integrity is essential to the proper discharge of the judicial office.

(iv) Propriety, and the appearance of propriety, are essential to the performance of all of the activities of the judge.

(v) Ensuring equality of treatment to all before the courts is essential to the due performance of the judicial office.

(vi) Competence and diligence are prerequisites to the due performance of judicial office.

The worked-out expression of those principles may be seen at: http://www.judiciary.gov.uk/Resources/JCO/Documents/Guidance/guide-judicial-conduct-aug2011.pdf

In relation to matters of discipline, the Constitutional Reform Act 2005 gave powers to both the Lord Chancellor and the Lord Chief Justice. Consistent with previous provisions, the position of all senior judicial office-holders is protected, and removal from office of any judge in the High Court or above is only possible following resolutions in both the House of Commons and the House of Lords. Under s 108 CRA, the Lord Chief Justice was given new powers enabling him to:

- advise;
- warn; or
- formally reprimand judicial office-holders.

He may also suspend them in certain circumstances, mainly regarding allegations relating to criminal offences. Such powers are subject to the agreement of the Lord Chancellor. The Lord Chief Justice may, again with the agreement of the Lord Chancellor, make regulations and rules about the disciplinary process.

The Office for Judicial Complaints

The Constitutional Reform Act 2005 also established the Office for Judicial Complaints (OJC) and gave the Lord Chancellor and the Lord Chief Justice joint responsibility for a new system for dealing with complaints about the personal conduct of all judicial office-holders in England and Wales. The OJC was set up in April 2006 to handle these complaints and provide advice and assistance to the Lord Chancellor and Lord Chief Justice in the performance of their new joint role.

In its annual report for the year 2010/11 the OJC revealed that, over the period, it had received 1,638 separate complaints against judicial office-holders, although 1,046 of these (64 per cent) related to judicial decisions, which are outside its remit. Unless there are elements of misconduct included in the complaint, issues can only be challenged through an appeal process.

The most common complaint, numbering 456 in total, related to inappropriate behaviour or comments. The next most frequent complaint, 30 in total, related to the non-performance of a judicial duty. Complaints relating to discrimination fell from 83 to 24.

Out of the 106 judicial office-holders subject to disciplinary action, 17 were from the mainstream judiciary, two were coroners, 16 were tribunals judiciary and 71 were magistrates. This total represents approximately 0.25 per cent of the 39,600 judicial office-holders.

The 29 judicial office-holders were removed from office for the following reasons:

- 9 for not fulfilling their judicial duties;
- 5 as a result of civil proceedings or criminal convictions;
- 7 for inappropriate behaviour or comments;
- 5 for professional misconduct;
- 2 for motoring offences;
- 1 for misuse of judicial status.

In addition:

- 28 judicial office-holders received a reprimand;
- 12 received formal advice/warning;
- there were 25 resignations during conduct investigations;
- the remaining 12 received formal guidance.

In June 2009, in rejecting an appeal by the *The Guardian* newspaper under the Freedom of Information Act 2001, the Information Tribunal decided that the Ministry of Justice does not have to disclose the names of judges disciplined following complaints on the basis that 'Disclosure would risk undermining a judge's authority while carrying out his or her judicial function.'

9.7.1 REMOVAL OF JUDGES

Reference has already been made to the need, with of course the exception of the Lord Chancellorship, to protect the independence of the judiciary by making it difficult for a discomfited government to remove judges from their positions on merely political grounds. The actual provision is that judges of the House of Lords, the Court of Appeal and the High Court hold their office during good behaviour, subject to the proviso that they can be removed by the Crown on the presentation of an address by both Houses of Parliament. In actual fact, this procedure has never been used in relation to an English judge, although it was once used in 1830 to remove an Irish judge who was found guilty of misappropriating funds.

Judges below the level of the High Court do not share the same degree of security of tenure as their more senior colleagues, and can be removed, on grounds of misbehaviour or incapacity, by the action of the Lord Chancellor subject to the approval of the Lord Chief Justice.

In practice only two judges have been removed on the grounds of misbehaviour. In 1983 Circuit Judge Bruce Campbell was removed after being found guilty of smuggling tobacco and alcohol into England from Guernsey. Then in 2009 District Judge Margaret Short was removed for behaviour that was 'inappropriate, petulant and rude' with regard to one incident, according to the Office for Judicial Complaints, and 'intemperate and ill-judged' with regard to another.

In a letter circulated in July 1994, Lord Mackay asked that judges inform him immediately if they are ever charged with any criminal offence other than parking or speeding violations. The Lord Chancellor stated that he wished to make it clear that a conviction for drink-driving would amount, *prima facie*, to misbehaviour. Causing offence on racial or religious grounds could also be seen as misbehaviour, as could sexual harassment.

The discretionary power of the Lord Chancellor not to extend the appointment of a recorder, without the need to explain or justify his action, has previously provided grounds for criticism and accusations of political interference on the part of the Lord Chancellor.

Stipendiary magistrates are subject to removal by the Crown on the recommendation of the Lord Chancellor and lay magistrates are subject to removal by the Lord Chancellor without cause or explanation.

9.8 JUDICIAL IMMUNITY FROM SUIT

A fundamental measure to ensure the independence of the judiciary is the rule that they cannot be sued in relation to things said or acts done in their judicial capacity in good faith. The effect of this may be seen in *Sirros v Moore* (1975), in which a judge wrongly ordered someone's detention. It was subsequently held by the Court of Appeal that, although the detention had been unlawful, no action could be taken against the judge as he had acted in good faith in his judicial capacity. Although some judges on occasion may be accused of abusing this privilege, it is nonetheless essential if judges are to operate as independent representatives of the law, for it is unlikely that judges would be able to express their honest opinions of the law, and the situations in which it is being applied, if they were to be subject to suits from disgruntled participants.

Given the increased use of the doctrine of *ultra vires* to justify legal action by way of judicial review against members of the executive, it is satisfyingly ironic that at least one judge, Stephen Sedley, who now sits in the Court of Appeal, sees the possibility of a similar *ultra vires* action providing grounds for an action against judges in spite of their previously assumed legal immunity. As he expressed the point in the *London Review of Books* of April 1994:

> Judges have no authority to act maliciously or corruptly. It would be rational to hold that such acts take them outside their jurisdiction and so do not attract judicial immunity.

No doubt such a suggestion would be anathema to the great majority of the judiciary, but the point remains: why should judges be at liberty to abuse their position of authority in a way that no other public servant can?

Before 1991, magistrates could be liable for damages for actions done in excess of their actual authority, but the CLSA 1990 extended the existing immunity from the superior courts to cover the inferior courts, so magistrates now share the same protection as other judges.

It is worth stating at this point that this immunity during court proceedings also extends as far as advocates and witnesses, and of course jurors, although the controls of *perjury* and *contempt of court* are always available to cover what is said or done in the course of court proceedings.

Related to, although distinct from, the principle of immunity from suit is the convention that individual judges should not be subject to criticism in parliamentary debate, unless subject to an address for their removal: legal principles and the law in general can be criticised, but not judges.

9.9   MAGISTRATES

The foregoing has concentrated attention on the professional and legally qualified judges. It should not be forgotten, however, that there are some 27,000 unpaid part-time lay magistrates, 141 full-time professional magistrates (known as district judges (magistrates' courts)) and 134 deputy district judges (magistrates' courts) operating within some 330 or so magistrates' courts in England. These magistrates are empowered to hear and decide a wide variety of legal matters and the amount and importance of the work they do should not be underestimated: as much as 95 per cent of all criminal cases are dealt with by the magistrates' courts. The operation of the magistrates' courts and the powers of magistrates have been considered in detail above at 4.3 and 9.2. Since April 2005, magistrates' courts in England and Wales have been administered by Her Majesty's Courts Service (HMCS, now the HMCTS). This amalgamation ended the previously long-standing separation between magistrates' courts, which were administered by a total of 42 independent local committees, and the government-run Court Service that ran the Court of Appeal, the High Court and all Crown and county courts.

It remains, however, to examine the manner in which they are appointed to their positions.

There is no requirement for lay magistrates to have any legal qualifications. On being accepted onto the bench, however, magistrates undertake a training process, under the auspices of the JSB. Magistrates are required to attend training courses, with a special emphasis being placed on Equal Treatment Training. The way in which the training programme seeks to overcome conceptions as to the politically narrow nature of the magistracy is evident in the content of the extensive training materials produced for the magistrates. These include modules on: raising awareness and challenging discrimination; discretion and decision-making; prejudice and stereotype; thus, the overall emphasis may be seen to be on equality of people, and equality of treatment. There is, however, a new emphasis on the practical skills involved in performing the duties placed on magistrates, and consequently much of the training will actually be based on sitting as magistrates with the input of specially trained mentors to give guidance and advice on how the new magistrates perform their tasks and fulfil their roles. About 12–18 months after appointment the new magistrate is appraised against a set of the competences covering each courtroom role from basic magistrates to chairmen in adult, youth and family courts. Competences include a checklist of observable behaviour and knowledge.

The training course is designed to give new magistrates an understanding of the functions and powers of the bench generally, and to locate that understanding within the context of national practice, particularly with regard to sentencing. On the topic of discretion and sentencing, Lord Irvine provided the magistrates with the following strong advice, not to say warning:

> You . . . must exercise your discretion in individual cases with great care within a system that needs to secure continuing public confidence. This is what makes the sentencing guidelines produced by the Magistrates' Association so important. They are guidelines – they do not curtail your independent discretion to impose sentences you think are right, case by case. But the guidelines exist to help you in that process, to give you more information in reaching your decision. And they help to assist the magistracy, to maintain an overall consistency of approach . . . I urge you to follow the guidelines, which are drawn up for your benefit and the magistracy as a whole [Speech to the Council of Magistrates' Association, March 1999].

One aspect of sentencing that merits attention arises in relation to the increasingly important area of environmental crime. In response to this, and to make magistrates fully aware of its importance, the Magistrates Association website made available an extremely useful guidance entitled 'Costing the Earth – guidance for sentencers'.

Justices' Clerk

Although particular key legal issues may be considered in the course of the training, it is not the intention to provide the magistrate with a complete grasp of substantive law and legal practice. Indeed, to expect such would be to misunderstand both the role of the magistrates and the division of responsibility within the magistrates' court. Every bench of magistrates has a legally qualified justices' clerk, whose function it is to advise the bench on questions of law, practice and procedure, leaving matters of fact to magistrates to decide upon (see above, at 6.2). This division of powers raises a further possible area of contention with regard to the operation of magistrates' courts, for in the case of some particularly acquiescent benches, the justices' clerks appear to run the court, and this leads to the suspicion that they actually direct the magistrates as to what decisions they should make. This perception is compounded by the fact that the bench is entitled to invite their clerk to accompany them when they retire to consider their verdicts. A *Practice Direction (Justices: Clerks to the Court)* (2000) set out the role and functions of the clerk to the court. Thus, the clerk, or legal adviser who stands in for the clerk, is stated to be responsible for providing the justices with any advice they require to properly perform their functions, whether or not the justices have requested that advice, on the following matters:

- questions of law (including ECHR jurisprudence and those matters set out in s 2(1) of the HRA 1998);
- questions of mixed law and fact;
- matters of practice and procedure;
- the range of penalties available;
- any relevant decisions of the superior courts or other guidelines; other issues relevant to the matter before the court;
- the appropriate decision-making structure to be applied in any given case; and
- in addition to advising the justices, it shall be the legal adviser's responsibility to assist the court, where appropriate, as to the formulation of reasons and the recording of those reasons.

As regards when and where this advice should be given, the *Practice Direction* states that:

> At any time, justices are entitled to receive advice to assist them in discharging their responsibilities. If they are in any doubt as to the evidence which has been given, they should seek the aid of their legal adviser, referring to his/her notes as appropriate. This should ordinarily be done in open court. Where the justices request their adviser to join them in the retiring room, this request should be made in the presence of the parties in court. Any legal advice given to the justices other than in open court should be clearly stated to be provisional and the adviser should subsequently repeat the substance of the advice in open court and give the parties an opportunity to make any representations they wish on that provisional advice.

In October 2007 the senior presiding judge for England and Wales issued new guidelines for the conduct of justices' clerks and assistant justices' clerks. These emphasise

the independence and impartiality of clerks (they may be seen at http://www.judiciary.
gov.uk/Resources/JCO/Documents/Guidance/guidance-justice-clerks-codeconduct_
updated_Oct07.pdf).

9.9.1 APPOINTMENT

Under the Justices of the Peace Act 1997, magistrates are appointed to, and indeed
removed from, office by the Lord Chancellor on behalf of the Queen, after consultation
with local advisory committees. Following the Constitutional Reform Act 2005 it was the
intention for the Judicial Appointments Commission eventually to deal with the appointment of magistrates. However, at least for the moment, the Ministry of Justice handles
such appointments. In this interim period recommendations on the appointment of
magistrates continue to be made by local advisory committees. These are then passed to
the Lord Chief Justice for approval, before being submitted to the Lord Chancellor to
make the appointment.

Section 50 of the Employment Rights Act 1996 provides that employers are
obliged to release their employees, for such time as is reasonable, to permit them to serve
as magistrates. In the event of an employer refusing to sanction absence from work to
perform magistrate's duties, the employee can take the matter before an employment
tribunal. Understandably, there is no statutory requirement for the employer to pay their
employees in their absence, but magistrates are entitled to claim expenses for loss of
earnings in the exercise of their office.

Once candidates of a suitable quality have been identified, the local advisory
committee is placed under the injunction to have regard to the need to ensure that
the composition of the bench broadly reflects the community that it serves in terms
of gender, ethnic origin, geographical spread, occupation and political affiliation.
It may even be that individuals who are otherwise suitably qualified may not be
appointed if their presence would exacerbate a perceived imbalance in the
existing bench. Nonetheless, there remains a lingering doubt, at least in the minds of
particular constituencies, that the magistracy still represents the values, both moral and
political, of a limited section of society. A further significant step towards opening up the
whole procedure of appointing magistrates was taken when local advisory committees
were granted the power to advertise for people to put themselves forward for selection.
As the chairman of the Mid-Staffordshire Magistrates' Bench stated in a local
newspaper, although previously rank and social position were the main qualifications,
nowadays:

> . . . it is important a bench has a balance of sexes, professions and political
> allegiances.

In March 1999, the LCD launched a campaign to attract a wider section of candidates to
apply to be magistrates. In announcing the campaign, Lord Irvine stated that:

> Magistrates come from a wide range of backgrounds and occupations. We
> have magistrates who are dinner ladies and scientists, bus drivers and
> teachers, plumbers and housewives. They have different faiths and come
> from different ethnic backgrounds, some have disabilities. All are serving
> their communities, ensuring that local justice is dispensed by local people.
> The magistracy should reflect the diversity of the community it serves . . .
> Rest assured appointments are made on the merit, regardless of educational
> background, social class or ethnic background.

The campaign was supported by adverts in some 36 newspapers and magazines, from
broadsheets to tabloids, from TV listings to women's magazines. The campaign was
particularly aimed at ethnic minorities, its adverts being carried in such publications as
the *Caribbean Times*, the *Asian Times* and *Muslim News*. The 1999 campaign was
followed in 2001 by a *Judiciary for All* scheme, which aimed to encourage more people
from ethnic minority groups to apply to become magistrates. The next initiative to make
the Bench more reflective of the public was the 'National Strategy for the Recruitment of
Lay Magistrates' announced by Lord Falconer in October 2003. As he stated:

> I consider it particularly important that the magistracy is seen to be repre-
> sentative of all sections of our society and that no one group of people
> should feel that they are under-represented on the magistrates' bench. My
> Department is already involved with a number of initiatives aimed at encour-
> aging young people and minority ethnic groups to become involved in the
> judicial process and, although the ethnic make up of the magistracy country-
> wide is close to the national average for cultural representation per head of
> population there are still regional variations, both in age and ethnicity, that
> need to be addressed.

The statistics demonstrate that the gender balance and ethnic mix of the magistracy does not appear to pose a problem, but the same cannot be said in terms of its class
mix. However, in 1998, the LCD issued a consultation paper relating to the political
balance in the lay magistracy, which suggested that political affiliation was no longer a
major issue, and therefore did not have to be controlled in relation to the make-up of
benches of magistrates. As support for its suggestion, the consultancy document made
three points. First, that actually ensuring a political balance on the bench raises:

> . . . the danger of creating a perception that politics do play a part in the
> administration of justice, notwithstanding that it is agreed on all sides that,
> in a mature democracy, politics have no place in the court room.

Second, that advisory committees:

> ... have increasingly found that many magistrates have declined to provide the information [relating to their political allegiance] or classed themselves as 'uncommitted'.

Third, it claimed that in any case, 'geodemographic classification schemes', based on an analysis of particular personal attributes such as ethnicity, gender, marital status, occupation, home ownership and car-owning status, are much more sensitive indicators for achieving social balance on benches than stated political allegiance.

Such 'geodemographics' might well represent the emergence of the truly classless society. Alternatively, they might represent a worrying denial of the importance of political attitudes within law generally, and the magistrates' bench in particular.

In any case, in March 2001, Jane Kennedy MP, Parliamentary Secretary to the LCD, announced that, at least for the moment, the Lord Chancellor had reluctantly decided that political balance would have to remain an issue. This statement was made in response to the disclosure that the Magistrates' Advisory Committee in Stoke-on-Trent had sent out a letter to several local organisations, which stated that:

> ... whilst the overriding criterion for appointment is always the suitability of the candidate, the Advisory Committee is particularly keen to receive applications from members of ethnic minorities, shop floor workers, the unemployed and Labour Party supporters.

In answering charges that such a letter was politicising the magistracy, Ms Kennedy pointed out that:

> Public confidence in lay magistrates is vital. This is achieved, first and foremost, by individual magistrates discharging their duties effectively. It is also achieved when Benches reflect the diversity of the communities which they serve. In Stoke-on-Trent the Labour vote is significantly under-reflected on the magistrates' Bench. Of those who expressed political affiliation 40 per cent were Labour, compared to 60 per cent who voted Labour in the area at the last General Election. This compares to 47 per cent of the Bench being acknowledged Conservative voters, compared to 27 per cent in the area.

The Advisory Committee was simply and correctly trying to attract more Labour voters to apply to become magistrates, in order that the composition of the Bench more broadly reflected the local voting pattern.

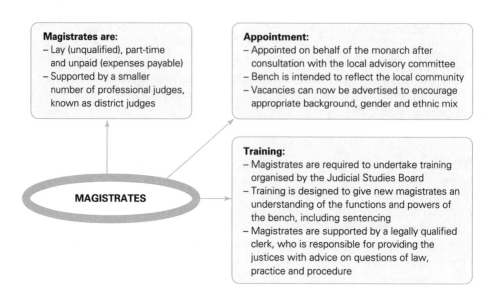

Magistrates are:
– Lay (unqualified), part-time
  and unpaid (expenses payable)
– Supported by a smaller
  number of professional judges,
  known as district judges

Appointment:
– Appointed on behalf of the monarch after
  consultation with the local advisory committee
– Bench is intended to reflect the local community
– Vacancies can now be advertised to encourage
  appropriate background, gender and ethnic mix

MAGISTRATES

Training:
– Magistrates are required to undertake training
  organised by the Judicial Studies Board
– Training is designed to give new magistrates an
  understanding of the functions and powers of
  the bench, including sentencing
– Magistrates are supported by a legally qualified
  clerk, who is responsible for providing the
  justices with advice on questions of law,
  practice and procedure

FIGURE 9.1 *Magistrates: an aide-mémoire.*

The age profile of magistrates

If the class make-up of the magistracy is possibly a problem, then a look at the current statistics will immediately show that the age profile and distribution of the current magistrates is certainly a matter for concern: 52 per cent of magistrates are aged 60 or above, 82 per cent of magistrates are at least 50 and only 4 per cent are below the age of 40. The average age was given as 57 in a parliamentary answer. Given the strictures that are involved in being a magistrate, it is obvious that the older members of society are more likely to have time to offer their services as magistrates, especially those who have retired. However, the inescapable question arises as to the representative nature of such a body, especially when the core clientele is likely to be a great deal younger than they are. It was an attempt to address this problem, at least of perception if not substance, that the age for service as a magistrate was reduced from 27 to 18 in 2003. Statistics on the magistracy are available at: http://www.judiciary.gov.uk/publications-and-reports/statistics/magistrates-statistics

9.9.2 THE FUTURE OF THE MAGISTRATES' COURTS

In December 2000, the results of a report, *The Judiciary in the Magistrates' Courts*, were published. The extensive report was jointly commissioned by the Home Office and the LCD and provided an extremely valuable comparison between the lay magistracy and stipendiaries, now known as District Judges (Magistrates' Courts). It found as follows.

As regards the lay magistracy:

- they are drawn overwhelmingly from professional and managerial ranks;
- 40 per cent of them are retired from full-time employment;
- the cost of an appearance before lay magistrates was £52.10 per hour.

As regards the stipendiaries:

- they are younger, but are mostly male and white;
- they hear cases more quickly;
- they are more likely to refuse bail and to make use of immediate custodial sentences;
- they are less likely to need legal advisers;
- the cost of an appearance before stipendiary magistrates was £61.78 per hour.

In the following January, 2001, a report entitled *Community Justice* by Professor Andrew Sanders for the Institute for Public Policy Research called for the replacement of panels of lay justices by panels composed of district judges, the former stipendiary magistrates, assisted by two lay magistrates. According to Professor Sanders:

> These proposals would increase public confidence, and they would enhance the contribution ordinary members of the public make to our justice system.

The Magistrates' Association took a rather different view and saw the proposals as an attack on what was already an extremely representative system of justice. According to its then Chair, Harry Mawdsley, the proposed scheme would cost around £30 million annually in salaries alone, but apart from costs:

> Lay magistrates provide community justice: they are ordinary people who live and work in the local community and who have an intimate knowledge of that community.

Although praising the magistracy's gender and ethnic make-up, Mr Mawdsley neverthe-less recognised the need to recruit more magistrates from working-class backgrounds.

When the Auld Report into the criminal court system was issued later that year, it suggested a compromise between these two positions: the retention of the magistrates' courts as one division in a unified criminal court, with the creation of a new District Division, made up of a district judge and two magistrates, to hear mid-range either way offences (the third division, the Crown Division, retained the role of the current Crown Court). In the event, the government declined to adopt the Auld recommendations in this regard, but instead proposed to increase the sentencing powers of the magistrates to 12 months in detention in s 154 of the Criminal Justice Act 2003. As Lord Irvine told the Magistrates' Association in October 2002:

> What the Government's proposals cement and enhance is your position at the heart of a reformed and more joined-up Criminal Justice System; one in which we have better pre-trial preparation; a more efficient trial process; and effective and appropriate sentencing.

Nonetheless, he felt required to re-emphasise how the magistrates should use their new sentencing power:

> I cannot emphasise this to you too strongly: your greater sentencing powers are to be exercised with restraint and in accordance with these principles: 'imprisonment only when necessary and for no longer than necessary'. The proposed new Sentencing Framework aims to encourage you to make full use of community sentences; and to reserve custodial sentences for serious, dangerous and persistent offenders.

However, as yet, the increased sentencing power under s 154 of the Criminal Justice Act 2003 has not been implemented. The Justice Ministry had intended to remove this power to increase the sentencing powers of magistrates and included a section to that end in its Legal Aid, Sentencing and Punishment of Offenders Bill. However, following the riots that took place across England in the summer of 2012, the Attorney General, Dominic Grieve, put himself at odds with the then Justice Minster, Ken Clarke, by suggesting that increasing the sentencing powers of magistrates would make the court system more efficient. To the pleasure of the Magistrates' Association, Grieve would appear to have won any argument that took place as the proposal was omitted from the subsequent Legal Aid, Sentencing and Punishment of Offenders Act 2012.

In an article in *Criminal Law & Justice Weekly* in September 2010, entitled 'The future of the magistracy', Noel Cox used some recent changes in New Zealand practice to offer some suggestions as to the way that the role of the magistrates may evolve in England and Wales.

He sees two related processes emerging. Firstly, the jurisdiction of magistrates has expanded in terms of number and complexity over the past few decades as a result either of existing crimes being downgraded to either summary, or offences triable either way, with new offences tending to be categorised in that way from the outset. However, the increased use of fixed penalties for minor summary offences (see below) is a related, if apparently contradictory, development in that it reduces the number of less serious cases coming before the magistrates' courts. It should also be remembered that, to a very large extent, the role of the magistrates' courts as licensing bodies has been removed.

Consequently there has been a radical shift of work to magistrates' courts and one that Cox sees as likely to continue. The threat for the lay magistracy is that the increase in the seriousness and complexity of the cases dealt with in their courts will lead, necessarily, to the further professionalisation of the magistracy in the form of increased use of district judges, and their role will be reduced to that of almost lay assessors or jury members, rather than judges.

Cox's conclusion, although not amounting to a death sentence, will raise concerns among the magistracy. As he sees it:

> In England and Wales the work of District Judges is currently expanding and their importance is likely to increase, as trial by jury is effectively restricted to the most serious cases. It is also possible that the powers of justices' clerks will continue to expand. They have acquired case management powers that were once reserved to magistrates and the Justices' Clerks Society have argued that its members should sit as chairmen of the bench.
>
> The days of the justice of the peace as an active lay magistrate may be drawing to a close. As a consequence, a long tradition of voluntary community service may be lost. But it would be premature to toll the death knell of the lay magistracy.

9.9.3 MAGISTRATES' COURTS AND NON-COURT DISPOSAL OF CRIMINAL OFFENCES

In 2005 the government issued its *Supporting Magistrates' Courts to Provide Justice* initiative, which went out of its way to assure the magistracy of its support. However, in July 2006 a three-department initiative involving the then Constitutional Affairs, the Home Office and the Attorney General announced a new initiative: *Criminal Justice: simple, speedy, summary* or *CJSS*.

- *Simple* – dealing with some specific cases transparently by way of warning, caution or some effective remedy to prevent re-offending without the court process;
- *Speedy* – those cases that need the court process will be dealt with fairly but as quickly as possible;
- *Summary* – a much more proportionate approach still involving due process – dealing with cases during the same week.

The intention was to improve the procedure within the lower courts so that those who pleaded guilty were dealt with as quickly as possible and those who elected to go for trial did not have to wait as long as previously for their hearing. The apparent success of *CJSS* in four pilots led to its rollout to all magistrates' courts.

However, at the same time the government was pursuing the increased use of non-court procedures for dealing with low-level criminal behaviour and disorder such as fixed penalty notices, penalty notices for disorder, simple and conditional cautioning.

Fixed Penalty Notices

Similar to the already common road traffic fixed penalty notices, these generally deal with environmental offences such as litter, graffiti, fly posting and dog fouling. They can be issued to anyone over 10 years old by police, local authority officers and police community support officers.

Penalty Notices for Disorder

These procedures were introduced to address low-level anti-social behaviour, while also reducing police bureaucracy and paperwork. They can be issued to anyone over 16 years old. The Home Office suggests that such orders may be issued in relation to:

- intentionally harassing or scaring people;
- being drunk and disorderly in public;
- destroying or damaging property;
- petty shoplifting;
- selling alcohol to underage customers;
- selling alcohol to somebody who is obviously drunk;
- using fireworks after curfew.

Although not the same as criminal convictions, failure to pay the penalty may result in higher fines or imprisonment.

Simple Cautions

These are used to deal quickly and simply with those who commit less serious crimes without the need to take them through the court procedure. A caution is not a criminal conviction, but it will be recorded on the police database and may be used in court as evidence of bad character, or as part of an anti-social behaviour order application (see 1.3.5 above). Cautions are issued where:

- there is evidence of criminal activity;
- the offender is 18 years of age or over (under the Crime and Disorder Act 1998 younger offenders are given 'reprimands' and 'final warnings' instead of simple cautions);
- the offender admits they committed the crime;
- the offender agrees to be given a caution; if they refuse they may be charged instead.

The use of cautions rather than court proceedings is at the discretion of senior police officers. However, the more serious crimes like robbery or assault must be referred to the Crown Prosecution Service.

Conditional Cautions

These were introduced in the Criminal Justice Act 2003 and differ from simple cautions to the extent that the recipient must comply with certain conditions to receive the caution and to avoid prosecution for the offence allegedly committed. Currently they can only be made against people 18 or older. However, although not yet in force, s 48 of the Criminal Justice and Immigration Act 2008 extends the conditional caution procedure to children below that age.

The nature of the conditions that can be attached to a conditional caution must have one or more of the following objectives:

- rehabilitation – such conditions are aimed at helping to change the behaviour of the offender, in order to reduce the likelihood of their re-offending or help to reintegrate the offender into society. They may require attendance at drug or alcohol misuse programmes, or interventions tackling other addictions or personal problems, such as gambling or debt management courses;
- reparation – conditions that aim to repair, or compensate for, the damage done either directly or indirectly by the offender;
- retribution – conditional cautions can include punitive elements, which are designed to penalise the offender for their criminal activity. Such conditions, introduced in the Police and Justice Act 2006, may require: the payment of a financial penalty, unpaid work for a period not exceeding 20 hours, attendance at a specified place for a period not exceeding 20 hours.

The recipient of the caution must admit their guilt or they will be charged and face trial. As with the simple caution, a conditional caution is not a criminal conviction as such. However, it will be recorded on the police database and may be considered in court in the event of another offence. In addition the record will remain on the police database along with photographs, fingerprints and any other samples taken at the time. If the recipient breaches the condition then they may be arrested and charged with the original offence.

It has been suggested that in the early enthusiasm for the *CJSS* programme the magistracy had not paid sufficient attention to the 'simple' aspect of *CJSS* as set out above. However, it was not long until the magistrates and their associaton were complaining about the bypassing of the courts through the use of the non-court procedures.

The suspicion of the magistrates appears to be that the use of alternative mechanisms meant that incidents that should have been heard by them were being dealt with inappropriately and perhaps more leniently than they should have been in order to save police time and State money: it was estimated in October 2009 that only half the 1.4 million offenders dealt with by the justice system each year were actually prosecuted in the courts.

Magistrates' anger reportedly increased to a fury when, in October, it emerged that Norfolk police had used its powers under the Community Safety Accreditation Scheme (CSAS), introduced by the Police Reform Act 2002, to give nightclub doormen the power to issue fixed penalties and that, under the same scheme, staff at Addenbrooke's Hospital in Cambridge had also been empowered to issue on-the-spot fines to people on the hospital premises. The deputy chairman of the Magistrates' Association, John Howson, was reported to have protested to the Justice Minister Jack Straw, stating that 'Our concern is that here we have essentially a "third-tier" police force that is now including security guards and door supervisors.' His response to the claim of the Director of Public Prosecutions, Keir Starmer, that on-the-spot fines helped lighten the load of courts was that 'The DPP should not be considering what is expedient but what is just.'

If the concern of the magistrates was at least partly that some offenders were escaping with a lesser punishment than they might otherwise have received had their case been treated with the severity it actually warranted, a completely different, not to say contrary, view was set out in a report published in August 2008 by the Centre for Crime and Justice Studies at King's College London. Entitled 'Summary Justice: fast – but fair?' the report, written by Professor Rod Morgan, argued that the government policies aimed at diverting minor offences from court had actually resulted in an extensive widening of the criminal net, with individuals being brought within the ambit of the criminal justice system who would have previously been ignored or dealt with informally.

The report highlighted a rise in the numbers of convictions for violent offences, but much larger rises in the resort to cautions. Thus, convictions for serious indictable violence offences were 11 per cent higher in 2006 compared with 2001, but cautions increased by 92 per cent. The comparable figures for less serious indictable offences included a rise of 19 per cent for convictions but 195 per cent for cautions. Such findings would appear to suggest that cautions have been issued where previously no official sanction would have been applied. It also suggested that regional differences in the use of summary powers, and the fact that decision-making was made in private rather than in open court, resulted in an 'accountability deficit'.

However, in line with the Magistrates' Association, the report insisted that there was a need for a thorough review of the government's approach. As Professor Morgan put it:

> The increased use of pre-court summary justice is one of the most important elements in the government's strategy for modernising the criminal justice system. The implementation of the strategy has received virtually no research, inspectoral or parliamentary scrutiny. The trend towards pre-court summary justice should more incisively be scrutinised to ensure that justice is being meted out fairly and effectively. We cannot be wholly confident that it is so.

The concerns of the magistracy were heightened further when, in October 2009, the Director of Public Prosecutions issued a draft code for consultation that would give crown prosecutors wider discretion over sending people to trial. Amongst a number of reasons, trials might not be pursued if they would be a disproportionate response – even if a hearing might otherwise be in the public interest. The proposals were reported as being 'intended to encourage common sense in the justice system and are aimed at balancing the cost and time involved in bringing a prosecution with the seriousness of a crime'. Other reasons for not pursuing an offence to trial included where the offence was committed as a result of a genuine mistake or misunderstanding, or where the court was likely to impose a nominal penalty, or where the defendant was already subject to a sentence and the further offence would not add to it.

Once again John Howson, deputy chairman of the Magistrates' Association, responded vigorously, claiming that the new code seemed to be:

part of the complete muddle in the way we treat offenders and over the boundaries between where the prosecutors and the courts lie . . . If someone has offended, they should be brought before the courts, where we have a range of penalties from an absolute discharge to custody. The job of prosecutors is to find the evidence, not to assess the weight of it.

In December 2011, the coalition Minister for Policing, Nick Herbert, addressed the National Council of the Magistrates' Association on the issue of summary justice in which he addressed some of the major concerns.

He recognised the need to ask fundamental questions about the system of summary justice in order to reverse the proliferation of administrative disposals that had taken place over the last few years. He also insisted that the magistracy should have an early role in overseeing how out-of-court sanctions are applied within their locality. He even suggested that magistrates could exercise a triage function outside of the court and could possibly pass immediate sentence in certain non-contested cases.

To quote him:

> 'Summary justice' was the misnomer given to the previous government's programme of administrative justice which saw an unprecedented growth in out-of-court disposals, exacerbated by the pursuit of targets. I know many of you will share my unease about the way out-of-court disposals have been used. . . Let us be clear: out-of-court disposals are not an acceptable way of dealing with persistent offenders. Such misuse risks undermining public confidence in our entire system of justice. And it gives rise to serious questions about the effectiveness of low-level sanctions. We must take action to tackle the inappropriate use of such sanctions and restore public confidence. . . . As I have said, we want to ensure that the out-of-court arena is far more transparent and accountable than is currently the case. I believe that the magistracy has a vital role to play here. I want to see, as has already happened in some police-force areas, magistrates given a supervisory role in overseeing how out-of-court sanctions are applied locally. . . I am very keen to think about how we put this into practice. I would welcome your views today.

It is hardly surprising that the Chairman of the Magistrates' Association, John Fassenfelt, almost immediately issued the following short press statement:

> The Magistrates' Association is very pleased that the valuable role of magistrates in community justice has been recognised. We have been raising concerns about the misuse and abuse of out-of-court disposals for the past three years and we are delighted that the Government has acted. We look forward to taking part in dissuasions regarding the details of these proposals.

In July 2012 Herbert announced the publication of a White Paper, 'Swift and Sure Justice: the Government's Plans for Reform of Criminal Justice', in which the points sketched out in his original speech to the MA were expanded on. As the title suggested, the White Paper set out a programme of reform based, it claimed, on some of the lessons learned from the response to the previous year's disturbances and during which 'the police, prosecutors and courts worked together – and offenders were brought to justice within days, sometimes even hours'.

Some of the points made included:

- local magistrates to be given a supervisory role in scrutinising the use of summary justice by officers;
- magistrates courts may conduct trials in the evenings and at weekends;
- magistrates, sitting alone, to deal with certain low-level uncontested cases;
- some cases to be heard outside traditional magistrates' court buildings;
- community sentences to include a punitive element;
- a speeding up of the criminal justice system through the use of more video-link technology.

Once again the Chair of the Magistrates' Association welcomed the anticipated changes, but warned:

> While most of our members will be pleased to see a role for single justices to deal with low-level uncontested cases, we are concerned about . . . judicial independence and that such powers for this role should be for the judiciary only and not delegated to justices' clerks.

In September 2012, at the time of the major reshuffle, Nick Herbert left the Justice Ministry. It remains to be seen what will become of his initiatives.

CHAPTER SUMMARY: THE JUDICIARY

THE CONSTITUTIONAL ROLE OF THE JUDICIARY

Judges play a central role in the UK constitution. The doctrine of the separation of powers maintains that the judicial function be kept distinct from the legislative and executive functions of the State.

THE CONSTITUTIONAL ROLE OF THE LORD CHANCELLOR

The Lord Chancellor held an anomalous position in respect of the separation of powers within the UK constitution, in that he was at one and the same time: the most senior member of the judiciary and can hear cases in the House of Lords as a court; a member of the legislature as Speaker of the House of Lords as a legislative assembly; and a member of the executive holding a position in the government. The Constitutional Reform Act 2005 dealt with the problem and subsequently the Lord Chancellor's Department has been replaced by a Ministry of Justice.

JUDICIAL OFFICES

The main judicial offices are the Lord Chancellor, the Lord Chief Justice, the Master of the Rolls, the President of the Family Division, the Vice Chancellor and the Senior Presiding Judge. Law Lords are referred to as Lords of Appeal in Ordinary. Court of Appeal judges are referred to as Lords Justices of Appeal.

APPOINTMENT OF THE JUDICIARY

The Constitutional Reform Act 2005 brought about a Judicial Appointment Commission, to replace the much-maligned previous system based on alleged secret soundings of the judiciary. However, the first appointments of the Commission have themselves been subjected to some criticisms for the conservative nature of the appointments made.

TRAINING OF THE JUDICIARY

Training of English judges is undertaken under the auspices of the Judicial Studies Board. Judges from the highest Law Lord to the lowest magistrate are subject to training. It is gratifying to note that anti-discriminatory training is a priority, although some have continued to express doubt about judicial attitudes in this regard. General training focuses on various aspects of discrimination and special training was undertaken in relation to the Woolf reforms and the introduction of the Human Rights Act. This being said, it remains arguable that the training undergone by UK judges is not as rigorous as the training of judges on the continent.

REMOVAL OF JUDGES

Senior judges hold office subject to good behaviour. They can be removed by an address by the two Houses of Parliament.

Judges below High Court status can be removed by the Lord Chancellor on grounds of misbehaviour or incapacity and he can remove magistrates without the need to show cause.

JUDICIAL IMMUNITY

To ensure judicial integrity, it is provided that judges cannot be sued for actions done or words said in the course of their judicial function.

This immunity extends to trial lawyers, witnesses and juries.

MAGISTRATES

Magistrates have powers in relation to both criminal and civil law.

District Judges (Magistrates' Courts) are professional and are legally qualified.

Lay magistrates are not paid and they are not legally qualified.

Magistrates are appointed by the Lord Chancellor.

Important issues relate to the representative nature of the magistracy.

THE CONSTITUTIONAL REFORM ACT

The essential features of the Act were designed to inspire transparency, openness and greater public confidence in Britain's constitution. Government ministers are now under a statutory duty to uphold the independence of the judiciary and are specifically barred from trying to influence judicial decisions through any special access to judges. The post of Lord Chancellor has been transformed with transfer of his judicial functions to the President of the Courts of England and Wales, the Lord Chief Justice. He will be responsible for the training, guidance and deployment of judges. He will also be responsible for representing the views of the judiciary of England and Wales to Parliament and ministers.

A new, independent Supreme Court, separate from the House of Lords, was established in 2009.

A new system of appointing judges, independent of the patronage of politicians, has been established. Appointments will be solely on the basis of merit and solely on the recommendation of the newly constituted Judicial Appointments Commission.

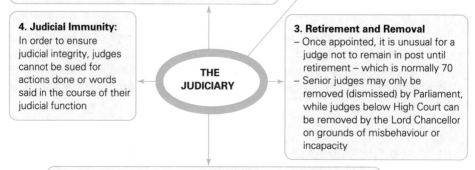

1. Selection and Appointment: Responding to criticism, the CLSA, 1990, introduced major change to judicial appointment, opening up the judiciary to non-barristers, with senior judges appointed by the Crown on the advice of the Prime Minister and High Court judges and below appointed on the advice of the Lord Chancellor. Transparency is encouraged, with vacancies for circuit judges and below, being advertised. The CRA introduces a *Judicial Appointments Commission* who will report to the Lord Chancellor, who continues to make recommendations to the Monarch

2. Training: Overseen and provided by the Judicial Studies Board, with emphasis on anti-discrimination training and application of the Human Rights Act. Still criticised for not being sufficiently rigorous in comparison to other European jurisdictions

4. Judicial Immunity: In order to ensure judicial integrity, judges cannot be sued for actions done or words said in the course of their judicial function

THE JUDICIARY

3. Retirement and Removal
– Once appointed, it is unusual for a judge not to remain in post until retirement – which is normally 70
– Senior judges may only be removed (dismissed) by Parliament, while judges below High Court can be removed by the Lord Chancellor on grounds of misbehaviour or incapacity

5. Criticisms: Commonly criticised as being 'white, middle class, middle aged to elderly men', which it has been argued may lead to bias and lack of social awareness

FIGURE 9.2 *The Judiciary: an aide-mémoire.*

FOOD FOR THOUGHT

1. Much has been made of the creation of a new Supreme Court but the issue to consider is whether, as has been suggested, a first-class Appeal Court has been replaced by a second-class Supreme Court. In particular, what distinguishes the UK Supreme Court from, for example, the Supreme Court of the USA?

2. Consider whether judicial training should be for a profession in its own right, rather than as an adjunct to another profession, such as the Bar.

3. In the context of the magistrates' courts, consider whether there is a place for non-legally qualified judges and whether the age of most magistrates leads to particular problems.

4. Following the English riots of summer 2011, there was some accusation of heavy-handed sentencing policy in the magistrates' courts. This raises questions as to whether magistrates' current sentencing powers should be raised from six to 12 months. Consider the pros and cons of any such change.

FURTHER READING

Bell, J and Engle, G (Sir), *Cross on Statutory Interpretation*, 1995, London: Butterworths

Bennion, F, *Statutory Interpretation*, 1992, London: Butterworths

Bindman, G, 'Lessons of Pinochet' (1999) 149 NLJ 1050

Bindman, G, 'Lessons of history' (2009) 159 NLJ 1110

Blom-Cooper, L, 'Age of judicial responsibility' [2009] PL 429–30

Cox, N, 'The future of magistracy' (2010) CLJ Weekly, Sept 18

Denning (Lord), *Due Process of Law*, 1980, London: Butterworths

Denning (Lord), *The Discipline of Law*, 1979, London: Butterworths

Dowell, K, 'Neuberger gains political clout after attacking Supreme Court' (2009) 23(35) Lawyer 48

Hunter, R, McGlynn, C and Rackley, E, *Feminist Judgments: From Theory to Practice*, 2010, Oxford: Hart Publishing

Manchester, C, Salter, D, Moodie, P and Lynch, B, *Exploring the Law*, 2000, London: Sweet & Maxwell

Parker, C, 'Judicial decision making' (1999) 149 NLJ 1142

Pearl, D, 'Judging success' (2009) Counsel 13–14

Pickles, J, *Straight from the Bench*, 1987, London: Hodder and Stoughton

Reid (Lord), 'The judge as law maker' (1972) 12 JSPTL 22

Weinreb, L, *Legal Reason: The Use of Analogy in Legal Argument*, 2004, Cambridge: CUP

USEFUL WEBSITES

http://webarchive.nationalarchives.gov.uk/+/http://www.dca.gov.uk/judges/diversity.htm

An archived webpage on information regarding the Lord Chancellor's commitment to ensuring 'a judiciary of the highest calibre, with candidates drawn from the widest possible range of available talent'.

www.judiciary.gov.uk

The official website for the Judiciary of England and Wales.

www.justice.gov.uk

Justice Ministry website

www.supremecourt.gov.uk

Official website of the Supreme Court

http://www.justice.gov.uk/downloads/publications/policy/moj/judicial-diversity-report-2010.pdf

Improving Judicial Diversity: Progress towards delivery of the 'Report of the Advisory Panel on Judicial Diversity 2010' May 2011

COMPANION WEBSITE

Now visit the companion website to:

- test your understanding of the key terms using our Flashcard Glossary;
- revise and consolidate your knowledge of 'The judiciary' using our Multiple Choice Question testbank;
- view all of the links to the Useful Websites above.

www.routledge.com/cw/slapper

JUDICIAL REASONING AND POLITICS

10

The popular perception of the judicial process is described by David Kairys as government by law, not people, together with the understanding that law is separate from, and superior to, politics, economics, culture and the values and preferences of judges. This perception is based on particular attributes of the decision-making process itself, which Kairys suggests comprises, among other things: the judicial recognition of their subservient role in constitutional theory; their passive role in the operation of the doctrine of precedent; their subordinate role in the determination and interpretation of legislation; and the '*quasi-scientific*, objective nature of legal analysis, and *technical* expertise of judges and lawyers' (*The Politics of Law: A Progressive Critique* (1982)). To the extent that law is generally portrayed as quasi-scientific, the operation of objective, technical and hence supposedly neutral rules, to that degree, the decisions that judges make are accepted as legitimate by the public. It is necessary, therefore, to consider the nature of reasoning in general and the extent to which judges make use of such reasoning, before considering the social location of the judges. It is only on the basis of the *nonexistence* of distinct and strictly applied principles of legal reasoning that the *existence* of judicial creativity and the *possibility* of judicial bias come into consideration.

There is a long-running controversy as to the relationship of law and logic and the actual extent to which legal decisions are the outcome of, and limited by, logical processes. At times, lawyers have sought to reject what is seen as the rigid inflexibility inherent in logical reasoning in favour of flexibility and discretion. As the American Supreme Court Judge, eminent legal writer and proponent of *Legal Realism*, Oliver Wendel Holmes expressed it: 'The life of the law has not been logic, it has been experience' (*The Common Law* (1881)).

The implication of this position is that the law is no more than a mechanism for solving particular problems and that judges should operate in such a way as to ensure the best possible result, even if this means ignoring previously established legal rules.

At other times, however, the courts have appeared to base and justify their decisions on the working out of deterministic formal rules of law, categorised in such phrases as 'The Law is the Law' and 'The Law must run its course'. The suggestion behind such expressions of the *Declaratory Theory of Law* is that the judge is no more than the voice of an autonomous legal system that he, through his legal training, is able to gain access to but is in no way able to influence. If, as the declaratory theory of law maintains, judges do no more than give expression to already existing legal principles and rules, then the particular views, opinions or prejudices of the judiciary are of absolutely no consequence. If such a representation were accurate, then the logical conclusion would be that judges could be replaced by a computerised *expert system*, which could be programmed to make decisions on the basis of a strict application of general rules. It is doubtful, however, if anyone would actually accept such a suggestion. It cannot be denied that the bulk of cases are decided on the simple application of the legal rules to the particular facts of the case with little or no consideration of the legal principles. In other cases, however, the straightforward and automatic application of a legal rule might lead to the possibility of injustice.

(For those particularly interested in the possibility of developing computer models of judicial reasoning and decision-making, see Allen, Aikenhead and Widdison, 'Computer Simulation of Judicial Behaviour', http://webjcli.ncl.ac.uk/1998/issue3/allen3.html.)

Hard cases are decided on the basis of judicial reaction to the immediate facts of the case. Such a situation, however, is clearly antithetical to the declaratory theory of law.

These *hard cases* demand a consideration of the legal principles involved in order to achieve a just result. They may therefore be decided other than on the strict application of the law as it had been previously expressed. It should be pointed out that such cases are usually the province of the higher courts and of particularly active judges within those courts. The old maxim/cliché that '*hard cases make bad law*' should also be borne in mind. (The career of Lord Denning might be cited as an example of this procedure and its shortcomings. Reference should be made to material covered previously in Chapter 3 of this book for a more detailed consideration of the problems inherent in judicial law-making and reform.)

10.3   REASONING IN GENERAL

In order to assess this apparent tension, if not divergence, of approach to the question whether legal reasoning is logical or not, it is necessary first of all to engage, at least minimally, in a consideration of what is to be understood by reasoning generally and logical reasoning in particular.

10.3.1   DEDUCTIVE REASONING

As regards reasoning in general, there is a division between deductive and inductive reasoning. *Deductive reasoning* may be categorised as reasoning from the whole to the part;

from the general to the particular. Deductive reasoning finds its simplest and yet most powerful expression in the Aristotelian syllogism. The syllogism takes the following form:

> Major premise: A = B for example, All men are mortal.
>
> Minor premise: B = C for example, Socrates is a man.
>
> Conclusion: therefore A = C that is, Socrates is mortal.

The power of the syllogism lies in its certainty. If the premises are true, then the conclusion cannot be false. The reason for this is that the conclusion is actually contained in the premises and amounts to no more than a restatement of those premises.

With regard to syllogisms, however, it is important to distinguish between *validity* of form and *truth* of content. It is quite possible for a syllogism to be logically valid but false. An example of this would be:

> Major premise: A = B for example, All men are pigs.
>
> Minor premise: B = C for example, Socrates is a man.
>
> Conclusion: therefore A = C that is, Socrates is a pig.

The logical form of this argument, as represented in alphabetical terms is valid, but the conclusion is not true. The reason for this is obviously that the major premise is false: the statement that all men are pigs is simply not true.

It is also possible for a syllogism to be both true and valid yet still be based on a false premise. An example of this would be:

> Major premise: A = B for example, All men are Greek.
>
> Minor premise: B = C for example, Socrates is a man.
>
> Conclusion: therefore A = C that is, Socrates is Greek.

Once again, the logical form expressed in alphabetical terms is valid, and once again the major premise is false. On this occasion, however, the conclusion is true.

To reiterate the essential point, all that the syllogistic form of reasoning maintains is that *if the premises are true then the conclusion cannot be false*; in itself, it states nothing as to the truth of those premises or the truth of the conclusion derived from them. As will be considered below, much legal argument is about the truth of particular premises rather than the validity of the logical form being operated.

Deductive reasoning can take another form as follows:

> If X then Y: If it rains, you will get wet.
>
> X: It is raining.
>
> Therefore, Y: You will get wet.

Again, the conclusion is contained in the premises, but equally again, if the premises are false, the conclusion may also be false.

10.3.2   INDUCTIVE REASONING

The second classic form of reasoning, *inductive reasoning*, may be described as arguing from the part to the whole; from the particular to the general. Inductive reasoning differs from deductive reasoning in two major respects:

1.   It reaches a conclusion that is *not* simply a restatement of what is already contained in the basic premises.
2.   It is *less certain* in its conclusions than deductive logic.

An example of this type of reasoning would be:

> The sun has always risen in the east.
> Therefore, the sun will rise in the east tomorrow.

If the premise is true, then the conclusion is probably true, but not 100 per cent necessarily so because the conclusion is not contained in the premise, but is a projection from it. On the basis of past experience, we can reasonably expect the sun to rise in the east tomorrow, but there is the possibility, no matter how remote it might be, that something might happen to the sun, or indeed the earth, to prevent its appearance tomorrow. The point is that we cannot predict with 100 per cent accuracy what will happen in the future just because it happened in the past. Because the inductive argument goes beyond the content of its premises, it provides the power to predict events, but it gives predictive power at the expense of certainty in its conclusion.

An alternative example of this type of inductive reasoning would be:

> John is lying dead with a bullet in his head.
> Jane is standing over him with a smoking gun in her hand.
> Therefore, it can be concluded that Jane shot John.

Now, the conclusion may be reasonable under the circumstances, but there are other possible explanations for the scene. Jane may have simply picked up the gun after someone else had shot John. We cannot actually tell who killed John, but we may reasonably suspect Jane of the crime and she would be the first person to be questioned to confirm either her guilt or innocence. The investigation of this event would use a form of reasoning equivalent to scientific reasoning. From available data, a hypothesis would be formed; in this case, that Jane killed John. Investigations would then be undertaken to test the validity of the hypothesis. Depending on the outcome of the investigation, the original hypothesis would be either accepted, rejected or refined.

10.3.3   REASONING BY ANALOGY

A third type of reasoning is *reasoning by example or analogy*. If deductive reasoning involves reasoning from the whole to the part, and inductive reasoning involves reasoning from the part to the whole, then reasoning by analogy involves reasoning from part to part.

An example of this type of reasoning would be:

Wood floats on water.
Plastic is like wood.
Therefore, plastic floats on water.

Or similarly:

Wood floats on water.
Stone is like wood.
Therefore, stone floats on water.

It can be seen that the truth of the conclusion depends completely on the accuracy of the analogy. The connection between the two objects that are being compared depends on weighing up and assessing their similarities and their differences. Only some characteristics are similar, and the question is whether those are more important than the differences between the two objects. If the analogy is valid, then the conclusion may very well be equally valid, although not necessarily correct, but, if it is not valid, then the conclusion will certainly be wrong, as the above examples demonstrate.

10.4 JUDICIAL REASONING

It is now appropriate to determine whether, or to what extent, judges use logical reasoning in reaching their decisions in particular cases and to determine which forms, if any, they make use of.

10.4.1 THE SYLLOGISM IN LAW

Some statutory provisions and also some common law rules can be expressed in the form of a syllogism. For example, the offence of theft may be reduced into such a formulation:

If A dishonestly appropriates B's property with the intention of permanently depriving B of it, *then* A is guilty of theft.
A has done this.
Therefore, A is guilty of theft.

This, however, represents an oversimplification of the structure of statute but, more importantly, the effect of concentrating on the logical form of the offence tends to marginalise the key issues in relation to its actual application. As has been stated previously, the great majority of cases are decided on the *truth* of the premises rather than the formal *validity* of the argument used. In other words, argument will concentrate primarily on whether A actually did the act or not and, second, on whether A appropriated the property either 'dishonestly' or 'with the intention of permanently depriving' B of it. Those are questions of fact, not logic.

10.4.2 THE LOGICAL FORM OF PRECEDENT

The operation of the rules of precedent appears, at first sight, to involve a similar operation of deductive logic to that applied in statute law: the judge merely applies the legal principle established in the precedent to the facts in hand to determine the outcome of the case. Thus:

> *Precedent*: in case X involving particular circumstances, legal principle Y was applied leading to conclusion Z.
>
> *Instant case*: in case W, similar circumstances to those in X have occurred.
>
> *Therefore*: principle Y must be applied to reach a conclusion similar to Z.

A closer consideration of the actual procedure involved in precedent, however, will reveal that it is not totally accurate to categorise precedent as a form of deductive reasoning.

In looking for a precedent on which to base a decision, judges are faced with a large number of cases from which to select. It is extremely unlikely that judges will find an authority that corresponds precisely to the facts of the case before them. What they have to do is to find an analogous case and use its reasoning to decide the case before them. This use of analogy to decide cases is prone to the same shortcomings as were revealed in the previous consideration of reasoning from analogy in general. The major difficulty is the need to ensure the validity of the analogy made, if the conclusion drawn is to be valid. There is, no doubt, considerable merit in the wish for similar cases to be treated similarly, but given the lack of precision that is inherent in the process of reasoning by analogy, it is not altogether certain that such a wish will be met.

A further reason why the operation of precedent cannot simply be considered as an example of deductive reasoning relates to the process through which the precedent is actually determined once an analogous case has been selected. The binding element in any precedent is the *ratio decidendi* of the decision. In delivering his decision, the judge does not separate the *ratio* of the case from other *obiter* comments. As has been considered previously, the *ratio* is a legal abstraction from the concrete facts of the case in which it appears, and in practice, it is for judges in subsequent cases to determine the *ratio* of any authority. The determination of the *ratio* and thus the precedent in a previous case may be seen as a process of *inductive reasoning*, in that the judge in the present case derives the *general* principle of the *ratio* from the *particular* facts of the previous case. This move from the particular to the general is by its nature inductive. The point to be remembered here is that, as was considered in relation to reasoning in general, the use of inductive reasoning cannot claim the certainty inherent in the use of deductive reasoning. The introduction of this increased element of uncertainty is inescapable and unconscious, but it is also appropriate to note that the determination of precedent by later courts gives the later judges scope to *consciously* manipulate precedents. This is achieved by the later judges formulating the *ratio* of a previous case in the light of their opinion as to what it *should* have been, rather than what it might actually have been. In other words, they have the scope to substitute their version of the *ratio*, even if it contradicts what the original judge thought the *ratio* was.

Thus, the apparent deductive certainty of the use of precedent is revealed to be based on the much less certain use of inductive reasoning and reasoning by analogy, with even the possibility of personal views of the judges playing some part in deciding cases. This latter factor introduces the possibility that judges do not in fact use any form of logical reasoning to decide their cases, but simply deliver decisions on the basis of an intuitive response to the facts of the case and the situation of the parties involved. The suggestion has been made that judges decide the outcome of the case first of all and only then seek some *post hoc* legal justification for their decision; and given the huge number of precedents from which they are able to choose, they have no great difficulty in finding such support as they require. The process of logical reasoning can be compared to the links in a chain, one following the other, but a more fitting metaphor for judicial reasoning would be to compare it with the legs of a chair: forced into place to support the weight of a conclusion reached *a priori*. Some critics have even gone so far as to deny the existence of legal reasoning altogether as a method of determining decisions, and have suggested that references to such are no more than a means of justifying the social and political decisions that judges are called upon to make.

In conclusion, however, it is not suggested that legal reasoning does not employ the use of logic, but neither can it be asserted that it is only a matter of logic. Perhaps the only conclusion that can be reached is that legal reasoning as exercised by the judiciary is an amalgam; part deductive, part inductive, part reasoning by analogy, with an added mixture of personal intuition, not to say personal prejudice.

10.4.3 LEGAL REASONING AND RHETORIC

Following on from the previous questioning of the logical nature of legal reasoning, it might be valuable to consider further the claim that legal decisions are not the outcome of a process of logical reasoning, but are in fact the products of a completely different form of communication. According to Peter Goodrich (*Reading the Law* (1986) at 171):

> . . . the legal art is an art of interpretation; it is concerned not with a necessary or scientific logic, but with probable arguments, with evaluative reasoning and not with absolute certainty. Rhetoric is the discipline which most explicitly studies the techniques relevant to presenting and evaluating,

affirming or refuting, such probable arguments . . . rhetoric, here, is defined as the reading of legal texts as acts of communication, as discourse designed to influence, to persuade and to induce action.

Goodrich analysed the use of rhetoric in law, from ancient Greece until the present time, in Chapter 6 of his book. In so doing, he revealed the specific rhetorical devices that judges bring to bear in their decisions in order to persuade their audience as to the objective validity of their decisions.

The question, however, is as to who constitutes the audience that the judiciary addresses. In the case of summings-up to juries, the answer is obvious, but there is still an audience being addressed when the judge delivers a judgment in any case. That audience, it is suggested, is the community at large, but with the community not as an active participant in the legal process, but as a passive body that merely has to be persuaded of the inherent and unquestionable validity of the judge's decision in any particular case.

As Goodrich points out (1986 at 188):

> The language of the legal decision strives for the appearance of objectivity and the exclusion of dialogue in favour of monologue. Its principal aim and function is that of achieving an image of incontestable authority and of correct legal meanings. Such a task is, essentially, a rhetorical one: the monologue is the language-usage of authority, it precludes dialogue or any questioning of the meanings given, and it closes legal discourse by privileging the voice of the judicial author as the supreme arbiter of meanings.

Rather than being presented as a particular individual's opinion, the legal text is typically expressed as in the language of objectivity. The use of such terms as 'thus', 'because', 'for the reason that', 'in spite of' indicates the voice of necessity, not of choice. When this is combined with the use of terms such as 'therefore' or 'consequently', the outcome is to reinforce the impression that the judge is merely engaged in a working out and presentation of the formal operation of the objective system that is law. In this fashion, the language of apparently objective, and logically determined, legal categories is revealed to be a mere rhetorical device marshalled by judges to provide their particular decisions with the justification of pseudo-objectivity. This process is complemented by the use of axioms; unquestioned and apparently unquestionable self-evident truths, to which the judiciary frequently have recourse in order to validate, without justifying, their own assumptions and presumptions. One should be on one's guard when one reads judges referring to principles that are 'so fundamental that they need not be debated', or where conclusions follow 'as a matter of course' on the basis of 'well-settled principle'. The question is whether such claims merely appeal to uncorroborated precedents and unsubstantiated prejudices.

One further aspect of the rhetorical nature of the judicial presentation directly relates to the inherently political nature of judicial decision-making. It is almost a commonplace in the most politically sensitive cases that the judges involved will ritually intone the mantra to the effect that, 'it is fortunate that the court does not have to consider the political aspects of this case . . .', before going on to make what cannot but be a political decision. To the contrary, as this book maintains, all judicial decisions are political in that they reflect a disposition as to where power should be located in any particular situation.

Judgments, and judicial presentations to juries, therefore are not merely statements of law; they are equally, if not more fundamentally, exercises in rhetoric. To read a judgment in this way is to see it in a new revelatory light that shows the justificatory, if not manipulative, use of language and linguistic devices that are an essential element of the judgment. It has to be pointed out, however, that the nature and use of rhetoric has changed over time. The difference between the operation of rhetoric in the ancient world and its use by the judiciary today is that, whereas in the ancient world it was used as a means of *persuading* an audience to reach a particular decision, its contemporary role is that of justifying the decision that the judge has taken. The judge speaks, the audience listens and is persuaded: the role of the audience as a participant has been removed and it now merely exists as the passive receiver of the court's decision.

In *R (Smeaton) v Secretary of State for Health* ([2002] EWHC 610, paras 46 and 47) which considered the legality of the morning after contraceptive pill, Munby J stated:

> I have said that this case raises moral and ethical questions of great importance. It would be idle to suggest otherwise. For those who view such matters in religious terms it raises religious and theological questions of great =N and, to some, transcending =N importance. But I must emphasise that, so far as the court is concerned, this case has nothing to do with either morality or religious belief. The issue which I have to decide is not whether the sale and use of the morning-after pill is morally or religiously right or wrong, nor whether it is socially desirable or undesirable. *What I have to determine is whether it may constitute an offence under the 1861 Act.*
>
> Cases such as this, and others in the field of medicine (one thinks of cases such as *Airedale NHS Trust v Bland* [1993] AC 789 and *Re A (Conjoined Twins: Medical Treatment)* [2001] Fam 147), raise moral, religious and ethical issues on which, as Lord Browne-Wilkinson pointed out in Bland at pp 879E, 880A, 'society is not all of one mind' and on which indeed 'society as a whole is substantially divided'. Our society, including the most thoughtful and concerned sections of our society, are deeply troubled by, and indeed deeply divided over, such issues. These are topics on which men and women of different faiths, or indeed of no faith at all, may and do hold, passionately and with the utmost sincerity, starkly differing views. *All of those views are entitled to the greatest respect but it is not for a judge to choose between them. The days are past when the business of the judges was the enforcement of morals or religious belief* (emphases added).

With the greatest of respect to Munby J, what he seeks to avoid is exactly what he is forced to do in making his 'legal' decision.

10.5   JUDICIAL REVIEW

The effect of the HRA on the interface between the judiciary and the executive has been considered previously at 2.5, but that Act merely heightened the potential for conflict in a relationship that was already subject to some tension as a consequence of the operation of judicial review. If the interface between judiciary and executive tends now to be most sharply defined in human rights actions, the previous and continued role of judicial review in that relationship should not be underestimated.

The growth in applications for judicial review prior to the HRA was truly startling, as individuals and the judiciary recognised its potential utility as a means of challenging administrative decisions. The records show that in 1980, there were only 525 applications for judicial review; in 1996, 4,586; in 1997, 4,636 such applications; and by 1998, applications had passed the 5,000 mark and continued to rise.

At the outset, it should be noted that although this section focuses on those instances where the judiciary have decided against the exercise of executive power in a particular way, it has to be emphasised that the vast majority of judicial review cases are decided in favour of the executive. This may be significant when the views of Professor Griffith are examined at 10.7.1 below.

The remedies open to anyone challenging the decisions or actions of administrative institutions or public authorities can be divided into *private* or *public* law remedies.

10.5.1   PRIVATE LAW REMEDIES

There are three private law remedies:

10.5.1.1   Declaration

This is a definitive statement, by the High Court or county court, of what the law is in a particular area. The procedure may be used by an individual or body to clarify a particularly contentious situation. It is a common remedy in private law, but it also has an important part to play in regard to individuals' relations with administrative institutions. This can be seen, for example, in *Congreve v Home Office* (1976), where the Court of Appeal stated that it would be unlawful for the Home Office to revoke annual television licences after only eight months because they had been bought in anticipation of an announced price rise but before the expiry of existing licences.

Declarations, however, cannot be enforced either directly or indirectly through the contempt of court procedure. Public authorities are, as a matter of course, expected to abide by them.

Usually, an injunction seeks to restrain a person from breaking the law; alternatively, however, a mandatory injunction may instruct someone to undo what they have previously done, or alternatively to stop doing what they are doing. Both types of injunction may be sought against a public authority. See *Attorney General v Fulham Corp* (1921), in which a local authority was ordered to stop running a laundry service where it only had the power to establish laundries for people to wash their own clothes.

Damages cannot be awarded on their own in relation to administrative misconduct, but may be claimed in addition where one of the other remedies considered above is sought, as, for example, in *Cooper v Wandsworth Board of Works* (1863). In this case, a builder had put up a building without informing the Board of Works as he was required to do. When the Board demolished the building, he nonetheless recovered damages against them on the basis that the Board had exceeded its powers by not allowing him to defend or explain his actions.

In order to seek one of these private law remedies, an individual merely had to issue a writ against a public authority in their own name. They did not require the approval of the court.

10.5.2 THE PREROGATIVE ORDERS

The prerogative orders are so-called because they were originally the means whereby sovereigns controlled the operation of their officials. As a consequence, the prerogative orders cannot be used against the Crown, but they can be used against individual ministers of State and, since *R v Secretary of State for the Home Department ex p Fire Brigades Union* (1995), considered at 10.6.1 below, it is clear that ministers cannot avoid judicial review by hiding behind the cloak of prerogative powers. The prerogative orders are as follows:

A quashing order, formerly known as *certiorari*, is the mechanism by means of which decisions of inferior courts, tribunals and other authoritative bodies are brought before the High Court to have their validity examined. Where any such decision is found to be invalid, it may be set aside. An example of this can be seen in *Ridge v Baldwin* (1964). Here, the plaintiff had been dismissed from his position as Chief Constable without having had the opportunity to present any case for his defence. The House of Lords held that the committee that had taken the decision had acted in breach of the requirements of natural justice and granted a declaration that his dismissal was null and void.

A prohibiting order, formerly known as *prohibition*, is similar to *certiorari* in that it relates to invalid acts of public authorities, but it is different to the extent that it is pre-emptive and prescriptive in regard to any such activity and operates to prevent the authority from taking invalid decisions in the first place. An example of the use of the order arose in *R v Telford Justices ex p Badham* (1991). In this case, an order was issued to stop committal proceedings in relation to an alleged rape that had not been reported until some 14 years after the alleged incident. The delay meant that the defendant would have been unable to prepare a proper defence against the charge.

A *mandatory order*, formerly known as *mandamus*, may be seen as the obverse of a prohibiting order, in that it is an order issued by the High Court instructing an inferior court or some other public authority to carry out a duty laid on them. Such an order is frequently issued in conjunction with an order of *certiorari*, to the effect that a public body is held to be using its powers improperly and is instructed to use them in a proper fashion. In *R v Poplar BC (Nos 1 and 2)* (1922), the court ordered the borough council to pay over money due to the county council and to levy a rate to raise the money if necessary. Failure to comply with the order led to the imprisonment of some of the borough councillors.

In *O'Reilly v Mackman* (1982), however, the House of Lords decided that issues relating to *public* rights could *only* be enforced by means of the judicial review procedure, and that it would be an abuse of process for an applicant to seek a declaration by writ in relation to an alleged breach of a public duty or responsibility by a public authority. In deciding the case in this way, the House of Lords did much to demarcate and emphasise the role of judicial review as the method of challenging public authorities in their performance of their powers and duties in public law.

10.5.3   GROUNDS FOR APPLICATION FOR JUDICIAL REVIEW

Judicial review allows people with a sufficient interest in a decision or action by a public body to ask a judge to review the lawfulness of:

(a)   an enactment; or

(b)   a decision, action or failure to act in relation to the exercise of a public function.

However, it is not an appeal on the merits of a decision. The grounds of application can be considered under two heads: *procedural ultra vires* and *substantive ultra vires*:

Procedural ultra vires, as its name suggests, relates to the failure of a person or body, provided with specific authority, to follow the procedure established for using that power. It also covers instances where a body exercising a judicial function fails to follow the requirements of natural justice by acting as prosecutor and judge in the same case or not permitting the accused person to make representations to the panel deciding the case.

Substantive ultra vires occurs where someone does something that is not actually authorised by the enabling legislation. In *Associated Provincial Picture House v Wednesbury Corp* (1947), Lord Greene MR established the possibility of challenging discretionary decisions on the basis of unreasonableness.

Lord Greene's approach was endorsed and refined by Lord Diplock in *Council of Civil Service Unions v Minister for the Civil Service* (1984), in which he set out the three recognised grounds for judicial review, namely:

- illegality;
- irrationality;
- procedural impropriety.

Lord Diplock, however, introduced the possibility of a much more wide-ranging reason for challenging administrative decisions: namely, the doctrine of *proportionality*. Behind this doctrine is the requirement that there should be a reasonable relation between a decision and its objectives. It requires the achievement of particular ends by means that are not more oppressive than they need be to attain those ends. The potentially innovative aspect of this doctrine is the extent to which it looks to the substance of the decisions rather than simply focusing on the way in which they are reached.

Lord Diplock's listing of proportionality within the grounds for judicial review was controversial, if not at the very least arguably mistaken. Proportionality, however, is a key principle within the jurisdiction of the ECtHR, and is used frequently to assess the validity of State action which interferes with individual rights protected under the Convention. Consequently, as the HRA has incorporated the European Convention into UK law, proportionality will be a part of UK jurisprudence and legal practice, at least in cases that fall within the scope of the HRA. Although HRA cases and judicial review are different and distinct procedures, nonetheless, it is surely a mere matter of time before the doctrine of proportionality is applied by the judges in judicial review cases unrelated to the Convention.

Indeed, such an approach was supported by Lord Slynn in *R v Secretary of State for the Environment, Transport and the Regions ex p Holding and Barnes* (2001), in which he stated ([2001] 2 All ER 929 at 975):

> The European Court of Justice does of course apply the principle of proportionality when examining such acts and national judges must apply the same principle when dealing with Community law issues. There is a difference between that principle and the approach of the English courts in *Associated Provincial Picture Houses Ltd v Wednesbury Corporation* [1948] 1 KB 223. But the difference in practice is not as great as is sometimes supposed. The cautious approach of the European Court of Justice in applying the principle is shown *inter alia* by the margin of appreciation it accords to the institutions of the Community in making economic assessments. I consider that even without reference to the Human Rights Act the time has come to recognise that this principle is part of English administrative law, not only when judges are dealing with Community acts but also when they are dealing with acts subject to domestic law. Trying to keep the *Wednesbury* principle and proportionality in separate compartments seems to me to be unnecessary and confusing. Reference to the Human Rights Act however makes it necessary that the court should ask whether what is done is compatible with Convention rights. That will often require that the question should be asked whether the principle of proportionality has been satisfied . . .

However, in *Frank Cowl v Plymouth City Council* (2001), the Court of Appeal held that judicial review was not necessarily the proper way in the face of alternatives. The claimant had sought to use judicial review as a means of challenging the council's decision to close a residential care home for the elderly, even though the council had said it was willing to consider his situation as part of a statutory complaints procedure. According to Lord Woolf:

> The courts should not permit, except for good reason, proceedings for judicial review to proceed if a significant part of the issues between the parties could be resolved outside the litigation process. The disadvantages of doing so are limited. If subsequently it becomes apparent that there is a legal issue to be resolved, that can thereafter be examined by the courts which may be considerably assisted by the findings made by the complaints panel . . . This case will have served some purpose if it makes it clear that the lawyers acting on both sides of a dispute of this sort are under a heavy obligation to resort to litigation only if it is really unavoidable. If they cannot resolve the whole of the dispute by the use of the complaints procedure they should resolve the dispute so far as is practicable without involving litigation.

10.5.4   THE EXCLUSION OF JUDICIAL REVIEW

As will be considered in Chapter 12, one of the reasons for the setting up of extensive systems of administrative tribunals was precisely the wish to curb the power of the judges. It was felt that judges, and indeed the common law itself, tended to be more supportive of *individual* rights and freedoms as opposed to *collective* notions of welfare pursued by post-war governments, and that they would not administer such policies sympathetically. The judges, however, asserted their ultimate control over such tribunals generally through the use of judicial review. There have been various attempts by parliamentary drafters to exclude the judiciary from certain areas by wording provisions in such a way as to deny the possibility of judicial review. These attempts, however, have mainly proved to be in vain and have been rendered ineffective by the refusal of the courts to recognise their declared effect. Examples are:

10.5.4.1   'Finality' or 'ouster' clauses

There is a variety of possible wordings for these clauses. For example, the legislation might provide that 'the minister's [or the tribunal's] decision shall be final', or alternatively it might attempt to emphasise the point by stating that the decision in question 'shall be final and conclusive', or it might even provide that 'it shall be final, conclusive and shall not be questioned in any legal proceedings whatsoever'. Unfortunately for the drafter of the legislation and the minister or tribunal in question, all three formulations are equally likely to be ineffective. The courts have tended to interpret such phrases in a narrow way, so as to recognise the exclusion of an appeal procedure but to introduce the possibility of judicial review, as distinct from appeal. The classic case on this point is *R v Medical Appeal Tribunal ex p Gilmore* (1957), in which Lord Denning stated that, 'The word "final" . . . does not mean without recourse to *certiorari*'. This, however, raised the point of provisions which expressly sought to exclude *certiorari*.

In *South East Asia Fire Bricks Sdn Bhd v Non-Metallic Mineral Products Manufacturing Employees Union* (1980), the Privy Council decided that a Malaysian statute was sufficiently detailed in its wording to effectively exclude *certiorari for an error of law on the face of the record*. The Privy Council pointed out, however, that the exclusion could not be effective to prevent judicial review where the institution in question had acted *ultra vires* or in breach of natural justice.

The fury of the judiciary against the government's statutory proposals found its fullest expression in respect of the Asylum and Immigration (Treatment of Claimants etc) Bill. The Bill, which was designed to speed up asylum and immigration procedures by curtailing the appeal structure, introduced the most wide-ranging of ouster clauses to the effect that no court shall have any supervisory or other jurisdiction in relation to the Asylum and Immigration Tribunal. In particular, the original cl 11 of the Bill stated that the courts could not question the decisions of the tribunal even in the event of:

- lack of jurisdiction;
- irregularity;
- error of law;
- breach of natural justice; or
- any other matter.

As was stated at the time, such a proposal was the 'mother and father' of all ouster clauses. The judiciary were extremely vocal in their opposition to cl 11, which they saw, and publicly represented, as an attack on the rule of law in its refusal to allow access to the ordinary courts. When it became apparent that the Bill was not going to pass through the House of Lords, Lord Falconer made it known that the government would change the appeal procedure to allow appellants some sort of access to the courts. Although the Lord Chancellor did not state the details of the new proposals, his promise was sufficient to win the approval of the House of Lords.

10.5.4.2 Partial exclusion clauses

Where legislation has provided for a limited time period within which parties have to apply for judicial review, then applications outside of the period will not be successful. In *Smith v East Elloe Rural DC* (1956), the House of Lords, although only by 3:2 majority, recognised the effectiveness of a six-week limitation clause in the Acquisition of Land (Authorisation Procedure) Act 1946. Although that case was subject to criticism in

Anisminic Ltd v Foreign Compensation Commission (1969), it was explained and followed in *R v Secretary of State for the Environment ex p Ostler* (1976).

In response to the Franks Committee's recommendation that judicial review should not be subject to exclusion, s 14(1) of the Tribunals and Inquiries Act 1971 was enacted to that end. Unfortunately, it only applies to pre-1958 legislation.

In November 2012 the David Cameron announced that his government intended to 'get a grip' on people forcing unnecessary delays to government policy by cracking down on the 'massive growth industry' of judicial review.

In December 2012 the government, in the form of the Justice Ministry, announced a consultation on a proposal to reduce the number of judicial review cases. The announcement stated that the Government was seeking views on a package of measures to stem the growth in applications for judicial reviews. The measures aimed to tackle the alleged burden that such growth had placed on stretched public services whilst protecting access to justice and the rule of law.

The engagement exercise sought views on proposals in three key areas;

- reducing the time limits for bringing a judicial review relating to procurement or planning from the current three months to six, or even four weeks;

- removing the right to an oral hearing where a judge refuses permission where there has been a prior judicial process, or where the claim was judged to be totally without merit. Consequently any right to appeal to the Court of Appeal would be on the papers.

- the introduction of a new fee for an oral renewal so that fees charged in Judicial Review proceedings better reflect the costs of providing the service. Currently, the fee for an application for permission in the High Court is £60, and where permission is granted a further fee of £215 is payable by the applicant for the matter to proceed to a trial. The consultation document proposed an increase in the initial fee to £215–£235. However it also proposed to waive the trial fee if the issue successfully proceeds to a hearing.

10.6 POLITICS AND THE JUDICIARY

Law is an inherently and inescapably political process. Even assertions as to the substantive autonomy of law (see Chapters 1 and 3) merely disguise the fact that, in making legal decisions, judges decide where the weight of public approval is to be placed and which forms of behaviour are to be sanctioned (see, for example, *R v Brown* (1993), where the House of Lords criminalised the sexual activities of consenting sadomasochists, arguably without fully comprehending some aspects of what was going on).

There is, however, an increasingly apparent tendency for contemporary judges to become actively, directly and openly engaged in more overtly political activity. The 1955 Kilmuir rules, named after the Lord Chancellor who introduced them, were designed to control the instances when the judiciary could express opinion in the media. The rules were abrogated in 1987 by Lord Mackay and, since then, the judiciary have been more forthcoming in expressing their views, not just on matters strictly related to their judicial functions but also on wider political matters.

As has been stated, the HRA merely heightened the potential for conflict between the judges and the executive and Parliament, but the relationship was already subject to some tension as a consequence of the operation of judicial review, as can be seen in a number of cases.

In *M v Home Office* (1993), the House of Lords decided that the court has jurisdiction in judicial review proceedings to grant interim and final injunctions against officers of the Crown, and to make a finding of contempt of court against a government department or a minister of the Crown in either his personal *or his official capacity*.

M v Home Office is of signal importance in establishing the powers of the courts in relation to the executive. It is also interesting to note that in delivering the leading speech, Lord Woolf quoted extensively from, and clearly supported, Dicey's view of the rule of law as involving the subjection of all, including State officials, to the ordinary law of the land (see Chapter 2).

In November 1994, the government suffered two damaging blows from the judiciary. In *R v Secretary of State for Foreign Affairs ex p World Development Movement Ltd* (1995), the Queen's Bench Divisional Court held that the Secretary of State had acted beyond his powers in granting aid to the Malaysian government in relation to the Pergau Dam project. The financial assistance was given, not for the promotion of development *per se*, as authorised by s 1 of the Overseas Development and Co-operation Act 1980, but in order to facilitate certain arms sales. As Rose LJ stated ([1995] 1 All ER 611 at 626):

> Whatever the Secretary of State's intention or purpose may have been, it is, as it seems to me, a matter for the courts and not for the Secretary of State to determine whether, on the evidence before the court, the particular conduct was, or was not, within the statutory purpose.

In *R v Secretary of State for the Home Department ex p Fire Brigades Union* (1995), the Court of Appeal held that the Home Secretary had committed an abuse of power in implementing a scheme designed to cut the level of payments made to the subjects of criminal injuries. The court held that he was under an obligation, under the CJA 1988, to put the previous non-statutory scheme on a statutory basis. It was not open for the Secretary of State to use his prerogative powers to introduce a completely new tariff scheme contrary to the intention of Parliament as expressed in the CJA 1988. The decision of the Court of Appeal was confirmed by a 3:2 majority in the House of Lords in April 1995, the majority holding that the Secretary of State had exceeded or abused powers granted to him by Parliament. It is of interest to note that in his minority judgment Lord Keith warned that to dismiss the Home Secretary's appeal would be:

> ... an unwarrantable intrusion into the political field and a usurpation of the function of Parliament.

In 1997, in *R v Secretary of State for the Home Department ex p Venables and Thompson*, the House of Lords decided that the Home Secretary had misused his powers in relation to two juveniles who had been sentenced to detention during Her Majesty's pleasure.

Even Lord Chancellors have not escaped the unwanted control of judicial review, and in March 1997, John Witham successfully argued that the Lord Chancellor had exceeded his statutory powers in removing exemptions from court fees for those in receipt of State income support (*R v Lord Chancellor ex p Witham* (1997)).

The change of government in 1997 did nothing to stem the flow of judicial review cases, with the occasional embarrassing defeat for the executive. Thus, in *R v Secretary of State for Education and Employment ex p National Union of Teachers* (2000), the Divisional Court held that the Secretary of State for Education had exceeded his statutory powers in seeking to alter teachers' contracts of employment, particularly by introducing threshold standards in relation to a new scheme of performance-related pay. He had sought to introduce the changes in the Education (School Teachers' Pay and Conditions) (No 2) Order 2000 after only four days' consultation with the trade union. The court held that although the Secretary of State had the statutory powers to alter the contracts of employment under the Teachers' Pay and Conditions Act 1991, he had not adopted the correct procedure for doing so as set out in that Act. Consequently, the Education (School Teachers' Pay and Conditions) (No 2) Order was quashed. Although this decision represented a victory for the Union and an embarrassment for the Secretary of State, it was only temporary in nature and the new contracts were subsequently introduced following the proper statutory procedure.

Given its centrality in the operation of the criminal justice system and immigration, it is hardly surprising that the Home Department is subject to more claims for judicial review than any other ministry, nor is it surprising that some of them go against it.

In *Alvi v Secretary of State for the Home Department* (2012), the Supreme Court ruled that the Home Secretary could not introduce substantive immigration requirements through policy decisions, guidance or instructions, rather than in the body of the immigration rules themselves. The list of skilled occupations used to assess immigration requests was held not to be part of the Immigration Rules, as the document in which that list was set out had not been laid before Parliament as was required under section 3(2) of the Immigration Act 1971. Although similar to *R v Secretary of State for Education & Employment ex p NUT*, the consequence of the decision had important implications for the operation of immigration policy and was not likely to be so easily remedied. As the Supreme Court acknowledged in reaching its conclusion:

> ... the volume of material that will now have to be laid to give effect to the court's judgment will impose a heavy burden on Parliament and on the Secondary Legislation Scrutiny Committee of the House of Lords in particular.

Although it did offer a possible solution requiring a change in parliamentary procedure:

> Methods of communication today are very different from what they were in 1971 when the statutory requirement, which involves laying hard copies of every paper that has to be laid in each House, was introduced. The court questions whether the current system, which is now over forty years old, is still fit for its purpose today. But any changes to it must be a matter for Parliament.

It can be seen from the foregoing that judicial review provided the judiciary with the means for addressing the potential for abuse that followed on from the growth of discretionary power in the hands of the modern State, particularly if it was operated on the basis of the doctrine of proportionality. Alongside the growth in the number of applications, there were also indications that at least some of the higher judiciary saw it as part of their function to exercise such control over the executive. For example, the former Master of the Rolls and former Lord Chief Justice, Lord Bingham, was quoted in *The Observer* newspaper of 9 May 1993 as saying that:

> Slowly, the constitutional balance is tilting towards the judiciary. The courts have reacted to the increase in powers claimed by the government by being more active themselves.

Judicial review is a delicate exercise and by necessity draws the judiciary into the political arena, using the word 'political' in its widest, non-party sense. That the judges were aware of this is evident from the words of Lord Woolf in the same article. As he recognised:

> Judicial review is all about balance: between the rights of the individual and his need to be treated fairly, and the rights of government at local and national level to do what it has been elected to do. There is a very sensitive and political decision to be made.

However, another former Law Lord, Lord Browne-Wilkinson, observed on a BBC radio programme, admittedly before his elevation to the House of Lords, that a great void was apparent in the political system, deriving from the fact that no government had a true popular majority and yet all governments were able to carry Parliament in support of anything they wanted. He went on to express the view that Parliament was not a place where it was easy to get accountability for abuse or misuse of powers. According to Lord Browne-Wilkinson, while judicial review could not overcome the will of Parliament, judges had a special role because *democracy was defective*. He then asked a rhetorical question as to who else but the judges could ensure that executive action is taken in accordance with law, *and not abused by increasingly polarised political stances*.

Such thinking is also evident in an article by Mr Justice Stephen Sedley (as he was then) in the May 1995 edition of the *London Review of Books*, in which he asserted that after decades of passivity, there is a new 'culture of judicial assertiveness to compensate for, and in places repair, dysfunctions in the democratic process', and that the last three decades of the twentieth century may have seen the UK constitution being refashioned by judges 'with sufficient popular support to mute political opposition'.

The Impact of the Human Rights Act 1998

As has been seen at 2.5 above, the introduction of the HRA greatly increased judicial power in relation to the other two branches of the constitution.

Initially the judges were reluctant to use their new powers, especially the Court of Appeal and the House of Lords, although the courts below them, and notably Collins J in the SIAC adopted a much more robust approach.

This initial position was set by Lord Irvine in his inaugural Human Rights Lecture at the University of Durham:

> It is all about balance. The balance between intense judicial scrutiny and reasonable deference to elected decision-makers is a delicate one to strike. But the judiciary have struck it well: and I welcome that. Whilst scrutiny is undoubtedly an important aid to better governance, there are areas in which decisions are best taken by the decision-makers entrusted by Parliament to make them. This may be for reasons of democratic accountability, expertise or complexity.

The former Lord Chancellor may well have been of the view that the judges had got it right, but his views did not sound in harmony with those of his ex-colleague, the former Home Secretary, David Blunkett, who was a consistent source of attack on the judiciary. Perhaps his most severe attack came after Collins J's decision in *R (on the Application of Q) v Secretary of State for the Home Department* (2003), which declared unlawful his power under s 55 of the Nationality, Immigration and Asylum Act 2002 to refuse to provide assistance to those who had not immediately declared their intention to claim asylum when they arrived in the UK. In the press, the then Home Secretary was quoted as saying:

> Frankly, I am fed up with having to deal with a situation where Parliament debates issues and judges then overturn them. We were aware of the circumstances, we did mean what we said and, on behalf of the British people, we are going to implement it.

Of even more concern were the reports that the then Prime Minister was 'prepared for a showdown with the judiciary to stop the courts thwarting government's attempts to curb the record flow of asylum seekers into Britain', and that he was looking into the possibility of enacting legislation to limit the role of judges in the interpretation of international human rights obligations and reassert the primacy of Parliament. There were even reports that the Prime Minister was considering withdrawing completely from the ECHR, rather than merely issuing derogations where it was thought necessary.

Given such pressure, it is perhaps not surprising that when the Court of Appeal heard the *Q* case, while it supported Collins J's decision, it went out of its way to provide the Home Secretary with advice on how to make the Act, and the procedures under it, compatible with ECHR rights.

In an article in *The Guardian* newspaper in November 2001, the commentator Hugo Young expressed his puzzlement about the Home Secretary's behaviour as follows:

> The judges have not been immune to the demands of the security state. Given what they are sometimes prepared to do to assist the executive, it is not easy to understand why Blunkett has marked his tenure by regularly casting aspersions on them.

It might not be too cynical to suggest that the continued favourable outcome was the justification for the continued attack. It might even not be overly cynical to suggest that the senior judiciary had been extremely circumspect in actually using their new powers, and had not been willing to use them to the extent they might have under other circumstances, when they have been generally accepted by both Parliament and the public. In April 2003, Lord Irvine entered the dispute when he offered an implicit, if no doubt stinging, criticism of the Home Secretary in his appearance before the select committee on the LCD. As he stated:

> When the judiciary gives decisions that the executive does not like, as in all governments, some ministers have spoken out against . . . [them] . . . I disapprove of that. I think it undermines the rule of law.

Not long after that statement, Lord Irvine was no longer Lord Chancellor, replaced by Lord Falconer, but for the time being David Blunkett remained as Home Secretary. It has been suggested that many of the fears among the senior judiciary in relation to the proposals in the Constitutional Reform Bill reflected a distrust of the Home Secretary and a lack of confidence in Lord Falconer's power to withstand his anti-judicial rhetoric and pressure.

Still, as Lord Woolf presciently recognised in a speech to the Royal Academy, which linked the HRA, judicial review and the rule of law, the possibility of a major confrontation between the judges and the executive still remained:

Just as the development of judicial review in the final quarter of last century improved administration in our increasingly complex society, so will the existence of the [HRA] protect our individual interests, which are so easily lost sight of in meeting the demands of the global economy. The real test of the [HRA] arises when individuals or minorities attract the antagonism of the majority of the public. When the tabloids are in full cry. Then, the courts must, without regard for their own interests, make the difficult decisions that ensure that those under attack have the benefit of the rule of law. At the heart of the [HRA] is the need to respect the dignity of every individual by ensuring he or she is not subject to discrimination. (Partly reported in the *Daily Mail*, 17 October 2002.)

Just such circumstances arose in the related cases of *A v Secretary of State for the Home Department* (2004) and *A v Secretary of State for the Home Department* (2005) (both considered extensively at 2.5.2) and as has been seen, the judges' response has been forthright in the preference for human rights over the expediencies of State control. The response of David Blunkett to those cases was not canvassed, as he had had to resign from his post as Home Secretary before the House of Lords' decision in the first case; and coincidentally, he had had to resign for a second time from the post as Secretary of State for Pensions before the second case was decided.

Critique of Judicial Activism

The fact that the judges increasingly see it as incumbent upon them to use judicial review and the HRA as the means of questioning and controlling what they see as the abuse of executive power does, at the very least, raise very serious questions in relation to their suitability for such a role. These doubts can be set out in terms of:

Competence

This refers to the question whether the judges are sufficiently competent to participate in deciding the substantive issues that they have been invited to consider under the guise of judicial review, and may be entitled to consider under the HRA. Judges are experts in law; they are not experts in the various and highly specialised areas of policy that by definition tend to be involved in judicial review cases. They may disagree with particular decisions, but it has to be at least doubted that they are qualified to take such policy decisions. A classic example of this difficulty was the 'fares' fair' cases (*Bromley London BC v GLC* (1983) and later, *R v London Transport Executive ex p GLC* (1983)), in which the courts got involved in deciding issues relating to transport policy for London on the pretext that they were judicially defining the meaning of particular words in a statute. As was considered in Chapter 6, the apparently technocratic, and hence neutral, application of rules of interpretation simply serves to disguise a political procedure and, in these cases, the policy issue concerned was certainly beyond the scope of the judges to determine. In *Bellinger v Bellinger* (2003), the House of Lords, although obviously sympathetic to the case, admitted their incompetence as regards deciding issues relating to the rights of transsexuals. For that reason, they issued a declaration of incompatibility under the HRA 1998 and thus passed the matter to Parliament for review and appropriate reform.

Constitutionality

This refers to the wider point that the separation of powers applies equally to the judiciary as it does to the executive. In interfering with substantive decisions and involving themselves in political matters, albeit on the pretence of merely deciding points of law, the judiciary may be seen to be exceeding their constitutional powers. It has to be remembered that judges are unelected and unaccountable.

Partiality

This refers to the possibility of individual, and indeed corporate, bias within the judiciary, as will be considered at 10.7.1 below.

The foregoing has indicated that the relationship between the State and the courts may, on occasion, involve a measure of tension, with the courts attempting to rein in the activities of the State. The relationship between the judiciary and the executive is well summed up in the words of Lord Justice Farquharson, again taken from an *Observer* article:

> We have to be very careful: the executive is elected. We have a role in the Constitution but, if we go too far, there will be a reaction. The Constitution only works if the different organs trust each other. If the judges start getting too frisky, there would be retaliation, renewed attempts to curb the judiciary.

Although no longer in force, the Kilmuir rules did have a valid point to make:

> . . . the overriding consideration . . . is the importance of keeping the judiciary in this country isolated from the controversies of the day. So long as a judge keeps silent, his reputation for wisdom and impartiality remains unassailable; but every utterance which he makes in public . . . must necessarily bring him within the focus of criticism.

When considering the role which the judiciary play in the process of applying the law, or indeed the process already adverted to in Chapter 3, whereby they actually make the law, criticism is usually levelled at the particular race, class and gender position of the majority of the judges. It is an objective and well-documented fact that the majority of judges are 'white, middle-class, middle-aged to elderly men', but the question that has to be considered is whether this *necessarily* leads to the conclusion that judges reach inherently biased decisions. It is always possible, indeed the newspapers make it relatively easy, to provide anecdotal evidence that apparently confirms either the bias or the lack of social awareness of the judiciary, but the fundamental question remains as to whether these cases are exceptional or whether they represent the norm.

Why should judges' class/race/gender placement make them less objective arbiters of the law? It is worth considering the fact that *unsupported* general assertions as to the inherently partial approach of the judiciary is itself partial. Simon Lee, not totally fatuously, has highlighted the logical flaw in what he refers to as the 'Tony Benn thesis' (Benn, the former left-wing Labour Party Member of Parliament who created history by being the first hereditary peer to renounce his peerage in order to remain in the House of Commons). Just because judges are old, white, rich, upper middle class, educated at public school and Oxbridge does not mean that they all necessarily think the same way; after all, Benn was a product of the same social circumstances. There is, of course, the point that people from that particular background *generally* tend to be conservative in outlook, and the apparent validity of Lee's argument is clearly the product of logic-chopping that reverses the accepted relationship and uses the exception as the rule, rather than seeing the exception as proving/testing the rule. Nevertheless, Lee's point remains true: that proof of judicial bias is needed.

As previous sections of this book have pointed out, if law were completely beyond the scope of judges to manipulate to their own ends, then the race, class and gender placement of individual judges would be immaterial, as they would not be in any position to influence the operation of the law. As was demonstrated in Chapter 3, however, the way in which the doctrines that set the limits within which the judiciary operate are by no means as rigid and restrictive as they might at first appear. It was seen that, although judges are supposed merely to apply rather than create law, they possess a large measure of discretion in determining which laws to apply, what those laws mean, and how they should be applied. In the light of this potential capacity to create law, it is essential to ensure that the judiciary satisfactorily represent society at large in relation to which they have so much power, and to ensure further that they do not merely represent the views and attitudes of a self-perpetuating elite.

The limited class background of the judiciary was confirmed in figures issued by the Lord Chancellor's office on 17 May 1995, which revealed that 80 per cent of Lords of Appeal, Heads of Division, Lord Justices of Appeal and High Court justices were educated at Oxford or Cambridge. In justifying the figures, the Lord Chancellor's Permanent Secretary, Sir Thomas Legg, showing insouciance to the level of arrogance, simply stated that: 'It is not the function of the professional judiciary to be representative of the community.' Such a response, even if it is true, let alone acceptable, must surely undermine the right of such an unrepresentative body to take action in the name of the majority, as the courts do in their use of judicial review.

Unfortunately, the continuing social imbalance among the senior judiciary was further confirmed in a report on judicial appointments by the Commons Home Affairs Committee, presented in June 1996. It revealed that four-fifths of judges went to both public schools and Oxbridge colleges, that only seven out of 96 High Court judges were women, and that only five out of the 517 circuit judges were black or Asian. Nevertheless, the Committee rejected proposals for positive discrimination or even for the establishment of a judicial appointments committee to replace the present informal system under the control of the Lord Chancellor.

Instead of things improving under new Labour, if one actually has the temerity to consider it an improvement to have fewer Oxbridge men on the bench, a Labour Research investigation found that things were actually getting worse in terms of the wider representational make-up of the judiciary. Still, Lord Irvine held fast to appointment solely on merit, which appeared wholly commendable, but, as has been stated before, who decides on merit, and what qualities are they actually measuring?

A Nuffield Foundation-funded report produced in November 1999 by Professor Hazel Genn in conjunction with the National Centre for Social Research, entitled *Paths to Justice*, revealed a truly remarkable lack of general confidence in the judiciary. The research surveyed a random selection of 4,125 people, from which total 1,248 people who had had experience of legal problems were selected for more detailed interview, with a smaller group of 48 being extensively interviewed. The results suggest that two out of three people think that judges are out of touch with ordinary people's lives, but more worryingly, only 53 per cent thought that they would get a fair hearing if they ever went to court. Disappointingly, at the launch of the report, Lord Woolf claimed that this 'misconception' was due to 'irresponsible media reporting' and stated that:

> It behoves the media to learn from this and recognise the dangers posed to confidence in the judicial system.

Surely, it more behoves the judiciary and the Justice Ministry to do more to redress this negative perception than simply blame the media for focusing on silly judge stories of which, unfortunately, there are still too many.

One of the findings of the report was that judges could improve their image by getting rid of their wigs and gowns. Perish the thought: there are standards and distinctions to be maintained. Thus, in *Practice Direction (Court Dress) (No 3)* (1998), the Lord High Chancellor, Lord Irvine of Lairg, provides:

> Queen's Counsel wear a short wig and silk (or stuff?) gown over a court coat; junior counsel wear a short wig and stuff gown with bands; solicitors and other advocates authorised under the Courts and Legal Services Act 1990 wear a black stuff gown, *but no wig* [emphasis added].

The issue of wigs resurfaced in March 2006 when once again a proposal was put forward to consider getting rid of them. Somewhat surprisingly and counter-intuitively, some supported wigs as a means of benefiting the justice system by protecting the anonymity of counsel and providing suitable gravitas to the less experienced members of the barrister's profession.

In July 2008 the Lord Chief Justice issued a Practice Direction which introduced the wearing of a new civil robe in civil and family law cases together with the announcement that wigs will no longer be worn in such courts. The reforms, which took effect from 1 October 2008, do not apply in criminal cases. Justices of the Supreme Court do not wear wigs or gowns when hearing cases.

10.7.1 CRITICISMS

The treatment of some aspects of potential bias within the judiciary has already been dealt with at 9.2.3 above, but this section addresses a more amorphous form of prejudice, and therefore one that is correspondingly more difficult to recognise or deal with. Given the central position of judges in the operation of law and the legal system, particularly with regard to the growth in judicial review and their new role in relation to giving effect to the HRA, the question these reports raise is whether the social placement of the judiciary leads to any perceptible shortfall in the provision of justice. The pre-eminent critic of the way in which the judiciary permit their shared background, attitudes and prejudices to influence their understanding and statement of the law is Professor JAG Griffith. According to Griffith, bias can occur at two levels:

> **Personal bias**
> Personal bias occurs where individual judges permit their own personal prejudices to influence their judgment and thus the effective application of the law. It is relatively easy to cite cases where judges give expression to their own attitudes and in so doing exhibit their own prejudices. As examples of this process, two cases can be cited which consider the rule of natural justice, that a person should not be both the accuser and judge in the same case. In *Hannam v Bradford Corp* (1970), the court held that it was contrary to natural justice for three school governors to sit as members of a local authority education disciplinary committee, charged with deciding whether or not to uphold a previous decision of the governors to dismiss a teacher. This was so even though the three governors had not been present at the meeting where it was decided to dismiss the teacher. On the other hand, in *Ward v Bradford Corp* (1971), the Court of Appeal refused to interfere with a decision by governors of a teacher training college to confirm the expulsion of a student, although they had instituted the disciplinary proceedings and three members of the governors sat on the original disciplinary committee. What possible explanation can there be for this discrepancy?

The only tenable explanation is to be found in the latter court's disapproval of the plaintiff's behaviour in that case. The truly reprehensible judgment of Lord Denning concludes that the student lost nothing, as she was not a fit person to teach children in any case. Can such a conclusion be justified on purely legal grounds or is it based on individual morality? Lord Denning did his best to buttress his judgment with spurious legal reasoning, but it could be suggested that, in so doing, he merely brought the process of legal reasoning into disrepute and revealed its fallaciousness.

Courts have also been notoriously unsympathetic to victims of rape and have been guilty of making the most obtuse of sexist comments in relation to such victims. Nor can it be claimed that depreciatory racist remarks have been totally lacking in court cases.

Such cases of bias are serious and reprehensible, but the very fact that the prejudice they demonstrate appears as no more than the outcome of particular judges, who are simply out of touch with current standards of morality or acceptable behaviour, suggests that it might be eradicated by the Lord Chancellor exercising stricter control over such mavericks and appointing more appropriate judges in the first place. Professor Griffith, however, suggests that there is a further type of bias that is actually beyond such relatively easy control.

Corporate bias

Corporate bias involves the assertion that the judges *as a body* decide certain types of cases in a biased way. This accusation of corporate bias is much more serious than that of personal bias, for the reason that it asserts that the problem of bias is *systematic* rather than merely limited to particular maverick judges. As a consequence, if such a claim is justified, it has to be concluded that the problem is not susceptible to treatment at the level of the individual judge, but requires a complete alteration of the whole judicial system. Griffith claims that, as a consequence of their shared educational experience, their shared training and practical experience at the Bar and their shared social situation as members of the Establishment, judges have developed a common outlook. He maintains that they share homogeneous values, attitudes and beliefs as to how the law should operate and be administered. He further suggests that this shared outlook is inherently conservative, if not Conservative in a party-political sense.

Griffith's argument is that the highest judges in the judicial hierarchy are frequently called upon to decide cases on the basis of a determination of what constitutes the public interest and that, in making that determination, they express their own corporate values, which are in turn a product of their position in society as part of the ruling Establishment. Griffith maintains that judges can be seen to operate in such a way as to maintain the status quo and resist challenges to the established authority. Underlying this argument is the implication that the celebrated independence of the judiciary is, in fact, a myth and that the courts will tend to decide cases in such a way as to buttress the position of the State, especially if it is under the control of a Conservative government.

In an attempt to substantiate his claims, Griffith examines cases relating to trade union law, personal rights, property rights and matters of national security, where he claims to find judges consistently acting to support the interests of the State over the rights of the individual. Some of the concrete examples he cites are the withdrawal of trade union rights from GCHQ at Cheltenham (*Council of Civil Service Unions v Minister for Civil Service* (1984)); the banning of publishing any extracts from the *Spycatcher* book (*AG v Guardian Newspapers Ltd* (1987)); and the treatment of suspected terrorists.

There certainly have been some overtly right-wing decisions taken by the courts, and the history of trade union cases is replete with them even at the highest level. The greater strength of Griffith's argument, however, would appear to be in the way that the courts have understood and expressed what is to be meant by 'public interest' in such a way as to reflect conservative, but not necessarily illiberal, values. It is surely only from that perspective that the higher judiciary's antagonistic response to some of the electorally driven policy decisions in relation to the legal system by *both* Conservative and New Labour administrations can be reconciled.

As would be expected, Griffith and other academics associated with the left, have expressed their reservations about the extent to which the HRA will hand power to an unelected, unaccountable, inherently conservative and unreformed body, as they claim the judiciary is.

A notable, if somewhat complacent, response to Griffith's book was provided by Lord Devlin, who pointed out that, in most cases and on most issues, there tended to be plurality rather than unanimity of opinion and decision among judges. He also claimed that it would be just as possible for a more conservatively minded person than Griffith to go through the casebooks to provide a list of examples where the courts had operated in an over-liberal manner. Lord Devlin also adopted a different explanation of the judiciary's perceived reluctance to abandon the status quo. For him, any conservatism on the part of judges was to be seen as a product of age rather than class. In conclusion, he asserted that even if the judiciary were biased, their bias was well known and allowances could be made for it.

The issue of the way in which the criminal appeal procedure dealt with suspected terrorist cases is of particular relevance in the light of the Runciman Commission Report. General dissatisfaction with the trials and appeals involving suspected terrorists such as the Maguire Seven, the Birmingham Six, the Guildford Four, the Tottenham Three, Stefan Kiszko and Judith Ward helped to give rise to the widespread impression that the UK criminal justice system, and in particular the British appeal system, needed to be considered for reform.

In the light of the fact that the appeal system did not seem to be willing to consider the possibility of the accused's innocence once they had been convicted, the Runciman

Commission's recommendation that a Criminal Case Review Authority be established, independent of the Home Office, was widely welcomed and resulted in the establishment of the CCRC in the Criminal Appeal Act 1995 (see 6.9). The question still remains, however, whether those earlier cases reflect an inherently and inescapably conservative judiciary, or were they simply unfortunate instances of more general errors of the system, which the implementation of the CCRC can overcome? And perhaps more importantly, will the Court of Appeal give a fair hearing to the cases referred to it by the CCRC?

It is apparent from the statistics produced by the DCA cited previously that senior judges are still being appointed from the same limited social and educational elite as they always have been. This gives rise to the suspicion, if not the reality, that the decisions that this elite make merely represent values and interests of a limited and privileged segment of society rather than society as a whole. Even if the accusations levelled by Professor Griffith are inaccurate, it is surely still necessary to remove even the possibility of those accusations.

It is not a little ironic that, in spite of the potential shortcomings that arise from the social composition of the current judicial body, there seems to be a distinct alteration in attitudes to the judiciary among those of a politically left-leaning persuasion. Following the introduction of the Human Rights Act and especially the decisions of the House of Lords in *A v Secretary of State for the Home Department* (2004) and *A v Secretary of State for the Home Department* (2005), many on the left now apparently see the courts as the bulwark of civilised society; against which beats the persistent tide of authoritarian legislation: the judges are now celebrated as the custodians of the rule of law, protecting the general populace from the depredations of the all-encompassing state. Thus, from previously being seen from this perspective, as reactionary, the courts are now seen as the appropriate defenders of generally accepted, and generally to be defended, liberal values.

In support of this odd transition may be cited a series of BBC radio programmes delivered, at the end of the summer 2009, by the liberal barrister and Labour peer Helena Kennedy. In the second programme she examined the shifting history of attacks on judicial independence, admitting that in the 1970s and 1980s, it was she and a generation of liberal lawyers who attacked the judiciary for being too *right wing* and out of touch. Now, however, right-wing critics have taken up their language but with the twist that they now attack the judiciary for being too *liberal* and out of touch.

In the third programme she focused on the way in which restraining orders to protect the victims of domestic violence, once again championed by liberal lawyers like her, have in recent years been broadened in scope and application, in such a way as to operate as mechanisms for politic control (see 1.3.5 above for a consideration of this particular issue and also a relevant newspaper article at www.guardian.co.uk/uk/2009/oct/27/high-court-injunctions-protests).

One would not have to be a confirmed cynic to recognise the dangers in such an approach. Those wishing to make radical changes in social order should not rely on the judges for support, nor place too much power in their hands. That is surely Griffith's underlying thesis?

It remains to be seen how the new coalition government will get on with the senior judiciary. The courts in recent times have stood out against the encroachments of the state under New Labour, and no doubt the courts would continue such a policy. However, the underlying policy of the coalition government seems to be the reduction of state activity and its replacement by private institutions, both profit and charity based. In that light, and it should not be forgotten that the Human Rights Act, the favoured means of protecting rights, is itself founded on the assertion of *individual* rights and is addressed toward *public* authorities, it is to be doubted that the courts will be found in the front-line of the fight against the accelerated privatisation of public service provision. Whether they would want to or not is another question. Perhaps *YL v Birmingham City Council* (see Chapter 2.5) represents the future.

10.7.2   THE POLITICS OF JUDICIAL INQUIRIES

During the summer of 2003, following the war in Iraq, the government established an inquiry to investigate the reasons why a British civil servant working for the Ministry of Defence (Dr David Kelly) apparently killed himself. The inquiry chairman was Lord Hutton, a Law Lord, and his task was set by the government as one to 'urgently conduct an investigation into the circumstances surrounding the death of Dr Kelly'. This prompts consideration of the judicial inquiry, and its place in the English legal system.

An inquiry is different from a tribunal, another quasi-judicial body with which it is sometimes compared. A tribunal is a permanent body whereas an inquiry is set up on an *ad hoc* basis to deal with one particular problematic issue. Tribunals are empowered to make decisions that affect the parties to the issue, whereas inquiries can only publish their 'findings' and make recommendations that might be implemented by the government.

A 'statutory inquiry' is one that is established because an Act permits or requires it to be set up in certain circumstances. For example, under s 78 of the Town and Country Planning 1990 Act, someone who seeks planning permission but is refused by his local planning authority has the right to appeal to the Secretary of State. In order to help decide the case, the Secretary can ask for a local public inquiry to be held.

A 'non-statutory inquiry' is one that has been set up by the government in order to examine matters of substantial public interest like disasters or scandals. Senior members of the judiciary usually, but not necessarily, chair these.

There are, importantly, two sorts of such judicial inquiry. First, there are those that are established under the Tribunals of Inquiry (Evidence) Act 1921. Such inquiries are similar in their formality and rules of procedure to court cases. The chair can summon witnesses under threat that they will commit an offence if they do not turn up to give evidence, and the chair can demand that documents be made available to the hearing. This type of inquiry can be established only upon a resolution of both houses of Parliament. The Bloody Sunday Inquiry into the killing of 13 Catholic civilians by British paratroopers in Derry in 1972 and chaired by Lord Saville of Newdigate was established under the 1921 Act. Similarly, the inquiry into the Dunblane shootings, in which many children at a primary school in Scotland were shot and killed in 1996, was also established under the 1921 Act.

Second, there are those judicial inquiries in which a judge is simply appointed by the government to chair the process but without the full powers of running it as a court case. For example, Lord Denning investigated aspects of the Profumo affair, a scandal in 1963 involving the Secretary of State for War at the time. Lord Scarman conducted the inquiry into the Brixton riots of 1981, Lord Justice Taylor examined the safety of sports grounds following the Hillsborough stadium disaster in 1991, and Lord Justice Scott inquired into the arms-for-Iraq affair in 1994. Such investigations, however, are not necessarily conducted by a judge, as may be seen from the pertinent example of the Franks Report on the conduct of the Falklands War in 1983.

However, judges have often been selected to chair inquiries into matters of public importance because they are expert in conducting fair and methodical hearings, and are generally regarded as wise people who are well versed in using rules of evidence justly to evaluate competing arguments. The Hutton Inquiry into the death of Dr Kelly was of this second sort.

Lord Hutton conducted his inquiry in a scrupulously forensic manner and, while it was ongoing, the press was particularly effusive in its praise of him. It was only with the release of the final report, which totally exonerated all members of the New Labour government and its entourage and castigated the BBC, that suggestions emerged that the Law Lord actually might not have been the best equipped person to undertake such a politically sensitive inquiry, at least from the point of view of those who were opposed to the actions of the government. For example, an article in *The Guardian* newspaper of 29 January 2004 stated that: 'Lord Hutton's report caused little surprise yesterday among lawyers who know the newly retired Law Lord. Most describe him as an establishment man and not one to rock the boat. When he set out on his task, they predicted that he would keep his remit as narrow as possible. That prediction has been proved right.'

Anthony Scrivener QC, a former chairman of the Bar, said: 'You get a conventional, conservative with a small "c" judge. You ask whether the Prime Minister and other members of the government have been lying through their teeth. As a conventional judge he applies the criminal standard of proof. You give him no right to get documents so he only sees the documents you give him. The result is entirely predictable.'

One senior QC said: 'I think the report reflects his establishment background. He is a trusting man as far as officialdom is concerned.'

Another, who knows him personally and has appeared before him, said: 'There are judges in the House of Lords who are liberal and progressive and might possibly shake the establishment branches, but not Brian Hutton.'

Whether the Hutton Report provides evidence to support Professor Griffith's thesis as to the inherently establishment nature of the judiciary as a body is a moot point, but it certainly caused Lord Woolf to question the wisdom of using members of the senior judiciary in such situations. In a *New Statesman* journal interview in February 2004, the Lord Chief Justice was quoted as disapproving of the present system. He said, 'In America they are not keen on judges doing this sort of thing', and that inquiries conducted by non-judges 'might be a better way of doing it'.

It could, once again, only be the unwonted, not to say hostile, publicity that led the Lord Chief Justice to such a conclusion: a conclusion that might suggest that judges should not be seen to be meddling in the political arena, but might also carry the implication that what is wrong is not so much the interference in itself, as the being seen to be interfering.

The Inquiries Act 2005
This new Act repeals the *Tribunals of Inquiry (Evidence) Act 1921*. Under the new Act:

- The inquiry and its terms of reference are to be decided by the executive in the form of the Minister of State responsible for the issue under investigation. That Minister may amend the terms of reference at any time if they consider that the public interest so requires. The terms of reference of the inquiry are defined as including:

  (i)   the matters to which the inquiry relates;

  (ii)   any particular matters as to which the inquiry panel is to determine the facts;

  (iii)   whether the inquiry panel is to make recommendations;

  (iv)   any other matters relating to the scope of the inquiry that the Minister may specify.

- In setting or amending the terms of reference, the Minister must consult the chair, but is not obliged to consult any other person.

- The chair of the inquiry is appointed by the Minister and the Minister has the discretion to dismiss any member of the inquiry.

- The decision whether the inquiry, or any individual hearings, should be held in public or private is also at the discretion of the Minister.

- The Minister may terminate an inquiry at any time. If they do so before the inquiry has delivered its report, the Minister must consult the chair, set out the reasons, and notify Parliament.

- Inquiries must deliver a report to the Minister setting out the facts determined by the inquiry panel and their recommendations. There is no provision for dissenting reports, but if the panel is not unanimous the report must reasonably reflect any disagreements.

- The chair is responsible for publishing the report, unless the Minister decides to take over that responsibility. Reports should be published in full but the person responsible for publishing a report may withhold material:

  (i)   as is required by any statutory provision, enforceable Community obligation or rule of law; or

  (ii)   as the person considers to be necessary in the public interest.

- Any decision to issue restrictive notices to block disclosure of evidence is also to be taken by the Minister.

- Any judicial review of a decision made by a Minister in relation to an inquiry or by the inquiry itself must be lodged within 14 days, which is shorter than the usual time limit of three months.

Critique of the Inquiries Act

In a trenchant assessment of the Inquiries Act 2005, the British and Irish Rights Watch, an independent human rights organisation, expressed the view that:

> The Inquiries Act has brought about a fundamental shift in the manner in which the actions of government and public bodies can be subjected to scrutiny in the United Kingdom. The powers of independent chairs to control inquiries has been usurped and those powers have been placed in the hands of government Ministers. The Minister:
>
> - decides whether there should be an inquiry;
> - sets its terms of reference;
> - can amend its terms of reference;
> - appoints its members;
> - can restrict public access to inquiries;
> - can prevent the publication of evidence placed before an inquiry;
> - can prevent the publication of the inquiry's report;
> - can suspend or terminate an inquiry; and
> - can withhold the costs of any part of an inquiry which strays beyond the terms of reference set by the Minister.
>
> Parliament's role has been reduced to that of the passive recipient of information about inquiries, whereas under the 1921 Act reports of public inquiries were made to Parliament. Now, not only is there no guarantee that any inquiry will be public, but inquiry reports will go to the Minister.
>
> The Minister's role is particularly troubling where the actions of that Minister or those of his or her department, or those of the government, are in question. In effect, the state will be investigating itself. In our view, the Inquiries Act is at odds with the United Nations' updated set of principles for the protection and promotion of human rights through action to combat impunity.
>
> Where Article 2 of the European Convention on Human Rights (which protects the right to life) is engaged, the Inquiries Act is at variance with the United Nations' Principles on the Effective Prevention and Investigation of Extra-legal, Arbitrary and Summary Executions. Indeed, we doubt that the Inquiries Act can deliver an effective investigation in compliance with Article 2. The Minister's powers to interfere in every important aspect of an inquiry robs it of any independence. Even if a Minister were to refrain from exercising those powers that are discretionary, s/he still has absolute power over whether there should be an inquiry at all and over its terms of reference. There is no scope for victims to be involved in or even consulted about the process. (http://www.birw.org/legislation_InquiriesActSummary.html)

In support of their view the organisation cited the views of Lord Saville, who chaired one of the most complex public inquiries in UK legal history, the Bloody Sunday Inquiry, who publicly expressed grave reservations about the Act. As they claim, in a letter to Baroness Ashton at the Department of Constitutional Affairs, dated 26 January 2005, he stated his opinion that:

> I take the view that this provision makes a very serious inroad into the independence of any inquiry and is likely to damage or destroy public confidence in the inquiry and its findings, especially in cases where the conduct of the authorities may be in question.

He added that such ministerial interference with a judge's ability to act impartially and independently of government would be unjustifiable. He further stated that neither he nor his fellow judges on the Bloody Sunday Inquiry would be prepared to be appointed as a member of an inquiry that was subject to a provision of that kind.

The Inquiries Act came under critical attention in July 2008 when the United Nations Human Rights Committee issued its concluding observations on the UK's periodic report under the UN Covenant on Civil and Political Right. As it stated:

> The Committee remains concerned that, a considerable time after murders (including of human rights defenders) in Northern Ireland have occurred, several inquiries into these murders have still not been established or concluded, and that those responsible for these deaths have not yet been prosecuted. Even where inquiries have been established, *the Committee is concerned that instead of being under the control of an independent judge, several of these inquiries are conducted under the Inquiries Act 2005 which allows the Government minister who is responsible for establishing an inquiry to control important aspects of that inquiry.* (Art 6)

The Leveson Inquiry

In July 2011 Lord Justice Leveson was appointed, under the Inquiries Act 2005, as chairman of an inquiry into the role of the press and police in the recent phone-hacking scandal. The inquiry opened in November 2011 and finished gathering formal evidence by the examination of witnesses in July 2012. The inquiry was established to examine the culture, practices and ethics of the media and, in particular, the relationship of the press with the public, police and politicians. Lord Leveson was assisted by a panel of six independent assessors with expertise in key issues being considered by the Inquiry and teams of assistants and counsel led by Robert Jay QC, who conducted the actual questioning.

When Leveson's report was issued, towards the end of November 2012, its most significant recommendation was the establishment of a new independent press regulator to replace the ineffective Press Complaints Commission. Although still independent and organised by the press industry, the new regulatory body was to be backed by statutory authority, thus introducing legal regulation into the operation of the press for the first time since the 17th century. It was this element of the report which generated the most heated debate, with the prime minister, David Cameron, declaring his lack of support for such a measure.

Leveson proposed that the new watchdog should have sufficient powers to carry out investigations into suspected serious or systemic breaches of its code of conduct, with the power to levy fines of 1% of turnover, up to a maximum of £1m. The report also recommended that the proposed regulator should have a fair, quick and inexpensive arbitration process in relation to civil legal claims against its members,

Although membership of the regulatory authority would not be a legal requirement for the press, Leveson suggested that the use of exemplary damages against non-members would go a long way to encourage membership.

CHAPTER SUMMARY: JUDICIAL REASONING AND POLITICS

REASONING IN GENERAL

Deductive reasoning is reasoning from the whole to the part; from the general to the particular. The syllogism is a form of deductive reasoning. Inductive reasoning is reasoning from the part to the whole; from the particular to the general. Reasoning by analogy is reasoning from part to part.

JUDICIAL REASONING

Laws can be presented in the form of syllogisms but do not actually focus on questions of deductive reasoning. The doctrine of judicial precedent appears at first sight to involve deductive reasoning, but is in fact based on the much less certain use of inductive reasoning and reasoning by analogy.

JUDICIAL REVIEW

Under the constitution of the UK, and within the doctrine of the separation of powers, judges and the executive have distinct but interrelated roles.

Judicial review remedies are the prerogative remedies of *quashing orders, mandatory orders* and *prohibiting orders*, together with the private law remedies of declaration, injunction and damages. Private law remedies cannot be used in relation to public law complaints.

Increased judicial activity in relation to State programmes raises questions about the competence and authority of judges to act, as well as raising doubts as to their political views.

POLITICS OF THE JUDICIARY

Judges have a capacity to make law – the question is, do they exercise this power in a biased way?

Bias can take two forms: personal and corporate.

Accusations of corporate bias suggest that, as a group, judges represent the interest of the status quo and decide certain political cases in line with that interest. However, more recently there has been a reliance on the judiciary as the protectors of human rights.

FOOD FOR THOUGHT

1.   Should the membership of the judiciary reflect the underlying social structure? In other words do the class, race and gender of the judiciary matter, and if so, why?

2.   Consider the extent to which the growth of judicial review and human rights actions are increasingly involving the judiciary in political decisions, and whether or not that is a good thing. In the words of the late Lord Denning, 'Someone must be trusted. Let it be the judges.' Is such an assertion valid in the light of the unrepresentative nature of the judiciary? As Lord Justice Laws has recently asked with regard to the HRA:

'Why should judges decide matters of social policy at all? The political rights, Articles 8–12, with the right set out in the first part and the derogation in the second, create a structure which means that a very large number of legal debates is about how the balance between private right and public interest should be struck. But what authority, expertise, do lawyers have to strike that balance, that is special to them?'

FURTHER READING

Baldwin, J, 'The social composition of magistrates' (1976) 16 British J of Criminology 171

Blom-Cooper, L, 'Bias: malfunction in judicial decision-making' [2009] PL 199–204

Browne-Wilkinson, N (Sir), 'The independence of the judiciary in the 1980s' [1988] PL 4

Clayton, R, 'Decision-making in the Supreme Court: new approaches and new opportunities' [2009] PL 682–5

Crawford, L, 'Race awareness training and the judges' (1994) Counsel 11

Griffith, JAG, *The Politics of the Judiciary*, 5th edn, 1997, London: Fontana

Hailsham (Lord), 'The office of Lord Chancellor and the separation of powers' (1989) 8 Civil Justice Quarterly 308

Lee, S, *Judging Judges*, 1988, London: Faber & Faber

MacCormick, N, *Legal Rules and Legal Reasoning*, 1978, Oxford: Clarendon

Mackay (Lord), *The Administration of Justice*, 1994, London: Sweet & Maxwell

Malleson, K, *The New Judiciary – The Effect of Expansion and Activism*, 1999, Aldershot: Ashgate

McLachlin, B, 'The role of judges in modern Commonwealth society' [1994] LQR 260

Murdoch, S, 'Judges use discretion over discharges' (2009) 940 EG 131

Pannick, D, *Judges*, 1987, Oxford: OUP

Parker, H *et al, Unmasking the Magistrates*, 1989, Milton Keynes: OUP

Royal Commission on Criminal Justice, *Runciman Report*, Cm 2263, 1995, London: HMSO

Rutherford, A, 'Judicial training and autonomy' (1999) 149 NLJ 1120

Skordaki, E, *Judicial Appointments*, Law Society Research Study No 5, 1991, London: HMSO

Smith, R, 'Judging the judges' (2009) 159 NLJ 1154

Stevens, R, *The Independence of the Judiciary*, 1993, Oxford: OUP

Stevens, R, *The English Judge: Their Role in the Changing Constitution*, 2002, Oxford: Hart Publishing

See, in addition, reading for Chapter 2

USEFUL WEBSITE

www.bailii.org/databases.html

A list of the databases that BAILII holds.

COMPANION WEBSITE

Now visit the companion website to:

- test your understanding of the key terms using our Flashcard Glossary;
- revise and consolidate your knowledge of 'Judicial reasoning and politics' using our Multiple Choice Question testbank;
- view the link to the Useful Website above.

www.routledge.com/cw/slapper

THE JURY

11

It is generally accepted that the jury of '12 good men and true' lies at the heart of the British legal system. The implicit assumption is that the presence of 12 ordinary lay-persons, randomly introduced into the trial procedure to be the arbiters of the facts of the case, strengthens the legitimacy of the legal system. It supposedly achieves this end by introducing a democratic humanising element into the abstract impersonal trial process, thereby reducing the exclusive power of the legal professionals who would otherwise command the legal stage and control the legal procedure without reference to the opinion of the lay majority.

According to EP Thompson:

> The English common law rests upon a bargain between the law and the people. The jury box is where the people come into the court; the judge watches them and the jury watches back. A jury is the place where the bargain is struck. A jury attends in judgement not only upon the accused but also upon the justice and humanity of the law [*Writing by Candlelight*].

Few people have taken this traditional view to task but, in a thought-provoking article in the Criminal Law Review ([1991] Crim LR 740), Penny Darbyshire did just that. In her view, the jury system has attracted the most praise and the least theoretical analysis of any component of the criminal justice system. As she correctly pointed out, and as will be shown below, juries are far from being either a random or a representative section of the general population. In fact, Darbyshire goes so far as to characterise the jury as 'an anti-democratic, irrational and haphazard legislator, whose erratic and secret decisions run counter to the rule of law'. She concedes that while the twentieth-century lay justices are not representative of the community as a whole, neither is the jury. She points out that jury equity, by which is meant the way in which the jury ignores the law in pursuit of justice, is a double-edged sword which may also convict the innocent; and counters examples such as the *Clive Ponting* case with the series of miscarriages of justice relating to suspected terrorists in which juries were also involved.

Darbyshire is certainly correct in taking to task those who would simply endorse the jury system in an unthinking, purely emotional manner. With equal justification, she criticises those academic writers who focus attention on the mystery of the jury to the exclusion of the hard reality of the magistrates' court. It is arguable, however, that she goes to the other extreme. Underlying her analysis and conclusions is the idea that 'the jury trial is primarily ideological' and that 'its symbolic significance is magnified beyond its practical significance by the media, as well as academics, thus unwittingly misleading the public'. While one might not wish to contradict the suggestion that the jury system operates as a very powerful ideological symbol, supposedly grounding the criminal legal system within a framework of participative democracy and justifying it on that basis, it is simply inadequate to reject the practical operation of the procedure on that basis alone. Ideologies do not exist purely in the realm of ideas, they have real, concrete manifestations and effects; in relation to the jury system, those manifestations operate in such a way as to offer at least a vestige of protection to defendants. In regard to the comparison between juries and the summary procedure of the magistrates' courts, Darbyshire puts two related questions. First, she asks whether the jury system is more likely to do justice and get the verdict right than the magistrates' courts; then she goes on to ask why the majority of defendants are processed through the magistrates' courts. These questions are highly pertinent; it is doubtful, however, whether her response to them is equally pertinent. Her answers would likely be that the jury does not perform any better than the magistrates and, therefore, it is immaterial that the magistrates deal with the bulk of cases. Her whole approach would seem to be concentrated on denigrating the performance of the jury system. A not untypical passage from her article admits that, in relation to the suspect terrorist miscarriages of justice, juries 'were not to blame for these wrongful convictions'. However, she then goes on in the same sentence to accuse the juries of failing 'to remedy the lack of due process at the pre-trial stage', and thus blames them for not providing 'the brake on oppressive State activity claimed for the jury by its defenders'.

Although there is most certainly scope for a less romantic view of how the jury system actually operates in practice, Darbyshire's argument seems to be that the magistrates are not very good but then neither are the juries; and as they only operate in a small minority of cases anyway, the implication would seem to be that their loss would be no great disadvantage. Others, however, would maintain that the jury system does achieve concrete benefits in particular circumstances and would argue further that these benefits should not be readily given up. Among the latter is Michael Mansfield QC who, in an article in response to the Runciman Report, claimed that the jury 'is the most democratic element of our judicial system' and the one that 'poses the biggest threat to the authorities'. (These questions will be considered further in relation to the Report of the Runciman Commission and the Criminal Justice (Mode of Trial) Bills, at 11.7.1 below.)

Having defended the institution of the jury generally, it has to be recognised that there are particular instances that tend to bring the jury system into disrepute. For example, in October 1994, the Court of Appeal ordered the re-trial of a man convicted of double murder on the grounds that four of the jurors had attempted to contact the alleged

THE ROLE OF THE JURY

victims using a Ouija board in what was described as a 'drunken experiment' (*R v Young* (1995)). A second convicted murderer appealed against his conviction on the grounds of irregularities in the manner in which the jury performed its functions. Among the allegations levelled at the jury was the claim that they clubbed together and spent £150 on drink when they were sent to a hotel after failing to reach a verdict. It was alleged that some of the jurors discussed the case against the express instructions of the judge and that on the following day, the jury foreman had to be replaced because she was too hung-over to act. One female juror was alleged to have ended up in bed with another hotel guest.

A truly remarkable case came to light in December 2000 when a trial, which had been going on for 10 weeks, was stopped on the grounds that a female juror was conducting what were referred to as 'improper relations' with a male member of the jury protection force who had been allocated to look after the jury during the trial. The relationship had become apparent after the other members of the jury had found out that they were using their mobile phones to send text messages to one another during breaks in the trial. That aborted trial was estimated to have cost £1.5 million, but it emerged that this was the second time the case had to be stopped on account of inappropriate behaviour on the part of jury members. The first trial had been abandoned after some of the jury were found playing cards when they should have been deliberating on the case.

Another example of the possible criticisms to be levelled against the misuse of juries occurred in Stoke-on-Trent, where the son of a court usher and another six individuals were found to have served on a number of criminal trial juries. While one could praise the public-spirited nature of this dedication to the justice process, especially given the difficulty in getting members of jury panels, it might be more appropriate to condemn the possibility of the emergence of a professional juror system connected to court officials. Certainly, the Court of Appeal was less than happy with the situation, and overturned a conviction when the Stoke practice was revealed to it.

Over the past 15 years, the operation of the jury system has been subject to one Royal Commission (Runciman), one review (Auld) and several statutory attempts to alter it. An examination of these various endeavours will be postponed until the end of this chapter; for the moment, attention will be focused on the jury system as it currently functions.

11.2 THE ROLE OF THE JURY

It is generally accepted that the function of the jury is to decide on matters of fact, and that matters of law are the province of the judge. Such may be the ideal case, but most of the time, the jury's decision is based on a consideration of a mixture of fact and law. The jurors determine whether a person is guilty on the basis of their understanding of the law as explained to them by the judge.

The oath taken by each juror states that they 'will faithfully try the defendant and give a true verdict according to the evidence', and it is contempt of court for a juror subsequent to being sworn in to refuse to come to a decision. In 1997, Judge Anura Cooray sentenced two women jurors to 30 days in prison for contempt of court for their failure to deliver a verdict. One of the women, who had been the jury foreman, claimed that the case, involving an allegation of fraud, had been too complicated to understand,

and the other had claimed that she could not ethically judge anyone. Judge Cooray was quoted (*The Guardian*, 26 March 1997) as justifying his decision to imprison them on the grounds that:

> I had to order a re-trial at very great expense. Jurors must recognise that they have a responsibility to fulfil their duties in accordance with their oath.

The women only spent one night in jail before the uproar caused by Cooray's action led to their release and the subsequent overturning of his sentence on them.

It should be appreciated that serving on a jury can be an extremely harrowing experience. Jurors are the arbiters of fact, but the facts they have to contend with can be horrific. Criticisms have been levelled at the way in which the jury system can subject people to what in other contexts would be pornography, of either a sexual or violent kind, and yet offer them no counselling when their jury service comes to an end. Many jurors fear reprisals from defendants and their associates. In April 2003, two illegal immigrants, Baghdad Meziane and Brahim Benmerzouga, were convicted of various offences under the Terrorism Act 2000. It appears that they had raised hundreds of thousands of pounds for Al Qa'ida and other radical Islamic organisations. The trial at Leicester Crown Court became a 'drama unprecedented in legal history' (S Bird, 'Jurors too scared to take on case', *The Times*, 2 April 2003):

> The case began in February, amid extraordinary security arrangements. A jury was sworn in and retired overnight . . . The next morning one frightened female juror had worked herself up into such a state that she vomited in the jury room. Two others burst into tears . . . The jury was dismissed – as was a second after a male juror expressed fears for his family's safety.

The third jury was down to nine members when it was time to deliver a verdict, which it duly did: a verdict of guilty, the accused receiving sentences of 11 years.

The only recognition currently available is that the judge can exempt them from further jury service for a particular period. Many would argue that such limited recognition of the damage that jurors might sustain in performing their civic duty is simply inadequate. Jury service can make excessive (many would say unreasonable) demands on jurors. In May 2005 a fraud trial collapsed after jurors had spent almost two years at the Old Bailey in London (see further, at 11.6.2.2).

11.3   THE JURY'S FUNCTION IN TRIALS

Judges have the power to direct juries to acquit the accused where there is insufficient evidence to convict them, and this is the main safeguard against juries finding defendants guilty in spite of either the absence, or the insufficiency, of the evidence. There is, however, no corresponding judicial power to instruct juries to convict (*DPP v Stonehouse* (1978); *R v Wang* (2005)). That being said, there is nothing to prevent the judge summing up in such a way as to make it evident to the jury that there is only one decision that can reasonably be made, and that it would be perverse to reach any other verdict but guilty.

What judges must not do is overtly put pressure on juries to reach guilty verdicts. Finding of any such pressure will result in the overturning of any conviction so obtained. The classic example of such a case is *R v McKenna* (1960), in which the judge told the jurors, after they had spent all of two and a quarter hours deliberating on the issue, that if they did not come up with a verdict in the following 10 minutes, they would be locked up for the night. Not surprisingly, the jury returned a verdict; unfortunately for the defendant, it was a guilty verdict; even more unfortunately for the judicial process, the conviction had to be quashed on appeal for clear interference with the jury.

In the words of Cassels J:

> It is a cardinal principle of our criminal law that in considering their verdict, concerning, as it does, the liberty of the subject, a jury shall deliberate in complete freedom, uninfluenced by any promise, unintimidated by any threat. They stand between the Crown and the subject, and they are still one of the main defences of personal liberty. To say to such a tribunal in the course of its deliberations that it must reach a conclusion . . . is a disservice to the cause of justice . . . [*R v McKenna* [1960] 1 All ER 326 at 329].

Judges do have the right, and indeed the duty, to advise the jury as to the proper understanding and application of the law that it is considering. Even when the jury is considering its verdict, it may seek the advice of the judge. The essential point, however, is that any such response on the part of the judge must be given in open court, so as to obviate any allegation of misconduct (*R v Townsend* (1982)).

In *R v Arshid Khan* (2008) Khan appealed against convictions on the ground that the judge at his trial had permitted new evidence to be put to the jury after it had retired to consider its verdict. The situation arose as a result of the jury returning to the court to ask for clarification of evidence relating to mobile phone calls. After the judge had answered the jury's questions, one of Khan's lawyers made further investigations which revealed that the evidence presented to the jury was inaccurate. The judge was informed of this fact and the jury was re-assembled within two hours of it having been given the information in answer to its questions.

The judge then informed the jury that some of the information may not have been correct. The jury were then told to go home and to return the following morning to resume their deliberations.

Further investigations revealed that the evidence presented to the jury was in fact inaccurate. On the following morning Khan's lawyers discussed the results of the investigation with him. And on the understanding that the new evidence might strengthen his case, he agreed that it should be put before the jury. Nonetheless, the jury returned guilty verdicts in relation to the charges against Khan, who subsequently appealed on the ground that the judge had erred in law in permitting the additional evidence to be put before the jury after it had retired.

In rejecting the appeal the Court of Appeal found that there was no reason in principle why the judge should not have agreed to allow the new evidence to be put before the jury. On the contrary, as they stated:

> we can see every reason why he should have allowed this evidence to go before the jury. The defence invited the judge to do so on the basis that the evidence assisted the appellant's case. It was evidence which trial counsel believed was capable of supporting the appellant's case in an area which both counsel felt the appellant's evidence was weak and required some support. We have no doubt that the appellant agreed to this course of action.

On that basis the court rejected Khan's appeal.

The decision in *Khan* reflects the changed approach of the courts to such situations as historically the authorities support the view that there was an absolute principle that no further evidence should be given after the judge's summing-up has been concluded and the jury has retired. Thus in *R v Owen* (1952), in which the trial judge allowed a doctor who had already given evidence in the case to be recalled to give evidence in answer to a question raised by the jury after their retirement, the subsequent conviction was quashed. The reason stated by Lord Goddard CJ was that: 'once the summing up is concluded, no further evidence ought to be given. The jury can be instructed in reply to any question they may put on any matter on which evidence has been given, but no further evidence should be allowed'.

However, subsequently, in *R v Sanderson* (1953), the Court of Criminal Appeal, including Lord Goddard CJ, held that it was permissible for the evidence of a witness for the defence to be taken after the summing up had been completed, *but before the jury had retired* and the 'very strict rule' that no evidence whatever must be introduced after the jury had retired was reiterated by Lord Parker CJ in *R v Gearing* (1968).

However, the introduction of the proviso under s 2(1) of the Criminal Appeal Act 1968 (see 6.5.2 above) led to a change in approach and in *R v Davis* (1976), the absolute nature of the rule was questioned and such an approach was approved of in *R v Karakaya* (2005).

More recently in *R v Hallam* (2007) the Court of Appeal actually held that a verdict was unsafe because a judge had refused to permit the jury to see a photograph which could potentially have assisted the appellant's defence, but which had come to light only after the summing-up. In that case the court defined the principle as follows:

> It used to be understood that there was a very firm rule that evidence cannot be admitted after the retirement of the jury, but more recent authorities

confirm that there is no absolute rule to that effect. The question is what justice requires.

In criminal cases, even perversity of decision does not provide grounds for appeal against acquittal. There have been occasions where juries have been subjected to the invective of a judge when they have delivered a verdict with which he disagreed. Nonetheless, the fact is that juries collectively, and individual jurors, do not have to justify, explain or even give reasons for their decisions. Indeed, under s 8 of the Contempt of Court Act 1981, it would be a contempt of court to try to elicit such information from a jury member in either a criminal or a civil law case.

In *Attorney General v Associated Newspapers* (1994), the House of Lords held that it was contempt of court for a newspaper to publish disclosures by jurors of what took place in the jury room while they were considering their verdict, unless the publication amounted to no more than a re-publication of facts already known. It was decided that the word 'disclose' in s 8(1) applied not just to jurors, but to any others who published their revelations.

In an interview for *The Times* in January 2001, the Lord Chief Justice, Lord Woolf, expressed himself very strongly in favour of lifting the ban on jury research, though he emphasised that great care was needed in the conduct of any such research.

These factors place juries in a very strong position to take decisions that are 'unjustifiable' in accordance with the law, for the simple reason that they do not have to justify the decisions. Thus, juries have been able to deliver what can only be described as perverse decisions. In *R v Clive Ponting* (1985), the judge made clear beyond doubt that the defendant was guilty, under the Official Secrets Act 1911, of the offence with which he was charged: the jury still returned a not guilty verdict. Similarly, in the case of Pat Pottle and Michael Randall, who had openly admitted their part in the escape of the spy George Blake, the jury reached a not guilty verdict in open defiance of the law.

In *R v Kronlid* (1996), three protestors were charged with committing criminal damage, and another was charged with conspiracy to cause criminal damage, in relation to an attack on Hawk Jet aeroplanes that were about to be sent to Indonesia. The damage to the planes allegedly amounted to £1.5 million and they did not deny their responsibility for it. They rested their defence on the fact that the planes were to be delivered to the Indonesian State, to be used in its allegedly genocidal campaign against the people of East Timor. On those grounds, they claimed that they were in fact acting to prevent the crime of genocide. The prosecution cited assurances, given by the Indonesian government, that the planes would not be used against the East Timorese, and pointed out that the UK government had granted an export licence for the planes. As the protestors did not deny what they had done, it was apparently a mere matter of course that they would be convicted as charged. The jury, however, decided that all four of the accused were innocent of the charges laid against them. A government Treasury minister, Michael Jack, subsequently stated his disbelief at the verdict of the jury. As he stated:

> I, and I am sure many others, find this jury's decision difficult to understand. It would appear there is little question about who did this 25damage. For whatever reason that damage was done, it was just plain wrong [(1996) *The Independent*, 1 August].

As stated above, jurors swear to return 'a true verdict according to the evidence'. Such verdicts may be politically inconvenient.

It is perhaps just such a lack of understanding, together with the desire to save money on the operation of the legal system, that has motivated the government's expressed wish to replace jury trials in relation to either way offences (see below, at 11.8). In any event, juries continue to reach perverse decisions where they are sympathetic to the causes pursued by the defendants. Thus, in September 2000, 28 Greenpeace volunteers, including its executive director Lord Melchett, were found not guilty of criminal damage after they had destroyed a field containing genetically modified maize. They had been found not guilty of theft in their original trial in April of that year. Judge David Mellor told the jury:

> It is not about whether GM crops are a good thing for the environment or a bad thing. It is for you to listen to the evidence and reach honest conclusions as to the facts.

However, the jury seemed to have adopted a different approach.

Fear of not achieving a successful conviction also appears to be the reason behind the CPS's belated decision, in February 2004, not to pursue the prosecution of Katherine Gun. Gun was the former GCHQ translator who revealed that the UK and the USA were involved in spying on members of the United Nations before a crucial vote on whether the 2003 war on Iraq would be sanctioned by the UN. Although she admitted she was the source of the leak and was consequently, at least *prima facie*, in breach of the Official Secrets Act, her prosecution was dropped after she had put forward the defence of necessity. The decision was apparently taken on the guidance of the Attorney General who was involved in the Iraq question from the beginning, being the source of the government's advice that the war was legal without the need for a specific resolution to that effect by the United Nations. In September 2008, six Greenpeace climate change activists were cleared of causing £30,000 of criminal damage at a coal-fired power station in Kent. They had admitted trying to shut down the station by occupying the smokestack and painting the word 'Gordon' down the chimney. However, the jury found them not guilty on the basis of their defence, which was that they were justified in their action as they were acting to prevent climate change causing greater damage to property around the world. In his summing-up at the end of an eight-day trial, the judge, David Caddick, said the case centred on whether or not the protesters had a lawful excuse for their actions and the jury found that they did.

A non-political example of this type of case can be seen in the jury's refusal to find Stephen Owen guilty of any offence after he had discharged a shotgun at the driver of a lorry that had killed his child. And, in September 2000, a jury in Carlisle found Lezley Gibson not guilty on a charge of possession of cannabis after she told the court that she needed it to relieve the symptoms of the multiple sclerosis from which she suffered. The tendency of the jury occasionally to ignore legal formality in favour of substantive justice is one of the major points in favour of its retention, according to its proponents.

11.3.1   APPEALS FROM DECISIONS OF THE JURY

In criminal law, it is an absolute rule that there can be no appeal against a jury's decision to acquit a person of the charges laid against him. Although there is no appeal as such against acquittal, there does exist the possibility of the Attorney General referring the case to the Court of Appeal, to seek its advice on points of law raised in criminal cases in which the defendant has been acquitted. This procedure was provided for under s 36 of the CJA 1972, although it is not commonly resorted to. It must be stressed that there is no possibility of the actual case being reheard or the acquittal decision being reversed, but the procedure can highlight mistakes in law made in the course of Crown Court trial and permits the Court of Appeal to remedy the defect for the future. (See *Attorney General's Reference (No 1 of 1988)* (1988) for an example of this procedure, in the area of insider dealing in relation to shares on the Stock Exchange. This case is also interesting in relation to statutory interpretation. See also *Attorney General's Reference (No 3 of 1999)*, considered above, at 9.3.2.)

In civil law cases, the possibility of the jury's verdict being overturned on appeal does exist, but only in circumstances where the original verdict was perverse, that is, no reasonable jury properly directed could have made such a decision.

11.3.2   MAJORITY VERDICTS

The possibility of a jury deciding a case on the basis of a majority decision was introduced by the CJA 1967. Prior to this, the requirement was that jury decisions had to be unanimous. Such decisions are acceptable where there are:

- not less than 11 jurors and 10 of them agree; or
- there are 10 jurors and nine of them agree.

Where a jury has reached a guilty verdict on the basis of a majority decision, s 17(3) of the Juries Act (JA) 1974 requires the foreman of the jury to state in open court the number of jurors who agreed and the number who disagreed with the verdict. See *R v Barry* (1975), where failure to declare the details of the voting split resulted in the conviction of the defendant being overturned. In *R v Pigg* (1983), the House of Lords held that it was unnecessary to state the number who voted against where the foreman stated the number in favour of the verdict, and thus the determination of the minority was a matter of simple arithmetic.

However, in *R v Mendy* (1992), when the clerk of the court asked the foreman of the jury how a guilty decision had been reached, he replied that it was 'by the majority of us all'. The ambiguity of the reply is obvious when it is taken out of context and this was relied on in a successful appeal. It was simply not clear whether it referred to a unanimous verdict, as the court at first instance had understood it, or whether it referred to a real majority vote, in which case it failed to comply with the requirement of s 17(3) as applied in *R v Barry*. The Court of Appeal held that in such a situation, the defendant had to be given the benefit of any doubt and he was discharged.

The Court of Appeal adopted a different approach in *R v Millward* (1999). The appellant had been convicted, at Stoke-on-Trent Crown Court, of causing grievous bodily harm. Although the jury actually had reached a majority decision, the foreman in response to the questioning of the clerk of the court mistakenly stated that it was the verdict of them all. The following day, the foreman informed the judge that the verdict had in fact been a majority verdict of 10 for guilty and two against.

The Court of Appeal met the subsequent challenge with the following exercise in sophisticated reasoning. The court at first instance had apparently accepted a unanimous verdict. Therefore, s 17 had not been brought into play at all. And, bearing in mind s 8 of the Contempt of Court Act 1981, discouraging the disclosure of votes cast by jurors in the course of their deliberations, the issue had to be viewed under the policy of the law. It would set a very dangerous precedent if an apparently unanimous verdict of a jury delivered in open court, and not then challenged by any juror, was reopened and subjected to scrutiny. It would be difficult to see how the court could properly investigate a disagreement as to whether jurors had dissented or not. In the instant case, there was a proper majority direction and proper questions asked of the jury and apparently proper and unambiguous answers given without challenge. Therefore, there should be no further inquiry.

There is no requirement for the details of the voting to be declared in a majority decision of not guilty.

11.3.3   DISCHARGE OF JURORS OR THE JURY

The trial judge may discharge the whole jury if certain irregularities occur. These would include the situation where the defendant's previous convictions are revealed inadvertently during the trial. Such a disclosure would be prejudicial to the defendant. In such a case, the trial would be ordered to commence again with a different jury. Individual jurors may be discharged by the judge if they are incapable of continuing to act through illness 'or for any other reason' (s 16(1) of the Juries Act (JA) 1974). Where this happens, the jury must not fall below nine members.

11.4   THE SELECTION OF THE JURY

In theory, jury service is a public duty that citizens should readily undertake. In practice, it is made compulsory, and failure to perform one's civic responsibility is subject to the sanction of a £1,000 fine.

In 2010, 373,650 juror summonses were issued and 181,281 people actually served as jurors (see the end of this section for an explanation of the difference in these figures). The JA 1974, as amended by the CJA 1988 and the CJA 2003, sets out the law relating to juries. Prior to the JA 1974, there was a property qualification in respect to jury service that skewed jury membership towards middle-class men. Now, the legislation provides that any person between the ages of 18 and 70, who is on the electoral register and who has lived in the UK for at least five years, is qualified to serve as a juror.

The procedure for establishing a jury is a threefold process:

- An officer of the court summons a randomly selected number of qualified individuals from the electoral register.
- From that group, panels of potential jurors for various cases are drawn up.
- The actual jurors are then randomly selected by means of a ballot in open court.

As has been pointed out, however, even if the selection procedure were truly random, randomness does not equal representation. Random juries, by definition, could be: all male, all female, all white, all black, all Conservative or all members of the Raving Loony Party. Such is the nature of the random process; the question that arises from the process is whether such randomness is necessarily a good thing in itself, and whether the summoning officer should take steps to avoid the potential disadvantages that can result from random selection.

As regards the actual random nature of the selection process, a number of problems arise from the use of electoral registers to determine and locate jurors:

- Electoral registers tend to be inaccurate. Generally, they misreport the number of younger people who are in an area simply because younger people tend to move about more than older people and therefore tend not to appear on the electoral roll of the place in which they currently live.
- Electoral registers tend to underreport the number of members of ethnic minorities in a community. The problem is that some members of the ethnic communities, for a variety of reasons, simply do not notify the authorities of their existence.
- The problem of non-registration mentioned above was compounded by the disappearance of a great many people from electoral registers in order to try to avoid payment of the former poll tax. It has been suggested that the current government's proposals to alter registration procedure to an individual voluntary process from a compulsory household process would have an even greater impact on the register of voters.

Prior to the CJA 2003, the general qualification for serving as a juror was subject to a number of exceptions.

A variety of people were deemed to be ineligible to serve on juries on the basis of their employment or vocation. Among this category were: judges; Justices of the Peace; members of the legal profession; police and probation officers; and members of the clergy or religious orders. Those suffering from a mental disorder were also deemed to be ineligible. Paragraph 2 of Sched 33 to the CJA 2003 removes the first three groups of persons ineligible – the judiciary, others concerned with the administration of justice, and the clergy – leaving only mentally disordered persons with that status.

This reform came into effect in April 2005. The extent to which 'ordinary' jurors will be influenced by contact with solicitors, barristers and judges remains to be seen (assuming that research into such matters is eventually permitted). In any event the provisions of the CJA 2003 as regards eligibility to serve were challenged, as being contrary to Art 6 of the ECHR, in *R v (1) Abdroikov (2) Green (3) Williamson* (2005), three otherwise unrelated cases. Each of the appellants appealed against their convictions on the grounds that the jury in their respective trials had contained members who were employed in the criminal justice system. The juries in the trials of the first and second appellants had contained serving police officers. The jury in the trial of the third appellant had contained a person employed as a prosecuting solicitor by the CPS. Their proposal was that, as prior to the CJA 2003 there would have been no doubt that the presence of such people on juries would have been unlawful, so their presence in the current cases ran contrary to the need for trials to be free from even the taint of apparent bias.

The Court of Appeal rejected such arguments as spurious, holding that the expectations placed on ordinary citizens in relation to jury service had to be extended to members of the criminal justice system.

However, by a majority of three to two the House of Lords held that the appeals of Green and Williamson should succeed, but that Abdroikov's appeal must fail. Lords Rodger and Carswell, in the minority, held that all appeals should fail. In reaching its decision the majority looked at the reports of previous committees that had been tasked with examining the operation of juries. Thus they referred to the findings of the 1965 committee chaired by Lord Morris of Borth-y-Gest, which recommended that the police and those professionally concerned in the administration of the law should continue to be ineligible. Then in 2001, Auld LJ reviewed the issue and recommended that everyone should be eligible for jury service save for the mentally ill. He recognised that the risk of bias could not be totally eradicated and envisaged that any question about the risk of bias on the part of any juror could be resolved by the trial judge on the facts of the case. His recommendation was given effect by the Criminal Justice Act 2003 s 321. However, as the House of Lords made clear, Auld LJ's expectation that each doubtful case would be resolved by the trial judge could not be met if neither the judge nor counsel knew that the juror was a police officer or CPS solicitor. The House of Lords recognised that there were situations where police officers and CPS solicitors would meet the tests of impartiality, however, that did not mean they would always do so automatically.

However, according to Lords Rodger and Carswell in the minority, Parliament had endorsed the view that universal eligibility for jury service was to be regarded as appropriate. In reaching that conclusion Parliament had to be taken to have been aware of the test for apparent bias. It must, therefore, be taken to have considered that the risk of bias in the case of serving police officers or CPS solicitors was manageable within the system of jury trial. The consequence of the House of Lords majority decision was pointed out by Lord Rodger in the clearest of terms:

> I can see no reason why the fair-minded and informed observer should single out juries with police officers and CPS lawyers as being constitutionally incapable of following the judge's directions and reaching an impartial verdict. It must be assumed, for instance, that the observer considers that there is no real possibility that a jury containing a gay man trying a man accused of a homophobic attack will, for that reason alone, be incapable of reaching an unbiased verdict, even though the juror might readily identify with a fellow gay man. Despite this – if Mr Green's appeal is to be allowed – the observer must be supposed to consider that there is, inevitably, a real possibility that a jury will have been biased in a case involving a significant conflict of evidence between a police witness and the defendant, just because the witness and a police officer juror serve in the same borough or the juror serves in a force which commits its work to the trial court in question. Similarly, if Mr Williamson's appeal is allowed, the observer must be taken to consider that the same applies to any jury containing a CPS lawyer whenever the prosecution is brought by the CPS. In my view, an observer who singled out juries with these two types of members would be applying a different standard from the one that is usually applied. For no good reason, the observer would be virtually ignoring the other 11 jurors ... your Lordships' decision to allow two of the appeals will drive a coach and horses through Parliament's legislation and will go far to reverse its reform of the law, *even though the statutory provisions themselves are not said to be incompatible with Convention rights.* Moreover, any requirement for police officers and CPS lawyers balloted to serve on a jury to identify themselves routinely to the judge would discriminate against them by introducing a process of vetting for them and them alone. Parliament cannot have considered that such a requirement was necessary since it did not impose it. The rational policy of the legislature is to decide who are eligible to serve as jurors and then to treat them all alike.

The issue of apparent juror bias on account of their occupation was considered further by the Court of Appeal in six conjoined cases in March 2008: *R v Khan* (2008). The occupations involved were those of serving police officers, employees of the CPS, although on this occasion in a prosecution brought by the Department of Trade and Industry, and prison officers. The judgment of the Court of Appeal was delivered by the then Lord Chief Justice, Lord Phillips, in the course of which he explained that, although the Criminal Justice Act 2003 had abolished automatic disqualification from jury service on account of an occupation associated with the administration of justice, it had not made those persons immune to claims of apparent bias and that 'the nature of some occupations is such that there is an obvious danger that the circumstances of a prosecution will give rise to an appearance of bias in relation to those who belong to them'. In its consideration of the issues, the Court of Appeal distinguished between apparent bias towards *a party* in the case and apparent bias towards *a witness* in the case. In the former instance should it become apparent during a trial that a juror is partial then they should be discharged. If the bias only becomes apparent after the verdict, then the conviction must be quashed. However, the Court held that apparent bias towards *a witness* does not, automatically, have those consequences, and will do so only if it would appear to the fair-minded observer that the juror's apparent bias may affect, or have affected, the outcome of the trial. The fair-minded observer test was established in the House of Lords in *Porter v Magill* (2001).

As regards serving police officers, the Court of Appeal could find no clear principles for identifying apparent bias from the majority judgments in *R v Abdroikov*, but went on to hold that although such jurors may seem likely to favour the evidence of a fellow police officer, that would not automatically lead to the appearance that they favoured the prosecution. For example if the police evidence was not challenged or was not an important part of the prosecution case, then there would be no reason to suspect bias on the part of the juror. It would only be appropriate to question a conviction for apparent bias if, and only if, the effect of the juror's partiality towards a fellow officer put in doubt the safety of the conviction and thus rendered the trial unfair.

More specifically, the court rejected the proposition that the mere fact that a police officer had taken part in operations involving the type of offence with which a defendant was charged gave rise, of itself, to an appearance of bias on the part of the police officer. As the court pointed out, police officers are likely to have had experience of most of the common types of criminal offence, not least drug dealing. Finally as regards police jurors, the fact that the jury was told that a defendant had a previous conviction for assaulting a police officer would not of itself raise the issue of apparent bias.

As seen above, in *Abdroikov*, the majority of the House of Lords held that a juror who was a member of the Crown Prosecution Service had the appearance of bias where they acted as a juror in a case prosecuted by their employer. However, the Court of Appeal distinguished the situation under its consideration from that case in holding that there could be no objection to a member of the Crown Prosecution Service sitting in a case prosecuted by some other authority, in this particular instance the Department of Trade and Industry.

With regard to the possibility of prison guards acting as jurors, the Court of Appeal made it clear that the mere suspicion that a juror might, by reason of employment in a prison where a defendant had been held, have acquired knowledge of that defendant's bad character could not, of itself, lead an objective observer to conclude that the juror had an appearance of bias. Where the juror had no knowledge of the defendant, there could be no objective basis for imputing bias towards the defendant. Indeed, even actual knowledge of a defendant's bad character would not automatically result in the juror ceasing to qualify as independent and impartial.

In concluding his judgment, Lord Phillips emphasised the court's concern with the need to regularise, and thus avoid appeals from, cases raising the issue of juror bias in relation to particular occupations. As he put it:

It is undesirable that the apprehension of jury bias should lead to appeals such as those with which this court has been concerned. It is particularly undesirable if such appeals lead to the quashing of convictions so that re-trials have to take place. In order to avoid this it is desirable that any risk of jury bias, or of unfairness as a result of partiality to witnesses, should be identified before the trial begins. If such a risk may arise, the juror should be stood down . . . It is essential that the trial judge should be aware at the stage of jury selection if any juror in waiting is, or has been, a police officer or a member of the prosecuting authority, or is a serving prison officer. Those called for jury service should be required to record on the appropriate form whether they fall into any of these categories, so that this information can be conveyed to the judge. We invite all of these authorities and Her Majesty's Court Service to consider the implications of this judgment and to issue such directions as they consider appropriate.

In an endeavour to maintain the unquestioned probity of the jury system, certain categories of persons are disqualified from serving as jurors. Among these are anyone who has been sentenced to a term of imprisonment, or youth custody, of five years or more. In addition, anyone who, in the past 10 years, has served a sentence, or has had a suspended sentence imposed on them, or has had a community punishment order made against them, is also disqualified. The CJA 2003 makes a number of amendments to reflect recent and forthcoming developments in sentencing legislation. Thus, juveniles sentenced under s 91 of the Powers of Criminal Courts (Sentencing) Act 2000 to detention for life, or for a term of five years or more, will be disqualified for life from jury service. People sentenced to imprisonment or detention for public protection, or to an extended sentence under ss 227 or 228 of the Act are also to be disqualified for life from jury service. Anyone who has received a community order (as defined in s 177 of the Act) will be disqualified from jury service for 10 years. Those on bail in criminal proceedings are disqualified from serving as a juror in the Crown Court.

Certain people were excused as of right from serving as jurors on account of their jobs, age or religious views. Among these were members of the medical professions, Members of Parliament and members of the armed forces, together with anyone over 65 years of age. Paragraph 3 of Sched 33 to the CJA 2003 repeals s 9(1) of the JA 1974 and consequently no one will in future be entitled to excusal as of right from jury service.

It has always been the case that if a person who has been summoned to do jury service could show that there was a 'good reason' why their summons should be deferred or excused, s 9 of the JA 1974 provided discretion to defer or excuse service. With the abolition of most of the categories of ineligibility and of the availability of excusal as of right, it is expected that there will be a corresponding increase in applications for excusal or deferral under s 9 being submitted to the Jury Central Summoning Bureau (see below).

Grounds for such excusal or deferral are supposed to be made only on the basis of good reason, but there is at least a measure of doubt as to the rigour with which such rules are applied.

A Practice Note issued in 1988 (now *Practice Direction (Criminal: Consolidated)* [2002] 1 WLR 2870, para 42) stated that applications for excusal should be treated sympathetically and listed the following as good grounds for excusal:

(a)   personal involvement in the case;

(b)   close connection with a party or a witness in the case;

(c)   personal hardship;

(d)   conscientious objection to jury service.

However, a new s 9AA, introduced by the CJA 2003, placed a statutory duty on the Lord Chancellor, in whom current responsibility for jury summoning is vested, to publish and lay before Parliament guidelines relating to the exercise by the Jury Central Summoning Bureau of its functions in relation to discretionary deferral and excusal.

The guidelines, available at http://www.official-documents.gov.uk/document/other/9780108508400/9780108508400.pdf, were issued in 2004 and make clear that only in extreme circumstances should a person be excused from jury service. They require summoning officers to refuse requests in the absence of 'good reason'. Even where 'good reason' is shown why the person should not sit on the date they have been summoned, deferral should always be considered in the first instance. Excusal from jury service should be reserved only for those cases where the jury summoning officer is satisfied that it would be unreasonable to require the person to serve at any time within the following 12 months.

The previous, somewhat antiquated procedure for selecting potential jury members, with its accompanying disparity of treatment, was modernised by the introduction of a Central Summoning Bureau based at Blackfriars Crown Court Centre in London. The Bureau uses a computer system to select jurors at random from the electoral registers and issue the summonses, as well as dealing with jurors' questions and requests. The jury summoning system is linked to the national police records system to allow checks to be made against potentially disqualified individuals.

However, severe doubts have been expressed as to the accuracy of the police national computer (PNC), which might not only render the checks on juries inaccurate, but might actually contravene the Data Protection Act 1998. When the Metropolitan Police conducted an audit of the PNC in 1999, it was found to have 'wholly unacceptable' levels of inaccuracy, with an overall error rate of 86 per cent. In one case in 2000 at Highbury Corner magistrates' court in north London, a man charged with theft of £2,700 was granted bail on the grounds that the PNC showed that he had no previous convictions. In fact, he was a convicted murderer released from prison on licence.

It has to be stated that, as reported in a parliamentary answer in February 2007, the Secretary of State for the Home Department intimated that later audits carried out in August 2002 had indicated that the general position on data accuracy was far more favourable than had previously been suggested. According to his statement, the exercise

TABLE 11.1 *Reproduced from Ministry of Justice Report*

Crown Court
Jury Central Summoning Bureau figures,[1] 2007–2011

	2007	2008	2009	2010	2011
Total number of summons issued[2,3] (r)	388,362	395,503	373,871	373,650	343,949
Total number of jurors supplied to the court	182,661	183,506	176,351	181,281	170,421
Deferred to serve at a later date	66,174	66,806	61,892	62,051	57,982
Number refused deferral	122	103	87	78	54
Excused by right having served in past two years	4,518	4,244	3,470	3,881	3,331
Excused for other reasons[4]	103,064	104,290	96,563	93,782	76,008
All excused	**107,582**	**108,534**	**100,033**	**97,663**	**79,339**
Number refused excusal	1,641	1,515	1,342	1,485	1,303
Disqualified – residency, mental disorders, criminality	94,171	96,325	92,704	96,482	89,668
Disqualified – on selection	58,900	59,017	56,967	56,871	52,115
Disqualified – failed Police National Computer check	207	225	220	215	239
Failed to reply to summons	40,635	45,192	49,086	47,221	43,663
Summons undelivered	18,325	17,603	13,646	12,916	12,583
Postponed by Jury Central Summoning Bureau	7,274	9,621	7,439	6,569	4,937

Source:
Jury Central Summoning Bureau
Notes:
[1] Numbers do not add up to the overall total within a given year as the data reflect rolling 12-month periods with 'carry-over' rules applied to certain rows in the table. For example, the number of disqualifications reported for a given year may include disqualifications for summons that were issued in previous years.
[2] Previously published figures for 2007 to 2009 double-counted summons that were re-issued due to a change in court venue. In this publication, these figures have been revised to remove any double counting.
[3] This figure represents the number of summons that were issued in a year and not the number of people that actually served on a jury in that year. For example, a person summoned for jury service in 2011 may not actually serve until 2012.
[4] Including childcare, work commitments, medical issues, language difficulties, student status, moved from area, travel difficulties and financial hardship.

found that in 94 per cent of cases, the key information was recorded entirely accurately, and that in the remaining 6 per cent some inaccuracies were found but, in the majority of instances, the inaccuracy was not critical.

Statistics relating to juries are contained in the Ministry of Justice 'Judicial and Court Statistics 2011 report available at: http://www.justice.gov.uk/publications/ statistics-and-data/courts-and-sentencing/ judicial-annual.htm

In 2011, 343,949 juror summonses were issued. Of these, 79,339 were excused: 3,331 were excused as they had already served in the last two years and 76,008 were excused for other reasons including childcare, work commitments, medical issues, language difficulty, student status, changes in residency, travel difficulties and financial hardship. The number of people who failed to reply to their summons, together with the number returned as undelivered, totalled 52,246, a remarkably high number.

11.4.3   DISABILITY AND JURY SERVICE

It is to be hoped that the situation of people with disabilities has been altered for the better by the CJPOA 1994, which introduced a new s 9B into the JA 1974. Previously, it was all too common for judges to discharge jurors with disabilities, including deafness, on the assumption that they would not be capable of undertaking the duties of a juror.

Under this provision, where it appears doubtful that a person summoned for jury service is capable of serving on account of some physical disability, that person, as previously, may be brought before the judge. The new s 9B, however, introduces a presumption that people should serve and provides that the judge shall affirm the jury summons unless he is of the opinion that the person will not be able to act effectively.

It would appear, however, that the CJPOA 1994 does not improve the situation of profoundly deaf people who could only function as jurors with the aid of a sign language interpreter. That was the outcome of a case decided in November 1999 that profoundly deaf Jeff McWhinney, Chief Executive of the British Deaf Association, could not serve as a juror. For him to do so would have required that he had the assistance of an interpreter in the jury room and that could not be allowed as, at present, only jury members are allowed into the jury room.

Any person who has suffered from 'a disorder or disability of the mind' and, because of that condition, regularly visits a medical practitioner for treatment, is precluded from jury service. As campaigners have pointed out, many people are being excluded from jury service after being treated for conditions such as depression, schizophrenia and bipolar disorder, which are all perfectly manageable through medication. As they also point out, one in four Britons suffers from mental illness at some point in their lives, and one in 10 is prescribed antidepressants.

In 2012 Gavin Barwell MP introduced a Private Member's Bill, the Mental Health (Discrimination) Bill, which looked to outlaw discrimination against people who have experienced mental ill health, including jury service and membership of the House of Commons.

That juries can be 'self-selecting' provides grounds for concern as to the random nature of the jury, but the traditional view of the jury is further and perhaps even more fundamentally undermined by the way in which both prosecution and defence seek to influence its constitution.

Under s 12(6) of the JA 1974, both prosecution and defence have a right to challenge the array where the summoning officer has acted improperly in bringing the whole panel together. Such challenges are rare, although an unsuccessful action was raised in *R v Danvers* (1982), where the defendant tried to challenge the racial composition of the group of potential jurors.

11.4.4.1 Challenge by the defence

Until the CJA 1988, there were two ways in which the defence could challenge potential jurors:

- *Peremptory challenge*

  The defence could object to any potential jury members, up to a maximum number of three, without having to show any reason or justification for the challenge. Defence counsel used this procedure in an attempt to shape the composition of the jury in a way they thought might best suit their client, although it has to be said that it was an extremely inexact process, and one that could upset or antagonise rejected jurors. In spite of arguments for its retention on a civil liberties basis, the majority of the Roskill Committee on Fraud Trials (January 1986, HMSO) recommended that the right be abolished, and abolition was provided for in the CJA 1988.

- *Challenge for cause*

  The defence retains the power to challenge any number of potential jurors for cause, that is to say that there is a substantial reason why a particular person should not serve on the jury to decide a particular defendant's case. A simple example would be where the potential juror has had previous dealings with the defendant or has been involved in the case in some way. There may be less obvious grounds for objection, however, which may be based on the particular juror's attitudes, or indeed political beliefs. The question arises whether such factors provide grounds for challenge. In what is known as *The Angry Brigade* case in 1972 (see *The Times*, 10–11 December 1971; *The Times*, 12–15 December 1972), a group of people were charged with carrying out a bombing campaign against prominent members of the Conservative government. In the process of empanelling a jury, the judge asked potential jurors to exclude themselves on a variety of sociopolitical grounds, including active membership of the Conservative Party. As a consequence of the procedure adopted in that case, the Lord Chief Justice issued a practice direction in which he made it clear that potential jurors were not to be excluded on account of race, religion, politics or occupation. Since that practice direction, it is clear that the challenge for cause can only be used within a restricted sphere, and this makes it less useful to the defence than it might otherwise be if it were to operate in a more general way.

It has been argued that the desire of civil libertarians to retain the right of the defence to select a jury that might be more sympathetic to its case is contradictory, because although in theory they usually rely on the random nature of the jury to ensure the appearance of justice, in practice they seek to influence its composition. When, however, the shortcomings in the establishment of panels for juries is recalled, it might be countered that the defence is attempting to do no more than counter the inbuilt bias that ensues from the use of unbalanced electoral registers.

11.4.4.2   Challenge by the prosecution

If the defence attempts to ensure that any jury will not be prejudiced against its case, if not predisposed towards it, the same is true of the prosecution. However, the prosecution has a greater scope to achieve such an aim. While the prosecution has the same right as the defence to challenge for cause, it has the additional option of excluding potential jury members by simply asking them to stand by until a jury has been empanelled. The request for the potential juror to stand by is only a provisional challenge and, in theory, the person stood by can at a later time take their place on the jury if there are no other suitable candidates. In practice, of course, it is unlikely in the extreme for there not to be sufficient alternative candidates to whom the prosecution do not object and prefer to the person stood by.

When the Roskill Committee recommended the removal of the defence's right to pre-emptive challenge, it recognised that, in order to retain an equitable situation, the right of the Crown to ask potential jurors to stand by should also be withdrawn. Unfortunately, although the government of the day saw fit to follow the Committee's recommendation in relation to the curtailment of the defence rights, it did not feel under the same obligation to follow its corresponding recommendation to curtail the rights of the prosecution. Thus, the CJA 1988 made no reference to the procedure and, in failing to do so, established a distinct advantage in favour of the prosecution in regard to selecting what it considered to be suitable juries.

The manifest unreasonableness of this procedure led to the Attorney General issuing a practice note (1988) to the effect that the Crown should only exercise its power to stand by potential jurors in the following two circumstances:

- To prevent the empanelment of a 'manifestly unsuitable' juror, with the agreement of the defence. The example given of 'manifest unsuitability' is an illiterate person asked to sit in a highly complex case. It is reasonable to doubt the ability of such a person to follow the process of the case involving a number of documents, and on that basis they should be stood by.

- In circumstances where the Attorney General has approved the vetting of the potential jury members and that process has revealed that the particular juror in question might be a security risk. In this situation, the Attorney General is also required to approve the use of the 'stand by' procedure.

11.4.4.3   Jury vetting

Jury vetting is the process by which the Crown checks the background of potential jurors to assess their suitability to decide particular cases. The procedure is clearly contrary to the ideal of the jury being based on a random selection of people, but it is justified on the basis that it is necessary to ensure that jury members are not likely to divulge any secrets made open to them in the course of a sensitive trial or, alternatively, on the ground that jurors with extreme political views should not be permitted the opportunity to express those views in a situation where they might influence the outcome of a case.

The practice of vetting potential jurors developed after the *Angry Brigade* trial in 1972, but it did not become public until 1978. In that year, as a result of an Official Secrets Act case, known by the initials of the three defendants as the ABC trial, it became apparent that the list of potential jurors had been checked to establish their 'soundness'. As a consequence of that case, the Attorney General published the current guidelines for vetting jury panels. Since that date, the guidelines have been updated and the most recent guidelines were published in 1988. These guidelines maintain the general propositions that jury members should normally be selected at random from the panel and should be disqualified only on the grounds set out in the JA 1974. The guidelines do, however, make reference to exceptional cases of public importance where potential jury members might properly be vetted. Such cases are broadly identified as those involving national security, where part of the evidence may be heard on camera, and terrorist cases.

Vetting is a twofold process. An initial check into police criminal records and police Special Branch records should be sufficient to reveal whether a further investigation by the security services is required. Any further investigation requires the prior approval of the Attorney General.

In addition to vetting properly so-called, the Court of Appeal in *R v Mason* (1980) approved the checking of criminal records to establish whether potential jurors had been convicted of criminal offences in the past and therefore were not eligible to serve as jurors. The Runciman Commission recommended that this process of checking on those who should be disqualified on the basis of previous criminal conviction should be regularised when the collection and storage of criminal records is centralised. This was achieved when the Criminal Records Bureau was established as a result of Part V of the Police Act 1997.

11.4.4.4   The racial mix of the jury

In *R v Danvers* (1982), the defence had sought to challenge the array on the basis that a black defendant could not have complete confidence in the impartiality of an all-white jury. The question of the racial mix of a jury has exercised the courts on a number of occasions. In *R v Ford* (1989), the trial judge's refusal to accept the defendant's application for a racially mixed jury was supported by the Court of Appeal on the grounds that, 'fairness is achieved by the principle of random selection' as regards the make-up of a jury, and that to insist on a racially balanced jury would be contrary to that principle, and would be to imply that particular jurors were incapable of impartiality. A similar point was made in *R v Tarrant* (1997), in which a person accused of drug-related offences was convicted by a jury that had been selected from outside the normal catchment area for the court. The aim of the judge had been to minimise potential jury intimidation, but nonetheless, the Court of Appeal overturned the conviction on the grounds that the judge had deprived the defendant of a randomly selected jury.

To deny people the right to have their cases heard by representatives of their own race, on the basis of a refusal to recognise the existence of racial discriminatory attitudes, cannot but give the appearance of a society where such racist attitudes are institutionalised. This has particular resonance given the findings of the Macpherson Inquiry that the police force was 'institutionally racist'. Without suggesting that juries as presently constituted are biased, it remains arguable that if, in order to achieve the undoubted appearance of fairness, jury selection has to be manipulated to ensure a racial mix, then it should at least be considered.

An interesting case study in this respect is the trial in 1994 of Lakhbir Deol, an Asian who was accused of the murder of a white youth in Stoke-on-Trent in 1993. Mr Deol's lawyers sought to have the case moved from Stafford to Birmingham Crown Court on the grounds that Stafford has an almost completely white population, whereas Birmingham has an approximately 25 per cent ethnic minority population. Mr Justice McKinnon repeatedly refused the request and the trial was heard in Stafford as scheduled. Mr Deol was acquitted, so his fears were proved groundless, but surely the worrying fact is that he had those fears in the first place.

In February 2010 the report on empirical research carried out by Professor Cheryl Thomas for the Ministry of Justice stated that:

> While these findings strongly suggest that racially balanced juries are *not needed* to ensure fair decision-making in jury trials with BME (black and minority ethnic) defendants, concerns about *the appearance of fairness* with all-white juries may still remain (emphasis added).

It is heartening to note that the Runciman Commission fully endorsed the views expressed above and recommended that either the prosecution or the defence should be able to insist that up to three jury members be from ethnic minorities, and that at least one of those should be from the same ethnic minority as the accused or the victim. Sir Robin Auld, in his review of the criminal courts, also recommended that provision should be made to enable ethnic minority representation on juries where race is likely to be relevant to an important issue in the case.

In *R v Smith* (2003), the Court of Appeal reaffirmed the traditional view in holding that it had not been unfair for Smith to be tried by a randomly selected all-white jury. In addition, however, the Court held that the selection process had not infringed Smith's rights under Art 6 of the ECHR.

Another case that raised a human rights issue was *R v Mushtaq* (2002), in which the defendant appealed against his conviction for conspiracy to defraud. He had admitted to police that he had played a minor part in the conspiracy, but later claimed that his confession had been obtained by oppression. The judge ruled during the trial that Mushtaq's confession had not been obtained by oppression and was therefore admissible, and in his summing-up to the jury, he emphasised that the confession was central and crucial to the case. Mushtaq claimed that the judge's direction to the jury was in breach of Art 6 of the ECHR and that the jury, *as a separate and distinct public authority*, had a duty to protect his rights. The Court of Appeal dismissed the appeal, holding that the separate functions allocated to the judge and the jury in relation to disputed confessions had significant advantages for ensuring that justice was done. The admissibility of a confession was a matter for the judge and if the prosecution failed to satisfy the judge that a confession was not obtained by oppression, the jury would not hear it. This division of function between judge and jury complied with the requirement to provide an adequate safeguard for a defendant's Art 6 rights, and it could not be said that the jury was a separate public authority having a distinct and separate duty from the judge to protect Mushtaq's rights. In a criminal trial, it was the court acting collectively that had the shared responsibility of ensuring a fair trial.

11.5 RACIAL BIAS IN JURIES

If the law does not allow for the artificial creation of ethnic balance in juries, then it must ensure that ethnically unbalanced juries do not become ethnically biased ones.

In May 2000, the ECtHR held by a majority of 4:3 that the right of a British Asian to be tried by an impartial tribunal had been violated on the basis of alleged racism within the jury that had convicted him. Kuldip Sander had been charged with conspiracy to commit fraud and was tried at Birmingham Crown Court in March 1995. During the trial, one of the jurors sent a note to the judge stating:

> I have decided I cannot remain silent any longer. For some time during the trial I have been concerned that fellow jurors are not taking their duties seriously. At least two have been making openly racist remarks and jokes and I fear are going to convict the defendants not on the evidence but because they are Asian. My concern is the defendants will not therefore receive a fair verdict. Please could you advise me what I can do in this situation.

The judge adjourned the case, but kept the juror who had written the letter apart from the other jurors while he listened to submission from counsel in open court. The defence asked the judge to dismiss the jury on the ground that there was a real danger of bias. The judge, however, decided to call the jury back into court, at which stage the juror who had written the complaint joined the others. The judge read out the complaint to them and told them the following:

> I am not able to conduct an inquiry into the validity of those contentions and I do not propose to do so. This case has cost an enormous amount of money and I am not anxious to halt it at the moment, but I shall have no compunction in doing so if the situation demands . . . I am going to ask you all to search your conscience overnight and if you feel that you are not able to try this case solely on the evidence and find that you cannot put aside any prejudices you may have will you please indicate that fact by writing a personal note to that effect and giving it to the jury bailiff on your arrival at court tomorrow morning. I will then review the position.

The next morning, the judge received two letters from the jury. The first letter, which was signed by all the jurors including the juror who had sent the complaint, refuted any allegation of racial bias. The second letter was written by a juror who appeared to have thought himself to have been the one who had been making the jokes. The juror in question stated that he was sorry if he had given any offence, that he had many connections with people from ethnic minorities and that he was in no way racially biased.

The judge decided not to discharge the jury and it went on to find the applicant guilty, although it acquitted another Asian defendant. The applicant's appeal, partly on the grounds of bias on the part of the jury, was dismissed by the Court of Appeal.

The majority of the ECtHR, however, held that the trial was conducted contrary to Art 6(1) of the ECHR. The Court considered that the allegations contained in the note were capable of causing the applicant and any objective observer to have legitimate doubts as to the impartiality of the court, which neither the collective letter nor the redirection of the jury by the judge could have dispelled.

In reaching its decision, the Court distinguished the decision in the similar case of *Gregory v UK* (1998). In the *Gregory* judgment, there was no admission by a juror that he had made racist comments, in the form of a joke or otherwise; there was no indication as to who had made the complaint and the complaint was vague and imprecise. Moreover, in the present case, the applicant's counsel had insisted throughout the proceedings that dismissing the jury was the only viable course of action.

The Court accepted that, although discharging the jury might not always be the only means to achieve a fair trial, there were certain circumstances where this was required by Art 6(1) of the ECHR. As the Court stated:

> Given the importance attached by all Contracting States to the need to combat racism, the Court considers that the judge should have reacted in a more robust manner than merely seeking vague assurances that the jurors could set aside their prejudices and try the case solely on the evidence. By failing to do so, the judge did not provide sufficient guarantees to exclude any objectively justified or legitimate doubts as to the impartiality of the court. It follows that the court that condemned the applicant was not impartial from an objective point of view.

The Court, however, refused his claim for compensation of some £458,000, which suggests that it was not convinced that a substitute jury would not have convicted him as well.

It has already been seen that s 8 of the Contempt of Court Act 1981 prevents investigation into what occurs in the privacy of the jury room and such prohibition applies equally to judges. In *R v Qureshi* (2001), the defendant had been convicted of arson and of attempting to attain property by deception. Three days after the verdict, a juror in the trial informed the court that some members of the jury had been racially prejudiced against Qureshi and had decided he was guilty from the outset of the trial. Qureshi's application for permission to appeal against his conviction was rejected by the Court of Appeal on the grounds that the complaint did not arise during the trial, but only after an apparently regular verdict had been delivered. In order to pursue the allegation, the court would have had to investigate what had happened in the jury room and that was precluded by s 8 of the Contempt of Court Act 1981. In reaching this decision, the Court of Appeal distinguished *Sander*, where the complaint arose during the trial, and followed *R v Miah* (1997), where the complaint arose after the event. In the latter case, it was stated that the rule against breaching jury secrecy applied to 'anything said by one juror to another about the case from the moment the jury is empanelled, at least provided what is said is not overheard by anyone who is not a juror'. It has to be asked whether such a rule is acceptable, especially when it conceals possible injustice. For a detailed analysis of these cases, see P Robertshaw, 'Responding to bias amongst jurors' (2002) 66(1) Journal of Criminal Law 84–95.

In June 2007, the Department of Justice published an extremely illuminating report of the results of a series of four linked empirical studies into the operations of juries in the English and Welsh Crown Courts. The report, entitled 'Diversity and Fairness in the Jury System', was produced by academic Cheryl Thomas, with the assistance of Nigel Balmer.

The four studies had conducted:

- a survey of the socioeconomic background of all jurors summoned in England and Wales in one week in 2003 and one week in 2005, involving a total of 15,846 jurors;

- a survey of the socioeconomic background of all jurors in jury pools, on jury panels and juries at three Crown Courts over a four-week period, involving 640 jurors;

- a case simulation study with real jurors exploring whether ethnicity affects jury verdicts or juror votes, involving 28 juries with a total of 319 jurors. While this allowed the study to examine whether ethnicity affected jury decision-making, its use of simulation meant that it did not contravene s 8 of the Contempt of Court Act 1981;

- a study of the relationship between jury verdicts, the composition of juries and the ethnicity of defendants in actual cases at three Crown Courts, involving 186 verdicts.

The final report claimed to be the first study to compare the ethnic profile of jurors summoned and serving at each Crown Court in England and Wales with the ethnic population profiles for the areas in which each court operated.

Concern about ethnic minority under-representation on juries implicitly assumes that the ethnic composition of juries may affect jury verdicts, and this is the first research conducted in this country to examine whether the research used case simulation with real jurors, along with a study of jury verdicts in real cases.

Despite its scope and innovation, none of the research required exemption from, and illustrates just how much jury research can be conducted in this country within existing restrictions.

The studies set themselves the task of challenging various assumptions about the representative nature of jury service, which have influenced reviews of the jury system and policy development in that area. As the report stated: 'most of these assumptions paint a picture of widespread jury service avoidance and unrepresentative jurors'.

However, somewhat surprisingly, the report claimed to establish that most of those assumptions about jury service were based on myth, rather than reality, as substantiated by the following conclusions it reached, that:

- there was no significant under-representation of black and minority ethnic (BME) groups among those summoned for jury service at virtually all Crown Courts in England and Wales;

- ethnic minorities are summoned in proportion to their representation in the local population in virtually all Crown Courts in England and Wales. However, racially mixed juries are only likely to exist in courts where BME groups make up at least 10 per cent of the entire juror catchment area. The report explained that this was simply the consequence of BME population levels in these catchment areas and the process of random selection;

- while there was some evidence that BME jurors on jury panels appeared to be selected to serve on juries less often than white panel members, but the report put this down to 'court clerks inadvertently avoiding reading out juror names that are difficult to pronounce';

- in addition, jury pools were found to closely reflect the local population in terms of gender and age, and the self-employed are represented among serving jurors in direct proportion to their representation in the population;

- the main factor affecting non-responses to summonses is high residential mobility, not ethnicity;

- there was no significant difference between BME and white respondents in their willingness to do jury service or indeed support for the jury system, which was strongly supported by both groups;

- the most significant factors predicting whether a summoned juror will serve or not were not ethnicity but income and employment status (those summoned for jury service who are economically inactive or in lower income brackets are far less likely to serve). Where ethnic minorities did not serve, this was primarily due to ineligibility or disqualification (residency or language);

- there is no mass avoidance of jury service by the British public (85 per cent of those summoned replied to their summonses and the vast majority served);

- the middle classes or 'the important and clever in society' do not avoid jury service. In fact the studies showed the contrary, that the highest rates of jury service are among middle to high-income earners and higher status professions. Again, perhaps surprisingly, the employed are over-represented among serving jurors, and the retired and unemployed are under-represented;

- the changes to juror eligibility under the Criminal Justice Act 2003 increased the proportion of those summoned who actually served, from 54 per cent to 64 per cent. Significantly, the proportion of serving jurors between 65 and 69 years of age doubled from 3 per cent in 2003 to 6 per cent in 2005, after their right of excusal was removed.

Perhaps the most controversial study informing the report was the research into the relationship of race and jury decision-making.

As the report recognised, the unstated but underlying assumption for those arguing possible under-representation of ethnic minorities on juries assumes that the ethnic composition of juries can affect jury outcomes.

- The research used case simulation with real jurors, supplemented by a study of jury verdicts in actual cases.

- The simulations were based on a real case, filmed in a real courtroom, with a real judge, barristers, court staff, police and witnesses. Real jurors were the study participants, jury panels were selected by the Court Service random selection programme, all juries included enough jurors to constitute a valid jury (10–12 jurors) and they deliberated in a real deliberating room.

All juries saw a film of an identical case where the defendant was charged with causing actual bodily harm (ABH), but where specific case elements were altered for different juries (race of defendant, victim and charges).

In examining the conclusions of the report it is important to distinguish between the decisions of individual jurors and the decision of the jury that they were a member of.

The main finding in relation to juries was that the verdicts of racially mixed *juries* did not discriminate against defendants based on the defendant's race. In the 28 separate jury verdicts, outcomes for the White, Black and Asian defendants were remarkably similar.

However, as regards the voting of individual jurors on racially mixed juries, even though the defendant's ethnicity did not have an impact on jury verdicts, the research found that in certain cases ethnicity did have a significant impact on the individual decisions of some jurors. Indeed, the report claimed that 'in certain cases BME jurors were significantly less likely to vote to convict a BME defendant than a white defendant'.

However, any 'same race leniency' among BME jurors was only found when race was not an explicit element of the case and that where the prosecution was racially aggravated ABH, BME jurors and white jurors had similar conviction rates for both the White and BME defendants. The report suggested that such leniency among BME jurors reflected their belief that the courts treat ethnic minority defendants more harshly than white defendants. Somewhat disconcertingly, while both black and Asian jurors showed leniency for the black defendant, there was apparently no leniency for the Asian defendant by either Asian or Black jurors.

The report also claimed to find evidence of race leniency among white jurors, but again only in cases where race was not an issue in the case. As the report stated: 'In non-race salient cases, white jurors had very low conviction rates for the white defendant, despite consistently stating that they did not believe his evidence and felt he was dishonest.'

Nonetheless, even in the face of these findings the report was confident that any same race leniency did not have an impact on the verdicts of the juries of which they were members on the basis that '12 jurors must jointly try to reach a decision and that majority verdicts are possible meant that more verdicts were achieved and individual biases did not dictate the decision-making of these racially mixed juries'. However, it was careful to warn that: 'If juries were smaller or if unanimous verdicts were required, then individual juror bias might potentially have a greater impact on jury verdicts.'

In February 2010 a second report for the Ministry of Justice by Professor Thomas, entitled 'Are juries fair?', concluded that, in essence, they were, that there was 'little evidence that juries are not fair' and that 'juries overall appear efficient and effective'.

The specific findings concluded that:

- there were no courts with a higher jury acquittal than conviction rate, and this dispels the myth that there are courts where juries rarely convict;

- all-white juries did not discriminate against BME defendants;

- differences in jury conviction rates for different specific offences suggest that juries try defendants on the evidence and the law;

- contrary to popular belief and previous government reports, juries actually convict more often than they acquit in rape cases (55% jury conviction rate);

- while over half of the jurors perceived the judge's directions as easy to understand, only a minority (31%) actually understood the directions fully in the legal terms used by the judge;

- younger jurors were better able than older jurors to comprehend the legal instructions, with comprehension of directions on the law declining as the age of the juror increased.

11.6 THE DECLINE OF THE JURY TRIAL

Many direct attempts have been made in the recent past to reduce the operation of the jury system within the English legal system. These particular endeavours, however, have to be understood in the context of the general historical decline in the use of the jury as the mechanism for determining issues in court cases. Perhaps the heat engendered in the current debate is a consequence of the fact that the continued existence of the jury as it is presently constituted cannot be taken for granted.

11.6.1 THE JURY TRIAL IN CIVIL PROCEDURE

There can be no doubt as to the antiquity of the institution of trial by jury, nor can there be much doubt as to its supposed democratising effect on the operation of the legal system. Neither, unfortunately, can there be any grounds for denying the diminishment that has occurred in the fairly recent past in the role of the jury as the means of determining the outcome of trials, nor can the continued existence of the jury as it is presently constituted be taken for granted.

In respect of civil law, the use of juries has diminished considerably and automatic recourse to trial by jury is restricted to a small number of areas and, even in those areas, the continued use of the jury is threatened. Prior to 1854, all cases that came before the common law courts were decided by a judge and jury. The Common Law Procedure Act of that year provided that cases could be settled without a jury where the parties agreed, and since then, the role of the jury has been gradually curtailed until, at present, under s 69 of the Senior Courts Act 1981, the right to a jury trial is limited to only four specific areas: fraud, defamation (i.e. libel and slander), malicious prosecution and false imprisonment. (Similar provisions are contained in the County Courts Act 1984.) Clause II of the Defamation Bill 2012 proposes to remove libel and slander from these lists. Even in these areas, the right is not absolute and can be denied by a judge under s 69(1) where the case involves 'any prolonged examination of documents or accounts or any scientific or local investigation which cannot conveniently be made with a jury'. (See *Beta Construction Ltd v Channel Four TV Co Ltd* (1990) for an indication of the factors that the judge will take into consideration in deciding whether a case should be decided by a jury or not.)

The question of whether or not juries should be used in libel cases gained wider consideration in the case involving McDonald's, the fast-food empire, and two environmentalists, Dave Morris and Helen Steel. McDonald's claimed that their reputation was damaged by an allegedly libellous leaflet issued by members of an organisation called London Greenpeace including Morris and Steel, which linked McDonald's' products to heart disease and cancer as well as the despoliation of the environment and the exploitation of the Third World. In a preliminary hearing, later confirmed by the Court of Appeal, it was decided that the evidence to be presented would be of such scientific complexity that it would be beyond the understanding of a jury (see *The Times*, 10 June 1997).

The right to jury trial in defamation cases has been the object of particular criticism. In 1975, the Faulks Committee on the Law of Defamation recommended that the availability of jury trial in that area should be subject to the same judicial discretion as all other civil cases. In its conclusions, the Faulks Report shared the uncertainty of the Court of Appeal in *Ward v James* (1965) as to the suitability of juries to determine the level of damages that should be awarded. Support for these views has been provided by a number of defamation cases decided since then, such as *Sutcliffe v Pressdram Ltd* (1990), in which the wife of a convicted serial killer was awarded damages of £600,000. She eventually settled for £60,000 after the Court of Appeal stated that it would reassess the award.

In *Aldington v Watts and Tolstoy* (1990), damages of £1.5 million were awarded. This huge award was subsequently held by the ECtHR to be so disproportionate as to amount to a violation of Tolstoy's right to freedom of expression under Art 10 of the ECHR (*Tolstoy Miloslavsky v UK* (1995)). Domestic law has also sought to deal with what could only be seen as excessive awards of damages in defamation cases, even prior to the HRA, which makes the ECtHR *Tolstoy* decision and Art 10 of the ECHR binding in UK law.

Section 8 of the CLSA 1990 gave appeal courts the power to alter damages awards made by juries to a level that they felt to be 'proper'. Nonetheless, the question of what actually constitutes a proper level of damages continued to present problems for juries, which continued to award very large sums. The problem arose from the limited guidance that judges could give juries in making their awards. In *Rantzen v Mirror Group Newspapers* (1993), the Court of Appeal stated that judges should advise juries, in making their awards, to consider the purchasing power of the award and its proportionality to the damage suffered to the reputation of the plaintiff, and should refer to awards made by the courts under s 8 of the CLSA (Rantzen's original award of £250,000 was reduced to £110,000). Still, extremely large awards continued to be made, and in *John v MGN Ltd* (1996), the Court of Appeal stated that past practice should be altered to allow juries to refer to personal injury cases to decide the level of award, and that the judge could indicate what sort of level would be appropriate (John's awards of £350,000 for the libel and £275,000 in exemplary damages were reduced to £75,000 and £50,000, respectively).

In 1996, statute law intervened in the form of the Defamation Act, which was designed to simplify the procedure of defamation cases. The main provisions of the Act are:

(a)   a one-year limitation period for defamation claims;

(b)   a statutory defence based on responsibility for publication. This replaces the common law defence of innocent dissemination;

(c)   an updating of defences in relation to privilege, that is, reporting on the proceedings and publications of, for example, the courts and government;

(d)   a streamlined procedure for dealing with a defendant who has offered to make amends. This would involve paying compensation, assessed by a judge, and publishing an appropriate correction and apology;

(e)   powers for judges to deal with cases without a jury. Under this provision, the judge can dismiss a claim if he considers it has no realistic prospect of success. Alternatively, if he considers there to be no realistic defence to the claim, he can award summary relief. Such relief can take the form of a declaration of the falsity of the statement; an order to print an apology; an order to refrain from repeating the statement; and damages of up to £10,000.

The most significant elements of the Defamation Act came into effect at the end of February 2000, but in January 2001 the Court of Appeal used its common law powers to completely overturn the award of damages in the case of *Grobbelaar v News Group Newspapers Ltd* (2001). Grobbelaar, an ex-football player, had been accused of accepting money to fix football matches. He had been found not guilty in a criminal case and had been awarded £85,000 damages for defamation in a related civil case against *The Sun* newspaper. On appeal, the Court of Appeal held that the newspaper could not rely on the defence of limited qualified privilege, as recently recognised in *Reynolds v Times Newspapers Ltd and Others* (1999), and could be held to account for such defamatory statements as could not be proved true. However, although the Court stated that it would be most reluctant to find perversity in a jury's verdict, it had such jurisdiction and, therefore, duty to consider that ground of appeal. The Court then went on to conclude that no reasonable jury could have failed to be satisfied on the balance of probabilities, and to a relatively high degree of probability, that Grobbelaar had been party to corrupt conspiracies. The court considered that the evidence led inexorably to the view that Grobbelaar's story was 'quite simply incredible. All logic, common sense and reason compelled one to that conclusion'.

As regards overturning the decision of the jury, in the words of Thorpe LJ:

> I recognise and respect the unique function of a jury that heard all of the evidence over some 16 days of trial, nevertheless it would be an injustice to the defendants to allow the outcome to stand.

On further appeal, the House of Lords held that the Court of Appeal was correct in holding that the jury's decision was open to review on the grounds of perversity. However, it found that the Court of Appeal had been wrong to overturn the jury's verdict on the grounds of perversity in this instance, as the verdict could have been explained in such a way that did not necessarily require the imputation of adversity. Grobbelaar's victory, however, was pyrrhic in the extreme; due to his breach of his legal and moral obligations, the damages awarded by the jury were quashed and substituted by the award of nominal damages of £1, with no costs awarded.

The extent of damages and, in particular, exemplary damages awarded against the police in a number of civil actions have also been problematic (see 5.10 for a consideration of types of damages). These actions have arisen from wrongful arrest, false imprisonment, assault and malicious prosecution and usually have involved connotations of racist behaviour on the part of the police. In setting the level of damages, juries have wished signally to demonstrate their disapproval of such police behaviour, but as the courts have correctly pointed out, any payments made come from the public purse, not from the individuals involved. The issue came to a head in *Thompson and Another v Commissioner of Police for the Metropolis* (1997), in which the Court of Appeal considered awards made to two plaintiffs. The first had been assaulted in custody and false evidence was used against her in a criminal trial during which she was held in prison. In a civil action, she was awarded £51,500 damages, of which £50,000 was exemplary damages. The second plaintiff was physically and racially abused by police when they broke into his house and arrested him. In a consequential civil action, he was awarded £220,000 for wrongful arrest, false imprisonment and assault, of which £200,000 was exemplary damages. On appeal, the Court of Appeal stated that in such cases, the judge should direct the jury that:

(i)   damages, save in exceptional circumstances, should be awarded only as compensation and in line with a scale which keeps the damages proportionate with those payable in personal injury cases;

(ii)   where aggravated damages are appropriate, they are unlikely to be less than £1,000, or to be more than twice the basic damages except where those basic damages are modest;

(iii)   in relation to the award of exemplary damages the jury should be told of the exceptional nature of the remedy, and told that the basic and aggravated damages together must be insufficient to punish the defendant before any exemplary damages can be considered. Where exemplary damages are appropriate they are unlikely to be less than £5,000. Conduct must be particularly deserving of condemnation to warrant an award of £25,000 and the absolute maximum should be £50,000. It would be unusual for such damages to be more than three times the basic damages being awarded unless those basic damages are modest.

In the two cases in question, the first exemplary award was reduced from £50,000 to £25,000; and in the second, the exemplary component was reduced from £200,000 to £15,000.

The reasoning in the *Thompson* case was followed in *Hill v Commissioner of Police for the Metropolis* (1998), where the plaintiff was awarded £45,600 for wrongful arrest, false imprisonment, assault and malicious prosecution. The most contentious award was that of exemplary damages, the bracket having been set by the judge as between £5,000 and £15,000, but the jury awarded the plaintiff £20,000. The Court of Appeal held that the jury had only gone beyond the guidelines to a limited extent and it was clear that they had taken a poor view of the police officers' conduct. In those circumstances, although the total award was high and might be seen to be out of proportion to awards made in personal injury cases, it was not seen as manifestly excessive in relation to Thompson's case.

If the extent of damages has been a particular problem in relation to defamation claims, especially when they are compared to the much smaller awards made in relation to personal injury, it should also be noted that public funding is not normally available in defamation cases, although it is available in relation to malicious falsehood. This effectively has made defamation a rich person's claim. As a consequence, people without the necessary wealth to finance legal proceedings find it extremely difficult to gain redress when they have suffered from what subsequently turns out to be false and damaging press coverage of their affairs. But of equal concern is the way some wealthy people were able and allowed to abuse the system. One example was the late and notorious publisher, Robert Maxwell, who often used libel proceedings or the threat of them to silence critics. As it turned out, much of what Mr Maxwell sought to prevent from becoming public knowledge was in fact illegal and harmful business conduct.

In 2011 a Defamation Bill was introduced by the Ministry of Justice, with the stated desire of reforming the law to strike the right balance 'between protection of freedom of speech and protection of reputation'. It has already been mentioned that clause 11 of the Bill effectively abolishes trial by jury in defamation cases by removing the presumption in favour of jury trial in such actions relating to libel and slander. In addition the Bill:

- includes a requirement for claimants to show that they have suffered serious harm before suing for defamation;
- introduces a defence of 'responsible publication on matters of public interest';
- provides increased protection to operators of websites that host user-generated content, providing they comply with the procedure to enable the complainant to resolve disputes directly with the author of the material concerned;
- introduces new statutory defences of truth and honest opinion to replace the common law defences of justification and fair comment.

Apart from the instances considered previously there is, therefore, a presumption against trial by jury in civil cases. However, under s 69(3) SCA 1981, the judge has the discretion to order a trial by jury. In *Ward v James* (1965), the Court of Appeal decided that a jury should be used in civil cases only in 'exceptional circumstances', although no exhaustive list as to what amounted to exceptional circumstances was provided.

11.6.2 JURIES IN CRIMINAL TRIALS

It has to be borne in mind that the criminal jury trial is essentially the creature of the Crown Court, and that the magistrates' courts deal with at least 95 per cent of criminal cases. In practice, juries determine the outcome of less than 1 per cent of the total of criminal cases for the reason that, of all the cases that are decided in the Crown Court, 71 per cent of defendants plead guilty on all counts and, therefore, have no need of jury trial. Initiatives in the Crown Court and other agencies, such as offering a discount on sentence for an early plea of guilty and providing early charging advice by the Crown Prosecution Service at police stations, have been put forward as reasons for this significant increase in the guilty plea rate.

It can be seen, therefore, that in absolute and proportional terms, the jury does not play a significant part in the determination of criminal cases.

If trial by jury is not statistically significant, it cannot be denied that it is of major significance in the determination of the most serious cases. Even this role, however, has not gone without scrutiny, as will be seen below.

It should not be forgotten that the right to jury trial has been abolished in Northern Ireland since 1973. In response to the problem of the intimidation of jury members, the *Report of the Commission to Consider Legal Procedures to Deal with Terrorist Activities in Northern Ireland*, headed by Lord Diplock, recommended that cases be decided without juries in particular situations. The so-called 'Diplock courts' operate in relation to certain 'scheduled offences', particularly, but not exclusively, associated with terrorism.

With regard to the continuation of no-jury trial in Northern Ireland, the United Nations Human Rights Committee, in its concluding observations on the UK's periodic report under the UN Covenant on Civil and Political Rights, stated its concern. In its words:

> The Committee remains concerned that, despite improvements in the security situation in Northern Ireland, some elements of criminal procedure continue to differ between Northern Ireland and the remainder of the State party's territory. In particular, the Committee is concerned that, under the Justice and Security (Northern Ireland) Act 2007, persons whose cases are certified by the Director of Public Prosecutions for Northern Ireland are tried in the absence of a jury. It is also concerned that there is no right of appeal against the decision made by the Director of Public Prosecutions for Northern Ireland.
>
> In October 2010 *The Guardian* newspaper reported that The Criminal Cases Review Commission (Chapter 6.9) had received applications from more than 200 people who claimed that they had suffered injustices under the Diplock trial system. By that time, the Court of Appeal in Belfast had overturned convictions in 24 of 26 cases referred to it by the Commission. The newspaper alleged that a number of men who served as detectives with the Royal Ulster Constabulary (RUC) claimed that senior officers 'encouraged the systematic mistreatment of suspects at Castlereagh interrogation centre in east Belfast' after the establishment of the Diplock courts in 1973. The accusation was that the officers took full advantage of the vague wording of emergency legislation in Northern Ireland, which allowed the courts to admit confessions as evidence, *providing there was no evidence* they had been obtained through the use of torture, or inhuman or degrading treatment. This issue clearly links back to the consideration of the use of torture in Chapter 2. A video report of the allegations may be seen at www.guardian.co.uk/uk/video/2010/oct/11/northern-ireland-police-torture.

11.6.2.1   Criminal Justice Act 2003: jury tampering

The term 'jury tampering' covers a range of circumstances in which the jury's independence is or may appear to be compromised. Such a situation could come about because of actual harm or threats of harm to jury members. It might equally involve intimidation or bribery of jury members. Alternatively, it could also include similar improper approaches to a juror's family or friends.

Sections 44 and 46 of the CJA 2003 provide for a trial on indictment in the Crown Court to be conducted without a jury where there is a danger of jury tampering, or continued without a jury where the jury has been discharged because of jury tampering. For an application under s 44 to be granted, the court must be satisfied that there is evidence of a real and present danger that jury tampering would take place. In addition, the court must also be satisfied that the danger of jury tampering is so substantial, notwithstanding any steps that could reasonably be taken to prevent it, as to make it necessary in the interests of justice for the trial to be conducted without a jury. Sub-section (6) sets out examples of what might constitute evidence of a real and present danger of jury tampering, which include:

- a case where the trial is a re-trial and the jury in the previous trial was discharged because jury tampering had taken place;
- a case where jury tampering has taken place in previous criminal proceedings involving the defendant or any of the defendants;
- a case where there has been intimidation, or attempted intimidation, of any person who is likely to be a witness in the trial.

Section 46 deals with trials already underway, where jury tampering has or appears to have taken place. In these circumstances, if the judge decides to discharge the jury, as he has a right to do in common law, and is satisfied that tampering has occurred, he may order that the trial should continue without a jury if he is satisfied that this would be fair to the defendant. On the other hand, if the judge considers it necessary in the interests of justice to terminate the trial due to tampering, he may order that the re-trial should take place without a jury.

In March 2010, after the first non-jury criminal trial for more than 350 years, four members of a gang were convicted of a £1.75m armed raid on a warehouse near Heathrow Airport in February 2004. Following three previous failed trials, the prosecution had applied for a non-jury trial on the grounds that the third trial had had to be halted because of alleged jury tampering.

In July 2010 Lord Judge CJ, in the Court of Appeal, handed down guidance on how the jury tampering provisions of the CJA 2003 were to be operated in two similar but unrelated cases, *R v J, S, M* (2010) and *R v KS* (2010). In overturning orders for non-jury trials Judge LCJ emphasised that the making of such an order:

> . . . remains and must remain the decision of last resort, only to be ordered when the court is sure (not that it entertains doubts, suspicions or reservations) that the statutory conditions are fulfilled. Save in extreme cases, *where the necessary protective measures constitute an unreasonable intrusion into the lives of the jurors,* for example, a constant police presence in or near their

homes, day and night and at the weekends, or police protection, which means that at all times when they are out of their homes, they are accompanied or overseen by police officers, again day and night and at the weekend, with its consequent impact on the availability of police officers to carry out their ordinary duties, the confident expectation must be that the jury will perform its duties with its customary determination to do justice [emphasis added].

However, in relation to s 46 powers he concluded that:

If during the course of this, or indeed any trial, attempts are made to tamper with the jury to the extent that the judge feels it necessary to discharge the entire jury, it should be clearly understood that the judge may continue with the trial and deliver a judgment and verdict on his own. The principle of trial by jury is precious, but in the end any defendant who is responsible for abusing this principle by attempting to subvert the process has no justified complaint that he has been deprived of a right which, by his own actions, he himself has spurned.

11.6.2.2   Criminal Justice Act 2003: complex fraud trials

In 1986, the Roskill Committee on Fraud Trials critically examined the operation of the jury in complex criminal fraud cases. Its report recommended the abolition of trial by jury in such cases. The Roskill Committee did not go as far as to recommend that all fraud cases should be taken away from juries, only the most complex, of which it was estimated that there were about two dozen or so every year. It was suggested that these cases would be better decided by a judge assisted by two laypersons drawn from a panel with specialist expertise. The government declined to implement the recommendations of the Roskill Committee, and instead introduced procedures designed to make it easier to follow the proceedings in complex fraud cases.

After being found not guilty of a £19 million fraud charge, George Walker, the former chief executive of Brent Walker, said: 'Thank God for the jury. It would be madness to lose the jury system.' This enthusiastic endorsement of the jury system is in no little way undercut, however, by the fact that Walker is reported as going on to state that he was sure the jury had not properly understood much of the highly detailed material in the trial, as he admitted: 'I didn't understand a lot of it, so I can't see how they could.'

Mr Walker's enthusiasm perhaps was not shared by his co-accused, Wilfred Aquilina, who was found guilty, on a majority verdict, of false accounting.

The Royal Commission on the Criminal Justice System of 1993 (the Runciman Commission) recognised the particular difficulties faced by jurors in fraud trials but, somewhat surprisingly in the light of its recommendations in relation to offences triable either way, it did not suggest the removal of the jury from such cases. It merely recommended that s 10(3) of the CJA 1988 should be amended to permit judges to put the issues before the jury at the outset of the trial.

In February 1998, the Home Office issued a Green Paper entitled *Juries in Serious Fraud Trials*. The Consultation Paper suggested the need for a new procedure in relation to complex fraud trials, due to the fact that 'the detection, investigation and trial of serious criminal fraud offences have presented certain difficulties not commonly found amongst other types of offences'. A variety of possible alternatives were put forward:

- *Special juries*: these would be made up of qualified people and might be drawn from a special pool of potential jurors. Alternatively, ordinary jurors would have to be assessed as to their competency to sit on the case.
- *Judge-run trials*: specially trained judges, either singly or in a panel, and possibly with the help of lay experts.
- *Fraud tribunals*: following Roskill, these would be made up of a judge and qualified lay members with the power to question witnesses.
- *Verdict-only juries*: in this situation, the judge would hear the evidence and sum up the facts, leaving the jury simply to vote on guilt or innocence.
- A *special juror*: here, 11 of the jury would be selected as normal, but number 12 would be specially qualified in order to be able to assist the others on complex points.

With respect to these alternatives, the government stated that it had no particular preference.

Subsequently, in April 1998, the Home Secretary requested the Law Commission to carry out a review of fraud trials, focusing particularly on whether the existing law was:

- readily comprehensible to juries;
- adequate for effective prosecution;
- fair to defendants; and
- able to cope with changes in technology.

However, in its response in Consultation Paper No 155, *Fraud and Deception* (1999), the Law Commission addressed only the issues of possible criminal offences and did not deal with any procedural issues.

In his extensive *Review of the Criminal Courts* (2001), Sir Robin Auld LJ recommended that in serious and complex frauds, the nominated trial judge should have the power to direct trial by himself and two lay members drawn from a panel established by the Lord Chancellor for the purpose or, if the defendant requested, by himself alone. However, in the White Paper preceding the CJA 2003, it was claimed that each year 15–20 complex fraud trials emerged that would be better dealt with by a judge sitting alone: Part 7 of the CJA 2003 provides for exactly that possibility. Section 43 allows the prosecution to apply for a serious or complex fraud trial on indictment in the Crown Court to proceed in the absence of a jury. Before granting the application, the Court has to be satisfied that the length or complexity of the trial is likely to make it so burdensome upon the jury that, in the interests of justice, serious consideration should be given to conducting the trial without a jury. Any order to that effect requires the approval of the Lord Chief Justice.

The CJA 2003 has thus introduced measures much more restrictive than any previous body had recommended, but, at least for supporters of juries, the situation could have been worse, as the initial Criminal Justice Bill proposed a similar potential curtailment in all complex or lengthy trials, not just fraud cases.

As part of the bargaining process at the end of the last parliamentary session in 2005, it was required that any move to bring the above contentious sections of the CJA 2003 into operation would require an affirmative, that is, a positive vote in favour, by both the House of Commons and the House of Lords.

The collapse of the longest ever jury trial, in March 2005, led to calls for the provisions of the CJA to be implemented. The case, relating to alleged bribery in contracts for the £3 billion extension of the London Underground Jubilee line, lasted for 21 months and cost an estimated £60 million. The trial only came to an end after protests by the jurors, who it was claimed were refusing to continue to participate in the trial. According to one juror, as reported in the *Observer* newspaper, 'It was a nightmare and a total waste of taxpayers' money.' As the newspaper ironically put it, 'Jurors do not usually discuss their experiences; but because this trial collapsed and, since their efforts were in vain, it has been hard to shut them up.'

The protestations of the long-suffering jury members led Lord Falconer to propose the expeditious implementation of the proposals of the CJA 2003. However, in November 2005 the Attorney General, Lord Goldsmith, confirmed that the government would not be pressing ahead with the proposal. In the face of the confirmed resistance, it recognised that it would certainly be unable to get such a vote in the House of Lords, even if it succeeded in the House of Commons, which was not at all certain. No proposed date for implementation has been suggested by the government since.

The Criminal Procedure Rules 2012 reaffirm the original protocol for the conduct of heavy fraud and other complex criminal cases issued by the Lord Chief Justice in 2005 (available at http://www.justice.gov.uk/courts/procedure-rules/criminal/pd-protocol/pd_protocol).

11.7 FUTURE JURY REFORM

The foregoing has considered the historical decline of the jury trial; it remains to consider its prospects for the future and the related matter of how and whether research can be conducted into the way in which juries operate in practice.

11.7.1 EITHER-WAY OFFENCES: THE ROLE OF THE JURY

In order to understand the full implications of the recommendation, it is necessary to reconsider points that have been discussed previously in Chapter 5.

It is essential to appreciate the distinction between offences to be tried only by summary procedure, offences to be tried only on indictment and offences triable 'either way'. Summary offences are those which are triable only in the magistrates' courts and cases which, as has been noted previously, magistrates decide on their own without the assistance of a jury. There are literally hundreds of summary offences; given the limitations on the sentencing powers of magistrates, they are by necessity the least serious of criminal acts, such as road traffic offences and minor assault. The most serious offences, such as major theft, serious assault, rape, manslaughter and murder, have to be tried on indictment before a jury in the Crown Court. There is, however, a third category, offences triable 'either way' which, as the name suggests, may be tried either summarily or on indictment.

The current way of determining how an offence triable 'either way' is actually heard is set out in the Magistrates' Courts Act (MCA) 1980. Under s 19 of that Act, the magistrates' court has to decide whether the offence is more suitable for summary trial or trial on indictment. In reaching that decision, the magistrates must take into account the nature of the case, its seriousness, whether the penalty they could impose would be adequate, and any other circumstances which appear to the court to make it more suitable for the offence to be tried one way rather than the other. If the accused agrees to a summary hearing, the trial goes ahead in the magistrates' court. If, however, the defendant objects to the summary procedure, the case goes on indictment to the Crown Court and the magistrates merely act as examining justices. It should be noted that the CJA 2003 alters the procedure in relation to the allocation of offences triable either way (see above, at 6.2.2).

The Royal Commission on Criminal Justice

The Runciman Commission's Report stated that defendants should not 'be able to choose their court of trial solely on the basis that they think that they will get a fairer hearing at one level than another' (see para 6.18 of the Report). The conclusion of the Commission seemed to be that, because defendants do not trust the magistrates' court, and there is some justification for this in respect of the rates of acquittal, and do have more faith in the Crown Court than is warranted in terms of sentencing, then they should be forced to use the magistrates' court. As the Report stated: 'Magistrates' courts conduct over 93 per cent of all criminal cases and should be trusted to try cases fairly' (see para 6.18 of the Report). It is at least arguable that in this conclusion, the Commission missed the point. Put starkly, the evidence supports the conclusion that defendants do not trust magistrates' courts. Indeed, the evidence as to the number of people changing their plea to guilty in the Crown Court would seem to support the conclusion, not so much that defendants trust juries, but more that they do not trust magistrates. This lack of trust in the magistracy is further highlighted by the fact that those who do not plead guilty would rather have their guilt or innocence determined by a jury.

Simply forcing such people to use the magistrates' courts does not address the underlying problem, let alone solve it.

It would have been possible for the Commission to have achieved its end by simply recommending that particular offences that are defined as triable 'either way' at present should be re-categorised as offences only open to summary procedure. That it did not do so further indicates the weakness of the underlying logic of its case for removing the right to insist on trial on indictment. The Commission rejected the reclassification of offences partly because of the difficulty and uncertainty inherent in the task. Additionally, and more importantly, however, it rejected this approach because it wished to leave available the possibility of the defendant successfully insisting on trial on indictment in the case of first offenders, where the consequences of loss of reputation would be significant. In the words of the Commission: 'Loss of reputation is a different matter, since jury trial has long been regarded as appropriate for cases involving that issue. But, it should only be one of the factors to be taken into account and will often be relevant only to first offenders' (see para 6.18 of the Report).

There are two assumptions in this proposal. First, there is the surely objectionable assumption that the reputation of anyone with a previous conviction is not important. But of even more concern is the fact that it is recognised that in the cases of first offenders, they should be permitted access to the jury. The question has to be asked: why should this be the case if juries do no more than magistrates do? It appears that in the instance of first offenders, it is recognised that juries do offer more protection than magistrates. Again, this demands the question: why should the extra protection not be open to all?

Criminal Justice (Mode of Trial) Bills

The Runciman Commission Report was produced under the auspices of a Conservative government operating under an economic imperative to reduce costs. If those who were opposed to its findings found comfort in the election of a New Labour government in 1997, they were soon to be disabused when the new (now former) Home Secretary, Jack Straw, announced his intention to reduce the rights to jury trials, essentially to the same end as the Runciman proposals. Thus, the first Criminal Justice (Mode of Trial) Bill was introduced in the parliamentary session of 1999–2000. This Bill sought to amend the MCA 1980 by introducing sections that gave the magistrates, rather than the accused, the power to decide whether a case should be tried summarily or on indictment. As Runciman's Report had been, so the new Bill was solicitous of the protection of those accused whose reputation 'would be seriously damaged as a result of conviction'. The Bill was generally criticised as an illiberal measure by civil liberties organisations and the legal professions, but was particularly attacked for the manner in which it sought to protect the rights of individuals with reputations to protect. Such solicitude for those with reputations to protect, apparently as opposed to the common majority of people, was seen as inherently unjust and dangerously class-based. The opposition to the Bill outside Parliament was matched, and more importantly so in relation to its legislative progress, by equal opposition within the House of Lords, which voted against its passage.

Undaunted by the rejection of his Bill, the Home Secretary reintroduced a reformed version of it in the Criminal Justice (Mode of Trial) (No 2) Bill. In acknowledgement of criticisms of the earlier Bill, the (No 2) Bill made it clear that the reputation, or any other personal characteristic, of the accused was not something to be taken into account by the magistrates in deciding on the mode of trial. Nonetheless, the Bill was once again defeated in the House of Lords in 2001.

Although the newly re-elected government insisted that it retained the power to use the Parliament Acts to force a mode of trial Bill through the House of Lords, its approach altered following the publishing of the report on the criminal courts conducted by Sir Robin Auld.

The Auld Review

In his extensive *Review of the Criminal Courts* (2001), Sir Robin Auld LJ included recommendations that were aimed specifically at the current operation of the jury within the criminal justice system. In summary, he recommended the following points:

- Jurors should be more widely representative than they are of the national and local communities from which they are drawn.

- No one in future should be ineligible for, or excusable as of right from, jury service. While those with criminal convictions and mental disorder should continue to be disqualified, any claimed inability to serve should be a matter for discretionary deferral or excusal.

- Provision should be made to enable ethnic minority representation on juries where race is likely to be relevant to an important issue in the case.

- The law should not be amended to permit more intrusive research than is already possible into the workings of juries, though in appropriate cases, trial judges and/or the Court of Appeal should be entitled to examine alleged improprieties in the jury room.

- The law should be declared, by statute if need be, that juries have no right to acquit defendants in defiance of the law or in disregard of the evidence.

- If the jury's verdict appears to be perverse, the prosecution should be entitled to appeal on the grounds that the perversity is indicative that the verdict is likely to be unfair or untrue.

- The defendant should no longer have an elective right to trial by judge and jury in 'either-way' cases.

- Trial by judge and jury should remain the main form of trial of the more serious offences triable on indictment, that is, those that would go to the Crown Division, subject to four exceptions:

    (i) defendants should be entitled, with the court's consent, to opt for trial by judge alone;

    (ii) in serious and complex frauds, the nominated trial judge should have the power to direct trial by himself and two lay members drawn from a panel established by the Lord Chancellor for the purpose (or, if the defendant requests, by himself alone);

    (iii) a Youth Court, constituted by a judge of an appropriate level and at least two experienced youth panel magistrates, should be given jurisdiction to hear all grave cases against young defendants;

    (iv) legislation should be introduced to require a judge, not a jury, to determine the issue of fitness to plead.

The Criminal Justice Act 2003

As has been seen, the CJA 2003 introduced significant changes in the role and place of juries in the criminal system, but it did so without addressing the contentious issue of either way offences. Perhaps this course of action was adopted in the belief that the increase in the sentencing power of the magistrates' courts to 12 months would reduce the pressure on the Crown Courts by cutting down the number of cases sent for sentencing. *It is unlikely, however, that the issue will have gone away forever.*

How true, but not particularly insightful or prescient, was the previous sentence, because within months of the installation of the coalition government, its 'victims' commissioner', Louise Casey, was calling for jury trial to be removed from petty criminals who were 'clogging up' the courts system and whose cases should be tried by magistrates. In her view, the right to opt for trial by jury in the Crown Court was a 'nicety' of the legal system and was being abused by criminals. As she was quoted as saying:

> In a time of cuts, we need to abandon some of the genteel traditions and niceties of the legal system. How can it be right that a jury can be made to convene to hear arguments about the theft of £20-worth of tea bags, as is the case now, when a magistrate could do the job justly but costing far less?

The simple answer is because it is of *crucial importance* to the person who is charged with the offence, no matter the cost to the state.

11.8 INVESTIGATION OF JURY BEHAVIOUR

The very first recommendation made by the Royal Commission on Criminal Justice was that s 8 of the Contempt of Court Act 1981 should be repealed to enable research to be conducted into juries' reasons for their verdicts. Section 8 makes it an offence to obtain, disclose or solicit any particulars of statements made, opinion expressed, arguments advanced or votes cast by members of a jury in the course of their deliberations in any legal proceedings.

In *Attorney General v Associated Newspapers* (1994), the House of Lords held that it was contempt of court for a newspaper to publish disclosures by jurors of what took place in the jury room while they were considering their verdict, unless the publication amounted to no more than a restatement of facts already known. It was decided that the word 'disclose' in s 8(1) applied not just to jurors, but to any others who published their revelations.

The continued legality of s 8 in the light of Art 6 of the ECHR was considered in *R v Mirza* in January 2004. The appellant Mirza had been convicted on six counts of indecent assault by a majority verdict of 10:2. He had arrived in the UK from Pakistan in 1988 and, during the trial, he had made use of an interpreter. During the course of the trial, the jury sent a note asking the interpreter whether it was typical of a man with Mirza's background to require an interpreter, despite having lived in the UK for so long.

It was explained to the jury that it was usual for people who were not fluent to have an interpreter in complicated and serious cases and, in his summing up, the judge directed the jury not to draw an adverse inference from Mirza's use of an interpreter.

Six days after the case finished, the defence counsel received a letter from one of the jurors claiming that some jurors had, from the beginning of the trial, believed that the use of the interpreter had been a devious ploy. The question of the interpreter was raised early during the jury's deliberations, and the letter writer was 'shouted down' when she objected and sought to remind the other members of the jury of the judge's directions. Members of the jury specifically refused to accept the judge's direction, and some regarded defence counsel's warnings against prejudice in her final speech as 'playing the race card'. The writer concluded that the decision of the jury was that of bigots who considered Mirza guilty because he used an interpreter in court after declining one for his police interviews.

When the case came on appeal to the House of Lords, it was confirmed by a majority of 4:1 that s 8 of the Contempt of Court Act 1981 prevented any investigation into what had taken place within the confines of the jury room. The majority also relied on a passage in *Gregory v UK* (1998), in which the ECtHR had previously approved the protection of jury secrecy under UK law in deciding that s 8 was not in conflict with Art 6 of the ECHR. In reaching its conclusion, the majority focused on the difficulties involved in assessing and investigating such matters of jury misbehaviour but, as Lord Steyn stated in his minority judgment:

> In my view it would be an astonishing thing for the ECtHR to hold, when the point directly arises before it, that a miscarriage of justice may be ignored in the interest of the general efficiency of the jury system. The terms of Art 6(1) of the ECHR, the rights revolution, and 50 years of development of human rights law and practice, would suggest that such a view would be utterly indefensible.

The issue was further considered by the House of Lords in *R v Smith (Patrick)* in 2005. That case related to a situation where, after a jury had begun its deliberations, the judge received a letter from one of the jurors claiming that some of the other members of the panel were disregarding the judge's directions on the law and were engaging in improper speculation over verdicts. Rather than discharge the jury, the judge, with the approval of the lawyers for both sides, had given further directions to the jury in which he clarified the burden of proof, and told them to decide the case on the evidence and not on speculation. He also stated the need for discussion, but told the jury members to resist being bullied into reaching a verdict they did not agree with. In the event the jury returned majority verdicts of guilty on all counts.

On allowing the appeal against conviction, the House of Lords held that the judge's directions had not been strong enough and that the jury had required much more emphatic and detailed guidance and instruction. The House of Lords held that, without such an emphatic reaffirmation of its role as was required after the allegation made by one of its members, it was difficult to be satisfied that the jury's discussions thereafter were conducted in the proper manner.

In reaching its unanimous decision the House affirmed Lord Carswell's judgment, in which he set out the circumstances that might be taken as undermining the propriety of jury verdicts and the common law principles governing the possibility of inquiring into jury verdicts. In so doing Lord Carswell set out six distinct situations:

(i)   The general rule is that the court will not investigate, or receive evidence about, anything said in the course of the jury's deliberations while they are considering their verdict in the jury room.

(ii)   An exception to the above rule may exist if an allegation is made which tends to show that the jury as a whole decided not to actually reach a decision at all, but decided the case by other means such as tossing a coin. As any such behaviour would be contrary to the function of a jury and the oath they took, any result decided in such a way could not be a proper decision at all (see *R v Young (Stephen)*, the Ouija board case).

(iii) There is a firm rule that after the verdict has been delivered evidence directed to matters intrinsic to the deliberations of jurors is inadmissible (but see *AG v Scotcher* (2005) below).

(iv)   The common exceptions to the general rule were confined to situations where the jury is alleged to have been affected by what are termed *extraneous* influences, e.g. contact with other persons who may have passed on information which should not have been before the jury. However those extraneous influences have been extended under the influence of new technology (see below). As an amusing sideline to this very serious issue, a Crown Court judge in 2006 made headline news in the papers by warning a jury that they were not to assume the proactive role that had been assumed by the hero of the popular television series *Judge John Deed*. In the television programme, the eponymous judge, whilst sitting on a jury, had personally entered into an active investigation of the situation he was supposed to be deciding on. It has to be said that the subsequent attempt by the legal adviser to the programme to justify its ludicrous travesty of the law was much more entertaining than the programme itself.

(v)   When complaints have been made during the course of trials of improper behaviour or bias on the part of jurors, judges have on occasion given further instructions to the jury and/or asked them if they feel able to continue with the case and give verdicts in the proper manner. This course should only be taken with the whole jury present and it is an irregularity to question individual jurors in the absence of the others about their ability to bring in a true verdict according to the evidence.

(vi)   Section 8(1) of the Contempt of Court Act 1981 is not a bar to the court itself carrying out necessary investigations of such matters as bias or irregularity in the jury's consideration of the case. If matters of that nature were raised by credible evidence the judge can investigate them and deal with the allegations as the situation may require.

While point (vi) in Lord Carswell's list was based on a well-established principle, it did not address the issue of a juror who wished to raise a matter of jury impropriety after the trial had been completed and the decision of the court recorded. However, just such a situation arose in *Attorney General v Scotcher* (2005). The defendant had been a member of a jury that reached a guilty verdict against two accused by a majority of 10:1. On the day after the case, Scotcher wrote an anonymous letter to the mother of one of the convicted men detailing improprieties that he alleged had taken place in the jury room. The letter stated, for example that ([2005] 3 All ER 1 at 6):

> Many changed their vote late on simply because they wanted to get out of the courtroom and go home . . . They just decide [sic] on prejudice and hearsay (and wanting to get home for tea!). I hope these are grounds in law to show that the verdict was unsafe. Don't know if it can be shown that the Judge misdirected the jury . . . Good luck.

The mother passed the letter on to her son's solicitor who raised it with the Court of Appeal, which in turn passed it on to the police who had no difficulty in tracing Scotcher, who was ultimately charged with contempt of court under s 8 of the Contempt of Court Act 1981. In rejecting his appeal against an earlier guilty verdict, the House of Lords upheld the principle that the secrecy of the jury room should remain paramount, but it also recognised, for the first time, the need to advise jurors as to what to do if they subsequently feel that they have participated in an unfair trial.

Prior to the judgment in *Scotcher*, jurors were advised by the judge that if they were concerned about the conduct of the jury itself, they could raise the issue with the judge *before* the verdict was passed, but they received no clear direction about what they could do *after* the trial. *Scotcher* set out a variety of options open to a juror in such a situation that did not render them vulnerable to prosecution for contempt of court. Thus jurors can safely alert the judicial authorities by contacting the clerk of the court or the jury bailiff, or even by sending a sealed letter to the court via an outside agency such as the Citizens' Advice Bureau.

The use of the internet and other electronic means of communication

There has always been a possibility of jurors being influenced by extraneous sources of information, such as press or other media sources, rather than solely relying on the evidence presented in the court. However, the growth of information technology has intensified the problem and generated particular difficulties in relation to juries. In *R v Adem Karakaya* (2005) the Court of Appeal held that material downloaded from the internet and taken into a jury room by one of the members of a jury was contrary to the general rule that jurors were not to rely on privately obtained information or to receive further information after it had retired.

Subsequently, in *R v Thakrar* (2008), a member of a jury supplied fellow jury members with information, again found on the internet, about the defendant's previous convictions. Unfortunately, the information was incorrect. Just over six weeks into the trial, and at the conclusion of the appellant's examination-in-chief, the jury passed a note to the judge, which revealed that they had received the information from the internet. The judge directed the jury in strong terms that they must disregard the internet information and they went on to find the accused guilty. However, on appeal it was held that there should be a retrial as under the circumstances there was a real possibility that a member, or members, of the jury did not follow the direction given by the judge.

The issue of jurors using the internet and mobile communications to research cases, and in particular details relating to the accused in cases, became a major issue in the course of 2010. In her report on the fairness of juries, released in February 2010, Cheryl Thomas found that, in high-profile cases almost three-quarters of jurors will be aware of media coverage of their case. However, the report raised questions about the issue of internet use by jury members in particular. The research revealed that:

- all jurors who looked for information about their case during the trial looked on the internet;
- more jurors said they saw information on the internet than admitted looking for it on the internet;
- in high-profile cases 26 per cent said they saw information on the internet, compared with 12 per cent who said they looked, whereas in standard cases 13 per cent said they saw information, compared with five per cent who said they looked.

As Thomas pointed out, as jurors were admitting to doing something they should have been told by the judge not to do, that may explain why more jurors said they 'just saw' reports on the internet than said they 'looked' on the internet.

Interesting and important as these findings were, they did not generate the same degree of heat that subsequent interventions did. In October 2010, a former Director of Public Prosecutions, now Lord Ken McDonald, engaged in a public debate on the matter by expressing the view that:

> This is a serious point and we struggled with it, in criminal justice, for years trying to protect juries from what they might read about a case on the internet, material they weren't supposed to know about while they were trying it . . . In essence, we're finally giving up and just concluding that you have to expect juries to try cases fairly and they're told to do that so I think

this is a serious issue around privacy, because policing the internet is really, I think, an unmanageable task. I don't think juries should be 'allowed' to do online research, but I do think we need to assume this will occasionally happen and that it should not invalidate a trial. We have to expect them to follow directions to try the case on the evidence. Otherwise, jury trial will go.

Lord McDonald's comments prompted the Lord Chief Justice to intervene with his own views in a lecture delivered to the Judicial Studies Board of Northern Ireland on 16 November 2010, entitled simply 'Jury trials' (available at www.judiciary.gov.uk/ NRrdonlyres/CBB8FE3E-ACEB-49EE-B004-A0AAD2AAC3F8/0/speechlcjjurytrial-sjsblecturebelfast.pdf).

In his speech Judge LCJ makes his view clear:

What we seem to do at the moment, is to assume that the occasions when jurors go to the internet for information are rare indeed. It is therefore easy to brush them aside as odd moments of aberration. I wonder whether we will still be thinking that in a year or two from now. Professor Thomas suggests that we should be thinking of it immediately. I respectfully agree.

I should just add that I must record my entire disagreement with the view of the former Director of Public Prosecutions in England and Wales, now Lord MacDonald, that judges are 'giving up trying to stop jurors using Google, Facebook and Twitter to access potentially false and prejudicial' information about defendants. He is reported as suggesting that a trial should not be invalidated if jurors are found to have conducted online research while a case is in progress.

Not only does Lord Judge appear to agree with Professor Thomas that there is a problem, but he also appears to agree with her proposed solution. As she suggested in her report:

To address both jury impropriety in general and juror use of the internet, the judiciary and HMCS should consider issuing every sworn juror with written guidelines clearly outlining the requirements for serving on a trial.

In the words of Judge LCJ:

I have to be blunt about this, but in my view, if the jury system is to survive as the system for a fair trial in which we all believe and support, the misuse of the internet by jurors must stop. And I think we must spell this out to them yet more clearly. It must be provided in the information received by every potential juror. It must be reflected in the video which jurors see before they start a trial. Judges must continue to direct juries in unequivocal terms from the very outset of the trial. And I should like the notice in jury rooms which identifies potential contempt of court arising from discussions outside the jury room of their debates, to be extended to any form of reference to the internet.

AG v Fraill & Sewart (2012)

The first defendant, Joanne Fraill, had been a juror in a case involving the second defendant as one of the accused in a prolonged drug case trial involving a number of charges against people. Sewart's partner, Gary Knox, was also accused of the drugs offences but was also charged with a distinct charge of conspiracy to commit misconduct in a public office together with a serving, although suspended, police officer, Philip Berry.

The judge gave the jury an unequivocal direction that they must not use the internet. He directed them as follows:

> You will make your decision about this case based solely upon the evidence which you hear during this trial, in this courtroom and upon nothing else. Most of us these days have access to the internet, it contains lots of fascinating information, some of it about the criminal justice system and some of it about specific criminal offences. If you do have access to the 'net, members of the jury, please do not go on the 'net during this trial to explore any issues which may arise. That would be wrong. As I have said, you must base your decision in this case solely on what you hear in this courtroom and upon nothing else.

The direction was repeated from time to time throughout the trial.

By 2 August Sewart had been acquitted of all three charges against her. Knox had been convicted on the conspiracy charge involving Berry, and had been acquitted on one other count. However, verdicts still had to be reached on three other counts. After her acquittal, Sewart continued to attend the ongoing trial of her partner, Knox.

On 4 August, it became apparent to the judge hearing the case that an unknown juror had been in Facebook contact with Sewart, commenting to the effect that she was pleased that Sewart had been acquitted because she was 'with her the whole of the way'. She also suggested that it was a pity that Sewart had not been in court when the verdicts involving Knox were announced because she was not able to see 'the look of delight' on Gary's face when he was acquitted on the remaining charge against him. Sewart had asked her Facebook friend about the conduct of the trial while it was ongoing.

On questioning the jurors individually, the judge established, through her owning up, that the juror in question was Joanne Fraill. Although the judge decided to continue the remainder of the hearings without Fraill's participation, he subsequently decided that the case could not proceed and discharged the rest of the jury.

Both Fraill and Sewart were subsequently found guilty of contempt of court in June 2011. The judgment against Fraill was so stark as to warrant quoting. As Judge LCJ stated, and the structure of what he says is significant:

> 55 . . . it is a feature of this case that when the question of Facebook contact was raised with her in the Crown Court, this woman of good character, immediately and unhesitantly admitted what she had done and apologised for it. During the subsequent investigation she provided evidence against herself of her misuse of the internet throughout the trial. In effect therefore she acknowledged her guilt at the earliest possible opportunity, and for some months now she has been waiting for the present proceedings to take place, and to know what the consequences of her contempt will be. The effect of all these stresses and strains was virtually palpable here in court.
>
> 56 . . . There will be an order for immediate custody for a period of 8 months.

Perhaps this is an example of Voltaire's maxim about English justice 'pour encourager les autres'; but it is hardly surprising that this statement was met with overwhelming distress and tears from Fraill. Sewart received a two-month custodial term, suspended for two years.

In November 2011 in *R v Mears*, evidence emerged that a member of the jury had been in mobile phone contact with her fiancé who had been sitting in the public gallery during a significant part of the trial and had observed proceedings which had taken place in the absence of the jury. A number of texts had been exchanged between them during the trial and the juror admitted receiving texts while in the jury room. One such text sent by the fiancé to the juror during the judge's summing-up read 'guilty'. Whilst the judge at the trial had refused a motion to discharge the jury, the Court of Appeal had no option but to overturn the conviction on the grounds of the risk of prejudice.

Finally in January 2012, a juror, Dr Theodora Dallas, was gaoled for 6 months for ignoring instructions to the contrary and conducting internet investigations into the accused person whose trial she was sitting on. When Dallas told the other jurors what she had found, that the accused had been previously accused of rape, they were concerned and informed the presiding judge, who halted the case.

11.9 CONCLUSION

It has been repeatedly suggested by those in favour of abolishing, or at least severely curtailing, the role of the jury in the criminal justice system, that the general perception of the jury is romanticised and has little foundation in reality. Runciman did not actually make this point explicitly, but it is implicit in his assessment of the jury system as against the magistrates' courts. Others have been more explicit; thus, the Roskill Committee expressed the view that:

> Society appears to have an attachment to jury trial which is emotional or sentimental rather than logical [para 8.21].

A similar point had been made previously by the Faulks Committee, but that report also recognised the source of the public's opinion and was careful not to dismiss it as unimportant:

> Much of the support for jury trials is emotional and derives from the undoubted value of juries in serious criminal cases where they stand between the prosecuting authority and the citizen [para 496].

The jury system certainly commands considerable public support. A survey published in January 2004, involving interviews with 361 jurors, found that, for the vast majority of respondents, juries were seen as an essential component of providing a fair and just trial process, and the diversity of the jury was seen as the best way of avoiding bias and arriving at a sound verdict. The major conclusions of the survey were as follows:

- The majority of respondents had a more positive view of the jury trial system after completing their service than they did before. Furthermore, despite the considerable personal inconvenience they may have suffered, virtually all jurors interviewed considered jury trials to be an important part of the criminal justice system.
- Confidence in the jury system was closely associated with the process, fairness, respect for the rights of defendants and ability of all the members of the jury to consider evidence from different perspectives. A jury's representation of a broad spectrum of views was a key factor in jurors' confidence in the Crown Court trial.
- Jurors were very impressed with the professionalism and helpfulness of the court personnel. In particular, they praised the judge's performance, commitment and competence.
- The main impediment to understanding proceedings was the use of legal terminology, although jurors also felt that evidence could sometimes be presented more clearly.
- Over half of the respondents said that they would be happy to do jury service again, while 19 per cent said that they 'would not mind' doing it again. The most positive aspects of engaging in jury service were reported to be having a greater

understanding of the criminal court trial, a feeling of having performed an important civic duty and finding the experience personally fulfilling.

The ideological power of the jury system should not be underestimated. It represents the ordinary person's input into the legal system and it is at least arguable that in that way, it provides the whole legal system with a sense of legitimacy. It is argued by some civil libertarians that the existence of the non-jury Diplock courts in Northern Ireland brings the whole of the legal system in that province into disrepute.

As Lord Devlin noted (*Trial By Jury*, 1966):

> The first object of any tyrant in Whitehall would be to make Parliament utterly subservient to his will; and the next to overthrow or diminish trial by jury, for no tyrant could afford to leave a subject's freedom in the hands of 12 of his countrymen.

Juror Satisfaction

It should also be noted that most jurors seem to be reasonably happy with the system despite the stress and inconvenience it can impose on them. The Justice Ministry carries out an annual survey to measure the expectations, attitudes and experiences of jurors (http://www.justice.gov.uk/downloads/publications/statistics-and-data/mojstats/crown-court-jurors-survey-2010.pdf). Jurors are asked to rate the service provided during the pre-court, at court and after court stages of their jury service. Amongst the findings are that:

- over three-quarters of jurors (77 per cent) said they were satisfied with their overall experience of jury service;
- 87 per cent stated that they were satisfied overall with the treatment they received from the Jury Summoning Bureau before they attended court;
- of those who had been on jury service before, 40 per cent felt their experience this time was better than last, while 14 per cent felt their experience was worse;
- 94 per cent were satisfied with both the politeness and helpfulness of staff, and thought that staff treated jurors fairly and sensitively.

However, only 43 per cent of jurors were satisfied with the time spent waiting to be selected for a trial, so this area clearly constitutes the major source of juror dissatisfaction.

Internet use

Although only a minority of 7 per cent of jurors contacted the Jury Central Summoning Bureau by email, this is a significant increase in numbers compared to 2009 (5%). One in 10 (10%) of those aged 18–34 used this method of communication. Nearly two-thirds of jurors were very satisfied with the information they received (65%) and the speed of the response (67%).

CHAPTER SUMMARY: THE JURY

THE JURY

The jury has come under close public scrutiny since the Runciman Commission's recommendation to curtail the right to jury trial. It is important to know the standard arguments in favour of the jury and also the arguments showing that it may not be truly random and representative. The detail of the jury's function in a trial and the extent to which its verdict can be appealed against are important. In what ways can the membership of the jury be challenged? Juries lie at the heart of the English criminal justice system but there is debate about whether juries provide any better justice than magistrates' courts or whether the role is purely symbolic.

THE ROLE OF THE JURY

To decide matters of fact, judges decide matters of law. Judges can instruct juries to acquit but not to convict. Juries do not have to give reasons for their decision. There is no appeal against an acquittal verdict, although points of law may be clarified by an Attorney General's reference. Civil cases can be overturned if perverse – but not criminal cases. Verdicts can be delivered on the basis of majority decisions. The use of juries has declined in relation to criminal and civil law.

SELECTION OF JURIES

Random in theory – selective in practice. All on the electoral register are liable to serve, but the registers tend to be inaccurate. Service is subject to exemption, excusal and disqualification. Defence and prosecution can challenge for cause. Prosecution can ask jurors to stand by. Jury vetting is checking that jurors are suitable to hear sensitive cases. If Runciman is followed, juries may be required to have a racial mix.

DECLINE IN JURY TRIALS

Under s 69 of the Senior Courts Act 1981, the right to a jury trial is limited to only four specific areas:

- fraud;
- defamation;
- malicious prosecution; and
- false imprisonment.

Even in these areas, the right is not absolute and can be denied by a judge under s 69(1) where the case involves 'any prolonged examination of documents or accounts or any scientific or local investigation which cannot conveniently be made with a jury'.

The Criminal Justice Act 2003 has potentially introduced restriction in jury trials in relation to:

- jury tampering;
- complex fraud cases.

INVESTIGATION OF JURY BEHAVIOUR

Section 8 of the Contempt of Court Act 1981 makes it an offence to obtain, disclose or solicit any particulars of statements made, opinion expressed, arguments advanced or votes cast by members of a jury in the course of their deliberations in any legal proceedings.

FOOD FOR THOUGHT

1. The essential feature of jury selection is randomness, but is that really a value in and of itself? Would an all-male jury be acceptable in a rape trial, even if that were the outcome of a random selection process. If not, why not? Similarly, would an all-black jury be acceptable in a case involving a member of the BNP? However, if these instances are thought to be problematic, why is this the case, and what implications does it have generally for juries' impartiality? Should what goes on in the jury room be sacrosanct, beyond investigation and subject to proceedings for contempt of court, even where the jurors may have engaged in prejudicial behaviour?

2. Some people are concerned that the jury selection process can quite easily result in unsuitable people serving as jurors and, for that reason, suggest that there should be some sort of minimum standard for serving as jurors. Do you agree?

3. In the context of recent development in information technology, should jurors be banned from investigating issues they are deciding about on the internet?

4. In the context of the cost involved, should all jury trials be abolished?

FURTHER READING

Airs, J and Shaw, A, 'Jury Excusal and Deferral' (1999), Home Office Research and Statistics Directorate Research Study No 102, 1999

Arce, R, 'Evidence evaluation in jury decision-making' (1995) Handbook of Psychology in Legal Contexts (Bull & Carson eds)

Baldwin, J and McConville, M, *Jury Trials*, 1979, Oxford: Clarendon Press

Barber, JW, 'The jury is still out: the role of jury science in the modern American courtroom' (1994) 31 Am Crim L Rev 1225

Broeder, DW, 'The University of Chicago jury project' (1959) 38 Nebraska LR 744

Carlton, Darbyshire, Harris, Hodgetts and Robbins, in separate articles (1990) 140 NLJ 1264–1276

Chada, R, 'Jury out on justice system' (2009) 106(28) Law Soc Gazette 8

Cornish, WR, *The Jury*, 1970, London: Allen Lane

Corrin, L, '12 heads better than one' (2009) 153(27) SJ 19

Darbyshire, P, 'The lamp that shows that freedom lives: Is it worth the candle?' (1991) Crim LR 740

Devlin, P, *Trial By Jury*, 1956, London: Stevens

Findlay, M and Duff, P, *The Jury Under Attack*, 1988, London: Butterworths

Finkel, NJ, *Common Sense Justice: Jurors' Notions of the Law*, 1995, Cambridge, MA: Harvard University Press

Gobert, J, *Justice, Democracy and the Jury*, 1997, Aldershot: Dartmouth

Griffiths, C, 'Jury trial' (1999) Counsel 14

Grove, T, *The Juryman's Tale*, 1998, London: Bloomsbury

Hastie, R, *Inside the Juror: The Psychology of Juror Decision-making*, 1993, Cambridge: CUP

Mathews, R, Hancock, L and Briggs, D, *Jurors' Perceptions: Understanding Confidence and Satisfaction in the Jury System – A Study in Six Courts*, 2004, London: Home Office

Sealy, AP and Cornish, WR, 'Jurors and their verdicts' (1973) 36 MLR 496

Vidmar, N (ed), *World Jury Systems*, 2000, Oxford: OUP

Wolchover, D, 'Twelve good men & true & safe' (2009) Counsel 28–30

USEFUL WEBSITES

www.justice.gov.uk/publications/docs/PagesfromJuries-report2-07C1.pdf
Diversity and fairness in the Jury System

www.justice.gov.uk/about/docs/are-juries-fair-research.pdf
Are juries fair?

www.judiciary.gov.uk/NR/rdonlyres/CBB8FE3E-ACEB-49EE-B004-A0AAD2AAC3F8/0/speechlcjju-rytrialsjsblecturebelfast.pdf
Jury Trials: Judge LCJ speech to Judicial Studies Board of Northern Ireland

COMPANION WEBSITE

Now visit the companion website to:

● test your understanding of the key terms using our Flashcard Glossary;

● revise and consolidate your knowledge of 'The jury' using our Multiple Choice Question testbank;

● view all of the links to the Useful Websites above.

www.routledge.com/cw/slapper

ARBITRATION, TRIBUNAL ADJUDICATION AND ALTERNATIVE DISPUTE RESOLUTION

12

12.1 INTRODUCTION

Law is one method of resolving disputes when, as is inevitable, they emerge. All societies have mechanisms for dealing with such problems, but the forms of dispute resolution tend to differ from society to society. In small-scale societies, based on mutual co-operation and interdependency, the means of solving disputes tend to be informal and focus on the need for mutual concessions and compromise to maintain social stability. In some such societies, the whole of the social group may become involved in settling a problem, whereas in others, particular individuals may be recognised as inter-mediaries, whose function it is to act as a go-between to bring the parties to a mutually recognised solution. The common factor remains the emphasis on solidarity and the need to maintain social cohesion. With social as well as geographical distance, disputes become more difficult to deal with.

It should not be thought that this reference to anthropological material is out of place in a book of this nature. It is sometimes suggested that law itself is a function of the increase in social complexity and the corresponding decrease in social solidarity; the oppositional, adversarial nature of law being seen as a reflection of the atomistic structure of contemporary society. Law as a *formal* dispute resolution mechanism is seen to emerge because *informal* mechanisms no longer exist or no longer have the power to deal with the problems that arise in a highly individualistic and competitive society. That is not to suggest that the types of mechanisms mentioned previously do not have their place in our own society: the bulk of family disputes, for example, are resolved through internal informal mechanisms without recourse to legal formality. It is generally recognised, however, that the very form of law makes it inappropriate to deal adequately with certain areas, family matters being the most obvious example. Equally, it is recognised that the formal and rather intimidatory atmosphere of the ordinary courts is not necessarily the most appropriate one in which to decide such matters, even where the dispute cannot be resolved internally. In recognition of this fact, various alternatives have been developed specifically to avoid the perceived shortcomings of the formal structure of law and court procedure.

In its 1999 Consultation Paper, *Alternative Dispute Resolution*, the Lord Chancellor's Department (LCD) redefined 'access to justice' as meaning:

> [W]here people need help there are effective solutions that are proportionate to the issues at stake. In some circumstances, this will involve going to court, but in others, that will not be necessary. *For most people most of the time, litigation in the civil courts, and often in tribunals too, should be the method of dispute resolution of last resort.*

That extremely useful Consultation Paper also set out the following list of types of alternative dispute resolution (ADR) mechanisms:

- *Arbitration* is a procedure whereby both sides to a dispute agree to let a third party, the arbitrator, decide. In some instances, there may be a panel. The arbitrator may be a lawyer or may be an expert in the field of the dispute. He will make a decision according to the law. The arbitrator's decision, known as an award, is legally binding and can be enforced through the courts.

- *Early neutral evaluation* is a process in which a neutral professional, commonly a lawyer, hears a summary of each party's case and gives a non-binding assessment of the merits. This can then be used as a basis for settlement or for further negotiation.

- *Expert determination* is a process where an independent third party who is an expert in the subject matter is appointed to decide the dispute. The expert's decision is binding on the parties.

- *Mediation* is a way of settling disputes in which a third party, known as a mediator, helps both sides to come to an agreement that each considers acceptable. Mediation can be 'evaluative', where the mediator gives an assessment of the legal strength of a case, or 'facilitative', where the mediator concentrates on assisting the parties to define the issues. When mediation is successful and an agreement is reached, it is written down and forms a legally binding contract unless the parties state otherwise.

- *Conciliation* is a procedure like mediation but where the third party, the conciliator, takes a more interventionist role in bringing the two parties together and in suggesting possible solutions to help achieve an agreed settlement. The term 'conciliation' is gradually falling into disuse and the process is regarded as a form of mediation.

- *Med-Arb* is a combination of mediation and arbitration where the parties agree to mediate, but if that fails to achieve a settlement, the dispute is referred to arbitration. The same person may act as mediator and arbitrator in this type of arrangement.

- *Neutral fact finding* is a non-binding procedure used in cases involving complex technical issues. A neutral expert in the subject matter is appointed to investigate the facts of the dispute and make an evaluation of the merits of the case. This can form the basis of a settlement or a starting point for further negotiation.

- *Ombudsmen* are independent office-holders who investigate and rule on complaints from members of the public about maladministration in government and, in particular, services in both the public and private sectors. Some Ombudsmen use mediation as part of their dispute resolution procedures. The powers of Ombudsmen vary. Most Ombudsmen are able to make recommendations; only a few can make decisions which are enforceable through the courts.

- *Utility regulators* are watchdogs appointed to oversee the privatised utilities such as water or gas. They handle complaints from customers who are dissatisfied by the way a complaint has been dealt with by their supplier.

While ADR is usually regarded as referring to arbitration and mediation and the operation of the Ombudsman scheme, this chapter will extend this meaning to allow an examination of the role of the various administrative tribunals that exercise so much power in contemporary society.

12.2 MEDIATION AND CONCILIATION

A number of alternatives to court proceedings have already been listed, but the two most common, or certainly the two that most immediately spring to mind when the topic of ADR is raised, are mediation and conciliation, and as a consequence, although distinct, they are dealt with together.

12.2.1 MEDIATION

Mediation is the process whereby a third party acts as the conduit through which two disputing parties communicate and negotiate, in an attempt to reach a common resolution to a problem. The mediator may move between the parties, communicating their opinions without their having to meet, or alternatively the mediator may operate in the presence of the parties, but in either situation the emphasis is on the parties themselves working out a shared agreement as to how the dispute in question is to be settled.

Before the Woolf reforms introduced the three-track system, the small claims process was referred to as mediation, due to its much less formal procedural rules and practices. Although the small claims track is still relatively informal in comparison with the other tracks (see Chapter 5.5 above), the Court Service introduced a distinct and specific mediation process as an alternative to the court-based procedure. This small claims mediation scheme is funded by HMCS and consequently is free to court users who have a defended small claim.

The scheme was assessed positively after a pilot at Manchester County Court, and in 2007 HMCS began to appoint a number of small claims mediators across England and Wales. By June 2008 each of the 23 HMCS Court Areas in England and Wales had an in-house small claims mediator to deal with appropriate cases (Small claims mediation service: http://www.direct.gov.uk/en/MoneyTaxAndBenefits/ManagingDebt/Makinga courtclaimformoney/DG_195936).

The small claims mediator settles the majority of disputes over the telephone without the need for either party to attend court, consequently reducing time and expense. However, if necessary, face-to-face mediation can be arranged, either on court premises or elsewhere as deemed appropriate. In the event of the parties not being able to reach a settlement at the mediation appointment, the case will be listed for a small claims hearing. As the mediation process is confidential, the judge who deals with the subsequent case in court will not be informed of the content of any discussions at any previous mediation proceedings.

Mediation is also available for higher value claims through the National Mediation Helpline, which, although not free, is much cheaper that making use of lawyers and going to court. Although the Helpline is mainly aimed at fast- and multi-track disputes (i.e. above £5,000), it can also deal with small claims.

The fees for using the National Mediation Helpline are:

Amount claimed	Fees (per party)	Length of session	Extra hours (per party)
£5,000 or less*	£50 + VAT	1 hour	£50 + VAT
	£100 + VAT	Up to 2 hours	
£5,000–£15,000	£300 + VAT	Up to 3 hours	£85 + VAT
£15,000–£50,000**	£425 + VAT	Up to 4 hours	£95 + VAT

The way in which mediation operates will become clear from the cases considered below. General information about the operation of mediation may be found at the National Mediation Helpline (www.nationalmediationhelpline.com) which is in itself an indication of the current importance of ADR as a means of resolving disputes. Equally helpful, with excellent flow diagrams on the relationship of ADR and court processes, is the *Civil Court Mediation Service Manual* produced by the Judicial Studies Board, which is available at http://www.judiciary.gov.uk/publications-and-reports/judicial-college/ Pre+2011/Court+Mediation+Service+Manual

12.2.2 MEDIATION IN DIVORCE

Mediation has an important part to play in family matters, where it is felt that the adversarial approach of the traditional legal system has tended to emphasise, if not increase, existing differences of view between individuals and has not been conducive to amicable settlements. Thus, in divorce cases, mediation has traditionally been used to enable the parties themselves to work out an agreed settlement rather than having one imposed upon them by the courts.

This emphasis on mediation was strengthened in the Family Law Act 1996 but it is important to realise that there are potential problems with mediation. The assumption that the parties freely negotiate the terms of their final agreement in a less than hostile manner may be deeply flawed, to the extent that it assumes equality of bargaining power and knowledge between the parties to the negotiation. Mediation may well ease pain, but unless the mediation procedure is carefully and critically monitored, it may gloss over and perpetuate a previously exploitative relationship, allowing the more powerful participant to manipulate and dominate the more vulnerable and force an inequitable agreement. Establishing entitlements on the basis of clear legal advice may be preferable to apparently negotiating those entitlements away in the non-confrontational, therapeutic, atmosphere of mediation.

Before receiving legal aid for representation in a divorce case a person is supposed to have a meeting with a mediator to assess whether mediation is a suitable alternative to court proceedings. The only exception to this requirement is in relation to allegations of domestic abuse. However, excluding those exempted for reasons of domestic abuse, only 20 per cent of people publicly funded in divorce proceedings actually get involved in mediation. In March 2007 the National Audit Office (NAO), an independent body responsible for scrutinising public spending on behalf of parliament, published the results of an investigation into this low take-up of mediation in this area. It was entitled *Legal aid and mediation for people involved in family breakdown*. Its findings were based on an 18-month period, from October 2004 to March 2006, and related to 4,000 people who had received legal aid in relation to marital breakdown proceedings. Those involved were also asked where they had first sought advice and whether their adviser had discussed mediation. Where mediation had been mentioned they were asked why they had either chosen or rejected mediation.

The report confirmed the statistic that only 20 per cent of people funded by legal aid for family breakdown cases presently opt for mediation and further found that:

- 33 per cent of those who did not try mediation said that their adviser had not told them about it. The NAO was particularly concerned at the proportion of legal advisers who failed to tell their clients about mediation, suggesting that the motivation for such failure was financial;
- 42 per cent of those who were not told about mediation would have been willing to try it had they known about it;
- the average cost of legal aid in mediated cases is £752, compared with £1,682 for non-mediated cases. Consequently, if all cases had been mediated the cost to the taxpayer would have been £74 million less and if 14 per cent of the cases that proceeded to court had been resolved through mediation, there would have been resulting savings equivalent to some £10 million a year;
- mediated cases are quicker to resolve, taking on average 110 days, compared with 435 days for non-mediated cases.

In April 2011 the scheme applying to those making use of legal aid was extended to all parties wishing to go to court to resolve children or property issues following a separation or divorce. Following changes to the Family Court Procedures it became compulsory to attend a Mediation Information and Assessment Meeting (MIAM). However, the parties were not actually required to commit to the mediation process if they did not wish to, or if their case was not suitable for mediation, such as those involving domestic violence. Where parties are not eligible for public funding, any charges made by the mediator for the meeting are the responsibility of the parties attending the MIAM.

In May 2006, the Family Mediation Helpline was officially launched. The Helpline is a public service designed to provide information on, and improve public access to, family mediation.

Its main purpose is to provide information on family mediation and to facilitate referrals to family mediators. The helpline provides: general information on family mediation; more specific information as to whether particular cases may be suitable for mediation; and some information on eligibility for public funding.

The helpline will put callers in touch with mediators in their local area and has a database containing over 600 mediation providers across England and Wales. The helpline number is 0845 60 26 627. There is also a supporting website at www. familymediationhelpline.co.uk. Users of the website can access a service finder, which identifies the mediation services in their local area. It is also possible for users of the website to contact the helpline operators using an online enquiry form.

12.2.3 CONCILIATION

Conciliation takes mediation a step further and gives the mediator the power to suggest grounds for compromise and the possible basis for a conclusive agreement. Both mediation and conciliation have been available in relation to industrial disputes under the auspices of the government-funded ACAS. One of the statutory functions of ACAS is to try to resolve industrial disputes by means of discussion and negotiation or, if the parties agree, the service might take a more active part as arbitrator in relation to a particular dispute.

The essential weakness in the procedures of mediation and conciliation lies in the fact that, although they *may* lead to the resolution of a dispute, they do not *necessarily* achieve that end. Where they operate successfully they are excellent methods of dealing with problems, as the parties to the dispute essentially determine their own solutions and feel committed to the outcome. The problem is that they have no binding power and do not always lead to an outcome. As a result, it is always possible that parties will go through the time and expense of mediation, only to find that, at the end of the procedure, one of them does not agree to a proposed resolution. As a result, the whole process ends up being longer and more expensive than it would have been if the dispute had been taken directly to court.

12.3 THE COURTS AND MEDIATION

The increased importance of ADR mechanisms has been signalled in both legislation and court procedures. For example, the Commercial Court issued a practice statement in 1993 stating that it wished to encourage ADR, and followed this in 1996 with a further direction allowing judges to consider whether a case is suitable for ADR at its outset, and to invite the parties to attempt a neutral non-court settlement of their dispute. In cases in the Court of Appeal, the Master of the Rolls now writes to the parties, urging them to consider ADR and asking them for their reasons for declining to use it. Also, as part of the civil justice reforms, the general requirement placed on courts to actively manage cases includes 'encouraging the parties to use an alternative dispute resolution procedure if the Court considers that to be appropriate and facilitating the use of such procedure'. Rule 26.4 of the Civil Procedure Rules (CPR) 1998 enables judges, either on their own account or at the agreement of both parties, to stop court proceedings where they consider the dispute to be better suited to solution by some alternative procedure, such as arbitration or mediation. CPR 44.3(2) provides that 'if the court decides to make an order about costs (a) the general rule is that the unsuccessful party will be ordered to pay the costs of the successful party; but (b) the court may make a different order'. CPR 44.3(4) provides that 'in deciding what order (if any) to make about costs, the court must have regard to all the circumstances, including (a) the conduct of the parties'. Rule 44.3(5) provides that the conduct of the parties includes '(a) conduct before, as well as during, the proceedings and in particular the extent to which the parties followed any relevant pre-action protocol'. If, subsequently, a court is of the opinion that an action it has been required to decide could have been settled more effectively through ADR, then under r 44.5 of the CPR, it may penalise the party who insisted on the court hearing by awarding them reduced or no costs should they win the case.

The potential consequences of not abiding by a recommendation to use ADR may be seen in *Dunnett v Railtrack plc* (2002). When Dunnett won a right to appeal against a previous court decision, the court granting the appeal recommended that the dispute should be put to arbitration. Railtrack, however, refused Dunnett's offer of arbitration and insisted on the dispute going back to a full court hearing. In the subsequent hearing in the Court of Appeal, Railtrack proved successful. The Court of Appeal, however, held that if a party rejected ADR out of hand when it had been suggested by the court, they would suffer the consequences when costs came to be decided. In the instant case, Railtrack had refused to even contemplate ADR at a stage prior to the costs of the appeal beginning to flow. In his judgment, Brooke LJ set out the modern approach to ADR ([2002] 2 All ER 850 at 853):

> Skilled mediators are now able to achieve results satisfactory to both parties in many cases which are quite beyond the power of lawyers and courts to achieve. This court has knowledge of cases where intense feelings have arisen, for instance in relation to clinical negligence claims. But when the parties are brought together on neutral soil with a skilled mediator to help them resolve their differences, it may very well be that the mediator is able to achieve a result by which the parties shake hands at the end and feel that they have gone away having settled the dispute on terms with which they are happy to live. A mediator may be able to provide solutions which are beyond the powers of the court to provide . . . It is to be hoped that any publicity given to this part of the judgment of the court will draw the attention of lawyers to their duties to further the overriding objective in the way that is set out in Part 1 of the Rules and to the possibility that, if they turn down out of hand the chance of alternative dispute resolution when suggested by the court, as happened on this occasion, they may have to face uncomfortable costs consequence.

The Court of Appeal subsequently applied *Dunnett* in *Leicester Circuits Ltd v Coates Brothers plc* (2003) where, although it found for Coates, it did not award it full costs on the grounds that it had withdrawn from a mediation process. The Court of Appeal also dismissed Coates' claim that there was no realistic prospect of success in the mediation. As Judge LJ stated (para 27):

> We do not for one moment assume that the mediation process would have succeeded, but certainly there is a prospect that it would have done if it had been allowed to proceed. That therefore bears on the issue of costs.

It is possible to refuse to engage in mediation without subsequently suffering in the awards of costs. The test, however, is an objective rather than a subjective one, and a difficult one to sustain, as was shown in *Hurst v Leeming* (2002). Hurst, a solicitor, started legal proceedings against his former partners and instructed Leeming, a barrister, to represent him. When the claim proved unsuccessful, Hurst sued Leeming in professional negligence. When that claim failed, Hurst argued that Leeming should not be awarded costs, as he, Hurst, had offered to mediate the dispute, but Leeming had rejected the offer. Leeming cited five separate justifications for his refusal to mediate. These were:

- the heavy costs he had already incurred in meeting the allegations;
- the seriousness of the allegation made against him;
- the lack of substance in the claim;
- the fact that he had already provided Hurst with a full refutation of his allegation;
- the fact that, given Hurst's obsessive character, there was no real prospect of a successful outcome to the litigation.

Only the fifth justification was accepted by the court, although even in that case it was emphasised that the conclusion had to be supported by an objective evaluation of the situation. However, in the circumstances, given Hurst's behaviour and character, the conclusion that mediation would not have resolved the complaint could be sustained objectively.

In *Halsey v Milton Keynes General NHS Trust* (2004), the Court of Appeal emphasised that the criterion was the reasonableness of the belief.

In the *Halsey* appeal, the only ground of appeal was that the judge at first instance had been wrong to award the defendant, the Milton Keynes General NHS, its costs, since it had refused a number of invitations by the claimant to mediate. As the court emphasised, in deciding whether to deprive a successful party of some or all of their costs on the grounds that they have refused to agree to ADR, it must be borne in mind that such an order is an exception to the general rule that costs should follow the event. In demonstrating such exceptional circumstances, in the view of the Court of Appeal, the burden is to be placed on the unsuccessful party to the substantive action to show why there should be any departure from that general rule. Lord Justice Dyson said (para 28):

It seems to us that a fair . . . balance is struck if the burden is placed on the unsuccessful party to show that there was a reasonable prospect that media-tion would have been successful. This is not an unduly onerous burden to discharge: he does not have to prove that a mediation would *in fact* have succeeded. It is significantly easier for the unsuccessful party to prove that there was a reasonable prospect that a mediation would have succeeded than for the successful party to prove the contrary.

In taking such a stance, the Court of Appeal was sensitive to the possibility, as it implic-itly suggested was the case in relation to the claimants in the *Halsey* case, that (para 18):

. . . there would be considerable scope for a claimant to use the threat of costs sanctions to extract a settlement from the defendant even where the claim is without merit. Courts should be particularly astute to this danger. Large organisations, especially public bodies, are vulnerable to pressure from claimants who, having weak cases, invite mediation as a tactical ploy. They calculate that such a defendant may at least make a nuisance-value offer to buy off the cost of a mediation and the risk of being penalised in costs for refusing a mediation even if ultimately successful . . .

As regards the power of the courts to order mediation, the Court of Appeal declined to accept such a proposition, finding it to be contrary to both domestic and ECHR law. As Dyson LJ stated in delivering the decision of the Court (para 9):

We heard argument on the question whether the court has power to order parties to submit their disputes to mediation against their will. It is one thing to encourage the parties to agree to mediation, even to encourage them in the strongest terms. It is another to order them to do so. It seems to us that to oblige truly unwilling parties to refer their disputes to mediation would be to impose an unacceptable obstruction on their right of access to the court. The court in Strasbourg has said in relation to Article 6 of the European Convention on Human Rights that the right of access to a court may be waived, for example by means of an arbitration agreement, but such waiver should be subjected to 'particularly careful review' to ensure that the claimant is not subject to 'constraint . . . If that is the approach of the ECtHR to an *agreement* to arbitrate, it seems to us likely that *compulsion* of ADR would be regarded as an unacceptable constraint on the right of access to the court and, therefore, a violation of Article 6.

It is clear that a party can refuse to accept an offer to participate in mediation, but any such refusal must be reasonable. Unfortunately, what counts as reasonable cannot be defined with certainty, but its centrality is evident in the two cases below.

In *Rolf v De Guerin* (2011) the claimant succeeded to a degree in her claim but only recovered a small proportion of the amount claimed (£2,500 against a claim of £92,515) and failed on a number of her main allegations. On such grounds the court at first instance decided that the costs should not 'follow the event' in this case and awarded costs to the unsuccessful defendant.

On appeal, the Court of Appeal took into account Rolf's repeatedly stated willingness to settle the dispute through mediation. The defendant had refused mediation until it was too late to be effective and the Court of Appeal denied the validity of his reasons for refusal. As the reasons for refusal were unreasonable, the Court of Appeal held that each party should bear their own individual costs.

Subsequently, however, in *Swain Mason v Mills & Reeve* (2012), the Court of Appeal reaffirmed the decision in *Halsey* that under certain circumstances parties could refuse to engage in mediation. On the issue of refusal to mediate, the Court of Appeal took a different view from the trial judge in holding that the defendants had not unreasonably refused to mediate. In reaching its decision the Court of Appeal provided a gloss on *Halsey v Milton Keynes General NHS Trust*, holding that it was authority for the following:

- parties should not be compelled to mediate;
- mediation and other ADR processes do not offer a panacea and can have disadvantages as well as advantages and are not appropriate for every case;
- a party's reasonable belief that it has a strong case is a factor in deciding whether it was unreasonable to refuse mediation;
- where a party reasonably believes that it has a watertight case that may well be a sufficient justification for a refusal to mediate;
- account needs to be taken of whether a meditation would succeed, given the parties' stances;
- the court should be astute to the danger of parties being wrongly put under costs pressure as regards mediation.

As Davis LJ put it:

> The fundamental question remains as to whether it had been shown by the unsuccessful party (the claimants) that the successful party (the defendant) had acted *unreasonably* in refusing to agree to a mediation. In my view, that could not be shown here; and I therefore think that the judge was wrong to bring into account, adversely to the defendant, the defendant's attitude to mediation in deciding what costs overall should be awarded.

The Court of Appeal, taking a broad-brush approach, substituted an order that the defendants recover 60 per cent as opposed to the original court decision to award only 50 per cent of its costs.

In May 2007, the Ministry for Justice published the results of a research project conducted by Professor Dame Hazel Genn and colleagues. The report, entitled '*Twisting arms: court referred and court linked mediation under judicial pressure*' related to two pilot mediation schemes operated at the Central London County Court (CLCC). The first scheme involved Automatic Referral to Mediation (ARM). This was a quasi-compulsory mediation scheme that was operated between April 2004 and March 2005 and under it 100 cases each month were randomly selected for referral to mediation. The original intention was that if either or both of the parties involved in the dispute objected to the mediation, they would have had to justify their reluctance to a judge, who would have the power to override their objections if they felt that the case was suitable for mediation. However, following the *Halsey* decision the scheme had to be altered to allow potential participants to opt out of the scheme. The second scheme considered was the voluntary mediation scheme (VOL), which had been operating in the court since 1996.

In relation to the ARM scheme the research found that:

- by the end of the evaluation (10 months after termination of the pilot), only 22 per cent of ARM cases had a mediation appointment booked and only 14 per cent of those originally referred had actually been mediated;

- there was a high rate of objection to automatic referral throughout the pilot. In 81 per cent of cases, one or both parties objected to being referred to mediation;

- defendants were more likely than claimants to object to referral in both personal injury (PI) and non-PI cases;

- objections to ARM were raised more often in PI cases than non-PI cases;

- the settlement rate over the course of the year was 55 per cent where neither party objected to mediation, but only 48 per cent where the parties were persuaded to attend, having both originally objected to the referral;

- when parties were called on to explain their objections to a judge, judicial pressure was unlikely to persuade them to mediate;

- the majority of cases in the ARM scheme settled out of court anyway, without going to mediation;

- in cases where mediation took place, but which did not settle at mediation, parties found that they added £1,000–£2,000 to their costs;

- parties who settled during mediation were generally positive about the process whereas parties who failed to settle during mediation were negative;

- judicial time spent on mediated cases was lower, but administrative time was higher;

- there were no obvious factors in predicting whether or not a case would settle.

As regards the voluntary (VOL) scheme the research reported an increase in demand following *Dunnett v Railtrack*. However, personal injury cases continued to avoid the scheme, accounting for only 40 of over 1,000 cases mediated between 1999 and 2004. Despite the increase in the uptake of the VOL scheme, the settlement rate at mediation actually declined from the high of 62 per cent in 1998 to below 40 per cent in 2000 and 2003. Since 1998, the settlement rate has not exceeded 50 per cent.

As for users' experiences of the VOL scheme, one in four respondents cited court direction, judicial encouragement or fear of costs penalties as the principal reason for mediating. However, those involved were generally positive about their mediation experience, displaying confidence in mediators and their neutrality. The informality of the process was valued, as was the opportunity to be fully involved in the settlement of the dispute. While it was generally felt that *successful* mediation had saved costs and time, about half of those involved in *unsuccessful* mediations thought that legal costs had been increased. The most common complaints related to failure to settle, rushed mediation, facilities at the court and poor skills on the part of the mediator.

In stating what could be learned from the research, the report concluded:

- Information from both the ARM and VOL schemes suggests that the motivation and willingness of parties to negotiate and compromise is critical to the success of mediation. Facilitation and encouragement together with selective and appropriate pressure are likely to be more effective and possibly more efficient than blanket coercion to mediate.

- Given the persistent rejection of mediation in personal injury cases, a question arises about the value of investing resources in attempting to reverse this entrenched approach. The lack of interest in mediation on the part of defendant insurance companies is intriguing, given the potential for reducing overall costs through mediation.

- While the legal profession has more knowledge and experience of mediation than was the case a decade ago, it clearly remains to be convinced that mediation is an obvious approach to dispute resolution.

- There is a policy challenge in reaching out to litigants so that consumer demand for mediation can develop and grow. Courts wanting to encourage mediation must find imaginative ways of communicating directly with disputing parties.

- The evaluation of the ARM and VOL schemes, together with recent evaluations from Birmingham and Exeter, establish the importance of efficient and dedicated administrative support to the success of court-based mediation schemes, and the need to create an environment conducive to settlement.

- Where there is no bottom-up demand for mediation, demand can be created by means of education, encouragement, facilitation, and pressure accompanied by sanctions or incentives. The evidence of this report suggests that an effective mediation-promotion policy might combine education and encouragement through communication of information to parties involved in litigation; facilitation through the provision of efficient administration and good quality mediation facilities; and well-targeted direction in individual and appropriate cases by trained judiciary, involving some assessment of contraindications for a positive outcome. *A critical policy challenge is to identify and articulate the incentives for legal advisers to embrace mediation on behalf of their clients.*

The above findings assume additional significance in the light of the Justice Ministry's proposals to reduce the availability of legal aid for litigation in favour of mediation.

A Case Study in How Not to Do It: Burchell v Bullard [2005] EWCA Civ 358

This unfortunate case, for everyone apart perhaps for the lawyers engaged to pursue it, can be taken as a signal example of the dangers and inappropriateness of pursuing legal action in the courts when ADR is available and a better way of deciding the contended issue.

The appellant in the case was a builder who had contracted to build two large extensions onto the defendants' home. The dispute arose because the Bullards claimed that some of the work carried out by Burchell's subcontractor was substandard. As a result they refused to make a payment, due under the contract, until the allegedly defective work had been rectified. As a result, Burchell left the site. In an attempt to resolve the dispute, Burchell suggested that the dispute be referred to mediation, but on the advice of their chartered surveyor the Bullards refused to mediate, claiming that due to the complexity of the issues the case was not appropriate for mediation.

At first instance the judge, District Judge Tennant, was clear that (para 20):

> There are faults on both sides . . . [o]n balance however, I am satisfied that quite apart from the net amount actually recovered by the claimant, the defendants are more at fault than the claimant in the sense that they have conducted the litigation more unreasonably.

Nonetheless, he decided that each of the parties should pay the costs of the other in relation to the main claim in the action. Burchell subsequently appealed against those costs orders.

The attitude of the Court of Appeal is scathingly evident in the judgment of Ward LJ. As to the offer of mediation he stated that (para 3):

> [Burchell's] solicitors wrote sensibly suggesting that to avoid litigation the matter be referred for alternate dispute resolution through 'a qualified construction mediator'. *The sorry response* from the respondents' chartered building surveyor was that 'the matters complained of are technically complex and as such mediation is not an appropriate route to settle matters'. (Emphasis added.)

However, as Ward LJ pointed out, 'All the Bullards wanted was for the builder to complete the contract and rectify the defective work.' So what was the underlying 'technically complex' issue that prevented mediation?

As Ward LJ examined the facts of the case he found things, regrettably but not unexpectedly, getting worse (para 23):

> As we had expected, *an horrific picture emerges*. In this comparatively small case where ultimately only about £5,000 will pass from defendants to claimant, the claimant will have spent about £65,000 up to the end of the trial and he will also have to pay the subcontractor's costs of £27,500. We were told that the claimant might recover perhaps only 25 per cent of his trial costs, say £16,000, because most of the contest centred on the counter-claim. The defendants' costs of trial are estimated at about £70,000 and it was estimated the claimant would have to pay about 85 per cent, i.e. £59,500. *Recovery of £5,000 will have cost him about £136,000. On the other hand the defendants who lost in the sense that they have to pay the claimant £5,000 are only a further £26,500 out of pocket in respect of costs.* Then there are the costs of the appeal – £13,500 for the appellant and over £9,000 for the respondents. *A judgment of £5,000 will have been procured at a cost to the parties of about £185,000. Is that not horrific?* (Emphasis added.)

In examining the situation, Ward LJ emphasised the fact that the appellant's offer to mediate was made long before the action started, and long before the crippling costs had been incurred. The issue to be decided, therefore, was whether the respondents had acted unreasonably in refusing the offer of mediation. While Ward LJ recognised that *Halsey v The Milton Keynes General NHS Trust* had set out the manner in which such a question should be answered, he declined to follow it in the immediate case. His reasoning was as follows (para 42):

> It seems to me, therefore, that the *Halsey* factors are established in this case and that the court should mark its disapproval of the defendants' conduct by imposing some costs sanction. Yet I draw back from doing so. This offer was made in May 2001. The defendants rejected the offer on the advice of their surveyor, not of their solicitor. The law had not become as clear and developed as it now is following the succession of judgments from this court of which *Halsey* and *Dunnett v Railtrack plc (Practice Note)* [2002] 1 WLR 2434 are prime examples. To be fair to the defendants one must judge the reasonableness of their actions against the background of practice a year earlier than *Dunnett*. In the light of the knowledge of the times and in the absence of legal advice, I cannot condemn them as having been so unreasonable that a costs sanction should follow many years later.

However, Ward LJ was as emphatic as he was admonitory in his assessment of the present case and his view as to how future cases should be treated. As he put it (paras 41–43):

> ... *a small building dispute is par excellence the kind of dispute which, as the recorder found, lends itself to ADR.* Secondly, the merits of the case favoured mediation. The defendants behaved unreasonably in believing, if they did, that their case was so watertight that they need not engage in attempts to settle. They were counterclaiming almost as much to remedy *some* defective work as they had contracted to pay for the whole of the stipulated work. There was clearly room for give and take. *The stated reason for refusing mediation, that the matter was too complex for mediation is plain nonsense.* Thirdly, the costs of ADR would have been a drop in the ocean *compared with the fortune that has been spent on this litigation.* Finally, the way in which the claimant modestly presented his claim and readily admitted many of the defects, allied with the finding that he was transparently honest and more than ready to admit where he was wrong and to shoulder responsibility for it augured well for mediation. The claimant has satisfied me that mediation would have had a reasonable prospect of success. The defendants cannot rely on their own obstinacy to assert that mediation had no reasonable prospect of success ... *The profession must, however, take no comfort from this conclusion. Halsey has made plain not only the high rate of a successful outcome being achieved by mediation but also its established importance as a track to a just result running parallel with that of the court system.* Both have a proper part to play in the administration of justice. The court has given its stamp of approval to mediation and *it is now the legal profession which must become fully aware of and acknowledge its value.* The profession can no longer with impunity shrug aside reasonable requests to mediate ... These defendants have escaped the imposition of a costs sanction in this case *but defendants in a like position in the future can expect little sympathy if they blithely battle on regardless of the alternatives.* (Emphasis added.)

In the final analysis the Court of Appeal directed the defendants to pay 60 per cent of the claimant's costs of the original claim and counterclaim and related proceedings. However, there was still a sting in the tail for as Ward LJ stated (para 47):

> We have not heard argument on the costs of this appeal. In order that more costs are not wasted, I say that my preliminary view is that costs of the appeal should follow the event. The appellant has been successful and as at present advised and having regard to the checklist of relevant considerations set out in CPR 44.3, I can see no justification for his not having the costs of the appeal.

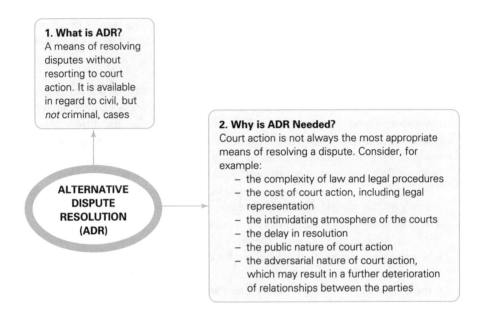

FIGURE 12.1 *Alternative Dispute Resolution (ADR): an aide-mémoire.*

So the Bullards faced even more costs for their failure to take advantage of the earlier offer of mediation. (For another case of money being thrown away in pursuit of a 'matter of principle', and perhaps even more scathing comments by Ward LJ, see *Egan v Motor Services (Bath) Ltd* (2007) in which a claim for about £6,000 damages cost £100,000 in fees.)

12.4 ARBITRATION

The first and oldest of these alternative procedures to the courts is arbitration. This is the procedure whereby parties in dispute refer the issue to a third party for resolution, rather than taking the case to the ordinary law courts. Studies have shown a reluctance on the part of commercial undertakings to have recourse to the law to resolve their disputes. At first sight, this appears paradoxical. The development of contract law can, to a great extent, be explained as the law's response to the need for regulation in relation to business activity, yet business declines to make use of its procedures. To some degree, questions of speed and cost explain this peculiar phenomenon, but it can be explained more fully by reference to the introduction to this chapter. It was stated there that informal procedures tend to be most effective where there is a high degree of mutuality and interdependency, and that is precisely the case in most business relationships. Businesses seek to establish and maintain long-term relationships with other concerns. The problem with the law is that the court case tends to terminally rupture such relationships. It is not suggested that, in the final analysis, where the stakes are sufficiently high, recourse will not be had to law, but such action does not represent the first or indeed the preferred option. In contemporary business practice, it is common, if not standard, practice for commercial contracts to contain express clauses referring any future disputes to arbitration. This practice is well established and its legal effectiveness has long been recognised by the law.

Thus in *Cable & Wireless Plc v IBM United Kingdom Ltd* (2002) the two parties had entered into a contractual agreement which provided that in the event of any dispute they:

> shall attempt in good faith to resolve the dispute or claim through an alternative dispute resolution procedure as recommended . . . by the Centre for Dispute Resolution ('CEDR'). However an ADR procedure which is being followed shall not prevent any party . . . from issuing proceedings.

However, when an issue arose the claimant declined to refer its claim to ADR, submitting that clause 41.2 was unenforceable because it lacked certainty due to its apparent contradictory wording, which suggested the possibility of both ADR and the issuing of court proceedings. It was suggested that the clause amounted to no more than an agreement to negotiate, which was not enforceable in English law. However, Colman J held that the issuing of proceedings was not inconsistent with the simultaneous conduct of an ADR procedure or with a mutual intention to have the issue finally decided by the courts only if the ADR procedure failed. He also concluded that the fact that the parties had identified a particular procedure from an experienced dispute resolution service provider indicated that they intended to be bound by the ADR provision. As regards the uncertainty issue, Colman J made a wider reference to the applicability of ADR agreements after *Dunnett v Railtrack*, holding that the English courts should not go out of their way to find uncertainty, and therefore unenforceability, in the field of ADR references. As he put it, 'For the courts now to decline to enforce contractual references to ADR on the grounds of intrinsic uncertainty would be to fly in the face of public policy.'

12.4.1 PROCEDURE

Section 1 of the Arbitration Act (AA) 1996 states that it is founded on the following principles:

(a)   the object of arbitration is to obtain the fair resolution of disputes by an impartial tribunal without necessary delay or expense;

(b)   the parties should be free to agree how their disputes are resolved, subject only to such safeguards as are necessary in the public interest;

(c)   in matters governed by this part of the Act, the court should not intervene except as provided by this part.

This provision of general principles, which should inform the reading of the later detailed provisions of the Act, is unusual for UK legislation, but may be seen as reflecting the purposes behind the Act, one major purpose of which was the wish to ensure that London did not lose its place as a leading centre for international arbitration. As a consequence of the demand-driven nature of the legislation, it would seem that court interference in the arbitration process has had to be reduced to a minimum and replaced by party autonomy. Under the 1996 Act, the role of the arbitrator has been increased and that of the court has been reduced to the residual level of intervention where the arbitration process either requires legal assistance or else is seen to be failing to provide a just settlement.

The Act, at least to a degree, follows the Model Arbitration Law adopted in 1985 by the United Nations Commission on International Trade Law (UNCITRAL), although it differs from the model code to the extent that it contains mandatory rules as well as provisions the parties can opt into or out of. For example, the power of the court to remove an arbitrator under s 24 cannot be overridden by the parties to the arbitration.

While it is possible for there to be an oral arbitration agreement at common law, s 5 provides that Part I of the 1996 Act only applies to agreements in writing. What this means in practice, however, has been extended by s 5(3) which provides that, where the parties agree to an arbitration procedure which is in writing, that procedure will be operative, even though the agreement between the parties is not itself in writing. An example of such a situation would be where a salvage operation was negotiated between two vessels on the basis of Lloyd's standard salvage terms. It would be unlikely that the actual agreement would be reduced to written form, but nonetheless, the arbitration element in those terms would be effective.

In analysing the AA 1996, it is useful to consider it in three distinct parts: autonomy of the parties; powers of the arbitrator and the court; and appellate rights:

- *Autonomy*

  It is significant that most of the provisions set out in the AA 1996 are not compulsory. As is clearly stated in s 1, it is for the parties to an arbitration agreement to agree what procedures to adopt. The main purpose of the Act is to empower the parties to the dispute and to allow them to choose how it is to be decided. In pursuit of this aim, the mandatory parts of the Act only take effect where the parties involved do not agree otherwise. It is actually possible for the parties to agree that the dispute should not be decided in line with the strict legal rules, but rather in line with commercial fairness, which might be a completely different thing altogether.

  In *Jivraj v Hashwani* (2011) the Supreme Court, in overruling the Court of Appeal, held that arbitrators were not employees and consequently the requirement to select arbitrators from a particular religious group (in this case the Ismaili community) did not breach the Employment Equality (Religion or Belief) Regulations 2003.

- *Powers of the arbitrator*

  Section 30 provides that, unless the parties agree otherwise, the arbitrator can rule on questions relating to jurisdiction, that is, in relation to:

(a)   whether there actually is a valid arbitration agreement;

(b)   whether the arbitration tribunal is properly constituted;

(c)   what matters have been submitted to arbitration in accordance with the agreement.

Section 32 allows any of the parties to raise preliminary objections to the substantive jurisdiction of the arbitration tribunal in court, but provides that they may only do so on limited grounds which require either: the agreement of the parties concerned; the permission of the arbitration tribunal; or the agreement of the court. Leave to appeal will only be granted where the court is satisfied that the question involves a point of law of general importance.

Section 28 expressly provides that the parties to the proceedings are jointly and severally liable to pay the arbitrators such reasonable fees and expenses as appropriate. Previously, this was only an implied term.

Section 29 provides that arbitrators are not liable for anything done or omitted in the discharge of their functions unless the act or omission was done in bad faith.

Section 33 provides that the tribunal has a general duty:

(a)   to act fairly and impartially between the parties, giving each a reasonable opportunity to state their case; and

(b)   to adopt procedures suitable for the circumstance of the case, avoiding unnecessary delay or expense.

Section 35 provides that, subject to the parties agreeing to the contrary, the tribunal shall have the following powers:

(a)   to order parties to provide security for costs (previously a power reserved to the courts);

(b)   to give directions in relation to property subject to the arbitration;

(c)   to direct that a party or witness be examined on oath, and to administer the oath.

The parties may also empower the arbitrator to make provisional orders (s 39).

Powers of the court

Where one party seeks to start a court action, contrary to a valid arbitration agreement, then the other party may request the court to stay the litigation in favour of the arbitration agreement under ss 9–11 of the AA 1996. Where, however, both parties agree to ignore the arbitration agreement and seek recourse to litigation, then, following the party consensual nature of the Act, the agreement may be ignored.

The courts may order a party to comply with an order of the tribunal and may also order parties and witnesses to attend and to give oral evidence before tribunals (s 43).

The court has power to revoke the appointment of an arbitrator on application of any of the parties where there has been a failure in the appointment procedure under s 18, but it also has powers to revoke authority under s 24. This power comes into play on the application of one of the parties in circumstances where the arbitrator:

(a)   has not acted impartially;

(b)   does not possess the required qualifications;

(c)   does not have either the physical or mental capacity to deal with the proceedings;

(d)   has refused or failed to properly conduct the proceedings, or has been dilatory in dealing with the proceedings or in making an award, to the extent that it will cause substantial injustice to the party applying for their removal.

Under s 45, the court may, on application by one of the parties, decide any preliminary question of law arising in the course of the proceedings.

Arbitrators

The arbitration tribunal may consist of a single arbitrator or a panel, as the parties decide (s 15). If one party fails to appoint an arbitrator, then the other party's nominee may act as sole arbitrator (s 17). Under s 20(4), where there is a panel and it fails to reach a majority decision, the decision of the chair shall prevail.

The tribunal is required to adopt procedures fairly and impartially, which are suitable to the circumstances of each case. It is also for the tribunal to decide all procedural and evidential matters. Parties may be represented by a lawyer or any other person and the tribunal may appoint experts or legal advisers to report to it.

Arbitrators will be immune from action being taken against them except in situations where they have acted in bad faith.

Appeal

The AA 1950 allowed for either party to the proceedings to have questions of law authoritatively determined by the High Court through the procedure of '*case stated*'. The High Court could also set aside the decision of the arbitrator on grounds of fact, law or procedure. Whereas the arbitration process was supposed to provide a quick and relatively cheap method of deciding disputes, the availability of the appeals procedures meant that parties could delay the final decision and in so doing increase the costs. In such circumstances, arbitration became the precursor to a court case rather than replacing it. The AA 1979 abolished the 'case stated' procedure and curtailed the right to appeal. The AA 1996 has reduced the grounds for appeal to the court system even further.

Once the decision has been made, there are limited grounds for appeal. The first ground arises under s 67 of the AA 1996 in relation to the substantive jurisdiction of the arbitral panel, although the right to appeal on this ground may be lost if the party attempting to make use of it took part in the arbitration proceedings without objecting to the alleged lack of jurisdiction. The second ground for appeal to the courts is on procedural grounds, under s 68, on the basis that some serious irregularity affected the operation of the tribunal. By serious irregularity is meant:

(a) failure to comply with the general duty set out in s 33;

(b) failure to conduct the tribunal as agreed by the parties;

(c) uncertainty or ambiguity as to the effect of the award;

(d) failure to comply with the requirement as to the form of the award.

Parties may also appeal on a point of law arising from the award under s 69. However, the parties can agree beforehand to preclude such a possibility, and where they agree to the arbitral panel making a decision without providing a reasoned justification for it, they will also lose the right to appeal.

12.4.2 RELATIONSHIP TO ORDINARY COURTS

The attitude of the courts generally to arbitration may be seen in the words of Mrs Justice Gloster in *Soeximex SAS v Agrocorp International PTE Ltd* [2011] EWHC 2743:

> The Commercial Court is very sensitive to the fact that parties have chosen to have their disputes resolved by an industry or trade arbitral tribunal, rather than by the Courts. As a matter of general approach, it tries to uphold arbitration awards and to read them in a sensible and commercial way. It is very mindful that the Court's role on a s 68 application is not to pick holes in an award, or to indulge in an over-nice analysis of what may be understandably brief reasons given by commercial men in areas with which they are far more familiar than the Court.

However where, as in the case in question, there are clearly legal issues to be addressed that were not dealt with in the arbitration, the court will allow an appeal and may impose its own, contrary, decision.

In general terms, therefore, the courts have no objection to individuals settling their disputes on a voluntary basis, but at the same time, they are careful to maintain their supervisory role in such procedures. Arbitration agreements are no different from other terms of a contract, and in line with the normal rules of contract law, courts will strike out any attempt to oust their ultimate jurisdiction as being contrary to public policy. Thus, as has been stated previously, arbitration proceedings are open to challenge through judicial review on the grounds that they were not conducted in a judicial manner.

In February 2008 the Archbishop of Canterbury, Rowan Williams, caused a furore when, in a speech, he suggested that the eventual use of Sharia law to deal with disputes was inevitable in the United Kingdom. His comment was taken out of context, but as some commentators pointed out, it was already possible for Sharia Councils to decide disputes on a informal non-compulsory basis using Sharia principles. Similarly, Jewish people have been able to use their own system of courts, the Beth Din, to decide issues on a voluntary basis.

12.4.3   ADVANTAGES

There are numerous advantages to be gained from using arbitration rather than the court system:

- *Privacy*

  Arbitration tends to be a private procedure. This has the twofold advantage that outsiders do not get access to any potentially sensitive information and the parties to the arbitration do not run the risk of any damaging publicity arising out of reports of the proceedings.

- *Informality*

  The proceedings are less formal than a court case and they can be scheduled more flexibly than court proceedings.

- *Speed*

  Arbitration is generally much quicker than taking a case through the courts. Where, however, one of the parties makes use of the available grounds to challenge an arbitration award, the prior costs of the arbitration will have been largely wasted.

- *Cost*

  Arbitration is generally a much cheaper procedure than taking a case to the normal courts. Nonetheless, the costs of arbitration and the use of specialist arbitrators should not be underestimated.

- *Expertise*

  The use of a specialist arbitrator ensures that the person deciding the case has expert knowledge of the actual practice within the area under consideration, and can form their conclusion in line with accepted practice.

It can be argued that arbitration represents a privatisation of the judicial process. It may be assumed, therefore, that of all its virtues, perhaps the greatest, at least as far as the government is concerned, is the potential reduction in costs for the State in providing the legal framework within which disputes are resolved.

12.5   ADMINISTRATIVE TRIBUNALS

Although attention tends to be focused on the operation of the courts as the forum within which legal decisions are taken, it is no longer the case that the bulk of legal and quasi-legal questions are determined within that court structure. There are, as an alternative to the court system, a large number of tribunals that have been set up under various Acts of Parliament to rule on the operation of the particular schemes established under those Acts. Almost one million cases are dealt with by tribunals each year, and as the Royal Commission on Legal Services (Cmnd 7648) pointed out in 1979, the number of cases then being heard by tribunals was six times greater than the number of contested civil cases dealt with by the High Court and county court combined. It is evident, therefore, that tribunals are of major significance as alternatives to traditional courts in dealing with disputes.

The generally accepted explanation for the establishment and growth of tribunals in Britain since 1945 was the need to provide a specialist forum to deal with cases involving conflicts between an increasingly interventionist welfare state, its functionaries and the rights of private citizens. It is certainly true that, since 1945, the welfare state has intervened more and more in every aspect of people's lives. The intention may have been to extend various social benefits to a wider constituency, but in so doing, the machinery of the welfare state, and in reality those who operate that machinery, have been granted powers to control access to its benefits, and as a consequence have been given the power to interfere in and control the lives of individual subjects of the state. By its nature, welfare provision tends to be discretionary and dependent upon the particular circumstance of a given case. As a consequence, state functionaries were extended discretionary power over the supply/withdrawal of welfare benefits. As the interventionist state replaced the completely free market as the source of welfare for many people, so access to the provisions made by the state became a matter of fundamental importance, and a focus for potential contention, especially given the discretionary nature of its provision. At the same time as welfare state provisions were being extended, the view was articulated that such provisions and projects should not be under the purview and control of the ordinary courts. It was felt that the judiciary reflected a culture that tended to favour a more market-centred, individualistic approach to the provision of rights and welfare and that their essentially formalistic approach to the resolution of disputes would not fit with the operation of the new projects.

12.5.1 TRIBUNALS AND COURTS

There is some debate as to whether tribunals are merely part of the machinery of *administration* of particular projects or whether their function is the distinct one of *adjudication*. The Franks Committee (Cmnd 218, 1957) favoured the latter view, but others have disagreed and have emphasised the administrative role of such bodies. Parliament initiated various projects and schemes, and included within those projects specialist tribunals to deal with the problems that they inevitably generated. On that basis, it is suggested that tribunals are merely adjuncts to the parent project and that this therefore defines their role as more administrative than adjudicatory.

If the foregoing has suggested the theoretical possibility of distinguishing courts and tribunals in relation to their administrative or adjudicatory role, in practice it is difficult to implement such a distinction for the reason that the members of tribunals may be, and usually are, acting in a quasi-judicial capacity. Thus, in *Pickering v Liverpool*

Daily Post and Echo Newspapers (1991), it was held that a mental health review tribunal was a court whose proceedings were subject to the law of contempt. Although a newspaper was entitled to publish the fact that a named person had made an application to the tribunal, together with the date of the hearing and its decision, it was not allowed to publish the reasons for the decision or any conditions applied.

If the precise distinction between tribunals and courts is a matter of uncertainty, what is certain is that tribunals are inferior to the normal courts. One of the main purposes of the tribunal system is to prevent the ordinary courts of law from being overburdened by cases, but a tribunal is still subject to judicial review on the basis of breach of natural justice, or where it acts in an *ultra vires* manner, or indeed where it goes wrong in relation to the application of the law when deciding cases.

In addition to the control of the courts, tribunals are also subject to the supervision of the Administrative Justice and Tribunals Council. Members of the Council are appointed by the Lord Chancellor and its role is to keep the general operation of the system under review.

12.5.2 THE LEGGATT REVIEW OF TRIBUNALS

In May 2000, the then Lord Chancellor, Lord Irvine, appointed Sir Andrew Leggatt to review the operation of the tribunal system, and the attendant Consultation Paper stated that:

> There are signs . . . that the complexity of the system (if indeed it amounts to a system at all), its diversity, and the separateness within it of most tribunals, may be creating problems for the user and an overall lack of coherence.

As Sir Andrew found, there were 70 different administrative tribunals in England and Wales, leaving aside regulatory bodies, and between them they dealt with nearly one million cases a year. However, of those 70 tribunals, only 20 heard more than 500 cases a year and many were, in fact, defunct. Sir Andrew's task was to rationalise and modernise the tribunal structure, and to that end, he made a number of proposals, including the following:

- *Making the 70 tribunals into one tribunals system*

    He suggested that the existing 'system' did not really merit that title and that combining the administration of the different tribunals was necessary to generate a collective standing to match that of the court system.

- *Ensuring that the tribunals were independent of their sponsoring departments by having them administered by one Tribunals Service*

    He thought that, as happened, where a Department of State may provide the administrative support for a tribunal, pay its fees and expenses, appoint some of its members, provide its IT support and possibly promote legislation prescribing the procedure that the tribunal was to follow, the tribunal neither appeared to be independent, nor was it independent in fact.

- *Improving the training of chairpersons and members in the interpersonal skills peculiarly required by tribunals*

  He saw the prime necessity for improved training in the interpersonal skills peculiar to tribunals so as to enable the users of the tribunals to cope on their own without the need for legal representation.

- *Ensuring that unrepresented users could participate effectively and without apprehension in tribunal proceedings*

  Following on from the previous finding, he felt that every effort should be made to reduce the number of cases in which legal representation was needed. He recognised, however, that there would always be a residual category of complex cases in which legal representation was necessary. Voluntary and community bodies should be funded so that they could provide such representation and only as a last resort should it be provided by public funding.

- *Providing a coherent appeal system*

  He found the current system to be confusing and some tribunals to have too many appeal stages, leading to long delays in reaching finality.

- *Reconsidering the position of lay members*

  He considered that there was no justification for any members to sit, whether expert or lay, unless they have a particular function to fulfil, as they do in the employment tribunal.

Subsequently, in March 2003, the Lord Chancellor's Office, as it then was, announced its intention to follow the Leggatt recommendation in establishing a new unified Tribunal Service. The details of the proposal were set out in a White Paper, *Transforming Public Services: Complaints, Redress and Tribunals*, in July 2004 and at its heart was the plan for a unified service, replacing the existing fragmented arrangement. The new organisation formally came into being in April 2005 and was launched operationally in April 2006.

According to its mission statement the Tribunals Service was focused on delivering real benefits to tribunal users, including:

- ensuring that tribunals are manifestly independent from those whose decisions are being reviewed;
- helping to provide better information to users and potential users;
- delivering greater consistency in practice and procedure; and
- making better use of existing tribunal resources.

On 1 April 2011 Her Majesty's Courts Service and the Tribunals Service were amalgamated into one integrated agency, Her Majesty's Courts and Tribunals Service (HMCTS), providing support for the administration of justice in courts (up to and including the

Court of Appeal) and most tribunals, but importantly not Employment Tribunals. The new Service operates as an agency of the Justice Ministry.

12.5.3 THE TRIBUNALS, COURT AND ENFORCEMENT ACT 2007

In further pursuance of the Leggatt review, the stated intention of this piece of legislation (TCEA 2007) was the creation of a new, simplified, statutory framework for tribunals, which was to be achieved not just by the bringing together of existing tribunal jurisdictions but by provision of a new structure of jurisdiction and new appeal rights.

- *Unified structure*

  The Act provides for the establishment of a new unified structure to subsume all tribunals, except for the Employment Tribunals, which will remain independent. This unification is to be achieved through the creation of two new tribunals, the First-tier Tribunal and the Upper Tribunal, and in pursuit of that end the Act gives the Lord Chancellor power to transfer the jurisdiction of existing tribunals to the two new tribunals. The Act also provides for the establishment within each tier of 'chambers', so that existing jurisdictions may be grouped together appropriately. Chambers at the first-tier level will hear cases initially and the role of the upper chambers will be mainly, but not exclusively, to hear appeals from the first tier. Each chamber will be headed by a Chamber President and the tribunals' judiciary, as the legal members of tribunals will now be entitled, will be headed by a Senior President of Tribunals.

- *Appeals*

  The Act specifically recognises and attempts to deal with the previous unclear and unsatisfactory routes of appeal in relation to tribunals' decisions. Under its provisions, in most cases, a decision of the First-tier Tribunal may be appealed to the Upper Tribunal and a decision of the Upper Tribunal may be appealed to the Court of Appeal. However, an appeal will not be allowed if such procedure is excluded by the specific Act or in any order made by the Lord Chancellor. However, it also provides that any such appeal must relate to a point of law and may only be exercised with permission from the tribunal being appealed from or the tribunal or court being appealed to.

- *Administration*

  The Act restated the role of the Tribunals Service, subsequently replaced by the amalgamated HMCTS, in the successful operation of the new unified system.

- *Supervision*

  Whereas previous tribunals came under the preview of the Council of Tribunals, the new Act replaced that body with the Administrative Justice and Tribunals Council (AJTC), an important new institution with responsibility not just for tribunals, as was the remit of the previous body, but with a wider overview and input into the operation of the administrative justice system as a whole.

- *Enforcement*

  In relation to enforcement, at present, tribunals have no enforcement powers of their own. Consequently, if a monetary award is not paid then the claimant must register the claim in the county court before seeking enforcement. Under the TCEA 2007, claimants will be able to go directly to the county court or High Court for enforcement.

Progress on the TCEA 2007

Sir Robert Carnwath, a Court of Appeal Judge, was appointed as the first Senior President of Tribunals. He has responsibility for representing the views of the tribunal judiciary to Ministers, Parliament and for training, guidance and welfare. In addition to the powers under the Act, the Lord Chief Justice has delegated to the Senior President some of his powers under the Constitutional Reform Act, particularly in relation to judicial discipline of most tribunal judges and members.

The following **Chambers within the First-tier** are operational:

- **General Regulatory Chamber**

  The General Regulatory Chamber (GRC) was established within the First-tier Tribunal on 1 September 2009. The GRC brings together tribunals that hear appeals on regulatory issues relating to the following specific areas:

  (a) Charity: the role of this tribunal is to hear appeals against the decisions of the Charity Commission and to consider references from the Attorney General or the Charity Commission on points of law.

  (b) Claims Management Services: the role of this tribunal is to hear appeals from businesses and individuals who provide claims management services in areas including:

  - personal injury;
  - criminal injuries compensation;
  - employment matters;
  - housing disrepair;
  - financial products and services;
  - industrial injury disablement benefits.

  The Tribunal considers cases where the Claims Management Regulator has refused them authorisation or imposed sanctions on them.

  (c) Consumer Credit: this tribunal hears appeals against decisions of the Office of Fair Trading relating to:

  - licensing decisions of the Office of Fair Trading made under the Consumer Credit Act 1974;
  - the imposition of requirements or a civil penalty on licensees under the Consumer Credit Act 1974;

    ○   the refusal to register, cancellation of registration or imposition of a penalty under the Money Laundering Regulations 2007.

(d)   Estate Agents: this tribunal hears appeals against decisions made by the Office of Fair Trading relating to, for example, orders prohibiting a person from acting as an estate agent where a person has been convicted of an offence involving fraud or other dishonesty.

(e)   Gambling: this tribunal hears appeal on issues such as the granting of operating licences by the Gambling Commission.

(f)   Immigration Services: this tribunal hears appeals against decisions made by the Office of the Immigration Services Commissioner and considers disciplinary charges brought against immigration advisors by the Commission.

(g)   Information Rights: this tribunal hears appeals from notices issued by the Information Commissioner under:

    ○   the Freedom of Information Act 2000;

    ○   the Environmental Information Regulations 2004;

    ○   the INSPIRE Regulations 2009 (these are the result of an EU Directive to establish an infrastructure for spatial information in Europe);

    ○   the Data Protection Act 1998;

    ○   the Privacy and Electronic Communications Regulations 2003;

    ○   the Data Protection Monetary Penalty Regulations 2010.

(h)   Local Government Standards in England: established to decide references and appeals about the conduct of members of local authorities.

(i)   Transport Functions: this tribunal decides appeals against decisions of the Registrar of Approved Driving Instructors. These appeals concern approved driving instructors, trainee driving instructors, and training provider appeals. It can also hear appeals for London service permits against decisions of Transport for London and resolve disputes over postal charges.

- **Social Entitlement Chamber**

The SEC Chamber deals with the following areas:

(a)   Asylum Support (it does not deal with asylum claims or other immigration matters).

(b)   Criminal Injuries Compensation.

(c)   Social Security and Child Support.

- **Health, Education and Social Care Chamber**

(a)   Care Standards (i.e. appeals from people who have received a decision issued by organisations concerned with children and vulnerable adults, and those which regulate the provision of social, personal and health care).

(b)　Special Education Needs and Disability.

(c)　Mental Health Review.

(d)　Primary Health Lists: this tribunal hears appeals/applications resulting from decisions made by Primary Care Trusts as part of the local management of such lists, which medical practitioners must be on in order to function.

● **Tax Chamber**

This Chamber has two specific areas of competence:

(a)　Tax, where it hears appeals against decisions relating to tax made by Her Majesty's Revenue and Customs (HMRC).

(b)　MPs' expenses, where it hears appeals against certain decisions made by the Compliance Officer. The Compliance Officer is appointed by the Independent Parliamentary Standards Authority (IPSA) and is responsible for determining and paying MPs' expenses. Appeals can be made by MPs under the Parliamentary Standards Act 2009.

● **War Pensions and Armed Forces Compensation Chamber**

As its title suggests this Chamber hears appeals from ex-servicemen or women who have had their claims for a war pension rejected by the Secretary of State for Defence.

The following is a list of the **Chambers within the Upper Tribunal** already operating:

● **Administrative Appeals Chamber**

This Chamber hears appeals from the present First-tier Tribunals; the General Regulatory Chamber, the Health, Education and Social Care Chamber, Social Entitlement Chamber, and the War Pensions and Armed Forces Compensation Chamber.

● **Tax and Chancery Chamber**

This Chamber hears appeals from the First-tier Tax Chamber Tribunal. This brought together the four existing tax tribunals to hear the full range of direct and indirect tax cases.

● **Lands Chamber (Lands Tribunal)**

In June 2009 the Lands Tribunal joined the tribunal system established by the TCEA when it became the Lands Chamber of the Upper Tribunal. As its functions have not changed, for the time being the Lands Chamber of the Upper Tribunal is still known as the Lands Tribunal.

● **Immigration and Asylum Chamber**

In February 2010, Immigration and Asylum Chambers were established in both tiers of the Unified Tribunals framework. The Upper Tribunal is a superior court of record dealing with appeals against decisions made by the First-tier Immigration and Asylum Chamber Tribunal.

Employment tribunals

The Employment Tribunal and the Employment Appeal Tribunal continue largely unchanged as a separate 'pillar' of the new system. They are subject to the authority of the Senior President for training and welfare purposes and are treated as having the same status as Chambers in the First-tier and Upper Tribunals.

Employment tribunals are governed by the Employment Tribunals Act 1996, which sets out their composition, major areas of competence and procedure. In practice, such tribunals are normally made up of a legally qualified chairperson, a representative chosen from a panel representing employers and another representative chosen from a panel representing the interests of employees. However, s 4(3) ETA details proceedings which may be heard by an Employment Judge sitting alone. In 2012 the list was extended to include actions in relation to unfair dismissal.

Employment tribunals have jurisdiction in relation to a number of statutory provisions relating to employment issues. The majority of issues arise in relation to such matters as disputes over the meaning and operation of particular terms of employment, disputes relating to redundancy payments, disputes involving issues of unfair dismissal, and disputes as to the provision of maternity pay.

They also have authority in other areas under different legislation. Thus, they deal with: complaints about racial discrimination in the employment field under the Race Relations Act 1976; complaints about sexual discrimination in employment under the Sex Discrimination Act 1975; complaints about equal pay under the Equal Pay Act 1970, as amended by the Sex Discrimination Act; complaints under the Disability Discrimination Act 1995; complaints about unlawful deductions from wages under the Wages Act 1986; and appeals against the imposition of improvement notices under the Health and Safety at Work Act 1974. There are, in addition, various ancillary matters relating to trade union membership and activities that employment tribunals have to deal with.

The tribunal hearing is relatively informal. As in arbitration hearings, the normal rules of evidence are not applied and parties can represent themselves or be represented by solicitors or barristers. And, as appropriate in an employment context, they may also be represented by trade union officials or representatives, or indeed by any other person they wish to represent them.

Appeal, on a point of law only, is to the Employment Appeal Tribunal, which also sits with lay representatives (see above, at 4.5.1).

Although less formal than ordinary courts, the process of taking a case to, or defending a case in, an employment tribunal can be time-consuming and expensive, and employers' representatives have complained about the increased use of tribunals. As an alternative to the formal hearing, Employment Tribunals offer a Judicial Mediation scheme. This was introduced as a pilot in 2006, and is now available throughout England and Wales. Judicial Mediation involves bringing the parties together for a Mediation Case Management Discussion before an employment judge who remains neutral and tries to assist the parties in resolving their disputes.

In a further attempt to remedy the alleged shortcomings in the Employment Tribunal process, the Advisory, Conciliation and Arbitration Service (ACAS) initiated a voluntary arbitration process for dealing with unfair dismissal claims as an alternative to using the employment tribunals. In the guide to the new scheme, ACAS states that:

> The intention is that the resolution of disputes under the Scheme will be confidential, relatively fast and cost-efficient. Procedures under the Scheme are non-legalistic and far more informal and flexible than the employment tribunal. The process is inquisitorial rather than adversarial with no formal pleadings or cross-examination by parties or representatives. Instead of applying strict law or legal tests the arbitrator will have regard to general principles of fairness and good conduct in employment relations including, for example, principles referred to in the ACAS Code of Practice Disciplinary and Grievance Procedures and the ACAS Handbook *Discipline at Work* which were current at the time of the dismissal. In addition, as it is only possible to appeal or otherwise challenge an arbitrator's award (decision) in very limited circumstances, the Scheme should also provide quicker finality of outcome for the parties to an unfair dismissal dispute.

However, even before it was introduced, the scheme came under attack from the Industrial Society. In a pamphlet entitled *Courts or Compromise? Routes to Resolving Disputes*, it argued that the new alternative to employment tribunals could well become as rigid, formal and almost as expensive as current tribunal and court processes, and claimed that in any event, the impact on the tribunal system was likely to be slight. While it recognised the advantages in such schemes, that they were faster, cheaper, more informal and flexible than tribunals, it also foresaw inherent risks. The pamphlet argued that ADR does not guarantee fairness or consistency in outcomes. In particular, it highlighted dangers where there is no appeal process, in lack of precedent, and where confidentiality is unjustifiable. It also pointed out the risk that compensation awarded through ADR might be less than in a tribunal or court. In conclusion, it warned that people who opt for ADR need to make sure that they understand the implications, for example, where the decision is binding and leaves no route to appeal.

12.5.4   COMPOSITION OF TRIBUNALS

Tribunals are usually made up of three members, only one of whom, the chair, is expected to be legally qualified. The other two members are lay representatives. The lack of legal training is not considered a drawback, given the technical, administrative, as opposed to specifically legal, nature of the provisions the members have to consider. Indeed, the fact of there being two lay representatives on tribunals provides them with one of their perceived advantages over courts. The non-legal members may provide specialist know-ledge and thus they may enable the tribunal to base its decision on actual practice as opposed to abstract legal theory or mere legal formalism.

The procedure for nominating tribunal members is set out in the parent statute, but generally it is the Minister of State with responsibility for the operation of the statute in question who ultimately decides the membership of the tribunal. As tribunals are established to deal largely with conflicts between the general public and government departments, this raises at least the possibility of suspicion that the members of tribunals are not truly neutral. In response to such doubts, the 1957 Franks Committee recommended that the appointment of the chairmen of tribunals should become the prerogative of the Lord Chancellor and that the appointment of the other members should become the responsibility of a Council on Tribunals. This recommendation was not implemented and ministers by and large still retain the power to appoint tribunal members. As a compromise, however, the minister selects the chairperson from a panel appointed by the Lord Chancellor.

12.5.5 DOMESTIC TRIBUNALS

The foregoing has focused on public administrative tribunals set up under particular legislative provisions to deal with matters of public relevance. The term 'tribunal', however, is also used in relation to the internal disciplinary procedures of particular institutions. Whether these institutions are created under legislation or not is immaterial; the point is that domestic tribunals relate mainly to matters of private rather than public concern, although at times the two can overlap. Examples of domestic tribunals are the disciplinary committees of professional institutions such as the Bar, The Law Society or the British Medical Association; trade unions; and universities. The power that each of these tribunals has is very great and it is controlled by the ordinary courts through ensuring that the rules of natural justice are complied with and that the tribunal does not act *ultra vires*, that is, beyond its powers. Matters relating to trade union membership and discipline are additionally regulated by the Employment Rights Act 1996.

12.5.6 ADVANTAGES OF TRIBUNALS

Advantages of tribunals over courts relate to such matters as:

- *Speed*

  The ordinary court system is notoriously dilatory in hearing and deciding cases. Tribunals are much quicker to hear cases. A related advantage of the tribunal system is the certainty that it will be heard on a specific date and not subject to the vagaries of the court system. This being said, there have been reports that the

tribunal system is coming under increased pressure and is falling behind in relation to its caseload.

- *Cost*

    Tribunals are a much cheaper way of deciding cases than using the ordinary court
    system. One factor that leads to a reduction in cost is the fact that no specialised
    court building is required to hear the cases. Also, the fact that those deciding the
    cases are less expensive to employ than judges, together with the fact that
    complainants do not have to rely on legal representation, makes the tribunal
    procedure considerably less expensive than using the traditional court system.
    These reductions are further enhanced by the additional facts that there are no
    court fees involved in relation to tribunal proceedings and that costs are not
    normally awarded against the loser.

- *Informality*

    Tribunals are supposed to be informal in order to make them less intimidating
    than full-blown court cases. The strict rules relating to evidence, pleading and
    procedure that apply in courts are not binding in tribunal proceedings. The lack
    of formality is strengthened by the fact that proceedings tend not to be inquisito-
    rial or accusatorial, but are intended to try to encourage and help participants to
    express their views of the situation before the tribunal. Informality should not,
    however, be mistaken for a lack of order, and the Franks Committee Report itself
    emphasised the need for clear rules of procedure. The provision of this informal
    situation and procedure tends to suggest that complainants do not need to be
    represented by a lawyer in order to present their grievance. They may represent
    themselves or be represented by a more knowledgeable associate such as a trade
    union representative or some other friend. This contentious point will be consid-
    ered further below.

- *Flexibility*

    Tribunals are not bound by the strict rules of precedent, although some pay more
    regard to previous decisions than others. It should be remembered that, as tribu-
    nals are inferior and subject to the courts, they are governed by the precedents
    made in the courts.

- *Expertise*

    Reference has already been made to the advantages to be gained from the partic-
    ular expertise that is provided by the lay members of tribunals, as against the
    more general legal expertise of the chairperson.

- *Accessibility*

    The aim of tribunals is to provide individuals with a readily accessible forum in
    which to air their grievances, and gaining access to tribunals is certainly not as
    difficult as getting a case into the ordinary courts.

- *Privacy*

    The final advantage is the fact that proceedings can be taken before a tribunal
    without necessarily triggering the publicity that might follow from a court case.

12.5.7 DISADVANTAGES OF TRIBUNALS

It is important that the supposed advantages of tribunals are not simply taken at face value. They represent significant improvements over the operation of the ordinary court system, but it is at least arguable that some of them are not as advantageous as they appear at first sight, and that others represent potential, if not actual, weaknesses in the tribunal system.

Tribunals are cheap, quick, flexible and informal, but their operation should not be viewed with complacency. These so-called advantages could be seen as representing an attack on general legal standards, and the tribunal system could be portrayed as providing a second-rate system of justice for those who cannot afford to pay to gain access to 'real law' in the court system. Vigilance is required on the part of the general community to ensure that such does not become an accurate representation of the tribunal system.

In addition to this general point, there are particular weaknesses in the system of tribunal adjudication. Some of these relate to the following:

- *Appeals procedures*

  Prior to the Franks Committee Report, tribunals were not required to provide reasons for their decisions and this prevented appeals in most cases. Subsequent to the Franks Report, however, most tribunals, although still not all of them, are required to provide reasons for their decisions under s 10 of the Tribunals and Inquiries Act 1992. The importance of this provision was that in cases where a tribunal had erred in its application of the law, the claimant could apply to the High Court for judicial review to have the decision of the tribunal set aside for error of law on the face of the record.

  The previous confusion and complexity relating to means and routes of appeal noted by Sir Andrew Leggatt have been remedied by the TCEA 2007.

- *Publicity*

  It was stated above that lack of publicity in relation to tribunal proceedings was a potential advantage of the system. A lack of publicity, however, may be a distinct disadvantage because it has the effect that cases involving issues of general public importance are not given the publicity and consideration that they might merit.

- *The provision of public funding*

  It was claimed previously that one of the major advantages of the tribunal system is its lack of formality and non-legal atmosphere. Research has shown, however, that individual complainants fare better where they are represented by lawyers. Additionally, as a consequence of the Franks recommendations, the fact that chairpersons have to be legally qualified has led to an increase in the formality of tribunal proceedings. As a result, non-law experts find it increasingly difficult in practice to represent themselves effectively. This difficulty is compounded when the body that is the object of the complaint is itself legally represented; although the parties to hearings do not have to be legally represented, there is nothing to prevent them from being so represented.

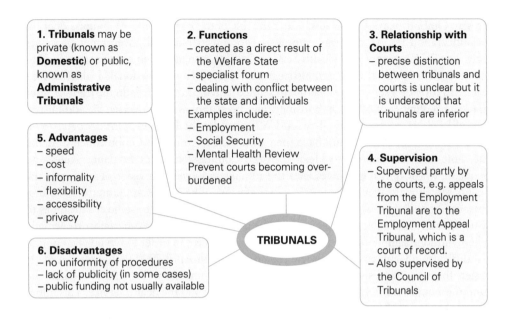

1. Tribunals may be private (known as **Domestic**) or public, known as **Administrative Tribunals**

5. Advantages
– speed
– cost
– informality
– flexibility
– accessibility
– privacy

6. Disadvantages
– no uniformity of procedures
– lack of publicity (in some cases)
– public funding not usually available

2. Functions
– created as a direct result of the Welfare State
– specialist forum
– dealing with conflict between the state and individuals
Examples include:
– Employment
– Social Security
– Mental Health Review
Prevent courts becoming over-burdened

3. Relationship with Courts
– precise distinction between tribunals and courts is unclear but it is understood that tribunals are inferior

4. Supervision
– Supervised partly by the courts, e.g. appeals from the Employment Tribunal are to the Employment Appeal Tribunal, which is a court of record.
– Also supervised by the Council of Tribunals

TRIBUNALS

FIGURE 12.2 *Tribunals: an aide-mémoire.*

12.6 OMBUDSMAN

As with tribunals, so the institution of the Ombudsman reflects the increased activity of the contemporary state. As the state became more engaged in everyday social activity, it increasingly impinged on, and on occasion conflicted with, the individual citizen. Courts and tribunals were available to deal with substantive breaches of particular rules and procedures, but there remained some disquiet as to the possibility of the adverse effect of the implementation of general state policy on individuals. If tribunals may be categorised as an ADR procedure to the ordinary court system in relation to *decisions taken in breach of rules*, the institution of the Ombudsman represents a procedure for the redress of complaints about *the way in which those decisions have been taken*. It has to be admitted, however, that the two categories overlap to a considerable degree. The Ombudsman procedure, however, is not just an alternative to the court and tribunal system; it is based upon a distinctly different approach to dealing with disputes. Indeed, the Parliamentary Commissioner Act 1967, which established the position of the first Ombudsman, provides that complainants with rights to pursue their complaints in either of those forums will be precluded from making use of the Ombudsman procedure. (Such a prohibition is subject to the discretion of the Ombudsman who tends to interpret it in a generous manner in favour of the complainant.)

The concept of the Ombudsman is Scandinavian in origin, and the function of the office-holder is to investigate complaints of *maladministration*; that is, situations where the performance of a government department has fallen below acceptable standards of administration. The first Ombudsman, appointed under the 1967 legislation, operated, and the present Ombudsman still operates, under the title of the Parliamentary Commissioner for Administration (PCA), and was empowered to consider central government processes only. The PCA also serves as Health Service Ombudsman, in which capacity they investigate complaints that hardship or injustice has been caused by the National Health Service's failure to provide a service, by a failure in service provided or by maladministration. Since that date, a number of other Ombudsmen have been appointed to oversee the administration of local government in England and Wales, under the Local Government Act 1974. Scotland and Northern Ireland have their own local government Ombudsmen fulfilling the same task. There are also Health Service Commissioners for England, Wales and Scotland, whose duty it is to investigate the administration and provision of services in the health service, and in October 1994, Sir Peter Woodhead was appointed as the first Prisons Ombudsman. This proliferation of Ombudsmen has led to some confusion as to which one any particular complaint should be taken to. This can be especially problematic where the complaint concerns more than one public body. In order to remedy this potential difficulty, a Cabinet Office review recommended in April 2000 that access be made easier through the establishment of one new Commission, bringing together the Ombudsmen for central government, local government and the health service. This initiative moved forward in August 2005 when the Cabinet Office published a *Consultation Paper on the Reform of Public Sector Ombudsmen Services in England*. As yet, the single Commission has not been brought into existence.

The Ombudsman system has also spread beyond the realm of government administration and there are Ombudsmen overseeing the operation of, among other things, legal services (see below, at 13.6.7 for details), banking and insurance. Some schemes, such as the legal services scheme, have been established by statute, but many others have been established by industry as a means of self-regulation. It is a peculiarity of the system that reference is always made to the Ombuds*man*, irrespective of the gender of the office-holder. The present Parliamentary Ombudsman is in fact Ann Abraham; however, as she was a previous Legal Services Ombudsman, she is no doubt used to the strange gender-specific title.

The European Parliament appointed an Ombudsman under the powers extended to it by the Treaty Establishing the European Community (EC Treaty) (Art 195, formerly 138(e)). The European Ombudsman has the function of investigating maladministration in all of the Community institutions, including the non-judicial operation of the European Court of Justice.

Before going on to consider the work of the Parliamentary Commissioner in some detail, mention should also be made of the various regulatory authorities that were established to control the operation of the recently privatised former State monopolies such as the water, gas, telephone and railway industries. Thus were OFWAT, OFGAS and OFTEL, and so on, set up, with part of their remit being to deal with particular consumer complaints, as well as the general regulation of the various sectors.

12.6.1 PROCEDURE

Although maladministration is not defined in the Parliamentary Commissioner Act 1967, it has been taken to refer to an error in the way a decision was reached rather than an error in the actual decision itself. Indeed, s 12(3) of the Parliamentary Commissioner Act 1967 expressly precludes the PCA from questioning the merits of particular decisions taken without maladministration. Maladministration therefore can be seen to refer to the procedure used to reach a result rather than the result itself. In an illuminating and much-quoted speech introducing the Act, Richard Crossman, the then leader of the House of Commons, gave an indicative, if non-definitive, list of what might be included within the term maladministration, and included within it: bias, neglect, inattention, delay, incompetence, ineptitude, perversity, turpitude and arbitrariness.

In his 1993 Annual Report, the then Ombudsman, Sir William Reid, added the following additional examples to Crossman's list:

- rudeness (though that is a matter of degree);
- unwillingness to treat the complainant as a person with rights;
- refusal to answer reasonable questions;
- neglecting to inform a complainant on request of his or her rights or entitlement;
- knowingly giving advice which is misleading or inadequate;
- ignoring valid advice or overruling considerations which would produce an uncomfortable result for the over-ruler;
- offering no redress or manifestly disproportionate redress;
- showing bias whether because of colour, sex, or any other grounds;
- omission to notify those who thereby lose a right of appeal;
- refusal to inform adequately of the right of appeal;
- faulty procedures;
- failure by management to monitor compliance with adequate procedures;
- cavalier disregard of guidance which is intended to be followed in the interest of equitable treatment of those who use a service;
- partiality; and
- failure to mitigate the effects of rigid adherence to the letter of the law where that produces manifestly inequitable treatment.

Members of the public do not have the right to complain directly to the PCA, but must channel any such complaint through a Member of Parliament. Complainants do not have to provide precise details of any maladministration. They simply have to indicate the difficulties they have experienced as a result of dealing with an agency of central government. It is the function of the PCA to discover whether the problem arose as a result of maladministration. There is a 12-month time limit for raising complaints, but the PCA has discretion to ignore this.

The powers of the PCA to investigate complaints are similar to those of a High Court judge to require the attendance of witnesses and the production of documents; wilful obstruction of the investigation is treated as contempt of court.

On conclusion of an investigation, the PCA submits reports to the Member of Parliament who raised the complaint, and to the principal of the government office that was subject to the investigation. The Ombudsman has no enforcement powers, but if their recommendations are ignored, and existing practices involving maladministration are not altered, they may submit a further report to both Houses of Parliament in order to highlight the continued bad practice. The assumption is that on the submission of such a report, Members of Parliament will exert pressure on the appropriate Minister of State to ensure that any changes needed in procedure are made.

Annual reports are laid before Parliament and a Parliamentary Select Committee exists to oversee the operation of the PCA. The operation of the PCA is subject to judicial review (*R v Parliamentary Commissioner for Administration ex p Balchin* (1997)).

12.6.2   CASE STUDIES

The relationship between the PCA and the government is highlighted by the following case studies:

12.6.2.1   Channel Tunnel Rail Link

As a consequence of the four-year delay on the part of the Department of Transport in deciding on a route for the Channel Tunnel Rail Link, the owners of properties along the various possible routes found the value of their properties blighted, or the property simply unsaleable. The situation was not finalised until the Department announced its final selection in 1994. According to the PCA:

> The effect of the Department of Transport's policy was to put the project in limbo, keeping it alive when it could not be funded.

As a consequence, he held that the Department:

> . . . had a responsibility to consider the position of such persons suffering exceptional or extreme hardship and to provide redress where appropriate. They undertook no such considerations. That merits my criticism.

The unusual thing about this case, however, was the reaction of the Department of Transport, which rejected the findings of the PCA and refused to provide any compensation. The refusal of the Department of Transport led the PCA to lay a special report before Parliament, consequent upon a situation where an 'injustice has been found which has not or will not be remedied' (s 10(3) of the Parliamentary Commissioner Act 1967). Even in the face of the implementation of this extremely rare form of censure, the government maintained its original policy that it was not liable for the consequences of either general or particular blight. The matter was then taken up by the Select Committee on the Parliamentary Commissioner for Administration, which supported the conclusions of the PCA and recommended that:

> . . . the Department of Transport reconsider its response to the Ombudsman's findings, accept his conclusions that maladministration had occurred . . . It would be most regrettable if the department were to remain obdurate. In such an event, we recommend that as a matter of urgency a debate on this matter be held on the floor of the House on a substantive motion in government time [*Sixth Report of PCA*].

Such a demonstration of solidarity between the PCA and the Committee had the desired effect, leading to the government's climbdown and payments of £5,000 to those property owners who had suffered as a consequence of the housing blight.

12.6.2.2   Trusting the pensions promise: government bodies and the security of
           final-salary occupational pensions

On 15 March 2006 the Ombudsman published the above named report on her investigation into the actions of government bodies in relation to the security of final-salary occupational pensions. She had received more than 200 complaints from MPs relating to the issue together with 500 direct complaints from members of the public. All of the complaints were against the Department for Work and Pensions, the Treasury, the former Occupational Pensions Regulatory Authority and the National Insurance Contributions Office. However, the claims actually related to some 85,000 people from 400 private pension schemes who had lost part or all of their occupational pensions as a result of their company becoming insolvent between 6 April 1997 and 31 March 2004. Additionally, people whose schemes finished between April 2004 and 31 March 2005 were affected.

The extensive report supported claims that government departments wrongly advised workers that their company pensions were safe and protected by law. In this regard the report focused on leaflets issued by the Department for Work and Pensions advising workers as to the security of their works pensions. Particular weight was placed on one leaflet, issued in January 1996, which proclaimed that the Pensions Act 1995 was introduced specifically because 'the government wanted to remove any worries people had about the safety of their occupational scheme following the "Maxwell affair"'. As a result of such information, many workers who lost out on company pension schemes when their employers went bust felt the government had failed to highlight the risks of occupational pensions.

It was also alleged that on a number of occasions, ministers and officials had ignored relevant evidence when taking policy and other decisions related to the protection of pension rights accrued in such schemes. Thus the government twice reduced the minimum funding requirement (MFR), a formula introduced in 1995 as a result of the Maxwell pensions scandal, designed to make final-salary schemes safer by setting out the level of funding occupational pension schemes were required to have. By reducing the MFR, the government reduced the burden on employers, but in so doing it also decreased the protection offered to members. Although the MFR was never intended to guarantee pensions, the complainants argued that the literature produced by the government agencies implied exactly that. Consequently, many workers thought their pensions were safer than they were.

The investigation uncovered evidence of real suffering, distress and uncertainty about the future among pension scheme members and their families, who had relied on government information when making choices about their future pension provision. Two people had actually committed suicide after learning they would not receive their full pensions.

The report found that official information about the security of final-salary occupational pension schemes provided over many years by the Department for Work and Pensions, the Occupational Pensions Regulatory Authority and other government bodies was *'inaccurate, incomplete, unclear and inconsistent'* and in her conclusion the Ombudsman stated that:

> *Government has a unique responsibility in these matters. Government set the pensions policy framework and took upon itself the responsibility of providing information for the public. The maladministration which my investigation has uncovered caused injustice to a large number of people who, as a result, lost the opportunity to make informed choices about their future.*

The report made the following five recommendations to the government:

- full restoration of all lost pensions plus any other benefits such as life cover, 'by whichever means is most appropriate, including if necessary by payment from public funds';
- making 'consolatory payments' in recognition of the 'outrage, distress, inconvenience and uncertainty' workers have endured;
- apologising to scheme trustees for the distress they have suffered;
- considering whether to compensate those who are not fully covered by her recommendations;
- reviewing what can be done to reduce the time taken to wind up final-salary schemes.

However, as the report itself revealed that ministers had not accepted the findings of the report and had informed the Ombudsman that they were likely to comply only with the last of her recommendations, she was left to conclude that:

Therefore, there is no basis on which I can be satisfied that the injustice I have identified will be remedied.

The estimation of costs of compensation was put between £5 billion and £10 billion to be paid over a period of some 40 years, a cost the government refused to meet. Whilst the then pensions minister, Stephen Timms, expressed his sympathy with the workers who lost their pensions, he stated that '. . . nobody ever said occupational schemes were guaranteed by the taxpayer'. He also claimed that the Ombudsman had made 'an implausible leap' when she suggested literature written by his department backing occupational schemes led to government liability. In his view:

> Responsibility must fall on those companies whose schemes were or are being wound up, and to the trustees who, with the benefit of professional advice, were responsible for protecting members' interests.

Subsequently the later pensions minister Peter Hain, towards the end of 2007, announced that the government intended to recompense most of the pensioners who had lost out in works' schemes.

12.6.2.3   Equitable Life: a decade of regulatory failure

This investigation originally took place into the role of the Financial Services Authority (FSA) and other authorities in regulating the conduct of the Equitable Life Assurance Society. In the 1950s the society started selling pension policies with a guaranteed annuity rate (GAR) that allowed policyholders to opt for minimum pension payouts and a bonus when their policy matured. Such policies were sustainable during the high inflation rates of the 1970s, but with current low inflation and interest rates Equitable found it hard to fund its commitments. Consequently, in an attempt to maintain payments to the majority of its customers who did not hold guarantees, it tried to withdraw the guaranteed payouts. However, in July 2000 the House of Lords ruled (in the *Hyman* litigation) that Equitable was required to make good its promises to the 90,000 holders of guaranteed annuity pension policies. As a consequence of this decision, it was apparent that Equitable was not in a position to maintain its payment to its policyholders; in December 2000 it closed its doors to new business and in July 2001 it announced that it was reducing the value of pension policies for with-profits policyholders by about 16 per cent. Later, in September 2001, Equitable published a compromise proposal for policyholders aimed at salvaging the company's finances and meeting its liabilities. This ensured that the existing GAR policyholders would get a 17.5 per cent increase in the value of their policies, but they would have to sign away their guaranteed pension rights. The other policyholders who were not GAR holders were offered a 2.5 per cent increase on the value of their policies, but they were required to sign away their rights to any legal claims. It has been estimated that some 800,000 policyholders have lost money as a result of the actions of Equitable. In August 2001, the government announced the independent Penrose Inquiry into events at Equitable Life; in October 2001, the then Parliamentary Ombudsman, Michael Buckley, announced that he would be carrying out a statutory investigation into the FSA's handling of events at Equitable Life beginning in 1999, when it had assumed responsibility for the prudential regulation of the life insurance industry. The investigation by the Ombudsman took 20 months, and when the report was issued by the Ombudsman in July 2003, it was not met with uniform approval. The Ombudsman 'found no evidence to suggest that the FSA ... had failed their regulatory responsibilities during the period under investigation'. As she pointed out:

> the responsibility for what individual potential investors were actually told when purchasing new policies or annuities was not a matter for the regulator. Given all the publicity surrounding Equitable's high-profile court case and their subsequent decision to put up the company for sale, I would have expected potential investors to have sought independent advice before investing in Equitable.

However, the investigation had highlighted a specific issue that she wished to draw to Parliament's attention. That was the apparent mismatch between public expectations of the role of the prudential regulator and what the regulator could reasonably be expected to deliver. It was never envisaged by those who framed the legislation establishing the regulatory regime that it would provide complete protection for all policyholders. The emphasis was on a 'light touch' approach to regulation and the avoidance of over-interference in a company's affairs. Referring to calls for her to extend her investigation to an earlier period, the Ombudsman stated that:

> I have the very deepest sympathy for those who have suffered financial loss as a result of events at Equitable. However, given my very limited remit and the conclusions I have drawn from the investigation, I do not believe that anything would be gained from my further intervention, nor do I believe I could meet the expectations of policyholders in terms of the remedies they are seeking. It would be offering policyholders false hope were I to suggest otherwise. I have therefore decided not to investigate further complaints about the prudential regulation of Equitable.

The placing of blame on the management of Equitable rather than on the regulator was confirmed when Lord Penrose issued his report in March 2004. The report laid the blame for the affair at the door of Equitable's management in its finding that 'a culture

In October 2009, in *Equitable Members Action Group (EMAG) v HM Treasury*, in a partial victory for EMAG, Lord Justice Carnwath and Mr Justice Gross, sitting in the Administrative Court, quashed the Treasury's decision to reject a number of findings of injustice and maladministration made by the Parliamentary Ombudsman on the basis of the date when State liability should start. Rather than start after 1995, as the Treasury had argued, the High Court held that the commencement date should be pushed back to 1991, thus greatly increasing the number of potential beneficiaries of compensation. The court gave the treasury 21 days to respond to the ruling and say what course of action they proposed to take and refused it permission to appeal.

In a subsequent Parliamentary statement the Chief Secretary to the Treasury, Liam Byrne, did not go out of his way to encourage the hopes of those waiting for payments:

> [Sir John Chadwick's] overall task remains the same, namely to advise the Government on those policyholders who have suffered disproportionate impact as a result of those cases of maladministration leading to injustice which the Government now accepts. The Government remains firmly committed to introducing a fair *ex gratia* payment scheme as soon as possible, taking benefit from Sir John's advice on the apportionment of responsibility and practicality of delivery, *and having taken account of the public finances*. Our goal is to introduce a scheme that is administratively quicker and simpler to deliver than that envisaged by the Ombudsman. (Emphasis added.)

One of the first measures announced by the new coalition government in May 2010 was that a scheme would be established to pay the claims in line with the Ombudsman's recommendations. The Equitable Life (Payments) Bill was introduced in July 2010 and was passed in December of that year. It gives the Treasury statutory authority to incur expenditure in making payments to Equitable Life policyholders. It was initially expected that the total could amount to £5 billion. However, following Chadwick's conclusion that even although people had lost £4.8bn in the debacle, compensation payments should only range between £400m and £500m, the coalition government was seen to withdraw from its original promise to the Equitable Life claimants. Thus, in October 2010 the Chancellor, George Osborne, announced that reparation of £1.5 billion would be made.

12.6.3 EVALUATION

All in all, the system appears to operate fairly well within its restricted sphere of operation, but there are major areas where it could be improved. The more important of the criticisms levelled at the PCA relate to:

- the retention of Members of Parliament as filters of complaints. It is generally accepted that there is no need for such a filter mechanism. At one level, it represents a sop to the idea of parliamentary representation and control. Yet at the practical level, PCAs have referred complaints made to them directly to the constituent's Member of Parliament, in order to have them referred back to them in the appropriate form. It is suggested that there is no longer any need or justification for this farce;

- the restrictive nature of the definition of maladministration. It is possible to argue that any procedure that leads to an unreasonable decision must involve an element of maladministration and that, therefore, the definition as currently stated is not overly restrictive. However, even if such reverse reasoning is valid, it would still be preferable for the definition of the scope of the PCA's investigations to be clearly stated, and be stated in wider terms than at present;

- the jurisdiction of the PCA. This criticism tends to resolve itself into the view that there are many areas that should be covered by the PCA, but which are not. For example, as presently constituted, the Ombudsman can only investigate the *operation* of general law. It could be claimed, and not without some justification, that the process of *making* law in the form of delegated legislation could equally do with investigation;

- the lack of publicity given to complaints. It is sometimes suggested that sufficient publicity is not given either to the existence of the various Ombudsmen or to the results of their investigations. The argument is that if more people were aware of the procedure and what it could achieve, then more people would make use of it, leading to an overall improvement in the administration of governmental policies;

- the reactive role of the Ombudsman. This criticism refers to the fact that the Ombudsmen are dependent upon receiving complaints before they can initiate investigations. It is suggested that a more *proactive* role, under which the Ombudsmen would be empowered to initiate investigation on their own authority, would lead to an improvement in general administration as well as increase the effectiveness of the activity of the Ombudsmen. This criticism is related to the way in which the role of the Ombudsmen is viewed. If they are simply a problem-solving dispute resolution institution, then a *reactive* role is sufficient; if, however, they are seen as the means of improving general administrative performance, then a more *proactive* role is called for.

CHAPTER SUMMARY: ARBITRATION, TRIBUNAL ADJUDICATION AND ALTERNATIVE DISPUTE RESOLUTION

ADR has many features that make it preferable to the ordinary court system in many areas.

Its main advantage is that it is less antagonistic than the ordinary legal system, and is designed to achieve agreement between the parties involved.

MEDIATION AND CONCILIATION

Mediation: the third party only acts as a go-between. The Family Law Act 1996 proposed a greater role for mediation in relation to divorce. However, following adverse trials, the Lord Chancellor announced in January 2001 that Part II of the Family Law Act would be repealed.

Conciliation: the third party is more active in facilitating a reconciliation or agreement between the parties.

ARBITRATION

This is the procedure whereby parties in dispute refer the issue to a third party for resolution, rather than take the case to the ordinary law courts. Arbitration procedures can be contained in the original contract or agreed after a dispute arises. The procedure is governed by the Arbitration Act 1996. The Act follows the Model Arbitration Law adopted by the United Nations Commission on International Trade Law (UNCITRAL). Arbitration awards are enforceable in the ordinary courts. They must be carried out in a judicial manner and are subject to judicial review.

Advantages over the ordinary court system are: privacy; informality; speed; lower cost; expertise; and it is less antagonistic.

ADMINISTRATIVE TRIBUNALS

These deal with cases involving conflicts between the State, its functionaries and private citizens. Domestic tribunals deal with private internal matters within institutions. Tribunals may be seen as administrative, but they are also adjudicative in that they have to act judicially when deciding particular cases. Tribunals are subject to the supervision of the Council on Tribunals, but are subservient to, and under the control of, the ordinary courts.

Usually, only the chair of a tribunal is legally qualified.

The tribunal structure has been altered by the Tribunals, Courts and Enforcement Act 2007, which introduced a two-tier system of original hearing and appeal.

Examples of tribunals are the: employment tribunal; social security appeals tribunal; mental health review tribunal; Lands Tribunal; and the Rent Assessment Committee.

Advantages of tribunals over ordinary courts relate to: speed; cost; informality; flexibility; expertise; accessibility; privacy.

Disadvantages relate to: the appeals procedure; lack of publicity; the lack of public funding in most cases.

OMBUDSMEN

The role of Ombudsmen is to investigate complaints of maladministration in various areas of State activity. Members of the public must channel complaints through a Member of Parliament.

The powers of the Parliamentary Commissioner for Administration to investigate complaints are similar to those of a High Court judge. The Ombudsman has no direct enforcement powers as such.

On conclusion of an investigation, he submits reports to the Member of Parliament who raised the complaint and to the principal of the government office that was subject to the investigation. He can also report to Parliament.

Shortcomings in the procedure: the Member of Parliament filter; uncertain, if not narrow, jurisdiction; lack of publicity; the reactive rather than proactive nature of the role.

FOOD FOR THOUGHT

1. One of the most frequently cited advantages of ADR is that it is cheaper than taking cases through the courts, but to what extent does that indicate that it is merely 'justice on the cheap'?

2. Given the much-vaunted advantages of ADR, should it really be made compulsory?

3. One of the most important previous complaints/concerns about administrative tribunals was their lack of independence from the institutions they were regulating/deciding on. Consider the extent to which the Tribunals Courts and Enforcement Act 2007 and the recently established unified courts and tribunals system has overcome this perception.

FURTHER READING

Abel, R, 'The comparative study of dispute institutions in society' (1973) 8 Law and Society Rev 217

Alle, T, 'Advancing ADR' (2009) 153(15) SJ 18–19

Baldwin, J, *The Small Claims Procedure and the Consumer*, 1995, London: Office of Fair Trading

Beale, H and Dugdale, T, 'Contracts between businessmen: planning and the use of contractual remedies' (1975) 2 British JLS 45

Court-based ADR Initiatives for Non-Family Civil Disputes: the Commercial Court and the Court of Appeal, 2002, London: Lord Chancellor's Department

Genn, H and Genn, Y, *The Effectiveness of Representation at Tribunals*, 1989, London: LCD

Hawkins, K, *Law as a Last Resort*, 2002, Oxford: OUP

JUSTICE, *Industrial Tribunals*, 1987, London: Sweet & Maxwell

Justice Mackay (Lord), *The Administration of Justice*, 1994, London: Sweet & Maxwell

Michaelson, J, 'An A–Z of ADR' (2003) 153 NLJ 101, 181 and 232

Payne, R, 'To counsel, not confront: the law on ADR' (1999) Counsel 30

Pedley, FH, 'The small claims process' (1994) 144 NLJ 1217

Qureshi, K, 'Absolute power' (2009) 159 NLJ 1393–4

Reid, V, 'ADR: an alternative to justice?' (2009) 39 Fam Law 981–3

USEFUL WEBSITES

www.cedr.co.uk

The official website for the Centre for Effective Dispute Resolution.

http://www.ciarb.org/

The website for the Chartered Institute of Arbitrators.

www.adrnow.org.uk

A useful website on ADR, run by the Advice Services Alliance.

http://www.justice.gov.uk/about/hmcts/index.htm

The website of the Tribunals Service

www.ombudsman.org.uk

Website of the Parliamentary and Health Service Ombudsman

http://www.justice.gov.uk/converged-sites/nmh/

Formally the National Mediation Helpline.

www.familymediationhelpline.co.uk

Useful helplines, as their names indicate.

COMPANION WEBSITE

Now visit the companion website to:

- test your understanding of the key terms using our Flashcard Glossary;
- revise and consolidate your knowledge of 'Arbitration, tribunal adjudication and alternative dispute resolution' using our Multiple Choice Question testbank;
- view all of the links to the Useful Websites above.

www.routledge.com/cw/slapper

LEGAL SERVICES 13

We are concerned here with a number of issues related to the provision and organisation of legal services, and issues of public access to legal services. The delivery of legal services at the outset of the twenty-first century looks very different from the way things were as recently as 1990. The legal profession has undergone a series of major changes as a result of the Courts and Legal Services Act (CLSA) 1990; the provision of public funding, advice and assistance has been drastically altered as a result of changes introduced in 1999; and the Legal Services Act 2007. The introduction of the 'conditional fee arrangement' (no win, no fee) in 1995 was another contentious issue in this area. In the 1950s, only a minute proportion of the population used lawyers to solve problems. Now, in the 21st century, a great many individuals, small businesses and organisations are using lawyers often as a matter of course.

The latest Law Society statistics *Trends in the solicitors' profession – statistical report 2011* show that there are 159,524 solicitors 'on the Roll', that is, people qualified to work as solicitors, of whom 121,933 have a current practising certificate (PC). This represents a growth of about 6 per cent 'on the Roll' and 41 per cent with a PC during the last 10 years. The number of women solicitors with PCs has increased over the same period by 75 per cent to 56,720. The percentage of PC holders drawn from minority ethnic groups has increased by 155 per cent over the same period to 14,600. The average age of a male solicitor with a practising certificate is 44.5 years and a female 38.4 years.

The geographical distribution of solicitors leaves much room for improvement. Of the 10,202 law firms in England and Wales, 27.4 per cent are in London, and 41.7 per cent of all firms are in a single region: the South-east. Firms in London employ 43.3 per cent of the 87,973 solicitors in private practice.

In 2010, there were 12,420 barristers in independent practice in England and Wales, of whom 8,443 were men and 3,977 were women. Queen's Counsel (QCs) are senior and distinguished barristers of at least 10 years' standing who, as a result of outstanding merit, have received a patent as 'one of her Majesty's counsel learned in the law'. The 2010 figures show there were 1,397 QCs, of whom 1,245 were men and 152 were women. In 2010, it was reported that the number of barristers called to the Bar had increased from 1,772 in 2009 to 1,852 in 2010 (Bar Council, *Annual Statistics*, 2010).

The professional work of lawyers continues to be very demanding. Of this there are various indices. In 2008, for example, a survey of lawyers found that 80 per cent had gone for a day without eating a single meal (eating only snacks) because of their heavy workloads ((2008) NLJ 1158).

The government's aim is to ensure that the professions are properly subject to competition. In most cases, the theory of modern capitalism is that open and competitive markets are the best way to ensure that consumers get the best possible service. On all the issues raised in this consultation, the government's position was that the market should be opened up to competition unless there existed strong reasons why that should not be the case, such as evidence that real consumer detriment might result from such a change. In 2004, the Secretary of State for Constitutional Affairs asked Sir David Clementi, a businessman, to review the regulation of the legal profession and to report to him with recommendations.

The main recommendations of the review included:

- The creation of a Legal Services Board, a new legal regulator that would supervise The Law Society, the Bar Council and all regulators of legal services.

- The creation of an Office for Legal Complaints, a single independent body that would handle consumer complaints against all providers of regulated legal services. Any discipline and conduct issues about solicitors would continue to be dealt with by The Law Society.

- The creation of Legal Disciplinary Partnerships (LDPs). These would be law practices that would enable lawyers from different professional backgrounds, for example solicitors and barristers, to work together, and which would permit non-lawyers to become involved in the management and ownership of legal practices.

The government accepted most of the Clementi recommendations and these are now incorporated in the Legal Services Act 2007. The main change in the Act, compared to Clementi's report, is the proposed new alternative business structures (ABSs), which permit the introduction of Multi-Disciplinary Practices (MDPs). MDPs would allow non-lawyer organisations (for example accountants and surveyors) to enter the legal market and offer their services to consumers alongside those of the legal profession.

The Legal Services Board agreed that ABSs would operate from 6 October 2011. The *Law Society Gazette* announced (6 September 2012) that the SRA has licensed 29 ABSs to date. LDPs came into existence from 31 March 2009 and as reported in The *Law Society Gazette* (9 April 2009) their creation has been fairly slow. There were just 497 according to the SRA Summary of Performance Measures and Statistics (July 2012).

The Legal Services Act 2007

The Legal Services Act 2007 heralds major change in the law. The changes prescribed in this new law are comprehensive and radical.

In July 2003, Sir David Clementi was appointed to carry out an independent review of the regulatory framework for legal services in England and Wales. In 2004, the Clementi Review's report was published. The government broadly accepted the main recommendations of the review. These were:

- A Legal Services Board – a new legal services regulator to provide consistent oversight regulation of 'front-line' regulators like those for solicitors (the Solicitors Regulation Authority) and those for barristers (the Bar Standards Board);

- Statutory objectives for the Legal Services Board, including promotion of the public and consumer interest;

- Front-line regulators to be required to make governance arrangements to separate their regulatory and representative functions;

- The Office for Legal Complaints – a single independent body to handle consumer complaints in respect of all members of front-line regulators, subject to oversight by the Legal Services Board;

- The facilitation of Alternative Business Structures that could see different types of lawyers and non-lawyers working together on an equal footing as well as providing for the possibility of external investment in the delivery of legal and other services.

The Legal Services Act was built on those recommendations. The Act will engineer major changes in many aspects of legal services – a £20 billion sector in the UK. It will also bring legal services in line with other professional services in the twenty-first century. The Act is designed to enable greater consumer choice and flexibility in legal services by removing restrictions on business structures, allowing lawyers and non-lawyers to set up businesses together for the first time, and enabling services to develop in what the Ministry of Justice described as 'new, consumer-friendly ways'.

The following measures are included in the Act:

- A single and fully independent **Office for Legal Complaints** (OLC) to remove complaints handling from the legal professions and restore consumer confidence. This established a new ombudsman scheme as a single point of entry for all consumer legal complaints. The Office commenced on 6 October 2010;

- **Alternative Business Structures** (ABSs), which will enable consumers to obtain services from one business entity that brings together lawyers and non-lawyers, increasing competitiveness and improving services. They will differ from the LDP in that substantial non-lawyer ownership will be permitted together with external investment. ABSs became operational from 6 October 2011 and Premier Property Lawyer, the conveyancing arm of myhomemove, was the first to register as such;

- LDPs have been permitted since 31 March 2009, with firms allowed to have up to 25 per cent non-lawyer or different kinds of lawyers as partners. In April 2010 the Bar announced that barristers could:

- ○   become managers of LDPs;
- ○   work in partnerships;
- ○   work in both a self-employed capacity and an employed capacity at the same time (although not in the same case);
- ○   hold shares in LDPs;
- ○   share premises and office facilities with others;
- ○   investigate and collect evidence and witness statements;
- ○   attend police stations;
- ○   conduct correspondence.

- A new **Legal Services Board** (LSB) to act as a single, independent and publicly accountable regulator with the power to enforce high standards in the legal sector, replacing a variety of regulators with overlapping powers. The supervision will extend to anyone providing legal services including claims handlers, notaries, licensed conveyancers, patent and trademark attorneys, and will writers. The chair of the Board will be a layperson;

- A clear set of **regulatory objectives** for the regulation of legal services which all parts of the system will need to work together to deliver, including promoting and maintaining adherence to professional principles.

These reforms come after extensive research and consultation, with input from a large cross-section of parties, including the Office of Fair Trading, consumer organisations, the legal professions and consumers themselves.

The Possible Effects of the Legal Services Act 2007

The Legal Services Board (LSB) announced that ABSs would commence from 6 October 2011. This will enable non-law firms to own legal practices and is commonly called by the media 'Tesco Law'. Whilst Tesco may well offer legal services, other large organisations have already stated their intention so to do. The Co-operative Society announced on 28 March 2012 that it had obtained a licence and become an ABS. The Halifax has also started supplying legal services via the internet, but has not, as yet, become an ABS. Slater and Gordon, the Australian quoted law firm, acquired the legal practice of Russell Jones & Walker in April 2012 following the SRA granting an ABS licence.

In a speech to the Birmingham Law Society, Lord Chancellor Kenneth Clarke referred to the 1986 deregulation of the stock exchange and financial services industry and said 'The financial community was changed forever by the "big bang". With the Legal Services Act, it's a whole new world – it could be the legal sector's equivalent of the big bang. It may well initially affect only some areas, but it's my feeling that this will fundamentally change the profession forever.' The speech was reported on the website thebusinessdesk.com. The website commented that 'some industry experts predict as many as 3,000 high street firms, or 35 per cent of the total may have to disappear . . .' The Law Society has not ignored this threat to its members and, in autumn 2008, commissioned a report by Lord Hunt, which was published on 5 October

2009 and titled 'The Hunt Review of the Regulation of Legal Services'. This is a lengthy report, which starts by considering the recent background to the legal profession and then considers various matters including professional regulation, education and training and ABS.

In his report (p. 102) Lord Hunt, in considering how ABS might work and be regulated, commented: 'How will the inevitable conflict between economic benefits and ethical concerns be resolved?' An example of this conflict might arise where a firm decided to settle a major piece of litigation, believing that it was in the best interest of the client to do so. The practice's shareholders might suffer a consequential loss of potential profit. Under company law the shareholder may be able to sue the directors for making such a decision. The Australian firm Slater and Gordon, the first legal practice in the Western world to be listed on a stock market, worked with its regulator to solve this conundrum. Its constitution states that: 'where an inconsistency or conflict arises between the duties of the company, the company's duty to the court will prevail over all duties'. This position has yet to be tested. As Stephen Mayson of the Legal Services Policy Institute of the College of Law pointed out in his excellent discussion paper on ABS and related issues:

> Experience in other jurisdictions (such as New South Wales) suggests that a focus on ethical behaviour and 'education for compliance' with regulation could pay dividends. Work commissioned by the Department for Constitutional Affairs also suggested that it is not the business structure that should be the principal cause for concern but rather the underlying incentives, and that 'traditional' structures and methods of practice involving only lawyers are just as likely to encourage unethical behaviour.

Slater and Gordon specialise as an insurance complainant practice and, compared with the top English law firms, are very small. Their turnover for the 2011 accounting year was Aus$ 182.3m (£119.2m) and profit Aus$ 27.9m (£18.2m), according to their published accounts. The Slater and Gordon business model may well be appropriate for similar practices in the UK, but it is probably less likely to be adopted by the large city corporate law practices.

Lord Hunt went on to say (p. 103):

> I still believe the 'poster boys' for ABS will not be those firms that look and behave least like traditional law firms; it will be those that demonstrate the most admirable qualities of a traditional law firm.

The former president of The Law Society, Robert Heslett, considered how ABS would apply in an article in *The Guardian* newspaper (9 June 2010) entitled 'What alternative business structures mean for the legal profession'. He stated that:

It is possible that the emergence of ABS will prove challenging for existing firms. There may be more competition for solicitors who are well established in what is an already competitive market place. But providing legal services is not the same as selling baked beans as a previous minister suggested. I believe most consumers will generally prefer solicitors, given their unique selling point of being trusted advisers. There is an opportunity for those providing legal services to develop new businesses, but there will also be a need to improve the way in which existing services are delivered in order to meet public needs.

A new franchise – QualitySolicitors – has recently been formed to enable law firms to become members and compete with the changes envisaged by the introduction of ABS. Their objective is to have member law firms across the country in every high street by October 2011. Andrew Holroyd, a former president of The Law Society (and partner in Jackson and Canter, which is now a member of QualitySolicitors) said in The *Law Society Gazette* (7 October 2010): 'the creation of a national legal services brand is essential if we are to compete with the new entrants to the market next year'.

Craig Holt, the chief executive of QualitySolicitors, told The *Law Society Gazette* (7 October 2010): 'massively increasing our number of fully branded firms will enable us to achieve our goal of becoming the first established household name brand for legal services'. According to their website (September 2012) they have over 200 members and over 150 legal access points at branches of WH Smith.

It is not only The Law Society that is concerned about the forthcoming changes brought about by the Legal Services Act 2007 (LSA 2007) but also other professions, including The Institute of Chartered Accountants in England and Wales (ICAEW). On its website the ICAEW considered the potential effects of the LSA 2007 on its members and commented:

A groundswell of general criticism led to the Clementi Report in 2004, and now the Legal Services Act 2007 which threatens to revolutionise the delivery of legal services. So it's about law and lawyers, isn't it? Why should accountants and other professionals be worried? Think of it as Professional Services Reform instead and the implications become more obvious. We have had MDPs in all but name for many years with skilled people without accountancy qualifications working in the accountancy profession at the highest level. Now lawyers can enter the MDP arena. By utilising the new business structures permitted in the Act solicitors can access new sources of external capital and expertise. External ownership is permitted for the very first time.

Will this give lawyers a competitive advantage? What if your most promising tax accountant is lured away by the offer of partnership in a revamped and expanded law firm (that could be funded and managed by venture capitalists), or a local solicitors practice gears up and takes on some accountants to compete directly with you?

The world of professional services delivery will be changing and it is impossible to predict what form those changes will take when the first ABS are licensed in autumn 2011. The ICAEW is engaging with the policymakers, regulators and other professions involved, ensuring that accountants are not disadvantaged and are given full opportunity to participate if they wish. According to the ICAEW website (September 2012) they are proposing to become a licensing authority of ABS and also seeking to become an approved regulator of the reserved legal services of probate.

In conclusion, the LSA 2007 and its potential effects are beginning to cause both legal and non-legal professions and individual firms to consider how to move forward and compete with the possible major changes from October 2011. It may be that after the initial interest shown by some businesses (e.g. Co-op and Halifax) there will be comparatively little change. Companies moving into legal services may ultimately find the work less profitable than anticipated and the risks of professional negligence claims against them may lead to such firms withdrawing from the market. An area of possible major change could be in the insurance claims market and firms seeking stock market listings like the Australian practice Slater and Gordon. There is also the potential for a legal insurer to acquire a legal practice to attempt to reduce costs of defending claims. The emergence of the QualitySolicitors franchise may help to protect the smaller high street practices against the new 'Tesco Law' type entrants into the market place. Further franchises and affiliations may possibly develop. Small to medium-sized law firms may consider mergers to create larger, more cost-efficient operations.

In early October 2011, Premier Property Lawyers, one of the largest conveyancing businesses in the UK and the conveyancing arm of myhomemove, was the first alternative business structure (ABS) to be licensed under the Legal Services Act.

A new pilot scheme for trainee solicitors has recently been started by a company called Acculaw, and approved by the SRA. Acculaw (now known as Accutrainee) will offer training contracts to law graduates and then second them to city law firms and in-house legal departments. Trainees will spend a minimum of three months with any firm and a maximum of three secondments. The trainees will be employed by Accutrainee rather than the law firms. It was announced (Legalweek.com, 20 September 2011) that Olswang became the first law firm to commit to the pilot scheme. The first trainee has recently joined the scheme (*Law Society Gazette*, 6 September 2012).

13.2   THE LEGAL PROFESSION

The English legal system is one of only three in the world to have a divided legal profession where a lawyer is either a solicitor or a barrister. Each branch has its own separate traditions, training requirements and customs of practice. It is important to remember that it is not only lawyers who regularly perform legal work. As one text noted (Bailey and Gunn, *Smith & Bailey on the Modern English Legal System* (1991), p 105):

> ... many non-lawyers perform legal tasks, some of them full time. For example, accountants may specialise in revenue law, trade union officials may appear regularly before industrial tribunals on behalf of their members, and solicitors may delegate work to legal executives. Conversely, many of the tasks performed by lawyers are not strictly 'legal'.

13.3   SOLICITORS

The solicitor can be characterised as a general practitioner: a lawyer who deals with clients direct and, when a particular specialism or litigation is required, will engage the services of counsel, that is, a barrister. Looking at the solicitor as a legal GP and the barrister as a specialist, however, can be misleading. Most solicitors, especially those in large practices, are experts in particular areas of law. They may restrict their regular work to litigation or commercial conveyancing or revenue work. Many barristers, on the other hand, might have a quite wide range of work including criminal, family matters and a variety of common law areas like tort and contract cases. The origins of the solicitor go back to the *attornatus*, or later the 'attorney', a medieval officer of the court whose main function was to assist the client in the initial stages of the case. One group of people practising in the Court of Chancery came to be known as 'solicitors'. Originally, they performed a variety of miscellaneous clerical tasks for employers such as landowners and attorneys. Their name was derived from their function of 'soliciting' or prosecuting actions in courts of which they were not officers or attorneys. Eventually, neither of these groups was admitted to the Inns of Court (where barristers worked); they merged and organised themselves as a distinct profession.

It was not, however, until 1831 that 'The Society of Attorneys Solicitors Proctors and Others not being Barristers Practising in the Courts of Law and Equity in the UK' was given its Royal Charter. This body emerged as the governing body of solicitors, the term 'attorney' falling from general use.

One very significant area of development and concern for solicitors at the beginning of the twenty-first century is the extent to which their monopolies of certain sorts of practice have been eroded. They have already lost their monopoly on conveyancing. Then, in 1999, the Access to Justice Act (see Chapter 14) introduced the provision that the Lord Chancellor would in future be able to authorise bodies other than The Law Society to approve of their members carrying out litigation. This, however, should be seen in the wider context of the policy to break down the historical monopolies of both branches of the legal profession. Thus, we can note the growth, since the CLSA 1990, of solicitors' rights of audience in court, and a corresponding anxiety at the Bar when these rights were granted.

The 1990 Act provides that every barrister and every solicitor has a right of audience before every court in relation to all proceedings. The right, however, is not unconditional. In order to exercise it, solicitors and barristers must obey the rules of conduct of the professional bodies and must have met any training requirements that have been prescribed, like the requirement to have completed pupillage in the case of the Bar, or to have obtained a higher courts advocacy qualification in the case of solicitors who wish to appear in the higher courts.

13.3.1 TRAINING

The standard route to qualification is a law degree followed by a one-year Legal Practice Course (LPC) and then a term as a trainee solicitor which, like the barrister's pupillage, is essentially an apprenticeship. The one-year LPC is slowly changing, with Linklaters starting a seven-and-a-half month course (from January 2011) and Clifford Chance a seven-month course one year later. According to LegalWeek.com (21 October 2010) only seven of the top 30 firms have so far adopted the shorter version of the LPC. Non-law graduates can complete the Postgraduate Diploma in Law in one year and then proceed as a law graduate. The Law Society has considered, backed by the Solicitors Regulation Authority (SRA), an aptitude test for all students wishing to undertake the LPC in a move to limit the numbers of students passing the course and failing to obtain a training contract. It was announced on 17 June 2011 that The Law Society will not be pursuing the aptitude test in light of the current review of education and training by the legal regulators. The Bar Standards Board, however, commenced a pilot scheme in September 2009 (with 300 volunteers) and a further pilot in 2010/11 with over 1,600 students and it will become compulsory in autumn 2012, subject to LSB approval. After completion of the LPC and traineeship, a trainee solicitor may apply to The Law Society to be 'admitted' to the profession. The Master of the Rolls will add the names of the newly qualified to the roll of officers of the Supreme Court. The requirement for a training contract may be removed or modified in the future. The SRA has investigated the need for a training contract and has proposed radical changes. In September 2008 a pilot scheme started with 46 firms taking part. There are two methods of training: the first is similar to the existing training contract, but the trainees (with a formal training contract) will not be guaranteed qualification as a solicitor if they do not meet the standards of rigorous testing to meet the objectives required and is referred to as 'work-based learning outcomes'. The second allows paralegals to qualify, without a training contract, whilst working in their current jobs. The pilot scheme finished in 2010 and 70 out of 79 students qualified. The results of the pilot scheme are currently being assessed. The SRA will not undertake further pilots before the Legal Education and Training Review has been completed. There are also proposals that qualification may in certain circumstances in the future take less than the current 24 months. To practise, a solicitor will also require a practising certificate issued by the SRA. This used to be a flat-rate annual fee, which in 2009 was £1,180. The SRA has changed the flat-fee method from 2010 to a four-part fee as listed below. The SRA's fee structure for 2012 will be:

Individual practising fee
A flat fee of £344 for every solicitor seeking a practising certificate.

Firm practising fee
A fee payable by every firm seeking or maintaining authorisation to practise. This is a turnover-based fee as shown in the table below.

Individual Compensation Fund contribution
A flat fee of £92 is payable by each individual.

Firm Compensation Fund contribution
A flat fee of £1,340 is payable by firms which hold client money.

Firm Practising Fee Calculation of Turnover for 2012.

Turnover range (A)	Pay per cent of turnover within band (B)	Minimum turnover in band (C)	Minimum fee in band (D)
£0–£19,999	0.86%	£0	£100
£20,000–£149,999	0.51%	£20,000	£272
£150,000–£499,999	0.49%	£150,000	£935
£500,000–£999,999	0.47%	£500,000	£2,650
£1,000,000–£2,999,999	0.45%	£1,000,000	£5,000
£3,000,000–£9,999,999	0.31%	£3,000,000	£14,000
£10,000,000–£29,999,999	0.26%	£10,000,000	£35,7000
£30,000,000–£69,999,999	0.23%	£30,000,000	£87,700
£70,000,000–£149,999,999	0.21%	£70,000,000	£179,700
£150,000,000+	0.08%	£150,000,000	£347,700

The firm fee is calculated by following the steps below:

- Identify which band the turnover (T) falls in from column A.
- Take T and subtract the figure in the corresponding column C.
- Multiply this figure by the corresponding percentage in column B.
- Finally add this figure to the corresponding figure in column D.
- Firm fee then needs to be rounded to the nearest pound (i.e. if less than 50p then round down and if equal to or more than 50p then round up).

Formula: (T – C) × B + D

Example for turnover of £200,000:
(£200,000 – £150,000) × 0.49% + £935 = £1,180.

Additionally, solicitors have to pay an annual premium for indemnity insurance.

All solicitors must now undergo regular continuing education, known as continuing professional development (CPD), which means attendance at non-examined legal courses designed to update knowledge and improve expertise. Each year solicitors are required to complete 16 hours of CPD training in the CPD year that currently runs from 1 November to 31 October each year. One CPD point equates to one hour's training. It is compulsory for all newly admitted solicitors to complete The Law Society's Management Course Stage 1 before the end of the third CPD year of the solicitor being admitted to the role.

This was the profession's governing body controlled by a council of elected members and an annually elected president. Its powers and duties derived from the Solicitors Act 1974. Complaints against solicitors used to be dealt with by the Solicitors' Complaints Bureau and the Solicitors' Disciplinary Tribunal, the latter having power to strike from the roll the name of an offending solicitor. It had been sometimes seen as worrying that the Society combined two roles with a possible conflict of interests: maintenance of professional standards for the protection of the public, and as the main professional association to promote the interests of solicitors. Consider a rather basic example. Acting for its members, The Law Society should perhaps try to ensure that insurance policies against claims for negligence are always available for solicitors even if they have been sued for this several times. For such insurance to be granted to someone with such a questionable professional record is, however, clearly not in the best interests of the public who use solicitors.

In 2006, The Law Society council began a debate on the future of the society. The question was whether the society should survive, if so in what shape, and what it should do for the solicitors who fund it. Reforms introduced in the Legal Services Bill 2006 have already led to changes, with the society hiving off, in January 2007, its regulation to the Solicitors' Regulation Authority and complaints handling to the Legal Complaints Service, which are new boards managed at 'arm's length' from the central body. The Law Society now deals with the interests of its members and will negotiate with and lobby the profession's regulators and government. The key roles of The Law Society now are to help, protect, promote, train and advise solicitors.

The profession is now four times the size it was 35 years ago, and with an ever-widening gap between the corporate giants and the legal aid firms, a substantial set of questions needed to be resolved.

Who will pay? In one Law Society survey, four in five solicitors believe that they should pay for at least some of the society's representative work; but they want a slimmed-down, leaner machine – a society that is more efficient, more responsive and decisive (Frances Gibb, *The Times*, 28 March, 2006). According to the society's 2011 financial report there were 1,023 (1,251 in 2010) staff costing £55 million (£63 million in 2010)out of the total annual overheads of £105 million (£104 million in 2010). . City solicitors – whom many feared would jump ship, preferring to use their own City of London Law Society – also want to keep a national voice. They appreciate the society's lobbying to open up markets overseas or on money laundering and company reform.

But only one in five law firms felt that all its needs were being met and 40 per cent felt 'few or none' of their needs were being met. A sizeable 37 per cent thought the society too expensive. The cost in 2005, through the practising certificate fee, was £1,020. The fee for 2006 was reduced to £950, but 34 per cent thought that still too high. It has since been increased to £1,180 for 2009, together with a contribution of up to £390 for the compensation fund. The fee structure since 2010 has been radically changed as shown in 13.3.1 above. Moreover, 47 per cent said that if membership of the new-style society was voluntary, they would not join. Another 31 per cent said that this would depend on cost.

Solicitors Regulation Authority (SRA)

The SRA is the independent regulatory body of The Law Society and was established in January 2007. It was formerly known as The Law Society Regulation Board, but changed its name so that it would be clear that it was independent of The Law Society. The SRA's job is to regulate and discipline all solicitors in England and Wales, who number in excess of 100,000, with its principal aim of giving the public confidence in the profession. The SRA's functions include:

- setting standards for qualifying as a solicitor and the requirements for solicitors' continuing professional development;
- monitoring the performance of organisations that provide legal training;
- monitoring solicitors and their firms to ensure compliance with rules;
- referring solicitors to the Solicitors Disciplinary Tribunal;
- running the compensation fund;
- drafting rules of professional conduct.

In carrying out its functions, the SRA consults with solicitors and other legal professionals, along with the public, consumer groups and the government.

The Compensation Fund was set up in 1941 by The Law Society to protect clients who lost money due to the dishonesty of their solicitor or their solicitor's failure to properly account for clients' money. The fund used to be supervised by the Consumer Complaints Service (CCS). However, the fund is now run by the SRA. Any person, and not just the client of a solicitor, may seek payment from the compensation fund providing the person has suffered financial loss due to the solicitor's dishonesty or financial hardship due to a solicitor's failure to pay over money that he has received. The loss must arise during the solicitor's normal work. As a general rule, a person must notify the SRA within six months after they discovered (or should have discovered) the loss. The SRA will require the person making the claim to complete an application form. A caseworker will then investigate the application and if necessary will request more information before an adjudicator or panel determines the application. The SRA will not normally sanction the payment of more than two million pounds including interest, costs and any other insurance or other payment the person who has suffered the loss may receive.

The Legal Complaints Service (LCS) may also direct a person to make a claim to the SRA's compensation fund. This may happen following the LCS directing a solicitor to pay compensation for poor service but are unable to pay it if their firm is insolvent, the SRA having intervened in the firm or their practice is closed.

The New Code of Conduct

On 1 July 2007 the Solicitors' Code of Conduct 2007 came into force which has now codified solicitors' conduct obligations. Rule 1 sets out six core duties which are fundamental rules and a breach could result in sanctions. Rules 2 to 25 are the rules that arise from the core duties and which basically put flesh on the bare bones of rule 1, breach of which may result in sanctions. After each rule there is guidance which is not mandatory and does not form part of the Code of Conduct.

Outcomes-focused regulation (OFR) is the SRA's new approach to regulation. OFR is a move away from a rules-based approach and instead focuses on high-level outcomes governing practice and the quality of outcomes for clients. The SRA has been implementing OFR since 6 October 2011.

Legal Complaints Service (LCS)

From 1 September 1996, the Solicitors' Disciplinary Tribunal continued to work as before, but the Office for the Supervision of Solicitors (OSS) took over the work of the Solicitors' Complaints Bureau, and the old organisation was abolished. The OSS was subsequently renamed in April 2004 as the Consumer Complaints Service (CCS). The CCS was replaced in January 2007 by the Legal Complaints Service (LCS), whose complaints handling is now operated by the Office for Legal Complaints (OLC) under the provisions of the Legal Services Bill. The OLC has in turn created the Legal Ombudsman (LO) as a single organisation (within the OLC) for all consumer legal complaints. The LO can, if it is agreed that there has been a problem with the lawyer's service, ask the lawyer or law firm to:

- apologise to you;
- return any documents you may need;
- put things right if more work can correct what went wrong;
- pay you back if you have lost out financially (up to £30,000, although most complaints involve much smaller amounts);
- pay compensation if you have lost out or been badly treated.

The OLC is funded by The Law Society. As an independent body, the OLC decides its own budget, which according to the LCS's chief executive, Deborah Evans (UK Legal News Analysis, 22/01/07), 'The Law Society's Council will rubberstamp'. According to Deborah Evans the LCS 'deals with 18,500 complaints a year and up to 700 inquiries a month, [their] direct costs are c£22.8m, but there is still debate about how some of the central costs are to be divided – which will boost this figure'. The OLC budget for 2012/13 is £17 million and to undertake 8,000 cases. Quarterly statistics are now issued by the OLC and in Q1 of 2012/13 there were 2,039 case closures at an average cost of £1,932.

The LO runs a remuneration scheme for any person dissatisfied with their solicitor's bill. This service is free, providing that the solicitor's bill does not include work for court proceedings. The LO will check the solicitor's bill to ensure that it is fair and reasonable. If the solicitor's work includes court proceedings then only the court can assess the bill.

The LO can also instruct a solicitor to pay compensation to their client for distress and inconvenience caused by poor service. If a person is dissatisfied with the service they received from their solicitor, they should first lodge a complaint with their solicitor or the solicitor's complaints handling partner. If the aggrieved party fails to receive a response, or a satisfactory response, they can complain to the LO. The LO can make an award of up to £30,000, including any extra expenses and losses. However, the average award is in the region of £450 and most are less than £250. The LO makes awards on the merits of each individual case.

Solicitors' Disciplinary Tribunal (SDT)

The Solicitors' Disciplinary Tribunal is constitutionally independent of The Law Society, although it is funded by them. The SDT's powers arise by virtue of the Solicitors Act 1974. The purpose of the SDT is to consider and determine applications involving allegations of professional misconduct of solicitors or breaches of their professional rules. Such allegations are brought to the attention of the SDT in one of three ways:

- by members of the public;
- on behalf of The Law Society by in-house solicitors/barristers;
- by independent prosecuting solicitors instructed by The Law Society.

In addition, the SRA may refer a case to the SDT if a solicitor's misconduct is likely to lead to a fine, suspension, being struck off or another power given to the SDT.

Whether a referral is made to the SDT depends on two tests being satisfied: the evidential test and the public interest test. The former test requires 'that there is enough evidence to provide a realistic prospect that the solicitor will be found guilty of misconduct' (Law Society, October 2006). The latter test involves considering the public interest once the evidential test is satisfied. For example, a case may be referred to the SDT if there are grounds for believing the conduct is likely to be continued or repeated, whereas a case may not be referred to the SDT if the misconduct was committed as a genuine mistake or misunderstanding or if the SDT is only likely to impose a small penalty.

The SDT can impose various sanctions which include the following:

- striking off the solicitor from the Roll;
- suspending the solicitor from practice for a fixed or indefinite period;
- ordering the solicitor to pay a penalty (to Her Majesty) not exceeding £5,000 for each allegation;
- reprimanding a solicitor.

As mentioned above, the LCS is (as the OLC will be) funded by The Law Society, so there will still be a serious question as to whether this body will be seen as sufficiently independent by the public.

The extent of solicitors' and their firm's potential liability can be illustrated by the following two cases. In *Wood v Law Society* (1995), the plaintiff (W) alleged that she was the victim of continuing misconduct by a firm of solicitors. She complained that H, a partner in a law firm, wrongly acted for both sides when arranging a series of loans for

W on the security of W's home, and that H failed to disclose that H's husband was a director of one of the lenders. H's firm acted for the lenders in issuing court proceedings and obtained possession of the cottage for them. After many complaints to them by W, The Law Society conceded, after much delay, that it had been 'unwise' for H's firm to act for the lenders and that this was 'conduct unbefitting a solicitor'. The Society issued a formal rebuke. W sought damages from The Law Society, arguing that, as a result of the Society's incompetence and delay, she lost the chance of avoiding repossession of her home and suffered anxiety and distress.

The Court of Appeal held that if there was a duty owed to W by the Society, *it did not include a duty to provide peace of mind or freedom from distress*. Even though the Society appeared not to have lived up to the standards reasonably to be expected of it, there was no prospect of establishing that its failure to properly or timely investigate her complaints could have any sounding in damages. The loss suffered by W was not directly caused by The Law Society's incompetence and delay.

Another case dealing with the liability of solicitors is *White v Jones* (1995). This decision arguably widened the liability of solicitors. The House of Lords decided that a solicitor owes a duty of care to the intended beneficiary of a will when instructed by the testator to draw up that will. A firm of solicitors had been instructed by a client to change his will so that his daughters (whom he had previously cut out of an inheritance) should each receive £9,000. The firm did not act promptly on these instructions and the father eventually died before the will had been changed. Thus, the daughters received nothing. The person actually acting in the matter was a legal executive, not a solicitor, but it was the liability of the firm which was in issue. The Court of Appeal allowed an appeal by the plaintiffs, and granted that they should be awarded damages from the firm of solicitors to cover the loss, that is, the amounts they would have inherited had the firm acted professionally. The House of Lords upheld this decision.

The case is an interesting illustration of the judicial development of the common law. There was no obvious way in which the claimants had an action. They could not sue the firm in contract because they had made no contract with the firm; only their father had done so. The daughters were outside of the arrangements between their father and his solicitors; they were third parties and the law did not at that time recognise a *ius quaesitum tertio* (a contractual right for the benefit of a third party). The precedents in the tort of negligence did not provide much assistance because, unlike the facts of those cases, the daughters here were not people who had relied upon the firm (as in a case like *Ross v Caunters* (1979)).

The leading opinion was given by Lord Goff who decided that there was a need to give people like the claimants a remedy in this sort of situation, a remedy that was not available according to technical rules of law. He thus favoured 'practical justice', recognising that:

> . . . cases such as these call for an appropriate remedy and that the common law is not so sterile as to be incapable of supplying that remedy when it is required [at p 777].

By a majority of 3:2, the Lords extended the duty of care owed by professionals as it had been expressed in *Hedley Byrne v Heller* (1963). They said that, where the loss suffered by the victim was purely economic, it would be possible to bring an action where the professional had given negligent advice or made negligent statements, but also extended this to the general principle that the provider of professional services could be liable for pure economic loss where his skills were being relied upon.

Solicitors play a very important part in modern life. Their clients are nearly always very concerned about the quality of work done because something important is at stake. People go to a solicitor often in circumstances where there is understandable intense concern – they might be facing a serious charge, a conviction for which would entail a long prison sentence, or lose their driving licence, or be in the throes of a divorce, or a neighbour dispute, or struggling with a commercial business problem. Even where the outcome of a legal event or transaction is good for the client – where he is buying a house or a flat, or a business – there is often heightened anxiety that everything goes as smoothly as possible. Solicitors need to make sure that, like other professions, if there are any bad practitioners among them, the consequential problems are dealt with as quickly and effectively as possible for the good of the legal profession at large. There is some evidence that this is not happening.

In 2006, The Law Society faced an unprecedented fine of up to £1 million after a legal ombudsman delivered a scathing attack on its handling of complaints from the public. The Society was accused of being too quick to 'rely on its budget and resources' to improve complaints handling, rather than looking at how it can be more efficient (F Gibb, *The Times*, 4 April 2006). The criticisms, from Zahida Manzoor, the Legal Services Complaints Commissioner, also castigated the society for failing to take appropriate action to make sure that people's complaints are handled speedily and efficiently. The society spent £19.3 million during the previous year on handling complaints over poor service, delays and lack of communication by solicitors. In 2008 the Legal Services Complaints Commissioner imposed a £275,000 fine on The Law Society for the inadequacies of its complaints handling plan for 2008/09, although The Law Society felt this was inappropriate as its performance had improved (D Hudson, 'An A-Grade Service' (2008) NLJ 833). See also 13.6.7 below. The Office of the Legal Services Complaints Commissioner ceased on 31 March 2010 when the Legal Services Board became fully operational.

13.3.3 THE INSTITUTE OF LEGAL EXECUTIVES

The Institute of Legal Executives (ILEX) represents over 10,000 legal executives employed in solicitors' offices. They are legally trained (the Institute runs its own examinations) and carry out much of the routine legal work that is a feature of most practices. The Institute was founded in 1892 and incorporated in 1963 with the support of The Law Society. The Managing Clerks' Association, from which ILEX developed, recognised that many non-solicitor staff employed in fee-earning work, and in the management of firms, needed and wanted a training route that would improve standards and award recognition for knowledge and skills. The education and training facilities ILEX offers have developed in number and diversity so that ILEX is able to provide a route to a career in law, which is open to all.

Legal executives are, in the phrase of the ILEX website (www.ilex.org.uk), qualified lawyers specialising in a particular area of law. They will have passed the ILEX Professional Qualification in Law in an area of legal practice to the same level as that required of solicitors. They will have at least five years' experience of working under the supervision of a solicitor in legal practice or the legal department of a private company or local or national government. Fellows are issued with an annual practising certificate, and only Fellows of ILEX may describe themselves as 'Legal Executives'. Specialising in a particular area of law, their day-to-day work is similar to that of a solicitor.

Legal executives might: handle the legal aspects of a property transfer; assist in the formation of a company; be involved in actions in the High Court or county courts; draft wills; advise clients accused of serious or petty crime, families with matrimonial problems and many other matters affecting people in their domestic and business affairs. Legal executives are fee earners – in private practice their work is charged directly to clients – making a direct contribution to the income of a law firm. This is an important difference between legal executives and other types of legal support staff who tend to handle work of a more routine nature. In March 2000, six legal executives qualified to become the first legal executive advocates under the CLSA 1990. The advocacy certificates were approved by the ILEX Rights of Audience Committee. The advocates now have extended rights of audience in civil and matrimonial proceedings in the county courts and magistrates' courts. In some circumstances, Fellows of ILEX can instruct barristers directly. BarDIRECT (the Bar Council's scheme by which barristers can be directly instructed by some professional and voluntary organisations, rather than by solicitors) enables legal executives to access a wide choice of legal advice and representation for their clients and their employers. In December 2010 the first member of ILEX was appointed a deputy district judge (*Law Society Gazette*, 27 January 2011).

13.4 BARRISTERS

The barrister is often thought of as primarily a court advocate, although many spend more time on drafting, pleadings (now called statements of case) and writing advice for solicitors. Professional barristers are technically competent to perform all advocacy for the prosecution or defence in criminal cases, and for a claimant or defendant in a civil claim. More generally, however, established barristers tend to specialise in particular areas of work. Over 60 per cent of practising barristers work in London.

The Bar had been organised as an association of the members of the Inns of Court by the fourteenth century. Today, there are four Inns of Court (Inner and Middle Temples, Lincoln's Inn and Gray's Inn), although there were originally more, including Inns of Chancery and Sergeants' Inns, the latter being an association of the king's most senior lawyers. Until the CLSA 1990, the barrister had a virtual monopoly on advocacy in all the superior courts (in some cases solicitors could act as advocates in the Crown Court). In most situations, they cannot deal direct with clients but must be engaged by solicitors (but see below at 13.6.2).

13.4.1 TRAINING

Entry to the Bar is now restricted to graduates and mature students. An aspirant barrister must register with one of the four Inns of Court in London. Commonly, a barrister will have a law degree and then undertake professional training (the Bar Practice Training Course (BPTC) formerly known as the Bar Vocation Course) for one year leading to the Bar Examinations. Alternatively, a non-law graduate can study for the Common Professional Examination for one year and, if successful in the examinations, proceed to the Bar Examinations. The Bar Standards Board is imposing an aptitude test from autumn 2012, subject to LSB approval, prior to a student undertaking the BPTC (see 13.3.1). The successful student is then called to the Bar by his or her Inn of Court. It is also a requirement of being called that, during study for the vocational course, the student attends his or her Inn to become familiar with the customs of the Bar. The student then undertakes a pupillage, essentially an apprenticeship to a junior counsel. Note that all barristers, however senior in years and experience, are still 'junior counsel' unless they have 'taken silk' and become Queen's Counsel (QCs). Barristers who do not intend to practise do not have to complete the pupillage.

13.4.2 THE INNS OF COURT

The Inns of Court are administered by their senior members (QCs and judges) who are called Benchers. The Inns administer the dining system and are responsible for calling the students to the Bar.

13.4.3 THE GENERAL COUNCIL OF THE BAR

The General Council of the Bar of England and Wales and of the Inns of Court (the Bar Council) is the profession's governing body. It is run by elected officials. It is responsible for the Bar's Code of Conduct, disciplinary matters and representing the interests of the Bar to external bodies like the Lord Chancellor's Department, the government and The Law Society. According to its own literature, this Council:

> ... fulfils the function of what might be called a 'trade union', pursuing the interests of the Bar and expanding the market for the Bar's services and is also a watchdog regulating its practices and activities.

13.4.4 EDUCATION

The Bar Standards Board (BSB) was established in January 2006 as a result of the Bar Council separating its regulatory and representative functions. That separation was to ensure that there was no conflict of interest between the people whose function was to represent the professional interests of barristers (as trade unions represent the interests of their members), and the people whose function is to regulate standards on behalf of the public and clients. As the independent regulatory board of the Bar Council, the BSB is responsible for regulating barristers called to the Bar in England and Wales. It takes decisions independently and in the public interest, and is not prejudiced by the Bar Council's representative function. The purpose of the BSB is 'to promote and maintain excellence in the quality of legal services provided by barristers to support the rule of law'. It does that by setting standards of entry to the profession and by ensuring that professional practice puts consumers first.

13.4.5 QUEEN'S COUNSEL

Queen's Counsel (QCs) are senior barristers of special merit. In 2010, the Bar had 1,397 QCs in practice, the status being conferred on about 45 barristers each year. They are given this status (known as 'taking silk' because a part of the robe they are entitled to wear is silk) by the Queen on the advice of the Lord Chancellor. There were, until the suspension of the system in 2003, annual invitations from the Lord Chancellor for barristers to apply for this title. Applicants needed to show at least 10 years of successful practice at the Bar. However, under arrangements announced recently a new independent selection procedure has replaced the widely criticised, former system, which relied on secret soundings among senior legal figures. Candidates will be chosen by the Lord Chancellor on the recommendation of an independent panel set up by The Law Society and the Bar Council. If appointed, the barrister will become known as a 'Leader' and he or she will often appear in cases with a junior. The old 'Two Counsel Rule', under which a QC always had to appear with a junior counsel, whether one was really required or not, was abolished in 1977. He or she will be restricted to high level work (of which there is less available in some types of practice) so appointment can be financially difficult but, in most cases, it has good results for the QC as he or she will be able to considerably increase fee levels. The first report by Sir Colin Campbell, First Commissioner of the Commission for Judicial Appointments, published at the end of 2002, revealed serious deficiencies in the previous system of appointment. The report upheld four complaints against the Lord Chancellor's Department and invited the Lord Chancellor (who is a member of the Cabinet, and thus could be seen as 'political') to reconsider his role in the appointments system. However, only 10 individuals made formal complaints from well over 3,000 unsuccessful applicants for judicial posts or for 'silk' (QC). Complaints were upheld on behalf of four people and rejected for two others. The four complaints were upheld on the basis of procedural and administrative failings, but did not go to the merits of any particular substantive decision. There are now almost 5,500 solicitor-advocates (*Law Society Gazette*, 10 March 2011) with more than 1,000 based in London. The number of solicitor-advocate QCs remains very low. The guidance of the new competition requires the comments of consultees on candidates to be supported by detailed reasons and to be based on recent experience. In addition, the 'sift panel' will include an independent assessor. In 2002, for the first time, the names of 55 commercial law firms who were consulted by the LCD about the suitability of applicants for silk were released. This sort of consultation has been used since

1999. There are, though, calls for even wider consultation of law firms, and even calls for all solicitors to be consulted (see *The Gazette*, 10 October 2002, p 29).

13.4.6 THE BARRISTER'S CHAMBERS

Barristers were not permitted to form partnerships (except with lawyers from other countries) until April 2010 when the Bar announced new rules following the LSA 2007; they work in sets of offices called chambers. Most chambers are run by barristers' clerks who act as business managers, allocating work to the various barristers and negotiating their fees. Imagine the situation where a solicitor wishes to engage a particular barrister for a case on a certain date and that barrister is already booked to be in another court three days before that date. The clerk cannot be sure whether the first case will have ended in time for the barrister to be free to appear in the second case. The first case might be adjourned after a day or, through unexpected evidential arguments in the early stages in the trial, it might last for four days. If the barrister is detained, then his brief for the second case will have to be passed to another barrister in his chambers very close to the actual trial. This is known as a late brief. Who will be asked to take the brief and at what point is a matter for the clerk. The role of the barrister's clerk is thus a most influential one. Since 2003, lay clients have been able to enjoy direct access to barristers: see www.barcouncil.org.uk, under 'BarDIRECT'. It is currently possible for barristers to accept instructions from some licensed organisations as opposed to the normal practice of being briefed by solicitors.

13.5   PROFESSIONAL ETIQUETTE

The CLSA 1990 introduced a statutory committee, the Lord Chancellor's Advisory Committee on Legal Education and Conduct (ACLEC), which, until recently, had responsibilities in the regulation of both branches of the profession.

As part of the government's reforms of legal services generally, and publicly funded legal advice specifically, the Access to Justice Act 1999 (s 35) has replaced the ACLEC (considered by some as slow and ponderous) with the Legal Services Consultative Panel, launched at the beginning of 2000. The Consultative Panel has: (a) the duty of assisting in the maintenance and development of standards in the education, training and conduct of persons offering legal services and, where appropriate, making recommendations to the Lord Chancellor; and (b) the duty of providing to the Lord Chancellor, at his request, advice about particular matters relating to any aspect of the provision of legal services (including the education, training and conduct of persons offering legal services).

The Law Society (through the Solicitors Regulation Authority) and the Bar Council (through the Bar Standards Board) exercise tight control over the professional conduct of their members. Barristers can only meet the client when the solicitor or his or her representative is present. This is supposed to promote the barrister's detachment from the client and his or her case, and thus lend greater objectivity to counsel's judgment. However, since April 2010 the Bar has relaxed the rules on the work a barrister can undertake (see 13.1). Barristers and solicitors must dress formally for court appearances, although solicitors, when appearing in the Crown, county or High Court, are required to wear robes but not wigs. A barrister not wearing a wig and robe cannot be 'seen' or 'heard' by the judge.

Traditionally, lawyers were not permitted to advertise their services, although this area has been subject to some deregulation in the light of recent trends to expose the provision of legal services to ordinary market forces. Solicitors can, subject to some regulations, advertise their services in print and on broadcast media.

13.5.1 IMMUNITY FROM NEGLIGENCE CLAIMS

Until recently barristers could not be sued by their clients for negligent performance in court or for work that was preparatory to court work (*Rondel v Worsley* (1969)); this immunity had also been extended to solicitors who act as advocates (*Saif Ali v Sidney Mitchell* (1980)). The client of the other side, however, may sue for breach of duty (*Kelly v London Transport Executive* (1982)). This was changed in a major case in 2000.

Advocates' Liability
Arthur JS Hall and Co v Simons and Other Appeals (2000)

Background

Lawyers are, for the general public, the most central and prominent part of the English legal system. They are, arguably, to the legal system what doctors are to the health system. For many decades, a debate had grown about why a patient injured by the negligence of a surgeon in the operating theatre could sue for damages, whereas a litigant whose case was lost because of the negligence of his advocate could not sue. It all seemed very unfair. Even the most glaringly obvious courtroom negligence was protected against legal action by a special advocates' immunity. The claim that this protection was made by lawyers (and judges who were lawyers) for lawyers was difficult to refute. In this House of Lords' decision, the historic immunity was abolished in respect of both barristers and solicitor-advocates (of whom there are now over 1,787 with higher courts rights of audience), and for both civil and criminal proceedings.

Facts

In three cases, all conjoined on appeal, a claimant raised a claim of negligence against a firm of solicitors, and in each case, the firms relied on the immunity attaching to barristers and other advocates from claims in negligence. At first instance, all the claims were struck out. Then, on appeal, the Court of Appeal said that the claims could have proceeded. The solicitors appealed to the Lords and two key questions were raised: should the old immunity rule be maintained and, in a criminal case, what was the proper scope of the principle against 'collateral attack'? A 'collateral attack' is when someone convicted in a criminal court tries to invalidate that conviction outside the criminal appeals process by suing his trial defence lawyer in a civil court. The purpose of such a 'collateral attack' is to win in the civil case, proving negligence against the criminal trial lawyer, and thus by implication showing that the conviction in the criminal case was unfair.

Held

The House of Lords held (Lords Hope, Hutton and Hobhouse dissenting in part) that, in the light of modern conditions, it was now clear that it was no longer in the public interest in the administration of justice that advocates should have immunity from suit for negligence for acts concerned with the conduct of either civil or criminal litigation.

Lord Hoffmann (with Lords Steyn, Browne-Wilkinson and Millett delivering concurring opinions) said that over 30 years had passed since the House had last considered the rationale for the immunity of the advocate from suit in *Rondel v Worsley*. Public policy was not immutable and there had been great changes in the law of negligence, the functioning of the legal profession, the administration of justice and public perceptions. It was once again time to re-examine the whole matter. Interestingly, Lord Hoffmann chose to formulate his opinion in a creative mode to reflect public policy, rather than in the tradition of what can be seen as slavish obedience to the details of precedent:

> I hope that I will not be thought ungrateful if I do not encumber this speech with citations. The question of what the public interest now requires depends upon the strength of the arguments rather than the weight of authority.

The point of departure was that, in general, English law provided a remedy in damages for a person who had suffered injury as a result of professional negligence. It followed that any exception that denied such a remedy required a sound justification. The arguments relied on by the court in *Rondel v Worsley* as justifying the immunity had to be considered. One by one, these arguments are evaluated and rejected.

Advocate's Divided Loyalty

There were two distinct versions of the divided loyalty argument. The first was that the possibility of being sued for negligence would actually inhibit the lawyer, consciously or unconsciously, from giving his duty to the court priority over his duty to his client. The second was that the divided loyalty was a special factor that made the conduct of litigation a very difficult art and could lead to the advocate being exposed to vexatious claims by difficult clients. The argument was pressed most strongly in connection with advocacy in criminal proceedings, where the clients were said to be more than usually likely to be vexatious.

There had been recent developments in the civil justice system designed to reduce the incidence of vexatious litigation. The first was r 24.2 of the Civil Procedure Rules, which provided that a court could give summary judgment in favour of a defendant if it considered that 'the claimant had no real prospect of succeeding on the claim'. The second was the changes to the funding of civil litigation introduced by the Access to Justice Act 1999, which would make it much more difficult than it had been in the past to obtain legal help for negligence claims that had little prospect of success.

There was no doubt that the advocate's duty to the court was extremely important in the English justice system. The question was whether removing the immunity would have a significantly adverse effect. If the possibility of being held liable in negligence was calculated to have an adverse effect on the behaviour of advocates in court, one might have expected that to have followed, at least to some degree, from the introduction of wasted costs orders (where a court disallows a lawyer from being able to claim part of a fee for work that is regarded as unnecessary and wasteful). Although the liability of a negligent advocate to a wasted costs order was not the same as a liability to pay general damages, the experience of the wasted costs jurisdiction was the only empirical evidence available in England to test the proposition that such liability would have an adverse effect upon the way advocates performed their duty to the court, and there was no suggestion that it had changed standards of advocacy for the worse.

The 'cab rank'

The 'cab rank' rule provided that a barrister could not refuse to act for a client on the ground that he disapproved of him or his case. The argument was that a barrister who was obliged to accept any client would be unfairly exposed to vexatious claims by clients for whom any sensible lawyer with freedom of action would have refused to act. Such a claim was, however, in the nature of things intuitive, incapable of empirical verification and did not have any real substance. This rule has been modified by the Bar Standards Board (*Law Society Gazette*, 2 August 2012). A barrister can now refuse to act when work is offered by firms on the List of Defaulting Solicitors.

The Witness Analogy

The argument started from the well-established rule that a witness was absolutely immune from liability for anything that he said in court. So were the judge, counsel and the parties. They could not be sued for libel, malicious falsehood or conspiring to give false evidence. The policy of the rule was to encourage persons who took part in court proceedings to express themselves freely. However, a witness owed no duty of care to anyone in respect of the evidence he gave to the court. His only duty was to tell the truth. There was no analogy with the position of a lawyer who owed a duty of care to his client. The fact that the advocate was the only person involved in the trial process who was liable to be sued for negligence was because he was the only person who had undertaken such a duty of care to his client.

Collateral Attack

The most substantial argument was that it might be contrary to the public interest for a court to retry a case which had been decided by another court. However, claims for negligence against lawyers were not the only cases that gave rise to a possibility of the same issue being tried twice. The law had to deal with the problem in numerous other contexts. So, before examining the strength of the collateral challenge argument as a reason for maintaining the immunity of lawyers, it was necessary to consider how the law dealt with collateral challenge in general.

The law discouraged re-litigation of the same issues except by means of an appeal. The Latin maxims often quoted were *nemo debet bis vexari pro una et eadem causa* and *interest rei publicae ut finis sit litium*. The first was concerned with the interests of the defendant: a person should not be troubled twice for the same reason. That policy had generated the rules that prevented re-litigation when the parties were the same: *autrefois acquit* (someone acquitted of a crime cannot be tried again for that crime); *res judicata* (a particular dispute decided by a civil court cannot be re-tried); and issue estoppel (a person cannot deny the fact of a judgment previously decided against him).

The second policy was wider: it was concerned with the interests of the State. There was a general public interest in the same issue not being litigated over again. The second policy could be used to justify the extension of the rules of issue estoppel to cases in which the parties were not the same, but the circumstances were such as to bring the case within the spirit of the rules. Criminal proceedings were in a special category, because although they were technically litigation between the Crown and the defendant, the Crown prosecuted on behalf of society as a whole. So, a conviction had some of the quality of a judgment *in rem*, which should be binding in favour of everyone.

Not all re-litigation of the same issue, however, would be manifestly unfair to a party or bring the administration of justice into disrepute. Sometimes there were valid reasons for rehearing a dispute. It was therefore unnecessary to try to stop any re-litigation by forbidding anyone from suing their lawyer. It was 'burning down the house to roast the pig; using a broad-spectrum remedy without side effects could handle the problem equally well'.

The scope for re-examination of issues in criminal proceedings was much wider than in civil cases. Fresh evidence was more readily admitted. A conviction could be set aside as unsafe and unsatisfactory when the accused appeared to have been prejudiced by 'flagrantly incompetent advocacy': see *R v Clinton* (1993). After conviction, the case could be referred to the Court of Appeal if the conviction was on indictment, or to the Crown Court, if the trial was summary, by the Criminal Cases Review Commission.

It followed that it would ordinarily be an abuse of process for a civil court to be asked to decide that a subsisting conviction was wrong. That applied to a conviction on a plea of guilty as well as after a trial. The resulting conflict of judgments was likely to bring the administration of justice into disrepute. The proper procedure was to appeal, or if the right of appeal had been exhausted, to apply to the Criminal Cases Review Commission. It would ordinarily be an abuse, because there were bound to be exceptional cases in which the issue could be tried without a risk that the conflict of judgments would bring the administration of justice into disrepute.

Once the conviction has been set aside, there could be no public policy objection to a claim for negligence against the legal advisers. There could be no conflict of judgments. On the other hand, in civil, including matrimonial, cases, it would seldom be possible to say that a claim for negligence against a legal adviser or representative would bring the administration of justice into dispute. Whether the original decision was right or wrong was usually a matter of concern only to the parties and had no wider implications. There was no public interest objection to a subsequent finding that, but for the negligence of his lawyers, the losing party would have won.

But again, there might be exceptions. The claim for negligence might be an abuse of process on the ground that it was manifestly unfair to someone else. Take, for example, the case of a defendant who published a serious defamation that he attempted unsuccessfully to justify. Should he be able to sue his lawyers and claim that if the case had been conducted differently, the allegation would have been proved to be true? It seemed unfair to the claimant in the defamation claim that any court should be allowed to come to such a conclusion in proceedings to which he was not a party. On the other hand, it was equally unfair that he should have to join as a party and rebut the allegation for a second time. A man's reputation was not only a matter between him and the other party; it represented his relationship with the world. So, it might be that in such circumstances, a claim for negligence would be an abuse of the process of the court.

Having regard to the power of the court to strike out claims that had no real prospect of success, the doctrine was unlikely in that context to be invoked very often. The first step in any application to strike out a claim alleging negligence in the conduct of a previous action had to be to ask whether it had a real prospect of success.

Lords Hope, Hutton and Hobhouse delivered judgments in which they agreed that the immunity from suit was no longer required in relation to civil proceedings, but dissented to the extent of saying that the immunity was still required in the public interest in the administration of justice in relation to criminal proceedings.

Comment

This decision is of major and historic importance in the English legal system for several reasons. It can be seen as a bold attempt by the senior judiciary to drag the legal profession (often a metonymy for the whole legal system) into the twenty-first century world of accountability and fair business practice. In his judgment, Lord Steyn makes this dramatic observation (*Arthur JS Hall & Co v Simons* [2000] 3 All ER 673 at 684):

> ... public confidence in the legal system is not enhanced by the existence of the immunity. The appearance is created that the law singles out its own for protection no matter how flagrant the breach of the barrister. The world has changed since 1967. The practice of law has become more commercialised: barristers may now advertise. They may now enter into contracts for legal services with their professional clients. They are now obliged to carry insurance. On the other hand, today we live in a consumerist society in which people have a much greater awareness of their rights. If they have suffered a wrong as the result of the provision of negligent professional services, they expect to have the right to claim redress. It tends to erode confidence in the legal system if advocates, alone among professional men, are immune from liability for negligence.

The case raises and explores many key issues of the legal system, including: the proper relationship between lawyers and the courts; the proper relationship between lawyers and clients; the differences between criminal and civil actions; professional ethics; the nature of dispute resolution and the circumstances under which the courts should make new law. Above all, however, the case has one simple significance: 'it will', in the words of Jonathan Hirst QC, a former Chairman of the Bar Council, 'mean that a claimant who can prove loss, as the result of an advocate's negligence, will no longer be prevented from making a claim. We cannot really say that is wrong' ((2000) *Bar News*, August, p 3).

13.6   THE COURTS AND LEGAL SERVICES ACT 1990

Both branches of the legal profession have traditionally enjoyed monopolies in the provision of certain legal services (for example, advocacy was reserved almost exclusively to barristers, while conveyancing was reserved to solicitors). In the 1980s, Lord Mackay, the then Lord Chancellor, argued that these monopolies did not best serve the users of legal services as they entailed unnecessarily limited choice and artificially high prices. The CLSA 1990 was introduced to reform the provision of legal services along such lines. Today, many of the old monopolies have been broken. Thus, we have solicitor-advocates and non-solicitor licensed conveyancers.

In 1990 in the CLSA, the government broke the solicitors' conveyancing monopoly by allowing licensed conveyancers to practise. There was initially evidence that this increased competition resulted in benefits to the consumer. From 1985, The Law Society had permitted solicitors to sell property, like estate agents, so as to promote 'one-stop' conveyancing. The Consumers' Association estimated that solicitors' conveyancing prices fell by a margin of 25–33 per cent before licensed conveyancers actually began to practise.

Under the CLSA 1990, apart from allowing the Bar Council and The Law Society to grant members rights of audience as before, The Law Society is able to seek to widen the category of those who have such rights. Applications are made to the Lord Chancellor, who refers the matter to his Advisory Committee. If the Committee favours the application, it must also be approved by four senior judges (including the Master of the Rolls and the Lord Chief Justice), each of whom can exercise a veto. The Director General of the Office of Fair Trading must also be consulted by the Lord Chancellor. All those who consider applications for extended rights of audience or the right to conduct litigation must act in accordance with the 'general principle' in s 17.

13.6.1 SECTION 17

The principle in s 17 states that the question of whether a person should be granted a right of audience or to conduct litigation is to be determined only by reference to the following four questions:

- Is the applicant properly qualified in accordance with the educational and training requirements appropriate to the court or proceedings?

- Are applicants members of a professional or other body with proper and enforced rules of conduct?

- Do such rules have the necessary equivalent of the Bar's 'cab rank rule', that is, satisfactory provision requiring its members not to withhold their services: on the ground that the nature of the case is objectionable to them or any section of the public; on the ground that the conduct, opinions or beliefs of the prospective client are unacceptable to them or to any section of the public; on any ground relating to the prospective client's source of financial support (for example, public funding)?

●   Are the body's rules of conduct 'appropriate in the interests of the proper and efficient administration of justice'?

Subject to the above, those who consider applications must also abide by s 17's 'statutory objective' of 'new and better ways of providing such services and a wider choice of persons providing them, while maintaining the proper and efficient administration of justice'.

Successful applications were made by The Law Society, the Head of the Government Legal Service and the Director of Public Prosecutions (DPP). The Advisory Committee, while rejecting the idea of an automatic extension of solicitors' rights of audience upon qualification (for example, guilty plea cases in Crown Courts), accepted the principle that they should qualify for enlarged rights after a course of advocacy training. Non-lawyers can also apply for rights of audience in the courts: the Chartered Institute of Patent Agents successfully applied for rights to conduct litigation in the High Court. Under s 12 of the CLSA 1990, the Lord Chancellor will use his power to enable lay representatives to be used in cases involving debt and housing matters in small claims procedures. Similarly, under ss 28 and 29 of the CLSA 1990, the right to conduct litigation is thrown open to members of any body that can persuade the Advisory Committee, the Lord Chancellor and the four senior judges that its application should be granted as the criteria set out in s 17 (above) are satisfied.

The historic monopoly of barristers to appear for clients in the higher courts was formally ended in 1994 when the Lord Chancellor approved The Law Society's proposals on how to certify its members in private practice as competent advocates. The innovation is likely to generate significant change in the delivery of legal services, especially in the fields of commercial and criminal cases. The prospective battle between solicitors and barristers for advocacy work can be simply characterised.

13.6.2 SOLICITORS' RIGHTS OF AUDIENCE

There are now almost 5,500 solicitors qualified as solicitor-advocates with rights to practise advocacy in some or most levels of the court structure (*Law Society Gazette*, 10 March 2011. This development began with changes in the 1990s. In February 1997, the Lord Chancellor, Lord Mackay, and the four designated judges (Lord Bingham, Lord Woolf, Sir Stephen Brown and Sir Richard Scott; see s 17 of the CLSA 1990) approved The Law Society's application for rights of audience in the higher courts for employed solicitors, but subject to certain restrictions.

Lord Phillips, the Lord Chief Justice, has put forward proposals that will allow solicitor-advocates to have the same dress code as barristers. The new reforms came into effect in 2008. Solicitor-advocates finally put on wigs in court (*Law Society Gazette*, 10 January 2008). Solicitor-advocates in criminal cases will be allowed to wear wigs, wing collars and bands. They can also wear stuff gowns. However, in civil and family proceedings the wigs and other regalia will no longer be worn. The dress code for judges was changed in 2008. The judge's robe, designed by Betty Jackson, received mixed reactions when it was unveiled in May 2008 ('Thumbs down for designer robe', *The Times*, 15 May 2008).

Under The Law Society's 1998 regulations approved by the Lord Chancellor's Department, some solicitors (those who are also barristers or part-time judges) are granted exemption from the new tests of qualification for advocacy. Others need to apply for the grant of higher courts qualifications, either in civil proceedings, criminal proceedings or in both. A holder of the higher courts (criminal proceedings) qualification has rights of audience in the Crown Court in all proceedings (including its civil jurisdiction) and in other courts in all criminal proceedings. A holder of the higher courts (civil proceedings) qualification may appear in the High Court in all proceedings and in other courts in all civil proceedings. On 1 April 2010 new rules came into force to for solicitors seeking higher rights of audience. The rules were amended on 1 September 2010. Qualification for higher rights is as follows:

- **Development route**

    (a) that they have undertaken training, assessment and experience in accordance with regulation 4; or

- **Qualifications gained in another jurisdiction**

    (b) that they may apply for a qualification to exercise rights of audience in all proceedings in the higher courts relying on qualification(s) gained in any comparable jurisdiction or a jurisdiction listed in Article 1 of the EC Parliament and Council Directive 98/5/EC by the Society under regulation 5; or

- **Exemptions under section 31C of the Courts and Legal Services Act 1990**

    (c) with respect to his or her entitlement to exercise a right of audience before a court in proceedings of a particular description, a solicitor or REL who is a person to whom, in respect of that court and that description of proceedings, section 31C of the Courts and Legal Services Act 1990 applies, shall have a higher courts advocacy qualification in respect of that entitlement under regulation 6; or

- **Conversion provision for RELs**

    (d) any REL who is granted a qualification listed in regulation 3.1 shall keep that qualification upon being admitted as a solicitor under regulation 7.

Large city firms of solicitors no longer need to take on small county court work as this experience is no longer required as a prerequisite for higher rights of audience under the new rules. All solicitors seeking these rights of audience have to pass an advocacy assessment based on higher rights of audience competency standards.

One benefit for law firms is that those that offer advocacy training are likely to attract the best graduates. This is a worry for the commercial Bar, as some graduates will see a training contract with an advocacy element as a better option than the less secure Bar pupillage. The Bar is determined that it will not lose any significant ground in the face of this new competition. Its representatives claim that solicitors will not be able to compete with barristers because of their much higher overheads.

From 2000, there have been three routes to qualification: the 'development' route leading to the all proceedings qualification; the 'accreditation' route appropriate for solicitors who have significant experience of the higher civil and/or higher criminal courts; and the 'exemption' route which has existed under both the 1992 and 1998 regulations. The accreditation and exemption routes were phased out in 2005, leaving now only the development route. The development route has three stages: training and assessment in procedure, evidence and ethics in the higher civil and higher criminal courts; training and assessment in advocacy skills; and experience of either civil or criminal proceedings, some of which may take place pre-admission. Trainee solicitors, therefore, can get training and assessment and up to six months' experience behind them during their training contract. However, this new fast track for novice lawyers has left The Law Society open to criticism of lowering standards and allowing inexperienced advocates into the higher courts without the necessary competence. The Law Society, however, recognises the need to maintain standards and believes that its proposals not only maintain standards, but have the capacity to enhance standards through the provision of advocacy services.

Many barristers are very worried about the threat to their traditional work. A potentially significant development is BarDIRECT, a pilot scheme set up in 1999 that enables certain professions and organisations to have direct access to barristers without referral through a solicitor. While this initiative could be one of the keys to the continuing success of the Bar, it is argued that it makes barristers no different from solicitors and could even encroach on the solicitors' market.

13.6.3 THE ACCESS TO JUSTICE ACT 1999 AND RIGHTS OF AUDIENCE

Lawyers' rights of audience before the courts were further addressed in Part III of the Access to Justice Act 1999. It replaces the Lord Chancellor's Advisory Committee on Legal Education and Conduct with a new Legal Services Consultative Panel:

- It provides that, in principle, all lawyers should have full rights of audience before any court, subject only to meeting reasonable training requirements.
- It reforms the procedures for authorising further professional bodies to grant rights of audience or rights to conduct litigation to their members; and for approving changes to professional rules of conduct relating to the exercise of these rights.

The Act also contains sections that:

- simplify procedures for approving changes to rules and the designation of new authorised bodies;
- give the Lord Chancellor power, with the approval of Parliament, to change rules that do not meet the statutory criteria set out in the CLSA 1990 as amended by these sections;
- establish the principle that all barristers and solicitors should enjoy full rights of audience; and
- establish the primacy of an advocate's ethical duties over any other civil law obligations.

The legislation enables employed advocates, including Crown Prosecutors, to appear as advocates in the higher courts if otherwise qualified to do so, regardless of any professional rules designed to prevent their doing so because of their status as employed advocates.

13.6.4 PARTNERSHIPS AND TRANSNATIONAL FIRMS

By virtue of s 66 of the CLSA 1990, solicitors are enabled to form partnerships with non-solicitors (multi-disciplinary partnerships or MDPs), and the section confirms that barristers are not prevented by the common law from forming such relationships. They are, however, prohibited from doing so (unless with a foreign lawyer) by the Bar. Solicitors are able, under s 89 of the CLSA 1990 (Sched 14), to form multinational partnerships (MNPs). The arrival of MNPs over the coming years will raise particular problems concerning the maintenance of ethical standards by the Solicitors' Regulation Authority over foreign lawyers. MDPs also raise potentially serious problems, as even in arrangements between solicitors and others, it will be likely that certain work (for example, the conduct of litigation) would have to be performed by solicitors.

The business organisation called the limited liability partnership (LLP) was introduced by the Limited Liability Partnership Act 2000. The new business form seeks to amalgamate the advantages of the company's corporate form with the flexibility of the partnership form. Although called a 'partnership', the new form is, in fact, a distinct legal entity that enjoys an existence apart from that of its members. The LLP can enter into agreements in its own name, it can own property, sue and be sued. Traditional partnerships by contrast entail liability for the partners as individuals. Although the LLP enjoys corporate status, it is not taxed as a separate entity from its members. Solicitors do not seem to have been keen to adopt these as their preferred form of firm. The growth in their popularity has been steady. In 2002, fewer than 100 from the then 8,300 law firms had become LPPs. Most were formed because of international constraints in mergers, that is, the foreign firm could not merge with the British one unless the British one became an LLP. By 2008, there were over 1,300 firms of solicitors (of 10,000 firms in England and Wales) practising as incorporated bodies, most of which were LLPs, and of those in *The Lawyer* Top 100 firms, only four of the top 25 remained as traditional partnerships (J Whittaker and J Machell, 'Covering all bases' (2008) NLJ 804–5).

Law Firms

Another feature of change is the evidently widening gap between the work and income of the top few hundred commercial firms and the 8,000 smaller high-street firms. A series of mergers has created a few relatively huge law firms, and the merger of an English firm with an American one produced the world's first billion-dollar practice. In 1999, partners at Clifford Chance voted to merge with the United States' Rogers & Wells, and Punders in Germany, to form a firm that now employs over 7,000 people in 30 offices worldwide. It specialises in corporate finance, commercial property, antitrust law and litigation. Keith Clark, senior partner (at the time) at Clifford Chance, explained that the aim of the merger was to create a truly international firm capable of offering an

1. Solicitors
- Often described as the 'general practitioners' of law, which may be misleading today, as solicitors in larger practices often specialise
- Rights of audience now extend to the senior courts, where a higher court advocacy qualification has been obtained
- In return solicitors have lost their monopoly in areas such as conveyancing
- Training involves a law degree (or GDL/CPE), followed by a Legal Practice Course (LPC) and two years as a trainee
- Supervised by the Solicitors' Regulation Authority, solicitors normally work together in partnerships, while complaints relating to maladministration in the legal profession can be made to The Legal Services Ombudsman

2. Barristers
- Often thought of as the 'specialists'; the academic stage of training is normally the same as for solicitors, but barristers complete a Bar Vocational Course (BVC), followed by a year's pupillage
- Barristers join one of the Inns of Court, which are responsible for 'calling' members to the Bar
- Supervised by the General Council of the Bar, barristers have rights of audience in all courts
- Senior barristers of merit may 'take silk', becoming Queen's Counsel (QCs)
- Barristers are normally, but not always, self-employed but share offices known as 'Chambers'

3. Legal Executives
The Institute of Legal Executives (ILEX), which was developed from the Managing Clerks Association, represents Legal Executives, who carry out the more routine legal work. Qualified lawyers, such practitioners will be specialists in a particular area of law and now have limited rights of audience in lower courts

THE LEGAL PROFESSION

4. Fusion of the Professions: The ELS is one of only three systems in the world that maintain a divided legal profession. Despite criticism of the present system, the legal professions have argued that fusion would lead to a fall in the quality of advocacy. It has, however, been claimed that there has been 'fusion by the backdoor', as the CLSA 1990 and the AJA 1999 have removed solicitors' monopolies over certain tasks such as conveyancing, as well as barristers' monopoly over advocacy in the senior courts

FIGURE 13.1 *A Breakdown of the Different Legal Professions.*

integrated legal service to an increasingly global business community. He has said, 'Clients don't want all the time delays and inefficiencies of dealing with half a dozen legal firms around the world. What they want is one firm which has the capacity to be a one-stop shop for all their corporate needs' (*The Times*, 12 July 1999). By 2006, the firm employed 3,200 lawyers and had 570 partners. In 2008, Clifford Chance retained its position as the world's largest law firm after announcing revenue of £1.33 billion for the previous financial year. Turnover at the firm rose 11 per cent in the year ended 30 April 2008. Its profit also jumped, with equity partners earning an average of £1.15 million, up 13 per cent on 2007 (Alex Spence and Michael Herman, 'Clifford Chance makes record £1.3bn as credit crunch provides more legal work', *The Times*, 30 May 2008). However, in 2009 the firm dropped to third position as revenue declined to £1.26 billion and average profit per equity partner (PEP) to £733,000 (The Lawyer.com UK 200 Annual Report 2009). The firm regained its top position in 2010 and maintained it in 2011 and 2012. The firm's turnover in 2012 was £1.303 billion and PEP £1,303,000. (*The Lawyer*, 3 July 2012). Whilst Clifford Chance remains the UK's largest firm, it has been overtaken globally by Baker & McKenzie, who reported a turnover for the year ended 30 June 2012 of $2.3bn, or £1.46bn (The Lawyer.com, 28 August 2012).

The trend of firms merging has continued. In 2008, it was found in one piece of research that more than 100 firms would be expecting to merge through merger or acquisition in the following year. The study found that 68 per cent of firms surveyed had talked about a merger with another firm in the previous year ((2008) NLJ 909).

13.6.5 EMPLOYED SOLICITORS

This is the fastest growing area of practice with more than one-fifth of those holding a practising certificate working outside private practice. Employed solicitors are professionals who work for salaries as part of a commercial firm, private or public enterprise, charity or organisation, as opposed to solicitors in private practice who take instructions from various clients. As Janet Paraskeva, The Law Society's Chief Executive, notes: 'In-house lawyers can provide cost-effective legal advice, and have an increasingly important role in corporate governance. [They] often act as co-ordinators for the outsourcing of legal work and become involved with public affairs, risk management and general business analysis' (*The Gazette*, 20 February 2003). In the decade 1994–2004, the numbers of employed solicitors grew from 10,910 to 21,678 – a 99 per cent increase. In fact, the number of solicitors working in the employed sector is likely to be much higher because the figures come from The Law Society list of those with practising certificates but, because of their employed status, many lawyers are not required to have such a certificate. In-house solicitors often enjoy more flexible working terms than their private practice counterparts, so it is probably no accident that 49.2 per cent of solicitors holding practising certificates in commerce and industry are women, while only 39.4 per cent of practising certificate holders in private practice are women (Law Society, *Key Facts 2006: The Solicitors' Profession*).

13.6.6 MONOPOLY CONVEYANCING RIGHTS

Historically, barristers, solicitors, certified notaries and licensed conveyancers enjoyed statutory monopolies, making it an offence for any other persons to draw up or prepare documents connected with the transfer of title to property for payment. The CLSA 1990 broke this monopoly by allowing any person or body not currently authorised to provide conveyancing services to make an application to the Authorised Conveyancing Practitioners' Board (established by s 34) for authorisation under s 37. The Board must be satisfied, before granting authorisation, that the applicant's business is, and will be, carried on by fit and proper persons, and must believe that the applicant will establish or participate in the systems for the protection of the client specified in s 37(7) including, for example, adequate professional indemnity cover and regulations made under s 40 concerning competence and conduct. Banks and building societies were in a privileged position (s 37(8)), since they were already regulated by statute. These institutions did not initially appear enthusiastic to compete with solicitors by establishing in-house lawyers. They have preferred instead to use panels of local practitioners.

The solicitors' monopoly on the grant of probate has also been abolished. Under ss 54–55 of the CLSA 1990, probate services were opened up to be available from approved bodies of non-lawyers. Grant of probate is the legal proof that a will is valid, which is needed for a person to put the will into effect. New probate practitioners directly compete with solicitors for probate work. The grant of probate is only a small part of the probate process, but when it was restricted as business that only a solicitor could perform, it effectively prevented others, except some banks, from being involved in probate. The banks seem best placed to take up work in this area as they already have trustee and executor departments. Like the slow take-up to do conveyancing work (there are still only relatively few commercial licensed conveyancers handling among them about 5 per cent of all conveyancing), enthusiasm to break into the probate business has been hard to detect.

In its Green Papers published in 1989, the government stated that the means it favoured to produce the most efficient and effective provision of legal services would be 'the discipline of the market'. This technique, however, has not been without its problems. There was not a rush to use the conveyancing services of solicitors who had made their prices very competitive in the wake of competition from licensed conveyancers. In one survey, The Law Society found that only 8 per cent of clients had opted for cheaper services (*The Lawyer*, 12 October 1993). More worrying is the allegation that a significant number of those offering 'cut-price' conveyancing are not producing a respectable quality of service. Tony Holland, a former president of The Law Society, argued that this is a result of a rush of inadequately trained persons to make money from that part of solicitors' erstwhile monopoly, which has been thrown open to non-lawyers ((1994) 144 NLJ 192). He noted, however, that at the time of writing the article he was engaged in giving expert testimony in no fewer than 19 actions for negligence arising from incompetent conveyancing.

Nevertheless, research published by the Department of the Environment, Transport and the Regions showed that conveyancing in England and Wales was the cheapest of the 10 European countries surveyed, even though it was the slowest. It takes an average of six to eight weeks for a contract to be exchanged in England and Wales, while in the United States and South Africa the average is a week. Even so, while the legal fee for conveyancing on a £60,000 house in England and Wales is about £1,500, the same service in France costs about £3,600 and in Portugal, it is about £6,000 (see News in Brief, 'Cheap conveyancing' (1998) 148 NLJ 8). The Lord Chancellor's Department's 2002 Consultation Paper on legal services, *In the Public Interest*, suggested that the introduction of the licensed conveyancer system has not worked well because licensed conveyancers are handling only 5 per cent of conveyancing services. The system has not, therefore, succeeded in providing real competition. There is a growing concentration of conveyancing into a small number of polarised firms (see, for example, NS Cobb (2002) 152 NLJ 1340) according to some observers of conveyancing.

13.6.7 THE LEGAL OMBUDSMAN

The post of Legal Services Complaints Commissioner (commonly known as Ombudsman (Legal Services Ombudsman)) was created in 1990 by s 21 of the CLSA 1990 and covered England and Wales. The Act provided that the LSO must not be a lawyer. The Access to Justice Act 1999 gave the LSO powers to make orders rather than recommendations requiring the legal professional bodies and individual practitioners to pay appropriate compensation to complainants.

The Legal Ombudsman (LO), replacing the previous LSO, was established by the Office for Legal Complaints (OLC) under the Legal Services Act 2007. It began accepting complaints in October 2010. The LO claims to be an independent, consumer-focused ombudsman scheme set up to resolve complaints about lawyers in England and Wales. It provides a free service to all members of the public, very small businesses, charities, clubs and trusts.

It deals with complaints about the following types of lawyers (and generally those working for them):

- barristers;
- solicitors;
- law costs draftsmen;
- legal executives;
- licensed conveyancers;
- notaries;
- patent attorneys;
- probate practitioners;
- registered European lawyers;
- trademark attorneys;

and deals with complaints relating to:

- buying and selling a house or property;
- family law such as divorce;
- wills;
- personal injury;
- intellectual property;
- criminal law;
- civil litigation;
- immigration;
- employment issues.

If the LO decides the service received by the complainant was unsatisfactory, it can require the lawyer to put it right. Although most complaints can be resolved informally, it is empowered to carry out a formal investigation.

The main area of debate on this theme is the best approach to supplying the highest number and widest range of people with legal services appropriate to what citizens need. How can the legal profession become more user-friendly? Have the changes made under the CLSA 1990 to increase competition in the provision of legal services been successful? Have the restrictive professional monopolies been properly broken and, if so, will the quality of services offered by non-lawyers (for example, conveyancing, probate, litigation) be reduced? Will the exclusion of millions of people from public funding eligibility have any serious consequences?

The impact of the conditional fee arrangements, the 1995 Green Paper on legal aid, and franchising are of special importance, but to deal with these issues properly, you need to be familiar with the details of how legal services are delivered in general.

THE LEGAL PROFESSION

The legal profession, although not fused, comprises solicitors and barristers whose work is becoming increasingly similar in many respects. Additionally, the ending of monopolies on litigation, probate and conveyancing has meant that lawyers' traditional work is increasingly becoming blurred with that of other professionals. The liabilities of lawyers for errors and negligence are key issues. Another is the way in which complaints are handled by the professions.

THE COURTS AND LEGAL SERVICES ACT 1990

The CLSA 1990 was passed 'to see that the public has the best possible access to legal services and that those services are of the right quality for the particular needs of the client'. The detail by which the Act sought to do this is very important, especially s 17 (general principle, litigation and rights of audience); s 11 (lay representatives); ss 28–29 (right to conduct litigation); s 66 (multi-disciplinary partnerships); s 89 (multinational partnerships); ss 34–37 (conveyancing); ss 21–26 (the Legal Services Ombudsman); and s 58 (conditional fee arrangements).

THE ACCESS TO JUSTICE ACT 1999

The 1999 Act makes many changes that will have an impact upon the professions. It articulates the principle that all lawyers should have full rights of audience before all courts, provided they have passed the relevant examinations. Also, by reforming the procedures for authorising further professional bodies to grant rights of audience, it signals a widening of those rights in the future.

IMMUNITY FROM NEGLIGENCE CLAIMS

Until recently barristers could not be sued by their clients for negligent performance in court or for work that was preparatory to court work (*Rondel v Worsley* (1969)); this immunity had also been extended to solicitors who act as advocates (*Saif Ali v Sidney Mitchell* (1980)). The client of the other side, however, may sue for breach of duty (*Kelly v London Transport Executive* (1982)). This was changed in a major case in 2000.

THE LEGAL OMBUDSMAN

An Ombudsman is a person independent of the government or a given field of activity, who investigates complaints of maladministration. The post of Legal Services Ombudsman is now operated under the LSA 2007 by the Office for Legal Complaints.

FOOD FOR THOUGHT

1. Why should the legal profession be divided into two discrete sectors? Whose interests does this really serve?

2. Why do barristers make the best judges, if they do?

3. Much is made of the need for greater access to the legal professions. However, given the increase in the number of law graduates and the restrictions in the number of training contracts and pupillages, is progression not a matter of 'who you know rather than what you know'?

4. In legal firms attention tends to be focused on the partners/solicitors, but what roles do the legal executives play?

5. Does the introduction of 'Tesco Law' (ABSs) necessarily mean a reduction in standards?

6. Consider the extent to which access to online provision reduces the need for legal professionals.

FURTHER READING

Abel, R, *The Legal Profession in England and Wales*, 1988, Oxford: Basil Blackwell

Baksi, C, 'Solicitor-advocates hit bar' (2008) Law Soc Gazette, 28 March

Browne, D, QC, 'A considered response' (2009) Counsel 3

Bryant, J, 'Proactive regulation will hit solicitors where it hurts' (2009) 23(40) Lawyer 6

Cocks, R, *Foundations of the Modern Bar*, 1983, London: Sweet & Maxwell

Farrow, A and Littler, R, 'Raising the bar' (2009) 153 (40) SJ 6

Genn, H and Genn, Y, *The Effectiveness of Representation at Tribunals*, 1989, London: LCD

Guise, T, 'Something for everyone' (2009) 153(41) SJ 19

Holroyd, A, 'Moving with the times' (2008) 105(2) Law Soc Gazette 16

Jackson, R, 'Disappointed litigants and doubtful actions' (1995) Counsel 16

Keogh, A, 'Power sharing' (2008) 158 NLJ 717

Money-Kyrle, R, 'Advocates' immunity after *Osman*' (1999) 149 NLJ 945 and 981

Underwood, K, 'Hope continues' (2007) 151(46) SJ 1542

Williamson, P, 'Open and accountable' (2007) 104(48) Law Soc Gazette 11

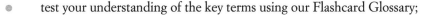

USEFUL WEBSITES

www.lawsociety.org.uk
The official site of The Law Society.

www.sra.org.uk
The official site of the Solicitors Regulation Authority.

www.barcouncil.org.uk
The official site of the Bar Council of England and Wales.

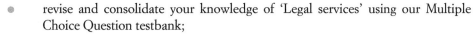

COMPANION WEBSITE

Now visit the companion website to:

- test your understanding of the key terms using our Flashcard Glossary;
- revise and consolidate your knowledge of 'Legal services' using our Multiple Choice Question testbank;
- view all of the links to the Useful Websites above.

www.routledge.com/cw/slapper

THE FUNDING OF LEGAL SERVICES

14

Legal aid (now called public funding) was introduced after the Second World War to enable people who could not otherwise afford the services of lawyers to be provided with those services by the State. The system and costs grew enormously over the decades. The system underwent various restrictions and cutbacks during the late 1990s and was replaced by other systems like the Community Legal Service (2000) and the Criminal Defence Service (2001). The term 'legal aid' is still used as a descriptive, non-technical term to refer to State-funded services. It is run by the Legal Services Commission (LSC) and assists over two million people each year. The annual legal aid budget for 2012–13 was £2 billion.

The importance of the system was neatly encapsulated by Tim Dutton, QC as Chairman of the Bar Council in 2008. He noted ((2008) NLJ 1031):

> In much the same way that the National Health Service has been held in high regard, we should be proud that our legal aid system has been considered one of the best at providing justice for the most vulnerable and needy in our society.

Following legal aid reforms suggested by Lord Carter in his report, 'Legal Aid – A market-based approach to reform', which was published on 13 July 2006, there were numerous changes made to the legal aid system (see 14.3). This chapter examines all the major elements of state-funded legal services. It also examines the alternative system of funding – conditional fee arrangements – under which payment to lawyers is made dependent on particular results.

In 2006, the government indicated it was determined to curb the spiralling cost of legal aid expenditure, which was £1.5 billion in 1996–97 and rose to almost £2.1 billion in

2003/04, where it peaked before decreasing slightly over the next few years to around £2 billion a year (Lord Hunt, *Hansard*, 19 February 2008, col 134). The cost of legal aid spending has risen sharply in recent years because of two areas of high expenditure; childcare proceedings where gross spending rose from £94 million in 1999/2000 to £209 million in 2005/06 and is expected to increase, and criminal cases. The legal aid bill for defendants in Crown Court cases rose by 125 per cent between 1995/96 and 2003/04.

The proposals in a report of a review team under Lord Carter of Coles (*Procurement of Criminal Defence Services: Market-based reform*, 2006) are being gradually implemented and are set to make substantial changes to the system. The system advocated by Carter is one where lawyers have to bid competitively to win contracts for doing criminal legal aid work. Under this new market-based model, all criminal legal aid lawyers are paid fixed fees – rather than being paid by time spent – and compete for contracts for work in police stations and courts.

The reforms prevent the highest-earning barristers being paid £1 million a year from legal aid, as used to be case. Such a reorganisation could halve the number of the 2,500 legal aid firms and cause wide-scale mergers.

Most criminal trials are now covered by fixed fees, but fees in the long and most complex criminal trials are still the subject of negotiation between the government and the professional bodies.

Legal aid work does not provide the lucrative million-pound briefs of the commercial or chancery bar. It is work done by about a third of the Bar – with a higher proportion of young, women and ethnic minority barristers. They choose it because they are committed, as Peter Lodder, QC puts it, 'to serving the public, are conscientious and prepared to put something back into the system' (Frances Gibb, 'Counting the cost of reforms', *The Times*, 11 September 2008).

There are several State-funded schemes to facilitate the provision of aid and advice. Each scheme has different rules relating to its scope, procedures for application and eligibility. Because of the importance of justice and access to the legal machinery, the idea behind legal aid is to give people who could otherwise not afford professional legal help the same services as more wealthy citizens. This raises important social, political and economic questions. Do poorer people deserve the same quality of legal advice as that which can be afforded by wealthy people? If so, how should such schemes be funded? The LSC, in its strategic plan published in April 2009 for the period 2009–2012, has a vision of 'fair access to justice to the people who need it but can least afford it'.

14.3   THE LEGAL AID SCHEME

The Access to Justice Act 1999 set up a new legal aid system and made provisions about rights to supply legal services (see Chapter 13), court procedure (see Chapter 6), magistrates and magistrates' courts (see Chapter 9). The provisions in the Act form part of the wide-ranging programme of reforms to legal services and the courts, described in the government's White Paper, *Modernising Justice*, published on 2 December 1998. Except where noted, the Act only affects England and Wales.

Part I of the 1999 Act established a Legal Services Commission (LSC) to maintain and develop the Community Legal Service (CLS) and the Criminal Defence Service (CDS), which replaced the Civil and Criminal Legal Aid schemes, respectively. The Act also enabled the Lord Chancellor to give the Commission orders, directions and guidance about how it should exercise its functions. The Community Legal Service Fund replaced the legal aid fund in civil and family cases. The Commission uses the resources of the Fund in a way that reflects priorities set by the Lord Chancellor, and its duty to secure the best possible value for money, to procure or provide a range of legal services. The Commission also has a duty to liaise with other funders of legal services to facilitate the development of co-ordinated plans for making the best use of all available resources. The strategy is to develop a network of legal service providers of assured quality, offering the widest possible access to information and advice about the law, and assistance with legal problems. The CDS is intended to ensure that people suspected or accused of a crime are properly represented, while securing better value for money than was possible under the legal aid scheme.

14.3.1 CONTROLLED AND LICENSED WORK

As noted at 14.2 above, legal aid funding was granted on a case-by-case basis until the system of franchising was introduced in August 1994, where firms of solicitors meeting certain requirements were able to contract to undertake certain cases without prior approval, and claim funding on a more advantageous basis than previously. This franchise or 'contract' system has formed the basis of the legal aid scheme.

Funded services for all civil contract work fall under the headings of 'controlled work' and 'licensed work'. In family cases controlled work covers legal help, family help (lower) and legal representation. In non-family cases there are three levels of service for controlled work: legal help, help at court and controlled legal representation, which includes legal representation before a mental health review tribunal or the Asylum and Immigration Tribunal. For controlled work the decision about whether to provide services in a particular case is made by the supplier, who is either a solicitor or a not-for-profit organisation, such as a law centre or Citizens' Advice Bureau (discussed below, at 14.10.2). They bid for a contract to provide legal services funded by the LSC to the Regional Legal Services Committees. Under the contract, the number of cases that may be undertaken by the suppliers is limited.

Licensed work is the equivalent of the case-by-case approval granted for all State-funded legal work prior to 1994 and all non-franchised work prior to the establishment of the LSC. Licensed work is administered through a certification process requiring the Commission's initial approval of the cost, timing and scope of each case. Once the licence is granted, it covers all legal representation before the courts, except for controlled legal representation or services funded by individual case contracts that are managed by the Commission, such as very expensive cases referred to as 'very high cost cases' (VHCC). In criminal work, the VHCC are those in which a solicitor is instructed with a criminal case that is likely to last 41 days or more at trial. There are other cases that fall into the VHCC category:

- Terrorism and Serious Fraud Office (SFO) if anticipated to last between 25 and 40 days and if two of the following apply:

    (a)   at least 10,000 pages of prosecution evidence;

    (b)   at least 10,000 pages of unused or third-party material;

    (c)   more than five defendants;

    (d)   fraud or serious drugs cases where the value of the fraud or drugs exceeds £1m.

Providers must notify the Complex Crime Unit (CCU) if they are instructed on VHCC criteria. A panel scheme commenced on 14 January 2008 for VHCC criminal cases and was suspended from 14 July 2010 when such cases became subject to an individual case contracting arrangement. Under the 2010 scheme organisations and individuals must obtain VHCC accreditation to undertake this work. VHCC was reintroduced in December 2006 for family cases. In civil cases, the LSC's Special Cases Unit (SCU) is responsible for managing VHCC, which fall into four categories:

- individual VHCC, which is where costs are expected to exceed £25,000, such as childcare proceedings;
- multi-party actions, which can range from 10 to 1,000 claimant actions;
- exceptional funding cases, which is where funding is approved outside the funding code;
- exceptional 'one-off' contracts with firms without franchises, such as where clients run out of money during a case and the firm has no franchise.

The VHCC is subject to a consultation for a new and better scheme that was due to be completed by 13 July 2009. The consultation has not been completed and the current interim scheme will continue for another year to allow further VHCC cases to be undertaken.

In family cases, licensed work covers family help (higher) and legal representation other than matters that are dealt with by an individual case contract. In non-family cases, legal representation can be either for investigative help or full representation.

14.3.2   CONTRACTING

The work that may be undertaken by a supplier, whether a solicitor or a not-for-profit organisation, covers a wide variety of categories. Civil legal aid work covers family, immigration, social welfare (which covers debt, employment, housing, community care and welfare benefits), mental health, personal injury, clinical negligence, consumer general contract, actions against police, public law and education. Criminal legal aid covers work in police stations, magistrates' courts, Crown Courts, VHCC and working within the criminal justice system.

The contract for civil work used to be carried out under a General Civil Contract under the CLS. However, this has now been replaced by a new Unified Contract, which is discussed below, at 14.3.3.

The current contract for criminal work is covered by a General Criminal Contract, under the CDS. This contract was in place prior to the legal aid reform programme. As a result of The Law Society's judicial review of the civil Unified Contract (see paragraph 14.3.3) this General Criminal Contract was terminated on 13 January 2008. An open tender process commenced in late September 2007 for a new six-month contract commencing 14 January 2008, which incorporated the new reforms for criminal legal aid. The LSC introduced the Unified Contract for criminal work in July 2008, and agreed a civil contract scheme in the same month ((2008) NLJ 494–5). All criminal legal aid providers had to sign a new contract from 14 July 2010 and on 1 September 2011 the LSC published amendments to the contract relating to fees that took effect from October 2011. The 2010 contract introduced standard terms that the LSC introduced to its three main contracts, namely civil, crime and VHCC (crime). The Unified Contract (Civil) will also be subject to changes to fees from 2011. The civil contract started on 14 October 2010. Both criminal and civil contracts are to run for three years and the LSC has a right to extend for a further two years. The LSC may terminate the contract for any reason at six months' notice and the providers at three months' notice. Key Performance Indicators (KPI) are now part of the contract and failure to comply will be a breach of contract. A further judicial review in September 2010 in relation to family legal aid was successful (see paragraph 14.3.3). This has prevented the start of the 2010 family contract. On 5 September 2011 the LSC published an invitation to tender for new contracts for Family Services and Family with Housing to commence in February 2012. This contact will now cease on 31 March 2013 and a new contract (with applications by 22 October 2012) will commence on 1 April 2013. This will cover the existing services together with Immigration and Asylum.

On 20 July 2009 the LSC published its response to the second stage of proposals to introduce Best Value Tendering (BVT). The plan was to set up BVT pilot schemes in Greater Manchester and Avon & Somerset for defence work in police stations and magistrates' courts. The pilot schemes were to commence in July 2010, fully evaluated and, if successful, will be introduced throughout the country by 2013. Following concerns of practitioners the LSC confirmed to The Law Society (by letter dated 13 August 2009 and published on The Law Society website) that they would extend the evaluation period and not extend it to other CJS areas before 2013. The Law Society then announced on 17 December 2009 that the government was going to drop the plans for the BVT pilot.

A contract may be awarded to allow a supplier to undertake work within one or more categories. The contract will state the categories and terms under which the supplier may provide legal advice and representation. The purpose of specifying categories in respect of civil contracts is to ensure an appropriate distribution of legal and advice services to meet demand in each region.

In order to assess demand and ensure that the right kind of services are available to meet the needs of a region, Community Legal Service Partnerships (CLSPs) were set up. The purpose of CLSPs is to provide a forum, in each local authority area, for the local authority and the LSC, and if possible other significant funders, to come together to co-ordinate funding and planning of local legal and advice services, to ensure that delivery of services better matches local needs. The Commission and the CLSPs were intended to encourage innovation by the voluntary sector in the delivery of advice, through increased use of information technology and mobile 'outreach' services providing help to people in remote communities.

Overall, the intention was to:

● make best use of all the resources available for funding legal services, by facilitating a co-ordinated approach to planning;

● improve value for money through contracting and the development of quality assurance systems;

● establish a flexible system for allocating central government funding, in a rational and transparent way within a controlled budget, so as to provide legal services where they are judged to be most needed; and

● ensure that the scheme is capable of adapting to meet changing priorities and opportunities.

The establishment of CLSPs was ahead of schedule. However, the LSC no longer facilitates CLSPs and the LSC has asked each CLSP to consider whether it has a viable role as a provider forum.

The service provided may be at different levels depending on the case. The different levels of service are:

Legal Help: this is the provision of initial advice and assistance.

Help at Court: this enables a solicitor or adviser to speak on behalf of a person at certain court hearings without formally acting for that person in the whole proceedings.

Approved Family Help: this is the provision of help in relation to family disputes including the resolution of the matter by negotiation or otherwise. This covers initial advice and assistance, issuing proceedings and representation where necessary in order to obtain disclosure of information from another party or to obtain a consent order when matters in dispute have been agreed. It is available in two forms: Help with Mediation where a person is attending mediation sessions and General Family Help.

Family Mediation: this covers mediation for a family dispute, including finding out whether mediation is suitable or not.

Legal Representation: under this, a person can be represented in court. It is available in two forms:

(i) *Investigative Help*: funding is limited to investigation of the strength of a claim.

(ii) *Full Representation*: funding is provided to represent people in legal proceedings.

Support Funding: this provides partial funding for very expensive cases, which are otherwise funded privately. It is available in two forms:

(i)   *Investigative Support*: funding is limited to investigation of the strength of a claim with a view to a conditional fee agreement.

(ii)   *Litigation Support*: this provides partial funding of high cost proceedings under a conditional fee agreement.

14.3.3 UNIFIED CONTRACT

Since 1 April 2007, Unified Contracts have replaced the General Civil Contract and Family Mediation Contracts, which expired on 31 March 2007. There was initial opposition to the new civil contract from practitioners. However, this has been mostly overcome and now in excess of 90 per cent of legal aid law firms have signed up to this new contract. The Unified Contract contains five key documents:

- The Contract for Signature. This specifies the contract term (which will initially run to 31 March 2010), the parties, the contract documents and authorised signatories. It also contains key information tables and annexes relevant to each particular provider, along with key performance indicators (KPI) and payment provisions. The new contract will run for three years from 14 October 2010 and KPIs will be part of the contract.

- Office Schedules. Every office of a provider will have a schedule to the contract (see below), which will run for a period of 12 months from 1 April to 31 March. This will contain details of matter starts, payment limits, outreach work and any special provisions applying to that particular office.

- Standard Terms. The new standard terms build on the terms of General Civil Contract and apply to all providers.

- Specification. This contains provisions about the performance of contract work and includes remuneration rates and runs alongside the Unified Contract standard terms. Since 1 October 2007, the General Civil Contract Specification has replaced the Unified Contract Specifications (Solicitor and NfP), which was in force from 1 April 2007. This has introduced new fee schemes, including fixed and graduated fees. The introduction of the new fee schemes is the result of legal aid reform recommended in Legal Aid: A market-based approach to reform in July 2006. It is anticipated that the new fee schemes will lead to greater competition among the providers, which in turn will produce good quality work and efficiency.

- Indemnities and Guarantees. The LSC may ask providers to give indemnities and guarantees.

- The LSC can terminate the contract for any reason at six months' notice and the providers at three months' notice.

According to the LSC website the Unified Contract (Civil) 2007 has been extended until 15 December 2010 for only the suppliers who currently deliver 'family only' and 'family and housing' publicly funded legal services. The quashing order issued by the High Court means that the LSC cannot proceed with awarding the 2010 Standard Civil Contracts in respect of those services to providers who were successful in the recent tender.

A new family contract commenced on 1 February 2012, but this will cease on 31 March 2013 and a new contract will commence the following day which will incorporate Immigration and Asylum work. All tenders for contracts and renewals must be submitted online.

The aim of the Unified Contract is to put not-for-profit advisers on the same footing as solicitors who carry out civil legal aid work and to create greater efficiency when working with providers. It is anticipated that one way this will be achieved is by requiring providers to work with the LSC by means of email to reduce administrative time and costs. In addition, providers will be required to meet certain standards that are contained in KPIs.

Another major change to this new system is the move away from issuing separate contracts to each office of a provider and instead issuing a contract to the whole organisation of the provider with each contract containing a schedule detailing the work that an individual office can undertake. The LSC will be able to stipulate a minimum and maximum number of cases that an individual office may start each year.

The Unified Contract introduces new provisions on equality and diversity, which is likely to be a major benefit to legal aid clients. According to the LSC Executive Director of Policy, Richard Collins, the new contract is not expected to reduce the legal aid costs, but to make available a greater proportion of the current budget available for civil legal aid.

The new contract introduces new payment on account provisions. It is no longer possible to receive the £250 automatic payment on account that was made once a legal aid certificate was issued. Instead a claim can now be made in the first three months.

14.3.4 QUALITY MARK

In order to be a supplier under either the CLS or the CDS, the solicitor or not-for-profit organisation must achieve the minimum standards under the respective Quality Marks. There are three kinds of Quality Mark: information, general help and specialist help, with a supplier displaying an appropriately endorsed logo on its premises. A supplier of information will typically be a library and provide leaflets, reference material and access to the CLS or CDS *Directory of Services*. A supplier of general help will provide information and advice and will be a Citizens' Advice Bureau or other advice agency. A supplier of specialist information will be a solicitor, a law centre, or some Citizens' Advice Bureaux, and it will be able to give information and advice on a complex problem in a specialist legal area, which will be shown next to the supplier's entry in the CLS or CDS *Directory*.

Since the introduction of Unified Contracts, suppliers will be required to meet the quality required under the key information tables set out in their contract. This Specialist Quality Mark is expected to be used by all providers (including those included on the Preferred Supplier Pilot) until the LSC only work with preferred suppliers. As part of the changes taking place in legal aid, the LSC set up a pilot preferred supplier scheme and now propose a national preferred supplier scheme. It is anticipated that having preferred suppliers will result in the consolidation of the market and improve value for money. The LSC proposes that the criteria for determining whether a supplier will qualify as a preferred supplier is by looking at KPIs such as success rates and bill assessment rates, file assessments and peer review.

There will be three Quality Marks applicable as follows.

SQM: Specialist Quality Mark. This will be for complex matters.

MQM: Family Mediation Quality Mark.

QMB: Quality Mark for the Bar.

14.4 THE LEGAL SERVICES COMMISSION

As from 1 April 2000, the Legal Services Commission replaced the Legal Aid Board. It was considered necessary to establish a new body to reflect the fundamentally different nature of the CLS when compared to civil legal aid. Within the broad framework of priorities set by the Lord Chancellor, the Commission is responsible for taking detailed decisions about the allocation of resources. It is also required to liaise with other funders to develop the CLS more widely. The Commission has a wider role in respect of the CDS than the Legal Aid Board did in respect of Criminal Legal Aid. The Board had very limited responsibilities for legal aid in the higher criminal courts. Membership of the Commission differs from that of the old Legal Aid Board, to reflect a shift in focus from the needs of providers to the needs of users of legal services. Also, the Commission is smaller than the Board: 7–12 members rather than 11–17. This is intended to facilitate 'focused decision-making'.

Legal aid has been one of the fastest growing parts of the public sector over the past 25 years, and expenditure has increased at almost 6 per cent per year in real terms, compared to similar increases in health and education of approximately 4 per cent and 2 per cent respectively. At approximately £38 per head of the population, the LSC also spends more in England and Wales than is spent by any other jurisdiction for which comparative data is currently available.

According to the LSC's annual report for 2011/12,

- legal aid funded over 2.476 million acts of assistance overall at a cost of £2,078 million;
- Criminal Defence Service (CDS see 14.7 below) providers delivered 1.39 million acts of assistance at a cost of £1,100 million;
- the LSC held 1,976 (including 265 by not-for-profit organisations) civil and 1,640 criminal contracts for legal aid focusing on areas of most need at 31 March 2012.

The LSC achieved four out of seven, largely achieved one, partially achieved one and missed one key performance indicators in the year.

14.5   THE COMMUNITY LEGAL SERVICE

The LSC has two main duties in respect of the CLS:

- First, it manages a CLS Fund (ss 4–11 of the 1999 Act), which has replaced legal aid in civil and family cases. The CLS Fund is used to secure the provision of appropriate legal services within the resources made available to it, and according to priorities set by the Lord Chancellor and by regional and local assessments of need. A Funding Code, drawn up by the Commission and approved by the Lord Chancellor, sets out the criteria and procedures for granting contracts and deciding whether to fund individual cases. As spending has been brought under better control, it has been possible to expand the scope of the fund into areas that were not covered by legal aid, in particular to alternatives to lawyers and courts, like mediation and advice agencies. Mediation is already a requirement in family matters (see Part III of the Family Law Act 1996).

- Second, as part of a wider CLS, the Commission has, in co-operation with local funders and interested bodies, developed local, regional and national plans to match the delivery of legal services to identified needs and priorities.

14.5.1   COMMUNITY LEGAL SERVICE CONTRACT

In carrying out the first duty of managing the CLS, the LSC developed the General Civil Contract to introduce contracting within the statutory framework created by the Access to Justice Act 1999, in effect since 1 January 2000. There are two versions of the General Civil Contract, one for solicitors and one for not-for-profit agencies, because of the differences in the terminology and methods of delivery used by these types of suppliers. An important aspect of the new scheme is that the right kind of services should be available to meet the needs of a region. In furtherance of this aim, the Commission published a Consultation Paper in 2002, setting out its proposals for establishing regional priorities for civil contracting through the production of Regional Legal Services Committees' reports, Regional Directors' contracting strategies and CLSPs. Following this consultation, the Commission has put in place a new process for the regional prioritisation of needs. As a result, new bid rules for the award of General Civil Contracts for Controlled Work apply as from 1 January 2003, although these were further revised on 1 April 2004 to reflect regional priorities and to hold a wider bidding process.

The new term for litigants who obtain LSC funding is 'LSC funded clients', and the fund out of which litigants who obtain LSC funding is referred to as the CLS Fund. Section 7 of the 1999 Act allows the Lord Chancellor, using regulations, to set financial eligibility limits. Therefore, an applicant must be able to show that his capital *and* income are within the current financial limits.

The Community Legal Service (Financial) (Amendment) Regulations 2007 (which amends the Community Legal Service (Financial) Regulations 2000) set out the thresholds for financial eligibility for all applications for funding made on or after 8 April 2008. The test uses the basic concepts of 'disposable income', that is, income available to a person after deducting essential living expenses; and 'disposable capital', that is, the assets owned by a person after essential items like a home. If a person could sell her home, pay off the mortgage and still have more than £100,000 left (called 'equity'), then she will not qualify for aid.

Certain services are free, regardless of financial resources, such as services consisting exclusively of the provision of general information about the law, legal system and availability of legal services, legal representation in some cases involving the Children Act 1989 and related proceedings, and representation at a mental health review tribunal. Some services are non-contributory and a client is either eligible or not, whereas others are contributory in accordance with a sliding scale, dependent on how much a client's income or capital exceeds a given threshold. There is a cap amount over which a person is ineligible for legal aid. In summary, the financial eligibility amounts for applications are as follows:

- For all levels of service, there is (as of April 2011) a gross income cap of £2,657 per month. This cap may be increased by £222 per month for each child in excess of four. A client who is directly or indirectly in receipt of Income Support or income-based Jobseeker's Allowance automatically satisfies the gross income test for all levels of service.

- For the service of Legal Help, Help at Court and Legal Representation before Immigration Adjudicators and the Immigration Appeal Tribunal, the disposable income must not exceed £733 per month. There is a capital limit of £3,000 for controlled legal representation in respect of immigration matters and £8,000 for all other levels of service. There is an intention that the £3,000 limit for immigration matters will be raised to £8,000 following consultation on a suitable scheme.

- For the service of Family Mediation, Help with Mediation and other Legal Representation (which may be subject to a contribution from income and capital), the disposable income must not exceed £733 per month and there is a capital limit of £8,000.

When assessing gross income and disposable income, State benefits under the Social Security Contributions and Benefits Act 1992 (Disability Living Allowance, Attendance Allowance, Constant Attendance Allowance, Invalid Care Allowance, Severe Disablement Allowance, Council Tax Benefit, Housing Benefit and any payment out of the social fund), back to work bonuses under the Jobseekers Act 1995, war and war widows' pensions and fostering allowances are disregarded.

The only level of service assessed by the supplier for which contributions can be sought is Legal Representation in Specified Family Proceedings. However, provided that the client's gross income is below the prescribed limit, clients with a disposable income of £315 or below per month will not need to pay any contributions from income, but may still have to pay a contribution from capital. A client with disposable income in excess of £315 and up to £733 per month will be liable to pay a monthly contribution of a proportion of the excess over £311, assessed in accordance with the following bands:

Band	Monthly disposable income	Monthly contribution
A	£316–£465	Quarter of income in excess of £311
B	£466–£616	£38.50 + third of income in excess of £465
C	£617–£733	£88.85 + half of income in excess of £616

A client whose disposable capital exceeds £3,000 is required to pay a contribution of either the capital exceeding that sum or the likely maximum costs of the funded service, whichever is the lesser.

For example, if disposable income is £480 per month, the contribution will be in Band B, the excess income is £15 (£480 – £465), the monthly contribution would therefore be £43.50 (£38.50 + £5 [a third of the excess income]). The Community Legal Advice website has an online legal aid eligibility calculator to enable people to check whether they are likely to qualify financially.

Provided it is not disregarded as subject matter of the dispute, a client's main or only dwelling in which he resides must be taken into account as capital, subject to the following rules:

(a)   The dwelling should be valued at the amount for which it could be sold on the open market.

(b)   The amount of any mortgage or charge registered on the property must be deducted, but the maximum amount that can be deducted for such a mortgage or charge is £100,000.

(c)   The first £100,000 of the value of the client's interest after making the above mortgage deduction must be disregarded.

The original proposal was that homeowners with £3,000 equity in their homes would be liable to make contributions to the cost of their legal aid. This was dropped following outrage by practitioners and legal interest groups, as it was said that such a move would effectively abolish legal aid for virtually all homeowners.

14.5.3   THE FUNDING CODE

In addition to financial eligibility, an applicant's case must also satisfy a new merits test. The Commission prepared a Code (2007) which replaces, and is intended to be more flexible than, the merits test that was used for civil legal aid. The Code sets out the criteria for determining whether services funded by the CLS Fund should be provided in a particular case and, if so, what services it is appropriate to provide. The Code also sets out the procedures for making applications. In drafting the Code, the Commission was required to consider the extent to which the criteria for assessment should reflect the following factors (s 8 of the Access to Justice Act 1999):

(a)   The likely cost of funding the services and the benefit which may be obtained by their being provided.

(b)   The availability of sums in the CLS Fund for funding the services and, having regard to the present and likely future demands on that Fund, the appropriateness of applying them to fund the services.

(c)   The importance of the matters in relation to which the services would be provided for the individual.

(d)   The availability to the individual of services not funded by the Commission and the likelihood of his being able to avail himself of them.

(e)   If the services are sought by the individual in relation to a dispute, the prospects of his success in the dispute.

(f)   The conduct of the individual in connection with services funded as part of the CLS (or an application for funding) or in, or in connection with, any legal proceedings.

(g)   The public interest.

(h)   Such other factors as the Lord Chancellor may by order require the Commission to consider.

The Code is required to reflect the principle that in many family disputes, mediation is more appropriate than court proceedings. This is intended to reinforce the development, under the Family Law Act 1996, of mediation as a means of resolving private law family disputes in a way that promotes as good a continuing relationship between the parties concerned as is possible in the circumstances. The government has argued that mediation is more constructive than adversarial court proceedings, and that litigation in these cases usually serves only to reinforce already entrenched positions and further damage the relationship between the parties. In addition, the cost of court proceedings is higher than that of mediation, and additional costs have to be borne by the property of the family, reducing the amount available to the parties and their children in future. The credibility of mediation as an appropriate forum for family matters in general suffered a blow in 1999, when the government abandoned plans to introduce the scheme related to divorce after pilot studies failed to produce good results.

The Commission revised the merits test for Controlled Legal Representation and issued guidance that came into force on 16 December 2002. The reform of the merits test, which regulates the demand that qualifies for help, is said by the government to complement the reforms of the supply of services – with the intention of creating a flexible system for deploying resources to meet a range of priorities within a controlled budget.

The Funding Code sets out general criteria in relation to services for all categories except very expensive cases, judicial review, claims against public authorities, clinical negligence, housing, family, mental health and immigration, for which there are criteria specific to the particular category. The Code defines which factors are relevant in a given category, how they should be taken into account, and what weight should be given to them. For example, standard criteria for the service of legal representation include: whether there is alternative funding available; whether there are alternatives to litigation; or whether the case could be allocated to the small claims track. For services in most categories, consideration must be given to whether there is sufficient benefit to the client in receiving a particular service and what the prospect of success is. Where this is a consideration, cases are put into one of six categories according to their chances of success as follows: very good (80 per cent or better chance of success); good (60–80 per cent); moderate (50–60 per cent); borderline (50 per cent); poor (less than 50 per cent); or unclear. The considerations are not the same for all services, categories or types of case within those categories: for example, prospects of success will not be a relevant factor in cases about whether a child should be taken into local authority care.

14.5.4 LEGAL SERVICES PROVIDED

Section 4 of the 1999 Act describes the services that may be provided under the CLS. These range from the provision of basic information about the law and legal services to providing help towards preventing or resolving disputes and enforcing decisions that have been reached. The scheme encompasses advice, assistance and representation by lawyers (which have long been available under the legal aid scheme), and also the services of non-lawyers. It will extend to other types of service including, for example, mediation in family or civil cases where appropriate.

Under Sched 2, restrictions are specified in respect of other services for certain categories. Only basic information and advice will be available for:

- disputes involving allegations of negligent damage to property or the person ('personal injury'), apart from those about clinical negligence. These cases are generally considered suitable for conditional fees;

- allegations of defamation or malicious falsehood. Generally, legal aid was not available for representation in defamation, but it was sometimes possible to get legal aid by categorising the case as one of malicious falsehood. The government's view is that these cases do not command sufficient priority to justify public funding; in any event, they may often be suitable for a conditional fee;

- disputes arising in the course of business. Legal aid was not available for firms and companies, but a sole trader could get legal aid to pursue a business dispute. Businessmen have the option of insuring against the possibility of having to take or defend legal action. The government does not believe that the taxpayer should meet the legal costs of sole traders who fail to do so;

- matters concerned with the law relating to companies or partnerships;

- matters concerned with the law of trusts or trustees; boundary disputes. The government does not consider that these command sufficient priority to justify public funding. In addition, funding for representation at proceedings before the Lands Tribunal or Commons Commissioners is no longer available. Other services, including assistance with preparing a case, continue to be available.

For some categories, subject to local priorities, a full range of services will be available, whereas for others, all services except representation at court by a lawyer may be obtained.

The Lord Chancellor can make directions bringing cases that would be excluded within the provisions of the Act in exceptional circumstances. For example, the Lord Chancellor may direct that personal injury cases (which are generally excluded by Sched 2, because most such cases are suitable for conditional fees) be funded by the CLS fund where exceptionally high investigative or overall costs are likely to be necessary, or where issues of wider public interest are involved. The LSC estimates that 200 cases per year are of wider public interest. The Consultation Paper, *Access to Justice with Conditional Fees* (Lord Chancellor's Department (LCD), 1998), notes that it will be necessary to decide what should constitute public interest (para 3.31). For example, a test case about a novel point of law might have no more than a 50 per cent chance of success, but the decision could impact on numerous future cases (in the way that recent cases involving sporting injuries have extended the duty of care owed by officials wider than was previously accepted: see *Vowles v Evans and Welsh Rugby Union* (2003)), or a claim for a relatively small sum in damages might benefit a large number of other people with a similar claim. Examples might be claims arising out of the use of pharmaceutical products and pollution of water supplies or the atmosphere. Very expensive cases often include this type of public interest aspect: they are expensive because they are novel and complex, or because their wide potential impact means that they are hard fought.

14.5.5 THE CLS FUND

The CLS Fund, as established under s 5 of the 1999 Act, is not uncapped, as was the old Legal Aid Fund. In the pre-1999 system, if more money was needed after the initial budgeting by the government, supplementary funding could be found. Today, the amount of the Fund is to be fixed each year by the Lord Chancellor, who takes account of the receipts from contributions (for example, from local authorities) with the balance from money voted by Parliament. The Lord Chancellor is able to direct the Commission to use specified amounts within the Fund to provide services of particular types (s 5(6)). The Lord Chancellor divides the Fund into two main budgets, for providing services in: (i) family; and (ii) other civil cases, while allowing the Commission limited flexibility to switch money between the two areas. The Lord Chancellor may set further requirements within these two budgets, by specifying the amount, or the maximum or minimum amount, that should be spent on, say, services from the voluntary advice sector, mediation or cases involving a wider public interest. The idea here is that in this way, it will be possible to ensure that resources are allocated in accordance with the government's priorities.

The Commission may use the CLS Fund to provide services (s 6(3)). These include making contracts with, or grants to, service providers, or employing staff to provide services directly to the public. These flexible powers are intended to give effect to one of the principal objectives of the reform of publicly funded legal services: that is, the ability to tailor the provision of services, and the means by which services are delivered, to the needs of local populations and particular circumstances. The Commission is allowed to test new forms of service provision through pilot projects such as the Family Advice and Information Networks Pilot Project (FAINS) and telephone advice service. The Commission is under a duty to obtain the best value for money – a combination of price and quality – when using the resources of the Fund to provide services.

In line with the principle of flexibility, it may be possible to exclude further categories that can generally be funded privately, as conditional fees, legal expenses insurance and other forms of funding develop more widely. Equally well, as resources become available through the greater control of spending and value for money provided by the new scheme and the development of private alternatives, it may be possible to extend the scheme's scope to cover services that are excluded now because, although they would command some priority, they are unaffordable.

14.5.6 EXTENSION OF FINANCIAL CONDITIONS ON AN ASSISTED PARTY

The 1999 Act extends the potential scope of financial conditions imposed on an assisted party in two ways, although there are no immediate plans to use either of these powers:

- It will be possible to make the provision of services in some types of case subject to the assisted person agreeing to repay an amount in excess of the cost of the services provided, in the event that their case is successful (s 10(2)). This might make it possible to fund certain types of case on a self-financing basis, with the additional payments from successful litigants applied to meet the cost of unsuccessful cases. It would also be possible to mix public funding with a private conditional fee arrangement, subject to the same conditions about the uplift to the costs in the event of a successful outcome. The government has suggested that this might be appropriate, for example, where a case could not be taken under a wholly private arrangement, because the solicitors' firm was not large enough to bear the risk of the very high costs likely to be involved.

- It will be possible (s 10(3), (4)) to require the assisted person to repay, over time and with interest, the full cost of the service provided (for example, through continuing contributions from income). This will make it possible to provide services in some categories of case in the form of a loan scheme.

Section 11 of the 1999 Act establishes limits on the liability of the person receiving funded services to pay costs to the unassisted party. The costs he must pay cannot go above what is 'reasonable' (s 11(1)), taking into account the financial resources of all parties. It also provides that regulations may specify the principles that are to be applied in determining the amount of any costs awarded against the party receiving funded services, and the circumstances in which a costs order may be enforced against the person receiving funded services.

Today, the regulations that limit the circumstances in which the costs order may be enforced against the person receiving funded services (or the liability of the Commission to meet any costs order on behalf of the person receiving funded services) are made on a more flexible basis. Previously, protection from costs was seen by governments to create too great an advantage in litigation for the person receiving legal aid.

When the scheme was proposed, government plans appeared so vague that some lawyers questioned the credibility of the service and warned that it ran the risk of being a 'leafleting service' (News, 'The legal profession and the Community Legal Service' (1999) 149 NLJ 1195). However, a report from the National Audit Office (NAO), *Community Legal Service: The Introduction of Contracting* (HC 89 2002/2003), identifies significant improvements that have taken place in the administration of civil legal aid, with better control, targeting and scrutiny of suppliers by the LSC since the CLS was created in April 2000 (see www. nao.gov.uk). In 2001/02, net expenditure borne by the CLS Fund totalled £734 million, with expenditure on licensed work totalling £476 million and expenditure on controlled work totalling £258 million. These positive points, though, should be read in the context of the general overspend on legal services cited at the outset of this chapter (14.1).

The LSC annual report (2011/12) noted that total resource spend from the CLS Fund during 2011/12 was £2.078m. Of this, £755m was spent on Licensed Work (below), and £223m was spent on Controlled Work (below); £1,100m was criminal and £82m was administration.

Licensed Work is work under the civil contract that covers all Legal Representation (representation by solicitors and barristers for civil cases which could go to court) except work covered by Controlled Work or Very High Cost Cases, which are managed under separate contracts. It was reported in Hansard (22 July 2010) that the cost of VHCC cases in 2009/10 was £95.6 million for criminal and £78.6 million for civil cases.

Controlled Work is work under the civil contract that covers the basic levels of legal advice and representation, including initial meetings and, in family cases, negotiations, and is referred to as Legal Help or as Family Help Lower. It also encompasses Help at Court and representation in front of Mental Health Review Tribunals and the Asylum and Immigration Tribunal. In Controlled Work an act of assistance is every instance in which a service provider gives legal help to a client, not including representation in court.

The NAO report also identifies some problems in the system. There is cause for concern about the volume of suppliers opting out of contracting in family work and the need for additional supply in high priority categories of law, such as community care, housing and mental health. Since the introduction of new contracting arrangements, there has been a decline in the number of solicitors' firms providing legal aid services from 4,866 in January 2000 to 4,427 by July 2002. However, the number of not-for-profit firms providing services rose from 344 to 402 over the same period. These numbers have since declined to 3,351 solicitors' firms undertaking legal aid and 265 not-for-profit firms (LSC Annual Report 2011/12). The reduction in the supplier base is partly a deliberate move away from reliance on a large number of generalist support firms towards a smaller number of specialist quality-assured providers. However, the reduction also reflects concern among some firms about the level of remuneration offered on civil legal aid work. The Commission has identified gaps in provision in some parts of the country, particularly in rural areas, and in some areas of law, for example, family law, but has had some success in attracting suppliers to immigration work.

14.6 COMMUNITY LEGAL ADVICE CENTRES AND NETWORKS

On 24 May 2007 the first Community Legal Advice Centre (CLAC) was officially opened in Gateshead, although it had been in operation since April 2007. The CLAC is funded jointly. Civil legal aid is funded by the LSC and social welfare services is funded by Gateshead Council. The Gateshead CLAC has a three-year budget of £2.6 million. Its aims include to provide help on social welfare, family matters, services to disadvantaged and vulnerable groups such as the young and old, and those living in run-down neighbourhoods, and services outside the scope of legal aid such as representation at employment tribunals.

CLACs have since been opened in a number of towns and cities, and it is anticipated that others will follow. While both CLACs and networks provide the same services with the same aims and objectives, they are delivered in different ways. CLACs are run by a single entity from a central office, along with outreach. Networks are where a group of providers come together and sign up to shared services. Anyone who contacts a network will therefore have full access to the range of services on offer. The LSC is currently working with Cornwall County Council to set up a Community Legal Advice network. As a minimum, every CLAC and network will provide advice and representation in community care, debt, employment, family, housing, welfare benefits and any public law relating to any of the foregoing.

The first Community Legal Advice Network (CLAN) opened in 2009/10. CLACs and CLANs will cease on 31 March 2013 and will be able to tender for a new contract to commence 1 April 2013.

14.7 THE CRIMINAL DEFENCE SERVICE

The Criminal Defence Service (CDS) uses criminal legal aid to help people who are under investigation or facing criminal charges. By ensuring that people accused of crimes have access to legal advice and representation, the CDS also helps the police and courts operate fairly and efficiently.

Criminal legal aid can offer:

- advice and assistance from a solicitor on criminal matters;
- free legal advice from a solicitor at the police station during questioning;

- the cost of a solicitor preparing a case and initial representation for certain proceedings at a magistrates' or Crown Court;
- full legal representation for defence in criminal cases at all court levels;
- a duty solicitor to provide free legal advice and representation at magistrates' court.

The Criminal Defence Service Act 2006 changed the arrangements for the grant of public funding for representation in criminal proceedings in England and Wales. It provides for the power to grant rights to representation to be conferred on the Legal Services Commission (LSC) instead of that being done by a court. It introduces a test of financial eligibility for the grant of such funding and, in cases where eligibility exists, contributions based on means.

The creation of the Criminal Defence Service (CDS) was part of the government's fundamental reform of the legal aid system, as set out in the Access to Justice Act 1999. The purpose of the CDS is to ensure access for individuals involved in criminal investigations or criminal proceedings to such advice, assistance and representation as the interests of justice require. The CDS was implemented and is managed by the LSC, which was also created by the Access to Justice Act 1999. Solicitors are required to work within quality assured contracts to perform CDS functions.

The LSC is responsible for funding legal representation under the Criminal Defence Service. However, under the old structure, it was the courts – and not the LSC – which were responsible for granting the right to have funding. Now the applications for funding are made centrally, not to a court.

The LSC awards CDS contracts to quality assured providers. At 31 March 2012, 2,309 solicitors' offices operated under a CDS contract, a net increase of 4.5 per cent on 2010/11.

The reduction in the number of contracts held reflects the trend over the last several years for offices doing small amounts of legal aid work to drop out of the market or merge with other offices, so that the work is done in larger volumes at fewer offices. As the LSC continues to pursue higher quality legal services, the number of providers is reducing (LSC Annual Report 2007/08, p 24). The LSC has stated that these trends have not significantly affected the ability of the public to obtain legal aid when they require it. That, however, is disputed by many lawyers (see www.lag.org.uk).

To get funding, an applicant must pass two tests: an 'interests of justice' test (that is, it is deemed to be in the interests of justice that society funds an applicant for his or her case), and a financial eligibility test.

The Interests of Justice Test

The 'interests of justice' test determines whether an applicant is entitled to a Representation Order based on the merits of the case. This is also known as the 'Widgery Criteria' (after the name of the judge in whose 1966 government report on legal aid they were originally formulated).

The applicant must indicate which of the following criteria they believe apply to their case:

- It is likely that I will lose my liberty.
- I have been given a sentence that is suspended or non-custodial. If I break this, the court may be able to deal with me for the original offence.
- It is likely that I will lose my livelihood.
- It is likely that I will suffer serious damage to my reputation.
- A substantial question of law may be involved.
- I may not be able to understand the court proceedings or present my own case.
- I may need witnesses to be traced or interviewed on my behalf.
- The proceedings may involve expert cross-examination of a prosecution witness.
- It is in the interests of another person that I am represented.
- Any other reasons.

If the applicant passes the 'interests of justice' test, he or she must also pass the means test to qualify for legal aid. The aid will be granted to an applicant who does not have the financial means to fund their own representation in a magistrates' court.

The means test in the magistrates' court establishes whether an applicant is financially eligible for legal aid. It only considers income and expenses – capital is not included.

Her Majesty's Courts Service (HMCS) staff apply the test once they receive a correctly completed application form.

So-called 'passported applicants' are those individuals who automatically pass the means test (for example because of the state benefits they are on). These applicants will still need to pass the interests of justice test to qualify for legal aid. The initial means test assesses the applicant's income and how this is spread between any partners and children.

A full means test is carried out if, through the initial means test, the applicant's adjusted income is calculated (after April 2008) to be more than £12,475 and less than £22,325. It works out an applicant's disposable income after deducting tax, maintenance and other annual costs from the gross annual income. There is also a complex means test for those who have complex financial circumstances. Hardship reviews can be carried out if an applicant can show they are genuinely unable to fund their own representation. A person may qualify for criminal legal aid if their annual disposable income exceeds £3,398, subject to making a contribution. This would be refunded if found not guilty. If found guilty and their capital exceeds £30,000, a contribution may be required.

In 2011/12, the public expenditure on the criminal defence service was £1,100m (LSC Annual Report, p 7). One service provided is known as 'CDS Direct'. It is a telephone helpline that provides non-means-tested legal advice direct to members of the public who are suspected of less serious criminal offences and detained by the police. In 2011/12 CDS Direct dealt with 143,602 cases, on issues like driving with excess alcohol, failure to provide a specimen and breach of bail conditions. In terms of response times, CDS Direct made over 98 per cent of outgoing calls to clients within 15 minutes (against a target of 90 per cent) and over 99 per cent within 30 minutes (against a target of 95 per cent). CDS Direct was expanded in early 2008 to cover own-client work as well as duty work for the same offences. This change, as well as providing better value for money, enables clients to receive quicker access to advice, which reduces their time in custody (LSC Annual Report 2007/08, p 25).

14.8   PUBLIC DEFENDER SERVICE

The Commission is piloting its own Public Defender Service (PDS). Section 13(2)(f) of the 1999 Act contains powers to enable the Commission to provide services through lawyers in its own employment. These powers are intended to provide flexibility if, for example, there is limited coverage by private lawyers in rural areas. Using employed lawyers should also, the government has argued, provide the Commission with better information about the real costs of providing these services. The Public Defender Service aims to:

- provide independent, high-quality value for money criminal defence services to the public;
- provide examples of excellence in the provision of criminal defence services nationally and locally;
- provide benchmarking information to be used to improve the performance of the contracting regime for private practice suppliers;
- raise the level of understanding within government and all levels and areas of the Commission of the issues facing criminal defence lawyers in providing high-quality services to the public;
- provide an additional option for ensuring the provision of quality criminal defence services in geographical areas where existing provision is low or of a poor standard;
- recruit, train and develop people to provide high-quality criminal defence services, in accordance with the PDS's own business needs, which will add to the body of such people available to provide criminal defence services generally; and share with private practice suppliers best practice in terms of forms, systems and so on, developed within the PDS to assist in the overall improvement of CDS provision locally.

The Public Defender Service (PDS) is the first salaried criminal provider in England and Wales.

There are currently four PDS offices: Cheltenham, Darlington, Pontypridd and Swansea.

The LSC directly employs the PDS staff of solicitors, accredited representatives and administrators. The PDS provides independent advice, assistance and representation on criminal matters. Lawyers are available 24 hours a day, seven days a week to give advice to people in custody, and represent clients in magistrates', Crown and higher courts where necessary. In 2011/12 the PDS opened 3,197 files.

14.9   THE MAGEE REVIEW 2009

In October, 2009 the Ministry of Justice announced a review of the way the £2 billion legal aid budget is delivered. The resultant conclusions could see separate civil and criminal funds run by different bodies (C Baksi, *Law Society Gazette*, 14 October 2009). The review was established while legal aid lawyers warned that firms providing social welfare legal services are at risk of collapse because of the 'artificial' way work is being distributed by the Legal Services Commission. Lord Bach, the minister for legal aid, appointed Sir Ian Magee, a former permanent secretary at the Department for Constitutional Affairs, to explore ways of optimising value for money in the way legal aid is administered.

Bach told the *Gazette* he was 'ruling nothing out and nothing in'. He said he would be surprised if the LSC ceased to exist, but said it could work alongside another body, with one administering the criminal budget and the other the civil budget. The two budgets could be ring-fenced.

The Law Society has warned that the LSC's policy of capping the number of new social welfare cases or 'matter starts' that a firm can take on could cause some firms to collapse. Nicola Mackintosh of legal aid firm Mackintosh Duncan questioned why the LSC was 'artificially limiting the number of clients who can get access to justice' by allocating firms only a set number of new cases (*Law Society Gazette*, 14 October 2009, p 1).

14.10   THE VOLUNTARY SECTOR

There are over 1,500 not-for-profit advice agencies in England and Wales. They receive their funding – over £150 million a year in total – from many different sources, mainly local authorities, but also charities including the National Lottery Charities Board, central government and the LSC. The provision of advice services is not spread consistently across the country. Some areas appear to have relatively high levels of both legal practitioners and voluntary outlets, while others have few or none. For example, the LSC's South East Area has one Citizens' Advice Bureau per 46,000 people, but, in the East Midlands, 138,000 people share a Citizens' Advice Bureau. The government believes that the fragmented nature of the advice sector obstructs effective planning and prevents local needs for legal advice and help from being met as rationally and fully as possible. The CAB helped 2.1 million people with 7.1 million problems in 2010/11 (CAB website).

14.10.1   LAW CENTRES

There are currently 55 Law Centres in England and Wales staffed by salaried solicitors, trainee solicitors and non-lawyer experts in other areas like debt management. They are funded by local and central government and charity. They have 'shop front' access and aim to be user-friendly and unintimidating. They are managed by committees and represented by the Law Centres' Federation (LCF). The first centre was established in England in North Kensington in July 1970 in the face of great opposition from The Law Society. Since then, the Society has developed a more tolerant stance to the centres as it acknowledges that they can confer benefits to local law firms through the referrals of clients.

Law Centres take on individual cases, providing, for example, advice on landlord and tenant matters and representing people at tribunals. Some centres also take on group work since quite often the problems of one client are part of a wider problem. This sort of work is controversial.

Law Centres co-operate with the LSC; however, this could end as a result of funding cuts and the introduction of fixed fees from 1 October 2007. John Fitzpatrick, the chairman of the LCF, was quoted in the *Law Society Gazette* (15/3/2007) as saying that fixed fees will effectively be 'dumbing down legal services'. He was of the opinion that 'there will be an irresistible pressure to push more simple cases through the Legal Aid system at the expense of the complex cases all Legal Aid lawyers try to take up, and that Law Centres specialise in'. The Secretary of State for Justice, Kenneth Clarke QC MP, announced on 30 June 2011 a fund of £20 million to assist Law Centres and not-for-profit advice organisations.

14.10.2 OTHER VOLUNTARY ADVICE

The Citizens' Advice Bureaux (CAB) have been assisting people since 1939 and there are now 394 CAB in England and Wales providing free, independent and impartial information and advice from over 3,300 locations. They deal with a high number of cases (over six million a year) and a very wide range of problems of which between one-third and one-half are legal problems. In 2005/06 the CAB clients' main problems were benefits, debt, employment, housing and legal. There are, however, very few trained lawyers working for the Bureaux, but over 20,000 volunteer helpers. In keeping with the changing technology of the modern world, the CAB now offers an online help service through its website providing independent advice on a range of topics such as money, family, consumer matters and civil rights.

The CLS launched CLS Direct in July 2004, a website providing free advice on a range of matters similar to the CAB. The website offers topics of the month on the home page such as redundancy rights. It also contains an online calculator to assist people to determine whether they qualify for legal aid. Legal information leaflets and factsheets are also available on this site.

The Bar Council supports a Free Representation Unit for clients at a variety of tribunals for which legal aid is not available. Most of the representation is carried out by Bar students supported and advised by full-time caseworkers. A special Bar unit based in London was formed in 1996 through which more senior barristers provide representation. Some colleges and universities also offer advice. For example, the College of Law in London operates a free advice service in which vocational students give advice on such matters as personal injury cases and employment law.

Both barristers and solicitors operate '*pro bono*' (from the Latin phrase *pro bono publico*, meaning for the public good) schemes under which legal work is done without charge or at reduced cost for members of the public ineligible for legal aid from the LSC but with limited means, or charitable and other non-profit-making organisations. Examples of *pro bono* activities include: solicitors attending advice sessions at Citizens' Advice Bureaux or other free services; free advice to members of organisations, for example, trade union general advice schemes; secondment to Law Centres; and free advice to charitable organisations.

14.11   CONDITIONAL FEE ARRANGEMENTS

These are sometimes known as 'no win, no fee' agreements. They are not used for family or criminal matters, but can be used in many types of civil action. In a 'no win, no fee' agreement, a litigant's solicitor will only be paid if the claim is successful. If so, the solicitor will also be entitled to an extra fee (known as a success fee). Both the basic fee and this extra fee are normally paid in whole or part by the losing party.

There are other incurred costs (such as court fees or the fee for a medical report). These are normally known as disbursements. Again, the losing party should pay all or part of these costs. A litigant is liable to pay his or her solicitor for any costs that the losing party is not ordered to pay.

If, under such an arrangement, a litigant's claim fails, they will not have to pay their own solicitor, but they will still probably have to pay the costs of the successful party – the other side. That is something, however, against which they can take out insurance. They will also have to pay any other incurred costs (such as court fees or the fee for a medical report). These are normally known as disbursements. The insurance in these circumstances is known as 'after the event' insurance. The client may have to pay the insurance premium.

Background

As part of the scheme to expose the provision of legal services to the full rigour of market forces, the then Lord Chancellor chose to devote an entire Green Paper in 1989 to *Contingency Fees*. Following a recommendation from the Civil Justice Review, the Paper had sought opinion on the funding of litigation on a contingent fee basis. This provides that litigation is funded by the claimant only if he wins, in which event, the lawyer claims fees as a portion of the damages payable to the claimant. The response to this idea was largely hostile.

The traditional opposition to contingency fees in the English legal system was that they were 'maintenance' (the financial support of another's litigation) and 'champerty' (taking a financial interest in another's litigation). Champerty occurs when the person maintaining another takes as his reward a portion of the property in dispute. It taints an agreement with illegality and renders it void (for a discussion of the principle, see *Grovewood Holding plc v James Capel & Co Ltd* (1995)). Section 14 of the Criminal Justice Act 1967 abolished maintenance and champerty as crimes and torts, but kept the rules making such arrangements improper for solicitors.

English litigation uses the Indemnity Rule, by which the loser pays the costs of the winner and thus puts him, more or less, in the position he enjoyed before the damage was done. Objectors to contingency fee agreements pointed out that such things were incompatible with the Indemnity Rule because, although the winner's costs would be paid for him by the other side, he would still have to pay for his lawyer from his damages (calculated to put him in the position he would have enjoyed if no wrong had been done to him) so he would not really be 'made whole' by his award. The position is different in the United States, where contingency agreements are common in personal injury cases, because there each side bears its own costs.

It was further contended by objectors to the contingency fee that the legal aid system adequately catered for those who were too poor to afford an ordinary private action. Even if there were people who were just above the legal aid financial thresholds but still too poor to pay for an action, this should be dealt with simply by changing the threshold.

Section 58 of the Courts and Legal Services Act (CLSA) 1990 permitted the Lord Chancellor to introduce conditional fee arrangements, although these cannot apply to criminal cases, family cases or those involving children (s 58(10)). However, there are a number of different arrangements for conditional fees, so one issue to be addressed was the type of conditional fee system that should be applied in England and Wales. The Scottish model, for which initially there was reasonable support, is that of the 'speculative fee', whereby the solicitor can agree with his client that he would be paid his ordinary taxed costs only if he won the case. Two other forms of contingency fee were rejected during the consultation period as being unsuitable. The first was a restricted contingency fee system in which the fee payable in the event of a successful action would be a *percentage of the damages*, but where the actual levels of recovery would be governed by rules. The second was an unrestricted contingency arrangement, similarly based on a percentage of damages, but at uncontrolled levels. These plans were rejected because it was thought that to give the lawyer a stake in the claimant's damages would be likely to create unacceptable temptations for the lawyer to behave unprofessionally in order to secure his fee.

The system eventually adopted is that where conditional fees are based on an 'uplift' from the level of fee the lawyer would normally charge for the sort of work in question. Originally, the maximum uplift was to be 20 per cent in order to induce lawyers to take on potentially difficult cases and to help finance lawyers' unsuccessful conditional fee cases. This would have meant they could charge the fee that they would normally charge for a given type of case, plus an additional fifth.

In August 1993, after a long process of negotiation with the profession, Lord Mackay, the then Lord Chancellor, finally announced that he would allow the conditional fee to operate on a 100 per cent uplift. Thus, solicitors receive no fee if they lose a case, but double what they would normally charge if they win the case. The Law Society had campaigned vigorously against the proposed 20 per cent uplift, arguing that such risks as the no win, no fee arrangement entailed would not be regarded as worth taking by many solicitors simply on the incentive that their fee for winning the case would be 20 per cent more than they would normally charge for such a case. The LCD originally decided to restrict the scheme to cases involving personal injury, insolvency and the European Court of Human Rights.

The system came into effect in June 1995. Such agreements are now legal, provided that they comply with any requirements imposed by the Lord Chancellor and are not 'contentious business agreements'. These are defined under s 59 of the Solicitors Act 1974 as agreements between a solicitor and his client made in writing by which the solicitor is to be remunerated by a gross sum, or a salary, at agreed hourly rates or otherwise, and whether higher or lower than that at which he would normally be remunerated. A valid CFA must comply with the LCD requirements, be in writing, stating the percentage uplift payable if successful (and 'must not exceed the percentage specified in relation to the description of proceedings to which the agreement relates by order made by the Lord Chancellor' – s 58(4)(c) CLSA 1990 as amended by s 27 of the Access to Justice Act 1999). A CFA cannot be used if proceedings do not allow an enforceable CFA.

The right to use 'no win, no fee' agreements to pursue civil law claims was extended by the Conditional Fee Agreements Order 1998. The Order allowed lawyers to offer conditional fee agreements to their clients in all civil cases excluding family cases. Speaking in the House of Lords on 23 July, the then Lord Chancellor, Lord Irvine, said:

> These agreements will result in a huge expansion of access to justice. Today, only the very rich or the very poor can afford to litigate. In future, everyone with a really strong case will be able to secure his rights free of the fear of ruin if he loses. They will bring the majority of our people into access to justice.

Conditional fees have been the means by which at least several hundred thousand personal injury cases have been brought, and many, in all likelihood, would not have been brought but for the existence of conditional fees. The Order retains the old rule that the maximum uplift on the fees lawyers can charge is 100 per cent. Thus, a lawyer may take on a claim against an allegedly negligent employer whose carelessness has resulted in the client being injured. The lawyer, who might normally charge £2,000 for such a case, can say 'I shall do this work for nothing if we lose, but £3,000 if we win'. In fact, as the price uplift can be up to 100 per cent of the normal fee, he can stipulate for up to £4,000 in this example. The Law Society has recommended an additional voluntary cap of 25 per cent of damages, and this has been widely accepted in practice.

The real problems continued to be:

(a)   that the new system, designed really to help the millions who have been regulated out of the legal aid system, does not help people whose cases stand only a limited chance of success, as lawyers will not take their cases; and

(b)   the difficulties of a claimant getting insurance to cover the costs that he will have to pay, if he loses the claim, for the other side's lawyers. Where a personal injury claim arises from a road traffic incident, it is almost always clear to a solicitor where blame and legal liability probably lie. Risks are therefore calculable by insurance companies, so one can presently insure against having to pay the other side's costs in the event of losing an action on a personal injury case for about £100 in a 'no win, no fee' arrangement. There are, however, many areas, and medical negligence cases are good examples, where the chances of success are notoriously difficult to predict. Thus, insurance against having to pay the other side's costs is prohibitively high, running into many thousands of pounds in some cases. It is quite unrealistic to assume that all such cases, arising often from highly distressing circumstances, will be dealt with in future on a 'no win, no fee' basis. Lawyers will generally not want to take on such cases on such a basis, and even where they do, clients will often not be able to afford the necessary insurance. As insurance to cover client costs in medical 'no win, no fee' cases has proven so expensive, legal aid continues to cover clinical negligence cases.

14.11.1 THE ACCESS TO JUSTICE ACT 1999

The Access to Justice Act 1999 (ss 27–31), together with the Conditional Fee Arrangements Regulations 2000 and the Collective Conditional Fee Agreements Regulations 2000, reformed the law relating to conditional fees to enable the court to order a losing party to pay, in addition to the other party's normal legal costs, the uplift on the successful party's lawyers' fees and, in any case where a litigant has insured against facing an order for the other side's costs, any premium paid by the successful party for that insurance. The intention was to:

- ensure that the compensation awarded to a successful party is not eroded by any uplift or premium. The party in the wrong will bear the full burden of costs;
- make conditional fees more attractive, in particular to defendants and to claimants seeking non-monetary redress (these litigants can rarely use conditional fees now, because they cannot rely on the prospect of recovering damages to meet the cost of the uplift and premium);
- discourage weak cases and encourage settlements;
- provide a mechanism for regulating the uplifts that solicitors charge. In future, unsuccessful litigants will be able to challenge unreasonably high uplifts when the court comes to assess costs.

In the first version of conditional fee arrangements, only people who expected to win money from their case could benefit from conditional fees. This was the only way that most people could afford to pay the success fee. There were also available insurance policies that could be taken out by someone contemplating litigation to cover the costs of the other party and the client's own costs (including, if not a conditional fee case, a client's solicitor's fees) if the case was lost. However, it meant that a successful litigant would not receive all the money he was awarded, so the government made provision in the Access to Justice Act 1999 to make it possible for the winning party to recover the success fee and any insurance premium from the losing party.

The rules, which had become very complex for all using them, were simplified in 2005. The Conditional Fee Agreements Regulations 2000 and the Collective Conditional Fee Agreements Regulations 2000 were revoked by the Conditional Fee Agreement (Revocation) Regulations 2005 (SI 2005/2305). The Access to Justice (Membership

Organisation) Regulations 2000 were revoked and replaced by the simpler Access to Justice (Membership Organisation) Regulations 2005 (SI 2005/2306).

The removal of the unnecessary regulation was applied to all CFAs across the range of civil cases, including commercial, insolvency, environmental, intellectual property, human rights, privacy, defamation and injury.

Announcing the simplified arrangements, Parliamentary Under Secretary of State Baroness Ashton of Upholland said (10 August, 2005):

> Conditional fee agreements play a valuable role in helping people with valid claims obtain access to justice. For many consumers and businesses this provides the only means of obtaining appropriate redress. A regime that is complex and opaque puts the consumer at a disadvantage. Revoking the existing regulations will help make CFA agreements a simpler product and in particular will help consumers to better understand the agreements they enter into and the risks they could face in contemplating litigation. Consumer safeguards will be improved as responsibility for proper advice falls on the solicitor.

Regulation of solicitors involved in CFA cases is the responsibility of the Solicitors' Regulation Authority. It is required to ensure that clients are fully informed about the strength of their case and prospects of success in clear, simple terms. This is designed to help to ensure that only well-founded claims proceed and benefit both claimants and defendants who will be spared the stress of avoidable court hearings.

Collective Conditional Fee Arrangements

Collective conditional fee agreements are designed specifically for mass providers and purchasers of legal services, such as trade unions, insurers or commercial organisations. A collective conditional fee agreement enables a trade union to enter into a single agreement with solicitors to govern the way in which cases for its members will be run and paid for; by simplifying the standard individual process, it reduces the cost of pursuing separate individual cases. The scheme also benefits commercial organisations which are able to enter collective conditional fee agreements to pursue or defend claims arising in the course of business.

14.11.2   THE ADVANTAGES OF CONDITIONAL FEE ARRANGEMENTS

For claimants, the advantages can be summarised as being:

- that lawyers acting in any case will be confident (they will have had to weigh carefully the chances of success before taking the case as their fee depends on winning) and determined;
- there will be freedom from the anxiety of having to pay huge fees;

- there will be no need to pay fees in advance; and
- there will be no delays or worries with legal aid applications.

For defendants there will be advantages too, as the contingency fee system will probably reduce the number of spurious claims. In a period where legal aid is being cut back so drastically, preventing so many people from going to law, this system can be seen as a way of preserving at least some limited access to the legal process. Losing parties will still be liable to pay the other side's costs, so it will be unlikely that people will take action unless they consider they have a good chance of success.

The taxpayer can also be given the advantage in the form of a significant reduction in the funding of the legal aid system. Furthermore, practitioners who are competent to assess and willing to take the risks of litigation will arguably enjoy a better fee-paying basis, increased fee income and overall business, fewer reasons for delay and more satisfied clients with fewer complaints.

Consider two examples. First, a middle-class couple consult their solicitor about injuries received in a road accident. Their joint income and savings put them outside the legal aid scheme. The proposed litigation is beset with uncertainties as the other driver's insurers have denied liability. The couple have to worry about their own expenses and the possibility under the Indemnity Rule of paying for the defendant's costs. Second, a young man who has been injured at work wants to sue his employer. The case will turn on some difficult health and safety law on which there are currently conflicting decisions. He is eligible for legal aid, but he will have to make substantial contributions because of his level of income, and if his claim fails, he will have to pay the same sum again towards the expenses of his employers. In both cases, the prospective litigants might well drop any plan to litigate. Both cases, however, might proceed expeditiously if they found a lawyer to act on a no win, no fee basis.

14.11.3 THE DISADVANTAGES OF CONDITIONAL FEE ARRANGEMENTS

Critics of the system argue that it encourages the sort of speculative actions that occur frequently in the United States, taken up by the so-called 'ambulance-chasing' lawyers. It can be argued that the system of contingency fees creates a conflict of interest between the lay client and the lawyer, with a consequential risk of exploitation of the client. Where a lawyer's fee depends on the outcome of a case, there is a greater temptation for him to act unethically. When the Royal Commission on Legal Services (1979) rejected the idea of contingent fees, it stated that such a scheme might lead to undesirable practices by lawyers including, 'the construction of evidence, the improper coaching of witnesses, the use of professionally partisan expert witnesses, especially medical witnesses, improper examination and cross-examination, groundless legal arguments designed to lead the courts into error and competitive touting'. If the case was won, the lawyer claimed a significant part of the damages, but there was also a real danger that lawyers would be pressured to settle too readily to avoid the costs of preparing for a trial that could be lost and therewith the fee. An example would be where an insurance company admits liability but contests the level of damages. The claimant might stand to get substantially higher compensation by contesting the case. Under the new system, however, his solicitor will have a strong interest in advising him to settle. A settlement would guarantee the solicitor's costs and the agreed 'mark-up' (up to 100 per cent more than a normal fee for such work), both of which would be completely lost if the case was fought and lost. This would not occur outside of a conditional fee arrangement. Although the conventional system of payment was not without problems, as Walter Merricks, then of The Law Society, has stated:

> ... when a lawyer is being paid by the hour, he may have a financial interest in encouraging his client to go on with an open-and-shut case, increasing his own fees.

The Law Society has argued that the system, if not properly regulated, could promote the sort of 'ambulance chasing' practised by American lawyers in the wake of the 1984 Bhopal disaster, in which over 2,500 people were killed by escaping gas from a US company (Union Carbide Corporation) plant in India. American lawyers flew out to act for victims and their relatives and some were reported to be taking fees of 50 per cent of the claimants' damages.

It was argued by some that by allowing lawyers to *double* their normal fee for certain cases, the Lord Chancellor risked eliminating any benefit speculative fees might bring. If the successful client was not to be able to recover the *uplift* from the other side, he would have to fund it himself out of the damages he had been awarded. In effect, this often resulted in his damages being halved. The uplift can now be recovered, subject to taxation (that is, court official approval), following changes made by the Access to Justice Act 1999.

It is not even clear that the main claim made for the system – that it increases access to the courts – is correct. The Scottish experience is that speculative cases do not exceed 1 per cent of the cases in the caseload of the Faculty of Advocates. One firm opponent of the system is Lord Justice Auld. He has argued that the system will eventually endanger the esteem in which lawyers are held by the public. He has doubted whether the scheme will produce greater commitment by lawyers to their cases: 'There is a distinction to be drawn between the lawyer's commitment to the case and his anxiety to recover his fees. The two do not always correspond.'

In 2008 the Minister of Justice, Jack Straw, announced that the government was considering placing a cap on the success fee that lawyers can charge for no-win no-fee work. He said he was concerned about soaring costs. He said 'It's claimed they have provided greater access to justice but the behaviour of some lawyers in ramping up their fees in these cases is nothing short of scandalous' ((2008) NLJ 1308).

14.12   REFORMS TO LEGAL AID

In 2005, Lord Falconer, the Lord Chancellor and Secretary of State for Constitutional Affairs asked Lord Carter of Coles to examine how to improve the arrangements for purchasing publicly funded legal services. Lord Carter was asked to produce a plan to implement a package of reforms to the way publicly funded legal advice and representation is procured by the state. The terms of reference can be found in the command paper 'Fairer Deal for Legal Aid' (Cm 6591). Reports of his review team, examined below, advance various schemes for such improvement.

It took Lord Carter a year to produce his final report, 'Legal Aid – A market-based approach to reform', which was published on 13 July 2006. In this report radical changes to the legal aid system were suggested. One of the main proposals Lord Carter suggested was the move away from hourly rates to a market-based system of competitive tendering. To prepare for these changes, new fixed and graduated fees are being introduced.

There has been a lot of criticism of the government's plans to implement the Carter legal aid reforms by the House of Commons Constitutional Affairs Committee. This is evidenced in their report, Implementation of the Carter Review of Legal Aid (HC 223, 1 May 2007) and can be summarised in their conclusion:

> **238.** The current proposed reforms to the Legal Aid system are radical and ambitious. They represent one of the most significant changes to the Legal Aid system in its history. We support the general aims of the reforms – there is a pressing need to limit the significant rise in expenditure on Legal Aid.
> **239.** The reform package is being implemented at too fast a speed. There has been no time for proper business planning by practitioners or even for them to understand the raft of proposals, counterproposals and consultations which have been emanating from the Legal Services Commission. Although it is clear that there is an urgent problem with Legal Aid expenditure, it is no solution to try to introduce changes in an atmosphere of panic.
> **240.** A major part of the proposals involves the introduction of transitional arrangements which are over complex and too rigid. We think that the Government should reconsider whether they are necessary. We doubt whether the risk to the supplier base which they pose justifies their introduction. We would prefer to see competitive tendering – insofar as that is a solution to the problem – implemented directly, once there has been adequate piloting.
> **241.** We are extremely concerned that the Department is trying to engage in such a far reaching change to the structure of Legal Aid on the basis of little or no evidence about which costs drivers have caused the problem or how its plans for a solution are likely to affect both suppliers and clients. We fear that if the reforms go ahead there is a serious risk to access to justice among the most vulnerable in society. It is clear that the Government has been unwise in attempting to reform the entire system rather than in concentrating on those areas which cause the problem: Crown Court and public law children cases.

In June 2007, the government responded to the Committee's report by publishing a report Implementing Legal Aid Reform. The government provided a summary overview of the programme for legal aid reform and responded in detail to the various points highlighted in the Committee's report. Despite the Committee's criticism, the government's response confirms its (and the LSC's) intention to proceed with the legal aid reforms as set out in Legal Aid Reform: the Way Ahead (Cm 6993, November 2006).

As mentioned earlier in the chapter, the introduction of the new legal aid reforms has not been without controversy. The Law Society sought a judicial review of the Unified Contract for civil work (see above, at 14.3.3) who challenged the legality of the 'amendment clause'. On 27 July 2007, Mr Justice Beatson gave judgment. The judge acknowledged that it was lawful for the LSC to amend the contract in respect of fees and structures. However, he ruled against them in respect of procurement requirements relating to the amendment of technical specifications (which includes KPIs and peer reviews) as the LSC did not comply with Public Contract Regulations 2006 and European Law. The judge stated that any changes should be restricted to those envisaged in the White Paper, 'Legal Aid Reform: the Way Ahead'.

14.12.1 MARKET-BASED REFORMS TO MAKE CRIMINAL LEGAL AID MORE EFFICIENT – THE CARTER REVIEW

Reforms to introduce a more sustainable market for publicly funded criminal defence services were proposed by Lord Carter of Coles as part of his review of legal aid procurement. The report, 'Procurement of Criminal Defence Services: Market Based Reform', recommends a phased transition towards a vibrant, good quality and efficient market nationwide by 2009. Since 1997, spending on criminal legal aid has risen by 37 per cent in real terms. The amount spent has increased from £730 million to nearly £1.2 billion. England and Wales have the highest per capita spend on criminal legal aid in the world at £22 per head.

Introducing his report, Lord Carter said (DCA Statement, 9 February 2006):

> We should be proud of our system of criminal legal aid. It ensures that everyone, whatever their wealth, has access to justice. But there are inherent inefficiencies in the way criminal legal aid work is procured that need addressing if we are to control increasing costs. Not withstanding the dedication and commitment of the profession, a significant amount of the criminal legal aid budget is spent on unproductive time and anomalies in the system. Moving to a sustainable market-based procurement system should help create a quality defence service that rewards the most efficient suppliers, provides clients with appropriate choice and brings greater predictability to cost.

Lord Carter's report acknowledges that moving towards competition is a significant departure from the present system. The report therefore recommends the reforms are introduced over a three-year period to ensure that suppliers of criminal defence services are able to adjust and prepare for the changes. This would involve the following three phases:

1. Fixed pricing for all criminal legal aid work, including that provided in police stations, magistrates' courts and Crown Courts.

2. A managed market, awarding contracts to efficient and good quality suppliers that can take on more cases, either individual firms or collections of firms formed to deliver the benefits of scale.

3. Managed price competition between efficient, good quality suppliers with safeguards to protect standards of quality, coverage in rural areas and diversity.

This phased approach fits with the Legal Service Commission's 'preferred supplier' strategy. The report also recommends that the proposals in this report should replace the Commission's original proposals for price competition in London. The timescale and managed criteria for delivering the market are very different. The flexible approach proposed in the report includes greater controls to manage the risks to suppliers and continuity of delivery of services, especially to black and minority ethnic communities.

The report was drawn up after extensive consultation with the judiciary, representatives of the legal profession and other leading players in the criminal justice system.

In an article following an interview with Lord Carter, Frances Gibb, Legal Editor of *The Times*, set the issues in a graphic context (*The Times*, 14 February 2006):

> What he found was a service that, if not quite dying, was time-limited because of the average age of practitioners – many in their fifties – and demoralised, with unfairnesses in the way that practitioners are paid. 'I was quite shocked, in certain parts, by the clear impoverishment of it. You do have incredible inequities in the system, some people do well and others are not doing very well at all. And there is a general sense of unhappiness.'
>
> Seeing first-hand how police stations work was an eye-opener. He saw the spectrum of clients: the first-timers in a state of shock, some of whom wanted legal advice, and the old hands. The Police and Criminal Evidence Act 1984, which governs what goes on at the station, worked well, he said:
>
>> But when you drill down into it, you find the help people get . . . is not from loyal Mr X from such and such a firm, who stays with you through the episode and sees the case to court and back. It's an agency business: people are processing these cases on behalf of firms – often former policemen or trainee lawyers, albeit accredited to do police station work, but not qualified solicitors. You think of these plucky, downtrodden solicitors out there, but in fact it's a bit like doctors using agencies at night.

As for the lawyers themselves, he found 'all types': 'many are dedicated, have done the work all their lives', for others it is 'just a job' and there is abuse – 'they have found techniques to "sweat" the file and exploit loopholes'. But that, in turn, reflects the low rates of pay for some work, he argues. It is like a constant game of dodge with the taxman: 'People find a way to maximise income, then that is closed and they find another – it's a determination to maintain income levels.' His aim is to end that battle and devise a system that is fairer to both sides.

The crunch question is whether a price-driven model can preserve quality and ensure no corner-cutting. He believes that it can: the professional bodies will be in charge of standards – peer review, he says, is the key. And price will be one factor, but not the only one – 'service will also be important'. The price at which a job can be fairly and properly done will be calculated, then firms asked what discount they can provide. 'But if we think 20% is the maximum reasonable discount, we'd not allow 30%. There will be a floor. We've got to be absolutely clear, nothing must undermine quality.'

Lord Carter's report notes that (page 4)

> The cost of legal aid has risen from 1.5 billion in 1997 to 2.1 billion today, an increase of 10% in real terms. Public spending in this area cannot be without limits. The growth of criminal legal aid (over half of the legal aid budget) is putting pressure on vital services for vulnerable people, provided through civil and family legal aid.

The report suggests that 'whole-system reform' is needed to deliver a system that is fair to all parties. The report says that a large amount of money is spent on unproductive time. Travel and waiting in police stations and magistrates' courts amounted to £90m in 2004/05. Part of this unproductive time is a result of inherent inefficiencies in the wider criminal justice system. There are approximately 2,500 suppliers of criminal defence services. The sheer number of suppliers in many urban areas makes it difficult for them to obtain volumes of work to structure themselves in the most efficient way. Many legal firms delivering legal aid complain about the bureaucratic costs they incur through the large amount of auditable information they must record as part of their duties. Approximately 1.5 million claims for payment are made every year.

The report recommends that the new market-based system should be dynamic. Rather than dealing with individual problems and anomalies of the scheme as they stand today, it argues that complete reform is needed. It notes that by 2009 a steady-state should have been reached, with a smaller number of large, more efficient, good quality suppliers who profit from increased volumes of work. It aims to provide (p 4):

an integrated system for delivering criminal justice services from the police station through to disposal in the Crown Court.

On completion of a series of phased reforms suppliers will be working under new contracting arrangements to deliver police station and associated magistrates' court and Crown Court work as a 'joined-up service'. The final phase of reforms will see contracts being tendered on quality (overseen by the professional regulating bodies), capacity and price. Contracts will cover a group of police stations and their associated magistrates' courts and Crown Court cases. Contracts will be competed for on a one- to two-year basis depending on the stability of the new market. This means that a smaller number of firms than now provide legal aid work will, if they have proved to the Legal Services Commission that they deserve 'preferred supplier' status, offer services to the public in future.

Payment for the provision of defence services in the police station will be by a block grant for the duration of the contract. So, a law firm winning an appropriate contract would have to provide all of the relevant defence services associated with that police station for a given period. Magistrates' court cases will be paid a fixed fee per case determined as part of the competition to award contracts. Contracts for police station work will also require the contractor to provide defence services for the majority of the Crown Court cases that come through their police station(s). Litigation and advocacy services in the Crown Court will be paid through a single graduated fee scheme determined as part of the competition to award police station contracts.

Defence services in very high-cost cases will be paid for under individual case contracts with single defence teams working to strict costs and case management rules. These defence teams will have to gain access to a specialist panel of suppliers. Teams will be required to pass an enhanced quality test demonstrating both expertise and experience to undertake this work. They will also need to have sufficient capacity to undertake cases at a competitive market rate. Lord Carter's report states that new auditing arrangements will ensure poor performing defence teams are penalised.

14.12.2 CIVIL LEGAL AID

In March 2006 the Department for Constitutional Affairs published a report suggesting that better co-ordinated delivery of legal advice could help resolve disputes about debt, housing, employment and other matters earlier and more effectively.

The report, *Getting Earlier, Better Advice To Vulnerable People*, set out a programme for co-ordinating and enhancing the role of independent advice across central and local government, and for using feedback from the process to help improve public services. It sought to develop a strategy for helping people, especially the vulnerable and socially excluded, to obtain such advice more easily.

The report suggested that such a strategy should address:

- the 'cluster' effect of problems, and stopping one problem escalating into other, often more serious, problems;

- quicker resolution of problems, enabling more people to be helped;
- more efficient use of limited resources in the advice sector; and
- ensuring that public services learn from mistakes, improving staff understanding, increasing efficiency, and reducing claims for compensation.

The Community Legal Service (CLS) strategy published in March 2006 set out how the Legal Services Commission (LSC) proposes to make the legally aided advice system more targeted to the socially excluded and others who really need advice.

A research paper, *Causes of Action*, 2006, suggests that the failure to resolve legal problems quickly and effectively can have wide-ranging and damaging effects on health, employment and domestic situations. It also has wider implications for public services, including significant costs for agencies such as the NHS, Department for Work and Pensions and the police, estimated to cost at least £3.5 billion each year.

More than half of civil legal problems lead to adverse outcomes such as ill-health, unemployment and homelessness, according to a study released today by the Legal Services Research Centre (LSRC).

The study is the most in-depth and long-term study into civil justice problems conducted in England and Wales. The research revealed a significant reduction in the number of people not taking action to resolve their problems in recent years. But around one in 10 people with legal problems are still not seeking advice, and around 15 per cent of those who seek advice fail to obtain any.

Other main findings:

- 30 per cent of civil justice problems affect people's health;
- 18 per cent of problems lead to stress-related ill-health;
- 6 per cent of problems lead to physical ill-health;
- of those who had physical health problems:

  (i)   1 in 5 needed medical treatment;

  (ii)   2 in 3 treated by GPs required an average of six appointments;

  (iii) 1 in 10 who are hospitalised spend an average of 9.5 days as inpatients;

- 16 per cent of problems lead to loss of income or employment;
- 6 per cent lead to loss of home.

The research found that civil problems can bring about and worsen social exclusion. Half of victims of crime also report a civil justice problem.

Three principal and distinct problem clusters can be identified. Clustering of problems occurs when there is a tendency for particular problems to be experienced simultaneously or in sequence by the same person. An understanding of clustering can help us to develop advice and legal services that address people's related needs. These are:

- 'Family' (domestic violence, divorce, relationship and children problems);
- 'Homelessness' (rented housing, homelessness and benefits);

●　　'Economic' (money and debt, consumer and employment problems).

Michael Bichard, LSC Chair said (LSC *Statement*, 23 March 2006):

> This research makes our challenge plain: get more legal advice to people and make it easy to find. The figures show that when people get early advice they will be healthier and happier. There is also a benefit to the public purse by avoiding the downstream cost of unsolved problems. The evidence of 'problem clusters' clearly shows the importance of joined up public services. Our new strategy for the Community Legal Service will make a real difference in tackling these challenges.

Client Case Study

The LSC *Statement* included this case study:

> Peter from Derby is disabled and found himself homeless because his rented accommodation wasn't properly adapted for wheelchair access. His housing application was denied because he was in arrears after not having received his Housing Benefit so he had to stay with his mother. A doctor confirmed that sleeping on the settee, having to crawl to the toilet and not being able to wash adequately was detrimental to his health.
>
> He has seen a huge improvement in his quality of life since the LSC granted legal aid to pay for help from Derbyshire Housing Aid. Legal work challenged the decisions made by a number of the local authority's departments, and Peter's needs were assessed again, he was rehoused into suitable adapted accommodation and he received £1,500 he was entitled to in Housing Benefit and £200 compensation.
>
> Peter said: 'I was really impressed by the level of advice and all the help that my advisor gave me. I now have no rent arrears and I am now happy in my new home, which is adapted for wheelchair use. Without the advice I would be homeless and in debt.'
>
> Many in the medical profession regularly see problems like Peter's. The following GPs refer patients to specialist advice on debt and accessing welfare benefits as part of a project funded by the Legal Services Commission involving six Northampton surgeries. The project has helped over 1,200 people since April 2002.

As part of the reforms to civil legal aid, fixed fees have been introduced with effect from 1 October 2007. The LSC also plans to introduce best value tendering (BVT) from 2009, and in the interim, to proceed with small scale tendering as part of the development of Community Legal Advice Centres and Networks for integrated social welfare law and family services. The LSC dropped the plans for BVT in December 2009.

Carolyn Regan, the LSC Chief Executive has commented that 'the new fixed fees will ensure greater value for money by moving from paying for inputs, like time spent and letters written, to outputs, like completed cases, which make a real difference for clients. The fees will also help providers adjust the way they work as they prepare for the introduction of best value tendering, when they will be bidding on the basis of a fixed fee for a specified amount of work'. She also commented that the 'changes are part of the overall reform of legal aid and will build on the improvements in quality of advice and value for money that the LSC and providers have achieved over recent years. They will enable us to continue increasing the number of people helped by civil legal aid by making best use of the funding available'.

Following the government's review of public expenditure, the Legal Services Commission will no longer be a Non-Departmental Public Body (NDPB), but will become an Executive Agency of the Ministry of Justice.

The Adam Smith Institute published a report on 26 August 2010 by Anthony Barton called 'Access to Justice – Balancing the Risks', and in conclusion stated:

> Both the legal aid and the CFA systems are flawed in that they give rise to situations which are not economically sustainable or politically acceptable. There is no prospect of expansion of civil legal aid – the indications are that there will be wide-ranging public sector cutbacks. The present CFA system allows overgenerous recovery of success fees and ATE insurance premium against defendants; this can be readily reformed. The risks of litigation can be apportioned fairly between the parties by capping the level of the success fee and the ATE insurance premium recoverable from the defendant; the claimant will have price incentives. A capping of additional costs liabilities can be probably achieved by secondary legislation and/or rules of court. Lord Justice Jackson's proposed shifting of additional costs liabilities is impractical and requires primary legislation. These cost-capping proposals will go some way to provide a system of funding access to justice that is simple, robust, fair, accessible, affordable and proportionate. The Government's proposed review of legal aid is part of a bigger scheme of public funding cuts. Accordingly it is crucial that any reform of civil costs regime in CFAs provides appropriate practical solutions. There should be an integrated review of funding access to civil justice which combines review of legal aid, reform of costs in CFAs and response to Lord Justice Jackson's *Review of Civil Litigation Costs*, and which addresses Lord Young's review of the operation of health and safety laws and the growth of the compensation culture.

The 2010 Government Papers

Governmental plans announced in November 2010 ('Legal aid cut to save taxpayer up to £400 million in a decade', Frances Gibb, *The Times*, 16 November) would, if implemented, severely affect the access to justice of a significant part of the population. The paper *Proposals for the Reform of Legal Aid in England and Wales*

Consultation Paper CP12/10, November 2010, would entail that more than 500,000 people would no longer qualify for legal aid in order to save up to £400 million over 10 years. Legal aid would be abolished for a range of problems including divorce, debt, employment, housing, welfare, immigration, clinical negligence and education.

In a severe reduction of lawyers' fees, barristers' earnings in civil and family cases would be cut by 42 per cent. Overall, lawyers' income would be reduced by up to £154 million over four years and the value of their caseloads by up to £275 million. Under the plans, only the most serious cases would be funded by legal aid, such as those where people's liberty or life is at risk, or where they are at risk of serious physical harm or immediate loss of their home. It would also remain for cases involving asylum, debt, housing where someone faces eviction, where children are liable to be taken into care and domestic violence.

The proposals were presented as beneficial as they would stop taxpayers' money being used in family disputes where couples squabble over children (saving £178 million a year); and for medical negligence claims, as well as immigration and welfare benefits, and what are sometimes seen as unwarranted human rights claims by prisoners. People who qualify for legal aid in civil matters will, if the plans are implemented, have to pay more towards their bills under changes to means-testing. Any state benefits will be taken into account and their capital will be taken to include equity in a property. A minimum contribution of £100 will be required from people who have more than £1,000 of disposable capital.

Fees across the board for all family and civil work will be cut by 10 per cent, but the impact on barristers doing civil work will be a '42 per cent reduction in income' and for those doing criminal work 'a 12 per cent reduction'.

Mr Clarke said: 'I strongly believe that access to justice is the hallmark of a civilised society but at more than £2 billion each year, we currently have one of the most expensive legal aid systems in the world. This cannot continue.'

Since its introduction in 1949 the scope had widened far beyond what had been intended, he said, adding: 'It cannot be right that the taxpayer is footing the bill for unnecessary court cases which would never have even reached the courtroom door, were it not for the fact that somebody else was paying.'

A second paper, *Proposals for Reform of Civil Litigation Funding and Costs in England and Wales Implementation of Lord Justice Jackson's Recommendations Consultation Paper* CP 13/10 (November 2010) outlined changes to curb the 'no win, no fee' system. People who sue successfully under such a deal will no longer be able to make the loser pay all their costs, including the 'success' fees charged by the 'no win' lawyers.

The sums awarded in damages would go up by 10 per cent – a figure that many lawyers argue is too low to pay for the cost of the fees that people would incur.

Legal aid will be retained for judicial review challenges against the State, inquests and for mediation, to encourage couples to resolve disputes out of court. It will also be available in exceptional cases such as a complex clinical negligence case involving a disabled claimant. The scope of criminal legal aid will remain the same.

The overhaul of the £2.1 billion legal aid scheme will mean that people will be forced to settle divorce disputes out of court and to take out private legal insurance to pursue their claims.

Vulnerable citizens will be likely to suffer, and the Citizens Advice Bureau warned that those with complex debt, benefit, housing and employment cases were threatened. Gillian Guy, its chief executive, said that in the past year, caseworkers, on legal aid, had dealt with more than 40,000 welfare benefit cases, almost 60,000 debt cases, more than 9,000 housing cases and 3,000 employment cases. 'If people can't access legal help,' she noted, 'the consequences can be dire: spiralling debt, homelessness, family breakdown, domestic violence, depression' (Frances Gibb, Sam Coates, '£350m cut in the legal aid budget "would limit access to justice"', *The Times*, 15 November, 2010).

CHAPTER SUMMARY: THE FUNDING OF LEGAL SERVICES

2. The Legal Aid Board
In 1989, the administration of legal aid was transferred from The Law Society to a new body known as the Legal Aid Board

1. The Background to Legal Aid
– Introduced in 1949 to assist those who would not otherwise have been able to afford legal advice and assistance
– Funded by the State and administered by The Law Society, it was often known as the 'second arm of the Welfare State'

PUBLIC FUNDING OF LEGAL SERVICES

3. The 'Old' System
Covered:
– Legal Advice and Assistance (the 'Green Form' scheme)
– Civil Legal Aid (available for most civil actions but not, for example, defamation. Merit and means-(tested)
– Criminal Legal Aid (granted by the court clerk in the 'interests of justice')

4. Impact of the Access to Justice Act 1999 and the 'New Legal Aid' Scheme: Due to the spiralling cost of legal aid, the provision of state funding was changed substantially by the introduction of:
– The *Legal Services Commission*, which replaced the Legal Aid Board
– The *Community Legal Service*, with responsibility for civil legal aid, and
– The *Criminal Defence Service* and the *Public Defender Service*

FIGURE 14.1 *Public Funding of Legal Services.*

1. The Legal Services Commission (LCS):
- Replaced the Legal Aid Board
- Maintains and supports two executive bodies: the Community Legal Service (civil) and the Criminal Defence Service (criminal), which replaced the Civil and Criminal Legal Aid schemes, respectively

2. The Community Legal Service:
- Primary responsibility is managing the *Community Services Fund*, a **capped**, government provided fund, in a manner that ensures value for money and best use of resources
- The funding may encompass advice, assistance and representation in areas covered
- Those providing publicly funded legal assistance must first have demonstrated their competence to do so

THE 'NEW LEGAL AID SCHEME': STATE FUNDED SERVICES

3. The Criminal Defence Service:
- Primary responsibility is to secure the provision of advice, assistance and representation, in the interests of justice, to those suspected of committing a crime. Funding is not capped
- The service encompasses the Duty Solicitor Schemes at both police stations and magistrates' courts
- In addition to contracting with solicitors in private practice to provide such assistance, the CDS has its own, employed lawyers under the Public Defender Service

FIGURE 14.2 *The 'New Legal Aid Scheme': State Funded Services.*

1. What are CFAs?
- Introduced by the CLSA 1990, and later reformed by the AJA 1999, they are an agreement between client and lawyer, which provides that an agreed fee will be paid ONLY if a case is won
- Also known as 'contingency fees' and 'no win, no fee' arrangements
- They cannot apply to criminal cases, only civil

2. What are the Advantages?
- Where publicly funded legal services are not available, conditional fees may provide the only way in which a litigant may be able to afford to bring an action – especially where state funding is no longer available, e.g. personal injury
- May remove some of the worry of losing a claim
- Reduces the number of spurious claims as lawyers will be unwilling to take up claims of little or no merit
- Reduction in the cost to the public purse

CONDITIONAL FEE ARRANGEMENTS

3. What are the Disadvantages?
- Argued that it may encourage speculative claims, 'ambulance chasing' and unethical behaviour

FIGURE 14.3 *Conditional Fee Arrangements.*

FOOD FOR THOUGHT

1. Are legal services really akin to health and social services? In any case should there be a limit to the funds that are expended on the provision of such services?

2. To what extent can voluntary services fill the gap left by professional legal advisors?

3. Anyone who has a phone has received a call from some ambulance-chasing claim firm. To what extent are such people providing a useful service?

4. Conditional fees were once seen as a way of reducing fees and costs, but are now attacked as having the opposite effect. Which version is true and why?

FURTHER READING

Butler, J, 'The funding drought' (2009) 63 Litigation Funding 16–17

Dutton, T, 'A public-private partnership' (2008) 158 NLJ 1013

Dutton, T, 'New year: new challenges' (2008) Counsel 3

Gilg, J-Y, 'Carolyn Regan: legal aid is the fourth plank of the welfare state' (2009) 153(29) SJ 10–11

Morris, A, 'Spiralling or stabilising? – the compensation culture and our propensity to claim damages for personal injury' (2007) 70(3) MLR 349–78

Morris, P *et al, Social Needs and Legal Action*, 1973, Oxford: Martin Robertson

Prior, S, 'Clinical negligence: the cost of claims' (2007) 52 Personal Injury Law Journal 11–13

Rhode, D, *Access to Justice*, 2004, Oxford: OUP

Robins, J, 'Are accident victims ill-served by "no win, no fee" agreements?' (2008) 158 NLJ 1125

Smith, R, 'Time to adjust' (2009) 159 NLJ 1271

Underhill, N *et al*, 'Law for free' (2003) Counsel 14

USEFUL WEBSITES

www.legalservices.gov.uk

The site of the Legal Services Commission, with links also to the Community Legal Service and the Criminal Defence Service.

COMPANION WEBSITE

Now visit the companion website to:

- test your understanding of the key terms using our Flashcard Glossary;
- revise and consolidate your knowledge of 'The funding of legal services' using our Multiple Choice Question testbank;
- view both the links to the Useful Websites above.

www.routledge.com/cw/slapper

THE EUROPEAN CONTEXT

15

As was stated in Chapter 3, it is unrealistic and indeed impossible for any student of English law and the English legal system to ignore the UK's membership of the European Union (EU). Nor can the impact of the European Court of Human Rights (ECtHR) be ignored, especially now that the Human Rights Act (HRA) 1998 has made the Articles of the European Convention on Human Rights (ECHR) directly applicable in the UK.

It is also essential to distinguish between the two different courts that operate within the European context: the Court of Justice of the European Union (CJEU), formerly the European Court of Justice (ECJ), which is the court of the EU, sitting in Luxembourg; and the ECtHR, which deals with cases relating to the ECHR and sits in Strasbourg.

The development of the European Union

The long-term process leading to the, as yet still to be attained, establishment of an integrated EU was a response to two factors: the disasters of the Second World War; and the emergence of the Soviet Bloc in Eastern Europe. The aim was to link the separate European countries, particularly France and Germany, together in such a manner as to prevent the outbreak of future armed hostilities. The first step in this process was the establishment of a European Coal and Steel Community. The next step towards integration was the formation of the European Economic Community (EEC) under the Treaty of Rome in 1957. The UK joined the EEC in 1973. The Treaty of Rome has subsequently been amended in the further pursuit of integration as the Community has expanded. Thus, the Single European Act (SEA) 1986 established a single economic market within the EC and widened the use of majority voting in the Council of Ministers. The Maastricht Treaty further accelerated the move towards a federal European supranational State, in the extent to which it recognised Europe as a social and political – as well as an economic – community. Previous Conservative governments of the UK resisted the emergence of the EU as anything other than an economic market and objected to, and resiled from, various provisions aimed at social, as opposed to economic, affairs. Thus, the UK was able to opt out of the Social Chapter of the Treaty of Maastricht. The new

Labour administration in the UK had no such reservations and, as a consequence, the Treaty of Amsterdam 1997 incorporated the European Social Charter into the EC Treaty which, of course, applies to the UK (see below).

As the establishment of the single market within the European Community progressed, it was suggested that its operation would be greatly facilitated by the adoption of a common currency, or at least a more closely integrated monetary system. Thus, in 1979, the European Monetary System (EMS) was established, under which individual national currencies were valued against a nominal currency called the ECU and allocated a fixed rate within which they were allowed to fluctuate to a limited extent. Britain was a member of the EMS until 1992, when financial speculation against the pound forced its withdrawal. Nonetheless, other members of the EC continued to pursue the policy of monetary union, now entitled European Monetary Union (EMU), and January 1999 saw the installation of the new European currency, the Euro, which has now replaced national currencies within what is now known as the Eurozone. The UK did not join the EMU at its inception and there is little chance that membership will appear on the political agenda for the foreseeable future, especially given the financial crisis that is enveloping many of the EMU states, particularly those on the periphery of the EU. It remains to be seen whether the ongoing financial crisis results in the break-up of the EMU, or its strengthening, as the current members may be forced to seek more economic unity to address its consequences.

In December 2000 the European Council met in Nice in the south of France. The Council consists of the heads of state or government of the member countries of the EU, and is the body charged with the power to make amendments to EU treaties (see below). The purpose of the meeting was to prepare the Union for expansion from its then 15 to 25 members by the year 2004, and so to its current 27 members. New members ranged from the tiny Malta with a population of 370,000 to Poland with its population of almost 39 million people. In order to accommodate this large expansion, it was recognised that significant changes had to be made in the institutions of the current Union, paramount among those being the weighting of the voting power of the Member States. Although parity was to be maintained between Germany, France, Italy and the UK at the new level of 29 votes, Germany and any two of the other largest countries gained a blocking power on further changes, as it was accepted that no changes, even on the basis of a qualified majority vote, could be introduced in the face of opposition from countries constituting 62 per cent of the total population of the Union. The recognition of such veto power was seen as a victory for national as against supranational interests within the Union and a significant defeat for the Commission. However, the number of matters subject to qualified majority voting was increased, although a number of countries, including the UK, refused to give up their veto with regard to the harmonisation of national and corporate tax rates. Nor would the UK, this time supported by Sweden, agree to give up the veto in relation to social security policy. Core immigration was another area in which the UK government retained its ultimate veto.

At the same time as these changes were introduced, the members of the Council of Europe also signed a new charter of fundamental rights. Among the rights recognised by the charter are included:

- right to life;
- respect for private and family life;
- protection of family data;
- right to education;
- equality between men and women;
- fair and just working conditions;
- right to collective bargaining and industrial action;
- right not to be dismissed unjustifiably.

It is significant that the charter was not included within the specific Treaty issues at Nice at the demand of the UK. The UK had also ensured that some of the references, particularly to employment matters, were subject to reference to domestic law.

In June 2001, Ireland caused a furore within the EU when its voters declined to ratify the Nice Treaty in a referendum. Perhaps not surprisingly, given the sensitivity of the issue, Ireland was the only Member State which made ratification a matter for its electorate, all the other Member States preferring to ratify the Treaty through their Parliaments. Following the vote, strong pressure was placed on the Irish government to ensure ratification at a later date, and at the Gothenburg summit meeting in the same month, the leaders of the EU made it clear that the expansion of the EU was irreversible. In 2002, the Irish electorate ratified the Treaty.

Although the Treaty of Nice was difficult and time-consuming in its formation, it looked for some time that its terms would be replaced before they had actually come into effect. This possibility came about as a result of the conclusions of the *Convention on the Future of Europe*, which was constituted in February 2002 by the then members to consider the establishment of a European Constitution. The Convention, which sat under the presidency of the former President of France, Valéry Giscard d'Estaing, produced a draft constitution, which it was hoped would provide a more simple, streamlined and transparent procedure for internal decision-making within the Union and to enhance its profile on the world stage. Among the proposals for the new constitution were the following:

- the establishment of a new office of President of the European Union;
- the appointment of an EU foreign minister;
- the shift to a two-tier Commission;
- fewer national vetoes;
- increased power for the European Parliament;
- simplified voting power;
- the establishment of an EU defence force by 'core members';
- the establishment of a charter of fundamental rights.

In the months of May and June 2005 the move towards the European Constitution came to a juddering halt when first the French and then the Dutch electorates voted against its implementation. Such a signal failure meant that it was not necessary for the UK government to conduct a referendum on the proposed constitution as it had promised. However, as with most EU initiatives, the new constitution did not disappear and re-emerged as the Treaty of Lisbon, signed by all the members in December 2007. Once again the UK government, together with the Polish one, insisted that a protocol, number 7, be appended to the treaty ensuring that the charter of fundamental rights could not create new rights in the UK. As usual the treaty had to be ratified by the members in the course of the next two years. The Lisbon Treaty gave rise to much ill-feeling in many states for the reason that it incorporated most of the proposals originally contained in the previously rejected constitutional proposal. In legal form, the Lisbon Treaty merely amended the existing treaties, rather than replacing them as the previous constitution had proposed. In practical terms, however, all the essential changes that would have been delivered by the constitution were contained in the treaty – a fact widely recognised by some EU leaders, although not the UK's. Thus Angela Merkel, Chancellor of Germany, was quoted in June 2007 in the *Daily Telegraph* as saying, 'The substance of the Constitution is preserved. That is a fact', and Valéry Giscard d'Estaing, Chairman of the Convention on the Future of Europe which drafted the Constitution was quoted, in a European Parliament press release on 17 July 2007, as saying, 'In terms of content, the proposals remain largely unchanged, they are simply presented in a different way . . . This text is, in fact, a rerun of a great part of the substance of the Constitutional Treaty.'

As a matter of interest and political significance, most member countries decided to ratify the new treaty through their legislatures rather than by hazarding it in a referendum, a decision that caused much discontent in many countries. In the UK, the government declined to have a referendum on the basis of the, not totally convincing, suggestion that the treaty was simply an amendment and a tidying-up measure and consequently did not need the confirmation of a referendum in the way necessary and promised for the constitution.

In June 2008 the Irish once again caused a furore in the EU when its electorate voted against the ratification of the Treaty of Lisbon. They were, of course, given a further opportunity to vote on the treaty and, in October 2009, following a number of concessions relating to taxation, 'family' issues, such as abortion, euthanasia and gay marriage and the traditional Irish state neutrality, approved it. Following the second Irish vote Poland's President, Lech Kaczynski, signed the treaty and that only left one member to fully ratify the treaty, the Czech republic. However, following the agreement that the Czechs could have the same protocol seven protections as the UK and Poland, President Vaclav Klaus signed the treaty, the Czech constitutional court dismissed an appeal against the treaty and the EU had a new treaty. It merely remained for the treaty to be put into effect. The necessary alterations to the fundamental treaties governing the EU, brought about by the Lisbon Treaty, were published at the end of March 2010 in the form of an updated *Treaty on European Union* (TEU), a newly named *Treaty on the Functioning of the European Union* (TFEU) (formerly the *Treaty Establishing the European Community*), together with *the Charter of Fundamental Rights of the European Union* (CFREU).

Tables of Equivalences, indicating where the provisions of previous iterations of the treaties are now located can be found at http://eur-lex.europa.eu/LexUriServ/LexUriServ.do?uri=OJ:C:2010:083:0361:0388:EN:PDF

1. The Council of Europe:	2. The European Court of Human Rights:	3. The European Union (EU):
– Set up in 1947 by European states following WWII, to protect human rights. It should be emphasised that this body is totally separate from the European Union – Enacted the **European Convention on Human Rights**, of which the UK is a signatory but which the UK has never fully incorporated into national law – **This body should not be confused with the European Council or the Council of the European Union**	– Established by the Council of Europe to enforce the rights contained in the European Convention on Human Rights – Following the enactment of the Human Rights Act in the UK, the decisions of this Court now have to be considered by our national courts – **This court should not be confused with the Court of Justice of the European Union (ECJ)**	– Originally known as the European Economic Community (EEC) when established by the Treaty of Rome 1957, it was created in order to ensure peace in Europe through economic integration of its Member States – The EEC was subject to a change of name following the Treaty on European Union, 1992 (TEU or Maastricht Treaty) after which it became known as the European Community (EC) – The TEU also created the European Union (EU) of which the EC was a component part – Since the enactment of the Lisbon Treaty in 2009, the EC no longer exists and all references should now be to the EU – The UK became a member in 1973, after the enactment of the **European Communities Act, 1972**

WHO'S WHO IN THE EUROPEAN CONTEXT

FIGURE 15.1 *Who's Who in the European Context.*

The Treaty on European Union (TEU)

The text of the treaty is divided into six parts as follows, with reference to some of the most important specific provisions:

1   *Common Provisions*

- Article 1 of this treaty makes it clear that 'The Union shall be founded on the present Treaty and on the Treaty on the Functioning of the European Union (hereinafter referred to as "the Treaties"). Those two Treaties shall have the same legal value. *The Union shall replace and succeed the European Community.*' This provision means that the previous confusion between when it was more appropriate to refer to EC rather than the EU has been removed and that it is now correct under all circumstances to refer to the EU. Article 47 provides further that the EU has legal personality, which means that the EU, as well as its constituent members, will be able to be a full member of the Council of Europe. As yet, the EU has not joined the Council, although an agreement to do so was established in July 2011.

- Article 2 establishes that the EU is 'founded on the values of respect for human dignity, freedom, democracy, equality, the rule of law and respect for human rights, including the rights of persons belonging to minorities'.

- Article 3 then states the aims of the EU in very general terms as follows:

  ○ the promotion of peace, its values and the well-being of its peoples; the assurance of freedom of movement of persons without internal frontiers but with controlled external borders;

  ○ the creation of an internal market . . . aiming at full employment and social progress, and a high level of protection and improvement of the quality of the environment;

  ○ the establishment of an economic and monetary union whose currency is the euro; the promotion of its values, while contributing to the eradication of poverty and observing human rights and respecting the Charter of the United Nations;

  ○ the sixth aim requires that the EU pursue its objectives by 'appropriate means'.

- Article 6 binds the EU to the Charter of Fundamental Rights of the European Union and the European Convention on Human Rights.

2   *Provisions on democratic principles*

- Article 9 establishes the equality of EU citizens and that every national of a Member State shall be a citizen of the Union. It makes clear that citizenship of the Union is *additional to* and does *not replace* national citizenship.

3   *Provisions on the institutions*

- Article 13 establishes the institutions in the following order and under the following names (except for the ECB these will be considered in detail below):

  ○ the European Parliament;
  ○ the European Council;
  ○ the Council;
  ○ the European Commission;
  ○ the Court of Justice of the European Union;
  ○ the European Central Bank;
  ○ the Court of Auditors.

- Article 15 establishes the President of the European Council.
- Articles 15(2) and 18 establish the High Representative of the Union for Foreign Affairs and Security Policy to conduct the Union's common foreign and security policy.

4   *Provisions on enhanced co-operations*

- Article 20 allows a number of Member States to co-operate in furthering integration in a particular area where other members are blocking full integration.

5   *General provisions on the Union's external action and specific provisions on the Common Foreign and Security Policy*

Articles 21–46 relate to the establishment and operation of a common EU foreign policy including:

- compliance with the UN charter, promoting global trade, humanitarian support and global governance;
- establishment of the European External Action Service, which will function as the EU's foreign ministry and diplomatic service;
- the furtherance of military co-operation including mutual defence.

6   *Final provisions*

- Article 47 establishes the legal personality of the EU.
- Article 48 deals with the method of treaty amendment; either through the ordinary or the simplified revision procedures.
- Articles 49 and 50 deal with applications to join the EU and withdrawal from it.

The Treaty on the Functioning of the European Union (TFEU)

This document, going back through several iterations to the original Treaty of Rome, contains the detail of the structure and operation of the European Union. (Once again it should be noted that a table of equivalences/destinations of previous provisions is available at http://eur-lex.europa.eu/LexUriServ/LexUriServ.do?uri=OJ:C:2010:083:0361:0388:EN:PDF.)

Article 2 of this treaty provides that:

> When the Treaties confer on the Union exclusive competence in a specific area, only the Union may legislate and adopt legally binding acts, the Member States being able to do so themselves only if so empowered by the Union or for the implementation of Union acts.

Article 3 specifies that the Union shall have exclusive competence in the following areas:

(a)   customs union;

(b)   the establishing of the competition rules necessary for the functioning of the internal market;

(c)   monetary policy for the Member States whose currency is the euro;

(d)   the conservation of marine biological resources under the common fisheries policy;

(e)   common commercial policy.

Article 3 provides that the Union shall also have exclusive competence for the conclusion of an international agreement when its conclusion is provided for in a legislative act of the Union or is necessary to enable the Union to exercise its internal competence, or in so far as its conclusion may affect common rules or alter their scope.

The provision of specific articles will be considered below.

The Charter of Fundamental Rights of the European Union (CFREU)

The Charter contains 54 Articles divided into seven titles. The first six titles deal with substantive rights relating to:

- *dignity*, including the right to life and the prohibition of torture and inhuman or degrading treatment or punishment;
- *freedom*, including the right to liberty and security of person, the right to engage in work and the freedom to conduct a business;
- *equality*, including equality before the law, and the right not to be discriminated against;
- *solidarity*, which emphasises workers' rights to fair working conditions, protection against unjustified dismissal, information and consultation within the undertaking, together with the right to engage in collective bargaining and to engage in industrial action;
- *citizens' rights*, including the right to vote and to stand as a candidate at elections; and finally
- *justice*, which includes the rights to a fair trial, the presumption of innocence and the right of defence.

The last title, Articles 51–54, deals with the interpretation and application of the Charter.

Many Member States, including the UK, have negotiated opt-outs of some of the provisions of the Charter.

15.1.1 PARLIAMENTARY SOVEREIGNTY, EUROPEAN UNION LAW AND THE COURTS

The doctrine of parliamentary sovereignty has already been considered with respect to the relationship between Parliament and the courts (see 2.3.2, above), and similar issues arise with regard to the relationship between EU law and domestic legislation. It has already been seen that the doctrine of parliamentary sovereignty is one of the cornerstones of the UK constitution. One aspect of the doctrine is that, as long as the appropriate procedures are followed, parliament is free to make such law as it determines. The corollary of that is that no current parliament can bind the discretion of a later parliament to make law as it wishes. The role of the court, as also has been seen, is merely to interpret the law made by parliament. Each of these constitutional principles is revealed as problematic in relation to the UK's membership of the EU and the relationship of domestic and EU law.

Before the UK joined the EU, its law was just as foreign as law made under any other jurisdiction. On joining the EU, however, the UK and its citizens accepted, and became subject to, EU law. This subjection to European law remains the case even where the parties to any transaction are themselves both UK subjects. In other words, in areas where it is applicable, European law supersedes any existing UK law to the contrary. The European Communities Act (ECA) 1972 gave legal effect to the UK's membership of the EEC, and its subjection to all existing and future Community/Union law was expressly stated in s 2(1), which provides:

> All such rights, powers, liabilities, obligations and restrictions from time to time created or arising by or under the Treaties, and all such remedies and procedures from time to time provided for by or under the Treaties, as in accordance with the Treaties *are without further enactment to be given legal effect or used in the UK* shall be recognised and available in law, and be enforced, allowed and followed accordingly [emphasis added].

Such statutory provision merely reflected the approach already adopted by the CJEU:

> By contrast with ordinary international treaties, the EC Treaty has created its own legal system which . . . became an integral part of the legal systems of the Member States and which their courts are bound to apply [*Costa v ENEL* (1964)].

The impact of Community/Union law on, and its superiority to, domestic law was clearly stated by Lord Denning MR thus:

> If on close investigation it should appear that our legislation is deficient or is inconsistent with Community law by some oversight of our draftsmen then it is our bounden duty to give priority to Community law. Such is the result of s 2(1) and (4) of the European Communities Act 1972 [*Macarthys Ltd v Smith* (1979)].

Thoburn v Sunderland CC (2002) appeared a simple enough case, but it raised some fundamental constitutional issues. It concerned a Sunderland greengrocer who sold fruit only by imperial weight. He was given a conditional discharge after his conviction under an Order in Council implementing a European Directive. He appealed by way of case stated, arguing that the Weights and Measures Act 1985 took precedence over European law or Orders in Council. His appeal failed, but in deciding the issue, Laws LJ rejected the argument that the overriding force of European law in the UK depends on its own principles as enunciated by the European Court in *Costa v ENEL*. Laws LJ stated that EU law could not entrench itself, because when Parliament enacted the ECA in 1972, it could not and did not bind subsequent Parliaments. The British Parliament, being sovereign, could not abandon its sovereignty, and there are no circumstances in which the jurisprudence of the Court of Justice could elevate Community law to a status within the corpus of English domestic law to which it could not aspire by any route of English law itself.

However, he went on, the traditional doctrine of parliamentary sovereignty has been modified by the common law, which has in recent years created classes of legislation that cannot be repealed by mere implication, that is, without express words to that effect. There now exists a clear hierarchy of Acts of Parliament – 'ordinary' statutes, which may be impliedly repealed, and 'constitutional' statutes, clearly including the ECA, which may not. The ECA is a constitutional statute and cannot be impliedly repealed, but that truth derives not from EU law but from the common law. In summary, the appropriate analysis of the relationship between EU and domestic law required regard to four propositions:

(i)   Each specific right and obligation provided under EC/EU law was, by virtue of the 1972 Act, incorporated into domestic law and took precedence. Anything within domestic law which was inconsistent with EC/EU law was either abrogated or had to be modified so as to avoid inconsistency.

(ii)   The common law recognised a category of constitutional statutes.

(iii)   The 1972 Act was a constitutional statute which could not be impliedly repealed.

(iv)   The fundamental legal basis of the UK's relationship with the EU rested with domestic rather than European legal powers.

Thus did Laws LJ maintain balance between the supremacy of EU law in matters of substantive law, and the supremacy of the UK Parliament in establishing the legal framework within which EU law operates. Clause 18 of the European Union Bill 2010/11 provides a statutory confirmation of Laws' reasoning.

An example of EU law invalidating the operation of UK legislation can be found in the *Factortame* cases. The Common Fishing Policy established by the EEC had placed limits on the amount of fish that any Member country's fishing fleet was permitted to catch. In order to gain access to British fish stocks and quotas, Spanish fishing boat owners formed British companies and reregistered their boats as British. In order to prevent what it saw as an abuse and an encroachment on the rights of indigenous fishermen, the British government introduced the Merchant Shipping Act 1988, which provided that any fishing company seeking to register as British would have to have its principal place of business in the UK and at least 75 per cent of its shareholders would have to be British nationals. This effectively debarred the Spanish boats from taking up any of the British fishing quota. Some 95 Spanish boat owners applied to the British courts for judicial review of the Merchant Shipping Act 1988 on the basis that it was contrary to Community law.

The High Court decided to refer the question of the legality of the legislation to the ECJ under Article 267 of the Treaty on the Functioning of the European Union (TFEU) (formerly Art 234 and Art 177 of previous versions of the treaty (see 15.3.6 below)), but in the meantime granted interim relief in the form of an injunction disapplying the operation of the legislation to the fishermen. On appeal, the Court of Appeal removed the injunction, a decision that was confirmed by the House of Lords. However, the House of Lords referred the question of the relationship of Community law and contrary domestic law to the ECJ. Effectively, they were asking whether the domestic courts should follow the domestic law or Community law. The ECJ ruled that the Treaty of Rome required domestic courts to give effect to the directly enforceable provisions of Community law and, in doing so, such courts are required to ignore any national law that runs counter to Community law. The House of Lords then renewed the interim injunction. The ECJ later ruled that in relation to the original referral from the High Court, the Merchant Shipping Act 1988 was contrary to Community law and therefore the Spanish fishing companies should be able to sue for compensation in the UK courts. The subsequent claims also went all the way to the House of Lords before it was finally settled in October 2000 that the UK was liable to pay compensation, which was estimated at between £50 million and £100 million.

The foregoing has demonstrated the way in which, and the extent to which, the fundamental constitutional principles of the UK are altered by its membership of the EU. Both the sovereign power of Parliament to legislate in any way it wishes and the role of the courts in interpreting and applying such legislation are now circumscribed by EU law. There remains one hypothetical question to consider and that relates to the power of Parliament to disapply legislation from the EU. While ECJ jurisprudence might not recognise such a power, it is certain that the UK Parliament retains such a power in UK law. If EU law receives its superiority as the expression of Parliament's will in the form of s 2 of the European Communities Act, as suggested by Lord Denning in *Macarthys*, it would remain open to a later Parliament to remove that recognition by passing new legislation. Such a point was actually made by the former Master of the Rolls in his judgment in that very case:

> If the time should come when our Parliament deliberately passes an Act with the intention of repudiating the Treaty or any provision in it or intentionally of acting inconsistently with it and says so in express terms then I should have thought that it would be the duty of our courts to follow the statute of our Parliament.

Article 10 (formerly 5) requires:

> Member States to take all appropriate measures, whether general or particular, to ensure fulfilment of the obligations arising out of this Treaty or resulting from action taken by the institutions of the Community. They shall facilitate the achievement of the Community's tasks. They shall abstain from any measure which could jeopardise the attainment of the objectives of this Treaty.

This Article effectively means that UK courts are now EU law courts and must be bound by, and give effect to, that law where it is operative. The reasons for the national courts acting in this manner were considered by John Temple Lang, Director in the Competition Directorate General, in an article entitled 'Duties of national courts under Community constitutional law' [1997] EL Rev 22. As he wrote:

> National courts are needed to give companies and individuals remedies which are as prompt, as complete and as immediate as the combined legal system of the Community and of Member States can provide. Only national courts can give injunctions against private parties for breach of Community law rules on, for example, equal pay for men and women, or on restrictive practices. Private parties have no standing to claim injunctions in the Court of Justice against a Member State; they can do so only in a national court. In other words, only a national court could give remedies to individuals and companies for breach of Community law which are as effective as the remedies for breach of national law.

European Union Act 2011

As was stated in Chapter 2, in September 2011 Parliament passed the European Union Act 2011. The main purpose of the Act was to make provision for the application of the post-Lisbon treaties. However, the Act also amended the European Communities Act (ECA) 1972 to ensure that any proposed future EU treaty, or amendment to the treaties, which purport to transfer competences or areas of power from the UK to the EU will have to be subject to a domestic referendum. Section 18 of the Act, for the first time, places the common law principle of parliamentary sovereignty on a statutory footing and states that all EU law takes effect in the UK only by virtue of the will of Parliament, as provided in the ECA 1972. Such measures were taken in an endeavour to provide clear statutory authority for the superiority of domestic law over EU law and to circumscribe any suggestion that EU law constitutes a new higher autonomous legal order in its own right. It has been suggested that these measures were a sop to the Eurosceptic wing of the Conservative Party within the coalition government and their precise effect remains to be seen.

15.2 SOURCES OF EUROPEAN UNION LAW

Community law, depending on its nature and source, may have direct effect on the domestic laws of its various members; that is, it may be open to individuals to rely on it without the need for their particular State to have enacted the law within its own legal system (see *Factortame*).

There are two types of direct effect. Vertical direct effect means that the individual can rely on EU law in any action in relation to their government, but cannot use it against other individuals. Horizontal direct effect allows the individual to use the EU provision in an action against other individuals. Other EU provisions only take effect when they have been specifically enacted within the various legal systems within the Community.

The sources of Community law are fourfold:

- internal treaties and protocols;
- international agreements;
- secondary legislation;
- decisions of the CJEU.

15.2.1 INTERNAL TREATIES

Internal treaties govern the Member States of the EU, and anything contained therein supersedes domestic legal provisions. Upon its joining the then Community, the Treaty of Rome was incorporated into UK law by the ECA 1972. Since that date the UK has been subject to the various iterations of the ruling treaties. As was considered previously, the ruling treaties are now:

- *Treaty on European Union* (TEU);
- *Treaty on the Functioning of the European Union* (TFEU);
- *Charter of Fundamental Rights of the European Union*.

As long as treaties are of a mandatory nature and are stated with sufficient clarity and precision, then they have both vertical and horizontal effect (*Van Gend en Loos* (1963)).

15.2.2 INTERNATIONAL TREATIES

International treaties are negotiated with other nations by the European Commission on behalf of the EU as a whole and are binding on the individual members of the EU.

Secondary legislation is provided for under Art 249 (formerly 189) of the Treaty of Rome. It provides for three types of legislation to be introduced by the European Council and Commission:

- *Regulations* apply to, and within, Member States generally, without the need for those States to pass their own legislation. They are binding and enforceable from the time of their creation and individual States do not have to pass any legislation to give effect to regulations. Thus, in *Macarthys Ltd v Smith* (1979), on a referral from the Court of Appeal to the ECJ, it was held that Art 157 (formerly 141) entitled the plaintiff to assert rights that were not available to her under national legislation, the Equal Pay Act 1970, that had been enacted before the UK had joined the EEC. Whereas the national legislation clearly did not include a comparison between former and present employees, Art 157's reference to 'equal pay for equal work' did encompass such a situation. Smith was consequently entitled to receive a similar level of remuneration to that of the former male employee who had done her job previously. The horizontal direct effect of regulations was confirmed by the ECJ in *Munoz y Cia SA v Frumar Ltd* (2002), in which it was held that the claimant was entitled to bring a civil claim against the defendant for failure to comply with EU labelling regulations.

  Regulations must be published in the *Official Journal* of the EU. The decision as to whether or not a law should be enacted in the form of a regulation is usually left to the Commission, but there are areas where the Treaty of Rome requires that the regulation form must be used. These areas relate to: the rights of workers to remain in Member States of which they are not nationals; the provision of State aid to particular indigenous undertakings or industries; the regulation of EU accounts and budgetary procedures.

- *Directives*, on the other hand, state general goals and leave the precise implementation in the appropriate form to the individual Member States. Directives, however, tend to state the means as well as the ends to which they are aimed and the CJEU will give direct effect to directives that are sufficiently clear and complete. See *Van Duyn v Home Office* (1974). Directives usually provide Member States with a time limit within which they are required to implement the provision within their own national laws. If they fail to do so, or implement the directive incompletely, then individuals may be able to cite and rely on the directive in their dealings with the State in question. Further, *Francovich v Italy* (1991) has established that individuals who have suffered as a consequence of a Member State's failure to implement Community law may seek damages against that State.

- *Decisions* on the operation of European laws and policies are not intended to have general effect but are aimed at particular States or individuals. They have the force of law under Art 288 (formerly 249).

- Additionally, Art 17(1) TEU (formerly 211 TEC) provides scope for the Commission to issue *recommendations* and *opinions* in relation to the operation of

Community law. These have no binding force, although they may be taken into account in trying to clarify any ambiguities in domestic law.

15.2.4 JUDGMENTS OF THE COURT OF JUSTICE OF THE EUROPEAN UNION

The CJEU is the judicial arm of the EU and, in the field of EU law, its judgments overrule those of national courts. Under Art 267 (formerly 234), national courts have the right to apply to the CJEU for a preliminary ruling on a point of Community law before deciding a case.

The mechanism through which Community law becomes immediately and directly effective in the UK is provided by s 2(1) of the ECA 1972. Section 2(2) gives power to designated ministers or departments to introduce Orders in Council to give effect to other non-directly effective Community law.

15.3   THE INSTITUTIONS OF THE EUROPEAN UNION

The major institutions of the EU are: the Council of Ministers; the European Parliament; the European Commission; and the CJEU.

15.3.1 THE COUNCIL OF THE EUROPEAN UNION

The Council is made up of ministerial representatives of each of the 27 Member States of the EU. The actual composition of the Council varies depending on the nature of the matter to be considered. When considering economic matters, the various States will be represented by their finance ministers or, if the matter before the Council relates to agriculture, the various agricultural ministers will attend. The organisation of the various specialist councils falls to the President of the Council and that post is held for six-monthly periods in rotation by the individual Member States of the EU. The Presidency of the Council is significant to the extent that the country holding the position can, to a large extent, control the agenda of the Council and thus can focus EU attention on areas that it considers to be of particular importance. The Foreign Affairs Council, that is, the meeting of national foreign ministers, is chaired by the Union's High Representative, who is currently Baroness Ashton.

The Council of Ministers is the supreme decision-making body of the EU and, as such, it has the final say in deciding upon EU legislation. Although it acts on recommendations and proposals made to it by the Commission, it does have the power to instruct the Commission to undertake particular investigations and to submit detailed proposals for its consideration.

Council decisions are taken on a mixture of voting procedures. Some measures only require a simple majority; in others, a procedure of qualified majority voting is used; and in yet others, unanimity is required. Qualified majority voting is the procedure in which the votes of the 27 member countries are weighted in proportion to their

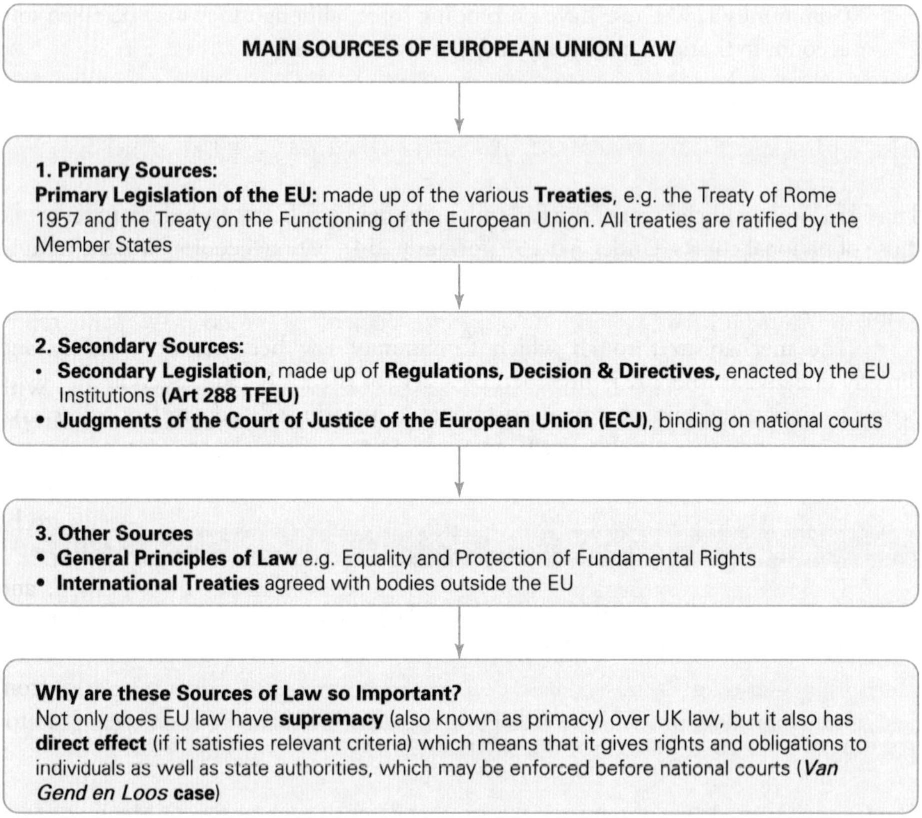

MAIN SOURCES OF EUROPEAN UNION LAW

1. Primary Sources:
Primary Legislation of the EU: made up of the various **Treaties**, e.g. the Treaty of Rome 1957 and the Treaty on the Functioning of the European Union. All treaties are ratified by the Member States

2. Secondary Sources:
• **Secondary Legislation**, made up of **Regulations, Decision & Directives,** enacted by the EU Institutions **(Art 288 TFEU)**
• **Judgments of the Court of Justice of the European Union (ECJ)**, binding on national courts

3. Other Sources
• **General Principles of Law** e.g. Equality and Protection of Fundamental Rights
• **International Treaties** agreed with bodies outside the EU

Why are these Sources of Law so Important?
Not only does EU law have **supremacy** (also known as primacy) over UK law, but it also has **direct effect** (if it satisfies relevant criteria) which means that it gives rights and obligations to individuals as well as state authorities, which may be enforced before national courts (*Van Gend en Loos* **case**)

FIGURE 15.2 *Sources of Community Law*

---

population from 29 down to three votes each: there are a total of 345 votes to be cast.

The SEA (a European treaty legislated into UK law as the European Communities (Amendment) Act 1986) extended the use of qualified majority voting and this was further extended under the Lisbon Treaty, but unanimity is still required in what can be considered as the more politically sensitive areas, such as those relating to the harmonisation of indirect taxation or the free movement of individuals. In addition to the need for unanimity in such sensitive areas, there is also the ultimate safeguard of what is known as the Luxembourg Compromise. This procedure, instituted at the behest of the French government in 1966, permits individual Member States to exercise a right of veto in relation to any proposals that they consider to be contrary to a 'very important interest' of theirs.

As the format of particular councils fluctuates, much of its day-to-day work is delegated to a Committee of Permanent Representatives, which operates under the title of COREPER.

15.3.2 THE EUROPEAN PARLIAMENT

The European Parliament is the directly elected European institution and, to that extent, it can be seen as the body that exercises democratic control over the operation of the EU. As in national Parliaments, members are elected to represent constituencies, the elections being held every five years.

The current total number of Members of the European Parliament (MEPs) is 754 and the distribution of representation is spread in relation to population. Thus Germany has 99 (reducing to 86 in 2014) MEPs, while the UK, France and Italy have 72 (temporarily rising to 73 for the UK and Italy and 74 for France). At the lower end of the representative scale, Luxembourg, Estonia and Cyprus have six representatives each and the smallest member of the Union, Malta, has five members (temporarily rising to six). With the accession of Bulgaria and Romania on 1 January 2007, the number of seats in the European Parliament was temporarily raised to 785 in order to accommodate MEPs from these countries. After the 2009 elections the number of seats was reduced to 736. However, the Treaty of Lisbon provides for a maximum number of 751 MEPs, to be temporarily raised to 754 until the next elections.

The European Parliament's general secretariat is based in Luxembourg, and although the Parliament sits in plenary session in Strasbourg for one week in each month, its detailed and preparatory work is carried out through 24 permanent committees, which usually meet in Brussels. These permanent committees consider proposals from the Commission and provide the full Parliament with reports of such proposals for discussion.

15.3.3 POWERS OF THE EUROPEAN PARLIAMENT

The powers of the European Parliament (the Parliament), however, should not be confused with those of national Parliaments, for the European Parliament is not a legislative institution and, in that respect, it plays a subsidiary role to the Council of Ministers. Originally its powers were merely advisory and supervisory.

In pursuance of its advisory function, the Parliament always had the right to comment on the proposals of the Commission and, since 1980, the Council has been required to wait for the Parliament's opinion before adopting any law. In its supervisory role, the Parliament scrutinises the activities of the Commission and has the power to remove the Commission by passing a motion of censure against it by a two-thirds majority.

The legislative powers of the Parliament were substantially enhanced by the SEA 1986. Since that enactment, it has had a more influential role to play, particularly in relation to the completion of the internal market. It can now negotiate directly with the Council as to any alterations or amendments it wishes to see in proposed legislation. It can also intervene to question and indeed alter any 'joint position' adopted by the Council on proposals put to it by the Commission. If the Council then insists on pursuing its original 'joint position', it can only do so on the basis of unanimity.

The SEA 1986 also required the assent of Parliament to any international agreements to be entered into by the EU. As a consequence, it has ultimate control not just in relation to trade treaties, but also as regards any future expansion in the EU's membership. The Lisbon Treaty has subsequently further increased the powers of the parliament, effectively giving it equal power of co-decision with the Council for most legislation, including the budget and agriculture.

The European Parliament is, together with the Council of Ministers, the budgetary authority of the EU. The budget is drawn up by the Commission and is presented to both the Council and the Parliament. As regards what is known as 'obligatory' expenditure, the Council has the final say, but in relation to 'non-obligatory' expenditure, the Parliament has the final decision whether to approve the budget or not. Such budgetary control places the Parliament in an extremely powerful position to influence EU policy, but perhaps the most draconian power the Parliament wields is the ability to pass a vote of censure against the Commission, requiring it to resign en masse.

The events of 1998/99 saw a significant shift in the relationship between the Parliament and the Commission. In December 1998, as a result of sustained accusations of mismanagement, fraud and cover-ups levelled against the Commission, the Parliament voted not to discharge the Commission's accounts for 1996. Such action was, in effect, a declaration that the Community's budget had not been properly handled and was tantamount to a vote of no confidence in the Commission. In January 1999, the Community's Court of Auditors delivered what can only be described as a devastating report on fraud, waste, mismanagement and maladministration on the part of the Commission. It was found that the Commission had understated its financial obligations by £3.3 billion, and was so lax in its control that it had not even noticed that its banks were not paying any interest on huge amounts of money they were holding. The report of the Court of Auditors led to a vote of no confidence in the Commission in early January 1999 and, although the Commission survived the vote by a majority of 293 to 232, it had to accept the setting-up of a 'committee of wise persons' to investigate and report on its operation. At the time, the appointment of this committee was thought to be a diplomatic fudge, allowing the Commission to carry on under warning as to its future conduct. However, when the committee submitted its report, it was so damning that it was immediately obvious that the Parliament would certainly use its power to remove the Commission. To forestall this event, the Commission resigned en masse.

However, by the first week of July 1999, a new Commission had been proposed and gained the approval of the European Parliament later that month.

15.3.4 ECONOMIC AND SOCIAL COMMITTEE

If the Parliament represents the directly elected arm of the EU, then the Economic and Social Committee represents a collection of unelected, but nonetheless influential, interest groups throughout the EU. This Committee is a consultative institution and its opinion must be sought prior to the adoption by the Council of any Commission proposal. The Economic and Social Committee represents the underlying 'corporatist' nature of the EU, to the extent that it seeks to locate and express a commonality of view and opinion on proposals from such divergent interest groups as employers, trade unions and consumers. It is perhaps symptomatic of the attitude of recent British governments to this underlying corporatist, essentially Christian Democratic, strand within the EU that it dispensed with its own similar internal grouping, the National Economic Development Council, in 1992.

15.3.5 THE EUROPEAN COMMISSION

The European Commission is the executive of the EU and, in that role, it is responsible for the administration of EU policies. There are 27 Commissioners chosen from the various Member States to serve for renewable terms of four years. Commissioners are appointed to head departments with specific responsibility for furthering particular areas of EU policy. Once appointed, Commissioners are expected to act in the general interest of the EU as a whole rather than in the partial interest of their own home country.

As a result of the Treaty of Nice, the five largest countries gave up one of their appointees in order that each of the then 25 Member States would be able to nominate a Commissioner. However, with further enlargement, it was intended that a system of rotation be implemented for the benefit of the smaller member countries, while preventing an increase in the number of Commissioners to match the new membership. However, such a procedure was not implemented when Bulgaria and Romania joined the European Union in 2007. So there are currently 27 Commissioners, although it still is proposed to introduce the system of rotation in the future.

In pursuit of EU policy, the Commission is responsible for ensuring that Treaty obligations between the Member States are met and that Union laws relating to individuals are enforced. In order to fulfil these functions, the Commission has been provided with extensive powers both in relation to the investigation of potential breaches of EU law and the subsequent punishment of offenders. The classic area in which these powers can be seen in operation is competition law. Under Arts 101 and 102 (formerly Arts 81 and 82) of the TFEU, the Commission has substantial powers to investigate and control potential monopolies and anti-competitive behaviour, and it has used these powers to levy what, in the case of private individuals, would amount to huge fines where breaches of EU competition law have been discovered. In November 2001, the Commission imposed a record fine of £534 million on a cartel of 13 pharmaceutical companies that had operated a price-fixing scheme within the EU in relation to the market for vitamins. The highest individual fine was against the Swiss company Roche, which had to pay £288 million, while the German company BASF was fined £185 million. The lowest penalty levelled was against Aventis, which was only fined £3 million due to its agreement to provide the Commission with evidence as to the operation of the cartel. Otherwise its fine would have been £70 million. The Commission took two years to investigate the operation of what it classified as a highly organised cartel, holding regular meetings to collude on prices, exchange sales figures and co-ordinate price increases.

In the following month, December 2001, Roche was again fined a further £39 million for engaging in another cartel, this time in the citric acid market. The total fines imposed in this instance amounted to £140 million.

In 2004 the then EU Competition Commissioner, Mario Monti, levied an individual record fine of €497 million (£340 million) on Microsoft for abusing its dominant position in the PC operating systems market. In addition, the Commissioner required Microsoft to disclose 'complete and accurate' interface documents to allow rival servers to operate with the Microsoft Windows system, or face penalties of €2 million (£1.4 million) for each day of non-compliance. In January 2006 Microsoft offered to make available part of its source code – the basic instructions for the Windows operating system. In an assertion of its complete compliance with Mario Monti's decision, Microsoft insisted it had actually gone beyond the Commission's remedy by opening up part of the source code behind Windows to rivals willing to pay a licence fee.

The offer, however, was dismissed by many as a public relations exercise. As a lawyer for Microsoft's rivals explained, 'Microsoft is offering to dump a huge load of source code on companies that have not asked for source code and cannot use it. Without a road map that says how to use the code, a software engineer will not be able to design inter-operable products.'

In February 2006 Microsoft repeated its claim that it had fully complied with the Commission's requirements. It also announced that it wanted an oral hearing on the allegations before national competition authorities and senior EU officials, a proposal that many saw as merely a delaying tactic postponing the imposition of the threatened penalties until the court of first instance has heard the company's appeal against the original allegation of abuse of its dominant position and, of course, the related €497 million fine. In July 2006, the Commission fined Microsoft an additional €280.5 million, €1.5 million per day from 16 December 2005 to 20 June 2006. On 17 September 2007, Microsoft lost their appeal and in October 2007, it announced that it would comply with the rulings.

However, in February 2008 Microsoft was fined an additional €899 million for failure to comply with the 2004 antitrust decision. In June 2012 Microsoft's appeal was rejected by the General Court of the EU (see below), although the total of the fine for non-compliance was reduced to €860. As a result, Microsoft has been fined a total of €1.64bn.

In May 2009 the Commission levied a new record individual fine against the American computer chip manufacturer Intel for abusing its dominance of the microchip market. Intel was accused of using discounts to squeeze its nearest rival, Advanced Micro Devices (AMD), out of the market. The amount of the fine was €1.06bn, equivalent to £950m, or $1.45bn. Intel appealed against the finding and the fine in July 2012. As yet, the appeal has not been decided.

The Commission also acts, under instructions from the Council, as the negotiator between the EU and external countries.

In addition to these executive functions, the Commission has a vital part to play in the EU's legislative process. The Council can only act on proposals put before it by the Commission. The Commission therefore has a duty to propose to the Council measures that will advance the achievement of the EU's general policies.

15.3.6 THE COURT OF JUSTICE OF THE EUROPEAN UNION

The CJEU is the judicial arm of the EU, and in the field of Community law its judgments overrule those of national courts. It consists of 27 judges, one from each Member State, assisted by eight Advocates General, and sits in Luxembourg. The Court may sit as a full court, in a Grand Chamber of 13 judges or in Chambers of three or five judges. The role of the Advocate General is to investigate the matter submitted to the Court and to produce a report, together with a recommendation, for the consideration of the Court. The actual Court is free to accept the report or not as it sees fit.

The SEA 1986 provided for a new Court of First Instance to be attached to the existing Court of Justice. Under the Treaty of Lisbon it was renamed the General Court. It has jurisdiction in first instance cases, with appeals going to the CJEU on points of law. The former jurisdiction of the Court of First Instance, in relation to internal claims by EU employees, was transferred to a newly created European Union Civil Service Tribunal in 2004. Together the three distinct courts constitute *the Court of Justice of the European Union*. The aim of introducing the two latter courts was to reduce the burden of work on the CJEU, but there is a right of appeal, on points of law only, to the full CJEU.

The Court of Justice performs two key functions:

> (a) It decides whether any measures adopted, or rights denied, by the Commission, Council or any national government are compatible with Treaty obligations. Such actions may be raised by any EU institution, government or individual.

In October 2000, the Court of Justice annulled EU Directive 98/43, which required Member States to impose a ban on advertising and sponsorship relating to tobacco products, because it had been adopted on the basis of the wrong provisions of the EC Treaty. The Directive had been adopted on the basis of the provisions of the Treaty relating to the elimination of obstacles to the completion of the internal market, but the Court decided that under the circumstances, it was difficult to see how a ban on tobacco advertising or sponsorship could facilitate the trade in tobacco products.

Although a partial prohibition on particular types of advertising or sponsorship might legitimately come within the internal market provisions of the Treaty, the Directive was clearly aimed at protecting public health and it was therefore improper to base its adoption on the freedom to provide services (*Germany v European Parliament and EU Council* (Case C-376/98)).

A Member State may fail to comply with its Treaty obligations in a number of ways. It might fail or indeed refuse to comply with a provision of the Treaty or a regulation; alternatively, it might refuse to implement a directive within the allotted time provided for. Under such circumstances, the State in question will be brought before the CJEU, either by the Commission or another Member State, or indeed individuals within the State concerned.

In 1996, following the outbreak of 'mad cow disease' (BSE) in the UK, the European Commission imposed a ban on the export of UK beef. The ban was partially lifted in 1998 and, subject to conditions relating to the documentation of an animal's history prior to slaughter, from 1 August 1999, exports satisfying those conditions were authorised for despatch within the Community. When the French Food Standards

Agency continued to raise concerns about the safety of British beef, the Commission issued a protocol agreement, which declared that all meat and meat products from the UK would be distinctively marked as such. However, France continued in its refusal to lift the ban. Subsequently, the Commission applied to the CJEU for a declaration that France was in breach of Community law for failing to lift the prohibition on the sale of correctly labelled British beef in French territory. In December 2001, in *Commission of the European Communities v France*, the CJEU held that the French government had failed to put forward a ground of defence capable of justifying the failure to implement the relevant Decisions and was therefore in breach of Community law.

France was also fined in July 2005 for breaching EU fishing rules. On that occasion the CJEU imposed the first ever 'combination' penalty, under which a lump-sum fine was payable, but in addition France is liable to a periodic penalty for every six months until it has shown it is fully complying with EU fisheries laws. The CJEU set the lump-sum fine at €20 million and the periodic penalty at €57.8 million.

The Court held that it is was possible and appropriate to impose both types of penalty at the same time, in circumstances where the breach of obligations has both continued for a long period and is inclined to persist.

(b) It provides authoritative rulings, at the request of national courts, under Art 267 (formerly 234) of the Treaty of Rome, on the interpretation of points of Community law. When an application is made under Art 267, the national proceedings are suspended until such time as the determination of the point in question is delivered by the CJEU. While the case is being decided by the CJEU, the national court is expected to provide appropriate interim relief, even if this involves going against a domestic legal provision, as in the *Factortame* case.

This procedure can take the form of a preliminary ruling where the request precedes the actual determination of a case by the national court.

Article 267 provides that:

The Court of Justice shall have jurisdiction to give preliminary rulings concerning:

(a)   the interpretation of treaties;

(b)   the validity and interpretation of acts of the institutions of the Union and of the European Central Bank;

(c)   the interpretation of the statutes of bodies established by an act of the Council, where those statutes so provide.

Where such a question is raised before any court or tribunal of a Member State, that court or tribunal may, if it considers that a decision on the question is necessary to enable it to give judgment, request the Court of Justice to give a ruling thereon.

> Where any such question is raised in a case pending before a court or tribunal of a Member State against whose decision there is no judicial remedy under national law, that court or tribunal shall bring the matter before the Court of Justice.

The question as to the extent of the CJEU's authority arose in *Arsenal Football Club plc v Reed* (2003), which dealt with the sale of football souvenirs and memorabilia bearing the names of the football club and consequently infringing its registered trademarks. On first hearing, the Chancery Division of the High Court referred the question of the interpretation of the Trade Marks Directive (89/104) in relation to the issue of trademark infringement to the CJEU. After the CJEU had made its decision, the case came before Laddie J for application, who declined to follow that decision. The grounds for so doing were that the ambit of the CJEU's powers was clearly set out in Art 234. Consequently, where, as in this case, the CJEU makes a finding of fact that reverses the finding of a national court on those facts, it exceeds its jurisdiction and it follows that its decisions are not binding on the national court. The Court of Appeal later reversed Laddie J's decision on the ground that the CJEU had not disregarded the conclusions of fact made at the original trial and, therefore, he should have followed its ruling and decided the case in Arsenal's favour. Nonetheless, Laddie J's general point as to the CJEU's authority remains valid.

It is clear that it is for the national court and not the individual parties concerned to make the reference. Where the national court or tribunal is not the 'final' court or tribunal, the reference to the CJEU is discretionary. Where the national court or tribunal is the 'final' court, then reference is obligatory. However, there are circumstances under which a 'final' court need not make a reference under Art 267 (formerly 234). These are:

- where the question of EU law is not truly relevant to the decision to be made by the national court;
- where there has been a previous interpretation of the provision in question by the CJEU so that its meaning has been clearly determined;
- where the interpretation of the provision is so obvious as to leave no scope for any reasonable doubt as to its meaning.

This last instance has to be used with caution given the nature of EU law; for example, the fact that it is expressed in several languages using legal terms that might have different connotations within different jurisdictions. However, it is apparent that where the meaning is clear, no reference need be made.

Reference has already been made to cases that have been referred under the Art 267 procedure. Thus, the first case to be referred to the CJEU from the High Court was *Van Duyn v Home Office* (1974), the first case to be referred from the Court of Appeal was *Macarthys Ltd v Smith* (1979), and the first from the House of Lords was *R v Henn* (1982).

Reference has already been made in Chapter 3 to the methods of interpretation used by courts in relation to Community law. It will be recalled that, in undertaking such a task, a purposive and contextual approach is mainly adopted, as against the more restrictive methods of interpretation favoured in relation to UK domestic legislation. The clearest statement of this purposive, contextualist approach adopted by the CJEU is contained in its judgment in the *CILFIT* case:

> Every provision of Community law must be placed in its context and inter-preted in the light of the provisions of Community law as a whole, regard being had to the objectives thereof and to its state of evolution at the date on which the provision in question is to be applied.

It can be appreciated that the reservations considered previously in regard to judicial creativity and intervention in policy matters in the UK courts apply *a fortiori* to the decisions of the CJEU.

Another major difference between the CJEU and the court within the English legal system is that the former is not bound by the doctrine of precedent in the same way as the latter is. It is always open to the CJEU to depart from its previous decisions where it considers it appropriate to do so. Although it will endeavour to maintain consistency, it has, on occasion, ignored its own previous decisions, as in *European Parliament v Council* (1990), where it recognised the right of the Parliament to institute an action against the Council.

The manner in which EU law operates to control sex discrimination through the Equal Treatment Directive is of significant interest and, in *Marshall v Southampton and West Hampshire Area Health Authority* (1993), a number of the points that have been considered above were highlighted. Ms Marshall had originally been required to retire earlier than a man in her situation would have been required to do. She successfully argued before the CJEU that such a practice was discriminatory and contrary to Community Directive 76/207 on the equal treatment of men and women.

The present action related to the level of compensation she was entitled to as a consequence of this breach. UK legislation, the Sex Discrimination Act 1975, had set limits on the level of compensation that could be recovered for acts of sex discrimination. Marshall argued that the imposition of such limits was contrary to the Equal Treatment Directive and that, in establishing such limits, the UK had failed to comply with the Directive.

The Court of Appeal referred the case to the ECJ, as it then was, under Art 267 (formerly 234) and the latter determined that the rights set out in relation to compensation under Art 5 of the Directive were directly effective, and that, as the purpose of the Directive was to give effect to the principle of equal treatment, that could only be achieved by either reinstatement or the awarding of adequate compensation. The decision of the ECJ therefore overruled the financial limitations placed on sex discrimination awards and effectively overruled the domestic legislation.

P v S and Cornwall CC (1996) extended the ambit of unlawful sex discrimination under the Directive to cover people who have undergone surgical gender reorientation (sex change). However, in *Grant v South West Trains Ltd* (1998), the ECJ declined to extend the Directive to cover discrimination on the grounds of sexual orientation (homosexuality), even though the Advocate General had initially supported the extension of the Directive to same-sex relationships. While *Grant* was in the process of being decided in the ECJ, a second case, *R v Secretary of State for Defence ex p Perkins (No 2)* (1998), had been brought before the English courts arguing a similar point, that discrimination on grounds of sexual orientation was covered by the Equal Treatment Directive. Initially, the High Court had referred the matter, under Art 267 (formerly 234), to the ECJ for decision, but on the decision in *Grant* being declared, the referral was withdrawn. In withdrawing the reference, Lightman J considered the proposition of counsel for Perkins to the effect that:

> ... there have been a number of occasions where the ECJ has overruled its previous decisions; that the law is not static; and, accordingly, in a dynamic and developing field such as discrimination in employment there must be a prospect that a differently constituted ECJ may depart from the decision in *Grant* ... But, to justify a reference, the possibility that the ECJ will depart from its previous decision must be more than theoretical: it must be a realistic possibility. The decision in *Grant* was of the full Court; it is only some four months old; there has been no development in case law or otherwise since the decision which can give cause for the ECJ reconsidering that decision ... I can see no realistic prospect of any change of mind on the part of the ECJ.

It could be pointed out that there could be no change in case law if judges such as Lightman J refused to send similar cases to the CJEU, but there may well be sense, if not virtue, in his refusal to refer similar cases to the court within such a short timescale.

15.3.7 THE COURT OF AUDITORS

Given the part that the Court of Auditors played in the 1998/99 struggle between the Parliament and the Commission, the role of this body should not be underestimated.

As its name suggests, it is responsible for providing an external audit of the EU's finances. It examines the legality, regularity and soundness of the management of all the EU's revenue and expenditure.

15.4 THE EUROPEAN COURT OF HUMAN RIGHTS

It has to be established and emphasised from the outset that the substance of this section has absolutely nothing to do with the EU as such; the Council of Europe, of which the

ECtHR is the legal institution, is a completely distinct organisation and, although membership of the two organisations overlap, they are not the same. The Council of Europe is concerned not with economic matters but with the protection of civil rights and freedoms.

It is gratifying, at least to a degree, to recognise that the ECHR and its Court (the ECtHR) are no longer a matter of mysterious external control, the HRA having incorporated the ECHR into UK law, making the ECtHR the supreme court in matters related to its jurisdiction. Much attention was paid to the ECHR and the HRA in Chapter 2 (see above, at 2.5), so it only remains to consider the structure and operation of the ECtHR. Two points should be emphasised at this juncture. First, although the number of domestic cases relating to the ECHR will continue to increase and consequently domestic human rights jurisprudence will emerge and develop, it should be borne in mind that in relation to these cases, the ultimate court of appeal remains the ECtHR. Second, as has been considered at 2.5, s 2 of the HRA requires previous decisions of the ECtHR to be taken into consideration by domestic courts, and this means *all* decisions of the ECtHR, not just the cases that directly involve the UK. Consequently, it remains imperative that students of the UK legal system be aware of, and take into consideration, the decisions of that court.

The Convention originally established two institutions:

(a)   The European Commission of Human Rights. This body was charged with the task of examining, and if need be investigating the circumstances of, petitions submitted to it. If the Commission was unable to reach a negotiated solution between the parties concerned, it referred the matter to the Court of Human Rights.

(b)   The ECtHR. The ECHR provides that the judgment of the Court shall be final and that parties to it will abide by the decisions of the Court. This body, sitting in Strasbourg, was, and remains, responsible for all matters relating to the interpretation and application of the current Convention.

However, in the 1980s, as the ECHR and its Court became more known and popular as a forum for asserting human rights, so its workload increased. This pressure was exacerbated by the break-up of the old Communist Eastern Bloc and the fact that the newly independent countries, in both senses of the words, became signatories to the Convention. The statistics support the view of the incipient sclerosis of the original structure.

Applications Registered with the Commission

Year	Number of applications registered
1981	404
1993	2,037
1997	4,750

Cases Referred to the Court

Year	Number of cases referred
1981	7
1993	52
1997	119

As a consequence of such pressure, it became necessary to streamline the procedure by amalgamating the two previous institutions into one Court. In pursuit of this aim, Protocol 11 to the Convention was introduced in 1994. The new ECtHR came into operation on 1 November 1998, although the Commission continued to deal with cases that had already been declared admissible for a further year.

The continuously increasing activity of the ECtHR has led to a large backlog of cases as may be seen from the court's own statistics for the year 2011:

> 64,500 applications were allocated to a judicial formation, an overall increase of 5 per cent compared with 2010 (61,300);
>
> 47,300 of these were identified as single-judge cases likely to be declared inadmissible (an increase of 11 per cent in relation to 2010);
>
> 17,200 were identified as Chamber or Committee cases (a decrease of 9 per cent);
>
> 52,188 applications were disposed of judicially, an increase of 27 per cent in relation to 2010.

However, the annual deficit, the difference between cases allocated and cases disposed of, was approximately 12,300 (i.e. a monthly deficit of more than 1,000). As a result the number of applications pending before a judicial formation rose by 9 per cent in 2011, from 139,650 to 151,600 (http://www.echr.coe.int/ECHR/EN/Header/Reports+and+Statistics/Statistics/Statistical+data/).

The foregoing statistics are understandable when it is realised that the ECtHR is accessible to some 800 million people from 47 different jurisdictions. Nonetheless, it is widely accepted that the court needs reform to allow it to function effectively under the ever-increasing burden of cases it has to deal with. The following are suggestions and actions to achieve this necessary reform.

The Woolf Report

In 2005 the former Lord Chief Justice of England, Lord Woolf, led a panel to consider what steps could be taken to deal with the ECtHR's current and projected caseload.

As the review, issued in December 2005, stated, the Court was a victim of its success. Nonetheless, it was faced with an enormous and ever-growing workload, thus it is quite clear that something had to be done, in the short term, if the Court was not to be overwhelmed by its own workload.

Among the Review's main recommendations were the following:

(i)   *The Court should redefine what constitutes an application*

It should only deal with properly completed application forms that contain all the information required for the Court to process the application.

(ii)   *Satellite Offices of the Registry should be established*

These would be located in key countries that produce high numbers of inadmissible applications. The satellite offices would provide applicants with information as to the Court's admissibility criteria, and the availability, locally, of ombudsmen and other alternative methods of resolving disputes. This could divert a significant number of cases away from the Court. Satellite offices would also be responsible for the initial processing of applications. They would then send applications, together with short summaries in either French or English, to the relevant division in Strasbourg. This would enable Strasbourg lawyers to prepare draft judgments more quickly.

(iii)   *Ombudsmen and other methods of Alternative Dispute should be used more*

Not surprisingly, given his championing of ADR in the English legal system, Lord Woolf's team recommended the encouragement of greater use of national Ombudsmen and other methods of ADR, thus diverting from the Court a large number of complaints that should never have come to it in the first place. As part of this approach the panel also recommended the establishment of a specialist 'Friendly Settlement Unit' in the Court Registry, to initiate and pursue proactively a greater number of friendly settlements.

(iv)   *The Court should deliver a greater number of pilot judgments*

Cases that are candidates for a pilot judgment should be given priority, and all similar cases stayed pending outcome of that case. The question of how much compensation to award successful litigants should, where possible, be remitted to domestic courts for resolution.

Protocol 14

Protocol 14 to the European Convention, adopted in May 2004, was designed to improve the efficiency of the Court through three provisions, which:

- allowed for a single judge, assisted by a non-judicial rapporteur, to reject cases where they are clearly inadmissible from the outset. This replaces the system where, previously, inadmissibility was decided by committees of three judges;
- allowed committees of three judges to give judgments in repetitive cases where the case law of the Court is already well-established, where such cases were previously heard by chambers of seven judges;
- introduced a new admissibility criterion in applicable cases where the applicant has not suffered a 'significant disadvantage'. There is the safeguard that the case must have already been duly considered by a domestic tribunal, with the

additional proviso that the case raises no general human rights concerns, requiring the case to be examined on its merits.

Given the continued delay on the part of the Russian Federation in ratifying Protocol 14, the other members of the European Council decided in May 2009 that the protocol should be adopted by all those countries willing to agree to its immediate implementation. Subsequently, the Russian Federation ratified the protocol in January 2010, and given the fact that Russia is the major source of applications coming before the ECtHR, this should have a considerable impact on the rate with which the court processes applications and cases.

The full text of the protocol may be read at http://conventions.coe.int/Treaty/EN/Treaties/html/194.htm.

Interlaken Declaration

In February 2010 human rights ministers from the 47 Member States of the Council of Europe met in Interlaken to discuss the future of the European Court of Human Rights. The ministers discussed reforms to ensure the long-term effectiveness of the Court, as well as ways of better monitoring the execution of its judgments and improving human rights protection at national level.

Noting that the number of applications brought before the Court and the deficit between applications introduced and applications disposed of continued to grow, the committee issued a declaration that additional measures were urgently required in order to:

(i)   achieve a balance between the number of judgments and decisions delivered by the Court and the number of incoming applications;

(ii)   enable the Court to reduce the backlog of cases and to adjudicate new cases within a reasonable time, particularly those concerning serious violations of human rights;

(iii) ensure the full and rapid execution of judgments of the Court and the effectiveness of its supervision by the Committee of Ministers.

Whilst recognising and upholding the right of individuals to petition the Court it saw the need to:

- improve the filtering out of inadmissible claims;
- reduce the number of repetitive cases;
- facilitate the adoption of friendly settlements;
- encourage the use of pilot cases to decide general issues.

As for the Court, it was invited to:

- avoid reconsidering questions of fact or national law that have been considered and decided by national authorities;
- apply uniformly and rigorously the criteria concerning admissibility and jurisdiction;

- consider the possibility of applying the principle *de minimis non curat praetor* (to the effect that the court should not bother with petty cases).

The Izmir Declaration

In April 2011, in Izmir, Turkey, the Committee of Ministers invited Member States to 'ensure that effective domestic remedies exist . . . providing for a decision on an alleged violation of the Convention and, where necessary, its redress', thus lessening the pressure on the ECtHR.

With respect to the need for adequate national measures to contribute to reducing the number of applications, the Committee of Ministers indicated that it continued to reflect on the advisability of introducing 'a procedure allowing the highest national courts to request advisory opinions from the [Strasbourg] Court concerning the interpretation and application of the Convention'.

The Brighton Declaration

On the setting up of a commission on the need for a UK Bill of Rights, chaired by Sir Leigh Lewis, in pursuit of a long-standing Conservative party suspicion of the very nature of the Human Rights Act, the first task the coalition government set the commission was to provide interim advice to the government on the ongoing Interlaken process to reform the ECtHR. The necessity for this advice was the fact that the UK would assume the Chairmanship of the Council of Europe from November 2011 to May 2012.

In April 2012 the Council of Europe met at Brighton and after a two-day conference issued the Brighton Declaration. This is an agreement designed to tackle perceived shortcomings in the operation of the court by:

- amending the convention to specifically include the principles of subsidiarity and the margin of appreciation. The declaration emphasised the fundamental importance of the principle of subsidiarity and pointed out that the ECtHR acts as a safeguard for violations that *have not been remedied at a national level*;
- amending the convention to tighten the admissibility criteria in order that trivial cases can be passed over to allow the court to focus on more serious abuses. The declaration recognised the significant steps already undertaken to achieve this end within the framework of Protocol No. 14;
- reducing the time limit for applications to the court from six months to four;
- improving the selection process for judges in recognition of their crucial role in deciding cases. It was emphasised that judgments of the court need to be clear and consistent in order to promote legal certainty. This was seen as helping national courts to apply the convention more precisely, and helping potential applicants decide whether they have grounds for making an application. However, it was also stressed that consistency in the application of the convention did not require the implementation of the convention uniformly through all 47 states, thus recognising the need to allow for a margin of appreciation;
- ensuring that state parties to the convention executed judgments of the court expeditiously by requiring the committee of minsters to take effective measures in

respect of any state party that failed to comply with its obligations under Article 46 of the convention;

- setting out a roadmap for further reform to anticipate future challenges and develop a vision for the future of the convention, so that future decisions can be taken in a timely and coherent manner.

Although the UK government expressed its satisfaction with the outcome of the Brighton conference, it has to be noted that the actual declaration fell considerably short of its original proposals contained in a draft document previously leaked in February 2012.

When the Commission on the UK Bill of Rights submitted its final report, 'A UK Bill of Rights? The Choice Before Us', in December 2012, it was much criticised for its lack of coherence. Not only did two of the eight members not agree that a UK bill of rights was needed, but the majority did not appear to have a unified approach to the question, let alone offer a consistent answer to the question posed.

Structure of the Court

The ECtHR consists of 47 judges, representing the number of signatories to the ECHR, although they do not have to be chosen from each State and, in any case, sit as individuals rather than representatives of their State. Judges are elected, by the Parliamentary Assembly of the Council of Europe, generally for six years, but arrangements have been put in place so that one-half of the membership of the judicial panel will be required to seek renewal every three years.

The Plenary Court elects its President, two Vice Presidents and two Presidents of Section for a period of three years. It is divided into four Sections, whose composition, fixed for three years, is geographically and gender balanced and takes account of the different legal systems of the Contracting States. Each Section is presided over by a President, two of the Section Presidents being at the same time Vice Presidents of the Court. Committees of three judges within each Section deal with preliminary issues and, to that extent, they do the filtering formerly done by the Commission. Cases are actually heard by Chambers of seven members chosen on the basis of rotation. Additionally, there is a Grand Chamber of 17 judges made up of the President, Vice Presidents and Section Presidents and other judges by rotation. The Grand Chamber deals with the most important cases that require a reconsideration of the accepted interpretations of the ECHR. Again, the Grand Chamber is established with a view to geographical balance and different legal traditions. The Section President and the judge elected in respect of the State concerned sit in each case. Where the latter is not a member of the Section, he sits as an *ex officio* member of the Chamber.

Procedure before the Court

Any individual or Contracting State may submit an application alleging a breach by a Contracting State of one of the ECHR rights. Individuals can submit applications themselves, but legal representation is recommended and is required for hearings. Although a legal aid scheme has been set up by the Council of Europe for applicants who cannot fund their cases, recovery is usual from any award of monetary compensation.

Hearings are public, unless the Chamber decides otherwise on account of exceptional circumstances, and all documents filed with the Court's Registry are accessible to the public. It is, however, quite common for negotiations towards a friendly settlement to take place during proceedings, with the Registrar acting as intermediary, and such negotiations are confidential.

Admissibility Procedure

Prior to Protocol 14 coming into full effect, each application was assigned to a Section whose President designated a rapporteur, who examined it and decided whether it should be dealt with by a three-member Committee or by a seven-member Chamber.

If passed to a Committee, it may decide, by unanimous vote, to declare inadmissible or strike out an application without further examination.

If not struck out, the case goes on to a Chamber for hearing on both admissibility and merits. The initial decisions of the Chamber on admissibility are taken by majority vote. They must contain reasons and be made public. The Chamber's decision to admit an application leads to a hearing as to the merits of the case.

Procedure on the Merits

The President of the Chamber may grant leave, or invite any Contracting State that is not party to the proceedings or any person concerned who is not the applicant, to submit written comments and, in exceptional circumstances, to make representations at the hearing. A Contracting State whose national is an applicant in the case is entitled to intervene as of right.

The Chamber hearing the case may at any time remit it to the Grand Chamber where it is concerned that it raises an important issue relating to the interpretation of the ECHR or a major extension of previous precedent.

In practice, only a minority of registered applications result in a judgment on the merits of the case. Other applications are completed at an earlier stage by being declared inadmissible, being otherwise struck out or following a friendly settlement. Examples of such friendly procedures are *Cornwell v UK* and *Leary v UK*, both reported in 2000. These cases both involved men whose wives died, leaving them solely responsible for their children. Had they been women in similar situations, they would have received benefits, namely a Widowed Mother's Allowance and a Widow's Payment, payable under the Social Security Contributions and Benefits Act 1992. The applicants complained that the lack of benefits for widowers under British social security legislation discriminated against them on grounds of sex, in breach of Art 14 (prohibition of discrimination) of the ECHR, taken in conjunction with both Art 8 (right to respect for private and family life) and Art 1 of Protocol No 1 (protection of property) of the ECHR. The cases were struck out following a friendly settlement in which Cornwell and Leary received back payment of monies due and further payments until the Welfare Reform and Pensions Act 1999 came into force, which equalised the position.

Judgments

Chambers decide by a majority vote and usually reports give a single decision. However, any judge in the case is entitled to append a separate opinion, either concurring or dissenting.

Within three months of delivery of the judgment of a Chamber, any party may request that a case be referred to the Grand Chamber if it raises a serious question of interpretation or application, or a serious issue of general importance. Consequently, the Chamber's judgment only becomes final at the expiry of a three-month period, or earlier if the parties state that they do not intend to request a referral. If the case is referred to the Grand Chamber, its decision, taken on a majority vote, is final. All final judgments of the Court are binding on the respondent States concerned. Responsibility for supervising the execution of judgments lies with the Committee of Ministers of the Council of Europe, which is required to verify that States have taken adequate remedial measures in respect of any violation of the ECHR.

In deciding cases, the ECtHR makes use of two related principles: the doctrine of the margin of appreciation; and the principle of proportionality.

Margin of Appreciation

This refers to the fact that the ECtHR recognises that there may well be a range of responses to particular crises or social situations within individual States, which might well involve some legitimate limitation on the rights established under the ECHR. The Court recognises that in such areas, the response should be decided at the local level, rather than being imposed centrally. The most obvious, but by no means the only, situations that involve the recognition of the margin of appreciation are the fields of morality and State security. For example, *Wingrove v UK* (1997) concerned the refusal of the British Board of Film Classification to give a certificate of classification to the video film, *Visions of Ecstasy*, on the grounds that it was blasphemous, thus effectively banning it. The applicant, the director of the film, claimed that the refusal to grant a certificate of classification to the film amounted to a breach of his rights to free speech under Art 10 of the ECHR. The Court rejected his claim, holding that the offence of blasphemy, by its very nature, did not lend itself to precise legal definition. Consequently, national authorities 'must be afforded a degree of flexibility in assessing whether the facts of a particular case fall within the accepted definition of the offence'. In reaching its decision, the Court clearly set out how the doctrine was to operate and its justifications. It also explained the different ranges of the margin of appreciation that will be allowed in different areas. Thus:

> Whereas there is little scope under Article 10 para 2 of the Convention (Art 10(2)) for restrictions on political speech or on debate of questions of public interest, a wider margin of appreciation is generally available to the Contracting States when regulating freedom of expression in relation to matters liable to offend intimate personal convictions within the sphere of morals or, especially, religion. Moreover, as in the field of morals, and perhaps to an even greater degree, there is no uniform European conception of the requirements of 'the protection of the rights of others' in relation to attacks on their religious convictions. What is likely to cause substantial offence to persons of a particular religious persuasion will vary significantly from time to time and from place to place, especially in an era characterised

by an ever growing array of faiths and denominations. By reason of their direct and continuous contact with the vital forces of their countries, State authorities are in principle in a better position than the international judge to give an opinion on the exact content of these requirements with regard to the rights of others as well as on the 'necessity' of a 'restriction' intended to protect from such material those whose deepest feelings and convictions would be seriously offended.

In *Civil Service Unions v UK* (1988), it was held that national security interests were of such paramount concern that they outweighed individual rights of freedom of association. Hence, the unions had no remedy under the ECHR for the removal of their members' rights to join and be in a trade union.

It should also be borne in mind that States can enter a derogation from particular provisions of the ECHR, or the way in which they operate in particular areas or circumstances. The UK entered such derogation in relation to the extended detention of terrorist suspects without charge under the Prevention of Terrorism (Temporary Provisions) Act 1989, subsequently replaced and extended by the Terrorism Act 2000. Those powers had been held to be contrary to Art 5 of the ECHR by the ECtHR in *Brogan v UK* (1989). The UK also entered a derogation in relation to the Anti-Terrorism, Crime and Security Act 2001, which was enacted in response to the attack on the World Trade Center in New York on 11 September of that year. The Act allows for the detention without trial of foreign citizens suspected of being involved in terrorist activities (see above, *A v Secretary of State for the Home Department* (2002) at 2.5.2).

One point to note in relation to the operation of the margin of appreciation is that, by definition, it is a rule of international law, in that it recognises the different approaches of distinct States. Consequently, it is limited in operation to the supranational ECtHR and not to national courts. The latter may follow precedents based on the doctrine, but it is difficult to see how they could themselves apply it in a national context, although it would appear that the domestic courts' development of the doctrine of deference achieves similar ends to those allowed under the margin of appreciation.

Proportionality

Even where States avail themselves of the margin of appreciation, they are not at liberty to interfere with rights to any degree beyond what is required, as a minimum, to deal with the perceived problem within the context of a democratic society. In other words, there must be a relationship of necessity between the end desired and the means used to achieve it.

As the ECtHR stated in *Chorherr v Austria* (1994):

The margin of appreciation extends in particular to the choice of the reasonable and appropriate means to be used by the authority to ensure that lawful manifestation can take place peacefully.

Proportionality has already been mentioned in relation to judicial review, where it was suggested that it might infiltrate the English legal system (see above, at 10.5.3). However, in relation to the HRA, proportionality is central to the jurisprudence of the ECtHR and as such is now central to the jurisprudence of the UK courts in relation to human rights issues. It is suggested that it will not be restricted to this limited sphere for long and that it will expand into judicial review and other areas as the HRA becomes increasingly understood and used.

It also has to be recognised that the ECHR as a legal document is not a fixed text. As Luzius Wildhaber, the former president of the Court, stated:

> On the question of evolutive interpretation, it is precisely the genius of the Convention that it is indeed a dynamic and a living instrument, which has shown its capacity to evolve in the light of social and technological developments that its drafters, however far-sighted, could never have imagined. The Convention has shown that it is capable of growing with society; and in this respect its formulations have proved their worth over five decades. It has remained a live and modern instrument. The 'living instrument' doctrine is one of the best known principles of Strasbourg case law, the principle that the Convention is interpreted 'in the light of present-day conditions', that it evolves, through the interpretation of the Court.

The recognition of this approach may be seen in the Court's legal recognition of transsexuals' new sexual identity in *Goodwin v UK* (2002). Until that decision, the Court had found that there was no positive obligation for the States to modify their civil status systems so as to have the register of births updated or annotated to record changed sexual identity. However, in *Goodwin*, the Court finally reached the conclusion that the fair balance now favoured the recognition of such rights, and ruled accordingly.

15.4.1 THE GENESIS OF THE REGULATION OF INVESTIGATORY POWERS ACT 2000

An examination of the list of cases decided by the ECtHR provides some interesting insights into the potential impact of the HRA now that it is open to UK courts to use the European Convention as a basis for their decisions.

One particular topic that has repeatedly drawn the attention of the ECtHR concerns the power of the police and security forces to collect incriminating information.

In *Malone v UK* (1984), the ECtHR decided that telephone tapping by the police, authorised by the UK government and condoned under common law powers by the High Court was in breach of Art 8 of the ECHR, which guarantees the right to respect for private life. The Article provides:

> There shall be no interference by a public authority with the exercise of this right except such as is in accordance with the law and is necessary in a democratic society in the interests of national security . . .

The ECtHR held that the tapping was in breach of Art 8(2), because it was not 'in accordance with law', but was rather governed by an unregulated discretion. It could not be 'necessary in a democratic society' as there were no constitutional safeguards against misuse of the power. The government reacted by introducing legislation to control telephone tapping by the police. The Interception of Communications Act (IOCA) 1985 limits telephone tapping to cases where the Home Secretary has issued a warrant and, to safeguard against arbitrary use, the warrant can only be issued in three specified circumstances, one of which is the prevention of serious crime. Further safeguards are provided by a tribunal to investigate complaints about the use of these powers and by the establishment of a Commissioner to review annually how the Home Secretary has exercised his powers.

However, perhaps the most surprising aspect of *Malone* was the recognition in the UK courts that telephone tapping could not be unlawful in the UK, as there was no right of privacy at common law that could be breached. And of course, the right of respect for private life provided by the European Convention was not justiciable in the UK courts at that time (*Malone v Metropolitan Police Commissioner* (1979)).

At least somewhat surprisingly, the IOCA 1985 only applied to interceptions on public telecommunications systems and did not regulate private systems such as internal works systems. As a consequence, the UK was also found in breach of Art 8 in *Halford v UK* (1997), where such a private system was abused to record conversations.

Even more surprising, not to say complacent, was the way in which the flaws inherent in the procedure relating to the interception of communication were not remedied in relation to the use of covert listening devices, commonly referred to as 'bugging'. Thus, a very similar situation, and corresponding decision, occurred in *Khan v UK* (2000). In *Khan*, the ECtHR held unanimously that there had been violations of Art 8 (right to respect for private and family life) and Art 13 (right to an effective remedy) of the ECHR, after the claimant had been convicted of drug dealing on the basis of evidence improperly obtained by a secret listening device installed by the police. As in *Malone*, the ECtHR held that, at the time in point, there was no statutory system to regulate the use of covert listening devices. As the Home Office Guidelines, which regulated such recordings, were neither legally binding nor publicly accessible, any such recording was consequently not 'in accordance with the law', as required by Art 8(2) of the ECHR. Khan had been arrested in 1993, but it was not until the enactment of the Police Act 1997 that a statutory basis for the authorisation of such surveillance operations was properly constituted, and that may have been instigated by a European Commission finding in *Govell v UK* (1997) that no existing statutory system governed the use of covert listening devices. Consequently, in the *Khan* case, there had been a breach of Art 8 of the ECHR because the tape-recording could not be considered to be 'in accordance with the law' as required by Art 8(2). The ECtHR found, however, that the use at the applicant's trial of the secretly taped material did not conflict with the requirements of fairness guaranteed by Art 6(1) of the ECHR. As the last court in the UK, the approach of the House of Lords is of some interest and reveals the frustration that the court felt in relation to the case, which no doubt it was aware would eventually be decided in a contrary manner by the ECtHR. As it stated, in English law, a breach of the provisions of Art 8 was not determinative of the outcome, and the judge's discretion to admit or exclude such evidence under s 78 of the Police and Criminal Evidence Act (PACE) 1984 was subject to common law rules that relevant evidence that was obtained improperly, or even unlawfully, remained admissible. As Lord Nolan expressed the situation:

> The sole cause of this case coming to your Lordships' House is the lack of a statutory system regulating the use of surveillance devices by the police. The absence of such a system seems astonishing, the more so in view of the statutory framework which has governed the use of such devices by the Security Service since 1989, and the interception of communications by the police as well as by other agencies since 1985. I would refrain from other comment because counsel for the respondent was able to inform us, on instructions, that the government proposes to introduce legislation covering the matter in the next session of Parliament.

One can almost hear the additional words 'and not before time', but unfortunately it was too late in the *Khan* case, which had to make its protracted way to the ECtHR. All of the preceding cases required action on the part of the UK government, and to that end the Regulation of Investigatory Powers Act (RIPA) was enacted in July 2000. That Act was specifically introduced to ensure that the investigatory powers of State authorities are used in accordance with human rights, but in so doing, it significantly increased the State's power in relation to surveillance.

Unfortunately, the RIPA 2000 was introduced too late to prevent the UK being found to be in breach of Art 8 of the ECHR in *Allan v UK* in 2002, which arose from covert bugging actions taken by the police.

15.5 THE EUROPEAN CONVENTION AND THE EUROPEAN UNION

Having started this section by stressing the fundamental distinction between the CJEU and the ECtHR, it is necessary to end it by blurring it and pointing out the various ways in which the EC, and then European Union, have expressly recognised the rights provided in the ECHR and the decisions made by the ECtHR. Thus, in a joint declaration delivered in 1997, the European Parliament, the Council and the Commission emphasised the prime importance they attached to the protection of fundamental rights:

> . . . as derived particularly from the constitution of the Member States and the European Convention for the Protection of Human Rights and Fundamental Freedoms [(1977) OJ C103].

Also, as has already been pointed out, Article 6 of the TEU binds the EU, not just to the Charter of Fundamental Rights of the European Union, which is founded on the European Convention on Human Rights, but also the ECHR itself.

The CJEU, in the same way as English courts, has equally been guided by the Convention where Community law is silent. It still remains possible, however, for cases to be brought to either, or both, judicial forums. Issues relating to discrimination are a case in point, by being potentially both in breach of employment law regulated by the EU, and fundamental human rights regulated by the ECHR. It is also an unfortunate fact that it is possible for at least a degree of incompatibility between the decisions of the two courts in relation to very similar matters (for example, see *SPUC v Grogan* (1991) and *Open Door and Well Women v Ireland* (1992)).

It is to be hoped that the fact that the TEU now provides for the EU having its own legal personality, thus allowing it to be a signatory member to the Convention, will remove any such potential incompatibilities.

CHAPTER SUMMARY: THE EUROPEAN CONTEXT

THE EUROPEAN UNION

UK law is now subject to European Union law in particular areas.

In practice, this has led to the curtailment of parliamentary sovereignty in those areas.

SOURCES OF EUROPEAN COMMUNITY LAW

The sources of EU law are:

- internal treaties and protocols – the TEU, TFEU, and Charter of Fundamental Rights are examples;
- international agreements;
- secondary legislation; and
- decisions of the European Court of Justice.

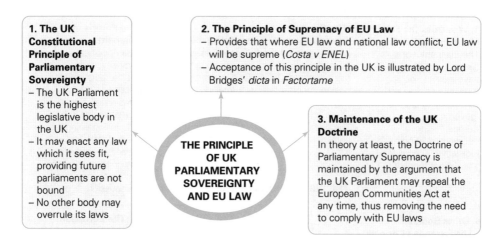

FIGURE 15.3 *The Principle of UK Parliamentary Sovereignty and EC Law.*

Secondary legislation takes three forms:

- regulations that are directly applicable;
- directives that have to be given statutory form; and
- decisions that are directly applicable.

MAJOR INSTITUTIONS

The major institutions of the European Union (EU) are:

- the Council of Ministers;
- the European Parliament;
- the Commission; and
- the European Court of Justice.

THE EUROPEAN COURT OF HUMAN RIGHTS

Refer to Chapter 2 above for a consideration of the effect of the ECHR on United Kingdom law.

The Council of Europe, the European Commission of Human Rights and the European Court of Human Rights are distinct institutions whose purpose is to regulate the potential abuse of human rights. They are not part of the EU structure.

Since the enactment of the Human Rights Act 1998, the European Convention on Human Rights has been incorporated into UK law. It remains to see what effect this has on domestic UK law, but it cannot but be significant.

1. Why Does the EU Need Institutions?
The EU Institutions (listed in Art 13 TEC) have a variety of functions as they act as the day-to-day 'government' of Europe, taking decisions relating to legislative, executive and judicial functions

2. The Council:
– A peripatetic body, representing the governments of the Member States. Its composition changes according to the subject matter under discussion
– It is an important decision-making body, with decisions normally taken by Qualified Majority Voting (QMV)
– The body is supported by a permanent body of staff known as COREPER

3. The European Parliament:
– A democratically elected body which represents the interests of EU citizens
– It has an important legislative role, which includes agreeing the EU Budget
– It also has supervisory functions, primarily in relation to the Commission

THE INSTITUTIONS OF THE EU

6. Other Bodies:
– **The European Council:** an Institution composed primarily of the heads of government of the States
– It is responsible for directing EU policy
- **The Court of Auditors:** an Institution which ensures EU money is spent in accor-dance with the EU's Budget
- **The European Central Bank:** works to maintain a stable financial system

5. The Court of Justice of the EU (ECJ):
– The ECJ is the judicial arm of the EU and is charged with ensuring that the law of the EU is observed (Art 19 TEU)
– It has the important function of interpreting EU law for the benefit of the Member States (Art 267 TFEU)
– It also hears actions relating to compliance with EU law by both the other Institutions (Art 263 TFEU) and the Member States (Art 258 TFEU)

4. The European Commission:
– The Commission represents the interests of the EU as a whole
– The Commission drafts EU legislation
– It also has a function in regard to the supervision of Member States, ensuring that they fulfil their EU obligations

FIGURE 15.4 *The Institutions of the EC/EU.*

FOOD FOR THOUGHT

1. Amongst the general public there is confusion between European Institutions, their courts and their laws and it is quite common for even politicians to confuse decisions of the Court of Justice of the EU and the European Court of Human Rights. It is essential that the two are not confused, but how can this be achieved?

2. Within the European Union there exists a tension between those countries who would support a more integrationist approach towards a federal state of Europe and those who would prefer to see the Union in purely economic market terms. Consider the current coalition government's approach to this issue, in light of the fundamentally different philosophies of the two constituent parties.

3. In the context of national sovereignty, consider whether the United Kingdom could leave the EU, either in theory or in practice.

4. The European Court of Human Rights is threatened with sclerosis if it does not deal with more cases, or deals with those cases differently. What reform is

necessary and how is it to be achieved, to ensure that the ECtHR continues to function adequately?

FURTHER READING

Benoetvea, J, *The Legal Reasoning of the European Court of Justice: Towards a European Jurisprudence*, 1993, Oxford: Clarendon

Borgsmit, K, 'The Advocate General at the European Court of Justice: a comparative study' (1988) 13 EL Rev 106

Boyes, R, Bremner, C, 'Czech President becomes last European leader to sign Lisbon treaty', *The Times*, 4 November 2009

Craig, P and de Búrca, G, *EU Law: Text, Cases and Materials*, 4th edn, 2007, Oxford: OUP

Davies, K, *Understanding EU Law*, 4th edn, 2010, Abingdon: Routledge

Dickson, B, *Human Rights and the European Convention*, 1997, London: Sweet & Maxwell

Dupre, C, 'Unlocking human dignity: towards a theory for the 21st century' (2009) 2 EHRLR 190–205

Editorial, 'Working time: worker sick while on holiday entitled to replacement leave' (2009) 887 IDS Emp L Brief 3–4

Foster, N, *EU Treaties and Legislation, 2007–2008*, 2007, Oxford: OUP

Gormsen, LL, 'The European Commission's priority guidelines on Article 82 EC' (2009) 14(3) Comms L 83–9

Harris, DJ, O'Boyle, M and Warbrick, C, *Law of the European Convention on Human Rights*, 1995, London: Butterworths

Kaczorowska, A, *EU Law*, 2nd edn, 2010, Abingdon: Routledge

Kennedy, T, *Learning European Law: A Primer and Vade-mecum*, 1998, London: Sweet & Maxwell

Lasok, KPE, *Law and Institutions of the European Union*, 7th edn, 2001, London: Butterworths

Neville Brown, L and Kennedy, T, *The Court of Justice of the European Communities*, 5th edn, 2000, London: Sweet & Maxwell

Shaw, J, *European Community Law*, 2nd edn, 1996, London: Macmillan

Ward, I, *A Critical Introduction to European Law*, 2nd edn, 2003, London: Butterworths

Weatherill, S and Beaumont, P, *EC Law*, 1993, London: Penguin

USEFUL WEBSITES

http://europa.eu.int/eur-lex/en/index.html

This site is the official database for all EU law. It includes the Official Journal, Treatises, recent case law, and legislation.

http://eur-lex.europa.eu/en/index.htm

EUR-Lex provides direct free access to European Union law.

http://curia.europa.eu

The official website for the Court of Justice of the European Communities.

www.echr.coe.int/echr

The official website of the European Court of Human Rights (ECHR).

COMPANION WEBSITE

Now visit the companion website to:

- test your understanding of the key terms using our Flashcard Glossary;
- revise and consolidate your knowledge of 'The European context' using our Multiple Choice Question testbank;
- view all of the links to the Useful Websites above.

www.routledge.com/cw/slapper

GENERAL LEGAL WEBSITES FOR THE ENGLISH LEGAL SYSTEM

www.bbc.co.uk

For general stories about the law, legal cases, political issues, and current affairs, the BBC site is an excellent source of information.

www.bailii.org

The British and Irish Legal Information Institute (BAILII) offers the most comprehensive set of primary legal materials that are available free and in one place on the internet. It includes 46 databases covering seven jurisdictions.

www.supremecourt.gov.uk

The Supreme Court is the final court of appeal in the UK for civil cases. It hears appeals in criminal cases from England, Wales and Northern Ireland. It hears cases of the greatest public or constitutional importance affecting the whole population.

www.timesonline.co.uk/tol/business/law/

The legal site of *The Times*. It is updated continuously every day, and contains a wide range of legal stories, analyses, and commentaries. Gary Slapper writes a weekly column for Times online. There are also over 500 of his articles in *The Times* online archive.

www.parliament.uk/judicial_work/judicial_work.cfm

This includes all the House of Lords' decisions since 14 November 1996.

www.uk-legislation.hmso.gov.uk/acts.htm

An excellent collection of contemporary and historical legislation. This site also houses Explanatory Notes for important legislation, and information about which sections of Acts have been brought into force.

www.direct.gov.uk

A helpful site from which you can find the 'A-Z of Government' (see the dedicated button on the DirectGov homepage) and scores of relevant organisations and departments.

www.justice.gov.uk

A good and regularly updated official coverage of all aspects of the justice system. The Ministry of Justice is one of the largest government departments. Every year around nine million people use its services in 900 locations across the United Kingdom, including 650 courts and tribunals and 139 prisons in England and Wales.

GENERAL READING

Archbold (Richardson, PJ (ed)), *Criminal Pleading, Evidence and Practice*, 2012, London: Sweet & Maxwell

Ashworth, A, *Sentencing and Criminal Justice*, 2010, Cambridge: Cambridge University Press

Bailey, SH, Gunn, MJ and Ormerod, D, *Smith & Bailey on The Modern English Legal System*, 5th ed, 2007, London: Sweet & Maxwell

Baldwin, J, 'Police interview techniques: establishing truth or proof?' (1993) 33 British J of Criminology 3

Baldwin, J, 'Power and police interviews' (1993) 143 NLJ 1194

Baldwin, J and Hill, S, *The Operation of the Green Form Scheme in England and Wales*, 1988, London: LCD

Baldwin, J and McConville, M, *Negotiated Justice: A Closer Look at the Implications of Plea Bargaining*, 1993, London: Martin Robertson

Baldwin, J and McConville, M, *Negotiated Justice: Pressures on Defendants to Plead Guilty*, 1977, London: Martin Robertson

Barnard, M, 'All bar none' (1999) 96/26 Law Soc Gazette 20

Bennion, F, 'A naked usurpation?' (1999) 149 NLJ 421

Bennion, F, 'Statute law obscurity and drafting parameters' (1978) British JLS 235

Bennion, F, *Statutory Interpretation*, 5th ed, 2008, London: Butterworths

Bindaman, D, 'Crown duals' (1999) Law Soc Gazette, 31 March

Bindman, G, 'Lessons of *Pinochet*' (1999) 149 NLJ 1050

Blackstone's Civil Procedure (Plant, C (ed)), 2010, Oxford: OUP

Blom-Cooper, L (ed), *The Law as Literature*, 1961, London: The Bodley Head

Bradley, A and Ewing, K, *Constitutional and Administrative Law*, 13th edn, 2003, London: Longman

Broadbent, G, 'Offensive weapons and the Criminal Justice Act' (1989) Law Soc Gazette, 12 July

Burns, R, 'A view from the ranks' (2000) 150 NLJ 1829–30

Burrow, J, 'Pre-committal custody time limits' (1999) 149 NLJ 330

Cane, P (ed), *Atiyah's Accidents, Compensation and the Law*, 6th ed, 2006, Cambridge University Press

Cape, E, 'Police interrogation and interruption' (1994) 144 NLJ 120

Card, R and Ward, R, *The Criminal Justice and Public Order Act 1994*, 1994, Bristol: Jordans

Clayton, R and Tomlinson, H, 'Arrest and reasonable grounds for suspicion' (1988) 32 Law Soc Gazette 22

Cragg, S, 'Stop and search powers: research and extension' (1999) Legal Action 3

Craig, P and de Búrca, G, *EU Law: Text, Cases and Materials*, 3rd edn, 2003, Oxford: OUP

Crawford, L, 'Race awareness training and the judges' (1994) Counsel 11

Croall, H, *Crime and Society in Britain*, 2008, London: Longman

Darbyshire, P, 'The lamp that shows that freedom lives – is it worth the candle?' [1991] Crim LR 740

De Sousa Santos, B, *Toward a New Common Sense*, 2002, London: Butterworths

Devlin (Lord), *Trial by Jury*, 1966, London: Stevens

Diamond, D, 'Woolf reforms hike costs' (1999) The Lawyer 2

Dicey, AV, *An Introduction to the Study of the Law of the Constitution* (1885), 10th edn, 1959, London: Macmillan

Dixon, D, Coleman, C and Bottomley, K, 'Consent and legal regulation of policing' (1990) 17 JLS 345

Exall, G, 'Civil litigation brief' (1999) SJ 32

Feldman, D, *Civil Liberties and Human Rights in England and Wales*, 1993, Oxford: OUP

Flemming, J, 'Judge airs concerns over Woolf reforms' (2000) Law Soc Gazette, 10 February

Freeman, M, *Law and Popular Culture*, 2005, Oxford: Oxford University Press

Frenkel, J, 'Offers to settle and payments into court' (1999) 149 NLJ 458

Frenkel, J, 'On the road to reform' (1998) Law Soc Gazette, 16 December

Genn, H, *Hard Bargaining: Out of Court Settlement in Personal Injury Claims*, 1987, Oxford: OUP

Genn, H and Genn, Y, *The Effectiveness of Representation at Tribunals*, 1989, London: LCD

Gibb, F, 'Rude judges must mind their language' (1999) *The Times*, 29 June

Gibb, F, 'Thatcher furious at "vindictive" Pinochet decision' (1999) *The Times*, 16 April

Gibb, F, 'Child killer Bell granted anonymity for life' (2003) *The Times*, 22 May

Gibb, F, 'Falconer takes an axe to legal tradition' (2003) *The Times*, 16 September

Gibb, F, 'Fee cuts prompt barristers to reject legal aid work' (2004) *The Times*, 5 April

Gibb, F, 'Commonwealth and common law: our imperial legacies' (2005) *The Times*, 13 September

Gibb, F, 'Some of the EU countries are hypocritical about human rights' (2006) *The Times*, 25 April

Gibb, F, 'Price is important, but quality can't be sacrificed' (2006) *The Times*, 14 February

Gibb, F, 'Legal profession set for historic reforms' (2009) *The Times*, 20 November

Gibb, F, 'Chilcot and legal advice' (2010) *The Times*, 3 February

Gibb, F, 'Gilderdale case prompts fresh calls to clarify the law on assisted dying' (2010) *The Times* 26 January

Gibb, F, 'Divorce courts may be thing of the past under radical overhaul of family justice' (2010) *The Times*, 21 January

Gibb, F, 'No win, no fee' deals cost taxpayers and insurers millions' (2010) *The Times* 15 January

Gibb, F, 'First criminal trial with no jury for 400 years starts' (2010) *The Times*, 13 January

Gibson, B, 'Why Bournemouth?' (1987) 151 JP 520

Glasser, C, 'Legal aid and eligibility' (1988) Law Soc Gazette, 9 March

Glasser, C, 'Legal services and the Green Papers' (1989) Law Soc Gazette, 5 April

Gold, S, 'Woolf watch' (1999) 149 NLJ 718

Goodhart, A, 'The *ratio decidendi* of a case' (1959) 22 MLR 117

Goodrich, P, *Reading the Law*, 1986, Oxford: Basil Blackwell

Grainger, I and Fealy, M, *An Introduction to the New Civil Procedure Rules*, 1999, London: Cavendish Publishing

Griffith, JAG, *The Politics of the Judiciary*, 5th edn, 1997, London: Fontana

Griffiths, C, 'Jury trial' (1999) Counsel 14

Hamer, P, 'Complaints: a new strategy' (1999) 149 NLJ 959

Harris, D *et al*, *Compensation and Support for Illness and Injury*, 1984, Oxford: Clarendon

Harrison, R, 'Appealing prospects' (2000) NLJ 1175–76

Harrison, R, 'Cry Woolf' (1999) 149 NLJ 1011

Harrison, R, 'Why have two types of civil court?' (1999) 149 NLJ 65

Hart, H, *The Concept of Law*, 1961, Oxford: OUP

Hayek, FA von, *The Road to Serfdom* (1971), 1994, London: Routledge and Kegan Paul

Hedderman, C and Moxon, C, *Magistrates' Court or Crown Court? Mode of Trial Decisions and Sentencing*, Home Office Study No 125, 1992, London: HMSO

HM Magistrates' Courts Service Inspectorate, *Annual Report 1997–98*, London: HMSO

Holdsworth, W, *A History of English Law*, 1924, London: Methuen

Holland, T, 'Cut price conveyancing' (1994) 144 NLJ 192

Hutchinson, A, *Evolution and the Common Law*, 2005, Cambridge: CUP

Irvine (Lord), 'Community vision under fire' (1999) Law Soc Gazette, 26 May

Jason-Lloyd, L, 'Section 60 of the Criminal Justice and Public Order Act 1994' (1998) 162 JP 836

JUSTICE, *Professional Negligence and the Quality of Legal Services – An Economic Perspective*, 1983, London: JUSTICE

Kadri, S, *The Trial: a history from Socrates to OJ Simpson*, 2005, London: HarperCollins

Kairys, D, *The Politics of Law: A Progressive Critique*, 1982, New York: Pantheon

Keating, D, 'Upholding the Rule of Law' (1999) 149 NLJ 533

Khan, S and Ryder, M, 'Police and the law' (1998) Legal Action 16

Law Society Civil Litigation Committee, 'Unravelling the enigma of *Thai Trading*' (2000) Law Soc Gazette, 9 June

Lee, S, *Judging Judges*, 1988, London: Faber & Faber

Legal Services Ombudsman, *Demanding Progress*, 1999–2000 Annual Report, London: HMSO

Lidstone, K, 'Entry, search and seizure' (1989) 40 NILQ 333

Lidstone, K (ed), *Prosecutions by Private Individuals and Non-Police Agencies*, 1980, London: HMSO

Lidstone, K and Palmer, C, *The Investigation of Crime*, 1996, London: Butterworths

Lord Chancellor's Department, *Judicial Statistics 2000*, Cm 3980, London: HMSO

Loughlin, M, *Sword and Scales*, 2000, Oxford: Hart

MacCallum, V, 'Learning lessons' (2001) Law Soc Gazette, 10 January

MacCormick, N, *Legal Rules and Legal Reasoning*, 1978, Oxford: Clarendon

Mackay (Lord), *The Administration of Justice*, 1994, Hamlyn Lectures, London: Sweet & Maxwell

Malleson, K, *The New Judiciary – The Effect of Expansion and Activism*, 1999, Aldershot: Ashgate

Malleson, K and Roberts, S, 'Streamlining and Clarifying the Appellate Process' (2002) Crim LR 272

Mansell, W and Meteyard, B, *A Critical Introduction to Law*, 2nd edn, 1999, London: Cavendish Publishing

Mayhew, L and Reiss, A, 'The social organisation of legal contacts' (1969) 34 American Sociological Rev 311

McConville, M, Sanders, A and Leng, R, *The Case for the Prosecution*, 1991, London: Routledge

McGrath, P, 'Appeals against small claims track decisions' (1999) 149 NLJ 748

McLaughlin, E and Muncie, J, *Controlling Crime*, 2001, London: Sage and the Open University

Money-Kyrle, R, 'Advocates' immunity after *Osman*' (1999) 149 NLJ 945 and 981

Montesquieu, C, *De l'Esprit des Lois* (1748), 1989, Cambridge: CUP

Morris, P, White, R and Lewis, P, *Social Needs and Legal Action*, 1973, London: Robertson

Motson, S, Stephenson, G and Williamson, T, ' The effects of case characteristics on suspect behaviour during police questioning' (1992) 32 British J of Criminology 23

Murphy, M, 'Civil legal aid eligibility' (1989) Legal Action 4

Napier, M, 'Conditional fees' (1995) 92/16 Law Soc Gazette 1626

News, 'The legal profession and the Community Legal Service' (1999) 149 NLJ 1195

News in Brief, 'Cheap conveyancing' (1998) 148 NLJ 8

Nobles, R, 'The Criminal Case Review Commission' (2005) Crim LR 173

Oliver, D and Drewry, G, *The Law and Parliament*, 1998, London: Butterworths

Pannick, D, *Advocates*, 1992, Oxford: OUP

Pannick, D, *Judges*, 1987, Oxford: OUP

Parker, C, 'Judicial decision making' (1999) 149 NLJ 1142

Parpworth, N, 'Breach of the peace: breach of human rights?' (1998) 152 JP 6

Payne, R, 'To counsel, not confront: the law on ADR' (1999) Counsel 30

Popplewell, O, *Benchmark: life, laughter, and the law*, 2003, London: Tauris

Purchas, F (Sir), 'What is happening to judicial independence' (1994) 144 NLJ 1306

Raz, J, 'The Rule of Law and its virtue' (1977) 93 LQR 195

Reid (Lord), 'The judge as law maker' (1972) 12 JSPTL 22

Reiner, R, *Crime, Order and Policing*, 1994, London: Routledge

Reiner, R, 'Responsibilities and reforms' (1993) 143 NLJ 1096

Reiner, R, *The Politics of the Police*, 2nd edn, 2000, Oxford: OUP

Richardson, J (ed), *Archbold on Criminal Pleading, Evidence and Practice*, 2012, London: Sweet & Maxwell

Robertshaw, P, *Rethinking Legal Need: The Case of Criminal Justice*, 1991, Aldershot: Dartmouth

Robertson, G, 'The Downey Report: MPs must realise they are not above the law' (1997) *The Guardian*, 4 July

Rutherford, A, 'Judicial training and autonomy' (1999) 149 NLJ 1120

Rutherford, A, 'Preserving a robust independence' (1999) 149 NLJ 908

Sanders, A, 'Class bias in prosecutions' (1985) 24 Howard J 17

Sanders, A, 'The silent code' (1994) 144 NLJ 946

Sanders, A and Young, R, *Criminal Justice*, 1995, London: Butterworths

Sanders, A and Young, R, 'Plea bargaining and the next Criminal Justice Bill' (1994) 144 NLJ 1200

Sanders, A *et al*, *Advice and Assistance at Police Stations and the 24 Hour Duty Solicitor Scheme*, 1989, London: LCD

Scrivener, A, 'The birth of a new language in the court room: English' (1999) *The Independent*, 26 April

Sedley, S (Sir), 'Human rights: a 21st century agenda' [1995] PL 386

Sidebottom, A, Belur, J, Bowers, K, Tompson, L and Johnson, SD, Theft in Price-Volatile Markets: On the Relationship between Copper Price and Copper Theft. (2011) 48(3) Journal of Research in Crime and Delinquency 396–418

Simpson, A, 'The *ratio decidendi* of a case' (1957) 20 MLR 413

Skordaki, E, *Judicial Appointments*, Law Society Research Study No 5, 1991, London: HMSO

Slapper, G, *Blood in the Bank*, 1999, Aldershot: Ashgate

Slapper, G, 'English legal system' (1999) 26 SLR 31

Slapper, G, *Organisational Prosecutions*, 2001, Aldershot: Ashgate

Smith, JC, 'Criminal appeals and the Criminal Cases Review Commission' (1995) 145 NLJ 534

Smith, R, 'Judicial statistics: questions and answers' (1994) 144 NLJ 1088

Smith, R, 'Politics and the judiciary' (1993) 143 NLJ 1486

Smith, R (ed), *Achieving Civil Justice*, 1996, London: LAG

Smith, R (ed), *Shaping the Future: New Directions in Legal Services*, 1995, London: LAG

St Luce, S, 'Cutting the lifeline' (1999) 149 NLJ 398

Steyn (Lord), 'The weakest and least dangerous department of government' [1997] PL 84

Temple Lang, J, 'The duties of national courts under Community constitutional law' [1997] EL Rev 22

Thomas, DA (ed), *Current Sentencing Practice*, 1999, London: Sweet & Maxwell

Thompson, P (ed), *The Civil Court Practice*, 1999, London: Butterworths

Trent, M, 'ADR and the new Civil Procedure Rules' (1999) 149 NLJ 410

Turner, AJ, 'Inferences under s 34 of the Criminal Justice and Public Order Act 1994: Part One' (1999) 163 JP, 27 March

Turner, AJ, 'Inferences under s 34 of the Criminal Justice and Public Order Act 1994: Part Two' (1999) 163 JP, 24 April

Twining, W, *Globalisation and Legal Theory*, 2000, Cambridge: Cambridge University Press

Twining, W and Meirs, D, *How To Do Things With Rules*, 5th ed, 2010, Cambridge: Cambridge University Press

Unger, R, *In Law and Modern Society*, 1976, New York: Free Press

Verkaik, R, 'Opinions on counsel' (1998) 95/04 Law Soc Gazette 22

Vignaendra, S, *Social Class and entry into the Solicitors' Profession: Research Study 41*, 2001, London: The Law Society

Wadham, J and Arkinstall, J, 'Human rights and crime' (1999) 149 NLJ 703

Watson, A, 'The right to elect trial by jury: the issue reappears' (1998) 163 JP 636

Weber, M, *Economy and Society (Wirtschaft und Gesellschaft)*, 1968, Roth, G and Widttich, C (trans), Berkeley: California UP

Wendel Holmes, O, *The Common Law* (1881), 1968, London: Macmillan

Williams, G, 'Letting off the guilty and prosecuting the innocent' [1985] Crim LR 115

Wolchover, D and Heaton-Armstrong, A, 'Jailing psychopaths and prison cell confessions' (1999) 149 NLJ 285

Woolf (Lord), 'Judicial review – the tensions between the executive and the judiciary' (1998) 114 LQR 579

Yarrow, S, *The Price of Success*, 1997, Grantham: Grantham

Yarrow, S and Abrams, P, *Nothing to Lose? Clients' Experiences of Using Conditional Fees*, Summary Report, 1999, London: University of Westminster

Zander, M, *A Matter of Justice*, 1989, Oxford: OUP

Zander, M, *Cases and Materials on the English Legal System*, 10th ed, 2007, Cambridge: Cambridge University Press

Zander, M, 'Costs of litigation – a study in the Queen's Bench Division' (1975) Law Soc Gazette, 25 June

Zander, M, 'How does judicial case management work?' (1997) 147 NLJ 353

Zander, M, 'Investigation of crime' [1979] Crim LR 211

Zander, M, *Legal Services for the Community*, 1978, London: Temple Smith

Zander, M, 'The trouble with fast track fixed costs' (1997) 147 NLJ 1125

Zander, M, 'The Woolf Report: forwards or backwards for the new Lord Chancellor' (1997) 16 Civil Justice Quarterly 208

Zander, M, 'Who goes to solicitors?' (1969) 66 Law Soc Gazette 174

Zander, M, 'Woolf on Zander' (1997) 147 NLJ 768

Zander, M and Henderson, P, *The Crown Court Study*, Royal Commission on Criminal Justice Study 19, 145, 1993, London: HMSO

INDEX